Morris—Const. & Am.Educ. ACB.—a

American Casebook Series

Hornbook Series and Basic Legal Texts

Nutshell Series

of

WEST PUBLISHING COMPANY

St. Paul, Minnesota 55102

ACCOUNTING

Fiflis and Kripke's Cases on Accounting for Business Lawyers, 687 pages, 1971.

ADMINISTRATIVE LAW

Davis' Basic Text on Administrative Law 3rd Ed., 617 pages, 1972.

Davis' Cases, Text and Problems on Administrative Law, 5th Ed., 650 pages, 1973.

Gellhorn's Administrative Law in a Nutshell, 336 pages, 1972.

ADMIRALTY

Healy and Currie's Cases on Admiralty, 872 pages, 1965.

AGENCY

Seavey and Hall's Cases on Agency, 431 pages, 1956.

Seavey's Text on Agency, 329 pages, 1964.

See Agency-Partnership.

AGENCY PARTNERSHIP

Henn's Cases on Agency, Partnership and Other Unincorporated Business Enterprises, 396 pages, 1972.

Seavey, Reuschlein & Hall's Cases on Agency and Partnership, 599 pages, 1962.

Steffen's Cases on Agency and Partnership, 3rd Ed., 733 pages, 1969.

ANTITRUST LAW

Oppenheim's Cases on Robinson-Patman Act, Pamphlet, 295 pages, 1967.

Oppenheim and Weston's Cases on Antitrust, 3rd Ed., 952 pages, 1968.

Oppenheim and Weston's Supplement, 1972.

BANKRUPTCY

MacLachlan's Text on Bankruptcy, 500 pages, 1956.

See Creditors' Rights.

Selected Commercial Statutes, 1016 pages, 1973.

BILLS AND NOTES

Aigler and Steinheimer's Cases on Bills and Notes, 670 pages, 1962.

Britton's Text on Bills and Notes, 2nd Ed., 794 pages, 1961.

See Commercial Transactions.

See Negotiable Instruments.

BUSINESS ORGANIZATIONS

See Agency-Partnership.

See Corporations.

CIVIL PROCEDURE

See Pleading and Procedure.

CLINICAL TEACHING

Freeman and Weihofen's Cases on Clinical Law Training—Interviewing and Counseling, 506 pages, 1972.

COMMERCIAL PAPER

See Bills and Notes.

See Commercial Transactions.

See Negotiable Instruments.

COMMERCIAL TRANSACTIONS

Speidel, Summers and White's Teaching Materials on Commercial Transactions, 1144 pages, 1969.

Murray and White's Problem Teaching Materials on Commercial Transactions, 292 pages, 1973.

White and Summers Text on the Uniform Commercial Code, 1054 pages, 1972.

Selected Commercial Statutes, 1016 pages, 1973

See Negotiable Instruments.

See Sales.

COMMON LAW PLEADING

Koffler and Reppy's Text on Common Law Pleading, 663 pages, 1969.

McBaine's Cases, Introduction to Civil Procedure, 399 pages, 1950.

Shipman's Text on Common Law Pleading, 3rd Ed., 644 pages, 1923.

COMMUNITY PROPERTY

Burby's Cases on Community Property, 4th Ed., 342 pages, 1955.

Huie's Texas Cases on Marital Property Rights, 681 pages, 1966.

Verrall and Sammis' Cases on California Community Property, 2nd Ed., 398 pages, 1971.

CONFLICT OF LAWS

Cramton and Currie's Cases—Comments—Questions on Conflicts, 915 pages, 1968.

Ehrenzweig's Text on Conflicts, 824 pages, 1962.

Ehrenzweig's Conflicts in a Nutshell, 3rd Ed., 432 pages, 1973.

Ehrenzweig and Louisell's Jurisdiction in a Nutshell, 3rd Ed., 291 pages, 1973.

Goodrich's Text on Conflict of Laws, 4th Ed., 483 pages, 1964.

Scoles and Weintraub's Cases on Conflict of Laws, 2nd Ed., 966 pages 1972.

CONSTITUTIONAL LAW

Engdahl's Constitutional Power in a Nutshell, 411 pages, 1974.

Lockhart, Kamisar and Choper's Cases — Comments — Questions on Constitutional Law, 3rd Ed., 1,487 pages, 1970.

Lockhart, Kamisar and Choper's Cases on The American Constitution, 3rd Ed., 1099 pages, 1970.

Lockhart, Kamisar and Choper's Annual Supplement.

See Constitutional Rights and Liberties.

CONSTITUTIONAL RIGHTS & LIBERTIES

Lockhart, Kamisar and Choper's Cases on Constitutional Rights and Liberties, 3rd Ed., 1118 pages, 1970.

Lockhart, Kamisar and Choper's Annual Supplement.

CONSUMER CREDIT

Kripke's Cases on Consumer Credit, 454 pages, 1970.

Schrag's Cases on Consumer Credit, 2nd Ed., Pamphlet reprint from Cooper, et al. Law and Poverty, 2nd Ed., 197 pages, 1973.

CONTRACTS

Calamari & Perillo's Text on Contracts, 621 pages, 1970.

Corbin's Cases on Contracts, 3rd Ed., 1381 pages, 1947. 1953 Supplement, 36 pages.

Corbin's Text on Contracts, Student Edition, 1224 pages, 1952.

Freedman's Cases on Contracts, 658 pages, 1973.

Fuller and Eisenberg's Cases on Contracts, 1043 pages, 1972.

Jackson's Cases on Contract Law in a Modern Society, 1404 pages, 1973.

Simpson's Cases on Contracts, 592 pages, 1956.

Simpson's Text on Contracts, 2nd Ed., 510 pages, 1965.

White and Summer's Text on the Uniform Commercial Code, 1054 pages, 1972.

COPYRIGHT

Nimmer's Cases on Copyright and Other Aspects of Law Pertaining to Literary, Musical and Artistic Works, 828 pages, 1971.

Nimmer's 1972 Supplement.

CORPORATIONS

Henn's Text on Corporations, 2nd Ed., 956 pages, 1970.

Henn's Cases on Corporations and Other Business Enterprises, about 1325 pages, 1974.

Henn's Statutory Supplement to Cases on Corporations, about 285 pages, 1974.

CORRECTIONS

Krantz' Cases on the Law of Corrections and Prisoners' Rights, 1130 pages, 1973.

Model Rules and Regulations on Prisoners Rights and Responsibilities, 212 pages, 1973.

CREDIT TRANSACTIONS

Maxwell & Riesenfeld's California Cases on Security Transactions, 371 pages, 1957.

Maxwell & Riesenfeld's Supplement, 68 pages, 1963.

CREDITORS' RIGHTS

Epstein's Teaching Materials on Debtor-Creditor Relations, 525 pages, 1973.

Epstein's Debtor-Creditor Relations in a Nutshell, 309 pages, 1973.

Riesenfeld's Cases on Creditors' Remedies and Debtors' Protection, 669 pages, 1967.

Riesenfeld's Case and Statutory Supplement, 1972.

CRIMINAL LAW

Dix and Sharlot's Cases on Criminal Law, 1360 pages, 1973.

LaFave and Scott's Text on Criminal Law, 763 pages, 1972.

Miller's Text on Criminal Law, 649 pages, 1934.

Stumberg's Texas Cases on Criminal Law, 505 pages, 1954.

Stumberg and Maloney's Texas Cases Supplement, 117 pages, 1965.

CRIMINAL PROCEDURE

Grano's Problems in Criminal Procedure, 171 pages, 1973.

Hall, Kamisar, LaFave and Israel's Cases on Modern Criminal Procedure, 3rd Ed., 1456 pages, 1969.

Hall, Kamisar, LaFave and Israel's Cases on Basic Criminal Procedure, 3rd Ed., 617 pages, 1969.

Hall, Kamisar, LaFave, and Israel's Annual Criminal Procedure Supplement.

Israels and LaFave's Constitutional Criminal Procedure in a Nutshell, 423 pages, 1971.

Federal Rules of Civil-Appellate-Criminal Procedure, Law School Edition, 206 pages, 1973.

DAMAGES

Crane's Cases on Damages, 3rd Ed., 337 pages, 1955.

McCormick's Text on Damages, 811 pages, 1935.

See Remedies.

DECEDENTS ESTATES

See Wills, Intestate Succession, Trusts, Gifts and Future Interests.

DICTIONARIES

Black's, one volume.
Bouvier's, two volumes.

DOMESTIC RELATIONS

Clark's Cases on Domestic Relations, 870 pages, 1965.

Clark's Text on Domestic Relations, 754 pages, 1968.

Paulsen's Cases on Family Law and Poverty, 2nd Ed., Pamphlet reprint from Cooper, et al. Law and Poverty, 2nd Ed., 200 pages, 1973.

See Juvenile Courts.

EDUCATION LAW

Morris' Cases on the Constitution and American Education, about 730 pages, 1974.

EQUITY

Cook's Cases on Equity, 4th Ed., 1192 pp., 1948.

Dobbyn's Injunctions in a Nutshell, about 265 pages, 1974.

McClintock's Text on Equity, 2nd Ed., 643 pages, 1948.

Van Hecke, Leavell and Nelson's Cases on Equitable Remedies and Restitution, 2nd Ed., 717 pages, 1973.

See Remedies.

EVIDENCE

Broun and Meisenholder's Problems in Evidence, 130 pages, 1973.

Cleary and Strong's Cases on Evidence, 967 pages, 1969.

McCormick, Elliott & Sutton's Cases on Evidence, 4th Ed., 1088 pages, 1971.

McCormick, Cleary, et al., Text on Evidence, 2nd Ed., 938 pages, 1972.

Rothstein's Evidence in a Nutshell, 406 pages, 1970.

FEDERAL ESTATE AND GIFT TAXATION

See Taxation.

FEDERAL INCOME TAXATION

See Taxation.

FEDERAL JURISDICTION AND PROCEDURE

Currie's Cases on Federal Courts, 823 pages, 1968.

Currie's Supplement, 1973.

Ehrenzweig and Louisell's Jurisdiction in a Nutshell, 3rd Ed., 291 pages, 1973.

Forrester, Currier and Moye's Cases on Federal Jurisdiction and Procedure, 2nd Ed., 933 pages, 1970.

Forrester, Currier and Moye's Supplement, 1973.

Merrill and Vetri's Problems in Federal Courts and Procedure, about 360 pages, 1974.

Wright's Text on Federal Courts, 2nd Ed., 745 pages, 1970.

Wright's Supplement, 1972.

FUTURE INTERESTS

Gulliver's Cases on Future Interests, 624 pages, 1959.

Powell's Cases on Future Interests, 3rd Ed., 1961.

Simes Text on Future Interests, 2nd Ed., 355 pages, 1966.

See Wills, Intestate Succession, Trusts, Gifts and Future Interests.

GRATUITOUS TRANSFERS

See Wills, Intestate Succession, Trusts, Gifts and Future Interests.

HOUSING AND URBAN DEVELOPMENT

Berger's Cases on Housing, 2nd Ed., Pamphlet reprint from Cooper, et al. Law and Poverty, 2nd Ed., 254 pages, 1973.

Krasnowiecki's Cases on Housing and Urban Development, 697 pages, 1969.

Krasnowiecki's Statutory Supplement 1969.

See Land Use.

INSURANCE

Keeton's Cases on Basic Insurance Law, 655 pages, 1960.

Keeton's Basic Text on Insurance Law, 712 pages, 1971.

Keeton's Case Supplement to Keeton's Basic Text, 398 pages, 1971.

Keeton's Programmed Problems in Insurance Law, 243 pages, 1972.

Keeton & Keeton's Compensation Systems, Pamphlet Reprint from Keeton & Keeton's Cases on Torts, 85 pages, 1971.

Vance's Text on Insurance, 3rd Ed., 1290 pages, 1951.

INTERNATIONAL LAW

Friedmann, Lissitzyn and Pugh's Cases on International Law, 1,205 pages, 1969.

Friedmann, Lissitzyn and Pugh's Supplement, 1972.

INTRODUCTION TO LAW

Fryer and Orentlicher's Cases on Legal Method and Legal System, 1,043 pages, 1967.

Kempin's Historical Introduction to Anglo-American Law in a Nutshell, 2nd Ed., 280 pages, 1973.

Kimball's Historical Introduction to Legal System, 610 pages, 1966.

Kinyon's Introduction to Law Study and Law Examinations in a Nutshell, 389 pages, 1971.

Smith's Cases on Development of Legal Institutions, 757 pages, 1965.

See Legal Method.

JUDICIAL ADMINISTRATION

Nelson's Cases on Judicial Administration and the Administration of Justice, about 1000 pages, 1974.

JURISPRUDENCE

Christie's Text and Readings on Jurisprudence—The Philosophy of Law, 1056 pages, 1973.

JUVENILE JUSTICE

Fox's Cases on Modern Juvenile Justice, 1012 pages, 1972.

Fox's The Law of Juvenile Courts in a Nutshell, 286 pages, 1971.

LABOR LAW

Oberer and Hanslowe's Cases on Labor Law, 1091 pages, 1972.

Oberer and Hanslowe's Statutory Supplement, 1972.

Sovern's Cases on Racial Discrimination in Employment, 2nd Ed., Pamphlet reprint from Cooper et al. Law and Poverty, 2nd Ed., 167 pages, 1973.

LAND USE

Beuscher and Wright's Cases on Land Use, 788 pages, 1969.

Hagman's Cases on Public Planning and Control of Urban and Land Development, 1208 pages, 1973.

Hagman's Text on Urban Planning and Land Development Control Law, 559 pages, 1971.

LEGAL BIBLIOGRAPHY

Cohen's Legal Research in a Nutshell, 2nd Ed., 259 pages, 1971.

How To Find The Law, with Special Chapters on Legal Writing, 6th Ed., 313 pages, 1965.

How To Find The Law Student Problem Book.

Rombauer's Legal Problem Solving, 2nd Ed., 212 pages, 1973.

Rombauer's Problem Supplement.

LEGAL ETHICS

Mellinkoff's Text on The Conscience of a Lawyer, 304 pages, 1973.

Pirsig's Cases on Professional Responsibility, 2nd Ed., 447 pages, 1970.

LEGAL HISTORY

Kempin's Historical Introduction to Anglo-American Law in a Nutshell, 2nd Ed., 280 pages, 1973.

Kimball's Historical Introduction to Legal System, 610 pages, 1966.

Radin's Text on Anglo-American Legal History, 612 pages, 1936.

Smith's Cases on Development of Legal Institutions, 757 pages, 1965.

LEGAL INTERVIEWING AND COUNSELING

See Clinical Teaching.

LAW SCHOOL PUBLICATIONS — Continued

LEGAL METHOD—LEGAL SYSTEM

Fryer and Orentlicher's Cases on Legal Method and Legal System, 1043 pages, 1966.
See Introduction to Law.

LEGAL PROCESS

See Legal Method.

LEGAL PROFESSION

See Legal Ethics.

LEGAL WRITING STYLE

Weihofen's Text on Legal Writing Style, 323 pages, 1961.
See Legal Bibliography.

LEGISLATION

Nutting, Elliott and Dickerson's Cases on Legislation, 4th Ed., 631 pages, 1969.

LOCAL GOVERNMENT LAW

Michelman and Sandalow's Cases on Government in Urban Areas, 1216 pages, 1970.
Michelman and Sandalow's 1972 Supplement.
Stason and Kauper's Cases on Municipal Corporations, 3rd Ed., 692 pages, 1959.
See Land Use.

MASS COMMUNICATION LAW

Gillmor and Barron's Cases on Mass Communication Law, 853 pages, 1969.
Gillmor and Barron's 1971 Supplement.

MORTGAGES

Osborne's Cases on Secured Transactions, 559 pages, 1967.
Osborne's Text on Mortgages, 2nd Ed., 805 pages, 1970.
See Sales.
See Secured Transactions.

MUNICIPAL CORPORATIONS

See Local Government Law.

NATURAL RESOURCES

Trelease, Bloomenthal and Geraud's Cases on Natural Resources, 1131 pages, 1965.

NEGOTIABLE INSTRUMENTS

Nordstrom and Clovis' Problems on Commercial Paper, 458 pages, 1972.
See Commercial Transactions.

OFFICE PRACTICE

A.B.A. Lawyer's Handbook, 557 pages, 1962.
See Clinical Teaching.

OIL AND GAS

Hemingway's Text on Oil and Gas, 486 pages, 1971.
Huie, Woodward and Smith's Cases on Oil and Gas, 2nd Ed., 955 pages, 1972.
See Natural Resources.

PARTNERSHIP

Crane and Bromberg's Text on Partnership, 695 pages, 1968.
See Agency-Partnership.

PATENTS

Choate's Cases on Patents, 1060 pages, 1973.

PERSONAL PROPERTY

Aigler, Smith and Tefft's Cases on Property, 2 Vols., 1339 pages, 1960.
Bigelow's Cases on Personal Property, 3rd Ed., 507 pages, 1942.
Fryer's Readings on Personal Property, 3rd Ed., 1184 pages, 1938.

PLEADING AND PROCEDURE

Brown, Karlen, Meisenholder, Stevens, and Vestal's Cases on Procedure Before Trial, 784 pages, 1968.
Cleary's Cases on Pleading, 2d Ed., 434 pages, 1958.
Cound, Friedenthal and Miller's Cases on Civil Procedure, 1075 pages, 1968.
Cound, Friedenthal and Miller's Cases on Pleading, Discovery and Joinder, 643 pages, 1968.
Cound, Friedenthal and Miller's Civil Procedure Supplement, 1972.
Ehrenzweig and Louisell's Jurisdiction in a Nutshell, 3rd Ed., 291 pages, 1973.
Elliott & Karlen's Cases on Pleading, 441 pages, 1961.
Hodges, Jones and Elliott's Cases on Texas Trial and Appellate Procedure, 2d Ed., about 775 pages, 1974.

PLEADING AND PROCEDURE—Cont'd

Hodges, Jones, Elliott and Thode's Cases on Texas Judicial Process Prior to Trial, 935 pages, 1966.

Karlen and Joiner's Cases on Trials and Appeals, 536 pages, 1971.

Karlen's Procedure Before Trial in a Nutshell, 258 pages, 1972.

McBaine's Cases on Introduction to Civil Procedure, 399 pages, 1950.

McCoid's Cases on Civil Procedure, about 850 pages, 1974.

McElhaney's Trials, Problems and Materials on Effective Litigation, about 290 pages, 1974.

Federal Rules of Civil-Appellate-Criminal Procedure, Law School Edition, 296 pages, 1973.

POVERTY LAW

Cooper, Dodyk, Berger, Paulsen, Schrag and Sovern's Cases on Law and Poverty, 2nd Ed., 1208 pages, 1973.

Cooper and Dodyk's Cases on Income Maintenance, 2nd Ed., Pamphlet reprint from Cooper, et al. Law and Poverty, 2nd Ed., 449 pages, 1973.

LaFrance, Schroeder, Bennett and Boyd's Text on Law and the Poor, 558 pages, 1973.

REAL PROPERTY

Aigler, Smith & Tefft's Cases on Property, 2 Vols., 1339 pages, 1960.

Browder, Cunningham & Julin's Cases on Basic Property Law, 2d Ed., 1397 pages, 1973.

Burby's Text on Real Property, 3rd Ed., 490 pages, 1965.

Moynihan's Introduction to Real Property, 254 pages, 1962.

Phipps' Titles in a Nutshell—The Calculus of Interests, 277 pages, 1968.

Smith and Boyer's Survey of the Law of Property, 2nd Ed., 510 pages, 1971.

See Housing and Urban Development.

REMEDIES

Cribbet's Cases on Judicial Remedies, 762 pages, 1954.

Dobb's Text, on Remedies, 1067 pages, 1973.

Dobbyn's Injunctions in a Nutshell, about 265 pages, 1974.

Van Hecke, Leavell and Nelson's Cases on Equitable Remedies and Restitution, 2nd Ed., 717 pages, 1973.

Wright's Cases on Remedies, 498 pages, 1955.

York and Bauman's Cases on Remedies, 2nd Ed., 1381 pages, 1973.

See Equity.

RESTITUTION

See Equity.

See Remedies.

REVIEW MATERIALS

Ballantine's Problems.

Burby's Law Refreshers.

Smith Reviews.

SALES

Nordstrom's Text on Sales, 600 pages, 1970.

Nordstrom and Lattin's Problems on Sales and Secured Transactions, 809 pages, 1968.

See Commercial Transactions.

SECURED TRANSACTIONS

Henson's Text on Secured Transactions, 364 pages, 1973.

See Commercial Transactions.

See Sales.

SEX BASED DISCRIMINATION

See Women and the Law.

SURETYSHIP AND GUARANTY

Osborne's Cases on Suretyship, 221 pages, 1966.

Simpson's Cases on Suretyship, 538 pages, 1942.

TAXATION

Chommie's Text on Federal Income Taxation, 2nd Ed., 1051 pages, 1973.

Chommie's Review of Federal Income Taxation, about 90 pages, 1973.

Hellerstein's Cases on State and Local Taxation, 3rd Ed., 741 pages, 1969.

Kragen & McNulty's Cases on Federal Income Taxation, 1,182 pages, 1970.

Lowndes, Kramer and McCord's Text on Federal Estate and Gift Taxes, 3rd Ed., about 950 pages, 1974.

McNulty's Federal Estate and Gift Taxation in a Nutshell, 343 pages, 1973.

McNulty's Federal Income Taxation in a Nutshell, 322 pages, 1972.

Rice's Problems in Federal Estate & Gift Taxation, 2nd Ed., 496 pages, 1972.

Rice's Problems in Federal Income Taxation, 2nd Ed., 589 pages, 1971.

Selected Federal Taxation Statutes and Regulations, 1130 pages, 1973.

TORTS

Green, Pedrick, Rahl, Thode, Hawkins and Smith's Cases on Torts, 1311 pages, 1968.

Green, Pedrick, Rahl, Thode, Hawkins and Smith's Cases on Injuries to Relations, 466 pages, 1968.

Keeton and Keeton's Cases on Torts, 1193 pages, 1971.

Prosser's Text on Torts, 4th Ed., 1208 pages, 1971.

TRADE REGULATION

See Anti-Trust Law.

See Unfair Trade Practices.

TRIAL AND APPELLATE PRACTICE

See Pleading and Procedure.

TRUSTS

Bogert's Text on Trusts, 5th Ed., 726 pages, 1973.

Powell's Cases on Trusts and Wills, 639 pages, 1960.

See Wills, Intestate Succession, Trusts, Gifts and Future Interests.

UNFAIR TRADE PRACTICES

Oppenheim's Cases on Unfair Trade Practices, 783 pages, 1965.

Oppenheim and Weston's Supplement.

Oppenheim's Robinson-Patman Act Pamphlet, 295 pages, 1967.

WATER LAW

Trelease's Cases on Water Law, 364 pages, 1967.

WILLS

Atkinson's Text on Wills, 2nd Ed., 975 pages, 1953.

Mennell's Cases on California Decedents' Estates, 566 pages, 1973.

Turrentine's Cases on Wills, 2nd Ed., 483 pages, 1962.

See Wills, Intestate Succession, Trusts, Gifts and Future Interests.

WILLS, INTESTATE SUCCESSION, TRUSTS, GIFTS AND FUTURE INTERESTS

Gulliver, Clark, Lusky and Murphy's Cases on Gratuitous Transfers: Wills, Intestate Succession, Trusts, Gifts and Future Interests, 1017 pages, 1967.

WOMEN AND THE LAW

Davidson, Ginsburg and Kay's Cases on Sex Based Discrimination, about 855 pages, 1974.

WORKMEN'S COMPENSATION

Malone and Plant's Cases on Workmen's Compensation, 622 pages, 1963.

THE CONSTITUTION

AND

AMERICAN EDUCATION

By

ARVAL A. MORRIS

Professor of Law

Adjunct Professor of Education

University of Washington

AMERICAN CASEBOOK SERIES

ST. PAUL, MINN.

WEST PUBLISHING CO.

1974

Morris—Const. & Am.Educ. ACB

FOR

LAURA

AND

HAL

SINE QUIBUS NON . . . .

*

PREFACE

Every author or editor has a view of his subject that informs his work, and I am no exception. Since it will facilitate understanding and put the reader in a better position to evaluate this book, I shall set forth my view and the constitutional principles upon which it rests.

American education is under attack. Perhaps it has always been a storm center, but currently America's schools are assailed from almost every direction and with almost every conceivable intention. Among the critics are some who are upset because the American school system has not eliminated poverty, war, injustice, disease, racial discrimination, slums, the disintegration of the family and a welter of other social problems. They point out that these social problems would remain even if the schools were abolished; so they ask, what good is American education? In the view of other critics students are prisoners of the state in schools where tyrants called teachers tyrannize them. Other critics indicate that the faults of the schools can be corrected only by a rigorous curriculum in which teachers are firmly in command. Other critics liken an educational system to the production line of a factory and insist that the proper focus is on "results" using the tool of performance contracting as the only business-like solution to the problem. Other critics see the schools as doing nothing other than keeping children in benevolent custody until they mature sufficiently to enter the work force. For them, the solution is to dismantle the American school system under the slogan, "Let Our Children Go."

Although frequently intemperate in tone, to my mind, many of the negative comments contain merit. More disturbing is that they all point to a similar conclusion: that the goals of American education no longer seem to be supported by a clear community consensus. Surely the life of any social institution is gravely endangered if it is under attack and the people have no clear idea of why, or whether, it should be supported. But, in order to know specifically what we want of our schools, we must first know what we want generally as a people. Some persons have argued that perhaps, the malaise affecting the schools is only an instance of the more general loss of goals by the American people. Although national goals are not absolutely clear, and agreed upon, I am not persuaded of the impossibility of a community consensus because I believe the American people share a fundamental set of common commitments that make education possible, and indeed, they require it.

PREFACE

The basic commitment of the American people is to their Constitution. The First Amendment to the Constitution of the United States plainly lays down the injunction that Congress shall make no law abridging the right of the people to freedom of speech or press. This provision simultaneously guarantees the right, and encourages every citizen to exercise his right, to express opinions on all aspects of public affairs. The underlying constitutional commitments are to a republican form of constitutional democracy in which the basic postulates are: (1) that the people of the United States are to be self-governing, controlling their government and not vice-versa, and (2) that the people are fully to engage in discussion and argument about the proper course of state in order to identify policies they want their representatives to follow for their common welfare. This vision lies at the core of the set of constitutional ideas expressed by the founding fathers, and their vision cannot be realized without an educated people. Citizens must be sufficiently educated in order to be able to think; to think clearly and discriminately, and to think independently for themselves. Thus, in outline form, it is possible to identify the constitutional criteria that are fundamental to the American political community and that are fundamental to the constituent elements of the concept of good citizenship. These criteria are also sufficient to identify a community consensus that will justify a system of American education.

Clearly, every American child must be educated in such a way that he is effectively afforded the opportunity to be the kind of citizen required by the First Amendment. At the very minimum this means that American schools must equip all students (1) with the tools of learning; (2) with curious minds that are open to new and different worlds in which they may live, and (3) with precise minds such that they can have a keen and profound understanding of their cultural heritage. These requirements go both to subject matter and to teaching methods. Moreover, although the First Amendment does not require that the people agree with each other, indeed it is assumed that they will not, it is essential that the people understand and communicate with each other. This means that the people must first learn to listen to one another, and hence another function of the American school can be identified.

It can be seen that the primary goals of the First Amendment are two, and that they are interconnected: to encourage the development in each citizen of the maximum amount of intelligent personality, and consequently, social diversity, within a social order that encourages the maximum amount of community citizenship, and consequently social unity. Obviously, the educational system has a vital role to play in helping the American people to realize these constitutional ideals. In this context then, the basic justification for an American school system is that it educate the next generation intelligently for good citizenship, as the concept of good citizenship is contemplated by the Constitution of the United States. In a profound sense therefore, American education is involved with the law.

A college or university justifiably can offer at least three courses on the intersections of law and education: (1) The Constitution and American Education; (2) School Law for Administrators and Teachers, and (3) The Law and Higher Education. The first course is the fundamental one, and it should analyze the basic constitutional framework within which law and education must function and then explore the constitutional problems and processes through which the constitution's ideals control various aspects of education. The second course for administrators and teachers would presuppose the first course, and it should explore the law in relation to topics such as the contract and tort liability of school districts, administrative officers and teachers; school board procedures, e. g., notice voting, public nature and recording requirements; school elections, e. g., petitions and notice for elections, ballots, qualifications for voting, the one person-one vote principle, whether school funds can be used to publicize elections, and a detailed analysis of the state and local administrative structures over education. The focus of the first two courses should be on elementary and secondary education, but that of the third course should be on higher education and the peculiar legal problems that it uniquely presents.

This book presents the basic information and problems necessary for a course on the Constitution and American Education. It can also be used in courses that seek to present law as part of the undergraduate curriculum. In the latter situation, the book has the advantage of its subject matter, with which students have had considerable experience and which experience can be brought to bear on the analyses of legal problems. Part I, The Constitutional Framework, provides a discussion of the origin and structure of the Constitution; an account of the court systems in the United States, and materials on the relationship between the Bill of Rights and the Fourteenth Amendment. I recommend that part one be covered as quickly as possible, especially in law courses where students have already taken courses in Constitutional Law and/or Federal Courts and the Federal System. Coverage of part one will probably be slower in courses with non-law students or with various mixtures of law and non-law students.

Once the constitutional framework has been set, part two of the book introduces the student to a series of cases, statutes and problems concerning education that present constitutional dimensions. The subjects of constitutional concern include constitutional limitations on a state's power to require schooling, the constitutional limitations on a state's power to require or disallow the expression of certain ideas in

PREFACE

either curricular or extra-curricular affairs, library censorship, the constitutional limitations on a state's power over students and faculty, desegregation and the constitutional right to equal educational opportunity. The overwhelming majority of the materials involve constitutional problems in elementary or secondary education, but I have not hesitated to include materials involving higher education wherever it appeared that their principles might apply to similar situations in the "common schools." I have tried to avoid presenting snippits of materials and over-editing the cases because I believe it is important for students to have a quantity sufficient for them to analyze and compare the underlying value premises and reasoning. Space considerations required that I choose between producing extensive notes and citations at the end of each section or producing occasional notes plus questions designed to aid student understanding of the materials and their interrelationships. While I chose the latter, the questions are neither comprehensive nor exhaustive, and they leave plenty of room for class discussion, which should be facilitated if students will prepare answers to the questions beforehand.

Before concluding these prefatory remarks I should like to thank some of the people who have helped make this book possible. I cannot trace my intellectual debts fully, but on any account I am especially indebted to Professors Ray O. Werner and Douglas J. Mertz of The Colorado College who thoroughly awakened my intellectual interests, and to Professors Rueben A. Zubrow and Morris Garnsey of the University of Colorado and Myres S. McDougal of the Yale Law School who, along with Professor Harold D. Evjen of Colorado, have helped me sustain my intellectual interests and curiosity. Finally, I am indebted to the late Gordon C. Lee who, as Dean of the College of Education at the University of Washington, introduced me to the importance of the impact of constitutional ideals on educational affairs. I also thank my students who have patiently suffered through experimental classes with these materials and particularly my students who in various ways have made direct contributions to this book, especially Earl O. Andrews, and Michael Hutton, Santiago Juarez, Sandra Ludes and Vernon Skeels. Furthermore, I thank Viola Bird, Eleanor Barrows, Maxine Dowd, Mary Hubert, Flora Meyerson, Harold Poole, Ann Van Hassel and Marian Gallagher for rendering their usual excellent library services. Of course, none of the persons named above is responsible for any of the shortcomings of this book. Finally, and especially, I thank Melody Walker and Diane Coleman who labored mightily and typed the entire manuscript and parts of it twice.

ARVAL A. MORRIS

Seattle, Washington
March, 1974

SUMMARY OF CONTENTS

*

TABLE OF CONTENTS

TABLE OF CONTENTS

CHAPTER III: THE BILL OF RIGHTS AND THE FOURTEENTH AMENDMENT—Continued

PART II: CONSTITUTIONAL CONTROLS AND EDUCATION

CHAPTER IV: CONSTITUTIONAL FREEDOM AND COMPULSORY EDUCATION 113

TABLE OF CONTENTS

TABLE OF CONTENTS

CHAPTER V: CONSTITUTIONAL FREEDOM AND GOVERN-
MENTAL POWER TO CONTROL THE EX-
PRESSION OF IDEAS—Continued

TABLE OF CONTENTS

TABLE OF CONTENTS

TABLE OF CONTENTS

TABLE OF CONTENTS

TABLE OF CONTENTS

TABLE OF CONTENTS

TABLE OF CONTENTS

*

TABLE OF CASES

The principal cases are in italic type. Cases cited or discussed are in roman type. References are to Pages.

TABLE OF CASES

TABLE OF CASES

TABLE OF CASES

†

THE CONSTITUTION
AND
AMERICAN EDUCATION

THE CONSTITUTION OF THE UNITED STATES OF AMERICA

We the people of the United States, in Order to form a more perfect
Union, establish Justice, insure domestic Tranquility, provide
for the common defence, promote the general Welfare, and secure
the Blessings of Liberty to ourselves and our Posterity, do ordain
and establish this Constitution for the United States of America.

ARTICLE I

SECTION 1. All legislative Powers herein granted shall be vested
in a Congress of the United States, which shall consist of a Senate and
House of Representatives.

SECTION 2. The House of Representatives shall be composed of
Members chosen every second Year by the People of the several States,
and the Electors in each State shall have the Qualifications requisite
for Electors of the most numerous Branch of the State Legislature.

No person shall be a Representative who shall not have attained to
the Age of twenty-five Years, and been seven Years a Citizen of the
United States, and who shall not, when elected, be an Inhabitant of
that State in which he shall be chosen.

Representatives and direct Taxes shall be apportioned among the
several States which may be included within this Union, according to
their respective Numbers, which shall be determined by adding to the
whole Number of free Persons, including those bound to Service for a
Term of Years, and excluding Indians not taxed, three fifths of all
other Persons. The actual Enumeration shall be made within three
Years after the first Meeting of the Congress of the United States, and
within every subsequent Term of ten Years, in such Manner as they
shall by Law direct. The Number of Representatives shall not exceed
one for every thirty Thousand, but each State shall have at Least one
Representative; and until such enumeration shall be made, the State
of New Hampshire shall be entitled to chuse three, Massachusetts
eight, Rhode Island and Providence Plantations one, Connecticut five,

New York six, New Jersey four, Pennsylvania eight, Delaware one, Maryland six, Virginia ten, North Carolina five, South Carolina five, and Georgia three.

When vacancies happen in the Representation from any State, the Executive Authority thereof shall issue Writs of Election to fill such Vacancies.

The House of Representatives shall chuse their Speaker and other Officers; and shall have the sole Power of Impeachment.

SECTION 3. The Senate of the United States shall be composed of two Senators from each State, chosen by the Legislature thereof, for six Years; and each Senator shall have one Vote.

Immediately after they shall be assembled in Consequence of the first Election, they shall be divided as equally as may be into three Classes. The Seats of the Senators of the first Class shall be vacated at the Expiration of the second Year, of the second Class at the Expiration of the fourth Year, and of the third Class at the Expiration of the sixth Year, so that one third may be chosen every second Year; and if Vacancies happen by Resignation, or otherwise, during the Recess of the Legislature of any State, the Executive thereof may make temporary Appointments until the next Meeting of the Legislature, which shall then fill such Vacancies.

No Person shall be a Senator who shall not have attained to the Age of thirty Years, and been nine Years a Citizen of the United States, and who shall not, when elected, be an Inhabitant of that State for which he shall be chosen.

The Vice President of the United States shall be President of the Senate, but shall have no Vote, unless they be equally divided.

The Senate shall chuse their other Officers, and also a President pro tempore, in the absence of the Vice President, or when he shall exercise the Office of President of the United States.

The Senate shall have the sole Power to try all Impeachments. When sitting for that Purpose, they shall be on Oath or Affirmation. When the President of the United States is tried, the Chief Justice shall preside: And no Person shall be convicted without the Concurrence of two thirds of the Members present.

Judgment in Cases of Impeachment shall not extend further than to removal from Office, and disqualification to hold and enjoy any Office of honor, Trust or Profit under the United States: but the Party convicted shall nevertheless be liable and subject to Indictment, Trial, Judgment and Punishment, according to Law.

SECTION 4. The Times, Places and Manner of holding Elections for Senators and Representatives, shall be prescribed in each State by the Legislature thereof; but the Congress may at any time by Law make or alter such Regulations, except as to the Places of Chusing Senators.

The Congress shall assemble at least once in every Year, and such Meeting shall be on the first Monday in December, unless they shall by Law appoint a different Day.

Section 5. Each House shall be the Judge of the Elections, Returns and Qualifications of its own Members, and a Majority of each shall constitute a Quorum to do Business; but a smaller Number may adjourn from day to day, and may be authorized to compel the Attendance of absent Members, in such Manner, and under such Penalties as each House may provide.

Each House may determine the Rules of its Proceedings, punish its Members for disorderly Behavior, and, with the Concurrence of two thirds, expel a Member.

Each House shall keep a Journal of its Proceedings, and from time to time publish the same, excepting such Parts as may in their Judgment require Secrecy; and the Yeas and Nays of the Members of either House on any question shall, at the Desire of one fifth of those Present, be entered on the journal.

Neither House, during the Session of Congress, shall, without the Consent of the other, adjourn for more than three days, nor to any other Place than that in which the two Houses shall be sitting.

Section 6. The Senators and Representatives shall receive a Compensation for their Services, to be ascertained by Law, and paid out of the Treasury of the United States. They shall in all Cases, except Treason, Felony and Breach of the Peace, be privileged from Arrest during their Attendance at the Session of their respective Houses, and in going to and returning from the same; and for any Speech or Debate in either House, they shall not be questioned in any other Place.

No Senator or Representative shall, during the Time for which he was elected, be appointed to any civil Office under the Authority of the United States, which shall have been created, or the Emoluments whereof shall have been encreased during such time; and no Person holding any Office under the United States, shall be a Member of either House during his Continuance in Office.

Section 7. All Bills for raising Revenue shall originate in the House of Representatives; but the Senate may propose or concur with Amendments as on other Bills.

Every Bill which shall have passed the House of Representatives and the Senate, shall, before it become a Law, be presented to the President of the United States; If he approve he shall sign it, but if not he shall return it, with his Objections to that House in which it shall have originated, who shall enter the Objections at large on their Journal, and proceed to reconsider it. If after such Reconsideration two thirds of that House shall agree to pass the Bill, it shall be sent, together with the Objections, to the other House, by which it shall likewise be reconsidered, and if approved by two thirds of that House, it shall become a Law. But in all such Cases the Votes of both Houses shall be determined by Yeas and Nays, and the Names of the Persons voting for and against the Bill shall be entered on the Journal of each House respectively. If any Bill shall not be returned by the President within ten Days (Sundays excepted) after it shall have been presented to him, the Same shall be a Law, in like Manner as if he had signed it, unless the Congress by their Adjournment prevent its Return, in which Case it shall not be a Law.

Every Order, Resolution, or Vote to which the Concurrence of the Senate and House of Representatives may be necessary (except on a question of Adjournment) shall be presented to the President of the United States; and before the Same shall take Effect, shall be approved by him, or being disapproved by him, shall be repassed by two thirds of the Senate and House of Representatives, according to the Rules and Limitations prescribed in the Case of a Bill.

SECTION 8. The Congress shall have Power To lay and collect Taxes, Duties, Imposts and Excises, to pay the Debts and provide for the common Defence and general Welfare of the United States; but all Duties, Imposts and Excises shall be uniform throughout the United States;

To borrow Money on the Credit of the United States;

To regulate Commerce with foreign Nations, and among the several States, and with the Indian Tribes;

To establish an uniform Rule of Naturalization, and uniform Laws on the subject of Bankruptcies throughout the United States;

To coin Money, regulate the Value thereof, and of foreign Coin, and fix the Standard of Weights and Measures;

To provide for the Punishment of counterfeiting the Securities and current Coin of the United States;

To establish Post Offices and post Roads;

To promote the Progress of Science and useful Arts, by securing for limited Times to Authors and Inventors the exclusive Right to their respective Writings and Discoveries;

To constitute Tribunals inferior to the supreme Court;

To define and punish Piracies and Felonies committed on the high Seas, and Offenses against the Law of Nations;

To declare War, grant Letters of Marque and Reprisal, and make Rules concerning Captures on Land and Water;

To raise and support Armies, but no Appropriation of Money to that Use shall be for a longer Term than two Years;

To provide and maintain a Navy;

To make Rules for the Government and Regulation of the land and naval Forces;

To provide for calling forth the Militia to execute the Laws of the Union, suppress Insurrections and repel Invasions;

To provide for organizing, arming, and disciplining the Militia, and for governing such Part of them as may be employed in the Service of the United States, reserving to the States respectively, the Appointment of the Officers, and the Authority of training the Militia according to the discipline prescribed by Congress.

To exercise exclusive Legislation in all Cases whatsoever, over such District (not exceeding ten Miles square) as may, by Cession of particular States, and the acceptance of Congress, become the Seat of the Government of the United States, and to exercise like Authority over all Places purchased by the Consent of the Legislature of the State in which the Same shall be, for the Erection of Forts, Magazines, Arsenals, dock-Yards, and other needful Buildings;—And

To make all Laws which shall be necessary and proper for carrying into Execution the foregoing Powers, and all other Powers vested by this Constitution in the Government of the United States, or in any Department or Officer thereof.

SECTION 9. The Migration or Importation of such Persons as any of the States now existing shall think proper to admit, shall not be prohibited by the Congress prior to the Year one thousand eight hundred and eight, but a Tax or duty may be imposed on such Importation, not exceeding ten dollars for each Person.

The privilege of the Writ of Habeas Corpus shall not be suspended, unless when in Cases of Rebellion or Invasion the public Safety may require it.

No Bill of Attainder or ex post facto Law shall be passed.

No capitation, or other direct, Tax shall be laid, unless in Proportion to the Census or Enumeration herein before directed to be taken.

No Tax or Duty shall be laid on Articles exported from any State.

No Preference shall be given by any Regulation of Commerce or Revenue to the Ports of one State over those of another; nor shall Vessels bound to, or from, one State, be obliged to enter, clear, or pay Duties in another.

No Money shall be drawn from the Treasury, but in Consequence of Appropriations made by Law; and a regular Statement and Account of the Receipts and Expenditures of all public Money shall be published from time to time.

No Title of Nobility shall be granted by the United States: And no Person holding any Office of Profit or Trust under them, shall, without the Consent of the Congress, accept of any present, Emolument, Office, or Title, of any kind whatever, from any King, Prince, or foreign State.

SECTION 10. No State shall enter into any Treaty, Alliance, or Confederation; grant Letters of Marque and Reprisal; coin Money; emit Bills of Credit; make any Thing but gold and silver Coin a Tender in Payment of Debts; pass any Bill of Attainder, ex post facto Law, or Law impairing the Obligation of Contracts, or grant any Title of Nobility.

No State shall, without the Consent of the Congress, lay any Imposts or Duties on Imports or Exports, except what may be absolutely necessary for executing its inspection Laws: and the net Produce of all Duties and Imposts, laid by any State on Imports or Exports, shall be for the Use of the Treasury of the United States; and all such Laws shall be subject to the Revision and Controul of the Congress.

No State shall, without the Consent of Congress, lay any duty of Tonnage, keep Troops, or Ships of War in time of Peace, enter into any Agreement or Compact with another State, or with a foreign Power, or engage in War, unless actually invaded, or in such imminent Danger as will not admit of delay.

ARTICLE II

SECTION 1. The executive Power shall be vested in a President of the United States of America. He shall hold his Office during the Term of four Years, and, together with the Vice President, chosen for the same Term, be elected, as follows

Each State shall appoint, in such Manner as the Legislature thereof may direct, a Number of Electors, equal to the whole Number of Senators and Representatives to which the State may be entitled in the Congress: but no Senator or Representative, or Person holding an Office of Trust or Profit under the United States, shall be appointed an Elector.

The Electors shall meet in their respective States, and vote by Ballot for two persons, of whom one at least shall not be an Inhabitant of the same State with themselves. And they shall make a List of all the Persons voted for, and of the Number of Votes for each; which List they shall sign and certify, and transmit sealed to the Seat of the Government of the United States, directed to the President of the Senate. The President of the Senate shall, in the Presence of the Senate and House of Representatives, open all the Certificates, and the Votes shall then be counted. The Person having the greatest Number of Votes shall be the President, if such Number be a Majority of the whole Number of Electors appointed; and if there be more than one who have such Majority, and have an equal Number of Votes, then the House of Representatives shall immediately chuse by Ballot one of them for President; and if no Person have a Majority, then from the five highest on the List the said House shall in like Manner chuse the President. But in chusing the President, the

Votes shall be taken by States, the Representation from each State having one Vote; A quorum for this Purpose shall consist of a Member or Members from two thirds of the States, and a Majority of all the States shall be necessary to a Choice. In every Case, after the Choice of the President, the Person having the greatest Number of Votes of Electors shall be the Vice President. But if there should remain two or more who have equal Votes, the Senate shall chuse from them by Ballot the Vice President.

The Congress may determine the Time of chusing the Electors, and the Day on which they shall give their Votes; which Day shall be the same throughout the United States.

No person except a natural born Citizen, or a Citizen of the United States, at the time of the Adoption of this Constitution, shall be eligible to the Office of President; neither shall any Person be eligible to that Office who shall not have attained to the Age of thirty-five Years, and been fourteen Years a Resident within the United States.

In Case of the Removal of the President from Office, or of his Death, Resignation, or Inability to discharge the Powers and Duties of the said Office, the same shall devolve on the Vice President, and the Congress may by Law provide for the Case of Removal, Death, Resignation or Inability, both of the President and Vice President, declaring what Officer shall then act as President, and such Officer shall act accordingly, until the Disability be removed, or a President shall be elected.

The President shall, at stated Times, receive for his Services, a Compensation, which shall neither be encreased nor diminished during the Period for which he shall have been elected, and he shall not receive within that Period any other Emolument from the United States, or any of them.

Before he enter on the Execution of his Office, he shall take the following Oath or Affirmation: "I do solemnly swear (or affirm) that I will faithfully execute the Office of President of the United States, and will to the best of my Ability, preserve, protect and defend the Constitution of the United States."

SECTION 2. The President shall be Commander in Chief of the Army and Navy of the United States, and of the Militia of the several States, when called into the actual Service of the United States; he may require the Opinion in writing, of the principal Officer in each of the executive Departments, upon any subject relating to the Duties of their respective Offices, and he shall have Power to Grant Reprieves and Pardons for Offenses against the United States, except in Cases of Impeachment.

He shall have Power, by and with the Advice and Consent of the Senate, to make Treaties, provided two thirds of the Senators present concur; and he shall nominate, and by and with the Advice and Consent of the Senate, shall appoint Ambassadors, other public Ministers and Consuls, Judges of the supreme Court, and all other Officers of the United States, whose Appointments are not herein otherwise provided for, and which shall be established by Law: but the Congress may by Law vest the Appointment of such inferior Officers, as they think proper, in the President alone, in the Courts of Law, or in the Heads of Departments.

The President shall have Power to fill up all Vacancies that may happen during the Recess of the Senate, by granting Commissions which shall expire at the End of their next Session.

SECTION 3.   He shall from time to time give to the Congress Information of the State of the Union, and recommend to their Consideration such Measures as he shall judge necessary and expedient; he may, on extraordinary Occasions, convene both Houses, or either of them, and in Case of Disagreement between them, with Respect to the Time of Adjournment, he may adjourn them to such Time as he shall think proper; he shall receive Ambassadors and other public Ministers; he shall take Care that the Laws be faithfully executed, and shall Commission all the Officers of the United States.

SECTION 4.   The President, Vice President and all civil Officers of the United States, shall be removed from Office on Impeachment for, and Conviction of, Treason, Bribery, or other high Crimes and Misdemeanors.

ARTICLE III

SECTION 1.   The judicial Power of the United States, shall be vested in one supreme Court, and in such inferior Courts as the Congress may from time to time ordain and establish.   The Judges, both of the supreme and inferior Courts, shall hold their Offices during good Behaviour, and shall, at stated Times, receive for their Services a Compensation which shall not be diminished during their Continuance in Office.

SECTION 2.   The judicial Power shall extend to all Cases, in Law and Equity, arising under this Constitution, the Laws of the United States, and Treaties made, or which shall be made, under their Authority;—to all Cases affecting Ambassadors, other public Ministers and Consuls;—to all Cases of admiralty and maritime Jurisdiction; —to Controversies to which the United States shall be a Party;—to Controversies between two or more States;—between a State and Citizens of another State;—between Citizens of different States;—between Citizens of the same State claiming Lands under Grants of different States, and between a State, or the Citizens thereof, and foreign States, Citizens or Subjects.

In all Cases affecting Ambassadors, other public Ministers and Consuls, and those in which a State shall be Party, the supreme Court shall have original Jurisdiction. In all the other Cases before mentioned, the supreme Court shall have appellate Jurisdiction, both as to Law and Fact, with such Exceptions, and under such Regulations as the Congress shall make.

The trial of all Crimes, except in Cases of Impeachment, shall be by Jury; and such Trial shall be held in the State where the said Crimes shall have been committed; but when not committed within any State, the Trial shall be at such Place or Places as the Congress may by Law have directed.

SECTION 3. Treason against the United States, shall consist only in levying War against them, or in adhering to their Enemies, giving them Aid and Comfort. No Person shall be convicted of Treason unless on the Testimony of two Witnesses to the same overt Act, or on Confession in open Court.

The Congress shall have power to declare the Punishment of Treason, but no Attainder of Treason shall work Corruption of Blood, or Forfeiture except during the Life of the Person attainted.

ARTICLE IV

SECTION 1. Full Faith and Credit shall be given in each State to the public Acts, Records, and judicial Proceedings of every other State. And the Congress may by general Laws prescribe the Manner in which such Acts, Records and Proceedings shall be proved, and the Effect thereof.

SECTION 2. The Citizens of each State shall be entitled to all Privileges and Immunities of Citizens in the several States.

A Person charged in any State with Treason, Felony, or other Crime, who shall flee from Justice, and be found in another State, shall on demand of the executive Authority of the State from which he fled, be delivered up, to be removed to the State having Jurisdiction of the Crime.

No Person held to Service or Labour in one State, under the Laws thereof, escaping into another, shall, in Consequence of any Law or Regulation therein, be discharged from such Service or Labour, but shall be delivered up on Claim of the Party to whom such Service or Labour may be due.

SECTION 3. New States may be admitted by the Congress into this Union; but no new State shall be formed or erected within the Jurisdiction of any other State; nor any State be formed by the Junction of two or more States, or parts of States, without the Consent of the Legislatures of the States concerned as well as of the Congress.

The Congress shall have Power to dispose of and make all needful Rules and Regulations respecting the Territory or other Property belonging to the United States; and nothing in this Constitution shall be so construed as to Prejudice any Claims of the United States, or of any particular State.

SECTION 4. The United States shall guarantee to every State in this Union a Republican Form of Government, and shall protect each of them against Invasion; and on Application of the Legislature, or of the Executive (when the Legislature cannot be convened) against domestic Violence.

ARTICLE V

The Congress, whenever two thirds of both Houses shall deem it necessary, shall propose Amendments to this Constitution, or, on the Application of the Legislatures of two thirds of the several States, shall call a Convention for proposing Amendments, which, in either Case, shall be valid to all Intents and Purposes, as part of this Constitution, when ratified by the Legislatures of three fourths of the several States, or by Conventions in three fourths thereof, as the one or the other Mode of Ratification may be proposed by the Congress; Provided that no Amendment which may be made prior to the Year One thousand eight hundred and eight shall in any Manner affect the first and fourth Clauses in the Ninth Section of the first Article; and that no State, without its Consent, shall be deprived of its equal Suffrage in the Senate.

ARTICLE VI

All Debts contracted and Engagements entered into, before the Adoption of this Constitution, shall be as valid against the United States under this Constitution, as under the Confederation.

This Constitution, and the Laws of the United States which shall be made in Pursuance thereof; and all Treaties made, or which shall be made, under the Authority of the United States, shall be the supreme Law of the Land; and the Judges in every State shall be bound thereby, any Thing in the Constitution or Laws of any State to the Contrary notwithstanding.

The Senators and Representatives before mentioned, and the Members of the several State Legislatures, and all executive and judicial Officers, both of the United States and of the several States, shall be bound by Oath or Affirmation, to support this Constitution; but no religious Test shall ever be required as a Qualification to any Office or public Trust under the United States.

ARTICLE VII

The Ratification of the Conventions of nine States shall be sufficient for the Establishment of this Constitution between the States so ratifying the Same.[a]

Done in Convention by the Unanimous Consent of the States present the Seventeenth Day of September in the Year of our Lord one thousand seven hundred and Eighty seven and of the Independence of the United States of America the Twelfth. In Witness whereof We have hereunto subscribed our Names. [Signatures omitted.]

ARTICLES IN ADDITION TO, AND AMENDMENT OF, THE CONSTITUTION OF THE UNITED STATES OF AMERICA, PROPOSED BY CONGRESS, AND RATIFIED BY THE LEGISLATURES OF THE SEVERAL STATES, PURSUANT TO THE FIFTH ARTICLE OF THE ORIGINAL CONSTITUTION.

AMENDMENT I

Congress shall make no law respecting an establishment of religion, or prohibiting the free exercise thereof; or abridging the freedom of speech, or of the press; or the right of the people peaceably to assemble, and to petition the Government for a redress of grievances.

AMENDMENT II

A well regulated Militia, being necessary to the security of a free State, the right of the people to keep and bear Arms, shall not be infringed.

AMENDMENT III

No Soldier shall, in time of peace be quartered in any house, without the consent of the Owner, nor in time of war, but in a manner to be prescribed by law.

AMENDMENT IV

The right of the people to be secure in their persons, houses, papers, and effects, against unreasonable searches and seizures, shall not be violated, and no Warrants shall issue, but upon probable cause, supported by Oath or affirmation, and particularly describing the place to be searched, and the persons or things to be seized.

[a] By July 26, 1788, eleven states had ratified the Constitution. On September 13, 1788, the Continental Congress (which had continued to function at irregular intervals) passed a resolution to put the new Constitution into operation. The first Wednesday, or January 17, 1789, was fixed as the day for choosing presidential electors, the first Wednesday of February for the meeting of electors, and the first Wednesday of March, i. e., March 4, 1789, for the opening of the new Congress.—Ed.

AMENDMENT V

No person shall be held to answer for a capital, or otherwise infamous crime, unless on a presentment or indictment of a Grand Jury, except in cases arising in the land or naval forces, or in the Militia, when in actual service in time of War or public danger; nor shall any person be subject for the same offence to be twice put in jeopardy of life or limb; nor shall be compelled in any criminal case to be a witness against himself, nor be deprived of life, liberty, or property, without due process of law; nor shall private property be taken for public use, without just compensation.

AMENDMENT VI

In all criminal prosecutions, the accused shall enjoy the right to a speedy and public trial, by an impartial jury of the State and district wherein the crime shall have been committed, which district shall have been previously ascertained by law, and to be informed of the nature and cause of the accusation; to be confronted with the witnesses against him; to have compulsory process for obtaining witnesses in his favor, and to have the Assistance of Counsel for his defence.

AMENDMENT VII

In suits at common law, where the value in controversy shall exceed twenty dollars, the right of trial by jury shall be preserved, and no fact tried by a jury, shall be otherwise re-examined in any Court of the United States, than according to the rules of the common law.

AMENDMENT VIII

Excessive bail shall not be required, nor excessive fines imposed, nor cruel and unusual punishments inflicted.

AMENDMENT IX

The enumeration in the Constitution, of certain rights, shall not be construed to deny or disparage others retained by the people.

AMENDMENT X

The powers not delegated to the United States by the Constitution, nor prohibited by it to the States, are reserved to the States respectively, or to the people.

AMENDMENT XI [1798]

The Judicial power of the United States shall not be construed to extend to any suit in law or equity, commenced or prosecuted against one of the United States by Citizens of another State, or by Citizens or Subjects of any Foreign State.

AMENDMENT XII [1804]

The Electors shall meet in their respective states and vote by ballot for President and Vice President, one of whom, at least, shall not be an inhabitant of the same state with themselves; they shall name in their ballots the person voted for as President, and in distinct ballots the person voted for as Vice President, and they shall make distinct lists of all persons voted for as President, and of all persons voted for as Vice President, and of the number of votes for each, which lists they shall sign and certify, and transmit sealed to the seat of the government of the United States, directed to the President of the Senate;—The President of the Senate shall, in presence of the Senate and House of Representatives, open all the certificates and the votes shall then be counted;—The person having the greatest number of votes for President, shall be the President, if such number be a majority of the whole number of Electors appointed; and if no person have such majority, then from the persons having the highest numbers not exceeding three on the list of those voted for as President, the House of Representatives shall choose immediately, by ballot, the President. But in choosing the President, the votes shall be taken by states, the representation from each state having one vote; a quorum for this purpose shall consist of a member or members from two-thirds of the states, and a majority of all the states shall be necessary to a choice. And if the House of Representatives shall not choose a President whenever the right of choice shall devolve upon them, before the fourth day of March next following, then the Vice President shall act as President, as in the case of the death or other constitutional disability of the President.—The person having the greatest number of votes as Vice President, shall be the Vice President, if such number be a majority of the whole number of Electors appointed, and if no person have a majority, then from the two highest numbers on the list, the Senate shall choose the Vice President; a quorum for the purpose shall consist of two-thirds of the whole number of Senators, and a majority of the whole number shall be necessary to a choice. But no person constitutionally ineligible to the office of President shall be eligible to that of Vice President of the United States.

AMENDMENT XIII [1865]

SECTION 1. Neither slavery nor involuntary servitude, except as a punishment for crime whereof the party shall have been duly convicted, shall exist within the United States, or any place subject to their jurisdiction.

SECTION 2. Congress shall have power to enforce this article by appropriate legislation.

AMENDMENT XIV [1868]

SECTION 1. All persons born or naturalized in the United States, and subject to the jurisdiction thereof, are citizens of the United States and of the State wherein they reside. No State shall make or enforce any law which shall abridge the privileges or immunities of citizens of the United States; nor shall any State deprive any person of life, liberty, or property, without due process of law; nor deny to any person within its jurisdiction the equal protection of the laws.

SECTION 2. Representatives shall be apportioned among the several States according to their respective numbers, counting the whole number of persons in each State, excluding Indians not taxed. But when the right to vote at any election for the choice of electors for President and Vice President of the United States, Representatives in Congress, the Executive and Judicial officers of a State, or the members of the Legislature thereof, is denied to any of the male inhabitants of such State, being twenty-one years of age, and citizens of the United States, or in any way abridged, except for participation in rebellion, or other crime, the basis of representation therein shall be reduced in the proportion which the number of such male citizens shall bear to the whole number of male citizens twenty-one years of age in such State.

SECTION 3. No person shall be a Senator or Representative in Congress, or elector of President and Vice President, or hold any office, civil or military, under the United States, or under any State, who, having previously taken an oath, as a member of Congress, or as an officer of the United States, or as a member of any State legislature, or as an executive or judicial officer of any State, to support the Constitution of the United States, shall have engaged in insurrection or rebellion against the same, or given aid or comfort to the enemies thereof. But Congress may by a vote of two-thirds of each House, remove such disability.

SECTION 4. The validity of the public debt of the United States, authorized by law, including debts incurred for payment of pensions and bounties for services in suppressing insurrection or rebellion shall not be questioned. But neither the United States nor any State shall assume or pay any debt or obligation incurred in aid of insurrection or rebellion against the United States, or any claim for the loss or emancipation of any slaves; but all such debts, obligations and claims shall be held illegal and void.

SECTION 5. The Congress shall have power to enforce, by appropriate legislation, the provisions of this article.

AMENDMENT XV [1870]

SECTION 1.   The right of citizens of the United States to vote shall not be denied or abridged by the United States or by any State on account of race, color, or previous condition of servitude.

SECTION 2.   The Congress shall have power to enforce this article by appropriate legislation.

AMENDMENT XVI [1913]

The Congress shall have power to lay and collect taxes on incomes, from whatever source derived, without apportionment among the several States, and without regard to any census or enumeration.

AMENDMENT XVII [1913]

The Senate of the United States shall be composed of two Senators from each State, elected by the people thereof, for six years; and each Senator shall have one vote.   The electors in each State shall have the qualifications requisite for electors of the most numerous branch of the State legislatures.

When vacancies happen in the representation of any State in the Senate, the executive authority of such State shall issue writs of election to fill such vacancies: *Provided,* That the legislature of any State may empower the executive thereof to make temporary appointments until the people fill the vacancies by election as the legislature may direct.

This amendment shall not be so construed as to affect the election or term of any Senator chosen before it becomes valid as part of the Constitution.

AMENDMENT XVIII [1919]

SECTION 1.   After one year from the ratification of this article the manufacture, sale, or transportation of intoxicating liquors within, the importation thereof into, or the exportation thereof from the United States and all territory subject to the jurisdiction thereof for beverage purposes is hereby prohibited.

SECTION 2.   The Congress and the several States shall have concurrent power to enforce this article by appropriate legislation.

SECTION 3.   This article shall be inoperative unless it shall have been ratified as an amendment to the Constitution by the legislatures of the several States, as provided in the Constitution, within seven years from the date of the submission hereof to the States by the Congress.

AMENDMENT XIX [1920]

The right of citizens of the United States to vote shall not be denied or abridged by the United States or by any State on account of sex.

Congress shall have power to enforce this article by appropriate legislation.

AMENDMENT XX [1933]

SECTION 1.   The terms of the President and Vice President shall end at noon on the 20th day of January, and the terms of Senators and Representatives at noon on the 3d day of January, of the years in which such terms would have ended if this article had not been ratified; and the terms of their successors shall then begin.

SECTION 2.   The Congress shall assemble at least once in every year, and such meeting shall begin at noon on the 3d day of January, unless they shall by law appoint a different day.

SECTION 3.   If, at the time fixed for the beginning of the term of the President, the President elect shall have died, the Vice President elect shall become President.   If a President shall not have been chosen before the time fixed for the beginning of his term, or if the President elect shall have failed to qualify, then the Vice President elect shall act as President until a President shall have qualified; and the Congress may by law provide for the case wherein neither a President elect nor a Vice President elect shall have qualified, declaring who shall then act as President, or the manner in which one who is to act shall be selected, and such person shall act accordingly until a President or Vice President shall have qualified.

SECTION 4.   The Congress may by law provide for the case of the death of any of the persons from whom the House of Representatives may choose a President whenever the right of choice shall have devolved upon them, and for the case of the death of any of the persons from whom the Senate may choose a Vice President whenever the right of choice shall have devolved upon them.

SECTION 5.   Sections 1 and 2 shall take effect on the 15th day of October following the ratification of this article.

SECTION 6.   This article shall be inoperative unless it shall have been ratified as an amendment to the Constitution by the legislatures of three-fourths of the several States within seven years from the date of its submission.

AMENDMENT XXI [1933]

SECTION 1.   The eighteenth article of amendment to the Constitution of the United States is hereby repealed.

SECTION 2. The transportation or importation into any State, Territory, or Possession of the United States for delivery or use therein of intoxicating liquors, in violation of the laws thereof, is hereby prohibited.

SECTION 3. This article shall be inoperative unless it shall have been ratified as an amendment to the Constitution by conventions in the several States, as provided in the Constitution, within seven years from the date of the submission hereof to the States by the Congress.

AMENDMENT XXII [1951]

SECTION 1. No person shall be elected to the office of the President more than twice, and no person who has held the office of President, or acted as President, for more than two years of a term to which some other person was elected President shall be elected to the office of the President more than once. But this Article shall not apply to any person holding the office of President when this Article was proposed by the Congress, and shall not prevent any person who may be holding the office of President, or acting as President, during the term within which this Article becomes operative from holding the office of President or acting as President during the remainder of such term.

SECTION 2. This article shall be inoperative unless it shall have been ratified as an amendment to the Constitution by the legislatures of three-fourths of the several States within seven years from the date of its submission to the States by the Congress.

AMENDMENT XXIII [1961]

SECTION 1. The District constituting the seat of Government of the United States shall appoint in such manner as Congress may direct:

A number of electors of President and Vice President equal to the whole number of Senators and Representatives in Congress to which the District would be entitled if it were a State, but in no event more than the least populous State; they shall be in addition to those appointed by the States, but they shall be considered, for the purposes of the election of President and Vice President, to be electors appointed by a State; and they shall meet in the District and perform such duties as provided by the twelfth article of amendment.

SECTION 2. The Congress shall have power to enforce this article by appropriate legislation.

AMENDMENT XXIV [1964]

SECTION 1. The right of citizens of the United States to vote in any primary or other election for President or Vice President, for electors for President or Vice President, or for Senator or Representative in Congress, shall not be denied or abridged by the United States or any State by reason of failure to pay any poll tax or other tax.

SECTION 2.   The Congress shall have power to enforce this article by appropriate legislation.

AMENDMENT XXV [1967]

SECTION 1.   In case of the removal of the President from office or of his death or resignation, the Vice President shall become President.

SECTION 2.   Whenever there is a vacancy in the office of the Vice President, the President shall nominate a Vice President who shall take office upon confirmation by a majority vote of both Houses of Congress.

SECTION 3.   Whenever the President transmits to the President pro tempore of the Senate and the Speaker of the House of Representatives his written declaration that he is unable to discharge the powers and duties of his office, and until he transmits to them a written declaration to the contrary, such powers and duties shall be discharged by the Vice President as Acting President.

SECTION 4.   Whenever the Vice President and a majority of either the principal officers of the executive departments or of such other body as Congress may by law provide, transmit to the President pro tempore of the Senate and the Speaker of the House of Representatives their written declaration that the President is unable to discharge the powers and duties of his office, the Vice President shall immediately assume the powers and duties of the office as Acting President.

Thereafter, when the President transmits to the President pro tempore of the Senate and the Speaker of the House of Representatives his written declaration that no inability exists, he shall resume the powers and duties of his office unless the Vice President and a majority of either the principal officers of the executive department or of such other body as Congress may by law provide, transmit within four days to the President pro tempore of the Senate and the Speaker of the House of Representatives their written declaration that the President is unable to discharge the powers and duties of his office.   Thereupon Congress shall decide the issue, assembling within forty-eight hours for that purpose if not in session.   If the Congress, within twenty-one days after receipt of the latter written declaration, or, if Congress is not in session, within twenty-one days after Congress is required to assemble, determines by two-thirds vote of both Houses that the President is unable to discharge the powers and duties of his office, the Vice President shall continue to discharge the same as Acting President; otherwise, the President shall resume the powers and duties of his office.

AMENDMENT XXVI [1971]

SECTION 1. The right of citizens of the United States, who are eighteen years of age or older, to vote shall not be denied or abridged by the United States or by any State on account of age.

SECTION 2. The Congress shall have power to enforce this article by appropriate legislation.

AMENDMENT XXVII (Proposed)

SECTION 1. Equality of rights under the law shall not be denied or abridged by the United States or by any state on account of sex.

SECTION 2. The Congress shall have the power to enforce, by appropriate legislation, the provisions of this article.

SECTION 3. This amendment shall take effect two years after the date of ratification.

NOTES AND QUESTIONS

1. What is the structural organization of the original document of 1787? Is it that basically, but not completely, each of the seven articles has its own subject area? Write out a brief description of the basic subject area for each of the seven articles.

2. Did the framers provide any one place where they set forth the entire powers of the states and their governments? The powers of the federal government? What are the likely consequences of such an apportionment of powers?

3. The framers divided the federal government into three separate and independent branches—the legislative, the excutive and the judiciary—and assigned a particular group of powers to each division. Identify the powers to be exercised by each branch of government. What reason accounts for the "separation of powers"? Distinguish the "separation of powers" from "checks and balances." Are these wise ideas? If you were creating a government, how would you do it? Why?

4. It is sometimes said that with one very important exception congress has no legislative powers except those that expressly are "herein granted" by the constitution. Explain the constitutional reasons why a person would make this statement and identify the "one very important exception." Do you agree?

5. Describe the way in which a bill would become a constitutionally valid law in the actual course of legislation. To what extent is the "separation of powers" involved? Indicate as many as you can of the president's functions in the legislative process. The judiciary's.

6. Give examples of cases that come under the jurisdiction of the federal courts. What, exactly, is the "judicial power"?

7. Article IV basically provides for constitutional relations between the states and the federal government and between the states themselves. What relations are provided? What are some of the limitations on the

"full faith and credit" clause? What procedure must Puerto Rico follow in order to become a state?

8. Article V basically provides two ways of amending the constitution. Describe each. Has each method been used in the past? Why or why not?

9. Article VI basically provides for the vindication of federal law. What methods are set forth? Are they adequate? "The powers of the national government are limited, but within the field of its power it is supreme, and this supremacy the state courts are bound to uphold." Explain the constitutional meaning and the importance of this quotation.

10. What are the limitations on the powers of the federal government that are found in the original constitution of 1787? What is the difference between a bill of attainder and an ex post facto law? What is a "writ of habeas corpus" and how does it function?

11. The first ten amendments—the Bill of Rights—were added on December 15, 1791. Analyze them carefully. Which amendments provide "substantive" protections and which provide "procedural" protections? Is the use of wire taps by police to obtain evidence a violation of any amendment; why or why not? Electronic eavesdropping?

12. Analyze the tenth amendment and the constitutional validity and significance of the statement: "The federal government is a government having only specifically delegated powers." What is the meaning of the statement: "The constitution sets up a limited government"? What are the constitutional limitations on government?

13. Evaluate the constitutional validity of this statement: "The fundamental civil and political rights of citizens stem from their State and not from their United States citizenship."

14. There are four fundamental categories relevant to the constitutional scheme of allocating power: (1) powers to be exercised exclusively by the federal government; (2) powers that may be exercised concurrently by the states and federal government; (3) powers to be exercised exclusively by the states, and (4) the denial of power and prohibiting their exercise by either federal governments, the states, or both. Identify the powers (or denials) that fall into each of the four categories and give your reasons for classifying each of them.

Part I

THE CONSTITUTIONAL FRAMEWORK

Chapter I

THE ORIGINS AND CREATION OF THE CONSTITUTION

The summer of 1787 was hot and wearying. If not for everyone, at least it was toilsome for the fifty-five men who had gathered together in Philadelphia. They did not all arrive at the same time. A few of the stragglers delayed coming until almost mid-summer; hence, their stay was a short one. But, for the others, the City of Brotherly Love offered its hospitality for a longer time, extending roughly from May 14 until September 17. The meetings were involved. The delegates debated, cajoled, provoked, threatened, and finally, somehow, they managed to compromise their differences. Their hard wrought labors have proved surprisingly successful and of crucial significance. For, just as the last jaded days of summer were beginning to pass away, these men completed their historic mission—the writing of the main body of the Constitution of the United States of America. Later, nine states had ratified it by June, 1788—the month it became effective. Today it is the world's oldest written constitution in force, having withstood that most acid of all tests—time.

The Philadelphia convention was a most historic event. It can be viewed as marking the end of one era of American history and the beginning of another. The first era includes all the events which occurred from the founding of Jamestown in 1607 to the successful conclusion of the Revolutionary War, and until the constitutional convention of 1787. Herein were witnessed the times and problems of the entire American colonial period. And within it, the colonists saw the disputes with the mother country slowly become ignited, and later, inflamed. Finally, a most unlikely spectacle came to pass—that of the colonies breaking with Britain. The Revolutionary War was fought and successfully concluded. It was followed by the arduous quest for national unity under the defective Articles of Confederation. As matters turned out, the search proved fruitless. The era came to a close with the advent of the constitutional convention. It gave birth to the body of our Constitution, and through it, the beginning of a new period of American history.

THE ARTICLES OF CONFEDERATION

The constitutional convention was a desperately needed meeting. The reason is simple: the then existing government was not working. It could not solve the problems which were facing the new nation. After the Revolutionary War, the country was governed by the Articles of Confederation to which the states had agreed on March 1, 1781. By and large, the Articles had done little more than give an official legal recognition to the already existing government which sprang up to fight, and win, the Revolutionary War. As its name implied, it was a confederacy, and, springing up from wartime needs, it was not designed to meet the peaceful demands of a new nation. At best, it was a loose association of sovereign states that jealously guarded their sovereignty.

The confederacy was weak and poorly planned to carry out necessary governing functions. No state considered itself necessarily obligated by the decisions of the confederate Congress, and most of the people who bothered to consider the matter believed that they had not surrendered any rights to the Congress. Hence, they believed the Congress possessed no direct powers over them, as individuals. Simply put, the confederacy had been conceived as a body of independent sovereign states more or less permanently, but loosely, united for purposes of joint action whenever a common meeting ground presented itself. As such, it could not cope with the daily demands made upon it by a young and vigorously growing American nation.

The Articles of Confederation had set up a single legislative chamber, known as the Continental Congress. There was no Senate nor House of Representatives. In addition, the Articles made no attempt to separate out any executive powers from those held by the Congress. The idea was that, from time to time, Congress would create the executive branch of government by appointing committees which would then perform the necessary executive duties. The influence of the British parliamentary system on the drafters of the Articles of Confederation is clearly reflected by these notions. Furthermore, the role of the confederate courts was most narrowly conceived. Ad hoc courts could be established by the Continental Congress, but only to try cases involving legal disputes between the sovereign states themselves. Also, permanent courts could hear certain other narrowly defined classes of cases which involved crimes or legal disputes relating to, or occurring upon, the high seas. All the remaining cases of national importance, consisting of a myriad of legal disputes, and which today make up much of the business of the federal courts, were to be handled and decided exclusively by the state courts.

The Continental Congress was further weakened because only the states possessed the power to vote. There was no representation of the people based directly upon the population living within the various states, but rather, representation, and the authority of the Congress, was based solely upon the state legislatures. The state legislatures elected the representatives, and they voted as a bloc representing the state. This meant that the state legislatures held final power, and not the people. The Articles had explicitly recognized the propriety of this situation when they declared that the separate states would continue to retain their "sovereignty, freedom and independence."

In addition to selecting its representative to the Continental Congress, each state legislature was required to pay the salary of its delegate. Salaries were not uniform, and the delegates were beholden, at least financially, to the state treasuries. Consequently, a delegate was most unlikely to take a national view of things, especially if such a view were contrary to his state's interest.

A two-thirds vote of Congress was necessary to pass a measure, except for amendments to the Articles, and they had to be approved unanimously. Important as these two defects were, and they would cripple any national government today, they were not, in themselves, the real reason why the confederacy failed. The prime reason lay in its lack of effective power.

The Continental Congress had been given several important powers. It was authorized to make war or to agree to a state of peace. Additionally, it could send emissaries to foreign nations and receive their ambassadors, and it could enter into treaties, coin money, establish a post office and seek to regulate Indian affairs. But that was just about all it could do. The Congress lacked three essential governmental powers: direct taxation, regulation of commerce, and power to enforce its laws. As a consequence of the lack of power to tax, the Continental Congress had to rely upon the states voluntarily to appropriate funds to meet its national budget. Needless to say, this scheme resulted in persistent financial chaos, especially when the Congress wanted to finance a measure which was unpopular with the states. The states simply refused to appropriate the money.

The lack of powers over commerce and law enforcement were equally devastating. The Continental Congress could make treaties with foreign nations on commercial matters, but it could not enforce them. The Congress had no direct power over citizens, but rather, it had to rely upon the state legislatures to carry out national policy. Congressional enactments under the Articles of Confederation were not the supreme law of the land. This meant that a state could defeat a Congressional treaty with a foreign country by retaliating openly against that foreign nation which may, because of the treaty, have discriminated against that state's trade. Or, a state could defeat a treaty by failing to prosecute one of its citizens who broke its requirements.

Under this state of affairs, the Articles of Confederation can hardly be described as setting up anything that modernly merits the label of efficient government capable of dealing with its problems. Nor had the colonists intended to set up a strong central government; their all too recent experiences with Great Britain cautioned them against this. They had instead, as the Articles themselves proclaimed, set up a "league of friendship" among sovereign states. But, it couldn't be made to work.

When it was discovered that the government was unable to perform its tasks, agitations grew up to amend the Articles of Confederation. Early in the confederate period, Alexander Hamilton had called for a "convention of all the states" in order to work out a scheme for a more perfect "general confederation." Tom Paine had done the same. New Jersey had sought an amendment which would place regulatory powers in Congress' hands, but failed. The Congress, itself, tried to establish an amendment which would give it power to levy a five per cent property tax on imports. But, Rhode Island voted against the measure. Finally, a Congressional committee recommended an amendment whereby the states would permit Congress to establish a revenue system, else the continued existence of the confederacy itself would be put in jeopardy. It appeared that agreement was about to be reached. However, New York, concerned about her business interests, scrapped the proposed amendment with her lone vote against it.

Thus, what started out as a "league of friendship" tended toward doom, largely because petty jealousies among the states resulted in a basic distrust. The general welfare was neglected. "State's rights" became all enveloping. This was particularly true whenever one state became suspicious of a proposed amendment because, conceivably, another state might secure a commercial advantage over her through it. By 1786, it appeared that the sun of hope had sunk into human frailty. The United States was at the brink of failure; some people still had visions, but others said prayers. The country was in a depression; the treasury was empty, and mobs of debt-ridden farmers refused to allow meetings of the county courts which would have entered judgments against them. And, pathetically, the Congress lacked the basic powers to meet national problems.

The leading statesmen were generally agreed that something more effective was required than the then prevailing state of affairs. The Articles of Confederation had been tried and found wanting. Charles Pinckney of South Carolina called upon the Congress to convene itself into a constitutional convention. But his motion failed. Then, as now, there were many people who had a vested interest in the status quo and preferred their own personal interests over the general welfare. However, Pinckney did salvage something—he managed to get the Congress to appoint a committee! Its task was first to meet and then to "report such amendments to the Continental Congress as it may be necessary to recommend to the several states." Ultimately, the committee reported that Congress be given powers over commerce and a limited power of taxation of imports. There was really nothing new in this report. Congress would still be more or less dependent upon the states for general appropriations. The scheme was obviously not what was needed, and Congress took no further action. Thus, stalemate grew.

But other events were taking place. Earlier, Maryland and Virginia had entered into an interstate agreement which put to rest a long standing dispute between the two states over the commercial regulation of the Potomac River. The technique used was a simple agreement between the states themselves. The Congress had been by-passed completely because it had little power over commerce. The interstate compact idea caught on. In fact, it promised to be such an attractive method of settling commercial problems between the states that a new proposal was under way. Maryland proposed that Virginia attend a general convention on commercial problems and that Delaware and Pennsylvania also be invited. The underlying thought was that the four states would now be able to compose their commercial problems into one harmonious interstate compact. Virginia thought the idea a good one, but countered Maryland's proposal with the suggestion that all the states of the union be asked to meet and consider the ground-rules for a commercial policy common to all the states. Her offer was accepted, at least by Maryland. The meeting was held at Annapolis, Maryland, in 1786, but only five states were in attendance. It appeared that this meeting, too, would be a failure because participation was so limited.

However, two of the prime movers responsible for the constitutional convention—James Madison and Alexander Hamilton—seized the opportunity and called for another convention. At their urging, even insistence, the Annapolis convention unanimously (five states) agreed to send delegates to a commercial convention to be held the following May in Philadelphia. The next step was to receive official Congressional approval, and in that way, hopefully, to achieve a full attendance of all states at the Philadelphia meeting. However, the Continental Congress was not committed to this notion, and besides, it too, was jealous lest another Annapolis convention sap its prerogative. Nevertheless, the need for a general conference on all matters of commerce could not be overlooked. After much maneuvering, the Congress finally was induced by the Virginia legislature to pass a resolution which recommended a convention, but it refused to acknowledge the proceedings of the Annapolis meeting. All the states nominated their delegates, except Rhode Island, which refused to attend and was never represented in Philadelphia at what turned out to be the historic constitutional convention.

THE CONSTITUTIONAL CONVENTION

———

Seventy-four men had been authorized as state delegates to the convention, but only fifty-five appeared. The heavy work was done by fewer still. The authority of the convention had been limited. It had not been directed to produce a new constitution for the United States of America. Far from it. Its purpose was much more modest. The convention was specifically empowered only to draft needed amendments for the Articles of Confederation. The basic idea was that, with a little tinkering here and there, the Articles could be made to work. All the delegates soon came to see the true purpose of the convention, but few of them saw it as soon, and as clearly, as did James Madison when he exclaimed from the convention floor that this meeting was "now to decide the fate of republican government." His vision proved itself, and because of his role at the convention he was later to be acclaimed as "the father of the constitution."

This was no usual convention, nor did it attract men of midget minds. Repeatedly, historians have wondered in awe how this infant nation of less than four million people huddled about the Atlantic coast could have produced men of such breadth of vision and intellect. Represented here were two university presidents, three professors and several others who had taught school at some time or other. Roughly half of them were college graduates, no mean feat for that day. One of them, William Samuel Johnson, held an Oxford degree of Doctor of Laws and was one of the most respected legal minds in America. Most of them were young with only twelve being fifty-four years or older, and six of them were under the age of thirty-one. Their average age was forty-two. More specifically, Alexander Hamilton had barely reached thirty, and James Madison, thirty-six. One member, Jonathan Dayton, was only twenty-seven.

Benjamin Franklin, at eighty-one, was the oldest representative, and he and George Washington were the most prestigious. Their talents as peacemakers proved useful. Besides including Franklin, the Pennsylvania delegation, along with the ones from Virginia, Connecticut and Massachusetts, was distinguished indeed. It included James Wilson, who, second only to Madison, was most instrumental during the convention. Additionally, there was the ever-brilliant Gouveneur Morris, a debater par excellence who made 173 speeches during the convention and actually wrote most of the finished Constitution; also present was the financier of the revolution, Robert Morris.

But several outstanding men of that day were missing from this "brain trust." John Jay, later to become the first Chief Justice of the United States Supreme Court, was the Secretary of Foreign Affairs and couldn't attend. Thomas Jefferson, who had written the Declaration of Independence eleven years earlier, at the age of thirty-six, was on a foreign mission to Europe. The same was true of John Adams and Tom Paine. Patrick Henry had "smelled a rat" in the agitations for the convention and had stayed at home. And missing too, were John Hancock and Richard Henry Lee. Had these men attended the convention, the present Constitution of the United States would have been different from the one that emerged.

The men who attended were independent minded and had differing notions about the form of the new government. Alexander Hamilton, a strong nationalist, wanted a strong presidency and a strong centralized government with unitary power over the states and the people, something akin to Great Britain's, which he believed to be almost perfect. But, his advocacy of what amounted to a constitutional monarchy placed him out of sympathy with the general sentiment of the convention, and he never came to play a role proportionate to his national stature. The newly independent America would have nothing to do with any ideas setting up anything akin to a monarchy.

Apart from Hamilton's ideas, two plans came to dominate the discussions. One of them, the plan of Virginia, provided for a strong national executive, judiciary and legislature, with the legislature entirely scaled in its representation according to population. It would have set up a firm central government resting directly on the vote of the people. Representation in the proposed national legislature would be only in accordance with population. Before debating this plan, the convention resolved itself into a committee of the whole house and registered a remarkable vote for nationalism by adopting the following resolution:

> That a *national* government ought to be established consisting of a *supreme* Legislative, Executive and Judiciary.

Thus, the convention aimed at remedying the defective Articles of Confederation, that "league of friendship" of sovereign states, by scrapping unlimited state sovereignty and the Articles entirely. But, in doing so, it had disregarded its own authority. Only Connecticut voted against this resolution. Thus, the formulation of a constitution for a new national government was set as the convention's goal.

If representation in the new legislature were based solely upon population, the smaller states, having a lesser population, came to see themselves dominated by the larger states. After all, the smaller states had enjoyed an equal status under the Articles of Confederation, and they argued that they should continue on an equal footing. Somehow, existing state equality had to be preserved. So, they submitted their own scheme, the New Jersey plan, and threatened to walk out on the convention if it were not accepted. Their scheme was little more than a re-hash of the Articles of Confederation. It did add an important provision that national law should be made the supreme law of the land. What these states wanted most was legislative representation based upon states, and not upon population.

Thus, the battle lines were drawn. Factions began to develop. Sectionalism between North-South, East-West, and prejudices between the commercial and agricultural groups and between the creditor and debtor groups also showed their seamy sides. However, surprisingly little was said about that peculiar institution of the South—slavery. But, sentiments ran deep on this issue too. July had brought the New Jersey plan, hot weather, hot tempers and heated deadlock. It also had produced a statement by Alexander Hamilton which summarized the state of affairs at Philadelphia: "It is a contest for power, not for liberty." The dogdayed pulse had taken hold, and deadlock appeared inevitable.

Compromise was needed, and fortunately, compromise came. The Connecticut delegation played an important role in it, and the so-called "Great Compromise" was reached. It revolved around representation, setting up two houses within a single legislature. The net result became the system of representation worked out for the Senate and the House of Representatives. Each state was to have an equal vote in the Senate, and this was accomplished by providing a term of six years for two senators from each state to be elected by the state legislature. (This was changed in 1913 by the adoption of the Seventeenth Amendment which provides that the Senators from each state shall be "elected by the people thereof.") It was agreed, however, that Senators must vote individually and not as a state bloc. Hence, the smaller states prevailed in part of their demands and were recognized as equals. To this extent the federal government rested upon the states, as it did under the Articles of Confederation. On the other hand, the House of Representatives was based upon population, each representative serving a two-year term; and there is the additional proviso that "all bills for raising revenue shall originate in the house of representatives . . . " Consequently, the larger states preserved much of their earlier position, and, at least to this extent, a national government was set up which rested its power directly upon the people.

This compromise was a needed agreement at the time, but like all compromises something had to be sacrificed. In this instance, it was a clear location of sovereignty. The locus of power was muddled. And today the United States has a form of government with dual sovereignty, and has two governments which are both supreme, within a single country. The national government is sovereign; yet, the states too are partially sovereign, within their respective spheres. The latter point is clear because, among others, there is the concession to state equality within the Senate. It has affirmed the principle of limited state sovereignty. In addition, as later set forth in the Ninth and Tenth Amendments to the Constitution, the powers not delegated to the Federal government nor reserved to the states are retained by the people. Thus, a legitimate claim of final sovereignty also can be said to rest with the people. The persistent problem which ever presents itself is what, exactly, should be the proper spheres enclosing the powers reserved to the people and what should be the proper spheres marking off the boundaries of national power? Federalism, under our constitution, does not provide a blueprint solution; instead, it provides guidelines for decision. It fails to spell out its one and only "true" meaning, once and for all time. This has been a source of both strengths and weaknesses. Hence, the Philadelphia convention scrapped a confederation and gave birth to a hybrid system of separation of powers and checks and balances—a federal system with fundamental rights and powers retained by the people; and federalism, without a clearcut delineation of powers between the people, state and federal government, has come to be a persistent feature of America's constitutional way of life.

The constitution is unique in other respects. It is the expression of an Eighteenth century ideal which placed its faith in man's enlightenment and in the final triumph of reason. This was the age of a grand political philosophy with enduring features: the compact theory of government, constitutional supremacy and limited legislative power, the separation of powers, checks and balances, and the doctrine of natural rights. All these notions found their way, in one manner or another, into the new federal constitution which sought to create a government of specially delegated powers—all other powers remaining either to the people or the state. This was the theoretical context; yet, the mood was practical and one of experience too.

The constitutional convention specifically addressed itself to most of the problems which had bedeviled the government under the Articles of Confederation. It decided to give the new Congress the power to tax and disburse funds for the general welfare. Where the Articles had failed to give power over commerce to the Congress, the new document was specifically designed to provide that:

> The congress shall have power: .   .   .   To regulate commerce with foreign nations, and among the several States, and with the Indian tribes. (Art. I, § 8, cl. 3)

And, very importantly, the document went on to provide a "necessary and proper" clause, the reach of which is not yet fully known:

> The congress shall have power: .   .   .   To make all laws which shall be necessary and proper for carrying into execution   .   .   .   powers vested by this Constitution in the government of the United States. (Art. I, § 8, cl. 17)

Where the Articles had narrowly restricted the federal courts, the Constitution now provided that "The judicial power of the United States shall be vested in one supreme court, and in such inferior courts as the Congress may, from time to time, ordain and establish." On the scope of the federal judicial power, the Constitution specifically said that:

> The judicial power shall extend to all cases in law and equity arising under this constitution, the laws of the United States,

and treaties made, or which shall be made, under their authority; to all cases affecting ambassadors, other public ministers, and consuls; to all cases of admiralty and maritime jurisdiction; to controversies to which the United States shall be a party; to controversies between two or more States, between a State and citizens of another State; between citizens of different States, between citizens of the same State claiming lands under grants of different States, and between a State, or the citizens thereof, and foreign states, citizens or subjects. (Art. III, § 2, cl. 1)

Under the Articles of Confederation, the national government had to rely upon the states to enforce national law. The thought then was that the states were fully independent sovereigns in their own rights. But, should they fail to enforce national law, there was no way in which national policy could be achieved because the Continental Congress had not been given power to coerce compliance from the sovereign states, nor to carry out its laws directly. The new document recognized and rectified this state of affairs by giving many powers of direct enforcement to Congress, and then it specifically provided a supremacy clause:

This constitution, and the laws of the United States which shall be made in pursuance thereof, and all treaties made, or which shall be made, under the authority of the United States shall be the supreme law of the land; and the judges in every State shall be bound thereby, anything in the constitution or laws of any State to the contrary notwithstanding. (Art. VI, cl. 2.)

Thus, the new constitution was adumbrated, and it slowly came into clear being. After more debate, it became a finished product. The convention decided that the document should be presented to the states for ratification, rather than to the Continental Congress. Its role was only that of sending the document to the States. The ratification of nine states was deemed necessary to establish the document as controlling the signing states. This procedure was not the one authorized for amending the provisions of the Articles of Confederation which had required unanimity. The proposed scheme was illegal, but effective.

Finally, in September, a vast majority of the remaining delegates voted to approve the final draft. The votes of approval included those from delegates who were strong nationalists and also those from delegates who were moderately, or more-so, in favor of states' rights. The delegates who represented the extreme states' rights position or those, like Hamilton, who espoused an extremely strong central government, had already given up in disgust, had left the convention and had gone home. Absenteeism had taken a heavy toll. Nevertheless, of the forty-two representatives who remained until the convention's end, thirty-nine delegates approved the document by signing the new constitution under the deceiving words: "Done in Convention by the Unanimous Consent of the states present . . . " Their signatures were affixed on September 17, 1787, and the convention adjourned. The delegates returned home to await the debates over ratification.

RATIFICATION

Most of the people living in the upland Alleghenies, and farther inland than fifty miles from the Atlantic coast, generally were anti-federalists and opposed to the proposed constitution. They were pioneers and farmers, and could not agree to the need for stronger national government. Notions of agrarianism dominated their minds as they faced the new frontier. They were not perplexed by problems of an expanding commerce and were openly hostile to the land speculators who needed a stable credit policy for their purposes. The pioneer farmers found that their monetary interest lay in favor of inflation because it helped to relieve them of their debts. Their interests were ones which a strong federal government would oppose.

The other people who lived within fifty miles of the sea coast primarily were federalists. These influential groups feared the growing power of the agrarian and unpropertied classes. By and large, these people were either influential men of wealth or influenced by them—the merchants, the land speculators, and the "city" dwellers. They wanted national protection for commerce and investment in western lands, and a lifting of trade barriers, especially interstate tariffs. They distrusted the unwashed masses and doubted the wisdom of even a limited democracy. One state, New York, was somewhat of an exception to the general pattern. Its government taxed interstate commerce and levied no land taxes for its support. Since the proposed constitution would disallow states the power to levy these tariffs, New York would have to turn to land taxes, which the powerful landed aristocracy vigorously opposed; hence, New York tended toward strong opposition of the new constitution.

The dream of a new constitution for America was not allowed to dictate its own rhythm. In less than two weeks after the end of the constitutional convention, the new document was submitted for ratification to the states by the Congress. Rhode Island refused to participate, and remained aloof. The remaining debates over ratification lasted ten months and were to drag the new document fully into the nakedness of light and expose its every provision.

The writings of this period are historic to the annals of government and are best exemplified by THE FEDERALIST PAPERS published by their authors under the pseudonym, Publius. They were actually written by John Jay (about five papers), James Madison

(about thirty), and Alexander Hamilton (about fifty). THE FED-
ERALIST PAPERS, produced during the ten-month struggle for
ratification, is a work of restrained partisanship, being doubly designed to win over the doubters and to defend the doctrine of a strong
federal government. The papers are clearly nationalistic in character and, in no small part, laid the foundations for future constitutional interpretation and development. They remain relevant to today's constitutional problems.

Richard Henry Lee of Virginia published THE LETTERS FROM
THE FEDERAL FARMER in 1787. They represented the strongest
challenges to the new constitution, scrutinizing its every detail from
an anti-federalist point of view. The work of Lee, THE FEDERA-
LIST PAPERS, and the debates over ratification have shown that the
new constitution was a serious matter and was not regarded as a mere
clotted parchment of meaningless blots and squiggles. Deeply vested
interests and grand principles were at stake. The Federalists favored
adoption and the Anti-federalists opposed. The controversies between
them were bitter, but the debates were thorough, dispelling all doubts
that the conventioneers might have tried to cast a dark-vowelled
spell over the country.

Striking first in Pennsylvania, the federalists pushed through an
election of a state convention before the anti-federalists could get
organized. Pennsylvania ratified the new constitution on December
18, 1787. Two days after the Congress had submitted the document
for ratification, the federalists of Pennsylvania moved for a state
convention which, hopefully, would ratify. The disorganized anti-
federalists resisted by absenting themselves from the legislative hall,
thereby preventing a quorum; hence, the delegation to consider the
constitution could not be chosen. But, the anti-federalists were unsuccessful:

> The sergeant-at-arms was sent to summon the delin-
> quents but they defied him, and so it was necessary to ad-
> journ until next morning .   .   .   Soon after breakfast next
> morning, two of them were visited by a crowd of men who
> broke into their lodgings and dragged them off to the State
> House, where they were forcibly held down in their seats,
> growling and muttering curses. This made a quorum, and
> the State Convention was immediately appointed .   .   .
> (John Fiske, The Critical Period of American History, p.
> 311. Reprinted by permission of the Houghton Mifflin Com-
> pany.)

Had Pennsylvania defeated the constitution, the defeat probably
would have killed it. But, irony runs deep, for had Pennsylvania followed the requirements of the proposed constitution and protected
the freedom of its two anti-federalist citizens, the United States might

never have come into being, and we would be without our constitution which seeks to promote human liberty!

Several of the smaller states soon followed suit, and ratified quickly. Massachusetts was the scene of the first real fight.

Cutting across factional lines was one repeated objection to the new constitution—it had no Bill of Rights. Thus, the rights of individual Americans were not safeguarded from depredations by the new government. The state constitutions had express provisions guaranteeing to each person certain rights, thereby insuring the people a moderate measure of security from tyrannical state action. But, the federal constitution contained no Bill of Rights to restrict the government; yet, it was designed to set up a strong government having a potential for tyranny. It was widely believed that an absence of a Bill of Rights would pave the way for steady, seeping encroachments upon the fundamental liberties of a free people.

The absence of a Bill of Rights proved to be a point of bargain and compromise. To meet this, and other objections, the federalists in Massachusetts drafted a Bill of Rights which was designed to accompany ratification of the constitution and which Massachusetts then could offer to other states. In addition, the federalists also agreed to support John Hancock's bid for governor if he would throw in with them. These two measures won over the doubters, and the Massachusetts convention ratified the constitution by the narrow margin of nineteen votes out of a total 355 cast. Other states followed, and by May of 1788, eight of the necessary nine states had ratified. But, the important states of New York and Virginia had not.

Virginia was the place of a pitched battle where anti-federalists met the federalists head-on, and on equal terms. Against the constitution were Patrick Henry, George Mason, James Monroe and Richard Henry Lee—formidable opposition. Favorable to it were James Madison, John Marshall, Edmund Pendleton and George Wythe. Patrick Henry's eloquent oratory blazed hot when he struck against the constitution as being undemocratic—it had no Bill of Rights—and he likened the presidency to an "American throne."

George Mason, another leader of the opposition had argued for a Bill of Rights at the constitutional convention, and he refused to sign the document without one. He had this to say:

> There is no declaration of rights: and the laws of the general government being paramount to the laws and constitutions of the several states, the declaration of rights, in the separate states, are no security . . . By requiring only a majority to make all commercial and navigation laws, the five southern states (whose produce and circumstances are totally different from those of the eight northern and eastern states) will be ruined: for such rigid and premature regulations may be made, as will enable the merchants

of the northern and eastern states not only to demand an exorbitant freight, but to monopolize the purchase of commodities, at their own price, for many years, to the great injury of the landed interest, and the impoverishment of the people . . .   There is no declaration of any kind for preserving the liberty of the press, the trial by jury in civil cases, nor against the danger of standing armies in time of peace . . .   This government will commence in a moderate aristocracy; it is at present impossible to foresee whether it will, in its operation, produce a monarchy, or a corrupt oppressive aristocracy; it will most probably vibrate some years between the two, and then terminate in one or the other.   (Pamphlets on the Constitution of the United States (P. L. Ford ed.) 1898, pp. 327–332).

Madison and Marshall countered. Following Massachusetts' example, they offered a Bill of Rights, and finally, on June 25, 1788, the Virginia federalists won out by the squeaky margin of ten votes, 89 to 79. Virginia made the tenth state to ratify, having been preceded a few days earlier by New Hampshire. A new nation had been born.

But New York had not yet ratified, and without that state, a huge gap of territory in the middle of the country would divide the new nation into incompleteness. The landed aristocracy was determined to resist, and the New York convention dragged on month after month. The basic line of division was New York City and the rest of the seaboard versus the interior. The promise of conciliatory amendments was not effective. Finally, Alexander Hamilton threatened to separate the state into two parts, detaching New York City and joining the Union. The plan would leave upstate New York to fend for itself without access to a seacoast. When it appeared that this threat was a genuine one, the New York convention ratified the constitution, albeit by the narrow margin of only three votes!

Only North Carolina and Rhode Island remained. North Carolina ratified in November of 1789, after the new federal government already had been set up and working. Rhode Island earlier had submitted the constitution to a vote of the people in their town meetings, where it was overwhelmingly defeated. But, later, on May 29, 1790, a new state assembly managed to ratify the constitution. Yet, it passed muster only by the margin of 34 to 32. This final action meant that all the states had ratified the new constitution.

NOT ONE BUT MANY CONSTITUTIONS

The entire document, as we know our constitution today, was not the work of the founding fathers at Philadelphia. Nor is it a single, unified document. There are at least two additional "constitutions," equally important in their own ways and for their own purposes. At Philadelphia, the founding fathers put together a formula for governing this new nation, at least in its basic and initial outlines. This "constitution" consists, in large part, of giving powers to the national government. Following on the heels of ratification, came the historic ten amendments known as the Bill of Rights. They had been the important vehicle of compromise during ratification debates. Their fundamental design is different. The Bill of Rights does not grant powers to government, but places limitations upon governmental powers in favor of individual rights and liberties. It can be looked upon as a separate document. Later, after the Civil War, came other historic amendments (Thirteenth, Fourteenth and Fifteenth). Unlike the Bill of Rights which limited federal powers, the Civil War Amendments primarily were designed to limit state powers and to increase federal powers to insure that the states would abide by the limitations. The Civil War Amendments enable the federal government to control the states on certain specified matters.

Viewing the constitution as a whole, it easily can be seen that some provisions of the constitution, the amendments, have been drafted by men who were not at the original constitutional convention, men who had aims different from those of the founding fathers, and who created amendments that are sometimes not consistent with each other or with the basic document itself. Yet, popular misconception has it that the current document is one single constitution produced at Philadelphia. Nothing is farther from the truth. From the viewpoint of constitutional origins, constitutional purposes, and the identity of the men who participated in its creation, it is useful to think of the constitution as a growing organic document having at least three separate, and sometimes inconsistent, sections. First of all, there is the basic document of 1787; then the Bill of Rights of 1791, and later, the Civil War Amendments of the late 1860's.

THE ORIGINAL BILL OF RIGHTS

It might seem odd that the initial version of the Constitution of the United States, drafted at Philadelphia, failed to include a Bill of Rights. Most of the state constitutions of that day included such provisions. Virginia adopted her Declaration of Rights on June 12, 1776 on the urgings of Thomas Jefferson, George Mason and James Madison; and Pennsylvania, on August 16, 1776, adopted provisions which were largely copied from the Declaration of Independence. John Adams was responsible for a notable Bill of Rights approved in 1780 by Massachusetts. All of these measures were enacted before the constitutional convention of 1787, and some of the men responsible for them, e. g., James Madison, attended the constitutional convention. The Bills of Rights were natural declarations for a people who so recently had freed themselves from the yoke of colonization. These people were interested in liberty and good government. As Jefferson said in a letter to Thomas Nelson on May 16, 1776, good government was the "whole object" of the Revolution, "for should a bad government be instituted for us in the future, it had been as well to have accepted at first the bad one offered to us from beyond the water without the risk and expense of contest."

We may never come to understand exactly what was intended to be encompassed within the words "good government," but one should be familiar with the political philosophy of the 18th century and its natural law doctrines. The ideas lying behind the Declaration of Independence and the Bill of Rights go back to a time well before the founding of the constitution. Aristotle, Rousseau and John Locke, and many others, all contributed in one way or another to the doctrine of natural rights. The American Bill of Rights truly has its origins deep in the history of mankind and its roots are lost in the antiquity and mists of time.

Today, however, the mind of America has a pragmatic bent and avidly avoids natural law thinking. The doctrine of natural rights has had so much scorn and cynical acid heaped upon it by our politicians and professors that the educated American public seems to have lost its perspective. We seem to have forgotten the great amount of truth in it, and also the tremendous role the doctrine played in shaping our constitutional heritage and our popular political theory. All squeezings from such aged lemons need not necessarily be sour.

The political theory of the revolutionary period and its heavy emphasis upon a person's natural rights were so much a part of the thinkers of that day that the Declaration of Independence refers to these rights as "self-evident." That document is still a rallying cry to the oppressed peoples of the world, and its success illustrates, as no other document has, the fundamental principles of a natural rights philosophy. The first notion imbedded in the political philosophy of the revolutionary era was that all men are by nature endowed with certain unalienable rights, the chief of these being the right to a fulfilling life itself. This philosophy posited that there existed a natural state of affairs which came into being between man and man before any civil government had been instituted. This philosophy suggested that men, as men, legitimately hold a body of natural rights, including the rights to "life, liberty and the pursuit of happiness." These pre-existing rights depend upon no government, nor upon any parchment or seal, but are self-evident and inherent in man himself, flowing from, as the Declaration stated, "the laws of nature and of nature's God."

In addition to locating a body of unalienable natural rights, this political philosophy held that the exercise of power by government over men could be legitimate only if that power derived from the consent of the men who were governed. The slogan of "no taxation without representation" is a striking example of the consent theory of government which epitomized men united in compact to carry out their common will. Only then, on their consent given through their representatives, could their taxation be justified. Since the colonists had no representation in Great Britain, their taxation had been unjustified. John Adams had declared that "where annual elections end, there tyranny begins."

A third, and related idea, concerns the proper end of government. Having been created by compact, government must seek for its object the achievement of general human development and well being within conditions of individual freedom. Otherwise, why should any government be instituted? The preamble to the Constitution clearly reflects these notions:

> We, the People of the United States, in Order to form a more perfect Union, establish Justice, insure domestic Tranquility, provide for the common defense, promote the general Welfare, and secure the Blessings of Liberty, to ourselves and our Posterity, do ordain and establish this Constitution for the United States of America.

Should a government clearly and continuously fail to serve the ends for which it was set up then that government has breached the compact which created it, and it has forfeited all rights to the loyalty of its citizens. Its authority is illegitimate. In such an extreme case, the people have a legitimate right to revolution, and the Declaration of Independence clearly formulated it by stating that:

> . . . . whenever any Form of Government becomes destructive of these ends, it is the Right of the People to alter or to abolish it, and to institute new Government, laying its foundation on such principles and organizing its powers in such form, as to them shall seem most likely to effect their Safety and Happiness.

In fact, "when a long train of abuses and usurpations, pursuing invariably the same object evinces a design to reduce them under absolute despotism, it is their right, it is their *duty*, to throw off such government." The right of revolution is deeply imbedded in the American fabric. Some writers have argued that the Second Amendment, providing that " . . . the right of the people to keep and bear arms, shall not be infringed," may represent a constitutional embodiment of this right of revolution.

The bundles of natural rights were considered the "unalienable possessions of every human being." The key to this philosophy lies in a deep and abiding respect for the equal rights of conscience, which reside, ultimately, in each human being. The highest value proclaimed is that of the equal dignity of the ordinary person as a person. The mood of that day was markedly against monarchy with its hierarchical structure. Instead, the mood emphasized human equality. Later, these ideas were to challenge slavery. Tom Paine wrote in his book COMMON SENSE, "Of more worth is one honest man to society . . . than all the crowned ruffians that ever lived." The Natural Rights philosophy turned and focused its attention onto the ordinary individual and his opportunities for self-realization as they might be played out within a cooperating society. Freedom is, of course, indivisible. The political philosophy of this age can be captured and aptly expressed by the Declaration in one of its most famous passages:

> We hold these truths to be self-evident, that all men are created equal, that they are endowed by their creator with certain unalienable Rights, that among these are Life, Liberty and the pursuit of Happiness. That to secure these rights, Governments are instituted among Men, deriving their just powers from the consent of the governed.

These ideas which were expressed so eloquently by the Declaration quite naturally came to translate themselves into Bills of Rights of Constitutions for many nations and organizations. Their most recent expression is found, in part, in the Declaration of Human Rights attached to the Charter of the United Nations. Individual freedom of religion, speech, press and association necessarily disallow governmental power to abridge these areas, and are legal reflections of the more basic notions. They express a respect for the individual and, further, they provide the basic groundrules for a practicing democracy. Could the people ever be paramount, and remain supreme without having the rights freely to associate and discuss the proper course of government, and its merits and demerits? But, the men who gathered at the constitutional convention did not see fit to include protection for these fundamental guarantees. In fact, several specific measures were presented to the convention, and they were defeated. Why?

The main reasons given for opposing federal Bills of Rights were simple ones. The federal government was created only as a government of specifically delegated powers. Since the federal constitution had granted the federal government no power over religion, press or speech, then, so the argument went, there was really no need for a Bill of Rights prohibiting these powers to the federal government. There could be no need to protect against a power which had not been delegated and could not be exercised. Actually, another argument continued, the inclusion of such provisions might prove to be self-defeating. If the founding fathers had specified exceptions and prohibitions on the exercise of powers not granted to the federal government, then this approach might allow someone to argue in the future that some general powers over these areas had actually been given to the federal government. That is, someone might imply their general existence from such exceptions and prohibitions. Else, why make the exceptions? Of course, the arguments overlooked the broad sweep of the "necessary and proper" clause of Article 1, section 8.

Alexander Hamilton stated one position with his characteristic clarity and vigor in *Federalist Paper* number eighty-four:

> For why declare that things shall not be done which there is no power to do? Why, for instance, should it be said that the liberty of the press shall not be restrained, when no power is given by which restrictions may be imposed? . . This may serve as a specimen of the numerous handles which would be given to the doctrine of constructive power, by an injudicious zeal for bills of rights.

However, the state ratifying conventions were not persuaded. They wanted a Bill of Rights. The demand became overwhelming, and the proponents of the new constitution, most of whom had never really been hostile to a Bill of Rights, acceded to the demands of the state legislatures. Collectively, the state assemblies during the ratification of the constitution proposed a total of twenty-two amendments. It was agreed that a Bill of Rights must be drafted during the first session of the new Congress and then sent immediately to the states for ratification as amendments to the Constitution of the United States.

When that Congress convened James Madison took the initiative, proposing certain constitutional amendments. He distilled them from the proposals submitted earlier by the states. Madison was morally committed to this course because he believed it to be the right one, but also, he undertook it in order to fulfill campaign promises. His election to Congress turned substantially on the fact that he had declared himself to be in favor of a federal Bill of Rights. Nevertheless, Madison satisfied scruples which must have been in addition to his own when he undertook the arduous and frequently thankless task of pushing the measures through the Congressional treadmill over the inertia and opposition of others. He proposed nine amendments, embodying nineteen substantive items. Madison clearly saw the real value of a Bill of Rights, and accurately predicted the critical role of the courts when they actually came to decide cases under these provisions. He said:

> If they are incorporated into the Constitution, independent tribunals of justice will consider themselves in a peculiar manner the guardians of those rights; they will be an impenetrable bulwark against every assumption of power in the Legislative or Executive; they will be naturally led to resist every encroachment upon rights expressly stipulated for in the Constitution by the declaration of rights. (Irving Brant, The Madison Heritage, 35 N.Y.U.L.Rev. 882, 889–900)

A federal judiciary must be committed to constitutional freedom, and it must also be independent if the constitution is to be realized. This commitment plus the independence of intelligent judges are absolutely necessary to achieve justice for individuals, insuring that they will be treated fairly and impartially in accordance with the requirements of our constitution. Without these conditions, judges can be subjected to pressures, sometimes overwhelming pressures, and the individual can be dealt with according to the whims of powerful politicians or of mobs, making a mockery of our ideal of equal treatment of all persons, high or low, under constitutional rules that apply to all who are similarly situated.

After long debates in committee and several rewritings of the amendments by both the House and Senate, twelve articles finally emerged from the Congress. They were sent by Thomas Jefferson, then Secretary of State, to the various state legislatures for ratification. Three-fourths of the thirteen states had to ratify in order to amend the new constitution. Two of the proposed twelve amendments failed and were not ratified. They dealt with the number and compensation of representatives in the House. The remaining ten amendments were ratified and became the American Bill of Rights. They became effective on December 15, 1791, when Virginia's ratification incorporated them into "the supreme law of the land." Belatedly, in 1939, Massachusetts, Connecticut and Georgia ratified the document, making ratification unanimous by the original thirteen states.

The general scheme of the Bill of Rights is one of prohibition, and the amendments themselves can be looked upon as being "substantive" or "procedural." The Bill of Rights enumerates a series of denials of powers to government by the substantive amendments, or prescribes certain procedures that must be followed, thereby denying others. These are considered some of the rights which have been retained by the people. They are secured to the people by the Constitution, but not granted by it because these rights are the natural rights of all men. The first of the ten amendments is a good example. Its structure illustrates the denial-of-power aspect, stating that:

> Congress shall make *no* law respecting the establishment of religion, or prohibiting the free exercise thereof; or abridging the freedom of speech, or of the press, or the right of the people peaceably to assemble, and to petition the Government for a redress of grievances.

By saying the Congress "shall pass *NO* law . . ." the first amendment denies all power to the government to abridge the subjects named, i. e., religion, speech, press and assembly. This amendment is not a qualified denial, but rather, its wording is a flat prohibition. The word used is "No." The amendment is substantive not procedural. The people have retained undeniable and unqualified rights to free speech, press and religion. But the amendment treats religion a bit differently from the remainder. The government is allowed to pass laws that promote and aid people to exercise their rights of free expression, e. g., speech, press, assembly, but not religion. When dealing with religion the government is flatly prohibited from establishing or abridging religion. It may not promote or aid religion, as it can free speech, press and assembly; that is, freedom of expression.

The United States Supreme Court, through Mr. Justice Jackson, has recognized this fundamental structure of a Bill of Rights and its denials of power. In 1943 in a famous case, Mr. Justice Jackson's Opinion of the Court said that:

> The very purpose of a Bill of Rights was to withdraw certain subjects from the vicissitudes of political controversy, to place them beyond the reach of majorities and officials and to establish them as legal principles to be applied by the courts. One's right to life, liberty, and property, to free speech, freedom of worship and assembly, and other fundamental rights may not be submitted to vote; they depend on the outcome of no election.

In short, these rights are personal; they are the fundamental rights of a free people held individually by them under the Bill of Rights. They are substantive rights.

The sixth amendment is a good example of a procedural amendment found in the Bill of Rights. Its aim is fairness, and this amendment requires that certain procedures must be followed in criminal cases, which, of course, means that other procedures cannot be used.

SIXTH AMENDMENT

> In all criminal prosecutions, the accused shall enjoy the right to a speedy and public trial, by an impartial jury of the State and district wherein the crime shall have been committed, which district shall have been previously ascertained by law, and to be informed of the nature and cause of the accusation; to be confronted with the witnesses against him; to have compulsory process for obtaining witnesses in his favor, and to have the Assistance of Counsel for his defence.

* * *

The general scheme of denying power to government within certain areas, or requiring certain fair procedures, is markedly in contrast with the structure of the main body of the constitution. With very few, but important, exceptions, the main body of the document consists of granting, not denying, powers to the government. The founding fathers were trying to create a new government, and they were allocating governmental powers. An instance in point is Article I, section 8, delegating power to Congress. One famous clause in this section indicates that Congress shall have power to regulate commerce with foreign nations and among the several states. Thus, there are at least two constitutional schemes—one granting power and the other denying power. Sometimes they are opposed to each other and, hence, come into conflict.

Suppose, for example, that Congress desires to establish a policy aimed at promoting the free flow of commerce. It has the constitutional power to do this. Congress might determine that "economic" strikes are within the usual tradition of American industrial development, and allow them. But, it might also decide that "political" strikes are alien to America's industrial way of life. That is, Congress might not attempt to hinder or promote those strikes which are designed to produce higher wages, better hours or improving the circumstance of work. But rather, strikes would be termed "political" only when their objectives were aimed at changing the form of government, or to serve ultimate revolutionary goals of their leaders by force. In particular, Congress might be concerned lest either corporations or labor unions come under the domination of communist, or other leaders who, by subterfuge, might subordinate legitimate economic ends to political ones and bring about obstructive lockouts, strikes, or work stoppages in favor of a foreign government. Seeking to implement its policy of free commerce for "economic" and not "political" ends, Congress might determine that each leader of industry, whether he be with corporate management or a union, must execute an affidavit stating: (1) that he is not now nor ever has been a member of the communist party or any other group or organization devoted to political change by force or violence, and (2) that he believes in the Constitution of the United States of America and will bear true faith to it, and (3) that his conscience forbids a belief in political strikes or overthrow of government by revolution, force or violence. If any person should fail to sign the statement, then Congress proclaims that the channels and benefits of interstate commerce would be closed to him and to their companies or unions, a devastating sanction.

Suppose, on the other hand, that two people, a corporate executive and a labor union leader of a teacher's union, are equally devout members of one of the Christian faiths. They refuse to execute the affidavit. It is their religious conviction that their belief is in God alone, and it is only to God that they will bear "true faith." They argue that the First Amendment has disallowed government all power over men's consciences, and also disallowed government power to compel anyone to declare a "belief." Beliefs are constitutionally protected and are an individual matter between each person and his God. They are not subject to governmental power. "Congress shall pass NO law . . . " Consequently, they argue that this law of Congress is really beyond its power to legislate and is, therefore, unconstitutional, and that, therefore, they need not execute the affidavit.

On the other hand, the government, after calling attention to that section of the constitution giving Congress power over commerce, advances the following argument: that the law is a reasonable exercise of Congressional power over commerce, designed to promote and protect commerce, and is, therefore, within Congressional power; hence, it is constitutional. Thus, the "commerce clause" comes into conflict with the First Amendment. Who is correct? Is the statute really constitutional? How can this problem be solved? A separate body— a court of law—is needed to adjudicate the issue, and without decision, we can only have stalemate, standoff and friction.

This example is a good illustration of the type of case which frequently confronts the nine Justices of the United States Supreme Court. Often, they are extremely important cases, calling for a deep insight and wisdom accompanied with a full understanding of our constitutional heritage and its potential future. These cases involve clashing constitutional provisions. But also, they are examples that the constitution is not fully harmonious within the four corners of the document. Nor should we expect it to be. It was drafted at different times by different men who sought different, and frequently conflicting, goals. There is not simply one constitution; there are several. And, it is the task of the United States Supreme Court to bring Constitutional order out of conflict.

THE CIVIL WAR AMENDMENTS

So far, two major divisions of the constitution have been considered—the original document of the founding fathers and the Bill of Rights. But there is at least one more major section of the constitution that continually commands attention, and remains for consideration. It consists of the Thirteenth, Fourteenth and Fifteenth Amendments which were added after the Civil War; hence, they carry as their name, the Civil War Amendments. These amendments are sometimes said to give rise to "civil rights"; whereas the Bill of Rights give rise to "civil liberties."

The issue of slavery ignited the Civil War, and it has repercussions today, long after the victorious North preserved the Union. Much of the modern impact of that war is felt through constitutional law. The Civil War Amendments have given the federal government certain powers over the states and prohibited others to them. For example, the Fourteenth Amendment's first section reads " . . . nor shall any state deprive any person of life, liberty or property, without due process of law; nor deny to any person within its jurisdiction the equal protection of the laws." The fifth section then provides a new power that: "The Congress shall have power to enforce, by appropriate legislation, the provisions of this article." Thus, the federal system is vitiated, at least in part, and Congress is given power to control the states in certain areas.

The Fourteenth Amendment is both a shield and a sword. By its own force it prohibits states from doing certain things, e. g., denying to any person within its borders the equal protection of its laws. The words are that: " . . . no *state* shall . . . ". Thus, the provision does not apply to individuals. Hence, a state may not discriminate in its laws or their applications, but a private person may. That is, an individual, when acting privately, whether he be a property owner, a businessman or an ordinary citizen, is free to practice whatever discriminations he might choose, and the federal constitution is no barrier. He is constitutionally free to discriminate privately, however benightedly, on the basis of race, creed or color, and can do so unless some law of Congress or of his state prohibits the discrimination. By its own force, the Fourteenth Amendment does not apply to him because it refers only to the *state*, which includes state officials, and therefore, requires some kind of "state action" before it can come into play. In this sense, then, the Fourteenth Amendment can be used as a shield; it shields the citizen from discriminatory practices by the state or its officials. The sweep is complete and runs throughout the Amendment.

On the other hand, the Civil War Amendments are more than a shield; they are also a sword. For example, Congress has been given the power to enforce the provisions of the Fourteenth Amendment. Even though that power might appear restricted to its subject matter which, again, must be the state and not a person, the Congress can pass a law applying to either a state or to an individual. For example, Congress might pass a law providing that any official of any state who has wilfully subjected any inhabitant of that state to the unequal protection of its laws or to the deprivation of any of his constitutional rights would be guilty of a federal crime. This law would tend to benefit individuals, as such. But, it should be noted that the object of congressional power is the state; in this instance, an official of the state, such as members of school boards. The individual benefit is a by-product. In this sense then, the Fourteenth Amendment can be used as a sword whereby Congress might pass laws insuring an individual's constitutional rights from being impinged upon by states or state officials.

Congress, under the Fourteenth Amendment, can also pass laws that apply directly to private persons acting in their private capacities, so long as those laws seek to achieve the goals of the amendment. For example, a major purpose of the Fourteenth Amendment was to protect the civil rights of all persons, especially Blacks, to own, buy, sell and rent all kinds of property free from racial discrimination. Thus, it is within the power of Congress to pass, as it has, a law making it illegal in almost all circumstances for a private person to discriminate against anyone on grounds of race when selling or renting a house or apartment. In this situation Congress has merely insured everyone's right to equal treatment and equal protection of the laws which is set forth in the Fourteenth Amendment, but Congress is doing so by a law that applied directly to the individual.

Prior to the Civil War Amendments, there were very few constitutional restraints on the actions of the states. As the history of slavery attests, the constitution had not undertaken to put beyond the grasp of the states the rights and liberties of all men which are commonly called "civil" and which the Declaration of Independence labelled "self-evident." Under slavery, Black men and women, and some Indians, were bought and sold as though they were garments or automobiles or household goods. Families were destroyed. People were considered "things." For example, the following advertisement was typical. It appeared in the New Orleans Bee, a newspaper of the times:

> "NEGROES FOR SALE—A negro woman, 24 years of age, and her two children, one eight and the other three years old. Said negroes will be sold *separately* or together, *as desired*. The woman is a good seamstress. She will be sold low for cash, or *exchanged for groceries*. For terms, apply to Matthew Bliss & Co." (Emphasis supplied.) (Wm. Goodell, THE AMERICAN SLAVE CODE, p. 54–55, N.Y. 1853, quoted in F. Tannenbaum "The Negro in the Americas" from SLAVE AND CITIZEN, Copyright © 1946 by Alfred A. Knopf, Inc.)

The laws of the southern states treated Blacks and some Indian slaves as objects of property, and these state laws were deemed constitutional. But then came the Civil War. And afterwards came the Civil War Amendments; no state could deny any of its inhabitants the equal protection of its laws.

The discussion of these amendments necessarily has been brief, but they will be the subjects of further explorations in later chapters. Suffice it here to say that these amendments, like those other portions of the constitution already discussed, have created their share of difficult constitutional problems. They too, have been products of yet another and different age having additional goals to achieve. They too, come into conflict with other sections of the constitution.

Again, what might appear as a clear constitutional provision can create difficult problems which must be resolved. The constitution itself must have a final arbiter. That body is, of course, the Supreme Court of the United States. Its task is crucial to our nation.

Chapter II

THE SUPREME COURT AND THE AMERICAN
LEGAL SYSTEMS

BACKGROUND

The legal systems of the United States baffle most foreign visitors. And not a few American citizens stand in awe of them. There is such a multiplicity of courts, laws and jurisdictions that even the perceptive observer frequently becomes lost in the legal maze. There are the legal systems, and subsystems, of the Fifty States. Then, of course, there are the Federal Court jurisdictions, the Federal administrative agencies and also the Military. Legal terminology appears impenetrable, and the law books foreboding. But, to some, what appears even more bewildering is the profuse expansion of American law, intruding during the last 100 years into almost every facet of everyday life. This has become particularly true with the rise of modern administrative agencies, some would say bureaucracies, which make their appearances at all levels: federal, state, and local.

The task of harnessing the fifty state-court systems and the federal court system, plus all the administrative agencies, state and federal, into a unified whole is difficult indeed. Yet, somehow, the American legal systems do manage to resolve their manifold complexities and to preserve the inner dynamics of an evolving American society. However, the niceties and refinements of the legal machinery must be fully comprehended to understand its total pervasiveness. But, an attempt to reduce the intricacies of the legal systems to one accurate summary would require many books and is a task fraught with peril. Perhaps, instead, a canvass of a few highpoints will suffice for the purposes at hand.

The Constitution's first three articles are devoted to setting up the federal legislature, the executive and the judiciary. These are the separate and coordinate branches of American government. The founding fathers were careful to provide for a separate and independent court system for the new federal government. Equally important, they determined that Congress might shape its contours to meet changing needs of the day. Early experiences, first in the colonies, and then under the Articles of Confederation, had taught them the wisdom of this course.

THE COLONIAL COURTS

During colonial days, there were neither federal courts nor fully independent colonial courts. The principal official in the colonies was the governor who represented the British Crown, and he acted as the chief executive. In addition, most of the colonies had a two-chambered legislature. The men serving in the upper house of the legislature, called councils, were usually selected by the British government, upon the recommendation of the governor. Representation in the lower house was usually by direct election, but coming solely from the propertied classes. Before one could qualify to be elected, he had to own a specified amount of property. This was the governmental climate within which the colonial legal institutions took root and grew. They influenced our present legal system.

The colonial courts were never very strong, nor independent. Usually, the council and/or the governor wielded final judicial authority. When life later became more complicated, and the colonies more populous, simple courts were set up whenever and wherever they were deemed necessary. Appeals were heard by the governor and the legislative council. It is true that, late in the colonial period, a few courts did come into continuous functioning on something other than an ad-hoc basis. But, their decisions were not always final. Their decisions could be overruled by the colonial legislative councils or, in some cases, by the governor.

Important cases could go higher up the legal ladder. During the colonial period, some appeals could be taken to the Privy Council in England, but not many of them actually got there. The British Privy Council had power to hear all final appeals in law cases coming from the American colonies, and also to review and nullify the laws which had been enacted by the colonial legislatures. Thus, justice in colonial America was fully supervised by the British parliament which, after all, might be the proper way to colonize. Frequently, the Privy Council gave legal effect to a British colonial policy which appeared not to enhance the interests of the colonists, but rather, to expand and protect the interests of the British Empire. These cases involved decisions which often, and understandably, met with colonial resistance.

With the Declaration of Independence, each of the colonies repudiated the lawful authority of the mother country. After a successful Revolutionary War this action had the legal effect of making each colony into a separate and independently sovereign country. In law, this meant that the court system of each colony became autonomous of Great Britain, and of the other colonies as well. For a short while then, North America really had thirteen separate nations, legally compartmentalized, and strung out along her Atlantic coastline. In legal theory, each was considered sufficient unto itself.

THE COURTS UNDER THE ARTICLES OF CONFEDERATION

———

The Articles of Confederation marked the beginning of the end of the thirteen separate nations. These Articles were a step toward American unity. The Articles made an attempt, albeit feeble, to set up a common legal system for the thirteen states. Basically, the document provided that the Continental Congress had the power to establish courts which could try "piracies and felonies committed on the high seas" and decide "appeals in all cases of captures." But, these courts had little real effect, and they could exercise only a group of narrowly limited powers. The Continental Congress itself was, as the Articles provided, "the last resort on appeal in all disputes . . . between two or more states concerning boundary jurisdiction or any other cause whatever."

THE SUPREME LAW OF THE LAND

———

The legal system established by the Articles was neither extensive nor adequate. Under it, the national government had to rely upon state courts to enforce national laws. The national situation then was similar to the international situation of today. The states were jealous of their new independence. Being enamored with their "rights of sovereignty," they refused to bind themselves cohesively into a common legal system. Under the Articles, the states remained almost fully sovereign. But, because of this, national solidarity and law were sacrificed at the altar of "states rights." Today, international world order fails in large part due to claims of national state sovereignty, "national rights," and jealously guarded national prerogatives.

Recognizing an inadequate court system as one of the many deficiencies of the Articles, the men who attended the Philadelphia convention took definite steps to assure that a federal court system would be created. In Article III of the Constitution, they provided that:

> The judicial power of the United States, shall be vested in one Supreme Court, and in such inferior courts as the Congress may from time to time ordain and establish.

A reading of this section reveals that, though definite in some respects, the Constitution really does not provide a blueprint for a new legal order. For example, although it does establish the Supreme

Court, it does not indicate how many men, termed "Justices," should be members of the Supreme Court, nor whether they must have a legal education or any education, nor does it disclose the nature or number of the other federal courts or their judicial compositions. It does, however, authorize and legitimize the existence of a federal court system. The federal judiciary is made, by the Constitution, into a separate and a coordinate branch of government, but Congress must pass laws necessary to establish courts inferior to the Supreme Court; to shape the contours of the judiciary's existence, and it must appropriate money for court operations. Hence, we can see that without the action of Congress and appointments by the President, there can be no federal court system because, under the Constitution, the lower federal courts remained to be created and all the judges, including those of the United States Supreme Court, remained to be appointed by the President on the advice and consent of the Senate. The constitutional convention entrusted these functions to the legislative and executive branches of government.

But, the men who gathered at Philadelphia did make sure that there would be only one paramount law. It is intended to govern these United States. They specifically included a supremacy provision in Article VI. Clearly and emphatically it declares that:

> This constitution, and the laws of the United States
> . . . and all treaties . . . shall be the supreme law
> of the land; and the judges in every state shall be bound
> thereby, anything in the constitution or laws of any state
> to the contrary notwithstanding.

When this supremacy clause is coupled with the provision setting forth the federal judicial power, it can be seen that the founding fathers worked a profound change in legal affairs from those existing under the Articles of Confederation. The thirteen countries ceased being independently sovereign. Instead, they were bound together by one supreme law; state judges were bound to apply the supreme law, and Congress was given power to create a system of courts which could give force and effect to that law. In short, the thirteen nations had become thirteen states within one federal nation, and had subjected themselves to a national government in order to promote their general welfare. The Constitution, the laws passed that conform to it and all its valid treaties are the "supreme law of the land," official and binding throughout the United States of America: East and West, North and South.

But, another question immediately presents itself. The individual states also retained their separate state courts. Thus, which court, state or federal, shall be selected to give effect to the supreme law? This question is crucial because the power of law interpretation is forceful indeed. Shall it be only the federal courts that shall declare and enforce the supreme law of the land, or shall it be only the state courts, or shall it, somehow, be both? The Constitution does not provide the complete answer, and the task of solving this problem falls to the lot of Congress. Of course, the solution must be fitted into our constitutional context, but, nonetheless, selection among the constitutionally permissible alternatives rests with Congress. It chose the third alternative.

A DUAL COURT SYSTEM FOR AMERICAN FEDERALISM

As previously indicated, the Constitution really has precious little to say about the exact form of our legal system. It simply declares that there shall be a Supreme Court, vesting judicial powers in it, and then delegates the task of setting up the rest of the legal system to Congress. Federal courts, inferior to the Supreme Court, may be created "as the Congress may from time to time ordain and establish." The First Congress exercised this power, and passed the Judiciary Act of 1789, setting up Federal courts that are inferior to the Supreme Court of the United States.

This famous law, like the Constitution itself, reflected a compromise between the federalists and the anti-federalists who had become members of the First Congress. The anti-federalists desperately wanted to minimize federal powers generally, including those of a federal judiciary. First, they tried to prevent the establishment of any inferior federal courts, but they failed. Secondly, conceding that if federal courts were to be established, then the anti-federalists favored giving them limited powers only to decide maritime and admiralty cases. This latter suggestion, if accepted, would have devised a federal inferior court system much akin to that which existed under the Articles of Confederation. The anti-federalists fought for their basic belief that the state courts, not federal courts, should exercise almost all judicial power, apply the supreme law of the land, and decide almost all cases containing federal constitutional and legal questions.

On the other hand, the federalists wanted to establish a complete system of federal courts, and with it, to supplant the states by nationalizing the entire administration of justice in America. They wanted the federal courts to exercise all federal judicial power which they had defined very broadly, and they wanted only federal courts to be allowed to decide cases involving the supreme law of the land: the constitution, federal law or treaty. The federalists did not think that it would be wise for each state court to have the powers to apply or construe the Constitution, the national laws and treaties. They thought that if state courts were allowed these powers, it would create the horrible possibility of sanctioning thirteen, perhaps conflicting, interpretations of the Constitution; and some of them by state courts that were hostile to Federal policies. The result of this conflict between the federalists and the anti-federalists was a compromise. It was agreed that there would be an extensive system of federal courts, but they would not be the only courts authorized to decide cases containing constitutional or federal law questions. The state courts also would be allowed to decide many of these cases. Thus, a dual system of courts, Federal and state, was created for the United States, and it exists today. The Federal courts are completely controlled by the Constitution and Congress; the state courts are controlled by state constitutions and state legislatures. State courts are separate and autonomous although they must comply with the applicable provisions of Federal statutes and the Constitution.

The Judiciary Act fixed six as the number of Justices of the Supreme Court and determined that it would have two sessions each year. The president appoints all federal judges with the advice and consent of the Senate. President Washington "packed" the Court when he staffed it for the first time. The Act then proceeded to set up the first inferior federal courts, the United States District Courts, which, in part, still serve as the foundation of current Federal court organization.

The Act of 1789, creating the federal court system, has been considered a success, and it is noteworthy to observe that the First Congress devised a federal court scheme which was to endure unchanged for almost one hundred years. Furthermore, the Judiciary Act allowed the Supreme Court to supervise the state courts, and thereby, to function as a key unifying force in United States history. The technique the Act used was that found in Section 25 which allowed cases to be appealed to the United States Supreme Court from state courts if the highest state court had ruled that a federal law was unconstitutional, or if it had ruled that a state law was constitutional after that state law had been attacked as being unconstitutional. This device meant that Federal policy could ultimately be vindicated by the Supreme Court of the United States and not defeated by hostile state court interpretations. Finally, the Act established the tradition of a dual court system in which federal courts operate alongside a system of state courts, with the Supreme Court at the top of the dual order. Thus, the Act preserved basic notions of federalism. The tradition was set, and it has grown.

Today we take for granted our dual system of courts—federal and state—which are found throughout the country. At present, the federal court system, like most state court systems, involves a three-layered arrangement. The bottom tier is populated by the trial courts. In the federal system they are officially known as the United States District Courts. Immediately above the trial courts is the first layer of appellate courts. In the federal system they are known as the United States Courts of Appeals. All state systems have a highest court, usually called a state supreme court. But, the paramount position in the American legal system is occupied by the Supreme Court of the United States which mainly decides cases coming to it from both the federal court system and from the state court systems. In short, it is the highest court in the land. Since the state court systems tend to be known, but not federal courts, a brief description of the federal court system might prove useful. State court systems are similarly structured usually having state trial courts, intermediate courts of appeal and a final court of appeal.

The United States District Courts are federal trial courts of original jurisdiction. This means that law suits having federal issues can be tried in them; this is their usual place of origin. Like state trial courts, the United States District Courts are where trials take place. Here, the judges and juries hear witnesses testify and consider other evidence which might be offered. They make the initial, and frequently the only, decision in a case, finally disposing of most of them. Most of the cases tried in federal trial courts fall into two broad classes: cases involving federal statutes or the Constitution (Federal question cases) and cases involving citizens of different states (diversity of citizenship cases). Criminal cases are tried here whenever a federal crime is involved such as those involving interstate commerce, counterfeiting or using the mail to defraud. Likewise, civil suits such as bankruptcy and copyright can be tried in the district courts. Appeals from their decisions may be taken to the United States Courts of Appeals, or, perhaps, in certain special instances, directly to the Supreme Court. At least one federal district court is located in each state, and the more populous states, having a greater volume of litigation, have more than one. Congress has power to create additional district courts as the need for them arises.

Each district court usually has one federal judge, who holds his tenure "during good behavior." This means that the appointment generally is for life. However, like all federal officials, these judges can be impeached for "treason, bribery or other high crimes and misdemeanors." Congress has not provided for their removal by any other means. The life appointment of these judges is important for two reasons. It tends to insure that the men holding the office will be independent of political forces so that they will be able to administer the laws fairly, as they honestly understand them. Secondly, life tenure tends to offset the somewhat low salaries of these judges. Their compensation, although improving, remains a problem and sometimes disallows capable men from accepting the office, much to the detriment of bench, bar, and society.

Most federal district court judges have been selected from the bar. That is, they are chosen from the practicing lawyers in the area. Only infrequently does an appointment come from among state court judges. Presently, these judges decide well over 100,000 cases a year. But, even so, the backlog of lawsuits is long, and the volume of cases is growing. Delay in the administration of justice usually means justice denied, and the increase in the number of federal district court judges has not tended to keep pace with the increase in the business of the federal courts. In recent years, this problem has been receiving increasing congressional attention.

The United States Courts of Appeals rank immediately above the federal district courts. Currently, the United States is divided into ten geographical areas called circuits. There is a separate Court of Appeals for each of the ten "circuits."

Each Court of Appeals is an intermediate court of review having a number of district courts under it. These courts were created in 1891 to relieve the United States Supreme Court of some of its workload. As their name implies, Courts of Appeals have only appellate jurisdiction. This means that cases are not started in these courts, nor do witnesses testify here, and they have no juries. Instead they function much like state supreme courts. The Courts of Appeals review the work of the lower federal courts as well as many of the decisions made by federal administrative agencies; agencies such as the National Labor Relations Board, the Federal Communication Commission, the Interstate Commerce Commission, etc. Usually, the court consists of a panel of three judges who carefully go over the record of the proceedings in the trial court in order to determine whether mistakes were made. They are guided by written and oral arguments of attorneys who direct judicial attention to the alleged errors.

It is important that, in addition to being independent, honest and fearless men, the judges of these appellate courts must have a realistic understanding of the nature of the federal district courts whose work they review. To meet this need, many of the men chosen as judges for Courts of Appeals have tended to come primarily from two sources, the federal district bench, and the lawyers who practice before the federal courts.

THE FEDERAL JUDICIAL POWER

Before considering the Supreme Court of the United States which sits at the top of the American legal systems, perhaps a few words should be said about the location and nature of the judicial powers exercised by the Federal Courts and how they differ from the powers of the courts which are found in the fifty states. Although the term "jurisdiction" can mean other things as well, one of its accepted meanings is power. The judicial powers given a court usually define its "jurisdiction." Geographical considerations are not important for our discussion. This is because a case must come within the jurisdictional powers of a court before a court can decide it and thereby render a lawful decision. Federal courts are courts of restricted, limited jurisdiction, but state courts have a broad, general jurisdiction.

The federal constitution has delegated only certain powers to the federal government, including the judicial powers. Thus, federal courts have only limited jurisdiction. The theory is that those powers not delegated to the federal government by the Constitution have been "reserved to the states respectively, or to the people." Thus, state courts can have a broad, general jurisdiction. But, the powers actually granted to the federal government have been described by words which are somewhat vague and loose. Hence, a continuing constitutional question presents itself. Exactly what judicial powers have been delegated to the federal courts, or, put another way, what classes of cases can be handled by federal courts? As always, the beginning point is the Constitution.

The judicial power is set forth in section 2 of Article III of the Constitution, stating that:

> The judicial power shall extend to all cases in law and equity arising under this constitution, the laws of the United States, and treaties made, or which shall be made, under their authority; to all cases affecting ambassadors, other public ministers, and consuls; to all cases of admiralty and maritime jurisdiction; to controversies to which the United States shall be a party; to controversies between two or more States; between a State and citizens of another State; between citizens of different States, between citizens of the same State claiming lands under grants of different States, and between a State, or the citizens thereof, and foreign States, citizens or subjects. (Art. III, sec. 2, cl. 1.)

This constitutional section sets forth "the judicial power"; i. e., Federal court jurisdiction, and the cases to which it may extend. There are several specific types of cases named plus a broad grant of jurisdiction to decide two kinds of cases: those that arise under the Constitution, treaties or Federal law (present a Federal question) and those that involve citizens of different states. The Constitution does not, itself, distribute judicial power, or any portion of it, among the various federal courts. The Constitution simply provides that this power shall reside in "one supreme court" and "in such inferior courts as the Congress may from time to time ordain and establish." The Constitution does not say that all of the judicial power automatically shall be given to each of the inferior federal courts. Nor does it say that this judicial power is only for the Federal courts, thereby excluding all state courts from exercising it. Congressional action is needed.

Nor is there any constitutional requirement that Congress must put all the judicial power in any one court which it may establish, say, for example, the federal district courts. Consequently, it is clear that, being created by Congress, the scope of the jurisdiction granted to the federal courts is dependent, in a major way, upon the laws passed by Congress, and not solely upon the Constitution. In fact, however, Congress has vested the bulk of the Federal judicial powers in the United States District Courts, and has provided for appeals to the United States Courts of Appeal, but Congress has not vested all the judicial power of Article III.

For example, although the Constitution states that the "judicial power shall extend to all cases between citizens of different States," Congress has required that these cases must involve more than $10,000 before they can be brought before a federal district court. If such a case does not involve that amount, then it must be decided, if at all, by the state courts. Suppose a citizen of New York is travelling to California and is in an automobile accident in Kansas, having been hit by a car driven by a citizen of Arizona. Assuming that the New Yorker wishes to sue, there clearly is, as the Constitution requires, a case "between citizens of different States." But, the federal district court has no jurisdiction to hear this case unless it involves more than $10,000. Congress has given the federal courts judicial power only in such instances.

Even if the lawsuit did involve more than $10,000, this does not mean it necessarily would be settled by a federal district court. Congress has not provided that these cases must come exclusively within federal judicial power. It has not specifically denied state courts the power to hear the type of case involved here. Hence, if the plaintiff from New York were willing, he could start his lawsuit in a court of the State of Kansas or Arizona, and it might decide the case, or he could choose the United States District Court, provided that more than $10,000 were involved.

The power of a federal court to decide a case must meet at least two tests. First a case must fit the type of power that has been delegated by Article III of the Constitution to the federal courts. This means that most cases must either be "diversity of state citizenship" cases or contain a substantial question of federal law. The usual marriage or divorce case, for example, generally involves the citizens of one state and state law only and does not contain a question of federal law. Consequently, typical marriage or divorce cases cannot be brought in the federal courts. One example that could possibly reach the Supreme Court of the United States would be a case in which it is claimed that the state divorce law was unconstitutional. Even in this example, however, the case would probably have been appealed from a state supreme court and would not have been started in the United States District Court. Secondly, and importantly, Congress has not vested all of the Constitution's judicial power in each of the federal courts; for example, consider the limitation of $10,000 on cases involving citizens of different states. Therefore, all cases brought in the federal courts must meet a second test: Is this case one of a type which Congress has empowered the federal courts to adjudicate? Jurisdiction then, in federal cases, involves both a constitutional and a federal statutory consideration. Both must be present, else the lawsuit cannot be decided by the federal courts.

This is decidedly not the situation regarding the state courts. Each state has its own court system which functions alongside the federal court system. Although subject to the Constitution, state courts are controlled by state constitutions and state legislatures. Except for the municipal courts of cities, and with minor specialized exceptions, such as the "family courts," the trial courts of the states usually are courts of "general jurisdiction." Usually, this means that state courts have the power to decide any and all questions which might be presented to them, and they can handle all sorts of lawsuits whether they involve one dollar or one million. That is, they derive their judicial powers broadly. State courts, with few exceptions, have general powers over two broad classes of cases. First, they can try cases involving only state law problems. Second, with certain important exceptions, state courts encompass within their jurisdiction the power to decide many cases which quite properly might be brought before the federal district courts. Thus, state courts have their own exclusive jurisdiction and a concurrent jurisdiction with federal courts. This situation exists because Congress has not required that each and every case involving a question of federal law exclusively be brought in the federal court system. Hence, in addition to possessing all the powers denied the federal government, the state courts also have the power to decide many of the so-called "federal" cases, as well. Their jurisdiction over the cases which could have been brought in a federal court continues in state courts so long as Congress sees fit not to withdraw it. If it so wished, Congress probably could put those powers in the federal courts. But, to date, Congress has not seen fit to do so. In some instances, Congress has done just the reverse. It has expressly conferred upon state courts additional powers to try cases involving federal issues. An example is that state courts have been given jurisdiction over legal actions brought by employees under the Federal Fair Labor Standards Act. When state courts decide cases that could not be presented to federal courts, they exercise a power that is possessed by the states exclusively, and the state courts are the final authorities in all cases involving only state, and not federal, matters. Generally speaking, cases involving only state problems cannot be brought in, or decided by, the federal courts, nor can they be appealed to the United States Supreme Court.

For example, the powers to decide marriage and divorce cases or to declare ownership of land traditionally have been powers held exclusively by the states. Suppose a case is brought between two citizens of the same state, A and B, involving a dispute over their prospective marriage. Suppose they want to marry but each is only thirteen years of age and that state law requires a person to be at least eighteen to marry. A and B sue the state Director of Marriage

Licenses asking that the court order the Director to issue them a license, but they make no claim or argument that the state law setting eighteen as the requisite age is unconstitutional. This case can be decided by the state courts; if so, that is the end of the matter. There is no federal or constitutional law problem. This type of case could not have been brought in a federal court, and it probably cannot be reviewed by the United States Supreme Court. There is no federal judicial power over the subject matter for no federal law questions or constitutional questions are presented by the case. The state court judgment is final, and that is the end of the matter.

Popular misconception has it that eventually every case can be appealed to the Supreme Court of the United States. But, this is certainly not true, especially when a case is properly within those powers "reserved to the states .   .   . or to the people." When cases properly fall into this area then state power is supreme. The federal government has been given no power over this area, and hence, the Supreme Court cannot entertain cases exclusively falling within it. Federal power does not reach so far.

This is not to say, however, that simply because a lawsuit involves a dispute over a marriage or divorce that there can be no possibility of that case ultimately being decided by the Supreme Court of the United States. It depends upon the nuances and facts of each case. Take, for example, the simple situation of marriage which seldom presents a case for the Supreme Court of the United States. Suppose A and B are both citizens of the same state, over twenty-one years of age, and that each wishes to marry the other. Suppose further, that A is black and B white and that the state legislature has passed an anti-miscegenation law which denies "Negroes" (variously defined) the right to marry caucasians, and vice-versa. Thus, under the law of the state, A and B cannot marry, regardless how much they want to. But, they could sue the Director of Marriage Licenses in a state court, asking the court to rule that he be required to issue them a marriage license.

With the exception of the federal question, this case is highly similar to the previous marriage case that could not have been appealed to the Supreme Court of the United States. Suppose the state courts apply the law of the state and refuse the request of A and B; even so, the state court's decision might not be the end of the matter. If A and B have argued that the state law disallowing Negroes and caucasians the right to marry violates the Fourteenth Amendment of our Constitution, then the Supreme Court may very well make the ultimate decision in this case. The Fourteenth Amendment is, of course, a federal law, supreme and binding upon all the states. It says " .   .   . nor shall any state .   .   . deny to any person within its jurisdiction the equal protection of the laws." In this situation, there clearly has been discrimination on the grounds of race, and A and B have been denied, by state law, the equal opportunity to marry any person in the state of their choosing. They have been denied the equal protection of state law, even though the law applies equally to caucasians and Negroes, within those classifications. The state law is based on a constitutionally suspect consideration—race, and before it could be upheld as constitutional the state would have to show an overriding and compelling interest that would justify the state classifying persons by state law on the basis of their race. If the purpose of the state law is only to keep the races apart, as did some anti-miscegenation laws in some southern states which have recently been declared unconstitutional, then that state interest, alone, is insufficient under our Constitution. (See, Loving v. Virginia, 388 U.S. 1 (1967).) Under our Constitution, the destiny of all Americans, of whatever races, is a common one, and compelling reasons, scrutinized by our federal courts, must be present before states can justifiably use race as a legal category classifying people. The case would be similar if the state law disallowed members of religious groups, e. g., Protestant, Catholic, Jew, from marrying each other.

The factor which has been added to the second case of marriage, but lacking in the first one, is that of racial discrimination based upon a constitutionally suspect ground, and it is the key that might bring the case before the United States Supreme Court. A federal law, the Fourteenth Amendment, is violated by the state law in the second example involving marriage. In fact, this second case probably could have originated in the federal court system as well as in the state court system. The basic points involved here are that the United States Supreme Court, and other federal courts, can decide only certain cases falling within their jurisdiction, and those cases which they can decide usually must present a substantial question of federal law, including, of course, Constitutional law, or involve diversity of state citizenship. In fact, very few of the total number of cases tried by the American legal systems could ever reach the Supreme Court. When someone has an ordinary case and says "I'll take my case to the Supreme Court!" you can be fairly sure that he probably will not.

JUDICIAL REVIEW

The Supreme Court has the power to make the final decisions in all cases presenting substantial questions about federal law, including constitutional law, whether or not the case involves an interpretation of the law or its proper application. It makes no difference whether the lawsuit was started in the state or federal courts, nor does it matter whether the federal law involved is the Constitution or treaty, or a law passed pursuant to the Constitution or a treaty, or an administrative or executive ruling. The Supreme Court of the

United States is the final authority on all questions of federal law. For example, in the second case about the marriage of A and B which involved the racially discriminatory state law, the Supreme Court would have to review the work product of a state legislature as well as that of a state court which had earlier passed on the same question, to see whether the statute and its interpretation were unconstitutional. This procedure is known as judicial review because it involves a judicial review of the laws passed by a legislature, either Congress or state, to determine whether they are unconstitutional. Since the Supreme Court has power only to decide "cases," judicial review can be exercised only when the proper "case" is brought before it. Judicial review is practiced by state and federal courts.

Judicial review is one of our bedrock ideas. Thus, it is most important to note that courts in the American legal systems really perform two prime, and different, functions. On the one hand, they decide individual lawsuits granting redress to private parties, or perhaps, punishing violators of law. This type of case constitutes their usual daily fare, and most of the lawsuits simply involve a selection of the governing law and an application of it to the facts of the case. But, on the other hand, the courts also decide cases in which an argument has been made that the law itself is not in keeping with the Constitution, or that the Constitution precludes a particular application of a law. In this second type of case, the courts perform a radically different function, they must determine whether a particular branch of government, say the legislature or the executive, has acted beyond the ambit of its constitutional powers. In these instances, the courts perform a supervisory function over the branches of government. This latter activity is known as judicial review. The court having the power to make the final decision on all questions concerning state constitutional questions is, of course, the highest state court, and the Court having the power to make the final decision on all questions concerning the United States Constitution is, of course, the Supreme Court of the United States. State constitutions, of course, must be consistent with our national Constitution and the United States Supreme Court can decide the cases where there is a conflict between the two. Thus a study of American Constitutional Law tends also to be a study of the Supreme Court of the United States.

The essence of judicial review has been cogently stated by Professor Charles L. Black of the Yale Law School in his interesting book, THE PEOPLE AND THE COURT. He says:

> In the course of a judicial proceeding, it may happen that one of the litigants relies on a statute or other governmental pronouncement which the other litigant contends to be repugnant to some provision of the Constitution. It is the task of the court to determine what the law is. If the Constitution is a law of superior status, then the rule

of the Constitution, and not the rule of the statute or other governmental pronouncement, is the correct rule of law for application to the case before the court. The Court, under our system, therefore considers itself bound to follow the rule of the Constitution, and so to treat the other rule as a nullity. (p. 12.) © Charles L. Black, Jr. 1960, The Mac-Millan Company, New York (1960).

Simply put, these notions are the hallmarks of judicial review. Whatever the final consensus of historical opinion about the American civilization, the role of the judiciary in interpreting and applying the Constitution to limit the powers of government will surely be a prime consideration for comment. Judicial review—that is, the power of American courts to set aside national and state legislation as unconstitutional—is one of the outstanding contributions of the United States to the science and art of government. Fundamentally, judicial review really accomplishes three things, each of which is vitally important. First, although the Supreme Court may say only that a law is "not unconstitutional," the public tends to believe that the Court places the stamp of legitimacy upon any law or practice that successfully passes its muster. Secondly, courts serve as a check on the otherwise unbridled power of the other branches of government whenever they seek to trespass onto territory forbidden them by the Constitution as it is interpreted by the Supreme Court. Thirdly, by fearlessly upholding a humane interpretation of our Constitution, the Supreme Court preserves, and requires the other branches of government to observe our great constitutional ideal of human dignity which otherwise might be forgotten.

THE JUSTIFICATION OF JUDICIAL REVIEW

Even though judicial review has been practiced at least since 1803, and even though it is a basic cornerstone of our constitutional order, nevertheless, the constitutional foundation of judicial review is not free from challenge. The reason is that there is no part of the Constitution that explicitly gives courts the power of judicial review; saying, for example, that the courts shall have the power to declare unconstitutional contravening laws that otherwise have been duly passed by legislatures, or contravening orders or actions of the executive. To the extent that there is a constitutional basis for judicial review, that basis must be inferred from the constitution. The continuing argument has been whether this inference properly can be made.

The Constitution in Article III, section 2, extends "the judicial power" "to *all* cases arising under this Constitution." Thus, the federal courts that exercise this "judicial power" can do so only in "cases." They have no judicial power to declare laws unconstitutional generally. The law or governmental action in question must be an integral part of a "case" between two adverse parties. There is no power to give an advisory opinion about the constitutionality of a law or a proposed law. The overriding requirement is that there must be an actual case between actual adverse litigants. It should be noted that not every controversy between two or more persons is a "case." The Supreme Court has evolved many technical rules of law for determining when a "case" is present. We need not consider them. For our more limited purposes, it is sufficient if we view a "case" as a lawsuit which exists between two honestly adverse parties each with an interest of his own to advance or protect in the lawsuit. The requirement that there be a "case" means then, that constitutional issues will not be decided by the "Article III" federal courts, including the Supreme Court, in friendly, non-adversary proceedings, or in advance of the necessity of actually deciding the specific issue, or in terms broader than those that are required to dispose of the issue presented by the facts of the case, or in lawsuits, where a person is not himself affected by the law or government action. These are some of the limitations placed on "the judicial power" by the constitution when it extended that power only to "cases".

Let us assume that there is a "case" presented to a federal court in which a state or federal law conflicts with the constitution. In this situation, the court must decide on the proper operation of each, because before a court can decide a case it must first say which law actually governs the case, and then it must apply that law to the case. As the Supreme Court said in a famous opinion in 1803:

> So, if a law be in opposition to the constitution; if both the law and the constitution apply to a particular case, so that the court must either decide that case conformably to the law, disregarding the constitution; or conformably to the constitution, disregarding the law; the court must determine which of these conflicting rules govern the case. This is the very essence of judicial duty. Marbury v. Madison, 1 Cranch 137.

There is no way a court can avoid this choice, and clearly, it must choose. How should it choose? Article VI, section 1, the supremacy clause, is helpful. Article VI states that the "Supreme Law of the Land" shall be the constitution; all "laws of the United States which shall be made in pursuance thereof," and all treaties made "under the authority of the United States." Not every federal "law" or "treaty" qualifies as the supreme law of the land. Before a federal law or treaty can be part of the "supreme law of the land" the substance of that law must have been made "in pursuance" of the constitution and the treaty made under the constitutional "authority of the United States." The words "in pursuance" are taken substantively and require that the supreme law of the land pursue the substantive ends set forth in the Constitution. Consequently, if a federal "law" or "treaty" were believed to be an integral part of a case, but either that "law" or "treaty" conflicted with the constitution, the judicial duty of the judge seems clear. The judge must resolve the conflict in favor of upholding the constitution. It seems clear that a power of judicial review can fairly be inferred from the constitution in circumstances where a "case" is presented to the federal courts for their exercise of "the judicial power."

But, what about state courts? Do they also have the power of judicial review?

The constitution is quite clear upon this point. In Article VI, section 1, the constitution declares that the constitution, the federal laws passed in pursuance of the constitution and all constitutionally authorized treatises are to be the "Supreme Law of the Land." Significantly, it continues stating explicitly that "the judges in every state shall be bound thereby, anything in the constitution or laws of any state to the contrary notwithstanding." Thus, it is clear that if a conflict exists between either a state law or a state governmental action, and the Constitution of the United States (the supreme law), then the state judge must choose to enforce the constitution. The same would be true if the conflict were between the constitution and a federal "law" or "treaty."

Judicial review seems to be inferred fairly from the textual meaning of the constitution. But a problem still remains. Nothing in the constitution expressly states that the Supreme Court of the United States should be the final arbiter of the meaning of the constitution. It should also be admitted that no fair inference can be made from the text of the constitution supporting the view that the Supreme Court shall be the final court to decide upon the meaning of the constitution. If this is true, why then, shouldn't each state court, each state governor, state administrator, and each federal court or each federal administrator be the final judge of the meaning and application of the constitution? Even though the Supreme Court as the final arbiter of the proper meaning and application of the constitution does not find its basis in the text of our constitution, the reason is found in wise policy. We simply need one, and only one, agency whose voice will be the final one, and the Supreme Court presents the best qualifications. It is a question of wise constitutional policy.

Atop the pinnacle of judicial review, and overlooking the American legal systems, sits our highest court of the land—the Supreme Court of the United States. Today, its nine members carry with them an immense measure of public esteem, and also, an equal measure of responsibility that wears weightily upon their collective shoulders. The Court is, as one perceptive scholar has put it, the umpire of our federal system. It is the final arbiter of the Constitution. Frequently, the Supreme Court must pass judgment on touchy matters of federalism which have been only tangentially resolved by the constitutional distribution of powers. In addition, the Court has inherited the task of resolving conflicts of opinion on constitutional questions among the appellate courts within the various federal circuits. It provides the critical functions of continuity and unity of constitutional interpretation for all the courts, federal and state, inferior to it. One can imagine what the condition of our federal statutory law and constitutional interpretation might be if there were no Supreme Court to generate harmony out of conflicting views. Close cases often produce differing results when they are judged by different courts in different federal circuits, or by different state judges in different states. This is due, in large measure, to the fact that law cases can be difficult and close, and that reasonable judges honestly can, and do, differ. It is not perversity. Without the harmonizing influence of the Supreme Court, it is likely that we would have differing statutory and constitutional interpretations in various federal circuits. This problem is rapidly aggravated when one considers the states. If the Court could not review the work of the state appellate courts whenever they pass upon federal constitutional questions, then our constitution could slip into a morass of uncertainty and confusion. If state court decisions were final, then there could possibly be fifty constitutional interpretations of each clause of the constitution, one for each state. Clearly, the review function of the Supreme Court is necessary, and a wise resolution of the issues must be reached by it. In short, the Supreme Court performs a vital job when it umpires our federal system and is the final arbiter of the meaning of the constitution. The Supreme Court and the individual Justices, when quite intelligent and strongly steeped in history and learning, have made a deep impress upon our social fabric as they have infused new ideas necessary to achieve enduring constitutional values in changing times. Some great Americans have sat on the Court, and they have contributed profoundly in shaping the contours of modern America—names springing to the fore are Marshall, Story, Taney, Miller, Harlan, Holmes, Brandeis, Black, Douglas, Frankfurter and Warren. The ideas of these Justices, and the functioning of the Court on which they sat, have not been fully satisfactory at all times to all people. Perhaps, no institution of government ever can be. But, one thing truly can be said, that despite the frailties found, the Supreme Court today better serves all its review functions within our scheme of government than could any other device which has been suggested as a substitute. Denude the Court of its powers and responsibilities of review and what shall be substituted in exchange? Discord? Anarchy? A chaos of conflicting legal decisions? Or a cry for arms? The Supreme Court is surely not beyond criticism, and constructive criticism helps it discharge its duties wisely. But, the broad good sense of the American people has never allowed any success to those persons who, in the past, have made narrowly partisan attacks upon the Court, and its high esteem which can properly be based only on the quality of its work. So long as the Justices and the work of the Court is of superior quality, the Court will probably be safeguarded from those people who attack it out of ignorance and bigotry.

WHAT STANDARD OF JUDICIAL REVIEW?

———

Another question about courts declaring laws or governmental actions unconstitutional has troubled some people. Simply put, the question is: what should be the appropriate standard of judicial review whenever a court makes a declaration of unconstitutionality? The usual rule is that legislation is *presumed* to be constitutional by courts, and the person attacking the constitutionality of a law has the burden of showing that the law is unconstitutional. But, according to what standard of unconstitutionality? Should the Supreme Court, or any court be willing to declare laws or governmental actions unconstitutional whenever they *may possibly* be unconstitutional, or when they *may* tend to be; or when they *actually tend* to be; or when, on close balance, they *preponderate* to be; or when they are *clearly and convincingly* shown to be; or only when there can be *absolutely no doubt* that the law or governmental action in question is unconstitutional—"so clear that it is not open to rational question"? Obviously, the role of the courts in our system of government would vary considerably depending which one of these standards is used. For example, courts would be most active under the first standard, declaring many laws and governmental actions unconstitutional, but they would be least active under the last standard when a court would not declare a law or act unconstitutional if there were any possible doubt. Under the last standard, so long as the government's choice could be shown to be rational then that choice would be constitutional. The question is: which standard should be used?

In times past, especially in the nineteenth century, most scholars, and the Supreme Court itself, argued for the last standard—a court should never make a declaration of unconstitutionality unless the matter is "so clear that it is not open to rational question." This rule and the presumption that a law is constitutional permit the widest latitude to other divisions of government, and, it is argued, that this rule is the only appropriate one for judicial review in a democracy. The people elect Congressmen and Presidents, but not Supreme Court Justices; therefore, it is argued, if America is to be ruled by a democracy, rather than by the Supreme Court, the Supreme Court, and other courts too, should declare governmental actions unconstitutional only when they are so clearly unconstitutional that the matter is not open to rational question. There is some merit in this view, but it is not the whole story.

This view has merit because the Constitution does give many powers to the various branches of government, and they are expected to use those powers for the general human welfare of all Americans. It would be intolerable for the Supreme Court to sit in judgment of every action, trying desperately to find something that was unconstitutional. It simply doesn't do this, and the other branches of government are allowed to interpret their constitutionally delegated powers broadly.

But, the American Constitutional scheme consists of more than a simple delegation of powers to government. In addition, there are certain matters which have not been delegated to government, but which have been retained by the people. There are many "no trespassing" signs in our constitution—areas where government is not allowed. Indeed, the Constitution expressly denies many powers to government, and that is the whole point of a Bill of Rights. Among others, it says that the people shall have certain constitutional rights—to speak, write, publish, read and associate freely—that is, without any governmental interference. In short, these rights are treasured rights. Shall the Supreme Court, when reviewing governmental actions dealing with these areas, especially freedom of thought and conscience, allow the governmental action to stand unless it is so clearly unconstitutional that the matter is not open to rational question? Or should some other standard of review be used by the Supreme Court in cases dealing with an American's fundamental rights and liberties?

It is obvious that two general types of issues are presented to the Supreme Court because of Constitutional structure. First, there is the type of case where the question is whether the Constitution has delegated a power to government to deal with a particular subject matter. For example, under Article I, section 8, of the Constitution a question can arise whether Congress has power to incorporate a national bank, or to tax gambling, or to regulate business and agriculture or to pass a law forbidding racial discrimination by motels and restaurants that are serving interstate travellers. The question in each of these cases is the reach of the delegated constitutional power: does it include this particular subject matter? Or is this subject matter solely for state legislation? In this first type of situation the political process can be relied upon. Lobbyists function and the elected politicians come from the state and are responsive to the people of the states. For this type of case the standard of review perhaps can appropriately be that the Supreme Court will declare a governmental action unconstitutional only when the matter is not open to rational question.

But, of course, a second general type of issue is presented to the Supreme Court. There are cases where the question for decision is whether an exercise of governmental power, state or federal, is contrary to a person's individual rights and liberties as they are set forth and protected by the Constitution? For example, the question may be whether governmental action infringes upon a person's rights to speak, to read, to publish, or to associate. In these cases, unlike the first type, the ordinary political processes cannot be relied upon. In a pure democracy the majority governs. For example, if the majority wanted to take away from some citizens the rights of free speech, press and association, then in a pure democracy, the majority can do so. But, that is not possible under the American Constitution. No American's rights to life, liberty, freedom of speech, press, association or worship can be submitted to a majority vote; no right protected by the Bill of Rights depends merely upon a political election. These rights have been withdrawn from the vicissitudes of everyday politics, and placed beyond the reach of simple majorities and elected or appointed officials. What is needed is a non-elected body; one not subject to the shifting winds of majority vote to protect these constitutional rights, and that is a primary task of all our courts, especially the Supreme Court.

Since the political process cannot be fully relied upon in this second type of case, and more reliance is placed on courts, the Supreme Court is justified in using a different standard of review and being more active. Its standard for reviewing governmental actions that allegedly invade fundamental liberties must be different. If the Court is to fulfill its role in this area it must act frequently and forcefully. It has done so; for example, it sometimes has relaxed the presumption of constitutionality or it has created a presumption against the constitutional validity of government actions alleged to invade fundamental American rights and liberties. This trend started with a famous footnote by Mr. Justice Stone:

> "There may be narrower scope for operation of the presumption of constitutionality when legislation appears on its face to be within a specific prohibition of the Constitution such as those of the first ten amendments, which are deemed equally specific when held to be embraced within the Fourteenth." (U. S. v. Carolene Products, 304 U.S. 144, 58 S.Ct. 778, 82 L.Ed. 1234 (1938)).

James Madison, the "father of our constitution," saw that American courts must necessarily play a more active role in cases involving human liberties and welfare than in other types of cases. During the Congressional deliberations in the first American Congress when the Bill of Rights was being formulated, James Madison said:

> If they are incorporated into the Constitution, independent tribunals of justice will consider themselves in a peculiar manner the guardians of those rights; they will be an impenetrable bulwark against every assumption of power in the Legislative or Executive; they will be naturally led to resist every encroachment upon rights expressly stipulated for in

the Constitution by the declaration of rights. (Irving Brant, The Madison Heritage, 35 N.Y.U. LAW REV. 882, 889–900.)

This role of the Supreme Court has caused some people to call it "activist." But would we want our liberties protected by a "passive" Court; one that would do so only when the unconstitutionality of the matter is not open to any rational question? Surely not. When dealing with this second general type of case, the Supreme Court, in a sense, acts as the constitutional conscience of our country, and rightly so. Recently, our courts, and especially the Supreme Court, have been dealing more and more with this second type of case involving human liberty, and less with the first type. Frequently, but not always, the Supreme Court and other courts have upheld our constitutional ideals of human liberty and human dignity with the result that they are greatly respected by the overwhelming majority of the American people. In doing so, the Supreme Court and the other courts are fulfilling their proper role in American society, and they are held in high esteem.

THE SUPREME COURT

The Supreme Court has not always been held in high esteem. On February 1, 1790, when the Supreme Court of the United States first convened in the Royal Exchange Building in New York City, it found that it had nothing to do. There were no cases to decide; so the Court adjourned. The next annual term of Court was held in Philadelphia's new City Hall. But again, there were no cases to decide; so after admitting some lawyers to practice before it, the Court adjourned. The Congress legislated, and the president administered, but the Court adjourned. During that ten-year period to 1800, it decided only fifty-six cases, and a scant few of them were of major significance. The importance of a Justice of the Supreme Court was not recognized, and it lay inchoate. The Court's role was slow to emerge.

In those days, being a Justice of the United States Supreme Court was seen by some people as having so little value and reward that John Jay, the Court's first Chief Justice, resigned to run for governor of the State of New York. His decision is really not surprising. It is understandable when one considers the nature of the early Court and its work, including the fact that the first courtroom in the Nation's capitol was so inadequate that it later became the office for the Marshal of the Court. In addition, these were the times when the Justices were required to "ride circuit" in order to handle certain aspects of judicial administration. Because of the inconveniences of transportation in those days Justice Iredell termed himself a "travelling postboy." His "circuit riding" necessitated a twice-a-year tour of Georgia and North and South Carolina plus a gruelling journey of two thousand miles twice a year, to and from Philadelphia. Riding circuit was so onerous and formidable that one of the early Justices, Johnson, resigned because of it. The rigors of this practice persisted well into the nineteenth century.

In 1800, an act of Congress created the District of Columbia and also created much work for the Supreme Court. The reason is simple. The Court now became the place of final resolution for all of the run-of-the-mill legal disputes of the people who lived in the District. Thus, the total business of the Supreme Court increased, but it tended to function more like a state court, rather than as the Supreme Court of the United States. This act of Congress pushed the Court towards becoming just another typical court of law deciding cases of contested wills, real estate and divorce. This state of affairs could not long endure for the pulse of America increased its beat.

Not only was the business of the Supreme Court to change, but so was its number of Justices. The Court has not always had nine Justices. When the Supreme Court first met in 1789 it had only five Justices, although six were authorized, and the next year it was expanded to six. The six Justices became seven in 1807; nine in 1834, and reached a historical high number of ten in 1863. The Court continued to have ten Justices until 1865 when Mr. Justice Catron died and his position was abolished by Congress, as was that of Mr. Justice Wayne who died in 1867. The reason Congress abolished both positions was to prevent President Johnson from filling them. In 1869, Congress created a new position making the Supreme Court consist of nine Justices, and nine has remained the number of Justices for over one hundred years. It is unlikely that the future will see a change in the number of Justices on the Court.

The nineteenth century saw the American people conquer a continent, spanning it by rail from coast-to-coast and creating new states where previously there had been territories. During the middle and latter portions of the nineteenth century thirty-five million uprooted immigrants migrated to these shores from Europe and Asia at great personal loss and suffering. With them came a new series of complicated legal problems wrapped together with all the constitutional issues inherent in a dynamic, and ofttimes exploitative, industrialism. And, of course, these were days of great domestic issues, generating their own constitutional problems, which culminated in the Civil War. No institution of government could fail to reverberate under the pulse of such pressure. The Supreme Court responded.

Long before 1875 the Court ceased to meet only to adjourn. That year it heard almost two hundred cases. That number is surely the maximum that can be heard and fully explored by nine Justices. These were important cases, befitting an expanding nation with its growing industrialism. Many of them involved the scope and nature of the freedom to be allowed interstate commerce; others dealt with Congressional powers to take lands previously in private ownership and develop them for public purposes, and other cases dealt with the right to trial by jury. In fact, the flow of cases came to be so great that Congress, in 1891, established the federal Courts of Appeal, thereby relieving the Supreme Court of what had grown to be an oppressive workload.

But, the pressures were relentless. By 1925, the total business of the Court had grown to such an extent that once again something had to be done about it. That something was known as the Judges' Bill because members of the Court prepared it, and Congress enacted it into law. Under the Act of 1925 the obligatory appeals jurisdiction was contracted and the Supreme Court was given almost complete discretion to choose among the many cases which compete to come to its courtroom either by way of appeal or certiorari. To a significant extent, this measure has been successful. The net result has been the establishment of a case selection process which has tended to stabilize the business of the Supreme Court, allowing the Court to hear and decide the most important constitutional, and other, cases of wide public interest. Occasionally, the Court uses its discretion not to consider a crucially important case, and it has been criticized for this practice. But, generally, the Supreme Court exercises its discretion to consider the most significant cases. This last point is not sufficiently understood and accounts for much of the popular ignorance. This selective process can produce an abnormal number of cases with stirring, controversial issues. The Court is repeatedly confronted with cases cluttered over with vested interests and in which public emotions run deep and prejudices are pronounced. In sum, then, these are controversial cases. It is no wonder that the Court frequently becomes a storm center for public discussion, and sometimes abuse, which defies quantitative description. Yet, only by deciding controversial cases can the Court continue to make its highest contribution to American life. That is its job, and this point is frequently overlooked by those who criticize the decision-making of the Court.

One point should be made clear. It concerns the cases in which the petitions have asked the Court for a hearing, but the Court refused; that is, *certiorari* has been denied. In these cases the decisions of the lower courts are not disturbed. It is important to note that the decisions are not "disturbed," and that the Supreme Court gave no view on the substantive merits or demerits of the lower court's decision, and that the only proper inference to be drawn is that the request for Court review of the case did not get the necessary four votes. No one knows exactly why the Justices refuse to vote to grant a full hearing to a case, and surely they can, and do, vote for different, and perhaps conflicting, reasons. The important point to remember is that a denial of certiorari does not mean that the Supreme Court agrees with the result reached by a lower federal or state court. Contrary to what might be reported by the media, a denial of certiorari means only that the case failed to get the necessary four votes for reasons that are unknown.

A slightly different circumstance prevails when the Supreme Court deals with a case that has come to it by appeal, rather than by certiorari. In the case of certiorari, the lawyers, in a sense, are standing outside petitioning the Court to open its doors to them and grant them a full hearing. Thus, a refusal to grant certiorari simply means that the case failed to get the necessary four votes to open the door and to get inside the Court. On the other hand, cases on appeal are, so to speak, already inside the Court, but the question is whether they can stay there and get a full hearing plus a decision on the merits. Cases on appeal contain the necessary federal question for obligatory appeals jurisdiction. But, many cases on appeal, like those on certiorari, border on the frivolous and represent a last-gasp attempt. If the federal question is insignificant or frivolous, the Court may not grant a full hearing to the case. Instead, it may dismiss the appeal for want of a substantial federal question, or perhaps, because the decision below was correct. In such circumstances the decision of the lower court is final, but the Supreme Court has also said that the federal question presented to it is "insubstantial." It did not say this in the cases that were denied certiorari. In appeals, also, as with certiorari, the final result is the same. The court has considerable leeway to pick and choose the cases which it will grant a full hearing, and then decide on the merits.

Currently, Supreme Court review is essentially as follows:

ON APPEAL (a review by right):

From state courts

1. Where a state court has held a federal statute or treaty provision unconstitutional.

2. Where a state court has upheld a state law or state constitutional provision arguably in conflict with the federal Constitution, laws, or treaties.

From federal courts of appeals

1. Where a federal law or treaty is held unconstitutional.

2. Where a state law or state constitutional provision is held invalid because it conflicts with a federal law, treaty, or constitutional provision.

From federal district courts (Direct appeal to Supreme Court)

1. Where a federal statute having a criminal penalty is held unconstitutional.

2. Where judgment has been rendered to enforce antitrust laws, the Interstate Commerce Act, or Title II of the Federal Communications Act.

3. Where a three-judge district court grants or denies an injunction restraining enforcement of state statutes or federal statutes, or orders of certain federal agencies.

ON CERTIORARI (a discretionary review granted or denied by vote of the Supreme Court):

From state courts

1. In cases involving federal questions where the decision was favorable to the federal claim made under federal law or Constitutional provisions.

From courts of appeals

1. Where a decision interprets or applies the Constitution or federal laws or treaties.

2. Where state laws or state constitutional provisions have been challenged as contrary to federal law, and the court of appeals has upheld the state provisions.

Decision-making by the Supreme Court is a group process. Solo performances are unknown. No single member, be he the Chief or Associate Justice, dictates his private reason or personal views to his independent-minded brethern. Individually and independently they work together to arrive at a group decision for the Court. The fact that the decisions of the Supreme Court are group decisions is trite, but easily overlooked. It is highly important and carries with it some interesting and frequently beneficial consequences. For example, one easily ignored implication is that a group decision probably produces a final judgment having a viewpoint of greater breadth and depth, and fewer extremes, than most individual decisions. This point is particularly applicable when one considers the quality of the individual members of the Supreme Court. When Justices are endowed with high-quality intellects and breadth of understanding, they can collectively bring to bear an awesome combination of sweeping brain power and extensive learning on a legal question.

Another feature frequently associated with the group decision process is that of stability. Because of this, the Supreme Court decisions tend to conform to the configurations of the past more than they otherwise might. Radical breaks with history seem not to appear often. Any Justice can raise a point of constitutional tradition and demand that it be met by his colleagues. Collectively, they can record doubts and qualifications which a person, working alone, can easily overlook. The fact that the Court must write group opinions, satisfactory to each member of the majority, although, perhaps, not fully satisfactory to each Justice entirely; the fact that the Court must justify its decisions within the framework of the constitution, and the fact that dissents to these opinions are freely filed, all go a long way toward insuring the integrity and reliability of the group decision process. This process can produce court opinions which are not fully satisfactory to the probing minds of legal scholars because the opinions must sometimes represent a compromise among some Justices, with no one Justice's view completely and rigorously followed. Occasionally, therefore, the group decision process can produce an unaesthetic opinion. But the group decision process also aids the Court to produce stable and, frequently, wise decisions which, in turn, are beneficial to our Nation and which can withstand the fickle breezes of a changing wind. One must always keep in mind: the judicial process in the Supreme Court is a group process. The Court does not function by using either committees or panels of Justices. Unless he disqualifies himself for some reason, each Justice passes on each case that seeks a hearing and on the merits of each case after the hearing has been held. The Constitution puts the judicial power in only one Supreme Court, not in its committees, panels or sections. One invariant rule prevails: judging is always an individual matter for each Justice and is never delegated; yet, too, the judicial process of the Supreme Court results in a group process.

What are the outlines of this judicial process? This question intrigues almost everyone who is seriously interested in the Supreme Court, and its answer is somewhat frustrating. The only honest answer is that no one, outside the Court members themselves, can be absolutely sure of everything that takes place inside the chambers. The reason for this situation is a simple one—the actual deliberations and intellectual interchanges of the Justices while they are in conference are, quite properly, not released to the press and are not made the subject of public curiosity. However, a few things are known, and they, in turn, allow some reasonable speculations regarding others.

A term of Court is well known, although its actual duration may vary slightly. It usually lasts about thirty-six weeks with the first session day being the first Monday of each October and continuing in session usually until about July 1. This means then, that, since the average Justice works six days a week and between eight and ten hours per day, each member of the Court puts in about 1,800 total hours per court term on court business. These hours are spent listening to lawyer arguments on cases, discussing court business in conference sessions, writing or studying opinions, reading other types of petitions, reading the briefs submitted by attorneys, and engaging in other collateral matters affecting the Court.

Officially, when the courtroom is open, the Court is in session only four days a week, Monday through Thursday, and the Justices listen to arguments only four hours per day. This schedule is usually followed by a recess period of about two weeks. During the days of argument the cases are called promptly, and the formal argument is held. Each case is usually given one hour for oral argument, one-half hour for each side. This is a critical time for the lawyer. He cannot read his argument to the Court. He must be able to pull together his side of a complex case, and to present it in a coherent and convincing way. Yet, there is a constant hurdle for him because he must also answer the probing questions which Justices ask, interrupting his argument, and which are based on their reading of the written materials in the case; that is, the briefs and other materials submitted by the attorneys. After hearing arguments, the Court recesses for two or three weeks for purposes of studying briefs, writing opinions and passing on other petitions.

One day has special significance for a student of the Supreme Court. Each Friday of the oral argument weeks finds the members of the Court in conference. During the usual conference session, the members of the Court spend most of their time discussing and voting, although they sometimes go over final drafts of opinions. The bulk of time in conference is probably spent on the cases which recently have been orally argued on their merits. Yet, the Court also must pass on those cases in which lawyers have asked that its discretion be exercised and that the case be granted a hearing by the Court. In these cases, the lawyers have asked that the Court grant their cases a hearing; that is, they have filed a petition requesting a grant of *certiorari,* or if the case is on appeal, they have filed a petition in support of the Court's jurisdiction over the case. The conference sessions begin sharply at eleven o'clock on Friday morning and last until five-thirty. One might be curious about what goes on in the conference.

On Fridays, at eleven, the Justices meet at their conference room which is a beautifully oak paneled chamber with one side lined with books from the floor to the ceiling. An exquisite marble fireplace is at one end of the chamber and over it hangs the only adornment in the room—a portrait of Mr. Chief Justice Marshall, the "Great Chief Justice." There is a rectangular table that stands in the middle of the conference room. The Justices are called to the conference by a buzzer that rings in each Justice's chamber about five minutes before the appointed hour. Religiously, the Justices follow a long held tradition. Meeting near Chief Justice Marshall's portrait, they greet each other in a friendly fashion and shake hands all around before beginning their work. The reason for this rite is that it helps to maintain the necessary working friendships among the Justices when they take up the court business which usually consists of very difficult and controversial cases. The observance is important. It shows that a harmony of aims if not views is the guiding principle of the Court. One should always remember that an independent Justice can be the possessor of a mind which has been honed to a keen cutting edge like a scalpel's, and, occasionally, he may have a rapier tongue to match. But reason prevails, and the Court deliberations seem not to get out of hand, despite the burning issues found in a case and the courage and convictions about them which a Justice may have. After cordialities have been exchanged, the members of the Court seat themselves around a large conference table. The session ensues.

Seated at the head of the table is the Chief Justice and directly across from him, at the other end of the table, sits the Senior Associate Justice. The rest of the members sit on either side of the table according to their rank in seniority, descending in seniority away from the Chief Justice. No one else ever is allowed in the room, and, if necessary, the most recently appointed Justice serves as a "messenger boy," carrying messages in and out of the conference room. This is a security device. It insures a full, frank and free discussion of all issues and ideas with the complete assurance of privacy. Consequently, no one, other than the Justices, really knows the substantive content of what actually transpires during a conference. However, it is known that each Justice has an agenda of the day's cases; that the Chief Justice calls the items on for discussion and that he has the first opportunity to discuss the matter, if he so chooses. Discussion of the matter under consideration then passes from Justice to Justice according to his seniority, those having more seniority speaking first, until each of them has said all that he wishes. After discussion, the Chief Justice calls for the vote. If the case is one that has already been accepted by the Court and has had its hearing it takes a majority vote, usually five of the nine votes, to dispose of the case on its merits. But, if the case is one in which the question is whether the Court will grant a full hearing, it takes only four votes to bring the case to the Court for its initial hearing. Thus, a vote of four Justices is necessary to fix the cases onto the calendar of the Supreme Court and a majority vote, usually a vote of five Justices, is necessary to decide the merits of the case removing it from the Court's calendar. If a Justice disqualifies himself in a case which has had a full hearing and if the remaining eight Justices split in their vote four-to-four, then the decision of the majority in the lower court is affirmed by the Supreme Court. While such a decision is binding on the parties, it does not become a precedent. Interestingly, the voting proceeds by an order opposite to that of the discussion. The first vote is cast by the Justice who has most recently been appointed to the Court and so on up the seniority ladder with the Chief Justice voting last. This procedure has been designed to eliminate the influence of a senior Justice's vote on a junior Justice. It should be noted that the discussion preceding the vote need not indicate the way a senior Justice will vote, but rather, it may very well consist only of an analytical and dispassionate discussion of the problems involved in a case as they have been seen by a Justice.

After the voting is concluded the case must be assigned to a Justice for opinion writing. This assignment is made by the Chief Justice if he has voted with the majority. If not, then the senior Justice voting with the majority assigns the case to a Justice for an opinion. The Justices are notified that evening by messenger of their assignments. No official assignments are made for dissenting or concurring opinions. These lie solely within the discretion of the Justices, and are freely filed. When the majority opinion has been written, to the satisfaction of the individual Justice doing the initial work, it is then circulated to the other members of the Court, majority and dissenting Justices, for their comments. This is a time of agonizing scrutiny. The cracks, crevices and loopholes of an opinion are revealed to its author by the discerning views of his brethren who pass on them with piercing eyes. Frequently, with due contrition, the opinion must be drastically rewritten by its original author and sent again upon its journey to the Justices. The dissenting opinions are also fully circulated among the Justices, and sometimes the dissenting opinions will change votes, occasionally enough votes to make that opinion the majority opinion. Before each Justice finally makes up his mind there has been a constant interchange among them by memoranda, telephone and at the lunch table. Majority opinions have been rewritten as many as ten to twenty times before final agreement was reached. Finally, after receiving approval from the majority, the opinion accompanied by its dissents, is filed in open court. Thus, in summary, it can be seen that the work of the Supreme Court Justices falls into four broad categories: reading various papers (petitions for certiorari, motions, etc.), listening to oral arguments, the conference and tentative voting, and writing opinions and ultimate decision.

Following is a description in quantitative terms of the business of the Supreme Court during the 1972 term. It provides another dimension showing the current workload of the Court. No attempt will be made to describe the legal complexity of any case, nor its controversial character. During that term, reaching roughly from October, 1972 to mid-1973, a record number of 3,748 cases were listed upon the Court's docket. The Court, as a unit, wrote full opinions, some of them from fifty to a hundred pages, or more, and, in addition, the individual Justices produced concurring and dissenting opinions. All in all, there were 182 full-blown Opinions of the Court written during the 1972 term. To gain a full perspective of the amount of work necessary to produce these opinions one should view them in the context of the additional demands upon members of the Court. Primarily, these additional demands are those of reading the briefs and petitions for certiorari, etc., which have been submitted; of hearing arguments; of participating in the deliberative sessions; and of researching and writing opinions. When these considerations are added to the other duties of a Justice, such as supervising a circuit, contributing to the legal education of both law students and members of the practicing bar, as well as conducting his private research and scholarly writing which is incidental to his own personal interests, then, it is clear that, once again, we have reached a point beyond which we cannot reasonably expect more.

CHART, FEDERAL COURT STRUCTURE AND FLOW OF CASES TO THE UNITED STATES SUPREME COURT

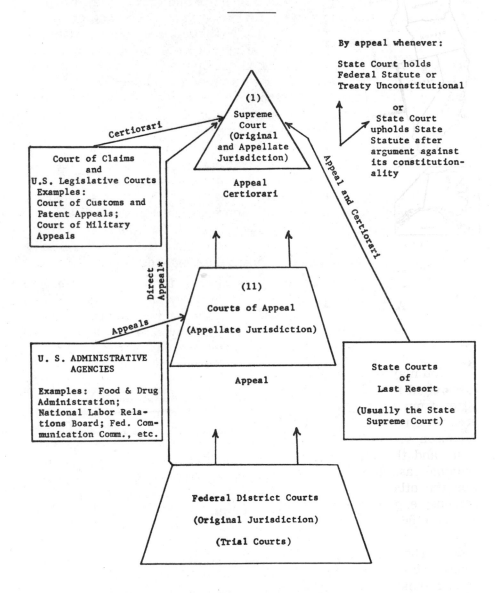

*(1) Holding Federal Statute unconstitutional.
*(2) Ruled against U.S. in criminal case.
*(3) Three-judge court enjoins Federal or state statute.
*(4) Rendering judgment enforcing Antitrust Act, I.C.C. or portions of F.C.C.A.

[A8692]

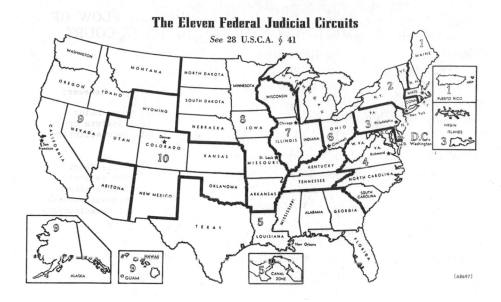

The Eleven Federal Judicial Circuits

See 28 U.S.C.A. § 41

A NOTE ON FINDING AND READING OF CASE OPINIONS

You may want to go to a law library and read the full reports of cases cited in this book. How will you find them? Legal citations differ from other citations, but are quite simple. Generally, cases are given the names of the parties to the law suit. An example is Adamson v. California. Adamson was the defendant in the lower court and the appellant in the Supreme Court, and since it was a criminal case, the State of California, represented by the prosecutor, was the other party. Civil cases usually carry the names of two persons; e. g., Baggett v. Bullitt, 377 U.S. 360, 84 S.Ct. 1316, 12 L.Ed. 2d 377 (1964), with the appellant's name appearing first. The numbers following the name of the case refer to volume and page in that order. The letters between the numbers refer to the title of the book where the opinion may be found. Frequently, the identical opinion can be found in more than one book. In this event, the official report of the case is always cited first. Thus, for Baggett v. Bullitt, the citation is to volume 377 of the official United States reports where the opinion is printed at page 360; it also refers you to volume 84 of the Supreme Court reporter (sometimes cited as S.Ct.), a publication of the West Publishing Company, where the identical opinion is printed at page 1316, and to volume 13 of the United States Supreme Court Reports, Lawyers Edition, second series, another private reporting company, where the identical opinion is printed at page 377. Finally,

(1964) is the date when the case was decided. The citations to state cases are similar. Books are cited similarly to cases: first comes the volume number, but only if the book has more than one volume, followed by the name of the author, then the title of the book, page, and finally the date of publication. Articles are similar: first is the name of the author, followed by the article's title, the volume number, then the title of the journal, followed by the page number, and lastly the date of publication.

Once you have found the opinion, whether in this book or the law library, what do you do with it? One suggestion comes from Karl Llewellyn's book, THE BRAMBLE BUSH, 1960, excerpts are from pp. 41–55:

". . . The first thing to do with an opinion, then, is read it. The next thing is to get clear the actual decision, the judgment rendered. Who won, the plaintiff or defendant? And watch your step here. You are after in first instance the plaintiff and defendant *below*, in the trial court. In order to follow through what happened you must therefore first know the outcome *below;* else you do not see what was appealed from, nor by whom. You now follow through in order to see exactly what *further* judgment has been rendered on appeal. The stage is then cleared of form—although of course you do not yet know all that these forms mean, that they imply. You can turn now to what you want peculiarly to know. Given the actual judgments below and above as your indispensable framework—what has the case decided, and what can you derive from it as to what will be decided later?

"You will be looking, in the opinion, or in the preliminary matter plus the opinion, for the following: a statement of the facts the court assumes; a statement of the precise way the question has come before the court—which includes what the plaintiff wanted below, and what the defendant did about it, the judgment below, and what the trial court did that is complained of; then the outcome on appeal, the judgment; and finally the reasons this court gives for doing what it did. This does not look so bad. But it is much worse than it looks.

"For all our cases are decided, all our opinions are written, all our predictions, all our arguments are made, on certain four assumptions. They are the first presuppositions of our study. They must be rutted into you till you can juggle with them standing on your head and in your sleep.

1) *The court must decide the dispute that is before it.* It cannot refuse because the job is hard, or dubious, or dangerous.

2) *The court can decide* only *the particular dispute which is before it.* When it speaks to that question it speaks ex cathedra, with authority, with finality, with an almost magic power. When it speaks to the question before it, it announces *law,* and if what it announces is new, it legislates, it *makes* the law. But when it speaks to any other

question at all, it says mere words, which no man needs to follow. Are such words worthless? They are not. We know them as judicial *dicta;* when they are wholly off the point at issue we call them *obiter dicta*—words dropped along the road, wayside remarks. Yet even wayside remarks shed light on the remarker. They may be very useful in the future to him, or to us. But he will not feel bound to them, as to his ex cathedra utterance. They came not hallowed by a Delphic frenzy. He may be slow to change them; but not so slow as in the other case.

3) *The court can decide the particular dispute only according to a general rule which covers a whole class of like disputes.* Our legal theory does not admit of single decisions standing on their own. If judges are free, are indeed forced, to decide new cases for which there is no rule, they must at least make a new rule as they decide. So far, good. But how wide, or how narrow, is the general rule in this particular case? That is a troublesome matter. The practice of our case-law, however, is I think fairly stated thus: it pays to be suspicious of general rules which look too wide; it pays to go slow in feeling *certain* that a wide rule has been laid down at all, or that, if seemingly laid down, it will be followed. For there is a fourth accepted canon:

4) *Everything, everything, everything, big or small, a judge may say in an opinion, is to be read with primary reference to the particular dispute, the particular question before him.* You are not to think that the words mean what they might if they stood alone. You are to have your eye on the case in hand, and to learn how to interpret all that has been said *merely* as a reason for deciding *that* case *that* way.

. . .

"What now of preparation for your case class? Your cases are assigned. Before they can be used they have to be digested. Experience shows that it is well to brief them. Briefing is valuable if only for the impending discussion. Briefing is well nigh essential when it comes to the review. . . .

". . . Briefing is also the saddest trap that ever awaited a law student, if he does not watch his step. For the practice under pressure of time, as eyes grow tired in the evening, or the movies lure, is to brief cases, *one by one,* and therefore blindly. Now if I have made one point in this discussion it should be this: that a case read by itself is meaningless, is nil, is blank, is blah . . . Briefing, I say again, is a problem of putting down what in the one case bears upon the problem stated by the other cases. Each brief should be in terms of *what this case adds to what I already know about* this subject. . . . What does the case *add, what difference does it make,* to what I already know? This is the keynote of the brief. . . .

"What, now, should a brief contain? (1) First, as a finder: the title and its page in the casebook. (2) Second, to orient it in the law, the state and date. From now on, the order becomes largely immaterial. I give you one possible and useful order. (3) What, precisely, did the plaintiff want? What did he ask for? This is one most vital and one almost regularly overlooked feature of a brief. This is the first start in coming to the *question*. (4) Contrariwise, what did the defendant want and how did the case come to an issue? (5) What did the trial court do; that is, what was the judgment below? (6) Finally, what action of the trial court is complained of? When you have these things in your brief, and only then, are you prepared to look for either relevant facts or relevant rules of law. When you have found these things, and only then, have you your cross-lines laid to spot *the question* in the case. (7) I find it useful to put down next the outcome of appeal. You see why that is useful. It at once makes clear whether the language of the court in a given passage was or was not necessary to the decision. (8) Then come the facts of the case as assumed by the court. I warn you, I warn you strongly, against cutting the facts down too far. If you cherish any hope of insight into *what difference the rules make* to people, you will have to keep an eye out to some of the more striking details of the facts, as the court gives them. I know you will lose patience with them. But observe this, my friends. *You will be impatient with the facts to the precise extent to which you need them.* If you do not need them, if you already have some knowledge of the background of the case, the facts will not be boring; they will interest you. If they pester and upset you, that is a sign that you know so little about what the case means in life that these facts need desperate study.

"Which facts, then, are significant? I recur again to my proposition. One case will not tell you. Only the group of cases will give you any start at solving that. The more cases you read, therefore, before you brief any, the better off you are, provided only that you brief them each one in the light of all.

"And finally, remember this: it is where the facts (as illumined, as *selected,* as *classified* in the light of other cases) *cross* with the issue given by the procedural set-up, that the narrow-issue question of the case is found. *And only there.*

(9) After the facts, the ratio decidendi, phrased preferably substantially along the lines taken by the court. (10) If you do not like the language of the court, in the light of the other cases, here is the place to note down how you think it should have phrased the rule.

"Beyond this, notes are a matter of discretion. (11) I have always found it useful to indicate something of the line of argument the court indulged in, for reasons which I hope to make appear. (12) A beginning law student, moreover, finds in the cases many remarks as to the law, which although they have no bearing on the subject he is studying, are highly interesting and informative. It was my practice when a student to note those down, but to note them by themselves, where they helped memory but did not get in the way of review.

"So much for the brief. And if you follow this advice you will discover that by the time the last brief is made the class is well prepared.   .   .   ."

Chapter III

THE BILL OF RIGHTS AND THE FOURTEENTH AMENDMENT

INTRODUCTION

The Bill of Rights became part of the Constitution of the United States because of the strong demands that were made for it in the several states during the ratification debates. These first ten amendments along with certain of the provisions of the original Constitution —the prohibitions on bills of attainder, ex post facto laws, impairment of the obligation of contract, suspension of the writ of habeas corpus (see, Art. I, secs. 9 and 10), plus careful procedures for, and a precise and narrow definition of, treason—were, and are, viewed as the fundamental liberties of a free people. They are viewed as fundamental freedoms because they place limitations on the powers of government. Because of these provisions government simply cannot do certain things; for example, it cannot pass a law abridging the freedom of speech; thus, the people constitutionally are free of government controls and within constitutional limits can speak freely, if they so choose. Initially, the Bill of Rights placed limitations only on the powers of the federal government, not on state governments. This view was the foundation of a ruling by the Supreme Court of the United States in Barron v. Baltimore, 7 Pet. 243, 8 L.Ed. 672 (1833). The basic idea was that the national Bill of Rights functioned as a limitation only on federal powers and the state bills of rights functioned as limitations on state powers; the national Bill of Rights did not control the states.

State bills of rights, while highly similar, are not uniform. More importantly, if a state fails to abide by its bill of rights there is little that can be done about it. One can appeal to the state courts that they enforce their limitations upon the powers of their state governments. But, if state courts do not enforce their bills of rights limiting state powers, then that is the end of the matter. Federal courts have no jurisdiction solely to enforce a state bill of rights against that state government. The state courts have the final word when construing and applying their state laws and constitutions, so long as no question of federal law is presented. Thus, when dealing with its own residents in situations not involving federal law, and when unchecked by state courts that fail to enforce their state bills of rights, a state can invade the liberties of its peoples with impunity.

The adoption of the Fourteenth Amendment in 1868 significantly changed this state of affairs by extending federal constitutional controls over the acts of the governments of the states. That amendment applies directly to the states declaring, among other matters, that "No state shall make or enforce any law which shall abridge the privileges or immunities of citizens of the United States; nor shall any State deprive any person of life, liberty or property, without due process of law; nor deny to any person within its jurisdiction the equal protection of the laws." By section five Congress is given power to pass all laws appropriate to implementing this provision. Since the Fourteenth Amendment and all of Congress' statutes under it are federal laws, they can be enforced directly by either state or federal courts having the proper jurisdiction.

One of the important problems posed for the Supreme Court by this amendment is its relationship to the national Bill of Rights. Basically, the Court has had to specify the meaning of the words "liberty" and "due process of law" in the provision of the Fourteenth Amendment declaring that no state shall "deprive any person of life, liberty or property, without due process of law." This provision is frequently referred to as the "due process" clause. But, what is the substantive content of this "liberty" and "due process," and does the Bill of Rights have some special relationship with the "liberty" and "due process" provisions of the Fourteenth Amendment? Three views of the proper relationship between the Bill of Rights and the Fourteenth Amendment have been expressed by Justices of the Supreme Court. They are. (1) The Fundamental Rights View; (2) The Complete Incorporation View, and (3) The Selective Incorporation View. The individual merits of each view have been debated at length, usually in dissenting or concurring opinions, and in the critical literature on the subject. Two additional views—The Complete Incorporation Plus Fundamental Rights View and The Selective Incorporation Plus Fundamental Rights View—set forth the possible breadth of the words "liberty" and "due process" of the Fourteenth Amendment.

THE FUNDAMENTAL RIGHTS VIEW

———

This view once prevailed in the Supreme Court, but no longer. However, some current Justices still adhere to it, and some recent opinions hanker for it to come back, at least in part. The "fundamental rights view" fails to find any necessary relationship between the Bill of Rights and the Fourteenth Amendment. It holds that the Fourteenth Amendment was intended to provide only for equal civil rights and did not directly concern itself with any of the civil liberties of the Bill of Rights. Under this view the "liberty" and the "due process" clauses incorporate only those principles that are "implicit in the concept of ordered liberty." Palko v. Connecticut, 302 U.S. 319, 58 S.Ct. 149, 82 L.Ed. 288 (1937). That is, no specific guarantee of the Bill of Rights is itself completely incorporated into the Fourteenth Amendment's guarantee of "liberty," but instead, only the vaguely defined traditional notions of due process of law are incorporated. The Bill of Rights is only one source of information. Thus, in 1949 in Wolf v. Colorado, 338 U.S. 25, 69 S.Ct. 1359, 93 L.Ed. 1782 (1949), the Supreme Court, in an Opinion by Mr. Justice Frankfurter, reaffirmed the Palko v. Connecticut approach, stating that the "security of one's privacy against arbitrary intrusion by the police—which is at the core of the Fourth Amendment—is basic to a free society. It is therefore implicit in 'the concept of ordered liberty' and as such enforceable against the States through the Due Process Clause." Note what is enforceable against the states. It is not the Fourth Amendment's verbatim provision that the "right of the people to be secure in their persons, houses, papers and effects, against unreasonable searches and seizures, shall not be violated," but rather, it is only the "core" of the Fourth Amendment: "the security of one's privacy against arbitrary intrusion by the police." This is the "fundamental right." Thus, on this view, an act of a state that violates one of the provisions of the national Bill of Rights is seen merely as an indicator that the concept of ordered liberty and a fundamental right may have been violated, but the violation of a guarantee of the Bill of Rights is not itself conclusive that the "liberty" provision of the Fourteenth Amendment has been violated. The ultimate decision would rest on the peculiarities of facts and the "totality of the circumstances" of each case. Thus, constitutional adjudication under the "fundamental rights view" is specifically placed on an ad hoc, case-by-case basis with different decisions turning on the various shadings of facts and different "totalities of circumstances" presented.

The "fundamental rights view" doesn't require that any of the specific, verbatim guarantees of the Bill of Rights be incorporated into the Fourteenth Amendment. On the other hand, it is not limited exclusively to the guarantees of freedom found in the Bill of Rights. So long as the right is "fundamental;" that is, "implicit in the concept of ordered liberty," then it is incorporated into the "liberty" provision of the due process clause, even though it may not be part of the Bill of Rights. Thus, using this view, a Justice could hold that a state was precluded from prosecuting women who had abortions during the first trimester, and doctors who aided them, because an adult woman has the "fundamental right" to ultimate control over her body, even though this "fundamental right" is nowhere explicitly stated as a guarantee of the Bill of Rights.

Judicial critics of the "fundamental rights view" have emphasized its ad hoc subjectivity. They argue that under this view the Justices of the Supreme Court have unconfined and unlimited powers and that such powers contradict the fundamental premise of a written constitution which is to set forth in writing the nature, scope and limits of a governmental power, including judicial power. Mr. Justice Black has stated that the "application of the 'vague contours of due process' depends entirely on the particular judge's idea of ethics and morals instead of requiring him to depend on the boundaries fixed by the written words of the Constitution." Duncan v. Louisiana, 391 U.S. 145, 88 S.Ct. 1444, 20 L.Ed.2d 491 (1968). Earlier in Rochin v. California, 342 U.S. 165, 72 S.Ct. 205, 96 L.Ed. 183 (1952), he said: "I believe that faithful adherence to the specific guarantees in the Bill of Rights insures a more permanent protection of individual liberty than that which can be afforded by the nebulous standards stated by the majority. What the majority hold is that the Due Process Clause empowers this Court to nullify any state law if its application 'shocks the conscience,' offends 'a sense of justice' or runs counter to the 'decencies of civilized conduct.' "

THE COMPLETE INCORPORATION VIEW

Some Justices, notably Mr. Justice Black, have argued that the Bill of Rights in its entirety, but nothing more, is incorporated into the Fourteenth Amendment. This view has never been the view of the Supreme Court, but several of the nine Justices, including Mr. Justice Douglas, serving concurrently have voted for it. This view is supported by its advocates on the grounds (1) that the intent of the makers of the Fourteenth Amendment was to apply the Bill of Rights to the states; (2) that it avoids the ad hoc subjectivity of the fundamental rights view because the Justices would be restricted to the specific wording of the guarantees of the Bill of Rights, and (3) that the Fourteenth Amendment expressly precludes a state from violating the "privileges and immunities of citizens of the United States" and that these privileges and immunities are the guarantees found in the Bill of Rights.

Judicial critics of the "complete incorporation view" dispute the meaning of the history about the intent of the framers of the Fourteenth Amendment, saying that it is not clear that the intent was to incorporate the entire Bill of Rights. They also hold that the "privileges and immunities" clause safeguards only the peculiar rights that inhere in the specific relationship between federal citizenship and the federal government. For example, absent unusual circumstances such as being infected by a severely contagious disease or being a convicted felon fleeing justice, a state could not prohibit a citizen of the United States from leaving its borders and traveling to Washington, D.C. They also argue that the due process clause of the Fourteenth Amendment merely restates one provision of the Fifth Amendment, and that it is the only provision applicable to the states, not the rest of the Bill of Rights. Finally, they hold that a full application of the Bill of Rights to the states would place excessive burdens on them and perhaps eliminate their opportunities for legal flexibility which could result in an extension of the area of human freedom beyond that guaranteed by the Bill of Rights.

THE SELECTIVE INCORPORATION VIEW

This is the current view of the Supreme Court on the relationship of the Bill of Rights to the Fourteenth Amendment, but it is not exhaustive of all the rights incorporated into the "liberty" and "due process" provisions of the Fourteenth Amendment. The "selective incorporation view" combines certain elements from the "complete incorporation view" with elements from the "fundamental rights view." The "selective incorporation view" holds that there is a necessary relationship between the Bill of Rights and the Fourteenth Amendment. In this respect it differs from the "fundamental rights view." It holds that the "liberty" provision of the Fourteenth Amendment necessarily, but selectively, incorporates only some of the verbatim guarantees of the Bill of Rights; those that are, in Mr. Justice Brennan's words, "of the very essence of the scheme of ordered liberty." See, Cohen v. Hurley, 366 U.S. 117, 81 S.Ct. 954, 6 L.Ed.2d 156 (1961). Thus, under this view the exact guarantee of one of the provisions of the Bill of Rights is incorporated, and not merely its "core." On the other hand, not all of the guarantees of the Bill of Rights are incorporated but only some of them are selected for incorporation; hence, the designation of this view as one of "selective incorporation." It also raises the questions: Which of the guarantees should be selected and according to what criteria?

Judicial advocates of this view argue that if a fundamental guarantee of the Bill of Rights is truly "implicit in the concept of ordered liberty" and fundamental to a free society, then that entire right as specifically guaranteed by the Bill of Rights should be incorporated. There should not be any chance that any right expressly stated by a provision of the Bill of Rights can be denied because its violation by the state did not lead inevitably to a violation of the ultimate principle of fundamental fairness and due process of law required by the "fundamental rights view." This latter possibility is open under the "fundamental rights view" because a violation of a Bill of Rights' guarantee by a state is not conclusive, and each case must be judged on its particular "totality of circumstances." Furthermore, they argue that the ad hoc, subjective nature of the "fundamental rights view" lacks the predictability which is present when the full guarantee of the Bill of Rights is incorporated, and that the predictability of law is one of its most desirable features.

Judicial critics have argued that the "selective incorporation view" is nothing more than a spurious compromise between the "fundamental rights view" and the "complete incorporation view" without having the logical or historical support of either. They also argue that when a Justice decides which of the guarantees of the Bill of Rights is to be incorporated, he is engaging in an ad hoc, subjective judgment fully equal to that of the "fundamental rights view." Moreover, they argue that there is no reliable historical evidence that indicates that the Fourteenth Amendment was designed to incorporate some, but not all, of the provisions of the Bill of Rights.

THE COMPLETE INCORPORATION PLUS FUNDAMENTAL RIGHTS VIEW

Although held by various Justices the "complete incorporation plus fundamental rights view" has never been the view of a majority of Justices on the Supreme Court. This view holds that the "liberty" provision of the Fourteenth Amendment not only incorporates the Bill of Rights in its entirety, but also that it includes certain additional "fundamental rights" that are not expressly set forth by the specific provisions of that document. The additional rights are those rights that are fundamental to a free society under the analysis of the "fundamental rights view." Judicial and other critics and supporters of this view rely upon the arguments set forth above.

THE SELECTIVE INCORPORATION PLUS FUNDAMENTAL RIGHTS VIEW

This is the current overall view of the Supreme Court on the "liberty" and "due process" provisions of the Fourteenth Amendment. This view holds that the "liberty" provision of the Fourteenth Amendment selectively incorporates those provisions of the Bill of Rights deemed "fundamental" or "implicit in the concept of ordered liberty," and it also includes other "fundamental rights" that are not expressly set forth in the Constitution. The additional "fundamental rights" are considered to have such a character that they cannot be denied without also violating the fundamental principles of justice that lie at the base of our civil and political institutions. When considering the validity of this view, one should recall the ninth amendment stating that the "enumeration in the Constitution, of certain rights, shall not be construed to deny or disparage others retained by the people." An example of this view is Roe v. Wade, 410 U.S. 113, 93 S.Ct. 705, 35

L.Ed.2d 147 (1973) in which the Supreme Court held certain anti-abortion laws unconstitutional:

". . . the Court has recognized that a right of personal privacy, or a guarantee of certain areas or zones of privacy, does exist under the Constitution. In varying contexts the Court of individual Justices have indeed found at least the roots of that right in the First Amendment, *Stanley v. Georgia,* 394 U.S. 557, 564 (1969); in the Fourth and Fifth Amendments, *Terry v. Ohio,* 392 U.S. 1, 8–9 (1968), *Katz v. United States,* 389 U.S. 347, 350 (1967), *Boyd v. United States,* 116 U.S. 616 (1886), see *Olmstead v. United States,* 277 U.S. 438, 478 (1928) (Brandeis, J., dissenting); in the penumbras of the Bill of Rights, *Griswold v. Connecticut,* 381 U.S. 479, 484–485 (1965); in the Ninth Amendment, *id.,* at 486 (Goldberg, J., concurring); or in the concept of liberty guaranteed by the first section of the Fourteenth Amendment, see *Meyer v. Nebraska,* 262 U.S. 390, 399 (1923). These decisions make it clear that only personal rights that can be deemed 'fundamental' or 'implicit in the concept of ordered liberty,' *Palko v. Connecticut,* 302 U.S. 319, 325 (1937), are included in this guarantee of personal privacy. They also make it clear that the right has some extension to activities relating to marriage, *Loving v. Virginia,* 388 U.S. 1, 12 (1967), procreation, *Skinner v. Oklahoma,* 316 U.S. 535, 541–542 (1942), contraception, *Eisenstadt v. Baird,* 405 U.S. 438, 453–454 (1972); *id.,* at 460, 463–465 (White, J., concurring), family relationships, *Prince v. Massachusetts,* 321 U.S. 158, 166 (1944), and child rearing and education, *Pierce v. Society of Sisters,* 268 U.S. 510, 535 (1925), *Meyer v. Nebraska, supra.*

"This right of privacy, whether it be founded in the Fourteenth Amendment's concept of personal liberty and restrictions upon state action, as we feel it is, or, as the District Court determined, in the Ninth Amendment's reservation of rights to the people, is broad enough to encompass a woman's decision whether or not to terminate her pregnancy."

Judicial and other critics and supporters of this view rely on the arguments set forth above.

Following are excerpts from opinions rendered in three Supreme Court cases. The extracts from the dissenting opinion in the first case, Adamson v. California, 332 U.S. 46, 67 S.Ct. 1672, 91 L.Ed. 1903 (1947), sets forth the view of complete incorporation plus fundamental rights. The second excerpt from Duncan v. Louisiana, infra, in footnotes 4 through 12 lists the decisions applying specific, whole provisions of the Bill of Rights to the states. They have been incorporated "selectively". The opinions in this case review the "incorporation controversy" but are not reprinted here. In addition to the specific guarantees and that incorporated by Duncan v. Louisiana, the double jeopardy prohibition was selectively incorporated and applied to the states in Benton v. Maryland, 395 U.S. 784, 89 S.Ct. 2056, 23 L.Ed.2d 707 (1969) in which the Court stated that "insofar as it is inconsistent with this holding, Palko v. Connecticut is overruled." The third excerpt from Griswold v. Connecticut, 381 U.S. 479, 85 S.Ct. 1678, 14 L.Ed.2d 510 (1965) provides the opportunity for reconsidering the controversy over "incorporation." When reading each of these extracts first identify each Justice with a view and then consider the following: (1) which view is the most objective, and why; (2) which view promotes the greatest predictability and certainty of the law, and why; (3) which view is most consistent with the Constitution, the Fourteenth Amendment and the value of Federalism, and why; and, (4) which view do you believe to be best, and why?

ADAMSON v. CALIFORNIA

Supreme Court of the United States, 1947.
332 U.S. 46, 67 S.Ct. 1672, 91 L.Ed. 1903.

Mr. Justice MURPHY, with whom Mr. Justice RUTLEDGE concurs, dissenting.

While in substantial agreement with the views of Mr. Justice BLACK, I have one reservation and one addition to make.

I agree that the specific guarantees of the Bill of Rights should be carried over intact into the first section of the Fourteenth Amendment. But I am not prepared to say that the latter is entirely and necessarily limited by the Bill of Rights. Occasions may arise where a proceeding falls so far short of conforming to fundamental standards of procedure as to warrant constitutional condemnation in terms of a lack of due process despite the absence of a specific provision in the Bill of Rights.

That point, however, need not be pursued here inasmuch as the Fifth Amendment is explicit in its provision that no person shall be compelled in any criminal case to be a witness against himself. That provision, as Mr. Justice BLACK demonstrates, is a constituent part of the Fourteenth Amendment. . . .

DUNCAN v. LOUISIANA

Supreme Court of the United States, 1968.
391 U.S. 145, 88 S.Ct. 1444, 20 L.Ed.2d 491, reh. den. 392 U.S. 947, 88 S.Ct. 2270,
20 L.Ed.2d 1412.

Mr. Justice WHITE delivered the opinion of the Court. . . .

The Fourteenth Amendment denies the States the power to "deprive any person of life, liberty, or property, without due process of law." In resolving conflicting claims concerning the meaning of this spacious language, the Court has looked increasingly to the Bill of Rights for guidance; many of the rights guaranteed by the first eight Amendments to the Constitution have been held to be protected against state action by the Due Process Clause of the Fourteenth Amendment. That clause now protects the right to compensation for property taken by the State;[4] the rights of speech, press, and religion covered by the First Amendment;[5] the Fourth Amendment rights to be free from unreasonable searches and seizures and to have excluded from criminal trials any evidence illegally seized;[6] the right guaranteed by the Fifth Amendment to be free of compelled self-incrimination;[7] and the Sixth Amendment rights to counsel,[8] to a speedy [9] and public [10] trial, to confrontation of opposing witnesses,[11] and to compulsory process for obtaining witnesses.[12]

The test for determining whether a right extended by the Fifth and Sixth Amendments with respect to federal criminal proceedings is also protected against state action by the Fourteenth Amendment has been phrased in a variety of ways in the opinions of this Court. The question has been asked whether a right is among those " 'fundamental principles of liberty and justice which lie at the base of all our civil and political institutions,' " Powell v. Alabama, 287 U.S. 45, 67 (1932);[13] whether it is "basic in our system of jurisprudence," In re Oliver, 333 U.S. 257, 273 (1948); and whether it is "a fundamental right, essential to a fair trial," Gideon v. Wainwright, 372 U.S. 335, 343–344 (1963); Malloy v. Hogan, 378 U.S. 1, 6 (1964); Pointer v. Texas, 380 U.S. 400, 403 (1965). The claim before us is that the right to trial by jury guaranteed by the Sixth Amendment meets these tests. The position of Louisiana, on the other hand, is that the Constitution imposes upon the States no duty to give a jury trial in any criminal

---

[4] Chicago, B. & Q. R. Co. v. Chicago, 166 U.S. 226 (1897).

[5] See, e. g., Fiske v. Kansas, 274 U.S. 380 (1927).

[6] See Mapp v. Ohio, 367 U.S. 643 (1961).

[7] Malloy v. Hogan, 378 U.S. 1 (1964).

[8] Gideon v. Wainwright, 372 U.S. 335 (1963).

[9] Klopfer v. North Carolina, 386 U.S. 213 (1967).

[10] In re Oliver, 333 U.S. 257 (1948).

[11] Pointer v. Texas, 380 U.S. 400 (1965).

[12] Washington v. Texas, 388 U.S. 14 (1967).

[13] Quoting from Hebert v. Louisiana, 272 U.S. 312, 316 (1926).

case, regardless of the seriousness of the crime or the size of the punishment which may be imposed. Because we believe that trial by jury in criminal cases is fundamental to the American scheme of justice, we hold that the Fourteenth Amendment guarantees a right of jury trial in all criminal cases which—were they to be tried in a federal court—would come within the Sixth Amendment's guarantee.[14] Since we consider the appeal before us to be such a case, we hold that the Constitution was violated when appellant's demand for a jury trial was refused.

[14] In one sense recent cases applying provisions of the first eight Amendments to the States represent a new approach to the "incorporation" debate. Earlier the Court can be seen as having asked, when inquiring into whether some particular procedural safeguard was required of a State, if a civilized system could be imagined that would not accord the particular protection. For example, Palko v. Connecticut, 302 U.S. 319, 325 (1937), stated: "The right to trial by jury and the immunity from prosecution except as the result of an indictment may have value and importance. Even so, they are not of the very essence of a scheme of ordered liberty. . . . Few would be so narrow or provincial as to maintain that a fair and enlightened system of justice would be impossible without them." The recent cases, on the other hand, have proceeded upon the valid assumption that state criminal processes are not imaginary and theoretical schemes but actual systems bearing virtually every characteristic of the common-law system that has been developing contemporaneously in England and in this country. The question thus is whether given this kind of system a particular procedure is fundamental—whether, that is, a procedure is necessary to an Anglo-American regime of ordered liberty. It is this sort of inquiry that can justify the conclusions that state courts must exclude evidence seized in violation of the Fourth Amendment, Mapp v. Ohio, 367 U.S. 643 (1961); that state prosecutors may not comment on a defendant's failure to testify, Griffin v. California, 380 U.S. 609 (1965); and that criminal punishment may not be imposed for the status of narcotics addiction, Robinson v. California, 370 U.S. 660 (1962). Of immediate relevance for this case are the Court's holdings that the States must comply with certain provisions of the Sixth Amendment, specifically that the States may not refuse a speedy trial, confrontation of witnesses, and the assistance, at state expense if necessary, of counsel. See cases cited in nn. 8–12, supra. Of each of these determinations that a constitutional provision originally written to bind the Federal Government should bind the States as well it might be said that the limitation in question is not necessarily fundamental to fairness in every criminal system that might be imagined but is fundamental in the context of the criminal processes maintained by the American States.

When the inquiry is approached in this way the question whether the States can impose criminal punishment without granting a jury trial appears quite different from the way it appeared in the older cases opining that States might abolish jury trial. See, e. g., Maxwell v. Dow, 176 U.S. 581 (1900). A criminal process which was fair and equitable but used no juries is easy to imagine. It would make use of alternative guarantees and protections which would serve the purposes that the jury serves in the English and American systems. Yet no American State has undertaken to construct such a system. Instead, every American State, including Louisiana, uses the jury extensively, and imposes very serious punishments only after a trial at which the defendant has a right to a jury's verdict. In every State, including Louisiana, the structure and style of the criminal process—the supporting framework and the subsidiary procedures—are of the sort that naturally complement jury trial, and have developed in connection with and in reliance upon jury trial.

GRISWOLD v. CONNECTICUT

Supreme Court of the United States, 1965.
381 U.S. 479, 85 S.Ct. 1678, 14 L.Ed.2d 510.

Mr. Justice DOUGLAS delivered the opinion of the Court.

Appellant Griswold is Executive Director of the Planned Parenthood League of Connecticut. Appellant Buxton is a licensed physician and a professor at the Yale Medical School who served as Medical Director for the League at its Center in New Haven—a center open and operating from November 1 to November 10, 1961, when appellants were arrested.

They gave information, instruction, and medical advice to *married persons* as to the means of preventing conception. They examined the wife and prescribed the best contraceptive device or material for her use. Fees were usually charged, although some couples were serviced free.

The statutes whose constitutionality is involved in this appeal are §§ 52–32 and 54–196 of the General Statutes of Connecticut (1958 rev.). The former provides:

"Any person who uses any drug, medicinal article or instrument for the purpose of preventing conception shall be fined not less than fifty dollars or imprisoned not less than sixty days nor more than one year or be both fined and imprisoned."

Section 54–196 provides:

"Any person who assists, abets, counsels, causes, hires or commands another to commit any offense may be prosecuted and punished as if he were the principal offender."

The appellants were found guilty as accessories and fined $100 each, against the claim that the accessory statute as so applied violated the Fourteenth Amendment. . . .

We think that appellants have standing to raise the constitutional rights of the married people with whom they had a professional relationship. . . . Certainly the accessory should have standing to assert that the offense which he is charged with assisting is not, or cannot constitutionally be, a crime. . . . The rights of husband and wife, pressed here, are likely to be diluted or adversely affected unless those rights are considered in a suit involving those who have this kind of confidential relation to them.

Coming to the merits, we are met with a wide range of questions that implicate the Due Process Clause of the Fourteenth Amendment. Overtones of some arguments suggest that Lochner v. New York, 198

U.S. 45, should be our guide.   But we decline that invitation.   .   .   .
We do not sit as a super-legislature to determine the wisdom, need, and
propriety of laws that touch economic problems, business affairs, or
social conditions.   This law, however, operates directly on an intimate
relation of husband and wife and their physician's role in one aspect
of that relation.

The association of people is not mentioned in the Constitution nor
in the Bill of Rights.   The right to educate a child in a school of the
parents' choice—whether public or private or parochial—is also not
mentioned.   Nor is the right to study any particular subject or any
foreign language.   Yet the First Amendment has been construed to
include certain of those rights.

By Pierce v. Society of Sisters, supra, the right to educate one's
children as one chooses is made applicable to the States by the force of
the First and Fourteenth Amendments   By Meyer v. Nebraska, supra,
the same dignity is given the right to study the German language in a
private school.   In other words, the State may not, consistently with
the spirit of the First Amendment, contract the spectrum of available
knowledge.   The right of freedom of speech and press includes not
only the right to utter or to print, but the right to distribute, the right
to receive, the right to read   .   .   .   and freedom of inquiry, freedom
of thought, and freedom to teach   .   .   .—indeed the freedom of the
entire university community.   .   .   .   Without those peripheral
rights the specific rights would be less secure.   .   .   .

In NAACP v. Alabama, 357 U.S. 449, 462, we protected the "freedom to associate and privacy in one's associations," noting that freedom of association was a peripheral First Amendment right.   Disclo
sure of membership lists of a constitutionally valid association, we
held, was invalid "as entailing the likelihood of a substantial restraint
upon the exercise by petitioner's members of their right to freedom of
association."   *Ibid.*   In other words, the First Amendment has a penumbra where privacy is protected from governmental intrusion.   In
like context, we have protected forms of "association" that are not
political in the customary sense but pertain to the social, legal, and
economic benefit of the members.   .   .   .   In Schware v. Board of
Bar Examiners, 353 U.S. 232, we held it not permissible to bar a lawyer
from practice, because he had once been a member of the Communist
Party.   The man's "association with that Party" was not shown to be
"anything more than a political faith in a political party"   .   .   .
and was not action of a kind proving bad moral character.   .   .   .

Those cases involved more than the "right of assembly"—a right
that extends to all irrespective of their race or ideology.   .   .   .   The
right of "association," like the right of belief   .   .   .   is more than
the right to attend a meeting;   it includes the right to express one's
attitudes or philosophies by membership in a group or by affiliation

with it or by other lawful means.   Association in that context is a form of expression of opinion; and while it is not expressly included in the First Amendment its existence is necessary in making the express guarantees fully meaningful.

The foregoing cases suggest that specific guarantees in the Bill of Rights have penumbras, formed by emanations from those guarantees that help give them life and substance.   . . .   Various guarantees create zones of privacy.   The right of association contained in the penumbra of the First Amendment is one, as we have seen.   The Third Amendment in its prohibition against the quartering of soldiers "in any house" in time of peace without the consent of the owner is another facet of that privacy.   The Fourth Amendment explicitly affirms the "right of the people to be secure in their persons, houses, papers, and effects, against unreasonable searches and seizures."   The Fifth Amendment in its Self-Incrimination Clause enables the citizen to create a zone of privacy which government may not force him to surrender to his detriment.   The Ninth Amendment provides: "The enumeration in the Constitution, of certain rights, shall not be construed to deny or disparage others retained by the people."

The Fourth and Fifth Amendments were described in Boyd v. United States, 116 U.S. 616, 630, as protection against all governmental invasions "of the sanctity of a man's home and the privacies of life." We recently referred in Mapp v. Ohio, 367 U.S. 643, 656, to the Fourth Amendment as creating a "right to privacy, no less important than any other right carefully and particularly reserved to the people." . . .

The present case, then, concerns a relationship lying within the zone of privacy created by several fundamental constitutional guarantees.   And it concerns a law which, in forbidding the *use* of contraceptives rather than regulating their manufacture or sale, seeks to achieve its goals by means having a maximum destructive impact upon that relationship.   Such a law cannot stand in light of the familiar principle, so often applied by this Court, that a "governmental purpose to control or prevent activities constitutionally subject to state regulation may not be achieved by means which sweep unnecessarily broadly and thereby invade the area of protected freedoms."   NAACP v. Alabama, 377 U.S. 288, 307.   Would we allow the police to search the sacred precincts of marital bedrooms for telltale signs of the use of contraceptives?   The very idea is repulsive to the notions of privacy surrounding the marriage relationship.

We deal with a right of privacy older than the Bill of Rights— older than our political parties, older than our school system.   Marriage is a coming together for better or for worse, hopefully enduring, and intimate to the degree of being sacred.   It is an association that promotes a way of life, not causes; a harmony in living, not political faiths, a bilateral loyalty, not commercial or social projects. Yet it is an association for as noble a purpose as any involved in our prior decisions.

Reversed.

Mr. Justice GOLDBERG, whom THE CHIEF JUSTICE [WARREN] and Mr. Justice BRENNAN join, concurring.

I agree with the Court that Connecticut's birth-control law unconstitutionally intrudes upon the right of marital privacy, and I join in its opinion and judgment. Although I have not accepted the view that "due process" as used in the Fourteenth Amendment incorporates all of the first eight Amendments, . . . I do agree that the concept of liberty protects those personal rights that are fundamental, and is not confined to the specific terms of the Bill of Rights. My conclusion that the concept of liberty is not so restricted and that it embraces the right of marital privacy though that right is not mentioned explicitly in the Constitution is supported both by numerous decisions of this Court, referred to in the Court's opinion, and by the language and history of the Ninth Amendment. In reaching the conclusion that the right of marital privacy is protected, as being within the protected penumbra of specific guarantees of the Bill of Rights, the Court refers to the Ninth Amendment, . . . I add these words to emphasize the relevance of that Amendment to the Court's holding.

The Court stated many years ago that the Due Process Clause protects those liberties that are "so rooted in the traditions and conscience of our people as to be ranked as fundamental." . . . In Gitlow v. New York, 268 U.S. 652, 666, the Court said:

> "For present purposes we may and do assume that freedom of speech and of the press—which are protected by the First Amendment from abridgment by Congress—are among the *fundamental* personal rights and 'liberties' protected by the due process clause of the Fourteenth Amendment from impairment by the States." (Emphasis added.)

And in Meyer v. Nebraska, 262 U.S. 390, 399, the Court, referring to the Fourteenth Amendment, stated:

> "While this Court has not attempted to define with exactness the liberty thus guaranteed, the term has received much consideration and some of the included things have been definitely stated. Without doubt, it denotes not merely freedom from bodily restraint but also [for example,] the right . . . to marry, establish a home and bring up children . . . ."

This Court, in a series of decisions, has held that the Fourteenth Amendment absorbs and applies to the States those specifics of the first eight amendments which express fundamental personal rights.

The language and history of the Ninth Amendment reveal that the Framers of the Constitution believed that there are additional fundamental rights, protected from governmental infringement, which exist alongside those fundamental rights specifically mentioned in the first eight constitutional amendments.

The Ninth Amendment reads, "The enumeration in the Constitution, of certain rights, shall not be construed to deny or disparage others retained by the people." The Amendment is almost entirely the work of James Madison. It was introduced in Congress by him and passed the House and Senate with little or no debate and virtually no change in language. It was proffered to quiet expressed fears that a bill of specifically enumerated rights could not be sufficiently broad to cover all essential rights and that the specific mention of certain rights would be interpreted as a denial that others were protected.

In presenting the proposed Amendment, Madison said:

"It has been objected also against a bill of rights, that, by enumerating particular exceptions to the grant of power, it would disparage those rights which were not placed in that enumeration; and it might follow by implication, that those rights which were not singled out, were intended to be assigned into the hands of the General Government, and were consequently insecure. This is one of the most plausible arguments I have ever heard urged against the admission of a bill of rights into this system; but, I conceive, that it may be guarded against. I have attempted it, as gentlemen may see by turning to the last clause of the fourth resolution [the Ninth Amendment]." I Annals of Congress 439 (Gales and Seaton ed. 1834).

Mr. Justice Story wrote of this argument against a bill of rights and the meaning of the Ninth Amendment:

"In regard to . . . [a] suggestion, that the affirmance of certain rights might disparage others, or might lead to argumentative implications in favor of other powers, it might be sufficient to say that such a course of reasoning could never be sustained upon any solid basis . . . .
But a conclusive answer is, that such an attempt may be interdicted (as it has been) by a positive declaration in such a bill of rights that the enumeration of certain rights shall not be construed to deny or disparage others retained by the people." II Story, Commentaries on the Constitution of the United States 626–627 (5th ed. 1891).

He further stated, referring to the Ninth Amendment:

"This clause was manifestly introduced to prevent any perverse or ingenious misapplication of the well-known maxim, that an affirmation in particular cases implies a negation in

all others; and, *e converso,* that a negation in particular
cases implies an affirmation in all others." Id., at 651.

These statements of Madison and Story make clear that the Framers
did not intend that the first eight amendments be construed to ex-
haust the basic and fundamental rights which the Constitution guaranteed to the people.

While this Court has had little occasion to interpret the Ninth
Amendment, "[i]t cannot be presumed that any clause in the constitution is intended to be without effect." Marbury v. Madison, 1
Cranch 137, 174. In interpreting the Constitution, "real effect should
be given to all the words it uses." . . . The Ninth Amendment to
the Constitution may be regarded by some as a recent discovery and
may be forgotten by others, but since 1791 it has been a basic part of
the Constitution which we are sworn to uphold. To hold that a right
so basic and fundamental and so deep-rooted in our society as the
right of privacy in marriage may be infringed because that right is
not guaranteed in so many words by the first eight amendments to
the Constitution is to ignore the Ninth Amendment and to give it no
effect whatsoever. Moreover, a judicial construction that this fundamental right is not protected by the Constitution because it is not
mentioned in explicit terms by one of the first eight amendments or
elsewhere in the Constitution would violate the Ninth Amendment,
which specifically states that "[t]he enumeration in the Constitution,
of certain rights, shall not be *construed* to deny or disparage others
retained by the people." (Emphasis added.)

A dissenting opinion suggests that my interpretation of the Ninth
Amendment somehow "broaden[s] the powers of this Court." . . .
With all due respect, I believe that it misses the import of what I am
saying. I do not take the position of my Brother BLACK in his dissent in Adamson v. California, . . . that the entire Bill of Rights
is incorporated in the Fourteenth Amendment, and I do not mean to
imply that the Ninth Amendment is applied against the States by the
Fourteenth. Nor do I mean to state that the Ninth Amendment constitutes an independent source of rights protected from infringement
by either the States or the Federal Government. Rather, the Ninth
Amendment shows a belief of the Constitution's authors that fundamental rights exist that are not expressly enumerated in the first
eight amendments and an intent that the list of rights included there
not be deemed exhaustive. As any student of this Court's opinions
knows, this Court has held, often unanimously, that the Fifth and
Fourteenth Amendments protect certain fundamental personal liberties from abridgment by the Federal Government or the States. . .
The Ninth Amendment simply shows the intent of the Constitution's
authors that other fundamental personal rights should not be denied
such protection or disparaged in any other way simply because they
are not specifically listed in the first eight constitutional amendments.

I do not see how this broadens the authority of the Court; rather it serves to support what this Court has been doing in protecting fundamental rights.

Nor am I turning somersaults with history in arguing that the Ninth Amendment is relevant in a case dealing with a *State's* infringement of a fundamental right. While the Ninth Amendment— and indeed the entire Bill of Rights—originally concerned restrictions upon *federal* power, the subsequently enacted Fourteenth Amendment prohibits the States as well from abridging fundamental personal liberties. And, the Ninth Amendment, in indicating that not all such liberties are specifically mentioned in the first eight amendments, is surely relevant in showing the existence of other fundamental personal rights, now protected from state, as well as federal, infringement. In sum, the Ninth Amendment simply lends strong support to the view that the "liberty" protected by the Fifth and Fourteenth Amendments from infringement by the Federal Government or the States is not restricted to rights specifically mentioned in the first eight amendments. . . .

In determining which rights are fundamental, judges are not left at large to decide cases in light of their personal and private notions. Rather, they must look to the "traditions and [collective] conscience of our people" to determine whether a principle is "so rooted [there] . . . as to be ranked as fundamental." . . . The inquiry is whether a right involved "is of such a character that it cannot be denied without violating those 'fundamental principles of liberty and justice which lie at the base of all our civil and political institutions'. . . ." . . . "Liberty" also "gains content from the emanations of . . . specific [constitutional] guarantees" and "from experience with the requirements of a free society." . . .

I agree fully with the Court that, applying these tests, the right of privacy is a fundamental personal right, emanating "from the totality of the constitutional scheme under which we live." . . . Mr. Justice Brandeis, dissenting in Olmstead v. United States, 277 U.S. 438, 478, comprehensively summarized the principles underlying the Constitution's guarantees of privacy:

"The protection guaranteed by the [Fourth and Fifth] Amendments is much broader in scope. The makers of our Constitution undertook to secure conditions favorable to the pursuit of happiness. They recognized the significance of man's spiritual nature, of his feelings and of his intellect. They knew that only a part of the pain, pleasure and satisfactions of life are to be found in material things. They sought to protect Americans in their beliefs, their thoughts, their emotions and their sensations. They conferred, as against the Government, the right to be let alone—the most comprehensive of rights and the right most valued by civilized men." . . .

In sum, I believe that the right of privacy in the marital relation is fundamental and basic—a personal right "retained by the people" within the meaning of the Ninth Amendment. Connecticut cannot constitutionally abridge this fundamental right, which is protected by the Fourteenth Amendment from infringement by the States. I agree with the Court that petitioners' convictions must therefore be reversed.

Mr. Justice HARLAN, concurring in the judgment.

I fully agree with the judgment of reversal, but find myself unable to join the Court's opinion. The reason is that it seems to me to evince an approach to this case very much like that taken by my Brothers BLACK and STEWART in dissent, namely: the Due Process Clause of the Fourteenth Amendment does not touch this Connecticut statute unless the enactment is found to violate some right assured by the letter or penumbra of the Bill of Rights.

In other words, what I find implicit in the Court's opinion is that the "incorporation" doctrine may be used to *restrict* the reach of Fourteenth Amendment Due Process. For me this is just as unacceptable constitutional doctrine as is the use of the "incorporation" approach to *impose* upon the States all the requirements of the Bill of Rights as found in the provisions of the first eight amendments and in the decisions of this Court interpreting them. . . .

In my view, the proper constitutional inquiry in this case is whether this Connecticut statute infringes the Due Process Clause of the Fourteenth Amendment because the enactment violates basic values "implicit in the concept of ordered liberty," Palko v. Connecticut, 302 U.S. 319, 325. For reasons stated at length in my dissenting opinion in Poe v. Ullman, . . ., I believe that it does. While the relevant inquiry may be aided by resort to one or more of the provisions of the Bill of Rights, it is not dependent on them or any of their radiations. The Due Process Clause of the Fourteenth Amendment stands, in my opinion, on its own bottom.

A further observation seems in order respecting the justification of my Brothers BLACK and STEWART for their "incorporation" approach to this case. Their approach does not rest on historical reasons, which are of course wholly lacking (see Fairman, Does the Fourteenth Amendment Incorporate the Bill of Rights? The Original Understanding, 2 Stan.L.Rev. 5 (1949)), but on the thesis that by limiting the content of the Due Process Clause of the Fourteenth Amendment to the protection of rights which can be found elsewhere in the Constitution, in this instance in the Bill of Rights, judges will thus be confined to "interpretation" of specific constitutional provisions, and will thereby be restrained from introducing their own notions of constitutional right and wrong into the "vague contours of the Due Process Clause." . . .

Judicial self-restraint will not, I suggest, be brought about in the "due process" area by the historically unfounded incorporation formula long advanced by my Brother BLACK, and now in part espoused by by Brother STEWART. It will be achieved in this area, as in other constitutional areas, only by continual insistence upon respect for the teachings of history, solid recognition of the basic values that underlie our society, and wise appreciation of the great roles that the doctrines of federalism and separation of powers have played in establishing and preserving American freedoms. See Adamson v. California, . . . (Mr. Justice Frankfurter, concurring). Adherence to these principles will not, of course, obviate all constitutional difference of opinion among judges, nor should it. Their continued recognition will, however, go farther toward keeping most judges from roaming at large in the constitutional field than will the interpolation into the Constitution of an artificial and largely illusory restriction on the content of the Due Process Clause.

Mr. Justice WHITE, concurring in the judgment.

In my view this Connecticut law as applied to married couples deprives them of "liberty" without due process of law, as that concept is used in the Fourteenth Amendment. I therefore concur in the judgment of the Court reversing these convictions under Connecticut's aiding and abetting statute.

It would be unduly repetitious, and belaboring the obvious, to expound on the impact of this statute on the liberty guaranteed by the Fourteenth Amendment against arbitrary or capricious denials or on the nature of this liberty. Suffice it to say that this is not the first time this Court has had occasion to articulate that the liberty entitled to protection under the Fourteenth Amendment includes the right "to marry, establish a home and bring up children," . . . and "the liberty . . . to direct the upbringing and education of children," . . . and that these are among "the basic civil rights of man." . . . These decisions affirm that there is a "realm of family life which the state cannot enter" without substantial justification. . . . Surely the right invoked in this case, to be free of regulation of the intimacies of the marriage relationship, "come[s] to this Court with a momentum for respect lacking when appeal is made to liberties which derive merely from shifting economic arrangements." . . .

Mr. Justice BLACK, with whom Mr. Justice STEWART joins, dissenting.

I agree with my Brother STEWART's dissenting opinion. And like him I do not to any extent whatever base my view that this Connecticut law is constitutional on a belief that the law is wise or that its policy is a good one. In order that there may be no room at all to doubt why I vote as I do, I feel constrained to add that the law is every bit as offensive to me as it is to my Brethren. . . . There is no single one of the graphic and eloquent strictures and criticisms fired at the policy of this Connecticut law either by the Court's opinion or by those of my concurring Brethren to which I cannot subscribe— except their conclusion that the evil qualities they see in the law make it unconstitutional.

Had the doctor defendant here, or even the nondoctor defendant, been convicted for doing nothing more than expressing opinions to persons coming to the clinic that certain contraceptive devices, medicines or practices would do them good and would be desirable, or for telling people how devices could be used, I can think of no reasons at this time why their expressions of views would not be protected by the First and Fourteenth Amendments, which guarantee freedom of speech. . . . But speech is one thing; conduct and physical activities are quite another. . . . The two defendants here were active participants in an organization which gave physical examinations to women, advised them what kind of contraceptive devices or medicines would most likely be satisfactory for them, and then supplied the devices themselves, all for a graduated scale of fees, based on the family income. Thus these defendants admittedly engaged with others in a planned course of conduct to help people violate the Connecticut law. Merely because some speech was used in carrying on that conduct—just as in ordinary life some speech accompanies most kinds of conduct—we are not in my view justified in holding that the First Amendment forbids the State to punish their conduct. Strongly as I desire to protect all First Amendment freedoms, I am unable to stretch the Amendment so as to afford protection to the conduct of these defendants in violating the Connecticut law. What would be constitutional fate of the law if hereafter applied to punish nothing but speech is, as I have said, quite another matter. . . .

One of the most effective ways of diluting or expanding a constitutionally guaranteed right is to substitute for the crucial word or words of a constitutional guarantee another word or words, more or less flexible and more or less restricted in meaning. This fact is well illustrated by the use of the term "right of privacy" as a comprehensive substitute for the Fourth Amendment's guarantee against "unreasonable searches and seizures." "Privacy" is a broad, abstract and ambiguous concept which can easily be shrunken in meaning but which can also, on the other hand, easily be interpreted as a constitutional ban against many things other than searches and seizures. I have expressed the view many times that First Amendment freedoms, for example, have suffered from a failure of the courts to stick to the simple language of the First Amendment in construing it, instead of invoking multitudes of words substituted for those the Framers used. . . . For these reasons I get nowhere in this case by talk about a constitutional "right of privacy" as an emanation from one or more constitutional provisions. I like my privacy as well as the next one, but I am nevertheless compelled to admit that government has a right to invade it unless prohibited by some specific constitutional provision. For these reasons I cannot agree with the Court's judgment and the reasons it gives for holding this Connecticut law unconstitutional.

This brings me to the arguments made by my Brothers HARLAN, WHITE and GOLDBERG for invalidating the Connecticut law. . . . I think that if properly construed neither the Due Process Clause nor the Ninth Amendment, nor both together, could under any circumstances be a proper basis for invalidating the Connecticut law. I discuss the due process and Ninth Amendment arguments together because on analysis they turn out to be the same thing—merely using different words to claim for this Court and the federal judiciary power to invalidate any legislative act which the judges find irrational, unreasonable or offensive.

The due process argument which my Brothers HARLAN and WHITE adopt here is based, as their opinions indicate, on the premise that this Court is vested with power to invalidate all state laws that it considers to be arbitrary, capricious, unreasonable, or oppressive, or on this Court's belief that a particular state law under scrutiny has no "rational or justifying" purpose, or is offensive to a "sense of fairness and justice." If these formulas based on "natural justice," or others which mean the same thing, are to prevail, they require judges to determine what is or is not constitutional on the basis of their own appraisal of what laws are unwise or unnecessary. The power to make such decisions is of course that of a legislative body. Surely it has to be admitted that no provision of the Constitution specifically gives such blanket power to courts to exercise such a supervisory veto over the wisdom and value of legislative policies and to hold unconstitutional those laws which they believe unwise or dangerous. I readily admit that no legislative body, state or national, should pass laws that can justly be given any of the invidious labels invoked as constitutional excuses to strike down state laws. But perhaps it is not too much to say that no legislative body ever does pass laws without believing that they will accomplish a sane, rational, wise and justifiable purpose. While I completely subscribe to the holding of Marbury v. Madison, 1 Cranch 137, and subsequent cases, that our Court has constitutional power to strike down statutes, state or federal, that violate commands of the Federal Constitution, I do not believe that we are granted power by the Due Process Clause or any other constitutional provision or provisions to measure constitutionality by our belief that legislation is arbitrary, capricious or unreasonable, or accomplishes no justifiable purpose, or is offensive to our own notions of "civilized standards of conduct." Such an appraisal of the wisdom of legislation is an attribute of the power to make laws, not of the power to interpret them. The use by federal courts of such a formula or doctrine or whatnot to veto federal or state laws simply takes away from Congress and States the power to make laws based on their own judgment of fairness and wisdom and transfers that power to this Court for ultimate determination—a power which was specifically denied to federal courts by the convention that framed the Constitution. . . .

My Brother GOLDBERG has adopted the recent discovery that the Ninth Amendment as well as the Due Process Clause can be used by this Court as authority to strike down all state legislation which this Court thinks violates "fundamental principles of liberty and justice," or is contrary to the "traditions and [collective] conscience of our people." He also states, without proof satisfactory to me, that in making decisions on this basis judges will not consider "their personal and private notions." One may ask how they can avoid considering them. Our Court certainly has no machinery with which to take a Gallup Poll. And the scientific miracles of this age have not yet produced a gadget which the Court can use to determine what traditions are rooted in the "[collective] conscience of our people." Moreover, one would certainly have to look far beyond the language of the Ninth Amendment to find that the Framers vested in this Court any such awesome veto powers over lawmaking, either by the States or by the Congress. Nor does anything in the history of the Amendment offer any support for such a shocking doctrine. The whole history of the adoption of the Constitution and Bill of Rights points the other way, and the very material quoted by my Brother GOLDBERG shows that the Ninth Amendment was intended to protect against the idea that "by enumerating particular exceptions to the grant of power" to the Federal Government, "those rights which were not singled out, were intended to be assigned into the hands of the General Government [the United States], and were consequently insecure." That Amendment was passed, not to broaden the powers of this Court or any other department of "the General Government," but, as every student of history knows, to assure the people that the Constitution in all its provisions was intended to limit the Federal Government to the powers granted expressly or by necessary implication. If any broad, unlimited power to hold laws unconstitutional because they offend what this Court conceives to be the "[collective] conscience of our people" is vested in this Court by the Ninth Amendment, the Fourteenth Amendment, or any other provision of the Constitution, it was not given by the Framers, but rather has been bestowed on the Court by the Court. This fact is perhaps responsible for the peculiar phenomenon that for a period of a century and a half no serious suggestion was ever made that the Ninth Amendment, enacted to protect state powers against federal invasion, could be used as a weapon of federal power to prevent state legislatures from passing laws they consider appropriate to govern local affairs. Use of any such broad, unbounded judicial authority would make of this Court's members a day-to-day constitutional convention. . . .

The late Judge Learned Hand, after emphasizing his view that judges should not use the due process formula suggested in the concurring opinions today or any other formula like it to invalidate legislation offensive to their "personal preferences," made the statement, with which I fully agree, that:

"For myself it would be most irksome to be ruled by a bevy of Platonic Guardians, even if I knew how to choose them, which I assuredly do not."

So far as I am concerned, Connecticut's law as applied here is not forbidden by any provision of the Federal Constitution as that Constitution was written, and I would therefore affirm.

Mr. Justice STEWART, whom Mr. Justice BLACK joins, dissenting.

Since 1879 Connecticut has had on its books a law which forbids the use of contraceptives by anyone. I think this is an uncommonly silly law. As a practical matter, the law is obviously unenforceable, except in the oblique context of the present case. As a philosophical matter, I believe the use of contraceptives in the relationship of marriage should be left to personal and private choice, based upon each individual's moral, ethical, and religious beliefs. As a matter of social policy, I think professional counsel about methods of birth control should be available to all, so that each individual's choice can be meaningfully made. But we are not asked in this case to say whether we think this law is unwise, or even asinine. We are asked to hold that it violates the United States Constitution. And that I cannot do.

In the course of its opinion the Court refers to no less than six Amendments to the Constitution: the First, the Third, the Fourth, the Fifth, the Ninth, and the Fourteenth. But the Court does not say which of these Amendments, if any, it thinks is infringed by this Connecticut law.

We *are* told that the Due Process Clause of the Fourteenth Amendment is not, as such, the "guide" in this case. With that much I agree. There is no claim that this law, duly enacted by the Connecticut Legislature, is unconstitutionally vague. There is no claim that the appellants were denied any of the elements of procedural due process at their trial, so as to make their convictions constitutionally invalid. And, as the Court says, the day has long passed since the Due Process Clause was regarded as a proper instrument for determining "the wisdom, need, and propriety" of state laws.   .   .   .

As to the First, Third, Fourth, and Fifth Amendments, I can find nothing in any of them to invalidate this Connecticut law, even assuming that all those Amendments are fully applicable against the States.   .   .   .

The Court also quotes the Ninth Amendment, and my Brother GOLDBERG's concurring opinion relies heavily upon it. But to say that the Ninth Amendment has anything to do with this case is to turn somersaults with history. The Ninth Amendment, like its companion the Tenth, which this Court held "states but a truism that all is retained which has not been surrendered," . . . was framed by James Madison and adopted by the States simply to make clear that the adoption of the Bill of Rights did not alter the plan that the *Federal* Government was to be a government of express and limited powers, and that all rights and powers not delegated to it were retained by the people and the individual States. Until today no member of this Court has ever suggested that the Ninth Amendment meant anything else, and the idea that a federal court could ever use the Ninth Amendment to annul a law passed by the elected representatives of the people of the State of Connecticut would have caused James Madison no little wonder.

What provision of the Constitution, then, does make this state law invalid? The Court says it is the right of privacy "created by several fundamental constitutional guarantees." With all deference, I can find no such general right of privacy in the Bill of Rights, in any other part of the Constitution, or in any case ever before decided by this Court.

At the oral argument in this case we were told that the Connecticut law does not "conform to current community standards." But it is not the function of this Court to decide cases on the basis of community standards. We are here to decide cases "agreeably to the Constitution and laws of the United States." It is the essence of judicial duty to subordinate our own personal views, our own ideas of what legislation is wise and what is not. If, as I should surely hope, the law before us does not reflect the standards of the people of Connecticut, the people of Connecticut can freely exercise their true Ninth and Tenth Amendment rights to persuade their elected representatives to repeal it. That is the constitutional way to take this law off the books.

NOTES AND QUESTIONS

1. What view is expressed by each Justice on the relationship of the Bill of Rights to the Fourteenth Amendment? What exact differences, if any, are there between the views of Justice Douglas (peripheries, penumbras, emanations); Justice Goldberg (Ninth Amendment, basic, fundamental, essential personal rights); Justice Harlan (basic values, implicit in the concept of ordered liberty); Justice White (due process); and Justice Black (complete incorporation but no more)? What difference do the differences make? Which view is correct? Why?

2. In Adamson v. California, 332 U.S. 46, 67 S.Ct. 1672, 91 L.Ed. 1903 (1947), Mr. Justice Black, joined by Mr. Justice Douglas, voted for the complete incorporation view. In Griswold, Black dissented from the Opinion of the Court written by Douglas. Considering the Griswold opinions, has either Black or Douglas changed his position on the complete incorporation view of the Bill of Rights? What does Black say? Do

you agree? In a footnote to his opinion in Roe v. Wade, 410 U.S. 113, 93 S.Ct. 705, 35 L.Ed.2d 147 (1973), Douglas writes about Griswold as follows:

"My Brother Stewart, writing in the present cases, says that our decision in *Griswold* reintroduced substantive due process that had been rejected in Ferguson v. Skrupa, 372 U.S. 726. *Skrupa* involved legislation governing a business enterprise; and the Court in that case, as had Mr. Justice Holmes on earlier occasions, rejected the idea that 'liberty' within the meaning of the Due Process Clause of the Fourteenth Amendment was a vessel to be filled with one's personal choices of values, whether drawn from the *laissez faire* school, from the socialistic school, or from the technocrats *Griswold* involved legislation touching on the marital relation and involving the conviction of a licensed physician for giving married people information concerning contraception. There is nothing specific in the Bill of Rights that covers that item. Nor is there anything in the Bill of Rights, that in terms protects the right of association or the privacy in one's association. Yet we found those rights in the periphery of the First Amendment. NAACP v. Alabama, 357 U.S. 449, 462. Other peripheral rights are the right to educate one's children as one chooses, Pierce v. Society of Sisters, 268 U.S. 510, and the right to study the German language, Meyer v. Nebraska, 262 U.S. 390. These decisions, with all respect, have nothing to do with substantive due process. One may think they are not peripheral rights to other rights that are expressed in the Bill of Rights. But that is not enough to bring into play the protection of substantive due process.

"There are of course those who have believed that the reach of due process in the Fourteenth Amendment included all of the Bill of Rights but went further. Such was the view of Mr. Justice Murphy and Mr. Justice Rutledge. See Adamson v. California, 332 U.S. 46, 123, 124 (dissenting). Perhaps they were right; but it is a bridge that neither I nor those who joined the Court opinion in *Griswold* crossed."

Do you agree? If so, how do you explain the Black-Douglas split in *Griswold?*

3. Douglas states in Griswold that the Supreme Court does "not sit as a super-legislature to determine the wisdom, need and propriety of laws that touch economic problems, business affairs, or social conditions," but does his Opinion for the Court assert that it sits as a "super-legislature" with respect to laws that "directly [affect the] intimate relation of husband and wife"? What evidence of this view is there in his opinion? Is it a constitutionally correct view? From which constitutional provision or provisions, and exactly how, according to Douglas, does the "right of marital privacy" emanate? Does any significant part of the decision in Griswold necessarily turn on the "marital" nature of the right to privacy? If not, what principle does Griswold stand for, and in what way is the principle of Griswold relevant to education?

4. Is there any evidence for the view that Douglas and Goldberg concede that the right to privacy can, but that the "right to marital privacy" cannot be found in the constitution? If this is so, can they avoid Black's charges against them?

5. Do you agree with Black that "constitutionally guaranteed" rights can be expanded or diluted by substituting "for the crucial word or words of a constitutional guarantee another word or words, more or less flexible and more or less restricted in meaning"? Is it easy "to stick to the simple language of the First Amendment in construing it, instead of invoking multitudes of words substituted for those the Framers used"? What is the obvious and clear meaning of the "simple language" of the Fourteenth Amendment's "due process clause"?

6. Which of the expressed views would, and which would not, hold unconstitutional a state law prohibiting: Abortion of married women? Abortion of single women? Voluntary euthanasia? Suicide? Adultery with contraceptives? Long-haired beards on high school students? Beards on public school teachers? Private possession in one's home of either marijuana, heroin or obscene films?

A NOTE ON STATE ACTION

Except for the first sentence, the rest of the first section of the Fourteenth Amendment is expressly qualified by a requirement that "state action" must be present before that amendment can apply; for example, ". . . nor shall any state deprive any person of life, liberty, or property, without due process of law. . . ." It does not apply to acts that are purely "private." But is the distinction so clear? What is "state action"?

State action is present whenever a state legislature passes a statute, or when a municipal legislature passes an ordinance, or whenever a State Board of Education or a Local School Board passes a rule or regulation applying to the operation of the public schools. State action is also present whenever a governor of a state acts, or whenever a superintendent, principal or, perhaps, a teacher acts pursuant to prior authorization by a state legislature or a school board. Thus, when in the classroom, the public-school teacher may be engaging in state action. Also, the teacher engages in state action whenever he or she carries out additional duties pursuant to a state law or a rule or regulation of a school board. The teacher is acting as an agent of the state, and his acts are "state action." But, does a teacher engage in state action if, when teaching class, he or she, without authorization, should suddenly hit a student with a club, yardstick or ruler? Or does a teacher engage in state action if while driving to school in the morning before classes, he stops his car four blocks from school and breaks up a fist fight between two pupils who are on their way to school? Is the teacher acting as a private citizen or as an agent of the state? Suppose he breaks up the fist fight after school hours and after the pupils have returned to their homes and have gone outside to play? Suppose the record reveals that a teacher systematically gives lower grades to minority pupils, is that teacher's grading subject to Fourteenth Amendment controls?

One case from the Supreme Court of the United States indicates that "private" schools, under certain circumstances, might possibly engage in "state action," with the result that the Fourteenth Amendment applies to them. In Burton v. Wilmington Parking Authority, 365 U.S. 715, 81 S.Ct. 856, 6 L.Ed.2d 45 (1961), a "private" restaurant obtained a twenty-year lease of some space within a building used for off-street automobile parking and which was owned and operated by the Wilmington Parking Authority, an agency of the State of Delaware. The "private" restaurant spent $220,000 of its money for improvements, redecorations and furnishings, all of which became the property of the Parking Authority; its main and marked public entrance was on the street, and there was no public entrance directly from the parking garage; the Delaware Supreme Court found only "private" action presented and that "the only connection Eagle [restaurant] has with the public facility .   .   . is the furnishing of the sum of $28,700 annually in the form of rent which is used by the Authority to defray a portion of the operating expenses of an otherwise unprofitable enterprise." Eagle restaurant practiced racial discrimination by refusing to serve Black people, and argued that it had a constitutional right to do so because it was "private," and the Fourteenth Amendment's prohibition of racial discrimination applied only to "state action." On appeal, the Supreme Court said: " .   .   . we cannot say that the [factual considerations] lead inescapably to the conclusion that state action is not present. Their persuasiveness is diminished when evaluated in the context of other factors which must be acknowledged.

"The land and building were publicly owned. As an entity, the building was dedicated to 'public uses' in performance of the Authority's 'essential governmental functions.' .   .   . The costs of land acquisition, construction, and maintenance are defrayed entirely from donations by the City of Wilmington, from loans and revenue bonds and from the proceeds of rentals and parking services out of which the loans and bonds were payable. Assuming that the distinction would be significant, cf. Derrington v. Plummer, 240 F.2d 922, 925, (5th Cir. 1956), the commercially leased areas were not surplus state property, but constituted a physically and financially integral and, indeed, indispensable part of the State's plan to operate its project as a self-sustaining unit. Upkeep and maintenance of the building, including necessary repairs, were responsibilities of the Authority and were payable out of public funds. It cannot be doubted that the peculiar relationship of the restaurant to the parking facility in which it is located confers on each an incidental variety of mutual benefits.

Guests of the restaurant are afforded a convenient place to park their automobiles, even if they cannot enter the restaurant directly from the parking area. Similarly, its convenience for diners may well provide additional demand for the Authority's parking facilities. Should any improvements effected in the leasehold by Eagle become part of the realty, there is no possibility of increased taxes being passed on to it since the fee is held by a tax-exempt government agency. Neither can it be ignored, especially in view of Eagle's affirmative allegation that for it to serve Negroes would injure its business, that profits earned by discrimination not only contribute to, but also are indispensable elements in, the financial success of a governmental agency.

"Addition of all these activities, obligations and responsibilities of the Authority, the benefits mutually conferred, together with the obvious fact that the restaurant is operated as an integral part of a public building devoted to a public parking service, indicates that degree of state participation and involvement in discriminatory action which it was the design of the Fourteenth Amendment to condemn. It is irony amounting to grave injustice that in one part of a single building, erected and maintained with public funds by an agency of the State to serve a public purpose, all persons have equal rights, while in another portion, also serving the public, a Negro is a second-class citizen, offensive because of his race, without rights and unentitled to service, but at the same time fully enjoys equal access to nearby restaurants in wholly privately owned buildings. As the Chancellor pointed out, in its lease with Eagle the Authority could have affirmatively required Eagle to discharge the responsibilities under the Fourteenth Amendment imposed upon the private enterprise as a consequence of state participation. But no State may effectively abdicate its responsibilities by either ignoring them or by merely failing to discharge them whatever the motive may be. It is of no consolation to an individual denied the equal protection of the laws that it was done in good faith. Certainly the conclusions drawn in similar cases by the various Courts of Appeals do not depend upon such a distinction. By its inaction, the Authority, and through it the State, has not only made itself a party to the refusal of service, but has elected to place its power, property and prestige behind the admitted discrimination. The State has so far insinuated itself into a position of interdependence with Eagle that it must be recognized as a joint participant in the challenged activity, which, on that account, cannot be considered to have been so 'purely private' as to fall without the scope of the Fourteenth Amendment.

"Because readily applicable formulae may not be fashioned, the conclusions drawn from the facts and circumstances of this record are by no means declared as universal truths on the basis of which every state leasing agreement is to be tested. Owing to the very 'largeness' of government, a multitude of relationships might appear to some to fall within the Amendment's embrace, but that, it must be remembered, can be determined only in the framework of the peculiar facts or circumstances present.   Therefore respondents' prophecy of nigh universal application of a constitutional precept so peculiarly dependent for its invocation upon appropriate facts fails to take into account 'Differences in circumstances [which] beget appropriate differences in law,' Whitney v. Tax Comm'n, 309 U.S. 530, 542. Specifically defining the limits of our inquiry, what we hold today is that when a State leases public property in the manner and for the purpose shown to have been the case here, the proscriptions of the Fourteenth Amendment must be complied with by the lessee as certainly as though they were binding covenants written into the agreement itself.

"The judgment of the Supreme Court of Delaware is reversed and the cause remanded for further proceedings consistent with this opinion.

"REVERSED AND REMANDED."

PROBLEM

Consider the following hypothetical set of facts in light of the Supreme Court's decision and reasoning in Burton v. Wilmington Parking Authority, supra.   The Sacred Heart Academy is a parochial school approved by the State Superintendent of Education for offering common-school education in grades one through twelve.   There is no doubt that the education offered has been certified by the State Superintendent of Education to serve a public purpose, and that the state has relied upon this instruction to service the educational needs of a large percentage of its school-age children; thus, the Academy is an integral part of the state's educational plan.   The Academy has two main buildings, one of which was recently built.   One, the recently constructed High School building, was constructed and furnished after the Board of Directors of the Sacred Heart Academy received a loan from the United States Office of Health, Education and Welfare to cover the entire cost of land acquisition, construction and furnishing. The loan carries the low interest rate of 1% per year, and is part of our Nation's policy of making low-interest funds available for school construction purposes.   The High School is fully equipped with a modern science center which was also purchased and is maintained with the money received from another loan for educational purposes from the federal government, and which carries .5% interest per year. Evidence shows that the Sacred Heart Academy receives tax exemptions from state, county and local property taxation; that it is exempt from Federal income taxation; that some of its required textbooks are supplied free of charge to its students by the State Office of Education; that its high school was constructed after receiving a zoning variance from the City Planning Commission which allowed the structure as an exception to the local zoning code, and that all of its teachers must, and do, have certification under state laws.   It cannot be doubted that the relationship between the Academy and the state is one which confers on each a variety of mutual benefits. The Academy's successes or failures are indispensable elements in the overall success or failure of the state's attempt to educate its children. The Sacred Heart Academy insists on teaching the scriptures of one religion as the revealed truth and as part of its required courses, and it admits all children except that it refuses to admit any children who themselves, or their parents, are of the Black Muslim faith or who are militant atheists. The Academy argues that its policies of discrimination on religious grounds and of promoting and furthering one specific religion are justifiable and are not subject to the Fourteenth Amendment because it is a "private" not a "public" school. Assume that you are the judge, what decision is proper? Would your decision be any different if the state also supplied and paid the salaries of all the science and mathematics teachers who taught at the Academy? If not, what more facts would be necessary before you would conclude that "state action" is present? Why? Assuming that you decide that "state action" is present at the Academy, at least with reference to the high school, would the Congress, the state legislature, or if properly authorized, the state board of education have power to enact rules and regulations controlling and prescribing the admission, and other, practices of the Sacred Heart Academy?

*

Part II

CONSTITUTIONAL CONTROLS AND EDUCATION

Chapter IV

CONSTITUTIONAL FREEDOM AND COMPULSORY EDUCATION

The importance of education is revealed by the fact that forty-eight of the 50 states have state constitutional provisions requiring that the state legislature create a system of public education. On the other hand, only one state (New York) has a constitutional provision requiring that the state provide a service other than education (welfare). Less than half of the state constitutions make specific reference to services, other than education, that a state may elect to provide. Thus, one can see the importance with which education is held, but the question remains: education for what? The answer from the state constitutions is that education is considered to be a vital part of the democratic process, so much so that without education the American political system could not function properly. Virginia, for example, historically recognized the special relationship between effective voting and education by its provision requiring that two-thirds of its poll tax be used "exclusively in aid of the free public schools." Constitution of Virginia, Article VIII, § 173, and see Harper v. Virginia Board of Elections, 383 U.S. 663, 664, 86 S.Ct. 1079, 1080, 16 L.Ed.2d 169 (1966). Minnesota's provision is not untypical:

> The stability of a republican form of government depending mainly upon the intelligence of the people, it shall be the duty of the legislature to establish a general and uniform system of public schools. (Constitution of Minnesota, Article VIII, § 1).

A citizen's willingness and ability to participate effectively in the social, civil and political life of the United States is uniquely dependent upon education.

The dominant purposes of compulsory education today are the development of good citizenship and the development of sufficient intellectual skills such that those capable of continuing on to higher education can do so; they can then supply the intellectual leadership needed for our society by becoming scholars, intellectuals and members of the learned professions. The overall goal seems to be the development of sufficient mind and character that will enable a person to know how to live and participate effectively in American democracy. "The modern public school derived from a philosophy of freedom reflected in the First Amendment," wrote Mr. Justice Frankfurter, adding that "the evolution of colonial education . . . into the public school system of today is the story of changing conceptions regarding the American democratic society, of the functions of State-maintained education in such a society and of the role therein of the free exercise of religion by the people." McCollum v. Bd. of Ed., 333 U.S. 203, 214, 68 S.Ct. 461, 466–467, 92 L.Ed. 649, 659–660 (1948):

> "The non-sectarian or secular public school was the means of reconciling freedom in general with religious freedom. The sharp confinement of the public schools to secular education was a recognition of the need of a democratic society to educate its children, insofar as the State undertook to do so, in an atmosphere free from pressures in a realm in which pressures are most resisted and where conflicts are most easily and most bitterly engendered. Designed to serve as perhaps the most powerful agency for promoting cohesion among a heterogeneous democratic people, the public school must keep scrupulously free from entanglement in the strife of sects. . . . This development of the public school as a symbol of our secular unity was not a sudden achievement nor attained without violent conflict." Id. at 216–217, 468, 661.

STATE AND FEDERAL CONTROL OF EDUCATION

Before the adoption of the Constitution of the United States, a child's education was the responsibility of his parents. This is the common-law rule—that parental control over a child extends to control the education of that child—and this rule of parental control still exists in the limited number of situations where it has not been modified by federal or state law. The United States Constitution is completely silent on the whole subject. It fails to make any direct references about education. Consequently, there is no specific constitutional directive about the purposes of education, nor are there any direct references about which of the two divisions of government, state or federal, shall have exclusive or shared constitutional responsibilities for education. The result has been that states primarily control and regulate public education for the following reasons.

In legal theory the federal government is looked upon as one of specifically delegated powers. Thus, for example, Congress can pass laws only by exercising the specific powers granted to it. The bulk of Congress' powers are set forth in Article I, Section 8, of the Constitution, and direct power over education is not among them. On the other hand, legal theory holds that the situation of a state government is just the opposite of that of the federal government. A state government possesses all the powers that are not specifically prohibited to it by either the federal or state constitutions. This broad, general reservoir of power that is possessed by a state is frequently referred to as the "police power," but the Supreme Court of the United States has never fully defined its scope and limits. In Mayor of the City of New York v. Miln, 11 Pet. 102, 9 L.Ed. 648 (1837), the Supreme Court said: "It [the police power] embraces every law which concerns the welfare of the whole people of the state or any individual within it, whether it relates to their rights or duties, whether it respects them as men or citizens of the state, whether in their public or private relations, whether it relates to the rights of persons or property of the whole people of the state or of any individual within it." In Hannibal & St. J. R. Co. v. Husen, 95 U.S. 465, 24 L.Ed. 527 (1877), it said: "The police power of a state extends to the protection of the lives, limbs, health, comfort, and quiet of all persons, and to the protection of all property, within the state, and hence to the making of all regulations promotive of domestic order, morals, health, and safety." The result is that state legislatures can legislate directly on the subject of education unless their state constitutions forbid them, because nothing in the federal constitution precludes state authority. The constitutions of most states require that their state legislatures create a system of public schools. This means then, that state legislatures generally have the power to see to it that schools are built; to require that certain persons attend school and to prescribe the curriculum, methods and goals of education. And state legislatures have exercised their powers extensively, establishing uniform, statewide systems of public education.

The traditional view that a state has extensive state power over education was set forth long ago, and has been reiterated by the Supreme Court of Indiana in State ex rel. Clark v. Haworth, 122 Ind. 462, 23 N.E. 946 (1890). The primary question presented to the court was whether jurisdiction over public education was a state or local governmental matter.

> " .   .   . Essentially and intrinsically, the schools in which are educated and trained the children who are to become the rulers of the commonwealth are matters of state, and not of local, jurisdiction. In such matters the state is a unit, and the legislature the source of power. The authority over schools and school affairs is not necessarily a distributive one, to be exercised by local instrumentalities; but, on the contrary, it is a central power residing in the legislature of the state. It is for the law-making power to determine whether the authority shall be exercised by a state board of education, or distributed to county, township, or city or-

ganizations throughout the state. With that determination the judiciary can no more rightfully interfere than can the legislature with a decree or judgment pronounced by a judicial tribunal. The decision is as conclusive and inviolable in the one case as in the other; and an interference with the legislative judgment would be a breach of the constitution which no principle would justify, nor any precedent excuse. . . . Judge Cooley has examined the question with care, and discussed it with ability; and he declares that the legislature has plenary power over the subject of the public schools. He says in the course of his discussion, that 'to what degree the legislature shall provide for the education of the people at the cost of the state, or of its municipalities, is a question which, except as regulated by the constitution, addresses itself to the legislative judgment exclusively.' Again, he says, 'The governing school boards derive all their authority from the statute and can exercise no powers except those expressly granted and those which result by necessary implication from the grant.' Const.Lim. (5th Ed.) p. 225, note 1. No case has been cited by counsel, and none has been discovered by us,—although we have searched the reports with care,—which denies the doctrine that the regulation of the public schools is a state matter, exclusively within the dominion of the legislature. . . ."

"As the [state] power over schools is a legislative one, it is not exhausted by exercise. The legislature, having tried one plan, is not precluded from trying another. It has a choice of methods, and may change its plans as often as it deems necessary or expedient; and for mistakes or abuses it is answerable to the people, but not to the courts. It is clear, therefore, that, even if it were true that the legislature had uniformly intrusted the management of school affairs to local organizations, it would not authorize the conclusion that it might not change the system. To deny the power to change, is to affirm that progress is impossible, and that we must move forever 'in the dim footsteps of antiquity.' But the legislative power moves in a constant stream, and is not exhausted by its exercise in any number of instances, however great. It is not true, however, that the authority over schools was originally regarded as a local one. On the contrary, the earlier cases asserted that the legislature could not delegate the power to levy taxes for school purposes to local organizations, but must itself directly exercise the power; thus denying, in the strongest possible form, the theory of local control. . . . All the public schools have been established under legislative enactments, and all rules and regulations have been made pursuant to statutory authority.

Every school that has been established owes its existence to legislation, and every school officer owes his authority to the statute.

"It is impossible to conceive of the existence of a uniform system of common schools without power lodged somewhere to make it uniform; and, even in the absence of express constitutional provisions, that power must necessarily reside in the legislature. If it does reside there, then that body must have, as an incident of the principal power, the authority to prescribe the course of study, and the system of instruction, that shall be pursued and adopted, as well as the books which shall be used. This general doctrine is well entrenched by authority. Hovey v. State, 119 Ind. 395, 21 N.E. Rep. 21; Hovey v. Riley, 119 Ind. 386, 21 N.E.Rep. 890; State v. Hawkins, 44 Ohio St. 98, 5 N.E.Rep. 228; State v. Harmon, 31 Ohio St. 250. Having this authority, the legislature may not only prescribe regulations for using such books, but it may also declare how the books shall be obtained and distributed. If it may do this, then it may provide that they shall be obtained through the medium of a contract awarded to the best or lowest bidder, since, if it be true, as it unquestionably is, that the power is legislative, it must also be true that the legislature has an unrestricted discretion, and an unfettered choice of methods. It cannot be possible that the courts can interfere with this legislative power, and adjudge that the legislature shall not adopt this method or that method; for, if the question is at all legislative, it is so in its whole length and breadth."

Finally, with respect to overall state authority over schools and school districts, Nebraska's Supreme Court said:

" . . . we have often held that the state is supreme in the creation and control of school districts, and may, if it thinks proper, modify or withdraw any of their powers, or destroy such school districts without the consent of the legal voters or even over their protests." Kosmicki v. Kowalski, 184 Neb. 639, 171 N.W.2d 172 (1969).

Must a state legislature having power over education exercise that power and create public schools? In the absence of a constitutional requirement to create schools a state legislature need not act. In such circumstances a state may have private schools but no public schools.

The constitutions of some states require their state legislatures to create a school system. Article 9, Section 5 of California's Constitution provides an example of a constitutional duty: "The legislature shall provide for a system of common schools by which a free school shall be kept up and supported in each district at least six months in

every year, after the first year in which a school has been established." When it is not defined by either constitution or statute, questions frequently arise concerning the scope and meaning of the term
"common schools". They are the schools that the legislature is obligated to establish. The distinctive elements of common schools are
"that they are free schools, open to all the children of proper school
age residing in the locality, and affording, so long as the term lasts,
equal opportunity for all to acquire the learning taught in the various
common school branches." City of Louisville v. Commonwealth, 134
Ky. 488, 121 S.W. 411 (1909), and see 47 Am.Jur., Schools, § 3, p. 298.
Included in the term "common schools" are the public elementary and
secondary grade schools, one through twelve. For example, the Supreme Court of Idaho in Paulson v. Minidoka County School Dist.,
93 Idaho 469, 463 P.2d 935 (1970), stated: "We hold that Minidoka
County High School is a 'common school' within the meaning . . .
of the Idaho Constitution. Because the appellants' high school is a
'common school' it must, by constitutional command, be 'free'." On
whether required textbooks and other needed materials must be supplied freely to pupils at state expense, see Bond v. Ann Arbor School
Dist., 18 Mich.App. 506, 171 N.W.2d 557 (1969) and Johnson v. New
York State Ed. Department, 449 F.2d 871 (2d Cir. 1971). Courts
have held that the term "common school" does not include kindergartens, Los Angeles County v. Kirk, 148 Cal. 385, 83 P. 250 (1905), nor
schools for adults or special education schools, such as a school for the
blind, Walls v. Board of Ed., 195 Ark. 955, 116 S.W.2d 354 (1938).
The duty of the legislature under this type of state constitutional provision extends only to establishing "common schools." On the other
hand, while not required by its state constitution to do so, if it chooses
to use it a state legislature has the power to establish free kindergartens, In re Kindergarten Schools, 18 Colo. 234, 32 P. 422 (1893),
free special education schools, or a free system of higher education.
State Bank of Commerce of Brockport v. Stone, 261 N.Y. 175, 184 N.E.
750 (1933).

State legislatures do not administer the daily affairs of the public schools. That would be an enormously unwieldly task, and legislatures would be free to do little else. Instead, state legislatures create
administrative agencies such as State Boards of Education; a chief
executive office commonly called the "State Superintendent of Public
Schools," and local school boards, and then delegate certain powers
to these sub-agencies to enable them to run the schools. The exact
statutory pattern varies from state to state. Courts refuse to allow
state legislatures to delegate their legislative powers to these administrative agencies because the state constitutions place the pure legislative power solely in the legislatures. The result is that so long as
state legislatures, by law, set forth clear and concise standards to
guide their administrative agencies, courts will allow legislatures
to delegate the authority necessary to enable administrative agencies
to make rules and regulations for running the day-to-day operations

of the schools. The power delegated includes the authority to perform legislative, executive and quasi-judicial functions. The State Board of Education usually functions as the legislative body that makes school policy; the State Superintendent usually functions as the highest administrative officer for the school system, and both may exercise quasi-judicial functions. Enactment of various rules and regulations is discretionary with the State Boards of Education. But, if rules or regulations are enacted, they must be made pursuant to, and be consistent with, the standards set forth by statute by the legislature.

So long as it follows the legislative standards and stays within its delegated powers, and it doesn't violate a constitutional limitation on them, the highest administrative agency, usually a State Board of Education, has the final authority on all matters of educational policy and on the ultimate administrative practices of a state's public schools. Its policy and administrative judgments will not be reviewed, nor reversed, by the courts unless bad faith, fraud or breach of trust can be shown as having been the basis for the policy of administrative judgments. The same situation prevails generally in the case of quasi-judicial rulings not involving a pure question of law. On the other hand, a State Board of Education cannot have the final word if only a pure question of law is involved, such as the proper interpretation of the law setting forth its controlling standards. The latter is a pure judicial function and there is no presumption in favor of a State Board's ruling; finality rests with the courts. See, Wilson v. Board of Ed., 234 Md. 561, 200 A.2d 67 (1964). But, when a case does not involve a pure question of law, a strong presumption favors the State Board's decision, and the courts generally will not substitute their decisions for those of State Boards by reversing the quasi-judicial rulings of a State Board of Education unless those rulings are arbitrary or capricious. This means that in all matters within its legal discretion that fairly and honestly admit of two or more opinions, the opinion of the State Board of Education is final and conclusive. For example, the Board of Trustees of a local Texas school district found the Superintendent of that district guilty of withholding, mishandling and misapplying school district funds, and ordered that he be discharged. The Superintendent of the district appealed the order to the State Superintendent of Public Instruction who, after a hearing, reversed the decision of the Board of Trustees and ordered that the Superintendent be reinstated. The Board of Trustees then appealed the State Superintendent's decision to the State Board of Education which reversed the State Superintendent's decision and affirmed the original order of the Board of Trustees calling for the discharge of the district Superintendent, who then brought an action in a court seeking to have his discharge order set aside. On appeal, the Court of Civil Appeals for Texas refused, stating:

"The question before the school board and the State Board of Education in the instant case was one of fact relating to the manner in which appellant was performing his duties as superintendent of schools in connection with the handling and application of the finances of the school district which had been entrusted to his care. There was no implication in the findings made by the school board that appellant had been guilty of an intentional misapplication of the funds belonging to the school district, or of an intention on his part to appropriate the funds of the school to his own use and benefit. The board simply found as a fact that appellant had 'withheld, mishandled and misapplied funds belonging to the Trinity Independent School District' which had been entrusted to his custody as superintendent of its schools and that he had 'failed to divulge material information relative to the handling of said funds to the trustees of the school district.' The question as to whether appellant should have been discharged for one or more of the reasons set out in the charges preferred against him were, we think, matters of fact relating to the internal affairs of the school and the efficient management thereof and 'came within the purview of the matters committed by the Legislature to such board for its determination' and the decision of the State Board that appellant had been properly discharged was final on that issue.

"Appellant's contention that the State Board of Education acted arbitrarily, capriciously, or fraudulently in affirming the judgment of the Board of Trustees of the Trinity Independent School District cannot be sustained. As stated by The Supreme Court in the case of Railroad Commission of Texas v. Shell Oil Co., Inc., et al., supra, it is generally recognized that where the order of the agency under attack involves the exercise of the sound judgment and discretion of the agency in a matter committed to it by the Legislature, the court will sustain the order if the action of the agency in reaching such conclusion is reasonably supported by substantial evidence, and, at the time such order was entered by the agency, there then existed sufficient facts to justify the entry of the order." Blair v. Board of Trustees, 161 S.W.2d 1030 (Texas, 1942).

A local government unit, such as a city or a town, has power over education only to the extent that the authority specifically has been delegated to it either by a statute of the state legislature or directly by the state constitution. "If a power is not given it is said it does not exist." Mosier v. Thompson, 216 Tenn. 655, 393 S.W.2d 734 (1965). Moreover, a state legislature can compel cities to levy taxes for school purposes in order "to supplement the fund paid to the [local school] district out of the state money" because education is a state, not a local, function. City of Louisville v. Commonwealth, 134 Ky. 488, 121 S.W. 411 (1909). A school district is also a local unit separate from a city or town, and it also is a creature of the state; thus, the state constitution and legislative statute creating the school district are the sources of that local district's powers. Its school board has no others. "A school district derives its existence and powers wholly from the General Assembly" said the Illinois court. Dato v. Village of Vernon Hills, 62 Ill.App.2d 274, 210 N.E.2d 626 (1965). A legislature can delegate certain broadly defined powers over education to a local school board. In such situations the school board is said to have discretionary authority within which it can make decisions or adopt additional rules and regulations that it deems necessary and wise, so long as they fall within the scope of the broadly defined powers delegated by the legislature. For example, it may have discretion to decide which teacher to hire or where to locate a school building. In addition to discretionary powers which require the exercise of judgment, a legislature can also require that a local (or state) school board act in very specific ways—ways that are ministerial and do not involve the exercise of judgment. For example, a local school board might be required to prepare a budget or accept the lowest bid on a contract. Thus, the powers of a local and state school board can be classified as discretionary or ministerial. Since education is primarily a state function and since members of state and local boards of education derive their offices and powers from the state, courts hold that members of State and local boards of education are state officers. Board of Ed. v. Society of Alumni of Louisville Male High, Ky., 239 S.W.2d 931 (1951).

Although the legal control of education is primarily a state function, no state legislature is absolutely free to do anything and everything with education that it may choose. Usually the courts will not interfere. But if a state should act in a manner that contravenes a constitutional limitation on its powers—say a provision of the Bill of Rights that has been incorporated into the Fourteenth Amendment—then courts do interfere. Also, Congress has vast power to regulate and control certain matters even though they might impinge upon education. If Congress properly exercises its constitutional powers and that exercise conflicts with a state constitution or statute, then that state law must give way because the federal law is the "Supreme Law of the Land." Moreover, Congress has power to affect education by taxing and then making the money available to the states for educational purposes so long as the states agree to comply with certain conditions set by Congress. Congress' power over these grant-in-aid programs derives from Article 1, Section 8, clause 1, of the Constitution of the United States which grants power to Congress "to lay and collect taxes, duties, imposts, and excises, to pay the debts and provide for the common defense and general welfare of the United States." Congress' powers to tax and to provide for "the general welfare" includes the power to provide for education through such means as making grants of funds available so long as the states agree to meet certain conditions. The result is that a complicated network of constitutional provisions, state and federal laws control or affect public education. A capsule description of one federal spending program follows. It is one example of the way in which Congress has affected education.

Congress enacted the Elementary and Secondary Education Act (ESEA) in 1965 (Pub.L.No. 89–10, 79 Stat. 27 (1965)). It is one of the most comprehensive attempts at the federal level to provide federal aid to elementary and secondary schools, public and private. There may be questions about the constitutionality of some of its provisions. Title I of ESEA sets up the largest and most pervasive program of the Act that has been funded by Congress. Under it, nine million students received over $1 billion aid during 1968–69. This title provides needed funds to the states for distribution to their local educational agencies for the creation and supplementation of programs to meet the special needs of educationally deprived children. However, before a state can distribute funds to one of its educational agencies, provision must first be made in that particular program for full participation of private schools, including parochial schools, that have deprived children in attendance. Title II of the Act provides funds to states to acquire textbooks, library resources and other instructional materials for the use of children in public and private, including parochial, elementary and secondary schools. Title III authorizes the Commissioner of Education to make direct grants to local educational agencies within a state for the construction and operation of educational centers, but first he must determine that the program of the local educational agency provides for the participation of children attending non-profit private schools as well as public schools. Title IV authorizes the Commissioner of Education to make grants to universities and colleges, including non-profit institutions for the purpose of advancing research in education.

NOTES AND QUESTIONS

1. Is the ultimate control over public education primarily a local function, a state function or a federal function? Why?

2. Does the state legislature have power to change or to abolish the system of public schools?

3. Does the state legislature have power to prescribe the curriculum and to select the books for public schools?

4. Does the state legislature have power to require that cities of a certain class, or counties, lay taxes and build and maintain public schools, even without a vote of the citizens within that city or county?

5. What is a "common school"? Is a community college a "common school"? A pre-school? A kindergarten? A school for the blind? A school for economically deprived children? A university?

6. What is "the police power"? If the legislature exercises its "police power" within its constitutional authority, will courts determine whether the legislation is good or bad, or wise or unwise?

7. If the State Constitution does not require its legislature to create a kindergarten, does it have power to do so? Could a legislature create a system of free community colleges?

8. Does the Constitution of the United States grant direct power over education to Congress? To the states? To municipalities?

9. When a school board adopts a curriculum plan is it exercising ministerial or discretionary powers?

10. Describe, in detail, the legal controls over the legislative and administrative structure of education in your state.

THE LEGAL OBLIGATION

The common-law responsibility of a parent for his child's education is owed not only to the child but to the state as well. The reason is that the state has an interest in having its children educated so that they can become good citizens and make up a body politic capable of solving new social problems in an intelligent and democratic way. To achieve these ends the common-law parental responsibility has been supplmented by state constitutional provisions and laws that apply to every child living within the state. Their overall constitutionality has been upheld. California's constitution provides an illustration, Article 9, Section 1, states: "A general difference of knowledge and intelligence being essential to the preservation of the rights and liberties of the people, the legislature shall encourage by all suitable means the promotion of intellectual, scientific, moral and agricultural improvement." These measures commonly provide for compulsory school attendance of children of specified ages and place an obligation upon parents, or their substitutes, to see to it that their children attend school regularly. By law, public school attendance officers have the duty of enforcing mandatory attendance at public and private schools. If parents should fail to meet their obligation by refusing to send a child to school, they can be subjected to civil or criminal penalties. If a child is sent to school but refuses to attend regularly thereby becoming an incorrigible truant, then states commonly provide that the child can be made a ward of the juvenile court to be supervised by a juvenile probation officer. Thus, state coercion is applied to enforce the duty to attend school. On this analysis, the common-school, public education provided for children by a state is primarily a duty imposed on the children and parents for the public good, and secondarily an individual right that they possess. Washington's law provides a typical example of the obligation to attend school.

"All parents, guardians and other persons in this state having custody of any child eight years of age and under fifteen years of age, or of any child fifteen years of age and under eighteen years of age not regularly and lawfully engaged in some useful and remunerative occupation or attending part-time school in accordance with the provisions of chapter 28A.28 RCW or excused from school attendance thereunder, shall cause such child to attend the public school of the district in which the child resides for the full time when such school may be in session or to attend a private school for the same time, unless the school district superintendent of the district in which the child resides shall have excused such child from such attendance because the child is physically or mentally unable to attend school or has already attained a reasonable proficiency in the branches required by law to be taught in the first nine grades of the public schools of this state. Proof of absence from any public or private school shall be prima facie evidence of a violation of this section. Private school for the purposes of this section shall be one approved or accredited under regulations established by the state board of education." RCW 28A.27.010.

Washington's law is typical in that it permits its requirements of compulsory school attendance to be satisfied by a child's regular attendance at either a public or an approved private school. Suppose, however, that the law were different and disallowed attendance at any private school from satisfying the obligation to attend school by requiring that the mandatory school attendance shall be only within the public schools provided by the state. Does a state constitutionally have such power?

————

PIERCE v. SOCIETY OF THE SISTERS OF THE HOLY NAMES OF JESUS AND MARY
PIERCE v. HILL MILITARY ACADEMY

Supreme Court of the United States, 1925.
268 U.S. 510, 45 S.Ct. 571, 69 L.Ed. 1070.

Mr. Justice McREYNOLDS delivered the opinion of the Court.

These appeals are from decrees, based upon undenied allegations, which granted preliminary orders restraining appellants from threatening or attempting to enforce the Compulsory Education Act adopted November 7, 1922, under the initiative provision of her Constitution by the voters of Oregon. Jud.Code, § 266. They present the same points of law; there are no controverted questions of fact. Rights said to be guaranteed by the federal Constitution were specially set up, and appropriate prayers asked for their protection.

The challenged Act, effective September 1, 1926, requires every parent, guardian or other person having control or charge or custody of a child between eight and sixteen years to send him "to a public school for the period of time a public school shall be held during the current year" in the district where the child resides; and failure to do so is declared a misdemeanor. There are exemptions—not specially important here—for children who are not normal, or who have completed the eighth grade, or who reside at considerable distances from any public school, or whose parents or guardians hold special permits from the County Superintendent. The manifest purpose is to compel general attendance at public schools by normal children, between eight and sixteen, who have not completed the eighth grade. And without doubt enforcement of the statute would seriously impair, perhaps destroy, the profitable features of appellees' business and greatly diminish the value of their property.

Appellee, the Society of Sisters, is an Oregon corporation, organized in 1880, with power to care for orphans, educate and instruct the youth, establish and maintain academies or schools, and acquire necessary real and personal property. It has long devoted its property and effort to the secular and religious education and care of children, and has acquired the valuable good will of many parents and guardians. It conducts interdependent primary and high schools and junior colleges, and maintains orphanages for the custody and control of children between eight and sixteen. In its primary schools many children between those ages are taught the subjects usually pursued in Oregon public schools during the first eight years. Systematic religious instruction and moral training according to the tenets of the Roman Catholic Church are also regularly provided. All courses of study, both temporal and religious, contemplate continuity of training under appellee's charge; the primary schools are essential to the system and the most profitable. It owns valuable buildings, especially constructed and equipped for school purposes. The business is remunerative—the annual income from primary schools exceeds thirty thousand dollars—and the successful conduct of this requires long time contracts with teachers and parents. The Compulsory Education Act of 1922 has already caused the withdrawal from its schools of children who would otherwise continue, and their income has steadily declined. The appellants, public officers, have proclaimed their purpose strictly to enforce the statute.

After setting out the above facts the Society's bill alleges that the enactment conflicts with the right of parents to choose schools where their children will receive appropriate mental and religious training, the right of the child to influence the parents' choice of a school, the right of schools and teachers therein to engage in a useful business or profession, and is accordingly repugnant to the Constitution and void. And, further, that unless enforcement of the measure is enjoined the corporation's business and property will suffer irreparable injury.

Appellee, Hill Military Academy, is a private corporation organized in 1908 under the laws of Oregon, engaged in owning, operating and conducting for profit an elementary, college preparatory and military training school for boys between the ages of five and twenty-one years. The average attendance is one hundred, and the annual fees received for each student amount to some eight hundred dollars. The elementary department is divided into eight grades, as in the public schools; the college preparatory department has four grades, similar to those of the public high schools; the courses of study conform to the requirements of the State Board of Education. Military instruction and training are also given, under the supervision of an Army officer. It owns considerable real and personal property, some useful only for school purposes. The business and incident good will are very valuable. In order to conduct its affairs long time contracts must be made for supplies, equipment, teachers and pupils. Appellants, law officers of the State and County, have publicly announced that the Act of November 7, 1922, is valid and have declared their intention to enforce it. By reason of the statute and threat of enforcement appellee's business is being destroyed and its property depreciated; parents and guardians are refusing to make contracts for the future instruction of their sons, and some are being withdrawn.

The Academy's bill states the foregoing facts and then alleges that the challenged Act contravenes the corporation's right guaranteed by the Fourteenth Amendment and that unless appellants are restrained from proclaiming its validity and threatening to enforce it irreparable injury will result. The prayer is for an appropriate injunction.

No answer was interposed in either cause, and after proper notices they were heard by three judges (Jud.Code § 266) on motions for preliminary injunctions upon the specifically alleged facts. The court ruled that the Fourteenth Amendment guaranteed appellees against the deprivation of their property without due process of law consequent upon the unlawful interference by appellants with the free choice of patrons, present and prospective. It declared the right to conduct schools was property and that parents and guardians, as part of their liberty, might direct the education of children by selecting reputable teachers and places. Also, that these schools were not unfit or harmful to the public, and that enforcement of the challenged statute would unlawfully deprive them of patronage and thereby destroy their owners' business and property. Finally, that the threats to enforce the Act would continue to cause irreparable injury; and the suits were not premature.

No question is raised concerning the power of the State reasonably to regulate all schools, to inspect, supervise and examine them, their teachers and pupils; to require that all children of proper age attend some school, that teachers shall be of good moral character and patriotic disposition, that certain studies plainly essential to good citizenship must be taught, and that nothing be taught which is manifestly inimical to the public welfare.

The inevitable practical result of enforcing the Act under consideration would be destruction of appellees' primary schools, and perhaps all other private primary schools for normal children within the State of Oregon. These parties are engaged in a kind of undertaking not inherently harmful, but long regarded as useful and meritorious. Certainly there is nothing in the present records to indicate that they have failed to discharge their obligations to patrons, students or the State. And there are no peculiar circumstances or present emergencies which demand extraordinary measures relative to primary education.

Under the doctrine of Meyer v. Nebraska, 262 U.S. 390, we think it entirely plain that the Act of 1922 unreasonably interferes with the liberty of parents and guardians to direct the upbringing and education of children under their control. As often heretofore pointed out, rights guaranteed by the Constitution may not be abridged by legislation which has no reasonable relation to some purpose within the competency of the State. The fundamental theory of liberty upon which all governments in this Union repose excludes any general power of the State to standardize its children by forcing them to accept instruction from public teachers only. The child is not the mere creature of the State; those who nurture him and direct his destiny have the right, coupled with the high duty, to recognize and prepare him for additional obligations.

Appellees are corporations and therefore, it is said, they cannot claim for themselves the liberty which the Fourteenth Amendment guarantees. Accepted in the proper sense, this is true. . . . But they have business and property for which they claim protection. These are threatened with destruction through the unwarranted compulsion which appellants are exercising over present and prospective patrons of their schools. And this court has gone very far to protect against loss threatened by such action. Truax v. Raich, 239 U.S. 33; Truax v. Corrigan, 257 U.S. 312; Terrace v. Thompson, 263 U.S. 197.

The courts of the State have not construed the Act, and we must determine its meaning for ourselves. Evidently it was expected to have general application and cannot be construed as though merely intended to amend the charters of certain private corporations, as in Berea College v. Kentucky, 211 U.S. 45. No argument in favor of such view has been advanced.

Generally it is entirely true, as urged by counsel, that no person in any business has such an interest in possible customers as to enable him to restrain exercise of proper power of the State upon the ground that he will be deprived of patronage. But the injunctions here sought are not against the exercise of any *proper* power. Plaintiffs asked protection against arbitrary, unreasonable and unlawful interference with their patrons and the consequent destruction of their business and property. Their interest is clear and immediate, within the rule approved in Truax v. Raich, Truax v. Corrigan and Terrace v. Thompson, supra, and many other cases where injunctions have issued to protect business enterprises against interference with the freedom of patrons or customers. . . .

The suits were not premature. The injury to appellees was present and very real, not a mere possibility in the remote future. If no relief had been possible prior to the effective date of the Act, the injury would have become irreparable. Prevention of impending injury by unlawful action is a well recognized function of courts of equity.

The decrees below are affirmed.

NOTES AND QUESTIONS

1. What facts of this case are precisely relevant to the Supreme Court's decision? Only these facts are called "the operative facts of the case," and they are the important ones.

2. What issues or questions were presented by this case for decision by the Supreme Court?

3. What was the ruling on the issues by the lower court?

4. What were the arguments presented to the Supreme Court by the lawyers for each party? Do you agree or disagree with the arguments? Why?

5. What decision was made by the Supreme Court on each issue presented? What reasoning is advanced by the Court to support its decisions? Do you agree or disagree with the reasoning of the Court? Why?

6. Do you believe that this case was rightly decided? Why or why not?

7. What proposition (or propositions) of law is illustrated by this case? (You should ask and answer each of the above seven questions in relation to every case opinion set forth in this book. It would be helpful to write them out.)

8. What right of the parent receives constitutional protection in this case: (1) the right of parents to direct the religious upbringing of their child, or (2) the right of parents to direct the education of their children during the early and formative years? Would the decision have been different if evidence had showed that the children wanted to go to public schools?

9. The Court states that "The child is not the mere creature of the State; those who nurture him and direct his destiny have the right, coupled with the high duty, to recognize and prepare him for additional obli-

gations." What additional obligations? See Wisconsin v. Yoder, infra, where the Court states that the "additional obligations" requirement "must be read to include the inculcation of moral standards, religious beliefs and elements of good citizenship." Is none of these the proper function of public education? Is each of these to be excluded from the obligation to attend public schools? If so, what is the purpose of the public schools?

10. If a State legislature can require that children in the State have a proper education, but if it has no power arbitrarily to conclude that a proper education can only be obtained at public schools, can it define the substantive content of a proper education and also the curriculum for achieving it, and then require that public and private schools follow that specific curriculum and no other? Consider especially the following language from the Supreme Court's opinion. Is it relevant? "The fundamental theory of liberty upon which all governments in this Union repose excludes any general power of the State to standardize its children by forcing them to accept instruction from public teachers only."

11. Does Pierce establish a constitutional right for the existence of private schools, including parochial schools?

12. Does Pierce establish that parents have a constitutional right to educate their children in their homes?

EDUCATION EQUIVALENT TO A PUBLIC SCHOOL

STATE OF WASHINGTON v. F. B. COUNORT

Supreme Court of Washington, 1912.
69 Wash. 361, 124 P. 910.

MORRIS, J.—Appellant was convicted of a violation of the school law in neglecting and refusing to cause his children, between the ages of eight and fifteen years, to attend the public school of the district in which he resides, or any approved private school, without obtaining an excuse for such failure and neglect to attend, from the county superintendent of schools. From such conviction he appeals.

The first error assigned is that the information does not charge a crime. The statute under which the information is drawn is Rem. & Bal. Code, § 4714:

"All parents, guardians and other persons in this state having or who may hereafter have immediate custody of any child between eight and fifteen years of age (being between the eighth and fifteenth birthdays), . . . shall cause such child to attend the public school of the district, in which the child resides, for the full time when such school may be in session or to attend a private school for the same time, unless the superintendent of the schools of the district in which the child resides, if there be such a superintendent, and in all other cases the county superintendents of common schools, shall have excused such child from such attendance because the child is physically or mentally unable to attend school or has already attained a reasonable proficiency in the branches required by law to be taught in the first eight grades of the public schools of this state as provided by the course of study of such school, or for some other sufficient reason. Proof of absence from public schools or approved private school shall be *prima facie* evidence of a violation of this section."

If we understand the objection made to the information, it is in the use of the word "approved," in charging the neglect or refusal to permit the children to attend an "approved private school." We can see no objection to the use of this word. The statute does not, in the first instance, provide that the private school shall be an approved one. The gist of the offense is in the failure to attend any school, either public or private, without having obtained an excuse for such failure from the superintendent of schools. The information clearly charges this refusal, and is sufficient.

The main assignments of error are in the admission and rejection of testimony, and as they all go to the same contention, they may be discussed together. The theory of appellant in this connection is that it would be a defense to this charge to show that he is experienced as a teacher and qualified to teach all branches required to be taught in the public schools of this state, and that he maintains a private school at his home for the instruction of his own children. We have no doubt many parents are capable of instructing their own children, but to permit such parents to withdraw their children from the public schools without permission from the superintendent of schools, and to instruct them at home, would be to disrupt our common school system and destroy its value to the state. This statute recognizes that adequate private schools may be maintained in any district to which parents may send their children without any violation of the law, and it would be a good defense to show attendance at such private school for the required time. We do not think that the giving of instruction by a parent to a child, conceding the competency of the parent to fully instruct the child in all that is taught in the public schools, is within the meaning of the law "to attend a private school." Such a requirement means more than home instruction; it means the same character of school as the public school, a regular, organized and existing institution making a business of instructing children of school age in the required studies and for the full time required by the laws of this state. The only difference between the two schools is the nature of the institution. One is a public institution, organized and maintained as one of the institutions of the state. The other is a private institution, organized and maintained by private individuals or corporations. There may be a difference in institution and government, but the purpose and end of both public and private schools must be the same—the education of children of school age. The parent who teaches his children at home, whatever be his reason for desiring to do so, does not maintain such a school. Undoubtedly a private school may be maintained in a private home in which the children of the instructor may be pupils. This provision of the law is not to be determined by the place where the school is maintained, nor the individuality or number of the pupils who attend it. It is to be determined by the purpose, intent and character of the endeavor. The evidence of the state was to the effect that appellant maintained no school at his home; that his two little girls could be seen playing about the house at all times during the ordinary school hours. No effort was made to refute this testimony. Appellant seemed to be impressed with the belief that, if he was a competent and qualified teacher and gave instruction to his children at his home, he maintained a private school within the meaning of the law. Such is not a compliance with the law.   .   .   .

The judgment is affirmed.

NOTES AND QUESTIONS

1. Where does Washington's statute provide that a private school must be "approved" and that the superintendent shall have the power of approval? What is Washington's definition of an "approved private school"?

2. Would this case have been decided differently if there had been evidence showing that Mr. Counort had eight of his children at home between the ages of eight and fifteen years? Would this number of "pupils" have converted his private home into a "private school"? If not, what more would be necessary?

3. Would this case have been decided differently if Mr. Counort had first obtained permission from the superintendent of schools to educate his children in his home? Why would the superintendent's permission have converted Mr. Counort's home into a "private school"? Isn't it the quality of the education that makes the difference rather than an official approval?

4. Do you believe that it is possible for a child to receive a proper education through home instruction? If the parent is a licensed teacher?

5. If one goal of education is to help a child to learn ways of living with others in a pluralistic society can home instruction provide the necessary group experiences or social viewpoints?

6. In another Washington case involving home instruction given by a mother who had no teaching license, the parents claimed the child was removed from school because their religion forbade eating of meat, fish, fowl or playing of music, and they did not want their child present where these activities took place. The Washington Supreme Court held that since there was no licensed teacher in the house, there was no possibility of the home instruction qualifying as an "approved private school." Shoreline School Dist. No. 412 v. Superior Court for King County, 55 Wash.2d 177, 346 P.2d 999 (1960).

7. Compare the following two cases, from New Jersey, with each other, and then with State v. Counort, supra. Would either constitute a "private school" in Washington?

STEPHENS v. BONGART

Juvenile and Domestic Relations Court of New Jersey, 1937.
15 N.J.Misc. 80, 189 A. 131.

SIEGLER, Judge. Helen Stephens, attendance officer of the school district of the town of West Orange in the county of Essex, filed her complaint against Gertrude R. Bongart and Benno Bongart, the defendants in this action, charging that they reside within the school district of the town of West Orange, and being the parents and having custody and control of William Bongart, aged twelve, and Robert Bongart, aged eleven, their children, have, since the 5th day of April 1936, failed to cause their said children regularly to attend the public schools of the school district of the said town of West Orange; further charging said defendants having neither caused said children to attend a day school in which there is given instruction equivalent to that provided in the public schools for children of similar grades and attainments, nor have they received equivalent instruction elsewhere than at school, contrary to the provisions of an act of the Legislature of the state of New Jersey entitled, "An Act to establish a thorough and efficient system of free public schools, and to provide for the maintenance, support and management thereof," approved October 19, 1903 (4 Comp.St. 1910, p. 4724, et seq., § 1 et seq.), and the Amendments thereof and Supplements thereto.

The act upon which these proceedings are based, chapter 307 of the Laws of 1931 (N.J.St.Annual 1931, § 185–165c), reads as follows: "Every parent, guardian or other person having custody and control of a child between the ages of seven and sixteen years shall cause such child regularly to attend the public schools of such district or to attend a day school in which there is given instruction equivalent to that provided in the public schools for children of similar grades and attainments or to receive equivalent instruction elsewhere than at school unless such child is above the age of fourteen years. . . . Such regular attendance shall be during all the days and hours that the public schools are in session in said school district, unless it shall be shown to the satisfaction of the board of education of said school district that the mental condition of the child is such that he or she cannot benefit from instruction in the school or that the bodily condition of the child is such as to prevent his or her attendance at school."

. . .

The second point for determination is whether or not the defendants provided instruction for their children equivalent to that provided in the public schools for children of similar grades and attainments.

This necessitates an analysis of the testimony. The proof is that the defendants' children, William, twelve, and Robert, eleven, were in the sixth and fifth grades, respectively, in the Washington Street School, West Orange, until April 3, 1936. From that date, these children failed to attend a public or day school, although proper notice was served upon the defendants to return the children to a school. The defendants admit they caused the children's withdrawal from the Washington School.

Since that time, the defendants claim that they instructed their children in their own home in the subjects taught in fifth and sixth grades. This instruction, they claim, is equivalent to that provided in the public schools for children of similar grades and attainments. The case turns on this factual situation. 2 Words and Phrases, Second Series, p. 312, defines the word equivalent as follows:

> " 'Equivalent' means 'equal in worth or value, force, power effect, import and the like.' " Citing McLean v. Moran, 38 Mont. 298, 99 P. 836, 837.

Quite definitely, the term refers to the giving of instruction equal in value and effect to that given in a public school. In determining this question, consideration must be given, first, to the matter of the ability of the parents to provide equivalent instruction, and, secondly, to a comparison of the quality, character, and methods of teaching employed by the defendants and that of the West Orange public school system. Mrs. Bongart was graduated from the Eastern District High School, New York City, in 1911. In 1917 she was a special student at Hunter College, evening course. This required three or four evenings a week, which she carried on for only two years. She studied economics, psychology, art, portrait work, charcoal work and painting; she majored in home economics. Mrs. Bongart had no teaching experience. She was married about fifteen years ago, and her chief employment was that of housewife. Mr. Bongart is a graduate of the University of Strassbourg, in the field of electrical and mechanical engineering. He never trained for teaching, but did have employment as a teacher at the New York Aerial School, Newark Technical School, and the Newark Junior High School until recently. He taught subjects in mechanical drawing and electrical engineering. The teachers in the elementary grades of the public schools, particularly the fifth and sixth grades in the West Orange school system, must have at least a high school education and three years at an approved normal school in the state of New Jersey.

The normal school curriculum includes a type of training and education intended to qualify students to teach in the elementary class in the subjects of English, history, science, sociology, civics, mathematics, hygiene, geography, art, music, and physical education. The major aim is to give the teachers training in techniques of presentation of material to elementary school students. That involves the proper selection of material, knowledge of children, and the organization of their work, so that every teacher should know the results which must be achieved in terms of knowledge, habits, skills, attitudes, and appreciations. Her training should qualify her to develop individuality and the personality of each child under her supervision. One of the major aims of our public school to-day is to teach the way in which the individual must fit into the social group. The evidence establishes that the teachers in the fifth and sixth grades of Washington School possess this training and qualify in these courses.

It is clear, upon comparison, that there is a substantial variance between the training, qualifications, and experience of the defendants and those obtaining in the public school system of West Orange.

Now, what was the instruction given by the defendants at their home? The children assemble, one in the dining room and the other in the front room, each morning at 9 o'clock, and continue until 12; they resume at 1 o'clock, and recess at 3 o'clock in the afternoon. They receive instruction in arithmetic, spelling, history, geography, language, and music. In the evening, the father instructs them in science between 7 and 9 o'clock.

In the study of arithmetic a text-book is used by Stone and Millis, dated 1914. There were no text-books for spelling, language, music, civics, hygiene, and art; while the text-books used were outmoded and outdated, the latest published in 1921 and the oldest in 1881, and all certainly of questionable value in the instruction of children. Spelling was taught without a book, the mother giving twenty words at random each week, which the children had to learn and place in a notebook. The other subjects were taught by assigning periods of 30 or 35 minutes for each. Language was taught largely through the reading of newspapers, the Literary Digest and the Saturday Evening Post. Poetry was principally taught by the use of an occasional piece of poetry out of the Sunday Times and the New York Daily News, a tabloid newspaper. No poems were memorized. Music was taught by listening to radio concerts. There were no song books or singing exercises. Mechanical drawing and current events were given by the father in the evening. The Newark Evening News and some other periodicals were sources from which current events were drawn for discussion. The Bible was read once in a while. The flag of the country was exhibited in front of the house on patriotic occasions. The mother spoke to them about hygiene and the danger of alcoholic beverages, but no hygiene textbook was used. There were no instructions in observance of patriotic holidays, and no observance of Arbor Day. There was no physical training except that which they got outside in the ordinary course of their play. They had membership in the Y.M.C.A., but failed to attend during September and October. Of this default the parents had no knowledge.

The instruction was interrupted from time to time by the mother's household duties, occasional shopping tours, and house callers.

The defendants had no definite schedule for daily instruction. The evidence indicates that the boys obtained from children in school, periodically, information as to the subjects they were studying in school, and transmitted that information to the mother, who guided herself in instructing the children, to some extent, by it. They had no marks for their work. There were no daily work papers, tests, or examinations; at least, there were none presented in evidence. In fact, the mother admits she had no standard by which to determine whether the children were absorbing the instruction she was attempting to give. There was no organized supervision over the teaching that the defendants gave; the work of the children, and the results accomplished, were never submitted to any other competent authority for supervision, criticism, or approval.

A summary of the methods of instruction at the Washington School of West Orange will be useful for comparative purposes. The elementary grades are supervised by a specially trained person, who has complete supervision over the courses of study, the textbooks used, and the methods employed by the teachers in transmitting knowledge and the building and developing of the personalities of the children. The school is organized as a miniature community center, a sort of city, where each child considers himself a citizen, with duties toward the community as is required on the outside. The educational structure thus developed is in the nature of a group enterprise, where the children work together for the common good. The teacher creates the atmosphere and becomes the guiding influence. A high discipline is maintained by strict attention to the development of habits, skills and attitudes. There is group discussion. The children bring in articles from the outside. They study the biographies of great men, and discuss their achievements. In the fifth and sixth grades, reading, writing, spelling, arithmetic, English, history, geography, civics, hygiene, safety education, music, art, and penmanship are taught. The children are taught to use the dictionary. The norm for instruction may be found in several monographs on each subject, provided by the state board of education, and strict adherence is required. In the fifth grade, there are seven text-books in daily use to cover the subjects. In the sixth grade, there are also seven text-books, supplemented by thirteen reference and reading books used in connection with their courses, and, in addition, the school library is available to them. Every text, reading, and reference book, 26 in number, produced in evidence, is carefully selected in accordance with the regulations of the state board of education and approved by the supervisor of the elementary grades and by the board of education of West Orange. There is a student schedule for the fifth and sixth grades, which provides for instruction from 8:45 a. m. until 3 p. m. from Monday to Friday, inclusive. The curriculum provides for instruction in the development of abilities, habits, and skills. Instruction is also given by way of travel lectures, picture studies, art and music, so that every child has something to talk about. Thus, an audience situation is created for the children, where each child is required to rise and speak to the entire group. This creates self-confidence, and tends to adjust the child to the social group.

One poem a week, and appreciation for the beauties of nature and literature are taught. Besides teaching arithmetic from texts, they instruct in practical matters requiring arithmetic. Geography is taught to meet life situations by creating interest in world travel and training the children to visualize, in their reading, places that they have studied. In music, each child is allowed to develop whatever talent he may possess. In art, each child learns the harmony of color in dress, interior decoration, and everyday life. Every morning the children have a reading from the Bible and recite the Lord's Prayer. They salute the flag and sing patriotic songs. They observe Arbor Day and all patriotic holidays. A course in safety education and fire prevention is pursued. The month of June is devoted to review. They have physical education four periods each week under a special supervisor. In the civics course, the children are on the lookout for all material in current events. There are three school magazines. Washington School has a monthly newspaper, and all children are eligible to participate in its columns.

The text-books used by the defendants are nine in number, and are as follows: Old Times in the Colonies, by Charles Carleton Coffin, 1881; an arithmetic book by Stone and Millis, 1914; A Manual of Child Development, 1927; The Home Kindergarten Manual, 1921 (2 volumes); How to Teach American History, by Wayland, 1914; Rabenort's Geography, 1921; American History, by Muzzey, 1911; The Teacher-Parent Guide to Character Building, 1926.

From this comparison and analysis of the evidence, I find (1) that the education, training, and equipment of the defendants are substantially inadequate, as compared with those of the public school teacher; (2) that the schedule of study and the program of activities of the defendant are irregular, uncertain, and without form, while the public school curriculum is definite and allots a specified time and, in most cases, a special teacher for every subject studied in the fifth and sixth grades; (3) that the instruction given by the defendants is without proper or modern text-books, lacks supervision by competent authorities of pupil and teacher, lacks a method, standard, or other means of determining the progress or attainments of the child; none of which deficiencies are present in the public school; (4) that the teaching of discipline and health habits lacks plan and a trained method, fixing responsibility on the child for its execution; while, at the school, it is part of a definite program of character education; (5) that the defendants cannot provide for group or class teaching, and lack the ability to develop attitudes and create a social setting so that the children may be trained to deal with their playmates and friends as a part of a social group; (6) that the public school system provides such social groups and lays emphasis on its development, and stresses the adjustment of the child to group life and group activity and a course of living that he will be required to follow and meet as he goes out into the world.

The primary function of education is to get an understanding and interpretation of modern civilization.   In the early days of the Republic, the idea that an educated citizenship lies at the very foundation of a democratic government has defined our philosophy of national development.   For these reasons, the maintenance of an adequate system of public education for youth is a fundamental responsibility of any commonwealth.   The public school system of New Jersey embodies the highest ideals of American democracy, and has developed a program which offers unusual opportunities to the children of our state.   All citizens have a deep interest in our public schools, and should take pride in the high rank which they occupy in the nation. To deny children instruction seems as unnatural as to withhold their necessary subsistence.   Education is brought, as it were, to the very door of all classes of society, and ignorance is quite inexcusable.   The failure of the parents to provide the child with the benefits of that opportunity should be a matter of great concern when at issue.   The education of youth is of such vast importance and of such singular utility in the journey of life that it obviously carries its own recommendation with it, for on it, in a great measure, depends all that we ever hope to be;   every perfection that a generous and well-disposed mind would gladly arrive at.   It is this that usually renders one man preferable to another.   And, as the great end of learning is to teach man to know himself and to fit him for life, so he who knows most is enabled to practice best and to be an example for those who know but little.

The schools, whose function frequently is thought of solely in material terms, have a far more important responsibility.   They must aid parents, not simply in the training of their children for the trades and professions, whose criterion of success too often is the amount of money they can make, but, rather, the training and development of men and women of character;   men and women whose minds have been trained to the understanding of basic principles and ideals, with the courage and strength of will to live up to and apply them in their daily lives.

I incline to the opinion that education is no longer concerned merely with the acquisition of facts;   the instilling of worthy habits, attitudes, appreciations, and skills is far more important than mere imparting of subject-matter.   A primary objective of education to-day is the development of character and good citizenship.   Education must impart to the child the way to live.   This brings me to the belief that, in a cosmopolitan area such as we live in, with all the complexities of life, and our reliance upon others to carry out the functions of education, it is almost impossible for a child to be adequately taught in his home. I cannot conceive how a child can receive in the home instruction and experiences in group activity and in social outlook in any manner or form comparable to that provided in the public school. To give him less than that is depriving the child of the training and development of the most necessary emotions and instincts of life. I cannot accept the theory asserted by Mr. Bongart that, "I am not interested in method, but in results." That theory is archaic, mechanical, and destructive of the finer instincts of the child. It does seem to me, too, quite unlikely that this type of instruction could produce a child with all the attributes that a person of education, refinement, and character should possess.

I have carefully observed the defendants' children in court, their demeanor, their responses under examination, and their reaction to the proceedings while in court, and there is clear evidence that it is their belief that they are on a "grand holiday," free from the restraints, discipline, and responsibility of other children in school attendance. All of this seems to me to be attributable to the course adopted and pursued by the parents. I have also carefully examined all the evidence and exhibits, and it is my opinion that the defendants have failed to give their children instruction equivalent to that provided with the public schools in the fifth and sixth grades, but, rather, have engaged in a haphazard and hit-or-miss kind of instruction, not calculated to conform with the provisions of the statute, and that both defendants actively and independently participated in causing their children not to go to the public school or a day school. I have been satisfied beyond a reasonable doubt by the evidence of the guilt of both defendants as charged. Both defendants are hereby deemed to be disorderly persons.

NOTES AND QUESTIONS

1. In this case Judge Siegler makes six findings of fact from which the court concludes that the defendant parents are criminally liable for keeping their children out of school while attempting to teach them at home. Are all six of the court's findings necessary to the result in the case? Which, if any, of the six findings of fact provide the strongest argument for bussing of school children to provide a racial balance?

2. Shirley Temple was a child actress who made films in Hollywood, California at an age when most other children were in a common school. The usual custom in the case of child actors who spent their days on the movie set instead of in a classroom is to provide special tutors, academically qualified, to educate such children. Would such a scheme meet the approval of Judge Siegler? Of State v. Counort? Why or why not?

3. True or false? Judge Siegler believed that the primary purpose of public education was to prepare one for later employment?

4. Could a child ever receive an adequate education at home in Judge Siegler's view? In yours? Explain.

STATE OF NEW JERSEY v. MASSA

Morris County Court, New Jersey, 1967.
95 N.J.Super. 382, 231 A.2d 252.

COLLINS, J. C. C.   This is a trial *de novo* on appeal from the Pequannock Township Municipal Court.   Defendants were charged and convicted with failing to cause their daughter Barbara, aged 12, regularly to attend the public schools of the district and further for failing to either send Barbara to a private school or provide an equivalent education elsewhere than at school, contrary to the provisions of N.J.S.A. 18:14–14.   The municipal magistrate imposed a fine of $2490 for both defendants.

Mr. and Mrs. Massa appeared *pro se*.   Mrs. Massa conducted the case; Mr. Massa concurred.

The State presented two witnesses who testified that Barbara had been registered in the Pequannock Township School but failed to attend the 6th grade class from April 25, 1966 to June 1966 and the following school year from September 8, 1966 to November 16, 1966— a total consecutive absence of 84 days.

Mrs. Massa testified that she had taught Barbara at home for two years before September 1965.   Barbara returned to school in September 1965, but began receiving her education at home again on April 25, 1966.

Mrs. Massa said her motive was that she desired the pleasure of seeing her daughter's mind develop.   She felt she wanted to be with her child when the child would be more alive and fresh.   She also maintained that in school much time was wasted and that at home a student can make better use of her time.

Mrs. Massa is a high school graduate.   Her husband is an interior decorator.   Neither holds a teacher's certificate.   However, the State stipulated that a child may be taught at home and also that Mr. or Mrs. Massa need not be certified by the State of New Jersey to so teach.   The sole issue in this case is one of equivalency.   Have defendants provided their daughter with an education equivalent to that provided by the Pequannock Township School System?

Mrs. Massa introduced into evidence 19 exhibits.   Five of these exhibits, in booklet form, are condensations of basic subjects, are concise and seem to contain all the basic subject material for the respective subjects.   Mrs. Massa also introduced textbooks which are used as supplements to her own compilations as well as for test material and written problems.

Mrs. Massa introduced English, spelling and mathematics tests taken by her daughter at the Pequannock School after she had been taught for two years at home.   The lowest mark on these tests was a B.

Other exhibits included one of over 100 geography booklets prepared by Mrs. Massa from National Geographic Magazine, each containing articles and maps concerning the topography and societies of a particular part of the world; a 1' wide and 30' long scroll depicting the evolution of life on earth commencing five billion years ago and continuing to the present, which appears to be a good visual aid not merely for children but adults as well; a series of 27 maps for study and memorization; textbooks used to supplement defendant's material; examples of books used as either references or historical reading, and photographs to show that the Massa family lives a normal, active, wholesome life. The family consists of the parents, three sons, (Marshall, age 16 and Michael, age 15, both attend high school; and William, age 6) and daughter Barbara.

There is also a report by an independent testing service of Barbara's scores on standard achievement tests. They show that she is considerably higher than the national median except in arithmetic.

Mrs. Massa satisfied this court that she has an established program of teaching and studying. There are definite times each day for the various subjects and recreation. She evaluates Barbara's progress through testing. If Barbara has not learned something which has been taught, Mrs. Massa then reviews that particular area.

Barbara takes violin lessons and attends dancing school. She also is taught art by her father, who has taught this subject in various schools.

Mrs. Massa called Margaret Cordasco as a witness. She had been Barbara's teacher from September 1965 to April 1966. She testified basically that Barbara was bright, well behaved and not different from the average child her age except for some trouble adjusting socially.

The State called as a witness David MacMurray, the Assistant Superintendent of Pequannock Schools. He testified that the defendants were not giving Barbara an equivalent education. Most of his testimony dealt with Mrs. Massa's lack of certification and background for teaching and the lack of social development of Barbara because she is being taught alone.

He outlined procedures which Pequannock teachers perform, such as evaluation sheets, lesson plans and use of visual aids. He also stressed specialization since Pequannock schools have qualified teachers for certain specialized subjects. He did not think the defendants had the specialization necessary to teach all basic subjects. He also testified about extra-curricular activity, which is available but not required.

The State placed six exhibits in evidence. These included a more recent mathematics book than is being used by defendants, a sample of teacher evaluation, a list of visual aids, sample schedules for the day and lesson plans, and an achievement testing program.

Leslie Rear, the Morris County Superintendent of Schools, then testified for the State. His testimony, like that of MacMurray, dealt primarily with social development of the child and Mrs. Massa's qualifications. He felt that Barbara was not participating in the learning process since she had not participated in the development of the material. Mrs. Massa, however, testified that these materials were used as an outline from which she taught her daughter and as a reference for her daughter to use in review—not as a substitute for all source material.

N.J.S.A. 18:14–14 provides:

"Every parent, guardian or other person having custody and control of a child between the ages of 6 and 16 years shall cause such child regularly to attend the public schools of the district or a day school in which there is given instruction equivalent to that provided in the public schools for children of similar grades and attainments *or to receive equivalent instruction elsewhere than at school.*" (Emphasis added)

State v. Vaughn, 44 N.J. 142, 207 A.2d 537 (1965), interpreted the above statute to permit the parent having charge and control of the child to elect to substitute one of the alternatives for public school. It is then incumbent upon the parent to introduce evidence showing one of the alternatives is being substituted. "If there is such evidence in the case, then the ultimate burden of persuasion remains with the State," . . .

N.J.S.A. 18:14–39 provides for the penalty for violation of N.J. S.A. 18:14–14:

"A parent, guardian or other person having charge and control of a child between the ages of 6 and 16 years, who shall fail to comply with any of the provisions of this article relating to his duties shall be deemed a disorderly person and shall be subject to a fine of not more than $5.00 for a first offense and not more than $25.00 for each subsequent offense, in the discretion of the court."

The statute subjects the defendants to conviction as a disorderly person, a quasi-criminal offense. In quasi-criminal proceedings the burden of proof is beyond a reasonable doubt. State v. Cestone, 38 N.J.Super. 139, 148, 118 A.2d 416 . . .

This case presents two questions on the issue of equivalency for determination. What does the word "equivalent" mean in the context of N.J.S.A. 18:14–14? And, has the State carried the required burden of proof to convict defendants?

In Knox v. O'Brien, 7 N.J.Super. 608, 72 A.2d 389 (1950), the County Court interpreted the word "equivalent" to include not only academic equivalency but also the equivalency of social development. This interpretation appears untenable in the face of the language of our own statute and also the decisions in other jurisdictions.

If the interpretation in *Knox,* were followed, it would not be possible to have children educated outside of school. Under the *Knox* rationale, in order for children to develop socially it would be necessary for them to be educated in a group. A group of students being educated in the same manner and place would constitute a *de facto* school. Our statute provides that children may receive an equivalent education elsewhere than at school. What could have been intended by the Legislature by adding this alternative?

The Legislature must have contemplated that a child could be educated alone provided the education was equivalent to the public schools. Conditions in today's society illustrate that such situations exist. Examples are the child prodigy whose education is accelerated by private tutoring, or the infant performer whose education is provided by private tutoring. If group education is required by our statute, then these examples as well as all education at home would have to be eliminated.

The court in State v. Counort . . . held that defendant had not complied with the state law on compulsory school attendance. The Washington statute, however, provided that parents must cause their child to attend public school or private school, or obtain an excuse from the superintendent for physical or mental reasons or if such child shall have attained a reasonable proficiency in the branches of learning required by law. The conviction was upheld because of the failure of the parents to obtain permission from the superintendent.

In discussing the nature of schools the court said, "This provision of the law [concerning what constitutes a private school] is not to be determined by the place where the school is maintained, *nor the individuality or number of pupils who attend it.*" . . . The court further said that the evidence of the state was to the effect that defendant maintained *no* school at his home. This is not the case here. Mrs. Massa was certainly teaching Barbara something.

The court in State v. Peterman, 32 Ind.App. 665, 70 N.E. 550, 551, . . . also commented on the nature of a school, stating, "We do not think that the number of persons whether one or many, makes a place where instruction is imparted any less or more a school." That case held that a child attending the home of a private tutor was attending a private school within the meaning of the Indiana statute.

This court agrees with the above decisions that the number of students does not determine a school and, further, that a certain number of students need not be present to attain an equivalent education.

A different form of legislative intention is illustrated by the case of People v. Turner, 121 Cal.App.2d 861, 263 P.2d 685   .   .   .   The California statute provided that parents must send their children to public school or a private school meeting certain prescribed conditions, or that the children be instructed by a private tutor or other person possessing a *valid state credential for the grade taught*. Defendants were convicted for failure to have such state credentials.

Other similar statutes are discussed in Rice v. Commonwealth, 188 Va. 224, 49 S.E.2d 342   .   .   .   where the Virginia law required certification of teachers in the home and specified the number of hours and days that the child was to be taught each year; Parr v. State, 117 Ohio St. 23, 15 N.E. 555   .   .   .   where the Ohio statute provided that a child would be exempted if he is being instructed at home by a *qualified* person in the subjects required by law.

Perhaps the New Jersey Legislature intended the word "equivalent" to mean taught by a certified teacher elsewhere than at school. However, I believe there are teachers today teaching in various schools in New Jersey who are not certified. The prosecutor stipulated, as stated above, that the State's position is that a child may be taught at home and that a person teaching at home is not required to be certified as a teacher by the State for the purpose of teaching his own children. Had the Legislature intended such a requirement, it would have so provided.

The other type of statute is that which allows *only* public school or private school education without additional alternatives.   .   .   .   Even in this situation, home education has been upheld as constituting a private school.   .   .   .

The case of Commonwealth v. Roberts, 159 Mass. 372, 34 N.E. 402   .   .   .   dealt with a statute similar to New Jersey's. The Massachusetts statute permitted instruction in school or academies in the same town or district, or instruction by a private tutor or governess, or by the parents themselves provided it is given in good faith and is sufficient in extent. The court stated that under this statute the parents may show that the child has been sufficiently and properly instructed. The object of the statute was stated to be that all children shall be educated, not that they shall be educated a particular way.

It is in this sense that this court feels the present case should be decided. The purpose of the law is to insure the education of all children. In State v. Peterman, supra, the court stated:

> "The law was made for the parent, who does not educate his child, and not for the parent   .   .   .   [who] places within the reach of the child the opportunity and means of acquiring an education equal to that obtainable in the public schools of the state."   .   .   .

People v. Levisen also commented on the spirit of the relevant statute stating:

> "The law is not made to punish those who provide their children with instruction equal or superior to that obtainable in public schools. It is made for the parent who fails or refuses to properly educate his child."   .   .   .

Faced with exiguous precedent in New Jersey and having reviewed the above cited cases in other states, this court holds that the language of the New Jersey statute, N.J.S.A. 18:14–14, providing for "equivalent education elsewhere than at school," requires only a showing of academic equivalence. As stated above, to hold that the statute requires equivalent social contact and development as well would emasculate this alternative and allow only group education, thereby eliminating private tutoring or home education. A statute is to be interpreted to uphold its validity in its entirety if possible. Rainbow Inn, Inc. v. Clayton Nat. Bank, 86 N.J.Super. 13, 205 A.2d 753 .   .   . This is the only reasonable interpretation available in this case which would accomplish this end.

Having determined the intent of the Legislature as requiring only equivalent academic instruction, the only remaining question is whether the defendants provided their daughter with an education equivalent to that available in the public schools. After reviewing the evidence presented by both the State and the defendants, this court finds that the State has not shown beyond a reasonable doubt that defendants failed to provide their daughter with an equivalent education.

The majority of testimony of the State's witnesses dealt with the lack of social development.

The other point pressed by the State was Mrs. Massa's lack of teaching ability and techniques based upon her limited education and experience. However, this court finds this testimony to be inapposite to the actual issue of equivalency under the New Jersey statute and the stipulations of the State. In any case, from my observation of her while testifying and during oral argument, I am satisfied that Mrs. Massa is self-educated and well qualified to teach her daughter the basic subjects from grades one through eight.

The remainder of the testimony of the State's witnesses dealt primarily with the child's deficiency in mathematics. This alone, however, does not establish an educational program unequivalent to that in the public schools in the face of the evidence presented by defendants.

Defendants presented a great deal of evidence to support their position, not the least of which was their daughter's test papers taken in the Pequannock school after having been taught at home for two years. The results speak for themselves. The evidence of the State which was actually directed toward the issue of equivalency in this case fell short of the required burden of proof.

The Massa family, all of whom were present at each of the hearings, appeared to be a normal, well-adjusted family. The behavior of the four Massa children in the courtroom evidenced an exemplary upbringing.

It is the opinion of this court that defendants' daughter has received and is receiving an education equivalent to that available in the Pequannock public schools. There is no indication of bad faith or improper motive on defendants' part. Under a more definite statute with sufficient guidelines or a lesser burden of proof, this might not necessarily be the case. However, within the framework of the existing law and the nature of the stipulations by the State, this court finds the defendant not guilty and reverses the municipal court conviction.

In view of the fact that defendants appeared pro se, the court suggests that the prosecutor draw an order in accordance herewith.

NOTES AND QUESTIONS

1. Why did Massa's home education qualify as "equivalent academic instruction" under the New Jersey statute but that of Bongart did not? Was the requirement of a "certified teacher" determinative? Peer socialization? Was the same meaning of the term "equivalent academic instruction" applied equally in the two cases? If not, and the meaning of the term varied between the two cases, what were the differences in meaning? Are the Washington and New Jersey statutes identical? If not, what difference does their differences make?

2. Did the court find as a fact that Mrs. Bongart was not and that Mrs. Massa was developing the individuality, personality and mentality of each child under her supervision? Do you agree? Why or why not? Was this consideration relevant in the same way to the decision in Massa? Should it have been?

3. Does the court's decision in Stephens v. Bongart ultimately rest on the view that home education is not equivalent to school education because home education fails to teach the individual how to fit into social groups? If so, could New Jersey's statute providing for "equivalent" education ever be satisfied by home education? Is the court consistent in Massa?

4. Do you agree that the factual distinctions between the Massa and the Bongart cases justified the different results? What precise facts? Why or why not?

5. Would the court's decision in the Massa case have been the same if there had been no evidence of the child's success on external examinations used by the public schools or by an independent testing service? Can there be true home education if the child is required to take periodic tests at a school?

6. Why didn't the Washington Court in State v. Counort, supra, consider the quality of the home education? Should it have? Why or why

not? If so, what are the specific criteria that make equivalent home instruction into a "private school"? Is association with other children from all walks of life a requirement?

7. Do you agree with the decisions and the reasoning in the Bongart, Massa and Counort cases? Which shows more insight into education? Why?

8. Why does the court in Massa require that the state carry the burden of proof? What was required in State v. Counort, supra? Why in Massa was the required standard of proof that the state had to meet the standard of "beyond a reasonable doubt" rather than the standard of "by a fair preponderance of the evidence"? What is the difference between these standards? Which would you require if you were the judge, and why?

9. Which of the decisions in the three cases is most promotive of and compatible with the views that "an educated citizenship lies at the very foundation of a democratic government" and that "a primary objective of education today is the development of character and good citizenship"? How can these objectives be achieved in school? In the home?

10. In relation to these three cases consider "The Dangers of Early Schooling" printed infra.

11. For discussion of state controls over private schools see, J. Elson, "State Regulation Of Nonpublic Schools: The Legal Framework," printed in D. A. Erickson (ed.), Public Control Of Nonpublic Schools (1969).

THE OBLIGATION TO ATTEND A DISTRICT SCHOOL

Taxpayers within a school district bear the burden of supporting the schools within their district. The courts usually hold that the "right" or "privilege" of being educated at public expense is restricted to the school-age children who are bona fide residents within that district. Thus, the obligation to attend a public school is further refined, obliging the parents residing in a school district to see to it that their children attend the public schools within that school district. The courts are not always agreed on the meaning of the term "residence," but usually a child takes the residence of his parents. If the parents reside in the school district that is usually sufficient. On the other hand, substantial questions can arise when the child lives in one school district and the parents in another.

PEOPLE ex rel. SAXE v. BOARD OF EDUCATION

Appellate Court of Illinois, 1917.
206 Ill.App. 381.

Mr. Justice HIGBEE delivered the opinion of the court.

This is an appeal from a judgment of the Circuit Court of Edwards county, directing that a writ of mandamus issue compelling appellant, the Board of Education of School District No. 36 in said county, to admit Edward J. Saxe, the relator, whom we will call the appellee, to the school of that district without the payment of tuition. The only question is whether appellee's residence in said school district No. 36 is such as to entitle him, under the law, to attend the school therein without the payment of the tuition required by the school board. By agreement the case was tried before the court without a jury.

Appellee is the eight-year-old son of William B. and Bessie Saxe. The City of Alton is within school district No. 36. William B. Saxe resides about six miles from Albion and without the boundaries of school district No. 36. In the fall of 1913 appellee entered the school of district No. 36, staying with his grandmother, Hannah Saxe, who was a widow sixty-six years of age and had lived in Albion by herself for some years. After the close of school in 1914, William B. Saxe, after some protest, paid appellee's tuition for the year 1913–1914, but subsequently refused to pay such tuition for the year 1914–1915. Appellee, by the direction of the school board, was refused admission to the school in 1915 unless his tuition was paid. It is the contention of appellee that soon after the opening of school in 1913, William B. Saxe and Bessie Saxe, his father and mother, entered into a verbal agreement with Hannah Saxe, his grandmother, the terms of which were, in substance, that he should live and have his home with his grandmother until her death or until he becomes twenty-one years of age; that she should have the absolute care, custody and control of him and should support and educate him at her own expense without any cost to his parents, and that, by virtue of such agreement, he is under the law entitled to attend school in district No. 36 without the payment of tuition. Appellants deny such an agreement was in fact made, and claim that even if made it was a mere subterfuge to avoid payment of tuition, and further that such an agreement, though made in good faith, would not entitle appellee to admission to the school without payment of tuition.

It becomes material in the first instance to determine whether the claimed agreement was in fact entered into, and if so whether it was made in good faith. If appellee was living with his grandmother for the primary purpose of attending the school, or if the agreement was not made, or was made as a subterfuge for the purpose of avoiding the payment of tuition, without question appellee would not be entitled to the writ. The father, mother and grandmother of appellee all testified to the making and terms of the agreement; that it was made soon after the opening of school in 1913; that the grandmother was lonesome and for some time had wanted appellee's parents to give him to her and allow him to live with her; that since the making of the contract the grandmother has had full custody and control of appellee and has clothed and maintained him; that he visited his parents' home at times between Fridays and Mondays during the school year and spent portions of his vacation period there; that the grandmother decided when he should come and go; that he made several trips with her and she paid his expenses. Appellants introduced evidence tending to prove contradictory statements by these witnesses; that appellee spent more time at his parents' home than claimed by them and that his father signed his report card. As a whole the proof shows the agreement was made as claimed by appellee; that it was made in good faith and not for the purpose of avoiding payment of tuition; that since the making thereof the grandmother has had full custody and control of appellee and has clothed and maintained him; that it was the intention of all parties that she should continue to do so and the child should live with her until her death, or he should reach the age of twenty-one years.

Counsel for appellants, however, contend, that even though the contract were made in good faith, appellee had not the right to attend the school without the payment of tuition for the reason that it is necessary to the right of a child to attend the public schools of the State, that it should have a legal domicile in the district in which the school is held, and that the legal domicile of a minor cannot be other than the domicile of the parents. As a general proposition of law it cannot be questioned that, during the lifetime of the parents, their domicile is the legal domicile of their minor child. It remains then to be determined in this case whether it is indispensable to the appellee's right to attend school in district No. 36 that his legal domicile be in that district. The very recent case of Ashley v. Board of Education, 275 Ill. 274, decided since this appeal was taken, is decisive of this question and also of this case, under the facts as above found. A reference to that case will render further discussion of the law unnecessary here. After considering the sections of the school law applicable to the facts, the court there said: "It is not essential to the right of a child to attend the public schools of the State that it should have a legal domicile in the place in which the school is held. The schools are required to be maintained for all persons in the district over the age of six and under twenty-one years of age. The residence required under this language is not such as would be required to establish a right to vote or which would fix the liability of a township or county for the support of a pauper. The right to attend school is not limited to the place of the legal domicile. A residence, even for a temporary purpose, in a school district is sufficient to entitle

children of school age to attend school. * * * The only requirement, so far as residence is concerned, is dwelling in the school district. Every child of school age in the State is entitled to attend the
public schools in the district in which it actually resides for the time
being, whether that be the place of its legal domicile or the legal
domicile of its parents or guardian, or not. For this has always been
the view which has been held, so far as we are informed, by those
charged with the administration of the school law." The court also
quoted with approval the following from Bateman's Common School
decisions . . . : "As a general rule, the residence of the parents
is the residence of their children. Boarding children in a district does
not, of itself, entitle them to the benefits of the free school in said
district. The mere temporary residence of a family in a district, solely
to enjoy the benefits of the free schools and with the intention of
removal as soon as that purpose is accomplished, does not entitle the
children to the privileges of said schools. The removal of a portion of
a family from the legal domicile to another district in order to send
to the free schools thereof does not confer the right to do so. As a
general rule, the residence of their parents is the residence of employees; hence the privilege of the free schools in another district is
not acquired by placing children temporarily at service in that district.
This includes those who are placed in families to attend school and
do chore work for their board, etc. The most liberal policy is, however, recommended towards this class of children. The State has as
much interest in their education as in that of the more favored, and,
although not legally eligible to attend free, the directors should permit them to do so, when not inconsistent with the rights of others
and the welfare of the school. Children who have been apprenticed
or adopted into a new family or who have been placed permanently in
the care of others with no intention of withdrawal, or those over whom
parents have relinquished all control from whatever cause, or those
who have no parents or guardians or whose parents or guardians live
in another State or country and exercise no control over their children,
or those who have no permanent abode but go from place to place in
search of employment and whose only home is where they find work,—
the children included in all the above classes are to be enumerated in
the district where they live and are entitled to all the rights and benefits of the free schools in said district."

This same principle is laid down in Board of Education v. Lease
. . . and Yale v. West Middle School Dist. . . . Under the
rule of law laid down in these authorities and the facts in this case,
appellee was entitled to attend the public school in district No. 36
without the payment of tuition, and the trial court did not err in
awarding the writ of mandamus.

. . . The judgment in this case should be and is affirmed.

NOTES AND QUESTIONS

1. The Court says that the state has a strong interest in educating all children within the state. Why? Do states show a comparably strong interest in the health and nutritional conditions of its children? Should these two interests be of equal state concern?

2. Under the law of this case a family cannot temporarily move to a school district "solely to enjoy the benefits of the free schools and with the intention of removal as soon as that purpose is accomplished . . . .". Why is it wrong for a family to move solely to take advantage of good, free public schools?

3. Why should actual residence in good faith be the requirement for allowing a child to attend a local public school? Is the justifying reason that the taxpayers of the district must pay the expenses for operating the schools? How persuasive is this reason in light of the large amounts of state and federal funds that go to local school districts?

GENTILE v. BOARD OF ED. OF CENTRAL H. S. DIST. NO. 2

Supreme Court, Special Term, Nassau County, Part I., 1968.
56 Misc.2d 216, 288 N.Y.S.2d 269.

JOSEPH A. SUOZZI, Justice. This is an application in the nature of a mandamus requiring the respondents to register one Marvin Jerome Short in New Hyde Park Memorial High School so that he may attend classes there as a full time, free tuition student.

The student for whom admission is sought is living in the home of the petitioners under the auspices of the Student Transfer Education Program (STEP), which is designed to enable selected children from southern communities to live with families in the north in order "to give academically talented students the opportunity to complete their last two years of college preparation in quality high schools."

This petition was instituted after the respondent school district in September of 1967 refused to register and admit the student. The student is presently registered and attending classes in New Hyde Park Memorial High School pursuant to a temporary order of a Justice of this Court pending the determination of this petition.

The pertinent provisions of the Education Law involved in this proceeding are subdivisions 2 and 5 of Section 3202, which provide as follows:

"2. Nonresidents of a district, if otherwise competent, may be admitted into the school or schools of a district or city, upon the consent of the trustees or the board of education, upon terms prescribed by such trustees or board."

"5. Children cared for in free family homes, and children cared for in family homes at board, when such family homes shall be the actual and only residence of such children or such children have been removed from the custody of their parents by order of the children's court, shall be deemed residents of the school district in which such family home is located. Other children cared for in family homes at board shall not be deemed residents of the school district in which such family homes are located, but shall receive free tuition in the school district in which such family homes are located, unless the trustees or board of education of such school district shall establish to the satisfaction of the commissioner of education that there is a valid and sufficient reason for refusal to receive such children or that the reception of such children in the school or schools imposes an unreasonable additional operating cost on such school district. In the latter case the commissioner of education may decide that tuition shall be paid for such children   *   *   * "

It is the respondents' contention that the child involved here is a non-resident, and that as such it is entirely within the province of the school board to decide whether or not he should be admitted at all, either as a tuition paying or free tuition student. Assuming without deciding that this contention is valid as to non-residents generally, as the Court reads this statute it is not valid as to non-residents who may qualify as "Other children cared for in family homes at board" in accordance with the second part of subdivision 5. Such children are presumptively entitled to admission and free tuition unless the school board can justify its refusal to the Commissioner of Education in accordance with the statute.

Dealing for a moment with the first part of subdivision 5, certainly on the facts revealed in this proceeding the child cannot be deemed a resident of the district. The petitioners' home in which the student is presently residing is not the actual or only residence of the child, and the child has not been removed from the custody of his parents by any order of the children's court.

Therefore the issue to be determined here is whether the child involved is or is not a child cared for in a family home at board within the meaning of the second part of this provision. This is a matter of statutory interpretation, and appropriately a judicial function.

It would appear from the legislative history, the social background and the context of this section that it was designed to remove obstacles in the use of family homes or foster homes in the care of dependent and deprived children, and it is undisputed that a foster child is a "child cared for in a family home at board" within the purview of this section. Admittedly the living arrangements which are the subject of this proceeding may not have been specifically contemplated by the Legislature when Section 3202(5) of the Education Law was originally enacted and later amended. However, this legislation basically reflects a concern of the Legislature that children who because of some deprivation or dependency live away from their parents would receive a proper and adequate education.

The relationship between this child and the petitioners is not dissimilar from that of a foster child and the foster parents with whom he resides. While it may not be a permanent arrangement, neither is that between a foster child and foster parents.

Whereas a foster child is placed with foster parents because of the inability of his natural parents to care for his physical needs, the child here has been placed with his host family presumably because of the inability of his natural parents, in the school district in which they reside, to provide him with an education in an environment in which he can develop his ability and talents to their best and fullest potential. The circumstances and conditions which impelled the boarding of this child with the petitioners reflect a situation of deprivation and dependency which is, in this Court's opinion, encompassed within the social philosophy which underlies this legislation.

In a similar situation, admission was recently sought for a child in the STEP program to a school in Port Washington. There the school district did not refuse admission, but offered to accept the child if tuition were paid. An appeal seeking free tuition was taken to the Commissioner of Education, who ruled that he was a child cared for in a family home at board located in the school district, and as such was entitled to free education since the school board had failed to show that his attendance at the school would impose an additional operating cost or demonstrate any other valid and sufficient reason for their refusal   .   .   .

A review of the Commissioner's decision was sought in the Supreme Court of Albany County. By granting the Commissioner of Education's motion for dismissal of the school board's petition, that Court upheld the Commissioner's decision. In so doing the Court, relying upon the Court of Appeals' holding in Matter of Board of Education of the City of New York v. Allen,   .   .   .   held that the decisions of the Commissioner of Education are final unless purely arbitrary, which the Court found was not the case   .   .   .   Although the Court did not make a specific ruling, there is implicit in its holding the Court's concurrence that the child involved was a child cared for in a family home at board within the purview of Section 3202(5).

On the basis of the broad language of the section, the failure of the Legislature to provide a more restrictive or precise definition of "a child cared for in a family home at board", and the related purposes and objectives of the foster home and the STEP program, the Court concludes and holds that the STEP child involved here is such a child within the meaning of this section.

This judicial determination that he comes within the purview of Section 3202(5) presumably entitles this child (1) to admission and

(2) to free tuition. However, this is not an absolute right since a school board may still refuse to admit such a child, but the statute imposes upon the board the burden of establishing to the satisfaction of the Commissioner of Education that there is some other valid and sufficient reason for refusal or that the admission imposes an un-reasonable additional operating cost on the school district.

Whether the school board has any such valid or sufficient reason or can establish an unreasonable burden upon the school district can-not be determined on the record before this Court. However, even if the full facts had been presented here, it would not be within the province and function of this Court to pass upon the sufficiency of the Board's purported justification for its refusal, since this is a mat-ter of educational policy exclusively within the province of the Com-missioner of Education. It is only when the Commissioner's decision, after an appeal pursuant to Section 310 of the Education Law, is found to be purely arbitrary that the courts may interfere.

If respondents persist in their refusal to admit the child, petition-ers will be required to pursue their appeal to the Commissioner of Education which is presently pending. In the meantime, since this child is presumptively entitled to admission and is presently attending the school, judgment is granted directing the respondents to allow him to continue to attend the school tuition free until such time as the Commissioner of Education may have adversely determined his right to such attendance, subject to such court review as may be available thereafter.

NOTES AND QUESTIONS

1. This was "an action in the nature of mandamus." What does that mean?

2. What are the implications of the Court's analogy between a foster child's right to free attendance in a local public school and the right of an out-of-state child similarly to attend tuition free? A child goes to a foster home because his minimum needs are not being pro vided for in his natural home, but the purpose of the STEP program is to develop a child's "ability and talents to their best and fullest potential," by allowing him to attend a better public school in another district than the district of his residence or domicile. No claim or argument was made that the minimum educational needs of the chil-dren in STEP were not being met. Would the case have been decided differently if this argument had been made? How convincing is the foster child analogy?

HOSIER v. EVANS

United States District Court, Virgin Islands, 1970.
314 F.Supp. 316 (D. St. Croix).

CHRISTIAN, District Judge. The plaintiffs herein are minor children of school age, each of whom has brought this action by "next friend," one of his parents. They are all aliens and the children of alien parents. They are all lawfully in the Virgin Islands as "non-immigrant" visitors. The period of the "visit" in some cases, approximates, or coincides with, the bonding period of those parents who are "non-immigrants," admitted on working bonds, i. e., six months. In the cases of those plaintiffs whose parents enjoy "immigrant" status, their visits are for such periods of time as the United States Immigration and Naturalization Service may grant. In any case the visiting period may be extended or renewed, and particularly in the cases of the non-immigrant parents, here on work bond, renewal follows as a matter of course unless the employer, for one reason or another cancels the bond.

Plaintiffs pray for declaratory and injunctive relief for themselves, and on behalf of all other non-citizen children, similary situated. They ask that the Court adjudge that they, as well as all members of the class on whose behalf they sue, are entitled to attend the public schools of the Virgin Islands, and that the Court also enjoin defendants to refrain from excluding plaintiffs and the members of their class from the said public schools. . . .

Defendants rely somewhat heavily on the nice legal distinctions revolving around residence, i. e., domicile. They would have this case turn on the implications, rights and limitations which flow from the concept of domicile. For the purpose of qualification or entitlement to public education, however, I disregard such formalistic distinctions as irrelevant and inapt, and I adhere to tthe concept of residence in the sense of physical presence in a place of abode. . . .

Of more than passing significance is the fact that the Virgin Islands Board of Education, the agency vested with the rule making authority in the Virgin Islands has promulgated no rules establishing residence requirements which must be met as a condition of enrollment in the public schools. It is, therefore, appropriate in the circumstances of this case that we hark back to the generally understood and accepted view, that a child becomes a resident, for the purpose of public school attendance, as soon as he acquires a home in a school district, be that home permanent or temporary in nature. . . .

We are here dealing with an aspect of twentieth century life so fundamental as to be fittingly considered the corner stone of a vibrant and viable republican form of democracy, such as we so proudly espouse, i. e., free and unrestricted public education. Following in the footsteps of our Federal Government, we too " * * * must consider public education in the light of its full development and its present place in American life. * * * " Brown v. Board of Education . . . . With like perception we must recognize that

> "Today, education is perhaps the most important function of state and local governments. Compulsory school attendance laws and the great expenditures for education both

demonstrate our recognition of the importance of education to our democratic society. * * * Today it is the principal instrument in awakening the child to cultural values, in preparing him for later professional training, and in helping him to adjust normally to his environment. In these days, it is doubtful that any child may reasonably be expected to succeed in life if he is denied the opportunity of an education. * * * " . . .

The foregoing, it will be remembered, was said by the Supreme Court of the United States with respect to black children, citizens of the United States, in striking down the "separate but equal," so-called, system of public education. Here we address ourselves to the problem of alien children in this territory, worse in plight, for they are offered no free, public education at all. As did the court in Brown v. Board of Education, supra, I hold that public education, " * * * where the state has undertaken to provide it, is a right which must be made available to all on equal terms."

Once we start from the premise posited by the Supreme Court of the United States in Levy v. Louisiana, 391 U.S. 68, 70 . . . as it spoke of illegitimate children, and take full cognizance of the fact that aliens, likewise, are not "non persons," but rather are " * * * humans, live, and have their being * * * " the conclusion is inescapable that alien children, lawfully within this territory, in the status of these plaintiffs, are unquestionably "persons" within the Equal Protection Clause of the Fourteenth Amendment.

So long settled as to be beyond the pale of controversy is the proposition that the long reach of the Fourteenth Amendment extends to the alien. Yick Wo v. Hopkins, 118 U.S. 356 . . . Limited only by a few exceptions, the non-citizen has a right to work at his calling. . . . But even those once hallowed preserves, historically "off limits" to the non-citizen, may have seen their best days. No longer is the right of an alien to own land open to serious question. . . . It is now far too late in the day to adopt a policy which acts as a government imposed stumbling block in his path as he reaches for an education, the better to enable him to engage in the productive endeavor by means of which he may become a land owner. Thus in Halaby v. Board of Directors, 162 Ohio St. 290, 123 N.E.2d 3 (1954) an attempt to set up "Municipal citizenship," in turn dependent upon United States Citizenship, as a qualifying condition for admission to a public institution (a universtiy in this case) and in this wise close the doors of the university to alien residents, was struck down. . . .

Defendants contend that the Legislature of the Virgin Islands is authorized to establish categories or classes of persons who may be admitted or excluded from the public schools so long as such classes or categories bear a reasonable relation to the power of the Legislature to enact laws for the protection of the public welfare. With this general principle, so well settled, none can quarrel, and it must be admitted that in this effort, a legislature is to be given great latitude. . . . This legislative power is not without its limitations, however, especially where basic civil rights are concerned, Skinner v. Oklahoma, 316 U.S. 535 . . . and those classifications which invade or restrain fundamental rights are to be " * * * closely scrutinized and carefully confined." Harper v. Virginia State Board of Elections, 383 U.S. 663, 670 . . ..

Defendants make much of the influx of aliens into the territory over the last few years and suggest that the cost of admitting these plaintiffs and all others in the class to the public schools would create an undue burden on the Government of the Virgin Islands. They would cover themselves with the cloak of "already severely inadequate" facilities which, by the granting of the relief here prayed for, would be rendered " * * * so chaotic as to totally destroy public education for all so entitled." The short answer to that argument is that fundamental rights guaranteed by the Constitution may be neither denied nor abridged solely because their implementation requires the expenditure of public funds. For such purposes, the Government must raise the funds. . . . What defendants advance as an inescapable conclusion—that relief must be denied—" * * * until such time as the educational facilities are adequate * * * " I reject out of hand as constitutionally impermissible, once the plaintiffs' right be established. These litigants may not be relegated to such a state of neglect, "benign" or otherwise.

Defendants stress that it is in the interest of the public weal that plaintiffs be debarred from the public schools, except upon such special conditions as they may prescribe. They would bottom this position with unbending reliance on the police power of the government. But what is in the public interest cannot be permanently catalogued on some motion of what was deemed best at a given time. The public's best interest inevitably changes with changing conditions and changing times. If ever sound public policy dictated that non-citizens be barred from the public schools, it can hardly be argued that the criteria and conditions which then dictated such policy still persist.

The exact number of children in the class represented by these plaintiffs has not been made known to the court. The Government has indicated that it can throw no light on this subject. Counsel for plaintiffs has informed the Court that in St. Croix alone upwards of three hundred and eighty alien children living on that island applied for and were denied admission to the public schools. An Office of Economic Opportunity survey of August 25, 1969, presumably covering the entire Virgins Islands was also made available to the court by plaintiffs' counsel. That study indicates that there are almost nine hundred alien children of school age living in the Virgin Islands and projects that figure into the thousands within the very near future. Without standing on the accuracy of those figures, it is safe to say that the class represented by these plaintiffs now number several hundred. It cannot be gainsaid that it is manifestly contrary to the public good in this territory to develop and foster a ghetto of ignorance, with countless numbers of untrained, untutored and perhaps untended children (since their parents are bonded workers) roaming the streets, this with the concomitant evils of crime, immorality and general social degeneracy. In the public interest a generation of illiterates is to be avoided, whatever the financial cost. I am of the opinion that the most compelling of public concern militates in favor of the prompt admission of these plaintiffs and all others of their class, to the public schools.

Defendants' "public welfare" argument may be considerably beside the point for I am not persuaded that we are dealing as much with an expressed policy of the Legislature of the Virgin Islands, as with principles laid down by the Virgin Islands Board of Education. Recognizing that the promulgated rules and regulations are accorded force of law, defendants go on to urge that the words of 17 V.I.C. Sec. 82 "All children * * *" are limited and qualified by Sec. 103–1 of the Regulations of the Department of Education. I am unable to agree with defendants that the words of 17 V.I.C. Sec. 82 are to be so restricted.

It is clear that the Board must have so construed the statute, but I find myself at loggerheads with that body. Allowing, as I must, great weight to that administrative agency's statutory construction, . . . its patent error, as I view it, gives me leave to disregard their judgment, . . . particularly since that administrative interpretation, is inconsistent with the obvious purpose of statute. . . .

Nowhere in Title 17 of the Virgin Islands Code or in its scant legislative history does one find a reliable clue to the legislative intent in the use of words "All children * * *" By the same token there is no justification for as narrow a reading of the words as, it seems, the Board has adopted. Since nothing in the statute points to the contrary I feel impelled to give the words their plain meaning, . . . and read them to mean "all children" living in the Virgin Islands. I would engraft no exceptions in addition to those specifically expressed. Had the Legislature intended to exclude resident "non-immigrant" children it should have, and I think certainly would have, said so. . . .

I am of the opinion that 17 V.I.C. Sec. 82, properly read and construed includes, rather than excludes, these plaintiffs among the children who must attend school. The construction advanced by defendants is unreasonable and unwarranted. Were I to so interpret the statute, and were it to be applied, I would be obliged to declare it invalid. That interpretation being far from compelled, I adopt the one which upholds the statute's validity.

Regulation 103–1 of the Virgin Islands Board of Education is another matter, however. Not only is it in conflict with 17 V.I.C.

Sec. 82, but it also imposes unreasonable and invidious discrimination on these plaintiffs and all members of their class and thus offends the equal protection clause of the Fourteenth Amendment of the Constitution of the United States. I declare that regulation null and void and conclude that the plaintiffs' motion for summary judgment should be granted.

NOTES AND QUESTIONS

1. The Court finds that education is a fundamental right guaranteed under the Constitution and that an abridgment of that right requires that government show more than a reasonable basis for so doing. Is this analysis correct? Is it consistent with the Supreme Court's decision in San Antonio School Board v. Rodriguez, infra?

2. In the alternative the Court finds that the denial of access by aliens to public schools is invidious discrimination violating the Fourteenth Amendment's equal protection clause. What is invidious discrimination? How does it differ from discrimination that is not invidious? By negative implication the Court in *Saxe,* supra, would not find invidious discrimination on its facts, although the school's attendance policy was a discriminatory act. How can Saxe and this case be reconciled or distinguished on this point?

PROBLEM

R. MANJARES v. DR. R. E. NEWTON

Supreme Court of California, 1966.
64 Cal.2d 365, 49 Cal.Rptr. 805, 411 P.2d 901.

"Plaintiffs live just off a county road in the Paloma Creek area of Monterey County. This is in the southeast corner of the school district, about 30 miles from the junior high school and about half that distance from the elementary school to which the children were assigned. For many years the district has provided bus transportation to students along certain county roads. The closest stop to plaintiffs' homes is at the Hastings Reservation, 6.2 miles away. The controversy between the parties involves the question whether the board is required to authorize transportation for this approximate six-mile distance.

"Each year the board reviews existing routes and decides whether to curtail, maintain, or extend them. In the three years prior to 1963, when plaintiffs moved into the area, there was a trend toward curtailing the routes for reasons of economy. The board's policy regarding transportation is contained in section 16B of its rules and regulations, which provides that, while it is the responsibility of students and their parents to arrange the daily travel between home and school, the board may assist in transporting pupils who live beyond two miles from a bus stop if road conditions, pupil density, or hazardous walking conditions make it advantageous, but that some areas will not be served by buses for reasons of safety. The section also provides that, if the distance from a regular bus stop to a student's home exceeds two miles, payments of six cents per additional mile may be authorized in lieu of transportation.

"As a result of plaintiffs' inability to provide transportation, the children did not attend school for the remainder of the 1963–64 school year. The district superintendent recommended to the county superintendent of schools that they be excused from compulsory school attendance under section 12153 of the Education Code, which provides that students residing more than two miles from school shall be exempted from compulsory attendance on the written approval of the county superintendent.

"In their complaint plaintiffs, after alleging their inability to secure transportation and the details of the Wallace proposal, asserted that the board's action resulted in excluding the minor plaintiffs from the public schools and in depriving them of their constitutional rights of due process of law and equal protection. They prayed for a restraining order compelling the board to furnish them with transportation to and from school."

Assume you are the Judge, what decision would you render in this case; following what precedents, and for what reasons?

NOTES AND QUESTIONS

1. What is the operational difference between not providing public transportation to students in order to enable them to receive a free public education and not providing specialized public education to students suffering from congenital or environmental learning disabilities such that they cannot take advantage of the usual curriculum of public education? Is the state legally obliged to provide the special education? Should it be? Who should bear its cost? Why? Should a school be legally obliged to provide for gifted children by creating "ability groups" or "tracking" within its curriculum? See, Hobsen v. Hansen, infra.

EARLY SCHOOLING OR EARLY LEARNING OR BOTH

STATE ex rel. SHINEMAN v. BOARD OF EDUCATION

Supreme Court of Nebraska, 1950.
152 Neb. 644, 42 N.W.2d 168.

SIMMONS, Chief Justice. In this action relators sought a writ of mandamus requiring the respondents to furnish and make available in the school operated by respondents a kindergarten or beginner grade for children who attained the age of five years but not six years on or before October 15, 1949. The trial court denied the writ. Relators appeal. We affirm the judgment of the trial court.

The relators are parents of children over five years of age, at the time this action was begun, not yet six years of age. They are residents of the city of Franklin and of School District No. 33 in Franklin County.

The respondents are the Board of Education of School District No. 33.

The district is a class III district as defined in section 79–102, R.S. Supp., 1949. The district has never maintained in its schools a kindergarten or beginner grade as distinguished from a first grade. Before the budget was adopted in June 1949, the question of establishing a kindergarten was considered but not adopted because of financial reasons and lack of available room. In August 1949, the Board of Education considered and denied a petition for the establishment of a kindergarten. At the beginning of the school term on September 12, 1949, the relators presented their children for admission as members of a kindergarten or beginner grade and were denied admission because such a grade was not maintained. It was stipulated that had the district provided a kindergarten grade the children would have been required to attend. Relators did not request that the children be admitted to the first grade. Shortly thereafter this action was begun for the writ and with the result above stated.

Relators rely upon the provisions of Article VII, section 6, of the Constitution and upon sections 79–802 and 79–444, R.S.Supp., 1949.

The constitutional provision is: "The legislature shall provide for the free instruction in the common schools of this state for all persons between the ages of five and twenty-one years."

The constitutional provision is clearly directed to the Legislature. We held in State ex rel. Walker v. Board of Commissioners, 141 Neb. 172, 3 N.W.2d 196, that a constitutional provision is not self-executing if the language of the Constitution is directed to the Legislature, or if it appears from the language used and the circumstances of its adoption that subsequent legislation was contemplated to carry it into effect. With reference to this provision we said in Affholder v. State, 51 Neb. 91, 70 N.W. 544, that the method and means to be adopted in order to furnish free instruction to the children of the state have been left by the Constitution to the Legislature. Clearly legislation is necessary to carry into effect the constitutional provision. It is not a self-executing provision. It follows that relators must find statutory authority to sustain their contention.

The Legislature has provided that "The district school boards and boards of education shall have the general care and upkeep of the schools, shall provide the necessary supplies and equipment, and, *except as herein otherwise provided, shall have the power to cause pupils to be taught in such branches and classified in such grades or depart-*

ments as may seem best adapted to a course of study which the school board or board of education shall establish with the consent and advice of the Superintendent of Public Instruction." (Emphasis supplied.)   § 79–443, R.S.Supp., 1949.

The statute places the general power in the school board with the consent and advice of the Superintendent of Public Instruction to establish such branches and grades as the board shall deem best adapted to the school. We find no indication in this record and it is not contended that the classification of grades in the school here involved is not in accord with the consent and advice of the Superintendent of Public Instruction.

Unless otherwise provided in the act, the determination of whether or not there shall be a kindergarten or beginner grade in the respondent school is to be determined by the board of education.

This brings us to the question of whether or not the two sections of the statutes, relied upon by relators, limit the power, for otherwise the respondents have determined the question here presented adverse to the desires of relators.

The act as it now stands (section 79–444, R.S.Supp., 1949) makes mandatory the age limits, subject to the exceptions, and makes for uniformity of age in the grades beginning with the first, in all the schools of the state. The Legislature did not undertake to say by this provision that all schools should provide a kindergarten or beginner grade.

The judgment of the district court is affirmed.

Affirmed.

NOTES AND QUESTIONS

1. What was "the law" before decision and at the time this case came before Nebraska's Supreme Court? Was "the law" clear on whether a five but not a six-year old child was entitled to early schooling? Was Nebraska's statute fully consistent with its constitutional provision? What was the actual decision in this case? Its reasoning? Is the decision educationally correct? Were the judges "bound" by law to decide this case the way in which they did? What was the "binding" rule of law? Could Nebraska's Supreme Court have decided this case other than the way it did? If so, by following what "law"? Do state supreme courts ever overrule their prior decisions? How would you have decided this case? Why?

2. If you were the lawyer arguing this case on behalf of Shineman, what legal arguments would you have made? What wise educational arguments about the benefits of early schooling would you have made? Would the latter be relevant, at least in part, to a wise decision by the court?

3. In Shineman the state constitution required the legislature to "provide for free instruction in the common schools . . . for all persons between the ages of five and twenty-one years." In turn, the legislature

delegated to district school boards and boards of education discretion on what pupils should be taught. Was this consistent with the state constitution? Who should control the content of the curriculum, the legislature, the school board, the teaching staff, the taxpayers or some other group?

4. Does the result of Shineman accord with wise educational policy? What is the relationship, if any, between the decision in Shineman and the following reading?

RAYMOND MOORE & DENNIS MOORE, THE DANGERS OF EARLY SCHOOLING

The idea that "the earlier a child starts school the better" is well on the way to becoming an unquestioned tenet of the conventional wisdom. Educators and legislators across the country are pressing for earlier and earlier schooling for *all* children, on the assumption that schools and teachers can do more for the child than parents can or will do. Parents themselves, bewildered over how best to meet their children's needs, not only have accepted this formulation but have agitated to be certain *their* children will not be left behind in the race to the schoolhouse.

In the face of this growing movement—and after exhaustive review of the research concerning early-childhood education—we contend that sending four-year-olds off to school results in far more harm than good. In fact, we argue that children probably shouldn't attend school until they are seven or eight years old.

There is simply no conclusive proof that even the best known early-schooling plans are working, and there is considerable evidence that most are not. Studies show that most of the extensive projects such as Head Start and Great Cities have failed to produce the expected growth in scholastic achievement. Furthermore, there is an impressive body of research indicating that the late starter generally does better through school than the child who starts early.

It may be that the sheer volume of professional and political propaganda—along with parental complacency and uncertainty—will sweep all four-year-olds into school regardless of what the facts are. Already there is considerable momentum: the National Education Association's Educational Policies Commission has called for public-supported education beginning with four-year-olds; the New York State Regents have recommended generalized schooling down to age three, to be achieved by 1973 or 1975; and California's state school superintendent is currently seeking legislation to authorize schooling for all four-year-olds. While the price to the taxpayer for such programs would be high, the costs could be even greater in damage to the very children who are supposedly being helped.

Most plans for early-childhood education seem to grow out of a genuine concern for children. The high caliber of people historically appointed to the Educational Policies Commission, for example, would suggest that only the highest motive stand behind its conclusions. Yet some of the older hands fear that many educators and media firms are moving rapidly into the field because, in the words of a key researcher, "that's where the money is."

Even the National School Public Relations Association might be forgiven for placing the movement for early-childhood education in a highly favorable light in its recent report, *Project Breakthrough*. Yet these leaders should be expected to provide hard evidence for their conclusions and recommendations, lest it be suggested their interest lies more in creating teacher jobs and government projects than in assuring the welfare of the child and his family. Indeed, one California state staffer expressed concern about teacher employment if research pointed away from early schooling.

Advocates of early schooling usually start from two well-proved points: the fact of incredibly rapid growth in the child's intelligence between birth and age five, and the need for the child's social development to keep pace with his intellectual maturity. But then they go on to make unfortunate twin assumptions: that a child's intelligence can be nurtured by organizing it, and that brightness means readiness for the world of schooling. In short, their happy vision is that early schooling offers the best garden for a child's budding intelligence and developing social awareness.

These assumptions, however comforting or promising, are contradicted by clear-cut experimental evidence. A wealth of research has established that one of a child's primary needs in these formative years is for an environment free of tasks that will tax his brain, and an equally important need is for a setting that provides warmth, continuity, and security. That normal school experience does not successfully meet these needs has been established by three different kinds of studies: those that compare early and later school entrants; those that explore important but little understood changes in the young child's brain; and those that compare the effectiveness of parents and teachers in the development of young children. All three lines of investigation point to a common conclusion: early schooling, far from being the garden of delights its advocates claim, may actually be a damaging experience.

Too Much Too Early

Investigators who have studied very young children in school overwhelmingly present a grim picture. The child too often stumbles insecurely through kindergarten and the early grades. His friends who were delayed a year or so quickly catch up and pass him—and usually become more stable and highly motivated. His learning retention frequently remains lower than that of his later-starting peers, regardless of how bright he is. In other words, it is hard to escape the conclusion that early schooling is little short of crippling. A few indicative studies by well-regarded researchers give a sense of the situation:

In an American Educational Research Association experiment with two groups of children matched by sex, age, intelligence, and home background, H. M. Davis reports: "One group began reading at the age of six, the other at the age of seven. In two years the late beginning group had caught up with the early beginning group. After the first two years, these two groups were joined in classes. At the end of their seventh school year the children who began a year later were one year ahead of the early beginners."

In Chula Vista, California, Margaret Gott compared kindergarten children who were about four years, nine months of age when enrolled, with those who were about five years, seven months. She found that, after six grades of schooling, the younger group achieved less well than the older group in all subjects at each grade level (except in one case where achievement was equal).

In Oak Ridge, Tennessee, Inez King reports, fifty-four children who were under six when they started school were compared with fifty children who started after age six. Stanford Achievement Tests at the end of grade six showed a distinct difference, strongly in favor of the older group.

Studies on how long and how well very young children retain their learning have been conducted in virtually all grades and socioeconomic levels with remarkably uniform results. B. U. Keister reported that even five-year-olds who developed enough skills to finish first-grade reading generally did not retain the learning through summer vacation. Other comparisons of reading achievements of early and late starters at third through sixth-grade levels all found that later entrants significantly excelled those who started earlier.

In Grosse Pointe, Michigan, Paul Mawhinney describes a study of children who were selected by psychologists because they were considered mature enough or bright enough to be admitted to kindergarten before age five. An evaluation of all those children remaining in the school system after fourteen years showed that more than one-fourth of the select group were below average or had repeated a grade.

Years ago, pioneer child researcher Arnold Gesell noted that school tasks such as reading, writing, and arithmetic "depend upon motor skills which are subject to the same laws of growth which govern creeping, walking, grasping." The awkwardness a young child may exhibit, he noted, "is often sadly overlooked by teachers and parents"—who should be as flexible in their attitudes toward the child's readiness to read as toward his readiness to walk.

Early Stress Can Injure

A second series of arguments against early schooling emerges from the studies of neurophysiologists, psychologists, and pediatricians concerned with the delicate harmonies at work in the development of the young child's brain. These investigators are in remarkable agreement in their timing of the stages at which children are normally ready to think abstractly, to organize facts, and to sustain and retain learning without undue damage or strain.

Research on brain development indicates that important changes are constantly underway in the normal child from birth into adolescence, including the shifting of control from the emotional centers to the reasoning centers The period at which "reason" develops, and the ability to organize facts emerges, normally comes between ages seven or eight and ten or eleven.

Numerous studies support the idea that the young child cannot meet the demands posed by schooling prior to the level of development usually achieved by age seven or eight. At Harvard, the work of Paul Yakovlev has shown that the nerve fibers between the thalamus and the cortex in a child's brain are not finished or fully insulated until after age seven. Likewise, it is only between the ages of seven and ten that the cerebral commissures (brain paths between the lobes) and the reticular formation (a primary arousing system) are fully developed.

A number of other studies have established that a child's visual and auditory systems reach maturity only gradually. This is of enormous consequence for tasks such as reading, where there are high demands for discrimination in sight and sound.

Luella Cola has observed that some children are unable to focus on objects at close range—as required for reading—until they are seven, eight, or even older. She reports that not more than 10 per cent of five-year-olds can perceive the difference between "d" and "b" or "p" and "q". Not until children are eight, she says, is it possible to "be perfectly certain the eyes are mature enough to avoid such confusions."

Hearing presents a similar situation. Luella Cola notes: "If [a child] has normal six-year-old ears he will still be unable to distinguish consistently between the sounds of 'g' and 'k', 'm' and 'n', 'p' and 'b' or any other pair of related sounds."

Dr. Henry L. Hilgartner, a Texas ophthalmologist, offers evidence of eye damage from early schooling. Noting that the eyes of young children focus better on distant objects than on close ones, he reported that the state's record prior to 1930 was 7.7 farsighted children to every nearsighted child. After 1930, when the Texas school-entry age was lowered from seven to six, the ratio shifted to five near-sighted children for every farsighted child.

Swiss psychologist Jean Piaget, one of the world's leading students of child development, long ago urged educators to concentrate on maximizing a child's development, not in accelerating it. He found that a child under age seven or eight relates quantity to shape and form of objects, but if the shape or form is changed, he becomes confused, assuming the quantity must also change. For instance, the four- or five-year-old seldom understands how a low, wide glass can hold as much water as a tall, narrow glass. Even after the water is poured from the tall glass into the wide one, he will usually insist that the tall one is larger and holds more. Not until he is seven or eight or older does he become a fully "reason-able" creature, able to reason abstractly instead of dealing solely with direct relationships.

On the Home Front

The third, and possibly the most important, conclusion to be drawn from research is that when a child is taken from the home for early schooling—or remains at home without loving care—he is vulnerable to mental and emotional problems that will affect his learning, motivation, and behavior. While many proponents of early schooling insist that the young child needs social contact outside the home—namely in the school—the lesson of numerous investigations is that this need ranks far behind the child's need for close parental contact. The teacher, in general, does not make a good surrogate mother.

Maternal deprivation, in the words of John Bowlby, a world authority on the subject, describes the extent to which a child does not experience "a warm, intimate, and continuous relationship with his mother (or permanent mother-substitute) in which both find satisfaction and enjoyment." As part of a 1951 World Health Organization study, Bowlby noted that "a child is deprived even though living at home if his mother (or permanent mother-substitute) is unable to give him the loving care small children need [or] . . . if for any reason he is removed from his mother's care." Today, he points out that in the Western world early childhood problems commonly result from "too little mothering, or . . . [from] mothering coming from a succession of different people." While a child is most vulnerable until age five, he can experience the effects of maternal deprivation until age eight.

In an experiment conducted in Uganda, Marcel Geber demonstrated that children who do not have continuous warm mothering are *less* sociable than those who do. Using standardized tests, Geber worked with babies from poor tribal families in which the mothers were child-centered, providing continual caressing, cuddling, and attention to their babies. He found these infants to be superior to Western children in sociability as well as in physiological maturation and coordination, adaptability, and language skills. While African children frequently mature earlier than Westerners, Geber also reported that babies from relatively well-to-do Uganda families, with less maternal contact but more formal training, were much less mature in these areas than the babies of poor families.

A more personal perspective on the socializing experience of early schooling is provided by M. W. Sullivan, a well-known educational programmer. He recalls that kindergarten only caused him to wet his pants. When the teacher sent him home he was so happy that he decided to keep on wetting his pants in school—until he was sent home for the year.

On the basis of such findings, it seems clear that for a child of this age, development at home is far more important than development in school. And if the parents' acceptance of their role is a key factor in the child's development, then it makes a great deal more sense to educate the parents to fulfill their proper role than to hire teachers to do an inadequate job of trying to substitute for them.

Traditionally, of course, school people have argued that parents simply don't care or are too ignorant or too obsessed with the desire to protect their own freedom to fulfill the needs of their children. Parents, for their part, have seldom contested this view, possibly out of feelings of uncertainty or inadequacy when confronted by the opinions of these professionals. The facts, however, as determined by a number of investigations of parental willingness to aid the development of their children, run counter to this conception. The vast majority of parents, regardless of socioeconomic status, stand ready to help their children in terms of home-education programs. While much of the justification for early-childhood education has grown from the belief that children from disadvantaged backgrounds in particular will benefit, studies have repeatedly shown that the home provides resources that should not be lightly dismissed.

On the basis of several studies, Bowlby insists that "children thrive better in bad homes than in good institutions." He goes on to observe: "It must never be forgotten   .   .   .   that even the bad parent who neglects her child is nonetheless providing much for him.   .   .   .   Except in the worst cases, she is giving him food and shelter, comforting him in distress, teaching him simple skills, and above all is providing him with that continuity of human care on which his sense of security rests."

In Flint, Michigan, Mildred Smith found that when she took study-help materials into disadvantaged homes and asked for parental help, 90 per cent of the families responded, and of these 99 per cent of the parents asked that the program be continued.

Burton Blatt and Frank Garfunkel found it necessary to reject the operating hypothesis of their own study—that preschool might be good for disadvantaged children who "were at least two years away entering the first grade." They concluded that (1) the home is more influential than the school; (2) the school can do little without strong home support; (3) disadvantaged parents "are often anxious to cooperate"; and (4) school organization and requirements are often "foreign" to these parents, who in turn are blamed by the school for not readily accepting them.

In all the investigations of early schooling, the only clear evidence proving its value is in the case of special child-care needs that are *not* common to most children—and even here the home should be the center of operation whenever possible. Special and early education is a benefit when it provides therapeutic help for the handicapped child—those with problems of vision, speech, hearing; or cerebral palsy, severe mental retardation, neurosis, psychoses, and advanced emotional problems. Likewise, in cases where the child may be severely deprived because his parents are mentally, physically, or emotionally unable to care for him, early schooling may provide an advantageous alternative to the home.

Yet one of the clear dangers of attempting to provide early schooling for all three- or four-year-olds is that these programs for the handicapped child, which are desperately needed, will be watered down. Sheldon White, a developmental psychologist at Harvard, fears that the early-schooling movement "will work itself into so much trouble within six years or so that it will wipe out the gains special education has made and possibly ruin the future of early-childhood education."

Most disturbing of all, the volume of research work that stands opposed to early-childhood education appears to have made hardly a dent in the enthusiasm of its proponents. The report of the California Task Force on Early Childhood Education, for example, loftily recommends early schooling as a way to prevent future "crime, poverty, addiction, malnutrition, and violence"—without pausing to notice that some of the studies it quotes in its support actually contradict its recommendations.

It appears, indeed, that many of the problems early schooling is supposed to solve actually exist because children right now are being forced into schooling too early. Throughout the experimental work in this area there is considerable evidence that early schooling and parental deprivation together are prime contributors to childhood maladjustment, motivational loss, poor retention, deterioration of attitudes, visual handicaps, and a wide variety of other physical and behavioral problems.

School in the Home

The question remains, of course, what is the alternative to early schooling? How are a bright child's enthusiasms and eagerness for learning to be met before he is eight years old and ready for school?

The most promising practical solution emerging from current research points to home-centered educational programs.

Susan Gray and Phyllis Levenstein, among others, are now experimenting with "home schools," the latter by means of a "Mother-Child Home Program." In this plan, teachers visit homes at regular intervals to work with parents in assessing a child's development and suggesting appropriate ways of nurturing his growth without taxing him. Essentially these visitors function less as traditional teachers and more as consultants or resource personnel, providing ideas and directions for the parents to use as they choose; in fact, to overcome parental fear of professional teachers, these visitors frequently refer to themselves as "toy demonstrators."

In terms of funds required, home-teaching programs avoid the need for heavy taxation to cover capital and operating costs that, for example, the California early-school proposal is certain to bring. The California planners are projecting a cost of $500 to $600 per child per year. New York state experts, however, point out that such programs must be funded at the rate of at least $1,800 per child annually, and that truly effective programs will cost "much more."

A central spokesman for the home-school approach is Earl Schaefer, Professor of Maternal and Child Health at the University of North Carolina and former chief of early child-care research at the National Institute of Mental Health. In a recent interview, Schaefer called home-centered programs, and particularly the work of Levenstein and Gray, "the current most likely solution" to the child-development dilemma. To its credit, the Office of Child Development in the Department of Health, Education and Welfare is embarking on a new project called Home Start, intended to redirect the focus of early-childhood education from the school to the home.

The home-school concept can be adapted to meet the growing national concern for children of working mothers. Neighborhood home centers could be established where the mothers (or other adults) providing care would be selected for their warmth, continuity, and dedication to the welfare of children. Where parents cannot afford the entire cost of these centers, the difference could be subsidized by the states. Traveling teachers or "toy demonstrators" on state or local payrolls could monitor these home "schools" to see that each was providing adequate care and equipment, and to coordinate them with existing social-service programs.

While the proposal is sketchy—and in any case may not provide the only answer to the country's child-care problem—it does establish a fruitful direction for exploration. After all, social policy must be a product of our best knowledge on public issues, or it runs the risk of plunging us even deeper into the problems we are attempting to escape. The clear lessons of scholarly research in the field of child development are that we must worry less about exploiting the child's intelligence and more about understanding it, and that schoolmen must realize that there is less value in attempting to substitute for the parent than in helping parents to help themselves and their children.

NOTES AND QUESTIONS

1. Do authors R. S. & D. R. Moore object to the dangers of early learning or early schooling, or both? Why? What difference does it make? What, precisely, is the recommendation made by the Moores? Do you agree? What is its implication, if any, for "headstart" programs?

2. Is there an actual difference between aiming education to develop the full potential of a child at a given stage of growth and development and aiming education to accelerate the stages of growth and development? Which is wiser? Do the Moores rely on either of these concepts? Is the latter one possible? With what consequences? If the former were thoroughly followed could schools have a rigorously regularized schedule for grades one through six?

3. Do the Moores invite you to reconsider your views about "equivalent home education" for children aged five through ten? In what way? What is your opinion on a child's obligation to attend school between the ages of five to eight? What would you anticipate to be the impact of the women's liberation movement on the recommendation made by the Moores?

4. For additional information and support of the Moores' thesis see, R. D. Hess and R. M. Bear, EARLY EDUCATION: CURRENT THEORY, RESEARCH AND ACTION (1968), and W. D. Rohwer, Jr. "Prime Time for Education: Early Childhood or Adolescence? 41 Harv.Ed. Rev. 316 (1971).

5. What limitations, if any, can you find in the Constitution of the United States limiting a state's power to require early schooling of every child? Suppose a state statute required that every child begin school at age 2 (3?) (4?), would such a statute be constitutional? Suppose a state's statute required schooling for everyone until age 21 (25?) (35?), would such a statute be constitutional? Why or why not?

VACCINATION

ARCHIE CUDE v. ARKANSAS

Supreme Court of Arkansas, 1964.
237 Ark. 927, 377 S.W.2d 816.

ROBINSON, Justice. The issue is the authority of the courts to appoint a guardian for children between the ages of 7 and 15, inclusive, who are not attending school, and to give the guardian custody of the children with directions to have them vaccinated to facilitate school attendance.

Appellants, Archie Cude and his wife, Mary Frances, are the parents of eight children, three of whom are between the ages of 7 and 15, inclusive. The children are Wayne Monroe, age 12, Delia Marie, 10, and Linda May, 8. Wayne went only to the second grade; the other two have not attended school at all. The children are not in school for the reason that the school authorities will not permit them to attend school because they have not been vaccinated against smallpox. The Cudes will not permit such vaccinations; they contend that it is contrary to their religion.

This litigation was commenced by Ben Core, Prosecuting Attorney for the Ninth Judicial District of the State of Arkansas, filing in the Probate Court of Polk County, on behalf of the State, a petition alleging that the three Cude children were not attending school; that the father, Archie Cude, had been fined on three occasions for violating the law requiring that parents send their children to school, and he has persisted in his refusal to have the children vaccinated so that they can attend school, and that the father has avowed that he will never permit the children to be vaccinated; that unless the children are removed from the custody of the natural parents they will not have all the benefits and advantages of a school education. The petition asks that the children be placed in the custody of the Child Welfare Division of the State Welfare Department.

The appellants responded, contending first, that the probate court did not have jurisdiction, and further, that vaccination of the children was against respondents' religious beliefs. There was a full scale hearing; it was shown that the children were not attending school because they had not been vaccinated; that the appellants would not permit them to be vaccinated because of their religious beliefs, and appellant, Archie Cude, testified that if the children were taken from him and vaccinated he would not accept them back.

The court appointed Miss Ruth Johnston, Director of the Child Welfare Division of the State Welfare Department, as guardian of the children. The order further provides: "Said guardian is authorized and directed to file a petition in the Chancery Court of Polk County, Arkansas, for the purpose of obtaining the physical control and custody of the children for the purpose of having such children properly vaccinated and immunized against the disease of smallpox, and thereafter enrolled in the public schools of this State, all in accordance with the laws of this State, and all to be done by qualified and licensed and practicing physicians of this State as soon as is reasonably possible after the said children are in the custody of said guardian. After the immunization of the said children, the guardian shall offer, through the office of the Prosecuting Attorney for the 9th Judicial Circuit, to deliver the said children back into the custody of the Defendants, and the guardian is authorized and directed to do so, and if the Defendants shall not accept the said children back into the home of the Defendants, then the said guardian is hereby authorized and empowered to consent to the subsequent adoption of the said children by a party or parties acceptable to the Guardian and to the Probate Court which may consent."

Pursuant to the foregoing order, the guardian, Ruth Johnston, filed a petition in the chancery court asking for custody of the children. Over appellants' protest the petition was granted. The Cudes have appealed.

Actually, there are two appeals; one from the order of the probate court appointing the guardian; the other from the order of the chancery court giving Miss Johnston custody of the children. The cases have been consolidated on appeal.

For the purposes of the appeal, we will assume that the Cudes, in good faith because of their religious beliefs, will not permit the children to be vaccinated. Then the question is whether they have the legal right to prevent vaccination. The answer is that they do not have such right.

There is no question that the laws of this State require parents to send to school their children between the ages of 7 and 15, inclusive. Ark.Stat.Ann. § 80–1502 (Repl.1960) provides: "Every parent, guardian, or other person residing within the State of Arkansas and having in custody or charge any child or children between the ages of seven [7] and fifteen [15], (both inclusive) shall send such child or children to a public, private, or parochial school under such penalty for noncompliance with this section as hereinafter provided."

The school administrative authorities of the State of Arkansas have adopted a regulation requiring vaccination as follows: "No person shall be entered as a teacher, employee or pupil in a public or private school in this state without having first presented to the principal in charge or the proper authorities, a certificate from a licensed and competent physician of this State certifying that the said teacher, employee or pupil has been successfully vaccinated; or in lieu of a certificate of successful vaccination, a certificate certifying a recent vaccination done in a proper manner by a competent physician; or a certificate showing immunity from having had smallpox. * * *"
There is no question about the validity of this regulation. .   .   .

It is clear that the law requires that the children attend school, and a valid regulation requires that they be vaccinated. The next question is: Are appellants, because of their religion, exempt from the law and the regulation requiring that the children be vaccinated so that they can go to school? It will be remembered that appellants do not object to the children going to school; it is the vaccination that is objectionable to them. But, according to a valid regulation, the children are not permitted to go to school without having been vaccinated.

Article 2, Sec. 24 of the Constitution of Arkansas provides: "All men have a natural and indefeasible right to worship Almighty God according to the dictates of their own consciences; no man can, of right, be compelled to attend, erect or support any place of worship; or to maintain any ministry against his consent. No human authority can, in any case or manner whatsoever, control or interfere with the right of conscience; and no preference shall ever be given, by law, to any religious establishment, denomination or mode of worship above any other." The foregoing provision of the Constitution means that anyone has the right to worship God in the manner of his own choice, but it does not mean that he can engage in religious practices inconsistent with the peace, safety and health of the inhabitants of the State, and it does not mean that parents, on religious grounds, have the right to deny their children an education.

The U. S. Supreme Court said in Prince v. Commonwealth of Massachusetts, 321 U.S. 158, 64 S.Ct. 438, 88 L.Ed. 645: "The right to practice religions freely does not include liberty to expose the community or the child to communicable disease or the latter to ill health or death.   *   *   *   Parents may be free to become martyrs themselves. But it does not follow they are free, in identical circumstances, to make martyrs of their children before they have reached the age of full and legal discretion when they can make that choice for themselves."

It is a matter of common knowledge that prior to the development of protection against smallpox by vaccination, the disease, on occasion, ran rampant and caused great suffering and sickness throughout the world. According to the great weight of authority, it is within the police power of the State to require that school children be vaccinated against smallpox, and that such requirement does not violate the constitutional rights of anyone, on religious grounds or otherwise. In fact, this principle is so firmly settled that no extensive discussion is required.

In the early case of Reynolds v. United States, 98 U.S. 145, 25 L.Ed. 244, the issue was whether a Mormon who believed in polygamy was immune from the operation of the statute forbidding the practice of multiple marriage. There, the court said: " *   *   *   the only question which remains is, whether those who make polygamy a part of their religion are excepted from the operation of the statute. If they are, then those who do not make polygamy a part of their religious belief may be found guilty and punished, while those who do, must be acquitted and go free. This would be introducing a new element into criminal law. Laws are made for the government of actions, and while they cannot interfere with mere religious belief and opinions, they may with practices. Suppose one believed that human sacrifices were a necessary part of religious worship, would it be seriously contended that the civil government under which he lived could not interfere and prevent a sacrifice? Or if a wife religiously believed it was her duty to burn herself upon the funeral pile of her dead husband, would it be beyond the power of the civil government to prevent her carrying her belief into practice?"

In cases too numerous to mention, it has been held, in effect, that a person's right to exhibit religious freedom ceases where it overlaps and transgresses the rights of others. We cite a few cases upholding the validity of statutes requiring vaccination, and affirming orders of courts authorizing blood transfusions, etc. In Re Whitmore, Dom. Rel.Ct.N.Y., 47 N.Y.S.2d 143; vaccination of school child. Sadlock v. Board of Education, 137 N.J.L. 85, 58 A.2d 218; vaccination of school child. State v. Perricone, 37 N.J. 463, 181 A.2d 751; giving blood transfusion to infant. City of New Braunfels v. Waldschmidt, 109 Tex. 302, 207 S.W. 303; vaccination of school child. Mosier v. Barren County Board of Health, 308 Ky. 829, 215 S.W.2d 967; vaccination of school child; Board of Education of Mountain Lakes v. Maas, 56 N.J. Super. 245, 152 A.2d 394; vaccination of school child. In Re Clark, Ohio Com.Pl., 185 N.E.2d 128; blood transfusion for three year old child.

This court said in Seubold v. Fort Smith Special School District, 218 Ark. 560, 237 S.W.2d 884: "In Jacobson v. Commonwealth of Massachusetts, 197 U.S. 11, 25 S.Ct. 358, 49 L.Ed. 643, the Supreme Court of the United States considered the matter of compulsory vaccination as infringing on rights claimed under the United States Constitution, and held that a State law requiring compulsory vaccination did not deprive a citizen of liberty guaranteed by the United States Constitution. More recently, in the case of Zucht v. King, 260 U.S. 174, 43 S.Ct. 24, 25, 67 L.Ed. 194, the United States Supreme Court again considered the matter of compulsory vaccination; and Mr. Justice Brandeis, speaking for the Court said: '* * * Long before this suit was instituted, Jacobson v. Massachusetts, 197 U.S. 11, 25 S.Ct. 358, 49 L.Ed. 643, 3 Ann.Cas. 765, had settled that it is within the police power of a state to provide for compulsory vaccination.'"

Appellant contends that in the circumstances of this case the probate court does not have jurisdiction to appoint a guardian. The Constitution of Arkansas, Article 7, Sec. 34 provides: "In each county the Judge of the court having jurisdiction in matters of equity shall be judge of the court or probate, and have such exclusive original jurisdiction in matters relative to * * * guardians * * *. *The judge of the probate court shall try all issues of law and of facts arising in causes or proceedings within the jurisdiction of said court, and therein pending.*" (Our italics).

It will be noticed that the above provision of the Constitution gives probate courts jurisdiction in matters relative to guardians, and provides that the probate court shall try all issues of law and facts in causes within the jurisdiction of the court and pending therein.

.   .   .

The issue of whether the three children of appellants were neglected was before the probate court in the proceeding for the appointment of a guardian, and the court had jurisdiction to determine that fact. The evidence that the parents would not permit vaccination and thereby enable the children to attend school is sufficient to base a finding of neglect. . . .

Appellants argue that Archie Cude has been fined on three occasions for not sending the children to school, and that the State has no other remedy. This action was not instituted for the purpose of punishing Cude, but to enable the children to obtain a reasonable education. The fact that Cude has been fined for violation of the law in not sending his children to school in no way benefited the children. It did not bring about the desired result of the children being sent to school. . . .

Affirmed.

JOHNSON, Justice (dissenting).

The only penalty which the legislature saw fit to provide for the failure to compel certain children to attend school is contained in Ark.Stat.Ann. § 80–1508 (Repl.1960) as follows:

> "Each day such persons violate the provisions of this act shall constitute a separate offense, and the penalty for the violation of such provision shall be a fine not to exceed ten dollars [$10.00] for each offense."

This penalty has been administered against appellants not because they have refused to comply with the compulsory attendance law but because they have refused to comply with an administrative regulation which resulted in the school authorities prohibiting their children's attendance.

It is well settled that penal statutes are to be strictly construed in favor of the accused and courts are not permitted to enlarge the punishment provided by the legislature either directly or by implication. . . .

While much of the logic contained in the majority opinion from a sociological standpoint appears to be unanswerable, nevertheless from a legal standpoint I have found no way to escape the conclusion that the trial court and this court on trial de novo on appeal are enlarging the penalty for failure to comply with the compulsory attendance law to an extent never dreamed of by the proper lawmaking body. In the absence of legislation to the contrary, I as a judge am not willing now or ever to say as a matter of law that the failure to comply with this one simple regulation of school administrative authorities constitutes such neglect of children so as to warrant the state administering the cruel and unusual punishment of depriving such children of their natural parents and depriving the natural parents of their children.

Some consolation may be derived from the fact that the children in the case at bar will be offered back to their parents when the State Welfare Department carries out the orders of the court. Even so, the precedent set here that permits the taking of the children *at all* is the vice that opens a Pandora's box which may haunt this court for years to come. In my view, one of the forseeable spectres is the unfettered interference by the State Welfare Department in areas where it has no legal standing whatsoever. In its apparent zeal to protect the immuned from the unimmuned I believe the majority has given meaning to the word *neglect* which no amount of rationalization can justify. This is the door that has been left open. History reveals that once a door is open to an administrative agency that door is not easily closed. Whose children under what pretext will be taken next? Will they be kept forever? For the reasons stated, I respectfully dissent.

NOTES AND QUESTIONS

1. In Mannis v. Arkansas, 240 Ark. 42, 398 S.W.2d 206 (1966), the Supreme Court of Arkansas applied and extended the *Cude* case, supra, holding that a parochial school was a "private school" within the meaning of its state laws requiring smallpox vaccinations of children attending public or private schools. What, if any, is the relationship between being vaccinated and obtaining an education?

2. North Carolina, like some other states, allows a statutory exemption for "members of a recognized religious organization whose teachings are contrary to the . . . [practice of vaccination]." See, State v. Miday, 263 N.C. 747, 140 S.E.2d 325 (1965). Is this desirable legislation? Why? What criteria should be used to determine which group is a "recognized religious" group?

3. As the *Cude* case demonstrates, parents do not have the legal right to prevent vaccination unless a law gives it to them. In the *Cude* case a school administrative authority adopted the regulation requiring the vaccination. By what authority do school boards or health boards have the power to adopt regulations requiring vaccinations as a condition precedent for school attendance? Was the act of the school administrative authority discretionary or ministerial? Could the school administrative authority adopt a regulation allowing an exemption from vaccination for certain members of religious faiths?

4. Could a state legislature, a school administrative authority or a state health board constitutionally require children to take an I.Q. test as a condition of entrance to a school? A personality test? Submit to a physical examination? To sex education? To the cutting of long hair? To blood sampling and typing? See, Streich v. Board of Ed., 34 S.D. 169, 147 N.W. 779 (1914), and also see Mathews v. Kalamazoo Board of Ed., 127 Mich. 530, 86 N.W. 1036 (1901) and Goldstein, "The Scope and Source of School Board Authority to Regulate Student Conduct and Status: A Nonconstitutional Analysis," 117 U. of Pa.Law Rev. 373, 387–411 (1969).

5. Is the decision in the Cude case consistent with the decision in Wisconsin v. Yoder, infra?

CONSTITUTIONAL LIMITATIONS ON THE OBLIGATION TO ATTEND SCHOOL

———

WISCONSIN v. YODER

Supreme Court of the United States, 1972.
406 U.S. 205, 92 S.Ct. 1526, 32 L.Ed.2d 15.

Mr. Chief Justice BURGER delivered the opinion of the Court.

On petition of the State of Wisconsin, we granted the writ in this case to review a decision of the Wisconsin Supreme Court holding that respondents' convictions for violating the State's compulsory school attendance law were invalid under the Free Exercise Clause of the First Amendment to the United States Constitution made applicable to the State by the Fourteenth Amendment. For the reasons hereafter stated we affirm the judgment of the Supreme Court of Wisconsin.

Respondents Jonas Yoder and Adin Yutzy are members of the Old Order Amish Religion, and respondent Wallace Miller is a member of the Conservative Amish Mennonite Church. They and their families are residents of Green County, Wisconsin. Wisconsin's compulsory school attendance law required them to cause their children to attend public or private school until reaching age 16 but the respondents declined to send their children, ages 14 and 15, to public school after completing the eighth grade. [The children, Frieda Yoder, aged 15, Barbara Miller, aged 15, and Vernon Yutzy, aged 14, were all graduates of the eighth grade of public school.] The children were not enrolled in any private school, or within any recognized exception to the compulsory attendance law, and they are conceded to be subject to the Wisconsin statute.

On complaint of the school district administrator for the public schools, respondents were charged, tried, and convicted of violating the compulsory attendance law in Green County Court and were fined the sum of $5 each. Respondents defended on the ground that the application of the compulsory attendance law violated their rights under the First and Fourteenth Amendments. [The First Amendment provides: "Congress shall make no law respecting an establishment of religion, or prohibiting the Free exercise thereof. . . . "] The trial testimony showed that respondents believed, in accordance with the tenets of Old Order Amish communities generally, that their children's attendance at high school, public or private, was contrary to the Amish religion and way of life. They believed that by sending their children to high school, they would not only expose themselves to the danger of the censure of the church community, but, as found

Morris—Const. & Am.Educ. ACB—12

by the county court, endanger their own salvation and that of their children.   The State stipulated that respondents' religious beliefs were sincere.

. . . . The history of the Amish sect was given in some detail, beginning with the Swiss Anabaptists of the 16th century who rejected institutionalized churches and sought to return to the early, simple, Christian life de-emphasizing material success, rejecting the competitive spirit, and seeking to insulate themselves from the modern world.   As a result of their common heritage, Old Order Amish communities today are characterized by a fundamental belief that salvation requires life in a church community separate and apart from the world and worldly influence.   This concept of life aloof from the world and its values is central to their faith.

A related feature of Old Order Amish communities is their devotion to a life in harmony with nature and the soil, as exemplified by the simple life of the early Christian era which continued in America during much of our early national life.   Amish beliefs require members of the community to make their living by farming or closely related activities.   Broadly speaking, the Old Order Amish religion pervades and determines the entire mode of life of its adherents.   Their conduct is regulated in great detail by the *Ordnung*, or rules, of the church community.   Adult baptism, which occurs in late adolescence, is the time at which Amish young people voluntarily undertake heavy obligations, not unlike the Bar Mitzvah of the Jews, to abide by the rules of the church community.

Amish objection to formal education beyond the eighth grade is firmly grounded in these central religious concepts.   They object to the high school and higher education generally because the values it teaches are in marked variance with Amish values and the Amish way of life; they view secondary school education as an impermissible exposure of their children to a "worldly" influence in conflict with their beliefs.   The high school tends to emphasize intellectual and scientific accomplishments, self-distinction, competitiveness, worldly success, and social life with other students.   Amish society emphasizes informal learning-through-doing, a life of "goodness," rather than a life of intellect, wisdom, rather than technical knowledge, community welfare rather than competition, and separation, rather than integration with contemporary worldly society.

Formal high school education beyond the eighth grade is contrary to Amish beliefs not only because it places Amish children in an environment hostile to Amish beliefs with increasing emphasis on competition in class work and sports and with pressure to conform to the styles, manners and ways of the peer group, but because it takes them away from their community, physically and emotionally, during the crucial and formative adolescent period of life.   During this period, the children must acquire Amish attitudes favoring manual work and self-reliance and the specific skills needed to perform the adult role of an Amish farmer or housewife. They must learn to enjoy physical labor. Once a child has learned basic reading, writing, and elementary mathematics, these traits, skills, and attitudes admittedly fall within the category of those best learned through example and "doing" rather than in a classroom. And, at this time in life, the Amish child must also grow in his faith and his relationship to the Amish community if he is to be prepared to accept the heavy obligations imposed by adult baptism. In short, high school attendance with teachers who are not of the Amish faith—and may even be hostile to it—interposes a serious barrier to the integration of the Amish child into the Amish religious community. Dr. John Hostetler, one of the experts on Amish society, testified that the modern high school is not equipped, in curriculum or social environment, to impart the values promoted by Amish society.

The Amish do not object to elementary education through the first eight grades as a general proposition because they agree that their children must have basic skills in the "three R's" in order to read the Bible, to be good farmers and citizens and to be able to deal with non-Amish people when necessary in the course of daily affairs. They view such a basic education as acceptable because it does not significantly expose their children to worldly values or interfere with their development in the Amish community during the crucial adolescent period. . . .

On the basis of such considerations, Dr. Hostetler testified that compulsory high school attendance could not only result in great psychological harm to Amish children, because of the conflicts it would produce, but would, in his opinion, ultimately result in the destruction of the Old Order Amish church community as it exists in the United States today. The testimony of Dr. Donald A. Erickson, an expert witness on education, also showed that the Amish succeed in preparing their high school age children to be productive members of the Amish community. He described their system of learning-through-doing the skills directly relevant to their adult roles in the Amish community as "ideal" and perhaps superior to ordinary high school education. The evidence also showed that the Amish have an excellent record as law-abiding and generally self-sufficient members of society.

. . . The Wisconsin Supreme Court, however, sustained respondents' claim under the Free Exercise Clause of the First Amendment and reversed the convictions. A majority of the court was of the opinion that the State had failed to make an adequate showing that its interest in "establishing and maintaining an education system overrides the defendants' right to the free exercise of their religion."

I

There is no doubt as to the power of a State, having a high responsibility for education of its citizens, to impose reasonable regulations for the control and duration of basic education. See, e. g., Pierce v. Society of Sisters, . . . Providing public schools ranks at the very apex of the function of a State. Yet even this paramount responsibility was, in *Pierce*, made to yield to the right of parents to provide an equivalent education in a privately operated system. There the Court held that Oregon's statute compelling attendance in a public school from age eight to age 16 unreasonably interfered with the interest of parents in directing the rearing of their offspring including their education in church-operated schools. As that case suggests, the values of parental direction of the religious upbringing and education of their children in their early and formative years have a high place in our society. . . . Thus, a State's interest in universal education, however highly we rank it, is not totally free from a balancing process when it impinges on other fundamental rights and interests, such as those specifically protected by the Free Exercise Clause of the First Amendment and the traditional interest of parents with respect to the religious upbringing of their children so long as they, in the words of *Pierce*, "prepare [them] for additional obligations." . . .

It follows that in order for Wisconsin to compel school attendance beyond the eighth grade against a claim that such attendance interferes with the practice of a legitimate religious belief, it must appear either that the State does not deny the free exercise of religious belief by its requirement, or that there is a state interest of sufficient magnitude to override the interest claiming protection under the Free Exercise Clause. . . .

The essence of all that has been said and written on the subject is that only those interests of the highest order and those not otherwise served can overbalance legitimate claims to the free exercise of religion. We can accept it as settled, therefore, that however strong the State's interest in universal compulsory education, it is by no means absolute to the exclusion or subordination of all other interests.

. . . .

II

We come then to the quality of the claims of the respondents concerning the alleged encroachment of Wisconsin's compulsory school attendance statute on their rights and the rights of their children to the free exercise of the religious beliefs they and their forebears have adhered to for almost three centuries. In evaluating those claims we must be careful to determine whether the Amish religious faith and their mode of life are, as they claim, inseparable and interdependent. A way of life, however virtuous and admirable, may not be interposed as a barrier to reasonable state regulation of education if it is based on purely secular considerations; to have the protection of the Religion Clauses, the claims must be rooted in religious belief. Although a determination of what is a "religious" belief or practice entitled to constitutional protection may present a most delicate question, the very concept of ordered liberty precludes allowing every person to make his own standards on matters of conduct in which society as a whole has important interests. Thus, if the Amish asserted their claims because of their subjective evaluation and rejection of the contemporary secular values accepted by the majority, much as Thoreau rejected the social values of his time and isolated himself at Walden Pond, their claim would not rest on a religious basis. Thoreau's choice was philosophical and personal rather than religious, and such belief does not rise to the demands of the Religion Clause.

Giving no weight to such secular considerations, however, we see that the record in this case abundantly supports the claim that the traditional way of life of the Amish is not merely a matter of personal preference, but one of deep religious conviction, shared by an organized group, and intimately related to daily living. That the Old Order Amish daily life and religious practice stems from their faith is shown by the fact that it is in response to their literal interpretation of the Biblical injunction from the Epistle of Paul to the Romans, "Be not conformed to this world. . . ." This command is <u>fundamental</u> to the Amish faith. Moreover, for the Old Order Amish, religion is not simply a matter of theocratic belief. As the expert witnesses explained, the Old Order Amish <u>religion pervades and determines virtually their entire way of life, regulating it with the detail of the Talmudic diet through the strictly enforced rules of the church community.</u>

The record shows that the respondents' religious beliefs and attitude toward life, family, and home have remained constant—perhaps some would say static—in a period of unparalleled progress in human knowledge generally and great changes in education. The respondents freely concede, and indeed assert as an article of faith, that their religious beliefs and what we would today call "life style" has not altered in fundamentals for centuries. Their way of life in a church-oriented community, separated from the outside world and "worldly" influences, their attachment to nature and the soil, is a way inherently simple and uncomplicated, albeit difficult to preserve against the pressure to conform. Their rejection of telephones, automobiles, radios, and television, their mode of dress, of speech, their habits of manual work do indeed set them apart from much of contemporary society; these customs are both symbolic and practical.

As the society around the Amish has become more populous, urban, industrialized, and complex, particularly in this century, government regulation of human affairs has correspondingly become more detailed and pervasive. The Amish mode of life has thus come into conflict increasingly with requirements of contemporary society exerting a hydraulic insistence on conformity to majoritarian standards. So long as compulsory education laws were confined to eight grades of elementary basic education imparted in a nearby rural schoolhouse, with a large proportion of students of the Amish faith, the Old Order Amish had little basis to fear that school attendance would expose their children to the worldly influence they reject. But modern compulsory secondary education in rural areas is now largely carried on in a consolidated school, often remote from the student's home and alien to his daily home life. As the record so strongly shows, the values and programs of the modern secondary school are in sharp conflict with the fundamental mode of life mandated by the Amish religion; modern laws requiring compulsory secondary education have accordingly engendered great concern and conflict. The conclusion is inescapable that secondary schooling, by exposing Amish children to worldly influences in terms of attitudes, goals and values contrary to beliefs, and by substantially interfering with the religious development of the Amish child and his integration into the way of life of the Amish faith community at the crucial adolescent state of development, contravenes the basic religious tenets and practice of the Amish faith, both as to the parent and the child.

The impact of the compulsory attendance law on respondents' practice of the Amish religion is not only severe, but inescapable, for the Wisconsin law affirmatively compels them, under threat of criminal sanction, to perform acts undeniably at odds with fundamental tenets of their religious beliefs. See Braunfeld v. Brown, 366 U.S. 599, 605 (1961). Nor is the impact of the compulsory attendance law confined to grave interference with important Amish religious tenets from a subjective point of view. It carries with it precisely the kind of objective danger to the free exercise of religion which the First Amendment was designed to prevent. As the record shows, compulsory school attendance to age 16 for Amish children carries with it a very real threat of undermining the Amish community and religious practice as it exists today; they must either abandon belief and be assimilated into society at large, or be forced to migrate to some other and more tolerant region.

In sum, the unchallenged testimony of acknowledged experts in education and religious history, almost 300 years of consistent practice, and strong evidence of a sustained faith pervading and regulating respondents' entire mode of life support the claim that enforcement of the State's requirement of compulsory formal education after the eighth grade would gravely endanger if not destroy the free exercise of respondents' religious beliefs.

III

.   .   .   Wisconsin concedes that under the Religion Clauses religious beliefs are absolutely free from the State's control, but it argues that "actions," even though religiously grounded, are outside the protection of the First Amendment.   But our decisions have rejected the idea that religiously grounded conduct is always outside the protection of the Free Exercise Clause.   It is true that activities of individuals, even when religiously based, are often subject to regulation by the States in the exercise of their undoubted power to promote the health, safety, and general welfare, or the Federal Government in the exercise of its delegated powers.   .   .   .   But to agree that religiously grounded conduct must often be subject to the broad police power of the State is not to deny that there are areas of conduct protected by the Free Exercise Clause of the First Amendment and thus beyond the power of the State to control, even under regulations of general applicability.   .   .   .   This case, therefore, does not become easier because respondents were convicted for their "actions" in refusing to send their children to the public high school; in this context belief and action cannot be neatly confined in logic-tight compartments.   .   .   .

Nor can this case be disposed of on the grounds that Wisconsin's requirement for school attendance to age 16 applies uniformly to all citizens of the State and does not, on its face, discriminate against religions or a particular religion, or that it is motivated by legitimate secular concerns.   A regulation neutral on its face may, in its application, nonetheless offend the constitutional requirement for governmental neutrality, if it unduly burdens the free exercise of religion. .   .   .   The Court must not ignore the danger that an exception from a general obligation of citizenship on religious grounds may run afoul of the Establishment Clause, but that danger cannot be allowed to prevent any exception no matter how vital it may be to the protection of values promoted by the right of free exercise.   By preserving doctrinal flexibility and recognizing the need for a sensible and realistic application of the Religion Clauses

> "we have been able to chart a course that preserved the autonomy and freedom of religious bodies while avoiding any semblance of established religion.   This is a 'tight rope' and one we have successfully traversed."   Walz v. Tax Commission, 397 U.S., at 672.

We turn, then to the State's broader contention that its interest in its system of compulsory education is so compelling that even the established religious practices of the Amish must give way.   Where fundamental claims of religious freedom are at stake, however, we cannot accept such a sweeping claim; despite its admitted validity in the generality of cases, we must searchingly examine the interests which the State seeks to promote by its requirement for compulsory education to age 16, and the impediment to those objectives that would flow from recognizing the claimed Amish exemption. .   .   .

The State advances two primary arguments in support of its system of compulsory education. It notes, as Thomas Jefferson pointed out early in our history, that some degree of education is necessary to prepare citizens to participate effectively and intelligently in our open political system if we are to preserve freedom and independence. Further, education prepares individuals to be self-reliant and self-sufficient participants in society. We accept these propositions.

However, the evidence adduced by the Amish in this case is persuasively to the effect that an additional one or two years of formal high school for Amish children in place of their long established program of informal vocational education would do little to serve those interests. Respondents' experts testified at trial, without challenge, that the value of all education must be assessed in terms of its capacity to prepare the child for life. It is one thing to say that compulsory education for a year or two beyond the eighth grade may be necessary when its goal is the preparation of the child for life in modern society as the majority live, but it is quite another if the goal of education be viewed as the preparation of the child for life in the separated agrarian community that is the keystone of the Amish faith. .   .   .

The State attacks respondents' position as one fostering "ignorance" from which the child must be protected by the State. No one can question the State's duty to protect children from ignorance but this argument does not square with the facts disclosed in the record. Whatever their idiosyncrasies as seen by the majority, this record strongly shows that the Amish community has been a highly successful social unit within our society even if apart from the conventional "mainstream." Its members are productive and very law-abiding members of society; they reject public welfare in any of its usual modern forms. The Congress itself recognized their self-sufficiency by authorizing exemption of such groups as the Amish from the obligation to pay social security taxes.

It is neither fair nor correct to suggest that the Amish are opposed to education beyond the eighth grade level. What this record shows is that they are opposed to conventional formal education of the type provided by a certified high school because it comes at the child's crucial adolescent period of religious development. Dr. Donald Erickson, for example, testified that their system of learning-by-doing was an "ideal system" of education in terms of preparing Amish children for life as adults in the Amish community, and that "I would be inclined to say they do a better job in this than most of the rest of us do." As he put it, "these people aren't purporting to be learned people, and it seems to me that the self-sufficiency of the community is the best evidence I can point to—whatever is being done seems to function well."

We must not forget that in the Middle Ages important values of the civilization of the western world were preserved by members of religious orders who isolated themselves from all worldly influences against great obstacles. There can be no assumption that today's majority is "right" and the Amish and others like them are "wrong." A way of life that is odd or even erratic but interferes with no rights or interests of others is not to be condemned because it is different.

The State, however, supports its interest in providing an additional one or two years of compulsory high school education to Amish children because of the possibility that some such children will choose to leave the Amish community, and that if this occurs they will be ill-equipped for life. The State argues that if Amish children leave their church they should not be in the position of making their way in the world without the education available in the one or two additional years the State requires. However, on this record, that argument is highly speculative. There is no specific evidence of the loss of Amish adherents by attrition, nor is there any showing that upon leaving the Amish community Amish children, with their practical agricultural training and habits of industry and self-reliance would become burdens on society because of educational shortcomings. Indeed, this argument of the State appears to rest primarily on the State's mistaken assumption, already noted, that the Amish do not provide any education for their children beyond the eighth grade, but allow them to grow in "ignorance." To the contrary, not only do the Amish accept the necessity for formal schooling through the eighth grade level, but continue to provide what has been characterized by the undisputed testimony of expert educators as an "ideal" vocational education for their children in the adolescent years.

There is nothing in this record to suggest that the Amish qualities of reliability, self-reliance, and dedication to work would fail to find ready markets in today's society. Absent some contrary evidence supporting the State's position, we are unwilling to assume that persons possessing such valuable vocational skills and habits are doomed to become burdens on society should they determine to leave the Amish faith, nor is there any basis in the record to warrant a finding that an additional one or two years of formal school education beyond the eighth grade would serve to eliminate any such problem that might exist.

Insofar as the State's claim rests on the view that a brief additional period of formal education is imperative to enable the Amish to participate effectively and intelligently in our democratic process, it must fall. The Amish alternative to formal secondary school education has enabled them to function effectively in their day-to-day life under self-imposed limitations on relations with the world, and to survive and prosper in contemporary society as a separate, sharply identifiable and highly self-sufficient community for more than 200 years in this country. In itself this is strong evidence that they are capable of fulfilling the social and political responsibilities of citizenship without compelled attendance beyond the eighth grade at the price of jeopardizing their free exercise of religious belief. . . .

The requirement for compulsory education beyond the eighth grade is a relatively recent development in our history. Less than 60 years ago, the educational requirements of almost all of the States were satisfied by completion of the elementary grades, at least where the child was regularly and lawfully employed. The independence and successful social functioning of the Amish community for a period approaching almost three centuries and more than 200 years in this country is strong evidence that there is at best a speculative gain, in terms of meeting the duties of citizenship, from an additional one or two years of compulsory formal education. Against this background it would require a more particularized showing from the State on this point to justify the severe interference with religious freedom such additional compulsory attendance would entail.

We should also note that compulsory education and child labor laws find their historical origin in common humanitarian instincts, and that the age limits of both laws have been coordinated to achieve their related objectives. In the context of this case, such considerations, if anything, support rather than detract from respondents' position. The origins of the requirement for school attendance to age 16, an age falling after the completion of elementary school but before completion of high school, are not entirely clear. But to some extent such laws reflected the movement to prohibit most child labor under age 16 that culminated in the provisions of the Federal Fair Labor Standards Act of 1938. It is true, then, that the 16-year child labor age limit may to some degree derive from a contemporary impression that children should be in school until that age. But at the same time, it cannot be denied that, conversely, the 16-year education limit reflects, in substantial measure, the concern that children under that age not be employed under conditions hazardous to their health, or in work that should be performed by adults.

The requirement of compulsory schooling to age 16 must therefore be viewed as aimed not merely at providing educational opportunities for children, but as an alternative to the equally undesirable consequence of unhealthful child labor displacing adult workers, or, on the other hand, forced idleness. The two kinds of statutes—compulsory school attendance and child labor laws—tend to keep children of certain ages off the labor market and in school; this in turn provides opportunity to prepare for a livelihood of a higher order than that children could perform without education and protects their health in adolescence.

In these terms, Wisconsin's interest in compelling the school attendance of Amish children to age 16 emerges as somewhat less substantial than requiring such attendance for children generally. For, while agricultural employment is not totally outside the legitimate concerns of the child labor laws, employment of children under parental guidance and on the family farm from age 14 to age 16 is an ancient tradition which lies at the periphery of the objectives of such laws. There is no intimation that the Amish employment of their children on family farms is in any way deleterious to their health or that Amish parents exploit children at tender years. Any such inference would be contrary to the record before us. Moreover, employment of Amish children on the family farm does not present the undesirable economic aspects of eliminating jobs which might otherwise be held by adults.

IV

Finally, the State, on authority of Prince v. Massachusetts, argues that a decision exempting Amish children from the State's requirement fails to recognize the substantive right of the Amish child to a secondary education, and fails to give due regard to the power of the State as *parens patriae* to extend the benefit of secondary education to children regardless of the wishes of their parents. .   .   .

Contrary to the suggestion of the dissenting opinion of Mr. Justice DOUGLAS, our holding today in no degree depends on the assertion of the religious interest of the child as contrasted with that of the parents. It is the parents who are subject to prosecution here for failing to cause their children to attend school, and it is their right of free exercise, not that of their children, that must determine Wisconsin's power to impose criminal penalties on the parent. The dissent argues that a child who expresses a desire to attend public high school in conflict with the wishes of his parents should not be prevented from doing so. There is no reason for the Court to consider that point since it is not an issue in the case. The children are not parties to this litigation. The State has at no point tried this case on the theory that respondents were preventing their children from attending school against their expressed desires, and indeed the record is to the contrary. [The only relevant testimony in the record is to the effect that the wishes of the one child who testified corresponded with those of her parents. Testimony of Frieda Yoder, Tr. 92–94, to the effect that her personal religious beliefs guided her decision to discontinue school attendance after the 8th grade. The other children were not called by either side.] The State's position from the outset has been that it is empowered to apply its compulsory attendance law to Amish parents in the same manner as to other parents—that is, without regard to the wishes of the child. That is the claim we reject today.

Our holding in no way determines the proper resolution of possible competing interests of parents, children, and the State in an appropriate state court proceeding in which the power of the State is asserted on the theory that Amish parents are preventing their minor children from attending high school despite their expressed desires to the contrary. . . .

The State's argument proceeds without reliance on any actual conflict between the wishes of parents and children. It appears to rest on the potential that exemption of Amish parents from the requirements of the compulsory education law might allow some parents to act contrary to the best interests of their children by foreclosing their opportunity to make an intelligent choice between the Amish way of life and that of the outside world. The same argument could, of course, be made with respect to all church schools short of college. There is nothing in the record or in the ordinary course of human experience to suggest that non-Amish parents generally consult with children up to ages 14–16 if they are placed in a church school of the parents' faith.

Indeed it seems clear that if the State is empowered, as *parens patriae,* to "save" a child from himself or his Amish parents by requiring an additional two years of compulsory formal high school education, the State will in large measure influence, if not determine, the religious future of the child. Even more markedly than in *Prince,* therefore, this case involves the fundamental interest of parents, as contrasted with that of the State, to guide the religious future and education of their children. The history and culture of western civilization reflect a strong tradition of parental concern for the nurture and upbringing of their children. This primary role of the parents in the upbringing of their children is now established beyond debate as an enduring American tradition. If not the first, perhaps the most significant statements of the Court in this area are found in Pierce v. Society of Sisters, in which the Court observed:

> "Under the doctrine of Meyer v. Nebraska, 262 U.S. 390, we think it entirely plain that the Act of 1922 unreasonably interferes with the liberty of parents and guardians to direct the upbringing and education of children under their control. As often heretofore pointed out, rights guaranteed by the Constitution may not be abridged by legislation which has no reasonable relation to some purpose within the competency of the State. The fundamental theory of liberty upon which all governments in this Union repose excludes any general power of the State to standardize its children by forcing them to accept instruction from public teachers only. The child is not the mere creature of the State; those who nurture him and direct his destiny have the right, coupled with the high duty, to recognize and prepare him for additional obligations." 268 U.S., at 534–535.

The duty to prepare the child for "additional obligations," referred to by the Court, must be read to include the inculcation of moral standards, religious beliefs and elements of good citizenship. *Pierce,* of course, recognized that where nothing more than the general interest of the parent in the nurture and education of his children is involved, it is beyond dispute that the State acts "reasonably" and constitutionally in requiring education to age 16 in some public and private school meeting the standards prescribed by the State.

However read, the Court's holding in *Pierce* stands as a charter of the rights of parents to direct the religious upbringing of their children. And, when the interests of parenthood are combined with a free exercise claim of the nature revealed by this record, more than merely a "reasonable relation to some purpose within the competency of the state" is required to sustain the validity of the State's requirement under the First Amendment. To be sure, the power of the parent, even when linked to a free exercise claim, may be subject to limitation under *Prince* if it appears that parental decisions will jeopardize the health or safety of the child, or have a potential for significant social burdens. But in this case, the Amish have introduced persuasive evidence undermining the arguments the State has advanced to support its claims in terms of the welfare of the child and society as a whole. The record strongly indicates that accommodating the religious objections of the Amish by foregoing one, or at most two, additional years of compulsory education will not impair the physical or mental health of the child, nor result in an inability to be self-supporting, or to discharge the duties and responsibilities of citizenship, or in any other way materially detract from the welfare of society.

In the face of our consistent emphasis on the central values underlying the Religion Clauses in our constitutional scheme of government, we cannot accept a *parens patriae* claim of such all-encompassing scope and with such sweeping potential for broad and unforeseeable application as that urged by the State.

V

For the reasons stated we hold, with the Supreme Court of Wisconsin, that the First and Fourteenth Amendments prevent the State from compelling respondents to cause their children to attend formal high school to age 16. Our disposition of this case, however, in no way alters our recognition of the obvious fact that courts are not school boards or legislatures, and are ill-equipped to determine the "necessity" of discrete aspects of a State's program of compulsory education. This should suggest that courts must move with great circumspection in performing the sensitive and delicate task of weighing a State's legitimate social concern when faced with religious claims for exemption from generally applicable educational requirements. It cannot be over-emphasized that we are not dealing with a way of life and mode of education by a group claiming to have recently discovered some "progressive" or more enlightened process for rearing children for modern life.

Aided by a history of three centuries as an identifiable religious sect and a long history as a successful and self-sufficient segment of

American society, the Amish in this case have convincingly demonstrated the sincerity of their religious beliefs, the interrelationship of belief with their mode of life, the vital role which belief and daily conduct play in the continued survival of Old Order Amish communities and their religious organization, and the hazards presented by the State's enforcement of a statute generally valid as to others. Beyond this, they have carried the even more difficult burden of demonstrating the adequacy of their alternative mode of continuing informal vocational education in terms of precisely those overall interests that the State advances in support of its program of compulsory high school education. In light of this convincing showing, one which probably few other religious groups or sects could make, and weighing the minimal difference between what the State would require and what the Amish already accept, it was incumbent on the State to show with more particularity how its admittedly strong interest in compulsory education would be adversely affected by granting an exemption to the Amish. Sherbert v. Verner.   .   .   .

Nothing we hold is intended to undermine the general applicability of the State's compulsory school attendance statutes or to limit the power of the State to promulgate reasonable standards that, while not impairing the free exercise of religion, provide for continuing agricultural vocational education under parental and church guidance by the Old Order Amish or others similarly situated. The States have had a long history of amicable and effective relationships with church-sponsored schools, and there is no basis for assuming that, in this related context, reasonable standards cannot be established concerning the content of the continuing vocational education of Amish children under parental guidance, provided always that state regulations are not inconsistent with what we have said in this opinion.

Affirmed.

Mr. Justice POWELL and Mr. Justice REHNQUIST took no part in the consideration or decision of this case.

Mr. Justice WHITE, with whom Mr. Justice BRENNAN and Mr. Justice STEWART join, concurring.   *   *   *

This would be a very different case for me if respondents' claim were that their religion forbade their children from attending any school at any time and from complying in any way with the educational standards set by the State.   *   *   *   There is evidence in the record that many children desert the Amish faith when they they come of age. A State has a legitimate interest not only in seeking to develop the latent talents of its children but in seeking to prepare them for the life style which they may later choose or at least to provide them with an option other than the life they have led in the past. In the circumstances of this case, although the question is close, I am unable to say that the State has demonstrated that Amish children who leave school in the eighth grade will be intellectually stultified or unable to acquire new academic skills later.   *   *   *

Decision in cases such as this and the administration of an exemption for Old Order Amish from the State's compulsory school attendance laws will inevitably involve the kind of close and perhaps repeated scrutiny of religious practices, as exemplified in today's opinion, which the Court has heretofore been anxious to avoid.   But such entanglement does not create a forbidden establishment of religion where it is essential to implement free exercise values threatened by an otherwise neutral program instituted to foster some permissible, nonreligious state objective.   I join the Court because the sincerity of the Amish religious policy here is uncontested, because the potential adverse impact of the state requirement is great and because the State's valid interest in education has already been largely satisfied by the eight years the children have already spent in school.

Mr. Justice DOUGLAS, dissenting in part.

I

I agree with the Court that the religious scruples of the Amish are opposed to the education of their children beyond the grade schools, yet I disagree with the Court's conclusion that the matter is within the dispensation of parents alone.   The Court's analysis assumes that the only interests at stake in the case are those of the Amish parents on the one hand, and those of the State on the other. The difficulty with this approach is that, despite the Court's claim, the parents are seeking to vindicate not only their own free exercise claims, but also those of their high-school-age children.

It is argued that the right of the Amish children to religious freedom is not presented by the facts of the case, as the issue before the Court involves only the Amish parents' religious freedom to defy a state criminal statute imposing upon them an affirmative duty to cause their children to attend high school.

First, respondents' motion to dismiss in the trial court expressly asserts, not only the religious liberty of the adults, but also that of the children, as a defense to the prosecutions.   .   .   .

Second,   .   .   .   no analysis of religious liberty claims can take place in a vacuum.   If the parents in this case are allowed a religious exemption, the inevitable effect is to impose the parents' notions of religious duty upon their children.   Where the child is mature enough to express potentially conflicting desires, it would be an invasion of the child's rights to permit such an imposition without canvassing his views.   .   .   .   As the child has no other effective forum, it is in this litigation that his rights should be considered.   And, if an Amish child desires to attend high school, and is mature enough to have that desire respected, the State may well be able to override the parents' religiously motivated objections.

Religion is an individual experience. It is not necessary, nor even appropriate, for every Amish child to express his views on the subject in a prosecution of a single adult. Crucial, however, are the views of the child whose parent is the subject of the suit. Frieda Yoder has in fact testified that her own religious views are opposed to high-school education. I therefore join the judgment of the Court as to respondent Jonas Yoder. But Frieda Yoder's views may not be those of Vernon Yutzy or Barbara Miller. I must dissent, therefore, as to respondents Adin Yutzy and Wallace Miller as their motion to dismiss also raised the question of their children's religious liberty.

II

This issue has never been squarely presented before today. Our opinions are full of talk about the power of the parents over the child's education. . . . Recent cases, however, have clearly held that the children themselves have constitutionally protectible interests.

These children are "persons" within the meaning of the Bill of Rights. We have so held over and over again. In Haley v. Ohio, 332 U.S. 596, we extended the protection of the Fourteenth Amendment in a state trial of a 15-year-old boy. In In re Gault, 387 U.S. 1, 13, we held that "neither the Fourteenth Amendment nor the Bill of Rights is for adults alone." In In re Winship, 397 U.S. 358, we held that a 12-year-old boy, when charged with an act which would be a crime if committed by an adult, was entitled to procedural safeguards contained in the Sixth Amendment.

In Tinker v. Des Moines School Dist., 393 U.S. 503, we dealt with 13-year-old, 15-year-old, and 16-year-old students who wore armbands to public schools and were disciplined for doing so. We gave them relief, saying that their First Amendment rights had been abridged.

"Students in school as well as out of school are 'persons' under our Constitution. They are possessed of fundamental rights which the State must respect, just as they themselves must respect the obligations to the State." . . .

. . . On this important and vital matter of education, I think the children should be entitled to be heard. While the parents, absent dissent, normally speak for the entire family, the education of the child is a matter on which the child will often have decided views. He may want to be a pianist or an astronaut or an ocean geographer. To do so he will have to break from the Amish tradition.

It is the future of the student, not the future of the parents, that is imperilled in today's decision. If a parent keeps his child out of school beyond the grade school, then the child will be forever barred from entry into the new and amazing world of diversity that we have today. The child may decide that that is the preferred course, or he may rebel. It is the student's judgment, not his parent's, that is essential if we are to give full meaning to what we have said about the Bill of Rights and of the right of students to be masters of their own destiny. If he is harnessed to the Amish way of life by those in authority over him and if his education is truncated, his entire life may be stunted and deformed. The child, therefore, should be given an opportunity to be heard before the State gives the exemption which we honor today.

The views of the two children in question were not canvassed by the Wisconsin courts. The matter should be explicitly reserved so that new hearings can be held on remand of the case.

III

I think the emphasis of the Court on the "law and order" record of this Amish group of people is quite irrelevant. A religion is a religion irrespective of what the misdemeanor or felony records of its members might be. I am not at all sure how the Catholics, Episcopalians, the Baptists, Jehovah's Witnesses, the Unitarians, and my own Presbyterians would make out if we were subjected to such a test. It is, of course, true that if a group or society was organized to perpetuate crime and if that is its motif, we would have rather startling problems akin to those that were raised when some years back a particular sect was challenged here as operating on a fraudulent basis. United States v. Ballard, 322 U.S. 78. But no such factors are present here, and the Amish, whether with a high or low criminal record, certainly qualify by all historic standards as a religion within the meaning of the First Amendment.

The Court rightly rejects the notion that actions, even though religiously grounded, are outside the protection of the Free Exercise Clause of the First Amendment. . . .

In another way, however, the Court retreats when in reference to Henry Thoreau it says his "choice was philosophical and personal rather than religious, and such belief does not rise to the demands of the Religion Clause." That is contrary to what we held in United States v. Seeger, 380 U.S. 163, where we were concerned with the meaning of the words "religious training and belief" in the Selective Service Act, which were the basis of many conscientious objector claims. We said:

" . . . Within that phrase would come all sincere religious beliefs which are based upon a power or being, or upon a faith, to which all else is subordinate or upon which all else is ultimately dependent. The test might be stated in these words: A sincere and meaningful belief which occupies in the life of its possessor a place parallel to that filled by the God of those admittedly qualifying for the exemption comes

within the statutory definition. This construction avoids imputing to Congress an intent to classify different religious
beliefs, exempting some and excluding others, and is in accord with the well-established congressional policy of equal
treatment for those whose opposition to service is grounded
in their religious tenets." Id., 176.

Welsh v. United States, 398 U.S. 333, was in the same vein, the Court
saying:

> " .   .   . In this case, Welsh's conscientious objection to
> war was undeniably based in part on his perception of world
> politics. In a letter to his local board, he wrote:

> " 'I can only act according to what I am and what I see.
> And I see that the military complex wastes both human and
> material resources, that it fosters disregard for (what I
> consider a paramount concern) human needs and ends; I see
> that the means we employ to "defend" our "way of life"
> profoundly change that way of life. I see that in our failure
> to recognize the political, social, and economic realities of
> the world, we, *as a nation,* fail our responsibility *as a na-
> tion.*' " Id., 342.

The essence of Welsh's philosophy on the basis of which we held
he was entitled to an exemption was in these words:

> "I believe that human life is valuable in and of itself;
> in its living; therefore, I will not injure or kill another hu-
> man being. This belief (and the corresponding 'duty' to ab-
> stain from violence toward another person) is not 'superior
> to those arising from any human relation.' On the contrary:
> *it is essential to every human relation.* I cannot, therefore,
> conscientiously comply with the Government's insistence that
> I assume duties which I feel are immoral and totally repug-
> nant." Id., 343.

I adhere to these exalted views of "religion" and see no acceptable alternative to them now that we have become a Nation of many
religions and sects, representing all of the diversities of the human
race. 380 U.S., at 192–193.

NOTES AND QUESTIONS

1. Whose case was before the Court for decision, that of the parents, the
    children, or both? What precisely, did the Court decide? Why was the
    religious belief upheld in Yoder but not in Cude's case, supra?

2. What is the right of the parents that is balanced against the state's
    interest in universal education of its population to the age of 16? Is
    it the right of parents to direct the religious upbringing of their chil-
    dren? Or the right of parents completely to direct the education of
    their children during their early and formative years? What differ-
    ence does it make if one or the other parental right is balanced?

3. According to the Court, what must necessarily be present before it will qualify as a bona fide assertion of a religious claim? In what way or ways does a valid religious claim differ from a claim based on philosophical beliefs about the ultimate being and destiny of man and the universe? Could a newly created religious group qualify under the Court's criteria? Why or why not?

4. What was Wisconsin's argument that was based on "actions" as distinguished from religious beliefs? Suppose an old religious order believed that a member would be purified by dancing in public with a live rattlesnake in one's mouth, and kept a supply of rattlesnakes for this purpose, would the religious act of dancing in public be constitutionally protected and immune from governmental regulation? The belief itself?

5. Did Yoder and the other defendants escape punishment precisely because they and other Amish were held to be "decent," "law abiding," "productive" and "sincere"? If not, what role did these characterizations play in the decision? What is Douglas' view on this point?

6. What were the two primary foundations of Wisconsin's argument that "its interest in its system of compulsory education is so compelling that even the established religious practices of the Amish must give away"? What was the Court's disposition of each argument? Do you agree or disagree with the Court's disposition of the arguments?

7. Suppose that the Amish believed that it was religiously improper to educate children beyond the sixth or third grade, would the decision of the Supreme Court have been the same? Why or why not? Suppose that the Amish did not believe in any formal education whatsoever, but believed that a child receives his necessary "equivalent" educational experience as he lives and works in the Amish community, would the decision of the Supreme Court have been the same? Why or why not? Does this Opinion speak to the notion of "equivalent education"? Does the Court hold that the Amish provide an equivalent and suitable alternative to public school education beyond the eighth grade? Does the decision in this case protect Indian or Chicano children and their beliefs and cultural values from the attack of mandatory education in strictly Anglo oriented schools?

8. Does a state have the absolute constitutional power without any limitation to require that each child within its borders receive formal elementary education for eight years in an approved school, all religious and other objections notwithstanding? What did the Supreme Court say about the constitutional power of a state to require compulsory education?

9. There are two phrases (called clauses) in the religious guarantee of the First Amendment; state them; which one was involved in this case?

10. Suppose that there had been evidence in this case showing (1) that up to 50%, and frequently 30%, of the Amish children abandoned their Amish way of life upon reaching adulthood and (2) that upon moving to urban areas those Amish peoples were relatively ill-prepared to be self-supporting, and were poorly prepared to participate in modern urban life and to discharge the responsibilities of citizenship. Would the Court's decision have been the same? Why or why not?

11. Suppose that this case also presented the interests of the Amish children, and that several of them testified that they wanted to go on to finish high school but that their parents on religious grounds forbade them to do so. Would the decision of the Court have been the same? Why or why not?

12. Should the Court have done what Mr. Justice Douglas suggested: required the Wisconsin court to canvass the opinions of the Amish children on whether or not they wanted to go to high school? Why or why not? Should the children have the right to choose to be or not to be a modern college-educated person, or should this be the parents' choice until children reach the legal age of adulthood? Upon reaching adulthood, how easily can a child who wants to be a modern person, undo the past decisions and overcome the lack of a high school education? See, Note, "The Right Not to be Modern Men: The Amish and Compulsory Education," 53 Va.L.Rev. 925 (1967).

13. In re Charlene Skipwith, 14 Misc.2d 235, 180 N.Y.S.2d 852 (1958), held that parents could not be constitutionally obligated by a state's compulsory education law to send their child to a school that offered educationally inferior opportunities as compared to the opportunities offered in other New York City schools whose pupil population was largely white.

COMMONWEALTH v. BEY

Superior Court of Pennsylvania, 1950.
166 Pa.Super. 136, 70 A.2d 693.

RENO, Judge. Appellants, husband and wife, were convicted in a summary proceeding before an alderman and on appeal in the court below of violating the compulsory attendance provisions of the School Code. . . .

The provision that children shall attend "continuously through the entire term" recognizes the obvious fact that each day's school work is built upon the lessons taught on the preceding day. It is virtually impossible properly to educate a child who is absent one day a week. Friday's instruction is the foundation for understanding Monday's lesson. By such regularly recurring absences the child loses not only one-fifth of the instruction, but the continuity of the course of study is broken and the pupil is not able to keep pace with his classmates. . . .

Appellants are Mohammedans, and they have persistently refused to send their children of compulsory attendance age to school on Fridays, the sacred day of that religion. They have sent them to the public schools on all other days except Friday. They invoke the guarantees of religious freedom contained in the State and Federal constitutions. Appellants were convicted for the same offense in 1943 and 1944. . . .

Judgment and sentence affirmed.

NOTES AND QUESTIONS

1. Assume that Commonwealth v. Bey, supra, has been appealed to the Supreme Court of the United States and that you are a Justice. In light of Wisconsin v. Yoder, what decision would be rendered? Why?

PARENTAL CONTROL OVER EDUCATION

PEOPLE ex rel. VOLLMAR v. STANLEY

Supreme Court of Colorado, 1927.
81 Colo. 276, 255 P. 610.

DENISON, J. . . . Mandamus was [asked], on the relation of Vollmar, to compel the respondents [Bd. of Ed.] to "revoke their said rule requiring the reading of the Bible as a portion of the morning exercises in the schools in which petitioners' children are in attendance and prohibit such religious exercises in the public schools of said school district."

An alternative writ was issued which required the above action. To this writ the respondents demurred, the demurrer was sustained, the cause was dismissed and comes here on error.

The writ recites that the . . . board of education of school district 118, Weld county, had promulgated and enforced a rule which required, as a part of the morning exercises in each classroom, the reading by the teacher of portions of King James version of the Bible without comment; that relators' children withdrew during such reading, and thereupon the respondents ruled that no pupil might leave the room during the reading.

The writ further states that the said version was a sectarian religious book, and was proscribed by the Roman Catholic Church, to which relator and his children belong; that the relator and his children conscientiously believe in the doctrines and worship of the Roman Catholic Church, which teaches that the King James translation is in part incorrect, is incomplete, and that the Scriptures ought not to be read indiscriminately nor without exposition by authorized teachers, and that other reading thereof is harmful rather than beneficial. It is further alleged that such reading is religious service and sectarian instruction.

The claim is made that the action of the respondents is contrary to section 1 of the Fourteenth Amendment to the national Constitution, and to article 2, § 4, and article 9, §§ 7 and 8, of the Colorado Constitution. The pertinent part of the Fourteenth Amendment is as follows: "Nor shall any state deprive any person of life, liberty or property without due process of law. * * * "

The powers of the state, the children and their parents over their education may be briefly but accurately stated thus:

1.   The state, for its own protection, may require children to be educated.   This needs no citation.

2.   Certain studies plainly essential to good citizenship must be taught.   .   .   .   And, as a corollary, such studies may be required of every child.

3.   Liberty is more than freedom from imprisonment.   The right to conduct a private school;   the right of parents to have their children taught where, when, how, what, and by whom they may judge best, are among the liberties guaranteed by section 1 of the Fourteenth Amendment of the United States Constitution.   Pierce v. Society of Sisters,   .   .   .

4.   But these rights are subject to the qualifications 1 and 2, above, and that teachers and places must be reputable and the things taught not immoral or inimical to the public welfare.   Pierce v. Society of Sisters,   .   .   .

5.   Conversely, the teaching of what is immoral or inimical to the public welfare may be forbidden by the state, even though taught as a moral and religious duty; e. g., polygamy.   Davis v. Beason, 133 U.S. 333.   .   .   .

It necessarily follows that, if parents can have their children taught what they please, they can refuse to have them taught what they think harmful, barring what must be taught; i. e., the essentials of good citizenship.   What these are the board of education of each district, primarily, and the courts ultimately, must decide.   So whether any study is immoral or inimical to the public welfare the board primarily and the courts ultimately must decide.   .   .   .

Some of the court think that,   .   .   .   the board has power to require attendance upon the study of any subject which they see fit to put on the course, and that the only remedy of parents is to put their children in a private school;   a majority of us, however, following, as we think, the above-cited decisions of the Supreme Court of the United States, hold that the right of the parents to select, within limits, what their children shall learn, is one of the liberties guaranteed by the Fourteenth Amendment to the national Constitution, and of which, therefore, no state can deprive them.

The parent has a constitutional right to have his children educated in the public schools of the state.   Colo.Const. art. 9, § 2.   He also has a constitutional right, as we have shown, to direct, within limits, his children's studies.   The school board, though with full power to prescribe the studies, cannot make the surrender of the second a condition of the enjoyment of the first.   They cannot say to him, "You have a constitutional right to deny your child the study of biology, and you have a constitutional right to have him taught in the public schools, but, if you are admitted to the latter, we shall deny you the former." This proposition has been more or less in doubt but is finally settled in Terral v. Burke Const. Co., 257 U.S. 529. . . .

In the final analysis there is but one point on which the members of this court disagree. The minority asserts, as they logically must to maintain their conclusion, that the parent has no right to deny his child the study of any subject which the school board may require, excepting, of course, such as are immoral or inimical to the public welfare. We concede that, if that is true, the board may require his child's attendance or deny him the school. We think, however, that the cases we have cited show that, within the limits we have stated, he has such right under the national Constitution. If that is true, then, since he has a right under the state Constitution to have his child attend the public schools, the requirement of study of a given subject or dismissal in effect makes the surrender of his right under the national Constitution a condition of his enjoyment of his rights under that of the state, which, as we have shown, cannot be done. The argument that he may send his child to a private school will not stand, for several reasons, the chief of which is because he will thus be forced to surrender his rights in the public schools. The provision that the school board "shall have control of instruction" should have a reasonable interpretation. It does not seem reasonable that every child should be required to take every subject which the board puts on the list. These conclusions are strengthened in the present case because the children in question have no parochial school within the district and because a great majority of children everywhere are, for one reason or another, dependent on the public schools for education.

It follows from the above that children cannot be compelled to take instruction not essential to good citizenship, and so, unless we hold the reading of King James Bible to be such, we cannot say that the board had power peremptorily to require attendance upon it. Unquestionably much in the Bible is essential to good citizenship, but that much can be taught otherwise than from between two particular covers; i. e., from between two other covers. We cannot say, then, that the book itself is so essential to good citizenship that parents may not exclude it from the instruction of their children. The conclusion must be, therefore, that children cannot be required, against the will of their parents or guardians, to attend its reading. It follows that the relator was entitled to relief to the extent of revocation of the order of compulsory attendance of which he complains, and the demurrer to the alternative writ should have been overruled. . . .

STATE ex rel. KELLEY v. FERGUSON

Supreme Court of Nebraska, 1914.
95 Neb. 63, 144 N.W. 1039.

FAWCETT, J. . . . [The allegations are that] prior to December 17, 1912, plaintiff had instructed his daughter Eunice Kelley "not to go to the class in domestic science; that said class was conducted in a building more than a mile distant from the Saratoga school which she was attending, and that the time consumed by said class was almost a half day, thereby causing the said Eunice Kelley to fall behind in her other studies for lack of time; that the respondents wrongfully and unlawfully and against the protests of relator required said Eunice Kelley to take said course in domestic science, and on the 17th day of December, 1912, the respondents wrongfully, unlawfully, and without cause therefor dismissed said Eunice Kelley from said school and refused and have ever since refused to allow her to attend school of said district, although since said time relator has several times made demand upon the said school board and its officers to reinstate her." The answer admits the formal allegations in the petition and alleges: That in the course of study adopted by the school district of Lincoln, which, it is alleged, is substantially the same as the courses of study in all other municipal school districts of the United States, there are eight grades below the high school; that Eunice Kelley is 12 years old and is a sixth grade pupil attending the Saratoga school; that all subjects in the sixth grade are required subjects, and one of these is domestic science; that no pupils are excused from taking any subjects in said grade except for good cause; that no cause was shown and none existed for excusing the said Eunice from attending said class; that the demand of the relator was arbitrary, unreasonable, and without just basis; that respondents could not comply with such arbitrary and unreasonable demand without undermining and destroying the discipline of the schools; that industrial training is essential to the welfare of the public, and it is the function of the state to require courses to be given affording industrial training; that in the exercise of this function a course in domestic science was prescribed for the sixth grade in the schools of the district; that in requiring attendance in classes in which this subject was taught the board of education was acting within its powers, and it could not excuse any pupils from taking said course unless a good and sufficient reason for such excuse was shown. The court found the facts as alleged . . . and awarded the writ. . . .

The issue presented by the pleadings and decided by the district court is clean cut and raises the single question: Can the parent of a child in a city graded school decide the question as to whether or not such child shall be required to carry any particular study which has been prescribed by the board of education; or does the power to make such decision rest entirely in such board? Or, to state it another way, has the parent a right to make a reasonable selection from the pre-scribed studies for his child to pursue, and, having done so, must this selection be respected by the board of education? If the parent has such right, and judgment in this case must be affirmed, for we do not think a case could be presented where a selection made by a parent would more clearly be a reasonable selection than the one attempted to be made in this case. The relator's child was a girl 12 years of age. She was in the sixth grade. The study which the relator directed her not to take was that of cooking, which is required under the subject of domestic science. The other studies which she was required to take and was taking were reading, spelling, arithmetic, geography, general lessons, drawing, and writing. The testimony of the father is that at the time the disagreement arose the daughter was studying music, which required not less than two hours a day. If the relator desired to have his daughter study music, he had the unquestionable right to have her do so, and if he thought that the taking of lessons in music, in addition to the studies she was taking in school, as above set out, was all she was able to carry, then, if he had a right to make a selection at all, it must be conceded that it was reasonable for him to select the lesson in domestic science, which took substantially one-tenth of her entire school time, as the lesson to be dropped, in order that she might continue her music. It is contended that this selection was not made by the relator in good faith but was made because of the fact that the school authorities declined to permit his daughter, at the close of the cooking lesson at the Capital school, to which the class were taken in a body by the teacher from the Saratoga school, to re-turn to her home on the Seventeenth Street car line instead of requir-ing her to return with the entire class to the Saratoga school and to be there dismissed. We do not think this fact, even if it were the cause which finally impelled relator to make his attempted selection, is very material. The important question to the school board and to parents generally is that of the right of a parent to make a reasonable selection from the prescribed studies for his child to pursue.

The question is not a new one. It was considered and decided by this court in State ex rel. Sheibley v. School District, 31 Neb. 552, 48 N.W. 393. In that case the father expressed a desire to have his daughter study grammar instead of rhetoric. His wish was respected and the change made. Subsequently he objected to her studying grammar and demanded that she be excused from continuing the study. When asked what reason he had for not wanting his daughter to pursue the study, he informed the board "that said study was not taught in said school as he had been instructed when he went to school." That was the only reason he would offer for not wanting his daughter to pursue the study. Under his direction the daughter re-fused to pursue the study, and as a result of such refusal she was ex-pelled. An original application for mandamus was made in this court, and the writ awarded. The syllabus holds: "The school trustees of a high school have authority to classify and grade the scholars in the district and cause them to be taught in such departments as they may deem expedient; they may also prescribe the courses of study and textbooks for the use of the school and such reasonable rules and regulations as they may think needful. They may also require prompt attendance, respectful deportment, and diligence in study. The parent, however, has a right to make a reasonable selection from the prescribed studies for his child to pursue, and this selection must be respected by the trustees, as the right of the parent in that regard is superior to that of the trustees and the teachers." * * * Now who is to determine what studies she shall pursue in school, a teacher, who has a mere temporary interest in her welfare, or her father, who may reasonably be supposed to be desirous of pursuing such course as will best promote the happiness of his child? The father certainly possesses superior opportunities of knowing the physical and mental capabilities of his child. It may be apparent that all the prescribed course of studies is more than the strength of the child can undergo; or he may be desirous, as is frequently the case, that his child, while attending school, should also take lessons in music, painting, etc., from private teachers. This he has a right to do. The right of the parent, therefore, to determine what studies his child shall pursue is paramount to that of the trustees or teacher. Schools are provided by the public in which prescribed branches are taught, which are free to all within the district between certain ages. But no pupil attending the school can be compelled to study any prescribed branch against the protest of the parent that the child shall not study such branch, and any rule or regulation that requires the pupil to continue such studies is arbitrary and unreasonable. There is no good reason why the failure of one or more pupils to study one or more prescribed branches should result disastrously to the proper discipline, efficiency, and well-being of the school. Such pupils are not idle but merely devoting their attention to other branches; and so long as the failure of the students, thus excepted, to study all the branches of the prescribed course does not prejudice the equal rights of other students, there is no cause for complaint." . . .

Wherever education is most general, there life and property are the most safe, and civilization of the highest order. The public school is one of the main bulwarks of our nation, and we would not knowingly do anything to undermine it; but we should be careful to avoid permitting our love for this noble institution to cause us to regard it as "all in all" and destroy both the God-given and constitutional right of a parent to have some voice in the bringing up and education of his children. We believe in the doctrine of the greatest good to the greatest number, and that the welfare of the individual must give way to the welfare of society in general. The whole current of modern thought and agitation is "onward." The people are beginning to realize as never before that, if we continue to jog along in the ruts our fathers before us have made, little will be accomplished in the way of national and social improvement. The state is more and more taking hold of the private affairs of individuals and requiring that they conduct their business affairs honestly and with due regard for the public good. All this is commendable and must receive the sanction of every good citizen. But in this age of agitation, such as the world has never known before, we want to be careful lest we carry the doctrine of governmental paternalism too far, for, after all is said and done, the prime factor in our scheme of government is the American home.   .   .   .

The judgment of the district court is therefore affirmed.

NOTES AND QUESTIONS

1. In Pierce v. Society of Sisters, supra, the Court stated: ". . . we think it entirely plain that the Act of 1922 unreasonably interferes with the liberty of parents and guardians to direct the upbringing and education of children under their control," and "The child is not the mere creature of the State; those who nurture him and direct his destiny have the right, coupled with the high duty, to recognize and prepare him for additional obligations." Does Pierce or Wisconsin v. Yoder provide the constitutional foundation for a parental right to control and direct the education of their children, or do the previous two cases involve legal rights of parents that are not constitutional rights?

2. Suppose a parent decided that his child should not participate in one of the following classes: reading, mathematics, chemistry, physical or sex education, would either Vollmar or Kelley v. Ferguson be determinative? What limitations are suggested by these two cases on the parental right to control and direct a child's education? Under the rule of these two cases could a parent refuse to allow his child to be taught "the essentials of good citizenship?" If not, is this then, the primary goal of the public schools? Who determines what subjects are essential for good citizenship? What were the conceptions of the political community and good citizenship that the Supreme Court allowed the Amish in Wisconsin v. Yoder? Is the conception the same or different in Pierce, Vollmar and Kelley v. Ferguson?

3. On the right of parents to control education see generally, School Board Dist. No. 18 v. Thompson, 24 Okl. 1, 103 P. 578 (1909); Hardwick v. Bd. of School Trustees, 54 Cal.App. 696, 205 P. 49 (1921); Sheibley v. School Dist., 31 Neb. 552, 48 N.W. 393 (1891) and compare, Samuel Benedict Memorial School v. Bradford, 111 Ga. 861, 36 S.E. 920 (1900), and State ex rel. Andrews v. Webber, 108 Ind. 31, 8 N.E. 708 (1886).

4. On the right of a parent to inspect his child's school records, see, Van Allen v. McCleary, 27 Misc.2d 81, 211 N.Y.S.2d 501 (S.Ct., 1961).

PROBLEM

An eighteen year old man, Peter Doe, has recently graduated from High School with a B minus grade average. He was never a discipline problem, and both he and his parents relied upon his grades—all of which were "C" or better. They believed that Peter Doe was learning when he attended school. They were shocked to discover that, after testing, Peter Doe's reading ability is only at the fifth-grade level, although his I.Q. is 100. Moreover, his language and writing abilities are only at the sixth grade level. Peter Doe is currently suing his teachers and the school district for $1 million. He contends that he was compelled by law to go to school; that compulsory education laws imply a duty on his teachers and on the school district to impart learning to him; that his teachers and the school district failed to impart learning to him; that his teachers and the school district mislead and deceived him and his family through his grades into believing that learning was imparted to him up to and through the 12th grade level when it wasn't, and that all of this amounts to negligence, malpractice and fraud by his teachers and by the school district to the detriment of Peter Doe.

Assume that you are the judge, how would you rule in this case and for what reason(s)?

WHAT IS THE PURPOSE OF THE PUBLIC SCHOOLS?

———

A carefully written legal obligation requiring that children attend public schools or their legal equivalent appears to be constitutionally valid. But, questions remain about the proper goals of public education. Is "schooling" properly to be distinguished from "education"? Clearly, the dominant political community should be required to justify its legal obligation to attend school and the prolonged detention of its children-citizens in a system of public, or equivalent, education. What then is the justifying purpose of modern compulsory schooling? A fair question is whether public education is any longer useful, and, if so, on what terms and conditions seeking what specific goals, and if not, then what is the alternative?

In McCollum v. Bd. of Ed., printed in Chapter 6, Mr. Justice Frankfurter stated that "the public school is at once the symbol of our democracy and the most pervasive means for promoting our common destiny." Frankfurter's belief, like Thomas Jefferson's before him, was that the two dominant purposes of compulsory public education are (1) to make the people capable of being guardians of their own liberties, and (2) to provide our society with intellectual leadership. The first purpose goes to effective citizenship. Compulsory public education should provide everybody with the intellectual resources, and particularly an effective command of the language, needed to separate public truths from half-truths or lies and thereby enabling everyone to participate effectively in the political processes and to defend themselves against demagogues and tyrants. Is one of the primary goals of modern education that of creating a political community, and, if so, how should that political community be defined? The second purpose of compulsory public education is to impart enough intellectual skills to students such that those capable of continuing can become scholars, intellectuals and members of the learned professions. This probably implies an elitist notion: that higher, non-compulsory education should be made available to men and women from all social classes, but only to those persons having a pronounced taste for intellectual matters; who are qualified for it, and who are committed to spending their lives in intellectual pursuits. Has the dream of making culture available to the masses, by making higher education widely available, failed? If so or if not, what are the implications for compulsory education in the "common schools"? Are the above two purposes the proper goals of compulsory education today?

What are the correct answers to the following questions? They are reprinted with permission from p. 18 of the April, 1973, issue of the *Center Report*, a publication of the Center for the Study of Democratic Institutions, Santa Barbara, California:

"I   Should the primary concern of education be the creation of a political community? If so, how shall the political community be conceived? As primarily economic, concerned mainly with the livelihoods of its members and with the productivity of the whole, or as requiring additional dimensions?

"A.   Questions regarding education in the context of a strict conception of political community:

"1.   Are universal literacy and numericity of sufficient importance in this decade to deserve the substantial share of educational funds and energies? Or should there be, for all students, a broader range of outcomes?

"2.   How shall the terminal point of public education be determined?

"3.   How shall assessed national needs and individual aspirations and propensities be reconciled when they are incongruent?

"4.   Are schools the appropriate institutions for career education (job training)? Or should training be on-the-job or in specially equipped and specially timed institutions supplementary to the schools?

"5.   Shall maximizing the educability of the deprived, least-schooled segments of our population be a matter of first priority? If so, what environmental deprivations are most deleterious and most capable of correction: e. g., parental expectations and rewards vs. richness of sensory imput in earliest years?

"6.   If the answer to question 5 is affirmative, is it also desirable that education of the less-deprived and the talented be refurbished and nurtured in the midst of emphasis on the deprived? If so, how maintain a maximum of the propinquities among socioeconomic classes and ethnic groups, if these are threatened by this dual emphasis?

"B.   Questions regarding education in the context of a broad conception of political community:

"1.   Shall schools be concerned with recast of values and loyalties and reformation of character?   If so, should the aim be one body of values, loyalties, and characteral traits or should a diversity be sought?   What are the components of the most desirable bodies of values, loyalties, character traits?

"2.   If this task is held inappropriate to the public schools, should it be undertaken at all?   If so, by what other means?

"3.   Shall the schools be concerned with imparting the arts of the 'practical,' i. e., the processes by which statute, moral precept, and scientific generality are brought to bear on concrete, particular situations, and consensus obtained?   Or should other instrumentalities for service be sought?   Or should these arts be left to those who seek them out in experience?

"4.   Concerning a common language, history, and culture: to what extent and in what form shall these be pursued?   What degree and form of patriotism?   How shall religion be treated?

"5.   What, if any, requirements of the community justify compulsory attendance?   To what age?

"6.   What, if any community requirements justify grades and credentials?

"7.   If the community believed that education (study) should be lifelong and made adequate provision for it, what would be the effect on all the preceding questions?

"II   Shall the public schools disavow restriction to political community narrowly conceived and concern itself as well with development of a wide range of human potentialities?   Should these potentialities be conceived as contributions to political community, as an added category of goods, or as the larger category within which membership in political community is one part?

"A.   Shall the public schools deepen their working definition of literacy to include perception of the terms, distinctions, and commitments to methods and principles which render a solution to a complex problem only one solution among several?   If pursued effectively, such a deepening of the notion of literacy will tend to blur the distinction between expert and layman, hence between ruler and ruled.   Is this wise?

"B.   Shall there be concern for individually different talents for satisfying activities unrelated to careers, e. g., appreciation and production of fine and applied arts?   If so, how can these individual differences be identified early?   What means are there for transforming fantasies about such activities, and limitations of the child's view of them imposed by limited experience, into trials of less fantastic and more varied resources of satisfaction?   How can such transformations be obtained while yet honoring individual differences in these respects?

"C.   If there shall be concern for individually different outcomes of education, what are the means for integrating individualized goals common to most or all recipients of education?

"D.   Should the schools, at every level, visibly as well as in fact, promise to each student a contribution to a then-felt want or need?

"E.   What of the educational responsibilities of other institutions: church, family, industry, the professions, institutions yet to be devised?"

Chapter V

CONSTITUTIONAL FREEDOM AND GOVERNMENTAL POWER TO CONTROL THE EXPRESSION OF IDEAS

INTRODUCTION

The First Amendment has been incorporated into the Fourteenth Amendment. Together, they protect a number of rights to free expression from abridgment by actions of Federal, state and local governments. These rights can be separated into two broad divisions: (1) the rights to religious expression and (2) the rights to non religious or "secular" free expression, including the freedoms of speech, press, assembly and the right to petition government for a redress of grievances. Because of the volume of litigation and the uniqueness of some of the problems, with few exceptions the guarantees of religious expression and their implications for education will be considered separately in the next chapter. This chapter will deal with the guarantees of freedom of secular expression as they function to limit government's power to require or promote the transmission of an official orthodoxy in public schools.

A fundamental cleavage exists regarding the ultimate purpose of education between those persons who, above all else, regard education as a means of instilling and propagating certain proper and officially approved or tolerated ideas, beliefs and values and those other people who, above all else, regard education as a means of producing a person with a disciplined and critical mind having the power of independent judgment and capable of choosing his own ideas, beliefs and values. The latter view is fully consistent with the requirements of a constitutional democracy, and it is helpful in defining the concept of "good citizenship." There is no reason to equate an "open mind" with an "empty mind".

Freedom in America implies a trust in the individual. The person is expected to think for himself and to come to his own conclusions. There is to be no censor of thoughts in America, and the founding fathers placed their trust in the ordinary person. They rejected forever the establishment of any authority over a person's mind or his conscience. A person's constitutional freedom to believe, and to say what he believes, does not depend upon what he believes or upon the rightness of what he believes, or upon obtaining prior permission from some superior authority. The American proposition of freedom is that a person is free to find and speak the truth that is in him and that the official views come afterward. The American trust in the free individual. On that we have staked our all.

This is not to say that the state can never place restraints on schools. We know that a complete absence of all restraints on all aspects of human liberty leads ultimately to the severest of restraints because the strong enslave the weak, and power, not reason, rules with the usual result that the powerfully intolerant destroy the tolerant and tolerance itself. On the other hand, it is to say that when the state places a restraint upon liberty that restraint, itself, must be justified before it can be allowed. Freedom is the fundamental preference and the basic postulate. Limitations on it must be justified and can be no broader than their justifications.

The next section contains several selections setting forth the fundamental theory of free expression generally, without special reference to education. They should be studied carefully, and after mastering their intrinsic merits, one should consider their implications for education. Two of the important questions are: (1) whether government has any power to suppress any substantive idea, and (2) whether government has any power to prohibit certain acts of free expression? These questions involving the substance of ideas should be distinguished from questions of procedure such as: Does the government have power fairly to regulate the time, place and manner of expressing ideas? Procedural regulations may not deny expression to any substantive idea or act, but may only regulate them. After all, it is difficult, if not impossible, to locate constitutional justification for a huge demonstration that seeks to express an idea, or protest a policy, at the busiest intersection of a community during the commuter rush hour. The community might justifiably require that the demonstration take place at another place or time, or perhaps, in another manner. But would the community, through its government, be justified in suppressing the idea in its entirety?

THE GENERAL THEORY OF FREE EXPRESSION

DECLARATION OF INDEPENDENCE
July 4, 1776.

When in the Course of human events, it becomes necessary for one people to dissolve the political bands, which have connected them with another, and to assume, among the powers of the earth, the separate and equal station, to which the Laws of Nature and of Nature's God entitle them, a decent respect to the Opinions of mankind requires that they should declare the causes which impel them to the separation.—We hold these truths to be self-evident, that all men are created equal, that they are endowed by their Creator with certain unalienable Rights, that among these are Life, Liberty and the pursuit of Happiness.—That to secure these rights, Governments are instituted among Men, deriving their just powers from the consent of the governed,—That whenever any Form of Government becomes destructive of these ends, it is the Right of the People to alter or to abolish it, and to institute new Government, laying its foundation on such principles and organizing its powers in such form, as to them shall seem most likely to effect their Safety and Happiness. Prudence, indeed, will dictate that Governments long established should not be changed for light and transient causes; and accordingly all experience hath shewn, that mankind are more disposed to suffer, while evils are sufferable, than to right themselves by abolishing the forms to which they are accustomed. But when a long train of abuses and usurpations, pursuing invariably the same Object evinces a design to reduce them under absolute Despotism, it is their right, it is their duty to throw off such Government, and to provide new Guards for their future security.—Such has been the patient sufferance of these Colonies; and such is now the necessity which constrains them to alter their former Systems of Government.

CONSTITUTION OF THE UNITED STATES

Preamble

We the People of the United States, in Order to form a more perfect Union, establish Justice, insure domestic Tranquility, provide for the common defence, promote the general Welfare, and secure the Blessings of Liberty to ourselves and our Posterity, do ordain and establish this Constitution for the United States of America. (March 4, 1789).

AMENDMENT I

Congress shall make no law   .   .   .   abridging the freedom of speech, or of the press; or the right of the people peaceably to assemble, and to petition the Government for a redress of grievances. (December 15, 1791).

AMENDMENT XIV

All persons born or naturalized in the United States, and subject to the jurisdiction thereof, are citizens of the United States and of the State wherein they reside. No State shall make or enforce any law which shall abridge the privileges or immunities of citizens of the United States; nor shall any State deprive any person of life, liberty or property, without due process of law, nor deny to any person within its jurisdiction the equal protection of the laws. (July 28, 1868).

JOHN STUART MILL, ON LIBERTY, 1859.

———

. . . The object of this Essay is to assert one very simple principle, as entitled to govern absolutely the dealings of society with the individual in the way of compulsion and control, whether the means used be physcial force in the form of legal penalties, or the moral coercion of public opinion. That principle is, that the sole end for which mankind are warranted, individually or collectively, in interfering with the liberty of action of any of their number is self-protection. That the only purpose for which power can be rightfully exercised over any member of a civilized community, against his will, is to prevent harm to others. His own good, either physical or moral, is not a sufficient warrant. He cannot rightfully be compelled to do or forbear because it will be better for him to do so, because it will make him happier, because, in the opinions of others, to do so would be wise, or even right. These are good reasons for remonstrating with him, or reasoning with him, or persuading him or entreating him, but not for compelling him, or visiting him with any evil, in case he do otherwise. To justify that, the conduct from which it is desired to deter him must be calculated to produce evil to someone else. The only part of the conduct of any one, for which he is amenable to society, is that which concerns others. In the part which merely con cerns himself, his independence is, of right, absolute. Over himself, over his own body and mind, the individual is sovereign.

It is, perhaps, hardly necessary to say that this doctrine is meant to apply only to human beings in the maturity of their faculties. We are not speaking of children, or of young persons below the age which the law may fix as that of manhood or womanhood. Those who are still in a state to require being taken care of by others, must be protected against their own actions as well as against external injury. . . . But as soon as mankind have attained the capacity of being guided to their own improvement by conviction or persuasion (a period long since reached in all nations with whom we need here concern ourselves), compulsion, either in the direct form or in that of pains and penalties for non-compliance, is no longer admissible as a means to their own good, and justifiable only for the security of others. . . .

. . . The only freedom which deserves the name, is that of pursuing our own good in our own way, so long as we do not attempt to deprive others of theirs, or impede their efforts to obtain it. . .

Though this doctrine is anything but new, and, to some persons, may have the air of a truism, there is no doctrine which stands more directly opposed to the general tendency of existing opinion and practice. Society has expended fully as much effort in the attempt (according to its lights) to compel people to conform to its notions of personal, as of social excellence. . . .

. . . If all mankind minus one, were of one opinion, and only one person were of the contrary opinion, mankind would be no more justified in silencing that one person, than he, if he had the power, would be justified in silencing mankind. Were an opinion a personal possession of no value except to the owner; if to be obstructed in the enjoyment of it were simply a private injury, it would make some difference whether the injury was inflicted only on a few persons or on many. But the peculiar evil of silencing the expression of an opinion is, that it is robbing the human race; posterity as well as the existing generation; those who dissent from the opinion, still more than those who hold it. If the opinion is right, they are deprived of the opportunity of exchanging error for truth: if wrong, they lose, what is almost as great a benefit, the clearer perception and livelier impression of truth, produced by its collision with error.

It is necessary to consider separately these two hypotheses, each of which has a distinct branch of the argument corresponding to it. We can never be sure that the opinion we are endeavoring to stifle is a false opinion; and if we were sure, stifling it would be an evil still.

First: the opinion which it is attempted to suppress by authority may possibly be true. Those who desire to suppress it, of course deny its truth; but they are not infallible. They have no authority to decide the question for all mankind, and exclude every other person from the means of judging. To refuse a hearing to an opinion, because they are sure that it is false, is to assume that *their* certainty is the same thing as *absolute* certainty. All silencing of discussion is an assumption of infallibility. Its condemnation may be allowed to rest on this common argument, not the worse for being common. . . .

. . . There is the greatest difference between presuming an opinion to be true because, with every opportunity for contesting it, it has not been refuted, and assuming its truth for the purpose of not permitting its refutation. Complete liberty of contradicting and disproving our opinion, is the very condition which justifies us in assuming its truth for purposes of action; and on no other terms can a being with human faculties have any rational assurance of being right. . . .

But, indeed, the dictum that truth always triumphs over persecution, is one of those pleasant falsehoods which men repeat after one another till they pass into commonplaces, but which all experience refutes. History teems with instances of truth put down by persecution. If not suppressed forever, it may be thrown back for centuries.   .   .   .   It is a piece of idle sentimentality that truth, merely as truth, has any inherent power denied to error, of prevailing against the dungeon and the stake. Men are not more zealous for truth than they often are for error, and a sufficient application of legal or even of social penalties will generally succeed in stopping the propagation of either. The real advantage which truth has, consists in this, that when an opinion is true, it may be extinguished once, twice, or many times, but in the course of ages there will generally be found persons to rediscover it, until some one of its reappearances falls on a time when from favorable circumstances it escapes persecution until it has made such head as to withstand all subsequent attempts to suppress it.   .   .   .

Let us now pass to the second division of the argument, and dismissing the supposition that any of the received opinions may be false, let us assume them to be true, and examine into the worth of the manner in which they are likely to be held, when their truth is not freely and openly canvassed. However unwillingly a person who has a strong opinion may admit the possibility that his opinion may be false, he ought to be moved by the consideration that however true it may be, if it is not fully, frequently, and fearlessly discussed, it will be held as a dead dogma, not a living truth.

There is a class of persons   .   .   .   who think it enough if a person assents undoubtingly to what they think true, though he has no knowledge whatever of the grounds of the opinion, and could not make a tenable defence of it against the most superficial objections. Such persons, if they can once get their creed taught from authority, naturally think that no good, and some harm, comes of its being allowed to be questioned. Where their influence prevails, they make it nearly impossible for the received opinion to be rejected wisely and considerately, though it may still be rejected rashly and ignorantly; for to shut out discussion entirely is seldom possible, and when it once gets in, beliefs not grounded on conviction are apt to give way before the slightest semblance of an argument. Waiving, however, this possibility—assuming that the true opinion abides in the mind, but abides as a prejudice, a belief independent of, and proof against, argument—this is not the way in which truth ought to be held by a rational being. This is not knowing the truth. Truth, thus held, is but one superstition the more, accidentally clinging to the words which enunciate a truth.

If the intellect and judgment of mankind ought to be cultivated .   .   .   on what can these faculties be more appropriately exercised by any one, than on the things which concern him so much that it is considered necessary for him to hold opinions on them? If the cultivation of the understanding consists in one thing more than in another, it is surely in learning the grounds of one's own opinions. Whatever people believe, on subjects on which it is of the first importance to believe rightly, they ought to be able to defend against at least the common objections.   .   .   .

If, however, the mischievous operation of the absence of free discussion, when the received opinions are true, were confined to leaving men ignorant of the grounds of those opinions, it might be thought that this, if an intellectual, is no moral evil, and does not affect the worth of the opinions, regarded in their influence on the character. The fact, however, is, that not only the grounds of the opinion are forgotten in the absence of discussion, but too often the meaning of the opinion itself.   .   .   .   The great chapter in human history which this fact occupies and fills, cannot be too earnestly studied and meditated on.   .   .   .

It still remains to speak of one of the principal causes which make diversity of opinion advantageous, and will continue to do so until mankind shall have entered a stage of intellectual advancement which at present seems at an incalculable distance. We have hitherto considered only two possibilities: that the received opinion may be false, and some other opinion, consequently, true; or that, the received opinion being true, a conflict with the opposite error is essential to a clear apprehension and deep feeling of its truth. But there is a commoner case than either of these; when the conflicting doctrines, instead of being one true and the other false, share the truth between them; and the nonconforming opinion is needed to supply the remainder of the truth, of which the received doctrine embodies only a part. Popular opinions, on subjects not palpable to sense, are often true, but seldom or never the whole truth. They are a part of the truth; sometimes a greater, sometimes a smaller part, but exaggerated, distorted, and disjoined from the truths by which they ought to be accompanied and limited. Heretical opinions, on the other hand, are generally some of these suppressed and neglected truths, bursting the bonds which kept them down, and either seeking reconciliation with the truth contained in the common opinion, or fronting it as enemies, and setting themselves up, with similar exclusiveness, as the whole truth. The latter case is hitherto the most frequent, as, in the human mind, one-sidedness has always been the rule, and many-sidedness the exception. Hence, even in revolutions of opinion, one part of the truth usually sets while another rises. Even progress, which ought to superadd, for the most part only substitutes one partial and incomplete truth for another; improvement consisting chiefly in this, that the new fragment of truth is more wanted, more adapted to the needs of the time, than that which it displaces. Such being the partial character of prevailing opinions, even when resting on a true foundation; every opinion which embodies somewhat of the portion of truth which the common opinion omits, ought to be considered precious, with whatever amount of error and confusion that truth may be blended. No sober judge of human affairs will feel bound to be indignant because those who force on our notice truths which we should otherwise have overlooked, overlook some of those which we see. Rather, he will think that so long as popular truth is one-sided, it is more desirable than otherwise that unpopular truth should have one-sided asserters too; such being usually the most energetic, and the most likely to compel reluctant attention to the fragment of wisdom which they proclaim as if it were the whole. . . .

. . . Before quitting the subject of freedom of opinion, it is fit to take some notice of those who say, that the free expression of all opinions should be permitted, on condition that the manner be temperate, and do not pass the bounds of fair discussion. Much might be said on the impossibility of fixing where these supposed bounds are to be placed; for if the test be offence to those whose opinion is attacked, I think experience testifies that this offence is given whenever the attack is telling and powerful, and that every opponent who pushes them hard, and whom they find it difficult to answer, appears to them, if he shows any strong feeling on the subject, an intemperate opponent. But this, though an important consideration in a practical point of view, merges in a more fundamental objection. Undoubtedly the manner of asserting an opinion, even though it be a true one, may be very objectionable, and may justly incur severe censure. But the principal offences of the kind are such as it is mostly impossible, unless by accidental self-betrayal, to bring home to conviction. The gravest of them is, to argue sophistically, to suppress facts or arguments, to misstate the elements of the case, or misrepresent the opposite opinion. But all this, even to the most aggravated degree, is so continually done in perfect good faith, by persons who are not considered, and in many other respects may not deserve to be considered, ignorant or incompetent, that it is rarely possible on adequate grounds conscientiously to stamp the misrepresentation as morally culpable; and still less could law presume to interfere with this kind of controversial misconduct. With regard to what is commonly meant by intemperate discussion, namely, invective, sarcasm, personality, and the like, the denunciation of these weapons would deserve more sympathy if it were ever proposed to interdict them equally to both sides; but it is only desired to restrain the employment of them against the prevailing opinion: against the unprevailing they may not only be used without general disapproval, but will be likely to obtain for him who uses them the praise of honest zeal and righteous indignation. Yet whatever mischief arises from their use, is greatest when they are employed against the comparatively defenceless; and whatever unfair advantage can be derived by any opinion from this mode of asserting it, accrues almost exclusively to received opinions. The worst offence of this kind which can be committed by a polemic, is to stigmatize those who hold the contrary opinion as bad and immoral men. To calumny of this sort, those who hold any unpopular opinion are peculiarly exposed, because they are in general few and uninfluential, and nobody but themselves feels much interest in seeing justice done them; but this weapon is, from the nature of the case, denied to those who attack a prevailing opinion: they can neither use it with safety to themselves, nor, if they could, would it do anything but recoil on their own cause. In general, opinions contrary to those commonly received can only obtain a hearing by studied moderation of language, and the most cautious avoidance of unnecessary offence, from which they hardly ever deviate even in a slight degree without losing ground: while unmeasured vituperation employed on the side of the prevailing opinion, really does deter people from professing contrary opinions, and from listening to those who profess them. For the interest, therefore, of truth and justice, it is far more important to restrain this employment of vituperative language than the other . . .

The liberty of the individual must be thus far limited; he must not make himself a nuisance to other people. But if he refrains from molesting others in what concerns them, and merely acts according to his own inclination and judgment in things which concern himself, the same reasons which show that opinion should be free, prove also that he should be allowed, without molestation, to carry his opinions into practice at his own cost. That mankind are not infallible; that their truths, for the most part, are only half-truths; that unity of opinion, unless resulting from the fullest and freest comparison of opposite opinions, is not desirable, and diversity not an evil, but a good, until mankind are much more capable than at present of recognizing all sides of the truth, are principles applicable to men's modes of action, not less than to their opinions. As it is useful that while mankind are imperfect there should be different experiments of living; that free scope should be given to varieties of character, short of injury to others; and that the worth of different modes of life should be proved practically, when any one thinks fit to try them. It is desirable, in short, that in things which do not primarily concern others, individuality should assert itself. Where, not the person's own character, but the traditions or customs of other people are the rule of conduct, there is wanting one of the principal ingredients of human happiness, and quite the chief ingredient of individual and social progress.

* * *

He who lets the world, or his own portion of it, choose his plan of life for him, has no need of any other faculty than the ape-like one of imitation. He who chooses his plan for himself, employs all his faculties. He must use observation to see, reasoning and judgment to foresee, activity to gather materials for decision, discrimination to decide, and when he has decided, firmness and self-control to hold to his deliberate decision. And these qualities he requires and exercises exactly in proportion as the part of his conduct which he determines according to his own judgment and feelings is a large one. It is possible that he might be guided in some good path, and kept out of harm's way, without any of these things. But what will be his comparative worth as a human being? It really is of importance, not only what men do, but also what manner of men they are that do it Among the works of man, which human life is rightly employed in perfecting and beautifying, the first in importance surely is man himself. Supposing it were possible to get houses built, corn grown, battles fought, causes tried, and even churches erected and prayers said, by machinery—by automatons in human form—it would be a considerable loss to exchange for these automatons even the men and women who at present inhabit the more civilized parts of the world, and who assuredly are but starved specimens of what nature can and will produce. Human nature is not a machine to be built after a model, and set to do exactly the work prescribed for it, but a tree, which requires to grow and develop itself on all sides, according to the tendency of the inward forces which make it a living thing.

.   .   .

———

ABRAMS v. UNITED STATES

Supreme Court of the United States, 1919.
250 U.S. 616, 629–631, 40 S.Ct. 17, 22, 63 L.Ed. 1173, 1180.

HOLMES, J.   . . .   In this case sentences of twenty years imprisonment have been imposed for the publishing of two leaflets that I believe the defendants had as much right to publish as the Government has to publish the Constitution of the United States now vainly invoked by them. Even if I am technically wrong and enough can be squeezed from these poor and puny anonymities to turn the color of legal litmus paper; I will add, even if what I think the necessary intent were shown; the most nominal punishment seems to me all that possibly could be inflicted, unless the defendants are to be made to suffer not for what the indictment alleges but for the creed that they avow—a creed that I believe to be the creed of ignorance and immaturity when honestly held, as I see no reason to doubt that it was held here, but which, although made the subject of examination at the trial, no one has a right even to consider in dealing with the charges before the Court.

Persecution for the expression of opinions seems to me perfectly logical. If you have no doubt of your premises or your power and want a certain result with all your heart you naturally express your wishes in law and sweep away all opposition. To allow opposition by speech seems to indicate that you think the speech impotent, as when a man says that he has squared the circle, or that you do not care whole-heartedly for the result, or that you doubt either your power or your premises. But when men have realized that time has upset many fighting faiths, they may come to believe even more than they believe the very foundations of their own conduct that the ultimate good desired is better reached by free trade in ideas—that the best test of truth is the power of the thought to get itself accepted in the competition of the market, and that truth is the only ground upon which their wishes safely can be carried out. That at any rate is the theory of our Constitution. It is an experiment, as all life is an experiment. Every year if not every day we have to wager our salvation upon some prophecy based upon imperfect knowledge. While that experiment is part of our system I think that we should be eternally vigilant against attempts to check the expression of opinions that we loathe and believe to be fraught with death, unless they so imminently threaten immediate interference with the lawful and pressing purposes of the law that an immediate check is required to save the country. I wholly disagree with the argument of the Government that the First Amendment left the common law as to seditious libel in force. History seems to me against the notion. I had conceived that the United States through many years had shown its repentance for the Sedition Act of 1798, by repaying fines that it imposed. Only the emergency that makes it immediately dangerous to leave the correction of evil counsels to time warrants making any exception to the sweeping command, "Congress shall make no law . . . abridging the freedom of speech." Of course I am speaking only of expressions of opinion and exhortations, which were all that were uttered here, but I regret that I cannot put into more impressive words my belief that in their conviction upon this indictment the defendants were deprived of their rights under the Constitution of the United States. . . .

WHITNEY v. CALIFORNIA

Supreme Court of the United States, 1927.
274 U.S. 357, 375–76, 47 S.Ct. 641, 648, 71 L.Ed. 1095, 1105–1106.

BRANDEIS, J. . . . Those who won our independence believed that the final end of the State was to make men free to develop their faculties; and that in its government the deliberative forces should prevail over the arbitrary. They valued liberty both as an end and as a means. They believed liberty to be the secret of happiness and courage to be the secret of liberty. They believed that freedom to think as you will and to speak as you think are means indispensable to the discovery and spread of political truth; that without free speech and assembly discussion would be futile; that with them, discussion affords ordinarily adequate protection against the dissemination of noxious doctrine; that the greatest menace to freedom is an inert people; that public discussion is a political duty; and that this should be a fundamental principle of the American government.[2] They recognized the risks to which all human institutions are subject. But they knew that order cannot be secured merely through fear of punishment for its infraction; that it is hazardous to discourage thought, hope and imagination; that fear breeds repression; that repression breeds hate; that hate menaces stable government; that the path of safety lies in the opportunity to discuss freely supposed grievances and proposed remedies; and that the fitting remedy for evil counsels is good ones. Believing in the power of reason as applied through public discussion, they eschewed silence coerced by law—the argument of force in its worst form. Recognizing the occasional tyrannies of governing majorities, they amended the Constitution so that free speech and assembly should be guaranteed.

Fear of serious injury cannot alone justify suppression of free speech and assembly. Men feared witches and burnt women. It is the function of speech to free men from the bondage of irrational fears. To justify suppression of free speech there must be reasonable ground to fear that serious evil will result if free speech is practiced. There must be reasonable ground to believe that the danger apprehended is imminent. There must be reasonable ground to believe that the evil to be prevented is a serious one. Every denunciation of existing law tends in some measure to increase the probability that there will be violation of it. Condonation of a breach enhances the probability. Expressions of approval add to the probability. Propagation of the criminal state of mind by teaching syndicalism increases it. Advocacy of law-breaking heightens it still further. But even advocacy of violation, however reprehensible morally, is not a justification for denying free speech where the advocacy falls short of incitement and there is nothing to indicate that the advocacy would be immediately acted on. The wide difference between advocacy and incitement, between preparation and attempt, between assembling and conspiracy, must be borne in mind. In order to support a finding of clear and present danger it must be shown either that immediate serious violence was to be expected or was advocated, or that the past conduct furnished reason to believe that such advocacy was then contemplated.

Those who won our independence by revolution were not cowards. They did not fear political change. They did not exalt order at the cost of liberty. To courageous, self-reliant men, with confidence in the power of free and fearless reasoning applied through the processes

[2] Compare Thomas Jefferson: "We have nothing to fear from the demoralizing reasonings of some, if others are left free to demonstrate their errors and especially when the law stands ready to punish the first criminal act produced by the false reasonings; these are safer corrections than the conscience of the judge." Quoted by Charles A. Beard, The Nation, July 7, 1926, vol. 123, p. 8. Also in first Inaugural Address: "If there be any among us who would wish to dissolve this union or change its republican form, let them stand undisturbed as monuments of the safety with which error of opinion may be tolerated where reason is left free to combat it."

of popular government, no danger flowing from speech can be deemed clear and present, unless the incidence of the evil apprehended is so imminent that it may befall before there is opportunity for full discussion. If there be time to expose through discussion the falsehood and fallacies, to avert the evil by the processes of education, the remedy to be applied is more speech, not enforced silence. Only an emergency can justify repression. Such must be the rule if authority is to be reconciled with freedom. Such, in my opinion, is the command of the Constitution. . . .

NOTES AND QUESTIONS

1. Mr. Justice Holmes' opinion in Abrams emphasizes the Millsian idea that "truth" is important and must be allowed to flourish in an open society without censorship so that in the long run the "truth" will be "accepted in the competition of the market" and an informed citizenry will then act according to the dictates of that known "truth." Are men such rational creatures after all? How would B. F. Skinner react to Holmes' views in Abrams? See B. F. Skinner, BEYOND FREEDOM AND DIGNITY (1971), chapters 1 and 2. For a discussion of anti-intellectualism in the twentieth century see Richard Hofstadter, ANTI-INTELLECTUALISM IN AMERICAN LIFE (1962) and Crane Brinton, IDEAS AND MEN—THE STORY OF WESTERN THOUGHT (1950), chapter 14. See also L. J. Henderson, PARETO'S GENERAL SOCIOLOGY (1935) for an exposition of human behavior at odds with the premise set out by J. S. Mill in ON LIBERTY.

2. In the Whitney case the defendant was convicted under a state syndicalism statute for forming an organization advocating violent overthrow of the government. The Supreme Court, speaking through Mr. Justice Sanford, affirmed with Mr. Justice Brandeis concurring in result. But, Brandeis disagreed with the majority's rationale that mere advocacy of violent overthrow of the government, standing alone, was sufficient to warrant the suppression of free speech. Is the Brandeis test for suppressing free speech reasonable? Workable? How could one know before hand whether his speech was protected or not under the Brandeis test? What difference does it make whether one knows if his speech will be protected? Whitney v. California was overruled in Brandenburg v. Ohio, 395 U.S. 444, 89 S.Ct. 1827, 23 L.Ed.2d 430 (1969), and Justice Brandeis' rationale for suppressing free speech is the current view of the Supreme Court.

3. The individual's right to freedom of speech is protected by the Constitution. But its contours might be defined, in part, by the public function of freedom of speech. The First Amendment protects the major public interest of self-governance requiring an integrated scheme of First Amendment freedoms: "The First Amendment does not protect a 'freedom to speak.' It protects the freedom of those activities of thought and communication by which we 'govern.' It is concerned, not with a private right, but with a public power, a governmental responsibility." A. Meiklejohn, The First Amendment Is an Absolute, 1961 Sup.Ct.Rev. 245, 255, and see, Brennan, The Supreme Court and the Meiklejohn Interpretation of the First Amendment, 79

Harv.L.Rev. 1 (1965). Meiklejohn first published his views at a period in our political history when "McCarthyism," then in its incipient stages, gave birth to the House of Representatives Committee on Unamerican Activities. A. Meiklejohn, Political Freedom (1948). What exactly is an "Unamerican Activity?" How do you suppose Meiklejohn viewed the McCarthy era? For a narrowing construction of the meaning of "unamerican activities" as it is used in the House of Representatives Unamerican Activities Committee see Barenblatt v. United States, 360 U.S. 109, 79 S.Ct. 1081, 3 L.Ed.2d 1115 (1960), and compare Watkins v. U. S., 354 U.S. 178, 77 S.Ct. 1173, 1 L.Ed.2d 1273 (1957).

THOMAS I. EMERSON, THE SYSTEM OF FREEDOM OF EXPRESSION

Selections from pages 6–15.

. . . The system of freedom of expression in a democratic society rests upon four main premises. These may be stated, in capsule form, as follows:

First, freedom of expression is essential as a means of assuring individual self-fulfillment. The proper end of man is the realization of his character and potentialities as a human being. For the achievement of this self-realization the mind must be free. Hence suppression of belief, opinion, or other expression is an affront to the dignity of man, a negation of man's essential nature. Moreover, man in his capacity as a member of society has a right to share in the common decisions that affect him. To cut off his search for truth, or his expression of it, is to elevate society and the state to a despotic command over him and to place him under the arbitrary control of others.

Second, freedom of expression is an essential process for advancing knowledge and discovering truth. An individual who seeks knowledge and truth must hear all sides of the question, consider all alternatives, test his judgment by exposing it to opposition, and make full use of different minds. Discussion must be kept open no matter how certainly true an accepted opinion may seem to be; many of the most widely acknowledged truths have turned out to be erroneous. Conversely, the same principle applies no matter how false or pernicious the new opinion appears to be; for the unaccepted opinion may be true or partially true and, even if wholly false, its presentation and open discussion compel a rethinking and retesting of the accepted opinion. The reasons which make open discussion essential for an intelligent individual judgment likewise make it imperative for rational social judgment.

Third, freedom of expression is essential to provide for participation in decision making by all members of society. This is particularly significant for political decisions. Once one accepts the premise of the Declaration of Independence—that governments "derive their just powers from the consent of the governed"—it follows that the governed must, in order to exercise their right of consent, have full freedom of expression both in forming individual judgments and in forming the common judgment. The principle also carries beyond the political realm. It embraces the right to participate in the building of the whole culture, and includes freedom of expression in religion, literature, art, science, and all areas of human learning and knowledge.

Finally, freedom of expression is a method of achieving a more adaptable and hence a more stable community, of maintaining the precarious balance between healthy cleavage and necessary consensus. This follows because suppression of discussion makes a rational judgment impossible, substituting force for reason; because suppression promotes inflexibility and stultification, preventing society from adjusting to changing circumstances or developing new ideas; and because suppression conceals the real problems confronting a society, diverting public attention from the critical issues. At the same time the process of open discussion promotes greater cohesion in a society because people are more ready to accept decisions that go against them if they have a part in the decision-making process. Moreover, the state at all times retains adequate powers to promote unity and to suppress resort to force. Freedom of expression thus provides a framework in which the conflict necessary to the progress of a society can take place without destroying the society. It is an essential mechanism for maintaining the balance between stability and change.

The validity of the foregoing premises has never been proved or disproved, and probably could not be. Nevertheless our society is based upon the faith that they hold true and, in maintaining a system of freedom of expression, we act upon that faith. The considerations just outlined thus represent the values we seek in a system of freedom of expression and the functions that system is intended to perform. It should be added that, while our current system of freedom of expression is a product of constitutional liberalism, the values and functions which underlie it are essential to any open society regardless of the particular form its political, economic and social institutions may take.

Two basic implications of the theory underlying our system of freedom of expression need to be emphasized. The first is that it is not a general measure of the individual's right to freedom of expression that any particular exercise of that right may be thought to promote or retard other goals of the society. The theory asserts that freedom of expression, while not the sole or sufficient end of society, is a good in itself, or at least an essential element in a good society. The society may seek to achieve other or more inclusive ends—such as virtue, justice, equality, or the maximum realization of the potentialities of its members. These are not necessarily gained by accepting the rules for freedom of expression. But, as a general proposition, the society may not seek them by suppressing the beliefs or opinions of individual members. To achieve these other goals it must rely upon other methods: the use of counter-expression and the regulation or control of conduct which is not expression. Hence the right to control individual expression, on the ground that it is judged to promote good or evil, justice or injustice, equality or inequality, is not, speaking generally, within the competence of the good society.

The second implication, in a sense a corollary of the first, is that the theory rests upon a fundamental distinction between belief, opinion, and communication of ideas on the one hand, and different forms of conduct on the other. For shorthand purposes we refer to this distinction hereafter as one between "expression" and "action." As just observed, in order to achieve its desired goals, a society or the state is entitled to exercise control over action—whether by prohibiting or compelling it—on an entirely different and vastly more extensive basis. But expression occupies an especially protected position. In this sector of human conduct, the social right of suppression or compulsion is at its lowest point, in most respects nonexistent. A majority of one has the right to control action, but a minority of one has the right to talk.

This marking off of the special status of expression is a crucial ingredient of the basic theory for several reasons. In the first place, thought and communication are the fountainhead of all expression of the individual personality. To cut off the flow at the source is to dry up the whole stream. Freedom at this point is essential to all other freedoms. Hence society must withhold its right of suppression until the stage of action is reached. Secondly, expression is normally conceived as doing less injury to other social goals than action. It generally has less immediate consequences, is less irremediable in its impact. Thirdly, the power of society and the state over the individual is so pervasive, and construction of doctrines, institutions, and administrative practices to limit this power so difficult, that only by drawing such a protective line between expression and action is it possible to strike a safe balance between authority and freedom.

The Dynamics of Limitation

In constructing and maintaining a system of freedom of expression the major controversies have arisen not over acceptance of the basic theory, but in attempting to fit its values and functions into a more comprehensive scheme of social goals. These issues have revolved around the question of what limitations, if any, ought to be imposed upon freedom of expression in order to reconcile that interest with other individual and social interests sought by the good society. Most of our efforts in the past to formulate rules for limiting freedom of expression have been seriously defective through failure to take into consideration the realistic context on which such limitations are administered. The crux of the problem is that the limitations, whatever they may be, must be applied by one group of human beings to other human beings.

First of all, it is necessary to recognize the powerful forces that impel men towards the elimination of unorthodox expression. Most men have a strong inclination, for rational or irrational reasons, to suppress opposition. On the other hand, persons who stand up against society and challenge the traditional view usually have similarly strong feelings about the issues they raise. Thus dissent often is not pitched in conventional terms, nor does it follow customary standards of polite expression. Moreover, the forces of inertia within a society ordinarily resist the expression of new ideas or the pressures of the underprivileged who seek a change. And the longer-run logic of the traditional theory may not be immediately apparent to untutored participants in the conflict. Suppression of opinion may thus seem an entirely plausible course of action; tolerance a weakness or a foolish risk.

Thus it is clear that the problem of maintaining a system of freedom of expression in a society is one of the most complex any society has to face. Self-restraint, self-discipline, and maturity are required. The theory is essentially a highly sophisticated one. The members of the society must be willing to sacrifice individual and short-term advantage for social and long-range goals. And the process must operate in a context that is charged with emotion and subject to powerful conflicting forces of self-interest.

These considerations must be weighed in attempting to construct a theory of limitations. A system of free expression can be successful only when it rests upon the strongest possible commitment to the positive right and the narrowest possible basis for exceptions. And any such exceptions must be clear-cut, precise, and readily controlled. Otherwise the forces that press toward restriction will break through the openings, and freedom of expression will become the exception and suppression the rule.

A second major consideration in imposing restrictions upon expression is the difficulty of framing precise limitations. The object of the limitation is usually not the expression itself but its feared consequences. Repression of expression is thus purely a preventive measure and, like all preventive measures, cuts far more widely and deeply than is necessary to control the ensuing conduct. Moreover, the infinite varieties and subtleties of language and other forms of communication make it impossible to construct a limitation upon expression in definite terms. Thus a wide area of expression is brought within reach of the limitation and enormous discretionary power placed in the hands of those who administer it.

Again, the apparatus of government required for enforcement of limitations on expression, by its very nature, tends towards administrative extremes. Officials charged with the duties of suppression already have or tend to develop excessive zeal in the performance of their task. The accompanying techniques of enforcement—the investigations, surveillance, searches and seizures, secret informers, voluminous files on the suspect—all tend to exert a repressive influence on freedom of expression. In addition, the restrictive measures are readily subject to distortion and to use for ulterior purposes.

Finally we must take into account the whole impact of restriction upon the healthy functioning of a free society. Limitations are seldom applied except in an atmosphere of public fear and hysteria. This may be deliberately aroused or may simply be the inevitable accompaniment of repression. Under such circumstances the doctrines and institutions for enforcing the limitations are subjected to intense pressures. Moreover, while some of the more hardy may be willing to defy the opposition and suffer the consequences, the more numerous are likely to be unwilling to run the risks. Similarly, persons whose cooperation is needed to permit the full flow of open discussion—those who own the means of publication or the facilities for communication—are likely to be frightened into withholding their patronage and assistance.

The lesson of experience, in short, is that the limitations imposed on discussion, as they operate in practice, tend readily and quickly to destroy the whole structure of free expression. They are very difficult to keep in hand; the exceptions are likely to swallow up the principle. Maintenance of a system of free expression, therefore, is not an easy task. This is especially true as we confront the conditions of today. We have tended over the years to refine and delineate more carefully the restrictions we seek to impose. But the new problems arising out of modern industrial society make the issues more delicate and troublesome than at any other time in our history.

ACADEMIC FREEDOM

AMERICAN CIVIL LIBERTIES UNION, ACADEMIC FREEDOM AND ACADEMIC RESPONSIBILITY

A.C.L.U., 156 Fifth Ave., N.Y.C., February 1956, pp. 5–16.

Academic Freedom and Academic Responsibility

Academic freedom and responsibility are here defined as the liberty and obligation to study, to investigate, to present and interpret, and to discuss facts and ideas concerning man, human society, and the physical and biological world in all branches and fields of learning.

They imply no limitations other than those imposed by generally accepted standards of art, scholarship, and science. They include the right within and without institutions of learning to be free from any special limitations of investigation, expression, and discussion. As citizens, students and teachers have the rights accorded to all citizens.

Outside the academic scene the teacher has no less freedom than other citizens. He is not required because of his profession to maintain a timorous silence as a price of professional status. On the contrary his greater knowledge imposes upon him the two-fold duty of advancing new and useful ideas and of helping to bury ideas which are outworn. However, since the public may judge his profession and his institution by his utterances, he should make every effort to maintain high professional excellence and at the same time to indicate that he does not speak for the institution which employs him. When he speaks or writes as an individual he should be free from both institutional and public censorship or discipline.

A time of crisis puts pressure on the schools to accept and inculcate current official interpretations of human behavior. Yet it is precisely in time of crisis that it is valuable democratic strategy to encourage the presentation of contrasting viewpoints and to cause students to realize that they are free to draw such conclusions as they think wise. As a member of an academic community and particularly as a teacher, the faculty member is free to present in the field of his professional competence his own opinions or convictions and with them the premises from which they are derived. It is his duty, on the other hand, not to advocate any opinions or convictions derived from a source other than his own free and unbiased pursuit of truth and understanding. Commitments of any kind which interfere with such pursuit are incompatible with the objectives of academic freedom. To the extent that activities of Communists or others represent violations of law the violators should be vigorously prosecuted. When we attempt to prevent divergent thought, however, we neither strengthen democracy nor weaken its enemies.

Anti-democratic groups can readily obtain a strong hold upon a society stricken with a fear of ideas. Unless we as a people give new enthusiasm and support to traditional American democratic principles and practices, we are in grave danger of being victimized by such groups.

The concept of academic freedom, like the concepts of most of our other freedoms, never remains static. It is continually reinterpreted in the light of changing events and conditions. Of recent years it has been extended in two notable and important directions.

1. It was held until about twenty-five years ago that academic freedom related chiefly to colleges and universities. Now, with increased awareness of the vital significance of each stage in the whole

educational process, we realize that all educational institutions must be assured of reasonable freedom.

2. It was earlier held that academic freedom concerned only the interests of teachers and that it only incidentally touched upon interests of students. Now we recognize that the indispensable basis of this liberty is freedom of inquiry and discussion within the whole institution and we realize that the distinction between teacher-freedom and student-freedom is artificial and should be discarded. It is to the interest of the public as a whole that this freedom be maintained for both students and teachers.

Our further discussion of academic freedom and responsibility falls into three sections. These restate ACLU interpretations of what academic freedom and responsibility mean (1) for students, (2) for teachers, and (3) for administrators and the community. . . .

The Meaning of Academic Freedom and Academic Responsibility for Teachers

Academic freedom and responsibility of teachers embraces two distinct areas: (1) the conduct of a teacher apart from specifically professional responsibilities and (2) his conduct in teaching and other activities directly related to professional responsibilities. An examination of the following principles reveals that the ACLU aligns itself with those adopted by the American Association of University Professors in 1947 and reaffirmed in 1950.

1. *When not engaged in specifically professional activities, the teacher should be able to function with the freedom of any other citizen*

a. *Freedom of Association:* In his private capacity the teacher should be as free as any other citizen to participate in political, religious, and social movements and organizations and in any other lawful activity, and to hold and to express publicly his political, religious, economic, and other views. The fact of his being a teacher should not debar him from any activities open to other citizens.

b. *Freedom of Expression:* The teacher should be as free as any other citizen to write on any subject which interests him. In the field of his professional competence he should speak and write mindful of the special responsibilities that professional standards impose. When acting as a private citizen, he should make it clear that he speaks, writes, and acts for himself and not for his institution. He should, however, be free to use his academic title for purposes of identification.

c. *Freedom to Organize:* Like any other professional or nonprofessional worker, the teacher should be free to organize with others to protect group interests, or to join existing unions or other organizations for such purposes. Any attempt on the part of an administration or other agency to prevent the establishment of such an organization, or to hamper its activities, or to discriminate against its members, is a serious infringement on the freedom of teachers.

d. *Oaths:* Teachers should not be required to take any special oath of loyalty to the government. We object to the irrelevance and futility of such special oaths and to their use as thought-control devices. No one should be subjected, as a condition of holding a teaching position, to any test of religious belief or of political belief other than his pledge to support the Constitution of his state and of the United States. A test oath is the first step toward tyranny.

2. *The criteria of performance for a teacher should be those associated with personal and professional integrity in a democractic society*

a. *Professional Independence:* The basic question in this regard is whether the schools and colleges of a democracy should be independent institutions guided by professional standards of learning and teaching and scholarship, or whether they should be instruments of current national policy or of other special interests. The ACLU takes the position that the educational system in a democracy should be independent of government policy or that of any other special interest and free to carry out its own highest standards.

b. *Criteria of Appointment and Tenure:* A teacher should be appointed on the basis of his teaching ability and his competence in his professional field, not on the basis of his race, nationality, creed, religious or political belief or affiliation; a proper exception exists in the right of a private institution of publicly declared faith, denomination or special function to select teachers on a basis harmonious with its public declaration. Continuation of appointment and the granting of continuing tenure should depend upon a teacher's performance as a teacher. None of the factors excluded from entering into appointment should influence continuation of appointment.

As a classroom teacher, the teacher should seek to promote an atmosphere of free and earnest inquiry. This should include discussion of controversial issues without the assumption that they are settled in advance or that there is only one "right" answer in matters of dispute. Studying a philosophy or a social theory for the purpose of approving or denouncing it is not studying it with an open mind. Such discussion should include presentation of divergent opinions and doctrines, past and present, on a given subject. The teacher's own judgment forms a part of this material. If his judgment is clearly stated, his students are better able to appraise it and differ from it on the basis of other materials and views placed at their disposal than they would be if he were to attempt to conceal his bias by a claim to "objective" scholarship. No set procedures for conduct of a class or for use of materials can guarantee the teacher's own integrity or take its place.

c. *Relationship of a Teacher's Views and Associations to his Teaching Position:* The central issue, in considering a teacher's fitness, is his own performance in his subject and his relationship with his students. The ACLU opposes as contrary to democratic liberties any ban or regulation which would prohibit the employment as a teacher of any person solely because of his views or associations, such as Communist or Fascist.

The ACLU does not oppose the ouster of any teacher found lacking in professional integrity. It will not defend a teacher duly discharged after proof that he has misused his position to pervert the academic process.

On the other hand, in the absence of substantial evidence of perversion of the academic process, the ACLU opposes the prohibition in educational employment of any person based even in part on his views or associations, such as Communist or Fascist. Even though a teacher may be linked with religious dogmatists or political authoritarians, the ACLU believes that he must nevertheless be appraised as an individual.

In advocating the principle of not imposing any tests on the beliefs or associations of teachers in public institutions the ACLU has been challenged by those who contend that a democratic society can not tolerate in its public schools teachers with anti-democratic beliefs or associations. The contention would be defensible if we could secure common agreement on what we mean by democratic and anti-democratic.

If we accept the views of dominant forces current at any one time or place there will be no end to the tests imposed on the fitness of teachers. If Communists are the main target today, as anarchists, socialists and the I.W.W. were a generation ago there will be some other main target tomorrow. What we do today to outlaw from teaching members of presently detested organizations creates the precedents by which all freedom of teaching can be destroyed. The ACLU stands on the principle that it is far better for our democracy to run the calculated risks of establishing freedom than to suffer the already proved dangers of repression.

Believing that an individualized judgment (as against generalized condemnation) is a basic democratic value, the ACLU urges the necessity for appraising the work of the individual teacher. The recent drives to discover Communist teachers illustrate the dangers of proceeding without specific charges that relate to a person's own conduct. In point of fact few Communists have been found in the nation's schools and colleges. But campaigns to expel Communists from educational posts have rarely stopped at their first objective; they have instead resulted in attacks upon persons who merely hold unpopular opinions. As a consequence, teachers everywhere have been made less courageous and less independent in the pursuit of truth, more cautious and more subservient.

The harm done by a few teachers who might be undetected in misusing their teaching positions for political or religious ends, is far less than the harm that is done by making all teachers less responsible and less courageous. The political or religious screening of all teachers is far more dangerous to education than the presence of the occasional teacher who is misusing his profession. Intelligent, qualified persons are discouraged from going into the teaching profession by the knowledge that they may be dismissed for nonconformity.

The ACLU will intervene in appropriate cases involving the discharge of a teacher when action is taken by administrative officials without a prior unfavorable judgment by the teacher's colleagues based on professional incompetence, immoral conduct, or perversion of academic process.

d. *Questioning of Teachers:* Where there is substantial evidence of perversion of the academic process, but only then, a committee of colleagues may in an academic hearing inquire into the beliefs and associations of a teacher, to the extent that they may be relevant to the asserted unprofessional conduct.

The refusal of a teacher to answer questions put by a legislative committee does not in itself constitute substantial evidence of perversion of the academic process. The ACLU does not question the right —many would say the obligation—of teachers to investigate charges of incompetence or perversion of the academic process made against one of their colleagues, whenever and however these may come into issue. But the Union does not believe that any such issue may be said to arise by reason of the refusal of a teacher to answer questions put by a legislative committee, however advisable or inadvisable such refusal may be for legal or other reasons.

A teacher asked about another teacher's views and associations should distinguish among the decisions to be made. He *may be required* to decide in terms of his legal position as a witness, and on this point he should seek legal advice. He *may wish* to decide by reference to his personal moral code and conscience. He *must* decide in terms of academic freedom because he is a teacher. The ACLU position is this: questions about another teacher's views or associations are always to be considered improper because they immediately subvert that sense of freedom which is the life center of the academic process.

e. *Campus Relations With Students Outside the Classroom:* The same standards of professional conduct which govern the teacher in the classroom should be observed by him elsewhere on the campus.

f. *Freedom of Research:* As a scholar and research worker, the teacher should be free to pursue truth in whatever form best expresses his convictions.

The Meaning of Academic Freedom and Academic Responsibility for
Administrators and for the Community

Students and teachers are the center of any educational institution. Academic freedom and responsibility therefore serve and benefit the community to the extent that they are regarded as the right and obligation of students and teachers. It is the duty of administrators to provide the atmosphere in which academic freedom will flourish.

Let us look at what academic freedom and academic responsibility should mean to administrators and to the community in terms of the relationships (1) between the community and the educational institution, (2) between the administrator and the community, and (3) between the administrator and students and teachers.

1. *The Community has the right to demand that the educational institution shall be competently staffed and capably administered*

a. *Control of Curriculum:* Matters of curriculum properly are the responsibility of the professional staff who are under obligation to be guided by high professional standards of scholarship and of teaching methods and by full awareness of the community's educational needs. The community has the right to expect that its youth will be made aware of the common principles underlying our general culture and civilization. It has neither the right to, nor indeed any social justification for, insistence that a discussion of deviations from accepted principles be excluded from the curriculum. It may properly insist that teachers do not present deviant ideas in such a manner as to imply that they are generally accepted.

b. *Personal Conduct of Teachers:* The community may properly expect of its teachers a standard of personal conduct comparable to that required of other responsible professional members of the community and a standard of public conduct harmonious with the teacher's position. The teacher must not be deemed to have sacrificed any of his rights as a private citizen. He should be as free as any other person to participate in his private capacity in political and social movements and in any other lawful activity and to hold and to express publicly his political, economic, religious and other views.

c. *Separation of Church and State:* Parents and citizens generally have a right to expect that in the public schools and colleges there will be no effort by the staff to offer instruction or to institute ritualistic or dramatic presentations of a sectarian nature. The United States Supreme Court has reaffirmed that in the public schools as elsewhere in our governmental life there must be a "wall of separation" between the churches and governmental agencies. Parents also have a right to anticipate that, when it is contrary to their religious convictions, their children will not be obliged to receive military education or to render flag salutes. It is of course equally valid that such parents should have no right to interfere with the requirement of such practices upon the part of other children.

d. *Curriculum Content by Legislation:* The ACLU looks with apprehension upon the practice of determining curriculum content by means of legislative statute. The ACLU feels that this opens up an avenue for powerful groups to impose their educational ideas upon an unsuspecting community.

2. *The administrator should serve and not dominate a school system or college*

a. *Creation of an Atmosphere of Freedom:* Administrators are often tempted to regard themselves as something more than facilitators of the study and teaching functions of their schools. Opportunism and considerations of expediency exert pressures upon them to restrict the areas of free investigation, discussion, and creation permissible to students and teachers. Our schools develop as mediums of growth and opportunity to the extent that administrators are able to resist the temptation to seek safety or prestige by emphasis upon their function as leaders.

b. *Liaison Functions:* Administrators, whether public or private, see themselves properly in two principal perspectives. On the one hand, the community entrusts them with the task of representing reasonable and legitimate community objectives in the administration of the schools. When special pressures bear heavily upon them, they can perform their proper role only by withstanding such pressures in the interests of broad and continuing community obligations. On the other hand, the community entrusts administrators with the task of serving as a liaison between itself and the desirable ferment to be found in a healthy body of students and teachers. In other words, the administrator should understand quite sympathetically and broadly the reasonable and legitimate objectives of both community and student-teacher body, and he should attempt as well as he can to facilitate the long-term aims of both. When there is a necessary choice, the freedom and responsibility of students and teachers should always have priority.

c. *Resistance to Pressure:* The administrator should resist the efforts of pressure groups which seek to eliminate experimental curriculums, or which seek to influence the curriculums in a particular direction against the advice of the professional staff.

JOINT STATEMENT ON RIGHTS AND FREEDOMS OF STUDENTS

AMERICAN ASSOCIATION OF UNIVERSITY PROFESSORS

Policy Documents and Reports 67–69 (1973).

In June, 1967, a joint committee, comprised of representatives from the American Association of University Professors, U. S. National Student Association, Association of American Colleges, National Association of Student Personnel Administrators, and National Association of Women Deans and Counselors, met in Washington, D.C., and drafted the Joint Statement on Rights and Freedoms of Students *published below.*

Since its formulation, the Joint Statement has been endorsed by each of its five national sponsors, as well as by a number of other professional bodies.

Preamble

Academic institutions exist for the transmission of knowledge, the pursuit of truth, the development of students, and the general well-being of society.   Free inquiry and free expression are indispensable to the attainment of these goals.   As members of the academic community, students should be encouraged to develop the capacity for critical judgment and to engage in a sustained and independent search for truth.   Institutional procedures for achieving these purposes may vary from campus to campus, but the minimal standards of academic freedom of students outlined below are essential to any community of scholars.

Freedom to teach and freedom to learn are inseparable facets of academic freedom.   The freedom to learn depends upon appropriate opportunities and conditions in the classroom, on the campus, and in the larger community.   Students should exercise their freedom with responsibility.

The responsibility to secure and to respect general conditions conducive to the freedom to learn is shared by all members of the academic community.   Each college and university has a duty to develop policies and procedures which provide and safeguard this freedom.   Such policies and procedures should be developed at each institution within the framework of general standards and with the broadest possible participation of the members of the academic community.   The purpose of this statement is to enumerate the essential provisions for student freedom to learn.

I.   Freedom of Access to Higher Education

The admissions policies of each college and university are a matter of institutional choice provided that each college and university makes clear the characteristics and expectations of students which it considers relevant to success in the institution's program. While church-related institutions may give admission preference to students of their own persuasion, such a preference should be clearly and publicly stated.   Under no circumstances should a student be barred from admission to a particular institution on the basis of race.   Thus, within the limits of its facilities, each college and university should be open to all students who are qualified according to its admission standards.   The facilities and services of a college should be open to all of its enrolled students, and institutions should use their influence to secure equal access for all students to public facilities in the local community.

II.   In the Classroom

The professor in the classroom and in conference should encourage free discussion, inquiry, and expression.   Student performance should be evaluated solely on an academic basis, not on opinions or conduct in matters unrelated to academic standards.

A.   *Protection of Freedom of Expression*

Students should be free to take reasoned exception to the data or views offered in any course of study and to reserve judgment about matters of opinion, but they are responsible for learning the content of any course of study for which they are enrolled.

B.   *Protection against Improper Academic Evaluation*

Students should have protection through orderly procedures against prejudiced or capricious academic evaluation.   At the same time, they are responsible for maintaining standards of academic performance established for each course in which they are enrolled.

C.   *Protection against Improper Disclosure*

Information about student views, beliefs, and political associations which professors acquire in the course of their work as instructors, advisers, and counselors should be considered confidential.   Protection against improper disclosure is a serious professional obligation.   Judgments of ability and character may be provided under appropriate circumstances, normally with the knowledge or consent of the student.

III.   Student Records

Institutions should have a carefully considered policy as to the information which should be part of a student's permanent educational record and as to the conditions of its disclosure.   To minimize the risk of improper disclosure, academic and disciplinary records should be separate, and the conditions of access to each should be set forth in an explicit policy statement. Transcripts of academic records should contain only information about academic status. Information from disciplinary or counseling files should not be available to unauthorized persons on campus, or to any person off campus without the express consent of the student involved except under legal compulsion or in cases where the safety of persons or property is involved. No records should be kept which reflect the political activities or beliefs of students. Provisions should also be made for periodic routine destruction of noncurrent disciplinary records. Administrative staff and faculty members should respect confidential information about students which they acquire in the course of their work.

IV.   Student Affairs

In student affairs, certain standards must be maintained if the freedom of students is to be preserved.

A.   *Freedom of Association*

Students bring to the campus a variety of interests previously acquired and develop many new interests as members of the academic community. They should be free to organize and join associations to promote their common interests.

1.   The membership, policies, and actions of a student organization usually will be determined by vote of only those persons who hold bona fide membership in the college or university community.

2.   Affiliation with an extramural organization should not of itself disqualify a student organization from institutional recognition.

3.   If campus advisers are required, each organization should be free to choose its own adviser, and institutional recognition should not be withheld or withdrawn solely because of the inability of a student organization to secure an adviser. Campus advisers may advise organizations in the exercise of responsibility, but they should not have the authority to control the policy of such organizations.

4.   Student organizations may be required to submit a statement of purpose, criteria for membership, rules of procedures, and a current list of officers. They should not be required to submit a membership list as a condition of institutional recognition.

5.   Campus organizations, including those affiliated with an extramural organization, should be open to all students without respect to race, creed, or national origin, except for religious qualifications which may be required by organizations whose aims are primarily sectarian.

B.   *Freedom of Inquiry and Expression*

1.   Students and student organization should be free to examine and discuss all questions of interest to them, and to express opinions

publicly and privately. They should always be free to support causes by orderly means which do not disrupt the regular and essential operation of the institution. At the same time, it should be made clear to the academic and the larger community that in their public expressions or demonstrations students or student organizations speak only for themselves.

2.   Students should be allowed to invite and to hear any person of their own choosing. Those routine procedures required by an institution before a guest speaker is invited to appear on campus should be designed only to insure that there is orderly scheduling of facilities and adequate preparation for the event, and that the occasion is conducted in a manner appropriate to an academic community. The institutional control of campus facilities should not be used as a device of censorship. It should be made clear to the academic and large community that sponsorship of guest speakers does not necessarily imply approval or endorsement of the views expressed, either by the sponsoring group or the institution.

C.   *Student Participation in Institutional Government*

As constituents of the academic community, students should be free, individually and collectively, to express their views on issues of institutional policy and on matters of general interest to the student body. The student body should have clearly defined means to participate in the formulation and application of institutional policy affecting academic and student affairs. The role of the student government and both its general and specific responsibilities should be made explicit, and the actions of the student government within the areas of its jurisdiction should be reviewed only through orderly and prescribed procedures.

D.   *Student Publications*

Student publications and the student press are a valuable aid in establishing and maintaining an atmosphere of free and responsible discussion and of intellectual exploration on the campus. They are a means of bringing student concerns to the attention of the faculty and the institutional authorities and of formulating student opinion on various issues on the campus and in the world at large.

Whenever possible the student newspaper should be an independent corporation financially and legally separate from the university. Where financial and legal autonomy is not possible, the institution, as the publisher of student publications, may have to bear the legal responsibility for the contents of the publications. In the delegation of editorial responsibility to students the institution must provide sufficient editorial freedom and financial autonomy for the student publications to maintain their integrity of purpose as vehicles for free inquiry and free expression in an academic community.

Institutional authorities, in consultation with students and faculty, have a responsibility to provide written clarification of the role of the student publications, the standards to be used in their evaluation, and the limitations on external control of their operation. At the same time, the editorial freedom of student editors and managers entails corollary responsibilities to be governed by the canons of responsible journalism, such as the avoidance of libel, indecency, undocumented allegations, attacks on personal integrity, and the techniques of harassment and innuendo. As safeguards for the editorial freedom of student publications the following provisions are necessary.

1. The student press should be free of censorship and advance approval of copy, and its editors and managers should be free to develop their own editorial policies and news coverage.

2. Editors and managers of student publications should be protected from arbitrary suspension and removal because of student, faculty, administrative, or public disapproval of editorial policy or content. Only for proper and stated causes should editors and managers be subject to removal and then by orderly and prescribed procedures. The agency responsible for the appointment of editors and managers should be the agency responsible for their removal.

3. All university published and financed student publications should explicitly state on the editorial page that the opinions there expressed are not necessarily those of the college, university, or student body.

V.   Off-Campus Freedom of Students

A.   *Exercise of Rights of Citizenship*

College and university students are both citizens and members of the academic community. As citizens, students should enjoy the same freedom of speech, peaceful assembly, and right of petition that other citizens enjoy and, as members of the academic community, they are subject to the obligations which accrue to them by virtue of this membership. Faculty members and administrative officials should insure that institutional powers are not employed to inhibit such intellectual and personal development of students as is often promoted by their exercise of the rights of citizenship both on and off campus.

B.   *Institutional Authority and Civil Penalties*

Activities of students may upon occasion result in violation of law. In such cases, institutional officials should be prepared to apprise students of sources of legal counsel and may offer other assistance. Students who violate the law may incur penalties prescribed by civil authorities, but institutional authority should never be used merely to duplicate the function of general laws. Only where the institution's interests as an academic community are distinct and clearly involved should the special authority of the institution be as-

serted. The student who incidentally violates institutional regulations in the course of his off-campus activity, such as those relating
to class attendance, should be subject to no greater penalty than would
normally be imposed. Institutional action should be independent of
community pressure. . . .

NOTES AND QUESTIONS

1. What part, or parts, if any, of the provisions in the above statements
    need revising? Why? Generally see, Note, Developments in the
    Law: Academic Freedom, 81 Harv.Law Rev. 1045 (1968).

2. Should any provision be changed in order to apply properly to a "com-
    mon school"? It is sometimes asserted that academic freedom stops
    with the university and does not extend to the common schools.
    What are the reasons that lead to this view? Is the view valid? Can
    it not be asserted that properly viewed the common school teacher
    and the university research scholar share the same ultimate faith?
    The task of the effective teacher is not only to disseminate available
    knowledge, but, more importantly, to teach the methods and criteria
    of objective inquiry and responsible evaluation. Of even greater im-
    portance is the task of the teacher to bring student awareness into
    full and profound appreciation and respect for objective fact and
    value and for intellectual clarity and integrity. Conceived properly,
    the aims of effective teaching are in harmony with those of the re-
    search scholar. Properly conceived and executed, teaching gives an
    enriched meaning to the life of the student. But it does more than
    this: it also is indispensable to achieving the proper goals of the
    University, and constitutes the means for achieving effective training
    for responsible citizenship and leadership in a free and democratic
    society. It should be noted that both research and teaching can be
    done excellently, or either can be done poorly, depending upon the
    abilities and talents of the person. But, while academic freedom
    might apply a bit differently to each of the grades of a common
    school, reason appears to insist that academic freedom extend
    throughout our school system—to the common schools as well as to the
    University. Is academic freedom protected by the constitution?

CONSTITUTIONAL PROTECTION OF THE RIGHT TO
ACADEMIC FREEDOM

SWEEZY v. NEW HAMPSHIRE

Supreme Court of the United States, 1957.
354 U.S. 234, 77 S.Ct. 1203, 1 L.Ed.2d 1311.

[Paul Sweezy, a former professor of economics at Harvard, describes himself as a "classical Marxist" and "Socialist." He has written books and articles on the general theme of the inevitable collapse
of capitalism and rise of socialism. He was invited to the University

of New Hampshire where he gave several lectures expressing his views. New Hampshire's Revised Statutes, 1955, ch. 588, § 1, provided, " 'Subversive person' means any person who commits, attempts to commit, or aids in the commission, or advocates, abets, advises or teaches, by any means any person to commit, attempt to commit, or aid in the commission of any act intended to overthrow, destroy or alter, or to assist in the overthrow, destruction or alteration of, the constitutional form of the government of the United States, or of the state of New Hampshire, or any political subdivision of either of them, by force, or violence; or who is a member of a subversive organization or a foreign subversive organization."

"Pursuant to an investigation of subversive activities authorized by a joint resolution of both houses of the New Hampshire Legislature, the State Attorney General subpoenaed petitioner [Sweezy] before him on January 8, 1954, for extensive questioning. Among the matters about which petitioner was questioned were: details of his career and personal life, whether he was then or ever had been a member of the Communist Party, whether he had ever attended its meetings, whether he had ever attended meetings that he knew were also attended by Party members, whether he knew any Communists in or out of the State, whether he knew named persons with alleged connections with organizations either on the United States Attorney General's list or cited by the Un-American Activities Committee of the United States House of Representatives or had ever attended meetings with them, whether he had ever taught or supported the overthrow of the State by force or violence or had ever known or assisted any persons or groups that had done so, whether he had ever been connected with organizations on the Attorney General's list, whether he had supported or written in behalf of a variety of allegedly subversive, named causes, conferences, periodicals, petitions, and attempts to raise funds for the legal defense of certain persons, whether he knew about the Progressive Party, what positions he had held in it, whether he had been a candidate for Presidential Elector for that Party, whether certain persons were in that Party, whether Communists had influenced or been members of the Progressive Party, whether he had sponsored activities in behalf of the candidacy of Henry A. Wallace, whether he advocated replacing the capitalist system with another economic system, whether his conception of socialism involved force and violence, whether by his writings and actions he had ever attempted to advance the Societ Union's 'propaganda line,' whether he had ever attended meetings of the Liberal Club at the University of New Hampshire, whether the magazine of which he was co-editor was 'a Communist-line publication,' and whether he knew named persons.

"[Sweezy] answered most of these questions, making it very plain that he had never been a Communist, never taught violent overthrow of the Government, never knowingly associated with Communists in the State, but was a socialist believer in peaceful change who had at one time belonged to certain organizations on the list of the United States Attorney General (which did not include the Progressive Party) or cited by the House Un-American Activities Committee. He declined to answer as irrelevant or violative of free speech guarantees certain questions about the Progressive Party and whether he knew particular persons. He stated repeatedly, however, that he had no knowledge of Communists or of Communist influence in the Progressive Party, and he testified that he had been a candidate for that Party, signing the required loyalty oath, and that he did not know whether an alleged Communist leader was active in the Progressive Party.

"Despite the exhaustive scope of this inquiry, the Attorney General again subpoenaed [Sweezy] to testify on June 3, 1954, and the interrogation was similarly sweeping. Petitioner again answered virtually all questions, including those concerning the relationship of named persons to the Communist Party or other causes deemed subversive under state laws, alleged Communist influence on all organizations with which he had been connected including the Progressive Party, and his own participation in organizations other than the Progressive Party and its antecedent, the Progressive Citizens of America. He refused, however, to answer certain questions regarding (1) a lecture given by him at the University of New Hampshire, (2) activities of himself and others in the Progressive political organizations, and (3) 'opinions and beliefs,' invoking the constitutional guarantees of free speech.

"The Attorney General then petitioned the Superior Court to order petitioner to answer questions in these categories. The court ruled that petitioner had to answer those questions pertaining to the lectures and to the Progressive Party and its predecessor but not those otherwise pertaining to 'opinions and beliefs.' Upon petitioner's refusal to answer the questions sanctioned by the court, he was found in contempt of court and ordered committed to the county jail until purged of contempt.

"The Supreme Court of New Hampshire affirmed the order of the Superior Court. It held that the questions at issue were relevant and that no constitutional provision permitted petitioner to frustrate the State's demands. . . .

"The questions that petitioner refused to answer regarding the university lecture, the third given by him in three years at the invitation of the faculty for humanities, were:

'What was the subject of your lecture?'

'Didn't you tell the class at the University of New Hampshire on Monday, March 22, 1954, that Socialism was inevitable in this country?'

'Did you advocate Marxism at that time?'

'Did you express the opinion, or did you make the statement at that time that Socialism was inevitable in America?'

'Did you in this last lecture on March 22 or in any of the former lectures espouse the theory of dialectical materialism?'

'I have in the file here a statement from a person who attended your class, and I will read it in part because I don't want you to think I am just fishing. "His talk this time was on the inevitability of the Socialist program. It was a glossed-over interpretation of the materialistic dialectic." Now, again I ask you the original question.'

"In response to the first question of this series, petitioner had said at the hearing:

'I would like to say one thing in this connection, Mr. Wyman. I stated under oath at my last appearance that, and I now repeat it, that I do not advocate or in any way further the aim of overthrowing constitutional government by force and violence. I did not so advocate in the lecture I gave at the University of New Hampshire. In fact I have never at any time so advocated in a lecture anywhere. Aside from that I have nothing I want to say about the lecture in question.'

"The New Hampshire Supreme Court, although recognizing that such inquiries 'undoubtedly interfered with the defendant's free exercise' of his constitutionally guaranteed right to lecture, justified the interference on the ground that it would occur 'in the limited area in which the legislative committee may reasonably believe that the overthrow of existing government by force and violence is being or has been taught, advocated or planned, an area in which the interest of the State justifies this intrusion upon civil liberties.' . . . According to the court, the facts that made reasonable the Committee's belief that petitioner had taught violent overthrow in his lecture were that he was a Socialist with a record of affiliation with groups cited by the Attorney General of the United States or the House Un-American Activities Committee and that he was co-editor of an article stating that, although the authors hated violence, it was less to be deplored when used by the Soviet Union than by capitalist countries.

"[Sweezy] stated, in response to questions at the hearing, that he did not know of any Communist interest in, connection with, influence over, activity in, or manipulation of the Progressive Party. He refused to answer, despite court order, the following questions on the ground that, by inquiring into the activities of a lawful political organization, they infringed upon the inviolability of the right to privacy in his political thoughts, actions and associations:

'Was she, Nancy Sweezy, your wife, active in the formation of the Progressive Citizens of America?'

'Was Nancy Sweezy then working with individuals who were then members of the Communist Party?'

'Was Charles Beebe active in forming the Progressive Citizens of America?'

'Did he work with your present wife—Did Charles Beebe work with your present wife in 1947?'

'Did it [a meeting at the home of one Abraham Walenko] have anything to do with the Progressive Party?'

"The Supreme Court of New Hampshire justified this intrusion upon his freedom on the same basis that it upheld questioning about the university lecture, namely, that the restriction was limited to situations where the Committee had reason to believe that violent overthrow of the Government was being advocated or planned. . . ."].

Mr. Chief Justice WARREN announced the judgment of the Court, and delivered an opinion in which Mr. Justices BLACK, DOUGLAS and BRENNAN joined.

. . . The State Supreme Court thus conceded without extended discussion that petitioner's right to lecture and his right to associate with others were constitutionally protected freedoms which had been abridged through this investigation. These conclusions could not be seriously debated. Merely to summon a witness and compel him, against his will, to disclose the nature of his past expressions and associations is a measure of governmental interference in these matters. These are rights which are safeguarded by the Bill of Rights and the Fourteenth Amendment. We believe that there unquestionably was an invasion of petitioner's liberties in the areas of academic freedom and political expression—areas in which government should be extremely reticent to tread.

The essentiality of freedom in the community of American universities is almost self-evident. No one should underestimate the vital role in a democracy that is played by those who guide and train our youth. To impose any strait jacket upon the intellectual leaders in our colleges and universities would imperil the future of our Nation. No field of education is so thoroughly comprehended by man that new discoveries cannot yet be made. Particularly is that true in the social sciences, where few, if any, principles are accepted as absolutes. Scholarship cannot flourish in an atmosphere of suspicion and distrust. Teachers and students must always remain free to inquire, to study and to evaluate, to gain new maturity and understanding; otherwise our civilization will stagnate and die.

Equally manifest as a fundamental principle of a democratic society is political freedom of the individual. Our form of government is built on the premise that every citizen shall have the right to engage in political expression and association. This right was enshrined in the First Amendment of the Bill of Rights. Exercise of these basic freedoms in America has traditionally been through the media of political associations. Any interference with the freedom of a party is simultaneously an interference with the freedom of its adherents. All political ideas cannot and should not be channeled into the programs of our two major parties. History has amply proved the virtue of political activity by minority, dissident groups, who innumerable times have been in the vanguard of democratic thought and whose programs were ultimately accepted. Mere unorthodoxy or dissent from the prevailing mores is not to be condemned. The absence of such voices would be a symptom of grave illness in our society.

Notwithstanding the undeniable importance of freedom in the areas, the Supreme Court of New Hampshire did not consider that the abridgment of petitioner's rights under the Constitution vitiated the investigation. In the view of that court, "the answer lies in a determination of whether the object of the legislative investigation under consideration is such as to justify the restriction thereby imposed upon the defendant's liberties." 100 N.H., at 113–114, 121 A.2d, at 791–792. It found such justification in the legislature's judgment, expressed by its authorizing resolution, that there exists a potential menace from those who would overthrow the government by force and violence. That court concluded that the need for the legislature to be informed on so elemental a subject as the self preservation of government outweighed the deprivation of constitutional rights that occurred in the process.

We do not now conceive of any circumstance wherein a state interest would justify infringement of rights in these fields. But we do not need to reach such fundamental questions of state power to decide this case. The State Supreme Court itself recognized that there was a weakness in its conclusion that the menace of forcible overthrow of the government justified sacrificing constitutional rights. There was a missing link in the chain of reasoning. The syllogism was not complete. There was nothing to connect the questioning of petitioner with this fundamental interest of the State.   .   .   .

The respective roles of the legislature and the investigator thus revealed are of considerable significance to the issue before us. It is eminently clear that the basic discretion of determining the direction of the legislative inquiry has been turned over to the investigative agency.   .   .   .

Instead of making known the nature of the data it desired, the legislature has insulated itself from those witnesses whose rights may be vitally affected by the investigation. Incorporating by reference provisions from its subversive activities act, it has told the Attorney General, in effect to screen the citizenry of New Hampshire to bring to light anyone who fits into the expansive definitions.

Within the very broad area thus committed to the discretion of the Attorney General there may be many facts which the legislature might find useful. There would also be a great deal of data which that assembly would not want or need. In the classes of information that the legislature might deem it desirable to have, there will be some which it could not validly acquire because of the effect upon the constitutional rights of individual citizens. Separating the wheat from the chaff, from the standpoint of the legislature's object, is the legislature's responsibility because it alone can make that judgment. In this case, the New Hampshire legislature has delegated that task to the Attorney General.

As a result, neither we nor the state courts have any assurance that the questions petitioner refused to answer fall into a category of matters upon which the legislature wanted to be informed when it initiated this inquiry. The judiciary are thus placed in an untenable position. Lacking even the elementary fact that the legislature wants certain questions answered and recognizing that petitioner's constitutional rights are in jeopardy, we are asked to approve or disapprove his incarceration for contempt.

In our view, the answer is clear. No one would deny that the infringement of constitutional rights of individuals would violate the guarantee of due process where no state interest underlies the state action. Thus, if the Attorney General's interrogation of petitioner were in fact wholly unrelated to the object of the legislature in authorizing the inquiry, the Due Process Clause would preclude the endangering of constitutional liberties. We believe that an equivalent situation is presented in this case. The lack of any indications that the legislature wanted the information the Attorney General attempted to elicit from petitioner must be treated as the absence of authority. It follows that the use of the contempt power, notwithstanding the interference with constitutional rights, was not in accordance with the due process requirements of the Fourteenth Amendment. . . .

The judgment of the Supreme Court of New Hampshire is

Reversed.

Mr. Justice FRANKFURTER, whom Mr. Justice HARLAN joins, concurring in the result.

. . . When weighed against the grave harm resulting from governmental intrusion into the intellectual life of a university, such justification for compelling a witness to discuss the contents of his lecture appears grossly inadequate. Particularly is this so where the witness has sworn that neither in the lecture nor at any other time did he ever advocate overthrowing the Government by force and violence.

Progress in the natural sciences is not remotely confined to findings made in the laboratory. Insights into the mysteries of nature are born of hypothesis and speculation. The more so is this true in the pursuit of understanding in the groping endeavors of what are called the social sciences, the concern of which is man and society. The problems are that the respective preoccupations and anthropology, economics, law, psychology, sociology and related areas of scholarship are merely departmentalized dealing, by way of manageable division of analysis, with interpenetrating aspects of holistic perplexities. For society's good—if understanding be an essential need of society—inquiries into these problems, speculations about them, stimulation in others of reflection upon them, must be left as unfettered as possible. Political power must abstain from intrusion into this activity of freedom, pursued in the interest of wise government and the people's well-being, except for reasons that are exigent and obviously compelling.

These pages need not be burdened with proof, based on the testimony of a cloud of impressive witnesses, of the dependence of a free society on free universities. This means the exclusion of governmental intervention in the intellectual life of a university. It matters little whether such intervention occurs avowedly or through action that inevitably tends to check the ardor and fearlessness of scholars, qualities at once so fragile and so indispensable for fruitful academic labor. One need only refer to the address of T. H. Huxley at the opening of Johns Hopkins University, the Annual Reports of President A. Lawrence Lowell of Harvard, the Reports of the University Grants Committee in Great Britain, as illustrative items in a vast body of literature. Suffice it to quote the latest expression on this subject. It is also perhaps the most poignant because its plea on behalf of continuing the free spirit of the open universities of South Africa has gone unheeded.

> "In a university knowledge is its own end, not merely a means to an end. A university ceases to be true to its own nature if it becomes the tool of Church or State or any sectional interest. A university is characterized by the spirit of free inquiry, its ideal being the ideal of Socrates—'to follow the argument where it leads.' This implies the right to examine, question, modify or reject traditional ideas and beliefs. Dogma and hypothesis are incompatible, and the concept of an immutable doctrine is repugnant to the spirit of a university. The concern of its scholars is not merely

to add and revise facts in relation to an accepted framework, but to be ever examining and modifying the framework itself.

.   .   .   .

"Freedom to reason and freedom for disputation on the basis of observation and experiment are the necessary conditions for the advancement of scientific knowledge. A sense of freedom is also necessary for creative work in the arts which, equally with scientific research, is the concern of the university.

.   .   .   .

".   .   . It is the business of a university to provide that atmosphere which is most conducive to speculation, experiment and creation. It is an atmosphere in which there prevail 'the four essential freedoms' of a university—to determine for itself on academic grounds who may teach, what may be taught, how it shall be taught, and who may be admitted to study." The Open Universities in South Africa 10–12. (A statement of a conference of senior scholars from the University of Cape Town and the University of the Witwatersrand, including A. v. d. S. Centlivres and Richard Feetham, as Chancellors of the respective universities.)

I do not suggest that what New Hampshire has here sanctioned bears any resemblance to the policy against which this South African remonstrance was directed. I do say that in these matters of the spirit inroads on legitimacy must be resisted at their incipiency. This kind of evil grows by what it is allowed to feed on. The admonition of this Court in another context is applicable here. "It may be that it is the obnoxious thing in its mildest and least repulsive form; but illegitimate and unconstitutional practices get their first footing in that way, namely, by silent approaches and slight deviations from legal modes of procedure."   .   .   .

In the political realm, as in the academic, thought and action are presumptively immune from inquisition by political authority. It cannot require argument that inquiry would be barred to ascertain whether a citizen had voted for one or the other of the two major parties either in a state or national election. Until recently, no difference would have been entertained in regard to inquiries about a voter's affiliations with one of the various so-called third parties that have had their day, or longer, in our political history.   .   .   . The implications of the United States Constitution for national elections and "the concept of ordered liberty" implicit in the Due Process Clause of the Fourteenth Amendment as against the States, Palko v. Connecticut,   .   .   . were not frozen as of 1789 or 1868, respectively. While the language of the Constitution does not change, the changing circumstances of a progressive society for which it was designed yield new and fuller import to its meaning. . . . Whatever, on the basis of massive proof and in the light of history, of which this Court may well take judicial notice, be the justification for not regarding the Communist Party as a conventional political party, no such justification has been afforded in regard to the Progressive Party. A foundation in fact and reason would have to be established far weightier than the intimations that appear in the record to warrant such a view of the Progressive Party. This precludes the questioning that petitioner resisted in regard to that Party.*

. . .

NOTES AND QUESTIONS

1. Was there a unifying rationale for the Court in the Sweezy case? How can one tell? Why is this an important question? Was the portent of Sweezy realized in the Keyishian case, infra?

2. In Shelton v. Tucker, 364 U.S. 479, 81 S.Ct. 247, 5 L.Ed.2d 231 (1960), all public school teachers were placed under an obligation by an Arkansas statute to file, each year, an affidavit listing all organizations to which they contributed funds and to which they belonged during the past five years. This law was declared unconstitutional because it was overly broad:

"The unlimited and indiscriminate sweep of the statute now before us brings it within the ban of our prior cases. The statute's comprehensive interference with associational freedom goes far beyond what might be justified in the exercise of the State's legitimate inquiry into the fitness and competence of its teachers." Moreover, the Supreme Court said:

"It is not disputed that to compel a teacher to disclose his every associational tie is to impair that teacher's right of free association, a right closely allied to freedom of speech and a right which, like free speech, lies at the foundation of a free society. . . . Such interference with personal freedom is conspicuously accented when the teacher serves at the absolute will of those to whom the disclosure must be made—those who any year can terminate the teacher's employment without bringing charges, without notice, without a hearing, without affording an opportunity to explain.

"The statute does not provide that the information it requires be kept confidential. Each school board is left free to deal with the information as it wishes. The record contains evidence to indicate that fear of public disclosure is neither theoretical nor groundless. Even if there were no disclosure to the general public, the pressure upon a teacher to avoid any ties which might displease those who control his professional destiny would be constant and heavy. Public exposure, bringing with it the possibility of public pressures upon school boards to discharge teachers who belong to unpopular or

* A dissenting opinion by Mr. Justice CLARK is omitted.

minority organizations, would simply operate to widen and aggravate the impairment of constitutional liberty.

"The vigilant protection of constitutional freedoms is nowhere more vital than in the community of American schools. . . ."

3. In Elfbrandt v. Russell, 384 U.S. 11, 86 S.Ct. 1238, 16 L.Ed.2d 321 (1966), Arizona required an oath of all state employees, including all school teachers, reading as follows:

"I, (type or print name) do solemnly swear (or affirm) that I will support the Constitution of the United States and the Constitution and laws of the State of Arizona; that I will bear true faith and allegiance to the same, and defend them against all enemies, foreign and domestic, and that I will faithfully and impartially discharge the duties of the office of (name of office) according to the best of my ability, so help me God (or so I do affirm)." Elfbrandt, a teacher and a Quaker, decided she could not in good conscience take the oath, not knowing what it meant and not having the opportunity for a hearing at which its precise scope and meaning could be determined. The Supreme Court held the oath requirement unconstitutional as an infringement of the First Amendment.

". . . One who subscribes to this Arizona oath and who is, or thereafter becomes, a knowing member of an organization which has as 'one of its purposes' the violent overthrow of the government, is subject to immediate discharge and criminal penalties. Nothing in the oath, the statutory gloss, or the construction of the oath and statutes given by the Arizona Supreme Court, purports to exclude association by one who does not subscribe to the organization's unlawful ends. Here as in Baggett v. Bullitt, [377 U.S. 360] the 'hazard of being prosecuted for knowing but guiltless behavior' (id., at 373) is a reality. People often label as 'communist' ideas which they oppose; and they often make up our juries. '[P]rosecutors too are human.' Cramp v. Board of Public Instruction, 368 U.S. 278, 287. Would a teacher be safe and secure in going to a Pugwash Conference? Would it be legal to join a seminar group predominantly Communist and therefore subject to control by those who are said to believe in the overthrow of the Government by force and violence? Juries might convict though the teacher did not subscribe to the wrongful aims of the organization. And there is apparently no machinery provided for getting clearance in advance.

"Those who join an organization but do not share its unlawful purposes and who do not participate in its unlawful activities surely pose no threat, either as citizens or as public employees. Laws such as this which are not restricted in scope to those who join with the 'specific intent' to further illegal action impose, in effect a conclusive presumption that the member shares the unlawful aims of the organization. See Aptheker v. Secretary of State, [378 U.S. 500]. The unconstitutionality of this Act follows a fortiori from Speiser v. Randall, 357 U.S. 513, where we held that a State may not even place on an applicant for a tax exemption the burden of proving that he has not engaged in criminal advocacy.

"This Act threatens the cherished freedom of association protected by the First Amendment, made applicable to the States through
the Fourteenth Amendment. . . . A statute touching those protected rights must be 'narrowly drawn to define and punish specific
conduct as constituting a clear and present danger to a substantial
interest of the State.' Cantwell v. Connecticut, 310 U.S. 296, 311.
Legitimate legislative goals 'cannot be pursued by means that broadly
stifle fundamental personal liberties when the end can be more narrowly
achieved.' Shelton v. Tucker, 364 U.S. 479, 488. . . . A law which
applies to membership without the 'specific intent' to further the illegal
aims of the organization infringes unnecessarily on protected freedoms.
It rests on the doctrine of 'guilt by association' which has no place here.
. . . Such a law cannot stand."

4.   In Barenblatt v. U. S., 360 U.S. 109, 79 S.Ct. 1081, 3 L.Ed.2d 1115
     (1959), an investigation case involving the then named House Com-
     mittee on Un-American Activities, currently renamed the House In-
     ternal Security Committee, the Supreme Court recognized: "Of course,
     broadly viewed, inquiries cannot be made into the teaching that is
     pursued at any of our educational institutions. When academic
     teaching-freedom and its corollary learning-freedom, so essential to
     the well-being of the Nation, are claimed, this Court will always be on
     the alert against intrusion by Congress into this constitutionally pro-
     tected domain."

KEYISHIAN v. BOARD OF REGENTS

Supreme Court of the United States, 1967.
385 U.S. 589, 87 S.Ct. 675, 17 L.Ed.2d 629.

Mr. Justice BRENNAN delivered the opinion of the Court.

. . . As faculty members of the State University [appel-
lants] continued employment was conditioned upon their compliance
with a New York plan, formulated partly in statutes and partly in administrative regulations, which the State utilizes to prevent the appointment or retention of "subversive" persons in state employment.

. . . Each . . . refused to sign, as regulations then in
effect required, a certificate that he was not a Communist, and that
if he had ever been a Communist, he had communicated that fact to
the President of the State University of New York. Each was notified that his failure to sign the certificate would require his dismissal.

. . .

Appellants brought this action for declaratory and injunctive relief, alleging that the state program violated the Federal Constitution
in various respects. . . .

We considered some aspects of the constitutionality of the New
York plan 15 years ago in Adler v. Board of Education, 342 U.S. 485.

That litigation arose after New York passed the Feinberg Law which added § 3022 to the Education Law. The Feinberg Law was enacted to implement and enforce two earlier statutes. The first was a 1917 law, now § 3021 of the Education Law, under which "the utterance of any treasonable or seditious word or words or the doing of any treasonable or seditious act" is a ground for dismissal from the public school system. The second was a 1939 law which . . . is now § 105 of that law. This law disqualifies from the civil service and from employment in the educational system any person who advocates the overthrow of government by force, violence, or any unlawful means, or publishes material advocating such overthrow or organizes or joins any society or group of persons advocating such doctrine.

The Feinberg Law charged the State Board of Regents with the duty of promulgating rules and regulations providing procedures for the disqualification or removal of persons in the public school system who violate the 1917 law or who are ineligible for appointment to or retention in the public school system under the 1939 law. The Board of Regents was further directed to make a list, after notice and hearing, of "subversive" organizations, defined as organizations which advocate the doctrine of overthrow of government by force, violence, or any unlawful means. Finally, the Board was directed to provide in its rules and regulations that membership in any listed organization should constitute prima facie evidence of disqualification for appointment to or retention in any office or position in the public schools of the State.

The Board of Regents thereupon promulgated rules and regulations containing procedures to be followed by appointing authorities to discover persons ineligible for appointment or retention under the 1939 law, or because of violation of the 1917 law. The Board also announced its intention to list "subversive" organizations after requisite notice and hearing, and provided that membership in a listed organization after the date of its listing should be regarded as constituting prima facie evidence of disqualification, and that membership prior to listing should be presumptive evidence that membership has continued, in the absence of a showing that such membership was terminated in good faith. Under the regulations, an appointing official is forbidden to make an appointment until after he has first inquired of an applicant's former employers and other persons to ascertain whether the applicant is disqualified or ineligible for appointment. In addition, an annual inquiry must be made to determine whether an appointed employee has ceased to be qualified for retention, and a report of findings must be filed.

Adler . . . held, in effect, that there was no constitutional infirmity in former § 12–a [the predecessor to § 105] or in the Feinberg Law on their faces and that they were capable of constitutional application. But the contention urged in this case that both § 3021 and § 105 are unconstitutionally vague was not heard or decided.

vagueness of language

.   .   .   Appellants in this case timely asserted below the unconstitutionality of all these sections on grounds of vagueness and that question is now properly before us for decision.   Moreover, to the extent that *Adler* sustained the provision of the Feinberg Law constituting membership in an organization advocating forceful overthrow of government a ground for disqualification, pertinent constitutional doctrines have since rejected the premises upon which that conclusion rested.   *Adler* is therefore not dispositive of the constitutional issues we must decide in this case.   .   .   .

Section 3021 requires removal for "treasonable or seditious" utterances or acts.   The 1958 amendment to § 105 of the Civil Service Law, now subdivision 3 of that section, added such utterances or acts as a ground for removal under that law also.   The same wording is used in both statutes—that "the utterance of any treasonable or seditious word or words or the doing of any treasonable or seditious act or acts" shall be ground for removal.   But there is a vital difference between the two laws.   Section 3021 does not define the terms "treasonable or seditious" as used in that section; in contrast, subdivision 3 of § 105 of the Civil Service Law provides that the terms "treasonable word or act" shall mean "treason" as defined in the Penal Law and the terms "seditious word or act" shall mean "criminal anarchy" as defined in the Penal Law.   .   .   .

Even assuming that "treasonable" and "seditious" in § 3021 and § 105, subd. 3, have the same meaning, the uncertainty is hardly removed.   .   .   .   The difficulty centers upon the meaning of "seditious."   Subdivision 3 equates the term "seditious" with "criminal anarchy" as defined in the Penal Law.   Is the reference only to Penal Law § 160, defining criminal anarchy as "the doctrine that organized government should be overthrown by force or violence, or by assassination of the executive head or of any of the executive officials of government, or by any unlawful means"?   But that section ends with the sentence "The advocacy of such doctrine either by word of mouth or writing is a felony."   Does that sentence draw into § 105, Penal Law § 161, proscribing "advocacy of criminal anarchy"?   If so, the possible scope of "seditious" utterances or acts has virtually no limit.   For under Penal Law § 161, one commits the felony of advocating criminal anarchy if he   "   .   .   .   publicly displays any book   .   .   . containing or advocating, advising or teaching the doctrine that organized government should be overthrown by force, violence or any unlawful means."   Does the teacher who carries a copy of the Communist Manifesto on a public street thereby advocate criminal anarchy?   It is no answer to say that the statute would not be applied in such a case.   We cannot gainsay the potential effect of this obscure wording on "those with a conscientious and scrupulous regard for such undertakings."   Baggett v. Bullitt, 377 U.S. 360, 374.   Even were it certain that the definition referred to in § 105 was solely Penal Law § 160, the scope of § 105 still remains indefinite.   The teacher cannot know the extent, if any, to which a "seditious" utterance must transcend mere statement about abstract doctrine, the extent to which it must be intended to and tend to indoctrinate or incite to action in furtherance of the defined doctrine. <u>The crucial consideration is that no teacher can know just where the line is drawn between "seditious" and nonseditious utterances and acts.</u>   .   .   .

Similar uncertainty arises as to the application of subdivision 1(b) of § 105. That subsection requires the disqualification of an employee involved with the distribution of written material "containing or advocating, advising or teaching the doctrine" of forceful overthrow, and who himself "advocates, advises, teaches, or embraces the duty, necessity or propriety of adopting the doctrine contained therein." Here again, mere advocacy of abstract doctrine is apparently included. And does the prohibition of distribution of matter "containing" the doctrine bar histories of the evolution of Marxist doctrine or tracing the background of the French, American, or Russian revolutions? The additional requirement, that the person participating in distribution of the material be one who "advocates, advises, teaches, or embraces the duty, necessity or propriety of adopting the doctrine" of forceful overthrow, does not alleviate the uncertainty in the scope of the section, but exacerbates it. Like the language of § 105, subd. 1(a), this language may reasonably be construed to cover mere expression of belief. For example, does the university librarian who recommends the reading of such materials thereby "advocate .   .   .   the   .   .   .   propriety of adopting the doctrine contained therein"?

.   .   .   In light of the intricate administrative machinery for its enforcement, this is not surprising. The very intricacy of the plan and the uncertainty as to the scope of its proscriptions make it a highly efficient *in terrorem* mechanism. It would be a bold teacher who would not stay as far as possible from utterances or acts which might jeopardize his living by enmeshing him in this intricate machinery. The uncertainty as to the utterances and acts proscribed increases that caution in "those who believe the written law means what it says." Baggett v. Bullitt, supra, at 374. The result must be to stifle "that free play of the spirit which all teachers ought especially to cultivate and practice.   .   .   ." That probability is enhanced by the provisions requiring an annual review of every teacher to determine whether any utterance or act of his, inside the classroom or out, came within the sanctions of the laws. For a memorandum warns employees that under the statutes "subversive" activities may take the form of "[t]he writing of articles, the distribution of pamphlets, the endorsement of speeches made or articles written or acts performed by others," and reminds them "that it is a primary duty of the school authorities in each school district to take positive action to eliminate from the school system any teacher in whose case there is evidence that he is guilty of subversive activity. School authorities are under obligation to proceed immediately and conclusively in every such case." . . .

Our Nation is deeply committed to safeguarding academic freedom which is of transcendent value to all of us and not merely to the teachers concerned. That freedom is therefore a special concern of the First Amendment, which does not tolerate laws that cast a pall of orthodoxy over the classroom. "The vigilant protection of constitutional freedoms is nowhere more vital than in the community of American schools." Shelton v. Tucker, . . . The classroom is peculiarly the "marketplace of ideas." The Nation's future depends upon leaders trained through wide exposure to that robust exchange of ideas which discovers truth "out of a multitude of tongues, [rather] than through any kind of authoritative selection." . . . In Sweezy v. New Hampshire, . . . we said:

"The essentiality of freedom in the community of American universities is almost self-evident. No one should underestimate the vital role in a democracy that is played by those who guide and train our youth. To impose any strait jacket upon the intellectual leaders in our colleges and universities would imperil the future of our Nation. No field of education is so thoroughly comprehended by man that new discoveries cannot yet be made. Particularly is that true in the social sciences, where few, if any, principles are accepted as absolutes. Scholarship cannot flourish in an atmosphere of suspicion and distrust. Teachers and students must always remain free to inquire, to study and to evaluate, to gain new maturity and understanding; otherwise, our civilization will stagnate and die."

We emphasize once again that "[p]recision of regulation must be the touchstone in an area so closely touching our most precious freedoms," N. A. A. C. P. v. Button, 317 U.S. 415, 438; "[f]or standards of permissible statutory vagueness are strict in the area of free expression. . . . Because First Amendment freedoms need breathing space to survive, government may regulate in the area only with narrow specificity." . . . New York's complicated and intricate scheme plainly violates that standard. When one must guess what conduct or utterance may lose him his position, one necessarily will "steer far wider of the unlawful zone. . . ." Speiser v. Randall, 357 U.S. 513, 526. For "[t]he threat of sanctions may deter . . . almost as potently as the actual application of sanctions." N. A. A. C. P. v. Button, supra, at 433. The danger of that chilling effect upon the exercise of vital First Amendment rights must be guarded against by sensitive tools which clearly inform teachers what is being proscribed. . . .

The regulatory maze created by New York is wholly lacking in "terms susceptible of objective measurement." Cramp v. Board of

Public Instruction, supra, at 286. It has the quality of "extraordinary ambiguity" found to be fatal to the oaths considered in Cramp and Baggett v. Bullitt. "[M]en of common intelligence must necessarily guess at its meaning and differ as to its application. . . ."
.   .   .   Vagueness of wording is aggravated by prolixity and profusion of statutes, regulations, and administrative machinery, and by manifold cross-references to interrelated enactments and rules.

We therefore hold that § 3021 of the Education Law and subdivisions 1(a), 1(b) and 3 of § 105 of the Civil Service Law as implemented by the machinery created pursuant to § 3022 of the Education Law are unconstitutional.

Appellants have also challenged the constitutionality of the discrete provisions of subdivision 1(c) of § 105 and subdivision 2 of the Feinberg Law, which make Communist Party membership, as such, prima facie evidence of disqualification. .   .   .   Subdivision 2 of the Feinberg Law was, however, before the Court in *Adler* and its constitutionality was sustained. But constitutional doctrine which has emerged since that decision has rejected its major premise. That premise was that public employment, including academic employment, may be conditioned upon the surrender of constitutional rights which could not be abridged by direct government action. Teachers, the Court said in *Adler,* "may work for the school system upon the reasonable terms laid down by the proper authorities of New York. If they do not choose to work on such terms, they are at liberty to retain their beliefs and associations and go elsewhere." 342 U.S., at 492. The Court also stated that a teacher denied employment because of membership in a listed organization "is not thereby denied the right of free speech and assembly. His freedom of choice between membership in the organization and employment in the school system might be limited, but not his freedom of speech or assembly, except in the remote sense that limitation is inherent in every choice."   .   .   .

We proceed then to the question of the validity of the provisions of subdivision 1(c) of § 105 and subdivision 2 of § 3022, barring employment to members of listed organizations. Here again constitutional doctrine has developed since *Adler*. Mere knowing membership without a specific intent to further the unlawful aims of an organization is not a constitutionally adequate basis for exclusion from such positions as those held by appellants.

In Elfbrandt v. Russell, 384 U.S. 11, we said, "Those who join an organization but do not share its unlawful purposes and who do not participate in its unlawful activities surely pose no threat, either as citizens or as public employees."   .   .   .   We there struck down a statutorily required oath binding the state employee not to become a member of the Communist Party with knowledge of its unlawful purpose, on threat of discharge and perjury prosecution if the oath were violated. We found that "[a]ny lingering doubt that proscrip-

tion of mere knowing membership, without any showing of 'specific intent,' would run afoul of the Constitution was set at rest by our decision in Aptheker v. Secretary of State, 378 U.S. 500."   .   .   .   In *Aptheker* we held that Party membership, without knowledge of the Party's unlawful purposes *and* specific intent to further its unlawful aims, could not constitutionally warrant deprivation of the right to travel abroad.   As we said in Schneiderman v. United States, 320 U.S. 118, 136, "[U]nder our traditions beliefs are personal and not a matter of mere association, and   .   .   .   men in adhering to a political party or other organization   .   .   .   do not subscribe unqualifiedly to all of its platforms or asserted principles."   "A law which applies to membership without the 'specific intent' to further the illegal aims of the organization infringes unnecessarily on protected freedoms.   It rests on the doctrine of 'guilt by association' which has no place here."
.   .   .   Thus mere Party membership, even with knowledge of the Party's unlawful goals, cannot suffice to justify criminal punishment, see Scales v. United States, 367 U.S. 203; Noto v. United States, 367 U.S. 290; Yates v. United States, 354 U.S. 298; nor may it warrant a finding of moral unfitness justifying disbarment.   Schware v. Board of Bar Examiners, 353 U.S. 232.   .   .   .

Measured against this standard, both Civil Service Law § 105, subd. 1(c), and Education Law § 3022, subd. 2, sweep overbroadly into association which may not be proscribed.   The presumption of disqualification arising from proof of mere membership may be rebutted, but only by (a) a denial of membership, (b) a denial that the organization advocates the overthrow of government by force, or (c) a denial that the teacher has knowledge of such advocacy.   .   .   .   Thus proof of nonactive membership or a showing of the absence of intent to further unlawful aims will not rebut the presumption and defeat dismissal.   This is emphasized in official administrative interpretations.   For example, it is said in a letter addressed to prospective appointees by the President of the State University, "You will note that .   .   .   both the Law and regulations are very specifically directed toward the elimination and nonappointment of 'Communists' from or to our teaching ranks.   .   .   .   "   The Feinberg Certificate was even more explicit: "Anyone who is a *member* of the Communist Party or of any organization that advocates the violent overthrow of the Government of the United States or of the State of New York or any political subdivision thereof cannot be employed by the State University."   .   .   .   This official administrative interpretation is supported by the legislative preamble to the Feinberg Law, § 1, in which the legislature concludes as a result of its findings that "it is essential that the laws prohibiting persons who are *members* of subversive groups, such as the communist party and its affiliated organizations, from obtaining or retaining employment in the public schools, be rigorously enforced."   .   .   .

Thus § 105, subd. 1(c), and § 3022, subd. 2, suffer from impermissible "overbreadth." . . . They seek to bar employment both for association which legitimately may be proscribed and for association which may not be proscribed consistently with First Amendment rights. Where statutes have an overbroad sweep, just as where they are vague, "the hazard of loss or substantial impairment of those precious rights may be critical," . . . since those covered by the statute are bound to limit their behavior to that which is unquestionably safe. As we said in Shelton v. Tucker, . . . "The breadth of legislative abridgment must be viewed in the light of less drastic means for achieving the same basic purpose."

We therefore hold that Civil Service Law § 105, subd. 1(c), and Education Law § 3022, subd. 2, are invalid insofar as they proscribe mere knowing membership without any showing of specific intent to further the unlawful aims of the Communist Party of the United States or of the State of New York.

The judgment of the District Court is reversed and the case is remanded for further proceedings consistent with this opinion.

Reversed and remanded.

Mr. Justice CLARK, with whom Mr. Justice HARLAN, Mr. Justice STEWART and Mr. Justice WHITE join, dissenting.

The blunderbuss fashion in which the majority couches "its artillery of words," together with the morass of cases it cites as authority and the obscurity of their application to the question at hand, makes it difficult to grasp the true thrust of its decision. . . .

It is clear that the Feinberg Law, in which this Court found "no constitutional infirmity" in 1952, has been given its death blow today. Just as the majority here finds that there "can be no doubt of the legitimacy of New York's interest in protecting its education system from subversion" there can also be no doubt that "the be-all and end-all" of New York's effort is here. And, regardless of its correctness, neither New York nor the several States that have followed the teaching of Adler v. Board of Education, 342 U.S. 485, for some 15 years, can ever put the pieces together again. No court has ever reached out so far to destroy so much with so little.

The section (§ 3021 of the Education Law) which authorizes the removal of superintendents, teachers, or employees in the public schools in any city or school district of New York for the utterance of any treasonable or seditious word or words is also struck down, even though it does not apply to appellants, as we shall discuss below.

Also declared unconstitutional are the subdivisions (1(a), 1(b) and 1(c) of § 105 of the Civil Service Law) which prevent the appointment and authorize the discharge of any superintendent, principal, or teacher in any part of New York's public education establishment who wilfully advocates, advises, or teaches the doctrine that the Government of the United States, or of any State or any political subdivision thereof should be overthrown by force, violence, or any other unlawful means (1(a)); or who prints, publishes, edits, issues, or sells any book, paper, document, or written or printed matter, in any form, containing such doctrine *and* "who advocates, advises, teaches, or embraces the duty, necessity or propriety of adopting the doctrine contained therein" (1(b)); or who organizes or helps to organize or becomes a member of any society or group which teaches or advocates such doctrine (1(c)). This latter provision was amended in 1958, while still part of § 12–a of the Civil Service Law, to make membership in the Communist Party prima facie proof of disqualification. The language "advocate, advise, teach," etc., obviously springs from federal statutes, particularly the Smith Act, § 2(a)(1), (2) and (3), 54 Stat. 671, which was approved by this Court in Dennis v. United States, 341 U.S. 494 (1951). State statutes of similar character and language have been approved by this Court.   .   .   .

Lastly stricken is the subdivision (3 of § 105) which authorizes the discharge of any person in the civil service of the State or any civil division thereof who utters any treasonable or seditious word or commits any treasonable or seditious act, although this subdivision is not and never has been a part of the Feinberg Law and New York specifically disclaims its applicability to the appellants. In addition, how can the Court pass upon this law *as applied* when the State has never attempted to and now renounces its application to appellants?

This Court has again and again, since at least 1951, approved procedures either identical or at the least similar to the ones the Court condemns today. In Garner v. Board of Public Works of Los Angeles, [341 U.S. 716] we held that a public employer was not precluded, simply because it was an agency of the State, "from inquiring of its employees as to matters that may prove relevant to their fitness and suitability for the public service."   .   .   . The oath there used practically the same same language as the   .   .   . statement here and the affidavit reflects the same type of inquiry as was made in the old certificate condemned here.   .   .   . Our late Brother Minton wrote for the Court:

> "A teacher works in a sensitive area in a schoolroom. There he shapes the attitude of young minds towards the society in which they live. In this, the state has a vital concern. It must preserve the integrity of the schools. That the school authorities have the right and the duty to screen the officials, teachers, and employees as to their fitness to maintain the integrity of the schools as a part of ordered society, cannot be doubted.   .   .   .

In view of this long list of decisions covering over 15 years of this Court's history, in which no opinion of this Court even questioned the validity of the *Adler* line of cases, it is strange to me that the

Court now finds that the "constitutional doctrine which has emerged since . . . has rejected [*Adler's*] major premise." With due respect, as I read them, our cases have done no such thing. . . .

    . . . The only portion of the Feinberg Law which the majority says was not covered there and is applicable to appellants is § 105, subd. 1(a), 1(b) and 1(c). These have to do with teachers who advocate, advise, or teach the doctrine of overthrow of our Government by force and violence, either orally or in writing. This was the identical conduct that was condemned in Dennis v. United States, supra. There the Court found the exact verbiage not to be unconstitutionally vague, and that finding was of course not affected by the decision of this Court in *Yates v. United States*, 354 U.S. 298. The majority makes much over the horribles that might arise from subdivision 1(b) of § 105 which condemns the printing, publishing, selling, etc., of matter containing such doctrine. But the majority fails to state that this action is condemned only *when and if* the teacher also personally advocates, advises, teaches, etc., the necessity or propriety of adopting such doctrine. This places this subdivision on the same footing as 1(a). And the same is true of subdivision 1(c) where a teacher organizes, helps to organize or becomes a member of an organization which teaches or advocates such doctrine, for scienter would also be a necessary ingredient under our opinion in *Garner*, supra. Moreover, membership is only prima facie evidence of disqualification and could be rebutted, leaving the burden of proof on the State. Furthermore, all of these procedures are protected by an adversary hearing with full judicial review.

    In the light of these considerations the strained and unbelievable suppositions that the majority poses could hardly occur. As was said in *Dennis*, supra, "we are not convinced that because there may be borderline cases" the State should be prohibited the protections it seeks. . . . Where there is doubt as to one's intent or the nature of his activities we cannot assume that the administrative boards will not give him full protection. Furthermore, the courts always sit to make certain that this is done.

    The majority says that the Feinberg Law is bad because it has an "over-broad sweep." I regret to say—and I do so with deference —that the majority has by its broadside swept away one of our most precious rights, namely, the right of self-preservation. Our public educational system is the genius of our democracy. The minds of our youth are developed there and the character of that development will determine the future of our land. Indeed, our very existence depends upon it. The issue here is a very narrow one. It is not freedom of speech, freedom of thought, freedom of press, freedom of assembly, or of association, even in the Communist Party. It is simply this: May the State provide that one who, after a hearing with full judicial review, is found to have wilfully and deliberately advocated, advised, or taught that our Government should be overthrown by force or violence or other unlawful means; or to have wilfully and deliberately printed, published, etc., any book or paper that so advocated *and to have personally* advocated such doctrine himself; or to have wilfully and deliberately become a member of an organization that advocates such doctrine, is prima facie disqualified from teaching in its university? My answer, in keeping with all of our cases up until today, is "Yes"!

I dissent.

NOTES AND QUESTIONS

1. In a dissent to the Adler decision, supra, which decision was overruled in Keyishian, Mr. Justice Douglas, joined by Mr. Justice Black, wrote:

   "The Constitution guarantees freedom of thought and expression to everyone in our society. All are entitled to it; and none needs it more than the teacher.

   "The public school is in most respects the cradle of our democracy. . . . the impact of this kind of censorship in the public school system illustrates the high purpose of the First Amendment in freeing speech and thought from censorship. . . .

   "The very threat of such a procedure is certain to raise havoc with academic freedom. . . . Fearing condemnation, [the teacher] will tend to shrink from any association that stirs controversy. In that manner freedom of expression will be stifled. . . .

   "There can be no real academic freedom in that environment. Where suspicion fills the air and holds scholars in line for fear of their jobs, there can be no exercise of the free intellect. . . .

   "This system of spying and surveillance with its accompanying reports and trials cannot go hand in hand with academic freedom. It produces standardized thought, not the pursuit of truth. Yet it was the pursuit of truth which the First Amendment was designed to protect. . . . We need be bold and adventuresome in our thinking to survive. . . . The Framers knew the danger of dogmatism; they also knew the strength that comes when the mind is free, when ideas may be pursued wherever they lead. We forget these teachings of the First Amendment when we sustain this law." Adler v. Board of Education, 342 U.S. 485 at 508–11, 72 S.Ct. 380 at 392–94, 96 L.Ed. 517 at 532–34 (1952), *passim.*

   Mr. Justice Frankfurter dissented on jurisdictional grounds but made special reference to "the teacher's freedom of thought, inquiry, and expression," and to "the freedom of thought and activity, and especially . . . the feeling of such freedom, which are, as I suppose no one would deny, part of the necessary professional equipment of teachers in a free society." Id. at 504–05.

2. In the same year that it decided the Adler case, the Supreme Court held unconstitutional an Oklahoma statute requiring all state employees, including teachers, to take a loyalty oath to the effect that for the preceding five years they were not members of organizations

listed as "subversive" or "communist front" by the United States
Attorney General. Mr. Justice Frankfurter wrote a concurring opinion joined by Mr. Justice Douglas:

". . . to require such an oath, on pain of a teacher's loss
of his position in case of refusal to take the oath, penalizes a teacher for exercising a right of association peculiarly characteristic of
our people. . . . Such joining is an exercise of the rights of
free speech and free inquiry. By limiting the power of the States
to interfere with freedom of speech and freedom of inquiry and
freedom of association, the Fourteenth Amendment protects all persons, no matter what their calling. But, in view of the nature of the
teacher's relation to the effective exercise of the rights which are
safeguarded by the Bill of Rights and by the Fourteenth Amendment, inhibition of freedom of thought, and of action upon thought,
in the case of teachers brings the safeguards of those amendments
vividly into operation. Such unwarranted inhibition upon the free
spirit of teachers affects not only those who, like the appellants, are
immediately before the Court. It has an unmistakable tendency to
chill that free play of the spirit which all teachers ought especially
to cultivate and practice; it makes for caution and timidity in their
associations by potential teachers. . . .

"That our democracy ultimately rests on public opinion is a
platitude of speech but not a commonplace in action. Public opinion
is the ultimate reliance of our society only if it be disciplined and
responsible. It can be disciplined and responsible only if habits of
open-mindedness and of critical inquiry are acquired in the formative years of our citizens. The process of education has naturally
enough been the basis of hope for the perdurance of our democracy
on the part of all our great leaders, from Thomas Jefferson onwards.

"To regard teachers—in our entire educational system, from
the primary grades to the university—as the priests of our democracy is therefore not to indulge in hyperbole. It is the special task
of teachers to foster those habits of open-mindedness and critical
inquiry which alone make for responsible citizens, who, in turn,
make possible an enlightened and effective public opinion. Teachers
must fulfill their function by precept and practice, by the very
atmosphere which they generate; they must be exemplars of open-
mindedness and free inquiry. They cannot carry out their noble
task if the conditions for the practice of a responsible and critical
mind are denied to them. They must have the freedom of responsible inquiry, by thought and action, into the meaning of social
and economic ideas, into the checkered history of social and economic dogma. They must be free to sift evanescent doctrine, qualified by time and circumstance, from that restless, enduring process
of extending the bounds of understanding and wisdom, to assure
which the freedoms of thought, of speech, of inquiry, of worship
are guaranteed by the Constitution of the United States against
infraction by national or state government.

"The functions of educational institutions in our national life
and the conditions under which alone they can adequately perform
them are at the basis of these limitations upon state and national

power." Wieman v. Updegraff, 344 U.S. 183 at 195–97, 73 S.Ct. 215 at 220–21, 97 L.Ed. 216 at 224–25 (1952).

3. Do these cases mean that public school teachers can no longer be disqualified from their jobs for any expression or association for which they could not be punished criminally?

4. May school administrators today constitutionally require a non-communist loyalty oath of teachers? May they inquire into a teacher's associations? With the communist party? Should a teacher be fired if he refuses to answer whether he is a communist or a member of the communist party? Why or why not? Why should secret membership in the communist party receive constitutional protection? Does it?

5. What, precisely, is the substantive content of the concept of Academic Freedom that is protected by the Constitution, and to whom does it apply and in what circumstances? Write it out on paper.

6. Should schools focus their teaching on those ideas that have won in the competition of the marketplace" or should they focus only on the ideas that have won the acceptance of scholars, or both? Why? What are the implications of your answer for the curriculum and teaching methods of a school?

7. Do "subversive activities" present special problems for schools justifying restraints on academic freedom? Is the problem any different for the "common schools" than for higher education?

PROBLEMS

In light of all the preceding materials, do you believe that any part of the following statutes from Florida, Louisiana and California are unconstitutional? If so, which part or parts? Why or why not?

Americanism vs. communism; required high school course

"(1) The legislature of the state hereby finds it to be a fact that

(a) The political ideology commonly known and referred to as communism is in conflict with and contrary to the principles of constitutional government of the United States as epitomized in its national constitution,

(b) The successful exploitation and manipulation of youth and student groups throughout the world today are a major challenge which the free world forces must meet and defeat, and

(c) The best method of meeting this challenge is to have the youth of the state and nation throughly and completely informed as to the evils, dangers and fallacies of communism by giving them a thorough understanding of the entire communist movement, including its history, doctrines, objectives and techniques.

"(2) The public high schools shall each teach a complete course of not less than thirty hours, to all students enrolled in said public high schools entitled "Americanism versus communism."

"(3) The course shall provide adequate instruction in the history, doctrines, objectives and techniques of communism and shall be for the primary purpose of instilling in the minds of the students a greater appreciation of democratic processes, freedom under law, and the will to preserve that freedom.

"(4) The course shall be one of orientation in comparative governments and shall emphasize the free-enterprise-competitive economy of the United States as the one which produces higher wages, higher standards of living, greater personal freedom and liberty than any other system of economics on earth.

"(5) The course shall lay particular emphasis upon the dangers of communism, the ways to fight communism, the evils of communism, the fallacies of communism, and the false doctrines of communism.

"(6) The state textbook council and the department of education shall take such action as may be necessary and appropriate to prescribe suitable textbook and instructional material as provided by state law, using as one of their guides the official reports of the house committee on un-American activities and the senate internal security subcommittee of the United States congress.

"(7) No teacher or textual material assigned to this course shall present communism as preferable to the system of constitutional government and the free-enterprise-competitive economy indigenous to the United States." Fla.Stat. § 233.064.

In 1962, Louisiana passed a similar statute directing the state department of education, in conjunction with the local school systems, to conduct seminars for "certain teachers and eleventh and twelfth grade high school students. . . . " The purpose of the seminars is to give their participants "a clear understanding of the fundamental principles of the American form of government, the evils of socialism and the basic philosophy of communism and the strategy and tactics used by the Communists in their efforts to achieve their ultimate goal of world domination."

California provides:

"No teacher giving instruction in any school, or on any property belonging to any agencies included in the public school system, shall advocate or teach communism with the intent to indoctrinate or to inculcate in the mind of any pupil a preference for communism.

"In prohibiting the advocacy or teaching of communism with the intent of indoctrinating or inculcating a preference in the mind of any pupil for such doctrine, the Legislature does not intend to prevent the teaching of the facts about communism. Rather, the Legislature intends to prevent the advocacy of, or inculcation and indoctrination into, communism as is hereinafter defined, for the purpose of undermining patriotism for, and the belief in, the government of the United States and of this state.

"For the purposes of this section, communism is a political theory that the presently existing form of government of the United States or of this state should be changed, by force, violence, or other unconstitutional means, to a totalitarian dictatorship which is based on the principles of communism as expounded by Marx, Lenin, and Stalin." West's Ann. Educ. Code of Calif. § 9031.

GOVERNMENTAL CONTROLS OVER THE CURRICULUM

INTRODUCTION

The term "curriculum" can be used in at least two senses. One sense refers to the studies prescribed for a given grade, the successful completion of which leads ultimately to a high school diploma. A second sense of the term refers to the whole life-experience program of the school; that is, "all of the experiences for which the school accepts responsibility." W. B. Ragan, MODERN ELEMENTARY CURRICULUM 5 (1966), and see, J. D. Mohler & E. C. Bolmeier, LAW OF EXTRACURRICULAR ACTIVITIES IN SECONDARY SCHOOLS (1968). In this sense, a school can be responsible for extra-curricular as well as curricular programs. Courts generally use the term "curriculum" in both senses, and indeed, occasionally in a third, and broader sense. They have infrequently used the term to apply to whatever happens in school, whether the authorities want to accept responsibility for it or not.

The federal government exerts considerable force on the curriculum by making grants of money available to states so long as they agree to provide certain programs. But the federal government has no direct control over the school curriculum. Within constitutional limitations, the state legislature has the power to control and to prescribe the subject matter of the curriculum, methods of instruction, and books to be used. The Supreme Courts of North Carolina and Tennessee have provided statements of the legislature's power:

> The General Assembly has the power, which we think cannot be questioned to prescribe by statute the subjects to be taught and the methods of instruction to be followed in the public schools of the state, whether such public schools be included within the uniform system required to be maintained by the Constitution, or whether they be public schools established for certain districts formed under the general school law by the state or under specific statutes. Posey v. Bd. of Ed., 199 N.C. 306, 154 S.E. 393 (1930).

> . . . That the state may establish a uniform series of books to be taught in the schools, which it provides and controls, seems to be a proposition as evident as that it may provide a uniform system of schools, which we take it is not now an open question; and while the selection of text-books may, in the earlier and cruder stages of the law, have been left to, and exercised by, local superintendents, directors, and teachers, it was not for want of authority in the state to prescribe a uniform system, but rather because the system had not reached that stage of development and progress that made it advisable, in the opinion of the legislature, to so provide. . . . We think it clear that the state itself might, if it saw proper, publish the books to be used in its public schools.
> . . .

> . . . The authority of the state over schools is a legislative one, and it is difficult to see how a uniform system can be maintained which will confer equal benefits upon all sections of the state, unless it is done by legislative action. If the authority to regulate and control schools is legislative, then it must have an unrestricted right to prescribe methods, and the courts cannot interfere with it, unless some scheme is devised which is contrary to other provisions of the constitution. . . . Leeper v. State, 103 Tenn. 500, 53 S.W. 962 (1899).

Methods of Instruction

State legislatures seldom prescribe the teaching methods that must be used in classroom teaching, leaving matters of pedagogy to school personnel. But, legislatures may speak to the subject generally, requiring that teachers carry out the prescribed teaching methods and courses of study; for example, Washington provides that

> "Certificated employees shall faithfully enforce in the common schools the course of study and regulations prescribed, whether regulations of the district, the superintendent of public instruction, or the state board of education, and shall furnish promptly all information relating to the common

schools which may be requested by the county or intermediate district superintendent.

"Any certificated employee who wilfully refuses or neglects to enforce the course of study or the rules and regulations as above in this section required, shall not be allowed by the directors any warrant for salary due until said person shall have complied with said requirements."   RCW 28A.-67.060.

Moreover, without reference to subject matter legislatures frequently direct teachers to impress certain values onto the minds of their students.   Again Washington provides a not unusual example:

"It shall be the duty of all teachers to endeavor to impress on the minds of their pupils the principles of morality, truth, justice, temperance, humanity and patriotism; to teach them to avoid idleness, profanity and falsehood; to instruct them in the principles of free government, and to train them up to the true comprehension of the rights, duty and dignity of American citizenship."   RCW 28A.67.110.

"No person, whose certificate or permit authorizing him to teach in the common schools of this state has been revoked due to his failure to endeavor to impress on the minds of his pupils the principles of patriotism, or to train them up to the true comprehension of the rights, duty and dignity of American citizenship, shall be permitted to teach in any common school in this state."   RCW 28A.67.030.

Can the above two statutes be enforced constitutionally?

The highest court in Massachusetts has sustained the right of school authorities to prescribe the teaching methods to be used in classroom teaching in a case involving a girl whose father refused to allow her to attend a bookkeeping class because she became upset when the teacher selected a rival pupil to aid in the correction of homework, and after a week's work on a problem the rival pupil marked her answer "wrong," but the teacher later marked it "correct":

The real and vital question is not whether the plaintiff was guilty of misconduct in refusing to attend her class, but whether a parent has the right to say a certain method of teaching any given course of study shall be pursued.   The question answers itself.   Were it otherwise, should several parents hold diverse opinions all must yield to one or confusion and failure inevitably follow.   The determination of the procedure and the management and direction of pupils and studies in this Commonwealth rests in the wise discretion and sound judgment of teachers and school committee, whose action in these respects is not subject to the supervision of this court.

The case at bar is one purely of administrative detail and its exercise violates no legal right of pupil or parent. The plaintiff was without right in requiring that the principal personally should attend to the supervision of her individual work, perhaps to the neglect of more important duties. Wulf v. Wakefield, 221 Mass. 427, 109 N.E. 358 (1915).

Qualified school administrators equally can have power over classroom teaching methods, but generally, members of boards of education do not.

The law does not contemplate that the members of a board of education shall supervise the professional work of teachers, principals, and superintendents. They are not teachers, and ordinarily, not qualified to be such. Generally they do not possess qualifications to pass upon methods of instruction and discipline. The law clearly contemplated that professionally trained teachers, principals, and superintendents shall have exclusive control of these matters. State ex rel. Rogers v. Board of Education, 125 W.Va. 579, 25 S.E.2d 537 (1943).

Generally, courts will not review a prescribed teaching method unless it raises a constitutional question or is "arbitrary or capricious," or raises other legal problems. For example, in State v. Avoyelles Parish School Bd., 147 So.2d 729 (La.1962), Louisiana's Supreme Court said that "It is not the function of a court to sit in judgment on the propriety of school curriculum, methods of teaching and demonstrations which school officials have determined necessary and proper."

Subjects Taught

The legislatures do not restrict themselves to presribing "academic" subjects. Legislatures also require that pupils engage in the study of thrift, Security Nat. Bank v. Bagley, 202 Iowa 701, 210 N.W. 947 (1926), driver education, Acorn Auto Driving School v. Board of Education, 27 Ill.2d 93, 187 N.E.2d 722 (1963) and health and physical education:

Various sections of our school law recognize the scope of physical training, or education; it has for many years formed a definite and integral part of the curriculum of the public schools. The school law . . . includes, in the course of study prescribed for the elementary public schools of the Commonwealth, instruction in 'health, including physical training,' as one of the required branches. For high schools, the State Council of Education determines the subjects to be taught based on statutory authority . . . . Physical training includes organized sports and athletic exercises. Athletics are important to the moral, physical and mental development of students. Appeal of Ganoposki, 332 Pa. 550, 2 A.2d 742 (1938).

Moreover, the sexism perhaps notwithstanding, a state legislature apparently can require that commercial and vocational courses be part of the curriculum:

> If this were a question of common school education, the proposition would probably not be questioned. But the power of the legislature to impose a system of public school education upon local communities is not limited to common branches alone. It is the judgment of the legislature that this state should now require public education in something more than the common branches; that it should provide for the public education of boys in that which pertains to successful agriculture, and of girls in that which pertains to successful housekeeping. The question whether the population and wealth of the state are such as to warrant such measures is a legislative and not a judicial question, a question of legislative policy, and not of legislative power. Associated Schools of Independent School Dist. No. 63 v. School Dist. No. 83, 122 Minn. 254, 142 N.W. 325 (1913).

What is the relationship of these subjects to "good citizenship"?

In practice, state legislatures mandate various subjects, requiring that they constitute a minimum part of the school curriculum, and then delegate powers to either State Boards of Education or Local School Boards, enabling them to prescribe and shape the remainder of the curriculum. Occasionally, an attempt will be made by either the legislature or school board to indoctrinate pupils into blindly holding only one point of view. At least three types of situations involving constitutional freedom can arise: (1) the situation of official indoctrination whereby either the legislature or school board not only requires that a certain subject be taught, but that it be taught uncritically or that only certain received "truths" be allowed; (2) the situation of official ignorance which is the converse of the situation of official indoctrination, whereby the legislature or school board disallows the teaching of a certain subject; e. g., man's evolution, usually because it is contrary to the received "truth," and finally (3) the rather common ambiguous situation in which no prior decision is made by the legislature or school board, but, for example, by a teacher who selects a book for a course or a method of teaching which is later attacked and sought to be suppressed because it is "dirty," or "improper" etc.

These three situations will be explored in the following materials, but first consider the illustrations excerpted from the New York legislature's prescription of curriculum. They are not untypical. What is their relationship to "good citizenship"? Section 3204(2) is a good example. Are New York's schools asked to do too much, or are they asked to do too much that is extraneous to quality education? Do these legislatively mandated requirements impair quality education?

Are they desirable? Are they constitutional? How can mathematics, science and other teachers fully comply with all the statutory requirements?

EDUCATION LAWS OF NEW YORK

§ 801. Courses of instruction in patriotism and citizenship and in certain historic documents

1. In order to promote a spirit of patriotic and civic service and obligation and to foster in the children of the state moral and intellectual qualities which are essential in preparing to meet the obligations of citizenship in peace or in war, the regents of The University of the State of New York shall prescribe courses of instruction in patriotism and citizenship, to be maintained and followed in all the schools of the state. The boards of education and trustees of the several cities and school districts of the state shall require instruction to be given in such courses, by the teachers employed in the schools therein. All pupils attending such schools, over the age of eight years, shall attend upon such instruction.

Similar courses of instruction shall be prescribed and maintained in private schools in the state, and all pupils in such schools over eight years of age shall attend upon such courses. If such courses are not so established and maintained in a private school, attendance upon instruction in such school shall not be deemed substantially equivalent to instruction given to pupils of like age in the public schools of the city or district in which such pupils reside. . . .

§ 802. Instruction relating to the flag; holidays

1. It shall be the duty of the commissioner of education to prepare, for the use of the public schools of the state, a program providing for a salute to the flag and a daily pledge of allegiance to the flag, for instruction in its correct use and display and such other patriotic exercises as may be deemed by him to be expedient, under such regulations and instructions as may best meet the varied requirements of the different grades in such schools.

2. It shall also be his duty to make special provision for the observance in the public schools of Lincoln's birthday, Washington's birthday, Memorial day and Flag day, and such other legal holidays of like character as may be hereafter designated by law when the legislature makes an appropriation therefor. . . .

§ 804. Instruction regarding nature of alcoholic drinks

1. The nature of alcoholic drinks and their effects on the human system shall be taught in connection with the various divisions of

physiology and hygiene, as thoroughly as are other branches in all schools under state control, or supported wholly or in part by public money of the state, and also in all schools connected with reformatory institutions.

2.   All pupils in the above-mentioned schools below the second year of the high school and above the third year of school work computing from the beginning of the lowest primary, not kindergarten, year, or in corresponding classes of ungraded schools, shall be taught and shall study this subject every year with suitable text-books in the hands of all pupils, for not less than three lessons a week for ten or more weeks, or the equivalent of the same in each year, and must pass satisfactory tests in this as in other studies before promotion to the next succeeding year's work; except that, where there are nine or more school years below the high school, the study may be omitted in all years above the eighth year and below the high school, by such pupils as have passed the required tests of the eighth year.   .   .   .

§ 804–a. Instruction regarding the nature and effects of narcotics and habit-forming drugs

1.   The courses of study beyond the first eight years of full time public day schools shall provide for instruction in the nature and effects on the human system of narcotics and habit-forming drugs, in accordance with the provisions of this section.   .   .   .

4.   Similar courses of instruction shall be prescribed and maintained in all private secondary schools in this state.   .   .   .

§ 805. Enforcement

1.   On satisfactory evidence that any teacher has wilfully refused to teach such subjects, as provided in sections eight hundred four and eight hundred four-a, the commissioner of education shall revoke the license of such teacher.   .   .   .

§ 806. Courses of instruction in highway safety and traffic regulation; school safety patrols

1.   The regents of The University of the State of New York shall prescribe courses of instruction in highway safety and traffic regulation, to be maintained and followed in all the schools of the state. The boards of education and trustees of the several cities and school districts of the state shall require instruction to be given in such courses, by the teachers employed in the schools therein. All pupils attending such schools shall attend upon such instruction.

Similar courses of instruction shall be prescribed and maintained in private schools in the state, and all pupils in such schools shall attend upon such courses. If such courses are not so established and maintained in a private school, attendance upon instruction in such school shall not be deemed substantially equivalent to instruction given to pupils of like grade in the public schools in the city or district in which such pupils reside.   .   .   .

§ 807.   Fire drills

1.   It shall be the duty of the principal or other person in charge of every public or private school or educational institution within the state, other than colleges or universities, having more than twenty-five pupils, or maintained in a building two or more stories high to instruct and train the pupils by means of drills, so that they may in a sudden emergency be able to leave the school building in the shortest possible time and without confusion or panic.   Such drills or rapid dismissals shall be held at least twelve times in each school year, eight of which required drills shall be held between September first and December first of each such year.   At least one-third of all such required drills shall be through use of the fire escapes on buildings where fire escapes are provided.   At least four additional drills shall be held in each school year during the hours after sunset and before sunrise in school buildings in which students are provided with sleeping accommodations. At least two additional drills shall be held during summer school in buildings where summer school is conducted, and one of such drills shall be held during the first week of summer school.   .   .   .

§ 808.   Instruction in fire prevention

1.   The commissioner of education is hereby directed to provide and prescribe a course of instruction in fire prevention relating to the protection of life and property against loss or damage as a result of preventable fire, for use in the schools of the state, as prescribed by this section.   .   .   .

§ 809.   Instruction in the humane treatment of animals and birds

The officer, board or commission authorized or required to prescribe courses of instruction shall cause instruction to be given in every elementary school under state control or supported wholly or partly by public money of the state, in the humane treatment and protection of animals and birds and the importance of the part they play in the economy of nature.   Such instruction shall be for such period of time during each school year as the board of regents may prescribe and may be joined with work in literature, reading, language, nature study or ethnology.   Such weekly instruction may be divided into two or more periods.   A school district shall not be entitled to participate in the public school money on account of any school or the attendance at any school subject to the provisions of this section, if the instruction required hereby is not given therein.   .   .   .

§ 810. Arbor and Wild Life day

1. The last Friday in April each year is hereby made and declared to be known as Arbor and Wild Life day, and observed in accordance with the provisions of this chapter.

2. It shall be the duty of the authorities of every public school in this state to assemble the pupils in their charge on that day in the school building, or elsewhere, as they may deem proper, and to provide for and conduct (1) such exercises as shall tend to encourage the planting, protection and preservation of trees and shrubs, and an acquaintance with the best methods to be adopted to accomplish such results, and (2) such lectures, pictures or tours, as shall tend to increase the interest and knowledge of such pupils in the wild life of the state. . . .

CONSTITUTIONAL LIMITATIONS ON GOVERNMENTAL CONTROLS OVER THE CURRICULUM

Education is an attempt by the community to form beliefs and habits that are consonant with the highest standards of knowledge and the best ideals of behavior. True as this statement is, it does not mean that schools are properly directed toward indoctrination or toward the preservation of the existing culture or any one political point of view. To hold that schools are to promote one, or a few, officially approved view, or views, is to hold to the totalitarian position, and that position is inconsistent with a democratic society. On the other hand, it is as unrealistic as it is evasive to hold that the curriculum and teachers must hold fast to neutrality whenever a controversial issue is presented, leaving the matter for the individual to decide. Diversity exists within America's democratic community, and it gives rise to controversial issues. A school is supposed to prepare the student for life in American democracy, and a school that failed openly to explore controversial questions would be a failure. It would not be a school at all, but more akin to a prison.

Yet, education necessarily involves some indoctrination. However, education is more than indoctrination, and not all indoctrination is inconsistent with the requirements of a democratic society. Indoctrination has at least two meanings. In one sense, indoctrination means the careful teaching of the fundamentals of a branch of knowledge as the basic principles have come to be accepted by scholars in that field of knowledge. Positive teaching may involve some indoctrination in this sense. In the beneficial use of the term the students are not equally competent as judges and a teacher's knowledge is to be conveyed. Yet, even here, the subject matter should be taught within an open atmosphere of challenge and criticism by students.

The goal is a critical and curious mind. "Indoctrination" can be used in a second, and obnoxious, sense, applying to a situation where there is a difference of opinion between equally competent judges on a matter of opinion such as religion. This is the area that needs a clear treatment showing a profound respect for matters of fact and value, and the methods of competent inquiry. It is a golden opportunity for the curriculum. In the obnoxious sense, indoctrination can occur when only one side of the matter is presented, or when the alternative sides are presented inadequately. Moreover, if there is not sufficient time for full exploration and development of the issue then obnoxious indoctrination will inevitably occur.

An indispensable function of the curriculum of the common school is to educate for good citizenship. In the American democracy this means education that is directed toward producing a mentality in all students such that they can distinguish fact from value and can critically evaluate values and rationally choose their own. It is education directed toward achieving a responsible freedom. Specifically it means that the educational process must itself respect the principles of the American constitution while teaching those principles, especially the principles and procedures of the American Bill of Rights. An educational curriculum based on these principles is not a catechism nor indoctrination in the obnoxious sense. This curriculum allows for differences of opinions where views can differ, and it would include a fair amount of discussion about political theory, alternative economic systems, government, contemporary affairs and literature. Its primary goal is the realization of the social purposes of American democratic society as they have been set forth in the Bill of Rights which constitutionally protects diversity. For further discussion see, I. B. Berkson, The Ideal And The Community 253–64 (1958).

FREEDOM FROM GOVERNMENTALLY COMPELLED BELIEFS

WEST VIRGINIA STATE BOARD OF EDUCATION v. BARNETTE

Supreme Court of the United States, 1943.
319 U.S. 624, 63 S.Ct. 1178, 87 L.Ed. 1628.

Mr. Justice JACKSON delivered the opinion of the Court.

Following the decision of this Court on June 3, 1940, in Minersville School District v. Gobitis, 310 U.S. 586, the West Virginia legislature amended its statutes to require all schools therein to conduct courses of instruction in history, civics, and in the Constitutions of the United States and of the State "for the purpose of teaching, fostering and perpetuating the ideals, principles and spirit of Americanism, and increasing the knowledge of the organization and machinery of the government." Appellant Board of Education was directed, with advice of the State Superintendent of Schools, to "prescribe the courses of study covering these subjects" for public schools. The Act made it the duty of private, parochial and denominational schools to prescribe courses of study "similar to those required for the public schools."

The Board of Education on January 9, 1942, adopted a resolution containing recitals taken largely from the Court's *Gobitis* opinion and ordering that the salute to the flag become "a regular part of the program of activities in the public schools," that all teachers and pupils "shall be required to participate in the salute honoring the Nation represented by the Flag; provided, however, that refusal to salute the Flag be regarded as an act of insubordination, and shall be dealt with accordingly."

The resolution originally required the "commonly accepted salute to the Flag" which it defined. Objections to the salute as "being too much like Hitler's" were raised by the Parent and Teachers Association, the Boy and Girl Scouts, the Red Cross, and the Federation of Women's Clubs. Some modification appears to have been made in deference to these objections, but no concession was made to Jehovah's Witnesses. What is now required is the "stiff-arm" salute, the saluter to keep the right hand raised with palm turned up while the following is repeated: "I pledge allegiance to the Flag of the United States of America and to the Republic for which it stands; one Nation, indivisible, with liberty and justice for all."

Failure to conform is "insubordination" dealt with by expulsion. Readmission is denied by statute until compliance. Meanwhile the expelled child is "unlawfully absent" and may be proceeded against as a delinquent. His parents or guardians are liable to prosecution, and if convicted are subject to fine not exceeding $50 and jail term not exceeding thirty days.

Appellees, citizens of the United States and of West Virginia, brought suit in the United States District Court for themselves and others similarly situated asking its injunction to restrain enforcement of these laws and regulations against Jehovah's Witnesses. The Witnesses are an unincorporated body teaching that the obligation imposed by law of God is superior to that of laws enacted by temporal government. Their religious beliefs include a literal version of Exodus, Chapter 20, verses 4 and 5, which says: "Thou shalt not make unto thee any graven image, or any likeness of anything that is in heaven above, or that is in the earth beneath, or that is in the water under the earth; thou shalt not bow down thyself to them nor serve them."

They consider that the flag is an "image" within this command. For this reason they refuse to salute it.

Children of this faith have been expelled from school and are threatened with exclusion for no other cause. Officials threaten to send them to reformatories maintained for criminally inclined juveniles. Parents of such children have been prosecuted and are threatened with prosecutions for causing delinquency.

The Board of Education moved to dismiss the complaint setting forth these facts and alleging that the law and regulations are an unconstitutional denial of religious freedom, and of freedom of speech, and are invalid under the "due process" and "equal protection" clauses of the Fourteenth Amendment to the Federal Constitution. . . .

This case calls upon us to reconsider a precedent decision, as the Court throughout its history often has been required to do. Before turning to the *Gobitis* case, however, it is desirable to notice certain characteristics by which this controversy is distinguished.

The freedom asserted by these appellees does not bring them into collision with rights asserted by any other individual. It is such conflicts which most frequently require intervention of the State to determine where the rights of one end and those of another begin. But the refusal of these persons to participate in the ceremony does not interfere with or deny rights of others to do so. Nor is there any question in this case that their behavior is peaceable and orderly. The sole conflict is between authority and rights of the individual. The State asserts power to condition access to public education on making a prescribed sign and profession and at the same time to coerce attendance by punishing both parent and child. The latter stand on a right of self-determination in matters that touch individual opinion and personal attitude.

As the present CHIEF JUSTICE said in dissent in the *Gobitis* case, the State may "require teaching by instruction and study of all in our history and in the structure and organization of our government, including the guaranties of civil liberty, which tend to inspire patriotism and love of country." . . .   Here, however, we are dealing with a compulsion of students to declare a belief. They are not merely made acquainted with the flag salute so that they may be informed as to what it is or even what it means. The issue here is whether this slow and easily neglected route to aroused loyalties constitutionally may be short-cut by substituting a compulsory salute and slogan. . . .

There is no doubt that, in connection with the pledges, the flag salute is a form of utterance. Symbolism is a primitive but effective way of communicating ideas. The use of an emblem or flag to symbolize some system, idea, institution, or personality, is a short cut from mind to mind. Causes and nations, political parties, lodges and ecclesiastical groups seek to knit the loyalty of their followings to a flag or banner, a color or design.   The State announces rank, function, and authority through crowns and maces, uniforms and black robes; the church speaks through the Cross, the Crucifix, the altar and shrine, and clerical raiment.   Symbols of State often convey political ideas just as religious symbols come to convey theological ones.   Associated with many of these symbols are appropriate gestures of acceptance or respect: a salute, a bowed or bared head, a bended knee.   A person gets from a symbol the meaning he puts into it, and what is one man's comfort and inspiration is another's jest and scorn.

Over a decade ago Chief Justice Hughes led this Court in holding that the display of a red flag as a symbol of opposition by peaceful and legal means to organized government was protected by the free speech guaranties of the Constitution.   Stromberg v. California, 283 U.S. 359.   Here it is the State that employs a flag as a symbol of adherence to government as presently organized.   It requires the individual to communicate by word and sign his acceptance of the political ideas it thus bespeaks.   Objection to this form of communication when coerced is an old one, well known to the framers of the Bill of Rights.

It is also to be noted that the compulsory flag salute and pledge requires affirmation of a belief and an attitude of mind.   It is not clear whether the regulation contemplates that pupils forego any contrary convictions of their own and become unwilling converts to the prescribed ceremony or whether it will be acceptable if they simulate assent by words without belief and by a gesture barren of meaning.   It is now a commonplace that censorship or suppression of expression of opinion is tolerated by our Constitution only when the expression presents a clear and present danger of action of a kind the State is empowered to prevent and punish.   It would seem that involuntary affirmation could be commanded only on even more immediate and urgent grounds than silence.   But here the power of compulsion is invoked without any allegation that remaining passive during a flag salute ritual creates a clear and present danger that would justify an effort even to muffle expression.   To sustain the compulsory flag salute we are required to say that a Bill of Rights which guards the individual's right to speak his own mind, left it open to public authorities to compel him to utter what is not in his mind.

Whether the First Amendment to the Constitution will permit officials to order observance of ritual of this nature does not depend upon whether as a voluntary exercise we would think it to be good, bad or merely innocuous.   Any credo of nationalism is likely to include what some disapprove or to omit what others think essential, and to give off different overtones as it takes on different accents or interpretations.   If official power exists to coerce acceptance of any patriotic creed, what it shall contain cannot be decided by courts, but must be largely discretionary with the ordaining authority, whose power to prescribe would no doubt include power to amend.   Hence validity of the asserted power to force an American citizen publicly to profess any statement of belief or to engage in any ceremony of assent to one, presents questions of power that must be considered independently of any idea we may have as to the utility of the ceremony in question.

Nor does the issue as we see it turn on one's possession of particular religious views or the sincerity with which they are held. While religion supplies appellees' motive for enduring the discomforts of making the issue in this case, many citizens who do not share these religious views hold such a compulsory rite to infringe constitutional liberty of the individual. It is not necessary to inquire whether non-conformist beliefs will exempt from the duty to salute unless we first find power to make the salute a legal duty.

The _Gobitis_ decision, however, _assumed_, as did the argument in that case and in this, that power exists in the State to impose the flag salute discipline upon school children in general. The Court only examined and rejected a claim based on religious beliefs of immunity from an unquestioned general rule. The question which underlies the flag salute controversy is whether such a ceremony so touching matters of opinion and political attitude may be imposed upon the individual by official authority under powers committed to any political organization under our Constitution. We examine rather than assume existence of this power and, against this broader definition of issues in this case, reexamine specific grounds assigned for the _Gobitis_ decision.

1. It was said that the flag-salute controversy confronted the Court with "the problem which Lincoln cast in memorable dilemma: 'Must a government of necessity be too _strong_ for the liberties of its people, or too _weak_ to maintain its own existence?'" and that the answer must be in favor of strength. . . .

We think these issues may be examined free of pressure or restraint growing out of such considerations.

It may be doubted whether Mr. Lincoln would have thought that the strength of government to maintain itself would be impressively vindicated by our confirming power of the State to expel a handful of children from school. Such oversimplification, so handy in political debate, often lacks the precision necessary to postulates of judicial reasoning. If validly applied to this problem, the utterance cited would resolve every issue of power in favor of those in authority and would require us to override every liberty thought to weaken or delay execution of their policies.

Government of limited power need not be anemic government. Assurance that rights are secure tends to diminish fear and jealousy of strong government, and by making us feel safe to live under it makes for its better support. Without promise of a limiting Bill of

Rights it is doubtful if our Constitution could have mustered enough strength to enable its ratification.   To enforce those rights today is not to choose weak government over strong government.   It is only to adhere as a means of strength to individual freedom of mind in preference to officially disciplined uniformity for which history indicates a disappointing and disastrous end.

The subject now before us exemplifies this principle.   Free public education, if faithful to the ideal of secular instruction and political neutrality, will not be partisan or enemy of any class, creed, party, or faction.   If it is to impose any ideological discipline, however, each party or denomination must seek to control, or failing that, to weaken the influence of the educational system.   Observance of the limitations of the Constitution will not weaken government in the field appropriate for its exercise.

2.   It was also considered in the *Gobitis* case that functions of educational officers in States, counties and school districts were such that to interfere with their authority "would in effect make us the school board for the country."   .   .   .

The Fourteenth Amendment, as now applied to the States, protects the citizen against the State itself and all of its creatures—Boards of Education not excepted.   These have, of course, important, delicate, and highly discretionary functions, but none that they may not perform within the limits of the Bill of Rights.   That they are educating the young for citizenship is reason for scrupulous protection of Constitutional freedoms of the individual, if we are not to strangle the free mind at its source and teach youth to discount important principles of our government as mere platitudes.

Such Boards are numerous and their territorial jurisdiction often small.   But small and local authority may feel less sense of responsibility to the Constitution, and agencies of publicity may be less vigilant in calling it to account.   The action of Congress in making flag observance voluntary and respecting the conscience of the objector in a matter so vital as raising the Army contrasts sharply with these local regulations in matters relatively trivial to the welfare of the nation.   There are village tyrants as well as village Hampdens, but none who acts under color of law is beyond reach of the Constitution.

3.   The *Gobitis* opinion reasoned that this is a field "where courts possess no marked and certainly no controlling competence," that it is committed to the legislatures as well as the courts to guard cherished liberties and that it is constitutionally appropriate to "fight out the wise use of legislative authority in the forum of public opinion and before legislative assemblies rather than to transfer such a contest to the judicial arena," since all the "effective means of inducing political changes are left free."   .   .   .

The very purpose of a Bill of Rights was to withdraw certain subjects from the vicissitudes of political controversy, to place them beyond the reach of majorities and officials and to establish them as legal principles to be applied by the courts. One's right to life, liberty, and property, to free speech, a free press, freedom of worship and assembly, and other fundamental rights may not be submitted to vote; they depend on the outcome of no elections.

In weighing arguments of the parties it is important to distinguish between the due process clause of the Fourteenth Amendment as an instrument for transmitting the principles of the First Amendment and those cases in which it is applied for its own sake. The test of legislation which collides with the Fourteenth Amendment, because it also collides with the principles of the First, is much more definite than the test when only the Fourteenth is involved. Much of the vagueness of the due process clause disappears when the specific prohibitions of the First become its standard. The right of a State to regulate, for example, a public utility may well include, so far as the due process test is concerned, power to impose all of the restrictions which a legislature may have a "rational basis" for adopting. But freedoms of speech and of press, of assembly, and of worship may not be infringed on such slender grounds. They are susceptible of restriction only to prevent grave and immediate danger to interests which the State may lawfully protect. It is important to note that while it is the Fourteenth Amendment which bears directly upon the State it is the more specific limiting principles of the First Amendment that finally govern this case.

Nor does our duty to apply the Bill of Rights to assertions of official authority depend upon our possession of marked competence in the field where the invasion of rights occurs. True, the task of translating the majestic generalities of the Bill of Rights, conceived as part of the pattern of liberal government in the eighteenth century, into concrete restraints on officials dealing with the problems of the twentieth century, is one to disturb self-confidence. These principles grew in soil which also produced a philosophy that the individual was the center of society, that his liberty was attainable through mere absence of governmental restraints, and that government should be entrusted with few controls and only the mildest supervision over men's affairs. We must transplant these rights to a soil in which the *laissez-faire* concept or principle of non-interference has withered at least as to economic affairs, and social advancements are increasingly sought through closer integration of society and through expanded and strengthened governmental controls. These changed conditions often deprive precedents of reliability and cast us more than we would choose upon our own judgment. But we act in these matters not by authority of our competence but by force of our commissions. We cannot, because of modest estimates of our competence in such specialties as public education, withhold the judgment that history authenticates as the function of this Court when liberty is infringed.

4.   Lastly, and this is the very heart of the *Gobitis* opinion, it reasons that "National unity is the basis of national security," that the authorities have "the right to select appropriate means for its attainment," and hence reaches the conclusion that such compulsory measures toward "national unity" are constitutional.   .   .   .   Upon the verity of this assumption depends our answer in this case.

National unity as an end which officials may foster by persuasion and example is not in question.   The problem is whether under our Constitution compulsion as here employed is a permissible means for its achievement.

Struggles to coerce uniformity of sentiment in support of some end thought essential to their time and country have been waged by many good as well as by evil men.   Nationalism is a relatively recent phenomenon but at other times and places the ends have been racial or territorial security, support of a dynasty or regime, and particular plans for saving souls.   As first and moderate methods to attain unity have failed, those bent on its accomplishment must resort to an ever-increasing severity.   As governmental pressure toward unity becomes greater, so strife becomes more bitter as to whose unity it shall be.   Probably no deeper division of our people could proceed from any provocation than from finding it necessary to choose what doctrine and whose program public educational officials shall compel youth to unite in embracing.   Ultimate futility of such attempts to compel coherence is the lesson of every such effort from the Roman drive to stamp out Christianity as a disturber of its pagen unity, the Inquisition, as a means to religious and dynastic unity, the Siberian exiles as a means of Russian unity, down to the fast failing efforts of our present totalitarian enemies.   Those who begin coercive elimination of dissent soon find themselves exterminating dissenters.   Compulsory unification of opinion achieves only the unanimity of the graveyard.

It seems trite but necessary to say that the First Amendment to our Constitution was designed to avoid these ends by avoiding these beginnings.   There is no mysticism in the American concept of the State or of the nature or origin of its authority.   We set up government by consent of the governed, and the Bill of Rights denies those in power any legal opportunity to coerce that consent.   Authority here is to be controlled by public opinion, not public opinion by authority.

The case is made difficult not because the principles of its decision are obscure but because the flag involved is our own.   Nevertheless, we apply the limitations of the Constitution with no fear that freedom to be intellectually and spiritually diverse or even contrary will disintegrate the social organization.   To believe that patriotism will not flourish if patriotic ceremonies are voluntary and spontaneous instead of a compulsory routine is to make an unflattering estimate of the appeal of our institutions to free minds.   We can have intellectual individualism and the rich cultural diversities that we owe to exceptional minds only at the price of occasional eccentricity and abnormal attitudes. When they are so harmless to others or to the State as those we deal with here, the price is not too great. But freedom to differ is not limited to things that do not matter much. That would be a mere shadow of freedom. The test of its substance is the right to differ as to things that touch the heart of the existing order.

If there is any fixed star in our constitutional constellation, it is that no official, high or petty, can prescribe what shall be orthodox in politics, nationalism, religion, or other matters of opinion or force citizens to confess by word or act their faith therein. If there are any circumstances which permit an exception, they do not now occur to us.

We think the action of the local authorities in compelling the flag salute and pledge transcends constitutional limitations on their power and invades the sphere of intellect and spirit which it is the purpose of the First Amendment to our Constitution to reserve from all official control.

The decision of this Court in Minersville School District v. Gobitis and the holdings of those few *per curiam* decisions which preceded and foreshadowed it are overruled, and the judgment enjoining enforcement of the West Virginia Regulation is

Affirmed.*

NOTES AND QUESTIONS

1. Would the decision in this case have been different if the plaintiffs had not been Jehovah's Witnesses? If so, what would have been the difference? Why? A teacher? See, Russo v. Central Sch. Dist., 469 F.2d 623 (2d Cir. 1972), cert. den., 411 U.S. 932.

2. Would the decision in this case have been different if the flag salute were optional rather than compulsory? Why? If a student, or teacher, refuses to salute the flag, can school authorities require that he leave the room or stand silently during the ceremony? See, Goetz v. Ansell, 477 F.2d 636 (2nd Cir. 1973).

3. Is it important to the decision in this case to distinguish between a person's action that affects others and a person's action that does not and concerns only that person's claim of free expression against the government?

4. Does this opinion set forth a constitutionally required theory and method of education? Regardless of the subject involved? If so, what is that theory and method? Is it "sound"? Why or why not? According to this opinion how should a teacher teach history, social studies, citizenship or current events?

5. Do you agree with the Court's decision and reasoning? Why or why not?

---

* The concurring opinion of Mr. Justice BLACK joined by Mr. Justice DOUGLAS and the dissenting opinion of Mr. Justice FRANKFURTER are omitted.

6. Why should "the test of legislation which collides with the Fourteenth Amendment, because it also collides with the principles of the First, [be] much more definite than the test when only the Fourteenth is involved"?

7. What was the "legislation" that collided with the Fourteenth Amendment? Is this a case of "legislation" or "state action"?

FREEDOM FROM GOVERNMENTALLY COMPELLED IGNORANCE

MEYER v. NEBRASKA

Supreme Court of the United States, 1923.
262 U.S. 390, 43 S.Ct. 625, 67 L.Ed. 1042.

Mr. Justice McREYNOLDS delivered the opinion of the Court.

Plaintiff in error [Meyer] was tried and convicted in the District Court for Hamilton County, Nebraska, under an information which charged that on May 25, 1920, while an instructor in Zion Parochial School, he unlawfully taught the subject of reading in the German language to Raymond Parpart, a child of ten years, who had not attained and successfully passed the eighth grade. The information is based upon "An act relating to the teaching of foreign languages in the State of Nebraska," . . .

"Section 1. No person, individually or as a teacher, shall, in any private, denominational, parochial or public school, teach any subject to any person in any language other than the English language.

"Sec. 2. Languages, other than the English language, may be taught as languages only after a pupil shall have attained and successfully passed the eighth grade as evidenced by a certificate of graduation issued by the county superintendent of the county in which the child resides.

"Sec. 3. Any person who violates any of the provisions of this act shall be deemed guilty of a misdemeanor and upon conviction, shall be subject to a fine of not less than twenty-five dollars ($25), nor more than one hundred dollars ($100) or be confined in the county jail for any period not exceeding thirty days for each offense.

"Sec. 4. Whereas, an emergency exists, this act shall be in force from and after its passage and approval."

The Supreme Court of the State affirmed the judgment of conviction. . . . It declared the offense charged and established was "the direct and intentional teaching of the German language as a distinct subject to a child who had not passed the eighth grade," in the parochial school maintained by Zion Evangelical Lutheran Congrega-

tion, a collection of Biblical stories being used therefor.   And it held
that the statute forbidding this did not conflict with the Fourteenth
Amendment, but was a valid exercise of the police power.   The following excerpts from the opinion sufficiently indicate the reasons
advanced to support the conclusion.

"The salutary purpose of the statute is clear.   The legislature
had seen the baneful effects of permitting foreigners, who had taken
residence in this country, to rear and educate their children in the
language of their native land.   The result of that condition was found
to be inimical to our own safety.   To allow the children of foreigners,
who had emigrated here, to be taught from early childhood the language of the country of their parents was to rear them with that
language as their mother tongue.   It was to educate them so that they
must always think in that language, and, as a consequence, naturally
inculcate in them the ideas and sentiments foreign to the best interests
of this country.   The statute, therefore, was intended not only to require that the education of all children be conducted in the English
language, but that, until they had grown into that language and until
it had become a part of them, they should not in the schools be taught
any other language.   The obvious purpose of this statute was that the
English language should be and become the mother tongue of all
children reared in this state.   The enactment of such a statute comes
reasonably within the police power of the state.   .   .   .

"It is suggested that the law is an unwarranted restriction, in
that it applies to all citizens of the state and arbitrarily interferes with
the rights of citizens who are not of foreign ancestry, and prevents
them, without reason, from having their children taught foreign languages in school.   That argument is not well taken, for it assumes that
every citizen finds himself restrained by the statute.   The hours which
a child is able to devote to study in the confinement of school are
limited.   It must have ample time for exercise or play.   Its daily
capacity for learning is comparatively small.   A selection of subjects
for its education, therefore, from among the many that might be
taught, is obviously necessary.   The legislature no doubt had in mind
the practical operation of the law.   The law affects few citizens, except
those of foreign lineage.   Other citizens, in their selection of studies,
except perhaps in rare instances, have never deemed it of importance
to teach their children foreign languages before such children have
reached the eighth grade.   In the legislative mind, the salutary effect
of the statute no doubt outweighed the restriction upon the citizens
generally, which, it appears, was a restriction of no real consequence."

The problem for our determination is whether the statute as
construed and applied unreasonably infringes the liberty guaranteed
to the plaintiff in error by the Fourteenth Amendment.   "No State
shall   .   .   .   deprive any person of life, liberty, or property, without
due process of law."

While this Court has not attempted to define with exactness the liberty thus guaranteed, the term has received much consideration and some of the included things have been definitely stated. Without doubt, it denotes not merely freedom from bodily restraint but also the right of the individual to contract, to engage in any of the common occupations of life, to acquire useful knowledge, to marry, establish a home and bring up children, to worship God according to the dictates of his own conscience, and generally to enjoy those privileges long recognized at common law as essential to the orderly pursuit of happiness by free men. . . . The established doctrine is that this liberty may not be interfered with, under the guise of protecting the public interest, by legislative action which is arbitrary or without reasonable relation to some purpose within the competency of the State to effect. Determination by the legislature of what constitutes proper exercise of police power is not final or conclusive but is subject to supervision by the courts. . . .

The American people have always regarded education and acquisition of knowledge as matters of supreme importance which should be diligently promoted. The Ordinance of 1787 declares, "Religion, morality, and knowledge being necessary to good government and the happiness of mankind, schools and the means of education shall forever be encouraged." Corresponding to the right of control, it is the natural duty of the parent to give his children education suitable to their station in life; and nearly all the States, including Nebraska, enforce this obligation by compulsory laws.

Practically, education of the young is only possible in schools conducted by especially qualified persons who devote themselves thereto. The calling always has been regarded as useful and honorable, essential, indeed, to the public welfare. Mere knowledge of the German language cannot reasonably be regarded as harmful. Heretofore it has been commonly looked upon as helpful and desirable. Plaintiff in error taught this language in school as part of his occupation. His right thus to teach and the right of parents to engage him so to instruct their children, we think, are within the liberty of the Amendment.

The challenged statute forbids the teaching in school of any subject except in English; also the teaching of any other language until the pupil has attained and successfully passed the eighth grade, which is not usually accomplished before the age of twelve. The Supreme Court of the State has held that "the so-called ancient or dead languages" are not "within the spirit or the purpose of the act." . . . Latin, Greek, Hebrew are not proscribed; but German, French, Spanish, Italian and every other alien speech are within the ban. Evidently the legislature has attempted materially to interfere with the calling of modern language teachers, with the opportunities of pupils to acquire knowledge, and with the power of parents to control the education of their own.

It is said the purpose of the legislation was to promote civic development by inhibiting training and education of the immature in foreign tongues and ideals before they could learn English and acquire American ideals; and "that the English language should be and become the mother tongue of all children reared in this State." It is also affirmed that the foreign born population is very large, that certain communities commonly use foreign words, follow foreign leaders, move in a foreign atmosphere, and that the children are thereby hindered from becoming citizens of the most useful type and the public safety is imperiled.

That the State may do much, go very far, indeed, in order to improve the quality of its citizens, physically, mentally and morally, is clear; but the individual has certain fundamental rights which must be respected. The protection of the Constitution extends to all, to those who speak other languages as well as to those born with English on the tongue. Perhaps it would be highly advantageous if all had ready understanding of our ordinary speech, but this cannot be coerced by methods which conflict with the Constitution—a desirable end cannot be promoted by prohibited means.

For the welfare of his Ideal Commonwealth, Plato suggested a law which should provide: "That the wives of our guardians are to be common, and their children are to be common, and no parent is to know his own child, nor any child his parent. . . . The proper officers will take the offspring of the good parents to the pen or fold, and there they will deposit them with certain nurses who dwell in a separate quarter; but the offspring of the inferior, or of the better when they chance to be deformed, will be put away in some mysterious, unknown place, as they should be." In order to submerge the individual and develop ideal citizens, Sparta assembled the males at seven into barracks and intrusted their subsequent education and training to official guardians. Although such measures have been deliberately approved by men of great genius, their ideas touching the relation between individual and State were wholly different from those upon which our institutions rest; and it hardly will be affirmed that any legislature could impose such restrictions upon the people of a State without doing violence to both letter and spirit of the Constitution.

The desire of the legislature to foster a homogeneous people with American ideals prepared readily to understand current discussions of civic matters is easy to appreciate. Unfortunate experiences during the late war and aversion toward every characteristic of truculent adversaries were certainly enough to quicken that aspiration. But the means adopted, we think, exceed the limitations upon the power of the State and conflict with rights assured to plaintiff in error. The interference is plain enough and no adequate reason therefor in time of peace and domestic tranquility has been shown.

The power of the State to compel attendance at some school and to make reasonable regulations for all schools, including a requirement that they shall give instructions in English, is not questioned. Nor has challenge been made of the State's power to prescribe a curriculum for institutions which it supports. Those matters are not within the present controversy. Our concern is with the prohibition approved by the Supreme Court. . . . No emergency has arisen which renders knowledge by a child of some language other than English so clearly harmful as to justify its inhibition with the consequent infringement of rights long freely enjoyed. We are constrained to conclude that the statute as applied is arbitrary and without reasonable relation to any end within the competency of the State.

As the statute undertakes to interfere only with teaching which involves a modern language, leaving complete freedom as to other matters, there seems no adequate foundation for the suggestion that the purpose was to protect the child's health by limiting his mental activities. It is well known that proficiency in a foreign language seldom comes to one not instructed at an early age, and experience shows that this is not injurious to the health, morals or understanding of the ordinary child.

The judgment of the court below must be reversed and the cause remanded for further proceedings not inconsistent with this opinion.

Reversed.

Mr. Justice HOLMES, with whom Mr. Justice SUTHERLAND concurred, dissented. His opinion appears in a companion case, Bartels v. Iowa, 262 U.S. 407 . . .

"We all agree, I take it, that it is desirable that all the citizens of the United States should speak a common tongue, and therefore that the end aimed at by the statute is a lawful and proper one. The only question is whether the means adopted deprive teachers of the liberty secured to them by the Fourteenth Amendment. It is with hesitation and unwillingness that I differ from my brethren with regard to a law like this but I cannot bring my mind to believe that in some circumstances, and circumstances existing it is said in Nebraska, the statute might not be regarded as a reasonable or even necessary method of reaching the desired result. The part of the act with which we are concerned deals with the teaching of young children. Youth is the time when familiarity with a language is established and if there are sections in the State where a child would hear only Polish or French or German spoken at home I am not prepared to say that it is unreasonable to provide that in his early years he shall hear and speak only English at school. But if it is reasonable it is not an undue restriction of the liberty either of teacher or scholar. No one would doubt that a teacher might be forbidden to teach many things, and the only criterion of his liberty under the Constitution that I can think of is 'whether, considering the end in view, the statute passes the bounds of reason and assumes the character of a merely arbitrary fiat.' . . . I think I appreciate the objection to the law but it appears to me to present a question upon which men reasonably might differ and therefore I am unable to say that the Constitution of the United States prevents the experiment being tried."

NOTES AND QUESTIONS

1. In Farrington v. Tokushige, 273 U.S. 284, 47 S.Ct. 406, 71 L.Ed. 646 (1927) the Supreme Court held unconstitutional the Foreign Language School Act of Hawaii which was similar to Nebraska's. See also, Mo Hock Ke Lok Po v. Stainback, 74 F.Supp. 852 (D.Hawaii 1947) which held unconstitutional subsequent legislation prohibiting the teaching of a foreign language to children below a specified age or grade, reversed on other grounds, 336 U.S. 368, 69 S.Ct. 606, 93 L.Ed. 741 (1949).

2. What educational ends are within the competency of the state according to this opinion?

EPPERSON v. ARKANSAS

Supreme Court of the United States, 1968.
393 U.S. 97, 89 S.Ct. 266, 21 L.Ed.2d 228.

Mr. Justice FORTAS delivered the opinion of the Court.

This appeal challenges the constitutionality of the "anti-evolution" statute which the State of Arkansas adopted in 1928 to prohibit the teaching in its public schools and universities of the theory that man evolved from other species of life. The statute was a product of the upsurge of "fundamentalist" religious fervor of the twenties. The Arkansas statute was an adaption of the famous Tennessee "monkey law" which that State adopted in 1925. The constitutionality of the Tennessee law was upheld by the Tennessee Supreme Court in the celebrated Scopes case in 1927.

The Arkansas law makes it unlawful for a teacher in any state-supported school or university "to teach the theory or doctrine that mankind ascended or descended from a lower order of animals," or "to adopt or use in any such institution a textbook that teaches" this theory. Violation is a misdemeanor and subjects the violator to dismissal from his position.

The present case concerns the teaching of biology in a high school in Little Rock. According to the testimony, until the events here in litigation, the official textbook furnished for the high school biology course did not have a section on the Darwinian Theory. Then, for the academic year 1965–1966, the school administration, on recommendation of the teachers of biology in the school system, adopted and prescribed a textbook which contained a chapter setting forth "the theory about the origin   *   *   *   of man from a lower form of animal."

Susan Epperson, a young woman who graduated from Arkansas' school system and then obtained her master's degree in zoology at the University of Illinois, was employed by the Little Rock school system in the fall of 1964 to teach 10th grade biology at Central High School. At the start of the next academic year, 1965, she was confronted by the new textbook (which one surmises from the record was not unwelcome to her). She faced at least a literal dilemma because she was supposed to use the new textbook for classroom instruction and presumably to teach the statutorily condemned chapter; but to do so would be a criminal offense and subject her to dismissal.

She instituted the present action in the Chancery Court of the State, seeking a declaration that the Arkansas statute is void and enjoining the State and the defendant officials of the Little Rock school system from dismissing her for violation of the statute's provisions. H. H. Blanchard, a parent of children attending the public schools, intervened in support of the action.

The Chancery Court, in an opinion by Chancellor Murray O. Reed, held that the statute violated the Fourteenth Amendment to the United States Constitution. The court noted that this Amendment encompasses the prohibitions upon state interference with freedom of speech and thought which are contained in the First Amendment. Accordingly, it held that the challenged statute is unconstitutional because, in violation of the First Amendment, it "tends to hinder the quest for knowledge, restrict the freedom to learn, and restrain the freedom to teach." In this perspective, the Act, it held, was an unconstitutional and void restraint upon the freedom of speech guaranteed by the Constitution.

On appeal, the Supreme Court of Arkansas reversed [in a two sentence opinion].   .   .   .   It sustained the statute as an exercise of the State's power to specify the curriculum in public schools. It did not address itself to the competing constitutional considerations. . . .

. . . It is of no moment whether the law is deemed to prohibit mention of Darwin's theory, or to forbid any or all of the infinite varieties of communication embraced within the term "teaching." Under either interpretation, the law must be stricken because of its conflict with the constitutional prohibition of state laws respecting an establishment of religion or prohibiting the free exercise thereof. The overriding fact is that Arkansas' law selects from the body of knowledge a particular segment which it proscribes for the sole reason that it is deemed to conflict with a particular religious doctrine; that is, with a particular interpretation of the Book of Genesis by a particular religious group.

The antecedents of today's decision are many and unmistakable. They are rooted in the foundation soil of our Nation. They are fundamental to freedom. . . .

Judicial interposition in the operation of the public school system of the Nation raises problems requiring care and restraint. Our courts, however, have not failed to apply the First Amendment's mandate in our educational system where essential to safeguard the fundamental values of freedom of speech and inquiry and of belief. By and large, public education in our Nation is committed to the control of state and local authorities. Courts do not and cannot intervene in the resolution of conflicts which arise in the daily operation of school systems and which do not directly and sharply implicate basic constitutional values. On the other hand, "[t]he vigilant protection of constitutional freedoms is nowhere more vital than in the community of American schools," Shelton v. Tucker, . . . As this Court said in Keyishian v. Board of Regents, the First Amendment "does not tolerate laws that cast a pall of orthodoxy over the classroom." . . .

The earliest cases in this Court on the subject of the impact of constitutional guarantees upon the classroom were decided before the Court expressly applied the specific prohibitions of the First Amendment to the States. But as early as 1923, the Court did not hesitate to condemn under the Due Process Clause "arbitrary" restrictions upon the freedom of teachers to teach and of students to learn. In that year, the Court, in an opinion by Justice McReynolds, held unconstitutional an Act of the State of Nebraska making it a crime to teach any subject in any language other than English to pupils who had not passed the eighth grade. The State's purpose in enacting the law was to promote civic cohesiveness by encouraging the learning of English and to combat the "baneful effect" of permitting foreigners to rear and educate their children in the language of the parents' native land. The Court recognized these purposes, and it acknowledged the State's power to prescribe the school curriculum, but it held that these were not adequate to support the restriction upon the liberty of teacher and pupil. The challenged statute it held, unconstitutionally interfered with the right of the individual, guaranteed by the Due Process Clause, to engage in any of the common occupations of life and to acquire useful knowledge. Meyer v. Nebraska, . . .

There is and can be no doubt that the First Amendment does not permit the State to require that teaching and learning must be tailored to the principles or prohibitions of any religious sect or dogma. . . .

. . . The State's undoubted right to prescribe the curriculum for its public schools does not carry with it the right to prohibit, on pain of criminal penalty, the teaching of a scientific theory or doctrine where that prohibition is based upon reasons that violate the First Amendment. It is much too late to argue that the State may impose upon the teachers in its schools any conditions that it chooses, however restrictive they may be of constitutional guarantees.   Keyishian v. Board of Regents,   . . .

In the present case, there can be no doubt that Arkansas has sought to prevent its teachers from discussing the theory of evolution because it is contrary to the belief of some that the Book of Genesis must be the execlusive source of doctrine as to the origin of man.   No suggestion has been made that Arkansas' law may be justified by considerations of state policy other than the religious views of some of its citizens.   It is clear that fundamentalist sectarian conviction was and is the law's reason for existence.   Its antecedent, Tennessee's "monkey law," candidly stated its purpose: to make it unlawful "to teach any theory that denies the story of the Divine Creation of man as taught in the Bible, and to teach instead that man has descended from a lower order of animals."   Perhaps the sensational publicity attendant upon the *Scopes* trial induced Arkansas to adopt less explicit language.   It eliminated Tennessee's reference to "the story of the Divine Creation of man" as taught in the Bible, but there is no doubt that the motivation for the law was the same: to suppress the teaching of a theory which, it was thought, "denied" the divine creation of man.

Arkansas' law cannot be defended as an act of religious neutrality. Arkansas did not seek to excise from the curricula of its schools and universities all discussion of the origin of man.   The law's effort was confined to an attempt to blot out a particular theory because of its supposed conflict with the Biblical account, literally read.   Plainly, the law is contrary to the mandate of the First, and in violation of the Fourteenth, Amendment to the Constitution.

The judgment of the Supreme Court of Arkansas is reversed.

Reversed.

Mr. Justice BLACK, concurring.   . . .

It is plain that a state law prohibiting all teaching of human development or biology is constitutionally quite different from a law that compels a teacher to teach as true only one theory of a given doctrine. It would be difficult to make a First Amendment case out of a state law eliminating the subject of higher mathematics, or astronomy, or biology from its curriculum.   And, for all the Supreme Court of Arkansas has said, this particular Act may prohibit that and nothing else. This Court, however, treats the Arkansas Act as though it made it a misdemeanor to teach or to use a book that teaches that evolution is true.   But it is not for this Court to arrogate to itself the power to determine the scope of Arkansas statutes.   Since the highest court of Arkansas has deliberately refused to give its statute that meaning, we should not presume to do so.

It seems to me that in this situation the statute is too vague for us to strike it down on any ground but that: <u>vagueness.</u>   Under this statute as construed by the Arkansas Supreme Court, a teacher cannot know whether he is forbidden to mention Darwin's theory, at all or only free to discuss it as long as he refrains from contending that it is true. It is an established rule that a statute which leaves an ordinary man so doubtful about its meaning that he cannot know when he has violated it denies him the first essential of due process. . . . Holding the statute too vague to enforce would not only follow long-standing constitutional precedents but it would avoid having this Court take unto itself the duty of a State's highest court to interpret and mark the boundaries of the State's laws. And, more important, it would not place this Court in the unenviable position of violating the principle of leaving the States absolutely free to choose their own curriculums for their own schools so long as their action does not palpably conflict with a clear constitutional command. . . .

Mr. Justice STEWART, concurring in the result.

The States are most assuredly free "to choose their own curriculums for their own schools." A State is entirely free, for example, to decide that the only foreign language to be taught in its public school system shall be Spanish. But would a State be constitutionally free to punish a teacher for letting his students know that other languages are also spoken in the world? I think not.

It is one thing for a State to determine that "the subject of higher mathematics, or astronomy, or biology" shall or shall not be included in its public school curriculum. It is quite another thing for a State to make it a criminal offense for a public school teacher so much as to mention the very existence of an entire system of respected human thought. That kind of criminal law, I think, would clearly impinge upon the guarantees of free communication contained in the First Amendment, and made applicable to the States by the Fourteenth.

The Arkansas Supreme Court has said that the statute before us may or may not be just such a law. The result, as Mr. Justice BLACK points out, is that "a teacher cannot know whether he is forbidden to mention Darwin's theory at all." Since I believe that no State could constitutionally forbid a teacher "to mention Darwin's theory at all," and since Arkansas may, or may not, have done just that, I conclude that the statute before us is so vague as to be invalid under the Fourteenth Amendment.*

NOTES AND QUESTIONS

1. The usual presumption attendant upon a state statute is that it is constitutional, and it is necessary for the party asserting its unconstitutionality to carry the burden of proof. In *Epperson* the Court assumed that the statute in question had a religious purpose and the

---

* A concurring opinion by Mr. Justice HARLAN is omitted.

burden of proving its constitutionality fell upon the state. Why should the Court reverse the presumption of constitutionality in this case?

2. Is the justifying rationale for the Epperson decision freedom of religion or academic freedom? What difference does it make? Should the rationale of decision have been unconstitutional vagueness? What difference would it make?

3. Do you believe that Mrs. Epperson was in danger of losing her job? No one had ever been prosecuted under the enforcement statute. Was this case a "tempest in a teapot"? Or was it worthwhile? Why?

4. Assuming that to some religious orders the teaching of the doctrine of evolution is "anti-religious", does the state have constitutional power to require or permit the teaching of a doctrine that is hostile to religion? Does the Epperson decision violate the religious freedom of those persons who consider the doctrine of evolution to be anti-religious?

5. A student teacher who, in response to questions from his students, stated that Darwin's theory of the origin of specie and the evolution of life is a valid one, and who stated he did not attend church, believe in life after death, nor in heaven or hell, was summarily discharged after a complaint had been lodged by parents. The court granted the teacher a judgment against school authorities ruling that the discharge was a violation of the establishment clause of the First Amendment. Moore v. Gaston Cty. Board of Education, 357 F.Supp. 1037 (W.D.N.Car.1973).

6. What are the implications of West Virginia v. Barnette, Meyer v. Nebraska and Epperson v. Arkansas for the teacher?

VALENT v. STATE BOARD OF EDUCATION

Superior Court of New Jersey, 1971.
114 N.J.Super. 63, 274 A.2d 832.

STAMLER, J. S. C. . . . Generally, plaintiffs [Valent] allege that a course entitled "Human Sexuality" given in the Parsippany-Troy Hills public schools requiring the attendance of their children violates the First, Ninth, Tenth and Fourteenth Amendments of the United States Constitution and Art. I, pars. 3 and 4 of the New Jersey Constitution. [Defendants moved for summary judgment.]

Collating the allegations of the verified complaint in each of its seven counts with the answers, there is but one area in which denials are found. . . . The local board does deny that the questioned course includes teachings and discussions of sexual intercourse, masturbation and contraception, contrary to religious beliefs of plaintiffs; that the course is critical of parental authority; that a *de facto* religion is created. . . .

We come through the years from 1878 to *Sherbert,* [374 U.S. 398] in 1963. A startling instruction by the United States Supreme Court for trial court conduct in "free exercise" cases appears between the lines. Mrs. Sherbert, a Seventh Day Adventist, was denied unemployment compensation because of her unwillingness to accept employment which required her to work on Saturday, a religious day. Mr. Justice Brennan, speaking for the Supreme Court, stated:

> It is basic that no showing merely of a rational relationship to some colorable state interest would suffice [to justify the denial]; in this highly sensitive constitutional area, "[o]nly the gravest abuses, endangering paramount interests, give occasion for permissible limitation." (374 U.S. at p. 406, 83 S.Ct. at p. 1795.)

Because the state had failed to carry its burden of showing clearly that an essential state interest would be jeopardized by non-compliance, Mrs. Sherbert prevailed. To put it another way, the impact of the questioned regulation upon her amounted to the loss of her living allowance, and the interest of the state was not particularly endangered. Additionally, an unquestioned, sincere religious belief was protected. . . .

The infant plaintiffs, speaking through their parents, state that they are sincere in their beliefs; that the program in "Human Sexuality" is derogatory to the beliefs that their religion requires them to entertain.

State v. Perricone, 37 N.J. 463, 181 A.2d 751 (1962), clearly exhibits that the trial court and our Supreme Court anticipated the *Sherbert* requirements of balancing. In *Perricone* the parents refused to grant permission for a blood transfusion for their infant son. The refusal was based upon their affiliation with and membership in Jehovah's Witnesses, whose dogma forbids the taking of blood or transferring it from one person to another. The trial court not only heard testimony of medical witnesses as to the child's condition, but also testimony of the parents as to the basis for the assertion of religious conscience. On appeal from an adverse decision at the trial level, the Perricones argued that their constitutional rights of parental care and religious freedom had been violated. . . .

In upholding the State's position, the Supreme Court concluded that the facts placed on the balance clearly evidenced a compelling necessity for the protection of the welfare of the child.

The intrusion into the religious life and parental authority in *Perricone* can be justified because the State, as *parens patriae,* is charged with protecting a child from "immediate and present danger," and the parents in the context of the case were unfit, cruel or neglectful. . . .

The questions to be answered in the present case are the extent of the governmental interest in promoting this program of "Human

Sexuality" and whether permitting a student to be excused therefrom will detract substantially from or prevent the success of an essential program. Plaintiffs' assertion of a right of conscience is more impressive than the scorecard which was presented by the defendant local board, that 70% of the Junior Chamber of Commerce poll thought sex education was a good idea.

Defendants attempt to persuade the court that because in the recent school board elections the "pro-sex-education" candidates defeated the "anti-sex-education" candidates, an over-riding governmental interest and necessity is clearly demonstrated. This is completely unacceptable. If majority rule were to govern in matters of religion and conscience, there would be no need for the First Amendment.

The First Amendment, and particularly the "free exercise clause," was adopted to protect the one percent, one individual, one person, who is sincere in a conscientious religious conviction. . . .

The case of Epperson v. Arkansas, 393 U.S. 97, 89 S.Ct. 266, 21 L. Ed.2d 228 (1968), the successor case to the Scopes trial, in which the Arkansas statute prohibiting the teaching of evolution was struck down, does not sustain defendants' position here.

There is nothing inherently evil from a constitutional standpoint in teaching evolution or comparative religions as historical fact. The disputed area of evolution, still disputed after all these years, is a matter of one belief in a scientific fact which does not intrude as long as other doctrine of genesis is given to the children. . . . *Epperson* does clearly state that the First Amendment mandate is absolute and "forbids alike the preference of a religious doctrine or the prohibition of theory which is deemed antagonistic to a particular dogma."
. . .

In the case at bar what is taught is operational—how best to plan a future life and what conduct is acceptable and which, according to plaintiff, is in direct conflict with or derogatory of plaintiffs' religious belief. The First Amendment stands ready, in the "free exercise" clause, to protect that person. Once it is shown that the state intrudes upon one's religious belief, the state, according to *Sherbert,* has the burden of showing an overriding need and that it has no other way to satisfy that need.

If the state can demonstrate that no satisfactory alternative exists, then the interest of the state and individual must be balanced. It may be that the individual's conscience may be fully protected by excusal from the program, or it may be that attendance is required because failure to perform the imposed duty has a harmful effect upon society generally and therefore involves a detriment to others. For example, a person may be required to take a smallpox or measles inoculation because failure to submit to injection may affect the health and welfare of many others in the community. There the state program is found to have an overriding purpose.

However, in dealing with persons who are fully consenting (unlike the situation in *Perricone,* supra), it may be that if an act is against religious belief and harms no other person, that person may be excused from submitting. For example, in the area of injections of penicillin and surgical procedures upon those people who practice Chistian Science. It should be apparent that, in a "free exercise" case requiring a balancing approach, judicial determinations are not solely answers to questions of law on summary judgment. Facts must either be proven or stipulated and then balanced before a legal standard can be applied and judgment rendered.

The motion of defendants for summary judgment is denied. . .

NOTES AND QUESTIONS

1. In this case the court denied a motion for summary judgment. A motion for summary judgment is a procedure used to determine whether there is an issue of any material fact in a lawsuit, and, if not, whether any of the parties is entitled to a judgment as a matter of law without going through a trial. In ruling on a motion for summary judgment the court does not resolve factual issues; rather, it determines whether there are any factual issues the resolution of which would materially effect the outcome of a trial. The court has no discretionary power to grant a motion for summary judgment but may do so only when, after weighing all the evidence most heavily against the moving party, it can state as a matter of law that one party must prevail. The purpose of the summary judgment procedure is to expedite the judicial process by disposing of frivolous law suits. A denial of a motion for summary judgment does not mean necessarily that at a subsequent trial on the merits the opposing party will prevail. Such denial only means that the court cannot rule as a matter of law that the moving party must prevail before factual issues are resolved by the triers of fact—jury or judge.

2. How do you think this case ought to be decided when tried on the merits?

FREEDOM FROM ARBITRARY TEACHING METHODS

———

WASILEWSKI v. BOARD OF SCHOOL DIRECTORS OF THE CITY OF MILWAUKEE

Supreme Court of Wisconsin, 1961.
14 Wis.2d 243, 111 N.W.2d 198.

CURRIE, Justice. . . .   May a teacher, such as relator, having tenure . . . be discharged for his conduct, in discussing matters of sex in his classes, which is alleged to transgress "good behavior" when the teacher has violated no rule promulgated by the superintendent or the board, and has received no advance warning that such conduct was disapproved by the school authorities?   .   .   .

Under the provisions of sec. 38.24(18), Stats., a teacher having tenure, such as relator, may only be discharged for conduct which transgresses the bounds of good behavior or constitutes inefficiency. The first issue to be considered is concerned only with the question of what bad behavior would be sufficient cause for discharge.   .   .

.   .   .   relator argues that the board's action in discharging him for interjecting matters of sex education into his speech classes was arbitrary, oppressive, and unreasonable.   However, such argument fails to recognize that the issue is not whether it was improper conduct for relator to discuss sex in his speech classes, but rather whether his handling of this topic was such a violation of recognized standards of propriety as to constitute bad behavior.   Thus, if relator's discourses on sex in his speech classes had been conducted in such a manner as to constitute proper conduct in a biology class, they would not automatically have been converted into misconduct warranting discharge by the happenstance that they took place in a speech class, absent any rule of the school authorities prohibiting the same or any specific warning to relator from the principal or superintendent that sex was not to be a subject of discussion in speech classes.   However, if relator's manner of discoursing on the topic of sex in his speech classes exceeded the bounds of the recognized standards of propriety, we deem that it constituted bad conduct which would warrant a discharge even though there was no express rule prohibiting it and he had received no warning to desist therefrom.   As an intelligent person trained to teach at the high school level, relator should have realized that such conduct was improper.   .   .   .

In reviewing this record we are satisfied that the following findings as to relator's acts in his speech classes, establish conduct transcending the contemporary standards of propriety of the community in which he taught: (1) That relator walked from desk to desk during a discussion of houses of prostitution and indicated to each student whether, in his opinion, such student was of such apparent age as to gain admittance to a house of prostitution;   (2) that he told the "Schultz" and "cow" vulgar stories;   (3) that he described the act of breaking the hymen of a virgin in such a manner as to give his students the impression that he was describing a personal experience— being an unmarried man he thereby may well have given the impression that he considered it proper conduct to violate the criminal statutes prohibiting fornication;   (4) that in discussing pre-marital sex relations, he indicated to his students that he believed in the same, although he qualified this view by stating that such relations might be objectionable under certain circumstances, such as where this practice violated religious beliefs;   and (5) that he discussed pre-marital sex relations without pointing out to the students that there were state statutes prohibiting the same.

In arriving at this conclusion we are unmindful of the fact that relator's speech classes were composed entirely of senior boys, and that the ages of such boys were from seventeen to nineteen years, inclusive.

There are sound reasons of policy why such conduct, by transcending the bounds of the standards of propriety of the contemporary community, constituted misconduct under sec. 38.24(18), Stats. As was well pointed out by the learned trial court in his memorandum opinion, a teacher exerts considerable influence in moulding the social and moral outlook of his students by his own precept, deportment, and example. This is especially true of a popular and effective teacher such as the record in this case discloses relator to have been. The importance of the teacher in moulding the social and moral views of his students is well stated in one of the texts on education as follows:

> "If we agree that the moral virtues are not taught and learned in the usual way, or at least not in the same way in which reading and writing and arithmetic are taught and learned, then they are incorporated into the pupil's system of values through practice, example, and emulation. With respect to moral formation the role of the teacher may not be minimized, for he is the chief creator of the student's educational environment and the main source of his inspiration."

In considering the immediately preceding issue, we have set forth certain conduct of the relator which has been determined to constitute misconduct warranting the discharge. Relator attacks the sufficiency of the evidence to sustain the findings of fact, whereby these enumerated activities were found to have occurred, as well as other additional findings of fact.

Our review of the testimony given at the hearing causes us to conclude that the board could reasonably make the findings which it did even though in some respects this court might have reached the opposite conclusion if it had been the trier of the facts. The applicable principle of law is well stated in State ex rel. Morehouse v. Hunt, 1940, 235 Wis. 358, 367, 291 N.W. 745, 749, as follows:

> "The case is *certiorari*. When *certiorari* is invoked to review the action of an administrative board, the findings of the board upon the facts before it are conclusive if in any reasonable view the evidence sustains them."

The testimony relating to certain of the matters covered in the findings is in sharp dispute. We can perceive of no useful purpose which would be served by recounting the testimony of the various witnesses.

. . . .

MARTIN, Chief Justice, and HALLOWS, Justice (concurring).

certiorari - case has been granted a hearing.

(extra verbiage used?)

We concur in the result but do not agree with much of the dicta and the reasoning of the majority. Much of what has been said would have been better off unsaid. We especially object to the proposition advanced that a teacher certified to teach history, English and speech can discuss a controversial subject of sex in his speech class as a teacher certified to teach biology might discuss it in a biology class in the absence of any rule of the school authorities or any specific warning that sex was not to be the subject of discussion in speech classes.

A teacher is hired for his competency to teach certain subjects. Sex education is a subject matter for which a teacher should be especially competent to teach. A parent and the school authorities have a right to expect that children are not going to be exposed to comments, discussions, and personal opinions of a teacher on sex who had not been certified to teach such subject in classes which do not relate to such subjects. There need be no rule of school authorities prohibiting the same or any specific warning to the teacher not to discuss sex in his classroom unless specifically authorized.

The majority opinion fails to recognize the right of the parent to determine whether his child shall be taught about sex in the public schools. The subject is optional. The concern of the parent as to who is to teach the subject and what his or her background and qualifications are, and the parent's right to visit the class in which the subject is discussed, are all ignored in the majority opinion. Only one qualified and so certified by the proper authorities should be allowed to undertake to teach this delicate subject and only in a class expressly held for that purpose.

A parent has the right to visit such a class to determine how such instructions are being given, who is giving the instructions, and in general know of the existing conditions. A parent should not be forced to visit each and every class which his child attends to determine whether sex education is being given and if it is, how it is being handled.

What has happened in this case may well be taken as an example of what we may expect if sex education is being given in classes other than those designated for that purpose.

Under the majority opinion, an unqualfied, unauthorized person, entirely unfit, may have his fling at teaching or instructing in sex education with little fear of the consequences, except perhaps a mild censure, unless the school board adopts a rule prohibiting such activity. It seems to us to be bad in itself, not bad because it is prohibited, mala in se, not mala prohibita.

NOTES AND QUESTIONS

1. The concurring opinion in this case says that the teacher's wrongful acts were "mala in se, not mala prohibita." What is the difference between these terms? See any Law Dictionary.

2. Does the reasoning of the concurring opinion suggest that a teacher of history would be forbidden to discuss the moral decay of the Roman Catholic Church in Europe prior to and during the Reformation because he isn't certified by the state to teach religion? Aren't school curriculum disciplines abstract categories which are compartmentalized for pedagogical purposes only? In fact, don't such disciplines flow into and affect each other so that a discussion about economics, for example, requires a knowledge of psychology, political science, mathematics and history? Could an economics teacher adequately teach economics without discussing the alternative and competing economic systems such as capitalism, socialism, communism? Would an economics teacher who discussed the economic system of communism be "teaching communism"?

3. California's law resolves the sex education question this way:

    "No governing board of a public elementary or secondary school may require pupils to attend any class in which human reproductive organs and their functions and processes are described, illustrated or discussed, whether such class be part of a course designated "sex education" or "family life education" or by some similar term, or part of any other course which pupils are required to attend.

    "If classes are offered in public elementary and secondary schools in which human reproductive organs and their functions and processes are described, illustrated or discussed, the parent or guardian of each pupil enrolled in such class shall first be notified in writing of the class. Sending the required notice through the regular United States mail, or any other method which such local school district commonly uses to communicate individually in writing to all parents, meets the notification requirements of this paragraph.

    "Opportunity shall be provided to each parent or guardian to request in writing that his child not attend the class. Such requests shall be valid for the school year in which they are submitted but may be withdrawn by the parent or guardian at any time. No child may attend a class if a request that he not attend the class has been received by the school.

    "Any written or audiovisual material to be used in a class in which human reproductive organs and their functions and processes are described, illustrated, or discussed shall be available for inspection by the parent or guardian at reasonable times and places prior to the holding of a course which includes such classes. The parent or guardian shall be notified in writing of his opportunity to inspect and review such materials.

"This section shall not apply to description or illustration of human reproductive organs which may appear in a textbook, adopted pursuant to law, on physiology, biology, zoology, general science, personal hygiene, or health.

"Nothing in this section shall be construed as encouraging the description, illustration, or discussion of human reproductive organs and their functions and processes in the public elementary and secondary schools.

"The certification document of any person charged with the responsibility of making any instructional material available for inspection under this section or who is charged with the responsibility of notifying a parent or guardian of any class conducted within the purview of this section, and who knowingly and willfully fails to make instructional material available for inspection or to notify such parent or guardian, may be revoked or suspended because of such act. The certification document of any person who knowingly and willfully requires a pupil to attend a class within the purview of this section when a request that the pupil not attend has been received from the parent or guardian may be revoked or suspended because of such act." West's Ann.Educ.Code of Calif. § 8506.

What are the merits and demerits of this statute? If you had been a California legislator would you have voted for this statute? Why or why not? Would it have been relevant to the decisions in the Wasilewski and Mailloux cases if it had been the law of those states at the time of decision? Why or why not?

MAILLOUX v. KILEY

United States District Court, 1971.
323 F.Supp. 1387 (D.Mass.), aff'd 448 F.2d 1242 (1st. Cir., 1971).

WYZANSKI, Chief Judge. This case involves an action by a public high school teacher against the City of Lawrence, the members of its school committee, the superintendent of its schools, and the principal of its high school. Plaintiff claims that in discharging him for his classroom conduct in connection with a taboo word the school committee deprived him of his rights under the First and Fourteenth Amendments to the United States Constitution, and that, therefore he has a cause of action under 42 U.S.C. § 1983 within this court's jurisdiction under 28 U.S.C. § 1343(3).

These are the facts as found by this court after a full hearing.

.   .   .   Defendant principal assigned plaintiff to teach basic English to a class of about 25 students, boys and girls 16 and 17 years of age, all in the junior class or 11th grade.

Plaintiff assigned to the class for outside reading chapters in a novel, The Thread That Runs So True, by Jesse Stuart. The novel describes an incident based on the experiences of the author as a young country school teacher in rural Kentucky. He had taken over a one-room school in which the class had been seated with boys on one side, and girls on the other side, of the room. He intermingled the sexes for seating. Some parents objected on the ground the new teacher was running a "courting school." Nowhere in the novel is there the word "fuck."

October 1, 1970, during a discussion of the book in class, some students thought the protest against changing the seating in the Kentucky classroom was ridiculous. Plaintiff said that other things today are just as ridiculous. He then introduced the subject of society and its ways, as illustrated by taboo words. He wrote the word "goo" on the board and asked the class for a definition. No one being able to define it, plaintiff said that this word did not exist in English but in another culture it might be a taboo word. He then wrote on the blackboard the word "fuck," and, in accordance with his customary teaching methods of calling for volunteers to respond to a question, asked the class in general for a definition. After a couple of minutes a boy volunteered that the word meant "sexual intercourse." Plaintiff, without using the word orally, said: "we have two words, sexual intercourse, and this word on the board *   *   *   one *   *   *   is acceptable by society *   *   *   the other is not accepted. It is a taboo word." After a few minutes of discussion of other aspects of taboos, plaintiff went on to other matters.

At all times in the discussion plaintiff was in good faith pursuing what he regarded as an educational goal. He was not attempting to probe the private feelings, or attitudes, or experiences of his students, or to embarrass them.

October 2, 1970, the parent of a girl in the class, being erroneously informed that plaintiff had called upon a particular girl in the class to define the taboo word, complained to the principal. He asked Miss Horner, the head of the English department, to investigate the incident. Plaintiff did admit that he had written on the board the taboo word. He also said he had "probably" called upon a specific girl to define the word. But this court is persuaded by all the testimony that he did not in fact call on any girl individually and that his statement to Miss Horner, repeated later to the union, of what he "probably" did is not an accurate statement of what he actually did. At his meeting with Miss Horner, plaintiff did not refer to the novel which the class had been discussing.

After plaintiff had been interviewed by Miss Horner, defendant superintendent on October 13, 1970 suspended him for seven days with pay.

Plaintiff engaged counsel who requested a hearing before the school committee, and a bill of particulars. The committee furnished particulars alleging that:

" *   *   * Mr. Mailloux did write a list of words on the chalkboard.

One of the words was 'fuck'."

A female student was asked to define the word 'fuck'."

"When confronted with the incident by the head of the department, Mr. Mailloux admitted that the incident was true." . . .

The committee gave plaintiff and his counsel a hearing on October 20, 1970.

October 21, 1970 the committee dismissed plaintiff on the general charge of "conduct unbecoming a teacher." It made no finding as to any specific particular.

Following his discharge, plaintiff brought this action seeking temporary and permanent relief. . . .

. . . . Upon the basis of [two] hearings this court makes the following additional findings.

1.   The topic of taboo words had a limited relevance to the Stuart novel which plaintiff's class was discussing, but it had a high degree of relevance to the proper teaching of eleventh grade basic English even to students not expecting to go to college and therefore placed in a "low track."

2.   The word "fuck" is relevant to a discussion of taboo words. Its impact effectively illustrates how taboo words function.

3.   Boys and girls in an eleventh grade have a sophistication sufficient to treat the word from a serious educational viewpoint. While at first they may be surprised and self-conscious to have the word discussed, they are not likely to be embarrassed or offended.

4.   Plaintiff's writing the word did not have a disturbing effect. A class might be less disturbed by having the word written than if it had been spoken. Most students had seen the word even if they had not used it.

5.   Plaintiff's calling upon the class for a volunteer to define the word was a technique that was reasonable and was in accordance with customs in plaintiff's class. It avoided implicating anyone who did not wish to participate.

6.   The word "fuck" is in books in the school library.

7.   In the opinion of experts of significant standing, such as members of the faculties of the Harvard University School of Education and of Massachusetts Institute of Technology, the discussion of taboo words in the eleventh grade, the way plaintiff used the word "fuck," his writing of it on the blackboard, and the inquiry he addressed to the class, were appropriate and reasonable under the circumstances and served a serious educational purpose. In the opinion of other qualified persons plaintiff's use of the word was not under the circumstances reasonable, or appropriate, or conducive to a serious educational purpose. It has not been shown what is the pre-

ponderant opinion in the teaching profession, or in that part of the profession which teaches English.

The parties have not relied upon any express regulation of the Lawrence School Committee or the Lawrence High School. The regulations set forth in an attachment to the complaint have no general or specific provisions relevant to this case.

We now turn to questions of ultimate fact and of law. . . .

The Fourteenth Amendment recognizes that a public school teacher has not only a civic right to freedom of speech both outside . . . the schoolhouse, but also some measure of academic freedom as to his in-classroom teaching. . . .

. . . cases . . . [uphold] two kinds of academic freedom: the substantive right of a teacher to choose a teaching method which in the court's view served a demonstrated educational purpose; and the procedural right of a teacher not to be discharged for the use of a teaching method which was not proscribed by a regulation, and as to which it was not proven that he should have had notice that its use was prohibited. . . .

The teaching methods plaintiff used were obviously not "necessary" to the proper teaching of the subject and students assigned to him, in the sense that a reference to Darwinian evolution might be thought necessary to the teaching of biology. See the concurrence of Mr. Justice Stewart in Epperson v. Arkansas, 393 U.S. 97, 116,
. . .

Here we have the use of teaching methods which divide professional opinion. There is substantial support from expert witnesses of undoubted competence that the discussion of taboo words was relevant to an assigned book, and, whether or not so relevant, was at least relevant to the subject of eleventh grade English, that "fuck" was an appropriate choice of an illustrative taboo word, and that writing it on the board and calling upon the class to define it were appropriate techniques. Yet there was also substantial evidence, chiefly from persons with experience as principals but also from the head of the English department at plaintiff's school, that it was inappropriate to use the particular word under the circumstances of this case. The weight of the testimony offered leads this court to make an ultimate finding that plaintiff's methods served an educational purpose, in the sense that they were relevant and had professional endorsement from experts of significant standing. But this court has not implied that the weight of opinion in the teaching profession as a whole, or the weight of opinion among English teachers as a whole, would be that plaintiff's methods were within limits that, even if they would not themselves use them, they would regard as permissible for others. To make a finding on that point would have required a more thorough sampling, especially of younger teachers, than the record offers.

.   .   .   the use in the classroom of the word "fuck" is not impermissible under all circumstances—as, for example when it appears in a book properly assigned for student reading.   But a teacher who uses a taboo sexual word must take care not to transcend his legitimate professional purpose.   When a male teacher asks a class of adolescent boys and girls to define a taboo sexual word the question must not go beyond asking for verbal knowledge and become a titillating probe of privacy.   He must not sacrifice his dignity to join his pupils as "frere et cochon."   Here it should be stated unequivocally, there is no evidence that this plaintiff transcended legitimate professional purposes.   Indeed, the court has specifically found he acted in good faith.   But the risk of abuse involved in the technique of questioning students precludes this court from concluding that the method was *plainly* permissible.   Too much depends on the context and the teacher's good faith.

Where, as here, a secondary school teacher chooses a teaching method that is not necessary for the proper instruction of his class, that is not shown to be regarded by the weight of opinion in his profession as permissible, that is not so transparently proper that a court can without expert testimony evaluate it as proper, but that is relevant to his subject and students and, in the opinion of experts of significant standing, serves a serious educational purpose, it is a heretofore undecided question whether the Constitution gives him any right to use the method or leaves the issue to the school authorities.   .   .

In support of a qualified right of a teacher, even at the secondary level, to use a teaching method which is relevant and in the opinion of experts of significant standing has a serious educational purpose is the central rationale of academic freedom.   The Constitution recognizes that freedom in order to foster open minds, creative imaginations, and adventurous spirits.   Our national belief is that the heterodox as well as the orthodox are a source of individual and of social growth.   We do not confine academic freedom to conventional teachers or to those who can get a majority vote from their colleagues.   Our faith is that the teacher's freedom to choose among options for which there is any substantial support will increase his intellectual vitality and his moral strength.   The teacher whose responsibility has been nourished by independence, enterprise, and free choice becomes for his student a better model of the democratic citizen.   His examples of applying and adapting the values of the old order to the demands and opportunities of a constantly changing world are among the most important lessens he gives to youth.

Yet the secondary school situation is distinguishable from higher levels of education.   .   .   .   There are constitutional considerations of magnitude which, predictably, might warrant a legal conclusion that the secondary school teacher's constitutional right in his classroom is only to be free from discriminatory religious, racial, political and like measure. Epperson v. Arkansas, supra, and from state action which is unreasonable, or perhaps has not even a plausible rational basis. . . .

The secondary school more clearly than the college or university acts *in loco parentis* with respect to minors. It is closely governed by a school board selected by a local community. The faculty does not have the independent traditions, the broad discretion as to teaching methods, nor usually the intellectual qualifications, of university professors. Among secondary school teachers there are often many persons with little experience. Some teachers and most students have limited intellectual and emotional maturity. Most parents, students, school boards, and members of the community usually expect the secondary school to concentrate on transmitting basic information, teaching "the best that is known and thought in the world," training by established techniques, and, to some extent at least, indoctrinating in the *mores* of the surrounding society. While secondary schools are not rigid disciplinary institutions, neither are they open forums in which mature adults, already habituated to social restraints, exchange ideas on a level of parity. Moreover, it cannot be accepted as a premise that the student is voluntarily in the classroom and willing to be exposed to a teaching method which, though reasonable, is not approved by the school authorities or by the weight of professional opinion. A secondary school student, unlike most college students, is usually required to attend school classes, and may have no choice as to his teacher.

Bearing in mind these competing considerations, this court rules that when a secondary school teacher uses a teaching method which he does not prove has the support of the preponderant opinion of the teaching profession or of the part of it to which he belongs, but which he merely proves is relevant to his subject and students, is regarded by experts of significant standing as serving a serious educational purpose, and was used by him in good faith the state may suspend or discharge a teacher for using that method but it may not resort to such drastic sanctions unless the state proves he was put on notice either by a regulation or otherwise that he should not use that method. This exclusively procedural protection is afforded to a teacher not because he is a state employee, or because he is a citizen, but because in his teaching capacity he is engaged in the exercise of what may plausibly be considered "vital First Amendment rights." Keyishian v. Board of Regents, 385 U.S. 489, 604, 87 S.Ct. 675, 684, 17 L.Ed.2d 629. In his teaching capacity he is not required to "guess what conduct or utterance may lose him his position," (Ibid). If he did not have the right to be warned before he was discharged, he might be more timid than it is in the public interest that he should be, and he might steer away from reasonable methods with which it is in the public interest to experiment. Ibid.

In the instant case it is not claimed that any regulation warned plaintiff not to follow the methods he chose. Nor can it be said that plaintiff should have known that his teaching methods were not permitted. There is no substantial evidence that his methods were contrary to an informal rule, to an understanding among school teachers of his school or teachers generally, to a body of disciplinary precedents, to precise canons of ethics, or to specific opinions expressed in professional journals or other publications. This was not the kind of unforeseeable outrageous conduct which all men of good will would, once their attention is called to it, immediately perceive to be forbidden. On this last point it is sufficient to refer to the testimony given by faculty members of Harvard University and M. I. T. who had prepared their students for secondary school teaching careers.

Finally, in the face of the record of judicial uncertainty in this case it cannot be held that it was self-evident that a teacher should not have used the methods followed by plaintiff. . . .

Inasmuch as at the time he acted plaintiff did not know, and there was no reason that he should have known, that his conduct was proscribed, it was a violation of due process for the defendants to suspend or discharge him on that account. . . .

. . . Nothing herein suggests that school authorities are not free after they have learned that the teacher is using a teaching method of which they disapprove, and which is not appropriate to the proper teaching of the subject, to suspend him until he agrees to cease using the method. . . .

NOTES AND QUESTIONS

1. If you had been the judge in the Mailloux case would you have decided it differently? Why or why not? In the Wasilewski case?

2. Do these cases involve constitutional law decisions? If so, what part of the constitution is relied upon?

3. What would have been the decision and rationale in the two cases if there had been a rule, regulation, policy or custom of the Board of Education prohibiting the classroom use of words like "fuck"? Would the Epperson case be relevant to such a problem? West Va. v. Barnette? Meyer v. Nebraska? Sweezy v. New Hampshire?

4. Would the decision in Mailloux have been any different if a book used in the class had been the subject of attack rather than the teaching method?

5. What are the implications of these cases for the future guidance of teachers?

FREEDOM FROM ARBITRARY CENSORSHIP OF CLASS MATERIALS

KEEFE v. GEANAKOS

United States Court of Appeals, 1969.
418 F.2d 359 (1st Cir.).

ALDRICH, Chief Judge. . . .   The plaintiff is the head of the English department and coordinator for grades 7 through 12 for the Ipswich (Massachusetts) Public School System, with part-time duties as a teacher of English. He has tenure, . . .

On the opening day of school in September 1969 the plaintiff gave to each member of his senior English class a copy of the September 1969 Atlantic Monthly magazine, a publication of high reputation, and stated that the reading assignment for that night was the first article therein. September was the educational number, so-called, of the Atlantic, and some 75 copies had been supplied by the school department. Plaintiff discussed the article, and a particular word that was used therein, and explained the word's origin and context, and the reasons the author had included it. The word, admittedly highly offensive, is a vulgar term for an incestuous son. Plaintiff stated that any student who felt the assignment personally distasteful could have an alternative one.

The next evening the plaintiff was called to a meeting of the school committee and asked to defend his use of the offending word. Following his explanation, a majority of the members of the committee asked him informally if he would agree not to use it again in the classroom. Plaintiff replied that he could not, in good conscience, agree. His counsel states, however, without contradiction, that in point of fact plaintiff has not used it again. No formal action was taken at this meeting. Thereafter plaintiff was suspended, as a matter of discipline, and it is now proposed that he should be discharged.

The Lifton article [The Young and the Old by Robert J. Lifton, psychiatrist and professor at Yale's Medical School] which we have read in its entirety, has been described as a valuable discussion of "dissent, protest, radicalism and revolt." It is in no sense pornographic. We need no supporting affidavits to find it scholarly, thoughtful and thought-provoking. The single offending word, although repeated a number of times, is not artificially introduced, but, on the contrary, is important to the development of the thesis and the conclusions of the author. Indeed, we would find it difficult to disagree with plaintiff's assertion that no proper study of the article could avoid consideration of this word. It is not possible to read the article, either in whole or in part, as an incitement to libidinous conduct, or even thoughts. If it raised the concept of incest, it was not to suggest

it, but to condemn it; the word was used, by the persons, described as
as a superlative of opprobrium. We believe not only that the article
negatived any other concept, but that an understanding of it would
reject, rather than suggest, the word's use.

With regard to the word itself, we cannot think that it is unknown to many students in the last year of high school, and we might
well take judicial notice of its use by young radicals and protesters
from coast to coast. No doubt its use genuinely offends the parents
of some of the students—therein, in part, lay its relevancy to the article.

Hence the question in this case is whether a teacher may, for
demonstrated educational purposes, quote a "dirty" word currently
used in order to give special offense, or whether the shock is too great
for high school seniors to stand. If the answer were that the students
must be protected from such exposure, we would fear for their future.
We do not question the good faith of the defendants in believing that
some parents have been offended. With the greatest of respect to
such parents, their sensibilities are not the full measure of what is
proper education.

We of course agree with defendants, that what is to be said or
read to students is not to be determined by obscenity standards for
adult consumption.   .   .   .   At the same time, the issue must be one
of degree. A high school senior is not devoid of all discrimination or
resistance. Furthermore, as in all other instances, the offensiveness
of language and the particular propriety or impropriety is dependent
on the circumstances of the utterance.

Apart from cases discussing academic freedom in the large, not
surprisingly we find no decisions closely in point.   .   .   .   We accept
the conclusion of the court below that "some measure of public regulation of classroom speech is inherent in every provision of public education." But when we consider the facts at bar as we have elaborated
them, we find it difficult not to think that its application to the present case demeans any proper concept of education. The general chilling effect of permitting such rigorous censorship is even more serious.

We believe it equally probable that the plaintiff will prevail on
the issue of lack of any notice that a discussion of this article with
the senior class was forbidden conduct. The school regulation upon
which defendants rely, although unquestionably worthy, is not ap-
posite. It does not follow that a teacher may not be on notice of
impropriety from the circumstances of a case without the necessity of
a regulation. In the present case, however, the circumstances would
have disclosed that no less than five books, by as many authors, containing the word in question were to be found in the school library.
It is hard to think that any student could walk into the library and
receive a book, but that his teacher could not subject the content to
serious discussion in class.

Such inconsistency on the part of the school has been regarded as fatal .   .   .

NOTES AND QUESTIONS

1. Should a faculty member have complete freedom to select classroom materials?

2. Could a parent sue to restrain the expenditure of tax funds to purchase this magazine? To remove the other "offensive" books from the library? Could the school board constitutionally instruct the librarian to remove the "offensive" books and to refrain from purchasing similar ones? Who properly censors the school library?

————

CENSORSHIP AND THE LIBRARY

"No text-book in any subject used in the public schools in this state shall contain any matter or statements of any kind which are seditious in character, disloyal to the United States or favorable to the cause of any foreign country with which the United States may be at war. The commission, consisting of the commissioner of education and of two persons to be designated by the regents whose duty it shall be on complaint to examine text-books used in the public schools of the state, in the subjects of civics, economics, English, history, language and literature, for the purpose of determining whether such text-books contain any matter or statements of any kind which are seditious in character, disloyal to the United States or favorable to the cause of any foreign country with which the United States may be at war, is hereby continued. Any person may present a written complaint to such commission that a text-book in any of the aforesaid subjects for use in the public schools of this state or offered for sale for use in the public schools of this state contains matter or statements in violation of this section, specifying such matter or statements in detail. If the commission determine that the text-book against which complaint is made contains any such matter or statements, it shall issue a certificate disapproving the use of such text-book in the public schools of this state, together with a statement of the reasons for its disapproval, specifying the matter found unlawful. Such certificate of disapproval of a text-book, with a detailed statement of the reasons for its disapproval, shall be duly forwarded to the boards of education or other boards or authorities having jurisdiction of the public schools of the school districts of this state, and after the receipt of such certificate the use of a text-book so disapproved shall be discontinued in such school district.

"Any contract hereafter made by any such board of education or other school authorities for the purchase of a text-book in any of such subjects, which has been so disapproved, shall be void. Any school officer or teacher who permits a text-book in any of such subjects, which has been so disapproved, to be used in the public schools of the state, shall be guilty of a misdemeanor."   Educ. Law of New York § 704.

ROSENBERG v. BOARD OF EDUCATION OF CITY OF NEW YORK

Supreme Court, Special Term, Kings County, N.Y., Part. I, 1949.
196 Misc. 542, 92 N.Y.S.2d 344.

DI GIOVANNA, Justice.   This is an application . . .   for review of a determination permitting and allowing the use of "Oliver Twist" by Charles Dickens and "The Merchant of Venice" by William Shakespeare, in the secondary schools of the City of New York as approved reading and study material. . . .

Petitioner charges that the two books are objectionable because they tend to engender hatred of the Jew as a person and as a race.

It is not contended herein that the respondents, collectively or individually, approved the books because of anti-religious or anti-racial inclinations.   As a matter of fact, because of public discussion concerning books of this nature, respondents have expressly required teachers to explain to pupils that the characters described therein are not typical of any nation or race, including persons of the Jewish faith, and are not intended and are not to be regarded as reflecting discredit on any race or national group.

Except where a book has been maliciously written for the apparent purpose of promoting and fomenting a bigoted and intolerant hatred against a particular racial or religious group, public interest in a free and democratic society does not warrant or encourage the suppression of any book at the whim of any unduly sensitive person or group of persons, merely because a character described in such book as belonging to a particular race or religion is portrayed in a derogatory or offensive manner.   The necessity for the suppression of such a book must clearly depend upon the intent and motive which has actuated the author in making such a portrayal.

Literary value of a work of fiction does not depend upon the religious or national origin of the characters portrayed therein.   If evaluation of any literary work is permitted to be based upon a requirement that each book be free from derogatory reference to any religion, race, country, nation or personality, endless litigation respecting many books would probably ensue, dependent upon sensibilities and views of the person suing.

Public education and instruction in the home will remove religious and racial intolerance more effectively than censorship and suppression of literary works which have been accepted as works of art and which are not per se propaganda against or for any race, religion or group. Removal from schools of these books will contribute nothing toward the diminution of anti-religious feeling; as a matter of fact, removal may lead to misguided reading and unwarranted inferences by the unguided pupil.

Educational institutions are concerned with the development of free inquiry and learning. The administrative officers must be free to guide teachers and pupils toward that goal. Their discretion must not be interfered with in the absence of proof of actual malevolent intent. Interference by the court will result in suppression of the intended purpose of aiding those seeking education.

The Court therefore finds that respondents, in exercising their judgment, did not abuse their discretion; that they acted in good faith without malice or prejudice and in the best interests of the school system entrusted to their care and control, and, therefore, that no substantial reason exists which compels the suppression of the two books under consideration. Motion for review is denied and the petition is dismissed.

NOTES AND QUESTIONS

1. What, if any, constitutional provision is the foundation of this opinion? If there is none, should there be one? If so, which one? Why?

2. What is the legal foundation for this opinion? Is it the administrative law standard of "arbitrary and capricious"?

3. Suppose a book is attacked by a Black because it sought to show the low I.Q. and inherent, constitutional inferiority of Blacks, what result?

4. Congress has provided that "no person in the United States shall, on the ground of race, color, or national origin, be excluded from participating in, be denied the benefits of, or be subjected to discrimination under any program or activity receiving Federal financial assistance." (42 U.S.C. § 2000d). Assuming New York's schools receive federal aid, should this statute have any bearing on the decision in the Rosenberg case, supra?

5. The Supreme Court denied certiorari in Presidents Council v. Community School Board, 409 U.S. 998, 93 S.Ct. 308, 34 L.Ed.2d 260 (1973); Mr. Justice Douglas dissented:

"A book entitled Down These Main Streets by Piri Thomas was purchased by the librarians of three junior high schools in School District 25 in Queens, New York. The novel describes in graphic detail sexual and drug related activities that are a part of everyday life for those who live in Spanish Harlem. Its purpose was to acquaint the youth of Queens with the problems of their contemporaries in this social setting. The book was objected to by some parents and after a public meeting the School Board by a vote of 5–3 banned it from the libraries. A later vote by the Board amended the order so the book is now kept on the shelves for direct loan to any parent who wants his or her children to have access to it. No child can borrow it directly.

"This suit was brought on behalf of a principal, a librarian, and various parents and children who request that the court declare the resolution adopted by the Board unconstitutional, and order the defendants to place the book on normal circulation in the libraries and enjoin them from interfering with other school libraries within their jurisdiction which desire to purchase the book.

"Actions of school boards are not immune from constitutional scrutiny, . . . The First Amendment involves not only the right to speak and publish but also the right to hear, to learn, to know. . . . And this Court has recognized that this right to know is "nowhere more vital than in our schools and universities," . . . The book involved is not alleged to be obscene either under the standards of Roth v. United States, 354 U.S. 476 (1957); or under the stricter standards for minors set forth in Ginsberg v. New York, 390 U.S. 629 (1968).

"The Board, however, contends that a book with such vivid accounts of sordid and perverted occurrences is not good for junior high students. At trial both sides produced expert witnesses to prove the value and/or harm of the novel. At school the children are allowed to discuss the contents of the book and the social problems it portrays. They can do everything but read it. This in my mind lessens somewhat the contention that the subject matter of the book is not proper.

"The First Amendment is a preferred right and is of great importance in the schools. In *Tinker*, the Court held that the First Amendment can only be restricted in the schools when a disciplinary problem is raised. No such allegation is asserted here. What else can the School Board now decide it does not like? How else will its sensibilities be offended? Are we sending children to school to be educated by the norms of the School Board or are we educating our youth to shed the prejudices of the past, to explore all forms of thought, and to find solutions to our world's problems?

"Another requirement of the First Amendment is that any statute that imposes restrictions on the freedoms it protects must be narrowly drawn so as to impose any limitation in only the least restrictive way. § 2590e(3) gives the Board power to 'determine matters relating to the instruction of students, including the selection of textbooks and other instructional materials . . . ,' provided they are approved by the Chancelor. The Commissioners' regulation says that secondary school book collections 'shall consist of books approved as satisfactory for (1) supplementing the curriculum (2) reference and general information (3) appreciation and (4) pleasure reading,' 8 N.Y.Code, Rules & Regs. Educ., § 91.1(b) (1966). Even a casual reading of these regulations show they contain no discreet limitations of the type spoken of in Cantwell v. Conn., Speiser v. Randall, or Shelton v. Tucker.

"Because the issues raised here are crucial to our national life, I would hear argument in this case.

"Mr. Justice STEWART would also grant the petition for certiorari and set the case for oral argument."

Assuming that the court had granted certiorari; what would have been the decision on the merits of this case and for what reasons?

THE LIBRARY BILL OF RIGHTS

Printed with permission of The American Library Association.

The Council of the American Library Association reaffirms its belief in the following basic policies which should govern the services of all libraries.

1. As a responsibility of library service, books and other library materials selected should be chosen for values of interest, information and enlightenment of all the people of the community. In no case should library materials be excluded because of the race or nationality or the social, political, or religious views of the authors.

2. Libraries should provide books and other materials presenting all points of view concerning the problems and issues of our times; no library materials should be proscribed or removed from libraries because of partisan or doctrinal disapproval.

3. Censorship should be challenged by libraries in the maintenance of their responsibility to provide public information and enlightenment.

4. Libraries should cooperate with all persons and groups concerned with resisting abridgment of free expression and free access to ideas.

5. The rights of an individual to the use of a library should not be denied or abridged because of his race, religion, national origins or social or political views.

6. As an institution of education for democratic living, the library should welcome the use of its meeting rooms for socially useful and cultural activities and discussion of current public questions. Such meeting places should be available on equal terms to all groups in the community regardless of the beliefs and affiliations of their members, providing that the meetings be open to the public.

(Adopted June 18, 1948. Amended February 2, 1961, and June 27, 1967, by the American Library Association Council).

PROBLEM

1. California's law provides:

"When, in the judgment of the State Board of Education, there exists sufficient evidence that a textbook offered and sold by a publisher for use as a textbook in any public high school in the state contains sectarian or denominational doctrine contrary to law or contains propaganda injurious to the welfare of the public schools, the board shall cause the book to be investigated by a committee of impartial experts. The committee shall be constituted and shall conduct its investigation under such rules and regulations as may be prescribed by the State Board of Education. If, in the opinion of the committee, the textbook does contain sectarian or denominational doctrine contrary to law or does contain propaganda injurious to the welfare of the public schools, or does not correctly portray the role and contribution of the American Negro and members of other ethnic groups in the total development of the United States and of the State of California, the Board of Education may order that the publisher shall cease to offer and sell such textbook for use as a textbook in any public high school in the state. If the State Board of Education shall make such an order, it shall be illegal for any district to purchase copies of such textbook for use as a textbook in any high school or to continue the use of the book as a textbook beyond the close of the current school year." West's Ann.Educ.Code of Calif. § 9959.

If you had been a member of California's legislature would you have voted for this statute? Why or why not? Is it constitutional?

CONSTITUTIONAL LIMITATIONS ON GOVERNMENTAL CONTROLS OVER IDEAS IN NON–CURRICULAR AFFAIRS

IN THE CLASSROOM

TINKER v. DES MOINES INDEPENDENT COMMUNITY SCHOOL DISTRICT

Supreme Court of the United States, 1969.
393 U.S. 503, 89 S.Ct. 733, 21 L.Ed.2d 731.

Mr. Justice FORTAS delivered the opinion of the Court.

Petitioner John F. Tinker, 15 years old, and petitioner Christopher Eckhardt, 16 years old, attended high schools in Des Moines, Iowa. Petitioner Mary Beth Tinker, John's sister, was a 13-year-old student in junior high school.

In December 1965, a group of adults and students in Des Moines held a meeting at the Eckhardt home. The group determined to publicize their objections to the hostilities in Vietnam and their support for a truce by wearing black armbands during the holiday season and by fasting on December 16 and New Year's Eve. Petitioners and their parents had previously engaged in similar activities, and they decided to participate in the program.

The principals of the Des Moines schools became aware of the plan to wear armbands. On December 14, 1965, they met and adopted a policy that any student wearing an armband to school would be asked to remove it, and if he refused he would be suspended until he returned without the armband. Petitioners were aware of the regulation that the school authorities adopted.

On December 16, Mary Beth and Christopher wore black armbands to their schools. John Tinker wore his armband the next day. They were all sent home and suspended from school until they would come back without their armbands. They did not return to school until after the planned period for wearing armbands had expired—that is, until after New Year's Day.

This complaint was filed in the United States District Court by petitioners, through their fathers, . . . It prayed for an injunction restraining the respondent school officials and the respondent members of the board of directors of the school district from disciplining the petitioners, and it sought nominal damages. . . . [T]he District Court dismissed the complaint. It upheld the constitutionality of the school authorities' action on the ground that it was reasonable in order to prevent disturbance of school discipline. . . . The court referred to but expressly declined to follow the Fifth Circuit's holding in a similar case that the wearing of symbols like the armbands cannot be prohibited unless it "materially and substantially interfere[s] with the requirements of appropriate discipline in the operation of the school." Burnside v. Byars, 363 F.2d 744, 749 (5th Cir. 1966). [But compare, Blackwell v. Issaquena Cty. Bd. of Education, 363 F.2d 749 (5th Cir. 1966).]

On appeal, the Court of Appeals for the Eighth Circuit considered the case *en banc*. The court was equally divided, and the District Court's decision was accordingly affirmed, without opinion. . . . We granted certiorari. . . .

The District Court recognized that the wearing of an armband for the purpose of expressing certain views is the type of symbolic act that is within the Free Speech Clause of the First Amendment. See West Virginia State Board of Education v. Barnette, . . . As we shall discuss, the wearing of armbands in the circumstances of this case was entirely divorced from actually or potentially disruptive conduct by those participating in it. It was closely akin to "pure speech" which, we have repeatedly held, is entitled to comprehensive protection under the First Amendment. . . .

First Amendment rights, applied in light of the special characteristics of the school environment, are available to teachers and students. It can hardly be argued that either students or teachers shed their constitutional rights to freedom of speech or expression at the school-house gate. This has been the unmistakable holding of this Court for almost 50 years. In Meyer v. Nebraska, . . .   this Court, . . . held that the Due Process Clause of the Fourteenth Amendment prevents States from forbidding the teaching of a foreign language to young students. Statutes to this effect, the Court held, unconstitutionally interfere with the liberty of teacher, student, and parent. . . .

. . .   On the other hand, the Court has repeatedly emphasized the need for affirming the comprehensive authority of the States and of school officials, consistent with fundamental constitutional safeguards, to prescribe and control conduct in the schools. . . .   Our problem lies in tthe area where students in the exercise of First Amendment rights collide with the rules of the school authorities.

The problem posed by the present case does not relate to regulation of the length of skirts or the type of clothing, to hair style, or deportment. . . .   It does not concern aggressive, disruptive action or even group demonstrations. Our problem involves direct, primary First Amendment rights akin to "pure speech."

The school officials banned and sought to punish petitioners for a silent, passive expression of opinion, unaccompanied by any disorder or disturbance on the part of petitioners. There is here no evidence whatever of petitioners' interference, actual or nascent, with the schools' work or of collision with the rights of other students to be secure and to be let alone. Accordingly, this case does not concern speech or action that intrudes upon the work of the schools or the rights of other students.

Only a few of the 18,000 students in the school system wore the black armbands. Only five students were suspended for wearing them. There is no indication that the work of the schools or any class was disrupted. Outside the classrooms, a few students made hostile remarks to the children wearing armbands, but there were no threats or acts of violence on school premises.

The District Court concluded that the action of the school authorities was reasonable because it was based upon their fear of a disturbance from the wearing of the armbands. But, in our system, undifferentiated fear or apprehension of disturbance is not enough to overcome the right to freedom of expression. Any departure from absolute regimentation may cause trouble. Any variation from the majority's opinion may inspire fear. Any word spoken, in class, in the lunchroom, or on the campus, that deviates from the views of another person may start an argument or cause a disturbance. But our Constitution says we must take this risk . . .   and our history says that it is this sort of hazardous freedom—this kind of openness —that is the basis of our national strength and of the independence and vigor of Americans who grow up and live in this relatively permissive, often disputatious, society.

In order for the State in the person of school officials to justify prohibition of a particular expression of opinion, it must be able to show that its action was caused by something more than a mere desire to avoid the discomfort and unpleasantness that always accompany an unpopular viewpoint. Certainly where there is no finding and no showing that engaging in the forbidden conduct would "materially and substantially interfere with the requirements of appropriate discipline in the operation of the school," the prohibition cannot be sustained. . . .

In the present case, the District Court made no such finding, and our independent examination of the record fails to yield evidence that the school authorities had reason to anticipate that the wearing of the armbands would substantially interfere with the work of the school or impinge upon the rights of other students. Even an official memorandum prepared after the suspension that listed the reasons for the ban on wearing the armbands made no reference to the anticipation of such disruption.

On the contrary, the action of the school authorities appears to have been based upon an urgent wish to avoid the controversy which might result from the expression, even by the silent symbol of armbands, of opposition to this Nation's part in the conflagration in Vietnam. It is revealing, in this respect, that the meeting at which the school principals decided to issue the contested regulation was called in response to a student's statement to the journalism teacher in one of the schools that he wanted to write an article on Vietnam and have it published in the school paper. (The student was dissuaded.)

It is also relevant that the school authorities did not purport to prohibit the wearing of all symbols of political or controversial significance. The record shows that students in some of the schools wore buttons relating to national political campaigns, and some even wore the Iron Cross, traditionally a symbol of Nazism. The order prohibiting the wearing of armbands did not extend to these. Instead, a particular symbol—black armbands worn to exhibit opposition to this Nation's involvement in Vietnam—was singled out for prohibition. Clearly, the prohibition of expression of one particular opinion, at least without evidence that it is necessary to avoid material and substantial interference with schoolwork or discipline, is not constitutionally permissible.

In our system, state-operated schools may not be enclaves of totalitarianism. School officials do not possess absolute authority over their students. Students in school as well as out of school are "persons" under our Constitution. They are possessed of fundamental rights which the State must respect, just as they themselves must respect their obligations to the State. In our system, students may not be regarded as closed-circuit recipients of only that which the State chooses to communicate. They may not be confined to the expression of those sentiments that are officially approved. In the absence of a specific showing of constitutionally valid reasons to regulate their speech, students are entitled to freedom of expression of their views. As Judge Gewin, speaking for the Fifth Circuit, said, school officials cannot suppress "expressions of feelings with which they do not wish to contend." Burnside v. Byars, supra, 363 F.2d at 749.

In Meyer v. Nebraska, supra, . . . Mr. Justice McReynolds expressed this Nation's repudiation of the principle that a State might so conduct its schools as to "foster a homogeneous people." He said:

> "In order to submerge the individual and develop ideal citizens, Sparta assembled the males at seven into barracks and intrusted their subsequent education and training to official guardians. Although such measures have been deliberately approved by men of great genius, their ideas touching the relation between individual and State were wholly different from those upon which our institutions rest; and it hardly will be affirmed that any Legislature could impose such restrictions upon the people of a state without doing violence to both letter and spirit of the Constitution."

This principle has been repeated by this Court on numerous occasions during the intervening years. In Keyishian v. Board of Regents, . . . Justice Brennan, speaking for the Court, said:

> " 'The vigilant protection of constitutional freedoms is nowhere more vital than in the community of American schools.' Shelton v. Tucker, . . . The classroom is peculiarly the 'marketplace of ideas.' The Nation's future depends upon leaders trained through wide exposure to that robust exchange of ideas which discovers truth 'out of a multitude of tongues, [rather] than through any kind of authoritative selection.' "

The principle of these cases is not confined to the supervised and ordained discussion which takes place in the classroom. The principal use to which the schools are dedicated is to accommodate students during prescribed hours for the purpose of certain types of activities. Among those activities is personal intercommunication among the students. This is not only an inevitable part of the process of attending school; it is also an important part of the educational process. A student's rights, therefore, do not embrace merely the classroom hours. When he is in the cafeteria, or on the playing field, or on the campus during the authorized hours, he may express his opinions, even on controversial subjects like the conflict in Vietnam, if he does so without "materially and substantially interfer[ing] with the requirements of appropriate discipline in the operation of the school" and without colliding with the rights of others. . . . But conduct by the student, in class or out of it, which for any reason—whether it stems from time, place, or type of behavior—materially disrupts classwork or involves substantial disorder or invasion of the rights of others is, of course, not immunized by the constitutional guarantee of freedom of speech. . . .

Under our Constitution, free speech is not a right that is given only to be so circumscribed that it exists in principle but not in fact. Freedom of expression would not truly exist if the right could be exercised only in an area that a benevolent government has provided as a safe haven for crackpots. The Constitution says that Congress (and the States) may not abridge the right to free speech. This provision means what it says. We properly read it to permit reasonable regulation of speech-connected activities in carefully restricted circumstances. But we do not confine the permissible exercise of First Amendment rights to a telephone booth or the four corners of a pamphlet, or to supervised and ordained discussion in a school classroom.

If a regulation were adopted by school officials forbidding discussion of the Vietnam conflict, or the expression by any student of opposition to it anywhere on school property except as part of a prescribed classroom exercise, it would be obvious that the regulation would violate the constitutional rights of students, at least if it could not be justified by a showing that the students' activities would materially and substantially disrupt the work and discipline of the school. . . . In the circumstances of the present case, the prohibition of the silent, passive "witness of the armbands," as one of the children called it, is no less offensive to the Constitution's guarantees.

As we have discussed, the record does not demonstrate any facts which might reasonably have led school authorities to forecast substantial disruption of or material interference with school activities, and no disturbances or disorders on the school premises in fact occurred. These petitioners merely went about their ordained rounds in school. Their deviation consisted only in wearing on their sleeve a band of black cloth, not more than two inches wide. They wore it to exhibit their disapproval of the Vietnam hostilities and their advocacy of a truce, to make their views known, and, by their example, to influence others to adopt them. They neither interrupted school activities nor sought to intrude in the school affairs or the lives of others. They caused discussion outside of the classrooms, but no interference with work and no disorder. In the circumstances, our Constitution does not permit officials of the State to deny their form of expression. . . .

Reversed and remanded.

Mr. Justice STEWART, concurring.

Although I agree with much of what is said in the Court's opinion, and with its judgment in this case, I cannot share the Court's uncritical assumption that, school discipline aside, the First Amendment rights of children are co-extensive with those of adults. Indeed, I had thought the Court decided otherwise just last Term in Ginsberg v. New York, 390 U.S. 629, ... I continue to hold the view I expressed in that case: "[A] State may permissibly determine that, at least in some precisely delineated areas, a child—like someone in a captive audience—is not possessed of that full capacity for individual choice which is the presupposition of First Amendment guarantees." Id., at 649–650, . . .

Mr. Justice WHITE, concurring.

While I join the Court's opinion, I deem it appropriate to note, first, that the Court continues to recognize a distinction between communicating by words and communicating by acts or conduct which sufficiently impinges on some valid state interest; and, second, that I do not subscribe to everything the Court of Appeals said about free speech in its opinion in Burnside v. Byars, . . . a case relied upon by the Court in the matter now before us.

Mr. Justice BLACK, dissenting.

The Court's holding in this case ushers in what I deem to be an entirely new era in which the power to control pupils by the elected "officials of state supported public schools * * * " in the United States is in ultimate effect transferred to the Supreme Court. The Court brought this particular case here on a petition for certiorari urging that the First and Fourteenth Amendments protect the right of school pupils to express their political views all the way "from kindergarten through high school." Here the constitutional right to "political expression" asserted was a right to wear black armbands during school hours and at classes in order to demonstrate to the other students that the petitioners were mourning because of the death of United States soldiers in Vietnam and to protest that war which they were against. Ordered to refrain from wearing the armbands in school by the elected school officials and the teachers vested with state authority to do so, apparently only seven out of the school system's 18,000 pupils deliberately refused to obey the order. One defying pupil was Paul Tinker, 8 years old, who was in the second grade; another, Hope Tinker, was 11 years old and in the fifth grade; a third member of the Tinker family was 13, in the eighth grade; and a fourth member of the same family was John Tinker, 15 years old, an 11th grade high school pupil. Their father, a Methodist minister without a church, is paid a salary by the American Friends Service Committee. Another student who defied the school order and insisted on wearing an armband in school was Christopher Eckhardt, an 11th grade pupil and a petitioner in this case. His mother is an official in the Women's International League for Peace and Freedom.

.   .   .

Assuming that the Court is correct in holding that the conduct of wearing armbands for the purpose of conveying political ideas is protected by the First Amendment, . . . the crucial remaining questions are <u>whether students and teachers may use the schools at their whim as a platform for the exercise of free speech</u>—"symbolic" or "pure"—<u>and whether the courts will allocate to themselves the function of deciding how the pupils' school day will be spent.</u> While I have always believed that under the First and Fourteenth Amendments neither the State nor the Federal Government has any authority to regulate or censor the content of speech, I have never believed that any person has a right to give speeches or engage in demonstrations where he pleases and when he pleases. This Court has already rejected such a notion. . . .

While the record does not show that any of these armband students shouted, used profane language, or were violent in any manner, detailed testimony by some of them shows their armbands caused comments, warnings by other students, the poking of fun at them, and a warning by an older football player that other, non-protesting students had better let them alone. There is also evidence that a teacher of mathematics had his lesson period practically "wrecked" chiefly by disputes with Mary Beth Tinker, who wore her armband for her "demonstration." Even a casual reading of the record shows that this armband did divert students' minds from their regular lessons, and that talk, comments, etc., made John Tinker "self-conscious" in attending school with his armband. . . . And I repeat that if the time has come when pupils of state-supported schools, kindergartens, grammer schools, or high schools, can defy and flout orders of school officials to keep their minds on their own schoolwork, it is the beginning of a new revolutionary era of permissiveness in this country fostered by the judiciary. The next logical step, it appears to me, would be to hold unconstitutional laws that bar pupils under 21 or 18 from voting, or from being elected members of the boards of education. . . .

In my view, teachers in state-controlled public schools are hired to teach there. Although Mr. Justice McReynolds may have intimated to the contrary in Meyer v. Nebraska, supra, certainly a teacher is not paid to go into school and teach subjects the State does not hire him to teach as a part of its selected curriculum. Nor are public school students sent to the schools at public expense to broadcast political or any other views to educate and inform the public. The original idea of schools, which I do not believe is yet abandoned as worthless or out of date, was that children had not yet reached the point of experience and wisdom which enabled them to teach all of their elders. It may be that the Nation has outworn the old-fashioned slogan that "children are to be seen not heard," but one may, I hope, be permitted to harbor the thought that taxpayers send children to school on the premise that at their age they need to learn, not teach. . . .

Change has been said to be truly the law of life but sometimes the old and the tried and true are worth holding. The schools of this Nation have undoubtedly contributed to giving us tranquility and to making us a more law abiding people. Uncontrolled and uncontrollable liberty is an enemy to domestic peace. We cannot close our eyes to the fact that some of the country's greatest problems are crimes committed by the youth, too many of school age. School discipline, like parental discipline, is an integral and important part of training our children to be good citizens—to be better citizens. Here a very small number of students have crisply and summarily refused to obey a school order designed to give pupils who want to learn the opportunity to do so. One does not need to be a prophet or the son of a prophet to know that after the Court's holding today some students in Iowa schools and indeed in all schools will be ready, able, and willing to defy their teachers on practically all orders. This is the more unfortunate for the schools since groups of students all over the land are already running loose, conducting break-ins, sit-ins, lie-ins, and smash-ins. Many of these student groups, as is all too familiar to all who read the newspapers and watch the television news programs, have already engaged in rioting, property seizures, and destruction. They have picketed schools to force students not to cross their picket lines and have too often violently attacked earnest but frightened students who wanted an education that the pickets did not want them to get. Students engaged in such activities are apparently confident that they know far more about how to operate public school systems than do their parents, teachers, and elected school officials. It is no answer to say that the particular students here have not yet reached such high points in their demands to attend classes in order to exercise their political pressures. Turned loose with lawsuits for damages and injunctions against their teachers as they are here, it is nothing but wishful thinking to imagine that young, immature students will not soon believe it is their right to control the schools rather than the right of the States that collect the taxes to hire the teachers for the benefit of the pupils. This case, therefore, wholly without constitutional reasons in my judgment, subjects all the public schools in the country to the whims and caprices of their loudest-mouthed, but maybe not their brightest, students. I, for one, am not fully persuaded that school pupils are wise enough, even with this Court's expert help from Washington, to run the 23,390 public school systems in our 50 States.   .   .   .   I dissent.

Mr. Justice HARLAN, dissenting.

.   .   .   I would, in cases like this, cast upon those complaining the burden of showing that a particular school measure was motivated by other than legitimate school concerns—for example, a desire to prohibit the expression of an unpopular point of view, while permitting expression of the dominant opinion.

Finding nothing in this record which impugns the good faith of respondents in promulgating the armband regulation, I would affirm the judgment below.

NOTES AND QUESTIONS

1. Would the decision have been different if teachers rather than students were involved? Why or why not? See, James v. Bd. of Ed., 461 F.2d 566 (2nd Cir. 1972), reh. den. 409 U.S. 1042. Suppose a local Board of Education passed a regulation prohibiting teachers from wearing political campaign buttons or armbands or any other similar type of insignia in the classroom, would this regulation be upheld? Consider the implications of the views of Mr. Justice Harlan as compared with those of the majority. What difference do they make? Which view do you agree with? Why?

2. Was the symbolic speech the free choice of the students or were they being "used" to further a "cause"? Should this consideration make any difference?

3. Suppose the school board had adopted a regulation to the effect that the wearing of armbands would be allowed on playfields, in the cafeteria and hallways, but not in the classrooms, would this regulation of the expression have been upheld?

4. Suppose the wearing of the armbands had provoked great student hostilities, including fist fights in classrooms, would the wearing of the armbands have been upheld in such circumstances? If not, does one's constitutional right to free expression depend upon the reception by others of the idea expressed? Isn't it true that the more unpopular the idea the greater is the reaction and the greater is the need for protection? Couldn't a determined group destroy one's rights simply by being hostile and violent? See, Melton v. Young, 465 F.2d 1332 (6th Cir. 1972), cert. den., 411 U.S. 951.

5. After the decision in *Tinker* do school boards have constitutional power to pass rules prohibiting students from wearing their hair longer than shoulder length? Beards? Micro-mini skirts? Dungarees?

6. After *Tinker* could a student stand quietly at the side of his desk as a symbolic protest of America's "Military-Industrial-Academic" complex even though there was a school board regulation requiring that students be seated in the classroom during class except for reasons of health?

7. The Supreme Court refused to grant certiorari to review Barker v. Hardway, Mr. Justice Fortas specifically stating:

    "I agree that certiorari should be denied. The petitioners were suspended from college *not* for expressing their opinions on a matter of substance, but for violent and destructive interference with the rights of others. An adequate hearing was afforded them on the issue of suspension. The petitioners contend that their conduct was protected by the First Amendment, but the findings of the District Court, which were accepted by the Court of Appeals, establish that the petitioners here engaged in an aggressive and violent demonstration and not in peaceful, nondisruptive expression, such as was involved in [Tinker]. The petitioners' conduct was therefore clearly not protected by the First and Fourteenth Amendments." Barker v. Hardway, 394 U.S. 905, 89 S.Ct. 1009, 22 L.Ed. 2d 217 (1969).

8. When deciding this type of a case should a court distinguish between disruptions of a school's curricular activities and disruptions of its extra-curricular activities? If so, why? Assuming that it is proper to distinguish curricular from extra-curricular activities, would that distinction have made any difference in the decision of this case?

PROBLEM

"The Court finds from this undisputed evidence that all of the plaintiffs are of Mexican descent and are referred to variously as 'Mexicans', 'Hispanos' and 'Chicanos'. In August of 1969, the plaintiff, Hernandez, spokesman for the plaintiffs, asked if plaintiffs would be permitted to wear black berets and long hair while in school. As reasons for the request, it was stated that the wearing of the berets would be a symbol of their Mexican culture; it would show unity among Mexicans; it would be a symbol of respect, and a symbol of their dissatisfaction with society's treatment of their race, and their desire to improve that treatment.

"Mr. Shannon, himself of Mexican descent, told the plaintiffs that he was a part of the same culture to which they referred and that he was sympathetic with their desire to generate respect for the Mexican culture. He told the plaintiffs that their request to wear long hair and black berets was new, but they would be permitted to do so and 'we would try and see if we could live with it.'

"In September, the plaintiffs requested permission to extend into the school system, a celebration of Independence Day of the Republic of Mexico (September 16) by having a walkout of students to participate in a parade and demonstration. Although this caused considerable apprehension among school officials and some students and parents, due to the fact that the previous spring, a demonstration at West High School in the Denver system had resulted in violence, destruction of property, and confrontations between students and police; nonetheless, Mr. Shannon not only granted the request, but he also arranged for assemblies at the school to explain the reason for and significance of the celebration on September 16 and to present appropriate Mexican entertainment.

".   .   .   The plaintiffs walked in the hallways during class time talking in loud voices and from time to time, shouting, 'Chicano power'; during passing periods, they congregated in the hallways to block the same from free passage by other students; they refused to give their names to the teachers and explain what they were doing in the hallways during class time;   .   .   .   when a teacher supervising the hallways gave some students directions, one of the plaintiffs stated: 'Don't listen to that old bag—the berets will take care of her';   .   .   .   they attempted to induce students in class to leave the classrooms and join them in the hallways; and they refused to obey a requirement of the School Board that material to be distributed on school property be submitted in advance to the principal." See Hernandez v. School District No. 1, 315 F.Supp. 289 (D.Colo.1970).

Assume that the plaintiffs have been suspended and that you are a judge, on the basis of all the materials studied, what decision would you make on the substantive merits and for what reasons? Compare Burnside v. Byars, 363 F.2d 744 (5th Cir. 1966) with Blackwell v. Issaquena County Bd. of Education, 363 F.2d 749 (5th Cir. 1966), and see also, Guzick v. Drebus, 305 F.Supp. 472 (N.D.Ohio 1969), aff'd 431 F.2d 594, cert. den. 401 U.S. 948.

OFF THE SCHOOL PREMISES

GRAYNED v. CITY OF ROCKFORD

Supreme Court of United States, 1972.
408 U.S. 104, 92 S.Ct. 2294, 33 L.Ed.2d 222.

Mr. Justice MARSHALL delivered the opinion of the Court.

Appellant Richard Grayned was convicted for his part in a demonstration in front of West Senior High School in Rockford, Illinois. Negro students at the school had first presented their grievances to school administrators. When the principal took no action on crucial complaints, a more public demonstration of protest was planned. On April 25, 1969, approximately 200 people—students, their family members, and friends—gathered next to the school grounds. Appellant, whose brother and twin sisters were attending the school, was part of this group. The demonstrators marched around on a sidewalk about 100 feet from the school building, which was set back from the street. Many carried signs which summarized the grievances: "Black cheerleaders to cheer too"; "Black history with black teachers"; "Equal rights, Negro counselors." Others, without placards, made the "power to the people" sign with their upraised and clenched fists.

In other respects, the evidence at appellant's trial was sharply contradictory. Government witnesses reported that the demonstrators repeatedly cheered, chanted, baited policemen, and made other noise that was audible in the school; that hundreds of students were distracted from their school activities and lined the classroom windows to watch the demonstration; that some demonstrators successfully yelled to their friends to leave the school building and join the demonstration; that uncontrolled latenesses after period changes in the school were far greater than usual, with late students admitting that they had been watching the demonstration; and that, in general, orderly school procedure was disrupted. Defense witnesses claimed that the demonstrators were at all times quiet and orderly; that they did not seek to violate the law, but only to "make a point"; that the only noise was made by policemen using loudspeakers; that almost no students were noticeable at the schoolhouse windows; and that orderly school procedure was not disrupted.

After warning the demonstrators, the police arrested 40 of them, including appellant. For participating in the demonstration, Grayned was tried and convicted of violating two Rockford ordinances, hereinafter referred to as the "anti-picketing" ordinance and the "anti-noise" ordinance. A $25 fine was imposed for each violation.   .   .   .

I.

At the time of appellant's arrest and conviction, Rockford's anti-picketing ordinance provided that

"A person commits disorderly conduct when he knowingly:

.   .   .   .

"(i) Pickets or demonstrates on a public way within 150 feet of any primary or secondary school building while the school is in session and one-half hour before the school is in session and one-half hour after the school session has been concluded, provided that this subsection does not prohibit the peaceful picketing of any school involved in a labor dispute .   .   .   ."

With the exception of two unimportant words, this ordinance is identical to the Chicago disorderly conduct ordinance we have today considered in Police Department of Chicago v. Mosley, ante. For the reasons given in Mosley, we agree with the dissenting Justice Schaefer below, and hold that § 18.1(i) violates the Equal Protection Clause of the Fourteenth Amendment. Appellant's conviction under this invalid ordinance must be reversed.

II.

The anti-noise ordinance reads, in pertinent part, as follows:

"[N]o person, while on public or private grounds adjacent to any building in which a school or any class thereof is in session, shall willfully make or assist in the making of any noise or diversion which disturbs or tends to disturb the peace or good order of such school session or class thereof .   .   .   ."   Code of Ordinances, c. 28, § 19.2(a).

Appellant claims that, on its face, this ordinance is both vague and overboard, and therefore unconstitutional. We conclude, however, that the ordinance suffers from neither of these related infirmities.

A. Vagueness

It is a basic principle of due process that an enactment is void for vagueness if its prohibitions are not clearly defined. Vague laws offend several important values. First, because we assume that man is free to steer between lawful and unlawful conduct, we insist that laws give the person of ordinary intelligence a reasonable opportunity to know what is prohibited, so that he may act accordingly. Vague laws may trap the innocent by not providing fair warning. Second, if arbitrary and discriminatory enforcement is to be prevented, laws must provide explicit standards for those who apply them. A vague law impermissibly delegates basic policy matters to policemen, judges, and juries for resolution on an *ad hoc* and subjective basis, with the attendant dangers of arbitrary and discriminatory application. Third, but related, where a vague statute "abut[s] upon sensitive areas of basic First Amendment freedoms," it "operates to inhibit the exercise of [those] freedoms." Uncertain meanings inevitably lead citizens to " 'steer far wider of the unlawful zone' . . . than if the boundaries of the forbidden areas were clearly marked."

Although the question is close, we conclude that the anti-noise ordinance is not impermissibly vague. The court below rejected appellant's arguments "that proscribed conduct was not sufficiently specified and that police were given too broad a discretion in determining whether conduct was proscribed." . . .

. . . we find no unconstitutional vagueness in the anti-noise ordinance. Condemned to the use of words, we can never expect mathematical certainty from our language. The words of the Rockford ordinance are marked by "flexibility and reasonable breadth, rather than meticulous specificity," . . . but we think it is clear what the ordinance as a whole prohibits. Designed, according to its preamble, "for the protection of Schools," the ordinance forbids deliberately noisy or diversionary activity which disrupts or is about to disrupt normal school activities. It forbids this willful activity at fixed times—when school is in session—and at a sufficiently fixed place—"adjacent" to the school. Were we left with just the words of the ordinance, we might be troubled by the imprecision of the phrase "tends to disturb." However, . . . the Supreme Court of Illinois construed a Chicago ordinance prohibiting, *inter alia*, a "diversion tending to disturb the peace," and held that it permitted conviction only where there was "*imminent* threat of violence." . . . we think it proper to conclude that the Supreme Court of Illinois would interpret the Rockford ordinance to prohibit only actual or imminent interference with the "peace or good order" of the school.

Although the prohibited quantum of disturbance is not specified in the ordinance, it is apparent from the statute's announced purpose that the measure is whether normal school activity has been or is about to be disrupted. We do not have here a vague, general "breach of the peace" ordinance, but a specific statute for the school context, where the prohibited disturbances are easily measured by their impact on the normal activities of the school. Given this "particular context," the ordinance gives "fair notice to whom [it] is directed." .   .   .

B. Overbreadth

A clear and precise enactment may nevertheless be "overbroad" if in its reach it prohibits constitutionally protected conduct. Although appellant does not claim that, as applied to him, the anti-noise ordinance has punished protected expressive activity, he claims that the ordinance is overbroad on its face. Because overbroad laws, like vague ones, deter privileged activity, our cases firmly establish appellant's standing to raise an overbreadth challenge. The crucial question, then, is whether the ordinance sweeps within its prohibitions what may not be punished under the First and Fourteenth Amendments. Specifically, appellant contends that the Rockford ordinance unduly interferes with First and Fourteenth Amendment rights to picket on a public sidewalk near a school. We disagree.

"In considering the right of a municipality to control the use of public streets for the expression of religious [or political] views, we start with the words of Mr. Justice Roberts that 'Wherever the title of streets and parks may rest, they have immemorially been held in trust for the use of the public and, time out of mind, have been used for purposes of assembly, communicating thoughts between citizens, and discussing public questions.' .   .   ." The right to use a public place for expressive activity may be restricted only for weighty reasons.

Clearly, government has no power to restrict such activity because of its message. Our cases make equally clear, however, that reasonable "time, place and manner" regulations may be necessary to further significant governmental interests, and are permitted. For example, two parades cannot march on the same street simultaneously, and government may allow only one. .   .   . Subject to such reasonable regulation, however, peaceful demonstrations in public places are protected by the First Amendment. Of course, where demonstrations turn violent, they lose their protected quality as expression under the First Amendment.

The nature of a place, "the pattern of its normal activities, dictates the kinds of regulations of time, place, and manner that are reasonable." Although a silent vigil may not unduly interfere with a public library, .   .   . making a speech in the reading room almost certainly would. That same speech should be perfectly appropriate in a park. The crucial question is whether the manner of expression is basically incompatible with the normal activity of a particular place at a particular time. Our cases make clear that in assessing the reasonableness of regulation, we must weigh heavily the fact that communication is involved; the regulation must be narrowly tailored to further the State's legitimate interest. "Access to [the streets, sidewalks, parks, and other similar public places] for the purpose of exercising [First Amendment rights] cannot constitutionally be denied broadly .   .   .   ." Free expression "must not, in the guise of regulation, be abridged or denied."

In light of these general principles, we do not think that Rockford's ordinance is an unconstitutional regulation of activity around a school. Our touchstone is Tinker v. Des Moines .   .   . in which we considered the question of how to accommodate First Amendment rights with the "special characteristics of the school environment." .   .   . *Tinker* held that the Des Moines School District could not punish students for wearing black armbands to school in protest of the Vietnam War. Recognizing that "wide exposure to .   .   . robust exchange of ideas" is an "important part of the educational process" and should be nurtured, .   .   . we concluded that free expression could not be barred from the school campus. We made clear that "undifferentiated fear or apprehension of disturbance is not enough to overcome the right to freedom of expression," .   .   . and that particular expressive activity could not be prohibited because of a "mere desire to avoid the discomfort and unpleasantness that always accompany an unpopular viewpoint," .   .   . But we nowhere suggested that students, teachers, or anyone else has an absolute constitutional right to use all parts of a school building or its immediate environs for his unlimited expressive purposes. Expressive activity could certainly be restricted, but only if the forbidden conduct "materially disrupts classwork or involves substantial disorder or invasion of the rights of others." .   .   . The wearing of armbands was protected in *Tinker* because the students "neither interrupted school activities nor sought to intrude in the school affairs or the lives of others. They caused discussion outside of the classrooms, but no interference with work and no disorder." .   .   .

Just as *Tinker* made clear that school property may not be declared off-limits for expressive activity by students, we think it clear that the public sidewalk adjacent to school grounds may not be declared off-limits for expressive activity by members of the public. But in each case, expressive activity may be prohibited if it "materially disrupts classwork or involves substantial disorder or invasion of the rights of others." .   .   .

We would be ignoring reality if we did not recognize that the public schools in a community are important institutions, and are often the focus of significant grievances. Without interfering with normal school activities, daytime picketing and handbilling on public grounds near a school can effectively publicize those grievances to pedestrians, school visitors, and deliverymen, as well as to teachers, administrators, and students.   Some picketing to that end will be quiet and peaceful, and will in no way disturb the normal functioning of the school.   For example, it would be highly unusual if the classic expressive gesture of the solitary picketer disrupts anything related to the school, at least on a public sidewalk open to pedestrians. On the other hand, schools could hardly tolerate boisterous demonstrators who drown out classroom conversation, make studying impossible, block entrances, or incite children to leave the schoolhouse.

. . .   Rockford's anti-noise ordinance goes no further than *Tinker* says a municipality may go to prevent interference with its schools. It is narrowly tailored to further Rockford's compelling interest in having an undisrupted school session conducive to the students' learning, and does not unnecessarily interfere with First Amendment rights. . . .   Rockford punishes only conduct which disrupts or is about to disrupt normal school activities.   That decision is made, as it should be, on an individualized basis, given the particular fact situation.   Peaceful picketing which does not interfere with the ordinary functioning of the school is permitted.   And the ordinance gives no license to punish anyone because of what he is saying.

We recognize that the ordinance prohibits some picketing which is neither violent nor physically obstructive.   Noisy demonstrations which disrupt or are incompatible with normal school activities are obviously within the ordinance's reach.   Such expressive conduct may be constitutionally protected at other places or other times,   . . . but next to a school, while classes are in session, it may be prohibited. The anti-noise ordinance imposes no such restriction on expressive activity before or after the school session, while the student/faculty "audience" enters and leaves the school.

. . .   Rockford's modest restriction on some peaceful picketing represents a considered and specific legislative judgment that some kinds of expressive activity should be restricted at a particular time and place, here in order to protect the schools.   Such a reasonable regulation is not inconsistent with the First and Fourteenth Amendments.   The anti-noise ordinance is not invalid on its face.

Mr. Justice BLACKMUN joins in the judgment and in Part I of the opinion of the Court.   He concurs in the result as to Part II of the opinion.

Mr. Justice DOUGLAS, dissenting in part [II].

. . .   We held in Cox v. Louisiana, 379 U.S. 536, 544–545, 85 S.Ct. 453, 458–459, 13 L.Ed.2d 471, that a State could not infringe a person's right of free speech and free assembly by convicting him under a "disturbing the peace" ordinance where all that the students in that case did was to protest segregation and discrimination against

Blacks by peaceably assemblying and marching to the courthouse where they sang, prayed, and listened to a speech, but where there was no violence, no rioting, no boisterous conduct.

The school where the present picketing occurred was the center of a racial conflict. Most of the picketers were indeed students in the school. The dispute doubtless disturbed the school; and the blaring of the loudspeakers of the police was certainly a "noise or diversion" in the meaning of the ordinance. But there was no evidence that appellant was noisy or boisterous or rowdy. He walked quietly and in an orderly manner. As I read this record the disruptive force loosened at this school was an issue dealing with race—an issue that is preeminently one for solution by First Amendment means. That is all that was done here; and the entire picketing, including appellant's part in it, was done in the best First Amendment tradition.

NOTES AND QUESTIONS

1. Suppose a city ordinance provided that a person is guilty of "disorderly conduct" if he knowingly "pickets or demonstrates on a public way within in 150 feet of any primary or secondary school building while the school is in session." Could this ordinance constitutionally be applied to the facts of the Grayned case? Why or why not? See Police Dept. of Chicago v. Mosley, 408 U.S. 92, 92 S.Ct. 2286, 33 L.Ed.2d 212 (1972), and Black, Equal But Inadequate Protection: A Look at Mosley and Grayned, 8 Harv.Civ.Rts. & Civ.Lib.L.Rev. 469 (1973).

FREEDOM OF ASSOCIATION

HEALY v. JAMES

Supreme Court of the United States, 1972.
408 U.S. 169, 92 S.Ct. 2338, 33 L.Ed.2d 266.

Mr. Justice POWELL delivered the opinion of the Court.   .   .   .

Petitioners are students attending Central Connecticut State College (CCSC), a state-supported institution of higher learning. In September 1969 they undertook to organize what they then referred to as a "local chapter" of Students for a Democratic Society (SDS). Pursuant to procedures established by the College, petitioners filed a request for official recognition as a campus organization with the Student Affairs Committee, a committee composed of four students, three faculty members and the Dean of Student Affairs. The request specified three purposes for the proposed organization's existence. It would provide "a forum of discussion and self-education for students developing an analysis of American society"; it would serve as "an agency for integrating thought with action so as to bring about constructive changes"; and it would endeavor to provide "a coordinating body for relating the problems of leftist students" with other interested groups on campus and in the community. The Committee, while satisfied that the statement of purposes was clear and unobjectionable on its face, exhibited concern over the relationship between the proposed local group and the National SDS organization. In response to inquiries, representatives of the proposed organization stated that they would not affiliate with any national organization and that their group would remain "completely independent."

In response to other questions asked by Committee members concerning SDS's reputation for campus disruption, the applicants made the following statements, which proved significant during the later stages of these proceedings:

"Q. How would you respond to issues of violence as other S.D.S. chapters have?

"A. Our action would have to be dependent upon each issue.

"Q. Would you use any means possible?

"A. No I can't say that; would not know until we know what the issues are.

"Q. Could you envision the S.D.S. interrupting a class?

"A. Impossible for me to say."

With this information before it, the Committee requested an additional filing by the applicants, including a formal statement regarding affiliations. The amended application filed in response stated flatly that "CCSC Students for a Democratic Society are not under the dictates of any National organization."   .   .   .

By a vote of six to two the Committee ultimately approved the application and recommended to the President of the College, Dr. James, that the organization be accorded official recognition.   .   .   .

Several days later, the President rejected the Committee's recommendation, and issued a statement indicating that petitioners' organization was not to be accorded the benefits of official campus recognition. His accompanying remarks, which are set out in full in the margin, indicate several reasons for his action. He found that the organization's philosophy was antithetical to the school's policies, and that the group's independence was doubtful. He concluded that approval should not be granted to any group that "openly repudiates" the College's dedication to academic freedom.   .   .   .

Their efforts to gain recognition having proved ultimately unsuccessful, and having been made to feel the burden of nonrecognition, petitioners resorted to the courts.   .   .   .

At the outset we note that state colleges and universities are not enclaves immune from the sweep of the First Amendment. "It can hardly be argued that either students or teachers shed their constitutional rights to freedom of speech or expression at the schoolhouse

gate." Tinker v. Des Moines Independent Community School District,
.   .   .   Of course, as Mr. Justice Fortas made clear in *Tinker*, First
Amendment rights must always be applied "in light of the special
characteristics of the   .   .   .   environment" in the particular case.
.   .   .   And, where state-operated educational institutions are involved, this Court has long recognized "the need for affirming the
comprehensive authority of the States and of school officials, consistent with fundamental constitutional safeguards, to prescribe and
control conduct in the schools."   .   .   .   Yet, the precedents of
this Court leave no room for the view that, because of the acknowledged need for order, First Amendment protections should apply with
less force on college campuses than in the community at large. Quite
to the contrary, "[t]he vigilant protection of constitutional freedoms
is nowhere more vital than in the community of American schools."
Shelton v. Tucker,   .   .   .   The college classroom with its surrounding environs is peculiarly the "market place of ideas" and we
break no new constitutional ground in reaffirming this Nation's dedication to safeguarding academic freedom. Keyishian v. Board of
Regents,   .   .   .

Among the rights protected by the First Amendment is the right
of individuals to associate to further their personal beliefs. While
the freedom of association is not explicitly set out in the Amendment, it has long been held to be implicit in the freedoms of speech,
assembly and petition.   .   .   .   There can be no doubt that denial
of official recognition, without justification, to college organizations
burdens or abridges that associational right. The primary impediment to free association flowing from nonrecognition is the denial of
use of campus facilities for meetings and other appropriate purposes.
The practical effect of nonrecognition was demonstrated in this case
when, several days after the President's decision was announced,
petitioners were not allowed to hold a meeting in the campus coffee
shop because they were not an approved group.

Petitioners' associational interests also were circumscribed by
the denial of the use of campus bulletin boards and the school newspaper. If an organization is to remain a viable entity in a campus
community in which new students enter on a regular basis, it must
possess the means of communicating with these students. Moreover,
the organization's ability to participate in the intellectual give and
take of campus debate, and to pursue its stated purposes, is limited by
denial of access to the customary media for communicating with the
administration, faculty members, and other students. Such impedi-
ments cannot be viewed as insubstantial.

Respondents and the courts below appear to have taken the view
that denial of official recognition in this case abridged no constitutional rights. The District Court concluded that

"President James' discretionary action in denying this application cannot be legitimately magnified and distorted into a constitutionally cognizable interference with the personal ideas or beliefs of any segment of the college students; neither does his action deter in any material way the individual advocacy of their personal beliefs; nor can his action be reasonably construed to be an invasion of, or having a chilling effect on academic freedom."

In that court's view all that was denied petitioners was the "administrative seal of official college respectability." . . . A majority of the Court of Appeals agreed that petitioners had been denied only the "college's stamp of approval." . . .

We do not agree with the characterization by the courts below of the consequences of nonrecognition. We may concede . . . that the administration "has taken no direct action . . . to restrict the rights of petitioners' members to associate freely." But the Constitution's protection is not limited to direct interference with fundamental rights. The requirement in *Patterson* that the NAACP disclose its membership lists was found to be an impermissible, though indirect, infringement of the members' associational rights. Likewise, in this case, the group's possible ability to exist outside the campus community does not ameliorate significantly the disabilities imposed by the President's action. We are not free to disregard the practical realities. Mr. Justice Stewart has made the salient point: "Freedoms such as these are protected not only against heavy-handed frontal attack, but also from being stifled by more subtle governmental interference." . . .

The opinions below also assumed that petitioners had the burden of showing entitlement to recognition by the College. While petitioners have not challenged the procedural requirement that they file an application in conformity with the rules of the College, they do question the view of the courts below that final rejection could rest on their failure to convince the administration that their organization was unaffiliated with the National SDS. For reasons to be stated later in this opinion, we do not consider the issue of affiliation to be a controlling one. But apart from any particular issue, once petitioners had filed an application in conformity with the requirements, the burden was upon the College administration to justify its decision of rejection. . . . It is to be remembered that the effect of the College's denial of recognition was a form of prior restraint, denying to petitioners' organization the range of associational activities described above. While a college has a legitimate interest in preventing disruption on the campus, which under circumstances requiring the safeguarding of that interest may justify such restraint, a "heavy burden" rests on the college to demonstrate the appropriateness of that action. . . .

These fundamental errors—discounting the existence of a cognizable First Amendment interest and misplacing the burden of proof—require that the judgments below be reversed. But we are unable to conclude that no basis exists upon which nonrecognition might be appropriate. Indeed, based on a reasonable reading of the ambiguous facts of this case, there appears to be at least one potentially acceptable ground for a denial of recognition. Because of this ambiguous state of the record we conclude that the case should be remanded and, in an effort to provide guidance to the lower courts upon reconsideration, it is appropriate to discuss the several bases of President James' decision. Four possible justifications for nonrecognition, all closely related, might be derived from the record and his statements. Three of those grounds are inadequate to substantiate his decision: a fourth, however, has merit.

A

From the outset the controversy in this case has centered in large measure around the relationship, if any, between petitioners' group and the National SDS. The Student Affairs Committee meetings, as reflected in its minutes, focused considerable attention on this issue; the court-ordered hearing also was directed primarily to this question. Despite assurances from petitioners and their counsel that the local group was in fact independent of the National organization, it is evident that President James was significantly influenced by his apprehension that there was a connection. Aware of the fact that some SDS chapters had been associated with disruptive and violent campus activity, he apparently considered that affiliation itself was sufficient justification for denying recognition.

Although this precise issue has not come before the Court heretofore, the Court has consistently disapproved governmental action imposing criminal sanctions or denying rights and privileges solely because of a citizen's association with an unpopular organization. . . . In these cases it has been established that "guilt by association alone, without [establishing] that an individual's association poses the threat feared by the Government," is an impermissible basis upon which to deny First Amendment rights. United States v. Robel, 389 U.S., at 265, ... The Government has the burden of establishing a knowing affiliation with an organization possessing unlawful aims and goals and a specific intent to further those illegal aims.

Students for a Democratic Society, as conceded by the College and the lower courts, is loosely organized, having various factions and promoting a number of diverse social and political views only some of which call for unlawful action. Not only did petitioners proclaim their complete independence from this organization, but they also indicated that they shared only some of the beliefs its leaders have expressed. On this record it is clear that the relationship was not an adequate ground for the denial of recognition.

B

Having concluded that petitioners were affiliated with, or at least retained an affinity for, National SDS, President James attributed what he believed to be the philosophy of that organization to the local group. He characterized the petitioning group as adhering to "some of the major tenets of the national organization," including a philosophy of violence and disruption. Understandably, he found that philosophy abhorrent. In an article signed by President James in an alumni periodical, and made a part of the record below, he announced his unwillingness to "sanction an organization that openly advocates the destruction of the very ideals and freedoms upon which the academic life is founded." He further emphasized that the petitioners' "philosophies" were "counter to the official policy of the college."

The mere disagreement of the President with the group's philosophy affords no reason to deny it recognition. As repugnant as these views may have been, especially to one with President James' responsibility, the mere expression of them would not justify the denial of First Amendment rights. Whether petitioners did in fact advocate a philosophy of "destruction" thus becomes immaterial. The College, acting here as the instrumentality of the State, may not restrict speech or association simply because it finds the views expressed by any group to be abhorrent. As Mr. Justice Black put it most simply and clearly:

> "I do not believe that it can be too often repeated that the freedoms of speech, press, petition and assembly guaranteed by the First Amendment must be accorded to the ideas we hate or sooner or later they will be denied to the ideas we cherish." Communist Party v. Subversive Activities Control Bd., 367 U.S. 1, 137 (1961).

C

As the litigation progressed in the District Court, a third rationale for President James' decision—beyond the questions of affiliation and philosophy—began to emerge. His second statement, issued after the court-ordered hearing, indicates that he based rejection on a conclusion that this particular group would be a "disruptive influence at CCSC." This language was underscored in the second District Court opinion. In fact, the [lower] Court concluded that the President had determined that CCSC–SDS's "prospective campus activities were likely to cause a disruptive influence at CCSC." . . .

If this reason, directed at the organization's activities rather than its philosophy, were factually supported by the record, this Court's prior decisions would provide a basis for considering the propriety of nonrecognition. The critical line heretofore drawn for determining the permissibility of regulation is the line between mere advocacy and advocacy "directed to inciting or producing imminent lawless action and .   .   . likely to incite or produce such action." Brandenburg v. Ohio, 395 U.S. 444, 447. .   .   . In the context of the "special characteristics of the school environment," the power of the government to prohibit "lawless action" is not limited to acts of a criminal nature. Also prohibitable are actions which "materially and substantially disrupt the work and discipline of the school." Tinker v. Des Moines Independent Community School District, .   .   . Associational activities need not be tolerated where they infringe reasonable campus rules, interrupt classes or substantially interfere with the opportunity of other students to obtain an education.

The "Student Bill of Rights" at CCSC, upon which great emphasis was placed by the President, draws precisely this distinction between advocacy and action. It purports to impose no limitations on the right of college student organizations "to examine and discuss *all* questions of interest to them." But it also states that students have no right (1) "to deprive others of the opportunity to speak or be heard," (2) "to invade the privacy of others," (3) "to damage the property of others," (4) "to disrupt the regular and essential operation of the college," or (5) "to interfere with the rights of others." The line between permissible speech and impermissible conduct tracks the constitutional requirement, and if there were an evidential basis to support the conclusion that CCSC–SDS posed a substantial threat of material disruption in violation of that command the President's decision should be affirmed.

The record, however, offers no substantial basis for that conclusion. .   .   .

D

These same references in the record to the group's equivocation regarding how it might respond to "issues of violence" and whether it could ever "envision .   .   . interrupting a class," suggest a fourth possible reason why recognition might have been denied to these petitioners. These remarks might well have been read as announcing petitioners' unwillingness to be bound by reasonable school rules governing conduct. The College's Statement of Rights, Freedoms and Responsibilities of Students, contains, as we have seen, an explicit statement with respect to campus disruption. The regulation, carefully differentiating between advocacy and action, is a reasonable one, and petitioners have not questioned it directly. Yet their statements raise considerable question whether they intend to abide by the prohibitions contained therein.

As we have already stated in Parts B and C, the critical line for First Amendment purposes must be drawn between advocacy, which is entitled to full protection, and action, which is not. Petitioners may, if they so choose, preach the propriety of amending or even doing away with any or all campus regulations. They may not, however, undertake to flout these rules. Mr. Justice Blackmun, at the time he was a circuit judge on the Eighth Circuit, stated:

> "We . . . hold that a college has the inherent power to promulgate rules and regulations; that it has the inherent power properly to discipline; that it has power appropriately to protect itself and its property; that it may expect that its students adhere to generally accepted standards of conduct."

. . .

Just as in the community at large, reasonable regulations with respect to the time, the place, and the manner in which student groups conduct their speech-related activities must be respected. A college administration may impose a requirement, such as may have been imposed in this case, that a group seeking official recognition affirm in advance its willingness to adhere to reasonable campus law. Such a requirement does not impose an impermissible condition on the students' associational rights. Their freedom to speak out, to assemble, or to petition for changes in school rules is in no sense infringed. It merely constitutes an agreement to conform with reasonable standards respecting conduct. This is a minimal requirement, in the interest of the entire academic community, of any group seeking the privilege of official recognition.

Petitioners have not challenged in this litigation the procedural or substantive aspects of the College's requirements governing applications for official recognition. Although the record is unclear on this point, CCSC may have, among its requirements for recognition, a rule that prospective groups affirm that they intend to comply with reasonable campus regulations. Upon remand it should first be determined whether the College recognition procedures contemplate any such requirement. If so, it should then be ascertained whether petitioners intend to comply. Since we do not have the terms of a specific prior affirmation rule before us, we are not called on to decide whether any particular formulation would or would not prove constitutionally acceptable. Assuming the existence of a valid rule, however, we do conclude that the benefits of participation in the internal life of the college community may be denied to any group that reserves the right to violate any valid campus rules with which they disagree.

We think the above discussion establishes the appropriate framework for consideration of petitioners' request for campus recognition. Because respondents failed to accord due recognition to First Amendment principles, the judgment below approving respondents' denial of recognition must be reversed. Since we cannot conclude from this record that petitioners were willing to abide by reasonable campus rules and regulations, we order the case remanded for reconsideration.

. . .

Reversed and remanded.

Mr. Chief Justice BURGER, concurring.

. . . It is within . . . the academic community that problems such as these should be resolved. The courts, state or federal, should be a last resort. Part of the educational experience of every college student should be an experience in responsible self-government and this must be a joint enterprise of students and faculty. It should not be imposed unilaterally from above, nor can the terms of the relationship be dictated by students. . . .

The relatively placid life of the college campus of the past has not prepared either administrators or students for their respective responsibilities in maintaining an atmosphere in which divergent views can be asserted vigorously, but civilly, to the end that those who seek to be heard accord the same right to all others. The "Statement of Rights, Freedoms and Responsibilities of Students," sometimes called the "College Bill of Rights," in effect on this campus, and not questioned by petitioners, reflected a rational adjustment of the competing interests. But it is impossible to know from the record in this case whether the student group was willing to acknowledge an obligation to abide by that "Bill of Rights." . . .

Mr. Justice DOUGLAS

While I join the opinion of the Court, I add a few words.

. . . the status quo of the college or university is the governing body (trustees or overseers), administrative officers, who include caretakers and the police, and the faculty. Those groups have well-defined or vaguely inferred values to perpetuate. The customary technique has been to conceive of the minds of students as receptacles for the information which the faculty have garnered over the years. Education is commonly thought as the process of filling the receptacles with what the faculty in its wisdom deems fit and proper.

Many inside and out of faculty circles realize that one of the main problems of faculty members is their own re-education or re-orientation. Some have narrow specialties that are hardly relevant to modern times. History has passed others by, leaving them interesting relics of a by-gone day. More often than not they represent those who withered under the pressures of McCarthyism or other forces of conformity and represent but a timid replica of those who once brought distinction to the ideal of academic freedom.

The confrontation between them and the oncoming students has often been upsetting. The problem is not one of choosing sides. Students—who by reason of the Twenty-sixth Amendment become eligible to vote when 18 years of age—are adults who are members of the college or university community. Their interests and concerns are often quite different from those of the faculty. They often have values, views, and ideologies that are at war with the ones which the college has traditionally espoused or indoctrinated. When they ask for change, they, the students, speak in the tradition of Jefferson and Madison and the First Amendment.

The First Amendment does not authorize violence. But it does authorize advocacy, group activities, and espousal of change.

The present case is miniscule in the events of the 60's and 70's. But the fact that it has to come here for ultimate resolution, indicates the sickness of our academic world, measured by First Amendment standards. Students as well as faculty are entitled to credentials in their search for truth. If we are to become an integrated, adult society, rather than a stubborn status quo opposed to change, students and faculties should have communal interests in which each age learns from the other. Without ferment of one kind or another, a college or university (like a federal agency or other human institution) becomes a useless appendage to a society which traditionally has reflected the spirit of rebellion. . . .

Mr. Justice REHNQUIST, concurring in the result.

While I do not subscribe to some of the language in the Court's opinion, I concur in the result that it reaches. . . .

I find the implication clear from the Court's opinion that the constitutional limitations on the government acting as administrator of a college differ from the limitations on the government acting as sovereign to enforce its criminal laws. The Court's quotations from Tinker v. Des Moines Independent Community School District, . . . to the effect that First Amendment rights must always be applied "in light of the special characteristics of the . . . environment," and from Esteban v. Central Missouri State College, 415 F.2d 1077, 1089 (CA8, 1969), to the effect that a college "may expect that its students adhere to generally accepted standards of conduct," emphasize this fact.

Cases such as United Public Workers v. Mitchell, 330 U.S. 75, . . . and Pickering v. Board of Education etc., 391 U.S. 563, . . . make it equally clear that the government in its capacity as employer also differs constitutionally from the government in its capacity as the sovereign executing criminal laws. The Court in *Pickering* said:

> "The problem in any case is to arrive at a balance between the interests of the teacher, as a citizen, in commenting upon matters of public concern and the interest of the State, as an employer, in promoting the efficiency of the public services it performs through its employees." . . .

Because of these acknowledged distinctions of constitutional dimension based upon the role of the government, I have serious doubt as to whether cases dealing with the imposition of criminal sanctions . . . are properly applicable to this case dealing with the government as college administrator. I also doubt whether cases dealing with the prior restraint imposed by injunctive process of a court, . . .

are precisely comparable to this case, in which a typical sanction imposed was the requirement that the group abandon its plan to meet in the college coffee shop.

Prior cases dealing with First Amendment rights are not fungible goods, and I think the doctrine of these cases suggests two important distinctions. The government as employer or school administrator may impose upon employees and students reasonable regulations that would be impermissible if imposed by the government upon all citizens. And there can be a constitutional distinction between the infliction of criminal punishment, on the one hand, and the imposition of milder administrative or disciplinary sanctions, on the other, even though the same First Amendment interest is implicated by each.

Because some of the language used by the Court tends to obscure these distinctions, which I believe to be important, I concur only in the judgment.

NOTES AND QUESTIONS

1. Would this case have been decided differently if (1) a "common school" rather than a university were involved, or if (2) the organization denied recognition were a teacher's organization rather than student? If so, why?

2. What are the constitutional rules governing school recognition of organizations? State them.

3. Does this case apply to secret societies? Would the decision have been different if a secret society were involved?

4. Assume you are the judge, and in light of Healy v. James, supra, would you have decided the following case differently than did Oregon's Supreme Court? If so, are the Oregon decision and its opinion fully consistent with Healy v. James? If not, where do they differ? Are these differings justifiable? Why or why not?

BURKITT v. SCHOOL DIST. NO. 1

Supreme Court of Oregon, 1952.
195 Or. 471, 246 P.2d 566.

LUSK, Justice. Since 1909 secret societies in the high schools of this state have been prohibited by law. The statute in O.C.L.A. so providing reads:

§ 111–3004. "Secret societies of every kind and character, including fraternities and sororities, so called, which may now or hereafter exist among the pupils of any of the public schools of this state, including high schools, either local or country, are hereby declared unlawful."

§ 111–3005.   "It is hereby made the duty of each school board within the state, to examine, from time to time, into the condition of all schools under its charge and to suppress all secret societies therein, and for this purpose such boards are hereby authorized to suspend or expel from school, in their discretion, all pupils who engage in the organization or maintenance of such societies."

§ 111–3006.   "This act shall not apply to either the state agricultural college or the state university."   .   .   .

.   .   .   .   the statute appears to have been more honored in the breach than the observance.   Until 1936 the school authorities seem to have done little if anything to discharge their statutory duty to "suppress all secret societies" in the high schools, although there were for many years in the high schools of Portland a number of secret fraternities and sororities, some of the former being local chapters of national organizations.   In 1936 a pledge system was inaugurated under which pupils and their parents were required to sign a pledge that the pupil was not and would not become a member of any such society. If it was discovered that a pupil had violated the pledge he was suspended; afterward he and a parent could come to the superintendent's office and agree that the pupil would resign from the organization, whereupon the suspension would be lifted.   The system was found only partially effective.   Sometimes, when the issue arose, parents protested that the particular organization involved was not a secret society and that it was not operating in the schools.   In 1943 and 1944 the school authorities, because of these protests from parents and their own feeling of uncertainty as to how far they could go in the enforcement of the law, abandoned the pledge system, and adopted a policy of ignoring the societies as long as they kept their activities out of the schools.   This did not work either; the pupils then began to wear fraternity and sorority pins openly and to engage in pledging, "dogging," and other activities peculiar to their organizations, in the schools.

It was against this background of experience with a problem which, as Mr. Jonathan W. Edwards, deputy superintendent of schools testified, "has existed in our schools for the last 35 or 40 years," and with the purpose of discharging the duty imposed upon them by law, that the board of directors of the school district on or about October 27, 1949, adopted a resolution by which were promulgated certain regulations prescribing the conditions under which clubs could be organized and conducted in the high schools of the district.   .   .   .

The resolution contains the following recitals:

"Whereas, secret societies of every kind and character, including fraternities and sororities, so called, are contrary to state law, and

"Whereas, the state law imposes upon the School Board the duty of suppressing such organizations within the public schools of this district and to that end authorizes the School Board to suspend or expel from schools in its discretion all pupils who engage in the organization or maintenance of such societies, and

"Whereas, clubs and organizations other than secret societies, organized and maintained by school pupils can become and be inimical to the best interest of the school pupils, the community or the effective operation of the schools."

The superintendent of schools is then directed to suppress secret societies "and also clubs and organizations other than secret societies which the Superintendent in his discretion considers inimical to the best interest of the school pupils, the community, or the effective operation of the schools, by suspending or expelling" pupils who are members thereof. It was further resolved that school clubs should not be banned which have been approved and chartered by the high school principal on conditions established by the superintendent of schools. These provisions are followed by what are termed "tentative conditions," which provide that all organizations of pupils must be approved by the central school administration and chartered by the particular school from which organized; that the application for a charter must show the sponsoring group, adult supervisor or advisors, the purposes of the organization and standards for membership, a list of officers and members, a copy of any ceremonial or initiation, and a pledge against secrecy. Then follow 18 rules designed to keep the school authorities advised of the membership and financial condition, and to regulate the activities of these chartered organizations. It is required that at all functions of the organizations adult advisors approved by the school principal shall be present; any initiation ceremonies not approved by the principal are prohibited, and such ceremonies are required to be open to the school staff and parents of inductees; no more than a two-thirds vote shall be required for admission to membership; hazing, "dogging" and all other types of pre-initiation activities, rush periods, and post-bid screening of members are prohibited. Membership in an organization not chartered is made a ground for suspension or expulsion.

The particular rule, however, which is involved in this case is No. 7, which reads as follows:

"Members of any chartered organizations shall be regularly enrolled high school students from one high school student body. Graduates or students who have dropped from school shall not be permitted to retain membership. Public school students who were bona fide members of an interschool club prior to October 27, 1949, may retain membership in any such club that qualifies for a charter."

The validity of this rule is the principal question in the case.
.   .   .

Plaintiffs are three adults and four minors. Of the adults one has
a son and a daughter attending Lincoln High School, a public school of
the district; another has a daughter attending St. Helen's Hall, a private school in Portland; and another has two daughters attending
St. Mary's Academy in Portland, erroneously referred to in the record
as a parochial school, actually a private school under Catholic auspices.
The two private schools give a high school education. Each of the
children of the adult plaintiffs is a member of one or another of the
four organizations named in the complaint whose status is here involved. Plaintiffs refer to these organizations as "unincorporated
clubs," defendants and intervenors as sororities and fraternities. We
shall call them simply "clubs." Each of the minor plaintiffs is a pupil
of a Portland public high school and a member and officer or representative of one or another of the following named clubs: Alpha
Sigma, Joma Joma, Wiki and Pierrette, and they appear on behalf,
not only of themselves, but of the clubs named and all other clubs
similarly situated. The defendants are the school district, its board
of directors, and school clerk.   .   .   .

The plaintiffs do not deny that there are secret societies in the
Portland high schools, or at least that there were on February 28,
1950, the day their complaint was filed.   .   .   .

The circuit judge found in his opinion that at least some of the
plaintiff clubs were secret societies. We think there is justification
in the evidence for that finding. Moreover, the evidence shows that
in organization, officers, types of records kept, rushing, pledging, initiation (with necessary variations as between fraternities and sororities) all the members of the Big Six followed somewhat of a pattern,
and that three members of the Big Six were chapters of national fraternities. We are inclined to the opinion that some elements of secrecy
were likewise common to all the Big Six societies. Indeed, if the
secret societies admitted to exist are not to be found among the un-
chartered members of the Big Six, we are at a loss to know where to
look for them. But in the view we take of the actual question for
decision, it is not necessary to determine which clubs are secret societies or whether the plaintiff clubs are among them. Much testimony was adduced upon that subject, and there has been extensive
argument respecting it. The basic questions, however, are whether
there is a secret society problem in the high schools of Portland, and,
if so, whether, by the adoption of Rule 7, along with the other so-called
"tentative conditions," the school board exceeded its authority; or
whether, on the other hand, Rule 7 is a reasonable regulation appropriate to accomplish the end expressed in the resolution of October 27, 1949, namely, the suppression of secret societies in the high
schools.   .   .   .

This court would be the last to sanction any unlawful interference with "the liberty of parents and guardians to direct the upbringing and education of children under their control."   Pierce v. Society of the Sisters,   . . .

The plaintiffs also rely on West Virginia State Board of Education v. Barnette,   . . .   Of course, no such question [of a compulsory flag salute] is involved here.

There is nothing in Rule 7, nor in any other of the rules adopted by the school board, which prevents the minor plaintiffs from assembling and associating freely at any time and place, outside of school hours, approved by their parents, with children from other high schools, public or private.   This is their constitutional right.   But they have no constitutional right to be members of clubs organized in the high schools, and composed of children attending different high schools, and which the school board may have substantial reason for believing to be inimical to the discipline and effective operation of the schools.   . . .   Nor does it make any difference that the minor plaintiffs may be required by law to attend some school, either public or private.   . . .   That obligation is likewise their opportunity to receive an education.   . . .   When they avail themselves of that opportunity they must, in the nature of things, submit to the discipline of the schools and to regulations reasonably calculated to promote such discipline and the high purpose for which the schools are established— the education of youth, which is not limited to the imparting of knowledge, but includes as well the development of character and preparation for the assumption of the responsibilities of citizenship in a democracy.   To attain these ends not the least in value of the lessons to be learned are the lessons of self-restraint, self-discipline, tolerance, and respect for duly constituted authority.   In this regard parents and the schools have their respective rights and duties, which complement one another, and may be exercised and discharged in cooperation for the welfare of the child and the state.

Here, as it seems to us, for the court to interfere with the action of the school authorities now challenged would be little less than to constitute ourselves a school board for all the schools of the state. This is something we have neither the right nor the inclination to do.

The provision of the resolution which invests the superintendent with the power to suppress nonsecret societies which in his discretion he considers inimical to the best interests of the school pupils, the community, or the effective operation of the schools, is attacked as a delegation of "unconstrained authority."   In connection with this claim attention is called to the fact that the superintendent has exempted from the ban clubs sponsored by national fraternal organizations, by religious organizations, national youth organizations, and civic organizations such as the Kiwanis Club.   . . .   If at any time the superintendent should be guilty of applying the regulation with "an unequal and oppressive mind," as in Yick Wo v. Hopkins, [118 U.S. 356] then the rule of that case could be invoked. We are unable to say from the record in this case that he has done so thus far. . . .

The foregoing considerations lead us to the conclusion that the defendant School Board, in adopting the regulations here in question, acted within its authority, and that the regulations, particularly Rule 7, are reasonable and constitute a measure taken in good faith for the purpose of stamping out secret societies in the high schools under the Board's jurisdiction, in accordance with the duty imposed upon it by law . . .

NOTES AND QUESTIONS

1. Is it possible that the statute and rule number 7 in this case if sought to be applied to adults would be an unconstitutional abridgment of the right to free and continuing secret association protected by the first amendment? See, NAACP v. Alabama, 357 U.S. 449, 78 S.Ct. 1163, 2 L.Ed.2d 1488 (1958). Cf. People of the State of New York ex rel. Bryant v. Zimmerman, 278 U.S. 63, 49 S.Ct. 61, 73 L.Ed. 184 (1928). What is the justification for the school district to ban secret associations? Is the statute and rule 7 overbroad?

2. Does the rationale of the court penalize students for their *status* as secret society members rather than for any *acts* as such members? Does the fact that their membership was voluntary affect your answer? Should it?

3. Should a constitutional distinction be drawn between public and secret association?

NEWSPAPERS

———

PAPISH v. BOARD OF CURATORS OF UNIVERSITY OF MISSOURI

Supreme Court of the United States, 1973.
410 U.S. 667, 93 S.Ct. 1197, 35 L.Ed.2d 618.

PER CURIAM.

Petitioner, a graduate student in the University of Missouri School of Journalism, was expelled for distributing on campus a newspaper "containing forms of indecent speech" in violation of the By-Laws of the Board of Curators. The newspaper, the Free Press Underground, had been sold on this state university campus for more than four years pursuant to an authorization obtained from the University Business Office. The particular newspaper issue in question was found to be unacceptable for two reasons. First, on the front cover the publishers had reproduced a political cartoon previously printed in another newspaper depicting policeman raping the Statue of Liberty and the Goddess of Justice. The caption under the cartoon read: " . . . With Liberty and Justice for All." Secondly, the issue contained an article entitled M_____ f_____ Acquitted," which discussed the trial and acquittal on an assault charge of a New York City youth who was a member of an organization known as "Up Against the Wall, M_____ f_____."

Following a hearing, the Student Conduct Committee found that petitioner had violated Paragraph B of Art. A of the General Standards of Student Conduct which requires students "to observe generally accepted standards of conduct" and specifically prohibits "indecent conduct or speech." [2] Her dismissal, after affirmance first by the Chancellor of the University and then by its Board of Curators, was made effective in the middle of the spring semester. Although she was then permitted to remain on campus until the end of the semester, she was not given credit for the one course in which she made a passing grade. . . . She claimed that her dismissal was improperly premised on activities protected by the First Amendment. The District Court denied relief, 331 F.Supp. 1321, and the Court of Appeals affirmed, one judge dissenting. 464 F.2d 136. . . .

The District Court's opinion rests, in part, on the conclusion that the banned issue of the newspaper was obscene. The Court of Appeals found it unnecessary to decide that question. Instead, assuming that the newspaper was not obscene and that its distribution in the community at large would be protected by the First Amendment, the court held that on a university campus "freedom of expression" could properly be "subordinated to other interests such as, for example, the conventions of decency in the use and display of language and pictures." . . . The court concluded that "[t]he Constitution does not compel the University [to allow] such publications as the one in litigation to be publicly sold or distributed on its open campus."

This case was decided several days before we handed down Healy v. James, 408 U.S. 169, 92 S.Ct. 2338, 33 L.Ed.2d 266 (1972), in which, while recognizing a state university's undoubted prerogative to enforce reasonable rules governing student conduct, we reaffirmed that "state colleges and universities are not enclaves immune from the sweep of the First Amendment." . . . See Tinker v. Des Moines Independent School District. . . . We think *Healy* makes it clear that the mere dissemination of ideas—no matter how offensive to good taste—on a state university campus may not be shut off in the name alone of "conventions of decency." Other recent precedents of this Court make it equally clear that neither the political cartoon nor

---

[2] In pertinent part, the By-Law states: "Students enrolling in the University assume an obligation and are expected by the University to conduct themselves in a manner compatible with the University's functions and missions as an educational institution. For that purpose students are required to observe generally accepted standards of conduct . . . . [I]ndecent conduct or speech . . . are examples of conduct which would contravene this standard . . . ." 464 F.2d, at 138.

the headline story involved in this case can be labelled as constitutionally obscene or otherwise unprotected. . . . There is language in the opinion below which suggests that the University's action here could be viewed as an exercise of its legitimate authority to enforce reasonable regulations as to the time, place, and manner of speech and its dissemination. While we have repeatedly approved such regulatory authority, . . . the facts set forth in the opinions below show clearly that petitioner was dismissed because of the disapproved *content* of the newspaper rather than the time, place, or manner of its distribution.

Since the First Amendment leaves no room for the operation of a dual standard in the academic community with respect to the content of speech, and because the state University's action here cannot be justified as a nondiscriminatory application of reasonable rules governing conduct, the judgments of the courts below must be reversed. Accordingly the petition for a writ of certiorari is granted, the case is remanded to the District Court, and that court is instructed to order the University to restore to petitioner any course credits she earned for the semester in question and, unless she is barred from reinstatement for valid academic reasons, to reinstate her as a student in the graduate program.

Reversed and remanded.

Mr. Chief Justice BURGER, dissenting.

I join the dissent of Justice REHNQUIST which follows and add a few additional observations. . . .

In theory, at least, a university is not merely an arena for the discussion of ideas by students and faculty; it is also an institution where individuals learn to express themselves in acceptable, civil terms. We provide that environment to the end that students may learn the self-restraint necessary to the functioning of a civilized society and understand the need for those external restraints to which we must all submit if group existence is to be tolerable.

. . . Students are, of course, free to criticize the university, its faculty, or the government in vigorous or even harsh terms. But it is not unreasonable or violative of the Constitution to subject to disciplinary action those individuals who distribute publications which are at the same time obscene and infantile. To preclude a university or college from regulating the distribution of such obscene materials does not protect the values inherent in the First Amendment; rather, it demeans those values. The anomaly of the Court's holding today is suggested by its use of the now familiar "code" abbreviation for the petitioner's foul language. . . .

Mr. Justice REHNQUIST, with whom THE CHIEF JUSTICE and Mr. Justice BLACKMUN join, dissenting. . . .

I continue to adhere to the dissenting views expressed in Rosenfeld v. New Jersey, 408 U.S. 901, 92 S.Ct. 2479, 33 L.Ed.2d 321 (1972),

that the public use of the word "M_____ f_____" is "lewd and obscene"   .   .   .   A state university is an establishment for the purpose of educating the State's young people, supported by the tax
revenues of the State's citizens. The notion that the officials lawfully charged with the governance of the university have so little control over the environment for which they are responsible that they
may not prevent the public distribution of a newspaper on campus
which contained the language described in the Court's opinion is quite
unacceptable to me and I would suspect would have been equally unacceptable to the Framers of the First Amendment. This is indeed a
case where the observation of a unanimous Court in *Chaplinski* that
"such utterances are no essential part of any exposition of ideas and
are of such slight social value as a step to truth that any benefit that
may be derived from them is clearly outweighed by the social interest in order and morality" applies with compelling force.

The Court cautions that "disenchantment with Miss Papish's performance, understandable as it may have been, is no justification for
denial of constitutional rights." Quite so. But a wooden insistence
on equating, for constitutional purposes, the authority of the State to
criminally punish with its authority to exercise even a modicum of control over the University which it operates, serves neither the Constitution nor public education well. There is reason to think that the
"disenchantment" of which the Court speaks may, after this decision,
become widespread among taxpayers and legislators. The system of
tax supported public universities which has grown up in this country is
one of its truly great accomplishments; if they are to continue to grow
and thrive to serve an expanding population, they must have something more than the grudging support of taxpayers and legislators.
But one can scarcely blame the latter, if told by the Court that their
only function is to supply tax money for the operation of the University, the "disenchantment" may reach such a point that they doubt
the game is worth the candle.

FUJISHIMA v. BOARD OF EDUCATION

United States Court of Appeals, 1972.
460 F.2d 1355 (7th Cir.).

SPRECHER, Circuit Judge. This suit challenges the constitutionality of section 6–19 of the rules of the Chicago Board of Education:

No person shall be permitted   .   .   .   to distribute on the
school premises any books, tracts, or other publications,
.   .   .   unless the same shall have been approved by the General Superintendent of Schools.

Plaintiffs are three high school students who were disciplined for violation of section 6–19. On behalf of themselves and of a class of all high school students in Chicago school districts, they sought declaratory and injunctive relief. They also asked for actual and exemplary damages.

Plaintiffs Burt Fujishima and Richard Peluso were seniors at Lane Technical High School. They were suspended for four and seven days respectively for distributing about 350 copies of *The Cosmic Frog*, an "underground" newspaper they and another student published. The papers were distributed free both before and between classes and during lunch breaks.

Plaintiff Robert Balanoff, a sophomore at Bowen High School, was suspended for two days for giving another student an unsigned copy of a petition calling for "teach-ins" concerning the war in Viet Nam. The exchange occurred in May of 1970 in a school corridor between classes.

In October 1970, Balanoff was suspended for five days for distributing leaflets about the war to 15 or 20 students. This distribution took place during a fire drill, while Balanoff and his classmates were in their assigned places across the street from the school. . . .

. . . Defendants' primary theory on the appeal is that section 6–19 is constitutionally permissible because it does not require approval of the *content* of a publication before it may be distributed. Unfortunately for defendants' theory, that is neither what the rule says nor how defendants have previously interpreted it. The superintendent must approve "the same," which refers back to "any books, tracts, or other publications." The superintendent cannot perform his duty under the rule without having the publication submitted to him. The principals believed the rule requires approval of the publication itself: the Fujishima and Peluso suspensions were for "distribution of unauthorized material in the school"; the Balanoff suspensions were for "distribution of unauthorized materials in the school building" and for "distributing unapproved literature in class during fire drill."

Because section 6–19 requires prior approval of publications, it is unconstitutional as a prior restraint in violation of the First Amendment. This conclusion is compelled by combining the holdings of Near v. Minnesota, 283 U.S. 697, . . . and Tinker v. Des Moines Independent Community School District, . . . *Tinker* held that, absent a showing of material and substantial interference with the requirements of school discipline, schools may not restrain the full First-Amendment rights of their students. *Near* established one of those rights, freedom to distribute a publication without prior censorship.

Other courts have held unconstitutional similar restraints on student distribution of underground newspapers and political literature.[3] In Riseman v. School Committee, 439 F.2d 148 (1st Cir. 1971), a rule directed against advertising and promoting on school grounds was used to deny permission to a student to distribute political litera- ture. The First Circuit invalidated the rule as vague, overbroad and impermissible as a prior restraint. The court said the school might regulate the time, manner and place of distribution, but could not require advance approval of the content of the material.

The Fourth Circuit in Quarterman v. Byrd, 453 F.2d 54 (1971), enjoined the enforcement of a rule which required prior permission from the principal before distributing any material. The court in Sullivan v. Houston Independent School District, 333 F.Supp. 1149 (S.D.Tex.1971), refused to permit the school to give even a one-day review to the principal; the school could not justify imposition of any prior restraint on distribution of underground newspapers.

The district court in Eisner v. Stamford Board of Education, 314 F.Supp. 832 (D.Conn.1970), reached the same result in invalidating a rule which required prior approval. On appeal the Second Circuit affirmed the invalidation, but modified the lower court's opinion so extensively as to obliterate it.   440 F.2d 803 (1971). The court al- lowed prior submission of publications if accompanied by elaborate procedural safeguards.

We believe that the court erred in *Eisner* in interpreting *Tinker* to allow prior restraint of publication—long a constitutionally pro- hibited power—as a tool of school officials in "forecasting" substantial disruption of school activities. In proper context, Mr. Justice Fortas' use of the word "forecast" in *Tinker* means a prediction by school officials that existing conduct, such as the wearing of arm bands—if allowed to continue—will probably interfere with school discipline. . . . *Tinker* in no way suggests that students may be required to announce their intentions of engaging in certain conduct beforehand so school authorities may decide whether to prohibit the conduct. Such a concept of prior restraint is even more offensive when applied to the long-protected area of publication.

This interpretation of the *Tinker* forecast rule is supported by this court's opinion in Scoville v. Board of Education, 425 F.2d 10 (7th Cir.), cert. denied, 400 U.S. 826, 91 S.Ct. 51, 27 L.Ed.2d 55 (1970). There the court applied the rule to a decision made by school officials

---

[3] In harmony with the cases cited in the text are these analogous cases: Anto- nelli v. Hammond, 308 F.Supp. 1329 (D. Mass.1970) (board could not require prior submission of material to be printed in college newspaper); Dickey v. Alabama State Board of Education, 273 F.Supp. 613 (M.D.Ala.1967) (student editor could not be expelled for inserting "CENSOR- ED" across blank columns where disap- proved editorial was to have run); Zuck- er v. Panitz, 299 F.Supp. 102 (S.D.N.Y. 1969) (students could purchase ad in high school paper to express feelings against the war); Brooks v. Auburn University, 296 F.Supp. 188 (M.D.Ala.), aff'd, 412 F.2d 1171 (5th Cir. 1969), and Snyder v. Board of Trustees, 286 F.Supp. 927 (N.D.Ill.1968) (banning certain speakers from appearing on campus was an un- constitutional prior restraint).

three days after publication and distribution of the newspaper. Even though *Grass High* contained articles critical of the school administration, this court found that the board could not reasonably have forecast substantial disruption and therefore could not expel the student authors.

The *Tinker* forecast rule is properly a formula for determining when the requirements of school discipline justify *punishment* of students for exercise of their First-Amendment rights. It is not a basis for establishing a system of censorship and licensing designed to *prevent* the exercise of First-Amendment rights.

Because we believe *Eisner* is unsound constitutional law, and because defendants in effect concede that they cannot require submission of publications before approval of distribution, we declare section 6–19 unconstitutional and remand the case for entry of an injunction against its enforcement.

Such injunction will not prevent defendants from promulgating reasonable, specific regulations setting forth the time, manner and place in which distribution of written materials may occur. This does not mean, as defendants' brief suggests, that the board may require a student to obtain administrative approval of the time, manner and place of the particular distribution he proposes. The board has the burden of telling students when, how and where they may distribute materials. *See* Sullivan v. Houston Independent School District, 307 F.Supp. 1328, 1340 (S.D.Tex.1969). The board may then punish students who violate those regulations. Of course, the board may also establish a rule punishing students who publish and distribute on school grounds obscene or libelous literature.

Plaintiff Balanoff's second suspension remains on his record. He was punished under section 6–19 for distributing leaflets to classmates during a fire drill. Because the rule is unconstitutional, his suspension under it cannot stand.

Defendants argue that the justification for the suspension is "self-evident" from the record. All that appears in the record are the following allegations by plaintiffs:

> At no time during the fire drill was there any disorder. The distribution of said leaflets did not disrupt classes; nor did it interfere with any other proper school activity, including the fire drill. At no time during the distribution was the Plaintiff asked to stop distributing the leaflets by any member of the Bowen faculty or administration.

Neither in the district court nor on appeal have defendants suggested that evidence exists to challenge those factual assertions.

The district court speculated that students might use a fire drill, or might even instigate one, to engage in disruptive activities. His error was similar to the district court's in Scoville v. Board of Education, . . . "No reasonable inference of [a showing that the action was taken on a reasonable forecast of a substantial disruption of school activity] can be drawn from the complaint. . . ."

The board might issue a rule prohibiting distribution of literature during a fire drill as a regulation of time and place, but it could not apply such a rule *ex post facto* to Balanoff.

The district court's order shall include a direction to expunge Balanoff's second suspension from his record.

NOTES AND QUESTIONS

1. Explain carefully the significance and different implications for a a system of free expression between a subsequent punishment for engaging in expression and a prior restraint on that expression. Which is more dangerous? Which was involved in each case?

2. In Baughman v. Freienmuth, 478 F.2d 1345 (4th Cir. 1973), the U. S. Court of Appeals held the Montgomery Bd. of Education's 'prior restraint regulation' unconstitutional and advanced the following propositions:

   (a) Secondary school children are within the protection of the first amendment, although their rights are not coextensive with those of adults.

   (b) Secondary school authorities may exercise reasonable prior restraint upon the exercise of students' first amendment rights.

   (c) Such prior restraints must contain precise criteria sufficiently spelling out what is forbidden so that a reasonably intelligent student will know what he may write and what he may not write.

   (d) A prior restraint system, even though precisely defining what may not be written is nevertheless invalid unless it provides for:

   (1) A definition of 'Distribution' and its application to different kinds of material;

   (2) Prompt approval or disapproval of what is submitted;

   (3) Specification of the effect of failure to act promptly; and,

   (4) An adequate and prompt appeal procedure.

   Is this case consistent with Fujishima v. Bd. of Ed.? See also, Sullivan v. Houston Independent School Dist., 475 F.2d 1071 (5th Cir. 1973).

3. California's law provides:

   "No bulletin, circular, publication, or article of any character, whose purpose is to spread propaganda, shall be distributed or displayed to anyone, or suffered to be distributed or displayed to anyone, for propaganda purposes on the school premises during school hours or within one hour before the time of opening or within one hour after the time of closing of the school, but such bulletin, circular, publication, or article may be used in school library collections and for legitimate instructional purposes. . . .

"The prohibition of this section shall not apply to bulletins or circulars concerning the meetings of organizations issued by any parent-teacher association or by any organization of parents formed for the purpose of cooperating with the school authorities in improving school conditions in the district." West's Ann.Educ.Code of Calif. § 9013.

Is any part of this statute unconstitutional? Why or why not?

CAMPUS SPEAKERS

———

"The board of trustees of each college or university which receives any State funds in support thereof, shall adopt and publish regulations governing the use of facilities of such college or university for speaking purposes by any person who:

"(1) Is a known member of the Communist Party;

"(2) Is known to advocate the overthrow of the Constitution of the United States or the State of North Carolina;

"(3) Has pleaded the Fifth Amendment of the Constitution of the United States in refusing to answer any question, with respect to Communist or subversive connections, or activities, before any duly constituted legislative committee, any judicial tribunal, or any executive or administrative board of the United States or any state.

"Any such regulations shall be enforced by the board of trustees, or other governing authority, of such college or university, or by such administrative personnel as may be appointed therefor by the board of trustees or other governing authority of such college or university" Gen.Stat.No.Carolina §§ 116–199, 116–200. For commentary on this statute, see, Pollitt, Campus Censorship, 42 No.C.L.Rev. 179 (1963).

———

DICKSON v. SITTERSON

United States District Court, 1968.
280 F.Supp. 486 (M.D.N.C.), aff'd 415 F.2d 228 (5th Cir. 1969).

EDWIN M. STANLEY, District Judge. The plaintiff seeks to declare unconstitutional and enjoin the enforcement of § 116–199 and § 116–200, General Statutes of North Carolina, statutes regulating the appearance of visiting speakers at State-supported colleges and universities. . . .

The basic facts are not in dispute, and are to be found in the complaint and answer, with exhibits attached, stipulated facts and documents, and depositions. . . .

At all times pertinent, the plaintiffs, except Wilkinson and Aptheker, were students duly enrolled and in good standing at the University of North Carolina at Chapel Hill, North Carolina. The student body consisted of approximately twelve thousand students and the plaintiff, Dickson, was the duly elected president of the student body. . . .

The plaintiff, Frank Wilkinson, is a citizen and resident of the State of California, and is Executive Director of the National Committee to Abolish the House Un-American Activities Committee.

The plaintiff, Herbert Aptheker, is a citizen and resident of the State of New York, and is Director of the American Institute for Marxist Studies. . . .

On January 3, 1966, the plaintiffs Matthews and Waller invited the plaintiff Wilkinson to speak on the campus of the University of North Carolina at Chapel Hill on March 2, 1966, and the plaintiff Aptheker to speak on March 9, 1966, under the sponsorship of the Students for a Democratic Society. These invitations were personally approved by the defendant Friday and by Chancellor Paul Sharp, who was then the Chancellor of the University of North Carolina at Chapel Hill, but no official action was taken.

On or about February 1, 1966, the plaintiffs Dickson, Nicholson and McCrary invited the plaintiff Aptheker to speak on the University campus on March 9, 1966, under the sponsorship of the Student Government, the Carolina Forum, and *The Daily Tar Heel*. The invitation was accepted by plaintiff Aptheker on February 3, 1966. . . .

On February 7, 1966, the Executive Committee of the Board of Trustees of the University reconvened in the office of the Governor of North Carolina, at which time the following resolutions were adopted:

"RESOLUTION No. 1

The Executive Committee of the Board of Trustees of the University of North Carolina deny the use of University facilities for speaking purposes for the scheduled appearances of Herbert Aptheker and Frank Wilkinson. . . .

The plaintiffs Wilkinson and Aptheker had previously spoken on many university campuses throughout the country on the subjects on which they were invited to speak at the University of North Carolina at Chapel Hill. During the month of March, 1966, they both spoke on these subjects on the campus of Duke University, Durham, North Carolina.

The University of North Carolina has hundreds of visiting speakers on its campuses each year, some invited by student organizations and some by faculty groups. . . .

Because Wilkinson has pleaded the Fifth Amendment in refusing to answer any questions with respect to Communist or subversive connections or activities before a duly constituted legislative committee, and because Aptheker admits being a member of the Communist Party of the United States, both are within the classifications set forth in G.S. § 116–199 and § 116–200, and the rules and regulations established by the defendants pursuant to said statutes.   .   .   .

This Court is not blind to world affairs, and can understand and appreciate the vital concern of the people of the State of North Carolina over the unregulated appearance of dedicated members of the Communist Party on the campuses of its State-supported institutions. The record in this case clearly establishes that the Communist conspiracy is dedicated to the destruction of freedom, and attempts to achieve its goals of world conquest through discord, deceit and untruths.   The record further establishes that the use of college campuses affords the Communist Party with an optimum chance of reaching and influencing a maximum number of young people.   Certainly, the State is under no obligation to provide a sanctuary for the Communist Party, or a platform for propagandizing its creed.

It is beyond question that boards of trustees of State-supported colleges and universities have every right to promulgate and enforce rules and regulations, consistent with constitutional principles, governing the appearance of all guest speakers.   Institutions of higher learning are engaged in the education of students, rather than satisfying their whimsical curiosity.   There are undoubtedly many speakers, both as individuals and with respect to the causes they espouse, who add nothing whatever to the educational process.   No one has an absolute right to speak on a college or university campus, but once such institution opens its doors to visiting speakers it must do so under principles that are constitutionally valid.   .   .   .

It is firmly established that a statute "which either forbids or requires the doing of an act in terms so vague that men of common intelligence must necessarily guess at its meaning and differ as to its application   *   *   *" violates the due process clause of the Fourteenth Amendment because of vagueness.   .   .   .   Moreover, standards of permissible statutory vagueness are particularly strict when First Amendment rights are involved.   .   .   .   While the question of vagueness has most frequently arisen in criminal prosecutions, it has been applied in a variety of other situations where the obedience to a rule or standard has been exacted.   .   .   .

The first provision of the statute under attack covers a "known member of the Communist Party."   "Known" to whom, and to what degree of certainty?   "Known" according to what standard?   A "member" in what sense?   Does it include membership in a Communist "front" organization?   Is it a matter of general reputation or rumor, or the personal knowledge of the Chancellor?   The statutes and regulations provide no clues to any of these questions. Without such answers, neither those who must obey nor those who must enforce the statutes and regulations can determine the extent of their obligation.

The next provision of the statute requires regulations covering visiting speakers who are "known to advocate the overthrow of the Constitution of the United States or the State of North Carolina." Does it mean with force and arms or is the advocacy of ideas sufficient? Must the advocacy be public or private? Is the advocacy of peaceful change included? It is sufficient to say that reasonable men might differ on the answers to these questions.

The third section of the statute covers speakers who have "pleaded the Fifth Amendment of the Constitution of the United States." Presumably, this means the "self-incrimination" class, although this is a matter of conjecture. What is meant by "subversive connections?" Here again, since reasonable men might differ, the statute is unconstitutionally vague. Moreover, the imposition of any sanction by reason of the invocation of the Fifth Amendment is constitutionally impermissible. . . .

Loyalty oaths have recently been declared unconstitutional because of vagueness in the cases of Baggett v. Bullitt, 377 U.S. 360, . . . and Elfbrandt v. Russell, 384 U.S. 11, . . . In Whitehill v. Elkins, 389 U.S. 54, . . . (1967), the Supreme Court, in another teacher oath case, again emphasized the need for "precision and clarity" in the "sensitive and important First Amendment area." Similarly, in Keyishian v. Board of Regents, 385 U.S. 589, . . . the Supreme Court, in striking down certain New York statutes and administrative regulations dealing with the employment or retention of State employees because of vagueness, stated:

> "There can be no doubt of the legitimacy of New York's interest in protecting its education system from subversion. But 'even though the governmental purpose be legitimate and substantial, that purpose cannot be pursued by means that broadly stifle fundamental personal liberties when the end can be more narrowly achieved.' Shelton v. Tucker, 364 U.S. 479, . . .

> We emphasize once again that '[p]recision of regulation must be the touchstone in an area so closely touching our most precious freedoms,' . . . '[f]or standards of permissible statutory vagueness are strict in the area of free expression. * * * Because First Amendment freedoms need breathing space to survive, government may regulate in the area only with narrow specificity.' . . . New York's complicated and intricate scheme plainly violates that standard. When one must guess what conduct or utterance may lose him his position, one necessarily will 'steer far wider of the unlawful zone * * *.' . . . For '[t]he threat of sanctions may

deter   *   *   *   almost as potently as the actual application of sanctions.'   .   .   .   The danger of that chilling effect upon the exercise of vital First Amendment rights must be guarded against by sensitive tools which clearly inform teachers what is being proscribed.   .   .   .

The regulatory maze created by New York is wholly lacking in 'terms susceptible of objective measurement.' Cramp v. Board of Public Instruction,   .   .   .   It has the quality of 'extraordinary ambiguity' found to be fatal to the oaths considered in *Cramp* and Baggett v. Bullitt. '[M]en of common intelligence must necessarily guess at its meaning and differ as to its application   *   *   *.'   Baggett v. Bullitt, supra [377 U.S.] at 367   .   .   .   Vagueness of wording is aggravated by prolixity and profusion of statutes, regulations, and administrative machinery, and by manifold cross-references to interrelated enactments and rules."

When the statutes and regulations in question are applied to the unbroken line of Supreme Court decisions respecting the necessity for clear, narrow and objective standards controlling the licensing of First Amendment rights, the conclusion is inescapable that they run afoul of constitutional principles.   .   .   .

BROOKS v. AUBURN UNIVERSITY

United States District Court, 1969.
296 F.Supp. 188 (M.D.Ala.), aff'd 412 F.2d 1171 (5th Cir., 1969).

JOHNSON, Chief Judge.   In this class action plaintiffs seek to have this Court issue a preliminary injunction restraining defendants from interfering with a scheduled speaking appearance at Auburn University of the Reverend William Sloan Coffin.   Plaintiffs also seek a declaratory judgment of the unconstitutionality of certain regulations, rules, and guidelines concerning inviting speakers to the Auburn University campus.   .   .   .

Plaintiffs in this action are students and faculty members of Auburn University, and the Human Rights Forum, an officially chartered Auburn University student organization.   Defendants are Auburn University, a state-operated institution of higher learning located at Auburn, Alabama, Dr. Harry M. Philpott, individually and as President of Auburn University, and Frank P. Samford, Sr., Chairman of the Board of Trustees of Auburn University.

The events immediately triggering this action commenced November 13, 1968, when the Chairman of the Human Rights Forum, David Jeffers, made a written request to the Public Affairs Seminar Board requesting $650 to pay the Reverend William Sloan Coffin to speak at the University on February 7, 1969. The Public Affairs Seminar Board was chartered by Auburn University for the purpose of "allocating funds to departments or groups for the presentation of seminars, conferences, individual lecturers, or other activities which encouraged the worthwhile discussion of public affairs." The Public Affairs Seminar Board met on November 20 and approved unanimously the Human Rights Forum's request. . . .

On November 22 President Philpott told the Chairman of the Public Affairs Seminar Board that the Reverend Mr. Coffin would not be allowed to come to the Auburn University campus because he might advocate breaking the law and because he was a convicted felon. . . .   President Philpott then laid down what the plaintiffs have termed "the oral Philpott rules" relative to inviting outside speakers. These rules consist of three provisions:

> Student organizations could not invite (a) a speaker that could reasonably be expected to advocate breaking a law, (b) a speaker who had been previously convicted of a felony, and (c) a speaker of the type as the Reverend Mr. Coffin because it would be tantamount to Auburn University's sanctioning what the Reverend Mr. Coffin advocated.

On December 4 the Public Affairs Seminar Board met with President Philpott at his request. . . .   At this meeting President Philpott handed out "Guidelines for Issuing Invitations to Outside Speakers." He stated these were for study and discussion only and were not being handed out as "rules." . . .   The most relevant guideline for present purposes is guideline 2 which provides:

> "Invitations to speak at Auburn University should not be extended to persons who by prior expression might reasonably be expected to advocate:
>
> a. Disregard for the laws of our society or the breaking of these laws.
>
> b. The violent overthrow of our government."

Several other background facts are worthy of note. The Reverend William Sloan Coffin is the active Chaplain of Yale University and has been an outspoken leader of the opposition to American involvement in the Vietnam war. In connection with these activities, the Reverend Mr. Coffin has been arrested and has been convicted by a United States District Court in Massachusetts for conspiracy to counsel and aid and abet young men in resisting the draft. That conviction is currently on appeal. The Reverend Mr. Coffin has frequently lectured on college campuses in the last twelve months.

Prior to the invitation to the Reverend Mr. Coffin, Auburn University had no written or orally announced policy or guidelines for inviting speakers to the campus. In the last several years speakers have been invited, some at University expense, to speak to student and faculty groups on campus.   Among others, these speakers includ-ed Whitney Young, George C. Wallace, Admiral John Crommelin, and Lurleen B. Wallace.

President Philpott has made it clear that the fact that the funds of the Public Affairs Seminar Board were to be used to pay the Rev-erend Mr. Coffin was a significant consideration but was not critical to his decision.   It also seems clear that the ban is not based upon the probability of violence, riots, or other disorders accompanying the proposed speech.   It is also clear from Dr. Philpott's testimony that the scheduled appearance of the Reverend Mr. Coffin would not unduly interfere with the discipline or the orderly operation of Au-burn University.   In short, the basic reasons Dr. Philpott advances in support of his decision to ban the Reverend Mr. Coffin's appear-ance and payment therefor at Auburn University are based upon a "philosophical concept" and his decision in the matter constitutes a "philosophical decision."   .   .   .

There can no longer be much doubt that constitutional freedoms must be respected in the relationships between students and faculty and their university.   .   .   .

.   .   .   Auburn University is, of course, a state agency, and in terms of freedom of expression what is true of elementary and secon-dary education must be true *a fortiori* of colleges and universities. Indeed, it could be argued that an open forum is even more important on a campus than among the public generally.   Chief Justice Warren seemed to be suggesting just that in Sweezy v. New Hampshire, 354 U.S. 234, 250   .   .   .   when he stated:

> "The essentiality of freedom in the community of Amer-ican universities is almost self-evident.   * * *   Teachers and students must always remain free to inquire, to study and to evaluate, to gain new maturity and understanding; other-wise our civilization will stagnate and die."

It is these considerations which have repeatedly led courts to strike down restrictions on First Amendment rights in this context.   .   .   .

Given that students and faculty are not second class citizens, one can turn to the many cases and scholarly articles from which emerge the nature and scope of their First Amendment rights.

The broad issue of whether Auburn might close its campus alto-gether to outside speakers is not raised in this case.   Rather, we have a situation similar to that facing a New York court in which the ob-servation was made:

> "The over-riding issue as to use of school facilities for non-academic purposes is not raised.   Thus, while there may be no duty to open the doors of the school houses for uses other than academic—and I have some doubt even as to this

proposition—once they are opened they must be opened under conditions consistent with constitutional principle."   Buckley v. Meng, supra, 230 N.Y.S.2d at 933.   .   .   .

   .   .   .   Among other things, plaintiffs contend that Auburn's rules are vague and overbroad.   Certainly they are that.   In barring anyone who "advocates" breaking of the laws, the regulations run afoul of the almost constitutional ambiguity of "advocate."   .   .   .

In barring all speakers convicted of a felony, the regulations run afoul of the ambiguity of "convicted."   In most instances lawyers would use "convicted" to refer to a final conviction after all appeals had been exhausted.   The meaning must be unclear, however, since here President Philpott has applied it to a speaker whose conviction is still on appeal.   .   .   .   As stated earlier, the Reverend Mr. Coffin has been "convicted" of a felony in a United States District Court in Massachusetts.   This conviction is presently on appeal, and although there is no testimony on this particular point it is common knowledge that the matter will be, if necessary, litigated through the courts, including the Supreme Court of the United States.   This Court is of the opinion that the present status of the criminal prosecution against the Reverend Mr. Coffin cannot be used as a justification for the regulations in question.   .   .   .

The vice in these regulations, however, is really far more basic than their just being vague and overbroad.   *These regulations of Dr. Philpott are not regulations of conduct at all.*   That would presuppose that they dealt with activities which the state had a legitimate interest in restricting.   No such interest has been suggested here. Rather, we have here direct regulation of speech, regulations which on their face restrict the nature and source—both the medium and the message—to which these student and faculty plaintiffs may be exposed.   In plain words these regulations must fall because they constitute blatant political censorship.   .   .   .   The State of Alabama cannot, through its President of Auburn University, regulate the content of the ideas students may hear.   To do so is illegal and thus unconstitutional censorship in its rawest form.   In reaching this conclusion upon the facts in this case, this Court makes no new law and advances no novel constitutional concepts to support its decision.   The cases on similar questions are practically unanimous in holding and declaring that such action as attempted by President Philpott in this case is unconstitutional censorship in violation of the First Amendment.   .   .   .

There is no doubt that the powers and responsibilities of a university president are awesome and extensive.   Those powers include wide discretion in dealing with allocating funds, with educational policy, with the requirements of campus order and discipline, and with the time, place, and manner of extracurricular lectures. This Court will not ordinarily sit to review the wisdom with which that discretion is exercised.

It is the duty of this Court, however, to review the exercise of governmental power where there is a tenable claim that it has been exercised in a manner inconsistent with the Constitution of the United States. The point which defendants have forgotten, as persons in authority are wont to forget, is that the First and Fourteenth Amendments are *limitations on governmental power*. They were intended to have and do have the force of law. If Acts of Congress, state statutes, or administrative actions conflict with these limitations, they must yield; the Constitution is the supreme law of the land.

Thus, while it can be said that President Philpott has the ultimate power to determine whether a speaker is invited to the campus, the First Amendment right to hear of the students and faculty of Auburn University means that this determination may not be made for the wrong reasons or for no reason at all. . . .

If the banning of the right to hear this speaker be seen as independent of the stated reasons, as indicated by the testimony to the effect that Dr. Philpott had not seen fit to apply these reasons to those who fit within the loose criteria as well as the Reverend Mr. Coffin, it must fall because it becomes the act of an unbridled censor. The arbitrary acts of a censor cannot be tolerated; not because arbitrary power will be abused in every case but because of its inherent potential for discrimination against unorthodox views. . . .

The prohibition on arbitrary or discriminatory action also relates to President Philpott's power to control the use of University facilities and funds where that control affects the right to listen. In this case it is clear that the University authorities allocated $10,000 from student fees to be used to pay speakers invited to campus by student organizations.

. . . Having allocated the money, however, and having paid other speakers with no questions asked, Auburn may not in this instance, for no constitutionally acceptable reason, withhold the funds for the Reverend Mr. Coffin as a censorship device.

Nor may Auburn withhold available facilities. While Auburn may establish neutral priorities and require adequate coordination, this Court is clear to the conclusion that it cannot altogether close its available facilities to outside speakers. But here there is no claim that space would not be available, and it is clear that facilities have always been available to speakers invited by student groups. Suitable space must be provided the Reverend Mr. Coffin too.

In the oft quoted words of Judge Learned Hand:

> "It [the First Amendment] presupposes that right conclusions are more likely to be gathered out of a multitude of

tongues, than through any kind of authoritative selection. To many this is, and always will be, folly; but we have staked upon it our all." United States v. Associated Press, 52 F. Supp. 362, 372 (S.D.N.Y.1943).

This Court is aware of the many forces which tend to foster the fear that the First Amendment is "folly". The paranoia of living under a nuclear balance of terror, the divisiveness of an unpopular war, the racial tensions existing throughout the country, the economic and social deterioration of our inner cities, and the insecurity of unprecedented technological change are but a few of the forces which continue to threaten our constitutional form of government. If our First Amendment's freedom to speak and freedom to listen are unduly infringed, our plan of self-government is seriously weakened.

.   .   .   Conflicting points of view on sensitive current topics must be—where people want to hear them—afforded a forum. The denial of the right to hear these conflicting views—even though those in authority believe them to be unwise or un-American—violates the very ideas of our government. As Alexander Meikeljohn wrote:

> "When men govern themselves, it is they—and no one else—who must pass judgment upon unwisdom and unfairness and danger. And that means that unwise ideas must have a hearing as well as wise ones, unfair as well as fair, dangerous as well as safe, un-American as well as American. * * * "

The denial of that right to hear:

> " *   *   *   is that mutilation of the thinking process of the community against which the First Amendment to the Constitution is directed."   .   .   .

NOTES AND QUESTIONS

1. Dickson dealt with a law seeking to keep certain members of named classes of persons off the campus. Brooks did not deal with a named class of persons but with a criterion based on what a speaker might be expected to say as evidenced by his past expression. Is there any constitutional difference presented by the two cases? Do both involve a prior restraint or a subsequent punishment? Would these cases have been decided differently if (1) a common school were involved, or if (2) teachers rather than students wanted to invite the speakers? If so, why?

2. What are the constitutional rules governing off-campus speakers? State them.

3. Do these cases hold that any speaker whomsoever can come onto a campus and speak, if properly invited, and if space is available?

4. Suppose a person is not invited, can he come onto the campus and give a nondisruptive speech on a public open space away from classrooms?

5. Do these cases hold that if a speaker is properly invited, the speaker's audience can be limited by administrative authorities to (1) the students who gave the invitation; (2) all students; (3) all students and faculty; or must the speech be open to the general public if so requested? Which should be the rule? Why?

6. Under what circumstances can an off-campus speaker be barred? Why?

7. If an invited, off-campus speaker attempts to speak on campus but is denied the opportunity by a rude portion of the students and faculty because of their loud hooting, catcalls, heckling and similar behavior, have they unconstitutionally denied the speaker freedom of speech and denied the other members of the audience the freedom to hear? If so, could they be subjected to discipline by a local board of education or its agent for depriving others of their constitutional rights?

SOLICITATION

KATZ v. McAULAY

United States Court of Appeals, 1971.
438 F.2d 1058 (2d Cir.) cert. den. 405 U.S. 933, 92 S.Ct. 930, 30 L.Ed.2d 809.

ANDERSON, Circuit Judge. The New York Board of Regents has a rule, some forty-seven years old, which prohibits "soliciting funds from the pupils in the public schools." Plaintiffs, four students at Ardsley High School, a public school in Westchester County, New York, brought this civil rights action for anticipatory relief against enforcement of that rule. Their action arose when school officials threatened plaintiffs with expulsion if they distributed on school premises leaflets soliciting funds from their fellow students.

More specifically, on February 6 and 9, 1970, plaintiffs distributed in the high school corridors a one-page leaflet entitled "Join the Conspiracy." In it they decried the prosecution of eight defendants then on trial in the District Court for the Northern District of Illinois and solicited funds for the "activists'" defense. The leaflet stated:

"More than $33,000 per month is spent on their defense. Money is desperately needed to give these people a just trial. Money is needed to pay for transcripts. PLEASE contribute and/or buy a button from Jane Katz, Carey Marvin, Greg Gottlieb or anyone else who is helping out."

The dissemination of leaflets occurred before the school day began, and the affidavits of school officials contain no evidence of a specific instance of interference by the plaintiffs with the operation of the school or of any demonstration collision with the rights of other students to be let alone. Nonetheless, school officials warned plaintiffs that their circulation of leaflets violated the Board of Regents rule and a local Board of Education rule forbidding any "outside or-

ganization * * * to use this School * * * for the dissemination or release of information by flyers * * * " without first obtaining written approval of the Board.

Asserting the First Amendment overbreadth of both rules, plaintiffs sought a declaratory judgment declaring that "the policies, regulations and actions of the defendants * * * are unconstitutional"
and preliminary and permanent injunctions restraining defendants
from taking disciplinary action against students distributing this leaflet or any other leaflet soliciting funds for causes involving "matters of
public interest."   . . .

An application for a preliminary injunction is addressed to the
judicial discretion of the district court, and this court will not set
aside the disposition of such an application unless erroneous as a
matter of law or the result of an abuse of judicial discretion.   . . .
We therefore go no further into the merits of this action than is necessary to determine whether the trial court's assessment of the relative
importance, on the one hand, of the rights asserted and, on the other,
of the governmental interest the rule purports to protect, constituted
an abuse of discretion.   In this connection consideration must be given
to the irreparable nature of the injury allegedly flowing from the
denial of preliminary relief and the likelihood of the applicants' ultimate success on the merits.   . . .

The constitutional guarantee of free speech limits state power to
regulate the personal intercommunication of secondary school pupils.
Tinker v. Des Moines Independent Community School District,   . . .
From this premise plaintiffs contend the distribution of leaflets which
"communicat[e] thoughts between citizens, and discuss   . . .
public questions,"   . . .   is protected expression and that such expression is no less protected by virtue of the fact that solicitation of
contributions is an integral part thereof.   . . .

Assuming that plaintiffs' activity was "speech" within the meaning of the First Amendment, school officials had the burden of showing governmental interests which might justify their interference with
that "speech."   . . .   The Supreme Court has repeatedly affirmed
that such an interest lies in the implementation of "the comprehensive
authority of the States and of school officials, consistent with fundamental constitutional safeguards, to prescribe and control conduct in
the schools."   . . .   The exercise of such authority may not, however,
abridge the free expression of students in the public high schools unless that expression "materially and substantially interfere[s] with
the requirements of appropriate discipline in the operation of the
school."   . . .

Though the skeletal evidentiary matter before the trial court disclosed minimal potential interference at most, the probability that
plaintiffs' overbreadth contention would prevail at trial is so slight
that the denial of preliminary relief cannot be held to have constituted

an abuse of discretion. . . . the Board of Regents' rule articulated its proscription in terms of those non-expressive features of student conduct which raise a sufficiently high probability of harm—i. e. the pressures upon students of multiple solicitations—to justify the Board's interference with such communicative conduct.

Pupils are on school premises in response to the statutory requirement that they attend school for the purpose of formal education. Where outside organizations or individuals espousing various causes seek to take advantage of the required assemblage of secondary school pupils, as a captive audience, to solicit funds, either directly or through the agency of some of the pupils, for their particular project or cause, they are in effect in competition for the time, attention and interest of the pupils with those who are seeking to administer the school system. Whether it is done a few minutes before school opens or a few minutes after, its effect is not so limited in time and it is plainly harmful to the operation of the public schools. If there is no regulation against it, literally dozens of organizations and causes may importune pupils to solicit on their behalf; and it is foreseeable that pressure groups within the student body are likely to use more than polite requests to get contributions even from those who are in disagreement with the particular cause or who are, in truth, too poor to afford a donation. The Board's regulation appears to be reasonable and proper and has a rational relationship to the orderly operation of the school system.

The rule's focus upon a demonstrable harm rather than an undifferentiated fear of disturbance distinguishes plaintiffs' action from Scoville v. Board of Education, 425 F.2d 10 (7 Cir. 1970). There, the complaint of students disciplined by school authorities, who were unable to prove a reasonable likelihood of substantial disruption which would follow the students' distribution of an underground newspaper, was held to state a claim for damages and declarative and injunctive relief. Though the underground newspaper was sold to students, the defendant school authorities did not act pursuant to an anti-solicitation regulation comparable to the Board of Regents' rule. . . .

Affirmed.

J. JOSEPH SMITH, Circuit Judge (dissenting):

I respectfully dissent. I agree that there are possibilities of embarrassment and disruption of school functions in solicitation of school students which might justify regulation not sustainable as to the public at large. But I think that when related to public issues such as that involved in this case, solicitation of funds is an integral part of the propagandizing, as in the case of the religious colporteurs, and freedom to do one includes freedom to do the other, at least in the absence of a showing of gross disruption, so that complete prohibition as opposed to reasonable regulation, as of time and place, cannot be sustained. See Cantwell v. Connecticut, 310 U.S. 296, 306–307, 60 S.Ct. 900, 84 L.Ed. 1213 (1940). "[T]he pamphlets of Thomas Paine were not distributed free of charge." Murdock v. Pennsylvania, 319 U.S. 105, 111, 63 S.Ct. 870, 874, 87 LEd. 1292 (1943). So I think on a showing such as this the courts must protect the students in their efforts to communicate, misguided as we may consider them. I would reverse for issuance of a temporary injunction.

NOTES AND QUESTIONS

1. How important to the decision of this case is it that its context is of a request for a preliminary injunction?

2. Suppose instead of asking for a preliminary injunction, plaintiffs had solicited the funds and then had been expelled from school because of that solicitation, would the decision have been the same? Why or why not?

3. Suppose the rule of the Board of Regents had been modified to permit solicitation of funds by the Jr. Red Cross and Neighbors In Need, a local group devoted to providing food for the hungry, would these factors have altered the decision of the Court? Should they? Why or why not?

4. Suppose plaintiffs wanted to distribute copies of an "underground" newspaper at ten cents a copy, and the newspaper carried the same language as did the leaflet in this case, plus a statement that all the money collected from the sale of this issue of the newspaper would be sent to the defense fund, what decision would you render and for what reasons?

5. California's law provides:

"During school hours, and within one hour before the time of opening and within one hour after the time of closing of school, pupils of the public school shall not be solicited on school premises by teachers or others to subscribe or contribute to the funds of, to become members of, or to work for, any organization not directly under the control of the school authorities, unless the organization is a non-partisan, charitable organization organized for charitable purposes by an act of Congress or under the laws of the state, the purpose of the solicitation is non-partisan and charitable, and the solicitation has been approved by the county board of education or by the governing board of the school district in which the school is located.

"No person shall solicit any other person to contribute to any fund or to purchase any item of personal property, upon the representation that the money received is to be used wholly or in part for the benefit of any public school or the student body of any public school, unless such person obtains the prior written approval of either the governing board of the school district in which such solicitation is to be made or the governing board of the school district having jurisdiction over the school or student body represented to be benefited by such solicitation, or the designee of either of such boards.

"The prohibitions of this section shall not apply with respect to any solicitation or contribution the total proceeds of which are delivered to a public school, nor to a solicitation of a transfer to be effected by a testamentary act." West's Ann.Educ. Code of California §§ 9021, 9022.

Is any part of these statutes unconstitutional? Why or why not?

6. An article dealing with many questions raised by this chapter is Charles A. Wright "The Constitution On The Campus," 22 Vanderbilt Law Rev. 1042 (1969).

BONNER–LYONS v. SCHOOL COMMITTEE OF BOSTON

United States Court of Appeals, 1973.
480 F.2d 442 (1st Cir.).

McENTEE, Circuit Judge. Plaintiffs, members of The Ad Hoc Parents' Committee for Quality Education, alleging violations of their first amendment and equal protection rights, initiated this action under 42 U.S.C. § 1983 to enjoin defendants, the members of the School Committee of the City of Boston, from using the internal distribution system of the City's schools to disseminate notices opposing the use of bussing to achieve school integration. In the alternative, plaintiffs sought an order compelling defendants to allow them to use this same system to distribute communications publicizing pro-bussing rallies. The trial court denied repeated requests for preliminary injunctive relief and this appeal followed. Since we conclude that by disseminating the notices in question the defendants utilized the school distribution system to support and promote the views of one group while denying the use of this system to groups representing other points of view, we reverse and grant the injunctive relief specified below.

The following facts are not in dispute. On March 29, 1973, defendants adopted an official resolution authorizing the distribution of notices to all Boston parents urging them to support a march and rally to be held at the Massachusetts State House on April 3. The purpose of this rally was to express opposition to the retention of the Massachusetts "Racial Imbalance Law," 9 M.G.L.A. c. 71, §§ 37C–37D, and to the use of forced bussing as a tool to achieve racial integration in the schools. When plaintiffs requested defendants either to abandon this planned distribution or to permit the dissemination of pro-bussing notices, defendants refused to agree to either alternative. Plaintiffs then filed this suit and sought a temporary restraining order against the distribution. Thereafter, pursuant to defendants' resolution, on March 30 the following notice was distributed by means of the school system's "fan-out" distribution procedure to the approximately 97,000 students in the Boston system.[1]

---

[1] According to plaintiffs' counsel's affidavit, the system's "fan-out" distribution procedure operates in the following manner. A message which is ready for distribution is first transmitted by telephone from the Deputy Superintendent to six

"Dear Parents:

At a meeting on March 29, 1973, a resolution of the School Committee to support the Parents' March on the State House on Tuesday, April 3, 1973, at 10:00 A.M. was passed unanimously.

The purpose of the meeting is to inform the Governor and members of the Legislature that parents and the Boston School Committee stand united in opposition to forced busing and redistricting now being considered by the State Board of Education.

All parents are encouraged to write the Governor, the Senators and the Representatives in support of House Bill 3439 which opposes busing without the written consent of the parents."

On April 3 the anti-bussing rally was held as scheduled and, on the following day, plaintiffs' initial appeal from the denial of a temporary restraining order to prevent the distribution of these notices was dismissed as moot. On April 13, 1973, however, plaintiffs filed a further motion for injunctive relief seeking in particular an order requiring defendants to make the school distribution system available for the dissemination of notices concerning a pro-bussing rally tentatively set for late April. Due to difficulties in obtaining a hearing, however, this motion was not heard until April 30 and the proposed rally had to be postponed and ultimately cancelled. Thereafter, the trial court, finding, *inter alia,* that plaintiffs had failed to establish either that defendants had interfered with their first amendment rights or that a federal question was presented, issued a brief order denying the requested preliminary injunction.

On this background we find ourselves unable to agree with this disposition. As we read the March 30 notice, it seems apparent that this message tended to lend support and to mobilize opinion in favor of the position of those private parties who sponsored the April 3 "Parents' March on the State House." Under these circumstances, we conclude that defendants, by authorizing this distribution, sanctioned the use of the school distribution system as a forum for discussion of at least those issues which were treated in this notice.[2]

area Assistant Superintendents and then by them to the individual schools in their charge. At the schools the message is typed, reproduced, and distributed to teachers who then deliver it to each individual student.

[2] We are further buttressed in our conclusion that defendants have made available the school distribution system as a forum for the discussion of the possible repeal of the "Racial Imbalance Act" and the forced bussing of school children by the indication in the record that on April 30, 1973, defendants apparently authorized the distribution of a second set of notices, publicizing an anti-bussing rally scheduled to be held on May 2. While the record has not been fully developed with regard to this incident, we note that defendants state that these notices were not prepared by them but rather by the Home and School Association which they describe as "a private group." If these

When defendants' refusal to allow plaintiffs access to this system is considered in light of this conclusion, the trial court's error becomes manifest since it is well settled that once a forum is opened for the expression of views, regardless of how unusual the forum, under the dual mandate of the first amendment and the equal protection clause neither the government nor any private censor may pick and choose between those views which may or may not be expressed. See, e. g., Police Department of Chicago v. Mosley . . . National Socialist White People's Party v. Ringers, 473 F.2d 1010, infra.

Under these circumstances and particularly in light of the fact that defendants refused to represent either in the trial court or in oral argument on appeal that no further notices of this type would be distributed, we remand with directions that the defendants, their agents, servants, or employees be enjoined from causing or directing administrators or teachers employed in the Boston Public Schools from distributing, in classrooms or on school premises during the hours of required school attendance, to pupils enrolled in said schools, notices calling the attention of their parents or others to or inviting them to attend particular rallies, meetings or other activities designed to support a particular viewpoint on so-called racial imbalance legislation now pending in the General Court, or soliciting them to engage in letter-writing or activity in support of a particular viewpoint on such legislation, unless fair and reasonable timely opportunity is afforded to others having differing views to use the same channels to invite attendance at or call attention to rallies and activity in furtherance of such differing views.

Remanded for proceedings, consistent with this opinion.

AFTER HOUR USE OF SCHOOL FACILITIES

NATIONAL SOCIALIST WHITE PEOPLE'S PARTY v. RINGERS

United States Court of Appeals, 1973.
473 F.2d 1010 (4th Cir.).

The facts underlying this controversy have been stipulated by the parties: The Party, a successor to the American Nazi Party, is a non-profit corporation, incorporated in Virginia. A charter purpose of the Party is to gain political power by all legal and non-violent means, including the elective process. Party membership is limited only to whites of any religion who embrace its views. No Negro has ever held membership in the Party.

representations are found to be true, a clearer example of an impermissible selective opening of a forum to a group whose views are favored is difficult to imagine.

The Board, an arm of the State of Virginia, has responsibility for schools, grounds, and related property. State law permits the Board to rent high school auditoriums during non-school hours "for any legal assembly," . . . "as will not impair the efficiency of the schools." . . . Pursuant to this statutory authority, the Board has promulgated regulations under which it leases school property to organizations in "good standing." By regulation, an organization possesses "good standing" if it has "no previous record of abuse of school facilities." The Board has for some time, and on a regular basis, granted permits to use the auditorium to a wide variety of public and private groups on a first-come first-served basis. The Board has granted such permits to organizations which exclude certain racial, religious, or sexual groups. Except for a few instances involving groups which had previously damaged school property, no group has been denied the use of an available auditorium except the Party.

The Board has consistently refused to rent available auditoriums to the Party, although the Party has no previous record of abuse to school property. . . .

The Board's repeated exercise of its discretionary authority to rent the Yorktown High School auditorium for a nominal fee during non-school hours to public and private groups for public and private meetings on a first-come first-served basis, to the extent that the auditorium is not needed for school purposes and that non-school uses will not endanger the property, constitutes, in our view an effective dedication of the auditorium for the exercise of the first amendment rights of freedom of speech, association and assembly. This partial dedication as a forum for the exercise of first amendment rights makes the school auditorium conceptually indistinguishable for first amendment purposes as a "public place" from streets and parks, which too, are acquired and maintained at public expense. There can be little doubt that streets and parks are recognized forums for the exercise of first amendment rights. In Hague v. C. I. O. . . . Mr. Justice Roberts wrote:

> Wherever the title of streets and parks may rest, they have immemorially been held in trust for the use of the public and, time out of mind, have been used for purposes of assembly, communicating thoughts between citizens, and discussing public questions. Such use of the streets and *public places* has, from ancient times, been a part of the privileges, immunities, rights, and liberties of citizens. The privilege of a citizen of the United States to use the streets and parks for communication of views on national questions may be regulated in the interest of all; it is not absolute, but relative, and must be exercised in subordination to the general comfort and convenience, and in consonance with peace and good order; but it must not, in the guise of regulation, be abridged or denied. (emphasis added).

By the same token, we conclude that the school auditorium, since it has effectively been partially dedicated for first amendment uses, may be used for purposes of assembly, communicating thoughts between citizens and discussing public questions. In a public place regularly used for the exercise of free speech and the exchange of ideas, we do not see how walls and a roof can insulate against the reach of the first amendment's commands. That amendment's protections cannot be made to turn on the structural distinctions between, for example, an open public park, a public amphitheatre, a public stadium, or an enclosed public auditorium. While limitations on its use as a forum to permit it to serve its prime function (school purposes), to serve the general comfort and convenience, and to preserve peace and good order, including the protection of property, may be sustained, a regulation which limits the exercise of first amendment guarantees should be stricken down.

There is no dispute that the first amendment protects from state interference the expression in a public place of the unpopular as well as the popular and the right to assemble peaceably in a public place in the interest and furtherance of the unpopular as well as the popular. Specifically, the expression of racist and anti-semitic views in a public place and the right to assemble in a public place for the purpose of communicating and discussing racist and anti-semitic views are protected activities and may not be circumscribed by the state, except where "advocacy is directed to inciting or producing imminent lawless action and is likely to incite or produce such action." Brandenburg v. Ohio . . . or where "there are special, limited circumstances in which speech is so interlaced with burgeoning violence that it is not protected by the broad guarantee of the First Amendment," Carroll v. Princess Anne, 393 U.S. 175, . . . Under the stipulated facts, the Party presented no such danger.

Certainly the ability to meet in public places is fundamental to the exercise of first amendment freedoms. If the state denies that opportunity to an unpopular group, the first amendment will be substantially emasculated. The very recent case of Healy v. James . . . held that the first amendment requires a state-supported college to recognize a student political group (SDS) and to afford it the use of campus facilities for communication and association, unless it was shown that the group, in addition to mere advocacy of radical doctrines, would likely "infringe reasonable campus rules, interrupt classes or substantially interfere with the opportunity of other students to obtain an education." . . . The basis of the Court's reasoning was the inescapable link between the denial of campus facilities for communication and assembly and prior restraint of unpopular ideas. Thus, the Court stressed that: "Among the rights protected by the First Amendment is the right of individuals to associate to further their personal beliefs. . . . There can be no doubt that denial of official recognition, without justification, to college organizations burdens or abridges that associational right. The primary impediment to free association flowing from nonrecognition is the denial of use of campus facilities for meetings and other appropriate purposes." . . . Later, the Court expressed the point more directly: "It is to be remembered that the effect of the College's denial of recognition was a form of prior restraint, denying to petitioners' organization the range of associational activities described above." . . .

Since the first amendment prohibits the state from interfering with the expression of unpopular, indeed, offensive, views, and with assembly and association for the purpose of exchanging and furthering them, we think that the first amendment protects the expression of such views in those public places dedicated to the exercise of first amendment rights by groups which implement them by restrictive membership policies. We therefore, conclude that the School Board's denial of the use of a public forum because of the Party's discriminatory membership policies constitutes as much of an invalid prior restraint as if it had denied the Party the use of the forum on the basis of the controversial beliefs which the Party would express at that place. . . .

We are confident that if the high school auditorium is made available to all groups, the very diversity and complexity of the views expressed, taken in bulk, will cure any incidental official identification attendant upon the use of the building for the articulation of extreme or abusive speech. At least that is the principle on which we have staked our all. As Mr. Justice Brandeis said years ago, "If there be time to expose through discussion the falsehood and fallacies, to avert the evil by the processes of education, the remedy to be applied is more speech, not enforced silence." . . . We conclude therefore that, considering all the factors in this case, the School Board has not overcome the "heavy presumption" against its effective prior restraint on the Party's right to free speech. . . .

BUTZNER, Circuit Judge (concurring in part and dissenting in part).

. . . Were this case concerned solely with prior restraint on freedom of speech and assembly, I would not dissent. But this appeal does not turn on the right to preach racial hatred and religious bigotry. The first amendment clearly grants this right whether the speech is made in a park, on a street, or in a building that has been designated as a public forum. It is the Party's exclusion of black citizens, not its message, that justified the Board's refusal to rent the auditorium.

Contrary to the Party's assertion, its first amendment rights are not so overriding that its racially discriminatory membership policy is irrelevant. Freedom of speech, assembly, and association are guaranteed by the first amendment to political organizations. Healy v. James, . . . Indeed, these rights are indispensable to a democracy.   Nevertheless, the guarantee of first amendment freedoms does not compel a state to nurture racially discriminatory political parties. Just the opposite is true.

In a long line of cases, the Supreme Court has construed the fourteenth and fifteenth amendments to prohibit a wide variety of devices designed to keep black citizens from participating in political parties and the election process.   As the abolition of white primaries attests, the state, acting through political parties or political associations, cannot abridge the right of a citizen to vote on account of race or deny him the equal protection of the laws.   While some of these cases involve the fourteenth amendment and others the fifteenth, the distinction is not critical to this appeal because both amendments bar discrimination that is tainted by state action.   These cases demonstrate that careful scrutiny of the state's involvement is demanded when the state aids political associations that discriminate on racial grounds.   They teach, albeit implicitly, that when state action is united with a political party or association that bars black people from full participation in its affairs, the union is illegal despite the first amendment rights possessed by white members of the organization.   These cases provide no valid distinction between a political party which has enjoyed success and one that has not.   To permit the Party to use the school auditorium now, but to refuse it access in the future when it achieves success is simply locking the barn door after the horse has been stolen.   .   .   .

Less my dissent provoke misunderstanding, I repeat that it is based on the racially discriminatory practices of the Party, not its speeches.   A political party's rhetoric cannot be equated with its rules. Though politicians of every persuasion are entitled to freedom of speech and assembly, their exclusion of people from party membership on account of race is a tactic that has been expressly condemned by the Supreme Court.   The Constitution's requirement of unrestricted membership is calculated to encourage, not suppress, free discussion and association.   By declaring that political parties must be open to all citizens, the Court has wisely assigned priority to the political rights secured by the fourteenth and fifteenth amendments.   Experience has shown this primacy affords ample accommodation for first amendment rights, and I see no reason in this appeal to encroach upon it.   The Party's exclusion of black citizens from membership is the decisive step beyond advocacy that justified the district court's dismissal of its complaint.

Chapter VI

CONSTITUTIONAL
FREEDOM AND RELIGION

INTRODUCTION

One definition of "religion" is that any "individual or group belief is religious if it occupies the same place in the lives of its adherents that orthodox beliefs occupy in the lives of their adherents. Four characteristics should be present: (1) a belief regarding the meaning of life; (2) a psychological commitment by the individual adherent (or if a group, by the members generally) to this belief; (3) a system of moral practice resulting from adherence to this belief; and, (4) an acknowledgement by its adherents that the belief (or belief system) is their exclusive or supreme system of ultimate beliefs. Note, Defining Religion, 32 U. of Chi.L.Rev. 533, 550–51 (1965).

Religion can be a strong force, and it can serve either to unify or to divide a people. If a country is strongly of one predominating faith, and if there is a union of church and state, that faith frequently, but not always, functions as a unifying societal force. But the United States does not rely upon any one religious viewpoint. There is no one "official" religion. In the United States church and state are separate, and many different religions are represented on its soil. Thus, religions in America coexist with each other within a secular state. This is the American Hertiage, and while harmony usually prevails, it is sometimes a heritage of friction.

Some religions have chosen to establish separate and independent parochial school systems. *however* Pierce v. Society of Sisters, supra, clearly recognizes that religious and other private groups have a constitutional right to establish separate, private schools, so long as they comply with the constitutional regulations of the schools set by state legislatures and state boards of education.

THE SEPARATION OF CHURCH AND STATE

The First Amendment provides that "Congress shall make no law respecting an establishment of religion, or prohibiting the free exercise thereof . . ." It has been incorporated into the Fourteenth Amendment and applies to the states and their subdivisions. The first prohibition is called the "establishment" clause, and the second the "free exercise clause." Thus, the guarantee of religious freedom has a double aspect. The Establishment clause prohibits legal compulsion requiring that anyone accept any belief or creed or the practice of any form of worship. The Free Exercise clause safeguards the free exercise of a chosen form of religion. Together these two clauses should maintain what the Supreme Court calls a "wholesome neutrality" the existence of which it tests by this formula: "What are the purposes and primary effects of the enactment? If either is the advancement or inhibition of religion then the enactment exceeds the scope of legislative power as circumscribed by the Constitution." When fully implemented, these two clauses of the First Amendment will produce a separation of church and state in the United States. In an educational context, three general types of constitutional law problems have arisen: (1) those concerning attempts to prescribe religion as part of the public school curriculum; (2) those concerning attempts to obtain public tax funds for the support of parochial schools, and (3) those concerning a public school curriculum requirement that is alleged to violate a pupil's right to the free exercise of his religion.

THE HERITAGE

EVERSON v. BOARD OF EDUCATION

Supreme Court of the United States, 1947.
330 U.S. 1, 67 S.Ct. 504, 91 L.Ed. 711, rehearing denied 330 U.S. 855, 67 S.Ct. 962, 91 L.Ed. 1297.
[The majority opinion in this case is printed infra, at p. 410].

Mr. Justice RUTLEDGE, with whom Mr. Justice FRANKFURTER, Mr. Justice JACKSON and Mr. Justice BURTON agree, dissenting.

"Congress shall make no law respecting an establishment of religion, or prohibiting the free exercise thereof. . . . " U.S.Const., Amend. I. . . .

This case forces us to determine squarely for the first time what was "an establishment of religion" in the First Amendment's conception. . . .

Not simply an established church, but any law respecting an establishment of religion is forbidden. The Amendment was broadly but not loosely phrased. It is the compact and exact summation of its author's views formed during his long struggle for religious freedom. In Madison's own words characterizing Jefferson's Bill for Establishing Religious Freedom, the guaranty he put in our national charter, like the bill he piloted through the Virginia Assembly, was "a Model of technical precision, and perspicuous brevity." Madison could not have confused "church" and "religion," or "an established church" and "an establishment of religion."

The Amendment's purpose was not to strike merely at the official establishment of a single sect, creed or religion, outlawing only a formal relation such as had prevailed in England and some of the colonies. Necessarily it was to uproot all such relationships. But the object was broader than separating church and state in this narrow sense. It was to create a complete and permanent separation of the spheres of religious activity and civil authority by comprehensively forbidding every form of public aid or support for religion. In proof the Amendment's wording and history unite with this Court's consistent utterances whenever attention has been fixed directly upon the question.

"Religion" appears only once in the Amendment. But the word governs two prohibitions and governs them alike. It does not have two meanings, one narrow to forbid "an establishment" and another, much broader, for securing "the free exercise thereof." "Thereof" brings down "religion" with its entire and exact content, no more and no less, from the first into the second guaranty, so that Congress and now the states are as broadly restricted concerning the one as they are regarding the other.

No one would claim today that the Amendment is constricted, in "prohibiting the free exercise" of religion, to securing the free exercise of some formal or creedal observance, of one sect or of many. It secures all forms of religious expression, creedal, sectarian or nonsectarian, wherever and however taking place, except conduct which trenches upon the like freedoms of others or clearly and presently endangers the community's good order and security. For the protective purposes of this phase of the basic freedom, street preaching, oral or by distribution of literature, has been given "the same high estate under the First Amendment as . . . worship in the churches and preaching from the pulpits." And on this basis parents have been held entitled to send their children to private, religious schools. Pierce v. Society of Sisters, 268 U.S. 510. Accordingly, daily religious education commingled with secular is "religion" within the guaranty's comprehensive scope. So are religious training and teaching in whatever form. The word connotes the broadest content, determined not by the form or formality of the teaching or where it occurs, but by its essential nature regardless of those details.

"Religion" has the same broad significance in the twin prohibition concerning "an establishment." The Amendment was not duplicitous. "Religion" and "establishment" were not used in any formal or technical sense. The prohibition broadly forbids state support, financial or other, of religion in any guise, form or degree. It outlaws all use of public funds for religious purposes.

II.

No provision of the Constitution is more closely tied to or given content by its generating history than the religious clause of the First Amendment. It is at once the refined product and the terse summation of that history. The history includes not only Madison's authorship and the proceedings before the First Congress, but also the long and intensive struggle for religious freedom in America, more especially in Virginia, of which the Amendment was the direct culmination. In the documents of the times, particularly of Madison, who was leader in the Virginia struggle before he became the Amendment's sponsor, but also in the writings of Jefferson and others and in the issues which engendered them is to be found irrefutable confirmation of the Amendment's sweeping content.

For Madison, as also for Jefferson, religious freedom was the crux of the struggle for freedom in general. . . . Madison was coauthor with George Mason of the religious clause in Virginia's great Declaration of Rights of 1776. He is credited with changing it from a mere statement of the principle of tolerance to the first official legislative pronouncement that freedom of conscience and religion are inherent rights of the individual. He sought also to have the Declaration expressly condemn the existing Virginia establishment. But the forces supporting it were then too strong.

Accordingly Madison yielded on this phase but not for long. At once he resumed the fight, continuing it before succeeding legislative sessions. As a member of the General Assembly in 1779 he threw his full weight behind Jefferson's historic Bill for Establishing Religious Freedom. That bill was a prime phase of Jefferson's broad program of democratic reform undertaken on his return from the Continental Congress in 1776 and submitted for the General Assembly's consideration in 1779 as his proposed revised Virginia code. With Jefferson's departure for Europe in 1784, Madison became the Bill's prime sponsor. Enactment failed in successive legislatures from its introduction in June, 1779, until its adoption in January, 1786. But during all this time the fight for religious freedom moved forward in Virginia on various fronts with growing intensity. Madison led throughout, against Patrick Henry's powerful opposing leadership until Henry was elected governor in November, 1784.

The climax came in the legislative struggle of 1784–1785 over the Assessment Bill. . . . This was nothing more nor less than a taxing measure for the support of religion, designed to revive the payment of tithes suspended since 1777. So long as it singled out a particular sect for preference it incurred the active and general hostility of dissentient groups. It was broadened to include them, with the result that some subsided temporarily in their opposition. As altered, the bill gave to each taxpayer the privilege of designating which church should receive his share of the tax. In default of designation the legislature applied it to pious uses. But what is of the utmost significance here, "in its final form the bill left the taxpayer the option of giving his tax to education."

Madison was unyielding at all times, opposing with all his vigor the general and nondiscriminatory as he had the earlier particular and discriminatory assessments proposed. The modified Assessment Bill passed second reading in December, 1784, and was all but enacted. Madison and his followers, however, maneuvered deferment of final consideration until November, 1785. And before the Assembly reconvened in the fall he issued his historic Memorial and Remonstrance.

This is Madison's complete, though not his only, interpretation of religious liberty. It is a broadside attack upon all forms of "establishment" of religion, both general and particular, nondiscriminatory or selective. Reflecting not only the many legislative conflicts over the Assessment Bill and the Bill for Establishing Religious Freedom but also, for example, the struggles for religious incorporations and the continued maintenance of the glebes, the Remonstrance is at once the most concise and the most accurate statement of the views of the First Amendment's author concerning what is "an establishment of religion." Because it behooves us in the dimming distance of time not to lose sight of what he and his coworkers had in mind when, by a single sweeping stroke of the pen, they forbade an establishment of religion and secured its free exercise, the text of the Remonstrance is appended at the end of this opinion for its wider current reference, together with a copy of the bill against which it was directed.

The Remonstrance, stirring up a storm of popular protest, killed the Assessment Bill. It collapsed in committee shortly before Christmas, 1785. With this, the way was cleared at last for enactment of Jefferson's Bill for Establishing Religious Freedom. Madison promptly drove it through in January of 1786, seven years from the time it was first introduced. This dual victory substantially ended the fight over establishments, settling the issue against them.

The next year Madison became a member of the Constitutional Convention. Its work done, he fought valiantly to secure the ratification of its great product in Virginia as elsewhere, and nowhere else more effectively. Madison was certain in his own mind that under the Constitution "there is not a shadow of right in the general government to intermeddle with religion" and that "this subject is, for the honor of America, perfectly free and unshackled. The government has no jurisdiction over it. . . . " Nevertheless he pledged that he would work for a Bill of Rights, including a specific guaranty of religious freedom, and Virginia, with other states, ratified the Constitution on this assurance.

Ratification thus accomplished, Madison was sent to the first Congress. There he went at once about performing his pledge to establish freedom for the nation as he had done in Virginia. Within a little more than three years from his legislative victory at home he had proposed and secured the submission and ratification of the First Amendment as the first article of our Bill of Rights.

All the great instruments of the Virginia struggle for religious liberty thus became warp and woof of our constitutional tradition, not simply by the course of history, but by the common unifying force of Madison's life, thought and sponsorship. He epitomized the whole of that tradition in the Amendment's compact, but nonetheless comprehensive, phrasing.

As the Remonstrance discloses throughout, Madison opposed every form and degree of official relation between religion and civil authority. For him religion was a wholly private matter beyond the scope of civil power either to restrain or to support. Denial or abridgment of religious freedom was a violation of rights both of conscience and of natural equality. State aid was no less obnoxious or destructive to freedom and to religion itself than other forms of state interference. "Establishment" and "free exercise" were correlative and coextensive ideas, representing only different facets of the single great and fundamental freedom. The Remonstrance, following the Virginia statute's example, referred to the history of religious conflicts and the effects of all sorts of establishments, current and historical, to suppress religion's free exercise. With Jefferson, Madison believed that to tolerate any fragment of establishment would be by so much to perpetuate restraint upon that freedom. Hence he sought to tear out the institution not partially but root and branch, and to bar its return forever.

In no phase was he more unrelentingly absolute than in opposing state support or aid by taxation. Not over "three pence" contribution was thus to be exacted from any citizen for such a purpose   .   .   . Tithes had been the lifeblood of establishment before and after other compulsions disappeared. Madison and his coworkers made no exceptions or abridgments to the complete separation they created. Their objection was not to small tithes. It was to any tithes whatsoever. "If it were lawful to impose a small tax for religion, the admission would pave the way for oppressive levies." Not the amount but "the principle of assessment was wrong." And the principle was as much to prevent "the interference of law in religion" as to restrain religious intervention in political matters. In this field the authors of our freedom would not tolerate "the first experiment on our liberties" or "wait till usurped power had strengthened itself by exercise, and entangled the question in precedents. "   .   .   .

In view of this history no further proof is needed that the Amendment forbids any appropriation, large or small, from public funds to aid or support any and all religious exercises. But if more were called for, the debates in the First Congress and this Court's consistent expressions, whenever it has touched on the matter directly, supply it.

By contrast with the Virginia history, the congressional debates on consideration of the Amendment reveal only sparse discussion, reflecting the fact that the essential issues had been settled. Indeed the matter had become so well understood as to have been taken for granted in all but formal phrasing. Hence, the only enlightening reference shows concern, not to preserve any power to use public funds in aid of religion, but to prevent the Amendment from outlawing private gifts inadvertently by virtue of the breadth of its wording. . . .

ATTEMPTS TO ESTABLISH RELIGION IN PUBLIC SCHOOLS

[In addition to the materials appearing in this section, consider also, Epperson v. Arkansas printed supra.]

McCOLLUM v. BOARD OF EDUCATION

Supreme Court of the United States, 1948.

333 U.S. 203, 68 S.Ct. 461, 92 L.Ed. 649.

Mr. Justice BLACK delivered the opinion of the Court.

This case relates to the power of a state to utilize its tax-supported public school system in aid of religious instruction insofar as that power may be restricted by the First and Fourteenth Amendments to the Federal Constitution.

The appellant, Vashti McCollum, began this action for mandamus against the Champaign Board of Education in the Circuit Court of Champaign County, Illinois. Her asserted interest was that of a resident and taxpayer of Champaign and of a parent whose child was then enrolled in the Champaign public schools. Illinois has a compulsory education law which, with exceptions, requires parents to send their children, aged seven to sixteen, to its tax-supported public schools where the children are to remain in attendance during the hours when the schools are regularly in session. Parents who violate this law commit a misdemeanor punishable by fine unless the children attend private or parochial schools which meet educational standards fixed by the State. District boards of education are given general supervisory powers over the use of the public school buildings within the school districts. . . .

Although there are disputes between the parties as to various inferences that may or may not properly be drawn from the evidence concerning the religious program, the following facts are shown by the record without dispute. In 1940 interested members of the Jewish, Roman Catholic, and a few of the Protestant faiths formed a voluntary association called the Champaign Council on Religious Education. They obtained permission from the Board of Education to offer classes in religious instruction to public school pupils in grades four to nine

inclusive.   Classes were made up of pupils whose parents signed printed cards requesting that their children be permitted to attend;   they
were held weekly, thirty minutes for the lower grades, forty-five
minutes for the higher.   The council employed the religious teachers
at no expense to the school authorities, but the instructors were subject to the approval and supervision of the superintendent of schools.
The classes were taught in three separate religious groups by Protestant teachers, Catholic priests, and a Jewish rabbi, although for the
past several years there have apparently been no classes instructed in
the Jewish religion.   Classes were conducted in the regular classrooms
of the school building.   Students who did not choose to take the religious instruction were not released from public school duties;   they
were required to leave their classrooms and go to some other place in
the school building for pursuit of their secular studies.   On the other
hand, students who were released from secular study for the religious
instructions were required to be present at the religious classes.   Reports of their presence or absence were to be made to their secular
teachers.

The foregoing facts, without reference to others that appear in the
record, show the use of tax-supported property for religious instruction
and the close cooperation between the school authorities and the religious council in promoting religious education.   The operation of the
state's compulsory education system thus assists and is integrated
with the program of religious instruction carried on by separate religious sects.   Pupils compelled by law to go to school for secular education are released in part from their legal duty upon the condition
that they attend the religious classes.   This is beyond all question a
utilization of the tax-established and tax-supported public school system to aid religious groups to spread their faith.   And it falls squarely
under the ban of the First Amendment   .   .   .   "Neither a state
nor the Federal Government can set up a church.   Neither can pass
laws which aid one religion, aid all religions, or prefer one religion
over another.   Neither can force or influence a person to go to or to
remain away from church against his will or force him to profess a
belief or disbelief in any religion.   No person can be punished for
entertaining or professing religious beliefs or disbeliefs, for church
attendance or non-attendance.   No tax in any amount, large or small
can be levied to support any religious activities or institutions, whatever they may be called, or whatever form they may adopt to teach
or practice religion.   Neither a state nor the Federal Government can,
openly or secretly, participate in the affairs of any religious organizations or groups and *vice versa*.   In the words of Jefferson, the clause
against establishment of religion by law was intended to erect 'a wall
of separation between church and State'."   .   .   .

To hold that a state cannot consistently with the First and Fourteenth Amendments utilize its public school system to aid any or all
religious faiths or sects in the dissemination of their doctrines and

ideals does not, as counsel urge, manifest a governmental hostility to religion or religious teachings. A manifestation of such hostility would be at war with our national tradition as embodied in the First Amendment's guaranty of the free exercise of religion. For the First Amendment rests upon the premise that both religion and government can best work to achieve their lofty aims if each is left free from the other within its respective sphere. . . . the First Amendment has erected a wall between Church and State which must be kept high and impregnable.

Here not only are the State's tax-supported public school buildings used for the dissemination of religious doctrines. The State also affords sectarian groups an invaluable aid in that it helps to provide pupils for their religious classes through use of the State's compulsory public school machinery. This is not separation of Church and State.

The cause is reversed and remanded to the State Supreme Court for proceedings not inconsistent with this opinion.

Reversed and remanded.*

ZORACH v. CLAUSON

Supreme Court of the United States, 1952.
343 U.S. 306, 72 S.Ct. 679, 96 L.Ed. 954.

Mr. Justice DOUGLAS delivered the opinion of the Court.

New York City has a program which permits its public schools to release students during the school day so that they may leave the school buildings and school grounds and go to religious centers for religious instruction or devotional exercises. A student is released on written request of his parents. Those not released stay in the classrooms. The churches make weekly reports to the schools, sending a list of children who have been released from public school but who have not reported for religious instruction.

This "released time" program involves neither religious instruction in public school classrooms nor the expenditure of public funds. All costs, including the application blanks, are paid by the religious organizations. The case is therefore unlike McCollum v. Board of Education, 333 U.S. 203, which involved a "released time" program from Illinois. In that case the classrooms were turned over to religious instructors. We accordingly held that the program violated the First Amendment which (by reason of the Fourteenth Amendment) prohibits the states from establishing religion or prohibiting its free exercise.

_____

* The concurring opinions of Mr. Justices Frankfurter and Jackson and the dissenting opinion of Mr. Justice Reed are omitted.

Appellants, who are taxpayers and residents of New York City and whose children attend its public schools, challenge the present law, contending it is in essence not different from the one involved in the *McCollum* case. Their argument, stated elaborately in various ways, reduces itself to this: the weight and influence of the school is put behind a program for religious instruction; public school teachers police it, keeping tab on students who are released; the classroom activities come to a halt while the students who are released for religious instruction are on leave; the school is a crutch on which the churches are leaning for support in their religious training; without the cooperation of the schools this "released time" program, like the one in the *McCollum* case, would be futile and ineffective. . . . .

The briefs and arguments are replete with data bearing on the merits of this type of "released time" program. Views *pro* and *con* are expressed, based on practical experience with these programs and with their implications. We do not stop to summarize these materials nor to burden the opinion with an analysis of them. For they involve considerations not germane to the narrow constitutional issue presented. They largely concern the wisdom of the system, its efficiency from an educational point of view, and the political considerations which have motivated its adoption or rejection in some communities. Those matters are of no concern here, since our problem reduces itself to whether New York by this system has either prohibited the "free exercise" of religion or has made a law "respecting an establishment of religion" within the meaning of the First Amendment.

It take obtuse reasoning to inject any issue of the "free exercise" of religion into the present case. No one is forced to go to the religious classroom and no religious exercise or instruction is brought to the classrooms of the public schools. A student need not take religious instruction. He is left to his own desires as to the manner of time of his religious devotions, if any.

There is a suggestion that the system involves the use of coercion to get public school students into religious classrooms. There is no evidence in the record before us that supports that conclusion. The present record indeed tells us that the school authorities are neutral in this regard and do no more than release students whose parents so request. If in fact coercion were used, if it were established that any one or more teachers were using their office to persuade or force students to take the religious instruction, a wholly different case would be presented. Hence we put aside that claim of coercion both as respects the "free exercise" of religion and "an establishment of religion" within the meaning of the First Amendment.

Moreover, apart from that claim of coercion, we do not see how New York by this type of "released time" program has made a law respecting an establishment of religion within the meaning of the First Amendment. There is much talk of the separation of Church and State in the history of the Bill of Rights and in the decisions clustering around the First Amendment. . . . There cannot be the slightest doubt that the First Amendment reflects the philosophy that Church and State should be separated. And so far as interference with the "free exercise" of religion and an "establishment" of religion are concerned, the separation must be complete and unequivocal. The First Amendment within the scope of its coverage permits no exception; the prohibition is absolute. The First Amendment, however, does not say that in every and all respects there shall be a separation of Church and State. Rather, it studiously defines the manner, the specific ways, in which there shall be no concert or union or dependency one on the other. That is the common sense of the matter. Otherwise the state and religion would be aliens to each other—hostile, suspicious, and even unfriendly. Churches could not be required to pay even property taxes. Municipalities would not be permitted to render police or fire protection to religious groups. Policemen who helped parishioners into their places of worship would violate the Constitution. Prayers in our legislative halls; the appeals to the Almighty in the messages of the Chief Executive; the proclamations making Thanksgiving Day a holiday; "so help me God" in our courtroom oaths —these and all other references to the Almighty that run through our laws, our public rituals, our ceremonies would be flouting the First Amendment. A fastidious atheist or agnostic could even object to the supplication with which the Court opens each session: "God save the United States and this Honorable Court."

We would have to press the concept of separation of Church and State to these extremes to condemn the present law on constitutional grounds. The nullification of this law would have wide and profound effects. A Catholic student applies to his teacher for permission to leave the school during hours on a Holy Day of Obligation to attend a mass. A Jewish student asks his teacher for permission to be excused for Yom Kippur. A Protestant wants the afternoon off for a family baptismal ceremony. In each case the teacher, in order to make sure the student is not a truant, goes further and requires a report from the priest, the rabbi, or the minister. The teacher in other words cooperates in a religious program to the extent of making it possible for her students to participate in it. Whether she does it occasionally for a few students, regularly for one, or pursuant to a systematized program designed to further the religious needs of all the students does not alter the character of the act.

We are a religious people whose institutions presuppose a Supreme Being. We guarantee the freedom to worship as one chooses. We make room for as wide a variety of beliefs and creeds as the spiritual needs of man deem necessary. We sponsor an attitude on the part of government that shows no partiality to any one group and that lets each flourish according to the zeal of its adherents and the appeal of its dogma. When the state encourages religious instruction or cooperates with religious authorities by adjusting the schedule of public events to sectarian needs, it follows the best of our traditions. For it then respects the religious nature of our people and accommodates the public service to their spiritual needs. To hold that it may not would be to find in the Constitution a requirement that the government show a callous indifference to religious groups. That would be preferring those who believe in no religion over those who do believe. Government may not finance religious groups nor undertake religious instruction nor blend secular and sectarian education nor use secular institutions to force one or some religion on any person. But we find no constitutional requirement which makes it necessary for government to be hostile to religion and to throw its weight against efforts to widen the effective scope of religious influence. The government must be neutral when it comes to competition between sects. It may not thrust any sect on any person. It may not make a religious observance compulsory. It may not coerce anyone to attend church, to observe a religious holiday, or to take religious instruction. But it can close its doors or suspend its operations as to those who want to repair to their religious sanctuary for worship or instruction. No more than that is undertaken here.

This program may be unwise and improvident from an educational or a community viewpoint. That appeal is made to us on a theory, previously advanced, that each case must be decided on the basis of "our own prepossessions." See McCollum v. Board of Education, supra. Our individual preferences, however, are not the constitutional standard. The constitutional standard is the separation of Church and State. The problem, like many problems in constitutional law, is one of degree. . . .

In the *McCollum* case the classrooms were used for religious instruction and the force of the public school was used to promote that instruction. Here, as we have said, the public schools do no more than accommodate their schedules to a program of outside religious instruction. We follow the *McCollum* case. But we cannot expand it to cover the present released time program unless separation of Church and State means that public institutions can make no adjustments of their schedules to accommodate the religious needs of the people. We cannot read into the Bill of Rights such a philosophy of hostility to religion.

Affirmed.

Mr. Justice BLACK, dissenting.

McCollum ex rel. Illinois v. Board of Education, 333 U.S. 203, held invalid as an "establishment of religion" an Illinois system under which school children, compelled by law to go to public schools, were freed from some hours of required school work on condition that they attend special religious classes held in the school buildings. Although the

386 CONSTITUTIONAL FREEDOM & RELIGION   Part 2

classes were taught by sectarian teachers neither employed nor paid by the state, the state did use its power to further the program by releasing some of the children from regular class work, insisting that those released attend the religious classes, and requiring that those who remained behind do some kind of academic work while the others received their religious training. We said this about the Illinois system:

> "Pupils compelled by law to go to school for secular education are released in part from their legal duty upon the condition that they attend the religious classes. This is beyond all question a utilization of the tax-established and tax-supported public school system to aid religious groups to spread their faith. And it falls squarely under the ban of the First Amendment.   .   .   ."   McCollum v. Board of Education, supra.

I see no significant difference between the invalid Illinois system and that of New York here sustained. Except for the use of the school buildings in Illinois, there is no difference between the systems which I consider even worthy of mention. In the New York program, as in that of Illinois, the school authorities release some of the children on the condition that they attend the religious classes, get reports on whether they attend, and hold the other children in the school building until the religious hour is over. As we attempted to make categorically clear, the *McCollum* decision would have been the same if the religious classes had not been held in the school buildings. We said:

> "Here *not only* are the State's tax-supported public school buildings used for the dissemination of religious doctrines. The State *also* affords sectarian groups an invaluable aid in that it helps to provide pupils for their religious classes through use of the State's compulsory public school machinery. *This* is not separation of Church and State." (Emphasis supplied.)   McCollum v. Board of Education, supra.

McCollum thus held that Illinois could not constitutionally manipulate the compelled classroom hours of its compulsory school machinery so as to channel children into sectarian classes. Yet that is exactly what the Court holds New York can do.

I am aware that our *McCollum* decision on separation of Church and State has been subjected to a most searching examination throughout the country. Probably few opinions from this Court in recent years have attracted more attention or stirred wider debate. Our insistence on "a wall between Church and State which must be kept high and impregnable" has seemed to some a correct exposition of the philosophy and a true interpretation of the language of the First Amendment to which we should strictly adhere. With equal conviction and sincerity, others have thought the *McCollum* decision fundamentally wrong and have pledged continuous warfare against it. The opinions in the court below and the briefs here reflect these diverse viewpoints.   In dissenting today, I mean to do more than give routine approval to our *McCollum* decision.   .   .   .

The Court's validation of the New York system rests in part on its statement that Americans are "a religious people whose institutions presuppose a Supreme Being."   This was at least as true when the First Amendment was adopted; and it was just as true when eight Justices of this Court invalidated the released time system in *McCollum* on the premise that a state can no more "aid all religions" than it can aid one.   It was precisely because Eighteenth Century Americans were a religious people divided into many fighting sects that we were given the constitutional mandate to keep Church and State completely separate.   Colonial history had already shown that, here as elsewhere zealous sectarians entrusted with governmental power to further their causes would sometimes torture, maim and kill those they branded "heretics," "atheists" or "agnostics."   The First Amendment was therefore to insure that no one powerful sect or combination of sects could use political or governmental power to punish dissenters whom they could not convert to their faith.   Now as then, it is only by wholly isolating the state from the religious sphere and compelling it to be completely neutral, that the freedom of each and every denomination and of all nonbelievers can be maintained.   It is this neutrality the Court abandons today when it treats New York's coercive system as a program which *merely* "encourages religious instruction or co-operates with religious authorities."   The abandonment is all the more dangerous to liberty because of the Court's legal exaltation of the orthodox and its derogation of unbelievers.

Under our system of religious freedom, people have gone to their religious sanctuaries not because they feared the law but because they loved their God.   The choice of all has been as free as the choice of those who answered the call to worship moved only by the music of the old Sunday morning church bells.   The spiritual mind of man has thus been free to believe, disbelieve, or doubt, without repression, great or small, by the heavy hand of government.   Statutes authorizing such repression have been stricken.   Before today, our judicial opinions have refrained from drawing invidious distinctions between those who believe in no religion and those who do believe.   The First Amendment has lost much if the religious follower and the atheist are no longer to be judicially regarded as entitled to equal justice under law.

State help to religion injects political and party prejudices into a holy field.   It too often substitutes force for prayer, hate for love, and persecution for persuasion.   Government should not be allowed, under cover of the soft euphemism of "co-operation," to steal into the sacred area of religious choice.   .   .   .

Mr. Justice JACKSON, dissenting.

This released time program is founded upon a use of the State's power of coercion, which, for me, determines its unconstitutionality.

Stripped to its essentials, the plan has two stages: first, that the State compel each student to yield a large part of his time for public secular education; and, second, that some of it be "released" to him on condition that he devote it to sectarian religious purposes.

No one suggests that the Constitution would permit the State directly to require this "released" time to be spent "under the control of a duly constituted religious body." This program accomplishes that forbidden result by indirection. If public education were taking so much of the pupils' time as to injure the public or the students' welfare by encroaching upon their religious opportunity, simply shortening everyone's school day would facilitate voluntary and optional attendance at Church classes. But that suggestion is rejected upon the ground that if they are made free many students will not go to the Church. Hence, they must be deprived of freedom for this period, with Church attendance put to them as one of the two permissible ways of using it.

The greater effectiveness of this system over voluntary attendance after school hours is due to the truant officer who, if the youngster fails to go to the Church school, dogs him back to the public schoolroom. Here schooling is more or less suspended during the "released time" so the nonreligious attendants will not forge ahead of the churchgoing absentees. But it serves as a temporary jail for a pupil who will not go to Church. It takes more subtlety of mind than I possess to deny that this is governmental constraint in support of religion. It is as unconstitutional, in my view, when exerted by indirection as when exercised forthrightly.

As one whose children, as a matter of free choice, have been sent to privately supported Church schools, I may challenge the Court's suggestion that opposition to this plan can only be antireligious, atheistic, or agnostic. My evangelistic breathren confuse an objection to compulsion with an objection to religion. It is possible to hold a faith with enough confidence to believe that what should be rendered to God does not need to be decided and collected by Caesar.

The day that this country ceases to be free for irreligion it will cease to be free for religion—except for the sect that can win political power. The same epithetical jurisprudence used by the Court today to beat down those who oppose pressuring children into some religion can devise as good epithets tomorrow against those who object to pressuring them into a favored religion. And, after all, if we concede to the State power and wisdom to single out "duly constituted religious" bodies as exclusive alternatives for compulsory secular instruction, it would be logical to also uphold the power and wisdom to choose the true faith among those "duly constituted." We start down a rough road when we begin to mix compulsory public education with compulsory godliness.

A number of Justices just short of a majority of the majority that promulgates today's passionate dialectics joined in answering them in McCollum ex rel. Illinois v. Board of Education, 333 U.S. 203. The distinction attempted between that case and this is trivial, almost to the point of cynicism, magnifying its nonessential details and disparaging compulsion which was the underlying reason for invalidity. A reading of the Court's opinion in that case along with its opinion in this case will show such difference of overtones and undertones as to make clear that the *McCollum* case has passed like a storm in a teacup. The wall which the Court was professing to erect between Church and State has become even more warped and twisted than I expected. Today's judgment will be more interesting to students of psychology and of the judicial processes than to students of constitutional law.*

NOTES AND QUESTIONS

1. What were the precise facts on which the Court based its decision in McCollum v. Bd. of Ed.? Does its decision rest on the power of the state to compel school attendance? If so, how can the decision in Zorach v. Clauson be reconciled with it? If it cannot, what were the decisions in McCollum and Zorach based upon? Are the two cases hopelessly in conflict? What importance should be attached to the facts that Mr. Justice Black delivered the opinion for the Court in McCollum but dissented in Zorach?

2. Under the decisions in these two cases would a religious program be constitutional if it were conducted on a voluntary basis, in the school during school hours but during the time when the students would otherwise be "released" if the religions paid the school for the use of the facilities? Why or why not? Suppose the program took place in the school immediately after the end of the required school day and payment were made for use of the facilities? Reconsider your answers to these questions in light of the following materials in this section.

3. In a town with two schools, one parochial and one public, would it be constitutional for the two schools to have joint graduation ceremonies, including religious services, in the auditorium of the public high school? Why or why not? Suppose the parochial high school had no auditorium, could it constitutionally use the public school auditorium during or after the required public school hours for its functions, many involving religious services? Why or why not?

4. According to the Supreme Court, which is the First Amendment's purpose: (1) to forbid government from preferring one religion over another, or (2) to forbid impartial governmental aid to all religions? Why?

5. Are the basic theories of the First Amendment the same in McCollum and Zorach? Or does one case promote a "neutralist" theory and the other an "accommodation of religion" theory? If so, which case does

---

* A dissenting opinion by Mr. Justice Frankfurter is omitted.

what? In what way do these two theories of the First Amendment differ from a "secularist" theory, if at all? Which theory is correct? Why?

6. A "shared time" (dual enrollment) arrangement is one whereby some students attend part-time at a public school, e. g., for the science and mathematics courses, and are then "released" to spend the remainder of the school day at a private school; the remaining students attend the public school full-time. Is such a program constitutional? A regulation under the Federal Elementary and Secondary Education Act of 1965 defines "dual enrollment" as a "shared use of public facilities for instructional purposes under public auspices by teachers or students from public and private nonprofit schools" (45 C.F.R. 118.1), and the act provides funds to states for certain programs if they will participate in the shared-time programs, can they do so constitutionally? Does the Federal Act incorporate a "neutralist," a "secularist" or an "accommodationist" theory of the First Amendment?

ENGEL v. VITALE

Supreme Court of the United States, 1962.
370 U.S. 421, 82 S.Ct. 1261, 8 L.Ed.2d 601.

Mr. Justice BLACK delivered the opinion of the Court.

The respondent Board of Education of Union Free School District No. 9, New Hyde Park, New York, acting in its official capacity under state law, directed the School District's principal to cause the following prayer to be said aloud by each class in the presence of a teacher at the beginning of each school day:

"Almighty God, we acknowledge our dependence upon Thee, and we beg Thy blessings upon us, our parents, our teachers, and our Country."

This daily procedure was adopted on the recommendation of the State Board of Regents, a governmental agency created by the State Constitution to which the New York Legislature has granted broad supervisory, executive, and legislative powers over the State's public school system. These state officials composed the prayer which they recommended and published as a part of their "Statement on Moral and Spiritual Training in the Schools," saying: "We believe that this Statement will be subscribed to by all men and women of good will, and we call upon all of them to aid in giving life to our program."

Shortly after the practice of reciting the Regents' prayer was adopted by the School District, the parents of ten pupils brought this action in a New York State Court insisting that use of this official prayer in the public schools was contrary to the beliefs, religions, or religious practices of both themselves and their children. Among other things, these parents challenged the constitutionality of both the state law authorizing the School District to direct the use of prayer in public schools and the School District's regulation ordering the recitation of this particular prayer on the ground that these actions of official governmental agencies violate that part of the First Amendment of the Federal Constitution which commands that "Congress shall make no law respecting an establishment of religion"—a command which was "made applicable to the State of New York by the Fourteenth Amendment of the said Constitution." . . .

We think that by using its public school system to encourage recitation of the Regents' prayer, the State of New York has adopted a practice wholly inconsistent with the Establishment Clause. There can, of course, be no doubt that New York's program of daily classroom invocation of God's blessings as prescribed in the Regents' prayer is a religious activity. It is a solemn avowal of divine faith and supplication for the blessings of the Almighty. The nature of such a prayer has always been religious, none of the respondents has denied this and the trial court expressly so found:

> "The religious nature of prayer was recognized by Jefferson and has been concurred in by theological writers, the United States Supreme Court and State courts and administrative officials, including New York's Commissioner of Education. A committee of the New York Legislature has agreed.
>
> "The Board of Regents as *amicus curiae*, the respondents and intervenors all concede the religious nature of prayer, but seek to distinguish this prayer because it is based on our spiritual heritage. . . ."

. . . It is a matter of history that this very practice of establishing governmentally composed prayers for religious services was one of the reasons which caused many of our early colonists to leave England and seek religious freedom in America. The Book of Common Prayer, which was created under governmental direction and which was approved by Acts of Parliament in 1548 and 1549, set out in minute detail the accepted form and content of prayer and other religious ceremonies to be used in the established, tax-supported Church of England. The controversies over the Book and what should be its content repeatedly threatened to disrupt the peace of that country as the accepted forms of prayer in the established church changed with the views of the particular ruler that happened to be in control at the time. Powerful groups representing some of the varying religious views of the people struggled among themselves to impress their particular views upon the Government and obtain amendments of the Book more suitable to their respective notions of how religious services should be conducted in order that the official religious establishment would advance their particular religious beliefs. Other groups, lacking the necessary political power to influence the Government on the matter, decided to leave England and its established church and seek freedom in America from England's governmentally ordained and supported religion.

It is an unfortunate fact of history that when some of the very groups which had most strenuously opposed the established Church of England found themselves sufficiently in control of colonial governments in this country to write their own prayers into law, they passed laws making their own religion the official religion of their respective colonies. Indeed, as late as the time of the Revolutionary War, there were established churches in at least eight of the thirteen former colonies and established religions in at least four of the other five. But the successful Revolution against English political domination was shortly followed by intense opposition to the practice of establishing religion by law. This opposition crystallized rapidly into an effective political force in Virginia where the minority religious groups such as Presbyterians, Lutherans, Quakers and Baptists had gained such strength that the adherents to the established Episcopal Church were actually a minority themselves. In 1785–1786, those opposed to the established Church, led by James Madison and Thomas Jefferson, who, though themselves not members of any of these dissenting religious groups, opposed all religious establishments by law on grounds of principle, obtained the enactment of the famous "Virginia Bill for Religious Liberty" by which all religious groups were placed on an equal footing so far as the State was concerned. Similar though less far-reaching legislation was being considered and passed in other States.

By the time of the adoption of the Constitution, our history shows that there was widespread awareness among many Americans of the dangers of a union of Church and State. These people knew, some of them from bitter personal experience, that one of the greatest dangers to the freedom of the individual to worship in his own way lay in the Government's placing its official stamp of approval upon one particular kind of prayer or one particular form of religious services. They knew the anguish, hardship and bitter strife that could come when zealous religious groups struggled with one another to obtain the Government's stamp of approval from each King, Queen, or Protector that came to temporary power. The Constitution was intended to avert a part of this danger by leaving the government of this country in the hands of the people rather than in the hands of any monarch. But this safeguard was not enough. Our Founders were no more willing to let the content of their prayers and their privilege of praying whenever they pleased be influenced by the ballot box than they were to let these vital matters of personal conscience depend upon the succession of monarchs. The First Amendment was added to the Constitution to stand as a guarantee that neither the power nor the prestige of the Federal Government would be used to control, support or influence the kinds of prayer the American people can say—that the people's religions must not be subjected to the pressures of government for change each time a new political administration is elected to office.   Under that Amendment's prohibition against governmental establishment of religion, as reinforced by the provisions of the Fourteenth Amendment, government in this country, be it state or federal, is without power to prescribe by law any particular form of prayer which is to be used as an official prayer in carrying on any program of governmentally sponsored religious activity.

There can be no doubt that New York's state prayer program officially establishes the religious beliefs embodied in the Regents' prayer.   The respondents' argument to the contrary, which is largely based upon the contention that the Regents' prayer is "non-denominational" and the fact that the program, as modified and approved by state courts, does not require all pupils to recite the prayer but permits those who wish to do so to remain silent or be excused from the room, ignores the essential nature of the program's constitutional defects.   Neither the fact that the prayer may be denominationally neutral nor the fact that its observance on the part of the students is voluntary can serve to free it from the limitations of the Establishment Clause, as it might from the Free Exercise Clause, of the First Amendment, both of which are operative against the States by virtue of the Fourteenth Amendment.   Although these two clauses may in certain instances overlap, they forbid two quite different kinds of governmental encroachment upon religious freedom.   The Establishment Clause, unlike the Free Exercise Clause, does not depend upon any showing of direct governmental compulsion and is violated by the enactment of laws which establish an official religion whether those laws operate directly to coerce nonobserving individuals or not.   This is not to say, of course, that laws officially prescribing a particular form of religious worship do not involve coercion of such individuals.   When the power, prestige and financial support of government is placed behind a particular religious belief, the indirect coercive pressure upon religious minorities to conform to the prevailing officially approved religion is plain.   But the purposes underlying the Establishment Clause go much further than that.   Its first and most immediate purpose rested on the belief that a union of government and religion tends to destroy government and to degrade religion.   The history of governmentally established religion, both in England and in this country, showed that whenever government had allied itself with one particular form of religion, the inevitable result had been that it had incurred the hatred, disrespect and even contempt of those who held contrary beliefs.   That same history showed that many people had lost their respect for any religion that had relied upon the support of government to spread its faith.   The Establishment Clause thus stands as an expression of principle on the part of the Founders of our Constitution that religion is too personal, too sacred, too holy, to permit its "unhallowed perversion" by a civil magistrate.   Another purpose of the Establishment Clause rested upon an awareness of the historical fact that

neutrality
pg. 429

pg. 375

governmentally established religions and religious persecutions go hand in hand. The Founders knew that only a few years after the Book of Common Prayer became the only accepted form of religious services in the established Church of England, an Act of Uniformity was passed to compel all Englishmen to attend those services and to make it a criminal offense to conduct or attend religious gatherings of any other kind—a law which was consistently flouted by dissenting religious groups in England and which contributed to widespread persecutions of people like John Bunyan who persisted in holding "unlawful [religious] meetings . . . to the great disturbance and distraction of the good subjects of this kingdom. . . ." And they knew that similar persecutions had received the sanction of law in several of the colonies in this country soon after the establishment of official religions in those colonies. It was in large part to get completely away from this sort of systematic religious persecution that the Founders brought into being our Nation, our Constitution, and our Bill of Rights with its prohibition against any governmental establishment of religion. The New York laws officially prescribing the Regents' prayer are inconsistent both with the purposes of the Establishment Clause and with the Establishment Clause itself.

It has been argued that to apply the Constitution in such a way as to prohibit state laws respecting an establishment of religious services in public schools is to indicate a hostility toward religion or toward prayer. Nothing, of course, could be more wrong. The history of man is inseparable from the history of religion. And perhaps it is not too much to say that since the beginning of that history many people have devoutly believed that "More things are wrought by prayer than this world dreams of." It was doubtless largely due to men who believed this that there grew up a sentiment that caused men to leave the crosscurrents of officially established state religions and religious persecution in Europe and come to this country filled with the hope that they could find a place in which they could pray when they pleased to the God of their faith in the language they chose. And there were men of this same faith in the power of prayer who led the fight for adoption of our Constitution and also for our Bill of Rights with the very guarantees of religious freedom that forbid the sort of governmental activity which New York has attempted here. These men knew that the First Amendment, which tried to put an end to governmental control of religion and of prayer, was not written to destroy either. They knew rather that it was written to quiet well-justified fears which nearly all of them felt arising out of an awareness that governments of the past had shackled men's tongues to make them speak only the religious thoughts that government wanted them to speak and to pray only to the God that government wanted them to pray to. It is neither sacrilegious nor antireligious to say that each separate government in this country should stay out of the business of writing or sanctioning official prayers and leave that purely religious function to the people themselves and to those the people choose to look to for religious guidance.

It is true that New York's establishment of its Regents' prayer as an officially approved religious doctrine of that State does not amount to a total establishment of one particular religious sect to the exclusion of all others—that, indeed, the governmental endorsement of that prayer seems relatively insignificant when compared to the governmental encroachments upon religion which were commonplace 200 years ago. To those who may subscribe to the view that because the Regents' official prayer is so brief and general there can be no danger to religious freedom in its governmental establishment, however, it may be appropriate to say in the words of James Madison, the author of the First Amendment:

> "[I]t is proper to take alarm at the first experiment on our liberties. . . . Who does not see that the same authority which can establish Christianity, in exclusion of all other Religions, may establish with the same ease any particular sect of Christians, in exclusion of all other Sects? That the same authority which can force a citizen to contribute three pence only of his property for the support of any one establishment, may force him to conform to any other establishment in all cases whatsoever?"

The judgment of the Court of Appeals of New York is reversed and the cause remanded for further proceedings not inconsistent with this opinion.

Reversed and remanded*

ABINGTON SCHOOL DISTRICT v. SCHEMPP

MURRAY v. CURLETT

Supreme Court of the United States, 1963.
374 U.S. 203, 83 S.Ct. 1560, 10 L.Ed.2d 844.

Mr. Justice CLARK delivered the opinion of the Court.

Once again we are called upon to consider the scope of the provision of the First Amendment to the United States Constitution. . . . These companion cases present the issues in the context of state action requiring that schools begin each day with readings from the Bible. While raising the basic questions under slightly different factual situations, the cases permit of joint treatment. In light of the history of the First Amendment and of our cases interpreting and applying its

* The concurring opinion of Mr. Justice
Douglas and dissenting opinion of Mr.
Justice Stewart are omitted.

requirements, we hold that the practices at issue and the laws requiring them are unconstitutional under the Establishment Clause, as applied to the States through the Fourteenth Amendment.

The Facts in Each Case: No. 142. The Commonwealth of Pennsylvania by law, 24 Pa.Stat. § 15–1516, as amended, Pub.Law 1928 (Supp.1960) Dec. 17, 1959, requires that "At least ten verses from the Holy Bible shall be read, without comment, at the opening of each public school on each school day. Any child shall be excused from such Bible reading, or attending such Bible reading, upon the written request of his parent or guardian." The Schempp family, husband and wife and two of their three children, brought suit to enjoin enforcement of the statute, contending that their rights under the Fourteenth Amendment to the Constitution of the United States are, have been, and will continue to be violated unless this statute be declared unconstitutional as violative of these provisions of the First Amendment. They sought to enjoin the appellant school district, wherein the Schempp children attend school, and its officers and the Superintendent of Public Instruction of the Commonwealth from continuing to conduct such readings and recitation of the Lord's Prayer in the public schools of the district pursuant to the statute. . . .

The appellees, Edward Lewis Schempp, his wife Sidney, and their children, Roger and Donna, are of the Unitarian faith and are members of the Unitarian Church in Germantown, Philadelphia, Pennsylvania, where they, as well as another son, Ellory, regularly attend religious services. . . .

On each school day at the Abington Senior High School between 8:15 and 8:30 a. m., while the pupils are attending their home rooms or advisory sections, opening exercises are conducted pursuant to the statute. The exercises are broadcast into each room in the school building through an intercommunications system and are conducted under the supervision of a teacher by students attending the school's radio and television workshop. Selected students from this course gather each morning in the school's workshop studio for the exercises, which include readings by one of the students of 10 verses of the Holy Bible, broadcast to each room in the building. This is followed by the recitation of the Lord's Prayer, likewise over the intercommunications system, but also by the students in the various classrooms, who are asked to stand and join in repeating the prayer in unison. The exercises are closed with the flag salute and such pertinent announcements as are of interest to the students. Participation in the opening exercises, as directed by the statute, is voluntary. The student reading the verses from the Bible may select the passages and read from any version he chooses, although the only copies furnished by the school are the King James version, copies of which were circulated to each teacher by the school district. During the period in which the exercises have been conducted the King James, the Douay and the Revised

Standard versions of the Bible have been used, as well as the Jewish Holy Scriptures.   There are no prefatory statements, no questions asked or solicited, no comments or explanations made and no interpretations given at or during the exercises.   The students and parents are advised that the student may absent himself from the classroom or, should he elect to remain, not participate in the exercises.

It appears from the record that in schools not having an intercommunications system the Bible reading and the recitation of the Lord's Prayer were conducted by the home-room teacher, who chose the text of the verses and read them herself or had students read them in rotation or by volunteers.   This was followed by a standing recitation of the Lord's Prayer, together with the Pledge of Allegiance to the Flag by the class in unison and a closing announcement of routine school items of interest.

At the first trial Edward Schempp and the children testified as to specific religious doctrines purveyed by a literal reading of the Bible "which were contrary to the religious beliefs which they held and to their familial teaching."   .   .   .   The children testified that all of the doctrines to which they referred were read to them at various times as part of the exercises.   Edward Schempp testified at the second trial that he had considered having Roger and Donna excused from attendance at the exercises but decided against it for several reasons, including his belief that the children's relationships with their teachers and classmates would be adversely affected.

Expert testimony was introduced by both appellants and appellees at the first trial, which testimony was summarized by the trial court as follows:

> "Dr. Solomon Grayzel testified that there were marked differences between the Jewish Holy Scriptures and the Christian Holy Bible, the most obvious of which was the absence of the New Testament in the Jewish Holy Scriptures.   Dr. Grayzel testified that portions of the New Testament were offensive to Jewish tradition and that, from the standpoint of Jewish faith, the concept of Jesus Christ as the Son of God was 'practically blasphemous.'   He cited instances in the New Testament which, assertedly, were not only sectarian in nature but tended to bring the Jews into ridicule or scorn.   Dr. Grayzel gave as his expert opinion that such material from the New Testament could be explained to Jewish children in such a way as to do no harm to them.   But if portions of the New Testament were read without explanation, they could be, and in his specific experience with children Dr. Grayzel observed, had been, psychologically harmful to the child and had caused a divisive force within the social media of the school.

> "Dr. Grayzel also testified that there was significant difference in attitude with regard to the respective Books of the

Jewish and Christian Religions in that Judaism attaches no special significance to the reading of the Bible *per se* and that the Jewish Holy Scriptures are source materials to be studied. But Dr. Grayzel did state that many portions of the New, as well as of the Old, Testament contained passages of great literary and moral value.

"Dr. Luther A. Weigle, an expert witness for the defense, testified in some detail as to the reasons for and the methods employed in developing the King James and the Revised Standard Versions of the Bible. On direct examination, Dr. Weigle stated that the Bible was non-sectarian. He later stated that the phrase 'non-sectarian' meant to him non-sectarian within the Christian faiths. Dr. Weigle stated that his definition of the Holy Bible would include the Jewish Holy Scriptures, but also stated that the 'Holy Bible' would not be complete without the New Testament. He stated that the New Testament 'conveyed the message of Christians.' In his opinion, reading of the Holy Scriptures to the exclusion of the New Testament would be a sectarian practice. Dr. Weigle stated that the Bible was of great moral, historical and literary value. This is conceded by all the parties and is also the view of the court." . . .

No. 119.   In 1905 the Board of School Commissioners of Baltimore City adopted a rule pursuant to Art. 77, § 202 of the Annotated Code of Maryland.   The rule provided for the holding of opening exercises in the schools of the city, consisting primarily of the "reading, without comment, of a chapter in the Holy Bible and/or the use of the Lord's Prayer."   The petitioners, Mrs. Madalyn Murray and her son, William J. Murray III, are both professed atheists. Following unsuccessful attempts to have the respondent school board rescind the rule, this suit was filed for mandamus to compel its recission and cancellation.   It was alleged that William was a student in a public school of the city and Mrs. Murray, his mother, was a taxpayer therein; that it was the practice under the rule to have a reading on each school morning from the King James version of the Bible; that at petitioners' insistence the rule was amended to permit children to be excused from the exercise on request of the parent and that William had been excused pursuant thereto; that nevertheless the rule as amended was in violation of the petitioners' rights "to freedom of religion under the First and Fourteenth Amendments" and in violation of "the principle of separation between church and state, contained therein. . . ." The petition particularized the petitioners' atheistic beliefs and stated that the rule, as practiced, violated their rights

"in that it threatens their religious liberty by placing a premium on belief as against non-belief and subjects their freedom of conscience to the rule of the majority; it pronounces belief in God as the source of all moral and spiritual values, equating these values with religious values, and thereby renders sinister, alien and suspect the beliefs and ideals of your Petitioners, promoting doubt and question of their morality, good citizenship and good faith."   . . .

The interrelationship of the Establishment and the Free Exercise Clauses was first touched upon by Mr. Justice Roberts for the Court in Cantwell v. Connecticut, [310 U.S. 296] at 303–304, where it was said that their "inhibition of legislation" had

"a double aspect. On the one hand, it forestalls compulsion by law of the acceptance of any creed or the practice of any form of worship. Freedom of conscience and freedom to adhere to such religious organization or form of worship as the individual may choose cannot be restricted by law. On the other hand, it safeguards the free exercise of the chosen form of religion. Thus the Amendment embraces two concepts,— freedom to believe and freedom to act. The first is absolute but, in the nature of things, the second cannot be."   . . .

The wholesome "neutrality" of which this Court's cases speak thus stems from a recognition of the teachings of history that powerful sects or groups might bring about a fusion of governmental and religious functions or a concert or dependency of one upon the other to the end that official support of the State or Federal Government would be placed behind the tenets of one or of all orthodoxies. This the Establishment Clause prohibits. And a further reason for neutrality is found in the Free Exercise Clause, which recognizes the value of religious training, teaching and observance and, more particularly, the right of every person to freely choose his own course with reference thereto, free of any compulsion from the state. This the Free Exercise Clause guarantees. Thus, as we have seen, the two clauses may overlap. As we have indicated, the Establishment Clause has been directly considered by this Court eight times in the past score of years and, with only one Justice dissenting on the point, it has consistently held that the clause withdrew all legislative power respecting religious belief or the expression thereof. The test may be stated as follows: what are the purpose and the primary effect of the enactment? If either is the advancement or inhibition of religion then the enactment exceeds the scope of legislative power as circumscribed by the Constitution. That is to say that to withstand the strictures of the Establishment Clause there must be a secular legislative purpose and a primary effect that neither advances nor inhibits religion.   . . .
The Free Exercise Clause, likewise considered many times here, withdraws from legislative power, state and federal, the exertion of any restraint on the free exercise of religion. Its purpose is to secure religious liberty in the individual by prohibiting any invasions thereof by civil authority. Hence it is necessary in a free exercise case for one

to show the coercive effect of the enactment as it operates against him in the practice of his religion. The distinction between the two clauses is apparent—a violation of the Free Exercise Clause is predicated on coercion while the Establishment Clause violation need not be so attended.

Applying the Establishment Clause principles to the cases at bar we find that the States are requiring the selection and reading at the opening of the school day of verses from the Holy Bible and the recitation of the Lord's Prayer by the students in unison. These exercises are prescribed as part of the curricular activities of students who are required by law to attend school. They are held in the school buildings under the supervision and with the participation of teachers employed in those schools. None of these factors, other than compulsory school attendance, was present in the program upheld in Zorach v. Clauson. The trial court in No. 142 has found that such an opening exercise is a religious ceremony and was intended by the State to be so. We agree with the trial court's finding as to the religious character of the exercises. Given that finding, the exercises and the law requiring them are in violation of the Establishment Clause.

There is no such specific finding as to the religious character of the exercises in No. 119, and the State contends (as does the State in No. 142) that the program is an effort to extend its benefits to all public school children without regard to their religious belief. Included within its secular purposes, it says, are the promotion of moral values, the contradiction to the materialistic trends of our times, the perpetuation of our institutions and the teaching of literature. The case came up on demurrer, of course, to a petition which alleged that the uniform practice under the rule had been to read from the King James version of the Bible and that the exercise was sectarian. The short answer, therefore, is that the religious character of the exercise was admitted by the State. But even if its purpose is not strictly religious, it is sought to be accomplished through readings, without comment, from the Bible. Surely the place of the Bible as an instrument of religion cannot be gainsaid, and the State's recognition of the pervading religious character of the ceremony is evident from the rule's specific permission of the alternative use of the Catholic Douay version as well as the recent amendment permitting nonattendance at the exercises. None of these factors is consistent with the contention that the Bible is here used either as an instrument for nonreligious moral inspiration or as a reference for the teaching of secular subjects.

The conclusion follows that in both cases the laws require religious exercises and such exercises are being conducted in direct violation of the rights of the appellees and petitioners. Nor are these required exercises mitigated by the fact that individual students may absent themselves upon parental request, for that fact furnishes no defense to a claim of unconstitutionality under the Establishment Clause.   .   .   . Further, it is no defense to urge that the religious practices here may be relatively minor encroachments on the First Amendment. The breach of neutrality that is today a trickling stream may all too soon become a raging torrent and, in the words of Madison, "it is proper to take alarm at the first experiment on our liberties." . . .

It is insisted that unless these religious exercises are permitted a "religion of secularism" is established in the schools. We agree of course that the State may not establish a "religion of secularism" in the sense of affirmatively opposing or showing hostility to religion, thus "preferring those who believe in no religion over those who do believe." . . . We do not agree, however, that this decision in any sense has that effect. In addition, it might well be said that one's education is not complete without a study of comparative religion or the history of religion and its relationship to the advancement of civilization. It certainly may be said that the Bible is worthy of study for its literary and historic qualities. Nothing we have said here indicates that such study of the Bible or of religion, when presented objectively as part of a secular program of education, may not be effected consistently with the First Amendment. But the exercises here do not fall into those categories. They are religious exercises, required by the States in violation of the command of the First Amendment that the Government maintain strict neutrality, neither aiding nor opposing religion.

Finally, we cannot accept that the concept of neutrality, which does not permit a State to require a religious exercise even with the consent of the majority of those affected, collides with the majority's right to free exercise of religion. While the Free Exercise Clause clearly prohibits the use of state action to deny the rights of free exercise to *anyone*, it has never meant that a majority could use the machinery of the State to practice its beliefs. Such a contention was effectively answered by Mr. Justice Jackson for the Court in West Virginia Board of Education v. Barnette, 319 U.S. 624, 638 (1943):

> "The very purpose of a Bill of Rights was to withdraw certain subjects from the vicissitudes of political controversy, to place them beyond the reach of majorities and officials and to establish them as legal principles to be applied by the courts. One's right to . . . freedom of worship . . . and other fundamental rights may not be submitted to vote; they depend on the outcome of no elections."

The place of religion in our society is an exalted one, achieved through a long tradition of reliance on the home, the church and the inviolable citadel of the individual heart and mind. We have come to recognize through bitter experience that it is not within the power of government to invade that citadel, whether its purpose or effect be to aid or oppose, to advance or retard. In the relationship between man and religion, the State is firmly committed to a position of neutrality. . . .*

NOTES AND QUESTIONS

1. Is the text of neutrality, that is, the "purpose and primary effect" test, clear? Can you use it? Present some hypothetical examples demonstrating its application. How can you determine the "purpose" of an enactment? How do you determine which effect is a statute's primary effect?

2. Would the decision in Engel have been any different if the prayer had not been composed by the New York Regents? Would it be constitutional for an elementary school to require its pupils each morning to utter the following verse:

> "We thank you for the flowers so sweet;
>
> "We thank you for the food we eat;
>
> "We thank you for the birds that sing;
>
> "We thank you for everything."

What decision under Engel and the "purpose and primary effect" test? Why? See, DeSpain v. DeKalb Comm. School Dist., 255 F. Supp. 655 (N.D.Ill.1966) cert. den. 390 U.S. 906 and Stein v. Oshinsky, 348 F.2d 999 (2d Cir. 1965).

3. What are the differences between the Abington and Murray cases? Should the differences have required differing applications of the neutrality test? Does an atheist have any claim under the First Amendment? If so, why? Which theory of the First Amendment supports an atheist's claim and which does not?

4. Assuming there is no state law or school regulation on the subject, can a teacher constitutionally begin class with prayers or a reading from the Bible? Can the teacher do so constitutionally if there is a state law or school regulation requiring the exercises?

5. After these cases, can a teacher constitutionally conduct a silent prayer in school? Is the following practice constitutional?
". . . in order to provide for a working accommodation, the School Board changed "the bell and beginning of school timing" as illustrated by the procedure inaugurated in the Sandy Hill School: at 8:40 A.M. a warning bell sounds, followed by another bell at 8:45 A.M. to indicate that the home rooms are open for the use of those children desiring to pray. At 8:50 A.M. a third bell rings, signifying the end of the voluntary prayer period and additionally, that school is about to begin. At 9:00 A.M. a bell signifying the actual start of the class day is rung.

"Plaintiffs object to these practices. . . .

"The policy initially proposed by defendants purported to establish a position of neutrality on the part of the Board of Education with respect to religion." See, Reed v. Van Hoven, 237 F.Supp. 48 (W.D.Mich.1965).

---

* Concurring opinions of Mr. Justices Douglas, Brennan and Goldberg are omitted as is a dissenting opinion by Mr. Justice Stewart.

6. Can the Bible constitutionally be part of the public school's library? If so, which version? May the Bible be distributed during school hours to all pupils who want a copy? May the Bible be used in the curriculum of public schools; if so, how?

CALVARY BIBLE PRESBYTERIAN CHURCH OF SEATTLE v. BOARD OF REGENTS OF THE UNIVERSITY OF WASHINGTON

Supreme Court of Washington, 1967.
72 Wash.2d 912, 436 P.2d 189, certiorari denied 393 U.S. 960,
89 S.Ct. 389, 21 L.Ed.2d 372.

WEAVER, J.—Since 1919, the Department of English of the University of Washington, a state tax-supported university, has offered an elective course of study presently designated "English 390: The Bible as Literature."

Two churches, incorporated organizations, and their respective ministers commenced this action against the Board of Regents of the University of Washington [asking]   .   .   .   for a "permanent injunction   .   .   .   restraining the Board of Regents from authorizing any course of instruction dealing with the historical, biographical, narrative or literary features of the Bible."

Plaintiffs contend that the teaching of English 390 is violative of article 1, section 11 and article 9, section 4 of the Washington State Constitution, which provide:

"No public money or property shall be appropriated for or applied to any religious worship, exercise or instruction .   .   .   .   (Const. art. 1, § 11)

"All schools maintained or supported wholly or in part by the public funds shall be forever free from sectarian control or influence." (Const. art. 9, § 4)

Plaintiffs also contend that the teaching of English 390 violates the first amendment to the United States Constitution ("Congress shall make no law respecting an establishment of religion, or prohibiting the free exercise thereof; .   .   .") as applied to the states through the Fourteenth Amendment.

Although the constitutional violations are urged, the major premise of plaintiffs' argument, as alleged in their amended complaint, is:

"That the manner in which said presentation is made [of English 390] is contrary to the religious beliefs of Plaintiffs, both individually and as church organizations and congregations. That said manner of presentation is in itself the presentation of a religious point of view, being one of several theological positions within the Protestant faith. .   .   ."

The trial court found: that English 390 concerns itself with the literary features of the Bible and, as a necessary part thereof, the history of ancient Israel; the authorship and treatment of the various books of the Bible, and their interpretation from a literary and an historical point of view, employing the same techniques of scholarship used in the study of any other literary or historical text; that the course is offered as part of a secular program of education to advance the knowledge of students and the learning of mankind; that it is taught by members of the English department who are competent literary scholars, qualified to teach in their respective fields of specialization. The course is not taught by theologians. One professor uses the Revised Standard Version of the Bible; another the Oxford Annotated Edition of the Revised Standard Version; a third, the King James version. Each makes his choice of the English translation for his own professional reasons.

Further, the court found that English 390 is taught as a study of the Bible for its literary and historic qualities and is presented objectively as a part of a secular program of education.

Finally, the court found that the course:

"does not promote a particular theology for purposes of religious indoctrination, nor is it slanted in a religious direction, nor does it induce any particular religious belief, nor does it advance any particular religious interests or theology.

.   .   .

"There is no evidence that English 390, as taught at the University of Washington, is intended to affect the religious beliefs of students taking the course or indoctrinate them in any particular religious belief, or that it has had that effect."

The trial court dismissed plaintiffs' complaint with prejudice.

.   .   .

The touchstone of the problem is the meaning attributed to "religious   .   .   .   instruction," as used in article 1, section 11 of our constitution. It must be kept in mind that the words appear after two more specific terms: "worship" and "exercise." This, we believe, is an indication that the framers of our constitution did not intend the word "instruction" to be construed without limit, but that the proscribed field be confined to that category of instruction that resembles worship, and manifests a devotion to religion and religious principles in thought, feeling, belief, and conduct, i. e., instruction that is devotional in nature and designed to induce faith and belief in the student.

There can be no doubt that our constitutional bars are absolute against *religious* instruction and indoctrination in specific religious beliefs or dogma; but they do not proscribe open, free, critical, and scholarly examination of the literature, experiences, and knowledge of mankind. If they did, many fields of scholarship—anthropology, zoology, the theory of evolution, astronomy, the germ theory of disease and medical cure, to mention only a few—would have to be removed from our university. It might be said that the objective examination of these theories conflicts with the religious beliefs of certain persons entertaining contrary beliefs based upon their religious convictions. This would, indeed, be true "sectarian control or influence," which is prohibited by article 9, section 4 of our constitution. It would, as Mr. Justice Brennan said so recently, "cast a pall of orthodoxy over the classroom." Keyishian v. Board of Regents, 385 U.S. 589, 87 S.Ct. 675, 17 L.Ed.2d 629 (1967).

The result advocated by plaintiffs would be catastrophic in the field of higher education. Would plaintiff have us strike the works of Milton, Dante, and the other ancient authors whose writings have survived the ages, because they wrote of religious theories with which plaintiffs quarrel? Our constitution does not guarantee sectarian control of our educational system.

In Illinois ex rel. McCollum v. Board of Education, 333 U.S. 203, 68 S.Ct. 461, 92 L.Ed. 649 (1948), Mr. Justice Jackson, in a concurring opinion, pointed out that:

> Music without sacred music, architecture minus the cathedral, or painting without the scriptural themes would be eccentric and incomplete, even from a secular point of view. . . . Even such a "science" as biology raises the issue between evolution and creation as an explanation of our presence on this planet. Certainly a course in English literature that omitted the Bible and other powerful uses of our mother tongue for religious ends would be pretty barren.

In the final analysis, plaintiffs contend: (1) That the Bible *cannot* be taught objectively as a course in literature for the attempt to do so violates their personal beliefs (sectarian); hence, the teaching is unconstitutional; (2) That the course is *not* taught objectively, but is slanted against plaintiffs' beliefs.

It is apparent that the two contentions overlap factually. The case was well presented to the court, although the evidence of the parties splashes over the guidelines set by the trial court. . . .

The testimony is fascinating reading for one interested in the subject. Competent scholars, educators, professors, ministers, theologians, and students who had taken the course testified. It would unduly extend this opinion to analyze the testimony of any group of witnesses, except, perhaps, to mention the testimony of the students.

There is competent testimony to support the trial court's conclusion that "English 390—The Bible as Literature" *can* be taught objectively in a course in literature, without religious implications, for the court found that the course does not promote a particular theology for purposes of religious indoctrination; that it is not slanted in a re-

ligious direction; that it does not induce any particular religious belief; and that it does not advance any particular religious interest or
theology. . . .

Experts may talk in the abstract, but the "proof of the pudding is
in the eating." Besides the experts, the following students who had
taken English 390 testified: one who had no personal religious beliefs;
a Catholic with a parochial school education; one who described herself as "a rather devout Methodist"; one a Christian Scientist; one a
member of a Jewish synagogue (an outstanding student and the University's nominee as a Rhodes scholar).

Telescoping their testimony, we find that English 390 was taught
in a completely objective manner; had no effect on religious beliefs;
was not slanted toward any particular theological or religious point of
view; did not indoctrinate anyone; did not enter into the realm of belief or faith; and was not taught from a religious point of view.

This, we believe, is sufficient to support the trial court's findings
and to justify its conclusion that "English 390—The Bible as Literature," as taught at the University of Washington, is not violative of
the constitutional provisions we have identified. . . .

Recently, the Supreme Court in Whitehill v. Elkins, 389 U.S. 54,
. . . (1967), quoted with approval from Sweezy v. New Hampshire, 354 U.S. 234, 250, . . . Although the facts are different, the
language has a bearing upon the problem before us. The court said:

> "The essentiality of freedom in the community of American
> universities is almost self-evident. No one should underesti-
> mate the vital role in a democracy that is played by those who
> guide and train our youth. To impose any straitjacket upon
> the intellectual leaders in our colleges and universities would
> imperil the future of our Nation. No field of education is so
> thoroughly comprehended by man that new discoveries can-
> not yet be made. *Particularly is that true in the social sci-
> ences, where few, if any, principles are accepted as absolutes.*
> Scholarship cannot flourish in an atmosphere of suspicion and
> distrust. Teachers and students must always remain free to
> inquire, to study, and to evaluate, to gain new maturity and
> understanding; otherwise our civilization will stagnate and
> die." (Italics ours.)

The judgment is affirmed. . . .

HUNTER, J. (dissenting)—I dissent. The main thrust of the majority opinion is that English 390 as taught at the University of Washington does not contravene our state constitutional prohibition against
religious instruction in public schools, article 1, section 11 and article
9, section 4; because it is a purely objective historical and literary
study of the Bible, and is not motivated by the purpose of religious indoctrination or inducement of any religious belief. Regardless of how

well intended the course may be, the record compels me to conclude that it is religious instruction and constitutes a direct attack upon the religious belief of many taxpayers of this state, who profess that the Bible is the "Revealed Word of God." This religious instruction and religious controversy in public schools is interdicted by our state constitution, supra.

The witnesses for both the appellants and respondents testified that within Christendom today there are two opposing religious views: (1) the traditional view that the Bible is the "Revealed Word of God," and (2) the liberal view that man is free to judge the genuineness and authority of the Bible. There can be no question from this record that the more liberal view is a part of the study for this course.

The outline written by Professor Fowler, as a study guide for the course, sets forth asserted facts inconsistent with Moses being the author of The Pentateuch; Isaiah as author of The Book of Isaiah; Daniel as author of The Book of Daniel; Paul, the Apostle, as author of The Pastoral Epistles; Peter as author of First Peter and Second Peter; and David as author of Psalms. It is conceded that the authorship of these books of the Bible is a matter of religious controversy.

The record, however, goes further. Dr. Wright, one of the instructors in the course, admitted that much of the factual material presented in the study outline was representative of the particular view of the Bible, held by Professor Fowler and himself, and also referred to as the Graf-Wellhausen hypothesis, the documentary hypothesis view, and the modernist view. Professor Fowler admitted his ideology was of the liberal view. Professor Irmscher, one of the instructors in English 390, admitted he instructed the students that the story of Adam and Eve in the Bible is a myth.

The following testimony of a student in the course further demonstrates the liberal point of view of the instructors:

Q. (by Mr. Smith) Did you have the impression that the course was slanted in a religious way? A. Yes, I did. Q. Could you state in what way? . . . A. It was slanted toward the liberal views of theology, specifically higher criticism, variously known, I believe as documentary hypothesis.

Also there was a certain amount of *making characters in the early parts of Genesis as myths, which would be the mythologizing of the scriptures.*

And he also felt that Paul in the New Testament was the one that emphasized and pushed the New Testament church; rather than using the teachings of Jesus, that Paul himself was the one that was the genius of the New Testament Church. (Italics mine.)

This direct attack on the integrity of the Bible unquestionably arouses deep resentment among those who adhere to the traditional view, and who are denied in this instance the assurance under our state constitution, article 1, section 11 and article 9, section 4, that their tax monies will never be used to support religious instruction. . . .

The majority further states that if this court holds that English 390 is constitutionally prohibited, such holding would result in the elimination of courses in many other fields of instruction, such as zoology, anthropology, theory of evolution, and astronomy, that may be inconsistent with the fundamentalist interpretation of the Bible. I can see no reason to raise this specter. Courses of this nature are not affected by the constitutional prohibitions in article 1, section 11 or article 9, section 4. These courses have no resemblance to religious instruction and in no manner come under the ambit of our constitutional prohibitions, supra.

In my judgment the majority has disregarded the basic purpose of the framers of our constitution in adopting article 1, section 11 and article 9, section 4 of our state constitution, . . .

> "We shall not go far afield when we suggest that it is a matter within the common knowledge of those who followed the discussion attending the framing of our constitution *that it was the purpose of the men of that time to avoid all of the evils of religious controversies,* the diversion of school funds to denominational schools and institutions, and the litigation that had occurred in other states. *For it was known that religious opinion is a thing that men will fight for, and sometimes in most insidious ways.* The question then was—and the people who adopted the constitution were so advised— whether we should adopt a constitution which provided *in terms that no religious instruction should ever be a part, directly or indirectly of the curriculum of our schools."* (Italics mine.)

What has happened in the present case is the very thing that the framers of our constitution sought to avoid: the unquestionable resentment of many of our citizens in knowing their tax dollars support a state university that tolerates religious instruction in a course that discredits the genuineness of a book *sacred* and *holy* to them.

I would reverse the trial court and grant the injunction prayed for.

NOTES AND QUESTIONS

1. Is this an "establishment" or "free exercise" case?
2. Is the Bible a religious or secular book? Does its character vary with the method of instruction?
3. Was this case decided correctly? Why or why not?

PUBLIC AID TO PAROCHIAL SCHOOLS

About five million students attend private or parochial schools in the United States. About ninety percent of these students attend Roman Catholic parochial schools. All these schools, private and parochial, have a constitutional right to exist under Pierce v. Society of Sisters, supra, Ch. 4. But parents of students attending these schools must pay tuition to these private schools, relief from which many parents, and their representatives, want. They seek to obtain this relief through a variety of legislative devices that would channel public tax funds to private and parochial schools thereby relieving parents of their need to pay tuition, in full or in part.

JACKSON v. CALIFORNIA

United States Court of Appeals, 1972.
460 F.2d 282 (9th Cir.).

PER CURIAM.

Appellants brought this action seeking injunctive relief from the operation of California's constitutional and statutory provisions limiting appropriation of public funds for education to the support of public schools. They seek to require the state to establish a system of "tuition grants" to parents of school-age children which the parents could then utilize to provide education for their children in nonpublic elementary and secondary schools. Appellants essentially contend that the present state provisions violate their right to free exercise of religion as granted by the First Amendment, and that they also violate the equal protection clause of the Fourteenth Amendment. They sought the convening of a three-judge District Court. This was denied on the ground that no substantial federal question was presented, and judgment was rendered for the state.

The precise questions noted above which are presented by this appeal have been decided adversely to appellants by a three-judge District Court convened in the Eastern District of Missouri. Brusca v. Missouri ex rel. State Board of Education, 332 F.Supp. 275 (E.D.Mo. 1971). We have deferred decision in this case awaiting the outcome of the appeal in *Brusca*. The Supreme Court has now affirmed the judgment of the District Court in that case. 405 U.S. 1050, 92 S.Ct. 1493, 31 L.Ed.2d 786 (1972).

On the authority of *Brusca*, judgment is affirmed.

EVERSON v. BOARD OF EDUCATION

Supreme Court of the United States, 1947.
330 U.S. 1, 67 S.Ct. 504, 91 L.Ed. 711.

Mr. Justice BLACK delivered the opinion of the Court.

A New Jersey statute authorizes its local school districts to make rules and contracts for the transportation of children to and from schools.[1] The appellee, a township board of education, acting pursuant to this statute, authorized reimbursement to parents of money expended by them for the bus transportation of their children on regular busses operated by the public transportation system. Part of this money was for the payment of transportation of some children in the community to Catholic parochial schools. These church schools give their students, in addition to secular education, regular religious instruction conforming to the religious tenets and modes of worship of the Catholic Faith. The superintendent of these schools is a Catholic priest.

The appellant, in his capacity as a district taxpayer, filed suit in a state court challenging the right of the Board to reimburse parents of parochial school students. He contended that the statute and the resolution passed pursuant to it violated both the State and the Federal Constitutions. . . .

Since there has been no attack on the statute on the ground that a part of its language excludes children attending private schools operated for profit from enjoying State payment for their transportation, we need not consider this exclusionary language; it has no relevancy to any constitutional question here presented.[2] Furthermore, if the

[1] "Whenever in any district there are children living remote from any schoolhouse, the board of education of the district may make rules and contracts for the transportation of such children to and from school, including the transportation of school children to and from school other than a public school, except such school as is operated for profit in whole or in part.

"When any school district provides any transportation for public school children to and from school, transportation from any point in such established school route to any other point in such established school route shall be supplied to school children residing in such school district in going to and from school other than a public school, except such school as is operated for profit in whole or in part."
New Jersey Laws, 1941, c. 191, p. 581; N.J.R.S.Cum.Supp., tit. 18, c. 14, § 8.

[2] Appellant does not challenge the New Jersey statute or the resolution on the ground that either violates the equal protection clause of the Fourteenth Amendment by excluding payment for the transportation of any pupil who attends a "private school run for profit." Although the township resolution authorized reimbursement only for parents of public and Catholic school pupils, appellant does not allege, nor is there anything in the record which would offer the slightest support to an allegation, that there were any children in the township who attended or would have attended, but for want of transportation, any but public and Catholic schools. It will be appropriate to consider the exclusion of students of private schools operated for profit when and if it is proved to have occurred, is made the basis of a suit by one in a position to challenge it, and New Jersey's highest court has ruled adversely to the challenger. Striking down a state law

exclusion clause had been properly challenged, we do not know whether New Jersey's highest court would construe its statutes as precluding payment of the school transportation of any group of pupils, even those of a private school run for profit. Consequently, we put to one side the question as to the validity of the statute against the claim that it does not authorize payment for the transportation generally of school children in New Jersey.

The only contention here is that the state statute and the resolution, insofar as they authorized reimbursement to parents of children attending parochial schools, violate the Federal Constitution in these two respects, which to some extent overlap. *First*. They authorize the State to take by taxation the private property of some and bestow it upon others, to be used for their own private purposes. This, it is alleged, violates the due process clause of the Fourteenth Amendment. *Second*. The statute and the resolution forced inhabitants to pay taxes to help support and maintain schools which are dedicated to, and which regularly teach, the Catholic Faith. This is alleged to be a use of state power to support church schools contrary to the prohibition of the First Amendment which the Fourteenth Amendment made applicable to the states.

First. The due process argument that the state law taxes some people to help others carry out their private purposes is framed in two phases. The first phase is that a state cannot tax A to reimburse B for the cost of transporting his children to church schools. This is said to violate the due process clause because the children are sent to these church schools to satisfy the personal desires of their parents, rather than the public's interest in the general education of all children. This argument, if valid, would apply equally to prohibit state payment for the transportation of children to any non-public school, whether operated by a church or any other non-government individual or group. But, the New Jersey legislature has decided that a public purpose will be served by using tax-raised funds to pay the bus fares of all school children, including those who attend parochial schools. The New Jersey Court of Errors and Appeals has reached the same conclusion. The fact that a state law, passed to satisfy a public need, coincides with the personal desires of the individuals most directly affected is certainly an inadequate reason for us to say that a legislature has erroneously appraised the public need.

. . . Changing local conditions create new local problems which may lead a state's people and its local authorities to believe that laws authorizing new types of public services are necessary to promote the general well-being of the people. The Fourteenth Amendment did

is not a matter of such light moment that it should be done by a federal court *ex mero motu* on a postulate neither charged nor proved, but which rests on nothing but a possibility. Cf. Liverpool, N. Y. & P. S. S. Co. v. Comm'rs of Emigration, 113 U. S. 33, 39.

not strip the states of their power to meet problems previously left for individual solution. . . .

It is much too late to argue that legislation intended to facilitate the opportunity of children to get a secular education serves no public purpose. Cochran v. Louisiana State Board of Education, 281 U.S. 370 . . . The same thing is no less true of legislation to reimburse needy parents, or all parents, for payment of the fares of their children so that they can ride in public busses to and from schools rather than run the risk of traffic and other hazards incident to walking or "hitchhiking." . . . Nor does it follow that a law has a private rather than a public purpose because it provides that tax-raised funds will be paid to reimburse individuals on account of money spent by them in a way which furthers a public program. . . . Subsidies and loans to individuals such as farmers and home-owners, and to privately owned transportation systems, as well as many other kinds of businesses, have been commonplace practices in our state and national history.

Insofar as the second phase of the due process argument may differ from the first, it is by suggesting that taxation for transportation of children to church schools constitutes support of a religion by the State. But if the law is invalid for this reason, it is because it violates the First Amendment's prohibition against the establishment of religion. . . .

This Court has previously recognized that the provisions of the First Amendment, in the drafting and adoption of which Madison and Jefferson played such leading roles, had the same objective and were intended to provide the same protection against governmental intrusion on religious liberty as the Virginia state [Virginia's Bill for Religious Liberty] Reynolds v. United States, supra, at 164; Watson v. Jones, 13 Wall. 679; Davis v. Beason, 133 U.S. 333, 342. . . .

The "establishment of religion" clause of the First Amendment means at least this: Neither a state nor the Federal Government can set up a church. Neither can pass laws which aid one religion, aid all religions, or prefer one religion over another. Neither can force nor influence a person to go to or to remain away from church against his will or force him to profess a belief or disbelief in any religion. No person can be punished for entertaining or professing religious beliefs or disbeliefs, for church attendance or non-attendance. No tax in any amount, large or small, can be levied to support any religious activities or institutions, whatever they may be called, or whatever form they may adopt to teach or practice religion. Neither a state nor the Federal Government can, openly or secretly, participate in the affairs of any religious organizations or groups and *vice versa*. In the words of Jefferson, the clause against establishment of religion by law was intended to erect "a wall of separation between Church and State." Reynolds v. United States, supra at 164.

We must consider the New Jersey statute in accordance with the foregoing limitations imposed by the First Amendment. But we must not strike that state statute down if it is within the State's constitutional power even though it approaches the verge of that power. . . New Jersey cannot consistently with the "establishment of religion" clause of the First Amendment contribute tax-raised funds to the support of an institution which teaches the tenets and faith of any church. On the other hand, other language of the amendment commands that New Jersey cannot hamper its citizens in the free exercise of their own religion. Consequently, it cannot exclude individual Catholics, Lutherans, Mohammedans, Baptists, Jews, Methodists, Non-believers, Presbyterians, or the members of any other faith, *because of their faith, or lack of it,* from receiving the benefits of public welfare legislation. While we do not mean to intimate that a state could not provide transportation only to children attending public schools, we must be careful, in protecting the citizens of New Jersey against state-established churches, to be sure that we do not inadvertently prohibit New Jersey from extending its general state law benefits to all its citizens without regard to their religious belief.

Measured by these standards, we cannot say that the First Amendment prohibits New Jersey from spending tax-raised funds to pay the bus fares of parochial school pupils as a part of a general program under which it pays the fares of pupils attending public and other schools. It is undoubtedly true that children are helped to get to church schools. There is even a possibility that some of the children might not be sent to the church schools if the parents were compelled to pay their children's bus fares out of their own pockets when transportation to a public school would have been paid for by the State. The same possibility exists where the state requires a local transit company to provide reduced fares to school children including those attending parochial schools, or where a municipally owned transportation system undertakes to carry all school children free of charge. Moreover, state-paid policemen, detailed to protect children going to and from church schools from the very real hazards of traffic, would serve much the same purpose and accomplish much the same result as state provisions intended to guarantee free transportation of a kind which the state deems to be best for the school children's welfare. And parents might refuse to risk their children to the serious danger of traffic accidents going to and from parochial schools, the approaches to which were not protected by policemen. Similarly, parents might be reluctant to permit their children to attend schools which the state had cut off from such general government services as ordinary police and fire protection, connections for sewage disposal, public highways and sidewalks. Of course, cutting off church schools from these services, so separate and so indisputably marked off from the religious function, would make it far more difficult for the schools to operate. But such is obviously not the purpose of the First Amendment. That

Amendment requires the state to be a neutral in its relations with groups of religious believers and non-believers; it does not require the state to be their adversary. State power is no more to be used so as to handicap religions than it is to favor them.

This Court has said that parents may, in the discharge of their duty under state compulsory education laws, send their children to a religious rather than a public school if the school meets the secular educational requirements which the state has power to impose. See Pierce v. Society of Sisters, 268 U.S. 510. It appears that these parochial schools meet New Jersey's requirements. The State contributes no money to the schools. It does not support them. Its legislation, as applied, does no more than provide a general program to help parents get their children, regardless of their religion, safely and expeditiously to and from accredited schools.

The First Amendment has erected a wall between church and state. That wall must be kept high and impregnable. We could not approve the slightest breach. New Jersey has not breached it here.

Affirmed.

Mr. Justice JACKSON, dissenting.

I find myself, contrary to first impressions, unable to join in this decision. I have a sympathy, though it is not ideological, with Catholic citizens who are compelled by law to pay taxes for public schools, and also feel constrained by conscience and discipline to support other schools for their own children. Such relief to them as this case involves is not in itself a serious burden to taxpayers and I had assumed it to be as little serious in principle. Study of this case convinces me otherwise. The Court's opinion marshals every argument in favor of state aid and puts the case in its most favorable light, but much of its reasoning confirms my conclusions that there are no good grounds upon which to support the present legislation. In fact, the undertones of the opinion, advocating complete and uncompromising separation of Church from State, seem utterly discordant with its conclusion yielding support to their commingling in educational matters. The case which irresistibly comes to mind as the most fitting precedent is that of Julia who, according to Byron's reports, "whispering 'I will ne'er consent,'—consented."

I

The Court sustains this legislation by assuming two deviations from the facts of this particular case; first, it assumes a state of facts the record does not support, and secondly, it refuses to consider facts which are inescapable on the record.

The Court concludes that this "legislation, as applied, does no more than provide a general program to help parents get their children, regardless of their religion, safely and expeditiously to and from accredited schools," and it draws a comparison between "state provisions intended to guarantee free transportation" for school children with services such as police and fire protection, and implies that we are here dealing with "laws authorizing new types of public services. . . . ." This hypothesis permeates the opinion. The facts will not bear that construction.

The Township of Ewing is not furnishing transportation to the children in any form; it is not operating school busses itself or contracting for their operation; and it is not performing any public service of any kind with this taxpayer's money. All school children are left to ride as ordinary paying passengers on the regular busses operated by the public transportation system. What the Township does, and what the taxpayer complains of, is at stated intervals to reimburse parents for the fares paid, provided the children attend either public schools or Catholic Church schools. This expenditure of tax funds has no possible effect on the child's safety or expedition in transit. As passengers on the public busses they travel as fast and no faster, and are as safe and no safer, since their parents are reimbursed as before.

In addition to thus assuming a type of service that does not exist, the Court also insists that we must close our eyes to a discrimination which does exist. The resolution which authorizes disbursement of this taxpayer's money limits reimbursement to those who attend public schools and Catholic schools. That is the way the Act is applied to this taxpayer.

The New Jersey Act in question makes the character of the school, not the needs of the children, determine the eligibility of parents to reimbursement. The Act permits payment for transportation to parochial schools or public schools but prohibits it to private schools operated in whole or in part for profit. Children often are sent to private schools because their parents feel that they require more individual instruction than public schools can provide, or because they are backward or defective and need special attention. If all children of the state were objects of impartial solicitude, no reason is obvious for denying transportation reimbursement to students of this class, for these often are as needy and as worthy as those who go to public or parochial schools. Refusal to reimburse those who attend such schools is understandable only in the light of a purpose to aid the schools, because the state might well abstain from aiding a profit-making private enterprise. Thus, under the Act and resolution brought to us by this case, children are classified according to the schools they attend and are to be aided if they attend the public schools or private Catholic schools, and they are not allowed to be aided if they attend private secular schools or private religious schools of other faiths. . . .

If we are to decide this case on the facts before us, our question is simply this: Is it constitutional to tax this complainant to pay the cost of carrying pupils to Church schools of one specified denomination?

II

Whether the taxpayer constitutionally can be made to contribute aid to parents of students because of their attendance at parochial schools depends upon the nature of those schools and their relation to the Church. The Constitution says nothing of education. It lays no obligation on the states to provide schools and does not undertake to regulate state systems of education if they see fit to maintain them. But they cannot, through school policy any more than through other means, invade rights secured to citizens by the Constitution of the United States. West Virginia State Board of Education v. Barnette, 319 U.S. 624. . . .

The function of the Church school is a subject on which this record is meager. It shows only that the schools are under superintendence of a priest and that "religion is taught as part of the curriculum." But we know that such schools are parochial only in name— they, in fact, represent a world-wide and age-old policy of the Roman Catholic Church. Under the rubric "Catholic Schools," the Canon Law of the Church, by which all Catholics are bound, provides:

"1215. Catholic children are to be educated in schools where not only nothing contrary to Catholic faith and morals is taught, but rather in schools were religious and moral training occupy the first place. . . . (Canon 1372.)"

"1216. In every elementary school the children must, according to their age, be instructed in Christian doctrine.

"The young people who attend the higher schools are to receive a deeper religious knowledge, and the bishops shall appoint priests qualified for such work by their learning and piety. (Canon 1373.)"

"1217. Catholic children shall not attend non-Catholic, indifferent, schools that are mixed, that is to say, schools open to Catholics and non-Catholics alike. The bishop of the diocese only has the right, in harmony with the instructions of the Holy See, to decide under what circumstances, and with what safeguards to prevent loss of faith, it may be tolerated that Catholic children go to such schools. (Canon 1374.)"

"1224. The religious teaching of youth in any schools is subject to the authority and inspection of the Church.

"The local Ordinaries have the right and duty to watch that nothing is taught contrary to faith or good morals, in any of the schools of their territory.

"They, moreover, have the right to approve the books of Christian doctrine and the teachers of religion, and to demand, for the sake of safeguarding religion and morals, the removal of teachers and books.   (Canon 1381.)"   (Woywod, Rev. Stanislaus, The New Canon Law, under imprimatur of Most Rev. Francis J. Spellman, Archbishop of New York and others, 1940.)

It is no exaggeration to say that the whole historic conflict in temporal policy between the Catholic Church and non-Catholics comes to a focus in their respective school policies.   The Roman Catholic Church, counseled by experience in many ages and many lands and with all sorts and conditions of men, takes what, from the viewpoint of its own progress and the success of its mission, is a wise estimate of the importance of education to religion. It does not leave the individual to pick up religion by chance.   It relies on early and indelible indoctrination in the faith and order of the Church by the word and example of persons consecrated to the task.

Our public school, if not a product of Protestantism, at least is more consistent with it than with the Catholic culture and scheme of values.   It is a relatively recent development dating from about 1840.   It is organized on the premise that secular education can be isolated from all religious teaching so that the school can inculcate all needed temporal knowledge and also maintain a strict and lofty neutrality as to religion.   The assumption is that after the individual has been instructed in worldly wisdom he will be better fitted to choose his religion.   Whether such a disjunction is possible, and if possible whether it is wise, are questions I need not try to answer.

I should be surprised if any Catholic would deny that the parochial school is a vital, if not the most vital, part of the Roman Catholic Church.   If put to the choice, that venerable institution, I should expect, would forego its whole service for mature persons before it would give up education of the young, and it would be a wise choice.   Its growth and cohesion, discipline and loyalty, spring from its schools. Catholic education is the rock on which the whole structure rests, and to render tax aid to its Church school is indistinguishable to me from rendering the same aid to the Church itself.

III

It is of no importance in this situation whether the beneficiary of this expenditure of tax-raised funds is primarily the parochial school and incidentally the pupil, or whether the aid is directly bestowed on the pupil with indirect benefits to the school.   The state cannot maintain a Church and it can no more tax its citizens to furnish free carriage to those who attend a Church.   The prohibition against establishment of religion cannot be circumvented by a subsidy, bonus or reimbursement of expense to individuals for receiving religious instruction and indoctrination.

The Court, however, compares this to other subsidies and loans to individuals and says, "Nor does it follow that a law has a private rather than a public purpose because it provides that tax-raised funds will be paid to reimburse individuals on account of money spent by them in a way which furthers a public program. . . . Of course, the state may pay out tax-raised funds to relieve pauperism, but it may not under our Constitution do so to induce or reward piety. It may spend funds to secure old age against want, but it may not spend funds to secure religion against skepticism. It may compensate individuals for loss of employment, but it cannot compensate them for adherence to a creed.

It seems to me that the basic fallacy in the Court's reasoning, which accounts for its failure to apply the principles it avows, is in ignoring the essentially religious test by which beneficiaries of this expenditure are selected. A policeman protects a Catholic, of course—but not because he is a Catholic; it is because he is a man and a member of our society. The fireman protects the Church school—but not because it is a Church school; it is because it is property, part of the assets of our society. Neither the fireman nor the policeman has to ask before he renders aid "Is this man or building identified with the Catholic Church?" But before these school authorities draw a check to reimburse for a student's fare they must ask just that question, and if the school is a Catholic one they may render aid because it is such, while if it is of any other faith or is run for profit, the help must be withheld. To consider the converse of the Court's reasoning will best disclose its fallacy. That there is no parallel between police and fire protection and this plan of reimbursement is apparent from the incongruity of the limitation of this Act if applied to police and fire service. Could we sustain an Act that said the police shall protect pupils on the way to or from public schools and Catholic schools but not while going to and coming from other schools, and firemen shall extinguish a blaze in public or Catholic school buildings but shall not put out a blaze in Protestant Church schools or private schools operated for profit? That is the true analogy to the case we have before us and I should think it pretty plain that such a scheme would not be valid.

The Court's holding is that this taxpayer has no grievance because the state has decided to make the reimbursement a public purpose and therefore we are bound to regard it as such. I agree that this Court has left, and always should leave to each state, great latitude in deciding for itself, in the light of its own conditions, what shall be public purposes in its scheme of things. . . . But it cannot make public business of religious worship or instruction, or of attendance at religious institutions of any character. There is no answer to the proposition, more fully expounded by Mr. Justice RUTLEDGE, that the effect of the religious freedom Amendment to our Constitution was to take every form of propagation of religion out of the realm of things which could directly or indirectly be made public business and thereby be supported in whole or in part at taxpayers' expense. That is a difference which the Constitution sets up between religion and almost every other subject matter of legislation, a difference which goes to the very root of religious freedom and which the Court is overlooking today. This freedom was first in the Bill of Rights because it was first in the forefathers' minds; it was set forth in absolute terms, and its strength is its rigidity. It was intended not only to keep the states' hands out of religion, but to keep religion's hands off the state, and, above all, to keep bitter religious controversy out of public life by denying to every denomination any advantage from getting control of public policy or the public purse. Those great ends I cannot but think are immeasureably compromised by today's decision.

This policy of our Federal Constitution has never been wholly pleasing to most religious groups. They all are quick to invoke its protections; they all are irked when they feel its restraints. This Court has gone a long way, if not an unreasonable way, to hold that public business of such paramount importance as maintenance of public order, protection of the privacy of the home, and taxation may not be pursued by a state in a way that even indirectly will interfere with religious proselytising.   .   .   .

But we cannot have it both ways. Religious teaching cannot be a private affair when the state seeks to impose regulations which infringe on it indirectly, and a public affair when it comes to taxing citizens of one faith to aid another, or those of no faith to aid all. If these principles seem harsh in prohibiting aid to Catholic education, it must not be forgotten that it is the same Constitution that alone assures Catholics the right to maintain these schools at all when predominant local sentiment would forbid them. Pierce v. Society of Sisters, 268 U.S. 510. Nor should I think that those who have done so well without this aid would want to see this separation between Church and State broken down. If the state may aid these religious schools, it may therefore regulate them. Many groups have sought aid from tax funds only to find that it carried political controls with it. Indeed this Court has declared that "It is hardly lack of due process for the Government to regulate that which it subsidizes." Wickard v. Filburn, 317 U.S. 111, 131.

    .   .   .   I cannot read the history of the struggle to separate political from ecclesiastical affairs .   .   .   without a conviction that the Court today is unconsciously giving the clock's hands a backward turn.

Mr. Justice RUTLEDGE, with whom Mr. Justice FRANKFURTER, Mr. Justice JACKSON and Mr. Justice BURTON agree, dissenting.

.   .   .

[The first portion of this opinion is printed supra.]

Does New Jersey's action furnish support for religion by use of the taxing power? Certainly it does, if the test remains undiluted as Jefferson and Madison made it, that money taken by taxation from one is not to be used or given to support another's religious training or belief, or indeed one's own. Today as then the furnishing of "contributions of money for the propagation of opinions which he disbelieves" is the forbidden exaction; and the prohibition is absolute for whatever measure brings that consequence and whatever amount may be sought or given to that end.

The funds used here were raised by taxation. The Court does not dispute, nor could it, that their use does in fact give aid and encouragement to religious instruction. It only concludes that this aid is not "support" in law. But Madison and Jefferson were concerned with aid and support in fact, not as a legal conclusion "entangled in precedents." . . . Here parents pay money to send their children to parochial schools and funds raised by taxation are used to reimburse them. This not only helps the children to get to school and the parents to send them. It aids them in a substantial way to get the very thing which they are sent to the particular school to secure, namely, religious training and teaching.

Believers of all faiths, and others who do not express their feeling toward ultimate issues of existence in any creedal form, pay the New Jersey tax. When the money so raised is used to pay for transportation to religious schools, the Catholic taxpayer to the extent of his proportionate share pays for the transportation of Lutheran, Jewish and otherwise religiously affiliated children to receive their non-Catholic religious instruction. Their parents likewise pay proportionately for the transportation of Catholic children to receive Catholic instruction. Each thus contributes to "the propagation of opinions which he disbelieves" in so far as their religions differ, as do others who accept no creed without regard to those differences. Each thus pays taxes also to support the teaching of his own religion, an exaction equally forbidden since it denies "the comfortable liberty" of giving one's contribution to the particular agency of instruction he approves.

New Jersey's action therefore exactly fits the type of exaction and the kind of evil at which Madison and Jefferson struck. Under the test they framed it cannot be said that the cost of transportation is no part of the cost of education or of the religious instruction given. That it is a substantial and a necessary element is shown most plainly by the continuing and increasing demand for the state to assume it. Nor is there pretense that it relates only to the secular instruction given in religious schools or that any attempt is or could be made toward allocating proportional shares as between the secular and the religious instruction. It is precisely because the instruction is religious and relates to a particular faith, whether one or another, that parents send their children to religious schools under the *Pierce* doctrine. And the very purpose of the state's contribution is to defray the cost of conveying the pupil to the place where he will receive not simply secular, but also and primarily religious, teaching and guidance. . . .

. . . transportation, where it is needed, is as essential to education as any other element. Its cost is as much a part of the total expense, except at times in amount, as the cost of textbooks, of school lunches, of athletic equipment, of writing and other materials; indeed of all other items composing the total burden. Now as always the core of the educational process is the teacher-pupil relationship. Without this the richest equipment and facilities would go for naught. . . .

For me, therefore, the feat is impossible to select so indispensable an item from the composite of total costs, and characterize it as not aiding, contributing to, promoting or sustaining the propagation of beliefs which it is the very end of all to bring about. Unless this can be maintained, and the Court does not maintain it, the aid thus given is outlawed. Payment of transportation is no more, nor is it any the less essential to education, whether religious or secular, then payment for tuitions, for teachers' salaries, for buildings, equipment and necessary materials. Nor is it any the less directly related, in a school giving religious instruction, to the primary religious objective all those essential items of cost are intended to achieve. No rational line can be drawn between payment for such larger, but not more necessary, items and payment for transportation. The only line that can be so drawn is one between more dollars and less. Certainly in this realm such a line can be no valid constitutional measure. . . . Now, as in Madison's time, not the amount but the principle of assessment is wrong. . . .

IV

. . . We have here then one substantial issue, not two. To say that New Jersey's appropriation and her use of the power of taxation for raising the funds appropriated are not for public purposes but are for private ends, is to say that they are for the support of religion and religious teaching. Conversely, to say that they are for public purposes is to say that they are not for religious ones.

This is precisely for the reason that education which includes religious training and teaching, and its support, have been made matters of private right and function, not public, by the very terms of the First Amendment. That is the effect not only in its guaranty of religion's free exercise, but also in the prohibition of establishments. It was on this basis of the private character of the function of religious education that this Court held parents entitled to send their children to private, religious schools. Pierce v. Society of Sisters, supra. Now it declares in effect that the appropriation of public funds to defray part of the cost of attending those schools is for a public purpose. If so, I do not understand why the state cannot go farther or why this case approaches the verge of its power.

In truth this view contradicts the whole purpose and effect of the First Amendment as heretofore conceived. The "public function"—"public welfare"—"social legislation" argument seeks, in Madison's words, to "employ Religion [that is, here, religious education] as an engine of Civil policy."   .   .   .   It is of one piece with the Assessment Bill's preamble, although with the vital difference that it wholly ignores what that preamble explicitly states.   .   .   .

It is not because religious teaching does not promote the public or the individual's welfare, but because neither is furthered when the state promotes religious education, that the Constitution forbids it to do so.   .   .   .   In failure to observe [this distinction] lies the fallacy of the "public function"—"social legislation" argument, a fallacy facilitated by easy transference of the argument's basing from due process unrelated to any religious aspect to the First Amendment.   .   .   .

The reasons underlying the Amendment's policy have not vanished with time or diminished in force. Now as when it was adopted the price of religious freedom is double. It is that the church and religion shall live both within and upon that freedom. There cannot be freedom of religion, safeguarded by the state, and intervention by the church or its agencies in the state's domain or dependency on its largesse.   .   .   .   The great condition of religious liberty is that it be maintained free from sustenance, as also from other interferences, by the state. For when it comes to rest upon that secular foundation it vanishes with the resting.   .   .   .   Public money devoted to payment of religious costs, educational or other, brings the quest for more. It brings too the struggle of sect against sect for the larger share or for any. Here one by numbers alone will benefit most, there another. That is precisely the history of societies which have had an established religion and dissident groups.   .   .   .   It is the very thing Jefferson and Madison experienced and sought to guard against, whether in its blunt or in its more screened forms.   .   .   .   The end of such strife cannot be other than to destroy the cherished liberty. The dominating group will achieve the dominant benefit; or all will embroil the state in their dissensions.   .   .   .

This is not therefore just a little case over bus fares. In paraphrase of Madison, distant as it may be in its present form from a complete establishment of religion, it differs from it only in degree; and is the first step in that direction.   .   .   .   Today as in his time "the same authority which can force a citizen to contribute three pence only   .   .   .   for the support of any one [religious] establishment, may force him" to pay more; or "to conform to any other establishment in all cases whatsoever." And now, as then, "either . . . we must say, that the will of the Legislature is the only measure of their authority; and that in the plenitude of this authority, they may sweep away all our fundamental rights; or, that they are bound to leave this particular right untouched and sacred."

. . .

Short treatment will dispose of what remains. Whatever might be said of some other application of New Jersey's statute, the one made here has no semblance of bearing as a safety measure or, indeed, for securing expeditious conveyance. The transportation supplied is by public conveyance, subject to all the hazards and delays of the highway and the streets incurred by the public generally in going about its multifarious business.

Nor is the case comparable to one of furnishing fire or police protection, or access to public highways. These things are matters of common right, part of the general need for safety. Certainly the fire department must not stand idly by while the church burns. Nor is this reason why the state should pay the expense of transportation or other items of the cost of religious education. . . .

I have chosen to place my dissent upon the broad ground I think decisive, though strictly speaking the case might be decided on narrower issues. The New Jersey statute might be held invalid on its face for the exclusion of children who attend private, profit-making schools. . . .

Two great drives are constantly in motion to abridge, in the name of education, the complete division of religion and civil authority which our forefathers made. One is to introduce religious education and observances into the public schools. The other, to obtain public funds for the aid and support of various private religious schools. . . . In my opinion both avenues were closed by the Constitution. Neither should be opened by this Court. The matter is not one of quantity, to be measured by the amount of money expended. Now as in Madison's day it is one of principle, to keep separate the separate spheres as the First Amendment drew them; to prevent the first experiment upon our liberties; and to keep the question from becoming entangled in corrosive precedents. We should not be less strict to keep strong and untarnished the one side of the shield of religious freedom than we have been of the other.

The judgment should be reversed.

NOTES AND QUESTIONS

1. What were the two issues in this case: How were they decided?

2. Were the two issues in Everson decided correctly? Why or why not? What is the majority's theory of the First Amendment? Is that theory faithfully applied by the majority? What proposition of the majority does Mr. Justice Jackson dispute? Is he correct or incorrect? Why?

Do you agree with Mr. Justice Rutledge that there is only one substantial issue in this case, and not two? Why or why not? Mr. Justice Rutledge argues (1) that it is impossible to separate out items of a school budget, all of which are thought essential for a child's education, and (2) that the public welfare or "child benefit" theory of the majority violates the intended purpose of the First Amendment; do you agree? Why or why not? What role should history play in the interpretation of the First Amendment? Did it play that role in the decision in this case?

3. Is Everson different in principle from the situation presented when police officers are required to be at street corners near parochial and private schools?

4. According to the dissenting opinions, would the expenditure of tax funds for public sidewalks that lead to a parochial school be a violation of the First Amendment? Should it be? Why or why not?

5. Under the public welfare theory of Everson is either the "purpose or primary effect" of New Jersey's statute considered to be (1) the transportation of the children, or (2) the protection of their "safety" when going to school?

6. The legal department of the National Catholic Welfare Conference states: "The rule of Everson . . . is plainly this: (1) Government may support the education of citizens in various ways. (2) 'Education of citizens' may take place in church-related schools. (3) Government may not support a religion or church, as such, but so long as its program confers directly and substantially a benefit to citizen education, that program is constitutionally unobjectionable, although benefit is at the same time incidentally conferred upon a religion or a church. . . ." Do you agree? The full position of the Legal Department is printed in 50 Geo.L.J. 397 (1961).

7. Under the Everson interpretation of the First Amendment could a state use tax funds to provide parochial schools with (1) fire extinguishers; (2) desks; (3) public health nurses; (4) school lunches; (5) science and mathematics teachers, or (6) textbooks? Why or why not?

Rev. Francis J. Connell, C. S. S. R., CENSORSHIP AND THE PROHIBITION OF BOOKS IN THE CATHOLIC CHURCH

Copyright © 1954 by Columbia Law Review.
Selections from Vol. 54, Columbia Law Review, pp. 699–709.

The Catholic Church approaches the problem of man's right to knowledge with the realization that in settling concrete problems relative to human freedom two fundamental principles must be observed: First, liberty is a most precious possession, based on the dignity of every human person as a creature of God destined to an everlasting existence; hence it must be respected and protected. Second, for the good of society as well as for the welfare of individuals, personal liberty must be curtailed in certain circumstances. This is particularly true when the limitation of liberty is required as a means of protecting individuals from sin or moral evil, which would constitute an impediment to the attainment of their final goal, eternal happiness with God. In determining the extent of man's rights in particular cases a just and reasonable mean must be observed between these two principles. If the first is overemphasized, liberty degenerates into license. If the second is stressed too much, authority becomes tyranny and the way is open to totalitarianism.

These two principles must be properly coordinated in one of the problems which the Church treats in detailed legislation—the problem of the right to read certain books and other forms of published literature, a problem with a direct bearing on the right to knowledge and its free use. . . .

The notion that people should be allowed to read everything they wish is quite common in our land, for we are a freedom-loving people, resenting any restriction of our freedom. How often do we hear the statement that reading will never cause the reader any harm! An example of this is a statement made by Verner W. Clapp, Acting Librarian of Congress:

> The notion that mankind is corrupted by books is, I believe, a notion held by those whose own reading has been largely of that enforced and unselective kind which the mass media provide. Books are corruptive only to those who seek to be corrupted; but they are already corrupt.

Despite the dogmatic assurance with which this statement is made, the fact is that people can be influenced to evil as well as to good by what they read. And while we justly uphold the ideals of freedom we must admit that freedom has its limitations. Catholics believe that the laws of their Church in regard to censorship and the prohibition of books represent a reasonable limitation of their freedom. And before passing an unfavorable judgment on the Church's legislation on this matter, one should examine the principles on which the Church bases its policy in restricting the right to read for those who are subject to the authority of the Church.

The Catholic Church believes that the chief purpose of man's earthly life is to prepare for an eternal life after death. Happiness in this everlasting existence is merited by living in this world a life in conformity with the commands of God; and it is supremely important to live this life in such a manner as to attain this goal. Whatever advantages may accrue through the exercise of personal freedom, they can have no real value if they impede or imperil the attainment of one's eternal destiny. Hence it is not an evil but a good when those in authority, whether parents, civil rulers or ecclesiastical authorities, regulate the exercise of freedom by those subject to their jurisdiction so as to aid them to observe God's law and to reach the eternal happiness which the Creator has appointed to every human being.

Everyone admits that it is perfectly reasonable to limit the freedom of individuals when the purpose of such limitations is to prevent them from doing physical harm to themselves or to others. If I refuse to give a person a gun with which he is likely to shoot himself or others I am indeed limiting his freedom, but no reasonable person will accuse me of doing wrong. Instead of hampering his proper use of freedom, I am preventing him from abusing it. The Catholic Church applies this same principle to the unrestricted right to read. There are books which would cause spiritual and moral harm to many persons if they were permitted to read them indiscriminately; hence the Church forbids the reading of such books.

Naturally it will be asked by what authority the Church claims the right to do this. The Church replies that it has received from God Himself the right to teach officially the truths of religion and morality and the right to legislate on matters pertinent to the spiritual welfare of those subject to its jurisdiction. . . .

Anyone who admits the existence of an intelligent and all-powerful Deity must grant that if He wills, He can authorize an organization on earth to represent Him in proposing to mankind the doctrines of religion and the principles of morality. For such a person, therefore, the vital question is whether or not the Almighty has acted thus in respect to the Catholic Church. . . .

As to the matter of religious belief, the Catholic Church is convinced that its duty of preserving in its members the faith in the truths which God has communicated to men calls for legislation against books that might endanger that faith. The Church is not motivated by a fear that the arguments brought against its teachings are sufficiently cogent in themselves to discredit Catholic teaching. Rather, the Church recognizes that many Catholics do not possess sufficient technical knowledge of the Catholic doctrine or of history to meet all the arguments that can be brought against Catholic belief; hence the Church legislates against books with such a purpose. . . .

BOARD OF EDUCATION v. ALLEN

Supreme Court of the United States, 1968.
392 U.S. 236, 88 S.Ct. 1923, 20 L.Ed.2d 1060.

Mr. Justice WHITE delivered the opinion of the Court.

A law of the State of New York requires local public school authorities to lend textbooks free of charge to all students in grade seven through 12; students attending private schools are included. This case presents the question whether this statute is a "law respecting an establishment of religion, or prohibiting the free exercise thereof," and so in conflict with the First and Fourteenth Amendments to the Constitution, because it authorizes the loan of textbooks to students attending parochial schools. We hold that the law is not in violation of the Constitution.

Until 1965, § 701 of the Education Law of the State of New York authorized public school boards to designate textbooks for use in the public schools, to purchase such books with public funds, and to rent or sell the books to public school students. In 1965, the Legislature amended § 701, . . . Beginning with the 1966–1967 school year, local school boards were required to purchase textbooks and lend them without charge "to all children residing in such district who are enrolled in grades seven to twelve of a public or private school which complies with the compulsory education law." The books now loaned are "textbooks which are designated for use in any public, elementary or secondary schools of the state or are approved by any boards of education," and which—according to a 1966 amendment—"a pupil is required to use as a text for a semester or more in a particular class in the school he legally attends."

Appellant Board of Education of Central School District No. 1 in Rensselaer and Columbia Counties, brought suit in the New York courts against appellee James Allen. The complaint alleged that § 701 violated both the State and Federal Constitutions; that if appellants, in reliance on their interpretation of the Constitution, failed to lend books to parochial school students within their counties appellee Allen would remove appellants from office; and that to prevent this, appellants were complying with the law and submitting to their constituents a school budget including funds for books to be lent to parochial school pupils. Appellants therefore sought a declaration that § 701 was invalid, an order barring appellee Allen from removing appellants from office for failing to comply with it, and another order restraining him from apportioning state funds to school districts for the purchase of textbooks to be lent to parochial students. . . .

Everson v. Board of Education, . . . is the case decided by this Court that is most nearly in point for today's problem. . . .

Everson and later cases have shown that the line between state neutrality to religion and state support of religion is not easy to locate. . . . "The test may be stated as follows: what are the purpose and the primary effect of the enactment? If either is the advancement or inhibition of religion then the enactment exceeds the scope of legislative power as circumscribed by the Constitution. That is to say that to withstand the strictures of the Establishment Clause there must be a secular legislative purpose and a primary effect that neither advances nor inhibits religion. . . ."

This test is not easy to apply. . . . The statute upheld in Everson would be considered a law having "a secular legislative purpose and a primary effect that neither advances nor inhibits religion."

We reach the same result with respect to the New York law requiring school books to be loaned free of charge to all students in specified grades. The express purpose of § 701 was stated by the New York Legislature to be furtherance of the educational opportunities available to the young. Appellants have shown us nothing about the necessary effects of the statute that is contrary to its stated purpose. The law merely makes available to all children the benefits of a general program to lend school books free of charge. Books are furnished at the request of the pupil and ownership remains, at least technically, in the State. Thus no funds or books are furnished to parochial schools, and the financial benefit is to parents and children, not to schools. Perhaps free books make it more likely that some children choose to attend a sectarian school, but that was true of the state-paid bus fares in Everson and does not alone demonstrate an unconstitutional degree of support for a religious institution.

Of course books are different from buses. Most bus rides have no inherent religious significance, while religious books are common. However, the language of § 701 does not authorize the loan of religious books, and the State claims no right to distribute religious literature. Although the books loaned are those required by the parochial school for use in specific courses, each book loaned must be approved by the public school authorities; only secular books may receive approval. . . . Absent evidence, we cannot assume that school authorities, who constantly face the same problem in selecting textbooks for use in the public schools, are unable to distinguish between secular and religious books or that they will not honestly discharge their duties under the law. In judging the validity of the statute on this record we must proceed on the assumption that books loaned to students are books that are not unsuitable for use in the public schools because of religious content.

The major reason offered by appellants for distinguishing free textbooks from free bus fares is that books, but not buses, are critical to the teaching process, and in a sectarian school that process is employed to teach religion. However, this Court has long recognized that religious schools pursue two goals, religious instruction and secular education. . . .

. . . private education has played and is playing a significant and valuable role in raising national levels of knowledge, competence, and experience. Americans care about the quality of the secular education available to their children. They have considered high quality education to be an indispensable ingredient for achieving the kind of nation, and the kind of citizenry, that they have desired to create. Considering this attitude, the continued willingness to rely on private school systems, including parochial systems, strongly suggests that a wide segment of informed opinion, legislative and otherwise, has found that those schools do an acceptable job of providing secular education to their students. This judgment is further evidence that parochial schools are performing, in addition to their sectarian function, the task of secular education.

Against this background of judgment and experience, . . . we cannot agree with appellants either that all teaching in a sectarian school is religious or that the processes of secular and religious training are so intertwined that secular textbooks furnished to students by the public are in fact instrumental in the teaching of religion. This case comes to us after summary judgment entered on the pleadings. Nothing in this record supports the proposition that all textbooks, whether they deal with mathematics, physics, foreign languages, history, or literature, are used by the parochial schools, to teach religion. No evidence has been offered about particular schools, particular courses, particular teachers, or particular books. We are unable to hold, based solely on judicial notice, that this statute results in unconstitutional involvement of the State with religious instruction or that § 701, for this or the other reasons urged, is a law respecting the establishment of religion within the meaning of the First Amendment.

Appellants also contend that § 701 offends the Free Exercise Clause of the First Amendment. However, "it is necessary in a free exercise case for one to show the coercive effect of the enactment as it operates against him in the practice of his religion," . . . and appellants have not contended that the New York law in any way coerces them as individuals in the practice of their religion.

The judgment is affirmed.

Mr. Justice Harlan, concurring. . . .

The attitude of government toward religion must, as this Court has frequently observed, be one of neutrality. Neutrality is, however, a coat of many colors. It requires that "government neither engage in nor compel religious practices, that it effect no favoritism among sects or between religion and nonreligion, and that it work deterrence of no religious belief." . . . Realization of these objectives entails "no simple and clear measure," . . . or which this or any case may readily be decided, but these objectives do suggest the principles which I believe to be applicable in the present circumstances. I would hold that where the contested governmental activity is calculated to achieve nonreligious purposes otherwise within the competence of the State, and where the activity does not involve the State "so significantly and directly in the realm of the sectarian as to give rise to . . . divisive influences and inhibitions of freedom," . . . it is not forbidden by the religious clauses of the First Amendment.

In my opinion, § 701 of the Education Law of New York does not employ religion as its standard for action or inaction, and is not otherwise inconsistent with these principles.

Mr. Justice BLACK, dissenting. . . .

The Everson and McCollum cases plainly interpret the First and Fourteenth Amendments as protecting the taxpayers of a State from being compelled to pay taxes to their government to support the agencies of private religious organizations the taxpayers oppose. To authorize a State to tax its residents for such church purposes is to put the State squarely in the religious activities of certain religious groups that happen to be strong enough politically to write their own religious preferences and prejudices into the laws. This links state and churches together in controlling the lives and destinies of our citizenship—a citizenship composed of people of myriad religious faiths, some of them bitterly hostile to and completely intolerant of the others. It was to escape laws precisely like this that a large part of the Nation's early immigrants fled to this country. It was also to escape such laws and such consequences that the First Amendment was written in language strong and clear barring passage of any law "respecting an establishment of religion."

It is true, of course, that the New York law does not as yet formally adopt or establish a state religion. But it takes a great stride in that direction and coming events cast their shadows before them. The same powerful sectarian religious propagandists who have succeeded in securing passage of the present law to help religious schools carry on their sectarian religious purposes can and doubtless will continue their propaganda, looking toward complete domination and supremacy of their particular brand of religion. And it nearly always is by insidious approaches that the citadels of liberty are most successfully attacked.

I know of no prior opinion of this Court upon which the majority here can rightfully rely to support its holding this New York law constitutional. In saying this, I am not unmindful of . . . Everson . . . . . . in which this Court, in an opinion written by me, upheld a New Jersey law authorizing reimbursement to parents for the transportation of children attending sectarian schools. That law did not attempt to deny the benefit of its general terms to children of any faith going to any legally authorized school. Thus, it was treated in the same way as a general law paying the streetcar fare *of all school children,* or a law providing midday lunches for all children or all school children, or a law to provide police protection for children going to and from school, or general laws to provide police and fire protection for buildings, including, of course, churches and church school buildings as well as others.

As my Brother Douglas so forcefully shows, in an argument with which I fully agree, upholding a State's power to pay bus or streetcar fares for school children cannot provide support for the validity of a state law using tax-raised funds to buy school books for a religious school. The First Amendment's bar to establishment of religion must preclude a State from using funds levied from all of its citizens to purchase books for use by sectarian schools, which, although "secular," realistically will in some way inevitably tend to propagate the religious views of the favored sect. Books are the most essential tool of education since they contain the resources of knowledge which the educational process is designed to exploit. In this sense it is not difficult to distinguish books, which are the heart of any school, from bus fares, which provide a convenient and helpful general public transportation service. . . .

. . . It requires no prophet to foresee that on the argument used to support this law others could be upheld providing for state or federal government funds to buy property on which to erect religious school buildings or to erect the buildings themselves, to pay the salaries of the religious school teachers, and finally to have the sectarian religious groups cease to rely on voluntary contributions of members of their sects while waiting for the Government to pick up all the bills for the religious schools. Arguments made in favor of this New York law point squarely in this direction, namely, that the fact that government has not heretofore aided religious schools with tax-raised funds amounts to a discrimination against those schools and against religion. And that there are already efforts to have government supply the money to erect buildings for sectarian religious schools is shown by a recent Act of Congress which apparently allows for precisely that. See Higher Education Facilities Act of 1963, 77 Stat. 363, 20 U.S.C. § 701 et seq.

I still subscribe to the belief that tax-raised funds cannot constitionally be used to support religious schools, buy their school books, erect their buildings, pay their teachers, or pay any other of their maintenance expenses, even to the extent of one penny. The First Amendment's prohibition against governmental establishment of religion was written on the assumption that state aid to religion and religious schools generates discord, disharmony, hatred, and strife among our people, and that any government that supplies such aids is to that extent a tyranny. And I still believe that the only way to protect minority religious groups from majority groups in this country is to keep the wall of separation between church and state high and impregnable as the First and Fourteenth Amendments provide. The Court's affirmance here bodes nothing but evil to religious peace in this country.

Mr. Justice DOUGLAS, dissenting. . . .

The statute on its face empowers each parochial school to determine for itself which textbooks will be eligible for loans to its students, for the Act provides that the only text which the State may provide is "a book which a pupil is required to use as a text for a semester or more in a particular class in the school he legally attends." . . .
This initial and crucial selection is undoubtedly made by the parochial school's principal or its individual instructors, who are, in the case of Roman Catholic schools, normally priests or nuns.

The next step under the Act is an "individual request" for an eligible textbook (§ 701, subd. 3), but the State Education Department has ruled that a pupil may make his request to the local public board of education through a "private school official." Local boards have accordingly provided for those requests to be made by the individual or "by groups or classes." And forms for textbook requisitions to be filled out by the head of the private school are provided.

The role of the local public school board is to decide whether to veto the selection made by the parochial school. This is done by determining first whether the text has been or should be "approved" for use in public schools and second whether the text is "secular," "non-religious," or "non-sectarian." The local boards apparently have broad discretion in exercising this veto power.

Thus the statutory system provides that the parochial school will ask for the books that it wants. Can there be the slightest doubt that the head of the parochial school will select the book or books that best promote its sectarian creed? . . .

Whatever may be said of Everson, there is nothing ideological about a bus. There is nothing ideological about a school lunch, or a public nurse, or a scholarship. The constitutionality of such public aid to students in parochial schools turns on considerations not present in this textbook case. The textbook goes to the very heart of education in a parochial school. It is the chief, although not solitary, instrumentality for propagating a particular religious creed or faith. How can we possibly approve such state aid to a religion? A parochial school textbook may contain many, many more seeds of creed and dogma than a prayer. Yet we struck down in Engel v. Vitale, . . . even though it was not plainly denominational. For we emphasized the violence done the Establishment Clause when the power was given religious-political groups "to write their own prayers into law." . . . That risk is compounded here by giving parochial schools the initiative in selecting the textbooks they desire to be furnished at public expense.

. . . The New York Legislature felt that science was a nonsectarian subject. . . . Does this mean that any general science textbook intended for use in grades 7–12 may be provided by the State to parochial school students? May John M. Scott's Adventures in Science (1963) be supplied under the textbook loan program? This book teaches embryology in the following manner:

> "To you an animal usually means a mammal, such as a cat, dog, squirrel, or guinea pig. The new animal or embryo develops inside the body of the mother until birth. The fertilized egg becomes an embryo or developing animal. Many cell divisions take place. In time some cells become muscle cells, others nerve cells, or blood cells, and organs such as eyes, stomach, and intestine are formed.

"The body of a human being grows in the same way, but it is much more remarkable than that of any animal, for the embryo has a human soul infused into the body by God. Human parents are partners with God in creation. They have very great powers and great responsibilities, for through their cooperation with God souls are born for heaven." (At 618–619.)

Comparative economics would seem to be a nonsectarian subject. Will New York, then, provide Arthur J. Hughes' general history text, Man in Time (1964), to parochial school students? It treats that topic in this manner:

"Capitalism is an economic system based on man's right to private property and on his freedom to use that property in producing goods which will earn him a just profit on his investment. Man's right to private property stems from the Natural Law implanted in him by God. It is as much a part of man's nature as the will to self-preservation." (At 560.)

"The broadest definition of socialism is government ownership of all the means of production and distribution in a country. . . . Many, but by no means all, Socialists in the nineteenth century believed that crime and vice existed because poverty existed, and if poverty were eliminated, then crime and vice would disappear. While it is true that poor surroundings are usually unhealthy climates for high moral training, still, man has the free will to check himself. Many Socialists, however, denied free will and said that man was a creation of his environment. . . . If Socialists do not deny Christ's message, they often ignore it. Christ showed us by His life that this earth is a testing ground to prepare man for eternal happiness. Man's interests should be in this direction at least part of the time and not always directed toward a futile quest for material goods." (At 561–564.)

Mr. Justice JACKSON said, ". . . I should suppose it is a proper, if not an indispensable, part of preparation for a wordly life to know the roles that religion and religions have played in the tragic story of mankind." . . . Yet, as he inquired, what emphasis should one give who teaches the Reformation, the Inquisition, or the early effort in New England to establish " 'a Church without a Bishop and a State without a King?' " . . . What books should be chosen for those subjects? . . .

Is the dawn of man to be explained in the words, "God created man and made man master of the earth" (P. Furlong, The Old World and America 5 (1937), or in the language of evolution (see T. Wallbank, Man's Story 32–35 (1961))? . . .

Is Franco's revolution in Spain to be taught as a crusade against anti-Catholic forces (see R. Hoffman, G. Vincitorio, & M. Swift, Man and His History 666–667 (1958)) or as an effort by reactionary elements to regain control of that country (see G. Leinwand, The Pageant of World History, supra, at 512)? Is the expansion of communism in select areas of the world a manifestation of the forces of Evil campaigning against the forces of Good? See A. Hughes, Man in Time, supra, at 565–568, 666–669, 735–748.

It will be often difficult, as Mr. Justice Jackson said, to say "where the secular ends and the sectarian begins in education." . . . But certain it is that once the so-called "secular" textbook is the price to be won by that religious faith which selects the book, the battle will be on for those positions of control. . . . It must be remembered that the very existence of the religious school—whether Catholic or Mormon, Presbyterian or Episcopalian—is to provide an education oriented to the dogma of the particular faith.

Father Peter O'Reilly put the matter succinctly when he disclosed what was happening in one Catholic school: "On February 24, 1954, Rev. Cyril F. Meyer, C. M., then Vice President of the University, sent the following letter to all the faculty, both Catholics and non-Catholics, even those teaching law, science, and mathematics:

" 'Dear Faculty Member"

" 'As a result of several spirited discussions in the Academic Senate, a resolution was passed by that body that a self-evaluation be made of the effectiveness with which we are achieving in our classrooms the stated objectives of the University. . . . The primacy of the spiritual is the reason for a Christian university. Our goal is not merely to equip students with marketable skills. It is far above this—to educate man, the whole man, the theocentric man. As you are well aware, we strive to educate not only for personal and social success in secular society, but far more for leadership toward a theocentric society. . . .

" 'May I, therefore, respectfully request that you submit answers as specific as possible to the following questions:

" '1. What do you do to make your particular courses theocentric?

" '2. Do you believe there is anything the Administration or your colleagues can do to assist you in presenting your particular courses more "according to the philosophical and theological traditions of the Roman Catholic Church"? Do not hesitate to let us know. There is no objective of our University more fundamental than this. We must all be aware that "the classroom that is not a temple is a den."

" 'Please try to have your answers, using this size paper, returned to me by March 10.' "

This tendency is no Catholic monopoly:

"The Presbyterian-affiliated Lewis and Clark College seems to have a similar interest in appearances of autonomy, with a view to avoiding possible legal bars to both federal funds and gifts from some foundations. The change, which legitimizes the college as an autonomous educational institution, removes the requirement that each presbytery in Oregon have at least one representative on the board, but it was made clear 'The college wishes to change *only its legal relationship* to the synod and *not its purposes*,' and promised that it still will elect a minister from each presbytery to the board on nomination of the synod, and will consult the synod before making any change in its statement of purpose, which defines it as a Presbyterian-related college."

The challenged New York law leaves to the Board of Regents, local boards of education, trustees, and other school authorities the supervision of the textbook program.

The Board of Regents (together with the Commissioner of Education) has powers of censorship over all textbooks that contain statements seditious in character, or evince disloyalty to the United States or are favorable to any nation with which we are at war. New York Education Law § 704. Those powers can cut a wide swath in many areas of education that involve the ideological element.

In general textbooks are approved for distribution by "boards of education, trustees or such body or officer as perform the functions of such boards. . . ." . . . These school boards are generally elected, . . . though in a few cities they are appointed. . . . Where there are trustees they are elected. . . . And superintendents who advise on textbook selection are appointed by the board of education or the trustees. . . .

The initiative to select and requisition "the books desired" is with the parochial school. Powerful religious-political pressures will therefore be on the state agencies to provide the books that are desired.

These then are the battlegrounds where control of textbook distribution will be won or lost. Now that "secular" textbooks will pour into religious schools, we can rest assured that a contest will be on to provide those books for religious schools which the dominant religious group concludes best reflect the theocentric or other philosophy of the particular church.

The states are now extremely high . . . to obtain approval of what is "proper." For the "proper" books will radiate the "correct" religious view not only in the parochial school but in the public school as well. . . .

. . . however the case be viewed—whether sectarian groups win control of school boards or do not gain such control—the principle of separation of church and state, inherent in the Establishment Clause of the First Amendment, is violated by what we today approve.

What Madison wrote in his famous Memorial and Remonstrance against Religious Assessments is highly pertinent here:

> "Who does not see that the same authority which can establish Christianity, in exclusion of all other Religions, may establish with the same ease any particular sect of Christians, in exclusion of all other Sects? That the same authority which can force a citizen to contribute three pence only of his property for the support of any one establishment, may force him to conform to any other establishment in all cases whatsoever?" . . .

Mr. Justice FORTAS, dissenting.

The majority opinion of the Court upholds the New York statute by ignoring a vital aspect of it. Public funds are used to buy, for students in sectarian schools, textbooks which are selected and prescribed by the sectarian schools themselves. . . . the transparent camouflage that the books are furnished to students, the reality is that they are selected and their use is prescribed by the sectarian authorities. The child must use the prescribed book. He cannot use a different book prescribed for use in the public schools. The State cannot choose the book to be used. It is true that the public school boards must "approve" the book selected by the sectarian authorities; but this has no real significance. The purpose of these provisions is to hold out promise that the books will be "secular" . . . but the fact remains that the books are chosen by and for the sectarian schools. . . .

This case is not within the principle of Everson. . . . Apart from the differences between textbooks and bus rides, the present statute does not call for extending to children attending sectarian schools the same service or facility extended to children in public schools. This statute calls for furnishing special, separate, and particular books, specially, separately, and particularly chosen by religious sects or their representatives for use in their sectarian schools. This is the infirmity, in my opinion. . . .

I would reverse the judgment below.

NOTE: SECTARIAN BOOKS, THE SUPREME COURT AND THE ESTABLISHMENT CLAUSE

Reprinted by permission of The Yale Law Journal Company and Fred B. Rothman & Company from *The Yale Law Journal*, Vol. 79, pp. 114–26.

In quoting with approval the interpretation given the Textbook Loan Law by the New York State Court of Appeals, the Supreme

Court reads the Act as " 'merely making available secular textbooks' " and not authorizing the loan of sectarian or religious books. Thus, approval or disapproval of a loan by public school authorities depends on whether the content of the requested book is of a secular or religious character.

This method review—reliance upon the content of the book—cannot directly accomplish the goals of the first amendment. Since the concern of the Establishment Clause is the government's propagation of religion, the effect of a government-purchased textbook *as it is used* should be the question facing reviewers. A seemingly neutral discussion within a book could be presented in the classroom in a way such that the book becomes a tool to promote religion or the views of a sect. In stating that the "meager record" before the Court did not justify a conclusion that "the processes of secular and religious training are so intertwined that secular textbooks furnished to students by the public are in fact instrumental in the teaching of religion," Justice White does imply that the loan of a book which is non-sectarian within its covers but which is nevertheless put to a religious use would violate the Establishment Clause. Nevertheless, the Court in *Allen*, by not requiring screeners to inquire into the use to which a book proposed for loan will be put, apparently accepts the presumption that a book which is secular within its covers will be put to a secular use, and that a religious book will not be used within a parochial school in a manner that will "cure" it of an impermissible effect. Guidelines issued by the New York State Commissioner of Education under the Textbook Loan Law entirely abandon a "use" approach, requiring that review depend entirely on the content of the book; they thus prohibit extending the scope of review even when there is evidence of a religious use.

Whether one talks of religious and secular *books* or religious and secular *uses*, the assumption that workable distinctions between "secular" and "religious" can be made is highly questionable. The Supreme Court gave assurances that the secular/religious distinction was a workable one: "Absent evidence, we cannot assume that school authorities, who constantly face the same problem in selecting textbooks for use in the public schools, are unable to distinguish between secular and religious books. . . ." The Court, however, as emphasized by the dissenters, declined to discuss the standards which textbook reviewers must apply. Thus, the defining of a standard which describes permissible state aid, as well as the application of that standard, was delegated to the supposedly expert local school authorities.

No federal court has been squarely confronted with the problem of deciding whether a particular book is sectarian. The question has, however, been the central issue of numerous state court cases testing the validity of public school Bible reading. The review criteria suggested by these state cases are based on the following questions:

1. What is a religion for the purposes of first amendment book review?

2. Does the book, overtly or convertly, present religious tenets which are not universally held?

3. Does the presentation of these tenets within the book take the form of advocacy?

These three questions provide a framework for analyzing textbook review for purposes of the Establishment Clause.

A. *Defining Religion or Sect*

It is clear that any book favoring the views of one sect over another should be rejected. . . . The most difficult theoretical problems in attempting to define "where the secular ends and the sectarian begins" in textbook review arise in answering the preliminary question of what is a religion or religious sect. Would a text advocating the tenets of the League of Spiritual Discovery be classified as a secular or sectarian book? What is the difference between a religion and an ideology? Would a book placing capitalism or democracy or individualism at the center of a world view run afoul of the Establishment Clause? Would a textbook advocating black separatism as a tenet of the Black Muslim religion be treated differently from a textbook advocating black separatism as the political philosophy of a black nationalist group? Is morality ever separable from religion? If a moral view is historically rooted in a religion, can its advocacy within a textbook ever escape the charge of being religious? Whose definition of religion should be controlling? . . .

The Court clearly did not regard the review process as necessarily excluding nearly every book from the approved list, but it failed even to suggest any less severe standard. In practice, most reviewers have been concerned only about favoritism between Catholics and Protestants or among Catholics, Protestants and Jews. The reviewers show little or no concern about propagation of views shared by these three religions but not by other sects or by nonbelievers. Thus, the reviewers are using a test that is workable, in the sense that books are being supplied, but one that fails to meet articulated requirements of the Establishment Clause. Furthermore, our study indicates that the review process has failed effectively to apply to the textbooks submitted for approval even the standard of favoritism among Catholics, Protestants and Jews.

B. *Identifying Non-Universal Tenets*

Religious References. Identifying overt references to religious doctrines, events, or objects which are not universally shared requires knowledge of the subject matter of the textbook and a thorough knowledge of religious doctrines. This expertise is usually not to be found in the New York officials charged with textbook review. . . . There is no reason to assume that the identification of even overt sectarian references is being competently done when it is entrusted by this Law to officials without needed qualifications and with extensive other duties.

Moral Undertone. Religious beliefs can also be advanced in a textbook by a sectarian moral or ethical undertone. . . . Given the constraints on the New York reviewers—limited time and lack of special knowledge—it is impossible for their inspections of contents consistently to expose the impermissible undertones which may be present. . . .

Certainly a cleric is capable of authoring a non-sectarian textbook. However, religious authorship does tend to indicate a sectarian content: there is a likelihood of at least subconscious bias, and a possibility that the fact of clerical authorship indicates that the book was written and published in the hope of having a particular appeal to parochial schools. But the regulations under the Textbook Loan Law declare that the reviewers' decisions must depend "entirely on content"; authorship cannot be considered. . . .

The regulations are thus handicapping the reviewers by simultaneously requiring that the decisions be based only on content, and forbidding the use of a valid indicator of hidden elements of content. A system in which reviewers would be permitted to look to authorship as an indirect indicator of content would more consistently detect impermissible textbooks. . . .

Church endorsement is another "exterior" characteristic which is treated irrationally. The regulations impose the opposite rule from that on religious authorship. The "imprimatur" and "nihil obstat" are symbols of Catholic Church approval which appear on the back of the frontispiece of the approved textbook. This endorsement, acquired after voluntary submission of the book to the church by the publisher, attests that the book is not offensive to the church, and is recommended for use in parochial schools.

As with clerical authorship, these notations should be seen as indirect indicia of sectarian content. The publisher's gaining of the "imprimatur" indicates his interest in appealing to Catholic readers. . . . However, unlike clerical authorship and cover pictures, the "imprimatur" and "nihil obstat" are not themselves elements of sectarian content: obscurely located and probably not understood by most readers, the endorsement notations cannot significantly affect the readers' response to the content.

The interpretation of the Textbook Loan Law by the New York State Education Department, through an Advisory Opinion of Counsel, is that the requirement that books be non-sectarian "eliminates denominational editions and those carrying the 'imprimatur' or 'nihil obstat' of a religious authority." Following this interpretation, sixty-three percent (29) of the school boards replied that the presence of an "imprimatur" would cause a history textbook to be rejected, and the same number replied that the presence of an "imprimatur" would cause a mechanical drawing textbook to be rejected. . . .

Thus, as evidenced by the treatment of both clerical authorship and imprimaturs, the absence of any workable standard applicable to content drives the authorities to adopt absolute rules. And the absolute rules adopted do not rationally discriminate among textbooks on any standard of sectarianism.

C. *Advocacy*

In describing what makes a book sectarian, screeners indicate the importance of the advocacy of religious tenets:

> "Primarily statements where only one side of a topic is present."

> "Rather than the presence of specific information, the absence of material pointing out another point of view. . . ."

> "[A]ny substantial treatment of a religious topic from the viewpoint of an adherent or advocate without presentation of other views."

Consistent replies reveal that sectarian references are defined as those religious references which are not objective or are not presented objectively within the book. An unobjective treatment is seen as advocacy.

A "secular" textbook is permitted to refer to religious events, and even to religious doctrine; but in each case the reference must be of a nature and in a context which eliminates any effect of promoting one religion over another, or of promoting religion over non-religion. Where the religious reference is not clearly called for by the context in which it appears, it must be balanced by references of equal emphasis to opposing beliefs or practices held by other religions or by the non-religious. Where the reference is justified by the context of the material being presented, compensating references may not be necessary, but the reference must be factual and in no greater or less detail than called for by the context. If the religious references appear in literary, artistic or musical works, the textbook will qualify as nonsectarian where the selections with religious themes, because of their power as art, do not have a primarily religious effect.

It is immediately apparent that decisions concerning advocacy will be heavily influenced by the personal bias of the reviewer. Furthermore, these distinctions are impossible without the experienced and knowledgeable reviewers which the Court postulated in *Allen*.

As has been asserted in discussions above, the officials charged with responsibility for review under the Textbook Loan Law generally lack the knowledge and expertise needed for determining sectarianism.

. . .

NOTES AND QUESTIONS

1. With which opinion of Everson and Board of Education v. Allen do you agree? Why?

2. Are the Everson and Allen cases fully consistent? Was the view of the court in Everson necessarily founded on the facts of that case that administered public funds paid on a non-discriminatory basis to all citizens who sent their children to school via public transportation systems owned and operated by public authorities? If so, is the analogous situation presented in Allen? Why or why not?

3. It is possible that a text book loan program, like the one approved in Bd of Ed. v. Allen, would be unconstitutional under a state's constitution. See, Dickman v. School Dist., 232 Or. 238, 366 P.2d 533 (1961) cert. den. 371 U.S. 823,

4. Do Everson and Allen authorize the payment of tax funds by public officials to hospitals run by religious orders so long as those hospitals perform a "public welfare" function?

5. Under Everson and Allen, could the federal government or a state pay tuition for students enrolled in institutions of higher education, including those enrolled in Schools of Theology?

6. Under Everson and Allen, could the federal government allow a full income tax deduction to all persons who paid tuition, whether it be to public or non-profit private schools, common or higher education?

7. If a text book loan program can comply with the First Amendment, could a teacher loan program? Are there any constitutional differences between making available bussing, textbooks or teachers for parochial school students? If a teacher loan program can comply with the First Amendment, could a program that paid parochial school salaries or provided funds for parochial school construction?

———

LEMON v. KURTZMAN

Supreme Court of the United States, 1971.
403 U.S. 602, 91 S.Ct. 2105, 29 L.Ed.2d 745,
rehearing denied 404 U.S. 876, 92 S.Ct. 24, 30 L.Ed.2d 123.

Mr. Chief Justice BURGER delivered the opinion of the Court.

These two appeals raise questions as to Pennsylvania and Rhode Island statutes providing state aid to church-related elementary and secondary schools. Both statutes are challenged as violative of the Establishment and Free Exercise Clauses of the First Amendment and the Due Process Clause of the Fourteenth Amendment. . . .

The Rhode Island Statute

The Rhode Island Salary Supplement Act was enacted in 1969. It rests on the legislative finding that the quality of education available in nonpublic elementary schools has been jeopardized by the rapidly rising salaries needed to attract competent and dedicated teachers. The Act authorizes state officials to supplement the salaries of teachers of secular subjects in nonpublic elementary schools by paying directly to a teacher an amount not in excess of 15% of his current annual salary. As supplemented, however, a nonpublic school teacher's salary cannot exceed the maximum paid to teachers in the State's public schools, and the recipient must be certified by the state board of education in substantially the same manner as public school teachers.

In order to be eligible for the Rhode Island salary supplement, the recipient must teach in a nonpublic school at which the average per-pupil expenditure on secular education is less than the average in the State's public schools during a specified period. Appellant State Commissioner of Education also requires eligible schools to submit financial data. If this information indicates a per-pupil expenditure in excess of the statutory limitation, the records of the school in question must be examined in order to assess how much of the expenditure is attributable to secular education and how much to religious activity.

The Act also requires that teachers eligible for salary supplements must teach only those subjects that are offered in the State's public schools. They must use "only teaching materials which are used in the public schools." Finally, any teacher applying for a salary supplement must first agree in writing "not to teach a course in religion for so long as or during such time as he or she receives any salary supplements" under the Act. . . .

The Pennsylvania Statute

Pennsylvania has adopted a program that has some but not all of the features of the Rhode Island program. The Pennsylvania Nonpublic Elementary and Secondary Education Act was passed in 1968 in response to a crisis that the Pennsylvania Legislature found existed in the State's nonpublic schools due to rapidly rising costs. The statute affirmatively reflects the legislative conclusion that the State's educational goals could appropriately be fulfilled by government support of "those purely secular educational objectives achieved through nonpublic education. . . ."

The statute authorizes appellee state Superintendent of Public Instruction to "purchase" specified "secular educational services" from nonpublic schools. Under the "contracts" authorized by the statute, the State directly reimburses nonpublic schools solely for their actual expenditures for teachers' salaries, textbooks, and instructional materials. A school seeking reimbursement must maintain prescribed accounting procedures that identify the "separate" cost of the "secular educational services." These accounts are subject to state audit. The funds for this program were originally derived from a new tax on horse and harness racing, but the Act is now financed by a portion of the state tax on cigarettes.

There are several significant statutory restrictions on state aid. Reimbursement is limited to courses "presented in the curricula of the public schools." It is further limited "solely" to courses in the following "secular" subjects: mathematics, modern foreign languages, physical science, and physical education. Textbooks and instructional materials included in the program must be approved by the state Superintendent of Public Instruction. Finally, the statute prohibits reimbursement for any course that contains "any subject matter expressing religious teaching, or the morals or forms of worship of any sect."   .   .   .

II

In Everson   .   .   .   Mr. Justice Black, writing for the majority, suggested that the decision carried to "the verge" of forbidden territory under the Religion Clauses.   .   .   .   Candor compels acknowledgment, moreover, that we can only dimly perceive the lines of demarcation in this extraordinarily sensitive area of constitutional law.   .   .   .

Every analysis in this area must begin with consideration of the cumulative criteria developed by the Court over many years. Three such tests may be gleaned from our cases. First, the statute must have a secular legislative purpose; second, its principal or primary effect must be one that neither advances nor inhibits religion,   .   .   . finally, the statute must not foster "an excessive government entanglement with religion."   .   .   .

Inquiry into the legislative purposes of the Pennsylvania and Rhode Island statutes affords no basis for a conclusion that the legislative intent was to advance religion.   .   .   .   A State always has a legitimate concern for maintaining minimum standards in all schools it allows to operate. As in Allen, we find nothing here that undermines the stated legislative intent; it must therefore be accorded appropriate deference.   .   .   .

.   .   .   We need not decide whether these legislative precautions restrict the principal or primary effect of the programs to the point where they do not offend the Religion Clauses, for we conclude that the cumulative impact of the entire relationship arising under the statutes in each State involves excessive entanglement between government and religion.   .   .   .

Our prior holdings do not call for total separation between church and state; total separation is not possible in an absolute sense. Some relationship between government and religious organizations is inevitable. . . .

In order to determine whether the government entanglement with religion is excessive, we must examine the character and purposes of the institutions that are benefited, the nature of the aid that the State provides, and the resulting relationship between the government and the religious authority. . . . Here we find that both statutes foster an impermissible degree of entanglement. . . .

(a) *Rhode Island program*

The District Court made extensive findings on the grave potential for excessive entanglement that inheres in the religious character and purpose of the Roman Catholic elementary schools of Rhode Island, to date the sole beneficiaries of the Rhode Island Salary Supplement Act.

The church schools involved in the program are located close to parish churches. This understandably permits convenient access for religious exercises since instruction in faith and morals is part of the total educational process. The school buildings contain identifying religious symbols such as crosses on the exterior and crucifixes, and religious paintings and statutes either in the classrooms or hallways. Although only approximately 30 minutes a day are devoted to direct religious instruction, there are religiously oriented extracurricular activities. Approximately two-thirds of the teachers in these schools are nuns of various religious orders. Their dedicated efforts provide an atmosphere in which religious instruction and religious vocations are natural and proper parts of life in such schools. Indeed, as the District Court found, the role of teaching nuns in enhancing the religious atmosphere has led the parochial school authorities to attempt to maintain a one-to-one ratio between nuns and lay teachers in all schools rather than to permit some to be staffed almost entirely by lay teachers.

On the basis of these findings the District Court concluded that the parochial schools constituted "an integral part of the religious mission of the Catholic Church." The various characteristics of the schools make them "a powerful vehicle for transmitting the Catholic faith to the next generation." This process of inculcating religious doctrine is, of course, enhanced by the impressionable age of the pupils, in primary schools particularly. In short, parochial schools involve substantial religious activity and purpose.

The substantial religious character of these church-related schools gives rise to entangling church-state relationships of the kind the Religion Clauses sought to avoid. . . .

The dangers and corresponding entanglements are enhanced by the particular form of aid that the Rhode Island Act provides. Our decisions from Everson to Allen have permitted the States to provide church-related schools with secular, neutral, or nonideological services, facilities, or materials.   Bus transportation, school lunches, public health services, and secular textbooks supplied in common to all students were not thought to offend the Establishment Clause. We note that the dissenters in Allen seemed chiefly concerned with the pragmatic difficulties involved in ensuring the truly secular content of the textbooks provided at state expense.

In Allen the Court refused to make assumptions, on a meager record, about the religious content of the textbooks that the State would be asked to provide. We cannot, however, refuse here to recognize that teachers have a substantially different ideological character from books. In terms of potential for involving some aspect of faith or morals in secular subjects, a textbook's content is ascertainable, but a teacher's handling of a subject is not. We cannot ignore the danger that a teacher under religious control and discipline poses to the separation of the religious from the purely secular aspects of precollege education. The conflict of functions inheres in the situation.

In our view the record shows there dangers are present to a substantial degree. The Rhode Island Roman Catholic elementary schools are under the general supervision of the Bishop of Providence and his appointed representative, the Diocesan Superintendent of Schools. In most cases, each individual parish, however, assumes the ultimate financial responsibility for the school, with the parish priest authorizing the allocation of parish funds. With only two exceptions, school principals are nuns appointed either by the Superintendent or the Mother Provincial of the order whose members staff the school. By 1969 lay teachers constituted more than a third of all teachers in the parochial elementary schools, and their number is growing. They are first interviewed by the superintendent's office and then by the school principal. The contracts are signed by the parish priest, and he retains some discretion in negotiating salary levels. Religious authority necessarily pervades the school system.

The schools are governed by the standards set forth in a "Handbook of School Regulations," which has the force of synodal law in the diocese. It emphasizes the role and importance of the teacher in parochial schools: "The prime factor for the success or the failure of the school is the spirit and personality, as well as the professional competency, of the teacher. . . ." The Handbook also states that "Religious formation is not confined to formal courses; nor is it restricted to a single subject area." Finally, the Handbook advises teachers to stimulate interest in religious vocations and missionary work. Given the mission of the church school, these instructions are consistent and logical. . . .

We need not and do not assume that teachers in parochial schools will be guilty of bad faith or any conscious design to evade the limitations imposed by the statute and the First Amendment. We simply recognize that a dedicated religious person, teaching in a school affiliated with his or her faith and operated to inculcate its tenets, will inevitably experience great difficulty in remaining religiously neutral. Doctrines and faith are not inculcated or advanced by neutrals. With the best of intentions such a teacher would find it hard to make a total separation between secular teaching and religious doctrine. . . .

A comprehensive, discriminating, and continuing state surveillance will inevitably be required to ensure that these restrictions are obeyed and the First Amendment otherwise respected. Unlike a book, a teacher cannot be inspected once so as to determine the extent and intent of his or her personal beliefs and subjective acceptance of the limitations imposed by the First Amendment. These prophylactic contacts will involve excessive and enduring entanglement between state and church.

There is another area of entanglement in the Rhode Island program that gives concern. The statute excludes teachers employed by nonpublic schools whose average per-pupil expenditures on secular education equal or exceed the comparable figures for public schools. In the event that the total expenditures of an otherwise eligible school exceed this norm, the program requires the government to examine the school's records in order to determine how much of the total expenditures is attributable to secular education and how much to religious activity. This kind of state inspection and evaluation of the religious content of a religious organization is fraught with the sort of entanglement that the Constitution forbids. It is a relationship pregnant with dangers of excessive government direction of church schools and hence of churches. The Court noted "the hazards of government supporting churches" . . ., and we cannot ignore here the danger that pervasive modern governmental power will ultimately intrude on religion and thus conflict with the Religion Clauses.

(b) *Pennsylvania program*

The Pennsylvania statute also provides state aid to church-related schools for teachers' salaries. The complaint describes an educational system that is very similar to the one existing in Rhode Island. According to the allegations, the church-related elementary and secondary schools are controlled by religious organizations, have the purpose of propagating and promoting a particular religious faith, and conduct their operations to fulfill that purpose. Since this complaint was dismissed for failure to state a claim for relief, we must accept these allegations as true for purposes of our review.

As we noted earlier, the very restrictions and surveillance necessary to ensure that teachers play a strictly nonideological role give rise to entanglements between church and state. The Pennsylvania statute, like that of Rhode Island, fosters this kind of relationship. Reimbursement is not only limited to courses offered in the public schools and materials approved by state officials, but the statute excludes "any subject matter expressing religious teaching, or the morals or forms of worship of any sect." In addition, schools seeking reimbursement must maintain accounting procedures that require the State to establish the cost of the secular as distinguished from the religious instruction.

The Pennsylvania statute, moreover, has the further defect of providing state financial aid directly to the church-related school. This factor distinguishes both Everson and Allen, for in both those cases the Court was careful to point out that state aid was provided to the student and his parents—not to the church-related school. . . .
. . ., the Court warned of the dangers of direct payments to religious organizations:

> "Obviously a direct money subsidy would be a relationship pregnant with involvement and, as with most governmental grant programs, could encompass sustained and detailed administrative relationships for enforcement of statutory or administrative standards. . . ."

The history of government grants of a continuing cash subsidy indicates that such programs have almost always been accompanied by varying measures of control and surveillance. The government cash grants before us now provide no basis for predicting that comprehensive measures of surveillance and controls will not follow. In particular the government's post-audit power to inspect and evaluate a church-related school's financial records and to determine which expenditures are religious and which are secular creates an intimate and continuing relationship between church and state.

A broader base of entanglement of yet a different character is presented by the divisive political potential of these state programs. In a community where such a large number of pupils are served by church-related schools, it can be assumed that state assistance will entail considerable political activity. Partisans of parochial schools, understandably concerned with rising costs and sincerely dedicated to both the religious and secular educational missions of their schools, will inevitably champion this cause and promote political action to achieve their goals. Those who oppose state aid, whether for constitutional, religious, or fiscal reasons, will inevitably respond and employ all of the usual political campaign techniques to prevail. Candidates will be forced to declare and voters to choose. It would be unrealistic to ignore the fact that many people confronted with issues of this kind will find their votes aligned with their faith.

Ordinarily political debate and division, however vigorous or even partisan, are normal and healthy manifestations of our democratic system of government, but political division along religious lines was one of the principal evils against which the First Amendment was intended to protect. .   .   .   The potential divisiveness of such conflict is a threat to the normal political process. .   .   .   To have States or communities divide on the issues presented by state aid to parochial schools would tend to confuse and obscure other issues of great urgency.   We have an expanding array of vexing issues, local and national, domestic and international, to debate and divide on. It conflicts with our whole history and tradition to permit questions of the Religion Clauses to assume such importance in our legislatures and in our elections that they could divert attention from the myriad issues and problems that confront every level of government.   The highways of church and state relationships are not likely to be one-way streets, and the Constitution's authors sought to protect religious worship from the pervasive power of government.   The history of many countries attests to the hazards of religion's intruding into the political arena or of political power intruding into the legitimate and free exercise of religious belief. .   .   .

The potential for political divisiveness related to religious belief and practice is aggravated in these two statutory programs by the need for continuing annual appropriations and the likelihood of larger and larger demands as costs and populations grow. .   .   .

In Walz it was argued that a tax exemption for places of religious worship would prove to be the first step in an inevitable progression leading to the establishment of state churches and state religion.   That claim could not stand up against more than 200 years of virtually universal practice imbedded in our colonial experience and continuing into the present.

The progression argument, however, is more persuasive here. We have no long history of state aid to church-related educational institutions comparable to 200 years of tax exemption for churches. Indeed, the state programs before us today represent something of an innovation.   We have already noted that modern governmental pro-grams have self-perpetuating and self-expanding propensities.   These internal pressures are only enhanced when the schemes involve in-stitutions whose legitimate needs are growing and whose interests have substantial political support.   Nor can we fail to see that in constitutional adjudication some steps, which when taken were thought to approach "the verge," have become the platform for yet further steps.   A certain momentum develops in constitutional theory and it can be a "downhill thrust" easily set in motion but difficult to retard or stop.   Development by momentum is not invariably bad; indeed, it is the way the common law has grown, but it is a force to be recog-nized and reckoned with.   The dangers are increased by the difficulty of perceiving in advance exactly where the "verge" of the precipice lies.   As well as constituting an independent evil against which the

Religion Clauses were intended to protect, involvement or entanglement between government and religion serves as a warning signal.

Finally, nothing we have said can be construed to disparage the role of church-related elementary and secondary schools in our national life.   Their contribution has been and is enormous.   Nor do we ignore their economic plight in a period of rising costs and expanding need.   Taxpayers generally have been spared vast sums by the maintenance of these educational institutions by religious organizations, largely by the gifts of faithful adherents.

The merit and benefits of these schools, however, are not the issue before us in these cases.   The sole question is whether state aid to these schools can be squared with the dictates of the Religion Clauses.   Under our system the choice has been made that government is to be entirely excluded from the area of religious instruction and churches excluded from the affairs of government.   The Constitution decrees that religion must be a private matter for the individual, the family, and the institutions of private choice, and that while some involvement and entanglement are inevitable, lines must be drawn. . . .

Mr. Justice DOUGLAS, whom Mr. Justice BLACK joins, concurring.

The analysis of the constitutional objections to these two state systems of grants to parochial or sectarian schools must start with the admitted and obvious fact that the raison d'etre of parochial schools is the propagation of a religious faith.   They also teach secular subjects; but they came into existence in this country because Protestant groups were perverting the public schools by using them to propagate their faith.   The Catholics naturally rebelled.   If schools were to be used to propagate a particular creed or religion, then Catholic ideals should also be served.   Hence the advent of parochial schools.

By 1840 there were 200 Catholic parish schools in the United States.   By 1964 there were 60 times as many.   Today 57% of the 9,000 Catholic parishes in the country have their church schools. "[E]very diocesan chancery has its school department, and it enjoys a primacy of status."   The parish schools indeed consume 40% to 65% of the parish's total income.   The parish is so "school centered" that "[t]he school almost becomes the very reason for being."

Early in the 19th century the Protestants obtained control of the New York school system and used it to promote reading and teaching of the Scriptures as revealed in the King James version of the Bible. The contests between Protestants and Catholics, often erupting into violence including the burning of Catholic churches, are a twice-told tale; the Know-Nothing Party, which included in its platform "daily Bible reading in the schools," carried three States in 1854—Massachusetts, Pennsylvania, and Delaware. Parochial schools grew, but not Catholic schools alone. Other dissenting sects established their own schools—Lutherans, Methodists, Presbyterians, and others. But the major force in shaping the pattern of education in this country was the conflict between Protestants and Catholics. The Catholics logically argued that a public school was sectarian when it taught the King James version of the Bible. They therefore wanted it removed from the public schools; and in time they tried to get public funds for their own parochial schools. . . .

The story of conflict and dissension is long and well known. The result was a state of so-called equilibrium where religious instruction was eliminated from public schools and the use of public funds to support religious schools was deemed to be banned.

But the hydraulic pressures created by political forces and by economic stress were great and they began to change the situation. Laws were passed—state and federal—that dispensed public funds to sustain religious schools and the plea was always in the educational frame of reference: education in all sectors was needed, from languages to calculus to nuclear physics. And it was forcefully argued that a linguist or mathematician or physicist trained in religious schools was just as competent as one trained in secular schools.

And so we have gradually edged into a situation where vast amounts of public funds are supplied each year to sectarian schools.

And the argument is made that the private parochial school system takes about $9 billion a year off the back of government—as if that were enough to justify violating the Establishment Clause.

While the evolution of the public school system in this country marked an escape from denominational control and was therefore admirable as seen through the eyes of those who think like Madison and Jefferson, it has disadvantages. The main one is that a state system may attempt to mold all students alike according to the views of the dominant group and to discourage the emergence of individual idiosyncrasies.

Sectarian education, however, does not remedy that condition. The advantages of sectarian education relate solely to religious or doctrinal matters. They give the church the opportunity to indoctrinate its creed delicately and indirectly, or massively through doctrinal courses. . . .

. . . we have never faced, until recently, the problem of policing sectarian schools. Any surveillance to date has been minor and has related only to the consistently unchallenged matters of accreditation of the sectarian school in the State's school system.

The Rhode Island Act allows a supplementary salary to a teacher in a sectarian school if he or she "does not teach a course in religion."

The Pennsylvania Act provides for state financing of instruction in mathematics, modern foreign languages, physical science, and physical education, provided that the instruction in those courses "shall not include any subject matter expressing religious teaching, or the morals or forms of worship of any sect."

Public financial support of parochial schools puts those schools under disabilities with which they were not previously burdened. For .   .   . governmental activities relating to schools "must be exercised consistently with federal constitutional requirements."
.   .   .

Sectarian instruction in which, of course, a State may not indulge, can take place in a course on Shakespeare or in one on mathematics. No matter what the curriculum offers, the question is, what is *taught*? We deal not with evil teachers but with zealous ones who may use any opportunity to indoctrinate a class.

It is well known that everything taught in most parochial schools is taught with the ultimate goal of religious education in mind.   .   .   .

One can imagine what a religious zealot, as contrasted to a civil libertarian, can do with the Reformation or with the Inquisition. Much history can be given the gloss of a particular religion. I would think that policing these grants to detect sectarian instruction would be insufferable to religious partisans and would breed division and dissension between church and state.   .   .   .

.   .   .   In the present cases we deal with the totality of instruction destined to be sectarian, at least in part, if the religious character of the school is to be maintained. A school which operates to commingle religion with other instruction plainly cannot completely secularize its instruction. Parochial schools, in large measure, do not accept the assumption that secular subjects should be unrelated to religious teaching.

Lemon [the Pennsylvania case] involves a state statute that prescribes that courses in mathematics, modern foreign languages, physical science, and physical education "shall not include any subject matter expressing religious teaching, or the morals or forms of worship of any sect." The subtleties involved in applying this standard are obvious. It places the State astride a sectarian school and gives it power to dictate what is or is not secular, what is or is not religious. I can think of no more disrupting influence apt to promote rancor and ill-will between church and state than this kind of surveillance and control. They are the very opposite of the "moderation and harmony" between church and state which Madison thought was the aim and purpose of the Establishment Clause.

The DiCenso cases have all the vices which are in Lemon, because the supplementary salary payable to the teacher is conditioned on his or her not teaching "a course in religion."

Moreover, the DiCenso cases reveal another, but related, knotty problem presented when church and state launch one of these educational programs. The Bishop of Rhode Island has a Handbook of School Regulations for the Diocese of Providence.

The school board supervises "the education, both spiritual and secular, in the parochial schools and diocesan high schools."

The superintendent is an agent of the bishop and he interprets and makes "effective state and diocesan educational directives."

The pastors visit the schools and "give their assistance in promoting spiritual and intellectual discipline."

Community supervisors "assist the teacher in the problems of instruction." .   .   .

These are only highlights of the handbook. But they indicate how pervasive is the religious control over the school and how remote this type of school is from the secular school. Public funds supporting that structure are used to perpetuate a doctrine and creed in innumerable and in pervasive ways. Those who man these schools are good people, zealous people, dedicated people. But they are dedicated to ideas that the Framers of our Constitution placed beyond the reach of government.

If the government closed its eyes to the manner in which these grants are actually used it would be allowing public funds to promote sectarian education. If it did not close its eyes but undertook the surveillance needed, it would, I fear, intermeddle in parochial affairs in a way that would breed only rancor and dissension.

We have announced over and over again that the use of taxpayers' money to support parochial schools violates the First Amendment, applicable to the States by virtue of the Fourteenth. .   .   .

Yet in spite of this long and consistent history there are those who have the courage to announce that a State may nonetheless finance the *secular* part of a sectarian school's educational program. That, however, makes a grave constitutional decision turn merely on cost accounting and bookkeeping entries. A history class, a literature class, or a science class in a parochial school is not a separate institute; it is part of the organic whole which the State subsidizes. The funds are used in these cases to pay or help pay the salaries of teachers in parochial schools; and the presence of teachers is critical to the essential purpose of the parochial school, viz., to advance the religious endeavors of the particular church. It matters not that the teacher receiving taxpayers' money only teaches religion a fraction of the time. Nor does it matter that he or she teaches no religion. The school is an organism living on one budget. What the taxpayers give for salaries of those who teach only the humanities or science without any trace of proseletyzing enables the school to use all of its own funds for religious training. As Judge Coffin said, 316 F.Supp.

112, 120, we would be blind to realities if we let "sophisticated book-keeping" sanction "almost total subsidy of a religious institution by assigning the bulk of the institution's expenses to 'secular' activities." And sophisticated attempts to avoid the Constitution are just as invalid as simple-minded ones. . . .

In my view the taxpayers' forced contribution to the parochial schools in the present cases violates the First Amendment.

Mr. Justice BRENNAN. . . .

I continue to adhere to the view that to give concrete meaning to the Establishment Clause "the line we must draw between the permissible and the impermissible is one which accords with history and faithfully reflects the understanding of the Founding Fathers. It is a line which the Court has consistently sought to mark in its decisions expounding the religious guarantees of the First Amendment. What the Framers meant to foreclose, and what our decisions under the Establishment Clause have forbidden, are those involvements of religious with secular institutions which (a) serve the essentially religious activities of religious institutions; (b) employ the organs of government for essentially religious purposes; or (c) use essentially religious means to serve governmental ends, where secular means would suffice. When the secular and religious institutions become involved in such a manner, there inhere in the relationship precisely those dangers—as much to church as to state—which the Framers feared would subvert religious liberty and the strength of a system of secular government." . . .

The common feature of all three statutes before us is the provision of a direct subsidy from public funds for activities carried on by sectarian educational institutions. . . .

The statutory schemes before us, however, have features not present in either the Everson or Allen schemes. For example, the reimbursement or the loan of books ended government involvement in Everson and Allen. In contrast each of the schemes here exacts a promise in some form that the subsidy will not be used to finance courses in religious subjects—promises that must be and are policed to assure compliance. Again, although the federal subsidy, similar to the Everson and Allen subsidies, is available to both public and nonpublic colleges and universities, the Rhode Island and Pennsylvania subsidies are restricted to nonpublic schools, and for practical purposes to Roman Catholic parochial schools. These and other features I shall mention mean for me that Everson and Allen do not control these cases. Rather, the history of public subsidy of sectarian schools, and the purposes and operation of these particular statutes must be examined to determine whether the statutes breach the Establishment Clause. . . .

Our opinion in Allen recognized that sectarian schools provide both a secular and a sectarian education. . . .

. . . I do not read Pierce or Allen as supporting the proposition that public subsidy of sectarian institution's secular training is permissible state involvement. I read them as supporting the proposition that as an identifiable set of skills and an identifiable quantum of knowledge, secular education may be effectively provided either in the religious context of parochial schools, or outside the context of religion in public schools. The State's interest in secular education may be defined broadly as an interest in ensuring that all children within its boundaries acquire a minimum level of competency in certain skills, such as reading, writing, and arithmetic, as well as a minimum amount of information and knowledge in certain subjects such as history, geography, science, literature, and law. Without such skills and knowledge, an individual will be at a severe disadvantage both in participating in democratic self-government and in earning a living in a modern industrial economy. But the State has no proper interest in prescribing the no precise forum in which such skills and knowledge are learned since acquisition of this secular education is neither incompatible with religious learning, nor is it inconsistent with or inimical to religious precepts.

When the same secular educational process occurs in both public and sectarian schools, Allen held that the State could provide secular textbooks for use in that process to students in both public and sectarian schools. Of course, the State could not provide textbooks giving religious instruction. But since the textbooks involved in Allen would, at least in theory, be limited to secular education, no aid to sectarian instruction was involved.

More important, since the textbooks in Allen had been previously provided by the parents, and not the schools, . . . no aid to the institution was involved. Rather, as in the case of the bus transportation in Everson, the general program of providing all children in the State with free secular textbooks assisted all parents in schooling their children. And as in Everson, there was undoubtedly the possibility that some parents might not have been able to exercise their constitutional right to send their children to parochial school if the parents were compelled themselves to pay for textbooks. However, as my Brother Black wrote for the Court in Everson, "[C]utting off church schools from these [general] services, so separate and so indisputably marked off from the religious function, would make it far more difficult for the schools to operate. But such is obviously not the purpose of the First Amendment. That Amendment requires the state to be a neutral in its relations with groups of religious believers and non-believers; it does not require the state to be their adversary. State power is no more to be used so as to handicap religions than it is to favor them." . . .

Allen, in my view, simply sustained a statute in which the State was "neutral in its relations with groups of religious believers and nonbelievers. The only context in which the Court in Allen employed the distinction between secular and religious in a parochial school was to reach its conclusion that the textbooks that the State was providing could and would be secular. The present cases, however, involve direct subsidies of tax monies to the schools themselves and we cannot blink the fact that the secular education those schools provide goes hand in hand with the religious mission that is the only reason for the schools' existence. Within the institution, the two are inextricably intertwined. . . .

I conclude that, in using sectarian institutions to further goals in secular education, the three statutes do violence to the principle that "government may not employ religious means to serve secular interests, however legitimate they may be, at least without the clearest demonstration that nonreligious means will not suffice." . . .

I, therefore, agree that the two state statutes that focus primarily on providing public funds to sectarian schools are unconstitutional. . . .

Mr. Justice WHITE, concurring. . . .

. . ., while the decision of the Court is legitimate, it is surely quite wrong in overturning the Pennsylvania and Rhode Island statutes on the ground that they amount to an establishment of religion forbidden by the First Amendment.

No one in these cases questions the constitutional right of parents to satisfy their state-imposed obligation to educate their children by sending them to private schools, sectarian or otherwise, as long as those schools meet minimum standards established for secular instruction. The States are not only permitted, but required by the Constitution, to free students attending private schools from any public school attendance obligation. Pierce v. Society of Sisters. . . . The States may also furnish transportation for students, Everson, . . . and books for teaching secular subjects to students attending parochial and other private as well as public schools, Board of Education v. Allen . . . ; we have also upheld arrangements whereby students are released from public school classes so that they may attend religious instruction. Zorach v. Clauson, . . .

Our prior cases have recognized the dual role of parochial schools in American society: they perform both religious and secular functions. . . . Our cases also recognize that legislation having a secular purpose and extending governmental assistance to sectarian schools in the performance of their secular functions does not constitute "law[s] respecting an establishment of religion" forbidden by the First Amendment merely because a secular program may incidentally benefit a church in fulfilling its religious mission. That religion may indirectly benefit from governmental aid to the secular activities of churches does not convert that aid into an impermissible establishment of religion. . . .

It is enough for me that the States . . . are financing a separable secular function of overriding importance in order to sustain the legislation here challenged. That religion and private interests other than education may substantially benefit does not convert these laws into impermissible establishments of religion. . . .

The Court . . . creates an insoluable paradox for the State and the parochial schools. The State cannot finance secular instruction if it permits religion to be taught in the same classroom; but if it exacts a promise that religion not be so taught—a promise the school and its teachers are quite willing and on this record able to give—and enforces it, it is then entangled in the "no entanglement" aspect of the Court's Establishment Clause jurisprudence. . . .

NOTES AND QUESTIONS

1. Carefully examine the above opinions. In what way, or ways, do they agree or disagree? Are the differing consequences to be drawn from each opinion important differences? Why or why not? With which opinion do you agree? Why? Are Mr. Justices Douglas's and Brennan's opinions consistent with Bd. of Ed. v. Allen? Is the majority opinion consistent with Allen? After Lemon v. Kurtzman what is the proper reading of Everson and Allen? Write out a statement of constitutional law that reconciles the three cases.

2. Compare Tilton v. Richardson, 403 U.S. 672, 91 S.Ct. 2091, 29 L.Ed.2d 790 (1971).

COMMITTEE FOR PUBLIC EDUCATION v. NYQUIST

Supreme Court of the United States, 1973.
413 U.S. 756, 93 S.Ct. 2955, 37 L.Ed.2d 948.

LEVITT v. COMMITTEE FOR PUBLIC EDUCATION

Supreme Court of the United States, 1973.
413 U.S. 472, 93 S.Ct. 2814, 37 L.Ed.2d 736.

SLOAN v. LEMON

Supreme Court of the United States, 1973.
413 U.S. 825, 93 S.Ct. 2982, 37 L.Ed.2d 939.

On June 25, 1973, the Supreme Court decided these three cases, summarized below. Each of them concern a state's attempt to aid private and/or parochial schools. A fourth case, Hunt v. McNair, 413 U.S. 734, 93 S.Ct. 2868, 37 L.Ed.2d 923 (1973), not set forth here, dealt with South Carolina's Educational Facilities Act which established a state authority to aid institutions of higher learning in construction, financing and refinancing projects by the issuance of revenue bonds. The only advantage obtained by the institution was that interest on bonds was not subject to income taxation and therefore the bonds carried a lower interest rate and were easier to sell.

In COMMITTEE FOR PUBLIC EDUCATION v. NYQUIST, the Supreme Court, in an Opinion by Mr. Justice Powell, struck down as a violation of the establishment clause three statutes of the State of New York each of which had a "secular legislative purpose"; collectively they tried to provide "financial assistance, in several ways, to nonpublic elementary and secondary schools." The first statute sought to establish a program whereby the state would provide grants of money to all nonprofit schools that served "a high concentration of pupils from low income families," and the tax money was to be used for the "maintenance and repair" of "school facilities and equipment to insure the health, welfare and safety of enrolled pupils." Schools falling into this category "are entitled to receive a grant of $30 per pupil per year, or $40 per pupil per year if the facilities are more than 25 years old [but] in no event may the grant to nonpublic qualifying schools exceed 50%" of "the average per-pupil cost for equivalent maintenance and repair services in the public schools."

"So long as expenditures do not exceed 50% of comparable expenses in the public school system, it is possible for a sectarian elementary or secondary school to finance its entire 'maintenance and repair' budget from state tax-raised funds. No attempt is made to restrict payments to those expenditures related to the upkeep of facilities used exclusively for secular purposes, nor do we think it possible within the context of these religion-oriented institutions to impose such restrictions. . . . it simply cannot be denied that this section has a primary effect that advances religion in that it subsidizes directly the religious activities of sectarian elementary and secondary schools." "The legislature's supposition might have been that at least 50% of the ordinary public school maintenance and repair budget would be devoted to purely secular facility upkeep in sectarian schools. The shortest answer to this argument is that the statute itself allows, as a ceiling, grants satisfying the entire 'amount of expenditures for maintenance and repair of such school' providing only that it is neither more than $30 or $40 per pupil nor more than 50% of the comparable public school expenditures. Quite apart from the language of the statute, our cases make clear that a mere statistical judgment will not suffice as a guarantee that state funds will not be used to finance religious education." "It takes little imagination to perceive the extent to which States might openly subsidize parochial schools under such a loose standard of scrutiny."

The second New York statute was "designed to allow direct, unrestricted grants of $50 to $100 per child (but no more than 50% of tuition actually paid) as reimbursement to parents in low-income brackets who send their children to nonpublic schools." This statute also violated the "effect" test: The "effect of the aid is unmistakably to provide desired financial support for nonpublic, sectarian institutions." The Opinion states that "There can be no question that these grants could not, consistently with the Establishment Clause, be given directly to sectarian schools, since they would suffer from the same deficiency that renders invalid the grants for maintenance and repair. [The Allen and Everson cases] make clear that, far from providing a per se immunity from examination of the substance of the State's program, the fact that aid is disbursed to parents rather than to the schools is only one among many factors to be considered." "The tuition grants here [as distinguished from Everson and Allen have no statutory restrictions] to guarantee the separation between secular and religious educational functions and to ensure that State financial aid supports only the former. Lemon v. Kurtzman . . . [38]

"Finally, the State argues that its program of tuition grants should survive scrutiny because it is designed to promote the free exercise of religion. The State notes that only 'low-income parents' are aided by this law, and without state assistance their right to have their children educated in a religious environment 'is diminished or even denied.' [Nevertheless, in the attempt by the State] to enhance the opportunities of the poor to choose between public and nonpublic education, the State has taken a step which can only be regarded as one 'advancing' religion."

The third New York statute involved the state's income tax and was "designed to yield a predetermined amount of tax 'forgiveness' " to parents of children enrolled in nonpublic schools who had an adjusted gross income less than $25,000, but who did not qualify for the tuition reimbursement because they earned more than $5,000. The Court said that "In practical terms there would appear to be little

[38] *Allen* and *Everson* differ from the present case in a second important respect. In both cases the class of beneficiaries included *all* school children, those in public as well as those in private schools. * * * We do not agree with the suggestion in the dissent of The Chief Justice that tuition grants are an analogous endeavor to provide comparable benefits to all parents of school children whether enrolled in public or nonpublic schools. The grants to parents of private school children are given in addition to the right that they have to send their children to public schools "totally at state expense." And in any event, the argument proves too much, for it would also provide a basis for approving through tuition grants the *complete subsidization* of all religious schools on the ground that such action is necessary if the State is fully to equalize the position of parents who elect such schools—a result wholly at variance with the Establishment Clause.

Because of the manner in which we have resolved the tuition-grant issue, we need not decide whether the significantly religious character of the statute's beneficiaries might differentiate the present case from a case involving some form of public assistance (e. g., scholarships) made available generally without regard to the sectarian-nonsectarian, or public-nonpublic nature of the institution benefitted. Thus, our decision today does not compel, as appellees have contended, the conclusion that the educational assistance provisions of the "G. I. Bill," impermissibly advance religion in violation of the Establishment Clause.

difference, for purposes of determining whether such aid has the effect of advancing religion, between the tax benefit allowed here and the tuition grant. . ." "The qualifying parent under either program receives the same form of encouragement and reward for sending his children to nonpublic schools. The only difference is that one parent receives an actual cash payment while the other is allowed to reduce by an arbitrary amount the sum he would otherwise be obliged to pay over to the State. . . . '[i]n both instances the money involved represents a charge made upon the state for the purpose of religious education.' "

[Addressing itself to Walz v. Tax Commission, 397 U.S. 664, 90 S.Ct. 1409, 25 L.Ed.2d 697 (1970) in which the Court upheld state laws allowing a tax exemption for church property, the Court said that] "tax exemptions for church property enjoyed an apparently universal approval in this country both before and after the adoption of the First Amendment. . . .

"But historical acceptance without more would not alone have sufficed. . . . It was the reason underlying that long history of tolerance of tax exemptions for religion that proved controlling. A proper respect for both the Free Exercise and the Establishment Clauses compels the State to pursue a course of 'neutrality' toward religion. Yet governments have not always pursued such a course, and oppression has taken many forms, one of which has been taxation of religion. Thus, if taxation was regarded as a form of 'hostility' toward religion, 'exemption constitute[d] a reasonable and balanced attempt to guard against those dangers.' Special tax benefits, however, cannot be squared with the principle of neutrality established by the decisions of this Court. To the contrary, insofar as such benefits render assistance to parents who send their children to sectarian schools, their purpose and inevitable effect are to aid and advance those religious institutions.

"Apart from its historical foundations, *Walz* is a product of the same dilemma and inherent tension found in most government-aid-to-religion controversies. To be sure, the exemption of church property from taxation conferred a benefit, albeit an indirect and incidental one. Yet that 'aid' was a product not of any purpose to support or to subsidize, but of a fiscal relationship designed to minimize involvement and entanglement between Church and State." "The granting of the tax benefit under the New York statute, unlike the extension of an exemption, would tend to increase rather than limit the involvement between Church and State.

"One further difference between tax exemptions for church property and tax benefits for parents should be noted. The exemption challenged in *Walz* was not restricted to a class composed exclusively or even predominantly of religious institutions. Instead the exemption covered all property devoted to religious, educational or charitable purposes. As the parties here must concede, tax reductions authorized by this law flow primarily to the parents of children attending sectarian, nonpublic schools. Without intimating whether this factor alone might have controlling significance in another context in some future case, it should be apparent that in terms of the potential divisiveness of any legislative measure the narrowness of the benefited class would be an important factor. . . .

"Because we have found that the challenged sections have the impermissible effect of advancing religion, we need not consider whether such aid would result in entanglement of the State with religion in the sense of '[a] comprehensive, discriminating, and continuing state surveillance.' Lemon v. Kurtzman. . . . But the importance of the competing societal interests implicated in this case prompts us to make the further observation that, apart from any specific entanglement of the State in particular religious programs, assistance of the sort here involved carries grave potential for entanglement in the broader sense of continuing political strife over aid to religion."

Although Chief Justice Burger and Justice Rhenquist joined the Court in its Opinion on the first New York statute concerning the "maintenance and repair" program, they, joined by Justice White, dissented from the Court's ruling on the tuition grant and tax benefit programs in an opinion by Burger, C. J.: "our cases do, it seems to me, lay down one solid, basic principle: that the Establishment Clause does not forbid governments, state or federal, from enacting a program of general welfare under which benefits are distributed to private individuals, even though many of those individuals may elect to use those benefits in ways that 'aid' religious instruction or worship. . . .

"This fundamental principle which I see running through our prior decisions in this difficult and sensitive field of law, and which I believe governs the present cases, is premised more on experience and history than on logic." "The only discernible difference between the programs in *Everson* and *Allen* and these cases is in the method of the distribution of benefits: here the particular benefits of the Pennsylvania and New York statutes are given only to parents of private school children, while in *Everson* and *Allen* the statutory benefits were made available to parents of both public and private school children. But to regard that difference as constitutionally meaningful is to exalt form over substance. It is beyond dispute that the parents of public school children in New York and Pennsylvania presently receive the 'benefit' of having their children educated totally at state expense; the statutes enacted in those States and at issue here merely attempt to equalize that 'benefit' by giving to parents of private school children, in the form of dollars or tax deductions, what the parents of public school children receive in kind. It is no more than simple equity to grant partial relief to parents who support the public schools they do not use.

" .   .   .   There are at present many forms of government assistance to individuals that can be used to serve religious ends, such as social security benefits or 'G. I. Bill' payments, which are not subject to nonreligious use restrictions.   Yet, I certainly doubt that today's majority would hold those statutes unconstitutional under the Establishment Clause."   "For purposes of constitutional adjudication of that issue, it should make no difference whether 5%, 20%, or 80% of the beneficiaries of an educational program of general application elect to utilize their benefits for religious purposes.   The 'primary effect' branch of our three-pronged test was never, at least to my understanding, intended to vary with the *number* of churches benefitted by a statute under which state aid is distributed to private citizens."

In a separate opinion Justice White, joined by Burger, C. J. and Rhenquist, J., wrote: "There is no doubt here that Pennsylvania and New York have sought in the challenged laws to keep their parochial schools system alive and capable of providing adequate secular education to substantial numbers of students.   This purpose satisfies the Court, even though to rescue schools that would otherwise fail will inevitably enable those schools to continue whatever religious functions they perform.   By the same token, it seems to me, preserving the secular functions of these schools is the overriding consequence of these laws and the resulting, but incidental, benefit to religion should not invalidate them.

"At the very least I would not strike down these statutes on their face.   The Court's opinion emphasizes a particular kind of parochial school, one restricted to students of particular religious beliefs and conditioning attendance on religious study.   Concededly, there are many parochial schools that do not impose such restrictions.   Where they do not, it is even more difficult for me to understand why the primary effect of these statutes is to advance religion."

Mr. Justice Rhenquist, joined by Burger, C. J. and White, J., wrote: "The Court's statement that 'special tax benefits, however, cannot be squared with the principle of neutrality established by decisions of this Court,' and that 'insofar as such benefits render assistance to parents who send their children to sectarian schools, their purpose and inevitable effect are to aid and advance those religious institutions,' are impossible to reconcile with *Walz*.   Who can doubt that the tax exemptions which that case upheld were every bit as much of a 'special tax benefit' as the New York tax deduction plan here, or that the benefits resulting from the exemption in *Walz* has every bit as much tendency to 'aid and advance   .   .   .   religious institutions' as did New York's plan here?

"The reimbursement and tax benefit plans today struck down, no less than the plans in *Everson* and *Allen,* are consistent with the principle of neutrality.   New York has recognized that parents who are sending their children to nonpublic schools are rendering the State a service by decreasing the costs of public education and by physically relieving an already overburdened public school system. Such parents are nonetheless compelled to support public school services unused by them and to pay for their own children's education. Rather than offering 'an incentive to send their children to sectarian schools,' as the majority suggests, New York is effectuating the secular purpose of the equalization of the costs of educating New York children that are borne by parents who send their children to nonpublic schools. As in *Everson* and *Allen*, the impact, if any, on religious education from the aid granted is significantly diminished by the fact that the benefits go to the parents rather than to the institutions."

In LEVITT v. COMMITTEE FOR PUBLIC EDUCATION, the Supreme Court in an Opinion written by Chief Justice Burger and relying on Nyquist, supra, held unconstitutional another New York statute that provided money payments to nonpublic schools in an attempt to reimburse them for administering examinations, making reports and for keeping other records each of which was required by state law. The law expressly forbade payments "for religious worship or instruction." Nevertheless, the Court invalidated the statute for it failed to include a "provision authorizing state audits of school financial records to determine whether a school's actual costs in complying with the mandated services are less than the annual lump sum payment. .   .   despite the obviously integral role of testing in the total teaching process, no attempt is made under the statute, and no means are available, to assure that internally prepared tests are free of religious instruction. We cannot ignore the substantial risk that these examinations, prepared by teachers under the authority of religious institutions, will be drafted with an eye, unconsciously or otherwise, to inculcate students in the religious precepts of the sponsoring church. .   .   the aid that will be devoted to secular functions is not identifiable and separable from aid to sectarian activities. .   .   .

"To the extent that appellants argue that the State should be permitted to pay for any activity 'mandated' by state law or regulation, we must reject the contention. State or local law might, for example, 'mandate' minimum lighting or sanitary facilities for all school buildings, but such commands would not authorize a State to provide support for those facilities in church-sponsored schools. The essential inquiry in each case, as expressed in our prior decisions, is whether the challenged state aid has the primary purpose or effect of advancing religion or religious education or whether it leads to excessive entanglement by the State in the affairs of the religious institution. .   .   That inquiry would be irreversibly frustrated if the Establishment Clause were read as permitting a State to pay for whatever it requires a private school to do." Justices Douglas, Brennan and Marshall concurred in the result, and Justice White dissented.

In SLOAN v. LEMON, the Supreme Court in an Opinion by Mr. Justice Powell found "no constitutionally significant difference" between the tuition grant program of New York and Pennsylvania's statute providing that regardless of income level the state would reimburse parents part of their costs incurred when sending their children to nonpublic schools. The Court held that Pennsylvania had "singled out a class of its citizens for a special economic benefit," and "whether that benefit be viewed as a simple tuition subsidy, as an incentive to parents to send their children to sectarian schools, or as a reward for having done so, at bottom its intended consequence is to preserve and support religion-oriented institutions."

NOTES AND QUESTIONS

1. Analyze and trace the position of each Justice in each of the cases beginning with Bd. of Ed. v. Allen. Which Justices are fully consistent and which not? What is the position of each Justice on the criterion of "the danger of political entanglement?"

2. Explain fully the current three-pronged constitutional test of religious establishment: purpose, effect and entanglement. How are these elements to be combined and weighed? Suppose an otherwise permissible statute had both a substantial sectarian and substantial secular effect, would it be upheld?

3. Is the wall of separation of church and state absolute in every respect? If not, identify the forms of state aid that would be constitutional and the reasons why. Would "voucher plans" pass constitutional muster? See infra ch. 11.

THE FREE EXERCISE OF RELIGION AND SCHOOLS

———

[Reconsider Wisconsin v. Yoder, supra, and Valent v. State Board of Education, supra.]

———

MITCHELL v. McCALL

Supreme Court of Alabama, 1962.
273 Ala. 604, 143 So.2d 629.

LIVINGSTON, Chief Justice. The appellant, petitioner below, commenced this action by a petition seeking an alternative writ of mandamus from the Circuit Court of Mobile County, directed to Mobile County School Board, the Superintendent of Education, and the Principal of Vigor High School, in the City of Prichard, Mobile

County, State of Alabama, or to appear before the Circuit Court of Mobile County to show cause why they should not so readmit said minor.

Respondents filed an answer to the petition.

The court denied the petition for writ of mandamus, and it is from this order that this appeal is taken.

Appellant's daughter, Eulene, was suspended from Vigor High School, a public school in Mobile County, for refusing to participate in the physical education program lawfully prescribed for that school. This refusal was originally based upon the three objections which follow:

A.   A refusal to wear the costume prescribed for the students while participating in the course on the ground that said costume is immodest and sinful according to the religious beliefs of the appellant.

B.   A refusal to perform certain physical exercises on the same grounds as listed above.

C.   A further refusal to attend the physical education course because such attendance would require appellant's daughter to be in the presence of the other girls and the instructress who wore the prescribed costume and performed all the exercises.

The school authorities offered to allow appellant's daughter to wear clothing which appellant would consider modest and suitable, and further agreed that she would not have to perform any exercises that seemed to her or her parents immodest for a girl to perform when clad in ordinary feminine clothing.

The court below incorporated these concessions in its decree and ordered the school authorities to readmit the girl on the further condition that she would attend the physical education course and participate therein subject to the concessions. Since these concessions were made by the school board and adopted by the lower court, and since no complaint is made of them here, this Court is not concerned with the concessions and expresses no opinion on their legality or illegality.

Appellant appeals from the decree of the lower court on the theory that the requirement that his daughter attend and participate in the course in the presence of the other girls and the instructress violates her freedom of religious belief secured to her by Art. 1, Sec. 3 of the Constitution of Alabama 1901, and the First and Fourteenth Amendments of the Constitution of the United States.

Appellant vigorously argues what he describes as his constitutional right to have his children educated in the public schools of the state. In this connection, it should be observed that the State of Alabama is under no constitutional obligation to provide public schools. . . .

Clearly, appellant's daughter does have a right to make use of such facilities if they are in fact provided by the state. However, appellant's daughter is free to refrain from attending the public schools since Alabama does not require public school attendance. . . . Her attendance in a public school is therefore voluntary. . . . .

Sec. 555 of Title 52, Code of Alabama 1940, provides as follows:

"Every public school and private or parochial school shall carry out a system of physical education, the character of which shall conform to the program or course outlined by the department of education."

The action of the appellees, of which appellant complains, was taken pursuant to the authority delegated to the department of education by this statute. Thus, the program of education prescribed under this delegated authority is legislative in nature and has the coercive effect of law. . . .

The legislation involved in the case at bar is unquestionably reasonable, and it touches only matters which are the legitimate concern and responsibility of the state and its agencies.

This is not the first instance of exacting obedience to general laws that have offended deep religious scruples. Compulsory vaccination, see Jacobson v. Massachusetts, 197 U.S. 11 . . . food inspection regulations, see Shapiro v. Lyle (D.C.Wash.) 30 F.2d 971; the obligation to bear arms, see Hamilton v. Regents of University of California, 293 U.S. 245 . . . testimonial duties, see Stansbury v. Marks, 2 Dall. 213, 1 L.Ed. 353; compulsory medical treatment, see People v. Vogelgesang, 221 N.Y. 290, 116 N.E. 977—these are but illustrations of conduct that has often been compelled in the enforcement of legislation of general applicability even though the religious consciences of particular individuals rebelled at the exaction.

Every precaution has been taken to insure that the course is conducted in a manner consistent with modesty and good taste. The classes which Eulene Mitchell, appellant's daughter, is required to attend are composed entirely of girls and the teacher is also a female. When the class is conducted in the gymnasium, the girls are completely excluded from male eyes, and when conducted outdoors, there is a school building between the girls and the boys. In spite of these facts, reasonable concession has been made to appellant's religious beliefs, and this Court therefore holds that the legislative policy overrides appellant's objections, and Art. 1, Sec. 3 of the Constitution of Alabama 1901 has not been violated.

It is the opinion of this Court that appellant's rights under the First and Fourteenth Amendments of the United States Constitution have not been infringed. In Hamilton v. Regents of University of California   .   .   ., supra, the Supreme Court of the United States unanimously held that a student attending a state-maintained university cannot refuse to attend required courses in military training on the ground that such courses offend his religious beliefs. Later, the Supreme Court of the United States held that the First and Fourteenth Amendments were violated by a West Virginia Statute which required all public school pupils to salute the flag of the United States and recite a pledge of allegiance. This requirement was held to violate the freedom of pupils who considered such conduct to be contrary to their religious beliefs. West Virginia State Board of Education v. Barnette,   .   .   . However, the Hamilton case, supra, was specifically distinguished on the basis that attendance at the state institution in question in that case was voluntary, and therefore a pupil could not refuse to comply with the reasonable conditions lawfully required and still demand admission. The Hamilton decision is therefore authority for the proposition that the State of Alabama can place reasonable, nondiscriminatory conditions on the privilege of attending public schools since such attendance is voluntary.

Moreover, even if this is not the case, West Virginia State Bd. of Education v. Barnette, supra, is clearly distinguishable on its facts. The statute involved in that case, as construed by the court, was invalid because it called for a compulsory statement of belief. There is nothing analogous to that in the case at bar. Indeed, the Barnette case, supra, would only be analogous if the complaining pupils in that case had further alleged that it was unconstitutional to require them to be present when other students professed their allegiance. The Alabama Constitution and the United States Constitution do not require such a result. Indeed, a decision supporting such an allegation would place an intolerable burden on the state and federal governments in the discharge of their responsibilities to the people of the state and the nation. Such a decision would give every citizen the power to nullify all state and federal legislation by simply asserting in a court of law that the behavior required is contrary to his religious beliefs. A power of nullification of such extreme scope would undermine the very foundation of our "democratic" institutions and undercut the very concept of ordered liberty protected by our state and federal constitutions.

Every reasonable concession has been made to the appellant in this case. This Court cannot go further and hold that appellant's religious belief that his daughter should not be placed in the presence of others whose dress and behavior is contrary to his scruples imposes upon the school the legal obligation to conduct a separate class in conformity with appellant's belief.

Appellant further complains that unless the school is required to conduct a separate class composed of those who share his and his daughter's belief that she will be made to appear a "speckled bird," and will be subject to the contumely of her fellow students.

All citizens in so far as they hold views different from the majority of their fellows are subject to such inconveniences. And this is especially true of those who hold religious or moral beliefs which are looked upon with disdain by the majority. It is precisely every citizen's right to be a "speckled bird" that our constitutions, state and federal, seek to insure. And solace for the embarrassment that is attendant upon holding such beliefs must be found by the individual citizen in his own moral courage and strength of conviction, and not in a court of law.

Our conclusion is, that in the posture of this case, the appellant's daughter is not required to participate in the exercises which would be immodest in ordinary apparel, nor is she required to wear the prescribed outfit. However, subject to these concessions previously made, she is obligated to attend the course in physical education.

. . .

NOTES AND QUESTIONS

1. Assume that Alabama had a compulsory school attendance like that found in most other states, what difference would this fact have made for the decision and reasoning in this case? Why should this make any difference? In Alabama does a child have a legal right to attend public school? If so, can that legal right be made available on the condition that the child give up his constitutional right to the free exercise of his religion?

2. What would be an example of a requirement of state law abridging the free exercise of a religious faith that the Alabama Supreme Court would hold "unreasonable"? Give several examples that should be held unreasonable.

3. Is this case fully consistent with the reasoning in Valent v. State Bd. of Ed., supra?

4. Consider California's approach to the question. Is it a proper approach in your opinion? Why?

    "Whenever any part of the instruction in 'health,' family life education, and sex education conflicts with the religious training and beliefs of the parent or guardian of any pupil, the pupil on written request of the parent or guardian, * * * shall be excused from the part of the training which conflicts with such religious training and beliefs.

    "As used in this section, 'religious training and beliefs' includes personal moral convictions." West's Ann.Educ.Code of Calif. § 8751.

Chapter VII

CONSTITUTIONAL FREEDOM AND GOVERNMENTAL CONTROLS OVER TEACHERS

CERTIFICATION

INTRODUCTION

Before a teacher lawfully can teach in a state's common schools that teacher must first be certified by that state. Thus, for example, Washington's law typically provides that "no person shall be accounted as a qualified teacher within the meaning of the school law who is not the holder of a valid teacher's certificate or permit issued by lawful authority of this state." RCW 28A.67.010. State legislatures and/or state boards of education have enacted laws governing the entire certification process. Immediately, a question is raised concerning student "practice teaching" because students do not meet the necessary conditions to be certificated, the purpose of which is to insure a minimum competency in classroom instructors and for which the student-teacher is preparing. Usually, this problem is met by statutes or rules and regulations of State Boards of Education that allow properly supervised practice teaching. In such situations the practicing teacher is considered to have volunteered his services and is entitled to no pay. See, Floyd County Board of Education v. Slone, 307 S.W.2d 912 (Ky.1957). The teaching certificate is a license, and is generally held not to be a contract between the teacher and the state. A valid certificate is evidence of teaching competency, and its absence is sufficient to uphold a finding of incompetency. Kobylski v. Board of Education, etc., 33 A.D.2d 603, 304 N.Y.S.2d 453 (1969).

A person is a "qualified teacher," in a legal sense, when that person has been certified and has a license to teach in the state's schools. Licenses can be restricted in various ways, and so may a teacher's "qualifications." Thus, a person can be certified to teach for only a period of time, or only to teach certain subjects, or only to teach in certain grades, etc. Furthermore, a state legislature can impose new or additional conditions that a teacher must satisfy in order to teach, and moreover, a teacher's license to teach can be revoked on prescribed grounds, so long as the grounds are constitutional. See, e. g., Keller v. Hewitt, 109 Cal. 146, 41 P. 871 (1895). Additionally, many states have a certificate renewal statute like California's which requires that a teacher have five years of successful teaching as a condition of renewal. These laws frequently lead to litigation because of differing opinions on what amounts to a "successful" teaching experience. For example, a California principal stated that he considered the performance of a teacher in his school to have been unsatisfactory, and her certificate was not renewed by the agency. She was dismissed. But California's court ruled that since she had been in that school system for ten years, and since no charges of incompetency had been brought against the teacher, her "successful" teaching experience would be presumed. Matteson v. State Bd. of Education, 57 Cal.App.2d 991, 136 P.2d 120 (1943).

While all states have laws requiring teacher certification, the laws vary greatly, from the overly specific to the broadly general. Thus, as with other matters, the same situation might receive different legal treatment in different states under different laws. It is essential that teachers know the specific law of their states. Nevertheless, one rule applicable in all states is that if a teacher meets all the conditions set forth for a certificate, the certifying agency has no power arbitrarily to refuse to issue the certificate, even though that agency might have discretionary powers delegated to it by the state legislature. Where states have delegated discretionary powers to a certifying agency, they sometimes include those allowing the agency to prescribe conditions for a teaching certificate in addition to those set forth by the legislature, and, of course, so long as the additionally prescribed conditions are properly within the agency's powers and are constitutional, they must be met before a certificate will issue. As in other matters, courts generally do not supervise the certification process, and tend not to interfere with the exercise of the discretionary powers of the certifying agency.

Can a certifying agency change its standards and then apply them to a person who began teacher training under the old standards? A Maryland case, Metcalf v. Cook, 168 Md. 475, 178 A. 219 (1935), is instructive. Maryland's legislature provided that a high school teacher's certificate "may be granted to persons who are graduates of a standard college or university, or who have had the equivalent in scholastic preparation." Under its discretionary powers, the state board of education promulgated a rule adding requirements to the state statute that "only such graduates as rank academically in the upper four-fifths of the Class and who make a grade of 'C' or better in practical teaching, shall be issued Maryland Teachers' Certificates." An applicant for a certificate ranked only in the lowest fifth of his class, and sued in the courts for a certificate after his application was refused by the state superintendent. The Court of Appeals of Maryland held:

> ". . . The provision . . . that a high school teacher's certificate 'may be granted,' to persons of the specified experience, is construed by the [applicant] as the equivalent of 'shall be granted,' and therefore as prohibiting a

choice among such persons by the board, limiting eligibility to those in the upper four-fifths of the classes. With this construction, too, the court is in disagreement. There seems to the court to be no intention manifested other than that of setting a minimum requirement for the board's selection of teachers. That seems to be a reasonable construction, in accord with the evident plan of the whole statute that the board shall be depended upon largely to make the educational system work properly. Discretion in selection from eligibles, whose fitness must differ greatly, would seem to be a very likely intention. And if the discretion is given, as we think it is, then when exercised it acquires by the express terms of the statute the force of law, not to be interfered with by the courts. . . .

"The [applicant] argues that exercise of the authority retroactively could not be intended, so that after a student has started on his preparation a higher test than that with which he was faced at the start could be imposed. The by-law makes no change in courses of study and preparation; it concerns only the diligence and ability of the student in it, and the contention seems to be that the student had a right to take his work more easily. We see no vested rights in the standards of work which might restrict retroactive by-laws. Before the student is selected as a teacher he has no contract with the state, and no vested rights. He is only the recipient of the state's bounty, with the state left unrestrained in adopting requirements it might find desirable at any time.

"A further objection, that no notice was given the [applicant] of the adoption of this by-law, is subject to the same criticisms. There is no requirement of notice to individuals. Publication of the by-law is required by the statute, and it is not denied that there was publication; and in that the full measure of the statutory requirements was met. Upon publication the by-law acquired the force of law."

In your opinion, could, and should, the new standard of the board of education constitutionally be applied to those teachers previously certified but who ranked only in the lowest fifth of their class? Why?

In addition to meeting required academic qualifications in most states an applicant must be of "good moral character," and that character must continue after certification otherwise the teacher may not be eligible for a renewal or continuation of his certificate. In the following case, was good moral character exhibited? Why or why not?

BAY v. STATE BOARD OF EDUCATION

Supreme Court of Oregon, 1963.
233 Or. 601, 378 P.2d 558.

PERRY, Justice.　Dean Norman Bay petitioned the circuit court of Union County for judicial review of the decision of appellant State Board of Education denying him issuance of a five-year elementary teacher's certificate.　From the decree of the circuit court reversing the Board's decision for lack of competent evidence, appeal is made to this court.

In December of 1953 petitioner was tried and convicted in the state of Washington for his acts of breaking, entering, and grand larceny of several stores, the American Legion Club, and the local high school, committed while employed as a night policeman.　At the time these acts were perpetrated, petitioner was 24 years old.　After serving 18 months of a two-year sentence, he was paroled.　He moved to La Grande, Oregon, where, in the fall of 1956 he enrolled at the Eastern Oregon College of Education.　In 1958 the state of Washington restored to him his full civil rights.

In 1960 petitioner was granted a one-year elementary teacher's emergency certificate by the Superintendent of Public Instruction, and taught elementary school while completing his fourth year at the college.　Following graduation he applied for a five-year elementary teacher's certificate, but his application was denied on June 14, 1961.

On September 13, 1961 a hearing was conducted before the Board, the primary purpose of which was to determine whether petitioner had furnished the evidence of good moral character which ORS 342.060(2) authorizes the superintendent to require of an applicant.　Whereas numerous witnesses appeared at the hearing to testify of petitioner's good character and over-all reputation in the community, the sole evidence of bad character introduced was the record of the prior conviction.　The Board concluded that petitioner had not met his burden of furnishing satisfactory evidence of good moral character and he thereupon petitioned the circuit court of Union County for review of the administrative order pursuant to ORS 183.-480.　The court held that evidence as to a prior conviction was irrelevant and immaterial in determining present character where not accompanied by other evidence which related the prior act to the present, and therefore adjudged there was no competent evidence to support the Board's findings.　The Board was ordered to issue petitioner the certificate, from which order this appeal is taken.　.　.　.

In order to properly discuss the issues presented it is first necessary to discuss the powers of the trial court in reviewing the Board's determination.

While the statute uses the language "as a suit in equity," it is quite clear that this language refers only to the fact that the review shall be made by the court, not a jury, and does not grant to a trial court the right on appeal to try the cause de novo. That is, the reviewing court is not granted the power to weigh the evidence and substitute its judgment as to the preponderance thereof for that of the agency. The extent to which a reviewing court should review the action of an administrative agency has been expressed by this court, as follows:

> " * * * Generally, they go no further than to determine whether the agency (1) acted impartially; (2) performed faithfully the duties delineated in the legislative acts which conferred jurisdiction upon it; (3) stayed within its jurisdiction; (4) committed no error of law; (5) exercised discretion judiciously and not capriciously; and (6) arrived at no conclusion which was clearly wrong." . . .

The learned trial court recognized these guide posts and reached the conclusion that the finding of the Board as to lack of good moral character could not be sustained by the record. This conclusion of the court is based upon a finding that there was no evidence of bad moral character at the time of application and therefore the Board's conclusion was clearly wrong.

Whether or not the Board arrived at a conclusion which was clearly wrong depends upon whether a review of the entire record discloses any facts from which the conclusion drawn by the Board could be reached by reasonable minds. . . . There must be evidence that is "more than a mere scintilla. It means such relevant evidence as a reasonable mind might accept as adequate to support a conclusion." . . . These thoughts are contained in and usually expressed as the "substantial evidence rule." . . .

The Board made the following findings of fact which are pertinent to this appeal:

> "1. That the applicant on December 9, 1953, was convicted of grand larceny on four counts in the Superior Court for Klickitat County, State of Washington and received a one to fifteen-year sentence by the said Court. That thereafter his sentence was fixed at a term of two years by the State Board of Terms and Parole of the State of Washington, and the applicant served an eighteen-month term at the Monroe Reformatory in the State of Washington.

> "2. Thereafter upon his release he was placed on parole for approximately a year and moved to the City of La Grande, Oregon, and in the fall of 1956 entered the Eastern Oregon College of Education and enrolled in a teacher education course.

"3. That by act of the Governor of the State of Washington full civil rights were restored to him on July 3, 1958.

*　　*　　*　　*　　*　　*　　*　　*　　*

"8. The Board further finds the offenses committed by Mr. Bay consisted of breaking and entering various stores in Goldendale, Washington and grand larceny, and included safe burglaries at the American Legion Club, the Goldendale High School. That at the time he committed the offenses for which he was imprisoned he had reached the age of 24 years; that his offenses numbered not one but several; that he was a man of superior intelligence as evidenced by his scores on intelligence tests in his subsequent college record.

"9. The Board further finds that at the time of the thefts he occupied a position of trust as a night policeman in the community and that while so engaged he committed the acts resulting in his conviction.

"10. That a teacher in a public school is the key factor in teaching by precept and example the subjects of honesty, morality, courtesy, obedience to law, and other lessons of a steadying influence which tend to promote and develop an upright and desirable citizenry, as required by ORS 336.240 and related statutes.

"11. That there has been no evidence submitted to the Board of any violations of law or deviations from normally considered moral conduct from the time of his release from the Monroe Reformatory to the present time."

The Board then made the following conclusions of law:

"1. That the applicant has not furnished evidence of good moral character deemed satisfactory and necessary by the Board to establish the applicant's fitness to serve as a teacher."

In resolving the question of moral character there must be kept in mind the distinction between character and reputation. "Character is what a man or woman is morally, while reputation is what he or she is reputed to be." .　.　.

"A person's 'character' is usually thought to embrace all his qualities and deficiencies regarding traits of personality, behavior, integrity, temperament, consideration, sportsmanship, altruism, etc. which distinguish him as a human being from his fellow men. His disposition toward criminal acts is only one of the qualities which constitute his character. The statute subjects an applicant's 'character' to scrutiny by the Commission; in the absence of a legislative directive to the narrow interpretation advanced by plaintiffs, courts must give to words their commonly understood definitions and in this case 'character' certainly embraces involvement in the litigation proved against the plaintiffs and their disposition not to be ingenuous and truthful concerning it."

.   .   .

Since the crux of the question before the Board was good moral character, the fact that he had been guilty of burglarizing properties while he held a position of trust was most pertinent. These actions of petitioner clearly evidenced a lack of the moral fiber to resist temptation. The trial court therefore erred in holding there was no evidence of lack of good moral character.

The petitioner offered numerous witnesses from which a conclusion might properly be reached that this lack of moral fiber no longer exists. However, this condition, having been shown to have existed, it became a matter of judgment as to whether it had been overcome.

The power to decide such an issue was delegated by the legislature to the Board of Education, therefore, as previously pointed out, the courts are not permitted to substitute their judgment for that of the Board where there is substantial evidence to support the agency.

The judgment of the trial court is reversed with instructions to enter findings of fact and conclusions of law sustaining the action of the Board of Education.

NOTES AND QUESTIONS

1. What was the scope of review by the Oregon Supreme Court? Why? Did its scope of review and the matters it considered within it differ from the scope of decision and the matters considered by the State Board of Education? Why? Do you agree with this procedure? Why or why not?

2. Do you agree with the decision of the State Board of Education? Do people change? Had the applicant changed? Is a conviction itself sufficient to show a lack of good moral character? Any conviction? Who among you has not committed a crime? Suppose the applicant had been convicted repeatedly of trespass, vagrancy and disorderly conduct because he repeatedly engaged in non-violent, civil-rights sit-in demonstrations against racial discriminators, or suppose he had been convicted of the private possession of marijuana, or of reckless driving, or of driving while intoxicated, would the decision have been the same? Should it be? Is it constitutionally required that in all cases the certifying agency must carefully consider (1) the nature of the conviction and whether it reveals items that would otherwise disallow the person from being a successful teacher, and (2) if so, whether that person has changed, or should the courts allow any conviction to support a certifying agency's decision of a lack of good moral character? If so, why? Is this what the Oregon Supreme Court did?

3. Define, precisely, what is meant by "good moral character" for a teacher. Should this standard be kept or eliminated? If a sexually active pedophile meets all the academic requirements for a teaching certificate, should he be issued one? Why or why not?

4. What is your legal opinion of the constitutionality of California's provision that:

"Whenever the holder of any credential, life diploma, or document issued by the State Board of Education has been convicted of any sex offense as defined in Section 12912 or narcotics offense as defined in Section 12912.5, the State Board of Education shall forthwith suspend the credential, life diploma, or document. If the conviction is reversed and the holder is acquitted of the offense in a new trial or the charges against him are dismissed, the Board shall forthwith terminate the suspension of the credential, life diploma, or document. When the conviction becomes final or when imposition of sentence is suspended the Board shall forthwith revoke the credential, life diploma, or document." West's Ann.Educ. Code of California § 13207. See, Vogulkin v. State Board of Education, 194 Cal.App.2d 424, 15 Cal.Rptr. 335 (1961), and State of Minnesota ex rel. Pearson v. Probate Court, 309 U.S. 270, 60 S.Ct. 523, 84 L.Ed. 744 (1940).

5. California also provides that:

"Except as provided in this code, no certification document shall be granted to any person unless and until he has subscribed to the following oath or affirmation: 'I solemnly swear (or affirm) that I will support the Constitution of the United States of America, the Constitution of the State of California, and the laws of the United States and the State of California, and will promote respect for the flag and respect for law and order and allegiance to the government of the United States of America.' The oath or affirmation shall be subscribed before any person authorized to administer oaths or before any member of the governing board of a school district or of any county board of education and filed with the commission or with the Board of Governors of the California Community Colleges, as the case may be. Any certificated person who is a citizen or subject of any country other than the United States, and who is employed in any capacity in any of the public schools of the state shall, before entering upon the discharge of his duties, subscribe to an oath to support the institutions and policies of the United States during the period of his sojourn within the state. Upon the violation of any of the terms of the oath or affirmation, the commission or the Board of Governors of the California Community Colleges, as the case may be, shall suspend or revoke the credential which has been issued." West's Ann.Educ.Code of California § 13165.

If a citizen refused to subscribe to this oath, does he lack good moral character? Is any part of this statute unconstitutional? Why or why not?

6. Could a state require a written, oral or performance examination of a prospective teacher as a condition of certification? A physical or

psychological examination? See, e. g., Crofts v. Board of Education, 105 Ill.App.2d 139, 245 N.E.2d 87 (1969); Corsover v. Board of Examiners, 59 Misc.2d 251, 298 N.Y.S.2d 757 (1968); Board of Trustees v. Porini, 263 Cal.App.2d 784, 70 Cal.Rptr. 73 (1968), and Nelson v. Board of Examiners, 21 N.Y.2d 408, 288 N.Y.S. 454, 235 N.E.2d 433 (1968).

7. Could the state require a personality test as a condition of certification? Why or why not? Is personality part of "good moral character"? Would Griswold v. Conn., supra, be relevant?

8. In 1967, a New York court required that an unsuccessful candidate for certification as a high school departmental chairman be given a model answer to the written examination questions on which his denial was based so the unsuccessful applicant would have some "objective" grounds for judging whether he was rightly denied the license. Schwartz v. Bogen, 28 A.D.2d 692, 281 N.Y.S.2d 279, modified 21 N.Y.2d 1020, 291 N.Y.S.2d 4, 238 N.E.2d 496 (1967). See also, Lubell v. Nyquist, 31 A.D.2d 569, 294 N.Y.S.2d 961 (1968).

DECERTIFICATION

———

Several states have statutes requiring the revocation of a teaching certificate under certain circumstances. So long as the decertifying grounds pass constitutional muster, decertification can take place. However, fair procedures must be followed. In Florida, for example, before decertifying can occur, the State board of education must conduct a preliminary investigation and a separate fair hearing before deciding whether a teacher is guilty of conduct amounting to "moral turpitude." Neal v. Bryant, 149 So.2d 529 (Fla.1962). Compare carefully the following two cases decided under the same statute. Are they consistent? What are the reasons accounting for the way in which California's Supreme Court, in Morrison, construed the statute? If the statute had not been construed this way, would a serious constitutional problem be presented? Why? If so, state the problem, and its probable resolution. Was this problem present in Sarac? If so, what was the court's resolution of it? With which case opinion do you agree? Why? What is the validity of Sarac after Morrison? Is Griswold v. Conn, supra, applicable to this type of situation?

———

SARAC v. STATE BOARD OF EDUCATION

Court of Appeals, Second District, 1967.
249 Cal.App.2d 58, 57 Cal.Rptr. 69.

COBEY, Associate Justice. This is an appeal from a judgment denying appellant's petition under Code of Civil Procedure,   .   .   .

for a writ of mandate against respondent compelling it to rescind its revocation of his general secondary teaching credential.

In reviewing this action of respondent, in proceedings in administrative mandamus, the trial court exercised its independent judgment on the weight of the evidence and its decision must be sustained if there is any credible competent evidence to support its findings. . . . Furthermore, all conflicts in evidence must be resolved in favor of respondent and all reasonable and legitimate inferences must be indulged in order to uphold the findings of the trial court. In short, the evidence must be viewed by us in light most favorable to respondent. . . . Likewise, respondent's determination of the penalty will not be disturbed unless an abuse of discretion in this respect is established. . . .

. . . All of the foregoing is, however, subject to the limitation that if appellant can show denial of an essential constitutional guaranty of fair trial or due process of law, the judgment of the trial court may become subject to reversal. . . .

The administrative proceedings under review began with the filing of an accusation by and before respondent against appellant, who is a male teacher. This pleading charged him in substance with having engaged in immoral and unprofessional conduct within the meaning of Education Code, section 13202, in having, on or about July 28, 1962, at a public beach in or about the City of Long Beach, "rubbed, touched and fondled the private sexual parts of one L. A. Bowers, a person of the masculine sex, with the intent to arouse and excite unnatural sexual desires in said L. A. Bowers and in the [appellant]." The accusation then went on to recite that by reason of this conduct appellant was arrested and charged with violation of Penal Code, section 647a and was on September 4, 1962, convicted in the Long Beach Municipal Court of violation of section 4130(a) of the Long Beach Municipal Code (Disorderly Conduct) upon his plea of guilty thereto. Lastly, the accusation charged that appellant was unfit for service in the public school system within the meaning of the just-mentioned statute because of this conduct by him on the beach, because of the just-mentioned criminal proceedings against him occasioned by such conduct, and because of two admissions he had made to the said Bowers on or about the said July 28, 1962, that he had had a homosexual problem since he was 20 years old and that the last time he had had sexual relations with a man was approximately three weeks earlier.

A hearing was thereafter duly held. . . . Following a decision and order adverse to appellant these mandamus proceedings were duly initiated. . . .

The trial court concluded as a matter of law that appellant had committed "a homosexual act involving moral turpitude" which conduct constituted both immoral and unprofessional conduct within the meaning of said Education Code, section 13202; that the decision of respondent revoking his general secondary teaching credential was correct in that appellant had demonstrated that he was unfit for service in the public school system within the meaning of the just-mentioned statute; that respondent's decision was supported by its findings of fact and that its findings of fact were supported by the weight of the evidence before it and that appellant had been afforded full and complete due process of law at all stages of the administrative proceedings before respondent.

On this appeal we are concerned solely and exclusively with the legal correctness of the judgment of the trial court in this case. Appellant attacks such judgment as being unconstitutional. More specifically he claims that the trial court relied in part upon appellant's conviction of a violation of a Long Beach municipal ordinance, which he asserts is unconstitutional for vagueness and uncertainty and because, as applied to the type of conduct involved here, its field of operation has been preempted by the State. He further contends that all three triers of fact found erroneously in accordance with the accusation that he had pled guilty to a violation of this ordinance, when in fact he had merely refrained from contesting the prosecution's case against him for such violation because he and his then counsel had made a deal with the prosecutor under which, in exchange for such conduct, he obtained a dismissal of the much more serious criminal proceedings against him charging violation of the above stated section of the Penal Code. He argues that this treatment of a nonadmission of guilt as if it had been an admission of guilt unconstitutionally prejudiced the three triers of fact against his credibility in view of the sharp conflict in the evidence between the two police officers on the one hand and himself, his psychiatric expert witness and his 23 character witnesses on the other. He also objects to the findings of fact below insofar as they found true the making by him of two admissions to the said L. A. Bowers of prior homosexual experience on his part. Finally, he says that respondent acted unconstitutionally in revoking his teaching credential because it failed to establish any rational connection between the homosexual conduct on the beach, of which he was found guilty by respondent, and immorality and unprofessional conduct as a teacher on his part and his fitness for service in the public schools; and as a consequence the penalty imposed upon him by respondent, the revocation of his general secondary teaching credential, deprived him of both liberty and property without due process of law, and constituted cruel, unusual and double punishment for the same offense.

We have pointed out that the trial court limited its conclusions of law, insofar as appellant's conduct was concerned, to his one homosexual act on the beach. This renders immaterial and irrelevant appellant's claims respecting the constitutionality of the Long Beach ordinance and the erroneous finding of what happened in the Long

Beach Municipal Court with respect to the basis of his conviction there of its violation. The same may be said in regard to his objections as to the inclusion in the court's findings of fact of his two admissions of prior homosexual experience. . . .

Our review of the record before us, under the rules of law enunciated at the outset of this opinion, convinces us that the testimony of Police Officer, L. A. Bowers, in and of itself, constitutes more than ample credible and competent evidence to support the findings of the trial court that on July 28, 1962, appellant committed a homosexual act on the public beach in Long Beach. Homosexual behavior has long been contrary and abhorrent to the social mores and moral standards of the people of California as it has been since antiquity to those of many other peoples. It is clearly, therefore, immoral conduct within the meaning of Education Code, section 13202. It may also constitute unprofessional conduct within the meaning of that same statute as such conduct is not limited to classroom misconduct or misconduct with children. . . . It certainly constitutes evident unfitness for service in the public school system within the meaning of that statute. . . . In view of appellant's statutory duty as a teacher to "endeavor to impress upon the minds of the pupils the principles of morality" (Ed. Code, § 7851) and his necessarily close association with children in the discharge of his professional duties as a teacher, there is to our minds an obvious rational connection between his homosexual conduct on the beach and the consequent action of respondent in revoking his secondary teaching credential on the statutory grounds of immoral and unprofessional conduct and evident unfitness for service in the public school system of this State. Needless to say, we find no abuse of discretion by respondent in the penalty it here imposed on appellant, nor any constitutional questions whatsoever with respect to such action on its part. . . .

MORRISON v. STATE BOARD OF EDUCATION

Supreme Court of California, 1969.
1 Cal.3d 214, 82 Cal.Rptr. 175, 461 P.2d 375.

TOBRINER, Justice. . . . For a number of years prior to 1964 petitioner worked as a teacher for the Lowell Joint School District. During this period, so far as appears from the record, no one complained about, or so much as criticized, his performance as a teacher. Moreover, with the exception of a single incident, no one suggested that his conduct outside the classroom was other than beyond reproach.

Sometime before the spring of 1963 petitioner became friends with Mr. and Mrs. Fred Schneringer. Mr. Schneringer also worked as a teacher in the public school system.   To the Schneringers, who were involved in grave marital and financial difficulties at the time, petitioner gave counsel and advice.   In the course of such counseling Mr. Schneringer frequently visited petitioner's apartment to discuss his problems.   For a one-week period in April, during which petitioner and Mr. Schneringer experienced severe emotional stress, the two men engaged in a limited, non-criminal physical relationship which petitioner described as being of a homosexual nature.   Petitioner has never been accused or convicted of any criminal activity whatever, and the record contains no evidence of any abnormal activities or desires by petitioner since the Schneringer incident some six years in the past.   Petitioner and Schneringer met on numerous occasions in the spring and summer after the incident and nothing untoward occurred.   When Schneringer later obtained a separation from his wife, petitioner suggested a number of women whom Schneringer might consider dating.

Approximately one year after the April 1963 incident, Schneringer reported it to the Superintendent of the Lowell Joint School District. As a result of that report petitioner resigned his teaching position on May 4, 1964.

Some 19 months after the incident became known to the superintendent, the State Board of Education conducted a hearing concerning possible revocation of petitioner's life diplomas.   Petitioner there testified that he had had some undefined homosexual problem at the age of 13, but that, with the sole exception of the Schneringer incident, he had not experienced the slightest homosexual urge or inclination for more than a dozen years.   Mr. Cavalier, an investigator testifying for the board, stated that the Schneringer incident "was the only time that [petitioner] ever engaged in a homosexual act with anyone."   No evidence was presented that petitioner had ever committed any act of misconduct whatsoever while teaching.

The Board of Education finally revoked petitioner's life diplomas some three years after the Schneringer incident.   The board concluded that that incident constituted immoral and unprofessional conduct, and an act involving moral turpitude, all of which warrant revocation of life diplomas under section 13202 of the Education Code.

Petitioner's actions cannot constitute immoral or unprofessional conduct or conduct involving moral turpitude within the meaning of section 13202 unless those actions indicate his unfitness to teach.

Section 13202 of the Education Code authorizes revocation of life diplomas for "immoral conduct," "unprofessional conduct," and "acts involving moral turpitude."   .   .   .   [W]e have given those terms more precise meaning by referring in each case to the particular profession or the specific governmental position to which they were applicable.   .   .   .

Board of Education v. Swan (1953) 41 Cal.2d 546, 261 P.2d 261, and Board of Trustees v. Owens (1962) 206 Cal.App.2d 147, 23 Cal. Rptr. 710, dealt with the term "unprofessional conduct" as applied to teachers. In *Swan* we stressed: "One employed in public service does not have a constitutional right to such employment and is subject to reasonable supervision and restriction by the authorized governmental body or officer *to the end that proper discipline may be maintained, and that activities among the employees may not be allowed to disrupt or impair the public service."* . . . In *Owens* the Court of Appeal held that in deciding whether certain conduct by a teacher constituted unprofessional conduct which warranted discipline, a trial court must inquire whether that conduct had produced "any disruption or impairment of discipline or the teaching process * * *."

In Orloff v. Los Angeles Turf Club (1951) 36 Cal.2d 734, 227 P.2d 449, we dealt with a statute authorizing the exclusion from theaters, museums, and race courses of persons of "immoral character." We reasoned that the objective of the statute was "the protection of others on the premises." (Id. at p. 740, 227 P.2d at p. 454.) Accordingly we held that a person might be excluded if, for example, he committed a lewd act or an act inimical to the public safety or welfare after gaining admittance to the place of entertainment. But we stressed that no sweeping inquiry could be made into the background and reputation of each person seeking admission. "[T]he private business, the personal relations with others, the past conduct not on the premises, of a person applying for or admitted to the [race] course, whether or not relevant to indicate his character, are immaterial in the application of the statutory standards * * *." . . .

In Jarvella v. Willoughby-Eastlake City School District (1967) 12 Ohio Misc. 288, 233 N.E.2d 143, the court faced the issue of whether a teacher could be dismissed for "immorality" merely because he had written a private letter to a friend containing language which some adults might find vulgar and offensive. The court held that Ohio Revised Code section 3319.16, authorizing dismissal for "immorality" did not cover the teacher's actions, and that he could not therefore be dismissed. The court explained, "Whatever else the term 'Immorality' may mean to many, it is clear that when used in a statute it is inseparable from 'conduct.' * * * But it is not 'immoral conduct' considered in the abstract. It must be considered in the context in which the Legislature considered it, as conduct which is hostile to the welfare of the general public; more specifically in this case, conduct which is hostile to the welfare of the school community. * * * In providing standards to guide school boards in placing restraints on conduct of teachers, the Legislature is concerned with the welfare of the school community. Its objective is the protection of students from corruption. This is a proper exercise of the power of a state to abridge personal liberty and to protect larger interests. But reasonableness must be the governing criterion. * * * Orloff v. Los Angeles Turf Club, Inc., 36 Cal.2d 734, 227 P.2d 449. * * * The private conduct of a man, who is also a teacher, is a proper concern to those who employ him only to the extent it mars him as a teacher * * *. Where his professional achievement is unaffected, where the school community is placed in no jeopardy, his private acts are his own business and may not be the basis of discipline." . . .

By interpreting these broad terms to apply to the employee's performance on the job, the decisions . . . give content to language which otherwise would be too sweeping to be meaningful. Terms such as "immoral or unprofessional conduct" or "moral turpitude" stretch over so wide a range that they embrace an unlimited area of conduct. In using them the Legislature surely did not mean to endow the employing agency with the power to dismiss any employee whose personal, private conduct incurred its disapproval. Hence the courts have consistently related the terms to the issue of whether, when applied to the performance of the employee on the job, the employee has disqualified himself.

In the instant case the terms denote immoral or unprofessional conduct or moral turpitude of the teacher which indicates unfitness to teach. Without such a reasonable interpretation the terms would be susceptible to so broad an application as possibly to subject to discipline virtually every teacher in the state. In the opinion of many people laziness, gluttony, vanity, selfishness, avarice, and cowardice constitute immoral conduct. . . . A recent study by the State Assembly reported that educators differed among themselves as to whether "unprofessional conduct" might include "imbibing alcoholic beverages, use of tobacco, signing petitions, revealing contents of school documents to legislative committees, appealing directly to one's legislative representative, and opposing major-[ity] *opinions* * * *." . . . We cannot believe that the Legislature intended to compel disciplinary measures against teachers who committed such peccadillos if such passing conduct did not affect students or fellow teachers. Surely incidents of extramarital heterosexual conduct against a background of years of satisfactory teaching would not constitute "immoral conduct" sufficient to justify revocation of a life diploma without any showing of an adverse effect on fitness to teach.

Nor is it likely that the Legislature intended by section 13202 to establish a standard for the conduct of teachers that might vary widely with time, location, and the popular mood. One could expect a reasonably stable consensus within the teaching profession as to what conduct adversely affects students and fellow teachers. No such consensus can be presumed about "morality." "Today's morals may be tomorrow's ancient and absurd customs." . . . And conversely, conduct socially acceptable today may be anathema tomorrow. Local boards of education, moreover, are authorized to revoke their own certificates and dismiss permanent teachers for immoral and unprofessional conduct . . . an overly broad interpretation of that authorization could result in disciplinary action in one country for conduct treated as permissible in another. . . . A more constricted interpretation of "immoral," "unprofessional," and "moral turpitude" avoids these difficulties, enabling the State Board of Education to utilize its expertise in educational matters rather than having to act "as the prophet to which is revealed the state of morals of the people or the common conscience." . . .

That the meaning of "immoral," "unprofessional," and "moral turpitude" must depend upon, and thus relate to, the occupation involved finds further confirmation in the fact that those terms are used in a wide variety of contexts. . . .

We therefore conclude that the Board of Education cannot abstractly characterize the conduct in this case as "immoral," "unprofessional," or "involving moral turpitude" within the meaning of section 13202 of the Education Code unless that conduct indicates that the petitioner is unfit to teach. In determining whether the teacher's conduct thus indicates unfitness to teach the board may consider such matters as the likelihood that the conduct may have adversely affected students or fellow teachers, the degree of such adversity anticipated, the proximity or remoteness in time of the conduct, the type of teaching certificate held by the party involved, the extenuating or aggravating circumstances, if any, surrounding the conduct, the praiseworthiness or blameworthiness of the motives resulting in the conduct, the likelihood of the recurrence of the questioned conduct, and the extent to which disciplinary action may inflict an adverse impact or chilling effect upon the constitutional rights of the teacher involved or other teachers. These factors are relevant to the extent that they assist the board in determining a teacher's fitness to teach, i. e., in determining whether the teacher's future classroom performance and overall impact on his students are likely to meet the board's standards.

If interpreted in this manner section 13202 can be constitutionally applied to petitioner.

Petitioner urges three substantive reasons to support his contention that section 13202 upon its face or as construed by the board deprived him of his constitutional rights. As we shall show, however, that section, as we have interpreted it, could constitutionally apply to petitioner.

Petitioner first suggests that the terms "unprofessional," "moral turpitude," and particularly "immoral" are so vague as to constitute a denial of due process. Civil as well as criminal statutes must be sufficiently clear as to give a fair warning of the conduct prohibited, and they must provide a standard or guide against which conduct can be uniformly judged by courts and administrative agencies. . . . The knowledge that he has erred is of little value to the teacher when gained only upon the imposition of a disciplinary penalty that jeopardizes or eliminates his livelihood. . . . Courts and commentators have exposed and condemned the uncertainty of words such as "unprofessional," "immoral," and "moral turpitude." Indeed, in Orloff v. Los Angeles Turf Club, supra . . . this court recognized that the term "immoral" might well be unconstitutionally vague. . .

. . . As we have explained above, the prohibitions against immoral and unprofessional conduct and conduct involving moral turpitude by a teacher constitutes a general ban on conduct which would indicate his unfitness to teach. This construction gives section 13202 the required specificity. Teachers, particularly in the light of their professional expertise, will normally be able to determine what kind of conduct indicates unfitness to teach. Teachers are further protected by the fact that they cannot be disciplined merely because they made a reasonable, good faith, professional judgment in the course of their employment with which higher authorities later disagreed. . . .

Petitioner secondly contends that the ban on immoral conduct in section 13202 violates his constitutionally protected right to privacy. It is true that an unqualified proscription against immoral conduct would raise serious constitutional problems. Conscientious school officials concerned with enforcing such a broad provision might be inclined to probe into the private life of each and every teacher, no matter how exemplary his classroom conduct. Such prying might all too readily lead school officials to search for "telltale signs" of immorality in violation of the teacher's constitutional rights. (Griswold v. Connecticut). . . . The proper construction of section 13202, however, minimizes the danger of such sweeping inquiries. By limiting the application of that section to conduct shown to indicate unfitness to teach, we substantially reduce the incentive to inquire into the private lives of otherwise sound and competent teachers.

Finally, petitioner urges that the board cannot revoke his life diplomas because his questioned conduct does not rationally relate to his duties as a teacher. No person can be denied government employment because of factors unconnected with the responsibilities of that employment. . . . Again, however, the proper construction of section 13202 avoids this problem, for that interpretation would bar disciplinary action against petitioner unless the record demonstrated that petitioner's conduct did indicate his unfitness to teach.

The record contains no evidence that petitioner's conduct indicated his unfitness to teach.

As we have stated above, the statutes, properly interpreted, provide that the State Board of Education can revoke a life diploma or other document of certification and thus prohibit local school officials from hiring a particular teacher only if that individual has in some manner indicated that he is unfit to teach. Thus an individual can be removed from the teaching profession only upon a showing that his retention in the profession poses a significant danger of harm to either students, school employees, or others who might be affected by his actions as a teacher. . . . Accordingly, we must inquire whether any adverse inferences can be drawn from that past conduct as to petitioner's teaching ability, or as to the possibility that publicity surrounding past conduct may in and of itself substantially impair his function as a teacher.

As to this crucial issue, the record before the board and before this court contains no evidence whatsoever. . . .

This lack of evidence is particularly significant because the board failed to show that petitioner's conduct in any manner affected his performance as a teacher. There was not the slightest suggestion that petitioner had ever attempted, sought, or even considered any form of physical or otherwise improper relationship with any student. There was no evidence that petitioner had failed to impress upon the minds of his pupils the principles of morality as required by section 13556.5 of the Education Code. There is no reason to believe that the Schneringer incident affected petitioner's apparently satisfactory relationship with his co-workers.

The board revoked petitioner's license three years after the Schneringer incident; that incident has now receded six years into the past. Petitioner's motives at the time of the incident involved neither dishonesty nor viciousness, and the emotional pressures on both petitioner and Schneringer suggest the presence of extenuating circumstances. Finally, the record contains no evidence that the events of April 1963 have become so notorious as to impair petitioner's ability to command the respect and confidence of students and fellow teachers in schools within or without the Lowell Joint School District.

Before the board can conclude that a teacher's continued retention in the profession presents a significant danger of harm to students or fellow teachers, essential factual premises in its reasoning should be supported by evidence or official notice. In this case, despite the quantity and quality of information available about human sexual behavior, the record contains no such evidence as to the significance and implications of the Schneringer incident. Neither this court nor the superior court is authorized to rectify this failure by uninformed speculation or conjecture as to petitioner's future conduct. . . .

Respondent relies heavily on Sarac v. State Bd. of Education. . . . The facts involved in *Sarac* are clearly distinguishable from the instant case; the teacher disciplined in that case had pleaded guilty to a criminal charge of disorderly conduct arising from his homosexual advances toward a police officer at a public beach; the teacher admitted a recent history of homosexual activities. The court's discussion in that case includes unnecessarily broad language suggesting that all homosexual conduct, even though not shown to relate to fitness to teach, warrants disciplinary action. . . . The proper construction of section 13202, however, as we have demonstrated, is more restricted than indicated by this dicta in *Sarac,* and to the extent that *Sarac* conflicts with this opinion it must be disapproved. . . .

Conclusion.

In deciding this case we are not unmindful of the public interest in the elimination of unfit elementary and secondary school teachers. . . . But petitioner is entitled to a careful and reasoned inquiry into his fitness to teach by the Board of Education before he is deprived of his right to pursue his profession. . . . "The right to practice one's profession is sufficiently precious to surround it with a panoply of legal protection" . . . and terms such as "immoral," "unprofessional," and "moral turpitude" constitute only lingual abstractions until applied to a specific occupation and given content by reference to fitness for the performance of that vocation. . . .

Our conclusion affords no guarantee that petitioner's life diplomas cannot be revoked. If the Board of Education believes that petitioner is unfit to teach, it can reopen its inquiry into the circumstances surrounding and the implications of the 1963 incident with Mr. Schneringer. The board also has at its disposal ample means to discipline petitioner for future misconduct.

Finally, we do not, of course, hold that homosexuals must be permitted to teach in the public schools of California. As we have explained, the relevant statutes, as well as the applicable principles of constitutional law, require only that the board properly find, pursuant to the precepts set forth in this opinion, that an individual is not fit to teach. . . .

SULLIVAN, Justice.

I dissent. . . .

. . . The precise question before us is this: Did the Board properly revoke petitioner's life diplomas upon determining that petitioner, while employed as a teacher, had committed homosexual acts and engaged in a homosexual relationship with a fellow teacher and that such acts constituted immoral and unprofessional conduct within the meaning the sections 13202 and 13209 of the Education Code?
. . .

. . . Homosexual behavior has long been contrary and abhorrent to the social mores and moral standards of the people of California as it has been since antiquity to those of many other peoples. It is clearly, therefore, immoral conduct within the meaning of Education Code, section 13202. It may also constitute unprofessional conduct within the meaning of that same statute as such conduct is not limited to classroom misconduct or misconduct with children. . . . It certainly constitutes evident unfitness for service in the public school system within the meaning of that statute. . . . In view of appellant's statutory duty as a teacher to 'endeavor to impress upon the minds of the pupils the principles of morality' (Ed.Code, § 7851) and his necessarily close association with children in the discharge of his professional duties as a teacher, there is to our minds an obvious rational connection between his homosexual conduct on the beach and the consequent action of respondent in revoking his secondary teaching credential on the statutory grounds of immoral and unprofessional conduct and evident unfitness for service in the public school system of this State." . . .

The majority argue that *Sarac* is distinguishable from the instant case on its facts. It is asserted that the teacher's homosexual conduct occurred on a public beach, whereas this petitioner's conduct occurred in the privacy of his apartment. Apparently this asserted difference reflects the view that, absent a criminal offense, petitioner's private life is his own business and the state " * * * must not arbitrarily impair the right of the individual to live his private life, apart from his job, as he deems fit. * * * " But the clandestine character of petitioner's acts did not render them any the less homosexual acts. These still remained, to borrow the language of *Sarac* " * * * contrary and abhorrent to the social mores and moral standards of the people of California * * *." . . . It would be fatuous to assume that such acts became reprehensible only if committed in public. One would not expect petitioner and Schneringer to commit the acts here involved (which, as I have said, need not be detailed) in full view of the citizenry.

It is also asserted by the majority that the teacher in *Sarac* pleaded guilty to and was convicted of a criminal charge. However, as I have pointed out, the accusation filed with the Board in that case was based primarily on the teacher's homosexual conduct, apart from his subsequent arrest, which fell within the compass of section 13202 and warranted revocation of his credentials. . . .

The court in *Sarac* also sustained the trial court's finding that the homosexual act there committed was one involving moral turpitude. As already stated, a similar finding and determination were made in the instant matter not only in the administrative proceedings but also in the superior court proceedings on review. The determination is unassailable. Although we have recognized on occasion that the problem of defining moral turpitude is not without difficulty . . . nevertheless this court has for many years . . . defined moral turpitude as " * * * everything done contrary to justice, honesty, modesty, or good morals. * * * " . . .

In sum, the majority opinion boils down to this: " * * * the Board failed to show that petitioner's conduct in any manner affected his performance as a teacher" and "petitioner is entitled to a careful and reasoned inquiry into his fitness to teach by the Board of Education before he is deprived of his right to pursue his profession." Taking this position, the majority remand this case to the superior court presumably, although they do not say so, to be remanded by that court in turn to the Board.

I feel it my duty to observe, with all due respect to the majority, that this action is taken without proper recognition of our function of review in cases of administrative boards. . . . To recapitulate: The Board in this case found on overwhelming evidence, indeed on the frank but unrepentent admissions of petitioner, that he had committed homosexual acts with another teacher and concluded that these acts constituted immoral and unprofessional conduct and acts involving moral turpitude. The trial court reached the same conclusion. The majority opinion is silent on this point. Yet I would respectfully suggest that it is an essential step in any process of reasoning which seeks to strike down the Board's action. Were petitioner's acts immoral or not? Or was he perhaps correct after all in maintaining they were not? The majority do not answer this question; nevertheless they reverse the judgment and remand the cause to the trial court for further proceedings. I would think that under the circumstances the question should be answered for the guidance of the court below on retrial; that court, as well as the Board, should be told whether or not they were in error in concluding that petitioner's homosexual acts were immoral and involved moral turpitude. As I said at the beginning, this is the pivotal question and I think it was correctly answered by the Board, the trial judge and the three appellate justices. . . .

In the instant case, both the Board and the trial court concluded that petitioner was unfit. I cannot say there is no rational connection between petitioner's homosexual acts and his fitness to teach. . . .

BURKE, Justice. . . .

. . . This case, and other recent cases, have involved the courts in the untenable position of attempting to assess factual issues of conduct, motive and intent that could better be left to the governmental agencies upon whom the discretion has been conferred by the Legislature. . . .

THE TEACHER'S CONTRACT

INTRODUCTION

If a person has been certified to teach in the common schools that does not mean he will automatically get a teaching position. It does mean that he has become a member of a "qualified" group, and can receive an offer of a job. In all states, statutes locate the power to make teaching contracts with qualified teachers in a school board, usually local boards. Similar to the certification process, school boards generally have power to promulgate legally valid rules and regulations that set forth the conditions under which a previously certified person becomes eligible for a contract. Thus, local boards establish qualifications for teachers through the contracting process that are in addition to those required for certification. Of course, the contractual conditions must themselves be constitutional; e. g., no local board could validly promulgate a rule denying contracts solely on the grounds of race, religion or political affiliation. But, what about union activities?

Only the board of education can enter into a binding contract. In the absence of a statute permitting that power to be delegated to someone else neither a State Superintendent, nor any other person, can validly make a contract with a teacher. Moreover, if there is no delegation of the power to contract, it follows that the Superintendent cannot terminate a contract, only the school board has the power to do so. Snider v. Kit Carson School District, 166 Colo. 180, 442 P.2d 429 (1968). The subject matter of teacher's contracts varies to a greater extent than certification requirements. A teacher can be employed to engage in a variety of activities that can be set forth in the contract. Thus, the contract is most important because it sets forth the rights and duties of the teacher and the school district. Moreover, contracts may be limited to a fixed period; thus, a teacher might have a lifetime certificate but only a one or three year contract. In such situations, after the time period has expired and both parties to the contract have performed, their relationship is at an end. The contract has expired.

At least two formal, legal requirements must be met before the teacher can be said to have a legally binding contract. First, the school board itself must have proceeded in such a way as to meet all the requirements for valid, legal action, thereby binding the school district. This means that the school board meeting where the action is taken to make an offer to a person, or to delegate that power (where permitted by statute), must conform to all the requirements of law, such as, having given proper notice; having a quorum present; having the meeting open, if required; following the technically correct procedures on the presentation of school board business, voting, etc. If the school board meeting does not comply with the requirements of law, then the school board, or its agent, has no lawful power to act, and in such circumstances, it cannot make a binding contract, and a teacher will not have a valid contract. Secondly, the teacher's contract must comply with the same general requirements of law that all contracts must satisfy. There must be (1) a specific and definite offer meeting the requirements of law and an unqualified acceptance of that offer; (2) legally competent persons capable of contracting, for example, a teacher without a valid teaching certificate may not be a competent person to contract with a board of education, this requirement can cause difficulty for persons who are graduating from a college or university and have obtained a teaching position before being certified; (3) consideration, i. e., something that is valuable, for example: the rendering of specified teaching services in exchange for money; (4) a legal subject matter, teaching is a lawful subject, but if it were not the contract would be declared void—could a school board validly contract with a minister to conduct religious services in school?; (5) a proper legal form; frequently States require that before a teacher's contract will be legally valid it must be in writing, especially tenure contracts.

If contracts required to be in writing are oral, then they are not enforceable; however, in such event, if a qualified teacher renders teaching services, courts allow him to recover a fair compensation for them, but not because he has a valid contract. See, e. g., Goose River Bank v. Willow Lake School Township, 1 N.D. 26, 44 N.W. 1002 (1890). Finally, in addition to the rules and regulations governing the qualifications for a contract, courts tend to hold that so long as the rules and regulations of the board of education do not conflict with the constitution, or other higher law, they, as well as the statutes of the state governing teacher behavior, are all part of the contract between the teacher and the school district. This last item can come as a surprise to many teachers who are ignorant of a local board's governing rules and regulations; for example, could a local board constitutionally provide that a teacher's contract would be terminated if he is absent from school for three months (Elder v. Board of Education, 60 Ill.App.2d 56, 208 N.E.2d 423 (1965)), or if he refused to sever his financial interests with a liquor store (Romeike v. Houston Independent School Dist., 368 S.W.2d 895 (Tex.1963)), or if he refused to engage in further professional training (Last v. Board of Education, 37 Ill.App.2d 159, 185 N.E.2d 282 (1962))?

At times local school boards, by contract, try to require that teachers go to rather drastic lengths in satisfying conditions that the board deems necessary for the efficient operation of the schools:

> "I promise to take a vital interest in all phases of Sunday-school work, donating of my time, service, and money without stint for the benefit and uplift of the community.

> "I promise to abstain from dancing, immodest dressing, and any other conduct unbecoming a teacher and a lady.

> "I promise not to go out with any young men except insofar as it may be necessary to stimulate Sunday-school work.

> "I promise not to fall in love, to become engaged or secretly married.

> "I promise to remain in the domitory or on the school grounds when not actively engaged in school or church work elsewhere.

"I promise not to encourage or tolerate the least familiarity on the part of any of my boy pupils . . ."

The above, taken from a teacher's contract in a North Carolina town, is set forth in Odegard, The American Public Mind 83 (1930), printed in Williams et al., Labor Relations and the Law. Boston: Little, Brown and Company, 1965, p. 751. Is such a contract constitutional? Is this type of contract a good argument for teachers' unions?

————

BIG SANDY SCHOOL DISTRICT NO. 100–J v. CARROLL

Supreme Court of Colorado, 1967.
164 Colo. 173, 433 P.2d 325.

McWILLIAMS, Justice. The central issue presented by this writ of error is whether a school board may delegate to its superintendent of schools the "power" and "duty" to employ teachers.

Before detailing some of the facts, it is deemed advisable to set forth at the very outset the particular statute with which we are here concerned. C.R.S.1963, 123–10–19, which pertains generally to the "powers of a school board," provides in part as follows:

"(1) *Every school board*, unless otherwise especially provided by law, *shall have power, and it shall be their duty:*

"(2) *To employ* or discharge *teachers,* mechanics and laborers, *and to fix* and order paid *their wages;* * * *"
(Emphasis added.)

The essential facts in the instant case are not really in dispute, although as to some peripheral matters there are some rather marked disputes. Sometime in June 1963 the five members of the school board for the Big Sandy School District No. 100–J "authorized" the superintendent of schools to "contact and employ" a combination principal and teacher for the high school in Simla. This "authorization" did not result from any formal action of the school board, but nonetheless was apparently acquiesced in by all five board members. The superintendent was advised as to the "salary limits" within which he could then fix the salary of the new principal-teacher, once he was located. Otherwise, there were no additional limitations or restrictions placed on the superintendent, and it was strictly up to him to find and hire a combination principal and teacher for the high school.

To facilitate the entire process, the President and Secretary of the school board signed "in blank" an employment contract form used by the District. In other words, the employment contract form signed by the President and Secretary of the Board did not, of course, designate the other contracting party, whose identity as of that time was unknown, or did it fix the salary or the dates the employment would either start or end.

In mid-August of 1963 Carroll first contacted the superintendent about possible employment as both the principal and a teacher in the Simla High School. On that occasion, Carroll and the superintendent conferred at some length about the teaching vacancy, and the two of them generally "came to terms" although Carroll said that he wanted to talk the matter over with his wife before he made any final decision. On this occasion the superintendent, in the presence of Carroll, typed in the "blanks" in the employment contract form theretofore signed in blank by the President and Secretary of the school board. Specifically, the superintendent typed in the name of "Barney Carroll" as the other party to the contract. The superintendent also typed in the salary as being "sixty-five hundred $6,500 dollars," payable in twelve monthly installments, as well as typing in the period of employment as "beginning August 21, 1963 and ending August 20, 1964."

According to Carroll, though this was denied by the superintendent, he (Carroll) called the superintendent on the following day and "accepted" the offer. Carroll testified that immediately thereafter he signed the original contract, and a copy thereof, both of which had been given him on the preceding day by the superintendent. Carroll retained the original of this contract and upon trial the document was offered and received into evidence. As concerns the copy of the aforementioned contract, Carroll testified that a few days after his telephone conversation with the superintendent he left the copy, signed by him, on the superintendent's desk. The superintendent testified, however, that he never found any such signed copy on his desk.

Without going into any great detail as to why he was relieved of his duties, Carroll was purportedly "discharged" by the superintendent some ten days later. It should be noted that the purported discharge occurred on the day before classes were to commence and was triggered by the fact that Carroll had "missed" the schools' registration day. However, no hearing was ever held as to whether this so-called discharge was "for cause," or not.

Carroll immediately brought suit against the District, alleging a contract of employment between himself and the District and a breach of that contract by the District when he was wrongfully discharged "without good cause shown or a hearing."

Upon trial of this matter the basic contention of the District was that the school board could not lawfully delegate to its superintendent 'he power to employ teachers and that accordingly there never was a valid contract between Carroll and the District. Though this case was tried to a jury, at the conclusion of all the evidence the trial court took the case from the jury on the premise that there were no issues of fact, only issues of law. The trial court then ruled that there was a valid contract of employment between Carroll and the District and that the District had breached the contract by summarily discharging Carroll without the benefit of any hearing as to whether there was "good cause" for his discharge. Judgment was then entered in Carroll's favor in the sum of $6,500 and interest from August 21, 1963. . . . Our study of the matter convinces us that under the circumstances there never was a valid and binding contract between Carroll and the District, and that the trial court therefore erred in its entry of judgment in behalf of Carroll.

The applicable statute not only empowers the school board to employ teachers and fix their wages, but goes on to declare that such is the *duty of the school board.* C.R.S.1963, 123–10–19. In other words, the power to employ teachers is exclusively vested by the legislature in the school board, and not in any other body or official. It being, then, the *duty* of the school board to employ teachers and fix their wages, the question is then raised as to whether the duty which has been thus placed by the legislature in the school board may be delegated, or on the contrary whether this is a non-delegable duty.

.   .   .

In our view the power to employ teachers and fix their wages is not a mere ministerial or administrative matter, where little or no judgment or discretion is involved, but on the contrary is a legislative or judicial power involving the exercise of considerable discretion. Hence, under the general rule, such power cannot be delegated. The power to employ teachers has been conferred by the legislature exclusively on the school board, and therefore it cannot be delegated. To hold to the contrary would thwart the obvious intent of the legislature and would amount to nothing more than pure judicial legislation. .   .   .

.   .   .   if this should be deemed a "hard" case, hard cases should not be allowed to make bad law. To permit Carroll to recover against the District would make some very bad law and would open the door to great abuse. In short, by statute the school board is empowered to hire teachers and while it may well want to act on the recommendation of its superintendent, it cannot escape this statutory duty by completely shifting the responsibility to its superintendent. This is so because that is the way the legislature wanted it.

The judgment is reversed. .   .   .

BUCKLEY v. COYLE PUBLIC SCHOOL SYSTEM

United States Court of Appeals, 10th Cir., 1973.
476 F.2d 92.

WILLIAM E. DOYLE, Circuit Judge. This is an appeal from the final judgment entered following the granting of defendants-appellees' motion for summary judgment. The plaintiff-appellant was a school teacher in the City of Coyle, Oklahoma Public School system. She was in her first year of employment and thus had no tenure. She was dismissed in accordance with a policy of the school system at the end of her sixth month of pregnancy. The action questioned the validity of this policy and of her termination pursuant to it.

The suit was brought under the Civil Rights Act of 1866 and of 1871, and also of 1964, Title VII.

. . . the trial court ruled that the action of the plaintiff-appellant was insufficient on its face and thus did not even merit preliminary inquiry, our problem is whether it does present a constitutional claim of sufficient substance to justify a hearing on the merits. We hold that the claim has apparent substance and more; that its nature and character are such as to make out a case of probable rather than merely possible recovery and, therefore, that it was error for the trial court to summarily throw it out, so to speak.

The plaintiff-appellant's contention is that the school policy calling for dismissal at the end of the sixth month of pregnancy discriminated against her solely on the basis of sex and in so doing violated the equal protection clause of the Fourteenth Amendment to the Constitution of the United States, plus the Civil Rights Act. She also maintains that she was discriminated against because of her exercise of First Amendment rights and also that she was the victim of discrimination based upon her color.

I.

We start with the most obvious of the alleged violations and that is the charge of discrimination based on sex. The trial court's attempted distinction between discriminatory and non-discriminatory regulations as being whether the condition involved is one which was involuntary must be rejected. The fact, if it be a fact, that pregnancy is a voluntary status really has nothing to do with the question. The point is that the regulation penalizes the feminine school teacher for being a woman and, therefore, it must be condemned on that ground.

Judge Brown dissented in one of the earlier cases, Phillips v. Martin-Marietta Corp., 416 F.2d 1257, 1259 (5th Cir. 1969), vacated per curiam, 400 U.S. 542 . . . a Title VII case in which the employer was willing to hire men with preschool age children for a certain position but not women, brought out the discriminatory nature of the regulation in these terms:

> The distinguishing factor seems to be motherhood versus fatherhood. The question then arises: Is this sex-related? To the simply query the answer is just as simple: Nobody —and this includes Judges, Solomonic or life-tenured—has yet seen a male mother. A mother, to oversimplify the simplest biology, must then be a woman.

So also in our case we have a regulation which bears down upon the person involved because she is a woman.

The Sixth Circuit has also considered the question in La Fleur v. Cleveland Bd. of Educ., 465 F.2d 1184 (6th Cir. 1972), wherein the regulation provided for maternity leave to be effective not less than five months before the expected date of the normal birth of the child. Certain other regulations which were not condemned required that notice be given of the condition and also that the notice be given two weeks before the effective date of the leave of absence. A great deal of evidence had been taken by the trial court and much of this had sought to justify the regulation, i. e., to show a rational basis for it. The court rejected these efforts saying that the rule was inherently based upon a classification by sex. The court (Judge Edwards writing) went on to mention the obvious truth that "male teachers are not subject to many types of illnesses and disabilities." The court continued: This record indicates clearly that pregnant women teachers have been singled out for unconstitutionally unequal restrictions upon their employment. Additionally, as we have observed, the rule is clearly arbitrary and unreasonable in its overbreadth. As the Supreme Court said in Wieman v. Updegraff, 344 U.S. 183 . . .

> "We need not pause to consider whether an abstract right to public employment exists. It is sufficient to say that constitutional protection does extend to the public servant whose exclusion pursuant to a statute is patently arbitrary or discriminatory."

The Fourth Circuit had a similar regulation before it in Cohen v. Chesterfield County School Bd., 5 EPD ¶ 7967 (4th Cir. 1972), rev'd en banc, 474 F.2d 395. In this case the regulation provided for the maternity leave to commence no later than the fifth month of pregnancy. A majority of the court in an opinion written by Chief Judge Haynsworth upheld the regulation as a reasonable classification. Judge Winter wrote the minority opinion which argued that the provision was discriminatory and in violation of the equal protection clause of the Fourteenth Amendment since there was neither medical reason nor administrative justification for the regulation; that there existed no valid reason for treating maternity leave differently from any other medical leave or any other medical disabilities. It is important to note that a full evidentiary hearing had been held and it thus differs from our situation in which the cause was summarily dismissed.

Appellees also rely on Schattman v. Texas Employment Comm'n, 459 F.2d 32, 42 (5th Cir. 1972), cert. denied 409 U.S. 1107, 93 S.Ct. 901, 34 L.Ed.2d 688. This case is factually different from ours in that the person was given a maternity leave instead of being discharged, and the leave commenced not later than two months before the expected delivery date. At least some effort was apparent in that case to develop a provision bearing some relationship to the realities of the pregnancy, and here also an extensive evidentiary hearing was had. In our case the policy of the Board appears drastic and categorical.

The classification here is at least susceptible to the charge leveled against it by appellant, namely, that it discriminates invalidly against womanhood, and that it invades plaintiff's privacy by requiring her to choose between employment and pregnancy, thus curtailing her interest in having a child—an interest recognized as constitutional in Skinner v. Oklahoma, 316 U.S. 535. . . . *Skinner* saw the interest in procreating as a basic one which is within the protection of the Fourteenth Amendment.

The remaining question is whether in determining the validity of the policy under consideration the trial court should apply the rational basis test enunciated in Dandridge v. Williams, 397 U.S. 471, . . . or the compelling state interest test of Shapiro v. Thompson, . . . We conclude that the state must demonstrate a compelling interest in order to justify its policy because the interest involved is a fundamental one in that 1) it concerns the acknowledged right of the plaintiff to bear children, and 2) it demands that a school teacher select either employment or pregnancy. In holding that compelling interest is the applicable test, we have in mind the matters just mentioned, plus the fact that plaintiff has alleged that her race was a factor in the application of this policy—that white teachers are not subjected to it in every instance. This is an allegation that must be supported by evidence in order to be entitled to recognition, but if it is true the compelling state interest approach is the appropriate one.

II.

The trial court was also in error when it summarily disposed of this action, notwithstanding appellant's allegation that the maternity regulation cloaks a more deep-seated policy of racial discrimination as well as reprisal resulting from appellant's First Amendment activities regarding library acquisitions. She is entitled to prove these charges, for it cannot be questioned that a teacher's exercise of First Amendment rights is not to be used as a ground for dismissal from public employment. . . .

While it is true that the appellant does not have a constitutional right to continue public employment, it cannot be gainsaid that she does have the right to be free from the imposition of unconstitutional conditions in connection with that employment. . . .

NOTES AND QUESTIONS

1. Mrs. Buckley was a probationary employee who was dismissed during her one-year contract period. What grounds do you believe the school board relied upon in order to terminate her contract before its termina-

tion date? Do you think the school rule on pregnancy was incorporated as part of Mrs. Buckley's contract? Did the court declare the school rule on pregnancy to be unconstitutional?

2. The court states that on retrial "the state must demonstrate a compelling interest in order to justify its policy" on pregnancy: Is this what the state usually must demonstrate in order to justify a rule of a school board? If not, what accounts for the use of a different requirement in this case?

3. Does the state have a compelling interest that would justify its policy on pregnancy? If not this specific policy, does a state have any compelling interest that would justify a rule on pregnancy? If so, what is that interest and what rule would it justify?

NOTE: See Cleveland Bd. of Ed. v. LaFleur, Supreme Court of the United States, 1974, Appendix at page 865, infra.

TEACHER TENURE

INTRODUCTION

Today, most state legislatures have passed teacher tenure laws which provide that after having served a satisfactory probationary period either a teacher's "position" or his "contract" will be a continuing one without a periodic need for renewal. In McSherry v. City of St. Paul, 202 Minn. 102, 277 N.W. 541 (1938), Minnesota's Supreme Court discussed the general history and purpose of tenure legislation:

"The education of our youth to fit them for the duties and responsibilities of citizenship in our state and nation was a matter of vital concern to our pioneers. This seems clear as we find that immediately upon statehood constitutional provision was made to accomplish that end. By article 8, §§ 1 to 7, inclusive, thereof provision was made for the establishment and maintenance of public education as a state system under its direction and control. Thus section 1 provides: 'The stability of a republican form of government depending mainly upon the intelligence of the people, it shall be the duty of the legislature to establish a general and uniform system of public schools.' . . .

"Teachers' tenure, like civil service and other similar movements, dates back now over a period of many years. The abuses existing by reason of the 'spoils system' which came into prominence during Jackson's administration, later followed by national and other administrations, led to much-deserved criticism. That is why on January 16, 1883 ('An act to regulate and improve the civil service of the United States,' 22 Stat. 403), the first civil service act was passed. In 1885, the National Education Association brought forth the question of tenure of school officials. A committee of that association studied the matter and later submitted a report. Generally speaking the tenure so sought was interpreted to mean, in substance, the application of the principles of civil service to the teaching profession. It was thought that for the good of the schools and the general public the profession should be made independent of personal or political influence, and made free from the malignant power of spoils and patronage. In 1886 the state of Massachusetts enacted a law 'relating to the tenure of office of teachers.' St.Mass.1886, c. 313. Thereunder school districts were permitted to enter into contracts with teachers for a longer period than one year. In 1889 the committee on rules of the Boston School Committee suggested a tenure law providing for a probationary period of one year, four years of annual elections, and thereafter permanent tenure subject to removal for cause after proper hearing. The bases for recommendations were that better talent would be attracted to the teaching profession; that annual contracts theretofore in vogue had not resulted in the elimination of poor, incompetent, and inefficient teachers; that the principle of annual election or appointment was not generally applied to policemen, firemen, or judicial officers, and in the very nature of things should not apply to teachers; that not infrequently the best teachers were discharged for inadequate reasons. (See report of Committee on Tenure of National Education Association for the year 1921.) Foreign countries have long recognized the principle of teachers' tenure. (See report of Committee on Tenure of National Education Association for the year 1936.) Since 1900 the principle of teachers' tenure in this country has developed more rapidly. In a general way it has followed the civil service plan. The objectives sought have been to protect the teachers against unjust removal after having undergone an adequate probationary period; that the movement itself has for its basis public interest, in that most advantages go to the youth of the land and to the schools themselves, rather than the interest of the teachers as such. (See report of Committee on Civil Service for Teachers of National Education Association for July, 1934.)

"Many states have adopted teachers' tenure acts. We shall not stop to enumerate them. The general purposes and advantages of these acts and the reasons therefor are interestingly set forth in 'Bulletin of National Education Association on Teachers' Tenure for 1937.'

"We refrain from making further comment on this phase, as every citizen knows and recognizes, not only as a matter of history, but also as a matter of personal experience, the great importance our schools have played and are playing in the furtherance of good citizenship by affording, generally, and to all our youth, opportunity to gain an education. . . .

"Plainly, the legislative purposes sought were stability, certainty, and permanency of employment on the part of those who had shown by educational attainment and by probationary trial their fitness for the teaching profession. By statutory direction and limitation there is provided means of prevention of *arbitrary* demotions or discharges by school authorities. The history behind the act justifies the view that the vicissitudes to which teachers had in the past been subjected were to be done away with or at least minimized. It was enacted for the *benefit and advantage of the school system* by providing such machinery as would tend to minimize the part that malice, political or partisan trends, or caprice might play. It established *merit* as the essential basis for the *right* of permanent employment. On the other hand, it is equally clear that the act does not impair *discretionary* power of school authorities to make the best selections consonant with the public good; but their conduct in this behalf is strictly circumscribed and must be kept within the boundaries of the act. The provision for a probationary period is intended for that very purpose. The right to demote or discharge provides remedies for safeguarding the future against incompetence, insubordination, and other grounds stated in the act. The act itself bespeaks the intent. Provisions for notice and hearing, the requirements of specified causes for discharge or demotion, are indicative of the general purpose. With these considerations in mind, it is our duty so to construe such parts of the act which on their face do not clearly delineate the legislative intent as will bring about a result in harmony with the expressed legislative policy. . . ."

Excerpts from Minnesota's current law applying to cities of the first class is an example of teacher tenure:

"All teachers in the public schools in cities of the first class during the first three years of consecutive employment shall be deemed to be in a probationary period of employment during which period any annual contract with any teacher may, or may not, be renewed as the school board shall see fit. The school board may, during such probationary period, discharge or demote a teacher for any of the causes as specified in this code. A written statement of the cause of such discharge or demotion shall be given to the teacher by the school board at least 30 days before such removal or demotion shall become effective, and the teacher so notified shall have no right of appeal therefrom.

"After the completion of such probationary period, without discharge, such teachers as are thereupon re-employed shall continue in service and hold their respective position during good behavior and efficient and competent service and shall not be discharged or demoted except for cause after a hearing.

"Any probationary teacher shall be deemed to have been re-employed for the ensuing school year, unless the school board in charge of such school shall give such teacher notice in writing before April 1 of the termination of such employment. In event of such notice the employment shall terminate at the close of the school sessions of the current school year.

"Causes for the discharge or demotion of a teacher either during or after the probationary period shall be:

(1) Immoral character, conduct unbecoming a teacher, or insubordination;

(2) Failure without justifiable cause to teach without first securing the written release of the school board having the care, management, or control of the school in which the teacher is employed;

(3) Inefficiency in teaching or in the management of a school;

(4) Affliction with active tuberculosis or other communicable disease shall be considered as cause for removal or suspension while the teacher is suffering from such disability; or

(5) Discontinuance of position or lack of pupils." M. S.A. § 125.17.

State tenure statutes may be broadly classified into three groups. One general type creates a "legislative status" for teachers by regulating the behavior of boards of education, but creates no contractual rights. Minnesota's statute, supra, is an example of this type of law. Its key word is "position," which refers to a teacher's relative rank, place or standing within a school system. Under it, local school boards have the power to transfer or assign teachers to positions for which they are qualified within the system so long as they act within their own rules and regulations and state law. This type of tenure statute confers a "position," not a contract right. In this circumstance, a state legislature is free to pass new laws amending the teacher-tenure statute; e. g., reducing salaries of tenured teachers or introducing new grounds for dismissal, without running afoul of Article I, section 10, of the United States Constitution, declaring that "No State shall . . . pass . . . any law impairing the obligation of contracts." See, Phelps v. Board of Education, 300 U.S. 319, 57 S.Ct. 483, 81 L.Ed. 674 (1937) and Dodge v. Board of Education, 302 U.S. 74, 58 S.Ct. 98, 82 L.Ed. 57 (1937).

A second general type of tenure statute creates a "contract status" for teachers, under which teachers have vested rights and state legislatures must conform all their future legislation to the requirements of Article I, section 10, of the Constitution of the United States. In 1927 Indiana's legislature passed a statute providing that "any person who has served . . . as a teacher in any school corporation in the State . . . for five or more successive years and who shall hereafter enter into a teacher's contract for further service with such corporation shall become a permanent teacher of such school corporation. . . . Upon the expiration of any contract between such school corporation and a permanent teacher, such contract shall be deemed to continue in effect for an indefinite period and shall be known as an indefinite contract . . .". Burns' Ind.Stat.Ann.Supp., 1929, § 6967.1. In 1933, Indiana's legislature tried to amend this statute by eliminating all township school corporations from its coverage, but not other types of school corporations. A teacher coming within the 1927 and 1933 laws brought suit, arguing that Indiana's 1933 amending statute was a violation of the constitutional clause prohibiting states from impairing the obligation of contracts. The Supreme Court of the United States agreed, holding that the teacher had a valid contract and that Indiana's 1933 amendment was an unconstitutional attempt to impair the obligation of that contract. State of Indiana ex rel. Anderson v. Brand, 303 U.S. 95, 58 S.Ct. 443, 82 L.Ed. 685 (1938). The Supreme Court did not say that a state legislature was fully disabled from passing all laws affecting teachers' contracts under tenure statutes. To the contrary, it stated:

> "Our decisions recognize that every contract is made subject to the implied condition that its fulfillment may be frustrated by a proper exercise of the police power [a state's legislative power] but we have repeatedly said that, in order to have this effect, the exercise of the power must be for an end which is in fact public and the means adopted must be reasonably adapted to that end, and the Supreme Court of Indiana has taken the same view in respect of legislation impairing the obligation of the contract of a state instrumentality. The causes of cancellation provided in the Act of 1927 and the retention of the system of indefinite contracts in all municipalities except townships by the Act of 1933 are persuasive that the repeal of the earlier Act by the latter was

not an exercise of the police power for the attainment of ends
to which its exercise may properly be directed."

Thus, the Court drew a line between the constitutional rights of a
person and the rights of all the people. If a new statute was passed
affecting Indiana's tenure statute and the contracts under it, but
whose purpose implemented the general welfare of the whole public
of the state then that new law would, presumably, be upheld as a reasonable and constitutional exercise of the legislature's powers.

A third general type of teacher tenure statute is one that expresses public policy. It neither creates a vested contract interest
nor a legislative position. It is a mere declaration of sentiment. Obviously, in this situation a state legislature is not bound by the clause
prohibiting the impairment of the obligation of contracts, and, perhaps, can repeal the law completely. See, Malone v. Hayden, 329
Pa. 213, 197 A. 344 (1938). Could the "practice" or "custom" of
Boards of Education under a statute merely declaring a public policy
in favor of tenure give rise to a legal interest similar to a property
interest, which is the teacher's? Why or why not?

PERRY v. SINDERMANN

Supreme Court of the United States, 1972.
408 U.S. 593, 92 S.Ct. 2694, 33 L.Ed.2d 570.

Mr. Justice STEWART delivered the opinion of the Court.

From 1959 to 1969 the respondent, Robert Sindermann, was a
teacher in the state college system of the State of Texas. After
teaching for two years at the University of Texas and for four years
at San Antonio Junior College, he became a professor of Government and Social Science at Odessa Junior College in 1965. He was
employed at the college for four successive years, under a series of
one-year contracts. He was successful enough to be appointed, for
a time, the cochairman of his department.

During the 1968–1969 academic year, however, controversy arose
between the respondent and the college administration. The respondent was elected president of the Texas Junior College Teachers
Association. In this capacity, he left his teaching duties on several
occasions to testify before committees of the Texas Legislature, and
he became involved in public disagreements with the policies of the
college's Board of Regents. In particular, he aligned himself with a
group advocating the elevation of the college to four-year status—a
change opposed by the Regents. And, on one occasion, a newspaper
advertisement appeared over his name that was highly critical of
the Regents.

Finally, in May 1969, the respondent's one-year employment
contract terminated and the Board of Regents voted not to offer him

a new contract for the next academic year. The Regents issued a press release setting forth allegations of the respondent's insubordination. But they provided him no official statement of the reasons for the nonrenewal of his contract. And they allowed him no opportunity for a hearing to challenge the basis of the nonrenewal.

The respondent then brought this action in a federal district court. He alleged primarily that the Regents' decision not to rehire him was based on his public criticism of the policies of the college administration and thus infringed his right to freedom of speech. He also alleged that their failure to provide him an opportunity for a hearing violated the Fourteenth Amendment's guarantee of procedural due process. The petitioners—members of the Board of Regents and the president of the college—denied that their decision was made in retaliation for the respondent's public criticism and argued that they had no obligation to provide a hearing. On the basis of these bare pleadings and three brief affidavits filed by the respondent, the District Court granted summary judgment for the petitioners. It concluded that the respondent had "no cause of action against the [petitioners] since his contract of employment terminated May 31, 1969, and Odessa Junior College has not adopted the tenure system.

The Court of Appeals reversed the judgment of the District Court. . . . First, it held that, despite the respondent's lack of tenure, the nonrenewal of his contract would violate the Fourteenth Amendment if it in fact was based on his protected free speech. Since the actual reason for the Regents' decision was "in total dispute" in the pleadings, the court remanded the case for a full hearing on this contested issue of fact. . . . Second, the Court of Appeals held that, despite the respondent's lack of tenure, the failure to allow him an opportunity for a hearing would violate the constitutional guarantee of procedural due process if the respondent could show that he had an "expectancy" of re-employment. . . .

The first question presented is whether the respondent's lack of a contractual or tenure right to re-employment, taken alone, defeats his claim that the nonrenewal of his contract violated the First and Fourteenth Amendments. We hold that it does not.

For at least a quarter century, this Court has made clear that even though a person has no "right" to a valuable governmental benefit and even though the government may deny him the benefit of any number of reasons, there are some reasons upon which the government may not act. It may not deny a benefit to a person on the basis that infringes his constitutionally protected interests—especially, his interest in freedom of speech. For if the government could deny a benefit to a person because of his constitutionally protected speech or associations, his exercise of those freedoms would in effect be penalized and inhibited. This would allow the government to "produce a result which [it] could not command directly."

. . . Such interference with constitutional rights is impermissible.

We have applied this general principle to denials of tax exemptions, . . . unemployment benefits, . . . and welfare payments, . . . But, most often, we have applied the principle to denials of public employment. . . . We have applied the principle regardless of the public employee's contractual or other claim to a job. . . .

Thus the respondent's lack of a contractual or tenure "right" to re-employment for the 1969–1970 academic year is immaterial to his free speech claim. Indeed, twice before, this Court has specifically held that the nonrenewal of a non-tenured public school teacher's one-year contract may not be predicated on his exercise of First and Fourteenth Amendment rights. . . .

In this case, of course, the respondent has yet to show that the decision not to renew his contract was, in fact, made in retaliation for his exercise of the constitutional right of free speech. The District Court foreclosed any opportunity to make this showing when it granted summary judgment. Hence, we cannot now hold that the Board of Regents' action was invalid.

But we agree with the Court of Appeals that there is a genuine dispute as to "whether the college refused to renew the teaching contract on an impermissible basis—as a reprisal for the exercise of constitutionally protected rights." . . . The respondent has alleged that his nonretention was based on his testimony before legislative committees and his other public statements critical of the Regents' policies. And he has alleged that this public criticism was within the First and Fourteenth Amendments' protection of freedom of speech. Plainly, these allegations present a *bona fide* constitutional claim. For this Court has held that a teacher's public criticism of his superiors on matters of public concern may be constitutionally protected and may, therefore, be an impermissible basis for termination of his employment. . . .

For this reason we hold that the grant of summary judgment against the respondent, without full exploration of this issue, was improper.

The respondent's lack of formal contractual or tenure security in continued employment at Odessa Junior College, though irrelevant to his free speech claim, is highly relevant to his procedural due process claim. But it may not be entirely dispositive.

We have held . . . that the Constitution does not require opportunity for a hearing before the nonrenewal of a nontenured teacher's contract, unless he can show that the decision not to rehire him somehow deprived him of an interest in "liberty" or that he had a "property" interest in continued employment, despite the lack of tenure or a formal contract. . . .

Similarly, the respondent here has yet to show that he has been deprived of an interest that could invoke procedural due process protection. As in *Roth,* the mere showing that he was not rehired in one particular job, without more, did not amount to a showing of a loss of liberty. Nor did it amount to a showing of a loss of property.

But the respondent's allegations—which we must construe most favorably to the respondent at this stage of the litigation—do raise a genuine issue as to his interest in continued employment at Odessa Junior College. He alleged that this interest, though not secured by a formal contractual tenure provision, was secured by a no less binding understanding fostered by the college administration. In particular, the respondent alleged that the college had a *de facto* tenure program, and that he had tenure under that program. He claimed that he and others legitimately relied upon an unusual provision that had been in the college's official Faculty Guide for many years:

> *"Teacher Tenure:* Odessa College has no tenure system. The Administration of the College wishes the faculty member to feel that he has permanent tenure as long as his teaching services are satisfactory and as long as he displays a co-operative attitude toward his co-workers and his superiors, and as long as he is happy in his work."

Moreover, the respondent claimed legitimate reliance upon guidelines promulgated by the Coordinating Board of the Texas College and University System that provided that a person, like himself, who had been employed as a teacher in the state college and university system for seven years or more has some form of job tenure. Thus the respondent offered to prove that a teacher, with his long period of service, at this particular State College had no less a "property" interest in continued employment than a formally tenured teacher at other colleges, and had no less a procedural due process right to a statement of reasons and a hearing before college officials upon their decision not to retain him.

We have made clear . . . that "property" interests subject to procedural due process protection are not limited by a few rigid, technical forms. Rather, "property" denotes a broad range of interests that are secured by "existing rules or understandings." . . . A person's interest in a benefit is a "property" interest for due process purposes if there are such rules or mutually explicit understandings that support his claim of entitlement to the benefit and that he may invoke at a hearing.

A written contract with an explicit tenure provision clearly is evidence of a formal understanding that supports a teacher's claim of entitlement to continued employment unless sufficient "cause" is shown. Yet absence of such an explicit contractual provision may not always foreclose the possibility that a teacher has a "property" interest in re-employment. For example, the law of contracts in most, if not all, [states] long has employed a process by which agreements, though not formalized in writing, may be "implied." . . . Explicit contractual provisions may be supplemented by other agreements implied from "the promisor's words and conduct in the light of the surrounding circumstances." . . . And, "[t]he meaning of [the promisor's] words and acts is found by relating them to the usage of the past." . . .

A teacher, like the respondent, who has held his position for a number of years, might be able to show from the circumstances of this service—and from other relevant facts—that he has a legitimate claim of entitlement to job tenure. Just as this Court has found there to be a "common law of a particular industry or of a particular plant" that may supplement a collective-bargaining agreement, . . . there may be an unwritten "common law" in a particular university that certain employees shall have the equivalent of tenure. This is particularly likely in a college or university, like Odessa Junior College, that has no explicit tenure system even for senior members of its faculty, but that nonetheless may have created such a system in practice. . . .

In this case, the respondent has alleged the existence of rules and understandings, promulgated and fostered by state officials, that may justify his legitimate claim of entitlement to continued employment absent "sufficient cause." We disagree with the Court of Appeals insofar as it held that a mere subjective "expectancy" is protected by procedural due process, but we agree that the respondent must be given an opportunity to prove the legitimacy of his claim of such entitlement in light of "the policies and practices of the institution." . . . Proof of such a property interest would not, of course, entitle him to reinstatement. But such proof would obligate college officials to grant a hearing at his request, where he could be informed of the grounds for his nonretention and challenge their sufficiency.

Therefore, while we do not wholly agree with the opinion of the Court of Appeals, its judgment remanding this case to the District Court is affirmed.

Affirmed.

Mr. Justice MARSHALL, dissenting in part. . . .

. . . I would modify the judgment of the Court of Appeals to direct the District Court to enter summary judgment for respondent entitling him to a statement of reasons why his contract was not renewed and a hearing on disputed issues of fact.

NOTES AND QUESTIONS

1. Would this case have been decided differently if the person involved had been a teacher in the "common schools"? Why or why not?

2. Is this case terminated, or is there another legal step? If so, what is it? What will be the issue(s) to be resolved?

3. This opinion addresses itself to two issues and has two major parts, one dealing with constitutionally protected free expression, and the other dealing with a quasi-property interest founded upon a reasonable and objective "expectancy" by the teacher. Carefully analyze the reasoning in each part. Do you agree or disagree? Why? What is the nature of the "expectancy"?

4. Does the Court hold that it would be constitutional to refuse to renew a teacher's contract on the ground that he published a paid advertisement highly critical of the Board of Regents or does it hold only that the teacher must be afforded a hearing in order to determine whether such non-renewal would be constitutional? Why? Suppose the teacher's contract were not renewed solely because he left his teaching duties in order to testify before a legislative committee, would the non-renewal be upheld without a hearing? Would a hearing have to be afforded? Would it be important whether the teacher was testifying on a school-related matter, or not? Suppose he was opposing federal aid to public schools? To private schools?

5. What type of tenure statute governed Odessa Jr. College? Did the Court say that this law did, or could, give rise to a legal interest in the teacher? If so, what would that interest be? What proof would have to be shown before the legal interest would be present? State what might be the "common law" of Odessa Jr. College. What is its relationship to the "expectancy" requirement set forth by the Court? Suppose the situation were one that a reasonably-minded teacher in the same or similar circumstances would reasonably and objectively believe that he had an expectancy of tenure, but in a specific case with a specific and skeptical teacher who subjectively did not have that belief, would the quasi-property interest exist? Why or why not?

6. A companion case decided with Sindermann, Board of Regents v. Roth, 408 U.S. 564, 92 S.Ct. 2701, 33 L.Ed.2d 584 (1972), involved the right to a hearing of a probationary teacher without tenure and on a one year contract at Wisconsin State University–Oshkosh. There was no statutory or administrative standards defining eligibility for re-employment. The Court stated that:

> "There might be cases in which a State refused to re-employ a person under such circumstances that interests in liberty would be implicated. But this is not such a case.

> "The State, in declining to rehire the respondent, did not make any charge against him that might seriously damage his standing and associations in his community. It did not base the nonrenewal of his contract on a charge, for example, that he had been guilty of dishonesty, or immorality. Had it done so, this would be a different case. For '[w]here a person's good name, reputation, honor, or integrity is at stake because of what the government is doing to him, notice and an opportunity to be heard are essential.' . . . In such a case, due process would accord an opportunity to refute the charge before University officials. In the present case, however,

there is no suggestion whatever that the respondent's interest in his 'good name, reputation, honor or integrity' is at stake.

"Similarly, there is no suggestion that the State, in declining to re-employ the respondent, imposed on him a stigma or other disability that foreclosed his freedom to take advantage of other employment opportunities. The State, for example, did not involve any regulations to bar the respondent from all other public employment in State universities. Had it done so, this, again, would be a different case. . . .

"Hence, on the record before us, all that clearly appears is that the respondent was not rehired for one year at one University. It stretches the concept too far to suggest that a person is deprived of 'liberty' when he simply is not rehired in one job but remains as free as before to seek another. . . .

"The Fourteenth Amendment's procedural protection of property is a safeguard of the security of interests that a person has already acquired in specific benefits. These interests—property interests—may take many forms. . . .

". . . To have a property interest in a benefit, a person clearly must have more than an abstract need or desire for it. He must have more than a unilateral expectation of it. He must, instead, have a legitimate claim of entitlement to it. It is a purpose of the ancient institution of property to protect those claims upon which people rely in their daily lives, reliance that must not be arbitrarily undermined. It is a purpose of the constitutional right to a hearing to provide an opportunity for a person to vindicate those claims.

". . . the respondent's 'property' interest in employment at the Wisconsin State University-Oshkosh was created and defined by the terms of his appointment. Those terms secured his interest in employment up to June 30, 1969. But the important fact in this case is that they specifically provided that the respondent's employment was to terminate on June 30. They did not provide for contract renewal absent 'sufficient cause.' Indeed, they made no provision for renewal whatsoever.

"Thus the terms of the respondent's appointment secured absolutely no interest in re-employment for the next year. They supported absolutely no possible claim of entitlement to re-employment. Nor, significantly, was there any state statute or University rule or policy that secured his interest in re-employment, or that created any legitimate claim to it. . . ."

7. Should a school district or a state legislature adopt the following rule? Why or why not? "In the event of a decision not to renew his contractual appointment, every faculty member shall be informed of the decision in writing by the State Superintendent and, if he so requests, he shall be advised of the reasons on which that decision is based".

8. Give several examples that would constitute improper grounds for non-renewal of a contract. Would any or all of the following be proper grounds for non-renewal, assuming they are part of a letter to the teacher from the State Superintendent: (a) we no longer have the necessary funds to employ you; (b) a majority of the tenured faculty, by secret ballot, voted not to retain you; (c) the staff I inherited from my predecessor was lazy and ineffective, and I had hoped that you would stimulate them to emulate your fine teaching practices, but instead, they have influenced you into bad habits, more of which I cannot afford, therefore, you will not be retained; (d) you have consistently annoyed parents, students and members of the Board of Education, and even though you have very high standards and are quite competent, I cannot, retain you; (e) your teaching colleagues and I think you're a phony; we haven't collected the evidence, but we can if we have to; anyway, you're fired; (f) according to the two department scoreboards, last year you got twenty-two student demerits and four stars, and fifteen administrative demerits and only two stars; as you know, you must have eight stars per year to be retained. . . .; (g) a more competent individual has applied for your job; and (h) all of the above!

BOARD OF EDUCATION v. WILLIAMS

Court of Appeals of Arizona, 1965.
1 Ariz.App. 389, 403 P.2d 324.

MALLOY, Judge. . . . The petitioner, prior to the institution of these proceedings, had been employed by the Board of Education of High School District No. 1, Pima County, for a number of year (sic). Under applicable law, we are concerned with four consecutive annual contracts, the first of such being for the 1959–1960 school year and the last one being for the 1962–1963 school year. In each of these documents it was stated that the contract was one between "John Wesley Williams, Teacher-Counselor" and the respondent, that the annual salary included a certain amount for "counseling," and that the time of employment was from a date approximately in mid-August until the end of the first week in June of the following calendar year. In the last of these contracts, the petitioner was employed at an annual salary of $8,731.00, which included $406.00 for counseling.

On March 22, 1963, the petitioner was asked to come to a conference at which the principal of his school and the respondent, Dr. Thomas Lee, Assistant Superintendent of Schools for Tucson High School District No. 1, were present. At this conference, the petitioner was told, and this communication was subsequently confirmed by a written memorandum, that:

"In view of the numerous instances of difficulties this year in your counseling and teaching work, to be effective with the 1963–64 school year we are relieving you of counseling duties and transferring you to another high school."

The written communication continued by saying that the action being taken:

" *   *   * should be regarded in the nature of a probationary move, because if your quality of teaching next year doesn't measure up to the quality expected in this district, we will recommend your termination."

Neither at this meeting, nor at a subsequent one with Dr. Lee called at the request of petitioner's counsel, were any specific written charges made against the petitioner nor were any witnesses called to substantiate any charges, though this was requested by the petitioner through counsel at the second conference.

Subsequently the petitioner was tendered a contract for the school year 1963–1964 at an annual salary of $8,675.00 ($56.00 less than the prior contract), which described the petitioner as a "teacher," and which, contrary to the previous contracts, did not have any indication that there was any special allowance for counseling. The new contract gave date of commencement as August 27, 1963, which was approximately two weeks later than the other contracts mentioned above.   .   .   .

The trial court found, and this court holds correctly, that the proffered contract which contained a salary reduction was a violation of the subject act.   Two pertinent provisions are these:

A.R.S. § 15–252:

"Subject to the provisions of § 15–257, the contract of employment of a probationary or continuing teacher for a school year shall be deemed *automatically renewed* for the next ensuing school year, unless, on or before March 15 immediately preceding the ensuing school year, the school board, a member thereof acting on behalf of the board, or the superintendent of the school district, gives notice to the teacher of the termination of his contract."   [Emphasis supplied]

A.R.S. § 15–257 [in part]:

"Nothing in this article shall be interpreted to prevent a school board from reducing salaries or eliminating teachers in a school district in order to effectuate economies in the operation of the district or to improve the efficient conduct and administration of the schools of the district, *but no reduction in the salary of a continuing teacher shall be made except in accordance with a general salary reduction in the school district by which he is employed,* and in such case the reduction shall be applied equitably among all such teachers.
*   *   * ".   [Emphasis supplied]

In this case, the petitioner was not notified prior to March 15 that his contract was not being renewed and there was no general salary reduction in the school district.

This court holds, therefore, that the petitioner was entitled to a renewal of his contract without a salary reduction. . . .

The tenure granted by the Act does not include the right to teach any particular class or classes nor to teach at any particular school. . . .

Under teacher's tenure statutes in other states, which do not contain an explicit prohibition against a salary reduction, several courts have come to the conclusion that the reduction in the "rank and grade" of a teacher, when attendant with a salary reduction, is a "dismissal," prohibited by the Act. . . . In a state such as ours, where there is a specific prohibition against reduction of salary, this court sees no need to extend the language of the Act so as to carry this implied prohibition against reduction in rank or grade. However, even if this be the law of this state, there is no showing here that a teacher is of any lower rank or grade than a counselor. The testimony of the petitioner was unequivocal that the additional pay was solely for the additional two weeks work. There is no showing that a counselor has any supervisory authority over other teachers nor that a counselor is regarded as of a higher professional stature than an ordinary teacher. Accordingly there has been no reduction in "rank and grade" of the petitioner. . . .

[A] "decision" in the "nature of a probationary move" is not one that is subject to being reviewed by a writ of certiorari. A writ of certiorari both at the common law and under our statute . . . is one that reviews the actions of an inferior tribunal while exercising judicial or quasi-judicial functions. . . . There was nothing judicial or quasi-judicial about [a teacher having a conference with a school administrator] . . . It [is] purely an administrative procedure. It must be remembered that a school board exercises administrative, legislative and quasi-judicial functions. The "triple personality" of such a board has been commented upon in this language:

> "A school board is a part of the executive department, but, in the operation of our public school system, it exercises not only purely administrative functions but others of a legislative character, and still others of a quasi judicial character. Of the administrative type are the hiring of teachers, their assignment in the school system, and their discharge, once the grounds therefor are established. Of the legislative type are the making of rules and the determination of policies governing such hiring, assignment, and discharge of teachers. Of the quasi judicial type is the power to hear and determine proceedings for the removal of teachers for cause.

* * * " State ex rel. Ging v. Board of Education of City of Duluth, 213 Minn. 550, 7 N.W.2d 544, 555 [1943].

Were the court to review "decisions" such as that taken at the subject conference, the court believes there would be no end to the judicial review of the multifarious administrative problems arising in school districts on a day-to-day basis. It is not felt that the judgment of the courts in connection with these problems of school administration would be any better than that of the officials elected to the positions of responsibility as to the particular school districts. The following additional quotation from the case of State ex rel. Ging v. Board of Education of City of Duluth, supra, is deemed pertinent:

> "The adoption of a liberal construction to combat the evils to which the law [Minnesota Teacher's Tenure Act] was directed does not permit a construction so benevolent toward teachers that, by eliminating one evil, we create another: that of transferring from the school boards, the duly elected representatives of the parents, taxpayers and other electors of the school district, to the teachers and the courts the management, supervision, and control of our school systems vested in such boards by other statutes." . . .

ROSENTHAL v. ORLEANS PARISH SCHOOL BOARD

Court of Appeals of Louisiana, 1968.
214 So.2d 203, app. den. 252 La. 963, 215 So.2d 130.

YARRUT, Judge. . . . Plaintiff is a tenured teacher. . .

In September, 1964, she was transferred by the School Board to the position of teacher of Biology at Benjamin Franklin Senior High School. On July 17, 1967, the Superintendent of The Orleans Parish School Board, notified Plaintiff, by letter, he planned to recommend to the School Board that she be transferred from the position of teacher of Biology at Franklin, to the position of teacher of Biology at Easton, reading:

> "At my request, Mr. Daniel A. Allain, Jr., Assistant Superintendent, conferred with you concerning your student grading procedures. During this conference, Mr. Allain brought to your attention the following facts:

> "1. Of the 55 pupils enrolled in your four sections of Biology during this past session, a total of 28 or 51 percent received final session grades of less than 80 percent.

> "2. At the start of the school session 67 pupils were enrolled in your classes. At the close of the year only 55 pupils remained. Twelve of the 23 Tenth Grade pupils to withdraw

from Franklin during the school year were assigned your course in Biology.

"3. The pupil-teacher ratio in your classes averaged 14.2 pupils per teacher.

"4. There was little improvement in the number of pupils receiving grades under 80 during the second semester in comparing the mid-year and final grades. The mid-term percentage was 56 percent and the final session percentage was 51 percent.

"5. During the 1965–1966 school session 41 percent of the pupils in your classes received final session grades of under 80 percent.

"It was your judgment in this conference that you do not have expectations of your students at Franklin which are unreasonable.

"After carefully weighing both perspectives and after reviewing your judgment in the context of the grades given by other teachers at Franklin, I conclude that your grading procedures do differ significantly from what is expected by both the administration of the school system and the great majority of the faculty at Franklin.

"The students at Franklin are required to maintain an overall average of 80, and are subject to removal if they do not. Consequently, if the grading procedures of any one teacher differs significantly from the grading procedures of the majority of the faculty, that one teacher will have an inordinate influence upon whether or not her students are allowed to remain at Franklin.

"For the foregoing reasons it is my opinion, and the opinion of the Director of Personnel, that the best interests of the school system will be served if you are transferred from the Benjamin Franklin Senior High School, to a position of equal rank, dignity and salary in another Senior High School in the system. . . .

. . . The general rule is:

"In the absence of constitutional or statutory limitations or restrictions, the employing school authorities usually have the power to assign, reassign, or transfer teachers, principals, and superintendents. * * *" . . .

Plaintiff contends that her transfer from the position of teacher of Biology at Franklin to the position of teacher of Biology at Easton, constitutes a removal from office which can be accomplished only if the provisions of [the teacher tenure code] are first complied with. . . .

The jurisprudence has established what does constitute such a removal under the above cited statute. In the case of State ex rel. McNeal v. Avoyelles Parish School Board, 199 La. 859, 7 So.2d 165, plaintiff resisted his transfer by the School Board from his position of a high school principal to the position of a teacher in a high school, at a reduced salary. The Court held that the School Board was without authority to demote plaintiff; and said:

> " 'Removed from office' is much broader in its scope than 'discharge' or 'dismiss.' It is well recognized in the jurisprudence of this country that the word 'removal' as used in statutes similar to our Teachers' Tenure Act includes a demotion in office by assigning the employee to a lower position in the same service at a lower rate of compensation. . . . "

The Supreme Court also cited with approval case of Board of Education of Richmond County v. Young, 187 Ga. 644, 1 S.E.2d 739, which held:

> " 'However, a demotion from one position to another, if and when accompanied by a substantial salary reduction, being in effect a removal from the original position . . . the board had no right, without assigning any cause and without a hearing, to accompany the demotion of this petitioner with a reduction in her salary from $2,200.00 to $1,400.00 per annum.' " . . .

Our jurisprudence established that the transfer of a teacher from one position to another, by a Parish School Board, does not constitute a removal from office, as prohibited by the Teachers' Tenure Law, unless: (1) A reduction in salary is involved; (2) the new position requires the teaching of subjects for which the teacher is not qualified; (3) the teacher must undergo additional training, at his expense, in order to obtain permanent certification in his new post; and (4) the transfer follows a dismissal without formal charges, or a hearing, and thus leaves a blot on the teacher's record. None of the foregoing exceptions are present in the instant case. . . .

The School Board has the duty to properly administer the Public School System, and necessarily has the right to transfer teachers from one school to another in the best interests of the pupils. This is the effect of the decision below for, if a teaching position at Franklin is of greater rank and dignity than a teaching position in the other Parish schools, then teachers assigned to Franklin cannot be transferred to any other school, for such a transfer would be a transfer to a position of lower rank and dignity. . . .

The only issue here is the relative rank and dignity of the positions of teacher of Biology at Franklin and at Easton. . . .

The students are selected for admission to Franklin based upon I.Q. and achievement, and are dismissed if they fail to mtaintain a high level of achievement. The teachers at Franklin are not selected on the basis of either their I.Q. or achievement. The tenure of teachers is not graded. Their transfer indicates nothing more nor less than the fact that those charged with the responsibility of running the School System feel that the service of such a teacher is needed more at some other school than at Franklin.

When Franklin was originally started the degree and experience requirements of teachers were higher than those required of teachers at other schools. However, some years before this suit was filed this differential in requirements was abolished.

While Franklin is an "exceptional school," since its students are required to have a minimum I.Q. and a minimum level of achievement, there is no evidence that the faculty at Franklin is any more exceptional than the faculty at any of the other senior high schools in the Orleans Parish School System. . . .

The Teachers' Tenure Act prevents a teacher from being "removed from office," without formal charges and a hearing. The Courts have found that being demoted constitutes being "removed from office." Before a teacher can be considered as having been demoted, she must have been assigned to a position of lower rank or dignity. It is submitted that the two teaching positions pay the same salary, and have the same rank and dignity. . . .

Accordingly, we must hold that the proposed transfer of Plaintiff from the position of teacher of Biology at the Benjamin Franklin Senior High School, to the position of teacher of Biology at the Warren Eastern Senior High School, does not amount to a demotion; and is not a removal from office; nor does it violate the Teachers' Tenure Act, nor any other statute of the State of Louisiana. . . .

REGAN, Justice (dissenting). . . .

. . . there is a very significant and pertinent letter in the record which also served to provoke this dissent. It is dated July 17, 1967, and it emanates from the Superintendent of the Orleans Parish School Board, Dr. Carl J. Dolce, and it is addressed to the plaintiff, Mrs. Rosenthal, wherein she is castigated and reprimanded in five distinct paragraphs of that letter for her "student grading procedure". In concluding this letter, Dr. Dolce was of the opinion that the best interests of the school system will be served if Mrs. Rosenthal is transferred from the Benjamin Franklin Senior High School to the Warren Easton Senior High School, and he finally expressed the hope that in her new assignment she would reexamine her "teaching techniques".

The only reasonable interpretation which can be drawn from the words forming the context of this letter is that Mrs. Rosenthal's transfer was simply a disciplinary measure neatly disguised in legalistic mumbo jumbo. A cursory reading of that letter will serve to confirm and emphasize this conclusion.

Hence, she is entitled to a hearing in conformity with the provisions of the Teachers' Tenure Law, . . .

NOTES AND QUESTIONS

1. Did Louisiana's court find that Carolyn Rosenthal had a constitutional right in this case, and then engage in a balancing process?

2. Was this case decided correctly? Why or why not? Should the court substitute its judgment for that of the school district if there is some substantial evidence supporting the finding of facts and decision of the school district?

3. Suppose Rosenthal had prevailed and the court decided this case was one of a teacher being "removed from office" or "demotion," what would the court have required under the teacher's tenure act before she could be either demoted or removed from office?

4. What role did tenure play in these two cases?

THE HEARING AND HEARING PROCEDURES

INTRODUCTION

Under the rulings of the Supreme Court of the United States, if a teacher insists, he clearly has a constitutional right to a hearing in the following situations: (1) decertification; (2) dismissal during a contractual term, and (3) dismissal if tenured. The hearing and the hearing procedures need not be those followed in a court of law. While variations of detail are permitted among the states in the three above situations, Supreme Court interpretation of the constitution requires: (1) that the teacher be given a clear statement of the charges against him and adequate opportunity to prepare his case; (2) that the standards under which he has been charged have been made publicly available to him and written in such a way that a man of ordinary intelligence can understand it, and (3) that a hearing be afforded where the teacher can be represented by a lawyer and have the opportunity to explain fully his side of the case. Following a hearing the hearing board must make specific findings of fact based upon the evidence presented during the hearing, indicating what evidence is relied upon to support which findings of fact. If the teacher relies on a constitutional right during the hearing, then that hearing must be of sufficient scope to allow for the full development of all the necessary facts and law in order to judge whether that constitutional right exists in the specific circumstances and whether it has been infringed. Automatic dismissal for exercising a constitutional right is clearly unconstitutional.   The overall impartiality and fairness of the hearing are the key considerations.

Most states have statutes affording a hearing in the case of decertification; dismissal during a contractual term or dismissal of a tenured teacher, and, of course, these statutes must be fully complied with.   Deviation from the statute means that the proceeding is not in accordance with law, and is invalid.   In such event, if a teacher has been suspended during this time, the school district must pay his salary.   The hearing is usually conducted by a state board of education, and if its findings of fact are later reviewed by a court, they are usually reviewed only to see whether they are supported by substantial evidence.   Courts generally prefer not to substitute their processes for those of the administrative agency's.   On the other hand, one of the major problems inherent in this procedure is insuring that the teacher has received an impartial and fair hearing.   The reason is that the board of education acts as prosecutor, judge and jury, and this situation sensitizes most courts.   Wherever courts doubt the overall fairness or impartiality of the hearing they will reverse the decision of the board of education.   The trend of court decision is toward requiring a hearing in a court of law rather than having the board of education function as prosecutor, judge and jury in the three types of circumstances mentioned above.   See, Osborne v. Bullitt County Board of Education, 415 S.W.2d 607 (Ky.1967).   In some states, statutes allow a "de novo" review in court to a teacher who has been decertified or dismissed.   This is a new trial, the court hearing is original, not appellate.

SLOCHOWER v. BOARD OF HIGHER EDUCATION

Supreme Court of the United States, 1956.
350 U.S. 551, 76 S.Ct. 637, 100 L.Ed. 602, reh. den. 351 U.S. 944,
76 S.Ct. 843, 100 L.Ed. 1470.

Mr. Justice CLARK delivered the opinion of the Court.

This appeal brings into question the constitutionality of § 903 of the Charter of the City of New York.   That section provides that whenever an employee of the City utilizes the privilege against self-incrimination to avoid answering a question relating to his official conduct, "his term or tenure of office or employment shall terminate and such office or employment shall be vacant, and he shall not be eligible to election or appointment to any office or employment under the city or any agency."   Appellant Slochower invoked the privilege against self-incrimination under the Fifth Amendment before an investigating committee of the United States Senate, and was summarily discharged from his position as associate professor at Brooklyn College, an institution maintained by the City of New York.   He now claims that the charter provision, as applied to him, violates both the

Due Process and Privileges and Immunities Clauses of the Fourteenth Amendment.

On September 24, 1952, the Internal Security Subcommittee of the Committee on the Judiciary of the United States Senate held open hearings in New York City. . . . Professor Slochower, when called to testify, stated that he was not a member of the Communist Party, and indicated complete willingness to answer all questions about his associations or political beliefs since 1941. But he refused to answer questions concerning his membership during 1940 and 1941 on the ground that his answers might tend to incriminate him. The Chairman of the Senate Subcommittee accepted Slochower's claim as a valid assertion of an admitted constitutional right. . . .

Shortly after testifying before the Internal Security Subcommittee, Slochower was notified that he was suspended from his position at the College; three days later his position was declared vacant "pursuant to the provisions of Section 903 of the New York City Charter."

Slochower had 27 years' experience as a college teacher and was entitled to tenure under state law. . . . Under this statute, appellant may be discharged only for cause, and after notice, hearing, and appeal. . . . The Court of Appeals of New York, however, has authoritatively interpreted § 903 to mean that "the assertion of the privilege against self incrimination is equivalent to a resignation." . . . Dismissal under this provision is therefore automatic and there is no right to charges, notice, hearing, or opportunity to explain. . . .

Slochower argues that § 903 abridges a privilege or immunity of a citizen of the United States since it in effect imposes a penalty on the exercise of a federally guaranteed right in a federal proceeding. . . . we conclude the summary dismissal of appellant in the circumstances of this case violates due process of law.

The problem of balancing the State's interest in the loyalty of those in its service with the traditional safeguards of individual rights is a continuing one. To state that a person does not have a constitutional right to government employment is only to say that he must comply with reasonable, lawful, and nondiscriminatory terms laid down by the proper authorities. . . .

Here the Board, in support of its position, contends that only two possible inferences flow from appellant's claim of self-incrimination: (1) that the answering of the question would tend to prove him guilty of a crime in some way connected with his official conduct; or (2) that in order to avoid answering the question he falsely invoked the privilege by stating that the answer would tend to incriminate him, and thus committed perjury. Either inference, it insists, is sufficient to justify the termination of his employment. . . .

At the outset we must condemn the practice of imputing a sinister meaning to the exercise of a person's constitutional right under the

Fifth Amendment. The right of an accused person to refuse to testify, which had been in England merely a rule of evidence, was so important to our forefathers that they raised it to the dignity of a constitutional enactment, and it has been recognized as "one of the most valuable prerogatives of the citizen." . . .   The privilege against self-incrimination would be reduced to a hollow mockery if its exercise could be taken as equivalent either to a confession of guilt or a conclusive presumption of perjury. . . .   a witness may have a reasonable fear of prosecution and yet be innocent of any wrongdoing. The privilege serves to protect the innocent who otherwise might be ensnared by ambiguous circumstances. See Griswold, The Fifth Amendment Today (1955).

With this in mind, we consider the application of § 903. As interpreted and applied by the state courts, it operates to discharge every city employee who invokes the Fifth Amendment. . . .   The heavy hand of the statute falls alike on all who exercise their constitutional privilege, the full enjoyment of which every person is entitled to receive. Such actions falls squarely within the prohibition of Wieman v. Updegraff, supra. . . .

. . . Since no inference of guilt was [constitutionally] possible from the claim before the federal committee, the discharge falls of its own weight as wholly without support. There has not been the "protection of the individual against arbitrary action" which Mr. Justice Cardozo characterized as the very essence of due process. . .

This is not to say that Slochower has a constitutional right to be an associate professor of German at Brooklyn College. The State has broad powers in the selection and discharge of its employees, and it may be that proper inquiry would show Slochower's continued employment to be inconsistent with a real interest of the State. But there has been no such inquiry here. We hold that the summary dismissal of appellant violates due process of law. . . .

Mr. Justice REED, with whom Mr. Justice BURTON and Mr. Justice MINTON join, dissenting. . . .

. . . We assert the contrary—the city does have reasonable ground to require its employees either to give evidence regarding facts of official conduct within their knowledge or to give up the positions they hold. . . .   Legally authorized bodies have a right to demand that citizens furnish facts pertinent to official inquiries. The duty to respond may be refused for personal protection against prosecution only, but such avoidance of public duty to furnish information can properly be considered to stamp the employee as a person unfit to hold certain official positions. Such a conclusion is reinforced when the claimant for protection has the role of instructor to youth. The fact that the witness has a right to plead the privilege against self-incrimination protects him against prosecution but not against the loss of his job. . . .

Mr. Justice HARLAN, dissenting.

I dissent because I think the Court has misconceived the nature of § 903 as construed and applied by the New York Court of Appeals, and has unduly circumscribed the power of the State to ensure the qualifications of its teachers. . . .

In effect, what New York has done is to say that it will not employ teachers who refuse to cooperate with public authorities when asked questions relating to official conduct. Does such a statute bear a reasonable relation to New York's interest in ensuring the qualifications of its teachers? The majority seems to decide that it does not. . . a State may properly make knowing membership in an organization dedicated to the overthrow of the Government by force a ground for disqualification from public school teaching. . . . A requirement that public school teachers shall furnish information as to their past or present membership in the Communist Party is a relevant step in the implementation of such a state policy, and a teacher may be discharged for refusing to comply with that requirement. . . . Moreover, I think that a State may justifiably consider that teachers who refuse to answer questions concerning their official conduct are no longer qualified for public school teaching, on the ground that their refusal to answer jeopardizes the confidence that the public should have in its school system. On either view of the statute, I think Dr. Slochower's discharge did not violate due process.

It makes no difference that the question which Dr. Slochower refused to answer was put to him by a federal rather than a state body.

. . .

NOTES AND QUESTIONS

1. What was the decision in this case and for what reason(s)? What does the term "summary dismissal" mean? Do you agree with the majority or the dissents? Why? Would the rule of this case apply equally to a probationary teacher in the same circumstances?

2. Would the decision have been different if a teacher in the "common schools" were involved? Would the decision have been different if the investigating committee had been one of the state rather than the federal government? Why? Would it be relevant to your answer to know whether the privilege against self-incrimination had been incorporated into the Fourteenth Amendment? Why or why not?

3. If a hearing had been held and the same facts had been developed at the hearing, could Slochower have been dismissed? Why or why not?

AYERS v. LINCOLN COUNTY SCHOOL DISTRICT

Supreme Court of Oregon, 1967.
248 Or. 31, 432 P.2d 170.

WOODRICH, Justice (pro tempore).   This is an appeal by the defendant school district from a judgment holding invalid the dismissal of a tenure teacher.   Hereafter, the word defendant will refer to the school district.   . . .

Plaintiff had been a regular teacher with the school district for a number of years.   She was subject to the Teacher Tenure Law.   On February 10, 1966, the district school superintendent, by letter to the plaintiff, advised her that he intended to recommend to the school board that she be dismissed as a permanent teacher and advised her of her right to have the proposed recommendation reviewed by a panel of the Professional Review Committee.

The teacher requested a review of the district superintendent's proposed recommendation by the Professional Review Committee pursuant to ORS 342.895(3).   Thereafter, the State Superintendent of Public Instruction designated the members of the panel to review the proposed recommendation of the district superintendent.

The Professional Review Committee met, heard witnesses, and examined documentary evidence.   The plaintiff and her attorney were excluded from the proceedings before the review panel, except for the specific time when she was allowed to present evidence and argument. The teacher and her attorney were not permitted to hear the testimony of the witnesses nor to cross-examine them.   Witnesses and evidence were presented and considered by the panel both before and after the teacher's testimony and argument.

Following the meeting of the Professional Review Committee, it entered its report on March 17, 1966, determining that the district superintendent was justified in recommending to the school board that plaintiff be dismissed for reason of physical incapacity, as authorized by ORS 342.865(1)(e), and that the grounds therefor were true and substantiated.

Thereafter, the plaintiff requested and was granted a hearing before the district school board, at which time testimony and documentary evidence was received by the board.   Following this hearing the board entered its resolution terminating the teacher.   The trial court on writ of review held the dismissal invalid.

This case involves the interpretation of ORS 342.905(2) and (3). These sections are a portion of the statute providing for the review of the superintendent's dismissal recommendation of a five-man panel of the Professional Review Committee, hereinafter called the "panel." The pertinent sections read, in part, as follows:

" *   *   *

"(2) As soon as possible after the time of designation, the panel shall elect a chairman and shall conduct such investigation as it may consider necessary for the purpose of determining whether the grounds for the recommendation are true and substantiated *   *   *.

"(3) The permanent teacher involved shall *have the right to meet with the panel accompanied by counsel* or other person of his choice *and to present any evidence and arguments which he considers pertinent."* (Emphasis supplied.)

This court is of the opinion that the legislature intended that the teacher's "right to meet with the panel" includes the right to be present throughout the hearing, personally and with counsel, to subpoena and cross-examine witnesses, present other evidence, and make arguments to the panel.

The type of hearings provided for in an administrative process is either an "adversary," trial-type hearing, or an "auditive," speech-making hearing. . . .   One indicia of the legislature's choice of hearing type is the nature of powers conferred on the agency in conducting its hearing. In this case the statutory powers conferred on the panel are those usually associated with the exercise of a judicial function.

" *   *   *   [T]he panel shall be furnished appropriate professional and other special assistance *   *   * shall be empowered to subpoena and swear witnesses and to require them to give testimony and to produce books and papers relevant to its investigation." ORS 342.905(2).

The function that the panel performs is essentially judicial. The panel is not called upon to make a policy decision or exercise discretion. It merely determines if the evidence substantiates the existence of one of several statutory grounds for dismissal. ORS 342.905(4).

The statute provides that a specific party, as distinguished from the public in general, has a right to appear and be heard. A provision for a general notice by publication stating that all who are interested may appear and be heard was held to evidence an intent to create an "auditive" type hearing. Mohr v. State Board of Education, supra.

Defendant contends that the panel proceedings are "investigatory" only, and because of that plaintiff may not complain over her exclusion. This argument would be more persuasive if plaintiff were given an effective opportunity at a later stage to test the basis for the panel's decision. The statutory procedure subsequent to the panel's decision does not protect that opportunity.

After the panel concludes its inquiry it must formalize its conclusions in a written report. ORS 342.905(4). Thereafter, the statutes provide two alternatives, depending on the findings of the panel. If the panel's report is unfavorable to the teacher, the report *must* be considered by the school board at its hearing, which hearing may be informal. At this informal hearing no explicit provision is made for subpoenaing witnesses, cross-examining witnesses, or making a record of the proceedings. ORS 342.925. There is no requirement that the report contain an accurate record of the evidence the panel considered. There is no provision for a transcript of the panel proceedings. If the panel report is favorable to the teacher, the report may, but need not necessarily, be considered by the board; it is merely made competent evidence at the board hearing.

The foregoing summary demonstrates the importance of the panel hearing and report in determining the ultimate outcome of the dismissal procedure. It is obviously of more significance to the teacher when adverse. In that event, unless the teacher has the right to participate fully in the proceedings before the panel, the teacher is effectively denied any opportunity to test the credibility and authenticity of the evidence which quite likely will be determinative of the ultimate result. The teacher is denied the right to know precisely what evidence has occasioned the dismissal. The teacher could not rebut by evidence or argue effectively against dismissal without such knowledge.

Because the statute was intended to afford the teacher the right to be present with counsel throughout all of the panel proceedings, it was error for the panel to exclude plaintiff and her attorney.

The judgment of the trial court is affirmed.

COMMENTS ON THE MODEL CODE OF PROCEDURES FOR ACADEMIC FREEDOM AND TENURE CASES

Draftsman of Model Code, Professor Arval A. Morris
School of Law, University of Washington
Seattle, Washington
Vol. 22 Journal of Legal Education pp. 222–234 (1968).

Any fair appraisal of the adequacy of any set of procedures in this area must proceed from one prime perspective: How well do the procedures actually protect academic freedom? What is desired is a fair, clear and orderly set of model procedures that allow for calm, clear and non-emotional decision making. This means, of course, that these procedures should be looked upon as "safeguards" or "procedural guarantees" conserving the interests of society and the faculty member in academic freedom; that is, both the "rights" and "duties" of academic freedom should be considered. Consequently, the procedures should be set forth in clear and consistent detail, and they should be incorporated into the governing code of the institution, and thereby, made mandatory. . . .

BACKGROUND EXPLANATION OF THE CODE
Informal Procedures

After failure of unstructured attempts satisfactorily to resolve a faculty personnel problem, the first phase of any faculty dismissal is, and should be, informal. Although this be true, it is wise, and necessary, that the procedures allowing for informal adjustment and settlement be structured and formally set forth. What should they be?

1. There should be a specific provision directing that a discussion, with the goal of amiable conciliation, be held between the faculty member and a representative of the administration. The code provision should specify that the purpose of this meeting is conciliatory, but that this end can only be reached if there is an honest and frank assessment of the situation followed by a sincere attempt to solve common problems. Naturally, such a conference must be held in good faith. Conducive to these ends is a code provision requiring that the administration representative produce a written statement of the facts so that a clear discussion can be had on this point. Also, a provision allowing a faculty member to present his view is necessary (this will, sometimes, persuade the administration not to review the faculty member's competence and integrity), and, conversely, there should be a provision whereby the administration presents its views to the faculty member (this may persuade a faculty member to cooperate with the administration).

2. There should be a code provision to the effect that, before the structured and informal conference is held, the administration must inform the faculty member, in writing, that any information or arguments yielded in the informal conference can be later used against him at a formal hearing.

3. The code should have a provision governing suspension during the hearing processes. A faculty member should be suspended from his assigned academic duties if, and only if, immediate harm to himself or others is threatened by his continuance. Suspension as an act to prevent immediate harm surely must be seldom, if ever. Suspension for any other reason profoundly affects the placing of burden of proof, etc., by prejudicing the minds of most persons with this question: "If faculty member 'X' really isn't guilty, then why was he immediately suspended, etc.?"

Formal Procedures

The procedures that are meant to govern formal hearings constitute the very heart of Academic Due Process. They are of extreme importance, and they should be carefully considered from all possible perspectives. What, in principle, ought they be?

The Hearing Committee

The hearing committee should be a standing committee of full-time teaching colleagues, without any administrative status or duties, who are democratically chosen by, and representative of the faculty, and selected by pre-established rules. The administration which is the "charging authority," i. e., by analogy only, "the prosecution," should completely disassociate itself from those performing a judicial function at the tenure hearing. The reason why the board must be all-faculty and all-faculty-elected is not that the faculty has greater wisdom, but rather that faculty points of view and judgment are needed, untinged by the appropriate but different contexts and value systems which might be applied by the administration and/or the ultimate perspectives play a role at a later stage. The problem of bias in the committee should be handled in the usual manner of peremptory challenges and challenges for cause.

Formal Procedures Prior to Hearing

The faculty member should receive from the administration an official statement that sets the formal machinery into operation, and this statement, the "complaint," should, in all particulars, meet the full demands of the principles of notice and confrontation. Within this framework the charge, or complaint, performs several other critical functions: it determines the boundaries of the hearing, usually dictating what can, and cannot, be contested, and, of course, it performs the function of adequate notice; thus, the complaint should embody:

1. A statement of the charges in the particular case, made in plain and simple English.

2. A detailed summary of the evidence upon which the charges are based.

3. A first list of witnesses to be called.

4. A statement setting forth the procedures the hearing body will follow, including a statement of the nature of the hearing body.

5. A formal invitation to the accused to attend the hearing with advisers and counselors.

6. A copy of relevant legislation, board or trustees bylaws and rulings, administrative rulings, faculty legislation, and so forth.

7. Assurance of adequate time for preparation of a defense.

8. An invitation to appropriate professional associations to send an observer.

Counsel: A faculty member (and administration) has need of two types of advice during a tenure hearing. One type, obviously, is legal, and for this service the faculty member needs a lawyer, or lawyers. Secondly, a faculty member (and administration) has need of advice on academic affairs, as well as a lawyer, and, like the lawyer, the academic adviser should be permitted to be present at all times. The same rights, of course, should apply to the administration as well as the faculty member in question.

Open or closed hearing? The tenure hearing should be private unless the faculty member requests otherwise. The decision about an open or closed hearing should be placed solely in the hands of the faculty member. His professional life, perhaps the whole future for himself and his family, may be at stake. These are great concerns and outweigh any consideration of possible embarrassment or pain to the institution, or to possible witnesses.

The Hearing

The main questions here are what, in principle, ought to be the procedures governing evidence and evidence gathering and testing techniques. I shall elaborate the major principles:

1. *Presence*: A faculty member and the administration, accompanied by their legal and academic adviser(s) ought to have full rights to be present at all times.

2. *Confrontation*: Faculty member and administration alike should not only be accorded full rights under the principle of notification, but, also, under the principle of confrontation, and each should have the fullest opportunity to present, deny, refute and rebut all the evidence produced by the other; this expressly includes the full and complete rights of cross-examination.

3. *Witnesses and Other Evidence*: Administration and faculty members should have complete rights to call witnesses and produce evidence in support of their position. The usual rules of evidence in law courts should not govern. The administration should make available to the faculty member whatever authority it possesses, under law, to require the presence of witnesses, production of other evidence, etc.

4. *Expert Witnesses*: If the charge is one of professional incompetency, there should be admitted as evidence, in addition to individual testimony, a formal report on the work of the faculty member by his departmental colleagues, and of cognate departments in the University, and, if the faculty member so requests, a report by a committee of fellow-specialists from other institutions, appointed by the Committee on Faculty Affairs, and, if the charges include one of classroom incompetency, then, in this event, and, only to the extent of classroom com-

petency, testimony from students taught by the faculty member may be elicited. Furthermore, any hearing committee judgment or professional competency must be restricted to the evidence described herein and cannot properly rest on any other considerations.

5. *The Hearing Committee Acting on Its Own Authority:* Prior to commencement of the hearing, the hearing committee should determine the order of proof; it may interrogate witnesses on its own when it believes either side has left a relevant matter lie dormant, and it may secure the presentation of evidence important to the case.

6. *Evidence Exempt from Cross-Examination:* The principle of confrontation should apply throughout the hearing and all evidence should be subjected to cross-examination. (There is only one conceivable ground that might be conceded here, and it is doubtful, but it is with respect to formal statements, depositions, of distant witnesses placed under oath, introduced under strict and exact rules of weight, openness to challenge, and every other safeguard needed to protect the faculty member).

7. *Burden of Proof:* The burden of proving the charges found in the complaint rests upon those who bring them, and that the burden of proving the charge shall be by a preponderance of the evidence relevant to each charge.

8. *The Record:* A full verbatim record of the proceedings shall be kept, the cost borne by the Institution, and that one full copy of said record be made available, at the same time, to the administration, to the faculty member involved and to the hearing committee.

9. *The Opinion:* In every case the tenure committee must write a full and adequate opinion setting forth its disposition of each issue in the case with its accompanying reasons relied upon to justify such disposition, and that one copy of this opinion be made available to the administration and the faculty member at the time when the tenure committee formally announces its decision in the case.

Appellate Review

The decision of the Hearing Committee, if it is to have effect, should be final and binding (not "advisory") on the faculty member and the administration, unless either party elects to appeal. If there is an appeal, there should only be an appeal directly to the governing board of the institution, the ultimate authority.

If the Board chooses to review the case, its first review should strictly be confined to the record made at the hearing, accompanied by argument, oral or written, or both, as the administration and faculty member, in their discretion, choose to make. The decision of the Hearing Committee should either be sustained by the Board, or the entire proceedings should then be returned to the Hearing Committee along with a statement of the objections specified in writing, and with certain instructions to that committee. In such event, the Hearing Committee should reconsider, taking into account the stated objections and receiving new evidence if necessary. It should render a new decision and a new opinion which then shall be binding and final, and the case returned to the Board. After study of the committee's reconsideration, plus arguments, oral or written, by the parties, the Board should make its final ruling in the case. Any subsequent recourse should be to the courts. This is the procedure that ought to be followed. It guarantees both faculty perspectives in the procedures governing academic due process, and leaves the final decision with the Board.

GROUNDS FOR DISMISSAL

INTRODUCTION

Decertification and teacher dismissal statutes set forth specific grounds for decertifying and dismissing teachers. These grounds usually apply not only to tenured teachers, but also to non-tenured probationary teachers. They too, may be dismissed during their contractual period on similar grounds. The courts tend to hold to the view that where a statute sets forth specific grounds, they are exclusive, and other grounds are precluded by implication. In other words, local school boards cannot discharge, and states may not decertify, on any other ground. From a practical point of view, this protection is slight because many state statutes, and many rules and regulations of state boards of education, specifically include such broad grounds as "immorality," "conduct unbecoming a teacher," "behavior detrimental to the efficient operation and administration of the schools," "insubordination" or "other just cause." These generalized and conclusory types of discharge provisions run a serious risk of being applied unconstitutionally, or of being declared unconstitutional by courts either because they are so broad that they include behavior that is constitutionally protected or because they are so vague that they fail to give an ordinary teacher an adequate appreciation of what is forbidden, thereby effectively disallowing him from conforming his behavior to the requirement of law. If the constitutionality of a statutory ground is challenged as being conclusory and indefinite as to time, place and circumstance, some courts may distinguish between probationary and tenured teachers. For example, Arizona's statute requires "a statement of reasons" to be given in the case of non-renewal of a contract of a probationary teacher. In the case of a probationary teacher whose contract was not renewed on the grounds of "lack of cooperation," and "insubordination," Arizona's Supreme Court distinguished tenured from probationary teachers, saying that in this case these grounds were constitutionally valid because the purpose of Arizona's statute requiring "a statement of reasons" for probationary teachers is "simply to point out the teacher's inadequacies in order that she may prevent them in the event of subsequent employment. Accordingly, a specification of details, such as time, place and circumstances, are unnecessary." One might wonder how a teacher can correct his inadequacies without a specification of the details. Arizona's court specifically commented on two reasons given for non-renewal, saying that:

> "Insubordination imports a willful disregard of express or implied directions of the employer and a refusal to obey reasonable orders, McIntosh v. Abbot, 231 Mass. 180, 120 N.E. 383, and lack of cooperation is characteristically a subtle species of insubordination. Both terms are descriptive of a class of censurable practices destructive of the efficiency of the employer's organization. Accordingly, where, as here, a probationary teacher's right to remain in public service is dependent upon whether the appointing officers are satisfied with the teacher's conduct and capacity, and they are, in law, the sole judges, we are reluctant to place an unduly narrow construction on the legislative language lest it defeat the salutary purpose of determining the fitness of a probationer to serve a school district." School Dist. v. Superior Ct. of Pinal Cty., 102 Ariz. 478, 433 P.2d 28 (1968).

The range of application of these generalized types of "grounds" can be wide indeed; for example, what type of behavior might fall within the category "lack of cooperation"?

———

F. Weaver, Jr., GROUNDS FOR REMOVAL OR SUSPENSION OF PUBLIC SCHOOL TEACHERS

Vol. 8 So. Dakota Law Review 138 (1963).

"Unprofessional conduct is a concept involving the ethics and standards of behavior that might reasonably be expected of a member in good standing in a profession; ". . . that which violates the rules or ethical code of a profession. . . ." Outside the classroom this ranges from making derogatory remarks at parent-teacher meetings to a refusal to answer questions posed by a State Senate Committee. The terms immorality or gross immorality are more popularly used to define such conduct. These terms are held to mean that which is flagrant, shameless, or indifferent to what is adjudged good moral conduct by respectable people in the community. Under statutes containing such terms, one teacher was fired for distributing and selling malt beverages, as a side line, under a fictitious name, and another intellectually competent teacher, of otherwise good moral character, was fired when his act of signing the nominating paper for a Communist Party candidate subsequently reached the newspapers.

Such acts led to this expression of concern in the area:

Professors need more than .   .   .   a guarantee that they will not be jailed for expressions of their thoughts. If they are to be encouraged to pursue the truth wherever it may lead .   .   .   they need protection from all more material sanctions, especially from dismissal. .   . .

.   .   .   [M]ore than in most other occupations, the dismissal of a professor jeopardizes or destroys his eligibility for another position in his occupation. If he loses his position for what he writes or says, he will, as a rule, have to leave his profession, and may no longer be able effectively to question and challenge accepted doctrines. And if some professors lose their positions for what they write or say, the effect on many other professors will be such that their usefulness to their students and to society will be gravely reduced. .   .   .

"In .   .   .   dismissal for cause, investigation into the conduct of the teacher is not limited solely to the classroom or the qualifying requisites of good teaching ability. The attempt is to protect the best interests of the school and its students at all times. The position taken is that the teacher's influence upon his students extends into the realm of his off-duty world. There, leadership qualities and general standing in the community may become assets or hindrances to his career, as the case may be.

It has always been the recognized duty of the teacher to conduct himself in such way as to command the respect and good will of the community, though one result of the choice of a teacher's vocation may be to deprive him of the same freedom of action enjoyed by persons in other vocations.

"As a result of this line of reasoning, teachers have been dismissed for a variety of outside activities completely dissociated from their normal teaching duties. Educators have been dismissed for writing messages congratulating a student on his failure to register for the draft, making public statements to the effect that one is not willing to aid the United States Government in war, gambling and drinking, being arrested, getting married, testifying before a Senate Committee in response to an official summons, becoming a candidate for public office, and becoming pregnant. It has been held that teachers have the right to unionize, but not to strike. Also, teachers who invoke the Fifth Amendment may be placing their positions in jeopardy, regardless of their valid reasons for having done so.

Board of Education v. Swan, . . . states:

One employed in public service does not have a constitutional right to such employment and is subject to reasonable supervision and restriction . . . to the end that proper discipline may be maintained and that activities among the employees may not be allowed to disrupt or impair the public service.

"The United States Supreme Court has allowed a certain amount of infringement upon individual rights by the state governments, providing the goal in mind is sufficiently important, thus, absolute constitutional protection for individual freedom depends upon the interests of the majority at stake. If state interests are sufficiently high, individual interests may be infringed upon. Although more liberality in allowing infringement of these rights has occurred in the situation where the state is the employer, the restrictions sought to be imposed must be construed narrowly, be of limited scope, and meet a specific need.

"In determining if the rights of the state are of sufficient magnitude to justify an encroachment of personal freedoms guaranteed in the First and Fourteenth Amendments to the United States Constitution, two basic methods have been advanced. Justice Holmes favored the 'Clear and Present Danger' test, in which, relative to freedom of speech, the question to be answered is '. . . whether the words used are of such a nature as to create a clear and present danger that they will bring about the substantive evils that Congress has a right to prevent.' If so, individual rights must yield. In applying this test it is necessary to determine whether the '. . . gravity of the evil, discounted by its improbability, justifies such invasion of free speech as is necessary to avoid the danger.' This principal is also applicable to controversies involving the states.

"Justice Frankfurter favored a balancing test, in which the state's interests are weighed against individual personal freedoms. The balancing test has been increasingly used in recent years, especially in cases involving compelled disclosure of membership in outside associations, although the clear and present danger test has been the general guide in the past.

"At any rate, the basic idea is to prevent strict application of the First Amendment from being a roadblock to free thinking, expression and reform. This might best be looked at by keeping in mind a clarification of the clear and present danger test espoused a number of years ago by Justice Brandeis:

The fact that speech is likely to result in some violence or in destruction of property is not enough to justify its suppression. There must be the probability of serious injury to the state.

Regardless of which test is applied, the process is still, in essence, one of balancing.

"If teaching be a profession, there is still no means for the profession, by itself, to control the conduct of its members. Control is left entirely to the statutes and the interpretation placed thereon by the courts, removal for cause outside the statutes generally being invalid. . . .".

THOMPSON v. PENDLETON COUNTY BOARD OF EDUCATION

Court of Appeals of Kentucky, 1935.
258 Ky. 843, 81 S.W.2d 863.

RATLIFF, Justice. The county board of education of Pendleton county employed the appellant, Forest S. Thompson, as teacher and principal of the Morgan High School of Pendleton County for the school year 1933–1934. In February, 1934, a number of the citizens and taxpayers of the school district petitioned the board of education for the removal of appellant as principal and teacher of said school on grounds of neglect of duty, immoral conduct, and incompetency. The board heard the evidence and sustained the charges and discharged appellant as teacher and principal of the school, and he then brought this action in the Pendleton circuit court seeking a mandatory injunction requiring the board to assemble and set aside their order of dismissal and reinstate him to his position. Upon a review of the record the trial court refused the relief sought. Hence this appeal.

It was charged that appellant had at various times absented himself from the school when it was in session, on an average of two hours per day three or four times each week, leaving no one in charge of the school. It was further charged that he became infatuated with a lady teacher of the school and persisted in paying her undue attentions; that he asked her for dates and social engagements and proposed to take her to distant cities and towns to picture shows and ball games; that he was a married man and did not propose or suggest that his wife or anyone accompany them on such proposed trips; that he would caress her and often kiss her hand and told her how much he loved her, and objected to her engagements or associations with her gentlemen friends, under threat of discharging her as a teacher if she did so. It was further charged, and so shown by the evidence, that during the campaign for the election of school trustees he demanded of this lady teacher that she contribute $25 to the candidacy of a certain trustee and coerced her to pay said sum under threat to discharge her as a teacher if she failed to do so. It is also charged and shown by the evidence that appellant went to the boarding houses or homes of two other lady teachers who were teaching in the rural schools of the county, and asked them for engagements and proposed to take them to distant cities and places, and engaged in conversation and conduct toward them similar to that detailed above with respect to the lady teacher of his school. Many other acts of similar conduct and incidents are detailed in the charges and evidence. It would serve no useful purpose to mention the names of these lady teachers or give further details of improper advances and conduct as above indicated. However, in justice to the lady teachers we deem it fair to them to say that there is nothing in the record that would in the least reflect on their moral character, integrity, or conduct as teachers or otherwise. In fact, in those respects their conduct and demeanor was, indeed, commendable. Neither is there any proof of actual immoral conduct on the part of the appellant, in the usual acceptation of that term. However, the evidence strongly tends to show that appellant's conduct and demeanor was improper, in view of the position he occupied, which, in the very nature of things, required discretion and exemplary conduct, especially toward the teachers and pupils of his school.

In Gover v. Stovall, 237 Ky. 172, 35 S.W.2d 24, 26, Gover was discharged as a teacher in a high school in Grayson county, Ky., upon charges and evidence no stronger nor of any more serious nature than the charges and evidence revealed in the instant case. After reciting many definitions of the words "bad behavior," "improper conduct," "mismanagement," and "wrong conduct," this court said: "Plaintiff in this case was a teacher in the public schools, and was so circumstanced as that both patrons and pupils regarded him in the light of an exemplar whose conduct might be followed by his pupils, and the law by necessary intendment demands and requires that he should not engage in any conduct inevitably calculated to invite criticism and of a nature and character justly productive of suspicions of immorality."

It is insisted for appellant that the members of the board of education who tried and discharged him were prejudiced and hostile and, therefore disqualified to try him. Conceding, without deciding, that the members of the board entertained such feeling toward appellant, that did not disqualify them to hear and try him on the charges, nor afford grounds of reversal or interference with their finding.

In Arbogast v. Weber, Mayor, 249 Ky. 20, 60 S.W.2d 144, it is held that city commissioners may not on grounds of bias or prejudice be enjoined from acting on charges against a co-member of their body for official misconduct, and if the commissioners acted arbitrarily in removing the accused from office he would have remedy as in other cases of improper action by administrative officers. See, also, to the same effect, Howard v. Bell County Board of Education, 247 Ky. 586, 57 S.W.2d 466.

In the cases, supra, the powers and authorities of the board of education are discussed and the law as pronounced in those cases is applicable to the instant case.

Section 4399a–7 of the Kentucky Statutes, under which the board acted, invested the board with such power and authority, and its findings are conclusive on the courts, unless it is clearly shown that the board exercised an abuse of discretion. Meade County Board of Education v. Powell, 254 Ky. 352, 71 S.W.2d 638.

Under the facts disclosed by this record, we do not think that the board exercised an abuse of discretion and that the charges and evidence are sufficient to sustain its finding.

Wherefore the judgment is affirmed. . . .

NOTES AND QUESTIONS

1. What, exactly, constituted the "unprofessional conduct" in the Thompson case? Why?

2. One of the fundamental premises of Thompson is that the teacher properly can be held to meet the standard of the exemplar; he should serve as a model even in his out-of-school activities. Is this premise consistent with the analysis of the Supreme Court of the United States in Pickering, infra? Does the Supreme Court say that the "teacher-as-exemplar" standard can never be used? If not, under what circumstances is it appropriate to hold a teacher to standards that are higher than those applied to citizens at large? Can the exemplar standard be applied to a teacher's activities outside of school? Should it be? See, Emerson & Haber, Academic Freedom of the Faculty Member As Citizen, 28 LAW & CONTEMP. PROBS. 525 (1963).

3. Suppose at a dismissal hearing "three police officers testified to different times they had arrested the plaintiff, and that she was intoxicated at those times, the last two being within the past school year. Their descriptions included statements that plaintiff's clothing, general appearance and hair were mussed, breath strong with liquor, equilibrium abnormal, speech vague, had to have assistance to keep from falling. On one occasion she spent the night in jail and missed three days of school. There was some other testimony that she had been seen unkempt, and that the arrests had been discussed by parents, teachers and pupils" (Scott v. Board of Education, 20 Ill.App.2d 292, 156 N.E.2d 1 (1969)), should this teacher be dismissed as having engaged in "unprofessional conduct"? Why or why not?

4. Suppose at a dismissal hearing the testimony established "complaints as that some children were not allowed to go to the restrooms without facing loss of recess time; a child who complained of excessive school bus speed was placed in the back of the bus; a child was taken from school property to the home of another parent in an attempt to resolve a disciplinary problem; a teacher under her supervision was allowed to spank a child on numerous occasions; and an alleged immoral act of one of the pupils was discussed with members of the community," and the "evidence disclosed that the [teacher] became the focus of a community squabble.

This arose out of the several incidents which are not sufficient to justify the discharge of a continuing teacher and in which the community apparently chose sides, some for and some against the teacher. The critical question in this appeal is whether being the 'center of controversy' constitutes 'good cause' under the Teacher Tenure Act. . . . " (Kersey v. Maine Consolidated School District, 96 Ariz. 266, 394 P.2d 201 (1964)), should this teacher be dismissed?

5. Would the following testimonial evidence justify discharging the teacher on any of the following grounds: immorality, incompetency, intemperance, cruelty, willful and persistent negligence, mental derangement, persistent and willful violation of school laws or unprofessional conduct?

"A witness testified as follows:

"Q. What, if anything, did you see Miss Horosko do with relation to this slot machine?

"Mr. Reedy: We object to that as irrelevant and immaterial.
"The Court: Objection overruled, with exception.

"Mr. Reedy: Answer the question. A. Well, she showed us how to put the nickels into the slot machine and how the machine paid for itself.

"Q. Were the school children present when this was done? A. Yes."
"The record shows that November 12, 1936, a warrant issued for Kearney's arrest on the oath of a constable charging that he did 'possess, promote or encourage a game or device of address or hazard, namely: 1 King Six Jr. 5¢–25¢ dice game and 1 'Bally' Pin-Ball Machine at which money or other valuable things were betted upon, staked, striven for, won or lost * * *' and that on December 24, 1936, Kearney pleaded guilty and paid a fine of $14. The evidence of this conviction, the learned trial judge said, he disregarded; when offered, it was received as affecting the teacher's credibility.

"A witness testified:

"Q. Whether or not there were any games played in this establishment, Mr. Flynn? A. Yes, sir.

"Mr. Reedy: Objected to as irrelevant and immaterial and the witness having answered we ask that the answer be stricken out.

"The Court: Objection overruled, with exception.

"Q. What was the nature of the games played?

"Mr. Reedy: We object to that too.

"The Court: Same ruling. A. Shaking dice.

"Q. Did you ever see Miss Horosko shake dice during this period? A. I have.

"Q. Ever shake dice with her? A. I have.
"Q. For what? A. Drinks."
"She [the teacher] testified that she never gambled but that:
"The only machine I know was in there was one of these pin-ball machines or amusement machines.

"Q. Were there any prizes offered for playing that? A. No, not the one I saw there.

"Q. Was it one of skill? A. Well, it was more of skill; amusement.

"Q. Did you ever play that in the presence of Mrs. Carley or anybody else?

A. I don't believe I did in her presence.

"Q. You recall Mrs. Carley testifying you showed her how to play it. Do you recall doing that? A. No, I do not.

"Q. If such a thing did occur was it played for money or anything of that kind? A. No." Horosko v. School District, 6 A.2d 866 (Pa. 1939).

OLIVER v. DONOVAN

Supreme Court of New York, 1969.
32 A.D.2d 1036, 303 N.Y.S.2d 779.

MEMORANDUM BY THE COURT.

In a proceeding pursuant to article 78 . . . to require respondents Donovan and Ferrerio to institute disciplinary proceedings against respondent Cooney, the principal of Public School 27, in Brooklyn, City of New York, petitioner appeals from a judgment of the Supreme Court, Kings County, entered January 21, 1969, which dismissed the petition.

Judgment affirmed, without costs and with leave to renew the application upon proper papers.

Petitioner is the mother of four school-age children, all attending P.S. 27 in School District 15. In addition, she is the chairman of the 'Education Action Board of School District 15", an unincorporated association of parents of children enrolled in schools in School District 15.

On September 28, 1968, petitioner and other representatives of the "Education Action Board" presented a "Statement of Charges" of misconduct and incompetence against respondent Cooney [Principal of Public School 27] to respondents Donovan, the Superintendent of Schools, and Ferrerio, the acting Superintendent of School District 15. Although the latter apparently recognized the "grave nature" of the matter, no action whatsoever was taken on the complaint.

Petitioner then commenced this proceeding to compel the institution of disciplinary proceedings against Miss Cooney. The Special Term dismissed the petition on the grounds that petitioner lacked standing to sue and had failed to state facts sufficient to state a cause of action.

On this appeal it is incumbent upon us to assume that the facts as set forth in the petition are true as alleged, and, in accordance with the general rule, every favorable inference must be drawn in petitioner's favor. . . .

The Statement of Charges contains 17 specifications of misconduct and incompetence on the part of respondent Cooney. Some of them relate to her conduct during the unfortunate school strike which paralyzed The New York City school system in the latter part of 1968. Several others relate to petitioner's dissatisfaction with certain purely educational decisions made by Miss Cooney. We are in agreement with the Special Term that petitioner has no standing with respect to these complaints and has failed to state a cause of action. . . .

However, the remainder of the allegations indicate that respondent Cooney has tolerated and condoned physical abuse of students and has failed to take action against an allegedly "alcoholic" school employee whose conduct is a continuing hazard to the health and safety of the children of the school. No fewer than seven assaults against children by school officials are alleged, including several requiring medical care and attention. It is contended that Miss Cooney, as principal of the school, has failed and refused to take disciplinary action against the school employees responsible and has accepted patently inadequate explanations of their conduct in complete vindication of their behavior.

In sum, we understand the thrust of these allegations to be that respondent Cooney has permitted a situation to develop which presents a continuing threat to the health, safety, and welfare of the students at the school, including petitioner's children. It is our view that this presents a judicially cognizable injury.

Petitioner has the duty to send her children to the public schools and the concomitant right to expect that they will not be subject to physical abuse and danger at the hands of the very school officials to whom petitioner has entrusted her children. . . .

However, parents do not enjoy a general power of supervision over the school authorities. Complaints pertaining solely to matters within the administrative expertise of the educational officials involved are not judicially cognizable. Proper avenues of appeal are available and the parent is constrained to employ them. . . . On the other hand, where, as here, the parent alleges that her children are daily being exposed to conditions which threaten their health, safety and welfare, a very different situation prevails. It is unnecessary for petitioner to allege that any of her children have been assaulted. In fact, it is the presence of impending or threatened injury which is the very basis of standing to sue. . . .

Respondents Donovan and Ferrerio contend that, even if petitioner herein has standing to sue, they are under no mandatory duty to institute disciplinary proceedings against the respondent Cooney. This is true. However, petitioner seeks the very limited relief of compelling Donovan and Ferrerio to exercise an "informed discretion" in determining whether or not such proceedings are necessary. It is settled that even in the exercise of discretion administrative agencies may not conduct themselves in an arbitrary and capricious manner. In view of the serious nature of the charges herein relating to the physical abuse of the students and the existence of dangerous conditions, there must be some explanation for the complete failure of the appropriate officials to respond in any manner. . . .

We cannot, however, grant the requested relief on the papers presented. CPLR 7804 (subd. d) requires that a petition in an article 78 proceeding must comply with the rules for a complaint in an action. These rules, generally, require that statements shall be sufficiently particular to give the court and parties notice of, *inter alia,* the material elements of each cause of action or defense (CPLR 3013). More precise information should be presented, including, but not limited to, the names of all parties, the dates of each of the incidents complained of, and the particular dangerous and unhealthy conditions which exist as a result of respondent Cooney's alleged misconduct. . . .

NOTES AND QUESTIONS

1. What will be the next step in this matter?
2. Is a law such as New York's wise? Would you vote for it if you were a member of the legislature? Why or why not?

CONSTITUTIONAL LIMITATIONS ON A STATE'S POWER TO DISMISS

PICKERING v. BOARD OF EDUCATION

Supreme Court of the United States, 1968.
391 U.S. 563, 88 S.Ct. 1731, 20 L.Ed.2d 811.

Mr. Justice MARSHALL delivered the opinion of the Court.

Appellant Marvin L. Pickering, a teacher in Township High School District 205, Will County, Illinois, was dismissed from his position by the appellee Board of Education for sending a letter to a local newspaper in connection with a recently proposed tax increase that was critical of the way in which the Board and the district superintendent of schools had handled past proposals to raise new revenue for the schools. Appellant's dismissal resulted from a determination by the Board, after a full hearing, that the publication of the letter was "detrimental to the efficient operation and administration of the schools of the district" and hence, under the relevant Illinois statute . . . that "interests of the school require[d] [his dismissal]."

Appellant's claim that his writing of the letter was protected by the First and Fourteenth Amendments was rejected. . . . For the reasons detailed below we agree that appellant's rights to freedom of speech were violated and we reverse.

In February of 1961 the appellee Board of Education asked the voters of the school district to approve a bond issue to raise $4,875,000 to erect two new schools. The proposal was defeated. Then, in December of 1961, the Board submitted another bond proposal to the voters which called for the raising of $5,500,000 to build two new schools. This second proposal passed and the schools were built with the money raised by the bond sales. In May of 1964 a proposed increase in the tax rate to be used for educational purposes was submitted to the voters by the Board and was defeated. Finally, on September 19, 1964, a second proposal to increase the tax rate was submitted by the Board and was likewise defeated. It was in connection with this last proposal of the School Board that appellant wrote the letter to the editor (which we reproduce in an Appendix to this opinion) that resulted in his dismissal.

Prior to the vote on the second tax increase proposal a variety of articles attributed to the District 205 Teachers' Organization appeared in the local paper. These articles urged passage of the tax increase and stated that failure to pass the increase would result in a decline in the quality of education afforded children in the district's schools. A letter from the superintendent of schools making the same point was published in the paper two days before the election and submitted to the voters in mimeographed form the following day. It was in response to the foregoing material, together with the failure of the tax increase to pass, that appellant submitted the letter in question to the editor of the local paper.

The letter constituted, basically, an attack on the School Board's handling of the 1961 bond issue proposals and its subsequent allocation of financial resources between the schools' educational and athletic programs. It also charged the superintendent of schools with attempting to prevent teachers in the district from opposing or criticizing the proposed bond issue.

The Board dismissed Pickering for writing and publishing the letter. Pursuant to Illinois law, the Board was then required to hold a hearing on the dismissal. At the hearing the Board charged that numerous statements in the letter were false and that the publication of the statements unjustifiably impugned the "motives, honesty, integrity, truthfulness, responsibility and competence" of both the Board and the school administration. The Board also charged that the false statements damaged the professional reputations of its members and of the school administrators, would be disruptive of faculty discipline, and would tend to foment "controversy, conflict and dissension" among teachers, administrators, the Board of Education, and the residents of the district. Testimony was introduced from a variety of witnesses on the truth or falsity of the particular statements in the letter with which the Board took issue. The Board found the statements to be false as charged. No evidence was introduced at any point in the proceedings as to the effect of the publication of the letter on the community as a whole or on the administration of the school system in particular, and no specific findings along these lines were made. [The Illinois Supreme Court upheld the action of the board] . . .

To the extent that the Illinois Supreme Court's opinion may be read to suggest that teachers may constitutionally be compelled to relinquish the First Amendment rights they would otherwise enjoy as citizens to comment on matters of public interest in connection with the operation of the public schools in which they work, it proceeds on a premise that has been unequivocally rejected in numerous prior decisions of this Court.   E. g., Wieman v. Updegraff, 344 U.S. 183 (1952); Shelton v. Tucker, 364 U.S. 479 (1960); Keyishian v. Board of Regents, 385 U.S. 589 (1967). "[T]he theory that public employment which may be denied altogether may be subjected to any conditions, regardless of how unreasonable, has been uniformly rejected."   Keyishian v. Board of Regents, supra, at 605–606.   At the same time it cannot be gainsaid that the State has interests as an employer in regulating the speech of its employees that differ significantly from those it possesses in connection with regulation of the speech of the citizenry in general. The problem in any case is to arrive at a balance between the interests of the teacher, as a citizen, in commenting upon matters of public concern and the interest of the State, as an employer, in promoting the efficiency of the public services it performs through its employees.

The Board contends that "the teacher by virtue of his public employment has a duty of loyalty to support his superiors in attaining the generally accepted goals of education and that, if he must speak out publicly, he should do so factually and accurately, commensurate with his education and experience."   Appellant, on the other hand, argues that the test applicable to defamatory statements directed against public officials by persons having no occupational relationship with them, namely, that statements to be legally actionable must be made "with knowledge that [they were] . . . false or with reckless disregard of whether [they were] . . . false or not," New York Times Co. v. Sullivan, 376 U.S. 254, 280 (1964), should also be applied to public statements made by teachers.   Because of the enormous variety of fact situations in which critical statements by teachers and other public employees may be thought by their superiors, against whom the statements are directed, to furnish grounds for dismissal, we do not deem it either appropriate or feasible to attempt to lay down a general standard against which all such statements may be judged.   However, in the course of evaluating the conflicting claims of First Amendment protection and the need for orderly school administration in the context of this case, we shall indicate some of the general lines along which an analysis of the controlling interests should run.

An examination of the statements in appellant's letter objected to by the Board reveals that they, like the letter as a whole, consist essentially of criticism of the Board's allocation of school funds between educational and athletic programs, and of both the Board's and the superintendent's methods of informing, or preventing the informing of, the district's taxpayers of the real reasons why additional tax revenues were being sought for the schools. The statements are in no way directed towards any person with whom appellant would normally be in contact in the course of his daily work as a teacher. Thus no question of maintaining either discipline by immediate superiors or harmony among coworkers is presented here. Appellant's employment relationships with the Board and, to a somewhat lesser extent, with the superintendent are not the kind of close working relationships for which it can persuasively be claimed that personal loyalty and confidence are necessary to their proper functioning. Accordingly, to the extent that the Board's position here can be taken to suggest that even comments on matters of public concern that are substantially correct—such as statements (1)–(4) of appellant's letter, see Appendix, infra, may furnish grounds for dismissal if they are sufficiently critical in tone, we unequivocally reject it.

We next consider the statements in appellant's letter which we agree to be false. The Board's original charges included allegations that the publication of the letter damaged the professional reputations of the Board and the superintendent and would foment controversy and conflict among the Board, teachers, administrators, and the residents of the district. However, no evidence to support these allegations was introduced at the hearing. So far as the record reveals, Pickering's letter was greeted by everyone but its main target, the Board, with massive apathy and total disbelief. The Board must, therefore, have decided, perhaps by analogy with the law of libel, that the statements were *per se* harmful to the operation of the schools.

However, the only way in which the Board could conclude, absent any evidence of the actual effect of the letter, that the statements contained therein were *per se* detrimental to the interest of the schools was to equate the Board members' own interests with that of the schools. Certainly an accusation that too much money is being spent on athletics by the administrators of the school system (which is precisely the import of that portion of appellant's letter containing the statements that we have found to be false, . . .) cannot reasonably be regarded as *per se* detrimental to the district's schools. Such an accusation reflects rather a difference of opinion between Pickering and the Board as to the preferable manner of operating the school system, a difference of opinion that clearly concerns an issue of general public interest.

In addition, the fact that particular illustrations of the Board's claimed undesirable emphasis on athletic programs are false would not normally have any necessary impact on the actual operation of the schools, beyond its tendency to anger the Board. For example, Pickering's letter was written after the defeat at the polls of the second proposed tax increase. It could, therefore, have had no effect on the ability of the school district to raise necessary revenue, since there was no showing that there was any proposal to increase taxes pending when the letter was written.

More importantly, the question whether a school system requires additional funds is a matter of legitimate public concern on which the judgment of the school administration, including the School Board, cannot, in a society that leaves such questions to popular vote, be taken as conclusive.   On such a question free and open debate is vital to informed decision-making by the electorate.   Teachers are, as a class, the members of a community most likely to have informed and definite opinions as to how funds allotted to the operation of the schools should be spent.   Accordingly, it is essential that they be able to speak out freely on such questions without fear of retaliatory dismissal.

In addition, the amounts expended on athletics which Pickering reported erroneously were matters of public record on which his position as a teacher in the district did not qualify him to speak with any greater authority than any other taxpayer.   The Board could easily have rebutted appellant's errors by publishing the accurate figures itself, either via a letter to the same newspaper or otherwise. We are thus not presented with a situation in which a teacher has carelessly made false statements about matters so closely related to the day-to-day operations of the schools that any harmful impact on the public would be difficult to counter because of the teacher's presumed greater access to the real facts.   Accordingly, we have no occasion to consider at this time whether under such circumstances a school board could reasonably require that a teacher make substantial efforts to verify the accuracy of his charges before publishing them.

What we do have before us is a case in which a teacher has made erroneous public statements upon issues then currently the subject of public attention, which are critical of his ultimate employer but which are neither shown nor can be presumed to have in any way either impeded the teacher's proper performance of his daily duties in the classroom or to have interfered with the regular operation of the schools generally.   In these circumstances we conclude that the interest of the school administration in limiting teachers' opportunities to contribute to public debate is not significantly greater than its interest in limiting a similar contribution by any member of the general public.

The public interest in having free and unhindered debate on matters of public importance—the core value of the Free Speech Clause of the First Amendment—is so great that it has been held that a State cannot authorize the recovery of damages by a public official for defamatory statements directed at him except when such statements are shown to have been made either with knowledge of their falsity or with reckless disregard for their truth or falsity. . . . It is therefore perfectly clear that, were appellant a member of the general public, the State's power to afford the appellee Board of Education or its members any legal right to sue him for writing the letter at issue here would be limited by the requirement that the letter be judged by the standard laid down in *New York Times*. . . .

While criminal sanctions and damage awards have a somewhat different impact on the exercise of the right to freedom of speech from dismissal from employment, it is apparent that the threat of dismissal from public employment is nonetheless a potent means of inhibiting speech. We have already noted our disinclination to make an across-the-board equation of dismissal from public employment for remarks critical of superiors with awarding damages in a libel suit by a public official for similar criticism. However, in a case such as the present one, in which the fact of employment is only tangentially and insubstantially involved in the subject matter of the public communication made by a teacher, we conclude that it is necessary to regard the teacher as the member of the general public he seeks to be.

In sum, we hold that, in a case such as this, absent proof of false statements knowingly or recklessly made by him, a teacher's exercise of his right to speak on issues of public importance may not furnish the basis for his dismissal from public employment. Since no such showing has been made in this case regarding appellant's letter . . . his dismissal for writing it cannot be upheld and the judgment of the Illinois Supreme Court must, accordingly, be reversed. . . .

APPENDIX TO OPINION OF THE COURT

A. *Appellant's letter*

LETTERS TO THE EDITOR

Graphic Newspapers, Inc.

Thursday, September 24, 1964, Page 4

Dear Editor:

I enjoyed reading the back issues of your paper which you loaned to me. Perhaps others would enjoy reading them in order to see just how far the two new high schools have deviated from the original promises by the Board of Education. First, let me state that I am referring to the February thru November, 1961 issues of your paper, so that it can be checked.

One statement in your paper declared that swimming pools, athletic fields, and auditoriums had been left out of the program. They may have been left out but they got put back in very quickly because Lockport West has both an auditorium and athletic field. In fact, Lockport West has a better athletic field than Lockport Central. It has a track that isn't quite regulation distance even though the board spent a few thousand dollars on it. Whose fault is that? Oh, I forgot, it wasn't supposed to be there in the first place. It must have fallen out of the sky. Such responsibility has been touched on in other letters but it seems one just can't help noticing it. I am not saying the school shouldn't have these facilities, because I think they should, but promises are promises, or are they?

Since there seems to be a problem getting all the facts to the voter on the twice defeated bond issue, many letters have been written to this paper and probably more will follow, I feel I must say something about the letters and their writers. Many of these letters did not give the whole story. Letters by your Board and Administration have stated that teachers' salaries total $1,297,746 for one year. Now that must have been the total payroll, otherwise the teachers would be getting $10,000 a year. I teach at the high school and I know this just isn't the case. However, this shows their "stop at nothing" attitude. To illustrate further, do you know that the superintendent told the teachers, and I quote, "Any teacher that opposes the referendum should be prepared for the consequences." I think this gets at the reason we have problems passing bond issues. Threats take something away; these are insults to voters in a free society. We should try to sell a program on its merits, if it has any.

Remember those letters entitled "District 205 Teachers Speak," I think the voters should know that those letters have been written and agreed to by only five or six teachers, not 98% of the teachers in the high school. In fact, many teachers didn't even know who was writing them. Did you know that those letters had to have the approval of the superintendent before they could be put in the paper? That's the kind of totalitarianism teachers live in at the high school, and your children go to school in.

In last week's paper, the letter written by a few uninformed teachers threatened to close the school cafeteria and fire its personnel. This is ridiculous and insults the intelligence of the voter because properly managed school cafeterias do not cost the school district any money. If the cafeteria is losing money, then the board should not be packing free lunches for athletes on days of athletic contests. Whatever the case, the taxpayer's child should only have to pay about 30¢ for his lunch instead of 35¢ to pay for free lunches for the athletes.

In a reply to this letter your Board of Administration will probably state that these lunches are paid for from receipts from the games. But $20,000 in receipts doesn't pay for the $200,000 a year they have been spending on varsity sports while neglecting the wants of teachers.

You see we don't need an increase in the transportation tax unless the voters want to keep paying $50,000 or more a year to transport athletes home after practice and to away games, etc. Rest of the $200,000 is made up in coaches' salaries, athletic directors' salaries, baseball pitching machines, sodded football fields, and thousands of dollars for other sports equipment.

These things are all right, provided we have enough money for them. To sod football fields on borrowed money and then not be able to pay teachers' salaries is getting the cart before the horse.

If these things aren't enough for you, look at East High. No doors on many of the classrooms, a plant room without any sunlight, no water in a first aid treatment room, are just a few of many things. The taxpayers were really taken to the cleaners. A part of the sidewalk in front of the building has already collapsed. Maybe Mr. Hess would be interest to know that we need blinds on the windows in that building also.

Once again, the board must have forgotten they were going to spend $3,200,000 on the West building and $2,300,000 on the East building.

As I see it, the bond issue is a fight between the Board of Education that is trying to push tax-supported athletics down our throats with education, and a public that has mixed emotions about both of these items because they feel they are already paying enough taxes, and simply don't know whom to trust with any more tax money.

I must sign this letter as a citizen, taxpayer and voter, not as a teacher, since that freedom has been taken from the teachers by the administration. Do you really know what goes on behind those stone walls at the high school?

Respectfully,

Marvin L. Pickering. . . .

Mr. Justice WHITE, concurring in part and dissenting in part.

The Court holds that truthful statements by a school teacher critical of the school board are within the ambit of the First Amendment. So also are false statements innocently or negligently made. The State may not fire the teacher for making either unless, as I gather it, there are special circumstances, not present in this case, demonstrating an overriding state interest, such as the need for confidentiality or the special obligations which a teacher in a particular position may owe to his superiors. The core of today's decision is the holding that Pickering's discharge must be tested by the standard of New York Times Co. v. Sullivan, 376 U.S. 254 (1964). To this extent I am in agreement. . . .

. . . As I see it, a teacher may be fired without violation of the First Amendment for knowingly or recklessly making false statements regardless of their harmful impact on the schools. As the Court holds, however, in the absence of special circumstances he may not be fired if his statements were true or only negligently false, even if there is some harm to the school system. . . . If Pickering's false statements were either knowingly or recklessly made, injury to the school system becomes irrelevant, and the First Amendment would not prevent his discharge. . . .

Nor can I join the Court in its findings with regard to whether Pickering knowingly or recklessly published false statements. . . .

NOTES AND QUESTIONS

1. What is the precise scope of the decision in Pickering and for what reason(s). Do you agree or disagree? State the principle of constitutional law that this case stands for. Should Pickering have been discharged?

2. Were the statements of Pickering made recklessly? Negligently? What difference would it make?

3. The Court stated that it would not "lay down a general standard against which all such statements [critical of school operation] may be judged" because there are an "enormous [possible] variety of fact situations." Present some hypothetical fact situations involving criticism that would be upheld by courts on the basis of the Pickering decision and other examples that would not.

4. Suppose Pickering had been dismissed for "incompetence," and the evidence of incompetence was the factual errors in the letter, would the Court's decision have been different? Why or why not?

5. Suppose a grievance procedure rule of the school board required teachers to submit complaints about school operations to their superiors for action thereon before bringing their complaints to the public, and suppose Pickering published his letter without first going through the grievance procedure, would the case have been decided the same way? Why or why not? At what point should a teacher be professionally free publicly to criticize the operations of his school?

6. Does the Supreme Court's decision in the Pickering case rest on the view that with respect to outside activities, even though involving a school, a teacher is to be treated like any other citizen, or does the Court's decision rest on the view that in such circumstances the teacher should be held to an exemplar standard and that Pickering met it?

7. In Finot v. Pasadena City Board of Education, 250 Cal.App.2d 189, 58 Cal.Rptr. 520 (1967), California's Court of Appeals held that a teacher had "a constitutional right [under the ninth and fourteenth amendments] to wear his beard while engaged in classroom teaching. . . ." Under the rule of this case, allowing the expression of one's personality, would a teacher have a constitutional right to wear dungarees, a daishiki, an Afro hairdo, a micro-mini skirt, or to teach braless? In Morrison v. Hamilton County Board of Education, —— Tenn. ——, 494 S.W. 2d 770 (1973) Tennessee's Supreme Court upheld the dismissal of a tenured teacher for wearing a beard. Compare Bishop v. Colaw, infra, Chapter 8.

PUENTES v. BOARD OF EDUCATION

Court of Appeals of New York, 1966.
18 N.Y.2d 906, 276 N.Y.S.2d 638, 223 N.E.2d 45.

Petitioner brought a proceeding . . . to review a determination of board of education that petitioner was guilty of conduct unbecoming a teacher and of insubordination under Education Law, . . . and suspending him, without pay, from his position as high school teacher. The petitioner wrote a letter, which was addressed to the board of education, and which was distributed to teachers and administrators within school district, as president of federation of teachers, criticizing failure on part of school administration to renew the employment of a certain probationary teacher. The first charge against the petitioner alleged that he was guilty of conduct unbecoming a teacher on ground that the letter contained defamatory accusations against administration of school district and school principal and was designed to hold them up to contempt and ridicule, to attack their professional integrity, and to create suspicion, dissension, and disharmony among board of education, administration, and faculty. The second charge alleged that petitioner was guilty of insubordination on ground that the letter encouraged a defiance and contempt of duly constituted authority and was contumacious in character, and that when petitioner was questioned by superintendent of school concerning the letter he refused to answer questions without advice of counsel. The board of education found that the letter had been written without consent of the probationary teacher referred to therein and after she had resigned and accepted employment elsewhere, and that it had not been authorized by a quorum of membership of federation of teachers, and that accusations contained therein were false, and that any qualified privilege was destroyed by malice because language used in letter allegedly was unreasonably vitriolic and because letter allegedly contained attacks wholly unrelated to incident complained of and was circulated beyond members of board of education so that it might come into hands of nonprofessional personnel and others. . . .

The Appellate Division entered an order by a divided court confirming the determination of the board of education. . . .

PUENTES v. BOARD OF EDUCATION

Court of Appeals of New York, 1969.
24 N.Y.2d 996, 302 N.Y.S.2d 824, 250 N.E.2d 232, rearg. dism. 25 N.Y.2d 930, 305 N.Y.S.2d 148, 252 N.E.2d 628.

Upon reargument: the order of the Appellate Division should be reversed, without costs, and the determination of respondent annulled.

Petitioner's letter was indiscreet and properly found to be embarrassing to the teacher on whose purported behalf it was sent. However, whatever factual inaccuracies were present in the letter related to teacher observation reports to which petitioner had no access. Hence, the inaccuracies were not the result of reckless or intentional falsehood. The other strident and, therefore, unnecessary comments were excessive characterizations and inferences and no worse. Since the letter's distribution was limited to the school system and the contents were arguably within the free speech protections laid down in Pickering v. Board of Educ., . . . there was lacking substantial evidence to warrant disciplinary action. . . .

There is no suggestion in the record that petitioner's indiscretions led to any deleterious effects within the school system, and it is unlikely that they should have. Indiscreet bombast in an argumentative letter, to the limited extent present here, is insufficient to sanction disciplinary action. Otherwise, those who criticize in an area where criticism is permissible would either be discouraged from exercising their right or would be required to do so in such innocuous terms as would make the criticism seem ineffective or obsequious.

Overall, a single incident was permitted by the petitioner, and later by the school administration, to be elevated into an issue quite disproportionate to the occasion. Concededly, petitioner's direct teaching and in-class performance were correct and were not affected by the writing or sending of the letter.

It should only be noted that petitioner's status as a union official did not give him, in this context, any greater privilege of speech or conduct than he had as an interested teacher, although such status was the occasion for his writing the letter. . . .

JASEN, Judge (dissenting). . . .

Since distribution of the letter was limited to the school system, and its contents were within the free speech protection laid down in Pickering v. Board of Educ., ... I agree with the holding of the majority insofar as it reverses appellant's suspension for writing and circulating the letter.

However, as to the second count of insubordination (i. e., refusing to answer the Superintendent's questions about the letter), I would affirm.

The Superintendent of Schools is the chief supervisory officer of the district and as such has a legitimate interest in the activities of the students, faculty and administration. Further, he has a duty to make inquiry into matters involving the district which warrant investigation.

Here, the Superintendent considered that the letter in question and its distribution to the School Board, the administrative officials and teachers, partly through the interschool mail system, required investigation. The charges made in the letter, if true, might have warranted action by the Superintendent to correct them. Furthermore, it was proper for the Superintendent to investigate whether the circulation of the letter was being carried on through school facilities on school time. Petitioner's signature on the letter indicated that the inquiry might properly begin with him.

However, appellant thwarted the investigation by refusing to answer any questions without the aid of counsel. . . .

. . . the board was completely justified in finding appellant insubordinate.

While the Constitution protects the individual's right to freedom of expression, it does not sanction every activity which may be tangentially related to that expression.

PROBLEM

VANCE v. BOARD OF EDUCATION

2 Ill.App.3d 745, 277 N.E.2d 337 (1971).

"The plaintiff [Vance] commenced teaching at Pekin Community High School on the designated contractual date of September 2, 1969. He taught courses in Economics and American Government. On September 29, 1969, the plaintiff was discharged from his teaching position by the defendant Board of Education. . . .

"The record discloses that during the short period the plaintiff taught in the Pekin Community High School a number of complaints were made against his methods of instruction and the type of discussions that were taking place in his classrooms. These complaints were made to a Mr. Holman, the school Superintendent, by parents, faculty members and school board members. Shortly after the plaintiff commenced his teaching duties the Student Council had under consideration a new constitution. A member of the Student Council gave the plaintiff a copy of the proposed constitution for the student body and after reading it he advised the members of his class that the document gave the students no voice in the operation of the school system. Members of the Student Council who were not enrolled as members of his regular classes were invited to attend such classes and further discussions ensued about the students having no voice in the operation of the school. For three days the plaintiff discussed with a large number of students the subject of 'student power' and how to achieve it. The plaintiff in discussing 'student power' with his pupils and members of the Student Council who were present in his classroom stated that the only way to get anything changed was through demonstrations such as 'walk outs.' The record discloses that during this period of time when the plaintiff was disseminating such information there was considerable unrest among the student body and it culminated in an attempted walk out on the part of the students. There is no evidence, however, in the record that would support a finding that the plaintiff ordered the 'walk out' or approved of it. However, never before in the school's history had such an atmosphere of unrest prevailed. . . .

"The sole question presented for review is whether the defendant Board of Education acted capriciously, maliciously or arbitrarily in dismissing the plaintiff and thereby breached the contract of employment."

1.   Does Pickering apply to this case?

2.   What decision would you render and for what reason(s)? See also, Watts v. Seward School Bd., Alaska, 421 P.2d 586 (1967), and 454 P.2d 732 (1969).

TEACHER ORGANIZATION

McLAUGHLIN v. TILENDIS

United States Court of Appeals, Seventh Circuit, 1968.
398 F.2d 287.

CUMMINGS, Circuit Judge. This action was brought under Section 1 of the Civil Rights Act of 1871 (42 U.S.C.A. § 1983) by John Steele and James McLaughlin who had been employed as probationary teachers by Cook County, Illinois, School District No. 149. Each sought damages of $100,000 from the Superintendent of School District No. 149 and the elected members of the Board of Education of that District.

Steele was not offered a second-year teaching contract and McLaughlin was dismissed before the end of his second year of teaching. Steele alleged that he was not rehired and McLaughlin alleged that he was dismissed because of their association with Local 1663 of the American Federation of Teachers, AFL–CIO. Neither teacher had yet achieved tenure.

In two additional Counts, Local 1663 and the parent union, through their officers and on behalf of all their members, sought an injunction requiring the defendants to cease and desist from discriminating against teachers who distribute union materials and solicit union membership.

The District Court granted the defendants' motion to dismiss the complaint, holding that plaintiffs had no First Amendment rights to join or form a labor union, so that there was no jurisdiction under the Civil Rights Act. The District Court's memorandum opinion did not consider the alternative defense presented in the motion that defendants were immune from suit under the Illinois Tort Immunity Act (Ill.Rev.Stats.1967, Ch. 85, Sec. 2–201). Concluding that the First Amendment confers the right to form and join a labor union, we reverse on the ground that the complaint does state a claim under Section 1983.

It is settled that teachers have the right of free association, and unjustified interference with teachers' associational freedom violates the Due Process clause of the Fourteenth Amendment. Shelton v. Tucker, 364 U.S. 479, 485–487. . . . Public employment may not be subjected to unreasonable conditions, and the assertion of First Amendment rights by teachers will usually not warrant their dismissal. Keyishian v. Board of Regents . . ., Pickering v. Board of Education. . . . Unless there is some illegal intent, an individual's right to form and join a union is protected by the First Amendment. Thomas v. Collins, 323 U.S. 516 . . ., Hague v. C.I.O., 307 U.S. 496 . . ., Griswold v. State of Connecticut . . ., Stapleton v. Mitchell, 60 F.Supp. 51, 59–60, 61 (D.Kan.1945; opinion of Circuit Judge Murrah), appeal dismissed, Mitchell v. McElroy, 326 U.S. 690, 66 S.Ct. 172, 90 L.Ed. 406. As stated in N.A.A.C.P. v. State of Alabama, 357 U.S. 449, 460, 78 S.Ct. 1163, 1171, 2 L.Ed.2d 1488:

> "It is beyond debate that freedom to engage in association for the advancement of beliefs and ideas is an inseparable aspect of the 'liberty' assured by the Due Process Clause of the Fourteenth Amendment, which embraces freedom of speech."

Even though the individual plaintiffs did not yet have tenure, the Civil Rights Act of 1871 gives them a remedy if their contracts were not renewed because of their exercise of constitutional rights.

. . .

Just this month the Supreme Court held that an Illinois teacher was protected by the First Amendment from discharge even though he wrote a partially false letter to a local newspaper in which he criticized the school board's financial policy. Pickering v. Board of Education. . . . There is no showing on this record that plaintiffs' activities impeded "[the] proper performance of [their] daily duties in the classroom." . . . If teachers can engage in scathing and partially inaccurate public criticism of their school board, surely they can form and take part in associations to further what they consider to be their well-being.

The trial judge was motivated by his conclusion that more than free speech was involved here, stating:

> "The union may decide to engage in strikes, to set up machinery to bargain with the governmental employer, to provide machinery for arbitration, or may seek to establish working conditions. Overriding community interests are involved. The very ability of the governmental entity to function may

> be affected. The judiciary, and particularly this Court, cannot interfere with the power or discretion of the state in handling these matters."

It is possible of course that at some future time plaintiffs may engage in union-related conduct justifying their dismissal. But the Supreme Court has stated that

> "Those who join an organization but do not share its unlawful purposes and who do not participate in its unlawful activities surely pose no threat, either as citizens or as public employees." Elfbrandt v. Russell, 384 U.S. 11, 17, . . .

Even if this record disclosed that the union was connected with unlawful activity, the bare fact that membership does not justify charging members with their organization's misdeeds. Idem. A contrary rule would bite more deeply into associational freedom than is necessary to achieve legitimate state interests, thereby violating the First Amendment.

Illinois has not prohibited membership in a teachers' union, and defendants do not claim that the individual plaintiffs engaged in any illegal strikes or picketing. Moreover, collective bargaining contracts between teacher's unions and school districts are not against the public policy of Illinois. . . . Illinois even permits the automatic deduction of union dues from the salaries of employees of local governmental agencies. . . . These very defendants have not adopted any rule, regulation or resolution forbidding union membership. Accordingly, no paramount public interest of Illinois warranted the limiting of Steele's and McLaughlin's right of association. Of course, at trial defendants may show that these individuals were engaging in unlawful activities or were dismissed for other proper reasons, but on this record we hold that the complaint sufficiently states a justifiable claim under Section 1983. There is nothing anomalous in protecting teachers' rights to join unions. Other employees have long been similarly protected by the National Labor Relations Act. . . .

The second ground of defendants' motion to dismiss was that they are protected against suit by the Illinois Tort Immunity Act (Ill. Rev.Stats.1967, Ch. 85, Sec. 2–201). Under the Supremacy Clause, that statute cannot protect defendants against a cause of action grounded, as here, on a federal statute. Legislators and judges have broad immunity under Section 1983 because in enacting that statute Congress did not intend to overturn their pre-existing defense. . . . However, other officials, such as present defendants, retain only a qualified immunity, dependent on good faith action. . . . In this Court and in their brief below the defendants also rely on common law immunity, but we rejected a similar contention in Progress Development Corp. v. Mitchell, 286 F.2d 222, 231 (7th Cir. 1961), where it was held that common law immunity did not extend to members of the Deerfield, Illinois, Park Board charged with discriminating against

Negroes. Unless they can show good faith action, the reach of that decision extends to the present defendants who are alleged to have discriminatorily discharged Steele and McLaughlin for their union membership. To hold defendants absolutely immune from this type of suit would frustrate the very purpose of Section 1983. . . .
At best, defendants' qualified immunity in this case means that they can prevail only if they show that plaintiffs were discharged on justifiable grounds. Thus here a successful defense on the merits merges with a successful defense under the qualified immunity doctrine.

. . .

The judgment of the District Court is reversed and the cause is remanded for trial.

NOTES AND QUESTIONS

1. Were tenured teachers involved in this case?

2. Did the court hold that teachers have a constitutional right to organize into unions in order to engage in lawful activities? If so, what activities? If so, what part of the constitution affords this right? Do you agree with the decision and the court's reasoning? Why or why not?

3. Could a tenured teacher, or a probationary teacher during the term of his contract, constitutionally be dismissed on the ground (1) that he is a member of a union; (2) that he is a member of a union that called for an illegal strike; or (3) that he is a member of a union that called for an illegal strike in which he participated?

4. What does the term "limited immunity from suit" mean?

5. What will be the issues to be resolved at the trial of this case? Suppose the school board shows by evidence other than union activities that the teachers were "insubordinate" or engaged in "unprofessional" activities, what result?

6. While essential to a complete understanding of the role of teacher organizations in education, a full development of all aspects of the law pertaining to teacher organization, collective bargaining, the right of public employees to strike, and their related considerations, is beyond the scope of this book. Only an introduction of the law will be set forth here. At present public employees do not come within the National Labor Relations Act; thus, teacher organization is dependent upon state statutes where they exist and upon the common law in the absence of state statutes. The usual steps of organizing are these. First of all are the initial organizing activities. They are usually carried on by rival organizations; e. g., the National Education Association and the American Federation of Teachers. The purpose of the organizing activity is to obtain approval from a majority of teachers in the district for the specific organization to represent them in negotiations with the school board. In some states, statutes lump teachers together with all other public employees, and allow only public-employee unions. In these situations, it still may be possible for teachers to obtain a separate union, or a separate division of a union, to repre-

sent them. Generally, an election is held to determine which organization shall be certified by the appropriate state agency as the collective bargaining representative. Assuming that a majority votes for one union and that state law is silent on the matter, a question can arise whether that organization shall be the exclusive bargaining agent or merely one of several. If the latter situation prevails then a board of education has the opportunity of pitting one group against another during negotiations and other activities. If one organization is designated the exclusive bargaining representative of the teachers then it will have the duty of fairly and honestly representing all the teachers, and not only those teachers who voted for it. Once the bargaining representative is selected the next step is to negotiate a collective agreement with the school board. This can be tricky, depending upon the exact way in which the law is worded and other factors. For example, suppose there is no legal authorization for a school board to negotiate, or if authorized, suppose there is no legal requirement that a school board negotiate and suppose it refuses to do so, or suppose it negotiates but refuses to do so in good faith? These are only some of the many problems that can arise. If the parties negotiate in good faith but an impasse develops, and the parties fail to resolve their differences, a specific problem can be submitted to mediation, and in some circumstances, to arbitration. Mediation involves bringing a powerless third party into the negotiations for the purposes of helping the negotiating parties modify their positions and reaching a voluntary agreement. Arbitration involves submitting the problem to arbitrators who, after a hearing on the issue, will decide the matter, and their decision will be binding, because, beforehand, the parties have agreed to be bound by it. Mediation and arbitration can also come into play when dealing with grievance concerns and other matters under a collective agreement. Assuming that a collective agreement is negotiated and that it comes into legal effect, it will create many rights and obligations between and among the school board, the teacher's organization and individual teachers. Basically, the style of decision-making within the district will change to meet the requirements of the collective agreement, affecting management decisions on such items as working conditions, salary levels, teacher assignment, transfer and dismissal. Additionally, collective agreements usually set up some type of grievance machinery through which teachers, the teacher organization and boards of education have access in order to complain. Many questions can arise; for example (1) what is the legal impact of an existing collective agreement on the power of the teachers to change their representative organization; (2) what is the legal validity of the existing collective agreement if the teachers change to another representative, or if there is a change in the employer because of school district reorganization? These and similar questions are beyond the scope of this book. The following materials illustrate some of the legal problems. Moreover, questions of constitutional freedom probably will also arise in the area of collective organization. For example, would a bargained for school board rule, or collective agreement provision be constitutional if it required all teachers to become members of and to contribute dues to a union that a majority of the teachers in that district selected as their bargaining representative? Could a teacher's union constitutionally contribute funds collected from all its members and then make contributions to support the election of a school board member who favored teacher unions or to support a political cause, both of which are opposed by some of the organization's members? Generally see, Wollett, The Coming Revolution In Public School Management, 67 Mich.L.Rev. 1017 (1969).

D. H. Wollett & R. H. Chanin, THE LAW AND PRACTICE OF TEACHER NEGOTIATIONS

Excerpts from pages 1–29.
Reprinted by permission from THE LAW AND PRACTICE OF TEACHER NEGOTIATIONS, by Donald H. Wollett and Robert H. Chanin, copyright © 1970 by The Bureau of National Affairs, Inc., Washington, D.C. 20037.

I. ORGANIZATIONAL ACTIVITY

Although there are some early court holdings to the effect that a school board may prohibit its employees from belonging to an employee organization, and some states even have enacted legislation to this effect, such restraints on the right of public employees to organize are clearly out of phase with the trends of decisional law in the past 20 years. Furthermore, they are very probably unconstitutional.

This latter conclusion is firmly supported by the logic of the following argument. Workers in the private sector are guaranteed by the First Amendment a "constitutional right . . . to assemble, to discuss and formulate plans for furthering their own self interest in jobs. . . ." The close nexus between freedom of speech and freedom of assembly means that the "right of free association . . . like free speech, lies at the foundation of a free society." In Brotherhood of Railroad Trainmen v. Virginia ex rel. Virginia State Bar [377 U.S. 1 (1964)], a case involving an effort to prevent a union from actively recommending lawyers to members with personal injury claims, the Supreme Court of the United States declared:

> "It cannot be seriously doubted that the First Amendment's guarantees of free speech, petition and assembly give railroad workers the right to gather together for the lawful purpose of helping and advising one another in asserting the rights Congress gave them in the Safety Appliance Act and the Federal Employers' Liability Act, statutory rights which would be vain and futile if the workers could not talk together freely as to the best course to follow."

The effort to interfere with the exercise of these rights was constitutionally proscribed because "the State . . . failed to advance any substantial regulatory interest, in the form of substantive evils flowing from . . . activities, which [could] . . . justify the broad prohibitions . . . imposed."

In Keyishian v. Board of Regents, the Court repudiated in its entirety the ancient distinction in constitutional status between public and private employees whereby "public employment, including academic employment, may be conditioned upon the surrender of constitutional rights which could not be abridged by direct government action." Indeed, adopting the language of the court below, the Supreme Court stated: "[T]he theory that public employment which may be denied altogether may be subjected to any conditions, regardless of how unreasonable, has been uniformly rejected." Public employees cannot be "relegated to a watered-down version of constitutional rights" solely because they are public employees.

The significance of this conclusion was graphically reflected in Pickering v. Board of Educ. . . .

In McLaughlin v. Tilendis [398 F.2d 287 (7th Cir. 1968)]. . . . The Seventh Circuit . . . conclud[ed] that "the First Amendment [of the United States Constitution] confers the right to form and join a labor union." The court said that "unless there is some illegal intent, an individual's right to form and join a union is protected by the First Amendment." Moreover, "[e]ven though the plaintiffs did not yet have tenure, the Civil Rights Act of 1871 gives them a remedy if their contracts were not renewed because of their exercise of constitutional rights." . . .

In American Federation of State, County and Municipal Employees, AFL–CIO v. Woodward [406 F.2d 137 (8th Cir. 1969)], the Eighth Circuit had the same question before it: Do public employees, discharged for membership in a labor union, have a cause of action for damages and injunctive relief under Section 1 of the Civil Rights Act of 1871? In reaching an affirmative answer, the court held that union membership is protected by the right of association under the First and Fourteenth Amendments. The court explicitly stated that "[t]he guarantee of the 'right of assembly' protects more than the 'right to attend a meeting; it includes the right to express one's attitudes or philosophies by membership in a group or by affiliation with it or by other lawful means.' "

Consistent with these holdings, a U. S. district court recently struck down the North Carolina statute referred to above, in an action for a declaratory judgment brought by a group of firemen, on the ground that it constituted on its face an unconstitutional abridgement of freedom of association protected by the First and Fourteenth Amendments to the Constitution of the United States.

There is a parallel and consistent line of cases from the state courts. See, for example, City of Springfield v. Clouse [356 Mo. 1239, 206 S.W.2d 539 (1947)], where the court stated:

"All citizens have the right, preserved by the First Amendment to the United States Constitution . . . to peaceably assemble and organize for any proper purpose, to speak freely and to present their views and desires to any public officer or legislative body. . . .

"Therefore, we start with the proposition that there is nothing improper in the organization of municipal employees into labor unions; and that no new constitutional provisions were necessary to authorize them."

In sum, it now seems clear that the constitutional rights of employees in the private sector extend to employees in the public sector, and that the latter have a federally protected right to form organizations and, through such organizations, to importune their employers for improvements in their terms and conditions of employment. However, the question remains as to whether these rights include the right to engage in what is generally referred to as collective negotiations.

II. COLLECTIVE NEGOTIATIONS

Historically many school boards were willing to listen to the presentations, proposals and requests of teacher organizations. The teachers' spokesman would make known the views of the professional staff in respect to salaries, sick leave, class size, etc., in an environment of unctuous gentility. There might or might not be a perceptible relationship between the actions ultimately taken by the school board and the proposals made by the teacher organization. This process has been derisively characterized as "collective begging."

Other school boards went beyond this, not only receiving the teachers' proposals but also reacting by asking questions about them, discussing their merits, or considering their practicability. The board might even promise to give the proposals study and consideration prior to reaching final decisions. Occasionally a teacher organization's proposal might find its way into a board policy or be reflected in a salary adjustment or an improvement in fringe benefits. This process has sometimes been referred to as "organized supplication."

Collective negotiations envisions something very different. The process is one of proposal and counterproposal, of action and reaction, of give and take—resulting finally in "deal" or "no deal," in mutual agreement or stalemate. The process also assumes parity of legal standing between the parties and rough parity of power. Bilateral determination of the terms and conditions of employment through the process of negotiations means that neither party has the ability to impose its will on the other, and that each is able, in law and in fact, to veto the proposals of the other.

Any movement to convert the relationship between teachers and boards of education from collective begging or organized supplication to "collective negotiations" was effectively blunted for many years by a multiplicity of legal and practical problems. Teacher apathy and timidity were inhibiting factors. Collective bargaining, trade-union style, was thought to be unprofessional and undignified. The myth that school boards, superintendents, principals, and teachers share a common bond—the desire to serve children—which unifies them in a single-minded enterprise manned by a work force whose ethic is punctuality, obedience, dedication and self-sacrifice was a powerful opiate.

Nor were the laws of any assistance. The term "employer" as used in the National Labor Relations Act excluded "any State or political subdivision thereof." The employees of such entities are also excluded. Similarly, those states with labor relations statutes usually limited coverage to private employees. Indeed, as previously noted, some states expressly prohibited public employees from organizing, under threat of criminal penalty, and declared collective bargaining illegal.

Thus, as the push for collective negotiations in public employment gathered momentum in the early 1960s, the efforts to make it a reality followed two channels. The first was to establish, in states which neither expressly permitted nor prohibited such activity, a formalized extralegal structure of bilateral decision-making by means of agreements between boards of education and teacher organizations on a district-by-district basis. The second was to press for the enactment of legislation which required school boards to negotiate collectively with teacher organizations.

A.   In the Absence of Express Statutory Authorization

In some states, the principal components of the state educational establishment, i. e., the state school boards association, the state association of school administrators (superintendents), and the state education association (with the approval, tacit or express, of the state board of education), have agreed to a set of policies concerning negotiations between local school boards and local teacher organizations.

Such documents have no binding effect on local school districts. They serve simply as guidelines which may be adopted in whole or in part. To the extent that such procedures have in fact been adopted, they have established an educational custom and practice which, while extralegal, should have an increasingly discernible impact on the development of statutory and decisional law.   .   .   .

In addition to these attempts at voluntarism on a state-wide basis, many local school boards and teacher organizations have entered into "professional communication" agreements or "working relations" agreements which establish, in varying degrees of detail and sophistication, some form of collective negotiations. These procedural agreements provide for school board recognition of an organizational representative, set up a framework for negotiations (including ground rules governing meetings), frequently contain a procedure for resolv-

ing individual teacher grievances, and sometimes include machinery
for resolving impasses over what the terms and conditions of employment should be. . . .

While these agreements are not substantive since they do not
prescribe policies in respect to salaries, fringe benefits, and other
terms and conditions of employment in the way that a comprehensive
collective agreement does, their significance should not be underesti-
mated. In the school year 1967–68, there were 2,212 school systems,
covering about 900,000 teachers, with some sort of negotiations agreement. Somewhere between 350,000 and 400,000 of these teachers
are probably covered by comprehensive substantive agreements. The
balance of 500,000 to 550,000 probably work under procedural agreements similar to the exhibits.

While there is a paucity of exact information, the probability is
that meeting and conferring, interacting, negotiating or whatever the
process is called under these procedural arrangements results in some
kind of agreement on substantive terms and conditions of employment.
Even though these agreements may never be memorialized in a bilat-
erally executed and enforceable "collective agreement," the process
may in fact have significant impact on school district policy-making
and administration.

Efforts to obtain a structure of collective negotiations by agreement are usually resisted on conceptual (policy) and legal grounds.
Each of these lines of resistance is examined in turn below.

1. *Conceptual Obstacles*

The unarticulated reason for resistance by many school boards to
voluntary acceptance of a structure of collective negotiations is obvious. Collective negotiations means bilateral decision-making in
respect to policy matters traditionally within the sole control of school
boards. It means that teachers will gain power at the expense of
those persons who now have power. History teaches that authority
is seldom relinquished without a struggle. Superintendents, to the
extent that they are *de facto* delegatees of board authority, can be
expected to be equally unenthusiastic about collective negotiations.
The resistance is seldom articulated in these terms. It is couched,
instead, in the liturgy of sovereignty, professionalism, democracy, and
selflessness . . .

2. *Legal Obstacles*

Where state law neither requires nor expressly permits collective
negotiations, efforts to establish a structured bargaining relationship
extralegally will predictably be met by objections predicated on the
ground that such a relationship is illegal. There are five standard
arguments.

First, a board of education is a body politic and corporate created
by the law of the state to aid in the administration of state govern-

ment. As such, it is charged with duties that are governmental in character. Such a public body has only such powers as are conferred upon it by law. It cannot, therefore, enter into collective negotiations in the absence of enabling legislation.

Second, the rights and obligations of a school board (e. g., to prescribe the duties, compensation and terms of employment of its employees") are derived by delegation from the legislature for exclusive exercise by the board and, therefore, cannot be delegated to or shared with a teacher organization through a process of give-and-take negotiations.

Third, collective negotiations is the same thing as collective bargaining. Collective bargaining requires that employees have the right to strike. Public school teachers do not have the right to strike. Ergo, they do not have the right to bargain or negotiate collectively.

Fourth, the working conditions of teachers are, to a large extent, fixed by statute (e. g., tenure, hiring and termination procedures, pension and retirement provisions, disability benefits, sick leave, job requirements, minimum salaries, medical insurance). Such matters cannot be the subject of local negotiations because their variance or modification is illegal.

Finally, a board of education, as a public employer performing governmental functions, cannot lawfully make a preferential or exclusive agreement with a particular organization in respect to any aspect of school district business. Therefore, it cannot recognize the organization chosen by the majority of the employees as the sole negotiating representative of all of the employees.

Court decisions pertinent to these issues are a mixed bag. . . .

3. *Pursuant to Express Statutory Authorization*

While some of the most effective systems of collective negotiations began as voluntary, extralegal arrangements (e. g., New York City, Rochester, N. Y., Newark, N. J., Detroit, Mich.) and others remain viable and functional in such states as Colorado, Illinois, Indiana, Kentucky, New Hampshire, Ohio, and Pennsylvania, despite the absence of legislation, a statutory structure is preferable for many reasons.

First, legislation provides an orderly method for resolving disputes over representation peaceably. Suppose, for instance, the teachers in a particular school district are demanding the establishment of a system of collective negotiations and recognition of either organization X or organization Y as the negotiating agent. The school board predictably will be reluctant to grant such demands because of self-concern over loss of power, because of doubts about legality, and because of considerations of "saving face" vis-a-vis its constituency. Such a dispute may rather quickly escalate into a confrontation involving public name-calling, demonstrations, and strike action on the one hand and disciplinary action and reprisals on the other. . . .

A statute takes the questions of "shall we do it and, if so, with whom" out of the arena of debate and provides a forum and a procedure for their resolution. Organized teachers need not resort to threats of strike action, and school boards no longer need fear cries of "sellout" from the taxpayers.

Second, legislation provides a basis for the orderly, equitable, and sensible resolution of the basic and subsidiary issues raised in a dispute over representation. These are especially delicate in situations where there are two or more organizations competing for status as the negotiating representative and the school board (absent legislation) finds itself in the middle. What should be the dimensions of the negotiating unit? Should supervisors be in or out? How about social workers and nurses? Are the decisions of the National Labor Relations Board appropriate analogies? Should there be an election to determine the wishes of the teachers, or is other evidence adequate? If there is an election, how many polling places should there be? Where should they be located? What should be the ground rules for the campaign, i. e., the use of school property and mail services? These are questions which cry for disposition by a neutral mechanism, i. e., a state agency or its designee, guided by agreed-upon (statutory) criteria.

Third, if the election is truly to reflect teacher free choice, and if the system of collective negotiations (assuming one emerges) is to function properly, it is desirable, if not essential, that the rights of teachers to organize, to participate in collective negotiations through a representative of their own choosing, and to engage in activities related to the negotiation process be protected against abridgment by denials of tenure, discriminatory transfers, adverse performance ratings, and all of the other repressive devices which are available to any employer who is free of countervailing force in the exercise of power over its employees.

Finally, there is the difficult problem of resolving disputes at the negotiating table equitably. For example, the Chicago Federation of Teachers initially achieved status as the negotiating representative on the condition that it agree, in the event of an impasse, that the decision of the school board would be final and binding without provision for any type of third-party intervention. Such a provision is repugnant to the principle of bilateralism which underlies collective negotiations.

While school boards have been willing to accept third-party intervention in some instances where legislation did not exist, it is not likely unless organized teachers resort to some species of self-help (e. g., a strike in Newark, N. J.; the submission of resignations *en masse* in Rochester, N. Y.).

The point is that boards of education are reluctant (indeed, may find it politically awkward, if not impossible) voluntarily to agree to some species of third-party intervention as the means for resolving negotiating impasses. They will either formally try to retain unilateral power to render the negotiating process a nullity or agree to such intervention only when all parties are *in extremis*.

It seems preferable to have some statutory machinery available if needed. This minimizes political embarrassment and, on the assumption that planning for crisis is better than reacting to crisis, may produce better results.

The impetus for the accelerated legislative activity in public-employee negotiations may be traced to Executive Order No. 10988, issued by President Kennedy on January 17, 1962, which established a new framework for employee-management relations in the federal service. Although it did not directly affect any teachers other than the 6,000 to 7,000 employed by the U. S. Department of Defense on military bases and the Department of the Interior on Indian Reservations, it signified a change in attitude toward negotiations in the public sector. The middle 1960s saw a spate of negotiations statutes enacted throughout the country and, at the time of this writing, a significant number of states have had proposals for such laws introduced into their legislatures. The basic structures of the statutes that have been enacted or proposed differ markedly, reflecting organizational philosophies, interorganizational rivalries, employer pressures and political realities.

In attempting to develop a system of negotiations in public education, it must be recognized that there are basic economic and political differences between public and private employment. Among these differences are the following:

A. Employers in the private sector act largely on the basis of a profit motive, whereas public employers function as the custodians of public funds. Accordingly, the motivation of the latter is essentially political rather than economic.

B. Fundamental to the collective bargaining process in the private sector is the virtually unlimited right of employees to strike and of management to lock out. This is not the situation in public employment.

C. In private collective bargaining, management has the power to make commitments and to carry them out. Many public agencies, on the other hand, do not have final authority to determine the size of their budget. To be most effective, therefore, negotiations must precede the adoption of the budget and the ability of the public agency to fulfill commitments made as to salaries and other economic items often will be dependent upon the subsequent appropriation of sufficient funds.

D.   Many conditions of public employment are dealt with by legislation. Thus, the protection provided for certain public employees in regard to retirement, tenure, sick leave and other matters is often influenced by political as well as economic factors.

The foregoing is not meant to imply that experience gained in the private sector is of no value here. The point is, rather, that analogies have limited application and the forms and procedures developed for private employment do not necessarily provide a monolithic model for public employment . . . Any attempt simply to bring public employees under the coverage of legislation designed to regulate bargaining in the private sector would prevent the flexibility necessary to develop such new procedures. It is generally accepted, therefore, that public employees should be covered by a separate statute which takes cognizance of and is structured to deal with the many unique aspects of public employment.

While there is relatively little dispute regarding this point, considerably more controversy surrounds the question of whether teachers should be included under a statute covering many categories of public employees or whether they should receive separate statutory treatment. Persons who take the latter view rest their case upon the proposition that teachers, by reason of their training and traditions, have an interest not necessarily shared by other public employees in the quality of the service provided by the enterprise of which they are a part. It is contended that this distinction, which allegedly has significance for a variety of legislative purposes, is obscured when teachers and other public employees are treated as equivalents legislatively. Although several states have enacted separate teacher negotiations laws, others apparently have concluded that the similarities among the various categories outweigh the dissimilarities and that a single statute creating the right to negotiate for many types of public employees, including teachers, is operationally more efficient.

It should be noted that there are intervening alternatives which accommodate to some extent the concerns of both groups. Thus, specific features relating to a particular category of public employees may be included within an all-inclusive statute. The recently enacted New Jersey statute, which covers many categories of public employees, illustrates the point. While granting public employees the virtually unlimited right to join any employee organization, the statute apparently recognizes policemen as occupying a somewhat unique position and prohibits them from joining "an employee organization that admits employees other than policemen to membership."

The various "teachers only" laws and the more inclusive statutes frequently share one common feature in regard to coverage—both exclude the principal executive officers of the employing agency. Thus, the all-inclusive New Jersey statute grants certain rights to public employees with the exception of "managerial executives" (Section 7) and the Maryland "teachers only" law applies to "any certificated professional person employed by a public school employer . . . *except the Superintendent of Schools*" (Section 1(a)(3)) (emphasis added).

One final point is perhaps worth mentioning in this connection— the distinction between statutory coverage and negotiating-unit structure. Coverage refers to the categories of employees over which the statute takes jurisdiction and is generally reflected in the definition of the word "employee." Negotiating unit has reference to the appropriate grouping of job categories among covered employees for purposes of dealing with the representatives of management.

A second basic question of approach concerns the method by which the statute is to be administered and enforced. Again, the existing laws show considerable diversity. California, Maryland, Minnesota and certain other states have enacted statutes setting forth mutual rights and obligations but have left their administration and enforcement to the traditional judicial processes. The reasons for taking this approach are presumably of a pragmatic nature—it is less expensive and does not require a special budgetary appropriation, and it avoids political opposition on the ground that the statute would contribute to an already overly-complex bureaucracy.

Many persons feel, however, that legislation of this type does not readily lend itself to self-implementation. Although it is conceded that in some instances teacher organizations and school boards have managed to agree upon the dimensions of the appropriate negotiating unit, to establish procedures for the management of an election and to define the scope of negotiations without undue conflict, they maintain that if these and other difficult questions are to be resolved in a fair and rational way, there should be some specific public agency responsible for their disposition. Moreover, experience has demonstrated that the mere passage of legislation does not necessarily mean the acceptance of the concept of negotiations, and attempts by teachers to implement such statutes have sometimes been met with resistance and repressive tactics. While court enforcement is an available avenue of redress, it is an expensive and time-consuming process with the result that teachers have, on occasion, been left dissatisfied or disillusioned or have been forced to resort to various forms of self-help in order to obtain their statutory rights.

Assuming that some specific agency is to be assigned the responsibility to administer and enforce the statute, the question that then arises is whether a special board or commission should be established or whether this responsibility should be vested in some existing agency. New York and Illinois are two of the relatively few states which have thus far established task forces to study in depth the problems involved in negotiations by public employees. It is noteworthy that both groups, after intensive study, concluded that the administration and enforcement of a negotiations statute should be vested in a specially created agency. Although the Illinois Legislature thus far has failed to enact any type of negotiations statute, the 1967 New York statute adopted this recommendation of Governor Rockefeller's Committee and established a separate Public Employment Relations Board.

Other states, such as Michigan, enacted legislation establishing collective negotiations for many types and categories of public employees and provided for administration by the same agency that handles collective bargaining in the private sector. It is noteworthy, however, that on July 29, 1966, Governor Romney of Michigan, alarmed by the number of public-employee strikes (primarily in education) that had occurred during the first year's operation of the statute, appointed an Advisory Committee on Public Employee Relations to study the problems and recommend changes needed in order to make the statute function more effectively. This committee, in its report dated February 15, 1967, urged, among other things, that fact-finding be taken away from the Michigan State Labor Mediation Board and given to a separate public employment relations panel. The committee reasoned that the designation of a separate panel would enhance the prestige and increase the effectiveness of the fact-finders, would assure the ready availability of competent persons to serve the fact-finding function, and would build up a body of experience which would be useful in view of the unique aspects of public-employee relations.

If the administration and enforcement are to be entrusted to some existing agency, the determination of which one would depend to a large extent upon the position taken in regard to coverage. Thus, if the statute applied only to teachers, the administration and enforcement might properly be vested in the State Department of Education or the Commissioner of Education. If, on the other hand, the statute covered a broader spectrum of employees, these functions could be assigned to the same agency that handles collective bargaining in the private sector (e. g., the Department of Labor; the State Mediation Board).

Regardless of the position taken with respect to the foregoing matter, there is merit to the point that the enforcement of the statute, including its unfair labor practice provisions, should be divorced from the negotiations-impasse-settlement function on the theory that vigorous discharge of the former responsibility will prejudice the ability of the agency to participate in the ameliorating processes of mediation and fact-finding. . . .

One further comment on legislation is in order here. Thus far, all legislative action regarding the negotiating rights of public school teachers has been on the state level. There has been some question as to the constitutional authority of the Federal Government to regulate the employment relationship between state and local governmental employees and their governmental employer. The negative answer has been predicated on the ground that school operations are not "commerce" which may be regulated by Congress. More specifically, it has been argued that there are three characteristics which remove the operation of schools from the reach of Congressional power: (1) education is a nonprofit operation; (2) it is a governmental function; and (3) it operates free of competition. Regulation would, therefore, be violative of the federal system. Recent developments, however, cast doubt on the validity of this position.

In 1966, the Fair Labor Standards Act [29 U.S.C. §§ 201 et seq.] was amended to apply the minimum wage and overtime provisions to certain employees of local public schools, hospitals and related institutions. An attack was made by several states upon the constitutionality of these amendments on the grounds set forth above. The district court holding that Congress had the power to pass the amendments was sustained by the Supreme Court [Maryland v. Wirtz, 269 F.Supp. 826 (D.Md.1967), aff'd, 392 U.S. 183 (1968)]. Although the district court was careful to point out that "Congress has not sought to cover doctors, nurses, principals, teachers, research assistants or the like," the basic premise underlying the holding would certainly seem to justify the application of federal power to those categories. Accordingly, federal regulation of teacher-school board relations must now be viewed as a realistic possibility.

ASSOCIATED TEACHERS OF HUNTINGTON v. BOARD OF EDUCATION

New York Supreme Court, 1969.
60 Misc.2d 443, 303 N.Y.S.2d 469.

WILLIAM R. GEILER, Justice. Application by respondent, Board of Education to stay arbitration proceedings commenced by claimant Associated Teachers of Huntington.

The respondent and claimant entered into a contract on June 10, 1968 with reference to the employment of teachers in the Union Free School District No. 3 within the Town of Huntington, Suffolk County.

The contract includes a procedure for the submission of grievances to arbitration and defines a grievance in Article II A(1) in the following terms:

"A grievance is a claim which involves the interpretation and application of the terms and provisions of this contract."

The contract also includes a provision for giving notice of termination of employment to non-tenure teachers. This provision is contained in Article XVIII, Section A, paragraph 3 of the agreement and provides:

> "Non-tenure teachers will be notified of termination of employment not later than March 1st, except that for the third year, the teacher will be notified not later than January 1."

The respondent, of May 1, 1969, sent a notice of termination of employment to a Samuel Grenz, a non-tenure teacher in his initial year of employment and a member of the claimant Teacher's Association. This notice was admittedly sent two months after the contractual requirement that all such notices be sent no later than March 1, 1969.

The claimant filed a demand for arbitration in accordance with Article II of the subject contract on the ground that there has been a violation of Article XVIII, Section A, paragraph 3 of the contract dealing with notice of termination of employment.

The respondent contends that this particular provision, governing the timing of termination notices to non-tenure teachers, is outside the scope of the grievance procedure and thus not subject to arbitration. The respondent Board, in support of this contention, cites Article XVIII, Section C of the contract, which provides:

> "No tenure teacher shall be disciplined, reprimanded, reduced in rank or compensation, suspended, demoted, transferred, terminated or otherwise deprived of any professional advantage without just cause. In no case shall this be done publicly unless so requested by the teacher. Any such action, including adverse evaluation of teacher performance or a violation of professional ethics asserted by the Board or any agent thereof, shall be subject to the grievance procedure set forth in this Agreement, provided that in the case of a non-tenure teacher, termination shall not be grievable."

The respondent Board also implies that Article XVIII, Section A paragraph 3 is contrary to certain statutory provisions of the State of New York and therefore is void.

Does the subject contract preclude arbitration with reference to the procedure used in terminating the employment of a non-tenure teacher?

The respondent, in arguing that the language of the contract precludes arbitration, relies primarily on Section C of Article XVIII, which deals not with the procedure to be followed in terminating employment of non-tenure teacher but with the right of the School Board to terminate a tenure teacher's employment for just cause. This particular provision, as indicated above, also provides that the Board may terminate the employment of a non-tenure teacher without having to demonstrate just cause in an arbitration proceeding.

There is no question that a non-tenure teacher, under Paragraph C of Article XVIII, is prohibited from challenging in arbitration the grounds for termination of employment and the claimant readily admits this fact. However, this prohibition, in and of itself, does not mean that a non-tenure teacher is barred from challenging the "procedure" used in terminating employment. Otherwise, Section A of Article XVIII would be meaningless and there is no language in the contract which declares or implies that this section dealing with notice of termination of employment of a non-tenure teacher was meant to be moot and unenforceable. The Court has been unable to find any language in the broad arbitration provisions set forth in Article II of the subject contract which would imply that the procedure used in the termination of a non-tenure teacher was prohibited from being the subject of an arbitration proceeding.

It has been the established law in this State that questions concerning arbitrability are to be resolved in arbitration and not in a court, unless there is a clear and unquestionable exclusion from arbitration. This basic rule of law was clearly enunciated . . . in the following language:

> "It is now a familiar rule that, where a labor agreement contains an arbitration provision, the presumption is that questions of arbitrability are for the arbitrator * * *. In the last analysis, arbitrations are the result of agreements between the parties and they draw their essence from those agreements. It is only where the parties have employed language which clearly rebuts the presumption of arbitrability * * * that the matter may be determined by the courts. In the absence of such unmistakably clear language * * * the matter is sent to the arbitrator for his determination on the merits."

The Court finds that there is no prohibition against submitting the question of the procedure used in terminating employment of a non-tenure teacher and the best that can be said for respondent's position herein is that there is doubt as to whether the provisions in question may or may not be arbitrable. In such circumstances, the question of arbitrability must be submitted to an arbitrator for resolution. . . .

Are school boards prohibited by law from agreeing to provide a notice of termination to non-tenure teachers? Is such an agreement unenforceable?

The respondent Board has advanced the argument that the notice of termination provision for non-tenure teachers is, even though freely agreed to by them, void on the following basis:

1) Section 3012 of the Education Law does not require notice by March 1, and therefore any such requirement in the subject contract is illegal.

2) The arbitration provisions under the subject contract, if they cover the subject grievance, is broader than Section 684 of the General Municipal Law and is therefore void.

Section 3012 of the Education Law provides in part:

"1. Teachers * * * shall be appointed by the board of education * * * for a probationary period of three years. The service of a person appointed to any of such positions may be discontinued at any time during such probationary period * * *.

"2. * * * Each person who is not to be recommended for appointment on tenure, shall be notified by the superintendent of schools in writing not later than sixty days immediately preceding the expiration of his probationary period."

There can be no dispute that this section allows termination of employment of a non-tenure teacher at any time during his probationary period without a hearing. It is also undisputable that this section does not forbid providing a non-tenure teacher with prior notice of termination. In fact, Paragraph 2 of Section 3012 supra, mandates sixty days notice of termination where the non-tenure teacher's employment is to be terminated after the full three year period. The statute, by requiring notice of termination "not later than sixty days" before termination, impliedly permits notice before that day. Certainly this statutory provision does not bar earlier notice.

The respondent seems to imply that any provision which is broader than the statutory benefits is invalid. In other words, the statutory minimum according to respondent's reasoning is also the maximum. Is a contract of employment invalid because it provides for a wage in excess of the minimum wage set by the State of New York? The position of the respondent is without legal foundation or rational basis.

There is also no legal basis for respondent's contention that Section 684 of the General Municipal Law prohibits the negotiation of a better or broader grievance procedure. In fact, Section 684 was never intended to provide the exclusive machinery for the resolution of grievances concerning public employees as can be seen from the following language contained in Section 684 of the General Municipal Law:

"Each government which, on or before October first, nineteen hundred sixty-three, has not established and does not thereafter maintain a two stage grievance procedure for all its employees shall, acting through the chief executive officer of each government establish and administer a basic grievance procedure for the employees of such government in accordance with the provisions of this section and section six hundred three of this article."

Thus, under this section, a board of education is free to adopt its own grievance procedure.

Certainly, after 1967, not only is the subject type of arbitration permissible, but it was mandated by the public policy of this State. In 1967 . . . the public policy of this State was set forth as follows in Section 200 of the Civil Service Law as amd.:

> "The legislature of the state of New York declares that it is the public policy of the state and the purpose of this act to promote harmonious and cooperative relationships between government and its employees * * * These policies are best effectuated by * * * (b) requiring the state, local governments and other political subdivisions to negotiate with, and enter into written agreements with employee organizations representing public employees * * * "

This Court would be remiss if it stayed the arbitration proceeding herein which is not prohibited by statute and which is in accordance with the public policy of this State. . . .

PINELLAS COUNTY CLASSROOM TEACHERS ASSOCIATION v. BOARD OF PUBLIC INSTRUCTION

Supreme Court of Florida, 1968.
214 So.2d 34.

THORNAL, Justice. . . . On January 11, 1967, the appellant, Pinellas County Classroom Teachers' Association, Inc., entered into a Professional Affairs Agreement with the appellee, Board of Public Instruction of Pinellas County. In this opinion we shall refer to the Agreement by that designation. The appellant association shall be called C.T.A., and the Board shall be so called. By the Agreement the Board shall be so called. By the Agreement the Board recognized C.T.A. as the organization with which it would negotiate concerning salaries and working conditions of teachers. Both parties accepted "their individual obligations to assure the uninterrupted operation of the School System." By its terms it remained effective until January 15, 1968. Numerous Conferences were held pursuant to the agreement. In April, 1967, new contracts were sent to all teachers employed on an annual contract basis and to those moving into a continuing contract or tenure status. Testimony was that not a single contract was returned to the Board with any statement of reservations. As a result, before the beginning of the 1967–68 school term, the Board had received executed contracts from every teacher who was returning to the system either under tenure or on an annual contract basis. In the former category there were 2,699, and in the latter, 1,073. Copies of the two types of contracts were attached to the complaint and a list of the names of all teachers who signed them was placed in evidence. Additionally, there were 252 teachers under so-called binder agreements. These were new teachers whose certification from the State had not yet been received. In this status they were not members of C.T.A. when suit was filed. However, each of these had previously *received* and *accepted* a formal "notification of appointment" which the chancellor correctly held constituted an enforceable agreement.

Each *annual contract* recited a base salary and then expressly provided that the Board agrees to employ the teacher "at a salary not less than that shown above, and in accordance with the officially adopted salary schedule." Each *continuing contract* provided that the teacher was employed on a continuing basis "at an annual salary schedule heretofore or hereafter adopted by the County Board." The so-called *binder agreement* stated that *"The signatures on this offer will indicate that this agreement is binding on the part* of the County Board and you." The binder provided also that "The salary scale for the coming school year recognizing certification, rank, and acceptable experience, will be observed." This was accepted by the 252 new teachers.

Normally, under state regulations the budget of the Board should have been submitted to the State Superintendent of Public Instruction by August 3, 1967. However, due to legislative delays occasioned by teacher salary problems at the time, the Board could not adopt its 1967–68 salary schedule until August 10, 1967. The Chancellor held that the delay was excusable and we agree.

At the August 10, 1967, Board Meeting the vice-president of C.T.A. read a prepared statement to the effect that the salary schedule was unacceptable despite increases in all categories. On August 15, 1967, the president of C.T.A. delivered to the County Superintendent a written communication to the effect that the teachers could not begin the performance of services until "such things as salaries and general working conditions could be agreed and incorporated in their respective contracts."

With schools scheduled for opening on August 16, 1967, and the announced intention of the teachers to stay away from the classrooms, the Board sought and obtained a temporary injunction to prohibit the strike. The temporary injunction was granted on August 15, 1967, and was made permanent on August 31, 1967, after two days of extensive hearings.

By the injunctive decree the Chancellor announced: "That the Pinellas County Classroom Teachers Association, Inc., and each of its members who hold an appointment with the Board of Public Instruction of Pinellas County, Florida, be and they are hereby permanently enjoined from striking, failing to report to work, stopping work, or failing to perform all or part of their duties of employment for the purpose of inducing, influencing or coercing a change in compensation or conditions of employment."

The Chancellor supplemented the formal decree with an explanatory opinion which was expressly incorporated into the decree. It is this decree which we now review on appeal.

Although appellants claim that the teachers were only negotiating and had never finalized contracts, this record is abundantly clear that all three classes of teachers had binding contracts with the Board. While the stipulated salaries were stated to be the minimums or those stated in the schedule to be adopted by the Board, the fact remains that all elements of a contract were present and agreed upon in writing. The Chancellor correctly held that all parties bound by his decree had valid and enforceable contracts. . . .

Appellants have come directly here, claiming that the trial judge passed directly on the validity of Fla.Stat. § 839.221 (1967), F.S.A. This statute, in effect, prohibits governmental officers and employees from participating in strikes against the government. It states that "no person shall accept or hold any * * * employment in the service of the state, of any county or of any municipality * * * " who participates in any strike against the governmental employer. The statute guarantees the right to bargain as a member of a uniform or labor organization but precludes the right to strike against government.

The Chancellor did not really pass on the validity of the statute. He recognized the statute and then announced that even if it were inapplicable, "a person holding a government position has no right to strike without clear and direct legislative authority to do so." He based his ultimate judgment on the general powers of equity to prevent the breakdown of an essential aspect of government because of an unauthorized work stoppage by its employees. In following this course the Chancellor relied upon sound concepts and precedents. . . .

The Chancellor did, however, construe the so-called "involuntary servitude" provisions of the state and federal Constitutions. Fla.Dec. of Rights § 19, F.S.A., provides in part: "Neither slavery nor involuntary servitude * * * shall ever be allowed in this state." Substantially identical proscriptions are announced by U. S. Const. amend XIII.

Appellants insist that the injunction requires involuntary servitude as proscribed by the foregoing provisions. The Chancellor specifically held that it does not. He clearly stated that involuntary servitude is not involved simply because all he was doing was prohibiting a strike by a group of teachers who had been duly appointed and who had not terminated their employment. The Chancellor did not force the teachers to work. He merely offered them alternatives, which were: (1) to work and thereby comply with their contracts; (2) resign in accordance with the terms of their contracts; or, (3) resign in violation of their contracts and subject themselves to the provisions of Fla.Stat. § 231.36 (1965), F.S.A., which would make them ineligible for employment in the school system for a period of one year from the date of such violation.

We are not here confronted by an arbitrary mandate to compel performance of personal service against the will of the employee. These people were simply told that they had contracted with the government and that they could, if they wished, terminate the contract legally or illegally, and suffer the results thereof. They could not, however, strike against the government and retain the benefits of their contract positions. . . .

A "strike is ordinarily thought of as the physical act of employees leaving their workbenches or office desks and departing from their place of employment, but not including in such departure a severance of the employer-employee relationship." . . . The teachers here were not quitting their jobs or severing the employer-employee relationship. They were free to do that before and after the injunction. What they were really attempting to do here was to exert pressure on the School Board by refusing to go to work, but at the same time laying claim to their positions and asserting the right to go back to work on terms more acceptable to them. This, indeed, was a typical strike. . . .

We affirm the holding of the Chancellor to the effect that in the absence of specific statutory authority an employee of government has no right to strike, as herein defined, in order to coerce a change in compensation or conditions of employment. To this end, we agree with the Chancellor when he stated:

> "To allow such action would permit the breakdown of governmental functions, would sanction the control of a governmental function for private gain; and further, to allow such action is the same as saying that governmental employees may deny the authority of government through its duly elected representatives. To permit this is to take the first step toward anarchy." . . .

NOTES AND QUESTIONS

1. What did the union want? Why? The school board? Why?

2. What was the issue(s) in this case and the reasons given by the court? Do you agree? Why or why not?

3. Suppose after this case, the teacher organization, through its parent organization, "sanctioned" the school district by black-listing it, would

such action be lawful? In the first appellate court opinion discussing blacklisting the Supreme Court of New Jersey said:

"And with respect to blacklisting of the school district and the scheme of 'sanctions' upon teachers who offer or take employment with a 'sanctioned' school board, it can escape no one that the purpose is to back up a refusal of others to continue to work. At a minimum the object is to withhold additional services a school district may need to discharge its public duty, which, as we have said, is no less illegal. Such an illegal agreement may come into being at time of the strike or may antedate it. If individuals enter into a union or association on terms that upon the occurrence of some stipulated event or signal they will impede government in its recruitment of services, that very arrangement constitutes an agreement the law denounces. An agreement not to seek, accept, or solicit employment in government whenever the upper echelon of the union makes a prescribed pronouncement is, no less, than an accomplished shutdown, a thrust at the vitality of government, and comes within the same policy which denounces a concerted strike or quit or slowdown or other obstruction of the performance of official duties." Board of Education v. New Jersey Ed. Assoc., 53 N.J.2d 29, 247 A.2d 867 (1969).

Do you agree? Should work stoppages, work slowdowns or blacklisting be treated, in law, like a strike? If so, what other powers do teacher's organizations possess to coerce recalcitrant school boards? Should they have any? Could the problem presented by strikes of public employees be correctly and constitutionally resolved by a state statute requiring that in the event the teacher organization and the school board reach an impasse and fail to agree on a matter, then that matter shall be submitted to compulsory, not voluntary, arbitration, and both parties shall be bound by the arbitrators' decision? Would it make any difference who the arbitrators were? Suppose there were a three member panel, and the teachers organization and the school board, in its discretion, selected one member each and the third member were selected by them jointly, or suppose all three members had to be selected jointly, which scheme is better; why? Is some other procedure better?

4.   Connecticut General Statutes, Title 10, provide:

"Sec. 10.153d. DUTY TO NEGOTIATE. The town or regional board of education and the organization designated or elected as the exclusive representative for the appropriate unit, through designated officials or their representatives, shall have the duty to negotiate with respect to salaries and other conditions of employment about which either party wishes to negotiate and such duty shall include the obligation of such board of education to meet at reasonable times, including meetings appropriately related to the budget-making process, and confer in good faith with respect to salaries and other conditions of employment, or the negotiation of an agreement, or any question arising thereunder and the execution of a written contract incorporating any agreement reached, if requested by either party, but such obligation shall not compel either party to agree to a proposal or require the making of a concession. The board of education of any town school district shall file forthwith a signed copy of any such contract with the town clerk. Any regional board of education shall file a signed copy of any such contract with the town clerk in each member town. The terms of such contract shall be binding on the legislative body of the town or regional school district, unless such body rejects such contract at a regular or special meeting called for such purpose within thirty days of the signing of the contract. Any regional board of education shall call a district meeting to consider such contract within such thirty-day period if the chief executive officer of any member town so requests in writing within fifteen days of the receipt of the signed copy of the contract by the town clerk in such town. The body charged with making annual appropriations in any school district shall appropriate to the board of education whatever funds are required to implement the terms of any contract not rejected pursuant to this section. If the legislative body rejects such contract within such period, the parties shall renegotiate the terms of the contract in accordance with the procedure in this section. The town or regional board of education, and its representatives, agents and superintendents shall not interfere, restrain or coerce employees in derogation of the rights guaranteed by sections 2 through 5 of this act and section 10–153c of the 1967 supplement to the general statutes, and, in the absence of any recognition or certification as the exclusive representative as provided by section 2 of this act, all organizations seeking to represent members of the teaching profession shall be accorded equal treatment with respect to access to teachers, principals, members of the board of education, records, mail boxes and school facilities and participation in discussions with respect to salaries and other conditions of employment.

"Sec. 10–153e. STRIKE PROHIBITED. No certified professional employee shall, in an effort to effect a settlement of any disagreement with his employing board of education, engage in any strike or concerted refusal to render services. This provision may be enforced in the Superior Court for any county in which said board of education is located by an ex parte temporary injunction issued by said court or a judge thereof; provided, however, that if such injunction is issued, such employee may file a motion to dissolve said injunction and a hearing upon said motion shall be held by the superior court not later than three days after service of said motion upon said board of education pursuant to an order of court or a judge thereof.

"Sec. 10f–153f. MEDIATION AND ARBITRATION OF DISAGREEMENTS. (a) The governor shall appoint not less than ten or more than twenty-five persons to serve on an arbitration panel as provided in subsection (c) of this section from the effective date of this act through December 31, 1970. Except as provided above, the governor shall appoint before the first day of December in the year of his election ten persons to serve on such panel, and he may appoint additional persons to the panel at any time provided the total number of persons serving on the panel shall not exceed twenty-five. Each appointee shall serve until the last day of December following the first gubernatorial election after his appointment. Persons appointed to the arbitration panel shall serve without compensation but each shall receive the per diem fee in lieu of expenses provided for arbitrators in section 31–94 for each day during which he is engaged in the arbitration of a dispute pursuant to this act. The parties to the dispute so arbitrated shall pay the fee in accordance with subsection (c) of this section. (b) If any town or regional board of education can not agree with the exclusive representatives of a teachers' or administrators' unit after negotiation concerning the terms and conditions of employment applicable to the employees in such unit, either party may submit the issues to the secretary for mediation. If the parties fail to initiate mediation and such failure is, in the opinion of the secretary, jeopardizing the education of the children in such school district, the secretary may order the parties to appeal before him for mediation of the dispute. In either case, the parties shall meet with him or his agents or a mediator designated by him from a panel of mediators selected by state board of education to assist him. For such purposes, the secretary may enter contracts for services with members of such panel, the terms of which shall be subject to approval by the state board of education. The parties shall provide such information as the secretary may require. The secretary may recommend a basis for settlement but such recommendations shall not be binding upon the parties. (c) If after mediation the parties have not reached agreement, the secretary may order the parties to appear before him on the fourth day next following the end of the mediation session. At such time the parties shall report their settlement of the dispute or each select and bring an arbitrator to such meeting. Such arbitrators may be members of the arbitration panel. Unless the parties have agreed to submit their dispute to one arbitrator, their designated arbitrators shall select a third arbitrator. If either party fails to bring an arbitrator, the secretary shall designate a member of the arbitration panel to serve and the two arbitrators shall select a third. If in either case the two arbitrators fail to agree on the selection of a third during such meeting, the secretary shall select the third from the arbitration panel. If both parties fail to bring an arbitrator and have not settled their dispute, the secretary shall designate one member of the arbitration panel to arbitrate the dispute. The arbitrators shall set the time and place for the hearing one week from the day on which the parties reported to the secretary except that if such day is Saturday, Sunday or a holiday, the hearing shall be held on the next Monday or the day following the holiday. After hearing all the issues, the arbitrators shall, within fifteen days, render a decision in writing, signed by a majority of the arbitrators, which states in detail the nature of the decision and the disposition of the issues by the arbitrators. The arbitrators shall file one copy of the decision with the secretary, each town clerk in the school district involved and the board of education and organization which are parties to the dispute. The decision of the arbitrators shall be advisory and shall not be binding upon the parties to the dispute. The parties shall each pay the fee of the arbitrator selected by or for them and share equally the fee of the third arbitrator and all other costs incidental to the hearing. . . ."

Is this a better solution to the problem than others? Why or why not? What happens if the report of the arbitrators is not accepted?

5. Suppose all the teachers in the Pinellas County case, supra, resigned after the decision in the case, and later the school board agreed to re-hire them, so long as each one "contributed" $100.00 to the school district's library fund, and suppose this condition of re-hiring were contested in court, what should be the court's decision; why?

NATIONAL EDUCATIONAL ASSOC. v. LEE COUNTY BD. OF PUBLIC INSTRUCTION

United States Court of Appeals, 5th Cir., 1972.
467 F.2d 447.

JOHN R. BROWN, Chief Judge. Having previously certified this case to the Supreme Court of Florida for an authoritative resolution of perplexingly difficult State law issues, we can now conclude with absolute assurance that despite a commendable effort the District Court incorrectly decided them. Since we are also convinced that the circumstances revealed by this record present no problem of Federal constitutional proportions, we reverse. . . .

Generally stated, the question is whether the Board of Public Instruction of Lee County, Florida may require individual payments of $100 as a condition for the reemployment with tenure of 425 public school teachers who had voluntarily submitted simultaneous mass resignations as a result of their disagreement with the State's educational policies. Deciding that the unilateral imposition of such a requirement violated both Florida law and the due process clause of the Fourteenth Amendment, the District Court granted the teachers' motion for summary judgment, directed the repayment of $100 to those teachers who had complied with the Board's demand, and ordered the reinstatement with back pay of those teachers who had not been re-hired because of their refusal to comply. . . .

We agree with the District Court that those teachers who accepted reemployment neither waived nor were thereafter estopped from asserting their right to contest the legality of the disputed payments. . . . But we do not agree that the Board's imposition of the $100 condition violated the teachers' Federal constitutional rights.

Essentially the teachers' theory is that the forced exaction of a $100 payment from each of them in exchange for their returning to work with their pre-resignation status intact amounted to a fine or penalty for a legislatively undefined wrong, violative of their right to procedural due process because they were afforded no hearing or other opportunity to protest the payments or to contest their legality.

Phrased another way, the argument is that the teachers were "punished" for their prior concerted efforts to effect changes in State school policies and that such "punishment," in the absence of traditional procedural safeguards, could not be made a condition for reemployment because it compelled the surrender of Fourteenth Amendment rights in return for a job in the Lee County school system.

Concededly it is now established to a point beyond all dispute that "public employment, including academic employment, may [not] be conditioned upon the surrender of constitutional rights which could not be abridged by direct governmental action." Keyishian v. Board of Regents . . .   Denial of a government job solely because an individual refuses to abjure the protection afforded by the United States Constitution amounts to nothing more than an attempt to accomplish indirectly an otherwise impermissible objective—penalization of conduct which is constitutionally insulated against punishment. . . .   Consequently, this Court has encountered no difficulty in holding that a Federal claim based upon the allegation that a State has denied public employment solely because of the exercise of a constitutional right will, if proven, entitle the plaintiff to appropriate relief. . . .

However, none of these cases have any application here unless the teachers were in fact compelled to forego the exercise of a Federal constitutional right in return for reemployment. The critical flaw in their argument is the uncritical (and, on this record, insupportable) assumption that the $100 payments constituted a *deprivation* of property without due process of law within the prohibition of the Fourteenth Amendment. The agreement clearly provided that the teachers would receive a benefit to which concededly they were not otherwise entitled—reemployment with full tenure rights and other accompanying privileges which they had enjoyed before their resignations— in return for a payment of $100. In substance, they were offered an opportunity to surrender one "property right" in order to acquire another "property right" that was plainly of greater value to them. Such a mutually advantageous exchange cannot be characterized as a *deprivation* of property, regardless of whether the teachers' payments are pejoratively denominated as "fines" and regardless of whether the subjective intention of the Board members who voted for it was to "punish" alleged past misconduct.

We do not dispute the District Court's conclusion that the payments were not "voluntary" in any meaningful sense. For that matter *all* exchanges of contractual consideration are "involuntary" to the extent that the contracting parties would much prefer to secure the benefits of the agreement without bearing the inevitable burdens. Likewise we may concede that the teachers here were involuntarily subjected to choosing between paying consideration for an employment benefit of at least equivalent value and foregoing employment altogether. The choice between these options was admittedly coerced. But regardless of whether it was accepted or rejected the Board's offer did not entail a deprivation of property. Accordingly, the payment of the $100 could not have involved the surrender of the right to protection of that property guaranteed by the due process clause of the Fourteenth Amendment.

Obviously the teachers would be in an entirely different position if they were somehow able to establish that they were legally entitled to tenure without payment of $100 and were therefore unilaterally deprived of that money without due process. Instead they are forced to concede that they had effectively resigned their positions and that the Board was not even legally obligated to rehire them at all. In such circumstances their claim fares no better than that of a teacher who, having neither *de facto* tenure nor an objective expectancy of reemployment, is discharged for unspecified reasons without notice or a hearing. . . . Absent the invasion of some protected Fourteenth Amendment right, neither notice nor hearing is required.

The same result obtains if approached outside of a concept of "exchange" of valuable rights. The key to decision, of course, is whether the teachers were forced to give up a constitutional right. Under Florida law they had no right to reemployment, either with or without tenure. Indeed, they had no right to reemployment with tenure. The loss of this right was not due to an exercise of First Amendment rights. It was the result of the purposeful resignations— a right which the earlier state court injunction expressly recognized was theirs The school authorities did not accede to the demands of the teachers, but it did not prior to the resignations or thereafter deny them any federal constitutional right or impede in any way the unrestricted assertion of them. The teachers sought reemployment and a return to the status of former tenure privileges, a status lost by the resignations. The Florida Supreme Court's obligatory ruling accords to the requirement of a $100 payment the exercise of reasonable judgment on the part of the school authorities and in its exercise we find no element of a denial of a federal right.

The judgment of the District Court is reversed and the cause remanded for entry of judgment in favor of the Lee County Board of Public Instruction.

Reversed and remanded.

NOTES AND QUESTIONS

1. Was the $100.00 payment a fine, an inducement for the board to rescind the resignations retroactively, or an "exchange of valuable rights"? If a fine, does a school board constitutionally have the power to "prosecute" a case, decide guilt or innocence, and levy a "fine"?

2. Under this case could a school board require that every teacher pay it $1,000.00 as a condition of obtaining tenure? Why or why not? Could

a school board constitutionally require that all teachers annually pay it $100.00 before obtaining their contracts to teach? Is a school board in the business of selling tenure or teacher's contracts?

3. Does this case raise a question of "the equal protection of laws"?

In the Matter of NEWARK TEACHERS UNION, LOCAL 481 AMERICAN FEDERATION OF TEACHERS AFL–CIO

Superior Court of New Jersey, 1972.
118 N.J.Super. 215, 287 A.2d 183.

PER CURIAM. During the 1971 Newark teachers strike which commenced February 2, 1971 and lasted until April 8, 1971, defendants were charged with contempt in that they willfully violated a final judgment of the Superior Court entered on February 27, 1970 which permanently enjoined the Newark Teachers Union, Local 481, its members, officers and directors, including certain named individuals, from participating in any strike, work stoppage, picketing, etc., against the Board of Education of Newark.

Hearings were held on the charges of contempt. At the conclusion thereof the trial court found in essence that each defendant had actual knowledge of the terms and conditions of the final judgment of February 27, 1970 but had nevertheless intentionally and deliberately participated in the 1971 strike activities and was guilty of the contempt charged. A fine, which ultimately amounted to $270,000, was imposed on the union. Twelve of the 15 individuals received six-month jail sentences and fines of $500. Defendant Fiorito, who was convicted of two separate contempts during the 1971 strike, was sentenced to two consecutive six-month jail terms and fined a total of $1,000. Defendants Bizzaro and Del Grosso received three-month terms and fines of $250.

We have carefully reviewed the entire record of proceedings *de novo,* and reach the following independent findings and conclusions as to guilt and punishment.

It is clear that each defendant had actual knowledge of the terms and provisions of the February 27, 1970 final judgment. That judgment in clear language manifested the intention of the court to prohibit participation in future strikes as well as the one then recently in progress. That that interpretation was not inadvertent is evidenced by the colloquy between the court and counsel for defendants at the time it was entered. The entry on February 3, 1971 of the cease and desist order and its subsequent service on the union and various individual defendants further emphasized and brought home to them the fact that the injunction was intended to apply to the 1971 strike. Nevertheless, they continued to defy its mandate. Thus, each of the defendants willfully and knowingly violated its terms by actually supporting and participating in the 1971 strike and is guilty of contempt. The record also establishes Fiorito's guilt of two separate contempts.

Defendants contend that regardless of their knowledge concerning its scope, the injunction was unconstitutional because (1) it was overbroad in that it barred future strikes, and (2) they were not given a hearing on the enforceability of the injunction where they might present new evidence. Both arguments are without merit.

We recognize that in the sensitive area of labor disputes the scope of the injunction should be carefully tailored to the factual situation from which the litigation sprang. Otherwise such injunctive orders may become overbroad or stale in their application to a later strike. Consequently, the better practice is for the employer to seek fresh relief. Thus, in the present case, when the 1971 strike materialized, it would have been better practice to file a new complaint with supporting affidavits setting forth the new factual situation and on this basis to seek a new injunction. However, we conclude that the 1970 final judgment, entered less than a year before the 1971 strike against the same union and its members, officers and directors, was efficacious in the particular circumstances here presented.

Defendants contend that they were entitled to a hearing on the enforceability of the injunction where they could present evidence that, in the negotiations for a new contract, the board of education was not bargaining in good faith and was using a strategy of forcing the teachers to strike so that they would lose public support.

If this was the board's plan it was reprehensible. However, assuming there was some basis for the teachers' contention, that was no excuse to violate the final judgment of February 27, 1970. The matter was not between private parties where issues of clean hands and good faith would be material. It concerned a public school system, and the continued public interest in having the schools remain open and the children educated.

As we have already noted, defendants had actual knowledge that the 1970 injunction was deemed applicable to the 1971 strike. If defendants intended to challenge its applicability to the 1971 context and, more specifically, to assert that a new situation had arisen with respect to the bargaining negotiations under the new contract, their remedy was to apply to the court to make that challenge before violating the outstanding injunction and to seek the court's assistance in requiring the board to negotiate in good faith. They were not free to defy the court order and take the law in their own hands. Walker v. City of Birmingham, 388 U.S. 307, 87 S.Ct. 1824, 18 L.Ed.2d 1210 (1967). . . .

We turn to the fines and jail sentences imposed by the trial court. It is clear that those participating in the 1971 strike have had brought home directly and emphatically the disastrous consequences of their illegal strike activity. However, of the 15 individual defendants herein, ten of them were also convicted of contempt in the 1970 strike proceedings. The union, of course, was also convicted in both the

1970 and 1971 contempt proceedings. We concur in the sentence imposed on the union by the trial court and adopt it as our own. Accordingly, a fine of $270,000 is hereby imposed on appellant Newark Teachers Union. Defendants Nicholas, Graves, Lasus, Lerman, Tur, Kirschbaum, Zimmer, Watkins and Washington, who were also convicted of contempt in 1970, are each hereby sentenced to three months in the Essex County Penitentiary and fined $500. Defendants Dasher, Koplin and Volpe, who, as officers of the union, were specifically named in the February 27, 1970 final judgment, are each hereby sentenced to three months in the Essex County Penitentiary and fined $500. Appellant Fiorito, who has been found guilty of two separate contempts during the 1971 strike and was also convicted of contempt during the 1970 strike, is hereby sentenced to a term of three months in the Essex County Penitentiary and fined $500 on each contempt. The jail terms hereby imposed on him run consecutively. His sentence will aggregate six months in jail and a total fine of $1,000. Defendants Bizzaro and Del Grosso are each hereby sentenced to one month in the Essex County Penitentiary and fined $250. Each individual defendant is placed on probation for one year. The only condition will be that the person refrain from participating in any illegal activity, including but not limited to striking or work stoppage in connection with his or her employment by the board of education.

It is unfortunate that resort must be had to contempt of court procedure in this type of situation. Jailing teachers is not the answer to school strikes. The solution is legislative. Public employees have the right to bargain collectively as to the terms and conditions of their employment but cannot do so on equal terms with their employment unit since they have no means of negotiating from a position of strength. If the present policy prohibiting strikes by public employees is to be continued, machinery for the compulsory settlement of deadlocked labor disputes involving public employees should be established. For a discussion of the problem and suggestions as to possible alternatives, see Comment, "Alternatives to the Strike in Public Labor Relations," 85 Harv.L.Rev. 459 (Dec.1971).

Judgment accordingly.

Chapter VIII

CONSTITUTIONAL FREEDOM AND GOVERNMENT CONTROLS OVER STUDENTS

FREEDOM OF DRESS AND APPEARANCE

BISHOP v. COLAW

United States Court of Appeals, 8th Cir., 1971.
450 F.2d 1069.

BRIGHT, Circuit Judge.   The school administration of St. Charles, Missouri, a suburb of St. Louis, Missouri, in March 1970, suspended fifteen year old Stephen Bishop from school attendance solely because his hairstyle violated provisions of the school dress code. Stephen and his parents brought this action seeking to obtain his readmission, and a declaratory judgment overturning the dress code regulations governing the hair length and style of male students.   Plaintiffs assert that these regulations violate Stephen's, and his parents', personal rights guaranteed by the United States Constitution.   .   .   .

The St. Charles high school administration incorporated the hair-length regulations into a dress code during the 1969–70 school year. The pertinent regulations in effect at the time of Stephen's expulsion provided as follows:

Section 4.   HAIR:

A.   All hair is to be worn clean, neatly trimmed around the ears and back of the neck, and no longer than the top of the collar on a regular dress or sport shirt when standing erect.   The eyebrows must be visible, and no part of the ear can be covered.   The hair can be in a block cut.

B.   The maximum length for sideburns shall be to the bottom of the ear lobe.

A few days after school opened in September 1969, the physical education teacher objected to Stephen's hairstyle because it was not tapered in the back and above the ears as was then required by the existing regulations.   Following several conferences involving Stephen, his parents, the principal, and the assistant principal, Stephen's hair was trimmed to conform to the regulations.   In November, the same teacher protested the length of Stephen's hair, and following additional conferences with the administration, Stephen again cut his hair.   In January 1970, after the hair-length regulations had been

583

modified to allow for a block cut, Stephen's mathematics teacher complained that Stephen's hair was too long in the back and over the ears. In response, Stephen trimmed his hair in back, and after additional conferences between the assistant principal and Stephen's father, Stephen's hair was made to comply with the regulations by also trimming it over the ears. Finally, in February 1970, Stephen and his parents refused to acquiesce in the further demands of the school administration that Stephen's hair be trimmed again. Stephen was suspended a few days later, and the instant litigation followed.

In recent years, the federal courts have found themselves increasingly embroiled in hair-length controversies resulting from the enforcement of regulations similar to that promulgated by the school administration of St. Charles High School. The Supreme Court has, on several occasions, refused to review the constitutional questions raised in this area. . . . What little guidance we have from the Court in this area is conflicting. Justice Black, writing as Circuit Justice in Karr v. Schmidt, 401 U.S. 1201 . . . took the position that state regulation of matters such as hair length raises no issue of constitutional dimensions calling for review by federal courts. On the other hand, Justice Douglas, dissenting from a denial of certiorari, argued that state regulation of hair length raises a serious equal protection question. Ferrell v. Dallas Independent School District, 393 U.S. 856 . . . In addition, several courts of appeals have considered the validity of hair regulations similar to those presented here against a broad range of constitutional attacks.

The Seventh Circuit has ruled in favor of the students, holding that a student's right to govern the style and length of his hair is a personal freedom protected under the Ninth Amendment and the Due Process Clause of the Fourteenth Amendment. Crews v. Cloncs, 432 F.2d 1259 (7th Cir. 1970); Breen v. Kahl, 419 F.2d 1034 (7th Cir. 1969), cert. denied 398 U.S. 937, 90 S.Ct. 1836, 26 L.Ed.2d 268 (1970). Under that circuit's decisions, the state carries a "substantial burden of justification" for regulations which infringe upon this freedom. . . .

The First Circuit has also concluded that students possess a constitutional right to wear their hair as they choose. Richards v. Thurston, 424 F.2d 1281 (1st Cir. 1970). The First Circuit's approach differed slightly, however, from that of the Seventh Circuit. In *Richards*, the court found that the right of students to determine their personal appearance is "implicit in the 'liberty' assurance of the Due Process Clause." . . . The court said:

> We do not say that the governance of the length and style of one's hair is necessarily so fundamental as those substantive rights already found implicit in the "liberty" assurance of the Due Process Clause, requiring a "compelling" showing by the state before it may be impaired. Yet "liber-

ty" seems to us an incomplete protection if it encompasses only the right to do momentous acts, leaving the state free to interfere with those personal aspects of our lives which have no direct bearing on the ability of others to enjoy their liberty. * * *

We think the Founding Fathers understood themselves to have limited the government's power to intrude into this sphere of personal liberty, by reserving some powers to the people. The debate concerning the First Amendment is illuminating. The specification of the right of assembly was deemed mere surplusage by some, on the grounds that the government had no more power to restrict assembly than it did to tell a man to wear a hat or when to get up in the morning. The response by Page of Virginia pointed out that even those "trivial" rights had been known to have been impaired —to the Colonists' consternation—but that the right of assembly ought to be specified since it was so basic to other rights. The Founding Fathers wrote an amendment for speech and assembly; even they did not deem it necessary to write an amendment for personal appearance. We conclude that within the commodious concept of liberty, embracing freedoms great and small, is the right to wear one's hair as he wishes.

The court went on to note that, although this right is not a "fundamental" freedom which can be impaired only by showing a compelling state interest, the burden of justifying restrictions on this freedom still rests with the state.

The Fifth, Sixth, and Ninth Circuits have sustained school codes regulating hair. Ferrell v. Dallas Independent School Dist., 392 F.2d 697 (5th Cir.), cert. denied . . . Gfell v. Rickelman, 441 F.2d 444 (6th Cir. 1971); Jackson v. Dorrier, 424 F.2d 213 (6th Cir.), cert. denied . . . King v. Saddleback Junior College Dist., 445 F.2d 932 (9th Cir. 1971). Each has adopted a different approach in sustaining these regulations.

In *King*, supra, 445 F.2d at 940, the Ninth Circuit held that students have no "substantial constitutional right" to wear their hair as they desire. As a consequence, school authorities need not present proof of actual classroom disruptions to support hair regulations. Mere opinion evidence of teachers or school administrators that long hair interferes with the educational process will suffice.

The Sixth Circuit, although not recognizing a specific constitutional right to determine one's hair length and style, requires proof that the appearance of the students caused classroom or other school disruptions. Implicit in these decisions is a recognition of the principle that the state has the burden of establishing the reasonableness of its regulations. . . .

The Fifth Circuit's decisions have turned on the reasonableness and necessity of the regulations. In *Ferrell* . . . the court, while recognizing the right of students to govern their personal appearance, held that this right was not unreasonably infringed because the school board was able to demonstrate a need for the regulations to control disruptions attributable to controversies over student hair lengths which departed from the more conventional styles. The court carefully disinguished a district court decision which had struck down a similar regulation because "[n]o suggestion was made that such [hairstyles] had any effect upon the health, discipline, or decorum of the institution."

In a subsequent decision, another panel of the Fifth Circuit did not hesitate to strike down a regulation restricting the style, rather than the length of hair. Griffin v. Tatum, 425 F.2d 201 (5th Cir. 1970). Later, in Stevenson v. Board of Education of Wheeler County, Georgia, 426 F.2d 1154 (5th Cir.), cert. denied . . . the court made clear that "[t]he touchstone for sustaining such regulations is the demonstration that they are necessary to alleviate interference with the educational process." . . .

Federal district courts generally, as well as those of this circuit, have disagreed about the validity of hair-length regulations. Aside from the instant case, two district courts in this circuit have upheld hair regulations against constitutional challenges. Carter v. Hodges, 317 F.Supp. 89 (W.D.Ark.1970); Giangreco v. Center School District, 313 F.Supp. 776 (W.D.Mo.1969). In both cases, however, the courts proceeded from the premise that the state carries the burden of demonstrating the reasonableness of the regulation. And, in both cases, the courts found that the students' appearance had, in fact, caused school disruptions.

The other district courts of this circuit which have considered the issue have followed the rationale of the First and Seventh Circuits in holding that students possess a constitutionally protected right to govern their personal appearance, and that the state must justify any infringement of this right. . . . In a comment typical of those made by other district judges of this circuit in rejecting the validity of hair regulations, Judge Eisele, in *Fry,* supra, said:

> The sincerity of the [school administrators] is not in in doubt. The Court believes that the "hair" rule was adopted because of the conviction of school authorities that to permit extreme hair styles would result in disruption or distraction in the classrooms.
>
> * * * But the facts do not appear to sustain the fear. Generally this fear is based upon the idea as stated by Mr. Swift, the superintendent, that anything out of the ordinary attracts attention and therefore could be disruptive of the educational process. This appears, however, to be more of

an educational philosophy than an established scientific fact. Students in our high schools and colleges must have some room within which to express their individual personalities.

With this background, we turn to the arguments advanced by appellants in this case.   The Bishops assert that the regulations violate: 1) Stephen's First Amendment right to "symbolic expression"; 2) his Fourteenth Amendment right to equal protection; 3) his Ninth and Fourteenth Amendment rights to govern his personal appearance; and 4) his parents' Ninth and Fourteenth Amendment rights to govern the raising of their family.

First Amendment

We deem the First Amendment contention to be without merit in the context of this case, since the record contains no evidence suggesting that Stephen's hairstyle represented a symbolic expression of any kind.   The appellants concede that Stephen never considered his hairstyle to be symbolic of any idea.   They argue, however, that a "[non-conforming hairstyle] need not symbolize anything at all * * * to be a constitutionally protected expression."   We cannot accept this unusually broad reading of the First Amendment.   Since all conduct cannot be labeled speech even when "the [actor] intends thereby to express an idea," United States v. O'Brien, 391 U.S. 367, 376, . . . certainly conduct not intended to express an idea cannot be afforded protection as speech.

Equal Protection

Dissenting in *Ferrell*, supra .   .   .   Judge Tuttle propounded an equal protection argument which Justice Douglas subsequently reiterated in dissenting from the Supreme Court's denial of certiorari Justice Douglas said:

> It comes as a surprise that in a country where the States are restrained by an Equal Protection Clause, a person can be denied education in a public school because of the length of his hair.   I suppose that a nation bent on turning out robots might insist that every male have a crew cut and every female wear pigtails.   But the ideas of "life, liberty, and the pursuit of happiness," expressed in the Declaration of Independence, later found specific definition in the Constitution itself, including of course freedom of expression and a wide zone of privacy.   I had supposed those guarantees permitted idiosyncrasies to flourish, especially when they concern the image of one's personality and his philosophy toward government and his fellow men.

The equal protection theory has been adopted in one circuit court decision.   In *Crews*, supra . . ., the Seventh Circuit found that male students were denied equal protection since females, who participated in substantially the same school activities as males, were not subject to the same hairstyle restrictions. Appellants have raised no question of sex discrimination. Their argument, cast as it is in terms of discrimination between males with differing hairlengths, does not fall within traditional concepts of invidious discrimination subject to the proscription of the Equal Protection Clause. Since we find in favor of appellants on other grounds, we do not pass upon this equal protection argument.

Parents' Rights

Stephen's parents argue that the regulations violate their constitutional right to govern the raising of their family. The thrust of their argument is that, although school authorities are vested with certain powers to maintain discipline, some room must be left for the exercise of parental control over a child's lifestyle. They assert that the Fourteenth Amendment forbids state intrusion, such as that attempted here, into the parent-child relationship. While there may be some merit to this assertion, we believe that this case is an inappropriate vehicle for making that determination. There is no indication in the record that Stephen's parents were responsible for his choice of hairstyle. Their role throughout has been limited to supporting Stephen's right to govern his personal appearance. The record, therefore, fails to establish any direct invasion of the parents' rights. We believe such a showing necessary to support a successful attack upon the regulations in question.

Stephen's Rights

We hold that Stephen possessed a constitutionally protected right to govern his personal appearance while attending public high school. In reaching this conclusion we find it necessary to determine the nature and source of this right. Among those courts which agree that this right exists, there is some disagreement as to its nature and source. . . . Some have referred to the right as "fundamental", others as "substantial", others as "basic", and still others as simply a "right". The source of this right has been found within the Ninth Amendment, the Due Process Clause of the Fourteenth Amendment, and the privacy penumbra of the Bill of Rights. A close reading of these cases reveals, however, that the differences in approach are more semantic than real. The common theme underlying decisions striking down hairstyle regulations is that the Constitution guarantees rights other than those specifically enumerated, and that the right to govern one's personal appearance is one of those guaranteed rights.

The existence of rights other than those specifically enumerated in the Constitution was recognized by the Supreme Court in Griswold v. Connecticut, 381 U.S. 479, ... Much of the present divergence of opinion as to the source of the right asserted here can be traced to the different approaches adopted by the Justices in *Griswold.* We see no point in rehashing these different approaches, since under any one of them, the conclusion follows that certain additional rights exist.

We believe that, among those rights retained by the people under our constitutional form of government, is the freedom to govern one's personal appearance. As a freedom which ranks high on the spectrum of our societal values, it commands the protection of the Fourteenth Amendment Due Process Clause. . . . The importance attached to such personal freedom has been long recognized. Writing in 1891, Justice Gray said:

> No right is held more sacred, or is more carefully guard-
> ed, by the common law, than the right of every individual to
> the possession and control of his own person, free from all
> restraint or interference of others, unless by clear and un-
> questionable authority of law. As well said by Judge Cooley,
> "The right to one's person may be said to be a right of com-
> plete immunity: to be let alone." [Union Pacific Ry. Co. v.
> Botsford, 141 U.S. 250, 251 . . .]

Our determination that Stephen possesses this personal freedom, however, does not end our inquiry into the constitutionality of the challenged regulations. Personal freedoms are not absolute; they must yield when they intrude upon the freedoms of others. Our task, therefore, is to weigh the competing interests asserted here. In doing so, we proceed from the premise that the school administration carries the burden of establishing the necessity of infringing upon Stephen's freedom in order to carry out the educational mission of the St. Charles High School. . . . Since our decision must turn on the necessity of the regulations, we review the evidence adduced in their support.

The record discloses that the St. Charles high school adminis-trators believed that the wearing of long hair caused disruption in the educational process. They asserted that the male students with long hair tended to be rowdy, created a sanitation problem in the swimming pool, caused a safety problem in certain shop classes, and tended to make poorer grades than those with shorter hair.

Mr. Lauer, the principal, testified that a group of about twenty-five boys and girls, who opposed the dress code, generally congregated at one table in the school cafeteria. According to Mr. Lauer, this group has been noisy and boisterous, and, on one occasion, disrespect-ful to a teacher. The boys in this group apparently wear their hair longer than most others in the school.

The principal expressed the opinion that without a dress code the students would polarize into camps of "long hairs" and "short hairs". Mr. Lauer also indicated that, in his opinion, if boys were allowed to wear long hair so as to look like girls, it would create problems with the continuing operation of the school because of confusion over appropriate dressing room and restroom facilities.

The school administrators offered evidence which indicated that a fight had occurred between a student with long hair and one with short hair at a nonschool function. The athletic director suggested that, although he had encountered no problems, long hair might affect sanitation in the swimming pool. He further commented that a boy wearing long hair and somewhat unusual attire had attracted attention and caused a commotion in the hallway of the school on one occasion. The shop teacher interjected that there was a risk of injury in his classes for a student wearing long hair. Another teacher testified that, in her opinion, students wearing long hair did not possess as good an attitude toward their studies as those with short hair. The school superintendent stressed in his testimony the possible reaction of other students, teachers, and the public as possibly jeopardizing the St. Charles educational program. He noted that the community favored the dress code and felt that this justified its imposition.

We find virtually no evidence in this record to support the school board's contention that the hair regulations are necessary to prevent disruptions at St. Charles High School. The primary weakness in the state's case is that the cited student behavorial problems existed even though all of the students, except Stephen, were in compliance with the regulations, albeit grudgingly in some instances. It is conceded that Stephen was not involved in any conduct which caused a disturbance. There was testimony that one young lady refused to wear a driving helmet which Stephen had previously worn, but there was no indication that this refusal was prompted by sanitary considerations. Stephen testified that he frequently washed his hair, and the school produced no evidence that his hair caused sanitation problems.

Passing to the other evidence presented, we note that much of the board's case rests upon conclusionary assertions that disruptions would occur without the hair regulations. Although we have construed the evidence most favorably to the trial court's findings in support of the regulations' validity, it is apparent that the opinion testimony of the school teachers and administrators, which lacks any empirical foundation, likely reflects a personal distaste of longer hairstyles, which distaste is shared by many in the older generation. We do not feel that the suggestion that a correlation exists between the length of a student's hair and his classroom performance requires a response. The assertion that the emergence of long hairstyles will lead to co-educational restrooms is equally untenable. Nor does the acceptance of the dress code by the majority of the St. Charles community and students justify the infringement of Stephen's liberty to govern his personal appearance. Toleration of individual differences is basic to our democracy, whether those differences be in religion, politics, or life-style.   Finally, we cannot accept the argument that uniformity of appearance must be maintained in order to prevent "polarization" in the St. Charles student body.

We find only two instances of actual disruption cited in the record.   The misconduct in the school cafeteria by students wearing longer hair than other students, but not longer than the school administration's edict, represents an isolated incident.   Moreover, its connection with long hair seems, at best, tenuous.   The disturbance in the hall related to a young man, wearing long hair and bizarre dress, who was not enrolled in school.   Of the justifications advanced by the school administrators in support of the regulations, only those relating to swimming pool sanitation and shop class safety bear any rational relation to the length of a student's hair.   The school administration has failed to show why these particular problems cannot be solved by imposing less restrictive rules, such as requiring students to wear swimming caps or shop caps.

In summary, the case presented by the school administrators fails to demonstrate the necessity of its regulation of the hair length and style of male students.   We hold this regulation invalid and its terms unenforceable.

We reverse and remand this case for the entry of judgment in conformity with this opinion.

ALDRICH, Circuit Judge (concurring).

A recent law review has concluded, after summarizing the cases,

> "What is disturbing is the inescapable feeling that long hair is simply not a source of significant distraction, and that school officials are often acting on the basis of personal distaste amplified by an overzealous belief in the need for regulations."   84 Harv.L.Rev. 1702 at 1715 (1971).

The connection between long hair and the immemorial problems of misdirected student activism and negativisim, whether in behavior or in learning, is difficult to see.   No evidence has been presented that hair is the cause, as distinguished from a possible peripheral consequence, of undesirable traits, or that the school board, Delilah-like, can lop off these characteristics with the locks.   Accepting as true the testimony that in St. Charles, Missouri, the longer the student's hair, the lower his grade in mathematics, it does not lead me to believe that shortening the one will add to the other.   Indeed, the very fact that such evidence is offered would seem to support the periodical's conclusion.

The area of judicial notice is circumscribed, but I cannot help but observe that the city employee who collects my rubbish has shoulder-length hair.   So do a number of our nationally famous Boston Bruins.   Barrel tossing and puck chasing are honorable pursuits, not to be associated with effeteness on the one hand, or aimlessness or indolence on the other. If these activities be thought not of high intellectual calibre, I turn to the recent successful candidates for Rhodes Scholarships from my neighboring institution. A number of these, according to their photographs, wear hair that outdoes even the hockey players. It is proverbial that these young men are chosen not only for their scholastic attainments, but for their outstanding character and accomplishments. What particularly impresses me in their case is that they feel strongly enough about their chosen appearance to risk the displeasure of a scholarship committee doubtless including establishmentarians who may be expected to find it personally distasteful.

It is bromidic to say that times change, but perhaps this is a case where a bromide is in order.

LAY, Circuit Judge (concurring).

I concur.

This case for me is not one of easy decision. On the surface, one can be somewhat troubled with the fact that overloaded federal dockets are further burdened with cases which center their controversies on the length of a school boy's hair. It may well seem appropriate that this issue does not involve a question of substantial constitutional dimension. Freeman v. Flake, 448 F.2d 258 (10 Cir. 1971), or that such problems should be left to local authorities, King v. Saddleback Jr. College District, 445 F.2d 932 (9 Cir. 1971). Nevertheless, a state's invasion into the personal rights and liberty of an individual, of whatever age or description, should present a justiciable issue worthy of federal review. There is little doubt that this regulation seeks to restrict a young persons' personal liberty to mold his own lifestyle through his personal appearance. To say that the issue is not "substantial" turns a deaf ear to the basic values of individual privacy and the freedom to caricature one's own image. Our institutions do not rely on submerging individual personality in order to create an "idealized" citizen. Cf. Meyer v. Nebraska, ... The abhorrence of such treatment stems from the enlightened philosophy that school children must be given every feasible opportunity to grow in independence, to develop their own individualities and to initiate and thrive on creative thought.

Moreover, to say simply that the problem is best left to local authorities bemeans the intrinsic constitutional issue involved. Such a rationale could sustain any school prohibition of the recognized constitutional rights of students. Tinker v. Des Moines Independent Community School District, . . .

The question confronting us is whether there exists any real educational purpose or societal interest to be served in the discipline the school has adopted. After due consideration I fail to find any rational connection between the health, discipline or achievement of a particular child wearing a hair style which touches his ears or curls around his neck, and the child who does not. The gamut of rationalizations for justifying this restriction fails in light of reasoned analysis. When school authorities complain variously that such hair styles are inspired by a communist conspiracy, that they make boys look like girls, that they promote confusion as to the use of restrooms and that they destroy the students' moral fiber, then it is little wonder even moderate students complain of "getting up tight." In final analysis, I am satisfied a comprehensive school restriction on male student hair styles accomplishes little more than to project the prejudices and personal distastes of certain adults in authority on to the impressionable young student.

———

BANNISTER v. PARADIS

United States District Court, D.N.H., 1970.
316 F.Supp. 185.

BOWNES, District Judge. This action was brought . . . by Kevin Bannister, a student at the Pittsfield Junior High School, through his mother . . . against the principal of the Pittsfield High School and the members of the Pittsfield School Board. The controversy centers on that portion of the Pittsfield dress code which provides as to boys: "Dungarees will not be allowed."

STIPULATED FACTS

Prior to hearing, the parties entered into a stipulation of facts as follows. Kevin Bannister is twelve years old and is a student in the sixth grade of the Pittsfield High School which runs from the fifth through the twelfth grades, and is a public school. The present version of the dress code was adopted unanimously by the School Board on April 27, 1970, and the only section of the dress code in issue is the section quoted above referring to dungarees. The plaintiff, however, does not agree that the dress code is constitutional as to its other provisions. Kevin was sent home for violation of the dress code because he was wearing blue jeans. At no time was force used to require Kevin to leave school.

FINDINGS

At the outset, the Court has had some difficulty defining the word "dungarees." The principal of the school defined "dungarees" as working clothes made of a coarse cotton blue fabric. The Chairman of the School Board defined "dungarees" as a denim fabric pant used for work with color of no significance. Webster's Third International Dictionary defines "dungarees" as heavy cotton work clothes usually made of blue dungaree. For purposes of this case, the Court finds that blue jeans and dungarees are synonymous and that Kevin Bannister deliberately violated the school dress code on at least two occasions by wearing blue jeans to school. These violations were with the full knowledge and consent, if not the actual urging, of Kevin's parents. At the time the violations occurred, the blue jeans were neat and clean, as was all of Kevin's ensemble.

There was no evidence that the wearing of dungarees of any color had ever caused any disturbance at the school or given rise to any disciplinary problems. Kevin's wearing of blue jeans did not cause any disturbance and there was no disciplinary problem involved except the one involving Kevin himself. It can be fairly concluded that wearing clean blue jeans does not constitute a danger to the health or safety of other pupils and that wearing them does not disrupt the other pupils.

The principal of the school, Mr. Paradis, who has had a total of seven years' experience in teaching and school administration, testified that discipline is essential to the educational process, and that proper dress is part of a good educational climate. It was his opinion that if students wear working or play clothes to school, it leads to a relaxed attitude and such an attitude detracts from discipline and a proper educational climate. Mr. Paradis stated further that students with patches on their clothes and students with dirty clothes, regardless of the type of clothing, should be sent home. The Court notes here that there is nothing in the dress code specifically stating that clothes should be neat and clean. The dress code, as to the boys, is directed primarily to specific prohibitions and does not promulgate any positive standards to follow. On cross-examination, the principal stated: "I apply the dress code as I see it. We don't define the term dungarees as to what it is."

The Chairman of the School Board, E. Windsor Burbank, testified that it was his opinion, and the opinion of the School Board, that the relaxed atmosphere induced by wearing work or play clothes to school does not fit into the atmosphere of discipline and learning. This opinion was based on the Chairman's assertion that California students had poor academic records and that this was due to the sloppy and casual attire worn by them to school. The Chairman is a full time pilot for TWA Airlines and his knowledge of the type of school dress worn by students in California was based on his observations at the times that his airplane schedule took him to various sections of California. The Chairman did not explain the basis for his assertion that California high school students have poor academic records.

Prior to the adoption of a revised dress code in 1970, the Student Council had recommended that the prohibition against dungarees be eliminated. The School Board did not accede to this request, but no reasons were given for its refusal.

RULINGS

.   .   .   New Hampshire Revised Statutes Annotated, Chapter 189, Section 15 provides:

> *Regulations.* The school board may, unless otherwise provided by statute or state board regulations, prescribe regulations for the attendance upon, and for the management, classification and discipline of, the schools; and such regulations, when recorded in the official records of the school board, shall be binding upon pupils and teachers.

There is no question, therefore, that the Pittsfield dress code is action by the State of New Hampshire. The serious question is whether or not the prohibition of wearing dungarees is a deprivation of any rights, privileges, or immunities secured by the Constitution of the United States. The Court has been unable to find any cases brought under the Civil Rights Act where the issue has been wearing apparel. Students and school boards seem to have become entangled in the hirsute aspect of school dress codes to the exclusion of almost everything else. The only case that comes close to the case before the Court is Westley v. Rossi, 305 F.Supp. 706 (D.Minn.1969), in which the plaintiff started out by violating several prohibitions of the dress code, but asserted in court that he was perfectly willing to comply with all of the rules and dress codes of his high school except for the length of his hair. This dearth of cases relative to wearing apparel in the Civil Rights field may be an indication that neither pupils nor school boards look on clothes with the same emotion and fervor with which they regard the length of a young man's hair or it may indicate, as the Court believes it does, that most school boards are no longer concerned with what a student wears to school as long as it is clean and covers adequately those parts of the body that, by tradition, are usually kept from public view.

There was no suggestion that the wearing of blue jeans, clean or otherwise, in any way constitutes a right of expression. The First Amendment, therefore, does not apply and is not an issue.

Certainly, the prohibition against the wearing of blue jeans or dungarees cannot by any stretch of the imagination touch the right of privacy as delineated in Griswold v. Connecticut, 381 U.S. 479, .   .

If it were not for the case of Richards v. Thurston, 424 F.2d 1281 (1st Cir. 1970), the Court might be tempted to dispose of this matter on the ground that there was no deprivation of any constitutional rights. The language and reasoning of that case, however, convinces us that a person's right to wear clothes of his own choosing provided that, in the case of a schoolboy, they are neat and clean, is a constitutional right protected and guaranteed by the Fourteenth Amendment.

Judge Coffin, in writing the opinion, quoted Union Pac. Ry. Co. v. Botsford, 141 U.S. 250, 251 . . . which stated:

> No right is held more sacred, or is more carefully guarded, by the common law, than the right of every individual to the possession and control of his own person, free from all restraint or interference of others, unless by clear and unquestionable authority of law.

Surely, the commodious concept of liberty invoked by Judge Coffin, embracing freedoms great and small, is large enough to include within its embrace the right to wear clean blue jeans to school unless there is an outweighing state interest justifying their exclusion. . . .

Since we have determined that a personal liberty is involved . . . we now consider the second question, and that is whether or not the regulations against the wearing of dungarees is justified under these circumstances. Going again to Richards v. Thurston, supra, for our guidelines, we take into account the nature of the liberty asserted, the context in which it is asserted, and the extent to which the intrusion on the liberty is confined to the legitimate public interest to be served.

On the scale of values of constitutional liberties, the right to wear clean blue jeans to school is not very high. There was no suggestion by the plaintiff that he could not afford pants other than blue jeans, although there was testimony by another parent that she had sent her son to school at the end of the year in blue jeans because she could not afford to buy him a pair of dress pants.

On the other hand, there was no showing that the wearing of dungarees in any way inhibited or tended to inhibit the educational process. The Court is, of course, mindful of the testimony of the principal and the Chairman of the School Board that wearing work clothes or play clothes is subversive of the educational process because students tend to become lax and indifferent. The Court confesses, however, that it has considerable difficulty accepting this proposition. There was no expert testimony to this effect with the exception of that of Mr. Paradis. While the Court realizes that Mr. Burbank's experience on the School Board of eight years' standing does give him certain credentials, it does not qualify him as an expert in the field of education and teaching. There was no evidence as to how many other school boards in the state followed a similar dress code nor, with the exception of Mr. Burbank's rather casual observations of the California school system, was there any testimony as to the type of dress worn by other pupils in any other schools.

In Breen v. Kahl, 419 F.2d 1034 (7th Cir. 1969), the Court pointed out at page 1037:

> Although schools need to stand in place of a parent, in regard to certain matters during the school hours, the power

must be shared with the parents, especially over intimately personal matters such as dress and grooming.

Quoting *Breen* again:

> To uphold arbitrary school rules which "sharply implicate basic constitutional values" for the sake of some nebulous concept of school discipline is contrary to the principle that we are a government of laws which are passed pursuant to the United States Constitution.

We realize that a school can, and must, for its own preservation exclude persons who are unsanitary, obscenely or scantily clad. Good hygiene and the health of the other pupils require that dirty clothes of any nature, whether they be dress clothes or dungarees, should be prohibited. Nor does the Court see anything unconstitutional in a school board prohibiting scantily clad students because it is obvious that the lack of proper covering, particularly with female students, might tend to distract other pupils and be disruptive of the educational process and school discipline.

While the Court recognizes that school boards do have power to adopt reasonable restrictions on dress as part of its educational policy and as an educational device, the school board's power must be limited to that required by its function of administering public education. The observation in Westley v. Rossi, supra, is pertinent.

> The standards of appearance and dress of last year are not those of today nor will they be those of tomorrow. Regulation of conduct by school authorities must bear a reasonable basis to the ordinary conduct of the school curriculum or to carrying out the responsibility of the school.

The Court rules that the defendants have not justified the intrusion on the personal liberty of Kevin Bannister, small as that intrusion may be, and that the prohibition against wearing dungarees is unconstitutional and invalid. The School Board and the principal of the Pittsfield High School are permanently enjoined from enforcing that portion of the dress code which prohibits boys from wearing dungarees. . . .

NOTES AND QUESTIONS

1. As a general proposition do courts endorse the view that local school boards have power to adopt reasonable rules and regulations governing students? Must these rules be reasonably related to proper functioning and welfare of the school? Give some examples that would and would not qualify. Does their reasonableness depend upon the circumstance; thus, a rule reasonable for a school's cafeteria would not be reasonable in its art class? Do the courts presume the validity of a rule or regulation of a local school board and require that the complaining party show that the rule is unreasonable? How can rules and regulations governing student behavior off school premises be justified as being reasonably re-

lated to the proper functioning and welfare of the school? Give some examples. In Sullivan v. Houston Ind. School Dist., 307 F.Supp. 1328 (S.D.Tex.1969) the court said:

"It is not clear whether the law allows a school to discipline a student for his behavior during free time away from the campus. . . . In this court's judgment, it makes little sense to extend the influence of school administration to off-campus activity under the theory that such activity might interfere with the function of education. School officials may not judge a student's behavior while he is in his home with his family nor does it seem to this court that they should have jurisdiction over his acts on a public street corner. A student is subject to the same criminal laws and owes the same civil duties as other citizens, and his status as a student should not alter his obligations to others during his private life away from the campus.

"Arguably, misconduct by students during non-school hours and away from school premises could, in certain situations, have such a lasting effect on other students that disruption could result during the next school day. Perhaps then administrators should be able to exercise some degree of influence over off-campus conduct. This court considers even this power to be questionable.

"However, under any circumstances, the school certainly may not exercise more control over off-campus behavior than over on-campus conduct. Serious disciplinary action concerning first amendment activity on or off campus must be based on the standard of substantial interference with the normal operations of the school."

2. Do you agree with the decisions and reasons in the above two opinions? Why or why not? Would these two cases have been decided differently by courts in the Fifth, Sixth and Ninth Circuits? Why? Is this result justifiable? Would the decisions have been the same if a teacher, rather than a student, had been involved? See, e. g., Finot v. Bd. of Ed., 250 Cal.App.2d 189, 58 Cal.Rptr. 520 (1967).

3. Does either court in Bishop or Bannister, supra, base its opinion on a constitutional provision? Is it the First Amendment? If not, which provision? Do you agree?

4. What reason(s) can you give justifying a school's interest in the way in which its students dress and in their overall appearance?

5. Suppose a school's regulation on hair styles pertains only to all students enrolled in either its shop, laboratory or art courses, requiring that (a) the ears shall not be covered below the lower parts of the earlobes; (b) hair at the back of the head shall not fall below the top of the dress shirt or blouse collar; (c) sideburns shall not extend below the bottom of the ear; and (d) the top of the eyebrow shall be the lower limit for the forehead, would this regulation be upheld? Suppose the school also required that all students take at least one shop, laboratory or art course, would this factor affect your reasoning? Why? See, Stull v. School Board, 459 F.2d 339 (3rd Cir. 1972).

6. Suppose a school's dress code provided that (1) students who ride bicycles to school shall not wear bell-bottomed slacks; (2) students who wear slacks shall not wear slacks that are so skintight and, therefore,

revealing as to provoke or distract students of the same or opposite sex; (3) no student shall wear bells, or other distractive devices, attached to the bottoms of slacks or other attire; (4) shirts and blouses must be tucked in at all times unless they are square cut in which case they can be left out; (5) metal cleats or taps are destructive of floor surfaces, and must not be worn; (6) no hairclips, hairrollers, haircurlers, kerchiefs or similar items may be worn; (7) sandals are not allowed; (8) neither micromini nor maxi skirts shall be worn; (9) all girls in high school shall wear brassieres, and (10) no partially bleached clothing shall be worn. Is any section of this code unenforceable because of constitutional reasons? If so, which one; why? See, e. g., Scott v. Board of Education, 61 Misc.2d 333, 305 N.Y.S.2d 601 (1969); Stromberg v. French, 60 N.D. 750, 236 N.W. 477 (1931); and Pugsley v. Sellmeyer, 158 Ark. 247, 250 S.W. 538 (1923).

7. Could a local board legally refuse to issue a diploma to a student on the ground that he would not wear a cap and gown, and did not participate in graduation ceremonies? See, Valentine v. School Dist., 191 Iowa 1100, 183 N.W. 434 (1921), and Ryan v. Board of Education, 124 Kan. 89, 257 P. 945 (1927).

FREEDOM FROM SEX DISCRIMINATION

BRENDEN v. INDEPENDENT SCHOOL DISTRICT 742

United States Court of Appeals, 8th Cir., 1973.
477 F.2d 1292.

HEANEY, Circuit Judge. This is a civil rights action brought under 42 U.S.C. § 1983 to enjoin enforcement of a rule promulgated by the Minnesota State High School League which bars females from participating with males in high school interscholastic athletics. The rule states:

"Girls shall be prohibited from participation in the boys' interscholastic athletic program either as a member of the boys' team or a member of the girls' team playing the boys' team.

"The girls' team shall not accept male members."

Minnesota State High School League Official Handbook, 1971–72.

Athletic Rules for Girls, Article III, Section 5.

The complaint charges that this rule discriminates against females in violation of the Equal Protection Clause of the Fourteenth Amendment to the United States Constitution.

The plaintiffs are Peggy Brenden and Antoinette St. Pierre, female high school students at Minnesota public high schools. . . . The plaintiffs desired to participate in non-contact interscholastic sports: Brenden in tennis; St. Pierre in cross-country skiing and cross-county running. Neither of their schools provided teams for females in the respective sports. They did, however, provide such teams for males. Both plaintiffs would have liked to qualify for positions on the teams which have been established for males, but they were precluded from doing so on the basis of the above quoted rule. The trial court found that both were excellent athletes, and that neither would be damaged by competition with males. The court, after a trial on the merits, granted relief . . .

The High School League first contends that there is no jurisdiction over it under 42 U.S.C. § 1983 because it is a voluntary organization not acting under the color of state law. However, the trial court specifically held that:

> " * * * Although the Minnesota State High School League is a voluntary organization, the original allowance for public high schools to join such an association or organization is authorized pursuant to Minnesota law. Minn.Stat.Ann. Section 192.12. In addition, the rules governing League members are promulgated pursuant to a procedure which integrally involves the member school districts in the decision-making process. Beyond this, the ultimate enforcement of the rules becomes the responsibility of the member school and the public officials of those schools and school districts. In such a situation, where there is a tremendous public interest in educational functions, and where the public school machinery of the state is so involved in the effectuation and enforcement of rules which bind all public high schools in the state, the Court is left with no conclusion other than that defendant Minnesota State High School League and the defendant school districts are acting under color of state law. * * * " (Footnote omitted.)

We agree with the trial court and affirm its decision in this regard.
. . .

We next turn to the merits. In evaluating a claim that state action violates the Equal Protection Clause, the following three criteria must be considered:

> " * * * [I] the character of the classification in question;
> [II] the individual interests affected by the classification;
> [III] and the governmental interests asserted in support of the classification. * * * "

In 1961, President Kennedy, having found that "prejudices and outmoded customs act as barriers to the full realization of women's basic rights," established the President's Commission on the Status of Women. Executive Order 10980 (December 14, 1961). That Commission, the President's Task Force on Women's Rights and Responsibilities, congressional hearings and critical studies have confirmed the serious nature of discrimination on account of sex.

In recent years, Congress and the Executive have acted to eliminate discrimination based on " 'stereotyped characterizations of the sexes',". See, Title VII of the Civil Rights Act of 1964, the Equal Pay Act, and Title IX of the Education Amendments of 1972. The jurisdiction of the Civil Rights Commission has been extended to include discrimination on the basis of sex. Finally, Congress has passed the Equal Rights Amendment and transmitted it to the states.

There is no longer any doubt that sex-based classifications are subject to scrutiny by the courts under the Equal Protection Clause and will be struck down when they provide dissimilar treatment for men and women who are similarly situated with respect to the object of the classification. . . . Furthermore, discrimination on the basis of sex can no longer be justified by reliance on "outdated images * * * of women as peculiarly delicate and impressionable creatures in need of protection from the rough and tumble of unvarnished humanity." In this case, it is unnecessary for this Court to determine whether classifications based on sex are suspect and, thus, can be justified only by a compelling state interest because the High School League's rule cannot be justified even under the standard applied to test nonsuspect classification.

The High School League contends that relief under the Civil Rights Act is inappropriate because participation in interscholastic sports is a privilege and not a right. We disagree. The Supreme Court has rejected "the concept that constitutional rights turn upon whether a governmental benefit is characterized as a 'right' or as a 'privilege.' * * *". The question in this case is not whether the plaintiffs have an absolute right to participate in interscholastic athletics, but whether the plaintiffs can be denied the benefits of activities provided by the state for male students.

Discrimination in high school interscholastic athletics constitutes discrimination in education. The Supreme Court of Minnesota has stated that:

> " * * * [I]nterscholastic activities * * * [are] to-
> day recognized * * * as an important and integral fac-
> et of the * * * education process, see, Bunger v. Iowa
> High School Athletic Assn, 197 N.W.2d 555 (Iowa 1972)."

Thompson v. Barnes, 200 N.W.2d 921, 926 n. 11 (Minn.1972). The court in *Thompson* pointed out that this was also the position of the Minnesota High School League. . . .

In view of these circumstances, we must conclude that at the very least, the plaintiffs' interest in participating in interscholastic sports is a substantial and cognizable one. Thus, this case is properly before a federal court to determine if the High School League's actions are in conformity with the Equal Protection Clause.

Because the defendant high schools have not provided teams for females in tennis and cross-country skiing and running, the effect of the High School League's rule is to completely bar Brenden and St. Pierre from competition in these non-contact interscholastic sports, despite their being fully qualified. The High School League argues, however, that its rule is justified in order to assure that persons with similar qualifications compete among themselves. They state that physiological differences between males and females make it impossible for the latter to equitably compete with males in athletic competition.

In evaluating the High School League's justification for their rule, we will, as we have indicated, apply the equal protection standard for evaluating non-suspect classifications. That standard is set forth in Reed v. Reed, [404 U.S. 71, 92 S.Ct. 251, 30 L.Ed.2d 225 (1971)]:

> " * * * A classification 'must be reasonable, not arbitrary, and must rest upon some ground of difference having a *fair and substantial* relation to the object of the legislation, so that all persons in similar circumstances shall be treated alike.' * * * "

We recognize that because sex-based classifications may be based on outdated stereotypes of the nature of males and females, courts must be particularly sensitive to the possibility of invidious discrimination in evaluating them, and must be particularly demanding in ascertaining whether the state has demonstrated a substantial rational basis for the classification. This is especially true where the classification involves the interest of females in securing an education.

We believe that in view of the nature of the classification and the important interests of the plaintiffs involved, the High School League has failed to demonstrate that the sex-based classification fairly and substantially promotes the purposes of the League's rule.

First, we do not believe the High School League has demonstrated a sufficient rational basis for their conclusion that women are incapable of competing with men in non-contact sports. . . .

Furthermore, the High School League failed to show that it had established any objective nondiscriminatory minimum standards for evaluating qualifications for non-contact interscholastic athletics. The record indicates, in fact, that the schools had adopted no cut policies allowing male students, no matter *how untalented,* to participate in the non-contact interscholastic sports involved here. . . .

Second, even if we assume, arguendo, that, on the whole, females are unlikely to be able to compete with males in non-contact interscholastic sports, this fact alone would not justify precluding qualified females like Brenden and St. Pierre from such competition. . . .

In our view, *Reed* precludes a state from using assumptions about the nature of females as a class, to deny to females an individualized determintation of their qualifications for a benefit provided by the state.

equal protection
and substantive right

In the present case, the underlying purpose of the High School League's rule is, as we have indicated, to insure that persons with similar qualifications will compete with each other. Yet, females, whatever their qualifications, have been barred from competition with males on the basis of an assumption about the qualifications of women as a class. The failure to provide the plaintiffs with an individualized determination of their own ability to qualify for positions on these teams is, under *Reed*, violative of the <u>Equal Protection Clause.</u>

The High School League argues that invalidation of its rule will have an adverse impact on the future development of opportunities for females in interscholastic sports. This argument is too speculative to have merit, particularly in view of the recent statement of the Minnesota State Board of Education calling on its local boards to provide equal education opportunity for females, . . . and the League's own stated commitment to interscholastic athletics for females. This argument certainly cannot be used to deprive Brenden and St. Pierre of their rights to equal protection of the law. With respect to these two females, the record is clear. Their schools have failed to provide them with opportunities for interscholastic competition equal to those provided for males with similar athletic qualifications. Accordingly, they are entitled to relief. . . .

NOTES AND QUESTIONS

1. What, and for what reasons, should be the decision of a court if instead of skiing, tennis and running, a contact sport such as football or wrestling is involved? Cf. Morris v. Michigan State Board of Education, 472 F. 2d 1207 (6th Cir., 1973).

2. Are physiological factors the only ones to be considered in these types of cases? Should courts consider psychological factors? Sexually erotic ones? Why or why not?

3. To afford "the equal protection of the laws" must, or may, a school select its athletic representatives on their abilities as judged in competitive events? If so, would a school be equally required to allow all male athletes to compete for positions on the "female" track, volleyball or swim teams?

FREEDOM FROM UNREASONABLE SEARCHES AND SEIZURES

PEOPLE v. OVERTON

Court of Appeals of New York, 1969.
24 N.Y.2d 522, 301 N.Y.S.2d 479, 249 N.E.2d 366.

BURKE, Judge. We ordered reargument in this case so that we might reconsider our initial determination . . . in light of the recent Supreme Court decision in Bumper v. North Carolina, 391 U.S.

543   .   .   .   The single issue before us is whether the search that was conducted in this case may be sustained without a warrant.

The facts, critical to our determination, are quite simple.   Three detectives of the Mount Vernon Police Department had obtained a warrant directing the search, *inter alia,* of two high school students and their lockers at the Mount Vernon High School.   The detectives presented the warrant to Dr. Adolph Panitz, the vice-principal of the school, who summoned the two students to his office.   The detectives searched the boys and found nothing.   After a brief interrogation, two of the detectives took one youth to his locker, leaving the defendant in the presence of the vice-principal and the remaining detective.   At this time, the defendant was asked if he had marijuana in his locker.   The youth did not answer, but merely nodded in an uncertain manner.   The detective persisted, so that the youth replied either "I guess so" or "Maybe".   The detective, Dr. Panitz, the school custodian and the defendant then went to the latter's locker.   Dr. Panitz opened the locker with his master key and the detective found marijuana cigarettes in the defendant's jacket.

Subsequently, it was held that the warrant was ineffective insofar as the search of the locker was concerned.   The defendant then moved to suppress the use of the cigarettes as evidence in a youthful offender proceeding.   The Trial Judge denied the motion, stating in part that "The Board of Education, through Dr. Panitz, retained dominion over the use of the lockers and the Court finds that the search was legal."   The Appellate Term disagreed, stating in a *Per Curiam* opinion that "The search was illegal and cannot be justified upon the theory of consent on the part of the vice-principal of said school"   .   .   .   .   In our initial determination, we reversed the Appellate Term and sustained the denial of the motion to suppress.   Judge Keating, writing for a majority of the court, concluded that Dr. Panitz consented to the search and that such consent was binding upon defendant.   In his opinion, he pointed out that the locker searched was assigned to defendant Overton at the beginning of the school year.   He was given a combination lock, but was required to disclose the combination to his official teacher.   In addition, both Dr. Panitz and the school custodian possessed a master key to all lockers in the school.   Also, regulations governed the use of this facility so that each student had exclusive possession of the locker only vis-a-vis other students.   In summarizing the supervisory position retained by the school, Judge Keating observed, "Not only have the school authorities a right to inspect but *this right becomes a duty when suspicion arises* that something of an illegal nature may be secreted there.   When Dr. Panitz learned of the detectives' suspicion, *he was obligated to inspect the locker.*   This interest, together with the nonexclusive nature of the locker, empowered him to consent to the search by the officers."   .   .   The dissenters argued that "the principal opened the door, not because he was exercising a free supervisory control over the locker in the interest of the school program, but because he felt the invalid warrant compelled him to do so." . . .

Following our decision, the Supreme Court decided Bumper v. North Carolina .   .   . .   Thereafter, a petition for certiorari was filed in the Supreme Court of the United States where, .   .   . vacated the judgment and remanded this case for further consideration in light of the *Bumper* decision. .   .   .

We are of the opinion that our initial decision, holding that the defendant is not entitled to suppress the cigarettes, was proper when rendered and is unaltered by the spirit, if not the language of Bumper v. North Carolina (supra).

The facts in *Bumper* illustrate the true meaning of what was written therein. In *Bumper,* an elderly Negro woman, living in a house located in a rural area at the end of an isolated mile-long dirt road in North Carolina, was confronted by four white law enforcement officials—the County Sheriff, two deputies and a State investigator—who claimed the right to enter her premises pursuant to a search warrant. The 66-year-old woman did not attempt to prevent them, as she meekly replied "Go ahead". In that case, as in the present situation, the prosecutor later attempted to sustain the search on the ground of consent. It was also argued that the search was valid because of what was uncovered. .   .   .   The Supreme Court rejected both arguments. In refusing to find a consent to the search, the court recited in detail the factual setting of the case and then declared that "When a law enforcement officer claims authority to search a home under a warrant, he announces that the occupant has no right to resist the search. The situation is instinct with coercion—albeit colorably lawful coercion. Where there is coercion there cannot be consent." .   .   .   As we indicated before, it is undisputed that these words, as presented in *Bumper,* seem applicable and thus determinative here.

A close analysis of the facts in this case, however, discloses that there is lacking here even the "lawful coercion" which was found objectionable in *Bumper*. In the City of Mount Vernon, title to all school buildings and properties is in the Board of Education. The administrators of the various schools operate them as representatives of the owner. Dr. Panitz, an experienced administrator and educator, is that representative in the Mount Vernon High School. Under his direction and supervision, desks and lockers are assigned to students for their use, under predetermined conditions, one of which prohibits the storage of material which violates the law. In this case, the detectives approached him and requested his permission to speak with the defendant. With his assistance, they first questioned the defendant and after the colloquy described above—wherein the defendant indicated that there was marijuana in his locker—Dr. Panitz opened the defendant's locker. Were we to apply *Bumper* literally to this situation, we would have to conclude, as the dissenters do, that Dr. Panitz was coerced into opening the locker. Should we do so, I feel we would be extending *Bumper* far beyond its logical applicability.

Dr. Panitz was in charge of the Mount Vernon High School and it was his duty to enforce the rules and regulations which were in existence. As we earlier observed, "this right becomes a duty when suspicion arises." Dr. Panitz expressed his awareness of the duties of his position when he testified that: "Being responsible for the order, assignment, and maintenance of the physical facilities, if any report were given to me by anyone of an article or item of the nature that does not belong there, or of an illegal nature, I would inspect the locker." As the designated representative of the people of Mount Vernon, Dr. Panitz opened the locker, which was certainly not the private property of the defendant, in fulfillment of the trust and responsibility given him by the city residents through the Board of Education. Coercion is absent in this setting, having been displaced by the performance of a delegated duty. While we did state in our prior opinion that Dr. Panitz was empowered to consent to the search, in retrospect, it should be noted that this consent was equated to a nondelegable duty, which had to be performed to sustain the public trust. Contrasting the facts in this case with those in *Bumper,* it does not require extensive analysis to conclude that the "situation instinct with coercion" which characterized the plight of Bumper's 66-year-old grandmother can not be discerned where we find a public official performing a delegated duty by permitting an inspection of public property. In sum, the factual disparities render the decision in *Bumper* inapplicable.

Accordingly, upon reargument, we should adhere to this court's original decision of July 7, 1967 reversing the order of Appellate Terms.

BERGAN, Judge (dissenting). The police presented to Dr. Panitz, the school vice-principal, a search warrant. The People concede it was a bad warrant. Possessed of the warrant they searched a locker which defendant had rented and which had been assigned personally to him.

The court is again holding, as it did when the case was here before, .   .   .   that, notwithstanding the purported authority of a bad search warrant, the search of defendant's locker was good because the principal who had general control of the school premises "consented" to the search.

No matter how the record is read, the coercive effect of this [illegal] search warrant on the principal as well as on the defendant is inescapable. Dr. Panitz himself testified that in permitting the search of defendant's locker he was "honoring the search warrant." .   .   .

There can be no doubt, therefore, that this was a search "in reliance upon a warrant" within the language of Bumper v. North Caro-

lina. . . . It must equally be said of this present situation, as
it was said in *Bumper*, that "the situation is instinct with coercion".
. . .

This means that if the bad search warrant played an effective
role in the invasion of defendant's privacy, the result is unlawful even
though the vice-principal also gave his "consent" to the search and
had a general authority in the school premises. . . .

Even if, on our own independent evalution of *Bumper,* we might
think it quite distinguishable from the present problem, there can be
no doubt that the Supreme Court saw an analogy between the cases
because, in vacating the judgment of the Appellate Term entered on
the remission from this court . . . it remanded the case back
to New York "for further consideration in the light of" its *Bumper*
decision. . . .

NOTES AND QUESTIONS

1. The Fourth Amendment protects the people in their "persons, houses,
   papers and effects," but the protection is only "against unreasonable
   searches and seizures." How can you identify whether a search or seizure is "reasonable" or "unreasonable"? Is a search conducted pursuant to a valid warrant reasonable? Can a warrantless search also be a
   "reasonable" search? What is required in order to get a warrant?

2. Does the court in this case hold that the Fourth Amendment applies to
   a student's locker but that the search was reasonable, or does it hold
   that the Fourth Amendment does not apply to student lockers? Would
   the Amendment apply to a teacher's desk or locker?

3. Would the decision in this case have been different if the students had
   rented the lockers for $30.00 for the school year and under the school
   rules no one else had access to them?

4. Suppose a student were wearing a jacket with marijuana cigarettes in
   a pocket (instead of in the locker), do the opinions hold that the principal could have consented to a search of the jacket? A student's pants
   pockets or purse? A faculty member's? Why or why not?

5. Suppose the principal refused to cooperate until after the police officers "ordered" him to open the locker, would the decision have been different? Why? Does the principal have a "duty" to open the locker and
   investigate after the police present him with uncorroborated but suspicious information? Will any "suspicion" do, or must it be supported by
   evidence? If so, how much evidence? Does a principal have a "duty" to
   frisk students? Faculty? Cf. Kansas v. Stein, 203 Kan. 638, 456 P.2d
   1 (1969).

6. What is the legal status of a faculty member's locker, closet, desk or
   chests that may be in the school building? Are they subject to the rule
   of this case? Why or why not?

FREEDOM OF OFF CAMPUS ACTIVITY

WOODS v. WRIGHT

United States Court of Appeals, 5th Cir., 1964.
334 F.2d 369.

JONES, Circuit Judge. The appellant, Linda Cal Woods, a Negro girl living in Birmingham, Alabama, was a pupil in Washington School, a public school of that City. . . . The complaint alleges that Linda Cal Woods participated in a peaceful demonstration against racial segregation on May 4, 1963, which was a Saturday and a school holiday. She was arrested and charged under Section 1159 of the Code of the City of Birmingham with parading without a license. On May 20, 1963, Linda Cal Woods was given a letter at her school directed to her father, Calvin Woods, signed by the school principal, suspending Linda and stating that she was requested not to return to school for the remainder of the school term. The letter stated that the action was taken under the terms of a letter to the principal from the Superintendent, who was the defendant below and is the appellee here. . . .

The appellant has specified as error that (a) the suspensions and expulsions without notice or hearing violated due process rights, (b) that the Superintendent's directive is a restraint upon First and Fourteenth Amendment rights of liberty of expression, and (c) that the suspension is a denial of due process because it results from an alleged violation of an unconstitutional ordinance. These questions, we think, are not properly before us for decision. The case comes to us on appeal from the refusal of the district court to grant a temporary restraining order. Our holding that this order has finality of a kind which gives it appealability, does not make the district court's ruling dispositive of the case or operative as a final judgment. These issues are, in the first instance, for the district court.

We are fully aware of the reluctance with which Federal Courts should contemplate the use of the injunctive power to interfere with the conduct of state officers. But when there is a deprivation of a constitutionally guaranteed right the duty to exercise the power cannot be avoided. See Dixon v. Alabama State Bd. of Education, 294 F.2d 150 (5th Cir. 1961), cert. den. 368 U.S. 930, 82 S.Ct. 368, 7 L.Ed. 2d 193. Where there is a clear and imminent threat of an irreparable injury amounting to manifest oppression it is the duty of the court to protect against the loss of the asserted right by a temporary restraining order. We think such an order should have been entered in this cause by the district court. . . .

The order denying a temporary restraining order will be reversed, and upon receipt of the mandate of this Court, a temporary restraining order will be entered by the district court enjoining, until its further order, Theo R. Wright, Superintendent of Schools of the City of Birmingham, his agents, employees, subordinates, successors, and all persons in active concert with him from enforcing and carrying into effect the order of the Board of Education issued by letter on May 20, 1963, which suspended or expelled the Negro minor plaintiff, Linda Cal Woods, and other pupils of the named class who received said letter, for parading without a permit. It will not be appropriate to say, at this juncture, that if the facts recited in the affidavit of Calvin Woods and filed in the district court on May 21, 1963, are established, the plaintiffs will be entitled to a preliminary injunction of substantially the same tenor as the preliminary injunction until the final disposition of the cause. . . .

PROBLEM

R. R. v. BOARD OF EDUCATION

Superior Court of New Jersey, 1970.
109 N.J.Super. 337, 263 A.2d 180.

LANE, J. S. C. . . . The essential facts are not in dispute. On January 20, 1970 R. R., aged 15, was a sophomore at the high school which is located in West Long Branch, New Jersey. After his dismissal from the high school at the end of the class day, he went to his home in a neighboring municipality, arriving about 3:30 P. M. Finding the door locked and no one at home, R. R. went across the street to the home of W. O. to see if his parents had left the key to the house there. When R. R. rang the doorbell, L. O., about 15 years old, came to the door and let R. R. in. It is not clear exactly what happened at this point. R. R. alleges that he was provoked into striking L. O. on the back of her head with a piece of wood that he was carrying. He claims that L. O. then picked up a knife and that during the ensuing scuffle in which he tried to get the knife away from her, she was cut in four places. Her version is that R. R. deliberately tried to stab her.

On January 21, 1970 Elbert M. Hoppenstedt, superintendent of the high school, was informed by the principal of the incident. Mr. Hoppenstedt immediately contacted the neighboring municipality's police department and was read a statement of L. O. which set forth her version of the incident. Based on this information and information from the principal and vice-principal of the school that R. R. had been engaged in less serious conflicts with other students (which R. R. denies), it was decided that R. R. should be suspended until the next meeting of the board of education. There was no specification as to such alleged "less serious conflicts." There was no hearing afforded to R. R.

On January 22, 1970 a complaint was signed by a representative of the neighboring municipality's police department against R. R. alleging a violation of N.J.S.A. 2A:90–1. The complaint was forwarded to the Juvenile and Domestic Relations Court on January 29, 1970. A plea of not guilty was entered on February 25, 1970. The matter is now scheduled before that court for a formal hearing on April 9, 1970.

On January 23, 1970 M. R., R. R.'s father, who had been out of the State on business before this date, called the vice-principal of the high school who informed him of R. R.'s suspension from the high school until further notice. The vice-principal told M. R. that the high school would try to get home instruction for R. R. during the period of his suspension. On his own initiative, M. R. had his son examined on January 26, 1970 by Dr. Frank Husserl, a well-qualified psychiatrist. Dr. Husserl requested that R. R. be examined by Dr. Edward Dengrove. This examination was completed but Dr. Dengrove requested an electroencephalograph. As a result of the report of Dr. Dengrove and the report of the electroencephalograph, which was normal, and based on his examination, Dr. Husserl under date of February 6, 1970 addressed a letter:

To Whom It May Concern:

I have examined the above named [R. R.] in my office on January 26, 1970.

It is my professional opinion that he may return to school without risk to the safety and security of others or himself. . . .

The court is informed that the board of education again considered the matter on February 25, 1970 and decided to keep the suspension in effect. No hearing was afforded to R. R.

The question before the court is whether public school officials can deprive a student of his right to attend school because of acts committed off school property and totally unrelated to school activities, and, if so, what procedural due process must the school officials afford to the student. . . .

Assume that you are the judge in this case, what decision will you render and for what reason(s)?

HOWARD v. CLARK

New York Supreme Court, 1969.
59 Misc.2d 327, 299 N.Y.S.2d 65.

W. VINCENT GRADY, Justice. This is an article 78 proceeding to compel respondents to reinstate the . . . petitioners as full time students in the New Rochelle High School. The . . . petitioners were suspended indefinitely pursuant to the New Rochelle School Board Resolution No. 69–323 on March 17, 1969, on the grounds that they had been arrested on March 10, 1969, by the Mamaroneck police and charged with the criminal possession of a hypodermic instrument. It is apparent that the Superintendent of Schools relied upon that portion of Board of Education Resolution No. 69–323 which mandates suspension of "any student upon his indictment or arraignment in any court * * * for any criminal act of a nature injurious to other students or school personnel. * * *"

Education Law Section 3214(6)(a) provides that suspension can only be invoked upon the following minors:

"The school authorities, the superintendent of schools, or district superintendent of schools may suspend the following minors from requiring attendance upon instruction:

"(1) A minor who is insubordinate or disorderly;

"(2) A minor whose physical or mental condition endangers the health, safety, or morals of himself or of other minors;

"(3) A minor who, as determined in accordance with the provisions of part one of this article, is feebleminded to the extent that he cannot benefit from instruction."

The respondents contend that the validity of the challenged resolution may not be lawfully determined in an article 78 proceeding and that petitioners have not exhausted their administrative remedies of appeal to the Commissioner of Education under Education Law Section 310. . . .

The question which is raised in this proceeding is whether the respondents in suspending the . . . petitioners under Resolution 69–323 of the New Rochelle Board of Education went beyond the powers conferred upon by the Superintendent of Schools and the Board of Education under section 3214(6)(a) of the Education Law.

Respondents argue that the Resolution was within the powers conferred by section 2503(2), (3) of the Education Law which gives power to the Board of Education to prescribe such regulations as may be necessary to make effectual the provisions of the Education Law for the general management operation, control maintenance and discipline of the schools. Since section 3214(6)(a) Education Law specifically defines the grounds for suspension of a student, the powers of the Board of Education are limited in suspension cases to these grounds.

The respondents allege that the Superintendent of Schools suspended petitioners for the reason that: "possession by a high school student of heroin and of a hypodermic syringe for injection of the drug into the blood stream regardless of where offense is committed identified offender as a person whose conduct and mental condition endanger the safety, morals, health and welfare of other high school students with whom he would associate in the school."

While the use of heroin by students off the high school premises bears a reasonable relation to and may endanger the health, safety and morals of other students, the bare charges against petitioners of possession of heroin do not justify suspension of petitioners on the grounds set forth in section 3214(6)(a) that they are insubordinate or disorderly; nor that their physical or mental condition endangers the health, safety or morals of themselves or other minors.

The court finds that the respondents have exceeded the powers conferred upon them by the Education Law in suspending the . . . petitioners on the ground that they have been accused of possession of heroin. Until the legislature amends the Education Law, suspension of a student should be done pursuant to a strict interpretation and application of section 3214(6)(a) of the Education Law.

The court need not decide the constitutional issues raised by petitioners since petitioners are entitled to the relief they seek on the ground that the New Rochelle Board of Education exceeded its powers under the Education Law in suspending the . . . petitioners.

The application of the intervenors to intervene in this proceeding is denied. However, since it appears that . . . Douglas Herman was suspended for five (5) days for being charged with possession of marijuana off school grounds, and his suspension has terminated, his intervention herein is now moot, but based on the within decision, the record of his suspension should be expunged from the school records.

The petition is granted and the Board of Education of the City of New Rochelle is ordered to permit petitioners to attend New Rochelle High School forthwith as full time students and the record of their suspensions should be expunged from the school records.

NOTES AND QUESTIONS

1. Like the laws of many states Kentucky Revised Statutes § 161.180, provide that "each teacher in the public schools shall hold pupils to a strict account for their conduct in school, on the way to and from school, on the playgrounds and during intermission or recess." Would the following properly come within such a statute: (a) teacher disciplining students for fist-fighting after they returned home and went out to play; (b) a school board regulation requiring that students go directly home at the close of the school day; (c) the disciplining of a student for smoking (drinking) (uttering profanities) while on a public street; or (d) a rule prohibiting students from attending films, shows or social events on any nights except Friday or Saturday?

2. Suppose a school board requires that students go directly home after school, but the custom, for years, has been for the students to "hang out" at a local business establishment after school, upon strict enforcement of the rule by a new principal the owner of the business sues the prin-

cipal for loss of profits, what decision? See, Jones v. Cody, 132 Mich. 13, 92 N.W. 495 (1902).

3. Repeated drinking of alcohol, smoking and late hours curtail or destroy an athlete's ability. Does a coach have the right to apply sanctions to these kinds of off-campus behavior?

4. Suppose a proprietor, Mr. Russell, opened a cafe on land adjacent to the school playground where students could be served without leaving school grounds. Also suppose the local board's regulation was designed to protect its lunchroom business: "No one, while in school, shall be allowed to enter the restaurant of Mr. Russell or any other business establishment in the town without permission from 8:45 a.m. until 3:00 p.m." and suppose the father of two students persisted in either taking them, or allowing them, to go to the Russell Cafe for lunch, could the students be subjected to discipline for this "off campus" activity? See, Casey County Board of Education v. Luster, 282 S.W.2d 333 (Ky.1955).

5. Suppose a local school board rule states that "No one shall leave the campus without permission or unless accompanied by a teacher from 9:00 a.m. until 3:00 p.m." and suppose a student was scheduled to take music lessons off-campus once a week during the school hours, but the school authorities refused to give permission; after being suspended, he now appeals—what decision for what reason(s)? See, Christian v. Jones, 211 Ala. 161, 100 So. 99 (1924).

6. In 1965 the American Civil Liberties Union revised its statement on "Academic Freedom and Civil Liberties of Students in Colleges and Universities" which now reads, in part, as follows:

> "A. *Non-Academic Activities*
>
> "In their non-academic life, private or public, students should be free from college control. On the other hand, the college should not be held responsible for the non-academic activities of its individual students.
>
> "The student, like the teacher, is a member not only of an academic community, but of the community at large and of other specific communities. His college must regard him as both a student and a private individual. It must recognize that his being a student is sometimes irrelevant to his private status. In this private status he should not be subject to punitive measures by the college, unless the college can prove (in the course of a hearing with due process safeguards as specified in IV) that he has acted in a way which adversely affects or seriously interferes with its normal educational function, or which injures or endangers the welfare of any of its other members.
>
> "B. *Off-Campus Activities*
>
> "No disciplinary action should be taken by a college against a student for engaging in such off-campus activities as political campaigns, picketing, or participating in public demonstrations, provided the student does not claim without authorization to speak or act in the name of the college or

one of its student organizations. Students should observe the same kind of self-discipline that their teachers accept when they speak as citizens and not as representatives of their educational institution.

"When students choose to participate in activities that result in police action, such as demonstrations against segregation, the civilian defense program or nuclear tests, it is an infringement of their liberty for the college to punish such activity. Students who violate a local ordinance or any law which they consider to be morally wrong, risk the legal penalties prescribed by the civilian authorities. Since not every conviction under law is for an offense with which an educational institution must concern itself, it is incumbent on the college to refrain from administrative decisions which would violate the students' academic freedom.

"In this connection, it is important to make clear that our discussion here concerns convictions. A record of mere arrest, not followed by conviction, should not be used by any educational institution to penalize a student in any way. As any other citizen, a student is presumed to be innocent until proven otherwise.

"And even in the case of conviction of a student for civil rights and other political activities such as those listed in paragraph B above, this should be distinguished by the college from convictions for criminal offenses not involving First Amendment considerations. In screening candidates for admission, college officials should take the position that the existence of an arrest or conviction record for civil rights and other political activities is irrelevant to the question of admission. However, even where the practice is to take cognizance of such records, this inclusion should not be permitted to affect adversely the student's chances of admission.

"When students run into police difficulties off the campus in connection with what they regard as their political rights—as, for example, taking part in sit-ins, picket lines, demonstrations, riding on freedom buses—the college authorities should take every practical step to assure themselves that such students are protected in their full legal rights, to wit: That they are given fair trials in a court of law where they are defended by counsel. That they are not abused by the police and that charges are brought against the police if the latter act wrongfully. That bail be sought and furnished. That they have speedy trials and that appeals be taken when necessary. Ideally, the college itself should provide such assistance. If this is not feasible, then the administration should permit and encourage individual faculty, student or alumni groups to render the help required.

"In order to protect the interests of students convicted for civil rights and other political activities, a college should separate the records of such convictions from other student records.   In other words, such records ought to be given a restricted status in order to obviate intentional or unintentional abuse.   In order further to protect the interests of students, an institution should not make the records in question available to prospective employers, graduate and professional schools, or government agencies, without the consent of students involved.

"Unless college authorities act in behalf of students, there is the very real danger of alienation: of the weakening of confidence in the university as a community and the resort by students to outside agencies—some of which may very well be self-serving—for support and defense.   College authorities have as much responsibility for maintaining that community—based upon mutual trust, respect, and forbearance—as do teachers and students.

"Both the United States Civil Service Commission and all similar state commissions require applicants to answer a question regarding arrests or convictions for any offense other than minor traffic violations.   Although we believe mere arrest records should not be used to penalize applicants, a student should answer such a question fully and accurately.   .   .   .

"C.   *Teacher Disclosure*

"Teachers who are asked to supply information to employers or prospective employers, governmental or private, about students or former students should be aware of the dangers to academic freedom inherent in this proliferating practice.   Since the best education calls for probing, sharing and hypothesizing, and for uninhibited expression and thinking out loud by the student, disclosure by the teacher to a source outside the college community of a student's expressed opinion, or the making of a statement based on such an opinion, becomes a threat to the educational process.   .   .   ."

FREEDOM OF MARRIAGE AND PARENTHOOD

BOARD OF EDUCATION OF HARRODSBURG v. BENTLEY

Court of Appeals of Kentucky, 1964.
383 S.W.2d 677.

DAVIS, Commissioner.   .   .   .   The Board of Education of Harrodsburg Independent School District (hereinafter designated as the Board) duly adopted the questioned resolution in 1957;   the text of the resolution is:

"Any student, either boy or girl, who marries, automatically must withdraw immediately from school and cannot re-enter school for one full year, and then only as a special student with permission of the principal. A special student cannot attend home room or study halls or enter into any class activities, social events or athletics. If, upon re-entering school after the year has elapsed, the student becomes pregnant, she will automatically withdraw until after the birth of the child." . . .

Appellee was a regularly enrolled student at Harrodsburg High School and a member of the junior class when she married April 10, 1964. The six-week term then current lacked one and a half weeks of completion. Appellee was permitted to remain as a student until the close of that six-week period; she was required to withdraw from school and dropped from its rolls April 24, 1964. . . .

It is recalled that the regulation in question provides for readmission of a married student after "one full year, and then only as a special student with permission of the principal." However, the record reflects that it has been the uniform policy in enforcement of the rule that the married student be permitted to complete the current six-week term. It was explained that the disruptive impact of student marriage is by reason of widespread student body discussion and excitement just prior to and just following the marriage. Apparently, the regulation as originally promulgated sought to alleviate the disruption generally said to be attendant at the time just before and just following the marriage. As noted, however, quite the opposite practice has been consistently followed. The pupil (including the present appellee) is allowed to remain actively in full school routine during the immediate time following the marriage—but no longer than the end of the then current six-week term. . . .

It is our conclusion that the decision of the trial court is correct; the instant regulation is arbitrary and unreasonable, and therefore void. The fatal vice of the regulation lies in its sweeping, advance determination that every married student, regardless of the circumstances, must lose at least a year's schooling. Moreover, the manner of enforcement of the regulation accentuates the fact that the regulation is not realistically related to its purported purpose. It is asserted for the Board that the most intense disruptive impact of a student marriage occurs during the time just preceding and just following the marriage. Yet, under the uniformly followed pattern of administration of this regulation, the married student is permitted to remain in school during all of the time preceding the marriage, and may remain for a maximum of six weeks thereafter. Such procedure, even though premised on the Board's commendable desire to permit the student to complete the current term, effectively frustrates the prime purpose of the regulation. Additionally, after it may be reasoned that the disturbing influence of the event has subsided, the situation is returned to the "spotlight" of student attendance by compelling withdrawal of the married student; after a year, assuming the principal is willing, the student is to be reinstated, thus injecting another occasion for student body agitation.

The regulation has a further inherent weakness in that it merely provides that a married student *may* be permitted to resume school if, but only if, the principal permits it. Of course, we will not assume that the principal would arbitrarily deny permission—but there is a complete absence of any standard or guideline for the principal; neither has the ousted student any gauge by which to estimate whether the principal's consent will be forthcoming after a year.

Implicit in this record is the desire of the Board to permit this appellee to "work something out" so that her education would not be interrupted. A review of the Board's minutes warrants the conclusion that the Board felt that its hands were tied—principally because it never had made any previous exception in such cases. The unreasonable and arbitrary effect of the regulation is thus demonstrated, since it imposes the identical result in every case, without regard to the circumstances of any case. The Board's discretion is foreclosed in advance, no matter what the facts. Such prejudgment is unreasonable and arbitrary.

We are not to be understood here as deciding that some reasonable and appropriate regulation in this area may not be adopted; we do hold the instant regulation invalid. . . .

STATE EX REL. BAKER v. STEVENSON

Court of Common Pleas of Ohio, 1962.
189 N.E.2d 181.

CRAMER, Judge.   Relator, a student in the senior class at Taft High School, Hamilton, Ohio, brings this action in mandamus to compel the respondents herein—Board of Education and Superintendent of Schools of the City of Hamilton, Ohio—to allow him, though married, to engage in extracurricular activities at the Taft High School.

Said relator, now seventeen years of age, became married at the age of sixteen in February, 1962. His wife, now age 17, also a student at Taft High School was pregnant at the time of her marriage and aged 16 years.

. . .   The relator herein, as a sophomore and junior was extremely active in a number of extracurricular activities, athletic and non-athletic alike. He was co-captain and an outstanding member of Taft High School basketball team last school year which won the State championship. He is an above average student, popular and well liked by his fellow students and teachers and has never been a disciplinary problem.

In May, 1962, the Respondent Board of Education of the City of Hamilton adopted what it termed a "Code of Ethics", governing the pupils of the schools under its supervision and control. This Code, also came as a product of the recommendations of a committee composed of a number of people in the community. They represented and are identified with various groups and agencies and included school teachers, principals and school administrators.

The organization of this committee came as a result of what was considered to be a "moral problem existing in the community"—particularly as it appeared in the high schools of the City of Hamilton. Various groups, parents, leaders of youth activities and organizations, P.T.A.s, civic and other organizations through their representatives, brought this matter to the Board's attention and requested the adoption of rules and regulations—a code of ethics—governing the conduct of pupils of and in the schools. . . .

The rule and regulation included within this "Code" with which we are here concerned is as follows:

"That married students in the Hamilton schools will not be permitted to participate in extra-curricular activities, effective as of the opening of the 1962–63 school year."

Extra-curricular activities are listed as including but not limited to the following:

(1) Leadership in school organizations or activities;

(2) Athletic activities;

(3) Scholarship activities;

(4) Member of band and glee club;

(5) Social events;

(6) Dramatic events and musical activities;

(7) Cheerleader;

(8) School sponsored trips.

The foregoing rule was adopted by the respondents herein. . . .

This particular rule is being attacked as arbitrary, unreasonable, and discriminatory as applied to relator; also as violative of public policy in that it penalizes marriage and, therefore, is void. . . .

Boards of education, rather than courts, are charged with the important and difficult duty of operating the public schools. So, it is not a question of whether this or that individual judge or court considers a given rule adopted by a board as expedient. The court's duty, regardless of its personal views, is to uphold the Board's regulation unless it is generally viewed as being arbitrary and unreasonable. Any other policy would result in confusion detrimental to the progress and efficiency of our public school system. . . .

We approach a consideration of the reasonableness and propriety of the rule under attack without any desire nor will we act as a super board of education and we have no right to substitute our judgment for that of the Board's. Our task is limited to a determination of whether, under the circumstances disclosed by the evidence, the action of the Respondent Board was unreasonable, arbitrary and constituted an abuse of discretion.

The presumption is always in favor of the reasonableness and propriety of any such rule duly adopted.

The burden, of course, is on the relator to prove, before he is entitled to the relief sought, that the complained of rule is unreasonable, arbitrary or violative of public policy.

Has such burden been discharged by him?

It clearly appears from the evidence that the Board, in adopting this particular rule, was motivated primarily by the desire to discourage juvenile marriages because such marriages result in student "drop outs."

The record here shows the following respecting the number of marriages in the two senior high schools in the City of Hamilton together with a number of married students who dropped out of school for the school years 1959–1960; 1960–1961; 1961–1962 and 1962–1963 (to date):

       1959–60, number of marriages, 42; drop outs, 41;
       1960–61, number of marriages, 53; drop outs, 50;
       1961–62, number of marriages, 53; drop outs, 51;
       1962–63, number of marriages, 52; drop outs, 41:

The number of students presently in both these senior high schools is approximately 2370.

It is thus seen that the number of married students who drop out of school is exceedingly high.

The Respondent Board, before adopting the rule here in question, was duly apprised, of course, of this situation. It was the Board's position—amply supported by the opinions expressed by those skilled in such matters who appeared before it, such as teachers, school principals, administrators and student and youth counselors, that those who dropped out of school seriously handicapped their future.

It took due notice of the fact that in our society today the boy or girl who is not a senior high school graduate suffers great disadvantages; that many will find that the only employment open to them is the "dead end job"; and they will be seriously limited in not only earning a livelihood but in making effective use of their full capacities; and are precluded from ever receiving a college education which today employers are insisting upon more and more.

The Respondent Board conceived it to be its duty to the pupils under its supervision and control to encourage them in every conceivable way, in the best interests of the students and our nation, to receive all that which a completed senior high school education admittedly furnishes them. . . .

It is a matter of common knowledge that the student who excels in athletics sets a pattern of conduct which his associates in the school are proud to follow. The "hero", in the eyes of his followers, "can do no wrong".

Our own observations and what we learn from the newspapers, student publications, books, magazines, movies, television and radio, convince us as to the truth of the foregoing. We have all witnessed the effect upon the entire student body caused when the "star" football or basketball player decides to adopt a manner of speech, type of haircut, wear a particular kind of clothing, eat a particular kind of food, expresses a preference for a definite song, singer, playing record, actor or performer and ad infinitum.

It is also a matter of common knowledge that a great segment of our adult population has likewise succumbed to the worship of the athlete. Many times the high school students have difficulty in securing seats at athletic contests because the adults have pre-empted their places.

Untold thousands upon thousands of dollars have been reaped by manufacturers from the sale of razor blades, lotions, hair tonic and creams, cigarettes and many, many other items made popular merely because used and consumed by Mickey Mantle, Frankie Robinson (we have yet to hear from Jerry Lucas), Oscar Robertson, Sam Snead, et al.

How much more susceptible, therefore, the high school student to the athletic "star".

Students today are, of course, more ready to accept the actions of their peers as the thing to do. If any married students are in a position of idolization, the more desirous is the group to mimic.

It is likewise apparent that the Board felt and took into consideration that married students need all the extra time available to provide a proper family life, and time spent in extra-curricular activities many times, is not conducive to this end.

Here, the evidence shows that relator, now that he is married and a father and expected to provide support for his wife and child is employed after school hours earning Twenty Dollars per week. Would not the required and regular basketball practice which takes place after school seriously interfere with his employment? Would not attendance at extra-curricular club meetings and affairs create a problem affecting his and his wife's family and home life?

While the school authorities discourage marriage by the high school student, once it occurs and the married student remains in school, the Board ought to be permitted to restrict the extra-curricular activities of such a student so as to prevent the marriage from being subjected to burdens additional to that of the youthfulness of the husband or wife. Should not the Board, in respect to such marriages, adopt such rules which, in its judgment, would be best designed and conducive to the preservation of the marriage? Can it be said that if a Board of Education, in the adoption of such rules, has such an objective in mind, it abuses its discretion? We think not.

In our opinion, it cannot be successfully claimed that the Respondent Board was unreasonable or arbitrary or abused its discretion, in concluding as it has, that marriage by the high school student causes the student to quit or drop out of school; nor in concluding that the married student engaging in extra-curricular activities sets a pattern which his or her fellow students follow; nor in concluding that participation by such a student in extra-curricular activities might interfere with and seriously affect that student's responsibilities as a husband and father; nor in concluding that the marriage has a better chance of lasting where interests of the husband or wife outside of and not connected with the home or marriage as such, are kept to a minimum. . . .

It remains for us now to determine whether the adoption of the rule here in question is violative of public policy in that it penalizes persons because of marriage.

It is indeed the policy of the law to look with favor upon marriage and to seek in all lawful ways to uphold this most vital social institution; every intendment being in favor of matrimony.

This policy, however, is referable to those of lawful age who enter into the marriage relationship (male, 18; female, 16 . . .). On the other hand, the legislative policy is otherwise in so far as an underage marriage is concerned. Marriages entered into by a male under the age of eighteen is prohibited by statute except in the instance which here took place. Under such circumstances, the consent of the juvenile judge must first be obtained. . . .

It thus appears that in this state it is clear that the public policy is not favorable to and in discouragement of "underage applicants" for matrimony.

The experience we gained, sitting as a trial judge in the divorce court in this county over a span of approximately eighteen years, reveals, at least to us, all too clearly the need to discourage those of immature years from entering into the marriage relationship. The life expectancy of such marriages is short indeed—the mortality rate thereof alarmingly high.

Any policy which is directed toward making juvenile marriages unpopular and to be avoided should have the general public's wholehearted approval and support. The school authorities, under whose supervision and control come the high school students, cannot be charged with abusing their discretion in promulgating rules which tend to make such marriages unpopular.

Is the rule void because it is retroactive in its effect on relator, since he was married prior to its adoption?

The evidence discloses that relator, by reasons of his high proficiency as a basketball player, has a college athletic scholarship potential. It is suggested that such potential is in danger unless he would be permitted to play basketball this, his last year in high school. It doesn't necessarily follow that his abstention from play during his senior year would diminish his athletic scholarship prospects. He might be injured during play this year; his responsibilities as a father and concern therefor might adversely affect his performance on the court; other things might occur in connection with his playing basketball which could easily affect, even destroy, his future as a college player, thus preventing his receipt of an athletic scholarship.

However, assuming that there would be such diminution of his prospects, this rule cannot be said to be retroactive and, therefore, in violation of law, because its application takes no vested right away from relator.

That which he contends for amounts to no more than a contingent or expectant right in contrast to a vested right which is an immediate, fixed right of present future enjoyment. . . .

It is, therefore, our opinion that this rule is not violative of the Constitution, State or Federal, because retroactive in its effect on relator.

Our attention has been called to an opinion of the Attorney General of Ohio on this subject being Opinion No. 2998, rendered May 15, 1962. It was his opinion that a board of education may not lawfully adopt a regulation prohibiting married students from participation in extra-curricular activities promoted by the school as a part of the regular school program. He made the observation that extracurricular activities "have become an integral part of contemporary education."

Even though the Attorney General states that "to deprive a student from participating in such activities (extra-curricular) for the dubious purpose of punishing marriage would amount to an abuse of discretion," it is apparent that he viewed the regulation under consideration as unwise and condemned it for that reason.

He thereby invaded a field of inquiry (the wisdom or unwisdom of the legislative act) denied, by law, both to him and this Court.

He apparently also found that the regulation was designed to "punish marriages." Such a motive is entirely absent here.

It is inconceivable to us, as it apparently was to the school experts who testified here,—and certainly a School Board does not abuse its discretion in not concluding—that, an athletic activity restricted to and participated in by but a mere "handful" of pupils (out of some 2370) as contrasted with a program of intramural athletics or physical education in which all students participate, regardless of their height, weight, ability to coordinate, agility or lack of either, is "an integral part of contemporary education", though very popular with and approved by school authorities, students and the public.

A board of education must not permit, as is evident in this instance this Board did not permit, its judgment as to what is beneficial or what is detrimental to the high school student, whose welfare and education have been entrusted to it by law, to be affected by the unrestrained enthusiasm of the adult population for athletic contests, events and those who excel in such sports, the "cheers" and sometimes the "boos" emanating from the high school stadium and gymnasium or the revenue derived from the turnstiles.   .   .   .

We find that the relator has failed to sustain this burden of showing that he has a clear right to the relief he seeks and that the writ of mandamus should be denied.   .   .   .

NOTES AND QUESTIONS

1. Do you agree with the decision and reasoning in these cases? Why or why not? Is the reasoning consistent in these cases?

2. Would the court have allowed the student to participate in extra-curricular activities if he had not been a "hero" or "star", but just another ordinary student without possibility of serving as a "model"?

3. Would this decision have been different if the state's compulsory education statutes expressly applied to married students? Should it? Why or why not?

4. Do you agree that by prohibiting married students from participating in extra-curricular activities school boards thereby deter student marriages?

5. Could the student have been dismissed from school? Does the reasoning of the court in this case apply to curricular as well as to non-curricular activities?

6. Would this decision have been different if the state's compulsory education law specifically applied to married students and broadly defined "curriculum" as "all activities and programs approved by the board of education"? Does this case present a question of "equal protection of the laws" under the Fourteenth Amendment?

CARROLLTON–FARMERS BRANCH INDEPENDENT SCHOOL DISTRICT v. KNIGHT

Court of Civil Appeals of Texas, 1967.
418 S.W.2d 535, ref. n. r. e.

FANNING, Justice. On January 13, 1967, Sallye Anne Thompson and Tex Lloyd Knight were married under a valid marriage license. Sallye Anne, a female, eighteen years of age, was under the laws of

Texas authorized to marry; Tex Lloyd Knight, a male, seventeen years of age, and having the required statutory parental consent to obtain a marriage license, was also duly authorized to marry. Such marriage was in all respects a valid and lawful marriage under the laws of Texas.

At said time Sallye Anne and Tex were students at R. L. Turner High School, which high school was under the jurisdiction of appellant school district.

On January 16, 1967, Sallye Anne and Tex were suspended from school because of their marriage on January 13, 1967, based upon certain regulations of the school board.

On January 18, 1967, the judge of the 68th District Court issued a temporary restraining order directed to appellant school district and the President of its Board of Trustees, permitting appellees Sallye Anne Thompson Knight and Tex Lloyd Knight to attend school for *scholastic purposes only.* . . .

The principal question involved here is whether the trial court did or did not abuse its discretion in granting the temporary injunction under the record in this case. Involved here is the question of whether marriage alone is sufficient grounds to suspend appellee students from attendance at a public free school in Texas, for scholastic purposes only, wherein appellee students were unquestionably carried as lawful scholastics for which the State of Texas had furnished funds in accordance with the laws of Texas. . . .

In Bd. of Education of Harrodsburg, Kentucky v. Bentley, 383 S.W.2d 677, . . . a student was required to withdraw from school for a year because of marriage. The court held the regulation was invalid and stated:

> "In 47 Am.Jur., Schools, § 155, it is said:
>
>> " 'However, a pupil may not be excluded from school because married, where no immorality or misconduct of the pupil is shown, nor that the welfare and discipline of the pupils of the school is injuriously affected by the presence of the married pupil.' " . . .

One of the first Texas cases dealing with married students was the case of Kissick v. Garland Independent School Dist., Tex.Civ.App., 330 S.W.2d 708 . . . (1959). This case involved the marriage of a sixteen year old boy and a fifteen year old girl. After his marriage Kissick was barred from further participation in athletic activities, but was allowed to continue his classroom work, pursuant to a regulation which provided that "married students or previously married students be restricted wholly to classroom work; that they be barred from participating in athletics or other exhibitions, and that they not be permitted to hold class offices or other positions of honor." The Dallas Court of Civil Appeals held that such regulation was reasonable in that the student was allowed to continue his classroom work.   Although the court in the Kissick case did not deal directly with complete suspension from school due to marriage, it said by way of dicta:

> "Apart from these considerations Jerry Kissick, Jr., had a *constitutional right* to attend the Garland School and take part in its functions subject to such reasonable rules and regulations as might be adopted by the School Board from time to time."   (Emphasis added.)   .   .   .

The latest Texas case dealing with aspects of the question here involved is Anderson v. Canyon Independent School Dist., by the Amarillo Court of Civil Appeals, Tex.Civ.App., 412 S.W.2d 387, no writ (1967), majority opinion by Chief Justice Denton, with Justice Northcutt dissenting.   The majority opinion held that the school board was without authority to adopt a rule that students who marry during the school term must withdraw from school for the remainder of the school year and that the board could not deny admission to the student because of the fact that she was married.   .   .   .

.   .   .   .   appellees were lawfully enrolled scholastics in R. L. Turner High School in appellant school district and possessed all the statutory requirements to attend said school as scholastics.   Their marriage was in all respects a legal marriage under the laws of Texas and such marriage being in all respects proper, legal and in compliance with the statutes of Texas could not be considered in any way to be against the public policy of the State of Texas.   The girl was 18 years of age and was of lawful age to marry; the boy was 17 years of age, and had the required statutory parental consent to marry and secure a valid marriage license.

There was no evidence that either of appellees were guilty of any "incorrigible" or improper conduct in any manner.   They were suspended from school merely because they married while being students at said school.

We think the weight of authority in Texas and in the United States is to the effect that marriage alone is not a proper ground for a school district to suspend a student from attending school for scholastic purposes only.

We hold that the trial court did not abuse its discretion in granting the temporary injunction against the appellant under the record in this cause.   All of appellant's points have been considered and are overruled.   .   .   .

DISQUALIFICATION

DAVIS, Justice.   The writer honestly feels that he should disqualify himself from the decision in the above and foregoing case for the following reasons:

.   I was one of seven children of tenant farmers.   My Mother passed away when I was only nine years of age.   It was always her ambition, and it became mine, to get an education and become a lawyer. I finshed Glenwood, unaffiliated, High School when I was 18 years old. I tried to enter college, but, met with two most embarrassing situations, and could not do so. I worked as a common laborer. Finally, I decided to get married, accumulate enough wealth to attend college, get a law degree and pursue my profession. I married on October 26, 1929. The Crash of 1929 was really felt in 1930. I was a tenant farmer and, although I was plagued with my difficulties, I managed to hold my own.

When I decided it was impossible for me to attend college, I decided to get my law degree by home study. I traded two "frying size chickens and a mess of turnip greens" for my first lawbook.

The only law that I know is what I have read from the lawbooks at home (many nights I have studied all night without any sleep), and have gained from experience. In 1934, I notified the Board of Legal Examiners that I was ready to take the examination for a license. In return, I was notified that I would have to finish an "AFFILIATED HIGH SCHOOL DIPLOMA", file an application, and then wait 27 months before I would be permitted to take the Bar Exams. No one can imagine the depressed feeling that was brought upon me. I was married, then the father of two children, and was too poor to think about going to school. After much serious consideration, and a talk with Superintendent Henry McClelland and Principal John W. Avery of the Gilmer Affiliated High School, I decided to make the race for Justice of the Peace. While serving as Justice of the Peace, I would get an affiliated high school diploma. To my surprise, they told me that I could attend the school without any payment of tuition whatever, if I had the ambition and the "Guts" to do it. I made the race and was elected. I entered Gilmer High School in the fall of 1935 and received my AFFILIATED HIGH SCHOOL DIPLOMA on June 1, 1936, at which time I was 27 years old, the father of three children and had another one on the way. I did not receive my license to practice law until April 29, 1940, at which time I was 31 years old.

I have always been taught that the best education that you can get, the better off you will be. To me, there is nothing immoral, wrong, or degrading about a legal and moral marriage. Of course, no one approves of the marriage of teen-agers, unless there is a good reason. My wife and I were teen-agers when we married. The school trustees of the Gilmer Affiliated Independent School District were so proud of the fact that I was attending the school because of my ambition that they did not charge any tuition. I was permitted the same privileges that were permitted all other school children. In the beginning, it was an awful experience. To me, any Board of Trustees who would do anything to punish or delay anyone that does not do anything that is morally wrong is not thinking in the terms of the Gospel.

As a result of my being permitted to attend High School, after I was married, I have served one term in the Texas Legislature, and I am now serving my third term on the Court of Civil Appeals. Although, I am not a perfect man, I am quite proud of the experience that I have had, and am still married to a wonderful woman and we have four children of whom we are justly proud.

Where would I be today if I had not been permitted to attend a high school because of my marriage? For this reason, I disqualify myself.

PERRY v. GRENADA MUNICIPAL SEPARATE SCHOOL DIST.

United States District Court, N.D.Miss., 1969.
300 F.Supp. 748.

ORMA R. SMITH, District Judge. On September 18, 1967, Clydie Marie Perry filed a complaint in the case sub judice seeking a preliminary and permanent injunction compelling the school district to admit her to the public schools of Grenada, Mississippi. The population of Grenada County, where the municipality of Grenada is located, is approximately 18,733 people. The plaintiff brought the action on behalf of all unwed mothers of school age residing in Grenada County who are affected by the policy of the school board of denying admission to unwed mothers. On November 30, 1967, an amended complaint was filed, adding another unwed mother, Emma Jean Wilson, as a party plaintiff. . . .

There are three issues before the Court: . . .

3) Whether the policy of the school board in excluding unwed mothers violates the Due Process Clause or the Equal Protection Clause of the Fourteenth Amendment of the Constitution. . . .

The crux of this cause is whether the policy of the school board of denying admission to unwed mothers violates the Equal Protection Clause of the Fourteenth Amendment of the Constitution. The case does not involve the curtailment of first amendment rights which has produced much litigation in recent years. . . . Neither does it fall within the ambit of cases involving whether a student received due process of law before being expelled from a school or university. . . . The case sub judice falls within the category of cases involving whether there is invidious discrimination which violates the Equal Protection Clause of the Fourteenth Amendment.

The standards of the Equal Protection Clause are broad; the generalities of the subject are not in dispute; the application of the Equal Protection Clause turns peculiarly on the particular circumstances of each case. . . . The Equal Protection Clause does not force the laws of each state in the Union into the same mold. A state may classify people but the classification must have some purpose and must not contain the kind of discrimination against which the Equal Protection Clause affords protection, . . . "Equal protection of the laws is something more than an abstract right." It is a command which the state must respect, the benefits of which every person may demand. Not the least merit of our constitutional system is that its safeguards extend to all—the least deserving as well as the most virtuous." . . .

The Supreme Court has laid down certain rules to test invidious discrimination:

> "The rules for testing a discrimination have been summarized as follows: 1. The equal protection clause of the Fourteenth Amendment does not take from the State the power to classify in the adoption of police laws, but admits of the exercise of a wide scope of discretion in that regard, and avoids what is done only when it is without any reasonable basis and therefore is purely arbitrary. 2. A classification having some reasonable basis does not offend against that clause merely because it is not made with mathematical nicety or because in practice it results in some inequality. 3. When the classification in such a law is called in question, if any state of facts reasonably can be conceived that would sustain it, the existence of that state of facts at the time the law was enacted must be assumed. 4. One who assails the classification in such a law must carry the burden of showing that it does not rest upon any reasonable basis, but is essentially arbitrary. . . .

> "To these rules we add the caution that 'Discriminations of an unusual character especially suggests careful consideration to determine whether they are obnoxious to the constitutional provision.' . . ." . . .

In the present age of enlightenment no one can deny the importance of education to our youth. As was stated in the Dixon case: "It requires no argument to demonstrate that education is vital and, indeed, basic to civilized society. Without sufficient education the plaintiffs would not be able to earn an adequate livelihood, to enjoy life to the fullest, or to fulfill as completely as possible the duties and responsibilities of good citizens." Dixon v. Alabama State Bd. of Education, 294 F.2d at 157.

The plaintiffs have introduced evidence which tends to show that unwed mothers, who are allowed to continue their education, are less likely to have a second illegitimate child. In effect the opportunity to pursue their education gives them a hope for the future so that they are less likely to fall into the snare of repeat illegitimate births. On the other hand the Court is aware of the defendants' fear that the presence of unwed mothers in the schools will be a bad influence on the other students vis-a-vis their presence indicating society's approval or acquiescence in the illegitimate births or vis-a-vis the association of the unwed mother with the other students.

The Court can understand and appreciate the effect which the presence of an unwed pregnant girl may have on other students in a school. Yet after the girl has the baby and has the opportunity to realize her wrong and rehabilitate herself, it seems patently unreasonable that she should not have the opportunity to go before some administrative body of the school and seek readmission on the basis of her changed moral and physical condition. Certainly this would be the cause if a girl had been raped and forced to bear the child of another.

Certainly school officials recognize the importance of education and the effect of a rigid rule which forever bars an individual from obtaining an education. The Court can appreciate that the Grenada School District might not have the funds to set up separate facilities for the education of pregnant girls. The purpose of excluding such girls is practical and apparent. But after the girl has the child, she should have the opportunity for applying for readmission and demonstrating to the school that she is qualified to continue her education. The continued exclusion of a girl without a hearing or some other opportunity to demonstrate her qualification for readmission serves no useful purpose and works an obvious hardship on the individual. It is arbitrary in that the individual is forever barred from seeking a high school education. Without a high school education, the individual is ill equipped for life, and is prevented from seeking higher education.

The Court would like to make manifestly clear that lack of moral character is certainly a reason for excluding a child from public education. But the fact that a girl has one child out of wedlock does not forever brand her as a scarlet woman undeserving of any chance for rehabilitation or the opportunity for future education. . . . the school is free to take reasonable and adequate steps to determine the moral character of a girl before she is readmitted to the school. If the board is convinced that a girl's presence will taint the education of the other students, then exclusion is justified. Nevertheless, the inquiry should be thorough and weighed in keeping with the serious consequences of preventing an individual from attaining a high school education.

In sum, the Court holds that plaintiffs may not be excluded from the schools of the district for the sole reason that they are unwed mothers; and that plaintiffs are entitled to readmission unless on a fair hearing before the school authorities they are found to be so lacking in moral character that their presence in the schools will taint the education of other students. . . .

CONFIDENTIALITY OF STUDENT RECORDS

ELDER v. ANDERSON

California District Court of Appeal, 1962.
205 Cal.App.2d 326, 23 Cal.Rptr. 48.

BROWN, Justice.   This action was brought by plaintiff's mother, Laura M. Elder, as guardian ad litem for her 17 year old son, for claimed damages from an alleged libelous statement made by five defendants who were all of the duly elected trustees of the Caruthers Union High School District, and defendant Harry R. Anderson, who was the superintendent and an employee of said district.   Said defendants were not named in their official capacities.   The alleged libel is part of an extensive Special Announcement mailed to many members of the general public within the boundaries of the school district.   The portion of the Announcement concerned and pleaded in the complaint is as follows:

> "At a special public meeting to be held Tuesday, November 24, 1959, in the Caruthers High School Gymnasium at 7:30 p. m. the Caruthers High School Board of Trustees, the administration, teachers and sponsors of the Los Angeles Band trip will bring the public in full focus of the serious violation of manners, morals and discipline that occurred in Los Angeles as the direct result of interference by the Elder and Fries boys who are now suspended from school."

However, although not complained of, the announcement continued:

> "These boys were not members of the Band, but were in Los Angeles on their own.   This is the issue that brought on this development; therefore, the full details will be open for all the public to hear and any other matter will be heard at this time, if desired."

The pretrial conference order stated that Harry Anderson was the superintendent and employee of the school district; that the other five defendants were the duly elected trustees of the school district; that the five trustees prepared the entire Special Announcement hereinabove referred to and mailed copies thereof to many members of the general public within the boundaries of the high school district; and that the said alleged libelous statement is contained in said Special Announcement.

Subsequently, the defendants filed a motion to dismiss plaintifff's complaint on the ground that said complaint was beyond the jurisdiction of the superior court, being barred by the doctrine of civil immunity.   .   .   .

Plaintiff claims that the doctrine of civil immunity does not apply to public officials if they are performing ministerial acts as opposed to discretionary acts, or if their acts are not within the course and scope of their authority.

Education Code, section 10751, specifically provides:

"No teacher, principal, employee, or governing board member of any public, private, or parochial school *shall give out any personal information concerning any particular minor pupil* enrolled in the school in any class of the twelfth grade or below or in the thirteenth or fourteenth grades of a public junior college to any person except under judicial process unless the person is one of the following:

"(a) A parent or guardian of such pupil.

"(b) A person designated by such parent or guardian in writing.

"(c) An officer or employee of a public, private, or parochial school where the pupil attends, has attended, or intends to enroll.

"(d) An officer or employee of the United States, the State of California, or a city, city and county, or county seeking information in the course of his duties.

"(e) An officer or employee of a public or private guidance or welfare agency of which the pupil is a client.

"Restrictions imposed by this act are not intended to interfere with the giving of information by school personnel concerning participation in athletics and other school activities, the winning of scholastic or other honors and awards, and other like information. Notwithstanding the restrictions imposed by this section, an employer or potential employer of the pupil may be furnished the age and scholastic record of the pupil and employment recommendations prepared by members of the school staff, and rosters or lists containing the names and addresses of seniors in public, private, or parochial high schools or junior colleges may be furnished to private business or professional schools and colleges." (Italics added.)

This section requires strict interpretation. It indicates by the exceptions that the legislative intent was to permit only the giving of personal information concerning the pupils involved in the participation of athletics and school activities, the winning of honors and awards and other similar information. It also permits the giving of personal information concerning the age and scholastic records of a pupil and lists of names and addresses of seniors in high schools to private business or professional schools and colleges. Thus, under no circumstances is any information to be given out by the school or its officials for any other purposes, whether beneficial or detrimental, except when waived in a public hearing under section 986 of the Education Code.

Plaintiff admits that the school board has the right and the discretion to determine whether or not to send out notices calling public meetings and also to send out announcements concerning activities of the school board, but that to insert such personal information in the announcements is an express violation of section 10751 of the Education Code.

Discretionary acts are those wherein there is no hard and fast rule as to the course of conduct that one must or must not take and, if there is a clearly defined rule, such would eliminate discretion.
. . .

. . . it is the plaintiff's contention that all matters in which discretion is not allowed are ministerial acts; that the prohibition expressed in section 10751 of the Education Code constitutes a mandatory, hard and fast rule; and that violation of that section eliminates the doctrine of sovereign immunity as far as the defendant trustees are concerned. With this we agree. . . .

In Lipman v. Brisbane Elementary School Dist., . . . 359 P.2d 465, the school trustees, outside of a meeting, made certain disparaging remarks concerning the superintendent of schools to members of the public. Such remarks were that the superintendent was dictatorial, operated a rubber stamp board, was overpaid, suppressed facts from the board, tampered with minutes of the meetings, received kickbacks from district employees, engaged in shady dealings and cleaned up on business transactions. The court said, . . .

"The statements allegedly made to the press and to members of the public were not confined to reports of charges that were being made; they purported to be statements of fact and were beyond the scope of the trustees' powers. In making these statements the three trustees were not within the immunity rule, and a cause of action is stated against them. The case of Hardy v. Vial, 48 Cal.2d 577, 311 P.2d 494, 66 A.L.R.2d 739, relied upon by defendants, is distinguishable because the school defendants involved there did not make statements to the public but only to three nonschool persons who filed false charges against the plaintiff with an appropriate administrative body in carrying out an alleged conspiracy with the officials. * * * They cannot claim immunity insofar as they made or caused to be made defamatory statements concerning plaintiff to members of the public which were not merely reports of official action but instead purported to be statements of fact within their personal knowledge."

The Lipman case . . . states that the school district, itself, is immune from "tort liability for the alleged acts of the trustees within the scope of their authority, and familiar principles of agency preclude its liability for acts outside the scope of their authority."

. . .

Was the Conduct of the Defendants
Beyond the Course and Scope
of Their Authority?

School boards have only such authority as is specifically granted by the Legislature, to be exercised in the mode and within the limits permitted by the statute. . . .

We think it is clear that no immunity exists for discretionary acts if the acts complained of are beyond the course and scope of the duties of the school trustees. . . .

The Special Announcement does not imply that the plaintiff was being charged with certain indiscretions, but states as a pure matter of fact that the plaintiff minor was involved in "serious violations of manners, morals and discipline that occurred in Los Angeles as the direct result of interference by the Elder [plaintiff] and Fries boys who are now suspended from school."

It is certainly true that governmental officials are not personally liable for discretionary acts within the course and scope of their authority, but, as the Lipman case provides . . .   " * * * this rule applies not only to acts essential to the accomplishment of the main purposes for which the office was created but also to acts which, although only incidental and collateral, serve to promote those purposes." We admit that the case before us may be an important one to all public officials. It is true that official bodies should obtain and retain outstanding citizens to hold public office, even though the positions may not have a great deal of monetary compensation but only the reward of public service. We borrow some of the language of Judge Learned Hand, stated in Gregoire v. Biddle, 2 Cir., 177 F.2d 579, 581. To subject citizens serving as public officers to suit and trial in every instance in which their good faith but mistaken actions caused injury to another "would dampen the ardor of all but the most resolute, or the most irresponsible, in the unflinching discharge of their duties." But here we find more than a good faith mistaken action. In this case defendants trustees violated a code section prohibiting dissemination of personal information concerning pupils, and thus stepped outside the protection of their office. . . .

We cannot tell from the general allegations in the complaint just exactly what Harry R. Anderson, as the superintendent of the school district, is alleged to have done, other than that generally alleged against all the other defendants. According to the Lipman case, supra, . . . Anderson cannot claim immunity insofar as he may have made or caused to be made defamatory statements concerning the plaintiff to members of the general public which were not merely reports of official action but instead, purported to be statements of fact within his personal knowledge. . . .

NOTES AND QUESTIONS

1. What is a discretionary act? A ministerial act? Which was involved in this case? What role did California's statute play in determining whether the act was ministerial or discretionary? Why did the statute require "strict interpretation"?

2. The court says that a violation of § 10751 "eliminates the doctrine of sovereign immunity as far as the defendant trustees are concerned." What is the "doctrine of sovereign immunity?" What would have been the result in this case if the doctrine of sovereign immunity had not been "eliminated"? What will "eliminate" that doctrine?

3. The court states "that governmental officials are not personally liable for discretionary acts within the course and scope of their authority." How can a school board official tell whether his actions are "within the course and scope of his authority"?

4. The court refused to dismiss plaintiff's complaint; what, normally, would be the next step in this case? What factors will be relevant when deciding whether Superintendent Anderson will be allowed to claim immunity? Will any of his, or the board's, statements be immune? Should they be? Why or why not? Could this law suit have been brought against a teacher if he had uttered the identical words to his class or to members of the community?

5. Assuming that plaintiffs prevail at trial, will the school district be obligated to pay the judgment? If not, who will be obligated to pay?

6. What would have been the decision in the following case, Marmo, if it had been decided in California in accordance with the principles of Elder v. Anderson?

MARMO v. NEW YORK CITY BD. OF EDUCATION

New York Supreme Court, 1968.
56 Misc.2d 517, 289 N.Y.S.2d 51.

BENJAMIN BRENNER, Justice. This is a proceeding, in the nature of mandamus, in which the petitioner seeks to compel the Board of Education to allow him to inspect the names and addresses of students who were in a particular class with him at Grover Cleveland High School in the academic year 1963–64, for the purpose of allowing him to prepare a defense in a pending criminal action.

The Board opposes on the grounds that such lists are privileged and confidential, and that an administrative ruling contained in the Board's Manual of School Office Procedures and Practices states:

"No information may be given to private detectives, solicitors, collectors or investigators for mercantile agencies, and the like, seeking to trace families through the medium of school records.   *   *   *   In cases where persons seek to trace families for personal reasons or where insurance agents are trying to prevent lapse of policy, the principal may authorize the mailing of a letter to the last known address of the family."

At common law the right to inspect records of a public nature, not detrimental to the public interest, exists as to persons who have sufficient interest in the subject matter.   .   .   .   It has even been held that one's interest in public records need not be of personal concern.   .   .   .   In certain instances, however, the policy of free inspection may be superseded by statute or otherwise to preserve the confidentiality of the records sought to be inspected where confidentiality weighs more heavily in the public interest than the right to inspect   .   .   .   .

Section 51 of the General Municipal Law provides for taxpayers' actions against and inspection of public records of subdivisions of the State.   In 1951 the Court of Appeals held that school districts were not within the purview of the section.   .   .   .   In 1962 the Section was amended to extend the right of inspection to the records of other "bodies corporate" possessing certain powers.   .   .   .   It is not clear whether the amendment effectively granted the right of inspection of school records, and thus the question remains whether petitioner's interest in the subject matter is sufficient under common-law rules to establish his right to the inspection   .   .

It should be observed that we are dealing with a record that may be helpful in defense of a criminal prosecution.   Thus, in Matter of Werfel v. Fitzgerald (supra), the Appellate Division, Second Department, said, with reference to the inspection of a record in a criminal proceeding by one not a party to the proceeding   .   .   . :

> "Indeed, as already noted, in the one specific instance which the petitioner alleges in his petition, the paper desired was a docket book which contained an entry of importance to a client represented by the petitioner—an address of a witness whose testimony would assist in the client's defense. Based on this allegation, we think that for a reason apart from the general right to inspect public records, the petitioner was entitled to examine the docket book. *Where the defense of a person accused of a crime requires access to public records or even to records sealed from general examination, the right of inspection has a greater sanction and must be enforced   .   .   .* "   (emphasis supplied).

It would seem, therefore, that in the case at hand the right of inspection to prepare a defense in a criminal prosecution has greater sanction than the right to close the record, based on the claim of confidentiality asserted by the Board of Education. I must add that the policy of the Board of Education as enunciated in the administrative ruling quoted is sound and ordinarily should be given sanction, even if it defeat the common-law right to inspect. However, that policy must yield in situations where, as here, an individual wishes a limited inspection of a specific class roll to obtain the name and address of a fellow classmate to assist him in defending a criminal indictment. Accordingly, petitioner's motion is granted.

NOTES AND QUESTIONS

1. Did the court follow the rule of the Board of Education? If not, did the court hold the rule invalid? What is the difference between "the common law rule" and the rule of the Board?

2. If the court held the rule of the Board of Education valid, why didn't the court follow the rule? State several other exceptions to the rule that the court would uphold. Why?

3. What would have been the decision of the court if instead of names and addresses of students the request had been for the reports and records of the school counselor? Why?

EINHORN v. MAUS

Civ. A. No. 69–1403
United States District Court, E.D.Pa., 1969.
300 F.Supp. 1169.

KRAFT, District Judge. This is a civil rights action brought by twelve minor plaintiffs and their parents to enjoin the defendant school officials from placing any notation upon the school record of any student who distributed literature or wore an arm band bearing the legend "HUMANIZE EDUCATION" at the graduation ceremonies of Springfield Township Senior High School on June 5, 1969.

Plaintiffs also seek to restrain defendants from communicating to any school, college, university, institution of higher learning or employer the fact that any student wore such an arm band or distributed such literature at the graduation ceremonies or that such students ignored an order of the school authorities not to engage in such activities.

Now before us is plaintiffs' motion for a preliminary injunction. At the hearing, the parties stipulated that for the purposes of this motion, the facts alleged in plaintiffs' complaint were to be taken as true. The Court approves the stipulation and adopts the allegations of fact in the complaint as its findings of fact.

At the hearing, the parties further stipulated that the only communication intended to be transmitted by defendants to the colleges and universities at which the minor plaintiffs hope to matriculate, respectively, in the fall is as follows:

> This letter is submitted to supplement the information we have furnished concerning _____. He/she was one of 22 seniors who wore arm bands at our Commencement Exercises *bearing the legend "Humanize Education"* as an indication of his/her concern regarding certain aspects of our educational program.

> These students wore arm bands even though they had been requested not to wear any insignia which deviated from the formal graduation attire. There was no disorder at the Commencement Exercises.

Counsel for the plaintiffs, at the hearing, agreed, in response to a question from the Court, that, if the defendants simply communicated to any such school a true factual account of what occurred at the graduation exercises, without expression of opinion as to the lawfulness or propriety of the demonstration, no constitutional invasion of plaintiffs' rights would occur. The proposed letter, supra, was first exhibited to the plaintiffs and their counsel at the hearing.

Since this is a motion for preliminary injunction it is fundamental that plaintiffs, in order to prevail, must demonstrate the likelihood of immediate, irreparable harm flowing from the defendants' proposed conduct.

An expression of opinion by students through the medium of arm bands in an orderly demonstration is constitutionally protected and cannot be circumscribed. Tinker v. Des Moines Independent Community School District. . . . .

The students here demonstrated in an orderly manner and simply publicized their views upon the humanizing of education by wearing arm bands. No disciplinary action whatsoever was taken by the school officials against the students, although they had been instructed not to deviate from the formal graduation attire.

We perceive no threatened irreparable harm flowing from the proposed letter nor have the plaintiffs offered any evidence to demonstrate any likelihood thereof. School officials have the right and, we think, a duty to record and to communicate true factual information about their students to institutions of higher learning, for the purpose of giving to the latter an accurate and complete picture of applicants for admission.

The contention that the defendant school officials *may* attempt to prevent succeeding graduates from expressing their views in graduation exercises in June, 1970 or thereafter does not warrant a grant now of extraordinary relief by this Court in the form of a preliminary injunction, since the action of the school officials alleged by plaintiffs *to be anticipated* does not pose a threat of immediate irreparable harm. What future graduating students may do or refrain from doing neither the Court nor the defendant school officials can forecast. When such student action or inaction becomes reasonably determinable we think, in light of the present suit, that the school officials then in charge will be guided in their actions by Tinker v. Des Moines Independent Community School District, supra, and any relevant interim decisions. If they fail so to do a remedy is not lacking.

. . .

NOTES AND QUESTIONS

1. Do you agree with the reasons of court in this case? Can school officials place anything they want onto a student's record? If not, why not?

2. Do you think that private and, perhaps, public institutions of higher learning would tend to refuse admission to these plaintiffs because they are "troublemakers"? If so, why should a person be denied admission for exercising his constitutional rights? Could a state institution constitutionally deny admission on this ground? If not, of what value will this information be to the institution? How may it be used constitutionally?

3. Is there any way, at the time of this case, that plaintiffs could have met the requirement of the court and "offered any evidence to demonstrate any likelihood" of threatened irreparable harm because of the letter?

4. Will the practice of sending this letter deter other students in the future from exercising their First Amendment rights? If so, what overriding justification is presented by the school district? What did the court say?

5. Could the Board of Education refuse to have issued the students a diploma because of their actions?

6. Do these cases apply to teachers' employment files?

CORPORAL PUNISHMENT

WARE v. ESTES

United States District Court, 1972.
328 F.Supp. 657 (N.D.Tex.), aff'd 458 F.2d 1360, cert. den. 409 U.S. 1027.

WILLIAM M. TAYLOR, Jr., District Judge. In this suit the Court is called upon to resolve another conflict between the Constitution and the campus. The plaintiffs seek to restrain the defendants from administering corporal punishment in the Dallas Independent School District without the prior permission of the parent or student on the grounds that it violates rights guaranteed by the

Eighth and Fourteenth Amendments to the United States Constitution. The cause is dismissed because the claims are not substantial.

The plaintiffs here undertake to represent a class consisting of all students and/or parents of students or those who may become parents or students in the Dallas Independent School District who are opposed to the use of corporal punishment as a method of discipline.

. . . .

According to the rules and policy of the Dallas Independent School District,

> "Principals are authorized to administer any reasonable punishment, including detention, corporal punishment, suspension for a period not to exceed ten school days at one time, or recommendation for expulsion from school."

The principal may delegate any of these duties to the assistant principal. The teacher is limited in his (her) use of corporal punishment.

> "Despite the best efforts of a teacher, there are students who cannot or will not control themselves and repeatedly disrupt the school program. These pupils are in serious need of guidance in progressing from the need for external controls to self-discipline and should be referred to the Pupil Personnel Committee for study. In the event the Committee determines that corporal punishment should be administered by the teacher it will be administered in the presence of an adult witness after receiving written permission from the child's parent."

After any corporal punishment has been administered, the principal is required to file a report with the assistant to the Associate Superintendent for Instruction.

The plaintiffs charge that any corporal punishment administered without parental or student consent deprives them of their rights to due process under the Fourteenth Amendment because any utilization of corporal punishment is arbitrary, capricious and unrelated to any legitimate educational purpose. They also charge that this corporal punishment, on its face, constitutes cruel and unusual punishment in violation of the Eighth Amendment as applied to the States through the Fourteenth Amendment.

The evidence has shown that corporal punishment is usually administered by hitting the student on his buttocks one or several times with a paddle. The paddle is a piece of wood about 2 feet long, ¼ to ½ inches thick, and 6 inches wide. There have also been incidents where the punishment has been administered with a tennis shoe. Plaintiffs have introduced testimony showing that corporal punishment has been administered by teachers without parental permission and even after permission has been denied by the parent. One of the plaintiffs, Roderick Oliver, was knocked unconscious by an Assistant

Principal when he allegedly directed an obscenity at the administrator.

From the evidence presented, the Court has no doubt that the
practice of corporal punishment has been abused by some of the seven
thousand odd teachers in the Dallas Independent School District.
This does not, however, show that the policy itself is unconstitutional.

Under the doctrine of Meyer v. Nebraska . . . the state
cannot unreasonably interfere with the liberty of parents and guardians to direct the upbringing and education of children under their
control. These parental rights are not beyond limitation. . . .
In order for a deprivation of due process under the Fourteenth Amendment to occur, the rules and policies of the school district must bear
"no reasonable relation to some purpose within the competency of the
State." Pierce v. Society of Sisters . . . .

According to the testimony, it cannot be said that the Dallas
Independent School District's policy on the use of corporal punishment bears no reasonable relation to some purpose within the competency of the state in its educational function. Dr. David Gil, an
expert in education and social policy, testified that according to tests
and studies he conducted there was a higher rate of delinquency
among those children exposed to physical discipline than there was
among children who were not physically chastised. It was his opinion
that corporal punishment is always detrimental to a child's development. Dr. Robert Dane, an assistant professor of psychology at a
nearby medical school, testified that there was evidence to show that
corporal punishment makes it difficult for a child to develop; however, he also said that there was evidence to the effect that corporal
punishment may be helpful to some children in the long run but not
for the majority. Dr. Nolan Estes, Superintendent of the Dallas Independent School District, testified that the District's policy on corporal punishment was adopted after a conference with Professor B.
F. Skinner of Harvard University, a recognized authority on child and
educational psychology. Dr. Estes stated that the District's policy on
corporal punishment reflects the philosophy of Dr. Skinner, i. e., in
some cases corporal punishment will be helpful.

Dr. Estes testified further that it was the District's policy that
corporal punishment be sparingly used and only as a last resort. For
this reason, it has to be recommended by a committee and approved
by the parent before a teacher can utilize it. He stated that these
prerequisites on the use of corporal punishment are not imposed upon
the principal or assistant principal because he has more resources at
his disposal to find out about the behavior and problems of the child
than does the teacher. With this in mind, it is then left up to his
professional judgment as to what he thinks is the best course of action.
Dr. Estes said that this policy on corporal punishment was recommended to him also by the principals and the classroom teachers as

the best interim measure at this time in light of the ultimate goal of complete self-discipline and individual education for the child.

It is not within this Court's function, or individual competence, to pass judgment upon the merits of corporal punishment as an educational tool or a means of discipline. The wisdom of the policy is not the Court's concern. The only judgment made is that the evidence has not shown this policy to be arbitrary, capricious, unreasonable or wholly unrelated to the competency of the state in determining its educational policy.

The plaintiffs have cited no authority for their allegation that they are somehow being denied due process except for the case of Murphy v. Kerrigan, CA No. 69–1174–W (D.Mass.1970). That case was a consent decree whereby both parties agreed that corporal punishment would be banned in the Boston Public Schools so long as the current Boston School Committee is in office. Being a consent decree, it has little, if any, precedential value. Other than the *Meyer* and *Pierce* cases, wherein the rights of the parents are subject to the reasonable regulations of the state, the Court knows of no such constitutional right.

The parents in the case of Cornwell v. State Board of Education, 314 F.Supp. 340 (D.Md.1969) aff'd 428 F.2d 471 (4th Cir. 1970), cert. denied, 400 U.S. 942, 91 S.Ct. 240, 27 L.Ed.2d 246, made a similar claim to that made by the parents in this case, i. e., that it was within their rights as parents to teach their children about sexual matters in their own homes and that this exclusive right would prohibit the teaching of sex in the schools. The law was found to be a valid and reasonable public health measure which outweighed claims based upon religious freedom and the right of parental control. Similarly, the judgment of the school board in the case at bar, having been found to be not unreasonable, outweighs any claims based upon parental rights.

While the School District here is certainly not compelled to use corporal punishment, they are allowed to use it by Texas Statute. Tex.Pen.Code Ann. art. 1142 (1961) immunizes teachers from assault and battery charges in the exercise of the right of moderate restraint given by law to "the teacher over the scholar" as well as "to the parent over the child." This statute has been construed as authorizing the school teacher to inflict moderate corporal punishment upon a pupil. . . .

> "The legislature [can] properly conclude that parents and others, *teachers for example*, who have this primary responsibility for children's well-being are entitled to the support of laws designed to aid discharge of that responsibility." . . .

The Court does not find that corporal punishment as authorized by the state law and the rules of the Dallas Independent School District amounts to cruel and unusual punishment. It must be pointed out in this context that if the corporal punishment is unreasonable or excessive, it is no longer lawful and the perpetrator of it may be criminally and civilly liable. The law and policy do not sanction child abuse.

In closing this opinion, the Court feels compelled to utter a general precept in light of the many cases it has had to entertain in the recent past embodying allegations of constitutional violations by the local school district. The following quote will succinctly and accurately describe the Court's attitude with respect to these cases.

"Judicial interposition in the operation of the public school system of the Nation raises problems requiring care and restraint. * * * By and large, public education in our Nation is committed to the control of state and local authorities. Courts do not and cannot intervene in the resolution of conflicts which arise in the daily operation of school systems and which do not directly and sharply implicate basic constitutional values." Epperson v. Arkansas . . .

Plaintiffs' complaint is hereby dismissed.

CITY OF MACOMB v. GOULD

Appellate Court of Illinois, 1969.
104 Ill.App.2d 361, 244 N.E.2d 634.

SCHEINEMAN, Justice. The defendant was found guilty of violating a city ordinance prohibiting fighting and was assessed a fine of $10.00. He appeals, contending the evidence is not sufficient to prove him guilty beyond a reasonable doubt as required in our present criminal code of procedure.

The occasion was at night at a high school football game. The defendant was on the teaching staff and was charged at the time with the duty of keeping the crowd away from the fence between the stands and the playing field. He proceeded to strike a 15-year old boy several times which brought on this charge. He defends on the ground that he was only enforcing discipline, and that as a teacher he had the right to use corporal punishment.

We have no doubt of the right of a teacher to inflict corporal punishment in the process of enforcing discipline. . . . The same cases state the limit of the right. He may not wantonly or maliciously inflict corporal punishment and may be guilty of battery if he does so. Whether he has done so may be inferred from the unreasonableness of the method adopted or the force employed under the circumstances. This presents a question of fact requiring reference to the evidence.

The complaining witness, Mike Daniels, testified that shortly before the half-time intermission a player was injured and was carried from the field on a stretcher. He was put down near the fence just below where Mike was sitting. Mike, and a number of others, went to the fence to learn something about the seriousness of the injuries. The defendant came along and ordered them back to their seats. Mike testifies the crowd started back, and as he turned to go back, the defendant took hold of him, turned him around, and started hitting him on the face, first with his fist, then continued with the flat of his hand. Another man (later identified as a campus policeman) stepped between him and defendant and stopped the striking. Mike stated he was not in any of the classes taught by the defendant but he recognized defendant and turned to obey him, and that he groaned a little as he turned but did not say anything.

The blow with the fist caused a red mark on the side of his face which he said diminished overnight to a small bruise so that he was not claiming any serious injuries. The defendant admitted some striking but denied using a fist. He asserted that he thought Mike was turning to go back to the fence when he turned Mike around. He testified Mike said "Ah, Gould." Some other teachers had seen part of the striking but minimized it, and one agreed with the defendant entirely that there was no blow with a fist.

The police officer saw the striking when it was going on and stepped in to stop it, but testified he could not see whether or not any blow was with a fist.

In addition to the complaining witness, there were five other prosecution witnesses who testified, not counting the policeman. One had not seen the preliminaries but looked up in time to see the defendant strike a blow with his fist, so there were six persons who testified to at least one blow with the fist, and five of them agreed that Mike was walking away when the defendant turned him or twirled him around to begin striking him on the face.

If it is believed that Mike was obeying orders, and was walking away when the defendant turned him around, was there any justification for physical acts of any kind? Furthermore, is a teacher ever justified in striking the face of a pupil with the fist?

Granting that a teacher may enforce discipline by punishing with a switch or a paddle, we would regard clubbing over the head as malicious and unreasonable force, but between these two extremes where is the line to be drawn between what is reasonable and what is malicious? We conclude that under the circumstances as attested by a number of witnesses, there was presented a question of fact to be resolved by the trier of fact, who would also have to consider the credibility of the various witnesses and to decide what facts were actually proved. It is not our province to override the trier of fact in these respects based on our reading of a transcript. . . . .

STOUDER, Justice (dissenting).

I cannot agree with the majority opinion. Under the cases decided in Illinois and relied upon in the majority opinion the law of

Illinois is quite clear. A teacher not only has the right but the duty to discipline children under his tutelage. Failure to do this is tantamount to the failure of a teacher to perform his function, that of teaching. The criteria established are that the discipline must not be actuated by malice and must not be excessively or wantonly administered. In spite of the conflicting evidence, there is no conflict in the fact that the defendant thought the child was being disobedient and rebellious and took steps to correct him. Evidence is lacking from which it may be inferred that the defendant acted maliciously or wantonly. The only question as to whether it was excessive is in how much force was used and the only evidence on this point is whether or not defendant used his fist to strike the child. A blow with a fist does not, necessarily, mean a more violent action than a slap with the hand. To suggest, as does the majority opinion that there was any clubbing about the head, is to utterly ignore the record. To question, as does the majority opinion whether a teacher is ever justified in striking the face of a pupil is only to question the method employed in performing a function admittedly within the province of the teacher.

I do not condone the methods here used. However, to say that because I would not use such methods should impose quasi criminal liability on the defendant would be to substitute my judgment for his in the performance of his duties. In the absence of any uniform recognition of what is and what is not acceptable discipline and on the basis of this record, I would reverse the judgment of the Circuit Court.

OWENS v. KENTUCKY

Court of Appeals of Kentucky, 1971.
473 S.W.2d 827.

STEINFELD, Judge. Appellant Ethel Owens, a 69-year-old schoolteacher of forty-eight years' experience, was adjudged guilty of assault and battery of a high school girl. She has appealed from the judgment, claiming only that the trial court erred in not instructing the jury that KRS 161.180 applies. We reverse.

The teacher had been warned of threats by certain pupils to injure her; wherefore, she carried a "sneeze gun", a small pencil-like device which, when activated, discharges a substance which causes temporary eye irritation to the person affected.

On the day preceding the alleged assault, Miss Owens had taken Brenda Hopkins to the office of the principal because she violated a school rule. The next morning the teacher arrived early at the school for the purpose of discussing the incident with the principal before classes started. Shortly thereafter, Brenda Hopkins and another girl stationed themselves at the door to Miss Owens' school room.   On several occasions when the teacher passed through the door to ascertain whether the principal had arrived, there were incidents of bodybumping with the two girls.   Finally, the general area was disturbed by loud remarks made by Miss Owens and by Brenda; whereupon, a large number of children gathered and other faculty and administrative personnel appeared.   Brenda was directed to go to the office in the company of a secretary and it was suggested that Miss Owens "quiet down".   Claiming that Miss Owens made vile remarks about her, Brenda left the secretary and returned to the place where Miss Owens was standing and almost immediately Brenda was sprayed with the "sneeze gun".

At the conclusion of the evidence, the court gave the jury the usual instructions in an assault and battery prosecution.   .   .   . One of the grounds asserted on the motion for a new trial was the failure of the court to " *   *   * advise the jury under KRS 161.180 that the defendant was empowered *   *   * to exercise such disciplinary force as was necessary to restrain and to hold the prosecuting witness, Brenda Hopkins, in strict account for her conduct at the Gallatin School building *   *   * "   KRS 161.180 reads:

> "Each teacher in the public schools shall hold pupils to a strict account for their conduct in school, on the way to and from school, on the playgrounds, and during intermission or recess."

A companion statute, KRS 161.190, provides:

> "No person shall upbraid, insult or abuse any teacher of the public schools in the presence of the school or in the presence of a pupil of the school."

It is our opinion that at all times related to this incident a student-teacher relationship existed between Brenda Hopkins and Miss Owens; therefore, the mandate of KRS 161.180 required that Miss Owens hold Brenda " *   *   * to a strict account for (her) conduct *   *   * " Carr v. Wright, 423 S.W.2d 521 (Ky.1968).   While we admit that the use of a weapon such as a "sneeze gun" is unusual and not to be encouraged, nevertheless, in this instance, threats of bodily harm being claimed, it may be justified.   It therefore appears that information with respect to the statutory duty of the teacher should have been given to the jury.

If this case is again tried and the evidence warrants, the court will repeat the instructions given in the first trial, except that Instruction No. 2 shall be given substantially as follows:

> Instruction No. 2: It is the duty of each teacher in the public school to hold pupils to a strict account for their conduct in school, on the way to and from school, on the playgrounds, and during intermission or recess. If the jury believe from the evidence in this case that at the time the de-

fendant sprayed, or caused to be sprayed the irritating substance as stated in Instruction No. 1, if she did so, the defendant was making a reasonable attempt to carry out that duty with respect to Brenda Hopkins; or if the jury believe from the evidence that the defendant had reasonable grounds to believe and did believe she was then and there about to be assaulted or have bodily harm inflicted on her and that it reasonably appeared to her to be necessary for her to so spray or cause to be sprayed the irritating substance in order to repeal such assault or prevent such infliction of such personal injury, the jury shall find the defendant not guilty. . . .

Aron & Katz

CORPORAL PUNISHMENT IN THE PUBLIC SCHOOLS

Vol. 6, Harv.Civ.Rts. & Civ.Lib.L.Rev. 583, 1971.

. . . The Common law does not protect students against all corporal punishment, the administration of which is governed in many jurisdictions by state statute or school board regulation. New Jersey is the only state to prohibit it by law. [Massachusetts joined New Jersey in 1972.] Statutes prohibiting cruelty to children and, more often, the common law of assault and battery provide some protection against abuses. Courts have held that corporal punishment of children must be administered without malice, be reasonable in light of the age, sex, size, and physical strength of the child; be proportional to the gravity of the offense; and be performed to enforce reasonable rules. In holdings governing corporal punishment, some courts have presumed the reasonableness of the teacher's actions. Permissible "unabusive" beatings with a ratan, strap, paddle, or hand, however, as well as beatings impermissible under common law, produce degradation and psychological reactions that provide the rationale for declaring all such punishments violative of the eighth and fourteenth amendments.

Corporal punishment in the public schools is ineffective and harmful. If mildly and irregularly applied, it is useless in controlling behavior. In order to prevent the recurrence of unwanted behavior, corporal punishment must either be applied continually, or its exemplary application must have a "terrifying and traumatic" effect. Not surprisingly, the National Education Association has concluded that corporal punishment is ineffective in reducing behavioral problems. Furthermore, an English study found that a deterioration of behavior and an increase in delinquency accompany increased use of corporal punishment.

Corporal punishment has further deleterious effects on children. Insofar as it relies on fear, it disrupts the learning process by repressing the natural tendency of children to explore. This fear may be channeled into aggression against the teacher, against the school, or against society. At the extreme, juvenile delinquency may result. Finally, and perhaps most seriously, the use of corporal punishment may inhibit the development of self-criticism and self-direction in the child. Corporal punishment may drive students to concentrate their energies on conflict with the teacher instead of encouraging them to adjust to their classroom situation.

While theoretically corporal punishment need not be brutal, there is no assurance that it will be inflicted moderately or responsibly. In the heat of anger, especially if provoked by personal abuse, some teachers are likely to exceed legal bounds. Moreover, if limited corporal punishment were permitted, controls would be unlikely to prevent the "really unmistakable kind of satisfaction which some teachers feel in applying the rattan." A total ban of this punishment would provide far more effective control.

Finally, corporal punishment undermines human dignity. Students are placed at the mercy of teachers who have the power to beat them without explanation or justification. In an institution which purports to inculcate the value of reason in human affairs and the worth of each individual in society, it is antithetical to educate by brutality and unreason.

Through the fourteenth amendment, the eighth amendment prohibition against cruel and unusual punishment has been applied to the official conduct of public school teachers and administrators. A teacher's resort to corporal punishment has been held to constitute "punishment" within the meaning of the amendment and is therefore subject to constitutional restraints. The question is whether corporal punishment is cruel and unusual within the meaning of the eighth amendment.

Although the Supreme Court has not provided any precise definition of these words, it has established certain guidelines to interpretation. It has held that underlying the amendment is "nothing less than the dignity of man." The Court has also declared that the scope of the clause extends beyond the prohibition of those punishments regarded in 1791 as cruel and unusual, holding that the amendment "must draw its meaning from the evolving standards of decency that mark the progress of a maturing society." The Court has approached eighth amendment challenges from two perspectives: first, whether the punishment is cruel and uncivilized, viewing only the punishment itself; and second, whether the punishment is clearly excessive in comparison to those meted out elsewhere for similar offenses.

In declaring disciplinary measures cruel and unusual, the Supreme Court has sought to express its concept of "civilized treatment." While it has tended to examine "historic usage of particular punishments, statutory authorization in other jurisdictions, and general public opinion," its inquiry has included "enlightened" as well as actual standards of decency. If the context in which a punishment is administered renders it degrading and subject to wanton—irregular and arbitrary—imposition, then under an enlightened standard such punishment should be presumed cruel and unusual.

The excessiveness principle could also serve as a basis for decision. Many American courts have misinterpreted the meaning of the cruel and unusual clause to prohibit only "cruel" and "barbaric" punishments, while the English history of the clause reveals "a general policy against excessiveness in punishments." Although courts refer to a principle relating the punishment to the offense charged, they appear reluctant to base conclusions on that ground. One reason may be the difficulty in determining in a specific context the sort of treatment which should be considered excessive, since penalties and their objectives for any given offense vary greatly from state to state. The difficulties of determining excessiveness are reduced in corporal punishment cases, however, because of the evolution of society's attitudes. For example, society no longer authorizes the corporal punishment of sailors, apprentices, domestic servants, women, and, more recently, convicts. The different treatment accorded students has been recognized and criticized for some time. The Supreme Court of Indiana declared as long ago as 1853:

> The public seem to cling to the despotism in thee government of schools which has been discarded everywhere else.
> . . . The husband can no longer moderately chastise his wife; nor . . . the master his servant or apprentice. Even the degrading cruelties of the naval service have been arrested. Why the person of the schoolboy . . . should be less sacred in the eye of the law than that of the apprentice or the sailor, is not easily explained.

When society becomes concerned about a group and begins to recognize its basic rights, it no longer subjects the group to corporal punishment. During the past few years the judiciary has become deeply involved in the recognition of students' rights. School regulations and procedures are being scrutinized intensely. . . .

A court which decides that corporal punishment in the public schools does not violate the eighth amendment's protections may still declare it unconstitutional as a violation of the due process clause of the fourteenth amendment. If the Supreme Court were to apply a limited standard of review, at it does in cases involving state economic regulation, corporal punishment would probably be upheld as a plausible, non-arbitrary method of maintaining discipline and order in a classroom. But when the Court has reviewed state actions that infringe upon rights protected by the first amendment or upon other fundamental interests, it has placed a more substantial burden of justification upon the state.

Physical integrity is such an interest. Although never confronting the question under the due process clause, the Court has suggested in recent cases challenging searches and seizures that the right of physical integrity is one of the underlying values of the fourth amendment. Corporal punishment, although neither a search nor a seizure under the fourth amendment, does directly infringe upon this underlying value, which is to be protected against state action. . . .

. . . a court should impose a greater burden than the mere rationality standard upon the state to justify the use of corporal punishment. Corporal punishment, like a search or seizure, infringes upon a value at the root of the fourth amendment—physical integrity. Insofar as the same values underlie the fourteenth amendment's due process clause, a court should test corporal punishment against a standard similar to that applied in cases involving search and seizure of the person. Extensive searches are permissible when a police officer arrests an individual with probable cause because he must protect himself and look for evidence which the suspect might destroy. Even in arrests, however, physical intrusion is limited by the requirements of the situation, especially when the intrusion is greater than a mere body search. In non-arrest situations, physical intrusion is even more strictly limited. Thus, in assessing corporal punishment, courts should require the states to demonstrate that there are no other effective means available which are less destructive of physical integrity. The burden of adducing evidence to uphold corporal punishment rests with the state. But to date, there is no empirical evidence to demonstrate that corporal punishment is necessary to maintain order in the classroom or to promote students' educational progress. If anything, the evidence suggests the contrary.

A less restrictive means test may sensibly be applied to corporal punishment in public schools. Because a state may pursue retribution as one of the aims of its penal laws, all penalties that do not violate the eighth amendment may be valid. Therefore, if a state prisoner were to argue that a five-year sentence provided as much deterrence and rehabilitation as the ten-year sentence he actually received, a court would be justified in refusing to declare the longer punishment unconstitutional. While corporal punishment in the schools is penal, in the sense that it seeks to correct the offender's future conduct and to deter others from acting in a similar manner, unlike a state penal code, such punishment is not properly directed toward retribution. Moreover, where criminal penalties are augmented because of the retributive element, such procedural safeguards as indictment, counsel, and jury trial—wholly inapposite in the school context—exist to guarantee the appropriateness of the penalty.

If corporal punishment is to be allowed at all, it must be administered only within the constraints of appropriate safeguards. Before taking certain disciplinary measures, public schools must provide students with an opportunity at least to hear and rebut charges before the proper authorities. Both colleges and public schools must accord students a hearing before suspending or dismissing them. Likewise, students subjected to disciplinary transfer, denied the right to participate in interscholastic athletics, or forbidden from taking a college qualifying examination, are entitled to hearings. Consideration of the procedural requisites of due process which should accompany disciplinary action necessitates an examination of the governmental function involved and the private interests affected.

As against a school's educational function, the interest of the student who is expelled or suspended is the impairment of his reputation, with serious economic and social consequences, especially when the action taken will be noted on his permanent record. The interest of the student subjected to corporal punishment involves his physical integrity and human dignity. The interest in each case is equally fundamental. Procedural safeguards in both, therefore, should prevent unwarranted punishment and those excessively administered.

Because tempers often flare in the classroom, it is important that the accuser, judge, and executioner not be the same person. The Supreme Court has recognized that the emotional involvement of the judge who declares a defendant in contempt disqualifies him from presiding when the contempt issue is tried. Similarly, the school official who prescribes corporal punishment, if it is permitted at all, should not be the one who applies it. At a minimum, for any offense serious enough to warrant corporal punishment, a child should have the opportunity to disclaim or justify his conduct before a teacher, parent, and impartial school officer, and the determination of the punishment should result from collaboration of the adults present. Such a requirement should be maintained because it is a guarantee of fairness and rationality which should be imported to an area in which students can be treated harshly.

The delay engendered by the imposition of procedural requirements between the misconduct and the punishment need not reduce the efficacy of the sanction, so long as the student fully comprehends the reason for his punishment. Even if the effectiveness were reduced, it might be the necessary cost of providing fair treatment. Schools would thereby demonstrate to their students that sound justifications should precede the use of physical force.

Once prevalent as a generally accepted means of controlling behavior, corporal punishment is officially sanctioned today only against children. It is inconsistent with modern educational theory and methods, which have progressed from a strict authoritarian concept of education to one emphasizing communication and rapport between teacher and student. The reliance on force, abusive and brutal at times, is a counterproductive means of achieving order in the schools. With an understanding of the effects of corporal punishment and an appreciation for the recently recognized status of students, courts should find corporal punishment cruel and unusual and a denial of due process of law.

PROBLEM

1. Assume that you are a member of a state legislature and must vote on the two statutes set forth below. How would you vote on them and for what reason(s)? For further discussion see, N.E.A. Report Of The Task Force On Corporal Punishment (1972).

New Jersey Statutes Annotated, sec. 18:19–1:

No person employed or engaged in a school or educational institution, whether public or private, shall inflict or cause to be inflicted corporal punishment upon a pupil attending such school or institution. But any such person may, within the scope of his employment, use and apply such amounts of force as is reasonable and necessary: (1) to quell a disturbance, threatening physical injury to others; (2) to obtain possession of weapons or other dangerous objects upon the person or within the control of a pupil; (3) for the purpose of self-defense; and (4) for the protection of persons and property; and such acts, or any of them shall not be construed to constitute corporal punishment within the meaning and intendment of this section. Every resolution, by-law, rule, ordinance, or other act or authority permitting or authorizing corporal punishment to be indicted upon a pupil attending a school or educational institution shall be void.

Code of Virginia, sec. 22–231.1:

In the maintenance of order and discipline, and in the exercise of a sound discretion, a principal or teacher in a public school or a school maintained by the state, may administer reasonable corporal punishment on a pupil under his authority, provided he acts in good faith and such punishment is not excessive.

FREEDOM FROM OVERLY BROAD AND VAGUE REGULATIONS

SULLIVAN v. HOUSTON INDEPENDENT SCHOOL DISTRICT

United States District Court, S.D.Tex., 1969.
307 F.Supp. 1328.

SEALS, District Judge. This action was instituted on behalf of two Houston high school students who were expelled from Sharpstown Junior/Senior High School for the remainder of the 1968–1969 term because of their involvement in the production and distribution of a "newspaper" called the *Pflashlyte* . . . which criticized school officials. . . .

Sharpstown Junior/Senior High School is one of Houston's newest [public] schools having opened only a year ago. Sharpstown is a large school with age levels varying from the seventh to the twelfth grade. This first year for Sharpstown was also the first experience for Mr. Coy P. Stewart as principal of a senior high school; he had just completed three years as principal of McReynolds Junior High when Sharpstown opened.

Dan Dullivan and Mike Fischer were seniors at Sharpstown during this first year—the 1968–1969 school term. Dan had attended Bellaire High School the previous year and Mike had gone to Lee High School. Both were "B" students. Their conduct records reflect a few minor infractions but neither student appears to have been a discipline problem. In fact, their conduct grade was "good." Their school records and their actions before this court point to the conclusion that Dan and Mike are rather typical young American men of high moral character.

After their first several months at Sharpstown, Dan and Mike along with some other students became concerned with the absence of any express school regulations governing student conduct. The complaint was, in essence, that a student never knew when he was violating "regulations" since no rules had ever been written down and distributed. Dan, for instance, was told that wearing a neckerchief around his neck violated "school regulations." Confusion also existed concerning the use of a park across from the school before classes began in the morning. Sometimes it was prohibited and sometimes it was not.

Concern for this problem led to the organization of a "rally" after school one day in the nearby park. Students and teachers were present and they all sat on the grass and listened to speeches by students who used the chance to air some grievances. The discussion was interrupted by the physical interference of certain Sharpstown High athletic coaches who threw books around the park, ripped up students' notebooks and accused students of being Communists and Fascists.

There were other incidents of harassment by gym coaches which added to the list of student complaints. On one occasion, Dan Sullivan was called into a coach's office and subjected to strong verbal abuse. When Dan stepped aside as someone entered the office door so that he had to lean against one of the coach's desks, the coach ordered him to get off that desk or he would get his "block knocked off."

In addition, it appears that some of the students in Mike Fischer's gym class who attended the rally were given "grade cuts." Mike's gym instructor later informed him that because of the present lawsuit Mike would receive an "F" in the course if the instructor could "get away with it."

After the incident at the "rally," some of the students decided to wear small American flags in their shirt lapels as a show of patriotism. Dan Sullivan had called the Houston office of the Federal Bureau of Investigation to ask if this was an acceptable way to display the flag and upon being assured that it was proper, he wore a flag to school. Dan was informed by a coach to remove the flag on penalty of suspension from school. The flag, the coach said, "was disruptive."

Another incident concerned solicitations for various fund-raising projects during school hours. Dan, Mike and a friend named Larry Craven approached Mr. Stewart about sponsoring a Red Cross drive for the starving people of Biafra. Dan had called the American Red Cross and they had expressed enthusiasm for the project. Mr. Stewart told the boys that such a program could not be allowed because it was explicitly prohibited by the downtown office to have any kind of solicitation from students during school time. The boys suggested small unobtrusive cans with slots to be placed on lunch tables. Stewart said this too was against "regulations." Dan later called the downtown office and was told that it was up to the principal to decide which fund drives should be allowed within the school.

Several weeks later, Mr. Stewart announced that as part of the senior project the school was to have a fund drive to collect $500.00 for the purchase of tropical plants, to be placed in a large planter box. Each student was expected to contribute twenty-five cents. Dan was asked by his physics teacher to make his contribution, not only during class time, but while an exam was in progress. When he refused to contribute saying it seemed somewhat hypocritical, Dan was lectured by the teacher and was told that his mind was being taken over by Communists.

Some time after these incidents, Mike and Dan decided they would put together a "newspaper" to voice their dissatisfactions and beliefs .   .   .

Mike and Dan began distribution of the introductory paper on February 27, 1969 and then continued on the 28th. The second edition was ready by the 28th so the students' efforts were directed at distributing it on that day, which was a Friday, and then again during the early part of the following week. Several other students helped Mike and Dan distribute the "newspaper" and they were instructed to not hand out the paper on school grounds or during school hours. They were also asked by Mike and Dan to tell students not to take the paper into the school with them but if they had to do so, to keep it in a notebook so that it would be out of sight. Distribution began in Landsdale Park just across the street from Sharpstown High. As students passed by on their way to classes they were given copies.

Issues were later handed out at Sharpstown Shopping Center and at various shops where students were known to congregate. About 1,000 copies of the second edition were eventually distributed. Most students did as Mike and Dan requested but others did not. In one boys' restroom, a stack of papers was found with a sign above it saying "take one." Copies were also placed in a paper towel dispenser and some were found inside sewing machines in a girls' homemaking class.

It also appears that some copies were found in classrooms during school hours. Teacher Don Ellisor found a student reading the *Pflashlyte* during class when she should have been working on an assignment. He took up the paper without disrupting the class. An English instructor, Mrs. Jeannine Wallace, had to take up papers from two students who were reading it during class. One student had laughed out-loud as she read and the teacher felt the need to take the paper from her. Mrs. Wallace had in the past taken up copies of the school-sponsored newspaper, *The Torch,* which students read in class. Mrs. Wallace also noticed somewhat more congestion in the halls as students made their way from one class to another.

Mrs. Woodie Kendall, a seventh grade teacher at Sharpstown, took up a copy of the "newpaper" from five boys who were reading it before class began for their homeroom period. She also noticed more congestion in the halls and added that movement through the school had been a problem since the school had opened because the halls were rather narrow. Mrs. Cyril Hosley, a typing instructor, observed an unusually large number of students tardy in arriving for class on February 28, 1969 and the following week, but she did not know a specific reason for the tardiness. Mrs. Hosley did see copies of the *Pflashlyte* in her room but did not take them up as they had not created any disturbance.

Math instructor Sidney Johnson was interrupted during a lecture by a student who twisted around in his seat to get a look at a copy of the paper held by the student behind him. Johnson immediately confiscated the copy, and sent both boys to the principal's office. Another of Johnson's classes was interrupted when a student tried to ask a question about the newspaper.

Charles Smith, also a math teacher at Sharpstown, was interrupted during his class lectures. Students wanted to talk about the *Pflashlyte* as often as twice a day for two or three days and then only once a day thereafter.

Assistant Principal Jackson attempted to summarize the disruptive effect on the school which resulted from the distribution of the *Pflashlyte:*

> Q. During that one-week period was there any disruption of the ordinary routine of the school or operations of the school which you believe is attributable to the fact that this paper was being circulated in the school? * * *

THE WITNESS: Sir, it will be virtually impossible for me to pinpoint a single incident. It would be my interpretation of the general attitude of the student body, which I couldn't say that at such-and-such a time that happened. I work with it every day.

THE COURT: You have a feeling for it?

THE WITNESS: Yes, sir, I do.

THE COURT: You have a feeling that the students' attitude was a certain way?

THE WITNESS: There seemed to be a difference in the attitude is the way I would say it, a marked difference.

Q.   (By Mr. Cook) In what way was it different from the ordinary attitude?

A.   Well—

Q.   Was it better or worse:

A.   Indifferent. I couldn't describe it as being better. There seemed to be, the attitude seemed to be, I don't know if its going to say what I, more concerned with something else. I wanted to say that you often see a group in the hall standing together and talking in between classes, passing time. You might see a group, a large group gathering at a lunch table. This in itself may or may not be attributed to something like this. It's difficult to say. There seemed to be, if I might describe it this way, there seemed to be something of concern that was generally among the student body.

Q.   Would you say that there prevailed an attitude of preoccupation of something that doesn't ordinarily go on in the school building?   *   *   *

THE COURT: Do you know a synonym for preoccupied?

THE WITNESS: I would say that they had been, let me think a minute. They had something on their minds that was causing them to be of great concern. That's my own choice of words.

Tr. at 550–53.

Sharpstown's principal, Mr. Coy P. Stewart, first learned of the presence of the *Pflashlyte* in the school building on Friday, February 28, 1969, the first day of large scale distribution. He received a copy of the short "introductory" issue in the mail and soon after classes began a teacher brought in a copy of the second edition which had been taken from a student. As more and more copies came to the administrative office, not only from teachers but from students, he became quite anxious about the situation and resolved that the students responsible would be expelled immediately. Stewart launched an investigation into the matter and he and other administrative personnel questioned students throughout the school trying to learn the identity of *Pflashlyte's* editors and distributors. He soon learned that two boys had been handing out the "newspaper" in Landsdale Park before school started in the morning. Stewart obtained descriptions of the boys as his investigation continued into the following week. By the middle of the week Stewart began to suspect Dan Sullivan and Mike Fischer. On Wednesday, March 5, 1969, Dan was called in by Mr. Stewart who began asking him random questions about his family, his teachers and about a theme paper Dan had written for an English class. It later developed that other Sharpstown students at the direction of administrative personnel had quietly filed past the open door of Stewart's office so that Dan could be viewed and identified as one of those who had distributed the *Pflashlyte*. Mr. Setwart made no mention of the "newspaper" to Dan.

On that Friday, March 7, 1969, Dan and Mike were called in separately to talk with Mr. Stewart and Assistant Principal Jackson. Both boys admitted that they had distributed the paper. Stewart advised them that their actions were serious violations of "school regulations" especially because of their involvement in a "secret organization." However, neither boy was informed of what disciplinary action, if any, would be taken nor were they offered the opportunity to cease their actions so as to mitigate their punishment.

The next contact Mike had with the administration was Wednesday, March 12, 1969. He came to the principal's office and found that his father was already conferring with Mr. Stewart. Mike was told he was being expelled for the remainder of his senior year. Dan was told the following day that he too, was expelled. Stewart phoned Dan's mother who came to the school for a conference. She asked if Dan could stay in school if the paper were discontinued, but Stewart said this was too serious. Mike Fischer spoke to Mr. Stewart again on Thursday, the 13th, and offered to cease all activities concerning the "newspaper" but Stewart refused saying Mike's "attitude" was bad.

It was clearly established that both boys were expelled solely for their involvement with the *Pflashlyte* and not for any previous misconduct. . . .

Finally, plaintiffs allege that certain regulations of the Houston Independent School District are unconstitutional under the Supreme Court's "void-for-vagueness" doctrine. . . .

The Supreme Court's "void-for-vagueness" doctrine has developed two distinct concepts. A statute is scrutinized first to determine if it is "overbroad"; could a reasonable application of its sanctions include conduct protected by the Constitution? . . .

A statute must also satisfy the "vagueness" standard of Connally v. General Construction Co., 269 U.S. 385, ... :

> [A] statute which either forbids or requires the doing of an act in terms so vague that men of common intelligence must necessarily guess at its meaning and differ as to its application violates the first essential of due process * * *
> . . .

In their General Order on Student Discipline, 45 F.R.D. 133, 146–47 (W.D.Mo.1968), the judges of the Western District of Missouri adopted the following view on this issue:

> Outstanding educational authorities in the field of higher education believe, on the basis of experience, that detailed codes of prohibited student conduct are provocative and should not be employed in higher education.

> For this reason, general affirmative statements of what is expected of a student may in some areas be preferable in higher education. Such affirmative standards may be employed, and discipline of students based thereon.

> The legal doctrine that a prohibitory statute is void if it is overly broad or unconstitutionally broad does not, in the absence of exceptional circumstances, apply to standards of student conduct. The validity of the form of standards of student conduct, relevant to the lawful missions of higher education, ordinarily should be determined by recognized educational standards.

However, in the case of Soglin v. Kauffman, 295 F.Supp. 978, 990 (W.D.Wis.1968) the court expressly rejected this view: "I cannot agree that university students should be deprived of these significant constitutional protections on so slender a showing." The court concluded that:

> The constitutional doctrines of vagueness and overbreadth are applicable, in some measure, to the standard or standards to be applied by the university in disciplining its students, and that a regime in which the term "misconduct" serves as the sole standard violates the due process clause of the Fourteenth Amendment by reason of its vagueness, or, in the alternative, violates the First Amendment as embodied in the Fourteenth by reason of its vagueness and overbreadth.

This court is persuaded by the *Soglin* decision. And in this court's judgment, these fundamental concepts of constitutional law must be applied "in some measure" even to high schools. The "measure" should reach only to rules the violation of which could result in expulsion or suspension for a substantial period of time. When faced with such drastic consequences, a high school student has no less a right to a clear, specific normative statement which does not infringe on free expression than does a university student or possibly even the accused in a criminal case. If the punishment could be this severe, there is no question but that a high school student as well as a university student might well suffer more injury than one convicted of a criminal offense. School rules probably do not need to be as narrow as criminal statutes but if school officials contemplate severe punishment they must do so on the basis of a rule which is drawn so as to reasonably inform the student what specific conduct is prescribed. Basic notions of justice and fair play require that no person shall be made to suffer for a breach unless standards of behavior have first been announced, for who is to decide what has been breached?

It is also clear that severe punishment may not be based on a rule which could reasonably be construed to embrace conduct protected by the first amendment. . . .

At the conclusion of the evidentiary hearing in this case the parties entered the following stipulation:

> The only written rule or regulation of the Houston Independent School District concerning the private publication and distribution of written material by students in secondary schools newspapers which are not published in the name of the school and which do not purport to be published under the auspices of any school is as follows:

> The school principal may make such rules and regulations that may be necessary in the administration of the school and in promoting its best interest. He may enforce obedience to any reasonable and lawful command.

It was further stipulated by the parties that Mr. Stewart had not made or announced any rule concerning the private publication or distribution of newspapers at Sharpstown Junior/Senior High School before the facts in question arose.

Lastly, the following was stipulated:

> [T]he rule * * * [quoted above] is construed by responsible officials of the Houston Independent School District to prohibit the type of publication and distribution engaged in by Michael Fischer and Dan Sullivan in February and March of 1969.

Since Mr. Stewart had not announced any rules regarding the private publication and distribution of newspapers and since he testified that he based his disciplinary action upon the rule quoted above, it must be assumed that this was the only standard available to students by which they could guide their conduct. The rule is, therefore, a proper subject for evaluation as to its vagueness and overbreadth.

Little can be said of a standard so grossly overbroad as "in the best interests of the school." . . . It cannot be contended that it supplies objective standards by which a student may measure his behavior or by which an administrator may make a specific ruling in evaluation of behavior. . . . It patently "sweeps within its broad scope activities that are constitutionally protected free speech and assembly." . . .

This is not meant in criticism of defendants. Generalities such as this one have been accepted for years as the proper sort of standard for our "unique educational environment." However, *Tinker* has tolled the beginnings of change. As Judge James Doyle wrote in Soglin v. Kauffman, 295 F.Supp. 978, 988 (W.D.Wisc.1968):

> I take notice that in the present day, expulsion from an institution of higher learning, or suspension for a period of time substantial enough to prevent one from obtaining academic credit for a particular term, may well be and often is in fact, a more severe sanction than a monetary fine or a relatively brief confinement imposed by a court in a criminal proceeding. The world is much with the modern state university. Some find this regrettable, mourning the passing of what is said to have been the old order. I do not share this view.

The high school too is changing and generalities can no longer serve as standards of behavior when the right to obtain an education hangs in the balance. This regulation is unconstitutional for both "vagueness" and "overbreadth" and plaintiffs are entitled to a declaratory judgment to that effect. *See generally* the article by Professor Charles Alan Wright entitled The Constitution On the Campus, 22 Vand.L.Rev. 1027 (1969).

Having concluded that defendants' regulation is overbroad, it falls upon the court to determine what equitable relief is proper protection for plaintiffs and their class. The determination of overbreadth coupled with the threat of further improper enforcement in the future clearly tends to "chill" the exercise of first amendment freedoms by students in Houston schools. . . .

In this court's judgment, further equitable relief is required by the facts of this case so as to provide adequate protection for plaintiffs' class. A permanent injunction will issue prohibiting the defendants from imposing serious disciplinary sanctions, in the absence of precise and narrowly drawn regulations, upon students who write, print, distribute or otherwise engage in the publication of newspapers either on or off of school premises during either school hours or nonschool hours unless such activities materially and substantially disrupt the normal operations of the school. . . .

Defendants will also be permanently enjoined from expelling or suspending for a substantial period of time secondary school students in the Houston School District who are guilty of any misconduct without compliance with minimal standards of procedural due process: (1) formal written notice of the charges and of the evidence against him must be provided to the student and his parents or guardian, (2) formal hearing affording both sides ample opportunity to present their cases by way of witnesses or other evidence, and (3) imposition of sanctions only on the basis of substantial evidence.

In 1943, Mr. Justice Jackson provided the principles which sustain this Court's decision today:

> The Fourteenth Amendment, as now applied to the states, protects the citizen against the State itself and all of its creatures—Boards of education not excepted. These have, of course, important, delicate, and highly discretionary functions, but none that they may not perform within the limits of the Bill of Rights. That they are educating the young for citizenship is reason for scrupulous protection of Constitutional freedoms of the individual, if we are not to strangle the free mind at its source and teach youth to discount important principles of our government as mere platitudes.

West Virginia State Board of Education v. Barnette, ...

NOTES AND QUESTIONS

1. What is the difference between an overly broad and a vague statute? What is the constitutional difficulty with each of them? See also, Shawley v. Northeast Ind. Sch. Dist., 462 F.2d 960 (5th Cir. 1972).

2. If you had been the judge in this case, how would you have decided it? Why? Do you believe the judges of the western district of Missouri are correct in holding "that detailed codes of conduct are provocative and should not be employed . . ."?

3. Would the following rule be upheld by court: "Any student who is on school premises and engages in conduct unbecoming a student shall be subject to discipline"? Is there any substantial difference between the above rule and one disciplining teachers for "unprofessional conduct" or for "actions tending to cause disrespect for the teaching profession"?

4. Does the rule supporting the decision in this case apply to: (a) suspension; (b) expulsion; (c) dismissal; or (d) reprimand? Compare, Murray v. West Baton Rouge Parish School Board, 472 F.2d 438 (5th Cir. 1973).

PROCEDURAL RIGHTS PRIOR TO SUSPENSION

S. v. BOARD OF EDUCATION

California Court of Appeal, 1971.
20 Cal.App.3rd 83, 97 Cal.Rptr. 422.

ELKINGTON, Associate Justice. The primary question on this appeal is whether Education Code, section 10607 (third paragraph), prescribing the procedure on suspension of a public school student, comports with state and federal constitutional requirements of due process of law.

A petition for writ of mandate was filed in the superior court on behalf of Charles S., a minor (whose full name for reasons which will become obvious is omitted), and all other persons similarly situated, including eight others expressly named. Each of the nine persons had been suspended from high school pending disposition of juvenile court proceedings against him.

The petitioners sought a court order: (1) terminating their suspensions pending a "full due process hearing," (2) that the school record of their illegal suspensions be expunged of "harmful notations," and (3) that additional educational programs be provided them "so that they can regain the valuable schooling missed as a result of the illegal disciplinary action."

They further sought a declaration of the superior court that "Section 10607 of the California Education Code requires a due process hearing within three days after the commencement of any school suspension from a California public school, or in the alternative that such statute is unconstitutional for not providing the nature of hearing required by due process, and further that this Court declare for the parties to this controversy what nature of hearing due process requires within three days of a suspension from a public high school."

. . .

The primary petitioner, 17 years old, and a California Youth Authority parolee, and the other eight named persons, 14 to 17 years of age were students of a San Francisco high school. During the month of September 1969, serious disturbances occurred at and around the school. At the time the nine juveniles were arrested for offenses ranging through kidnaping, rape, assault upon a police officer, assault with a bumper jack, assault resulting in the death of a boy whose head struck a sidewalk curb, carrying a concealed weapon, and disturbing the peace. The alleged offenses appear to have occurred at times when the students should have been in class. Juvenile court proceedings were instituted in each case. At about the same time each of the nine students was suspended from school for the reasons which brought about the juvenile court proceedings; these are the suspensions which are the basis of the instant action and appeal.

Although the evidence is to some extent in conflict, a serious doubt arises therefrom as to the fidelity with which the school authorities followed the requirements of the third paragraph of section 10607 relating to "meetings" with the parents or guardians of the suspended students. Petitioners, however, appear to make no real complaint over any such deficiency; they emphasize that the issue before us "is one of law, not of fact."

Before proceeding further it seems proper to dispose of petitioners' repeated and insistent claims that they were "indefinitely suspended." Such, if it were true, would be tantamount to expulsion from school—a denial of one's right to an education. . . . Obviously the demands of due process upon an expulsion must be stricter than upon a reasonably limited suspension. Indeed, in a case of expulsion section 10608 calls for a "hearing" and "decision" with the implied due process connotations of those terms.

But such claims of indefinite suspensions are wholly without support in the record. Furthermore, at the oral argument on this appeal it was conceded that each suspension terminated no later than the related decision of the juvenile court. Such terminations were in full compliance with Education Code, section 10607.5 authorizing extension of a suspension "until such time as the juvenile court * * * has rendered a decision in the action."

And we observe that the Education Code expressly forbids indefinite suspension of public school students. Teachers may suspend a pupil "for not exceeding one schoolday, plus the remainder of the schoolday during which the suspension is ordered, * * *" (§ 10601.) Suspension by a principal "shall not exceed 10 schooldays". (§ 10601.5.) Section 10607.5 provides, " * * * no student shall be suspended from school for more than 20 days in a school year," excepting cases of "transfer to another regular school for adjustment purposes, [in which case] additional days of suspension are limited to 10," and excepting also juvenile court cases, discussed *ante*. And even where the suspension is related to pending juvenile court proceedings, that court is admonished to be "expeditious" in the proceedings. . . .

We come now to petitioners' real contention. They argue that section 10607 does not meet "minimum requirements" of due process before a public school student's suspension will be permitted. These minimum requirements they insist, are: (1) The student must be given written notice of the pertinent charges and of his right to a hearing; (2) He must be allowed discovery of the school's evidence in order that his case be properly prepared; (3) A hearing must be held, at which he shall have the right (4) to counsel, (5) to an "impartial decision-maker," (6) to present evidence, (7) to confront and cross-examine adverse witnesses, (8) to written findings of fact based only upon substantial evidence produced at the hearing, and (9) to record the hearing at his own expense.

We first consider the contention that section 10607 denies due process of law to suspended public school students.

Due process of law is susceptible of no simple definition. We are well guided, however, by several writings of our state's Supreme Court.

"The various conflicting cases demonstrate that there is no rule of universal application concerning the right of an individual to present his views at a hearing prior to the institution of action affecting his substantial rights. What is due process depends on circumstances. It varies with the subject matter and the necessities of the situation. . . . Its content is a function of many variables, including the nature of the right affected, the degree of danger caused by the proscribed condition or activity, and the availability of prompt remedial measures. * * * " . . .

"The contours of due process * * * are not always the same. . . . 'The very nature of due process negates any concept of inflexible procedures universally applicable to every imaginable situation. * * * [C]onsideration of what procedures due process may require under any given set of circumstances must begin with a determination of the precise nature of the governmental function involved as well as of the private interest that has been affected by governmental action.' " . . .

" '[D]ue process is not interested in mere technical formalism. It is the substance that is determinative of whether due process has been afforded.' " . . .

"It has always been recognized that 'the more important the rights at stake the more important must be the procedural safeguards surrounding those rights.' . . . "

The courts have often spoken on the subject of due process in the application of sanctions for academic misbehavior. It has been said that any analogy of student discipline to adult or juvenile criminal proceedings is not sound, and both impractical and detrimental to the educational atmosphere and functions. . . . In the imposition of such sanctions a "full dress judicial hearing" is not required. . . . Further, such proceedings need not be adversary in nature. . . . It has been held in such cases that due process does not imply a right to counsel . . . nor right of cross-examination . . . nor right to a stenographic report of the proceedings . . . nor right to a separation of the "judging and prosecuting" function. . . .

We find further relevant judicial comment on due process as it relates to student disciplinary action.

"Law and order in the classroom should be the responsibility of our respective educational systems. The courts should not usurp this function and turn disciplinary problems, involving suspensions, into criminal adversary proceedings—which they definitely are not. * * *" . . .

"It may be conceded that a state college or university must necessarily possess a very wide latitude in disciplining its students and that this power should not be encumbered with restrictions which would embarrass the institution in maintaining good order and discipline among members of the student body and a proper relationship between the students and the school itself. It may be further conceded that it is a delicate matter for a court to interfere with the internal affairs and operations of a college or university, whether private or public, and that such interference should not occur in the absence of the most compelling reasons." (Knight v. State Board of Education, D. C., 200 F.Supp. 174, 179.)

"By judicial mandate to impose upon the academic community in student discipline the intricate, time consuming, sophisticated procedures, rules and safeguards of criminal law would frustrate the teaching process and render the institutional control impotent. This Court will not make such imposition." (Esteban v. Central Missouri State College, supra, 290 F.Supp. 622, 629.)

"Historically, the academic community has been unique in having its own standards, rewards and punishments. Its members have been allowed to go about their business of teaching and learning largely free of outside interference. To compel such a community to recognize and enforce precisely the same standards and penalties that prevail in the broader social community would serve neither the special needs and interests of the educational institutions, nor the ultimate advantages that society derives therefrom. Thus, in an academic community, greater freedoms and greater restrictions may prevail than in society at large, and the subtle fixing of these limits should, in a large measure, be left to the educational institution itself." (Goldberg v. Regents of the University of California, supra, 248 Cal. App.2d 867, 880, 57 Cal.Rptr. 463, 472.)

The cases we have cited deal generally with student expulsion or its equivalent, indefinite suspension. Reasonably the demands of due process in situations, as here, of student suspension for a limited period fixed by law, must be less rigid, certainly not greater. . . .

Two recent federal cases concerning due process requirements upon the limited suspension of public school students have come to our attention.

The first is Banks v. Board of Public Instruction of Dade County, supra, 314 F.Supp. 285. Under consideration was a "School Board Policy—Regulation 5114" which set forth procedure to be employed in the suspension of students. The regulation provided that on a suspension for up to ten days the school principal must forthwith send a notice of the suspension to the student's parents. The notice is required to contain the student's name and the reason for the suspension and to invite the parents to contact the school and discuss the matter more thoroughly with the authorities. The regulation further provided that every effort shall be made to contact the parents in order to inform them of the reason for the suspension and that a formal notice has been mailed. The regulation did not provide for a hearing prior to the suspension.

Contention was made that the regulation denied suspended students due process of law. The district court disagreed, finding the regulation not to be "facially unconstitutional."

The court pointed out that the legal processes due suspended students must be less exacting than those due a person charged with crime. But nevertheless it held . . . "that notice [must] be given, a hearing provided for, and that the hearing [must] include the rudimentary adversary elements. Thus, the students should be given specific notice of the charges, the names of witnesses with a summary of their testimony, and should be given the opportunity to refute the charges by oral or written testimony. * * *" Such a hearing, it was held, need not be *prior* to the suspension.

Turning to the regulation, the court stated . . . that it provided "for immediate notice of the suspension and the reasons therefor to be sent to the parents, and for the parents to be notified of the suspension before the student can be sent home. Moreover, the notice of suspension invites the parents to contact the school if they desire to discuss the matter. This procedure, which provides for a hearing after the fact upon request of the parents, while somewhat informal when contrasted with criminal procedure, is nonetheless consistent with the dictates of due process when examined in light of the public school setting."

Williams v. Dade County School Board, 5 Cir., 441 F.2d 299, is the second "suspension" case. It arose in the same jurisdiction and concerned the same school board policy regulation as did Banks v. Board of Public Instruction, supra . . . It appeared that the regulation also permitted an additional "30-day suspension" after the initial one of 10 days. Additional procedures were required in the implementation of the second suspension. It was provided that the superintendent of schools . . . "shall notify the parent by certified mail of the [additional 30-day] suspension and the basis for the action taken. * * *"

The court approved the result reached in Banks v. Board of Public Instruction, supra, and also found no constitutional fault in the "hearing after the fact" of the 10-day suspension. But it said . . . : "In the case at bar we have a much different situation. An additional 30-day suspension was added after tensions began to subside and a need for summary action could not be overriding. * * * [¶] We realize, of course, that it is not necessary that students be given the kinds of procedural protections reserved for those accused of serious crime. Nevertheless, we feel that a penalty of this magnitude ought not be imposed without proper notice of the charges, and at least an attempt to ascertain accurately the facts involved and to give the student an opportunity to present his side of the case."

The court then held that the rudimentary requirements of the Banks v. Board of Public Instruction, supra, "after the fact" hearing were required *before* imposition of an additional 30-day suspension. Those requirements, it recited, were that . . . : " * * * the students should be given specific notice of the charges, the names of witnesses with a summary of their testimony and should be given the opportunity to refute the charges by oral or written testimony."

We believe that *Banks* and *Williams* generally correctly state the due process requirements upon a student's suspension from public school. But we think that the requirement of "names of *witnesses*" with a "summary of their *testimony*" and an opportunity to refute by "oral and written *testimony*" suggest a formalistic judicial sort of hearing which appears unnecessary and unreasonable, and which was probably unintended. . . .

We think a better statement of the pertinent due process requirements was, as we have indicated . . . : "[W]e feel that a penalty of this magnitude ought not be imposed without proper notice of the charges, and at least an attempt to ascertain accurately the facts involved and to give the student an opportunity to present his side of the case."

Perlman v. Shasta Joint Jr. College Dist. Bd. of Trustees, supra, 9 Cal.App.3d 873, 88 Cal.Rptr. 563, appears to be the only California case involving a student suspension. (Section 10607 referring to primary and secondary schools was there inapplicable.) A college student was suspended for three days. It was urged that the requirements, discussed ante, of Dixon v. Alabama State Board of Education, supra, 294 F.2d 150, were applicable. The court disagreed . . . stating that the type of due process required in criminal court proceedings were unsuited to college suspension; and that "A reasonable rule would be that all that is required is that the student be given a fair notice and a fair hearing, the type of notice to depend upon the circumstances of the offense."

From the foregoing it becomes evident that in the case of public school student *suspensions*, a "full time process hearing" as elaborated and demanded by petitioners, is not constitutionally mandated.

Instead, our consideration of the pertinent fundamental principles, and the authority to which we have adverted, impels us to conclude that due process requirements, upon a suspension, are met by the following procedures:

(1) Notice by telephone, mail, or other appropriate method, to the parents or guardian within a reasonable time *after* the suspension,

advising of the fact of such suspension, its duration, and the reasons therefor, and further stating that if desired a prompt meeting or hearing will be held at which the suspension may be discussed with school officials.

(2) If requested, a meeting or hearing within a reasonable time, at which the suspended student may also be present, where the student shall be afforded an opportunity to present informal proof of his side of the case.

We advert now to section 10607. We consider its language and that which is necessarily implied therefrom. "[W]hatever is necessarily implied in a statute is as much a part of it as that which is expressed. * * * " . . . We should so construe the statute, if its language permits, as to render it valid and constitutional rather than invalid and unconstitutional. . . . And we must presume that the Legislature intended to enact a valid statute, and adopt an interpretation that, consistent with the statutory language and purpose, eliminates doubt as to its constitutionality. . . .

We restate here the pertinent provision of Education Code, section 10607: "On or before the third consecutive school day of any given period of suspension, the parent or guardian of the pupil involved shall be asked to attend a meeting with school officials, at which time the causes, the duration, the school policy involved, and other matters pertinent to the suspension, shall be discussed. If the parent or guardian fails to join in such a conference, the school officials shall send him by mail a letter stating the fact that suspension has been implemented and setting forth all other data pertinent to the action."

We note preliminarily that in two closely positioned Education Code sections dealing with closely related subject matter, the Legislature has used different terms. Section 10607, dealing with temporary suspension of students, calls for a "meeting" or "conference" with unspecified "school officials" for discussion of the suspension. Section 10608 . . . concerning "expulsion" of a student requires a "hearing" thereon before the "county board of education" which shall thereafter "render its decision." Such a radical change in the wording of adjacent code sections "cannot be deemed meaningless and without design." . . . " 'When different language is used in the same connection in different parts of a statute it is to be presumed the Legislature intended a different meaning and effect.' " . . .

In People v. Pennington . . . 426 P.2d 942, 951, it is said, "A 'hearing' is generally understood to be a proceeding where evidence is taken to the end of determining an issue of fact and a decision made on the basis of that evidence. * * * " It must reasonably be assumed that the Legislature in enacting section 10607 also understood the ordinary meaning of the word "hearing" and chose to mandate something less than a "full due process hearing" as the term is used by petitioners.

Adverting to section 10607 we observe that upon failure of the parent or guardian to attend the "meeting" with school officials, he shall be notified by letter that the "suspension has been implemented [i. e., carried into effect] and setting forth all other data" pertinent to the suspension. This must be construed as indicating that the suspension initially was provisional, to be confirmed and continued only in the absence of disclosure of good reason at the meeting why it should not.

We further construe the section to provide the following. On or before the third day of a student's suspension notice shall be given his parent or guardian by mail, telephone, or other reasonable means, of the fact of and reason for the suspension, with a request that the parent or guardian attend a meeting with the school officials concerning the suspension. The meeting shall be promptly held unless the parent or guardian shall otherwise request. At the meeting "the causes, the duration, the school policy involved, and other matters pertinent to the suspension, shall be discussed." The suspended student may of course attend the meeting. "Matters pertinent to the suspension" would include any reason, or informal proof, why the suspension should not continue, including, but not limited to, claims of mistaken identity or obviously false charges. If good reason to the contrary is not shown the suspension may then be implemented and continued. Upon failure of the parent or guardian to attend the meeting he shall be advised by "letter stating the fact that suspension has been implemented and setting forth all other data pertinent to the action."

So construed section 10607 affords to the suspended student "proper notice of the charges, and at least an attempt to ascertain accurately the facts involved and to give the student an opportunity to present his side of the case." . . . And it gives to the student "fair notice and a fair hearing" in the circumstances of limited suspension. . . .

We accordingly hold that section 10607, as interpreted by this court, meets the due process of law demands of the state and federal Constitutions.

PROCEDURAL RIGHTS PRIOR TO EXPULSION

TIBBS v. BOARD OF EDUCATION

Superior Court of New Jersey, 1971.
114 N.J.Super. 287, 276 A.2d 165.

PER CURIAM.

The expulsions of appellants are reversed and set aside for failure to produce the accusing witnesses for testimony and cross-examination.

The matters are remanded to the Commissioner of Education for rehearing *de novo* of the charges on which appellants were expelled should the local school authorities choose to prosecute them. No costs.

CONFORD, P. J. A. D. (concurring).

The *per curiam* opinion of the court represents what all the members of the court can agree upon. I herewith supplement that determination with my own reasons for joining therein and my own more specific views as to what the Commissioner of Education should do and the local school authorities may do at this juncture.

We granted leave to appeal an interlocutory decision of the State Commissioner of Education, but denied appellants' request for *ad interim* readmission to classes at Franklin High School from which they had theretofore been expelled or suspended for an alleged physical assault upon other students said to have occurred October 7, 1970. (All were ultimately expelled.) The Supreme Court on motion thereafter directed the appellants to be readmitted to school, subject to good behavior, pending determination of this appeal.

The sole issue presented is whether a high school student may be expelled from school on the charge of physical assault upon another student where the hearing conducted by the local board of education on the charge is not preceded by identification to the accused of the accusing student witnesses whose *ex parte* statements the school administration has relied on in bringing the disciplinary proceedings and where such witnesses do not appear to testify at the hearing. My view, and I believe that of the court, is that this procedure denies due process to the student so expelled, and this notwithstanding a determination by the local board, held warranted by the State Commissioner, that the student witnesses were afraid to testify because of fear of physical reprisal and should not be compelled to do so against their will.

On October 7, 1970, according to hearsay testimony adduced before the local board and the Commissioner, two students at the school, sisters, were assaulted by a group of others, all or mostly girls, while all were walking home after classes, a short distance from the school exits. They were struck with a stick, pushed to the ground and jumped upon or kicked, and some of their possessions were taken from them and purloined or scattered. One of them sustained the destruction of her eyeglasses. Both had minor injuries. They ran, crying, back to the guidance office at the school. It appears that neither could, or was willing to, identify any of the attackers. But a number of student witnesses volunteered statements to the school authorities identifying appellants and others (about ten in all) as involved in the episode. They were apparently assured, upon request, that they would not be identified to the accused students because of fear of physical retaliation.

The alleged assailants were, so far as available, called in for interviews, and generally denied complicity. But some stated they were in the vicinity and had seen part of the events. In the case of appellant Tanya Tibbs, statements of other students supporting her defense that she had seen but not participated in the occurrence were proffered to the school authorities by her parents, but investigation thereof failed to satisfy the authorities that the *prima facie* case against her had been impaired. We are informed that initial suspensions were imposed upon a total of ten students. After informal hearings the suspensions were lifted as to five of the accused, but the other five, including the four present appellants, were expelled by the board of education after hearings substantially of the kind afforded Tanya, and described hereafter.

Tanya was originally notified of a suspension to begin October 13, 1970 and to terminate November 16. (She remained out of school until the Supreme Court order of January 25, 1971.) Tanya's parents were given notice October 27, 1970 by the superintendent of schools that the board of education would meet November 2, 1970 for a full hearing to consider the recommendation of the school principal and himself that the girl be expelled from school for "assault upon a student of Franklin High School"; that they could be represented by an attorney; that the vice-principal and principal would testify and be subject to cross-examination, and that signed statements of student witnesses would be presented but that such students would not appear at the hearing. The accused pupil would have the right to present testimony of witnesses or a signed statement by any witness not desiring or able to attend.

The hearing was postponed to November 9, 1970 at the request of Tanya's attorney but the latter was informed that the statements of the student witnesses to be provided would not be signed or identified.

At the hearing before the board the principal and vice-principal of the high school testified concerning their investigation and the informal hearings they conducted as to the incident, resulting in findings and conclusions by them substantially to the effect indicated above, including that of Tanya's guilt. The principal also testified that he had received a telephone call from the mother of one of the accused students threatening the life of one of the prospective student witnesses. There was testimony that the student witnesses were in terror of retaliation if their identity was revealed to the accused students. The principal explained that the problem he faced in deciding whether to produce the children to testify was "a two-fold one: What happens within the confines of a racially tense school; and my own concern for the continued safety of the students involved." (It seems agreed there has been a history of racial conflicts at the school.) The board voted to accept into evidence unsigned and unidentified statements by student witnesses, and three such were read into the record. In each such statement Tanya was identified as one of those "doing the hitting." A statement by the victims, identified as the Cornwell sisters, was also read. This described the occurrence but omitted identification of any assailant.

The attorney for Tanya objected throughout the hearing to the failure to identify and produce and subject to cross-examination any of the accusing witnesses whose statements were read. On the basis of that deficiency he refused to adduce defensive testimony by or on behalf of his client. He had also at the outset of the hearing moved that two members of the board disqualify themselves as prejudiced because of public statements previously made by them concerning the incident and alleged antecedent related occurrences. The motion was denied.

The board of education thereupon voted Tanya guilty and then took testimony concerning her prior disciplinary record in school. This was generally poor. After argument by counsel against expulsion the board voted that determination.

Tanya filed an appeal against the expulsion with the Commissioner of Education and petitioned him for *ad interim* relief of admission to classes pending adjudication. A hearing on the petition was conducted November 20, 1970 before the Division of Controversies and Disputes at which the school principal testified to the substance of what had been adduced before the local board. On December 1, 1970 the Commissioner of Education denied *ad interim* relief. He expressly decided that the procedure used by the local board comported with due process and that he was satisfied by the testimony of the principal "that school officials had sufficient cause for concern regarding the safety of potential student witnesses" so as to justify not "releasing the students' names" or permitting their cross-examination.

It is not necessary here to pursue in detail the long and uneven development of the law over the past century concerning appropriate procedures in school and college student disciplinary proceedings.
.   .   .

To summarize briefly, the early cases, particularly in relation to proceedings below the college level, generally did not recognize due process concepts as appropriate to the exercise of discipline of students, even in the case of expulsion. The idea of the school administrators being *in loco parentis* to students of secondary and primary grade level held some sway. In the course of time, however, when the sanction applied for misconduct was expulsion or suspension of severe duration, especially in college-level cases, the decisions began to speak in terms of hearing requirements of due process. But a variety of expressions can be found in the cases as to the specifics of fair hearings or due process, particularly in relation to such claimed incidents as the right of counsel, personal appearances of accusing witnesses, and the right of cross-examination of such witnesses by the defense. The variations are probably explainable on the basis of the diversity of attendant circumstances in different cases—the nature of the offense; nature of the prosecuting and adjudicating entities; ages of the accused students and of witnesses; stage of the proceedings in the entirety of the process of investigation, punishment-treatment and review; and effect of statutory provisions, e. g., as to right to subpoena witnesses or to counsel, or the absence thereof, etc. See Madera v. Board of Education, City of New York, 386 F.2d 778 (2 Cir. 1967) cert. den. . . . Schwartz v. Schuker, 298 F.Supp. 238 (E.D.N.Y. 1969).

Our own statutes are rudimentary. N.J.S.A. 18A:37–2 provides that certain types of pupil misbehavior, including "d. physical assault upon another pupil * * *" may be attended by "suspension or expulsion from school." A principal may suspend any pupil "for good cause" but must report it forthwith to the superintendent of schools. The superintendent must report the suspension to the board of education at its next regular meeting. Either the principal or superintendent may reinstate the pupil prior to the second regular meeting of the board thereafter unless the board does so at its first meeting. N.J.S.A. 18A:37–4. No suspension may continue beyond the second regular meeting of the board after the suspension unless the board continues it, "and the power to reinstate, continue any suspension reported to it or expel a pupil shall be vested in each board." N.J.S.A. 18A:37–5. No hearing procedures attendant upon suspensions or expulsions are specified.

The leading decision of the modern era relating to fair procedures in college expulsion cases is Dixon v. Alabama State Board of Education, 294 F.2d 150 (5 Cir. 1961), cert. den. 368 U.S. 930, 82 S.Ct. 368, 7 L.Ed.2d 193 (1961). The guidelines there stated were quoted in full in R. R. v. Board of Education, Shore Reg. H.S., supra, (109 N.J.Super at 349, 263 A.2d 180) and need not be repeated here. . . . In contrast with the particular procedures followed here, the *Dixon* guidelines require affording the accused student in advance the names of the witnesses against him and a report of the facts they attest to.

Cross-examination of witnesses and a "full-dress judicial hearing" is said not to be necessary. . . . Some cases, however, seem to suggest the desirability of production of the accusatory witnesses at the hearing and allowance of their cross-examination. Esteban v. Central Missouri State College, 277 F.Supp. 649, 651–652 (W.D.Mo. 1967) . . .

In R. R. v. Board of Education, Shore Reg. H.S., supra, our Chancery Division held a *Dixon*-type hearing mandatory as a condition for suspension of indefinite duration of a high school student charged with an assault on another child (off-school premises). The New Jersey State Department of Education has heretofore recognized the general requirements of procedural due process in relation to school students facing severe disciplinary sanctions. Scher v. Board of Education, West Orange, 1968 School Law Decisions 92, 95.

There is no issue in the present case as to the necessity for a "fair hearing procedure" antecedent to imposition by a local board of education of the sanction of expulsion of a student for misconduct. Both sides agree on it. The issue is whether student witnesses against the accused must be identified to the accused and be produced and be subject to cross-examination, either (a) generally, or (b) under the circumstances of this case.

It is apparent from the decided cases that due process in the school or college context does not, by the weight of authority, require the production in person and right of cross-examination of adverse witnesses. It does call for identification of such witnesses and for supplying the accused with statements or affidavits by them verifying the charges in advance of the hearing. That much is minimally essential, in an issue over controverted objective conduct, as here, to give the accused a fair opportunity to meet and refute possibly mistaken or unfounded assertions of fact. If, despite the witnesses' fears, their identify must be revealed as a matter of minimum due process to the accused, there would seem little point in precluding the availability of the substantially more revealing personal testimony of the witnesses for the benefit both of the triers of the fact and the defense of the accused children in the search for the truth of the matter. Common experience, moreover, establishes that the right of cross-examination is almost always essential for assurance of an enlightened determination of a contested issue of fact. I therefore conclude that in the context of such a case as this not only should the accusing witnesses be identified in advance but also, as a general matter and absent the most compelling circumstances bespeaking a different course, be produced to testify and to be cross-examined.

Cross-examination of school children witnesses in proceedings like these should, however, be carefully controlled by the hearing officer or body, limited to the material essentials of the direct testimony and not be unduly protracted. Such a proceeding is decidedly not in the nature of a criminal trial nor to be encrusted with all the ordinary procedural and evidential concomitants of such a trial.

It remains to consider the particular objections raised by respondents to identification and examination at the hearing of the accusatory witnesses. I have no inclination to gainsay the determination of the local and state educational officials that these children were in a genuine state of fear over having their identity revealed. Whether the procedural policy adopted and approved at the administrative level for the handling of this matter would be justified, in the attendant circumstances, were the ultimate sanctions imposed substantially less than that of expulsion of the accused, is not the immediate issue here. I discuss that particular contingency later herein. We here confront a decision for expulsion—action which constitutes deprivation of a most drastic and potentially irreparable kind. In that setting compromise with punctilious procedural fairness becomes inacceptable. As was recently stated by a writer on the subject:

> The problem can be put in greater perspective by considering the importance of fair procedure to the student involved. He may have as much to fear from the arbitrary use of power at the secondary level as at the college or university level. This is particularly true where the misconduct may result in an expulsion or a lengthy suspension. The stigma of compulsory withdrawal may follow even a high school student for many years after the institution has considered the incident closed. Expulsion or suspension always involves a permanent notation on the student's record which may have long term effects on his ability to achieve entry into college or the job market. Moreover, if the child is unable to return to school, the economics of a premature withdrawal are startling and more tangible evidence of the burden that he must shoulder. . . .

At oral argument respondent conceded there was no assurance of early or favorable action on any application for reinstatement after expulsion which might be made by appellants, and it is apparent that admission to schools in other districts, if obtainable at all, would entail payment of a substantial nonresident fee these students could probably ill afford.

As against the interests of the pupils here accused in remaining in school, the school community must be content to deal with threats or intimidation of the kind allegedly encountered by invoking the jurisdiction of the law enforcement authorities who must be presumed equal to their responsibilities. . . .

KOLOVSKY, J. A. D. (concurring).

The State Commissioner of Education has heretofore recognized that in proceedings before a local board of education which may lead to the expulsion or suspension of a public school student for alleged misconduct—as contrasted with scholastic failure—due process requires, among other things, that the accused student be given at least the names of the witnesses against him and copies of the statements and affidavits of those witnesses. . . .

In my view, due process also requires that there be added to these minimal rights the right to demand that any such witness appear in person to answer questions. If the witness does not do so, his statement should not and may not be considered or relied on by the board.

. . . in this case the local board did not have to identify the witnesses against the accused students and could act on the basis of unsigned statements obtained from the witnesses. Justification therefor was found in the determination by the local board, based on the testimony of its investigatory staff, that the witnesses were afraid to testify for fear of physical reprisal.

In my opinion such fears afford no justification in any case for depriving the accused students of their constitutional right to be confronted by and to examine the witnesses against them. An ordered society cannot accept the view that the police and prosecuting authorities will be impotent to prevent and punish unlawful conduct of the kind which the witnesses allegedly fear, and on that basis deny the accused students their constitutional right to demand confrontation by the witnesses against them.

Such right is a fundamental aspect of due process, whatever other variant in the form of the hearing may be permitted where a public school student is charged with misconduct. . . .

It must be borne in mind that the action sought to be reviewed here is administrative action by a governmental agency, an agency which has the power to compel the attendance of witnesses. See N.J. S.A. 18A:6–20. Cases upholding expulsions or suspensions from schools or colleges that are not governmental agencies and whose administrators lack such power . . . are therefore of no precedential significance.

Rather, what is of controlling significance is the constitutional rule which mandates that a respondent charged with misconduct in a hearing before a governmental agency be given the opportunity to confront and cross-examine adverse witnesses where the decision of the governmental agency will turn on questions of fact. Goldberg v. Kelly, 397 U.S. 254, 269–270. . . .

My brother CONFORD suggests that such right of confrontation does not exist if the local board should decide that the penalty to be imposed on the accused students for the assaults and batteries with which they are charged is less than "expulsion or severe term of suspension."

I cannot agree. The constitutional rights of the accused students may not be dissipated by a decision by the local board in advance of a hearing that the penalty will not be "expulsion or a severe term of suspension." Moreover, it is evident that any suspension beyond the preliminary period of suspension which, under N.J.S.A. 18A:37–4, a principal may lawfully impose without a hearing, is a "severe term of suspension." . . .

CARTON, J. A. D. (concurring). . . .

I concur generally with the view expressed by Judge KOLOVSKY that in a disciplinary proceeding such as this which may result in expulsion, due process requires that the accused student be afforded an opportunity to confront and cross-examine adverse witnesses. However, I am concerned that our recognition of that right may be construed to mean that such a full-dress hearing is a necessary ingredient of procedural due process at the *local board level* or that our decision be interpreted to lay down the requirements of all such proceedings conducted at that level.

I would hold only that any procedures conducted by the local board must comply with the minimum requirements set forth in Dixon v. Alabama State Board of Education, 294 F.2d 150 (5 Cir. 1961), . . . The board should not be compelled, and due process does not require, the in-person production of adverse witnesses and the right of cross-examination at the local board hearing. Although cross-examination is a valuable method of developing the entire factual situation in a given case, it must be borne in mind that the proceeding is an administrative one conducted and controlled by boards of nine lay citizens ordinarily unfamiliar with legal procedures.

The courts cannot envision the whole range of situations which might arise in this administrative area. On the other hand, the Commissioner has an expertise in this field and by reason thereof is in an excellent position to develop and formulate workable and comprehensive procedures. Consequently, we should leave to his office the responsibility of determining the specific format of the hearings and the safeguards required at the board level in cases of this kind, subject of course to the fundamental requirements set forth in *Dixon*. . . .

TIBBS v. BOARD OF EDUCATION

Supreme Court of New Jersey, 1971.
59 N.J. 506, 284 A.2d 179.

PER CURIAM.

The judgment of the appellate Division is affirmed substantially for the reasons expressed in the opinion of Judge Kolovsky. (114 N.J. Super. 287, 276 A.2d 165.) . . .

PROCEDURAL RIGHTS PRIOR TO DISMISSAL

KNIGHT v. BOARD OF EDUCATION

United States District Court, E.D.N.Y., 1969.
48 F.R.D. 108.

WEINSTEIN, District Judge. This is a class action against the Board of Education of the City of New York and some of its officials by the seven named plaintiffs individually and on behalf of hundreds of fellow students allegedly dismissed from Franklin K. Lane High School on January 27, 1969. Two months after the event, March 28, the complaint was filed. It was not until April 17th that a proposed order was presented to this Court directing the defendants to show cause why a temporary injunction should not issue requiring the immediate readmission of these students. On request of the attorneys for the plaintiffs the order is not returnable until April 25, three months after the class was allegedly expelled. By telegram to counsel and individual defendants, the Court, on its own motion, ordered an appearance in Court at 9:00 A. M. today, Monday, April 21, for a conference pursuant to Rule 23 of the Federal Rules of Civil Procedure.

Allegations in the complaint and motion papers make out a prima facie failure by defendants to comply with elementary concepts of equal protection and due process in denying one of the necessities of our society—a sound high school education, important both for its own value and as a predicate for college. Defendants deny the charge, asserting that no students have been dismissed, that the school system has been, and is, making a determined and good faith attempt to provide meaningful education for all members of the class who wish it; and that it is providing intensive rehabilitative training and guidance to those members of the class, deficient in scholarship and delinquent in attendance, who are willing to prepare themselves to benefit from regular and full day-time high school attendance. The following statements of facts, except where specifically indicated, is based upon plaintiffs' contentions—strenuously controverted by defendants—and is intended only for purposes of the preliminary determinations made in this memorandum and order.

Franklin K. Lane High School (Lane) is an academic high school operated by the New York City Board of Education. On January 27, 1969, a total of 670 students were expelled from that school. Of this number, 412 were 17 years of age on April 1, 1969. Most of these 17-year olds have been discharged from the New York City Public School System and are presently receiving no public education; 258, who are under 17, were transferred to the jurisdiction of the Bureau of Attendance, an agency of the Board of Education. Many of those under 17 years of age are presently receiving instruction at an "annex" to Lane. This "annex" is inferior to Lane in physical facilities and educational exposure; it operates only three hours per day; no homework, examinations or grades are given.

It is the defendants' contention that approximately 600 students were involved; that each of them and their parents were contracted through a number of letters; and that many of the others were seen in repeated personal visits and interviews. Defendants submit that 165 students, who are over the age of 17, were voluntarily withdrawn from the school at the request of their parents; that 50 could not be located by mail or personal visitations although attempts are still being made to locate them; that 18 have returned to full-time instruction at Lane; that 70 are attending an annex of Lane where they are receiving intensive personal instruction in order to prepare them for full academic work at Lane; that 44, who are over 17, are now attending night high school; that 139, who are over 17, are still being investigated by the Bureau of Attendance although each has already received two letters and one visit; and that 112, who are under 17, are still being investigated, although each has already received two letters and one visit.

Plaintiffs assert that the only reason for this mass expulsion was the desire to relieve overcrowded conditions. No other high school in the City has found it necessary to embark upon a similar course. In effectuating the plan to relieve overcrowding, the following criteria were embodied in a mechanical rule: all students absent 30 days or more during the present school year and who had maintained an unsatisfactory academic record in the Autumn, 1968 semester, were to be dismissed from Lane.

Allegedly, no procedures were established to challenge the criteria or their application. No opportunity to adduce any mitigating circumstances or to appeal the decisions of the administrators was provided.

Among the seven named plaintiffs, the criteria were applied without regard to specific circumstances, and in a non-uniform manner. In several instances, the administrators of this program failed to adhere to their own criteria:

(1) Plaintiff Oscar Gonzalus had been absent less than 30 days in the Autumn, 1968 semester;

(2) Plaintiff Marcine Chestnut had maintained a satisfactory academic record during the Autumn, 1968 semester;

(3) Plaintiff Altamese Washington had maintained a satisfactory academic record, and had been absent less than 30 days during the Autumn, 1968 semester.

In addition, there was at least one instance in which the administrators of the program failed to take into account mitigating circumstances: Plaintiff Arthur Knight was absent from Franklin K.

Lane High School for the entire Autumn, 1968 semester because of a kidney ailment.

Three named plaintiffs meet the criteria and offer no mitigating circumstances. Plaintiffs Willie Chestnut, Joel Barry Shiggs, and Jacqueline Andrews did experience academic difficulties during the Autumn, 1968 semester, and each was absent for more than 30 days during that period.

Plaintiffs Knight and Shiggs are the only named plaintiffs under the age of 17; both are assigned to the "annex." Five of the named plaintiffs are above the age of 17. Of these, four are presently receiving no public education. Plaintiff Washington, a 17-year old senior, was readmitted to Lane on March 12, 1969. Her eligibility for June, 1969 graduation is now in doubt because of schooling she lost during her exclusion.

Plaintiffs allege that the Autumn, 1968 semester is not an appropriate time period to use in formulating criteria designed to measure desire for an education. During that semester there was a series of City-wide strikes by public school teachers; a disruptive student boycott of Lane; and disputes in several schools, among them Lane, about the propriety of establishing additional class days to compensate for those lost during the City-wide teachers' strike. Absences on "make-up" days were counted as absences on students' attendance records. During the Fall of 1968 there was also a severe influenza epidemic resulting in a large number of justifiable absences. . . .

Children have a right to due process and equal protection under the Constitution. . . . The right to attend a public school may not be denied without due process. . . .

Constitutional requirements of due process in the administration of public school systems are violated by the expulsion of students without affording them an opportunity for a hearing. . . .

Even if the criteria for expulsion were valid, lack of procedural due process, it is alleged, resulted in misapplication of the standards used. In the case of three of the named plaintiffs an opportunity to be heard might have revealed that they did not come within even the letter of the expulsion criteria; a fourth named plaintiff might well have been able to show that strict application of the guidelines would have been unjustified.

Once a state undertakes to provide free public education, it may not arbitrarily discriminate among its citizens in making it available. Brown v. Board of Education . . . New York State has assumed the task of providing free education to all those between the ages of five and 21 who wish to take advantage of the opportunity; attendance in New York City is compulsory between the ages of seven and 16. . . .

Beyond the issue of procedural due process, the facts alleged by the plaintiffs strongly suggest that hundreds of high school students may have been discriminated against by being denied the opportunity to obtain the free public education that is extended to other school-age youths in New York City. Some rational basis justifying this discrimination must be shown by the state. Hobson v. Hansen, 269 F. Supp. 401, 426, 429 (D.D.C.1967). None has yet been offered except that this action was taken to prevent overcrowding. Yet, other schools in New York City are apparently at least equally overcrowded. With the expulsion of these students, Lane has become only the second of all New York City's high schools which do not require the scheduling of "multiple sessions" to meet the demands of large numbers of students. Such discrimination, if it is proven—especially when no effective alternate educational opportunity is provided—must be considered invidious, and in violation of the requirements of the Equal Protection Clause of the Fourteenth Amendment.

The question of whether a case has been stated for a constitutionally prohibited discrimination within Lane between those students who have been retained and those who have been expelled, is closer. If it were really necessary to take such a drastic step to relieve overcrowding, it would be difficult to classify as unreasonable, arbitrary, or capricious a determination that only those who may benefit the most and who have shown the greatest interest may continue.

If, however, a determination based upon interest is made, it must be made in a reasonable manner and upon reasonable premises. The facts upon which the distinction has been based cannot be said, at this stage of the litigation, to be of unquestionable relevance. The disruptions that took place during the Fall period—a fact of which this Court must take judicial notice—were hardly conducive to the development of typical academic performances. Since the choice of a period upon which to base the figures which formed the criteria for expulsion may have been constitutionally irrational, productive of untypical and distorted results, the actions of the school authorities may have resulted in an invidious discrimination in violation of the Fourteenth Amendment guarantees of equal protection.

In sum, in addition to the legal problems created by the alleged denial of due process to those students who allegedly have been expelled, there are questions of denial of equal protection raised by the action of the school authorities. Serious questions arise on two levels. First, has the action of the Board of Education resulted in an arbitrary and forbidden discrimination between the students at Lane and the students of other high schools in the City of New York? Second, has there been an invidious discrimination within Lane, between those students expelled and those continued as pupils? Plaintiffs have asserted a valid cause of action entitling them to immediate consideration of their claim that unless this Court acts at once they will be seriously harmed by denial of their constitutional rights. . . .

MODEL SCHOOL DISCIPLINARY CODE
prepared by **Jeff Kobrick** with **Pat Lines**
Center for Law and Education, Harvard University.

Reprinted from INEQUALITY IN EDUCATION, #12, 1972, pp. 47–49,
a publication of the Center for Law and Education, Cambridge, Mass.

The model code which follows was prepared by lawyers at the Center for Law and Education as a guide to procedural due process . . . [for elementary and secondary schools]. It . . . would require some modification if it were to be used as state legislation. We thank Sue Martinez of the Youth Law Center and Ralph Faust of the Juvenile Law Center for their comments on earlier drafts.

Section 1.   The imposition of serious discipline upon any student including, but not limited to, suspension, transfer and expulsion, shall be governed by the provisions of this Code.

Section 2.   No student shall be suspended, transferred, expelled or otherwise seriously disciplined except on the basis of published and clear rules which reasonably inform students.

(a) of the specific kinds of conduct which can form the basis for punishment or discipline, and

(b) of the nature, and, in the case of a separation from school, duration of the punishment which can be imposed for each type of conduct which is prohibited by the rules.

Section 3.   Any rules which form the basis for discipline shall be distributed to students and their parents at the beginning of each school year and shall be posted in conspicuous places within each school throughout the school year.   Changes in the rules shall not take effect until they are distributed to students and parents.

Section 4.   No student shall be disciplined for, and no school rule or policy shall prohibit, impede or discourage, the exercise of constitutionally protected rights.

Section 5.   The principal or head administrative officer of each school shall have the sole power to initiate proceedings to suspend, transfer or expel any student.   If, upon receiving a complaint of possible student misconduct, the principal believes the matter is a potential disciplinary one, he shall fully investigate the facts.   Whenever possible, facts shall be obtained from those who directly observed them, and the student shall be allowed fully to explain his side of the story (although the student shall be advised that he has a right to remain silent if he wishes.)   The principal may hold a post-investigation conference with the student and his parents.

Section 6.   If, after full investigation, discussion, and attempted resolution of a complaint against a student, the principal finds

(a) that there is evidence that the student has actually committed the conduct charged, and

      (b) that the matter cannot be handled through discussion or counselling, he may initiate the hearing procedure, as provided below, to suspend, transfer, or expel any student.

The principal shall make every effort to resolve potential disciplinary matters through discussion and counselling.

Section 7.   Prior to the suspension, transfer, or expulsion of any student, except as provided in section 16 below, the student shall be accorded a due process hearing.   The hearing shall be before an impartial panel which shall consist of

      (a) an assistant superintendent, designated by the school committee;

      (b) a student designated by the student council or some other fairly representative student group within the school;

      (c) a teacher designated by the student who is charged with misconduct.

The principal shall be the charging party, and the assistant superintendent shall convene the hearing panel.   The principal shall not discuss the merits of the case with any member of the hearing panel prior or subsequent to the hearing.

Section 8.   The principal shall furnish the student written notice of the hearing sufficiently in advance to allow him adequately to prepare his defense.   The notice shall contain the following:

      (a) the time and place of the hearing;

      (b) a statement of the specific facts alleged against the student, the school rule(s) allegedly violated, and the proposed discipline;

      (c) the student's right to be represented by an advocate of his choosing (including counsel);

      (d) the student's right to present evidence, call witnesses, and cross-examine adverse witnesses; and

      (e) a copy of the school code of discipline.

Section 9.   All hearings shall be conducted as follows:

      (a) it shall be private, unless the student requests that it be public;

      (b) no evidence shall be offered against a student unless prior to the hearing the student is allowed to inspect written evidence and is informed of the names of witnesses against him and the substance of their testimony;

      (c) all parties shall have the right to present evidence, call witnesses, cross-examine adverse witnesses, and submit rebuttal evidence.   All testimony shall be given under oath;

      (d) the student shall have the right to be represented by an advocate of his choice (including counsel);

    (e) the student shall have the right to confront any witnesses against him;

    (f) the hearing panel or committee shall not be required to observe the same rules of evidence observed by the courts, but evidence may be admitted and given probative effect only if it is the kind of evidence on which reasonable persons are accustomed to rely in the conduct of serious affairs. The scope of the hearing shall be confined to the charges contained in the notice required by section 8;

    (g) the hearing panel or committee shall make a verbatim transcript or tape recording of the hearing, a copy of which shall be made available to the student;

    (h) the hearing panel or committee shall issue a written decision stating its findings of fact and the evidence upon which the findings are based. Findings shall be based solely on relevant evidence presented at the hearing.

Section 10.   No decision that disciplinary action is warranted shall be made unless the hearing panel first finds, upon the basis of clear and convincing evidence,

    (a) that the student has, in fact, committed the conduct charged;

    (b) that the student's conduct violated a published school rule; and

    (c) that the student had reasonable notice that his conduct was prohibited by a school rule.

If the panel so finds against the student, it shall, by majority vote, take such disciplinary action as it may deem appropriate; provided, however, that such action shall not be more severe than that recommended by the principal.

Section 11.   In any case where the hearing panel imposes a suspension or transfer of ten or more school days, or expulsion, the student shall have a right, upon request, to a hearing before the school committee, which shall be conducted according to the rules set forth in section 9.

The scope of the school committee hearing shall be confined to the charges contained in the notice required by section 8.

The student shall be allowed to attend his regularly-assigned school pending the school committee hearing unless the hearing panel below finds, on the basis of clear and substantial evidence, that his continued presence presents a threat to the physical safety of others or that his conduct is so extremely disruptive as to make his removal necessary to preserve the right of other students to pursue an education.

Where the student is out of school, the hearing before the school committee shall be held within seven days from the day of his exclusion or transfer, unless the student or his representative move for an extension of time to allow adequate preparation.

Section 12. No student shall be expelled from school unless both the hearing panel and the school committee find, beyond a reasonable doubt, that he has engaged in frequent and repetitive conduct of such an extreme and serious nature as to make his removal for the rest of the school year necessary to protect the physical safety of others or to preserve the right of other students to pursue an education.

Section 13. In expulsion cases the student shall be represented by counsel, and the school committee shall pay for, or retain counsel to represent the student at all stages of the proceedings where the student is, himself, unable to retain or pay for counsel (for whatever reason). The school committee shall also compel the attendance, both at the initial hearing and at the school committee hearing, of witnesses requested by the student who are employed in the school system.

Section 14. No expulsion shall last beyond the school year in which it is made. The school committee shall notify an expelled student by registered mail of his right to re-enroll in school at the beginning of the school year following the expulsion.

Section 15. In the event that disciplinary action is not found warranted by either the hearing panel or the school committee, all notations relating thereto shall be completely removed from all school records. Students shall have the right to inspect their school records to ensure that such matters are removed, and also so that they will have reasonable opportunity to bring to the attention of school authorities and to rebut or correct any mistaken or incorrect information or notation thereon.

Section 16. The principal of a school (or an impartial person designated by a school committee to take his place where he is a complaining party) may take emergency action, including temporary suspension, after making a finding, that

    (a) the student's conduct presents a clear threat to the physical safety of others, or is so extremely disruptive as to make the student's temporary removal necessary to preserve the right of other students to pursue an education;

    (b) it is impossible to hold the hearing described in section 9 because of the emergency nature of the situation.

The principal or impartial person shall do everything feasible to assure that the temporary action is based upon a clear factual situation warranting it, including questioning the student and the complaining party in the student's presence.

A temporary suspension or removal shall last no longer than necessary to avoid the dangers described in (a) of this section, and in such cases the principal or impartial person shall make a written report of his findings to the student and to the school committee. In no event shall a student be temporarily suspended under this section for more than three consecutive school days or more than a total of six school days in a school year without the full hearing provided for in sections 7–10 above.

NOTES AND QUESTIONS

1. Should any of the provisions in the above statement be revised? If so, how and why?

Chapter IX

CONSTITUTIONAL FREEDOM AND RACIAL DESEGREGATION

THE CONCEPT OF RACE

"Race" is not a sufficiently descriptive concept to be very helpful to physical anthropologists and to other physical scientists who study human populations from a genetic point of view. "Race" may be an important concept that can be culturally defined in various ways by sociologists, cultural historians or others who study people because people act in accordance with their cultural attitudes, whether their attitudes are well founded or not. But, as put by one eminent scholar:

> "The scientific study of human races is at least two centuries old. There are nevertheless few natural phenomena, and probably no other aspect of human nature, the investigation of which has so often floundered in confusion and misunderstanding." Dobzhansky, Mankind Evolving, 253 (Yale University Press, 1962).

The past history of racial classifications in the United States demonstrates that differently defined racial classifications were enacted into law during the height of this country's confusions and misunderstandings about race at a time of extreme social prejudice, and with the most deleterious social consequences. See, e. g., G. Myrdal, An American Dilemma: The Negro Problem and Modern Democracy (1944), and A. Montagu, Man's Most Dangerous Myth: The Fallacy of Race (1964).

It is now generally agreed that man, the genus *Homo,* is not more than a single specie to which all living races belong. Species are groups of inbreeding natural populations, reproductively isolated from other such groups. "Reproductive isolation" does not refer to spatial or geographical isolation, but rather to physical capacity. It refers to the *inability* to mate with other species and produce fertile progeny. A species, therefore is a genetically closed system since new genes, the biological units of inheritance, cannot be obtained from other groups and passed on through fertile hybrids. Thus, the species is the basic group for biological and anthropological classification.

See generally, Simpson, Principles of Animal Taxonomy 18, 148–152 (1961); Dobzhansky, supra (1962).

Between the individual organism—which is the basic unit of the species—and the species itself, is another layer of cultural, but not physical, classification known as race. These racial classifications are classifications based on population groups within the species, which because of social or geographical boundaries, have tended to inbreed among themselves over long periods of time. As a result of this endogamy, they tend to express certain similar physical and genetic characteristics. See Johnston, The Population Approach to Human Variation, 134 Annals of the New York Academy of Sciences, 507–515 (Feb. 28, 1966).

The process of classification and of the variability of racial classification has recently been described in this manner:

"A race of *Homo sapiens* is a Mendelian population, a reproductive community of individuals sharing a common gene pool. The level at which the reproductive community is defined depends upon the problem one is interested in investigating. There is no absolute, final or 'true' level at which these reproductive communities are defined. All members of our species belong to one Mendelian population, and its name is *Homo sapiens*. This large specie-wide Mendelian population may be divided into smaller Mendelian populations, for all practical purposes an infinitely large number of them . . . Races are open genetic systems, and as such they are quite different from species." Reuttner-Janusch, Book Review, American Journal of Physical Anthropology, 25:2, September 1966, p. 184.

The practical truth of the statement that the number of races can be infinite depending upon who is the classifier, is shown by Garn and Coon in an article, *On the Number of Races of Mankind*. (57 American Anthropologist 996 (1955)) Differing classificatory systems have listed as few as two races and as many as two hundred. The difference depends upon whether the classifier is a "lumper", one who groups a number of varieties into one broad category because the differences are considered too trivial to warrant special classification, or a "splitter", one who believes that distinctness and variety merit attention, but even in the latter case each minute distinction is not separately classed. Garn, Human Races 15 (3rd. ed. 1971). The usual approach to racial classifications is to focus on geography, either on a few geographical races, or on many local or microgeographical races.

A geographical race may be defined as "a collection of similar populations inhabiting a broad continental area or island chain."

A local race is a more neatly circumscribed physically or socially isolated inbreeding population group. If the classifier uses the geographical races, then depending upon the criteria used, the number can be "approximately six or seven." If the classifier uses local races, the number can be "upwards of thirty." Garn & Coon, supra 999. In other words, even at the level of greatest organization, the number is only an approximation. There is, of course, no agreement on the precise number of geographical races or of the peoples that properly should be included within them. See classifications noted in Comas, Manual of Physical Anthropology, 18–19, 303–309 (1960) and Dobzhansky, supra, 262–265. Geographical races, the type of concept that has been used most often in the United States, are merely "collections of convenience." Garn and Coon, supra, 1000. They have insufficient scientific accuracy for the population geneticist. This is not to say that racial classifications have had an unimportant social history in the United States.

Moreover, when an individual leaves his population group and mates with an individual in another group, the racial classification of the offspring is immediately put in question. When miscegenation —which within the last five centuries has risen to rates unprecedented in human history—becomes widespread, "classifications of convenience" become even more blurred, loose and inexact. This is the situation in the United States today. The point is that there is only one "race"—the human race. For excellent analysis of this subject, see, L. Morris, Human Populations, Genetic Variation and Evolution (1971); S. M. Garn, Human Races (3rd. ed., 1971), and R. A. Goldsby, Race and Races (1971).

RACIAL SEGREGATION

Although the concept of race lacks scientific validity, the Supreme Court of the United States approved the use of legislatively defined racial classification in 1896. In Plessy v. Ferguson, 163 U.S. 537, 16 S.Ct. 1138, 41 L.Ed. 256 (1896), the Court sustained the constitutional validity of a Louisiana statute requiring "equal but separate accommodations" for white and Negro railway passengers. The statute had been attacked as violative of the Fourteenth Amendment's prohibition that no state shall " . . . deny to any person within its jurisdiction the equal protection of the laws." In his Opinion for the Court, Mr. Justice Brown approved of the "separate but equal doctrine" holding that:

> "The object of the [Fourteenth] Amendment was undoubtedly to enforce the absolute equality of the two races

before the law, but in the nature of things it could not have been intended to abolish distinctions based upon color, or to enforce social, as distinguished from political equality, or a commingling of the two races upon terms unsatisfactory to either. Laws permitting, and even requiring, their separation in places where they are liable to be brought into contact do not necessarily imply the inferiority of either race to the other, and have been generally, if not universally, recognized as within the competency of the state legislatures in the exercise of their police power. The most common instance of this is connected with the establishment of separate schools for white and colored children, which has been held to be a valid exercise of the legislative power even by courts of States where the political rights of the colored race have been longest and most earnestly enforced. . . .

"[This] case reduces itself to the question whether the statute of Louisiana is a reasonable regulation, and with respect to this there must necessarily be a large discretion on the part of the legislature. In determining the question of reasonableness it is at liberty to act with reference to the established usages, customs and traditions of the people, and with a view to the promotion of their comfort, and the preservation of the public peace and good order. Gauged by this standard, we cannot say that [this law] is unreasonable, or more obnoxious to the Fourteenth Amendment than the acts of Congress requiring separate schools for colored children in the District of Columbia, the constitutionality of which does not seem to have been questioned, or the corresponding acts of state legislatures.

"We consider the underlying fallacy of the plaintiff's argument to consist in the assumption that the enforced separation of the two races stamps the colored race with a badge of inferiority. If this be so, it is not by reason of anything found in the act, but solely because the colored race chooses to put that construction upon it. The argument necessarily assumes that if, as has been more than once the case, and is not unlikely to be so again, the colored race should become the dominant power, and should enact a law in precisely similar terms, it would thereby relegate the white race to an inferior position. We imagine that the white race, at least, would not acquiesce in this assumption. The argument also assumes that social prejudices may be overcome by legislation, and that equal rights cannot be secured to the negro except by an enforced commingling of the two races. We cannot accept this proposition. If the two races are to meet upon terms of social equality, it must be the result of natural affinities, a mutual appreciation of each other's merits and a voluntary consent of individuals. . . . Legislation is powerless to eradicate racial instincts or to abolish distinctions based upon physical differences, and the attempt to do so can only result in accentuating the difficulties of the present situation. If the civil and political rights of both races be equal one cannot be inferior to the other civilly or politically. If one race be inferior to the other socially, the Constitution of the United States cannot put them upon the same plane."

The first Mr. Justice Harlan dissented, saying:

". . . It was said in argument that the statute of Louisiana does not discriminate against either race, but prescribes a rule applicable alike to white and colored citizens. But this argument does not meet the difficulty. Every one knows that [Louisiana's law] had its origin in the purpose, not so much to exclude white persons from railroad cars occupied by blacks, as to exclude colored people from coaches occupied by or assigned to white persons. . . . The thing to accomplish was, under the guise of giving equal accommodation for whites and blacks, to compel the latter to keep to themselves while travelling in railroad passenger coaches. No one would be so wanting in candor as to assert the contrary. The fundamental objection, therefore, to the statute is that it interferes with the personal freedom of citizens. . . .

"The white race deems itself to be the dominant race in this country. And so it is, in prestige, in achievements, in education, in wealth and in power. So, I doubt not, it will continue to be for all time, if it remains true to its great heritage and holds fast to the principles of constitutional liberty. But in view of the Constitution, in the eye of the law, there is in this country no superior, dominant, ruling class of citizens. There is no caste here. Our Constitution is color-blind, and neither knows nor tolerates classes among citizens. There is no caste here. . . . The destinies of the two races, in this country, are indissolubly linked together, and the interests of both require that the common government of all shall not permit the seeds of race hate to be planted under the sanction of law. What can more certainly arouse race hate, what more certainly create and perpetuate a feeling of distrust between these races, than state enactments, which, in fact, proceed on the ground that colored citizens are so inferior and degraded that they cannot be allowed to sit in public coaches occupied by white citizens?

That, as all will admit, is the real meaning of such legislation as was enacted in Louisiana. . . .

"The arbitrary separation of citizens, on the basis of race, while they are on a public highway, is a badge of servitude wholly inconsistent with the civil freedom and the equality before the law established by the Constitution. It cannot be justified upon any legal grounds. . . . The thin disquise of 'equal' accommodations for passengers in railroad coaches will not mislead anyone, nor atone for the wrong this day done. . . ."

NOTES AND QUESTIONS

1. What reason did the Court give as justification for its decision? Do you agree?

2. By what criteria can one accurately judge who is "white" or "Negro"? Plessy was alleged to have been "seven-eighths Caucasian and one-eighth African blood" and that "the mixture of colored blood was not discernible in him." Was Plessy "white" or "Negro"?

3. The Court drew a line between "social" and "political" equality, indicating that the Fourteenth Amendment's "equal protection" clause only applies to the latter. Is this distinction workable? Could the separate but equal doctrine be applied to a mixed jury, or would it require that the jury be of one "race"? Could the doctrine be applied and still allow for a mixed faculty?

4. What promotion of the public's welfare was achieved by Louisiana's law?

5. Is it possible for two educational facilities, one for black students and one for whites, ever to be equal? In faculty? In Library? In scientific laboratories? In other facilities? In equality of classroom instruction? In student populations? If not, what does "equal" in "separate but equal" mean? If one "race" is dominant in political and social power, will the "inferior race" actually enjoy "equal" educational, or other, opportunities?

6. How would you have decided this case and for what reason(s)?

"THE EQUAL PROTECTION OF THE LAWS"

BROWN v. BOARD OF EDUCATION

Supreme Court of the United States, 1954.
347 U.S. 483, 74 S.Ct. 686, 98 L.Ed. 873.

Mr. Chief Justice WARREN delivered the opinion of the Court.

These cases come to us from the States of Kansas, South Carolina, Virginia, and Delaware. . . .

segregation

In each of the cases, minors of the Negro race, through their legal representatives, seek the aid of the courts in <u>obtaining admission to the public schools of their community on a nonsegregated basis</u>. In each instance, they had been denied admission to schools attended by white children under laws requiring or permitting segregation according to race. This <u>segregation</u> was alleged to <u>deprive the plaintiffs of the equal protection of the laws under the Fourteenth Amendment</u>. In each of the cases other than the Delaware case, a three-judge federal district court denied relief to the plaintiffs on the so-called "separate but equal" doctrine announced by this Court in Plessy v. Ferguson, 163 U.S. 537. Under that doctrine, equality of treatment is accorded when the races are provided substantially equal facilities, even though these facilities be separate. In the Delaware case, the Supreme Court of Delaware adhered to that doctrine, but ordered that the plaintiffs be admitted to the white schools because of their superiority to the Negro schools.

The plaintiffs contend that <u>segregated public schools are not "equal" and cannot be made "equal", and that hence they are deprived of the equal protection of the laws.</u> . . .

. . . The most avid proponents of the post-[Civil] War Amendments undoubtedly intended them to remove all legal distinctions among "all persons born or naturalized in the United States." Their opponents, just as certainly, were antagonistic to both the letter and the spirit of the Amendments and wished them to have the most limited effect. What others in Congress and the state legislatures had in mind cannot be determined with any degree of certainty.

An additional reason for the inconclusive nature of the Amendment's history, with respect to segregated schools, is the status of public education at that time. In the South, the movement toward free common schools, supported by general taxation, had not yet taken hold. Education of white children was largely in the hands of private groups. Education of Negroes was almost nonexistent, and practically all of the race were illiterate. In fact, any education of Negroes was forbidden by law in some states. Today, in contrast, many Negroes have achieved outstanding success in the arts and sciences as well as in the business and professional world. It is true that public school education at the time of the Amendment had advanced further in the North, but the effect of the Amendment on Northern States was generally ignored in the congressional debates. Even in the North, the conditions of public education did not approximate those existing today. The curriculm was usually rudimentary; ungraded schools were common in rural areas; the school term was but three months a year in many states; and compulsory school attendance was virtually unknown. As a consequence, it is not surprising that there should be so little in the history of the

Fourteenth Amendment relating to its intended effect on public education.

.   .   .   The doctrine of "separate but equal" did not make its appearance in this Court until 1896 in the case of Plessy v. Ferguson, supra, involving not education but transportation.   American courts have since labored with the doctrine for over half a century.   In this Court, there have been six cases involving the "separate but equal" doctrine in the field of public education.   In Cumming v. County Board of Education, 175 U.S. 528, and Gong Lum v. Rice, 275 U.S. 78, the validity of the doctrine itself was not challenged.   In more recent cases, all on the graduate school level, inequality was found in that specific benefits enjoyed by white students were denied to Negro students of the same educational qualifications.   Missouri ex rel. Gaines v. Canada, 305 U.S. 337; Sipuel v. Oklahoma, 332 U.S. 631; Sweatt v. Painter, 339 U.S. 629; McLaurin v. Oklahoma State Regents, 339 U.S. 637.   In none of these cases was it necessary to re-examine the doctrine to grant relief to the Negro plaintiff.   And in Sweatt v. Painter, supra, the Court expressly reserved decision on the question whether Plessy v. Ferguson should be held inapplicable to public education.

In the instant cases, that question is directly presented.   Here, unlike Sweatt v. Painter, there are findings below that the Negro and white schools involved have been equalized, or are being equalized, with respect to buildings, curricula, qualifications and salaries of teachers, and other "tangible" factors.   Our decision, therefore, cannot turn on merely a comparison of these tangible factors in the Negro and white schools involved in each of the cases.   We must look instead to the effect of segregation itself in public education.

In approaching this problem, we cannot turn the clock back to 1868 when the Amendment was adopted, or even to 1896 when Plessy v. Ferguson was written.   We must consider public education in the light of its full development and its present place in American life throughout the Nation.   Only in this way can it be determined if segregation in public schools deprives these plaintiffs of the equal protection of the laws.

Today, education is perhaps the most important function of state and local governments.   Compulsory school attendence laws and the great expenditures for education both demonstrate our recognition of the importance of education to our democratic society.   It is required in the performance of our most basic public responsibilities, even service in the armed forces.   It is the very foundation of good citizenship.   Today it is a principal instrument in awakening the child to cultural values, in preparing him for later professional training, and in helping him to adjust normally to his environment.   In these days, it is doubtful that any child may reasonably be expected to succeed in life if he is denied the opportunity of an education.

Such an opportunity, where the state has undertaken to provide it, is a right which must be made available to all on equal terms.

We come then to the question presented: Does segregation of children in public schools solely on the basis of race, even though the physical facilities and other "tangible" factors may be equal, deprive the children of the minority group of equal educational opportunities? We believe that it does.

In Sweatt v. Painter, supra, in finding that a segregated law school for Negroes could not provide them equal educational opportunities, this Court relied in large part on "those qualities which are incapable of objective measurement but which make for greatness in a law school." In McLaurin v. Oklahoma State Regents, supra, the Court, in requiring that a Negro admitted to a white graduate school be treated like all other students, again resorted to intangible considerations: " . . . his ability to study, to engage in discussions and exchange views with other students, and, in general, to learn his profession." Such considerations apply with added force to children in grade and high schools. To separate them from others of similar age and qualifications solely because of their race generates a feeling of inferiority as to their status in the community that may affect their hearts and minds in a way unlikely ever to be undone. The effect of this separation on their educational opportunities was well stated by a finding in the Kansas case by a court which neverthless felt compelled to rule against the Negro plaintiffs:

> "Segregation of white and colored children in public schools has a detrimental effect upon the colored children. The impact is greater when it has the sanction of the law; for the policy of separating the races is usually interpreted as denoting the inferiority of the negro group. A sense of inferiority affects the motivation of a child to learn. Segregation with the sanction of law, therefore, has a tendency to [retard] the educational and mental development of negro children and to deprive them of some of the benefits they would receive in a racial[ly] integrated school system."

Whatever may have been the extent of psychological knowledge at the time of Plessy v. Ferguson, this finding is amply supported by modern authority.[11] Any language in Plessy v. Ferguson contrary to this finding is rejected.

[11] K. B. Clark, Effect of Prejudice and Discrimination on Personality Development (Midcentury White House Conference on Children and Youth, 1950); Witmer and Kotinsky, Personality in the Making (1952), c. VI; Deutscher and Chein, The Psychological Effects of Enforced Segregation: A Survey of Social Science Opinion, 26 J.Psychol. 259 (1948); Chein, What are the Psychological Effects of Segregation Under Conditions of Equal Facilities?, 3 Int.J.Opinion and Attitude Res. 229 (1949); Brameld, Educational Costs, in Discrimination and National Welfare (MacIver, ed., 1949), 44–48; Frazier, The Negro in the United States (1949), 674–681. And see generally Myrdal, An American Dilemma (1944).

We conclude that in the field of public education the doctrine of "separate but equal" has no place. Separate educational facilities are inherently unequal. Therefore, we hold that the plaintiffs and others similarly situated for whom the actions have been brought are, by reason of the segregation complained of, deprived of the equal protection of the laws guaranteed by the Fourteenth Amendment. This disposition makes unnecessary any discussion whether such segregation also violates the Due Process Clause of the Fourteenth Amendment.

Because these are class actions, because of the wide applicability of this decision, and because of the great variety of local conditions, the formulation of decrees in these cases presents problems of considerable complexity. On reargument, the consideration of appropriate relief was necessarily subordinated to the primary question—the constitutionality of segregation in public education. We have now announced that such segregation is a denial of the equal protection of the laws. In order that we may have the full assistance of the parties in formulating decrees, the cases will be restored to the docket, and the parties are requested to present further argument on [the question of an adequate remedy].

BROWN v. BOARD OF EDUCATION

Supreme Court of the United States, 1955.
349 U.S. 294, 75 S.Ct. 753, 99 L.Ed. 1083.

Mr. Chief Justice WARREN delivered the opinion of the Court.

These cases were decided on May 17, 1954. The opinions of that date, declaring the fundamental principle that racial discrimination in public education is unconstitutional, are incorporated herein by reference. All provisions of federal, state, or local law requiring or permitting such discrimination must yield to this principle. There remains for consideration the manner in which relief is to be accorded.

Because these cases arose under different local conditions and their disposition will involve a variety of local problems, we requested further argument on the question of relief. In view of the nationwide importance of the decision, we invited the Attorney General of the United States and the Attorneys General of all states requiring or permitting racial discrimination in public education to present their views on that question. The parties, the United States, and the States of Florida, North Carolina, Arkansas, Oklahoma, Maryland, and Texas filed briefs and participated in the oral argument. . . .

Full implementation of these constitutional principles may require solution of varied local school problems. School authorities have the primary responsibility for elucidating, assessing, and solving these problems; courts will have to consider whether the action of school authorities constitutes good faith implementation of the governing constitutional principles. Because of their proximity to local conditions and the possible need for further hearings, the courts which originally heard these cases can best perform this judicial appraisal. Accordingly, we believe it appropriate to remand the cases to those courts.

In fashioning and effectuating the decrees, the courts will be guided by equitable principles. Traditionally, equity has been characterized by a practical flexibility in shaping its remedies and by a facility for adjusting and reconciling public and private needs. These cases call for the exercise of these traditional attributes of equity power. At stake is the personal interest of the plaintiffs in admission to public schools as soon as practicable on a nondiscriminatory basis. To effectuate this interest may call for elimination of a variety of obstacles in making the transition to school systems operated in accordance with the constitutional principles set forth in our May 17, 1954, decision. Courts of equity may properly take into account the public interest in the elimination of such obstacles in a systematic and effective manner. But it should go without saying that the vitality of these constitutional principles cannot be allowed to yield simply because of disagreement with them.

While giving weight to these public and private considerations, the courts will require that the defendants make a prompt and reasonable start toward full compliance with our May 17, 1954, ruling. Once such a start has been made, the courts may find that additional time is necessary to carry out the ruling in an effective manner. The burden rests upon the defendants to establish that such time is necessary in the public interest and is consistent with good faith compliance at the earliest practicable date. To that end, the courts may consider problems related to administration, arising from the physical condition of the school plant, the school transportation system, personnel, revision of school districts and attendance areas into compact units to achieve a system of determining admission to the public schools on a nonracial basis, and revision of local laws and regulations which may be necessary in solving the foregoing problems. They will also consider the adequacy of any plans the defendants may propose to meet these problems and to effectuate a transition to a racially nondiscriminatory school system. During this period of transition, the courts will retain jurisdiction of these cases.

The judgments below, except that in the Delaware case, are accordingly reversed and the cases are remanded to the District Courts to take such proceedings and enter such orders and decrees consistent with this opinion as are necessary and proper to admit to public schools on a racially nondiscriminatory basis with all deliberate speed the parties to these cases. The judgment in the Delaware case—ordering the immediate admission of the plaintiffs to schools previously attended only by white children—is affirmed on the basis of the principles stated in our May 17, 1954, opinion, but the case is remanded to the Supreme Court of Delaware for such further proceedings as that Court may deem necessary in light of this opinion.

It is so ordered.

NOTES AND QUESTIONS

1. Identify precisely the specific reason(s) given by the Court as justification for its decision on the merits. Do you agree? Was the decision based on the social science information cited in footnote 11? Does it rest on accepted standards of right or wrong plus the view that racial segregation by law necessarily inflicts humiliation?

2. State the principle of law in Brown v. Board of Education. What set of circumstances must be present before it can apply to future cases?

3. Does the ruling in Brown prohibit: (1) all forms of racial segregation in education; (2) only all forms that are enforced by law; (3) only all forms that are enforced by law in the public schools; or (4) only pupil assignment to public schools on the basis of race, whether such assignment is required by law or not?

4. What is the nature of a child's constitutional right? Is it a right: (1) to an integrated education; (2) to a desegregated education; (3) to require that a school board create a desegregation plan; (4) to one of the above but only "with all deliberate speed"?

5. Is the phrase "with all deliberate speed" a contradiction? Does it really call for a speedy but orderly transition to be supervised by the federal courts? If so, a transition from a dual school system to what: (1) a unitary school system, meaning only that action must be taken to produce the absence of a dual school system, or (2)a unitary school system, meaning action must be taken to produce a fully integrated system? By what criteria would you judge a school system completely to be racially integrated? How would you recognize one if you saw it?

6. Do you agree with one court's interpretation of Brown v. Board of Education? In Briggs v. Elliott, 132 F.Supp. 776 (D.C.S.1955) the court said:

> "Whatever may have been the views of this court as to the law when the case was originally before us, it is our duty now to accept the law as declared by the Supreme Court.
>
> "Having said this, it is important that we point out exactly what the Supreme Court has decided and what it has not decided in this case. It has not decided that the federal courts are to take over or regulate the public schools of the states. It is not decided that the states must mix persons of different races in the schools or must require them to attend schools or must deprive them of the right of choosing the schools they attend. What it has decided, and all that it has decided, is that a state may not deny to any person on account of race the right to attend any school that it maintains. This, under the decision of the Supreme Court, the state may not do directly or indirectly; but if the schools which it maintains are open to children of all races, no violation of the Constitution is in-

volved even though the children of different races voluntarily attend different schools, as they attend different churches. Nothing in the Constitution or in the decision of the Supreme Court takes away from the people freedom to choose the schools they attend.

"It does not forbid such segregation as occurs as the result of voluntary action. It merely forbids the use of governmental power to enforce segregation. The Fourteenth Amendment is a limitation upon the exercise of power by the state or state agencies, not a limitation upon the freedom of individuals."

BOLLING v. SHARPE

Supreme Court of the United States, 1954.
347 U.S. 497, 74 S.Ct. 693, 98 L.Ed. 884.
[This case was decided on the same day as Brown I, supra.]

Mr. Chief Justice WARREN delivered the opinion of the Court.

This case challenges the validity of segregation in the public schools of the District of Columbia. The petitioners, minors of the Negro race, allege that such segregation deprives them of due process of law under the Fifth Amendment. They were refused admission to a public school attended by white children solely because of their race. They sought the aid of the District Court for the District of Columbia in obtaining admission. That court dismissed their complaint. . . .

We have this day held that the Equal Protection Clause of the Fourteenth Amendment prohibits the states from maintaining racially segregated public schools. The legal problem in the District of Columbia is somewhat different, however. The Fifth Amendment, which is applicable in the District of Columbia, does not contain an equal protection clause as does the Fourteenth Amendment which applies only to the states. But the concepts of equal protection and due process, both stemming from our American ideal of fairness, are not mutually exclusive. The "equal protection of the laws" is a more explicit safeguard of prohibited unfairness than "due process of law," and, therefore, we do not imply that the two are always interchangeable phrases. But, as this Court has recognized, discrimination may be so unjustifiable as to be violative of due process.

Classifications based solely upon race must be scrutinized with particular care, since they are contrary to our traditions and hence constitutionally suspect. As long ago as 1896, this Court declared the principle "that the Constitution of the United States, in its present form, forbids, so far as civil and political rights are concerned, discrimination by the General Government, or by the States, against any citizen because of his race." And in Buchanan v. Warley, 245 U.S. 60, the Court held that a statute which limited the right of a property owner to convey his property to a person of another race was, as an unreasonable discrimination, a denial of due process of law.

Although the Court has not assumed to define "liberty" with any great precision, that term is not confined to mere freedom from bodily restraint. Liberty under law extends to the full range of conduct which the individual is free to pursue, and it cannot be restricted except for a proper governmental objective. Segregation in public education is not reasonably related to any proper governmental objective, and thus it imposes on Negro children of the District of Columbia a burden that constitutes an arbitrary deprivation of their liberty in violation of the Due Process Clause.

In view of our decision that the Constitution prohibits the states from maintaining racially segregated public schools, it would be unthinkable that the same Constitution would impose a lesser duty on the Federal Government. We hold that racial segregation in the public schools of the District of Columbia is a denial of the due process of law guaranteed by the Fifth Amendment to the Constitution.

For the reasons set out in Brown v. Board of Education, this case will be restored to the docket for reargument.   .   .   .

It is so ordered.

NOTES AND QUESTIONS

1. In what way(s) is Bolling different from Brown I?

2. What justifying reason(s) is given by the Court for its decision? Do you agree? Is it that schools segregated by law are "so unjustifiable as to be violative of due process?" If so, what is the relationship between the equal protection clause and the due process clause? Is every violation of equal protection thereby a violation of due process? Is the justifying reason that "segregation in public education is not reasonably related to any proper governmental objective?" What about the governmental objective of maintaining the public peace approved in Plessy?

3. What is the status of Plessy after Brown v. Board of Education and Bolling v. Sharpe?

4. Would a desegregation plan meet the requirements of Brown if it permitted a student of a minority race voluntarily to transfer back to a school, where previously, his race was in the majority? Why? See, Goss v. Knoxville Board of Education, 373 U.S. 683, 83 S.Ct. 1405, 10 L.Ed.2d 632 (1963).

5. Would a desegregation plan meet Brown's requirements of "deliberate speed" if it desegregated one grade a year, assigning pupils in the non-desegregated grades on the basis of race? See, Rogers v. Paul, 382 U.S. 198, 86 S.Ct. 358, 15 L.Ed.2d 265 (1965).

6. Would a desegregation plan meet the requirements of Brown if students, or their parents, voluntarily could choose the school at which the child would attend?

GREEN v. COUNTY SCHOOL BOARD

Supreme Court of the United States, 1968.
391 U.S. 430, 88 S.Ct. 1689, 20 L.Ed.2d 716.

Mr. Justice BRENNAN delivered the opinion of the Court.

The question for decision is whether, under all the circumstances here, respondent School Board's adoption of a "freedom-of-choice" plan which allows a pupil to choose his own public school constitutes adequate compliance with the Board's responsibility "to achieve a system of determining admission to the public schools on a nonracial basis. . . ." Brown v. Board of Education, 349 U.S. 294, 300–301 (*Brown II*).

Petitioners brought this action in March 1965 seeking injunctive relief against respondent's continued maintenance of an alleged racially segregated school system. New Kent County is a rural county in Eastern Virginia. About one-half of its population of some 4,500 are Negroes. There is no residential segregation in the county; persons of both races reside throughout. The school system has only two schools, the New Kent school on the east side of the county and the George W. Watkins school on the west side. In a memorandum filed May 17, 1966, the District Court found that the "school system serves approximately 1,300 pupils, of which 740 are Negro and 550 are White. The School Board operates one white combined elementary and high school [New Kent], and one Negro combined elementary and high school [George W. Watkins]. There are no attendance zones. Each school serves the entire county." The record indicates that 21 school buses—11 serving the Watkins school and 10 serving the New Kent school—travel overlapping routes throughout the county to transport pupils to and from the two schools.

The segregated system was initially established and maintained under the compulsion of Virginia constitutional and statutory provisions mandating racial segregation in public education, Va.Const., Art. IX, § 140 (1902); Va.Code § 22–221 (1950). These provisions were held to violate the Federal Constitution in Davis v. County School Board of Prince Edward County, decided with Brown v. Board of Education, 347 U.S. 483, 487 (*Brown I*). The respondent School Board continued the segregated operation of the system after the *Brown* decisions, presumably on the authority of several statutes enacted by Virginia in resistance to those decisions. Some of these statutes were held to be unconstitutional on their face or as applied. One statute, the Pupil Placement Act, Va.Code § 22–232.1 et seq. (1964), not repealed until 1966, divested local boards of authority to assign children to particular schools and placed that authority in a State Pupil Placement Board. Under that Act children were each year automatically reassigned to the school previously attended unless upon their application the State Board assigned them to another school; students seeking enrollment for the first time were also assigned at the discretion of the State Board. To September 1964, no Negro pupil had applied for admission to the New Kent school under this statute and no white pupil had applied for admission to the Watkins school.

The School Board initially sought dismissal of this suit on the ground that petitioners had failed to apply to the State Board for assignment to New Kent school. However on August 2, 1965, five months after the suit was brought, respondent School Board, in order to remain eligible for federal financial aid, adopted a "freedom-of-choice" plan for desegregating the schools. Under that plan, each pupil, except those entering the first and eighth grades, may annually choose between the New Kent and Watkins schools and pupils not making a choice are assigned to the school previously attended; first and eighth grade pupils must affirmatively choose a school. .   .   .

The pattern of separate "white" and "Negro" schools in the New Kent County school system established under compulsion of state laws is precisely the pattern of segregation to which *Brown I* and *Brown II* were particularly addressed, and which *Brown I* declared unconstitutionally denied Negro school children equal protection of the laws. Racial identification of the system's schools was complete, extending not just to the composition of student bodies at the two schools but to every facet of school operations—faculty, staff, transportation, extracurricular activities and facilities. In short, the State, acting through the local school board and school officials, organized and operated a dual system, part "white" and part "Negro".

It was such dual systems that 14 years ago *Brown I* held unconstitutional and a year later *Brown II* held must be abolished; school boards operating such school systems were *required* by *Brown II* "to effectuate a transition to a racially nondiscriminatory school system." 349 U.S., at 301. It is of course true that for the time immediately after *Brown II* the concern was with making an initial break in a long-established pattern of excluding Negro children from schools attended by white children. The principal focus was on obtaining for those Negro children courageous enough to break with tradition a place in the "white" schools. See, e. g., Cooper v. Aaron, 358 U.S. 1. Under *Brown II* that immediate goal was only the first step, however. The transition to a unitary, nonracial system of public education was and is the ultimate end to be brought about; it was because of the "complexities arising from the transition to a system of public education freed of racial discrimination" that we provided for "all deliberate speed" in the implementation of the principles of *Brown I*. .   .   . Thus we recognized the task would necessarily involve solution of "varied local school problems."   .   .   .   In referring to the "personal interest of the plaintiffs in admission to public schools as soon as practicable on a nondiscriminatory basis," we also noted that "[t]o effectuate this interest may call for elimination of a variety of ob-

stacles in making the transition. . . ." . . . Yet we emphasized that the constitutional rights of Negro children required school
officials to bear the burden of establishing that additional time to
carry out the ruling in an effective manner "is necessary in the
public interest and is consistent with good faith compliance at the
earliest practicable date." . . . We charged the district courts in
their review of particular situations to

> "consider problems related to administration, arising
> from the physical condition of the school plant, the school
> transportation system, personnel, revision of school districts
> and attendance areas into compact units to achieve a system
> of determining admission to the public schools on a nonracial
> basis, and revision of local laws and regulations which may be
> necessary in solving the foregoing problems. They will also
> consider the adequacy of any plans the defendants may pro-
> pose to meet these problems and to effectuate a transition to
> a racially nondiscriminatory school system." . . .

It is against this background that 13 years after *Brown II* commanded the abolition of dual systems we must measure the effectiveness of respondent School Board's "freedom-of-choice" plan to achieve
that end. The School Board contends that it has fully discharged its
obligation by adopting a plan by which every student, regardless of
race, may "freely" choose the school he will attend. The Board attempts to cast the issue in its broadest form by arguing that its
"freedom-of-choice" plan may be faulted only by reading the Fourteenth Amendment as universally requiring "compulsory integration,"
a reading it insists the wording of the Amendment will not support.
But that argument ignores the thrust of *Brown II*. In the light of the
command of that case, which is involved here is the question whether
the Board has achieved the "racially nondiscriminatory school system"
Brown II held must be effectuated in order to remedy the established
unconstitutional deficiencies of its segregated system. In the context
of the state-imposed segregated pattern of long standing, the fact that
in 1965 the Board opened the doors of the former "white" school to
Negro children and of the "Negro" school to white children merely
begins, not ends, our inquiry whether the Board has taken steps adequate to abolish its dual, segregated system. *Brown II* was a call for
the dismantling of well-entrenched dual systems tempered by an
awareness that complex and multifaceted problems would arise which
would require time and flexibility for a successful resolution. School
boards such as the respondent then operating state-compelled dual systems were nevertheless clearly charged with the affirmative duty to
take whatever steps might be necessary to convert to a unitary system
in which racial discrimination would be eliminated root and branch.
. . . The constitutional rights of Negro school children articulated
in *Brown I* permit no less than this; and it was to this end that *Brown
II* commanded school boards to bend their efforts.

In determining whether respondent School Board met that command by adopting its "freedom-of-choice" plan, it is relevant that this first step did not come until some 11 years after *Brown I* was decided and 10 years after *Brown II* directed the making of a "prompt and reasonable start." This deliberate perpetuation of the unconstitutional dual system can only have compounded the harm of such a system. Such delays are no longer tolerable, for "the governing constitutional principles no longer bear the imprint of newly enunciated doctrine." . . . Moreover, a plan that at this late date fails to provide meaningful assurance of prompt and effective disestablishment of a dual system is also intolerable. "The time for mere 'deliberate speed' has run out," Griffin v. County School Board, 377 U.S. 218, 234; "the context in which we must interpret and apply this language [of *Brown II*] to plans for desegregation has been significantly altered." . . . The burden on a school board today is to come forward with a plan that promises realistically to work, and promises realistically to work *now*.

The obligation of the district courts, as it always has been, is to assess the effectiveness of a proposed plan in achieving desegregation. There is no universal answer to complex problems of desegregation; there is obviously no one plan that will do the job in every case. The matter must be assessed in light of the circumstances present and the options available in each instance. It is incumbent upon the school board to establish that its proposed plan promises meaningful and immediate progress toward disestablishing state-imposed segregation. It is incumbent upon the district court to weigh that claim in light of the facts at hand and in light of any alternatives which may be shown as feasible and more promising in their effectiveness. Where the court finds the board to be acting in good faith and the proposed plan to have real prospects for dismantling the state-imposed dual system "at the earliest practicable date," then the plan may be said to provide effective relief. Of course, the availability to the board of other more promising courses of action may indicate a lack of good faith; and at the least it places a heavy burden upon the board to explain its preference for an apparently less effective method. Moreover, whatever plan is adopted will require evaluation in practice, and the court should retain jurisdiction until it is clear that state-imposed segregation has been completely removed. . . .

We do not hold that "freedom of choice" can have no place in such a plan. We do not hold that a "freedom-of-choice" plan might of itself be unconstitutional, although that argument has been urged upon us. Rather, all we decide today is that in desegregating a dual system a plan utilizing "freedom of choice" is not an end in itself. As Judge Sobeloff has put it,

> " 'Freedom of choice' is not a sacred talisman; it is only a means to a constitutionally required end—the abolition of

the system of segregation and its effects. If the means prove effective, it is acceptable, but if it fails to undo segregation, other means must be used to achieve this end. The school officials have the continuing duty to take whatever action may be necessary to create a 'unitary, nonracial system'." Bowman v. County School Board, 382 F.2d 326, 333 (C.A.4th Cir. 1967) (concurring opinion).

. . . Where it offers real promise of aiding a desegregation program to effectuate conversion of a state-imposed dual system to a unitary, nonracial system there might be no objection to allowing such a device to prove itself in operation. On the other hand, if there are reasonably available other ways, such for illustration as zoning, promising speedier and more effective conversion to a unitary, nonracial school system, "freedom of choice" must be held unacceptable.

The New Kent School Board's "freedom-of-choice" plan cannot be accepted as a sufficient step to "effectuate a transition" to a unitary system. In three years of operation not a single white child has chosen to attend Watkins school and although 115 Negro children enrolled in New Kent school in 1967 (up from 35 in 1965 and 111 in 1966) 85% of the Negro children in the system still attend the all-Negro Watkins school. In other words, the school system remains a dual system. Rather than further the dismantling of the dual system, the plan has operated simply to burden children and their parents with a responsibility which *Brown II* placed squarely on the School Board. The Board must be required to formulate a new plan and . . . fashion steps which promise realistically to convert promptly to a system without a "white" school and a "Negro" school, but just schools.

. . . .

NOTES AND QUESTIONS

1. Green holds, inter alia, that all deliberate speed has run out and that the constitutional duty of a school board is to produce a unitary, "nondiscriminatory school system." Assume you are a local board member charged with describing to the board and to the public exactly what constitutes a unitary, "nondiscriminatory school system," what will you say?

2. How urgent is the constitutional duty of Green? Must a school board take *"whatever* steps might be necessary" to achieve a unitary, nondiscriminatory school system, or must it only approve of "alternatives which may be shown as feasible"?

3. Is the interpretation of the requirements of the equal protection clause in Green consistent with Brown I and II? Is the appropriate interpretation one that forbids only the use of a racial classification as the basis for student assignment to schools (a de jure approach), or is it one that focuses on the result requiring that a unitary, nondiscriminatory school system be achieved in fact (a de facto approach)?

4. Does Green require that boards of education create educational programs for educationally deprived children because of previous segregation? If so, can these programs be segregated? See, United States by Clark v. Plaquemines Parish School Board, 291 F.Supp. 841 (E.D. La.1967), mod. 415 F.2d 817 (5th Cir.).

5. Are the requirements of Green met by school board action to build a new school at a site that fails to make progress toward desegreation? See, Broussard v. Houston, 395 F.2d 817 (5th Cir. 1968) and United States v. Board of Public Instr. of Polk County, 395 F.2d 66 (5th Cir. 1968).

6. Does Green's constitutional duty apply to school boards that never operated a dual school system?

7. Could a state constitutionally pass a law allowing any or all counties to close any or all county schools if counties wanted to rather than comply with Brown and Green? See, Griffin v. County School Board, 377 U.S. 218, 84 S.Ct. 1226, 12 L.Ed.2d 256 (1964). Suppose instead of closing its schools a county simply gave large amounts of aid to nonsectarian, non-profit "private" schools, most of which were segregated?

ALEXANDER v. HOLMES COUNTY BOARD OF EDUCATION

Supreme Court of the United States, 1969.
396 U.S. 19, 90 S.Ct. 29, 24 L.Ed.2d 19, reh. den. 396 U.S. 976, 90 S.Ct. 437,
24 L.Ed.2d 447.

PER CURIAM. This case comes to the Court on a petition for certiorari to the Court of Appeals for the Fifth Circuit. The petition was granted on October 9, 1969, and the case set down for early argument. The question presented is one of paramount importance, involving as it does the denial of fundamental rights to many thousands of school children, who are presently attending Mississippi schools under segregated conditions contrary to the applicable decisions of this Court. Against this background the Court of Appeals should have denied all motions for additional time because continued operation of segregated schools under a standard of allowing "all deliberate speed" for desegregation is no longer constitutionally permissible. Under explicit holdings of this Court the obligation of every school district is to terminate dual school systems at once and to operate now and hereafter only unitary schools. Griffin v. County School Board, 377 U.S. 218, 234 (1964); Green v. County School Board of New Kent County, 391 U.S. 430, 438–439, 442 (1968). Accordingly, *It is hereby adjudged, ordered, and decreed*:

1. The Court of Appeals' order of August 28, 1969, is vacated, and the case is remanded to that court to issue its decree and order, effective immediately, declaring that each of the school districts here involved may no longer operate a dual school system based on race or color, and directing that they begin immediately to operate as unitary

school systems within which no person is to be effectively excluded from any school because of race or color.

2.   The Court of Appeals may in its discretion direct the schools here involved to accept all or any part of the August 11, 1969, recommendations of the Department of Health, Education, and Welfare, with any modifications which that Court deems proper insofar as those recommendations insure a totally unitary school system for all eligible pupils without regard to race or color.

The Court of Appeals may make its determination and enter its order without further arguments or submissions.

3.   While each of these school systems is being operated as a unitary system under the order of the Court of Appeals, the District Court may hear and consider objections thereto or proposed amendments thereof, provided, however, that the Court of Appeals' order shall be complied with in all respects while the District Court considers such objections or amendments, if any are made.   No amendment shall become effective before being passed upon by the Court of Appeals.

4.   The Court of Appeals shall retain jurisdiction to insure prompt and faithful compliance with its order, and may modify or amend the same as may be deemed necessary or desirable for the operation of a unitary school system.

5.   The order of the Court of Appeals dated August 28, 1969, having been vacated and the case remanded for proceedings in conformity with this order, the judgment shall issue forthwith and the Court of Appeals is requested to give priority to the execution of this judgment as far as possible and necessary.

SINGLETON v. JACKSON MUNICIPAL SEPARATE SCHOOL DIST.

United States Court of Appeals, 1970.
419 F.2d 1211 (5th Cir.), cert. den. 402 U.S. 944, 91 S.Ct. 1611, 29 L.Ed.2d 112.

PER CURIAM.   These appeals, all involving school desegregation orders, are consolidated for opinion purposes.   They involve, in the main, common questions of law and fact.   They were heard en banc on successive days.

Following our determination to consider these cases en banc, the Supreme Court handed down its decision in Alexander v. Holmes County Board of Education   .   .   .   That decision supervened all existing authority to the contrary.   It sent the doctrine of deliberate speed to its final resting place   .   .   .

The rule of the case is to be found in the direction to this court to issue its order "effective immediately declaring that each of the school districts   .   .   .   may no longer operate a dual school system based on race or color, and directing that they begin immediately to operate as unitary school systems within which no person is to be effectively excluded from any school because of race or color." We effectuated this rule and order in United States v. Hinds County School Board (5 Cir. (1969)), 417 F.2d 852. It must likewise be effectuated in these and all other school cases now being or which are to be considered in this or the district courts of this circuit.

The tenor of the decision in Alexander v. Holmes County is to shift the burden from the standpoint of time for converting to unitary school systems. The shift is from a status of litigation to one of unitary operation pending litigation. The new modus operandi is to require immediate operation as unitary systems. Suggested modifications to unitary plans are not to delay implementation. Hearings on requested changes in unitary operating plans may be in order but no delay in conversion may ensue because of the need for modification or hearing.

In Alexander v. Holmes County, the court had unitary plans available for each of the school districts. In addition, this court, on remand, gave each district a limited time within which to offer its own plan. It was apparent there, as it is here, that converting to a unitary system involved basically the merger of faculty and staff, students, transportation, services, athletic and other extra-curricular school activities. We required that the conversion to unitary systems in those districts take place not later than December 31, 1969. It was the earliest feasible date in the view of the court. United States v. Hinds County supra. In three of the systems there (Hinds County, Holmes County and Meridian), because of particular logistical difficulties the Office of Education (HEW) had recommended two-step plans. The result was, and the court ordered, that the first step be implemented not later than December 31, 1969, and the other beginning with the fall 1970 school term.

I

Because of Alexander v. Holmes County, each of the cases here, as will be later discussed, must be considered anew, either in whole or in part, by the district courts. It happens that there are extant unitary plans for some of the school districts here, either Office of Education or school board originated. Some are operating under freedom of choice plans. In no one of the districts has a plan been submitted in light of the precedent of Alexander v. Holmes County. That case resolves all questions except as to mechanics. The school districts here may no longer operate dual systems and must begin immediately to operate as unitary systems. The focus of the mechanics question is on the accomplishment of the immediacy requirement laid down in Alexander v. Holmes County.

Despite the absence of plans, it will be possible to merge faculties and staff, transportation, services, athletics and other extra-curricular activities during the present school term. It will be difficult to arrange the merger of student bodies into unitary systems prior to the fall 1970 term in the absence of merger plans. The court has concluded that two-step plans are to be implemented. One step must be accomplished not later than February 1, 1970, and it will include all steps necessary to conversion to a unitary system save the merger of student bodies into unitary systems. The student body merger will constitute the second step and must be accomplished not later than the beginning of the fall term 1970.[2] The district courts, in the respective cases here, are directed to so order and to give first priority to effectuating this requirement.

To this end, the district courts are directed to require the respective school districts, appellees herein, to request the Office of Education (HEW) to prepare plans for the merger of the student bodies into unitary systems. These plans shall be filed with the district courts not later than January 6, 1970, together with such additional plan or modification of the Office of Education plan as the school district may wish to offer. The district court shall enter its final order not later than February 1, 1970, requiring and setting out the details of a plan designed to accomplish a unitary system of pupil attendance with the start of the fall 1970 school term. Such order may include a plan designed by the district court in the absence of the submission of an otherwise satisfactory plan. A copy of such plan as is approved shall be filed by the clerk of the district court with the clerk of this court.[3]

The following provisions are being required as step one in the conversion process. The district courts are directed to make them a part of the orders to be entered and to also give first priority to implementation.

[2] Many faculty and staff members will be transferred under step one. It will be necessary for final grades to be entered and for other records to be completed, prior to the transfers, by the transferring faculty members and administrators for the partial school year involved. The interim period prior to February 1, 1970, is allowed for this purpose.

The interim period prior to the start of the fall 1970 school term is allowed for arranging the student transfers. Many students must transfer. Buildings will be put to new use. In some instances it may be necessary to transfer equipment, supplies or libraries. School bus routes must be reconstituted. The period allowed is at least adequate for the orderly accomplishment of the task.

[3] In formulating plans, nothing herein intended to prevent the respective school districts or the district court from seeking the counsel and assistance of State departments of education, university schools of education or of others having expertise in the field of education.

It is also to be noted that many problems of a local nature are likely to arise in converting to and maintaining unitary systems. These problems may best be resolved on the community level. The district courts should suggest the advisability of biracial advisory committees to school boards in those districts having no Negro school board members.

The respective school districts, appellees herein, must take the following action not later than February 1, 1970:

DESEGREGATION OF FACULTY AND OTHER STAFF

The school board shall announce and implement the following policies:

1. Effective not later than February 1, 1970, the principals, teachers, teacher-aides and other staff who work directly with children at a school shall be so assigned that in no case will the racial composition of a staff indicate that a school is intended for Negro students or white students. For the remainder of the 1969–70 school year the district shall assign the staff described above so that the ratio of Negro to white teachers in each school, and the ratio of other staff in each, are substantially the same as each such ratio is to the teachers and other staff, respectively, in the entire school system.

The school district shall, to the extent necessary to carry out this desegregation plan, direct members of its staff as a condition of continued employment to accept new assignments.

2. Staff members who work directly with children, and professional staff who work on the administrative level will be hired, assigned, promoted, paid, demoted, dismissed, and otherwise treated without regard to race, color, or national origin.

3. If there is to be a reduction in the number of principals, teachers, teacher-aides, or other professional staff employed by the school district which will result in a dismissal or demotion of any such staff members, the staff member to be dismissed or demoted must be selected on the basis of objective and reasonable nondiscriminatory standards from among all the staff of the school district. In addition if there is any such dismissal or demotion, no staff vacancy may be filled through recruitment of a person of a race, color, or national origin different from that of the individual dismissed or demoted, until each displaced staff member who is qualified has had an opportunity to fill the vacancy and has failed to accept an offer to do so.

Prior to such a reduction, the school board will develop or require the development of nonracial objective criteria to be used in selecting the staff member who is to be dismissed or demoted. These criteria shall be available for public inspection and shall be retained by the school district. The school district also shall record and preserve the evaluation of staff members under the criteria. Such evalu-

710 FREEDOM AND RACIAL DESEGREGATION Part 2

ation shall be made available upon request to the dismissed or demoted employee.

"Demotion" as used above includes any reassignment (1) under which the staff member receives less pay or has less responsibility than under the assignment he held previously, (2) which requires a lesser degree of skill than did the assignment he held previously, or (3) under which the staff member is asked to teach a subject or grade other than one for which he is certified or for which he has had substantial experience within a reasonably current period. In general and depending upon the subject matter involved, 5 years is such a reasonable period.

MAJORITY TO MINORITY TRANSFER POLICY

The school district shall permit a student attending a school in which his race is in the majority to choose to attend another school, where space is available, and where his race is in the minority.

TRANSPORTATION

The transportation system, in those school districts having transportation systems, shall be completely reexamined regularly by the superintendent, his staff, and the school board. Bus routes and the assignment of students to buses will be designed to insure the transportation of all eligible pupils on a nonsegregated and otherwise nondiscriminatory basis.

SCHOOL CONSTRUCTION AND SITE SELECTION

All school construction, school consolidation, and site selection (including the location of any temporary classrooms) in the system shall be done in a manner which will prevent the recurrence of the dual school structure once this desegregation plan is implemented.

ATTENDANCE OUTSIDE SYSTEM OF RESIDENCE

If the school district grants transfers to students living in the district for their attendance at public schools outside the district, or if it permits transfers into the district of students who live outside the district, it shall do so on a nondiscriminatory basis, except that it shall not consent to transfers where the cumulative effect will reduce desegregation in either district or reenforce the dual school system.

See United States v. Hinds County, supra, decided November 6, 1969. The orders there embrace these same requirements.

II

In addition to the foregoing requirements of general applicability, the order of the court which is peculiar to each of the specific cases being considered is as follows:

No. 26285—Jackson, Mississippi

This is a freedom of choice system. The issue presented has to do with school building construction. We enjoined the proposed construction pending appeal.

A Federal appellate court is bound to consider any change, either in fact or in law, which has supervened since the judgment was entered.   .   .   .   We therefore reverse and remand for compliance with the requirements of Alexander v. Holmes County and the other provisions and conditions of this order. Our order enjoining the proposed construction pending appeal is continued in effect until such time as the district court has approved a plan for conversion to a unitary school system.

No. 28261—Marshall County

*   *   *   *   *   *   *   *   *   *

III

In the event of an appeal or appeals to this court from an order entered as aforesaid in the district courts, such appeal shall be on the original record and the parties are encouraged to appeal on an agreed statement as is provided for in rule 10(d), Federal Rules of Appellate Procedure (FRAP). Pursuant to rule 2, FRAP, the provisions of rule 4(a) as to the time for filing notice of appeal are suspended and it is ordered that any notice of appeal be filed within 15 days of the date of entry of the order appealed from and notices of cross-appeal within 5 days thereafter. The provisions of rule 11 are suspended and it is ordered that the record be transmitted to this court within 15 days after filing of the notice of appeal. The provisions of rule 31 are suspended to the extent that the brief of the appellant shall be filed within 15 days after the date on which the record is filed and the brief of the appellee shall be filed within 10 days after the date on which the brief of appellant is filed. No reply brief shall be filed except upon order of the court. The times set herein may be enlarged by the court upon good cause shown.

The mandate in each of the within matters shall issue forthwith. No stay will be granting pending petition for rehearing or application for certiorari.

Reversed as to all save Mobile and St. John The Baptist Parish; affirmed as to Mobile with direction; affirmed in part and reversed in part as to St. John The Baptist Parish; remanded to the district courts for further proceedings consistent herewith.

SWANN v. CHARLOTTE–MECKLENBURG BOARD OF EDUCATION

Supreme Court of the United States, 1971.
402 U.S. 1, 91 S.Ct. 1267, 28 L.Ed.2d 554, cert. den. 403 U.S. 912, 91 S.Ct. 2200, 29 L.Ed.2d 689.

[These cases considered desegregation plans involving Charlotte, N. C. and its environs.   In 1969–70 the federal district court rejected three plans that had been proposed by the board of education (respondent) and then accepted a plan prepared at the court's request by "an expert in education administration," and issued a decree which later was partially modified by the court of appeals.   Later still, the district court rejected a plan prepared by HEW concluding that either the plan submitted by a minority of the school board or the one submitted by the court's expert was "reasonable and acceptable."]

Mr. Chief Justice BURGER delivered the opinion of the Court.

.   .   .

This case and those argued with it arose in States having a long history of maintaining two sets of schools in a single school system deliberately operated to carry out a governmental policy to separate pupils in schools solely on the basis of race.   That was what Brown v. Board of Education was all about.   These cases present us with the problem of defining in more precise terms than heretofore the scope of the duty of school authorities and district courts in implementing Brown I and the mandate to eliminate dual systems and establish unitary systems at once.   .   .   .

.   .   .   we should now try to amplify guidelines, however incomplete and imperfect, for the assistance of school authorities and courts.   The failure of local authorities to meet their constitutional obligations aggravated the massive problem of converting from the state-enforced discrimination of racially separate school systems. This process has been rendered more difficult by changes since 1954 in the structure and patterns of communities, the growth of student population, movement of families, and other changes, some of which had marked impact on school planning, sometimes neutralizing or negating remedial action before it was fully implemented.   Rural areas accustomed for half a century to the consolidated school systems implemented by bus transportation could make adjustments more readily than metropolitan areas with dense and shifting population, numerous schools, congested and complex traffic patterns.

The objective today remains to eliminate from the public schools all vestiges of state-imposed segregation.   .   .   .

If school authorities fail in their affirmative obligations   .   .   . judicial authority may be invoked.   Once a right and a violation have been shown, the scope of a district court's equitable powers to remedy past wrongs is broad, for breadth and flexibility are inherent in equitable remedies.

> "The essence of equity jurisdiction has been the power of the Chancellor to do equity and to mould each decree to the necessities of the particular case. Flexibility rather than rigidity has distinguished it. The qualities of mercy and practicality have made equity the instrument for nice adjustment and reconciliation between the public interest and private needs as well as between competing private claims."
>
> . . .

This allocation of responsibility once made, the Court attempted from time to time to provide some guidelines for the exercise of the district judge's discretion and for the reviewing function of the courts of appeals. However, a school desegregation case does not differ fundamentally from other cases involving the framing of equitable remedies to repair the denial of a constitutional right. The task is to correct, by a balancing of the individual and collective interests, the condition that offends the Constitution.

In seeking to define even in broad and general terms how far this remedial power extends it is important to remember that judicial powers may be exercised only on the basis of a constitutional violation. Remedial judicial authority does not put judges automatically in the shoes of school authorities whose powers are plenary. Judicial authority enters only when local authority defaults.

School authorities are traditionally charged with broad power to formulate and implement educational policy and might well conclude, for example, that in order to prepare students to live in a pluralistic society each school should have a prescribed ratio of Negro to white students reflecting the proportion for the district as a whole. To do this as an educational policy is within the broad discretionary powers of school authorities; absent a finding of a constitutional violation, however, that would not be within the authority of a federal court. As with any equity case, the nature of the violation determines the scope of the remedy. In default by the school authorities of their obligation to proffer acceptable remedies, a district court has broad power to fashion a remedy that will assure a unitary school system.

The school authorities argue that the equity powers of federal district courts have been limited by Title IV of the Civil Rights Act of 1964, 42 U.S.C. § 2000c. The language and the history of Title IV show that it was enacted not to limit but to define the role of the Federal Government in the implementation of the *Brown I* decision. It authorizes the Commissioner of Education to provide technical assistance to local boards in the preparation of desegregation plans, to arrange "training institutes" for school personnel involved in desegregation efforts, and to make grants directly to schools to ease the transition to unitary systems. It also authorizes the Attorney General, in specified circumstances, to initiate federal desegregation suits. Section 2000c(b) defines "desegregation" as it is used in Title IV:

> " 'Desegregation' means the assignment of students to public schools and within such schools without regard to their race, color, religion, or national origin, but 'desegregation' shall not mean the assignment of students to public schools in order to overcome racial imbalance."

Section 2000c–6, authorizing the Attorney General to institute federal suits, contains the following proviso:

> "nothing herein shall empower any official or court of the United States to issue any order seeking to achieve a racial balance in any school by requiring the transportation of pupils or students from one school to another or one school district to another in order to achieve such racial balance, or otherwise enlarge the existing power of the court to insure compliance with constitutional standards."

On their face, the sections quoted purport only to insure that the provisions of Title IV of the Civil Rights Act of 1964 will not be read as granting new powers. The proviso in § 2000c–6 is in terms designed to foreclose any interpretation of the Act as expanding the *existing* powers of federal courts to enforce the Equal Protection Clause. There is no suggestion of an intention to restrict those powers or withdraw from courts their historic equitable remedial powers. The legislative history of Title IV indicates that Congress was concerned that the Act might be read as creating a right of action under the Fourteenth Amendment in the situation of so-called "de facto segregation," where racial imbalance exists in the schools but with no showing that this was brought about by discriminatory action of state authorities. In short, there is nothing in the Act that provides us material assistance in answering the question of remedy for state-imposed segregation in violation of *Brown I*. The basis of our decision must be the prohibition of the Fourteenth Amendment that no State shall "deny to any person within its jurisdiction the equal protection of the laws."

We turn now to the problem of defining with more particularity the responsibilities of school authorities in desegregating a state-enforced dual school system in light of the Equal Protection Clause.

. . .

In *Green*, we pointed out that existing policy and practice with regard to faculty, staff, transportation, extracurricular activities, and facilities were among the most important indicia of a segregated system. . . . Independent of student assignment, where it is possible to identify a "white school" or a "Negro school" simply by reference to the racial composition of teachers and staff, the quality of school buildings and equipment, or the organization of sports activities, a *prima facie* case of violation of substantive constitutional rights under the Equal Protection Clause is shown.

When a system has been dual in these respects, the first remedial responsibility of school authorities is to eliminate invidious racial distinctions. With respect to such matters as transportation, supporting personnel, and extracurricular activities, no more than this may be necessary. Similar corrective action must be taken with regard to the maintenance of buildings and the distribution of equipment. In these areas, normal administrative practice should produce schools of like quality, facilities, and staffs. Something more must be said, however, as to faculty assignment and new school construction.

In the companion *Davis* case .   .   .   the Mobile school board has argued that the Constitution requires that teachers be assigned on a "color blind" basis. It also argues that the Constitution prohibits district courts from using their equity power to order assignment of teachers to achieve a particular degree of faculty desegregation. We reject that contention.

In United States v. Montgomery County Board of Education, 395 U.S. 225 (1969), the District Court set as a goal a plan of faculty assignment in each school with a ratio of white to Negro faculty members substantially the same throughout the system. This order was predicated on the District Court finding that:

> "The evidence does not reflect any real administrative problems involved in immediately desegregating the substitute teachers, the student teachers, the night school faculties, and in the evolvement of a really legally adequate program for the substantial desegregation of the faculties of all schools in the system commencing with the school year 1968–69." Quoted at 395 U. S., at 232. .   .   .

We [held] that the order of the District Judge

> "was adopted in the spirit of this Court's opinion in *Green* .   .   .   in that his plan 'promises realistically to work, and promises realistically to work *now*'." .   .   .

The construction of new schools and the closing of old ones are two of the most important functions of local school authorities and also two of the most complex. .   .   .   Over the long run, the consequences of the choices will be far reaching. People gravitate toward school facilities, just as schools are located in response to the needs of people. The location of schools may thus influence the patterns of residential development of a metropolitan area and have important impact on composition of innercity neighborhoods.

In the past, choices in this respect have been used as a potent weapon for creating or maintaining a state-segregated school system. In addition to the classic pattern of building schools specifically intended for Negro or white students, school authorities have sometimes, since *Brown*, closed schools which appeared likely to become racially mixed through changes in neighborhood residential patterns. This was sometimes accompanied by building new schools in the areas of white suburban expansion farthest from Negro population centers in order to maintain the separation of the races with a minimum departure from the formal principles of "neighborhood zoning." Such a policy does more than simply influence the short-run composition of the student body of a new school. It may well promote segregated residential patterns which, when combined with "neighborhood zoning," further lock the school system into the mold of separation of the races. Upon a proper showing a district court may consider this in fashioning a remedy.

In ascertaining the existence of legally imposed school segregation, the existence of a pattern of school construction and abandonment is thus a factor of great weight. In devising remedies where legally imposed segregation has been established, it is the responsibility of local authorities and district courts to see to it that future school construction and abandonment are not used and do not serve to perpetuate or re-establish the dual system. When necessary, district courts should retain jurisdiction to assure that these responsibilities are carried out. . . .

The central issue in this case is that of student assignment, and there are essentially four problem areas: . . .

(1) *Racial Balances or Racial Quotas*.

. . . . It would not serve the important objection of *Brown I* to seek to use school desegregation cases for purposes beyond their scope, although desegregation of schools ultimately will have impact on other forms of discrimination. We do not reach in this case the question whether a showing that school segregation is a consequence of other types of state action, without any discriminatory action by the school authorities, is a constitutional violation requiring remedial action by a school desegregation decree. This case does not present that question and we therefore do not decide it.

Our objective in dealing with the issues presented by these cases is to see that school authorities exclude no pupil of a racial minority from any school, directly or indirectly, on account of race; it does not and cannot embrace all the problems of racial prejudice, even when those problems contribute to disproportionate racial concentrations in some schools.

In this case it is urged that the District Court has imposed racial balance requirements of 71%–29% on individual schools. . . .

. . . . If we were to read the holding of the District Court to require, as a matter of substantive constitutional right, any particular degree of racial balance or mixing, that approach would be disapproved and we would be obliged to reverse. The constitutional command to desegregate schools does not mean that every school in every community must always reflect the racial composition of the school system as a whole.

.   .   . the use made of mathematical ratios was no more than a starting point in the process of shaping a remedy, rather than an inflexible requirement. From that starting point the District Court proceeded to frame a decree that was within its discretionary powers, as an equitable remedy for the particular circumstances. As we said in *Green*, a school authority's remedial plan or a district court's remedial decree is to be judged by its effectiveness. Awareness of the racial composition of the whole school system is likely to be a useful starting point in shaping a remedy to correct past constitutional violations. In sum, the very limited use made of mathematical ratios was within the equitable remedial discretion of the District Court.

(2) *One-race Schools.*

The record in this case reveals the familiar phenomenon that in metropolitan areas minority groups are often found concentrated in one part of the city. In some circumstances certain schools may remain all or largely of one race until new schools can be provided or neighborhood patterns change.   .   .   .

.   .   . No *per se* rule can adequately embrace all the difficulties of reconciling the competing interests involved; but in a system with a history of segregation the need for remedial criteria of sufficient specificity to assure a school authority's compliance with its constitutional duty warrants a presumption against schools that are substantially disproportionate in their racial composition. Where the school authority's proposed plan for conversion from a dual to a unitary system contemplates the continued existence of some schools that are all or predominately of one race, they have the burden of showing that such school assignments are genuinely nondiscriminatory. The court should scrutinize such schools, and the burden upon the school authorities will be to satisfy the court that their racial composition is not the result of present or past discriminatory action on their part.

An optional majority-to-minority transfer provision has long been recognized as a useful part of every desegregation plan. Provision for optional transfer of those in the majority racial group of a particular school to other schools where they will be in the minority is an indispensable remedy for those students willing to transfer to other schools in order to lessen the impact on them of the state-imposed stigma of segregation. In order to be effective, such a transfer arrangement must grant the transferring student free transportation and space must be made available in the school to which he desires to move.

.   .   .   .

(3) *Remedial Altering of Attendance Zones.*

The maps submitted in these cases graphically demonstrate that one of the principal tools employed by school planners and by courts to break up the dual school system has been a frank—and sometimes drastic—gerrymandering of school districts and attendance zones. An additional step was pairing, "clustering," or "grouping" of schools with attendance assignments made deliberately to accomplish the transfer of Negro students out of formerly segregated Negro schools and transfer of white students to formerly all-Negro schools. More often than not, these zones are neither compact nor contiguous; indeed they may be on opposite ends of the city. As an interim corrective measure, this cannot be said to be beyond the broad remedial powers of a court.

Absent a constitutional violation there would be no basis for judicially ordering assignment of students on a racial basis. All things beng equal, with no history of discrimination, it might well be desirable to assign pupils to schools nearest their homes. But all things are not equal in a system that has been deliberately constructed and maintained to enforce racial segregation. The remedy for such segregation may be administratively awkward, inconvenient, and even bizarre in some situations and may impose burdens on some; but all awkwardness and inconvenience cannot be avoided in the interim period when remedial adjustments are being made to eliminate the dual school systems.

No fixed or even substantially fixed guidelines can be established as to how far a court can go, but it must be recognized that there are limits. The objective is to dismantle the dual school system. "Racially neutral" assignment plans proposed by school authorities to a district court may be inadequate; such plans may fail to counteract the continuing effects of past school segregation resulting from discriminatory location of school sites or distortion of school size in order to achieve or maintain an artificial racial separation. When school authorities present a district court with a "loaded game board," affirmative action in the form of remedial altering of attendance zones is proper to achieve truly nondiscriminatory assignments. In short, an assignment plan is not acceptable simply because it appears to be neutral.

In this area, we must of necessity rely to a large extent, as this Court has for more than 16 years, on the informed judgment of the district courts in the first instance and on courts of appeals.

We hold that the pairing and grouping of noncontiguous school zones is a permissible tool and such action is to be considered in light of the objectives sought. Judicial steps in shaping such zones going beyond combinations of contiguous areas should be examined in light of what is said in subdivisions (1), (2), and (3) of this opinion concerning the objectives to be sought. Maps do not tell the whole story since noncontiguous school zones may be more accessible to each other in terms of the critical travel time, because of traffic patterns and good highways, than schools geographically closer together. Conditions in different localities will vary so widely that no rigid rules can be laid down to govern all situations.

(4) *Transportation of Students.*

. . . No rigid guidelines as to student transportation can be given for application to the infinite variety of problems presented in thousands of situations. Bus transportation has been an integral part of the public education system for years, and was perhaps the single most important factor in the transition from the one-room schoolhouse to the consolidated school. Eighteen million of the Nation's public school children, approximately 39%, were transported to their schools by bus in 1969–1970 in all parts of the country. . . .

The decree provided that the buses used to implement the plan would operate on direct routes. Students would be picked up at schools near their homes and transported to the schools they were to attend. The trips for elementary school pupils average about seven miles and the District Court found that they would take "not over 35 minutes at the most." This system compares favorably with the transportation plan previously operated in Charlotte under which each day 23,600 students on all grade levels were transported an average of 15 miles one way for an average trip requiring over an hour. In these circumstances, we find no basis for holding that the local school authorities may not be required to employ bus transportation as one tool of school desegregation. Desegregation plans cannot be limited to the walk-in school.

An objection to transportation of students may have validity when the time or distance of travel is so great as to either risk the health of the children or significantly impinge on the educational process. District courts must weigh the soundness of any transportation plan in light of what is said in subdivisions (1), (2), and (3) above. It hardly needs stating that the limits on time of travel will vary with many factors, but probably with none more than the age of the students. The reconciliation of competing values in a desegregation case is, of course, a difficult task with many sensitive facets but fundamentally no more so than remedial measures courts of equity have traditionally employed. . . .

. . . we are unable to conclude that the order of the District Court is not reasonable, feasible and workable. However, in seeking to define the scope of remedial power or the limits on remedial power of courts in an area as sensitive as we deal with here, words are poor instruments to convey the sense of basic fairness inherent in equity. Substance, not semantics, must govern, and we have sought to suggest the nature of limitations without frustrating the appropriate scope of equity.

At some point, these school authorities and others like them should have achieved full compliance with this Court's decision in *Brown I*. The systems would then be "unitary" in the sense required by our decisions in *Green* and *Alexander*.

It does not follow that the communities served by such systems will remain demographically stable, for in a growing, mobile society, few will do so. Neither school authorities nor district courts are constitutionally required to make year-by-year adjustments of the racial composition of student bodies once the affirmative duty to desegregate has been accomplished and racial discrimination through official action is eliminated from the system. This does not mean that federal courts are without power to deal with future problems; but in the absence of a showing that either the school authorities or some other agency of the State has deliberately attempted to fix or alter demographic patterns to affect the racial composition of the schools, further intervention by a district court should not be necessary. . . .

NOTES AND QUESTIONS

1. Do you agree with the opinion of the Supreme Court?

2. Is the constitution "color blind"?

3. Does this opinion indicate that the proper approach when deciding school desegregation cases is a result-oriented, de facto approach? If so, what standard should be used to judge whether the end sought has been achieved? Is it a "unitary" school system, or a unitary "non-discriminatory school system"? Does it make any difference whether the stress is on one or the other aspect of the formula?

4. Is Swann rigorously consistent with Green and Brown I and II?

5. Mr. Chief Justice Burger, speaking for the Court in Swann, states that "[a]n objection to transportation of students may have some validity when the time or distance of travel is so great as to . . . significantly impinge on the educational process." Suppose the following facts appear in a case before the Supreme Court: Past racial segregation in the schools of your school district has resulted in large discrepancies in educational achievement between students of the same grade but attending different de facto or de jure segregated schools within the district and that a bussing plan such as that offered in Swann was mandated. Suppose further that it was shown that because of the sudden integration of previously segregated students (who though in the same grade bring widely differing academic achievement to the now integrated classroom) the better prepared students will be slowed in their academic progress because of the presence of others who are less well prepared. Thus, integration may "significantly impinge on the educational process" as it affects the better prepared group. Proponents of the bussing plan, citing the above language from Swann, have appealed to the Supreme Court from a ruling of the federal circuit court of appeals holding the bussing plan invalid. Assume you are a member of the Supreme Court, what decision would you render and for what reason(s)?

6. What does the court say about de facto segregation?

7. The constitutional viability of a neighborhood school policy which causes, perpetuates or simply fails to eliminate racial imbalance has been the topic of considerable discussion. See generally, 1 U. S. Comm'n on Civil Rights, Racial Isolation in the Public Schools 219–29 (1967). If a school board follows a neighborhood school policy when drawing local school district lines, and it results in segregated schools, is this situation de jure segregation, coming within Brown I and II and Green?

KEYES v. SCHOOL DISTRICT NO. 1

Supreme Court of the United States, 1973.
413 U.S. 921, 93 S.Ct. 2686, 37 L.Ed.2d 548.

[This statement of facts is taken from the opinion of the Court of Appeals, 445 F.2d 990 (1971):

"In substance, the trial court found and concluded . . . that the named schools in Northeast Denver were segregated by affirmative state action. In its findings, the trial court noted specific instances of boundary gerrymandering, construction of a new school and classrooms, minority-to-majority transfers, and excessive use of mobile classroom units in this section of the district, all of which amount to unconstitutional state segregation. . . . On the second count, the court found that although the core area schools were not segregated by state action, fifteen designated schools should be granted relief because it was demonstrated that they were offering their pupils an unequal educational opportunity in violation of the Fourteenth Amendment equal protection clause. . . .

"The schools . . . are located in Northeast Denver in what is generally referred to as the Park Hill area. The schools are: East High School, Smiley and Cole Junior High Schools, Barrett, Stedman, Hallett, Park Hill and Philips Elementary Schools. Prior to 1950, the Negro population was centered in the Five Points area, near the northwest corner of City Park. Since 1940, the Negro population has steadily increased from 8,000 to 15,000 in 1950, to 30,000 in 1960, and to approximately 45,000 by 1966. The residential movement reflecting this growth has been eastward, down a 'corridor' which has fairly well defined north-south boundaries. In the early 1950, York Street (some 16 blocks west of Colorado Boulevard) was the east boundary of the residential expansion. Ten years later, the movement had reached and crossed Colorado Boulevard to a limited degree, and now the corridor of Negro residences extends from the Five Points area to the eastern city limits. The schools of concern are in and adjacent to this narrow strip of Negro residences.

"Barrett Elementary is located one block west of Colorado Boulevard in the heart of the Negro community. When it opened in 1960, the attendance lines were drawn to coincide almost precisely with the then eastern boundary of the Negro residential movement—Colorado Boulevard. When the school was being planned in 1958 and the sites for construction were being considered, the area west of Colorado Boulevard was already predominantly Negro; by 1960, when the school opened, the racial composition of the neighborhood which it was to serve was reflected in the 89.6% Negro student enrollment. In 1970, the racial and ethnic composition of the school was approximately 93% Negro, 7% Hispano.

"In addition, Barrett was built to accommodate only 450 students, a factor which manifestly precluded its use to substantially relieve the overcrowded conditions at adjacent schools. In 1960, Stedman (then predominantly Anglo), which was eight blocks due east of Barrett, was well over its intended capacity. Rather than constructing a larger physical plant at Barrett to accommodate part of Stedman's overflow, Barrett's size was restricted to serve only those pupils west of Colorado Boulevard.

"The trial court held that 'the positive acts of the Board in establishing Barrett and defining its boundaries were the proximate cause of the segregated condition which has existed in that school since its creation, which condition exists at present. * * * The action of the Board * * * was taken with knowledge of the consequences, and these consequences were not merely possible, they were substantially certain. Under such conditions we find that the Board acted purposefully to create and maintain segregation at Barrett.' . . .

"In 1960, Stedman was 96% Anglo, 4% Negro and was 20% above capacity. By 1962, it was 35 to 50% Anglo and 50 to 65% Negro. In 1963, it was 87.4% Negro and 18.6% Anglo, and still overcrowded. By 1968, this school was 94.6% Negro and 3.9% Anglo. Stedman is eight blocks due east of Barrett, and in 1960 the residential trend all but insured that in a few years it would be predominantly Negro. In 1962, three boundary changes were proposed to the Board which would have transferred students from Stedman to Smith, Hallett and Park Hill, each of which was predominantly Anglo. These three proposals were refused by the Board. In 1964, the Board made two boundary changes which affected Stedman: (1) a predominantly Anglo section of Stedman's school zone was detached to Hallett, and (2) the Park Hill-Stedman optional zone (96% Anglo) was transferred to Park Hill. To facilitate an expanding population at Stedman, which was overwhelmingly Negro, mobile units were erected.

"The trial court held: 'The actions of the Board with respect to boundary changes, installation of mobile units and repeal of Resolution 1531 shows a continuous affirmative policy designed to isolate Negro children at Stedman and to thereby preserve the "white" character of other Park Hill schools.' . . .

"In 1960, Park Hill and Philips Elementary Schools were predominantly Anglo. In 1968, Park Hill was 71% Anglo, 23.2% Negro and 3.8% Hispano; Philips was 55.3% Anglo, 36.6% Negro and 5.2% Hispano. Notwithstanding the Negro movement into this area, these two schools have continued to maintain a majority of Anglos in the student body.

"The court stated: 'In light of the natural and probable segregative consequences of removing the stabilizing effect of Resolution 1531 on Park Hill and Philips and re-establishing the original district boundaries, the Board must be regarded as having acted with a purpose of approving those consequences.' . . .

"In 1960, Hallett Elementary was 99% Anglo; in 1968 it was 90% Negro, 10% Anglo. The school is about 12 blocks due east of Stedman. When the Stedman boundary changes were considered in 1962, Hallett was under capacity and was 80 to 95% Anglo. The results of the boundary changes, had they occurred, would have brought Hallett up to capacity and would have had an integrative effect on the latter school. The 1964 Stedman boundary change that sent the predominantly Anglo section of Stedman to Hallett resulted in a 80% Anglo section of Hallett's attendance area being transferred to Philips. The effect of the Hallett to Philips transfer was a reduction in Anglo pupils at Hallett from 68.5 to 41.5%. By 1965, when four mobile units were built and additional classrooms constructed, Hallett was 75% Negro.

"The court said: 'The effect of the mobile units and additional classrooms was to solidify segregation at Hallett increasing its capacity to absorb the additional influx of Negro population into the area.'

. . .

"The feeder schools for Smiley Junior High School are Hallett, Park Hill, Smith, Philips, Stedman, Ashley and Harrington. By the established residential trend, Smiley will soon be all Negro. In 1968 there were 23.6% Anglo, 71.6% Negro and 3.7% Hispano, and there were 23 minority teachers. Only one other school in the entire Denver system, Cole Junior High, had more than six minority teachers. The court held: 'The effect of this repeal [of Resolutions 1520 and 1524] was to re-establish Smiley as a segregated school by affirmative Board action. At the time of the repeal, it was certain that such action would perpetuate the racial composition of Smiley at over 75 percent minority and that future Negro population movement would ultimately increase this percentage. * * * We, therefore, find that the action of the Board in rescinding Resolutions 1520 and 1524 was wilful as to its effect on Smiley.' . . .

"In 1969, East High School was 54% Anglo, 40% Negro and 7% Hispano. The court held that neither before nor after the passage of Resolution 1520 could East be considered segregated. But '[r]escission of these Resolutions might, through the feeder system, result in a segregated situation at East in the future. . . .   the trial court extended its findings of de jure segregation to East High and Cole Junior High: 'The effect of the rescission of resolution 1520 at East High was to allow the trend toward segregation * * * to continue unabated. The rescission of Resolution 1524 as applied to Cole Junior High was an action taken which had the effect of frustrating an effort at Cole which at least constituted a start toward ultimate improvement in the quality of the educational effort there. * * * We must hold then that this frustration of the Board plan which had for its purpose relief of the effects of segregation at Cole was unlawful.' "]

Mr. Justice BRENNAN delivered the opinion of the Court. . . .

Petitioners apparently concede for the purposes of this case that in the case of a school system like Denver's, where no statutory dual system has ever existed, plaintiffs must prove not only that segregated schooling exists but also that it was brought about or maintained by intentional state action. Petitioners proved that for almost a decade after 1960 respondent School Board had engaged in an unconstitutional policy of deliberate racial segregation in the Park Hill schools. Indeed, the District Court found that "[b]etween 1960 and 1969 the Board's policies with respect to those northeast Denver schools show an undeviating purpose to isolate Negro students" in segregated schools "while preserving the Anglo character of [other] schools." . . .   This finding did not relate to an insubstantial or trivial fragment of the school system. On the contrary, respondent School Board was found guilty of following a deliberate segregation policy at schools attended, in 1969, by 37.69% of Denver's total Negro school population, including one-fourth of the Negro elementary pupils, over two-thirds of the Negro junior high pupils, and over two-fifths of the Negro high school pupils. In addition, there was uncontroverted evidence that teachers and staff had for years been assigned on a minority teacher-to-minority school basis throughout the school system. Respondent argues, however, that a finding of state-imposed segregation as to a substantial portion of the school system can be viewed in isolation from the rest of the district, and that even if state-imposed segregation does exist in a substantial part of the Denver school system, it does not follow that the District Court could predicate on that fact a finding that the entire school system is a dual system. We do not agree. We have never suggested that plaintiffs in school desegregation cases must bear the burden of proving the elements of *de jure* segregation as to each and every school or each and every student within the school system. Rather, we have held that where plaintiffs prove that a current condition of segregated schooling exists within a school district where a dual system was compelled or authorized by statute at the time of our decision in Brown v. Board of Education, . . .   (*Brown I*), the State automatically assumes an affirmative duty "to effectuate a transition to a racially nondiscriminatory school system," . . . (*Brown II*), that is, to eliminate from the public schools within their school system "all vestiges of state-imposed segregation." . . .

This is not a case, however, where a statutory dual system has ever existed. Nevertheless, where plaintiffs prove that the school authorities have carried out a systematic program of segregation affecting a substantial portion of the students, schools, teachers and facilities within the school system, it is only common sense to conclude that there exists a predicate for a finding of the existence of a dual school system. Several considerations support this conclusion. First, it is obvious that a practice of concentrating Negroes in certain schools by structuring attendance zones or designating "feeder" schools on the basis of race has the reciprocal effect of keeping other nearby schools predominantly white. Similarly, the practice of building a school—such as the Barrett Elementary School in this case—to a certain size and in a certain location, "with conscious knowledge that it would be a segregated school," . . . has a substantial reciprocal effect on the racial composition of other nearby schools. So also, the use of mobile classrooms, the drafting of student transfer policies, the transportation of students, and the assignment of faculty and staff, on racially identifiable bases, have the clear effect of earmarking schools according to their racial composition, and this, in turn, together with the elements of student assignment and school construction, may have a profound reciprocal effect on the racial composition of residential neighborhoods within a metropolitan area, thereby causing further racial concentration within the schools. . . .

In short, common sense dictates the conclusion that racially inspired school board actions have an impact beyond the particular schools that are the subjects of those actions. This is not to say, of course, that there can never be a case in which the geographical structure of or the natural boundaries within a school district may have the effect of dividing the district into separate, identifiable and unrelated units. Such a determination is essentially a question of fact to be resolved by the trial court in the first instance, but such cases must be rare. In the absence of such a determination, proof of state-imposed segregation in a substantial portion of the district will suffice to support a finding by the trial court of the existence of a dual system. Of course, where that finding is made, as in cases involving statutory dual systems, the school authorities have an affirmative duty "to effectuate a transition to a racially nondiscriminatory school system." . . .

Plainly, a finding of intentional segregation as to a portion of a school system is not devoid of probative value in assessing the school authorities' intent with respect to other parts of the same school system. On the contrary, where, as here, the case involves one school board, a finding of intentional segregation on its part in one portion of a school system is highly relevant to the issue of the board's intent with respect to other segregated schools in the system. This is merely an application of the well-settled evidentiary principle that "the prior doing of other similar acts, whether clearly a part of a scheme or not, is useful as reducing the possibility that the act in question was done with innocent intent." . . . "Evidence that similar and related offenses were committed . . . tend[s] to show a consistent pattern of conduct highly relevant to the issue of intent." . . . Similarly, a finding of illicit intent as to a meaningful portion of the item under consideration has substantial probative value on the question of illicit intent as to the remainder. . . . And "[t]he foregoing principles are equally as applicable to civil cases as to criminal cases, . . ."

Applying these principles in the special context of school desegregation cases, we hold that a finding of intentionally segregative school board actions in a meaningful portion of a school system, as in this case, creates a presumption that other segregated schooling within the system is not adventitious. It establishes, in other words, a prima facie case of unlawful segregative design on the part of school authorities, and shifts to those authorities the burden of proving that other segregated schools within the system are not also the result of intentionally segregative actions. This is true even if it is determined that different areas of the school district should be viewed independently of each other because, even in that situation, there is high probability that where school authorities have effectuated an intentionally segregative policy in a meaningful portion of the school system, similar impermissible considerations have motivated their actions in other areas of the system. We emphasize that the differentiating factor between *de jure* segregation and so-called *de facto* segregation to which we referred in *Swann* is *purpose* or *intent* to segregate. Where school authorities have been found to have practiced purposeful segregation in part of a school system, they may be expected to oppose system-wide desegregation, as did the respondents in this case, on the ground that their purposefully segregative actions were isolated and individual events, thus leaving plaintiffs with the burden of proving otherwise. But at that point where an intentionally segregative policy is practiced in a meaningful or significant segment of a school system, as in this case, the school authorities can not be heard to argue that plaintiffs have proved only "isolated and individual" unlawfully segregative actions. In that circumstance, it is both fair and reasonable to require that the school authorities bear the burden of showing that their actions as to other segregated schools within the system were not also motivated by segregative intent.

This burden-shifting principle is not new or novel. There are no hard and fast standards governing the allocation of the burden of proof in every situation. The issue, rather, "is merely a question of policy and fairness based on experience in the different situations."

. . . . In the context of racial segregation in public education, the courts, including this Court, have recognized a variety of situations in which "fairness" and "policy" require state authorities to bear the burden of explaining actions or conditions which appear to be racially motivated. . . .

In discharging that burden, it is not enough, of course, that the school authorities rely upon some allegedly logical, racially neutral explanation for their actions. Their burden is to adduce proof sufficient to support a finding that segregative intent was not among the factors that motivated their actions. The courts below attributed much significance to the fact that many of the Board's actions in the core city area antedated our decision in *Brown*. We reject any suggestion that remoteness in time has any relevance to the issue of intent. If the actions of school authorities were to any degree motivated by segregative intent and the segregation resulting from those actions continues to exist, the fact of remoteness in time certainly does not make those actions any less "intentional."

This is not to say, however, that the prima facie case may not be met by evidence supporting a finding that a lesser degree of segregated schooling in the core city area would not have resulted even if the Board had not acted as it did. In *Swann*, we suggested that at some point in time the relationship between past segregative acts and present segregation may become so attenuated as to be incapable of supporting a finding of *de jure* segregation warranting judicial intervention. . . . We made it clear, however, that a connection between past segregative acts and present segregation may be present even when not apparent and that close examination is required before concluding that the connection does not exist. Intentional school segregation in the past may have been a factor in creating a natural environment for the growth of further segregation. Thus, if respondent School Board cannot disprove segregative intent, it can rebut the prima facie case only by showing that its past segregative acts did not create or contribute to the current segregated condition of the core city schools.

The respondent School Board invoked at trial its "neighborhood school policy" as explaining racial and ethnic concentrations within the core city schools, arguing that since the core city area population had long been Negro and Hispano, the concentrations were necessarily the result of residential patterns and not of purposefully segregative policies. We have no occasion to consider in this case whether a "neighborhood school policy" of itself will justify racial or ethnic concentrations in the absence of a finding that school authorities have committed acts constituting *de jure* segregation. It is enough that we hold that the mere assertion of such a policy is not dispositive where, as in this case, the school authorities have been found to have practiced *de jure* segregation in a meaningful portion of the school system by techniques that indicate that the "neighborhood school" concept has not been maintained free of manipulation. . . .

Thus, respondent School Board having been found to have practiced deliberate racial segregation in schools attended by over one-third of the Negro school population, that crucial finding establishes a prima facie case of intentional segregation in the core city schools. In such case, respondent's neighborhood school policy is not to be determinative "simply because it appears to be neutral." . . .

. . . the case is remanded to the District Court for further proceedings consistent with this opinion.

It is so ordered.

Mr. Chief Justice BURGER concurs in the result.

Mr. Justice WHITE took no part in the decision of this case.

Mr. Justice DOUGLAS.

While I join the opinion of the Court, I agree with my Brother POWELL that there is, for the purposes of the Equal Protection Clause of the Fourteenth Amendment as applied to the school cases, no difference between *de facto* and *de jure* segregation. The school board is a state agency and the lines that it draws, the locations it selects for school sites, the allocation it makes of students, the budgets it prepares are state action for Fourteenth Amendment purposes.

. . . segregated schools are often created, not by dual school systems decreed by the legislature, but by the administration of school districts by school boards. Each is state action within the meaning of the Fourteenth Amendment. "Here school authorities assigned students, faculty, and professional staff, employed faculty and staff; chose sites for schools; constructed new schools and renovated old ones; and drew attendance zone lines. The natural and foreseeable consequence of these actions was segregation of Mexican-Americans. Affirmative action to the contrary would have resulted in desegregation. When school authorities by their actions, contribute to segregation in education, whether by causing additional segregation or maintaining existing segregation, they deny to the students equal protection of the laws.

"We need not define the quantity of state participation which is a prerequisite to a finding of constitutional violation. Like the legal concepts of 'the reasonable man,' 'due care,' 'causation,' 'preponderance of the evidence,' and 'beyond a reasonable doubt,' the necessary degree of state involvement is incapable of precise definition and must be defined on a case-by-case basis. Suffice it to say that school authorities here played a significant role in causing or perpetuating unequal educational opportunities for Mexican-Americans, and did so on a system-wide basis."

These latter acts are often said to create *de facto* as contrasted with *de jure* segregation. But as Judge Wisdom observes, each is but another form of *de jure* segregation.

I think it is time to state that there is no constitutional difference between *de jure* and *de facto* segregation, for each is the product of state actions or policies. If a "neighborhood" or "geographical" unit has been created along racial lines by reason of the play of restrictive covenants that restrict certain areas to "the elite," leaving the "undesirables" to move elsewhere, there is state action in the constitutional sense because the force of law is placed behind those covenants.

There is state action in the constitutional sense when public funds are dispersed by urban development agencies to build racial ghettoes.

Where the school district is racially mixed and the races are segregated in separate schools, where black teachers are assigned almost exclusively to black schools, where the school board closed existing schools located in fringe areas and built new schools in black areas and in distant white areas, where the school board continued the "neighborhood" school policy at the elementary level, these actions constitute state action. They are of a kind quite distinct from the classical *de jure* type of school segregation. Yet calling them *de facto* is a misnomer, as they are only more subtle types of state action that create or maintain a wholly or partially segregated school system.

.   .   .

Mr. Justice POWELL concurring in part and dissenting in part.

.   .   .

This is the first school desegregation case to reach this Court which involves a major city outside the South. It comes from Denver, Colorado, a city and a State which have not operated public schools under constitutional or statutory provisions which mandated or permitted racial segregation. Nor has it been argued that any other legislative actions (such as zoning and housing laws) contributed to the segregation which is at issue.   .   .   .

In my view we should abandon a distinction which long since has outlived its time, and formulate constitutional principles of national rather than merely regional application. When Brown v. Board of Education,   .   .   .   was decided, the distinction between *de jure* and *de facto* segregation was consistent with the limited constitutional rationale of that case. The situation confronting the Court, largely confined to the southern States, was officially imposed racial segregation in the schools extending back for many years and usually embodied in constitutional and statutory provisions.

The great contribution of *Brown I* was its holding in unmistakable terms that the Fourteenth Amendment forbids state-compelled or authorized segregation of public schools.   .   .   .   Although some of the language was more expansive, the holding in *Brown I* was essentially negative: It was impermissible under the Constitution for the States, or their instrumentalities, to force children to attend segregated schools. The forbidden action was *de jure*, and the opinion in *Brown I* was construed—for some years and by many courts—as requiring only state neutrality, allowing "freedom of choice" as to schools to be attended so long as the State itself assured that the choice was genuinely free of official restraints.

But the doctrine of *Brown I*, as amplified by *Brown II*, . . . did not retain its original meaning. In a series of decisions extending from 1954 to 1971 the concept of state neutrality was transformed into the present constitutional doctrine requiring affirmative state action to desegregate school systems. The keystone case was Green v. County School Board, . . . where school boards were declared to have "the affirmative duty to take whatever steps might be necessary to convert to a unitary system in which racial discrimination would be eliminated root and branch." The school system before the Court in *Green* was operating in a rural and sparsely settled county where there were no concentrations of white and black populations, no neighborhood school system (there were only two schools in the county), and none of the problems of an urbanized school district. The Court properly identified the freedom of choice program there as a subterfuge, and the language in *Green* imposing an affirmative duty to convert to a unitary system was appropriate on the facts before the Court. . . .

Rather than continue to prop up a distinction no longer grounded in principle, and contributing to the consequences indicated above, we should acknowledge that whenever public school segregation exists to a substantial degree there is prima facie evidence of a constitutional violation by the responsible school board. It is true, of course, that segregated schools—wherever located—are not solely the product of the action or inaction of public school authorities. Indeed, as indicated earlier, there can be little doubt that principal causes of the pervasive school segregation found in the major urban areas of this country, whether in the North, West, or South, are the socio-economic influences which have concentrated our minority citizens in the inner cities while the more mobile white majority disperse to the suburbs. But it is also true that public school boards have continuing, detailed responsibility for the public school system within their district and, as Judge John Minor Wisdom has noted, "where the figures [showing segregation in the schools] speak so eloquently, a *prima face* case of discrimination is established." United States v. Texas Education Agency, 467 F.2d 848, 873 (C.A.5 *en banc* 1972). Moreover, as aforeshadowed in *Swann* and as implicitly held today, school boards have a duty to minimize and ameliorate segregated conditions by pursuing an affirmative policy of desegregation. It is this policy which must be applied consistently on a national basis without regard to a doctrinal distinction which has outlived its time.*

NOTES AND QUESTIONS

1. What are the ways in which courts allocate "burdens" (1) when dealing with a district that openly had operated a dual school system, and (2) when dealing with a district that had never openly operated a dual school system? What difference does the procedure make? Do you agree? Why? See also, Cisneros v. Corpus Christi Ind. Sch. Dist., 467 F.2d 142 (5th Cir. 1972).

2. What evidence in addition to de facto segregation would be required in order to show that a school offered educational opportunities inferior to those of other schools or intended to segregate? What are the implications of Keyes for "de facto segregation"?

3. Is it true that segregated education is necessarily inferior education and that integrated education is necessarily superior education? Is "race" the critical factor or socio-economic class? Consider the following: "Coleman on 'The Coleman Report'

    "The following letter, by Professor James Coleman, was sent to to the *New York Times* on April 13th. The *Times* having failed to find space for it, we are here inserting it into the public record of the debate on busing and school integration:

    "Dear Sirs:

    "Although I make it a practice to stay away from reporters, some statements of mine were printed in Sunday's (April 9) *Times*. I want to clarify several things concerning the findings of the so-called 'Coleman Report,' and the use of those findings by governmental institutions, including the courts:

    "1. The Report found, as I have testified in various court cases, and as has been confirmed by numerous further analyses of those same data, that the academic achievement of children from lower socio-economic backgrounds (black or white) was benefited by being in schools with children from higher socio-economic backgrounds (black or white).

    "2. This achievement increment is not nearly sufficient to overcome the educational disadvantage of children from lower socio-economic backgrounds.

    "3. This effect, however, was greater than those of other school resources of the kind ordinarily added by compensatory programs. The effects of these resources on achievement can hardly be found at all.

    "My opinion, with which others who have more experience in constitutional law than I may disagree, is that the results stated in 1 and 3 above have been used inappropriate-

---

* A dissenting opinion by Mr. Justice Rehnquist is omitted.

ly by the courts to support the premise that equal protection for black children is not provided unless racial balance is achieved in schools. I believe it is necessary to recognize that equal protection, in the sense of equal educational opportunity, cannot be provided by the State. Most of the inequality of opportunity originates in the home, through loving care and attention by parents—but differential care and attention, since parents differ—and the State can hope only to add opportunity in such a way that these inequalities are not increased but reduced. This does mean, of course, that actions of the State that have increased racial or socio-economic segregation should be corrected by the courts, but not on the mistaken assumption that they are thereby creating equal educational opportunity.

"While the issue of racial integration in schools does not, I believe, involve constitutional questions of equal protection for black children conditional upon increased achievement in integrated schools, it is a matter on which school boards and governmental authorities have a responsibility to take affirmative action—action with a less punitive and blunt quality than some court decisions, but affirmative action nevertheless. In the past 20 years, there has been an increasing self-segregation into homogeneous communities by those families that have greatest freedom to move. The result is an increasing social and economic segregation in the schools, which makes a mockery of the classic American conception of the common school attended by children of all social groups.

"Probably the most cogent recent statement on this issue is that made by the New York Board of Regents on March 24, in reaffirming its stand on school integration. The Board of Regents did not mention constitutional equal protection of black students because of greater achievement in integrated schools, but said rather, 'This Board cannot foresee any but the most sullen and corrosive scenarios of the future if the multicolored and multicultured children of this state and nation are not permitted to get to know one another as individuals.'

> "James S. Coleman
> "Professor of Social Relations"

From No. 28, the Public Interest 127–8 (Summer 1972), c. by National Affairs Inc., 1972, and see also, J. S. Coleman, et al., Equality of Educational Opportunity (1966).

4. Does a court have constitutional power to order socio-economic integration, as distinguished from racial desegregation? Does a school board? Why or why not? If most minority groups are poor does racial integration tend to produce socio-economic integration? Is this an objective school board should seek to accomplish? See, H. Walberg & A. Kopan, Rethinking Urban Education (1972).

5. Should school boards seek racial integration even if it could not be shown that students do better academically in racially integrated schools? Are there other proper objectives?

6. Can a school be desegregated in terms of its overall numbers, but segregated within its walls because of internal devices such as "ability grouping" or "tracking"? See, Hobson v. Hansen, infra, Ch. 10.

7. Does a Federal court have constitutional power to order a desegregation plan that joins together contiguous school districts thereby allowing desegregation of the districts—one mostly black and the other white? See, Bradley v. Milliken, 345 F.Supp. 914 (E.D.Mich., 1972).

————

BLACK SCHOOLS THAT WORK

Newsweek Magazine, Jan. 1, 1973.
Reprinted with permission Copyright, © Newsweek, Inc., 1973.

The Windsor Hills Elementary School in Los Angeles had a big problem. When city school officials disclosed in 1969 that its pupils had the highest average IQ scores in Los Angeles, Windsor Hills was threatened with inundation by parents from other districts who tried to enroll their children, sometimes going to the length of faking their home addresses. In response, the neighborhood formed a Parents for Quality Education committee to fight overcrowding. "We were out there every morning," recalls one of the parents, Mrs. Gwen Jackson, "taking down the license plates of those who didn't belong." That scene has been repeated many times in the unequal world of American education; at good schools, the "haves" always want to keep the "have-nots" out. What makes Windsor Hills extraordinary is the fact that its students body is 98 per cent black.

The school has gone through a racial transformation that is typical of many urban schools. A decade ago, most of its students were white. Then blacks began to move into the neighborhood, and in almost textbook fashion, the student body "tipped"; by 1965 it was half black, and three years later few whites were left. In most American schools, racial tipping is followed by a decline in educational quality . . . Instead, Windsor Hills improved dramatically. Once only average, it now ranks among the top 5 per cent of the city's schools in standard reading tests. Few predominantly black schools in the U. S. can match that record. But a handful do, and as black psychologist Kenneth Clark observes, "the fact that there are a few good black schools means that low quality is not inevitable."

Success: One of the things that make Windsor Hills a good school is that most of its pupils come from prosperous families. The parents are an upper-middle-class melange of doctors, lawyers and engineers, and the houses in the hilly neighborhood overlooking the Pacific are worth as much as $150,000. But there are other ingredients of the school's success, and these factors—unlike high family income—are common to all of the outstanding, predominantly black schools across the country.

One of the hallmarks is strict discipline and a strong focus on such fundamentals as reading and writing. "We are less permissive than other high schools," says Napoleon B. Lewis, the black principal of Howard D. Woodson High School in Washington, D. C. "I don't believe in crutches. The best thing you can do for a black kid is to have high expectations." "They need academic skills," adds Sondra Hirsch, a white teacher at P. S. 234 in New York's borough of the Bronx. "I'm a staunch supporter of innovation, but kids have to learn to read, and I expect them to do it." Father Paul Smith, the black principal of the Holy Angels Roman Catholic elementary school in Chicago, argues that permissive educators reflect "an Anglo-Saxon mentality of freedom. The black child in the inner city needs the tight system that we have here because of the chaos and disruption in the community where he lives." Father Smith's system is tight indeed. At Holy Angels, homework is mandatory every day, and the children are spanked when other forms of discipline fail.

Most children seem to respond well to such stern requirements. "The harder I work them, the more they like it," reports Mrs. Hirsch. "Third graders come back for homework, and second graders moan when there isn't any." "I'm a slow learner," admits a member of the junior class at Woodson. "I was going to drop out of my old school, but coming here changed my thoughts a little." Although some 70 percent of his schoolmates hope to go on to college, Jones wants to be an electrician, which is one of the many vocational skills taught at Woodson.

Sound: Stressing the basics does not mean that up-to-date teaching methods are ignored. New York's P.S. 234 uses a system developed by British mathematician Caleb Gattegno to teach reading and math. The reading program revolves around a large word chart, on which each of the 47 sounds in the English language is color-coded. The *u* in "up" is yellow, for example, as are the similar-sounding *o* in "done," the *oe* in "does" and the *oo* in "blood."

Like most urban schools, the best of the black institutions have crowded classrooms. At Windsor Hills, the first three grades average 28 children to a class, and grades four through six have about 35. What sets the better schools apart is that most of them have superior facilities, often due to Federal aid. Woodson's new $10 million, eight-story building includes a rifle range and an Olympic-size swimming pool. The top schools also manage to give their students individual attention, despite crowded classrooms. At the Woodland Elementary School in Kansas City, students in the first three grades take a reading course that allows each child to work through nineteen books at his own pace. "The slow ones aren't forced to go too fast," says reading teacher Dan Reuter, "and the bright ones aren't frustrated by being held back."

Successful schools also work hard at involving parents in their activities. In addition to its PTA, the Captain Arthur Roth Elementary School in Cleveland has a fathers' club that organizes recreation and trips—pointedly including children who don't have fathers of their own. At Woodland, a salaried "parent visitor," Mrs. Rose Fowler, calls on other parents who are suspicious or apathetic about the school. "We start with little things," says Mrs. Fowler, "like keeping a supply of underwear and socks for children whose parents can't afford to buy them." The PTA at Windsor Hills has such *esprit de corps* that the school auditorium can barely contain the turnout at its monthly meetings. In addition, more than 100 parents take part in a volunteer program, performing such jobs as running the mimeograph machine, keeping order in the corridors and tutoring slow students. There is also an advisory council of parents that takes part in the selection of new teachers. "We are so interested," reports one member of the panel, "that we even sent representatives to sit in when a man was interviewed for a new custodial post."

Another essential requirement, of course, is a competent and dedicated faculty. And somehow, amid all the frustrations of the urban educational scene, a few predominantly black schools have succeeded in assembling an impressive array of teaching talent. Before P. S. 234 opened in the fall of 1971, the community school board placed an advertisement in The New York Times asking for imaginative teachers. Nearly 250 people applied for the 85 jobs at P. S. 234 and a neighboring school, and principal Peter Negroni was able to handpick his staff. One of the successful candidates was Sondra Hirsch, who had just obtained her master's degree and who turned down a position in pastoral Vermont to come to the Bronx. "It's the best school in the city," maintains Mrs. Hirsch, who commutes to her job from suburban Long Island. "I wish my own kids were here instead of in Great Neck."

NOTES AND QUESTIONS

1. What factor(s) is responsible for the quality of these schools? Did the factor(s) play an important role in Brown v. Board of Education? Should it have?

2. What are the implications of these schools "that work" for desegregation? Socio-cultural integration? Headstart programs? Future court decisions?

3. In what way are these schools different from upper-middle class "white" schools?

4. Should these schools be desegregated?

NOTE ON ALTERNATIVES TO INTEGRATION

White resistance in the North and West as well as in the South to the Supreme Court's decision in Brown v. Board of Education has not abated. In some parts of the United States the white resistance has intensified and has assumed more subtle forms. Faced with continuing white resistance to integration many minority-group parents and leaders have tired. They no longer pursue methods designed to achieve integration in schools. Instead, they are trying to identify alternative ways in which minority-group children can actually be afforded equal educational opportunity in quality schools without concern whether the schools are integrated. Among the methods that are being tried are community control, various kinds of compensatory education schemes, free schools and equalized school funding. These, and other, techniques promise some measure of success in certain circumstances, but they raise major questions of adequacy when they are offered as alternatives to fully integrated schools for all minority groups as a whole. They also raise new and different legal problems. See, Bell, School Litigation Strategies for the 1970's: New Phases in the Continuing Quest for Quality Schools, 1970 Wis.L.Rev. 257.

Community Control

Many minority-group parents and leaders who are pursuing alternatives to integrated schools distinguish sharply between a "segregated" school and a school that is all, or predominantly, of one minority group; e. g., black. The ultimate difference between the two is said to be the quality of education offered. For example, some black parents and leaders hold that a "segregated" school is one that not only is populated with children who are all, or almost all, from one or more minority groups, but also, a "segregated" school is one that is controlled by whites. Blacks and other minority groups have no voice nor effective power over the substance of critical decisions, curriculum or other matters that count. Moreover, the white administrators and teachers in "segregated" schools are said not to understand fully their black, and other minority-group, children. All too often, the argument proceeds, the white faculty members and administrators operate on the basic belief that black children cannot be expected to learn very much because (1) black children are inferior in some basic way or (2) black children have suffered crippling blows from their culturally and economically deprived backgrounds. In both cases, the crucial consequences are identical. The teachers have low learning expectations for black and other minority group children which expectations, in turn, tend to fulfill themselves, because if the low expectations held by the teachers are conveyed to the children and they come to believe that they can't learn, then they do not, especially when combined with opinions of low self-esteem. See, e. g., R. Rosenthal & L. Jacobson, Pygmalian in the Classroom (1968).

There are at least three possible solutions to this problem. First, white administrators and teachers could change the message that they transmit. The feasibility of this solution is usually discounted on various grounds. Second, white children can be brought into the classrooms, thereby seeking to have the teachers and administrators elevate their expectations accordingly. This solution leads to integration strategies. As Dr. Kenneth Clark sees the matter: "It is not the presence of the white child per se that leads to higher achievement for the Negro child who associates with him in class; it is the quality of the education provided because the white child is there that makes the difference." (Clark, Fifteen Years of Deliberate Speed, *Saturday Review*, Dec. 20, 1969). This solution is discounted because of white resistance to integration. Third, black and other minority-group teachers and administrators can replace whites. The idea is that under community control, especially minority-group control of local school boards, the new teachers and administrators who will be appointed will be selected because they are sensitive to the needs of minority-group children and because they will create an atmosphere of mutual trust, pride and esteem that is more conducive to learning. This solution directly eliminates the low expectations and simultaneously affords minority-group school children with minority-group models of success which will serve to increase the children's pride and raise their low self-esteem which subverts their achievement potential. The community control solution is seen as providing the foundation for a "union of children, parents, teachers (specially trained to teach in such communities), social workers, psychologists, doctors, lawyers and community planners," which would "make the system a functioning, relevant part of the lives of the local people" and such "involvement is essential" to abate "the present situation of existing and growing alienation." Hamilton, Race and Education: A Search for Legitimacy, 38 Harv.Ed.Rev. 671 (1968). For further discussion see, M. Berobe and M. Gittell, Confrontation at Ocean Hill-Brownsville (1968); Edmonds, Judicial Assumptions on the Value of Integrated Education for Blacks, Proceedings, Nat'l Policy Conference on Education for Blacks 140 (1972); U.S. Senate Select Committee on Equal Educational Opportunity, Hearings, 5873–5874 (July 27, 1971); Kirp, Community Control, Public Policy and the Limits of Law, 68 Mich.L.Rev. 1355 (1970); Owens v. School Committee, 304 F.Supp. 1327 (D.Mass., 1969), and Oliver v. Donovan, 293 F.Supp. 958 (E.D. N.Y.1968).

Compensatory Education

Compensatory education programs take many forms. But commonly, they provide for more teachers with specialized teaching skills; for more and specialized teaching aids, and for more and specialized programs aimed at the specific problems of minority children, especially ghetto children. Compensatory education programs are costly, and usually local communities will not, or cannot, tax themselves sufficiently to finance them. Some compensatory education programs have been financed by the federal government under the largest compensatory education program ever attempted, authorized by Title I of the Elementary and Secondary Education Act of 1965 (79 Stat. 27–35, as amended, 20 U.S.C. §§ 236–244 (1965).

But problems have arisen. There have been repeated reports of corruption, waste, misuse and mismanagement of the federal monies. Far too often monies have been used to equalize state funding of schools rather than to increase the funding of ghetto schools that already should be receiving their equal share of funds, or monies have been used to upgrade the physical aspects of target schools rather than their educational programs. See, 1969 Civil Rights Commission Report 32. But probably the greatest obstacle to realizing fully the promise of compensatory educational programs is a failure of national will and funds. The magnitude of the need is great, and compensatory education is expensive. The Chairman of the Senate's Select Committee on Equal Educational Opportunity, Walter Mondale, stated that "with few exceptions, an annual Federal investment of $1.5 billion in compensatory education has little perceptible impact on mounting educational disadvantages." (New York Times, Feb. 27, 1972, E. 13, col. 8). But, the large scale resistance by whites to integration indicates that there is probably insufficient solid support for the needed compensatory education programs that would spend four times as much money on the education of minority-group children than on white education. See, Cohen, Policies for the Public Schools: Compensation and Integration, 38 Harv.Ed.Rev. 114 (1968).

Free Schools

Free schools, generally, are private schools that have been located in poor areas. They serve minority-group children primarily. They tend to be staffed by sensitive and committed teachers, to have exciting curricula especially designed for minority-group children, and they seem to be fun for the children and have a better-than-average rate of success. See, J. Kozol, Free Schools (1972), and G. Dennison, Lives of Children (1969). But free schools have many problems, probably the greatest of which is financing. Parents who are able to pay tuition pay it on a sliding scale basis, and sometimes there are additional funds that come from foundation grants and other sources. The free schools of the Black Muslims seek no outside sources of funds. These schools are characterized by strict segregation, strong discipline, attempts to generate feelings of racial pride and self-reliance, and the black children seem to achieve at, or above, their grade levels. See, The Muslim Way, *Newsweek*, 106 (Sept. 25, 1972). The Black Muslims, of course, have an intensity of commitment not easily duplicated. Dedication can be a second problem. In addition to funds, free schools also require large amounts of commitment, competence, courage and considerateness from their teachers which, often, are hard to sustain over long periods of time.

Equalized School Funding

The idea here is that state authorities should undertake to eliminate financial differences between school districts, especially the under-financed ghetto schools. Much financing of the common schools comes from local property taxes. The amount of funds raised varies widely among school districts because valuable properties and their assessed valuations and their property tax rates vary widely. Equalized school funding is explored in Chapter 10.

Voucher Education

Voucher education, or a system of tuition grants, has been proposed as an alternative to integrated education. See Sizer & Whitten, A Proposal for a Poor Children's Bill of Rights, Psychology Today 59 (Aug. 1968), and Sizer, The Case for a Free Market, Saturday Review 34 (Jan. 11, 1969). This scheme is the subject of Chapter 11. For a discussion of the constitutional and other problems presented by a voucher program compare King, Rebuilding the "Fallen House"— State Tuition Grants for Elementary and Secondary Education, 84 Harv.L.Rev. 1057 (1971) with Green, Education Vouchers, 6 Harv.Civ. Rights-Civ.Lib.L.Rev. 466 (1971), and see, Mecklenberger and Wilson, Learning C.O.D.—Can the Schools Buy Success?, *Saturday Review* 62 (Sept. 18, 1972).

CONSTITUTIONAL LIMITATIONS ON STATE AID TO RACIALLY DISCRIMINATORY PRIVATE SCHOOLS

NORWOOD v. HARRISON

Supreme Court of the United States, 1973.
413 U.S. 455, 93 S.Ct. 2804, 37 L.Ed.2d 723.

Mr. Chief Justice BURGER delivered the opinion of the Court.

. . .

Private schools in Mississippi have experienced a marked growth in recent years. As recently as the 1963–1964 school year, there were only 17 private schools other than Catholic schools; the total enrollment was 2,362 students. 916 students in these nonpublic schools were Negro, and 192 of these were enrolled in special schools for retarded, orphaned, or abandoned children. By September of 1970, the number of private non-Catholic schools had increased to 155 with a student population estimated at 42,000, virtually all white. Appellees do not challenge the statement, which is fully documented in appellants' brief, that "the creation and enlargement of these [private] academies occurred simultaneously with major events in the desegregation of public schools. . . . "

This case does not raise any question as to the right of citizens to maintain private schools with admission limited to students of particular national origins, race or religion or of the authority of a State to allow such schools. See Pierce v. Society of Sisters . . . The narrow issue before us, rather, is a particular form of tangible <u>assistance the State provides to students in private schools in common with all other students by lending textbooks</u> under the State's 33-year-old program for providing free textbooks to all the children of the State. The program dates back to a 1940 appeal for improved education facilities by the Governor of Mississippi to the state legislature. The legislature then established a state textbook purchasing board and authorized it to select, purchase, and distribute free textbooks for all school children through the first eight grades. In 1942, the program was extended to cover all high school students, and, as codified, the statutory authorization remains substantially unchanged. . . .

The District Court found that "34,000 students are presently receiving state-owned textbooks while attending 107 all-white, non-sectarian private schools which have been formed throughout the state since the inception of public school desegregation." During the 1970–1971 school year, these schools held 173,424 books for which Mississippi paid $490,239. The annual expenditure for replacement or new texts is approximately $6 per pupil or a total of approximately $207,000 for the students enrolled in the participating private segregated academies, exclusive of mailing costs which are borne by the state as well.

In dismissing the complaint the District Court stressed, first, that the statutory scheme was not motivated by a desire to further racial segregation in the public schools, having been enacted first in 1940, long before this Court's decision in Brown v. Board of Education, 347 U.S. 483 (1954), and consequently, long before there was any occasion to have a policy or reason to foster the development of racially segregated private academies. Second, the District Court took note that providing textbooks to private *sectarian* schools had been approved by this Court in Board of Education v. Allen, 392 U.S. 236 (1968), and that "the essential inquiry, therefore, is whether we should apply a more stringent standard for determining what constitutes state aid to a school in the context of the Fourteenth Amendment's ban against denial of equal protection that the Supreme Court has applied in the First Amendment cases." The District Court held no more stringent standard should apply on the facts of this case, since, as in *Allen,* the books were provided to the students and not to the schools. Finally, the District Court concluded that the textbook loans did not interfere with or impede the State's acknowledged duty to establish a unitary school system under this Court's holding in Green v. County School Board, . . .

This Court has consistently affirmed decisions enjoining state tuition grants to students attending racially discriminatory private schools. A textbook lending program is not legally distinguishable from the forms of state assistance foreclosed by the prior cases. Free textbooks, like tuition grants directed to private school students, are a form of financial assistance inuring to the benefit of the private schools themselves. An inescapable educational cost for students in both public and private schools is the expense of providing all necessary learning materials. When, as here, that necessary expense is borne by the State, the economic consequence is to give aid to the enterprise; if the school engages in discriminatory practices the State by tangible aid in the form of textbooks thereby gives support to such discrimination. Racial discrimination in state-operated schools is barred by the Constitution and "[i]t is also axiomatic that a state may not induce, encourage or promote private persons to accomplish what it is constitutionally forbidden to accomplish." . . .

We do not suggest that a State violates its constitutional duty merely because it has provided *any* form of state service that benefits private schools said to be racially discriminatory. Textbooks are a basic educational tool and, like tuition grants, they are provided only in connection with schools; they are to be distinguished from generalized services government might provide to schools in common with others. Moreover, the textbooks provided to private school students by the State in this case are a form of assistance readily available from sources entirely independent of the State—unlike, for example, "such necessities of life as electricity, water, and police and fire protection." . . . The State has neither an absolute nor operating monopoly on the procurement of school textbooks; anyone can purchase them on the open market.

The District Court laid great stress on the absence of showing by appellants that "any child enrolled in private school if deprived of free textbooks would withdraw from private schools and subsequently enroll in the public schools." We can accept this factual assertion; we cannot and do not know, on this record at least, whether state textbook assistance is the determinative factor in the enrollment of any students in any of the private schools in Mississippi. We do not agree with the District Court in its analysis of the legal consequences of this uncertainty, for the Constitution does not permit the State to aid discrimination even when there is no precise causal relationship between state financial aid to a private school and the continued well-being of that school. A State may not grant the type of tangible financial aid here involved if that aid has a significant tendency to facilitate, reinforce, and support private discrimination. "[D]ecisions on the constitutionality of state involvement in private discrimination do not turn on whether the state aid adds up to 51 per cent or adds up to only 49 per cent of the support of the segregated institution." . . .

The recurring theme of appellees' argument is a sympathetic one —that the State's textbook loan program is extended to students who attend racially segregated private schools only because the State sincerely wishes to foster quality education for all Mississippi children, and, to that end, has taken steps to insure that no sub-group of school children will be deprived of an important educational tool merely because their parents have chosen to enroll them in segregated private schools. We need not assume that the State's textbook aid to private schools has been motivated by other than a sincere interest in the educational welfare of all Mississippi children. But good intentions as to one valid objective do not serve to negate the State's involvement in violation of a constitutional duty. "The existence of a permissible purpose cannot sustain an action that has an impermissible effect." . . . The Equal Protection Clause would be a sterile promise if state involvement in possible private activity could be shielded altogether from constitutional scrutiny simply because its ultimate end was not discrimination but some higher goal. . . .

The District Court offered as further support for its holding the finding that Mississippi's public schools "were fully established as unitary schools throughout the state no later than 1970–71 [and] continue to attract 90% of the state's educable children." . . . We note, however, that overall statewide attendance figures do not fully and accurately reflect the impact of private schools in particular school districts. In any event, the constitutional infirmity of the Mississippi textbook program is that it significantly aids the organization and continuation of a separate system of private schools which, under the District Court holding, may discriminate if they so desire. A State's constitutional obligation requires it to steer clear not only of operating the old dual system of racially segregated schools but also of giving significant aid to institutions that practice racial or other invidious discrimination. That the State's public schools are now fully unitary, as the District Court found, is irrelevant.

Appellees and the District Court also placed great reliance on our decisions in Everson v. Board of Education . . . and Board of Education v. Allen . . . In *Everson,* we held that the Establishment Clause of the First Amendment did not prohibit New Jersey from "spending tax-raised funds to pay the bus fares of parochial school pupils as part of a general program under which it pays the fares of pupils attending public and other schools." . . . *Allen,* following *Everson,* sustained a New York law requiring school textbooks to be let free of charge to all students, including those in attendance at parochial schools, in specified grades.

Neither *Allen* nor *Everson* is dispositive of the issue before us in this case. Religious schools "pursue two goals, religious instruction and secular education." . . . And, where carefully limited so as to avoid the prohibitions of the "effect" and "entanglement" tests, States may assist church-related schools in performing their secular functions . . . not only because the States have a substantial interest in the quality of education being provided by private schools . . . but more importantly because assistance properly confined to the secular functions of sectarian schools does not substantially promote the readily identifiable religious mission of those schools and it does not interfere with the free exercise rights of others.

Like a sectarian school, a private school—even one that discriminates—fulfills an important educational function; however, the difference is that in the context of this case the legitimate educational function cannot be isolated from discriminatory practices—if such in fact exist. Under Brown v. Board of Education, supra, discriminatory treatment exerts a pervasive influence on the entire educational process. The private school that closes its doors to defined groups of students on the basis of constitutionally suspect criteria manifests, by its own actions, that its educational processes are based on private belief that segregation is desirable in education. There is no reason to discriminate against students for reasons wholly unrelated to individual merit unless the artificial barriers are considered an essential part of the educational message to be communicated to the students who are admitted. Such private bias is not barred by the Constitution, nor does it invoke any sanction of laws, but neither can it call on the Constitution for material aid from the State.

Our decisions under the Establishment Clause reflect the "internal tension in the First Amendment between the Establishment Clause and the Free Exercise Clause," . . . This does not mean, as we have already suggested, that a State is constitutionally obligated to provide even "neutral" services to sectarian schools. But the transcendent value of free religious exercise in our constitutional scheme leaves room for "play in the joints" to the extent of cautiously delineated secular governmental assistance to religious schools, despite the fact that such assistance touches on the conflicting values of the Establishment Clause by indirectly benefiting the religious schools and their sponsors.

In contrast, although the Constitution does not proscribe private bias, it places no value on discrimination as it does on the values inherent in the Free Exercise Clause. Invidious private discrimination may be characterized as a form of exercising freedom of association protected by the First Amendment, but it has never been accorded affirmative constitutional protections. And even some private discrimination is subject to special remedial legislation in certain circumstances under § 2 of the Thirteenth Amendment; Congress has made such discrimination unlawful in other significant contexts. However narrow may be the channel of permissible state aid to sectarian schools . . . it permits a greater degree of state assistance than may be given to private schools which engage in discriminatory practices that would be unlawful in a public school system. . . .

The judgment of the District Court is vacated and the case is remanded for further proceedings consistent with this opinion.

So ordered.

Mr. Justice DOUGLAS and Mr. Justice BRENNAN concur in the result.

NOTES AND QUESTIONS

1. Identify the types of aid that a state constitutionally can provide to a racially discriminatory private school? To a non-racially discriminatory private school that is also a parochial school? To a non-racially discriminatory, non-parochial private school?

2. Does the principle of this case apply to parochial schools that refuse to admit as students those persons who are not members of the school's religious faith?

3. What would be the application of the principle of this case to a state program that awarded tuition grants to all students in the state so that they could go to "any school of their choosing, public or private"? Cf. Coffey v. State Educational Fin. Comm., 296 F.Supp. 1389 (S.D. Miss.1969), app. dism., 398 U.S. 956, 400 U.S. 986. Suppose the Commissioner of Internal Revenue has awarded the schools in Norwood a tax-exempt status under § 501(c)(3) of the Federal Internal Revenue Code thus ensuring donors the right to deduct contributions to these schools, would a plaintiff be successful under the rule of this case in obtaining an injunction prohibiting these schools from being classified as tax-exempt? See, Green v. Kennedy, 309 F.Supp. 1127 (D.C.1970), and Comment, Segregation Academies And State Action, 82 Yale L.J. 1436 (1973).

INTEGRATION OF FACULTY

BAKER v. COLUMBUS MUNICIPAL SEPARATE SCHOOL DIST.

United States District Court, N.D.Miss.1971.
329 F.Supp. 706, aff'd 462 F.2d 1112.

ORMA R. SMITH, District Judge.

FINDINGS OF FACT ON COUNT ONE

1. Plaintiffs in Count One of this action are the National Education Association (NEA), the Mississippi Teachers Association (MTA), and eight Negro teachers who taught in the Columbus Municipal Separate School District during the academic year 1969–70 . . .

3. The defendants are the Columbus Municipal Separate School District of Lowndes County, Mississippi . . .

4. Count One of the amended complaint alleges that defendants have unlawfully refused to reemploy black teachers and to hire black applicants for teaching positions. . . .

6. During the academic year 1969–70, the student enrollment in the Columbus Public School was 8,865 students. The racial composition of the student body was approximately 5,392 white students or 61 per cent white, and approximately 3,473 black students or 39 per cent black.

7. At least until the commencement of the 1970–71 school year, the defendants operated a dual school system. . . .

9. Defendants intended to reduce the size of the faculty by three positions for the 1970–71 school year. On the day before school opened, however, Superintendent Goolsby advised the Court that there were 36 vacancies on his staff. Thus, the 1970–71 school year commenced with a faculty that was 39 persons below the faculty for the preceding academic year, 1969–70. In all, there were 376 faculty members in 1969–70 and 337 faculty members as of September 3, 1970.

10. Between the academic years 1969–70 and 1970–71, the racial composition of the faculty changed substantially. The number of black teachers dropped from 133 to 103 and the number of white teachers dropped from 243 to 234. Thus, the number of black teachers on the faculty declined by 22 per cent and the number of white teachers on the faculty declined by 3 per cent.

11. Through September 3, 1970, defendants had hired 44 new teachers for the 1970–71 academic year. All but one were white.

12. The marked changes in the racial composition of defendants' faculty between the academic years 1969–70 and 1970–71 coincide with the changes in defendants' hiring and retention policy. On January 12, 1970, the Board of Trustees modified the procedures and requirements for hiring and reelection of teachers by adding to those procedures and requirements, effective for the 1970–71 academic year, the following:

"Each classroom teacher that was employed to teach in the Columbus Public School System for the first time for the year 1969–1970 [shall] be required to have on file in the Superintendent's office a composite score of 1000 on the National Teachers Examination before they [shall] be considered for employment as a classroom teacher for the year 1970–71 and * * * all classroom teachers that were not employed by the Columbus Public Schools during the 1969–70 school year and all future classroom teachers that are employed [shall] be required to meet the above standards."

. . .

18. Also on or about March of each year, each principal has evaluated the teachers in his school on the basis of a rating form used throughout the school district. The principals rated the teachers on a scale of 0 to 5 with respect to each of 25 criteria:

Wholesome Personality
Appearance
Poise
Desirable Work Habits
Good Command of English
Good Physical and Mental Health

Proper Ethical Conduct
Interest in Self Improvement
Knowledge of Subject Matter and Methods of Instruction
Academic Requirements of Subject Matter or Grade Level
Willingness to Accept and Execute Policies and Assignments
Readiness to Share Ideas and Methods
Skill in Evaluating Pupils and Reporting to Parents
Willingness to Ask for and Accept Help
Participation in Professional Organizations and School Activities
Competency in Record Keeping
Follows Philosophy of Education for Columbus Public Schools
Concern for Physical Aspects of Room
Self-Discipline and Classroom Control
Consistency in Lesson Planning
Energy and Enthusiasm in Presenting Lesson
Skill in Giving Directions, Questioning and Testing
Use of Teaching Aids
Skill in Making Reasonable Homework and Research Assignments
Providing for Individual Instruction During Supervised Study
Period .   .   .

22.   The NTE cutoff score requirement had its origins in a merit pay program of defendants known as the "Voluntary Professional Enrichment Program" or "PEP".

23.   .   .   .   The PEP program was formulated by the Superintendent, who consulted with a committee of teachers belonging to the local white teacher association. No black teachers were consulted.

24.   Under PEP no teacher was eligible for merit pay unless he had filed an NTE score with the school district. In addition, a teacher had to earn 70 points to qualify for the minimum pay increment of $300; 75 points for an increment of $400; and 80 points for the maximum increment of $500.   .   .   .

27.   During the first year of PEP (1966–67), 59 teachers applied for merit pay and filed NTE scores. Five of the applicants were black. Fifty-two white teachers and one black teacher posted scores of 500 or more on one of the NTE examinations. Twenty-six applicants, all of whom were white, received merit pay.

28.   In the second year (1967–68) of PEP, 77 teachers applied for merit pay. Seven of these applicants were black. Sixty-eight white teachers and one black teacher posted scores of 500 or more on one of the NTE examinations. Forty-three of the applicants, all of whom were white, received merit pay.

29.   In the third year (1968–69) of PEP, 98 teachers applied for merit pay. Fifteen of these applicants were black. Seventy-nine white teachers and eight black teachers posted scores of 500 or

more in one of the NTE examinations. Fifty-six teachers, of whom four were black, received merit pay. . . .

33. On April 14, 1969, Mrs. Holloman moved the Board of Trustees "to require new teachers elected to the Columbus Public Schools faculty for the first time for the 1969–70 school session to file their National Teacher Examination scores by January 1, 1970." The motion carried. . . .

36. The NTE cutoff score requirement was invoked by defendants without investigating or studying the validity and reliability of the examination and the particular cutoff score as a means of selecting teachers for hiring and reelection for the Columbus system, and without consulting with the developer of the NTE. The Superintendent disavows any expertise with respect to the NTE.

37. The Board of Trustees, in adopting the cutoff score on January 12, 1970, was aware of the racially disparate results worked by the NTE requirements of the PEP program. The Superintendent also expected that the percentage of black teachers or applicants who would not qualify would be greater than the percentage of whites. . . .

The National Teachers Examination

39. Educational Testing Service (ETS), a non-profit corporation, produces and administers the National Teachers Examination. It also designs, produces and administers a broad range of other standardized testing programs, including the College Board Examinations, the Law School Aptitude Test, and the Graduate Record Examinations. ETS annually administers test programs to about five million individuals who are in or moving toward professional careers.

40. There are two major sections of the NTE: the Common Examination and the Teaching Area Examination. The Common Examination consists of a professional education test and a set of three general education tests which provide a general appraisal of the prospective teacher's basic professional preparation and general academic attainment. The Teaching Area Examinations test the candidate with respect to a particular academic discipline. There are about 20 different Teaching Area Examinations. Separate scores are reported by ETS for the Common Examination and for the Teaching Area Examination.

41. Plaintiffs presented as their expert witness Dr. James R. Deneen, Senior Program Director for Teacher Examinations of the ETS. Prior to joining ETS in 1969, Dr. Deneen was a full-time consultant to the Ford Foundation in matters of school administration. In earlier years, he was the Codirector of Education Study in the Catholic Archdiocese of New York; an Adjunct Professor at Fordham University, teaching school personnel administration; and Executive Secretary for the Superintendent of the National Catholic Education

Association; and between 1957 and 1966 the Superintendent of Schools for the Catholic Diocese of Evansville, Indiana, a system of 16,000 pupils.

42.   Defendants presented as their expert witness Dr. Stephen Knezevich, Professor of Education Administration at the University of Wisconsin. Prior to serving at the University of Wisconsin, Dr. Knezevich was associated with the American Association of School Administrators. In earlier years, he served as Professor and Department Head at Florida State University; Professor of Education at the University of Iowa; Associate Professor of Education at University of Tulsa; and Superintendent of Schools in Algoma, Wisconsin.

43.   Dr. Deneen's experience with the NTE has been in his present capacity as the supervisor of the program in which the NTE is developed and administered. Dr. Knezevich's direct experience with the NTE was in 1960 when he reviewed the test and prepared a paper on the subject. Since that time, his contact with the NTE has been limited to that stemming from his relationship to the process for admission of students for the Florida State Graduate School of Administration Supervision and Curriculum between 1961 and 1965. In admitting students, that graduate school relied in part on standardized test scores, most extensively the Graduate Record Examination score, but sometimes the NTE score. With the exception of a review of some NTE booklets in preparation for his testimony in this case, Dr. Knezevich has not had any contact with the NTE since 1965.

What the NTE Is Designed to Measure

44.   The primary purpose of the NTE is to measure the academic achievement of college seniors completing four years of teacher education. It is limited to the assessment of those aspects of teacher education which are validly and reliably measured by well-constructed, objective paper-and-pencil tests. The NTE are used primarily by state and local school systems, teacher education institutions, and other agencies concerned with the guidance, preparation, certification and employment of teachers for elementary and secondary schools.

45.   It is not known whether there is a relationship between academic preparation, as measured by the NTE, and effective teaching. Dr. Deneen testified that "We cannot demonstrate such a relationship," and Dr. Knezevich generally agreed with the conclusion. Thus, the reliability and validity of the NTE as a means of identifying effective teachers is unknown. There is no evidence developed to date of a correlation, positive or negative, between the NTE score and teacher effectiveness. The NTE does not claim predictive validity—i. e., "the ability to forecast teaching performance."

Defendants' Use of the NTE—Absence of Validation

46.   Defendants rely exclusively on the NTE in refusing to re-employ first-year teachers and to hire applicants who have not satisfied the 1000 cutoff score requirement.

47.   Use of the NTE with a cutoff score as a means of selecting teachers cannot be considered reasonable unless steps are first taken to relate the score to experience and needs in the particular school district. These steps include identification of the strengths and weaknesses of the school district's present staff; determination of the characteristics of teacher preparation programs in those colleges from which the district draws most of its teachers; determination of the composition and needs of the district's student body in relation to national and local education goals; and consultation with ETS regarding the uses to which the examination can be put in meeting the districts' goals and the tests' limitations.

48.   In making a decision not to reemploy an in-service teacher or not to employ an applicant solely on the basis of the NTE, an administrator runs great risks of arbitrary and unreasonable results in the absence of information which relates academic qualities to teaching success in his district.

49.   The defendants did not take the steps necessary to guard against arbitrary results in using cutoff scores on the NTE as a means of selecting teachers for reemployment and employment.

51.   The likelihood of arbitrary results from use of the NTE with a cutoff score is enhanced because the NTE measures only a fraction of the characteristics required for effective classroom performance.

52.   The NTE examinations are not measures of classroom teaching performance. Dr. Deneen testified: "The test does not get at, does not examine, * * * many areas which school superintendents or a state may wish to know about prospective teacher candidates. It cannot, for example, supply what one can learn uniquely through a personal interview."   Among the qualities required of teachers which the NTE does not measure are: possession of manual skills, attitudes about children, personal and social characteristics, ability to communicate with students, ability to motivate students, ability to discipline students, ability to evaluate students, capability to maintain satisfactory relationships with parents of students, capability to maintain satisfactory relationships with fellow teachers and, most important, whether the teacher can function effectively in the classroom.

53.   In his paper on the subject, Dr. Knezevich observed:

"The examinations do not purport to measure such things as personal and social characteristics. Those responsible for the examinations are quick to point these things out and urge the National Teacher Examinations result be supplemented with the result of other evaluations of techniques before any final decision is made to the prospective teacher's qualifications.

"The National Teacher Examinations were constructed to provide objective measures of some of the intellectual, academic, and cultural factors basis [sic] for teacher success. Any school official or other person who is judging the teacher fitness of a candidate should not use the National Teacher Examinations result as a sole basis for selection. Due cognizance should be taken of such factors as personality, social characteristics, training, experience, and classroom effectiveness. These should be evaluated independently by local school officials through interviews, observations of classroom procedures, and careful consideration of records and credentials."

54. The NTE tests in some degree for only four of the 25 criteria used by defendants to evaluate in-service teachers—namely, knowledge of subject matter and methods of instruction; academic requirements of subject matter or grade level; skill in giving directions, questioning and testing; and use of teaching aids. . . .

55. With respect to new hires, it was unreasonable for defendants to exclude teacher applicants on the sole basis of a score on the NTE which had never been validated.

56. With respect to in-service teachers, it was even less justifiable for defendants to exclude teachers from reemployment on the sole basis of a score on the NTE because other, more probative means of evaluation were available. As Dr. Deneen testified:

> The best indication that a teacher can teach well is that he has taught well. . . .

58. ETS made a computer check of the NTE scores achieved by students reporting attendance at predominately white and black institutions of higher learning in Mississippi during the four most recent administrations of the examination prior to the hearing in this case— July and November 1969, and January and April 1970. The racial make-up of these institutions was determined from the Department of Health, Education and Welfare's publication reporting the enrollment by race in Mississippi institutions.

59. ETS's study of scores at Mississippi institutions show that about 90 per cent of the students graduating from predominately white institutions score 1000 or better on the NTE, while 89 percent of the students graduating from predominately black institutions fail to attain a score of 1000.

60. Roughly 75 per cent of the teachers hired by defendants are graduates of Mississippi institutions of higher education.

61. The NTE cutoff score requirement will continue to disqualify substantially more black applicants for teaching positions in defendants' system than white applicants for the next few years. . . .

Unequal Application of the NTE Requirement

67. The NTE cutoff requirement has been applied in a racially discriminatory manner. One first-year white teacher who failed to attain the cutoff score was reemployed for the 1970–71 school year. No black teacher who failed to attain the NTE cutoff score was reemployed for 1970–71.

68. Two black teachers—plaintiffs Prowell and Hubbard—were nonrenewed on the basis of the NTE requirement, although they were not within the class of teachers to which the requirement applied. . . .

69. Defendants, on the day before school opened, had hired 43 new white teachers and one new black teacher. At that time, there were 36 vacancies on defendants' staff.

70. Five black applicants had filed satisfactory NTE scores with their applications to the Columbus School District prior to July 14, 1970. The number had increased from five to nine by September 3, 1970. None of the applicants had been employed by defendants prior to the time when this Court entered its preliminary injunction on September 3, 1970.

Conclusion

71. The facts surrounding the adoption and application of the NTE requirement demonstrate that defendants acted for the purpose of barring proportionately more black teachers than white teachers from reemployment and hiring by the Columbus School district.

72. The effect of the NTE cutoff score requirement has been to bar proportionately more black teachers than white teachers from reemployment and hiring by the Columbus School District. . . .

CONCLUSIONS OF LAW . . .

3. It is unconstitutional for public officials to discriminate on the basis of race in the hiring and retention of teachers in the public schools. . . .

4. In cases where discrimination is in issue, "statistics often tell much, and Courts listen." . . .

5. In the case at bar there has been a long history of racial discrimination by defendants in the conduct of the Columbus Municipal Separate School District. . . .

6. The inference that defendants acted with a racially discriminatory purpose in setting the requirement for a 1000 score on the NTE is concretely reinforced in this case by other facts. First, defendants knew from the experience with the PEP program that a 1000 cutoff score would eliminate proportionately a much higher percentage of black than white teachers and applicants. Second, defendants applied the NTE score requirement in an uneven fashion. Two black teachers who were employed prior to the 1969–70 school year and therefore were not subject to the NTE requirement were refused reemployment because they allegedly failed to qualify with a score of 1000. One white teacher in his first year was retained even though he did not attain a score of 1000. Third, defendants hired 44 new teachers, only one of whom was black. On the day before school opened, defendants have not offered jobs to nine black applicants who had attained and submitted NTE scores of 1000 or more even though there were 36 vacancies in defendants' system.

7. The inference of racial discrimination arising from the circumstances of this case "thrust[s] upon the School Board the burden of justifying its conduct by clear and convincing evidence."   .   .   .

8. Defendants have not shown by "clear and convincing evidence" that their failure to rehire black first-year teachers and to hire black applicants was not racially discriminatory.   .   .   .

9. The Court concludes that defendants in formulating and applying the NTE cutoff score requirement have purposely discriminated against black teachers and black applicants on account of their race.
.   .   .

13. In the case at bar, defendants have not discharged their "very heavy burden of justification"   .   .   .   and the Court, therefore, concludes that the NTE cutoff score requirement is an unconstitutional racial classification.   .   .   .

18. In the case at bar, defendants have failed to show a "manifest relationship" between the cutoff score used and job performance.

19. Although plaintiffs do not have the burden of proving that there is no "manifest relationship," the proof demonstrates as much. The NTE does not predict classroom effectiveness and does not even test for the great majority of factors that defendants believe are important in good teaching. The relationship between the test and teaching effectiveness is even more attenuated because defendants have used a cutoff score of 1000. There is no convincing evidence in the record showing any relationship between 1000 on the NTE and effective classroom teaching, and results worked by the use of the cutoff score indicate that no relationship can be established. The Superintendent admitted that the NTE would bar some good teachers and all the plaintiffs at bar were recommended for reelection by their principals, who made their evaluations on the basis of classroom

performance.   One of these plaintiffs ranked first on the faculty at his school.   .   .   .

21.   It is unlawful for public officials to exclude a person from practicing his profession in a manner or for reasons that contravene the Due Process or Equal Protection Clauses of the Fourteenth Amendment.   In this connection, the Supreme Court has ruled that "any qualification must have a rational connection with the applicant's fitness or capacity" to perform his occupation or profession.   .   .   . The Court concludes that, apart from its discriminatory aspects, the NTE cutoff score requirement is an arbitrary and unreasonable qualification for reemployment and employment as a teacher in the Columbut system and therefore violates the Due Process Clause   .   .   .   .

NOTES AND QUESTIONS

1.   Does the court say that NTE scores could never be used for purposes of salary increases and teacher retention, or not used in the way they were in this case?   If they can be used constitutionally, describe how.

2.   See also, United States v. Texas Ed. Agency, 459 F.2d 600 (5th Cir. 1972), and Armstead v. Starkville Mun. Sch. Dist., 461 F.2d 276 (5th Cir. 1972).

AFFIRMATIVE ACTION PROGRAMS

PORCELLI v. TITUS

United States Court of Appeals, 3rd Cir., 1970.
431 F.2d 1254, cert. den. 402 U.S. 944, 91 S.Ct. 1612, 29 L.Ed.2d 112.

PER CURIAM.

The plaintiffs herein, Victor Porcelli et al., ten white teachers employed by the Newark Board of Education, brought suit under the Civil Rights Act alleging that as of May 28, 1968, the defendant, Superintendent of Schools in the City of Newark, Franklyn Titus, acting under color of law for the Newark School System, subjected the plaintiffs to deprivation of their rights, privileges or immunities secured to them by the Constitution of the United States of America. This allegedly was accomplished by the abolition of a promotional list which had been in existence since 1953, which provided for oral and written examinations for anyone wishing to aspire to be principals or vice-principals in the System and which, it was contended by so doing, racially discriminated against whites whose names appeared on the promotional list for appointment.   At the time of the abolition or suspension of the said promotional list, the first fifteen thereon had been appointed, but Porcelli, Bigley and Shapiro, plaintiffs herein, though eligible, had not yet been appointed.

The school population in the City of Newark in October, 1961, was 67,134, of which the Negro population was 55.1%.   In September,

1968, the total school population was 75,876, with a Negro student population of 72.5% reflecting an increase in seven years of 8,742 students and a percentage increase of Negro students of 17.4%. During the school year 1967–1968, there were 249 administrative and supervisory positions (superintendents, principals and vice-principals, senior and junior high school principals, etc.), of which 27, or 10%, were held by Negroes. On August 22, 1968, only one Negro each for principal and vice-principal was eligible on the promotional list and of the 72 principals in the system none were Negro and of 67 vice-principals, 64 were white and 3 Negro. . . .

Under date of May 28, 1968, defendant Board of Education passed a resolution suspending and abolishing the making of appointments from this list and instead the defendant, Franklyn Titus, Superintendent of the School System in Newark, presented certain recommendations for the appointments of principals, vice-principals, senior and junior high school principals, which the Board adopted, representing a total of 35 white appointments and 20 Negro appointments. The appointments were designated as temporary appointments and the Board was to later review the appointments recommended, the criteria to be used by the Board having not as yet been finalized. In his recommendation to the Board the Superintendent candidly admitted that color was one of the criteria which he utilized, contending that the pattern by which principals, vice-principals and others were appointed reflected an era in 1953, when the promotional list was adopted, and as of 1968, conditions had so changed in the Newark School System that the promotional list had become outmoded by virtue of the changing population, community-wise and in the school system, which had occurred since its adoption.

This action was begun by a motion for summary judgment on the pleading, but the lower court denied it and ordered a full evidentiary hearing at which both sides were heard at great length. Superintendent Titus, one of the defendants, stated as one of his reasons for the abolition of the promotional list the fact that the Newark Public School System, especially in reading, was well below the national norm which obtained throughout the country; that there was such a great imbalance in the principal and vice-principal positions that, in his professional judgment, he felt that by adding a Negro who was qualified to these important positions, thus making the faculty more integrated, would the more readily lend itself to an upgrading of the Public School System in Newark. Although, as has been indicated, color was frankly admitted by all the witnesses for the appellees as being one of the factors in the selection of the principals and vice-principals, and one Simeon Moss, who was the assistant superintendent for elementary education who made the recommendations to the Superintendent for the appointments, stated that color was a prime factor, it was not the only factor, as the procuring of qualified individuals was the real objective. Plaintiffs' position was that this use of color in the selection of principals and vice-principals and the device used to achieve that selection by abolition or suspension of the promotional list was a violation of their Constitutional rights under the Fourteenth Amendment.

With this contention we do not agree. State action based partly on considerations of color, when color is not used per se, and in furtherance of a proper governmental objective, is not necessarily a violation of the Fourteenth Amendment. Proper integration of faculties is as important as proper integration of schools themselves.   .   .   . In Kemp v. Beasley, 389 F.2d 178, at 189 (8 Cir. 1968), the court held, where race was a consideration in the selection of teachers and faculties, "We reaffirm the principle that faculty selection must remain for the board and sensitive expertise of the School Board and its officials."   .   .   .   "The question thus becomes, when is there such faculty distribution as to provide equal opportunities to all students and to all teachers—whether white or Negro? Students in each school should have the same quality of instruction as in any other school. Every predominantly Negro school should have, wherever possible, substantially as integrated a faculty as the predominantly white school."

.   .   .

It would therefore seem that the Boards of Education have a very definite affirmative duty to integrate school faculties and to permit a great imbalance in faculties—as obtained on August 22, 1968, when a new plan was proposed to the School Board in Newark for the increasing of qualified Negro administrators—would be in negation of the Fourteenth Amendment to the Constitution and the line of cases which have followed Brown v. Board of Education, supra.

.   .   .

The judgment of the lower court will be affirmed.

NOTES AND QUESTIONS

1. Was this case one of de jure or de facto segregation? Did the board of education come within the affirmative duty imposed by Brown I and II and Green supra? Did Newark ever operate a dual school system?

2. Is the Porcelli case an example of an affirmative action program by a board of education; a program having been designed to relieve racial imbalances which the board did not create?

3. In Anderson v. San Francisco Unified School District, 357 F.Supp. 248 (N.D.Cal.1972), the court held unconstitutional a school district's plan to give preference in employment and promotions to members of ethnic minorities in administrative and supervisory positions—a plan designed to increase the numerical representation of ethnic minorities in the administration of the schools.

    Problem: A school district's special operative budget levy fails, requiring a 25% reduction in teaching staff within the district. The school board's established policy for not renewing teaching contracts in such an eventuality has been to decline to renew all the contracts of that 25% of the teaching staff most recently hired. However, the board of education observes that if such a practice is adopted now virtually all the present minority teachers will not be renewed because they were the most recently hired in the school because of the district's recent affirmative action program and so, under the old scheme, they would be the first to go. In the past minorities had been under represented on the teaching faculty; there has been no past practice of racial discrimination in hiring.   Now, wanting to maintain its newly increased minority representation on its staff, the school board has decided to divide the teaching staff into two classes, non-minority and minority, and not to renew 25% of those persons in each class who have the least seniority. Winefred White has four years seniority, and Betty Black has three years of seniority. But, because more than 25% of the minority staff has less than three years seniority, Betty Black's teaching contract is renewed. However, Winefred White's contract is not renewed because the 25% of non-minority staff most recently hired include all those with four years seniority or less. White brings an action against the school district in federal district court under the Civil Rights Act (42 U.S.C. §§ 1983 and 1985(3)), asking that her contract be renewed, claiming that she has been denied the due process and equal protection of the laws solely on the basis of her or another's race. You are the federal district court judge. What decision do you render and for what reasons? Cf. DeFunis v. Odegaard, 82 Wash.2d 11, 507 P.2d 1169 (1973), and Morris, "Equal Protection, Affirmative Action And Racial Preferences In Law Admissions: DeFunis v. Odegaard," 49 Wash.L.Rev. 1 (1973).

Chapter X

CONSTITUTIONAL FREEDOM AND EQUAL EDUCATIONAL OPPORTUNITY

INTRODUCTION

A state is not obligated by the Constitution of the United States to provide any educational opportunity for its children. However, if a state does provide any type of educational opportunity for its children, then the equal protection clause of the Fourteenth Amendment requires that the state provide that educational opportunity "equally" to all its children. This requirement provided the foundation for decision in the desegregation cases. Brown I declared that a state-operated dual school system that is based on race deprived the minority children of equal educational opportunity because "separate educational facilities are inherently unequal." They stigmatize minority children, branding them as inferior, and this "impact is greater when it has the sanction of the law." Thus, we know that racially separated education, by law, is constitutionally unequal education. But a problem arises when we try to go beyond race. What other types of educational opportunity might or might not qualify as being "equal" or "unequal"? That is the primary question posed by this chapter.

A second concept of equal educational opportunity, not involving race, derives from the principles of classical liberalism. According to this concept equal educational opportunity exists when each child has equal access to an equal amount of public school resources; i. e., when each child has equal educational facilities, an equal amount of school financing and equal services. The focus is on the schools and on an equality of inputs per student. In this sense, the input per student of the schools themselves is to be measured, and those inputs are to be made fully equal. But schools are not to be equalizers. The students are to be afforded equal access to equal amounts of public resources devoted to education, ignoring the unequal backgrounds and abilities that students may bring to the schools, unless they are gross.

A third concept of equal educational opportunity focuses primarily on the output of the schools, and schools are to be equalizers. According to this view, equal educational opportunity exists when each child is schooled in relation to his individual background and ability up to a minimum and when the consequences of schooling compensate for prior inequalities among students. Under this concept consequences are critical, and it would not be a violation of equal educational opportunity for one student to receive more school resources, finances and services than another student. A violation would occur when the constitutionally required minimum outcomes of schooling are unequal, and all school resources would be devoted to producing this minimum in all students. A variant of this concept does not require that all school resources be devoted exclusively to producing a constitutionally required minimum of education in each student. It does include the minimum outcome requirement, but also it allows for some school resources to be used for more than the minimum educational development of students of high ability who show promise. Under the variant concept, each student first is to be educated at least up to the constitutionally required minimum outcome, and, secondly, each student capable of it is to be educated beyond that minimum level in accordance with his innate capacities for educational growth and development. Thus, under the variant concept, the equality of consequence that is to be achieved beyond the minimum required of all, is the equally full educational development of the uniquely unequal talents that are innately found in each student whether he be rich or poor. Should the constitutionally required minimum, be defined as that education necessary for "good citizenship"? If so, what public justifications are there (1) for using the public's tax funds to educate some, but not all, students beyond that minimum, and (2) for requiring compulsory school attendance of students after they have attained the minimum level?

Three basic categories of equal educational opportunity can be identified which will include the alternative and competing concepts of equal educational opportunity: (1) equal treatment of races, (2) equal access to an equal amount of public school resources (input equality), and (3) equal outcomes from the effectiveness of school resources and processes (output equality). All present severe problems of accurate measurement. The latter two are the primary focus of this chapter. For discussion see, Yudoff, Equal Educational Opportunity and the Courts, 51 Texas L.Rev. 411 (1973), and Rand Corp., Report: How Effective Is Schooling? (1971), prepared for the President's Commission On School Finance, Dec. 1971.

THE PROBLEM

What is within a state's power to equalize? Does J. S. Coleman provide a beginning answer in his Foreword to J. Coons, W. H. Clune III and S. Sugarman, Private Wealth and Public Education (1970): "There is, of course, a broader sense of the term 'equality of educational opportunity' [than financial equality] which should be kept in mind: equality of *all* the effective resource inputs into education, not merely the financial ones. This equality can only be measured by equal effects for children of equal ability; but it clearly consists of a variety of input resources, not merely financial ones. The question about the state's provision of equal education opportunity becomes a difficult one: over which of these resources does the state have control, or should the state have control? Which of the resources can the state, through legal means, demand be redistributed equally? Certainly not the attentive help that some parents give their children in learning to read, nor the discipline some parents exert in enforcing the homework assignments of the school, nor the reinforcements by parents of the performance rewards given by the school. But the state has attempted to control the distribution of one educational resource, that is money—though, . . . this distribution is currently far from equal—and recently it has, in what might be seen as a radical venture into resource redistribution, attempted to control the distribution of educational resources embodied in classmates. The means, of course, has been racial and social class integration. In this second area of resources, it has been even more ineffective than in its attempt to redistribute financial resources. This [is a] second kind of educational resource, in the form of other children in a school. . . . Yet the attempt of the state to effect a redistribution focuses attention on the fact that financial resources are not the only ones. More fundamentally, it raises the question of just how far the state can go, and how far it should go, in redistributing educational resources to provide equal protection to the young in the form of equal educational opportunity. It is not a question that is easily answered. . . . ."

For an analysis concluding that the education actually received by students in American schools has failed to equalize Americans and to make us more equal in terms of income, social status and political power, see, Jencks et al., Inequality (1972). Granting this conclusion, does it follow that equal educational opportunity in the sense of equal school inputs per child also would probably fail to equalize socio-economic classes in this country? If so, is this an acceptable argument against providing equal schools to all children? Or is this an acceptable justification for constitutionally requiring an output measure of equal educational opportunity?

TOWARD EQUAL EDUCATIONAL OPPORTUNITY

United States Senate Select Comm. On Equal Educational Opportunity,
Report, 92nd Cong., 2nd Sess. Dec. 31, 1972.
Excerpts from pp. 9–13.

. . . About one-fifth, or 9.3 million of our Nation's 46.3 million students in public preschools and elementary and secondary schools, are members of minority groups. At the same time another 20 percent are from families with incomes under $5,000 a year, and about 4 million are from families with annual incomes less than $3,000 per year. Also, 12.2 million students are in families where the head of the household has no more than 8 years of school, and 10.5 million are children with unemployed or underemployed parents. These and other statistics—the 8.7 million children who arrive at school each day without a nutritious breakfast, the fact that at least 5 million children live in substandard housing units, and the high incidence of inadequate health care for perhaps as many as 21 million children of all ages—indicate the magnitude of disadvantaged among our Nation's school- and preschool-age population. We estimate that at least 12 million and perhaps as many as 20 million of the Nation's school-age population of 59 million, between 3 and 17, are from either economically or educationally disadvantaged homes.

For most of these children formal education is a yearly repetition of accelerating failure. Our public education system has failed and continues to fail successive generations of children from disadvantaged and minority group backgrounds—millions of children who leave school years behind in achievement and without the skills, knowledge or motivation they need to succeed in life. The result is that our public schools not only perpetuate but often exacerbate rather than help overcome the economic, social and racial inequalities in our society.

The typical child who is black, Mexican American, Puerto Rican, American Indian, a member of another racial- or language-minority group, or poor white and living in a rural community, is likely to achieve in school at two-thirds the rate of the average child. On entering the third grade he is often already a year behind. By the 12th grade he is likely to be 4½ years behind.

But the real story of educational failure was related to the committee in the testimony of witnesses, many of them professional educators, from communities across the country. It is a tale of devastating personal tragedy of enormous consequences to individual children. Here is a sampling of some of the things we heard about the performance of disadvantaged children.

- In the ghetto schools of Hartford, Conn., the average IQ scores of black elementary schoolchildren show a steady decline between the 4th and the 8th grade from 94 to 86. This 8th grade score is only 6 points above the IQ level at which the laws of Connecticut permit institutionalization in special schools for the mentally retarded.

- Similarly, at the preschool level, in the Edgewood school district of San Antonio, Tex., Chicano children at the age of 3 score an average of 104 in IQ tests. At age 4 their average is 90. By the time they are 5, and ready to enter the first grade, it is 70.

- In the typical Philadelphia inner city elementary school, 65 percent of the students score in the 16th percentile in the Iowa Test of Basic Skills—so low they are simply not functioning as students.

- Of the Mexican-American students in Texas, 56.8 percent leave school before completing the 8th grade; 78.9 percent drop out before high school graduation. One expert estimated 20 percent of migrant children never attend school at all.

- There are 7,800 Puerto Rican students in the public schools of Newark, N. J. Only 96 are in the 12th grade: in Boston between 1965 and 1969, only 4 out of 7,000 Puerto Rican schoolchildren graduated from high school; and in Chicago, the Puerto Rican dropout rate before high school graduation is 60 percent.

- Two-thirds of all American Indian adults have never gone beyond elementary school; 10 percent of those over 14 never went to school at all; and probably as many as half the American Indian children enrolled in school today will not finish high school.

These are but a few examples of the tragic educational failure of minority group and disadvantaged children.

THE ELEMENTS OF INEQUALITY IN EDUCATION

Today and throughout our history, where a person is born, his race, his native language, his cultural background and his parents' income and occupation are the principal factors that determine where he lives and the quality of his education. The child from a disadvantaged home usually enters school already behind in his ability to communicate and relate to the new world around him. He goes to school with others from similar backgrounds and often to a school with inadequate facilities. He is often taught by less-qualified teachers who are insensitive to his culture and background, and who label him as different, slow in learning and likely to fail. He is often tested and tracked in a class for slow learners. He is more likely than the child from an advantaged home to drop out before graduation. If he does graduate he is usually years behind in achievement; he seldom continues his education and is likely to return to all the handicaps of the environment into which he was born. This is the unequal life of the disadvantaged schoolchild.

There are three principal, interrelated ways in which the process of education in this Nation is unequal.

First, children from minority and economically disadvantaged families live their lives isolated from the rest of society. The fact is that education in this country is still—for the most part—segregated by race, economic and social class. By any reasonable measure, except in the 11 Southern States, we have hardly begun the task of eliminating the segregation of minority group and disadvantaged students in our Nation. Nationally, 5.9 million out of 9.3 million minority-group students, or more than 60 percent, still attend predominantly minority-group schools. At the same time 72 percent of the Nation's nonminority-group students attend schools which are at least 90 percent nonminority. Four million minority-group students attend schools which are 80 percent or more minority, and 2 million are in classes which are 99–100 percent minority. . . .

Minority-group children are more isolated in large school districts than in small ones. About one-half of the Nation's black students are in our 100 largest school districts. These school districts, which include all the Nation's large cities, are the most segregated in the Nation. Nearly 75 percent of the black students in these districts were in 80–100 percent minority schools, and 60 percent were in 95–100 percent minority schools in the Fall of 1971.

Second, minority and disadvantaged children are often treated in unequal ways by schools themselves.

Their performance, their aspirations and motivations are often adversely affected by the attitudes and expectations of their teachers—who often label them as inferior, and destined to fail. The disadvantaged child is often tracked in a class or other group of "slow learners" or "underachievers." In short, these children are subjected to a labeling process according to their background rather than their ability or potential—a process which deeply affects a child's attitudes about himself, his family, his culture and virtually assures school failure and a life of unequal opportunity after school.

One of our witnesses described these unequal practices as they affect Spanish-speaking children:

> The injuries of the Latin American child have been inflicted by those who have claimed to teach and motivate him, and who have, in reality, alienated him, and destroyed his identity through the subtle rejection of his language [which nobody speaks], his culture [which nobody understands], and ultimately him [whom nobody values].

Third, the financial resources for public elementary and secondary education are both raised and distributed inequitably so that the quality of a child's education is largely dependent upon the taxable wealth of each school district and its citizens. As a result, most children from low-income families and those who live in communities with low tax bases or high public service costs attend schools with fewer and lower quality educational services.

The disparities in school expenditures across the Nation can only be described as spectacular. They exist among States, among school districts within States and among schools within school districts. Among the 50 States the range of per-pupil expenditures is from

$1,429 in Alaska to $489 in Alabama. Within almost every State the highest spending school district spends at least twice as much as the lowest spending school district and variations of 3-, 4-, and 5-to-1 are not uncommon.

In short, poor children usually attend poor schools. They are the victims of the fact that most of the resources for education in this Nation are allocated in a manner which assures that the best education that money can buy is available to children in wealthy communities, and the lowest quality education goes to those in the poorest communities.

These three factors—segregation of minority-group and disadvantaged children in fact, if not in law; the unequal practices and treatment to which they are subjected, and the inequality in educational resources—combine to produce inequality in American public elementary and secondary education. Together they produce educational failure in the form of low aspirations and motivations, high dropout rates, and low achievement.

THE PRIMARY CAUSES OF EDUCATIONAL INEQUALITY

What these elements of educational inequality—segregation, economic discrimination, malnutrition and the unequal treatment of, and unequal resources for, minority-group and poor children—add up to is a system which is failing millions of children. The reasons for that failure are complex. But they add up to a central finding of our work:

It is not that children fail. It is our Nation that has failed them.

They are the victims—the victims of racial discrimination and class prejudice, poor schools, unfit housing, inadequate health care, malnutrition, unemployment and poverty. They are the victims of virtually every institution in our society—of which our public education system is among the most important—institutions that are insensitive and unresponsive to the needs of racial minorities and disadvantaged groups. The fact is that many of the school systems in this Nation that are confronted with children from families whose racial or cultural heritage or spoken language are different from those of most white middle-class American children are somehow institutionally unable to respond to their needs.   .   .   .

RECOMMENDATIONS

We believe that any system designed to make schools more responsive must have four key elements:

First, parents and students should become directly involved in school affairs.

Second, the fullest possible, accurate information must be publicly available on school performance and other essential aspects of school life.

Third, school principals should be relieved of many of their present administrative burdens so they can be more active participants in the educational process and made more responsible for the outcomes of their schools.

Fourth, all teachers must become sensitive to diversity and to the backgrounds of different children and be free to innovate, experiment and develop new instructional techniques.

THE OTHER MINORITY

A Preliminary Report on USOE's Effort To Help Our Most Promising Children
by
Dr. Harold C. Lyon, Jr.
Director of Education For The Gifted and Talented
U.S. Office of Education

.   .   .   there is another minority that has as much right to special attention—a minority denoted not by race, socio-economic background, ethnic origin or impaired faculties, but by their exceptionability.   They come from all levels of society, from all races and national origins, and are equally distributed among the sexes.

These children have an unusual endowment of talent. It may be intellectual. It may be aesthetic. It may be creative in an artistic or scientific or social way, or even in ways which neither the schools nor society yet understand. But whatever their talent, from their ranks will come the small percentage of humans who are truly great —not just capable performers in the sciences, the arts, and the professions, but those extraordinary few who will leave their disciplines, their societies, and perhaps even the human kind different because of their work. These are the future Beethovens; the Newtons, the Jeffersons, the Picassos, the Baldwins, the Ernesto Galarzas and the Martin Luther Kings.

These are gifted children—and, like the other minorities, they need help. Though the great men mentioned above had their painful struggles, history was generous to them, and it may be difficult to grasp why children with the potential to achieve a similar eminence should require special attention from our educational system. The explanation is that for every Einstein or Martin Luther King who emerges, it is likely that a dozen or more do not. Though it is impossible to offer scientific proof of this hypothesis—biographers, after all, do not study average men and women—the evidence that we have from the lives of great men and women as well as studies of school-age children back up this conclusion from a 1968 investigation of the gifted.

"We would even go so far as to say that, to a very considerable extent, those individuals who constitute the 'creative minority' in our society (or in *any* society) .   .   .

have achieved their eminence *in spite of,* rather than because of, our school system."

Thomas Edison's mother withdrew him from school after three months of the first grade because, his teacher said, he was "unable." Gregor Mendel, founder of the science of genetics, flunked his teacher's examination four times and gave up trying. Newton, considered a poor student in grammar school, left at 14, was sent back at 19 because he read so much, and graduated from Cambridge without any distinction whatever. Winston Churchill was last in his class at Harrow. Charles Darwin dropped out of medical school. Shelley was expelled from Oxford, James Whistler and Edgar Allen Poe from West Point. Gibbon considered his education a waste of time, and Einstein found grammar school boring; it was his uncle, showing the boy tricks with numbers, who stimulated his interest in mathematics.

For every genius who did poorly in school, one can cite another who did well. Yet this random sampling of academic misfits indicates that traditional academic programs are sometimes poorly suited to humans of extraordinary potential. One is left to wonder how many Churchills, how many Whistlers did not survive educational disaster —how many hatchlings (pronounced ugly ducklings) had the good luck and the persistence to continue seeking other ponds until they were recognized as swans.

Why should children with unusual ability experience trouble with ordinary school curricula?

Precisely because they are ordinary. Education is a mass enterprise, geared by economic necessity as well as politics to the abilities of the majority—and the majority are, by definition, average, but just as a child of less-than-average mental ability frequently has trouble keeping up with his classmates, so a child of above average ability has trouble staying *behind* with them. Mastering in a few days material that other children require weeks to understand, he or she becomes bored, restless, anxious to move on. Prevented from moving ahead by the rigidity of normal school procedures—assigned to a class with others of the same age, expected to devote the same attention to the *same* textbooks, required to be present for the same number of hours in the same seat—the gifted youngster typically takes one of two tacks: he or she conceals his or her ability, anxious not to embarrass others or draw their ridicule by superior performance; or, not understanding his or her frustration, becomes a discipline problem. Typical of the latter case was a troublesome seventh-grader whose baffled teacher reported that, while the girl claimed she could not understand simple fractions, she "delighted in working compound trigonometry fractions"; the same week that she failed a math test, this girl was caught in study hall "writing her own math textbook."

Uniformity of curriculum is not the only difficulty under which gifted children must work. Others include:

—*Failure to be identified:* The president of one State association for the handicapped reported that his staff members find "extremely gifted children among their target group *very* frequently," and another State found that 3.4 percent of its school dropouts had IQ's of 120 or higher. Of schools surveyed by the U.S. Office of Education during the 1969–70 school year, 57.5 percent reported that they had no gifted pupils .   .   . an indication that teachers and other staff simply did not know how to identify them.

—*Hostility of school staff:* For quite human reasons, including an impatience with the "unusual" child and an assumption that the gifted are a favored elite who deserve even less than normal consideration, some educational personnel actually resent them. One study, surprisingly, found "significantly greater hostility toward the gifted among school psychologists" than among school personnel.

—*Lack of attention to the gifted:* In only 10 State departments of education is there a professional assigned full-time responsibility for education of the gifted and talented; it is estimated that fewer than four percent of the Nation's gifted and talented students have access to special programs. Of these, the great majority are in the 10 States with a full-time professional responsible for programs in this area.

—*Lack of trained teachers:* Only 12 American Universities offer graduate programs to train teachers in educating the gifted and talented.

Most Americans by now accept the reality of racial, linguistic, socioeconomic, and physical handicaps, and back special educational efforts to help children overcome these obstacles to their self-realization. It is time for us to recognize that unusual ability can also prove a barrier to achievement, and that it is peculiarly in our national interest to assure the development of children who have potential to make extraordinary contributions to our common life.

CONSTITUTIONAL FREEDOM AND ABILITY GROUPING

HOBSON v. HANSEN

United States District Court, 1967.
269 F.Supp. 401, cert. dism. 393 U.S. 801, 89 S.Ct. 40, 21 L.Ed.2d 85.

[The opinion in this case is 119 pages; only excerpted portions dealing with ability grouping are reprinted here. The entire opinion merits careful study and is recommended.)

J. SKELLY WRIGHT, Circuit Judge. . . .

IV. THE TRACK SYSTEM

The District of Columbia school system employs a form of ability grouping commonly known as the track system, by which students at the elementary and secondary level are placed in tracks or curriculum levels according to the school's assessment of each student's ability to learn. Plaintiffs have alleged that the track system—either by intent or by effect—unconstitutionally discriminates against the Negro and the poor. . .   . . . As the evidence in this case makes painfully clear, ability grouping as presently practiced in the District of Columbia school system is a denial of equal educational opportunity to the poor and a majority of the Negroes attending school in the nation's capital, a denial that contravenes not only the guarantees of the Fifth Amendment but also the fundamental premise of the track system itself. What follows, then, is a discussion of that evidence—an examination of the track system: in theory and in reality.

B. *Track Theory.*

Basic to an understanding of the conflict between the parties in this lawsuit is an appreciation of the theory that motivates the track system as it operates in the District school system. The most comprehensive statement of that theory can be found in Dr. Hansen's book, FOUR TRACK CURRICULUM FOR TODAY'S HIGH SCHOOLS, published in 1964. Although Dr. Hansen disclaims full responsibility for creating the track system, a reading of his book leaves no doubt that it was his firm guiding hand that shaped that system in its essential characteristics. Thus, as principal architect of the track system and as Superintendent of Schools, Dr. Hansen presumably can be looked to as the authoritative spokesman on the subject.

Purpose and philosophy. Dr. Hansen believes that the comprehensive high school (and the school system generally) must be systematically organized and structured to provide differing levels of education for students with widely differing levels of academic ability.

This is the purpose of the track system. In expressing the track system's philosophy Dr. Hansen has said, "Every pupil in the school system must have the maximum opportunity for self-development and this can best be brought about by adjusting curriculum offerings to different levels of need and ability as the pupil moves through the stages of education and growth in our schools." . . . And he has identified as the two objectives on which the track system is founded: "(1) The realization of the doctrine of equality of education and (2) The attainment of quality education."

Student types. Within the student body Dr. Hansen sees generally four types of students: the intellectually gifted, the above-average, the average, and the retarded. He assumes that each of these types of students has a maximum level of academic capability and, most importantly, that that level of ability can be accurately ascertained. The duty of the school is to identify these students and provide a curriculum commensurate with their respective abilities. Dr. Hansen contends that the traditional school curriculum—including the usual two-level method of ability grouping—does a disservice to those at either end of the ability spectrum.

The gifted student is not challenged, so that he becomes bored, lazy, and perhaps performs far below his academic potential; his intellectual talents are a wasted resource. The remedy lies in discovering the gifted student, placing him with others of his own kind, thereby stimulating him through this select association as well as a rigorous, demanding curriculum to develop his intellectual talent. Indeed, "the academically capable student should be required as a public necessity to take the academically challenging honors curriculum."

On the other hand, continues Dr. Hansen, the retarded or "stupid" student typically has been forced to struggle through a curriculum he cannot possibly master and only imperfectly comprehends. Typically he is slow to learn and soon falls behind in class; he repeatedly fails, sometimes repeating a grade again and again; he becomes isolated, frustrated, depressed, and—if he does not drop out before graduation —graduates with a virtually useless education. Here the remedy is seen as separating out the retarded student, directing him into a special curriculum geared to his limited abilities and designed to give him a useful "basic" education—one which makes no pretense of equalling traditionally taught curricula.

In short, Hansen views the traditional school curriculum as doing too little for some students and expecting too much of others. As for the latter type, whom Dr. Hansen characterizes as "the blue-collar student," going to school—a "white-collar occupation"—can be an artificial experience. . . .

Tracking. In order to tailor the educational process to the level appropriate to each student. Dr. Hansen adopted the track system. Each track is intended to be a separate and self-contained curriculum, with the educational content ranging from the very basic to the very advanced according to the track level. In the elementary and junior high schools three levels are used: Basic or Special Academic (retarded students), General (average and above-average), and Honors (gifted). In the senior high school a fourth level is added: The Regular Track, a college-preparatory track intended to accommodate the above-average student.

The significant feature of the track system in this regard is its emphasis on the ability of the student. A student's course of instruction depends upon what the school system decides he is capable of handling. "It took a while for everybody on the [working] committee to understand that *ability was to be the primary key to the placement in a curriculum sequence, and that this factor, not the subject-matter emphasis, was one of the unique characteristics of the four-track system.*"

Flexibility. Dr. Hansen, while assuming that some students can be educated to their maximum potential in one of the four curricula, also anticipates that not all students will neatly or permanently fit into a track. Thus a second important assumption underlying the track system is that tracking will be a flexible process. Flexibility encompasses two things: First, although a student today may demonstrate an ability level which calls, for example, for placement in the General Track, a constant and continuing effort must be made to assure that he is at his true ability level. This calls for instruction directed toward correcting any remedial educational problems which account for the student's present poor performance; and it calls for close analysis and counselling to determine whether these remediable deficiencies exist and when they have been sufficiently corrected. When the latter is determined, the student is to be upgraded to the next higher track. Second, even though a student may not be in a position to make an across-the-board move from one track to another, his ability level may be such that he needs to take courses in two track levels on a subject-by-subject basis. This process, known as cross-tracking, is critical: it is the mechanism the system relies upon to assure that students whose ability levels vary according to particular subjects are not thwarted in developing their strong areas because their weak areas result in their being placed in a lower curriculum level. It also serves as a way of selectively raising the intensity of instruction on a subject-matter basis as a part of the process of gradually upgrading a student.

Fundamental assumptions. To summarize, the track system's approach is twofold. The separate curriculum levels are for some the maximum education their abilities permit them to achieve. For others, a track is supposed to be a temporary assignment during which a student's special problems are identified and remedied in whatever way possible. The express assumptions of this approach are three: *First*, a child's maximum educational potential can and will be accurately ascertained. *Second*, tracking will enhance the prospects for correcting a child's remediable educational deficiencies. *Third*, tracking must be flexible so as to provide an individually tailored education for students who cannot be pigeon-holed in a single curriculum. . . .

Having seen how the track system in practice has become a relatively rigid form of class separation, the court now turns to a discussion of the principal causes of this result. . . . Here the focus will be on the major institutional shortcomings that not only thrust the disadvantaged student into the lower tracks but tend to keep him there once placed. The first area of concern is the lack of kindergartens and Honors programs in certain schools; the second relates to remedial and compensatory programs for the disadvantaged and educationally handicapped student; and the third, and most important, involves the whole of the placement and testing process by which the school system decides who gets what kind of education. . . .

   3. *Placement and testing.*

What emerges as the most important single aspect of the track system is the process by which the school system goes about sorting students into the different tracks. This importance stems from the fact that the fundamental premise of the sorting process is the keystone of the whole track system: that school personnel can with reasonable accuracy ascertain the maximum potential of each student and fix the content and pace of his education accordingly. If this premise proves false, the theory of the track system collapses, and with it any justification for consigning the disadvantaged student to a second-best education. . . .

The court now turns to the crucial issue posed by plaintiffs' attack on defendants' use of tests: whether it is possible to ascertain with at least reasonable accuracy the maximum educational potential of certain kinds of schoolchildren. This question goes to the very foundation of the track system since . . . one of the fundamental premises of track theory is that students' potential can be determined. On this premise rests the practice of separating students into homogeneous ability groups; and most importantly, on this premise rests the sole justification for a student's being *permanently* assigned to lower track classes where the instructional pace and content have been scaled down to serve students of supposedly limited abilities. That is, according to track theory, those who remain in a lower curriculum remain *because they are achieving at their maximum level of ability*. They are not admitted to—or are at least discouraged from seeking admission to—a higher instructional level because the school system has determined that they cannot "usefully" and "successfully" rise above their present level. The evidence that defendants are in no position to make such judgments about the learning capacity of a majority of District schoolchildren is persuasive. Because of the importance of testing to the process of evaluating and programming students, the evidence has focused primarily on tests. However, necessarily bound up in the question of testing is the larger problem of the whole evaluation process—how the school goes about deciding who gets what kind of education. Plaintiffs' attack strikes at the heart of this process. . . .

Test structure.

(a) *The nature of scholastic aptitude tests.*

There are essentially two types of tests used in educational evaluation, achievement tests and scholastic aptitude tests. An *achievement* test is designed primarily to measure a student's level of attainment in a given subject, such as history, science, literature, and so on. The test presumes the student has been instructed in the subject matter; it seeks to find out how well he has learned that subject. Although achievement test scores play an important role in placement decisions, their use has not been seriously questioned by plaintiffs except to the extent the test scores tend to reinforce already erroneous decisions. Consequently, the discussion here will center on aptitude tests.

A *scholastic aptitude* test is specifically designed to predict how a student will achieve in the future in an academic curriculum. It does this by testing certain skills which have come to be identified as having a high correlation with scholastic achievement. Once a student's present proficiency in these skills is ascertained, an inference is drawn as to how well he can be expected to do in the future.

The skills measured by scholastic aptitude tests are verbal. More precisely an aptitude test is essentially a test of the student's command of standard English and grammar. The emphasis on these skills is due to the nature of the academic curriculum, which is highly verbal; without such skills a student cannot be successful. Therefore, by measuring the student's present verbal ability the test makes it possible to estimate the student's likelihood of success in the future.

Some aptitude tests may include questions that are nonverbal in content so as to circumvent possible verbal handicaps. Technically, nonverbal tests are nonlanguage tests of reasoning processes thought to be indicative of ability to handle academic tasks successfully. . . . The usual type of question consists of geometric symbols or drawings, the student being required to perceive and analyze relationships among a group of symbols. The process is variously termed "abstract reasoning," "spatial perception," or the like. As with verbal tests, prediction is based on how well a student is able to answer nonverbal questions. . . .

Whether a test is verbal or nonverbal, the skills being measured are *not* innate or inherited traits. They are learned, acquired through experience. It used to be the prevailing theory that aptitude tests—or "intelligence" tests as they are often called, although the term is obviously misleading—do measure some stable, predetermined intellectual process that can be isolated and called intelligence. Today, modern experts in educational testing and psychology have rejected this concept as false. Indeed, the best that can be said about intelligence insofar as testing is concerned is that it is whatever the test measures. . . . In plain words, this means that aptitude tests can only test a student's present level of learning in certain skills and from that infer his capability to learn further.

Of utmost importance is the fact that, to demonstrate the ability to learn, a student must have had the opportunity to learn those skills relied upon for prediction. In other words, an aptitude test is necessarily measuring a student's background, his environment. It is a test of his cumulative experiences in his home, his community and his school. Each of these social institutions has a separate influence on his development; one may compensate for the failings of the others, or all may act in concert and reinforce each other—for good or for ill.

(b) *Causes of low test scores.*

A low aptitude test score may mean that a student is innately limited in intellectual ability. On the other hand, there may be other explanations possible that have nothing to do with native intelligence. Some of those reasons are pertinent here.

. . . one of the important factors that could account for a low test score is the student's *environment*. If a student has had little or no opportunity to acquire and develop the requisite verbal or nonverbal skills, he obviously cannot score well on the tests.

Another source of variation is the student's *emotional or psychological condition* when he takes the test. He may have a poor attitude toward the test or the testing situation, generally characterized as apathy. This may be due to lack of motivation; or it may be a defensive reaction caused by worry or fear—what has been called "test anxiety". Anxiety can also cause extremely nervous reactions. All of these behavior patterns will cause the student to perform poorly on a test, either because he panics and forgets what he knows or rushes through the test skipping questions, guessing at answers, or otherwise acting carelessly.

Some tests are constructed to take account of some behavior variations. In general, however, every test score must be interpreted by those who intend to rely on them for making decisions about the individual student. Test publishers warn that scores must be evaluated in terms of the individual so as to discover, if possible, any nonintellectual variables that could have influenced the student's test score. . . .

Testing the Disadvantaged Child.

Having touched generally upon the technical aspects of scholastic aptitude testing, it is now possible to give attention to plaintiffs' specific arguments.   At base they are focusing on an area of educational testing that has been given close attention only in recent years: the testing of the disadvantaged child.   The issue plaintiffs have raised is whether standard aptitude tests are appropriate for making inferences about the innate intellectual capabilities of these children.

Although the term "disadvantaged" is by nature imprecise, a working definition adopted for purposes of discussing educational problems is commonly based on two factors: the child's socio-economic status, as measured by the family's annual income; and his cultural status, as measured by the number of years of schooling attained by his parents.   Both of these factors have been identified as having a high correlation with achievement both in school and in society generally, since they tend to reflect the kinds of background more or less conducive to developing scholastic-type skills.   There are also indications that racial factors may well have some separate bearing on whether a child can be considered disadvantaged.   .   .   .

(a) *Handicaps to learning.*

Disadvantaged children typically are saddled with tremendous handicaps when it comes to competing in the ethnocentric academic society of public schools.   That society, mirroring American society generally, is strongly influenced by white and middle class experiences and values.   While there is nothing necessarily wrong about this orientation, it does raise certain barriers for lower class and Negro children—barriers that are to be found in most aptitude tests as well.

1. *Environmental factors.*   The chief handicap of the disadvantaged child where verbal tests are concerned is in his limited exposure to people having command of standard English.   Communication within the lower class environment, although it may rise to a very complex and sophisticated level, typically assumes a language form alien to that tested by aptitude tests.   Slang expressions predominate; diction is poor; and there may be ethnically based language forms. The language spoken by Negro children in the ghetto has been classified as a dialect.   .   .   .

The disadvantaged child has little or no opportunity to range beyond the boundaries of his immediate neighborhood.   He is unfamiliar, therefore, with concepts that will expand both his range of experiences and his vocabulary.   He has less exposure to new things that he can reduce to verbal terms.   For example, one defense witness, a principal of a low-income Negro elementary school, told of how most of the children had never been more than a few blocks from home; they had never been downtown, although some had been to a Sears department store; they did not know what an escalator was, had not seen a department-store Santa Claus, had not been to a zoo. These experiences, common in the subject matter of tests and textbooks, were alien to the lives of these children.

The way in which environmental factors affect the development of nonverbal skills is not quite as clear. There is evidence that such factors are less of a handicap to scoring well on a nonverbal aptitude test than they are to scoring well on a verbal test. . . . Nonetheless, the child's environment remains very much a factor in the development of nonverbal skills. Defendants' expert, Dr. Dailey, was of the opinion that a nonlanguage test of abstract reasoning tests the same intellectual process required to read a paragraph and answer questions about it. Thus the skill a child develops in the process of reducing life experiences to verbal terms is really but another aspect of the process by which a child reasons abstractly about geometric symbols in nonlanguage terms. The less a child is exposed to situations in which he has the stimulation or the opportunity to deal with complex experiences or concepts, the more retarded both his verbal and nonverbal development will be—although the retarding effect may be greater in the case of verbal skills.

2. *Psychological factors.* Although any student taking a test may be subject to psychological influences of various sorts, there is a good deal of evidence that disadvantaged children and Negro children are more likely than others to suffer from influences that have a depressing effect on test scores. The problem can generally be described as one of low self-esteem, or lack of self-confidence.

i. *Socio-economic causes.* There is evidence that disadvantaged children, black or white, are those most likely to lack self-confidence in the school situation. This is due to a complex of causes, many of them directly related to the environmental factors already discussed. The disadvantaged child is made profoundly aware of this academic shortcoming as soon as he enters school. There is a great risk of his losing confidence in his ability to compete in school with children who are "better off." A frequent manifestation of this is for the child to become a discipline problem, as he goes through the process of rejecting a situation in which he feels inadequate. All of this can have a direct and significant effect on test performance as much as on scholastic performance.

ii. *Racial causes.* Apart from factors related to socio-economic status, there is striking evidence that Negro children undergo a special kind of psychological stress that can have a debilitating effect on academic and test performance. . . . Because of their race and the ever present reminders of being "different", Negro children generally are subject to very serious problems of self-identification. By the time the Negro child is about to enter school he has become very much racially self-conscious, which causes considerable psychological turmoil as he attempts to come to terms with his status as a Negro.

He tends to be imbued with a sense of worthlessness, of inferiority, of fear and despair which is transmitted to him primarily through his parents.

In this state of turmoil, many Negro children approach school with the feeling they are entering a strange and alien place that is the property of a white school system or of white society, even though the school may be all-Negro. And when the school *is* all-Negro or predominantly so, this simply reinforces the impressions implanted in the child's mind by his parents, for the school experience is then but a perpetuation of the segregation he has come to expect in life generally. Evidence of turmoil can be found in the inability of many Negro pre-schoolers and first graders to draw themselves as colored, or other than in an animal-like or caricature-like fashion. This general psychological phenomenon is not confined to the South but is common to Negroes throughout the country.   .   .   .

When economically based deprivation is combined with the traumas suffered simply because of being Negro, the psychological impact can be crushing.

iii. *Manifestations of low self-esteem: anxiety and apathy.* When a child lacks confidence in himself or is self-degrading, he is likely to manifest this during the test-taking experience. One reaction that has been identified has been called "test anxiety." The child, apprehensive about his ability to score well and fearful about what others—especially his teacher or principal—might see in the test score, reacts in a self-defeating manner: He becomes highly nervous, even "wildly rampant"; or he withdraws. Either reaction lowers his test score.   .   .   . Although both advantaged and disadvantaged children can experience test anxiety, in the opinion of Dr. Cline, plaintiffs' expert, the disadvantaged child—and particularly the disadvantaged Negro child—tend to be under much greater psychological stress in the testing situation and thus are more likely to show the effects in test performance.   .   .   . Several empirical studies support Dr. Cline's conclusion.   .   .   .

Aside from anxiety-caused withdrawal, a child may be apathetic about a test simply because he does not see it as important. Children who come from backgrounds lacking in parental and environmental support for academic achievement will be more prone to be apathetic about testing; and disadvantaged children are those most likely to have nonsupportive backgrounds. In general, the middle and upper class child is made aware of the importance and value of school and testing; this will make him take both more seriously in terms of his goals in life. The lower class child, and especially a Negro facing the fact of racial discrimination, is more likely to view school and testing as a waste of time. Those grown accustomed to lower horizons may find it hard to take seriously such things as aptitude tests.

(3) *Empirical confirmation.*

Empirical confirmation of the disadvantaged child's handicaps on aptitude tests can be found in the remarkably high degree of correlation between test scores on standard aptitude tests and the socio-economic status of the child. The more disadvantaged the child, the lower his test score will be. . . .

Defendants, while acknowledging the handicaps of the disadvantaged child, have steadfastly maintained that the cause of low test scores is strictly a matter of socio-economic status, not race. In their view, the fact that a child is Negro is irrelevant to test performance. The evidence, however, does not support such a definitive conclusion. Dr. Lennon testified that, in constructing sampling groups, socio-economic and cultural factors seem to account for any significant variances. And Dr. Dailey testified to having conducted a multiple regression study of District test results, finding that the race of the child had no observable impact on those particular test scores. . . . Nevertheless, Dr. Dailey later admitted that he has not firmly ruled out race as a wholly irrelevant factor. . . . Thus, what both he and Dr. Lennon left open was the possibility of an overlap between socio-economic and racial factors, the former in many instances masking the effects of the latter.

Certainly, given the persuasive evidence of the psychological impact of segregation and other forms of discrimination on the Negro, defendants' evidence falls far short of successfully eliminating racial factors as influential in test performance.

(4) *The influence of school.*

For the disadvantaged child, handicapped as he is by home and community circumstances, the school remains as the last hope for overcoming academic deficiencies. In recognition of this fact the urban schools, including the District school system, are giving more and more attention to providing compensatory education for these children, for it is the school that by definition is best suited to providing students with the opportunity to acquire and perfect the academic skills which the school itself demands. And if the school fails in this task, the disadvantaged child will remain handicapped both in class and in taking tests.

But the influence of the school is not confined to how well it can teach the disadvantaged child; it also has a significant role to play in shaping the student's emotional and psychological make-up. The formula for reaching a student who comes to school academically ill-equipped from the start, who is disposed to reject the whole educational complex because of feelings of fear, frustration and an abiding sense of futility, is still one of the unsolved problems in American education. What is clear is that the urban school treads a narrow and difficult path in trying to reach the disadvantaged child. If it missteps, the consequence can be a devastating reinforcement of the psychological handicaps that already plague these children.   .   .   .

.   .   .   The horrible consequence of a teacher's low expectation is that it tends to be a self-fulfilling prophecy. The unfortunate students, treated as if they were subnormal, come to accept as a fact that they *are* subnormal. They act out in their school behavior and in the testing situation what they have been conditioned to believe is their true status in life; and in conforming to expectations, they "confirm" the original judgment. A noted expert, Professor Kenneth Clark, has summed up the problem thusly:

> " * * * When a child from a deprived background is treated as if he is uneducable because he has a low test score, he becomes uneducable and the low test score is thereby reinforced. If a child scores low on an intelligence test because he cannot read and then is not taught to read because he has a low test score, then such a child is being imprisoned in an iron circle and becomes the victim of an educational self-fulfilling prophecy."

Aside from the influence of the teacher, the whole of the school experience will shape a student's behavior. If that experience is for one reason or another a negative one for the student, his performances will likewise be negative.   .   .   .

d. *Accuracy of test measurements.*

Plaintiffs charge that the disadvantaged child's handicaps—both environmental and psychological—are such that standard aptitude tests cannot serve as accurate measurements of innate ability to learn. In Dr. Cline's opinion these tests are worthless. The evidence that this is so is persuasive.

It will be recalled that a scholastic aptitude test is constructed to test present facility in verbal—and, sometimes, nonverbal—skills so as to make possible an inference about an individual's innate ability to succeed in school. The inference is expressed in the form of a test score which is a statement of how the individual student compares with the median score of the norming group. The median reflects an "average" ability to learn, a score above or below that average indicating superior or inferior ability. A crucial assumption in this comparative statement, however, is that the individual is fairly comparable with the norming group in terms of environmental background and psychological make-up; to the extent the individual is not comparable, the test score may reflect those differences rather than innate differences. For example, perhaps the most ideal circumstance for making an accurate estimate of innate ability from comparing test scores would be in the case of twins. If the twins were given the same test and one scored significantly higher than the other, a reasonable inference would be that the higher scoring twin had the superior innate ability; both children presumably would have had the same opportunity to learn the tested skills and both would probably have been subject to similar psychological influences.

Transferring this principle to standard aptitude tests in general, the best circumstance for making accurate estimates of ability is when the tested student is most like the typical norming student: white and middle class. Because the white middle class student predominates in the norming sample, it is possible to say the average student in that group will have had roughly the same opportunities to develop standard verbal and nonverbal skills as the rest of the group and will probably be psychologically similar as well. Thus the national median or norm is a reasonably accurate statistical statement of what the average American student ought to have learned in the way of verbal and nonverbal skills by a certain age and what can therefore be considered average intelligence or ability to learn. For this reason, standard aptitude tests are most precise and accurate in their measurements of innate ability when given to white middle class students.

When standard aptitude tests are given to low income Negro children, or disadvantaged children, however, the tests are less precise and less accurate—so much so that test scores become practically meaningless. Because of the impoverished circumstances that characterize the disadvantaged child, it is virtually impossible to tell whether the test score reflects lack of ability—or simply lack of opportunity. Moreover, the probability test scores of the Negro child or the disadvantaged child will be depressed because of somewhat unique psychological influences further compounds the risk of inaccuracy.

Lorton study. Striking evidence of the inaccuracy of standard tests is revealed in a study made in 1965 at the Lorton Youth Center, a penal institution set up under the Federal Youth Corrections Act and serving the District of Columbia. Inmates range in age from 18 to 26 years; 90% are dropouts from the District schools; and 95% of these are Negroes. Sixty-nine inmates enrolled in the Youth Center School pursuing a course of study leading to a high-school-equivalent diploma were examined as a follow-up to an earlier study to determine these inmates' educational progress under "ideal" educational circumstances. In the earlier study several factors had been identified as causing these inmates to underachieve in school and eventually to drop out; the second study was designed to measure achievement once those factors had been removed. . . . the major points of interest are these:

1) Two types of aptitude tests were used to measure ability, the Otis test used in District Schools, a verbal test; and the Revised Beta Examination, which is nonverbal. The IQ ranges for the two tests differed markedly. For the whole group of 69 inmates the range of IQ's obtained by using the Otis test was from 50 to 110; the average was 78, substantially below normal. Scores on the nonverbal Beta

test, however, were higher, ranging from 71 to 118; the average was 98—20 points higher than the Otis average, and a level considered to indicate average intelligence.

Twenty-four of the 69 inmates scored at 75 or below on the Otis test, the IQ's ranging from 50 to 75; the average was 62. Yet on the Beta test the range was from 71 to 112, the average being 91—or 29 points higher than the Otis average.

2) Gains in achievement in reading and arithmetic over a one-year period were measured using the Stanford Achievement Tests, one of the series used in the District schools. The expected gain for a student of average intelligence, according to Stanford norms, is 1.0 (i. e., a progress equivalent to one grade level in one year).

Reading. The average gain for all 69 inmates was 1.3 years, increasing from an average grade level equivalent of 6.9 (ninth month of the sixth grade) to 8.2 (second month of the eight grade). For the 24 inmates in the 75 or below range (Otis), the average gain also was 1.3 years, increasing from a grade level equivalent of 3.9 to 5.2.

Arithmetic. The average gain for all inmates was 1.8 years, increasing from 5.6 to 7.4. For the 24 low-scoring inmates the average gain was 1.8, increasing from 4.2 to 6.0.

This study reveals in hard fact that a disadvantaged Negro student with a supposedly low IQ can, given the opportunity, far surpass what might be expected of a truly "subnormal" student. It illustrates the principle that a standard verbal aptitude test—in this case the Otis test—can be a faulty predictor of actual achievement for disadvantaged students, and confirms Dr. Clines assessment of the disabilities of such tests in making accurate inferences about innate ability.

Local norms. Two techniques have been cited by plaintiffs that might help give a more accurate estimation of the ability of the disadvantaged child. One of these is the development of a locally standardized test. The principle is the same as that applied to the nationally standardized test, except that the test questions are made appropriate to the students being tested and the norm is ascertained from a group of similarly situated students—that is, those students within the local school system at the appropriate age levels. The purpose of the local norm is to produce test scores that will reflect what the child *has* had the opportunity to learn and to compare his achievement with that of others who have had comparable opportunities. Defendants have not availed themselves of this technique.
.   .   .

Another method of establishing a local norm is to use the standard aptitude test but to restandardize the median score according to local performances.   .   .   .

Empirical verification. A second method designed to assure accuracy of measurements, strongly recommended by educational test experts and test publishers alike, is for the school system to conduct an empirical study of the predictive validity of the aptitude tests it uses. Since there is a probability of error in prediction for any school population, it is desirable to obtain evidence as to how accurate the test is for the local student body. When the student body is highly dissimilar to the standardizing group it becomes even more desirable to verify the accuracy of the test's predictions. This is done by making a follow-up study of a group of students to see how much correlation there is between actual scholastic achievement and the initial test score. The District has not made any empirical studies of this sort, even though the student body and the system itself are admittedly "unique". . . .

Conclusion. In light of the above evidence regarding the accuracy of aptitude test measurements, the court makes the following findings. First, there is substantial evidence that defendants presently lack the techniques and the facilities for ascertaining the innate learning abilities of a majority of District school children. Second, lacking these techniques and facilities, defendants cannot justify the placement and retention of these children in lower tracks on the supposition that they could do no better, given the opportunity to do so.

Misjudgments and undereducation. Plaintiffs have alleged that the harm in using standard aptitude tests is not simply a matter of technical inability to estimate innate learning capacities of disadvantaged children. They go further and say that the false images test scores can project because of this disability will lead teachers —and principals, when they are involved in making the decision about proper track placement—into misjudging the capabilities of these children. The consequence is to create a substantial risk of underestimating and thus undereducating the disadvantaged child. . . .

OPINION OF LAW

. . .

VI. THE TRACK SYSTEM

. . . The evidence amassed by both parties with regard to the track system has been reviewed in detail . . . the court has already had occasion to note the critical infirmities of that system. The sum result of those infirmities, when tested by the principles of equal protection and due process, is to deprive the poor and a majority of the Negro students in the District of Columbia of their constitutional right to equal educational opportunities. . . .

Ability grouping is by definition a classification intended to discriminate among students, the basis of that discrimination being a student's capacity to learn. Different kinds of educational opportunities are thus made available to students of differing abilities. Whatever may be said of the concept of ability grouping in general, it has been assumed here that such grouping can be reasonably related to the purposes of public education. . . . the substance of plaintiffs' complaint is that in practice, if not by design, the track system—as administered in the District of Columbia public schools —has become a system of discrimination founded on socio-economic and racial status rather than ability, resulting in the undereducation of many District students.

As the court's findings have shown, the track system is undeniably an extreme form of ability grouping. Students are early in elementary school sorted into homogeneous groups or tracks (and often into subgroups within a track) thereby being physically separated into different classrooms. Not only is there homogeneity, in terms of supposed levels of ability—the intended result—but as a practical matter there is a distinct sameness in terms of socio-economic status as well. More importantly, each track offers a substantially different kind of education, both in pace of learning and in scope of subject matter. At the bottom there is the slow-paced, basic (and eventually almost purely low-skill vocational) Special Academic Track; at the top is the intense and challenging Honors program for the gifted student. For a student locked into one of the lower tracks, physical separation from those in other tracks is of course complete insofar as classroom relationships are concerned; and the limits on his academic progress, and ultimately the kind of life work he can hope to attain after graduation, are set by the orientation of the lower curricula. Thus those in the lower tracks are, for the most part, molded for various levels of vocational assignments; those in the upper tracks, on the other hand, are given the opportunity to prepare for the higher ranking jobs and, most significantly, for college.

In theory, since tracking is supposed to be kept flexible, relatively few students should actually ever be locked into a single track or curriculum. Yet, in violation of one of its principal tenets, the track system is not flexible at all. Not only are assignments permanent for 90% or more of the students but the vast majority do not even take courses outside their own curriculum. Moreover, another significant failure to implement track theory—and in major part responsible for the inflexibility just noted—is the lack of adequate remedial and compensatory education programs for the students assigned to or left in the lower tracks because of cultural handicaps. Although one of the express reasons for placing such students in these tracks is to facilitate remediation, little is being done to accomplish the task. Consequently, the lower track student, rather than obtaining an enriched educational experience, gets what is essentially a limited or watered-down curriculum.

These are, then, the significant features of the track system: separation of students into rigid curricula, which entails both physical segregation and a disparity of educational opportunity; and, for those consigned to the lower tracks, opportunities decidedly inferior to those available in the higher tracks.

A precipitating cause of the constitutional inquiry in this case is the fact that those who are being consigned to the lower tracks are the poor and the Negroes, whereas the upper tracks are the provinces of the more affluent and the whites. Defendants have not, and indeed could not have, denied that the pattern of grouping correlates remarkably with a student's status, although defendants would have it that the equation is to be stated in terms of income, not race. However, . . . to focus solely on economics is to oversimplify the matter in the District of Columbia where so many of the poor are in fact the Negroes. And even if race could be ruled out, which it cannot, defendants surely "can no more discriminate on account of poverty than on account of religion, race, or color." . . . As noted before, the law has a special concern for minority groups for whom the judicial branch of government is often the only hope for redressing their legitimate grievances; and a court will not treat lightly a showing that educational opportunities are being allocated according to a pattern that has unmistakable signs of invidious discrimination. Defendants, therefore, have a weighty burden of explaining why the poor and the Negro should be those who populate the lower ranks of the track system.

Since by definition the basis of the track system is to classify students according to their ability to learn, the only explanation defendants can legitimately give for the pattern of classification found in the District schools is that it does reflect students' abilities. If the discriminations being made are founded on anything other than that, then the whole premise of tracking collapses and with it any justification for relegating certain students to curricula designed for those of limited abilities. While government may classify persons and thereby effect disparities in treatment, those included within or excluded from the respective classes should be those for whom the inclusion or exclusion is appropriate; otherwise the classification risks becoming wholly irrational and thus unconstitutionally discriminatory. It is in this regard that the track system is fatally defective, because for many students placement is based on traits other than those on which the classification purports to be based.

The evidence shows that the method by which track assignments are made depends essentially on standardized aptitude tests which, although given on a system-wide basis, are completely inappropriate for use with a large segment of the student body. Because these tests are standardized primarily on and are relevant to a white middle class group of students, they produce inaccurate and misleading test scores when given to lower class and Negro students. As a result, rather than being classified according to ability to learn, these students are in reality being classified according to their socio-economic or racial status, or—more precisely—according to environmental and psychological factors which have nothing to do with innate ability.

Compounding and reinforcing the inaccuracies inherent in test measurements are a host of circumstances which further obscure the true abilities of the poor and the Negro. For example, teachers acting under false assumptions because of low test scores will treat the disadvantaged student in such a way as to make him conform to their low expectations; this acting out process—the self-fulfilling prophecy —makes it appear that the false assumptions were correct, and the student's real talent is wasted. Moreover, almost cynically, many Negro students are either denied or have limited access to the very kinds of programs the track system makes a virtual necessity: kindergartens; Honors programs for the fast-developing Negro student; and remedial and compensatory education programs that will bring the disadvantaged student back into the mainstream of education. Lacking these facilities, the student continues hampered by his cultural handicaps and continues to appear to be of lower ability than he really is. Finally, the track system as an institution cannot escape blame for the error in placements, for it is tracking that places such an emphasis on defining ability, elevating its importance to the point where the whole of a student's education and future are made to turn on his facility in demonstrating his qualifications for the higher levels of opportunity. Aside from the fact that this makes the consequences of misjudgments so much the worse, it also tends to alienate the disadvantaged student who feels unequal to the task of competing in an ethnocentric school system dominated by white middle class values; and alienated students inevitably do not reveal their true abilities—either in school or on tests.

All of these circumstances, and more, destroy the rationality of the class structure that characterizes the track system. Rather than reflecting classifications according to ability, track assignments are for many students placements based on status. Being, therefore, in violation of its own premise, the track system amounts to an unlawful discrimination against those students whose educational opportunities are being limited on the erroneous assumption that they are capable of accepting no more.

REMEDY

The remedy to be provided against the discriminatory policies of the defendants' school administration must center primarily on pupil assignment, teacher assignment and the track system.   .   .   .

.   .   .   with respect to the track system, the track system simply must be abolished.   .   .   .

Even in concept the track system is undemocratic and discriminatory. Its creator admits it is designed to prepare some children for white-collar, and other children for blue-collar, jobs. Considering the tests used to determine which children should receive the blue-collar special, and which the white, the danger of children completing their education wearing the wrong collar is far too great for this democracy to tolerate. Moreover, any system of ability grouping which, through failure to include and implement the concept of compensatory education for the disadvantaged child or otherwise, fails in fact to bring the great majority of children into the mainstream of public education denies the children excluded equal educational opportunity and thus encounters the constitutional bar. . . .

NOTES AND QUESTIONS

1. Did the court say that ability group tracking was unconstitutional per se, in all circumstances, or that it was unconstitutional only within the circumstances of this case? If only within this case, identify the critical circumstances. How would it have to be changed so as to make ability group tracking constitutional in Washington, D. C.? Why did the court hold that "the track system simply must be abolished"?

2. Did the court hold that ability group tracking is unconstitutional in Washington, D. C., because it denied equal educational opportunity irrespective of race, or because it was the functional equivalent of racial segregation enforced by public officials under law? What difference does the reason make? Did Washington, D. C., operate a dual school system before Brown I and II? If so, does this opinion merely extend Bolling v. Sharpe to ability group tracking?

3. Are the vices of segregation and ability group tracking as set forth by Judge J. Skelly Wright found equally in schools where de facto segregation exists? If so, would his opinion apply equally to de facto situations? Why or why not? Should your answer be yes, is it based on the view that the reasoning in this case is ultimately grounded on an unconstitutional denial of equal educational opportunity irrespective of race? How can equal educational opportunity be made available to all children? What about the "gifted" child? Shouldn't he have an honors program?

4. Can you accurately measure and predict a student's "maximum educational potential" one month into the future? Six months? One year? Three years? Five years? How? Do you agree with the court's reasoning on this point? If not, how can you accurately identify the retarded child, the gifted child, the superior child or the ordinary child?

5. In the Keyes case, supra, the court required proof that the racial imbalance "was caused by intentional state action," did the court require the same proof in Hobson v. Hansen? If not, why not? Do you agree?

6. Is Hobson v. Hansen an "equal protection" or "due process" case, or both? Why? What concept of equal educational opportunity does the decision rest on?

7. On appeal, the decision in Hobson v. Hansen was affirmed sub nom. in Smuck v. Hobsen, 408 F.2d 175 (D.C.Cir. 1969). On tracking the appellate court said: "The simple decree enjoining the 'track system' does not interpose any realistic barrier to flexible school administra-

tion by a school board genuinely committed to attainment of more quality and equality of educational opportunity." If you had been a member of the reviewing court, how would you have voted? Why? State the way(s) in which it would be possible to attain "more quality and equality of educational oporunity." See, Symposium, Equal Educational Opportunity, 61 Geo.L.J. 845 (1973).

8. It has been said that the superior student wastes half his time in the typical American school; that the gifted child wastes it all, and that the upper five to ten percent of America's school-age children are the most underprivileged group. For example at page 19 of The Gifted Child in the Regular Classroom (1953) Marian Scheifele states that "it is a shocking fact that many gifted children, in terms of [potential] achievement, are the most serious retarded pupils in our schools today." Moreover, there is reason to believe that the characteristics denoted as "giftedness" are equally distributed in children throughout the "racial" and socio-economic spectra. Thus, the minority or lower income class student who is "gifted" may be doubly at a disadvantage. The problem for our schools today is simply that of making available to ALL young people the sort of educational opportunity which an accurate appraisal of their capacities require, and boards of education (and teachers too) should see to it that universal education translates as honest educational opportunities commensurate with a child's genuine talent and potential. Assuming that this goal is valid and desirable, how can it be achieved while also achieving desegregation and the elimination of unconstitutional tracking systems?

CONSTITUTIONAL FREEDOM AND LANGUAGE MINORITIES

TOWARD EQUAL EDUCATIONAL OPPORTUNITY

United States Senate Select Comm. on Equal Educational Opportunity,
Report, 92nd Cong., 2nd Sess. Dec. 31, 1972.
Excerpts from Pp. 45–47, 49.

.   .   .   The American child whose first language is other than English suffers a double disadvantage. Like the black child and poor white child he is probably isolated in a rural slum or urban ghetto community where he was born and lives and goes to school. If he is poor, he probably attends a school with other poor children of the same racial or ethnic background. And often it is an older school with less qualified teachers and fewer resources.

But when he arrives at school he faces a special disadvantage, for his language and culture are different and they are often neither valued nor understood by those who teach him and run his school. Often his language is considered alien, his culture unimportant, and his manner unusual. He is probably told he must learn in English, a language which may be alien to him or at least is seldom spoken at home. He enters a new world where the values his parents taught him are now often rejected, tacitly if not explicitly. He may be asked to change into something different. He is sometimes even forbidden to speak his native language in school.

Unable to conform to his new world, the language-minority child is often labeled and stamped as inferior. He is tested. But the test he takes was probably designed for middle-class English-speaking "Anglo" children. If he fails or does poorly, he is then often tracked into a class with slow learners. He may then see himself as inferior. He soon learns that his heritage is not regarded by others as important, for there is little in his curriculum or his textbooks about his heroes or the history of his people. His world at home is simply excluded from this world at school.

This is the plight of hundreds of thousands of language-minority children—children whose heritage in Spanish, Mexican, Puerto Rican, Portuguese, Chinese, Japanese, Filipino, Korean, American Indian or whose forebears may be from any of a large number of other foreign lands.

Unfortunately, all too often fluency in a foreign language is looked upon by public school systems as a handicap for the child who is deficient in his ability to communicate in English. While detailed surveys have not been undertaken for language-minority groups, the U. S. Census Bureau estimates that of the 9.2 million Spanish-surnamed Americans in the United States, only half usually speak English at home. In a survey conducted by the U. S. Civil Rights Commission in 1969 it was estimated that nearly half the Mexican-American first graders in Arizona, California, Colorado, New Mexico and Texas are deficient in English when they arrive at school.

Even greater proportions of American Indian children are deficient in English. In its report, "Indian Education: A National Tragedy—A National Challenge," the Special Subcommittee on Indian Education concluded that more than half our Indian youths between the ages of 6 and 18 use their native language at home and that two-thirds of Indian children entering BIA schools have little or no skill in English.

The language-minority child not only arrives at school with this handicap, he is immediately subjected to practices and policies and sometimes even legal prohibitions which attempt to keep him from communicating in his native language. In fact, until recently, many States had legal prohibitions forbidding teaching in public schools in any language other than English.

But even in the absence of official State laws prohibiting foreign languages in schools there are still school districts which prohibit or discourage the speaking of foreign languages.

These rules are enforced, often rigidly, through various forms of punishment: Detention after school hours, the payment of a few pennies in fines for each word of Spanish spoken, suspension from school, and even, sometimes, corporal punishment.

The rejection of the minority child's language is also accompanied by the exclusion of his culture from the school curriculum. Most schools offer neither Spanish-surnamed, Indian, Oriental or other foreign language children an opportunity to learn about their heritage or folklore. Their textbooks either ignore the history of their people or present a distorted picture based on false stereotypes.

Witnesses before this and other committees described history texts with degrading characterizations of Hispanic, Oriental and American Indian peoples. They also described school censorship practices which deprive language-minority children of the opportunity for exposure to the conditions of their people in America today.

These are among the unequal practices to which the language-minority child is subjected in school. But they are perhaps only the symptoms of a more fundamental cause of educational inequality for the language-minority child—exclusion from the process by which decisions are made about the education of minority-group and disadvantaged children. For the language minorities and for other disadvantaged groups most public school systems are a closed society. All too often educational decisions are made about disadvantaged children without consultation with or explanation to those who are affected and in some school districts school officials are openly hostile to language-minority groups.

It is clear from all the testimony we have heard—from the educators, students and other observers from both minority and non-minority groups that unless ways can be found to involve minority groups in their own education and in their own schools, for them public education will remain unequal and their lives will remain a series of lost opportunities.   .   .   .

Bilingual Educational Personnel—The effectiveness of any bilingual education effort depends largely on the availability of teachers, principals, counselors and other educational personnel who are capable of meeting the needs of language-minority children. Only if educators are sensitive to the needs of these children, understand and respect the language they speak and the culture and heritage of which they are proud will education be a successful experience for minority-group children whose first language is not English.

There is presently a totally inadequate supply of trained teachers and other school personnel who are either themselves members of language-minority groups or who are adequately trained to meet the need for bilingual education.

There are a number of reasons for this lack of adequate personnel for bilingual education.

First, the recruitment and training of bilingual teachers and administrative personnel has been largely neglected by our public school systems and by teacher education institutions.

Second, there has been neither an adequate commitment nor sufficient resources for the recruiting and training of bilingual teacher aides and paraprofessionals from minority groups.

Third, State legal requirements which are designed to set minimum standards for the employment of educational personnel often operate to discriminate against language-minority educators.

We recommend that teacher training institutions in this country, particularly those in regions of the Nation containing substantial numbers of language-minority citizens, include in their curricula programs designed to acquaint prospective teachers with the culture and heritage of language-minority children. We recommend that teachers be encouraged to concentrate in this vital field and that a major effort be undertaken by teacher training institutions to recruit members of language-minority groups.

NOTE: See Lau v. Nichols, Supreme Court of the United States, 1974, Appendix at page 875, infra.

SERNA v. PORTALES MUNICIPAL SCHOOLS
United States District Court, D.N.Mex., 1972.
351 F.Supp. 1279.

Plaintiffs are minors of Spanish-surnamed heritage represented by their parents in this suit which they have brought as a class action. They seek declaratory and injunctive relief, invoking jurisdiction here under 28 U.S.C. Sections 1343, 2201 and 2203. Plaintiffs assert that defendants have discriminated against them and the members of the class they claim to represent in failing to provide learning opportunities which satisfy both their educational and social needs. They claim deprivation of due process and equal protection guaranteed by the Fourteenth Amendment of the United States Constitution and of their statutory rights under Title VI of the Civil Rights Act of 1964, specifically Section 601 (42 U.S.C. 2000(d)).

The City of Portales is divided by railroad tracks. The Spanish-surnamed population is concentrated on the North side of these tracks. One of the City's four elementary schools, Lindsey School, is located in that area. For the 1971–1972 school year Lindsey School had a student enrollment of 86.7% Spanish-surnamed students. The ethnic composition of the three elementary schools South of the tracks, Brown, James and Steiner, during the same year was predominately Anglo, with 78% to 88% Anglo enrollment. Spanish-surnamed children comprise 34.5% of the student population of the four elementary schools in the Portales school district. There is one junior high school and one senior high school in the district. The junior high school enrollment is 70.2% Anglo and 28.8% Spanish-surnamed.   In the senior high school, 82% of the students are Anglo and slightly over 17% are Spanish-surnamed.

The focal point of this action pivots around the education offered in the Lindsey School where the Spanish-surnamed children comprise a large majority. While plaintiffs assert that educational discrimination exists throughout the Portales school system, it is alleged to be most evident at Lindsey. Plaintiffs claim discrimination is the result of an educational program within the Portales school system which is tailored to educate the middle class child from an English speaking family without regard for the educational needs of the child from an environment where Spanish is the predominant language spoken. Such a program, it is claimed, is a denial of equal educational opportunity to the Spanish-surnamed children.

Plaintiffs do not claim that the program in the Lindsey School is inferior to that offered in any other school within the district. In fact plaintiffs contend that the educational program at Lindsey is substantially the equivalent of that offered at the Brown, James and Steiner schools. It is the similarity of these programs which is the crux of plaintiffs claim of inequality of educational opportunity.

Although the programs offered at Lindsey are similar in many regards with programs offered at Brown, James and Steiner, plaintiffs are not correct in their assertion that the education offered at Lindsey is the same as that offered in the other schools. In the current school year, six Spanish-American teachers are employed at Lindsey. The school is continuing a bilingual-bicultural program for first graders which was instituted in the 1971–1972 school year and also provides a limited program in English as a second language which reaches approximately 40 students in the second through sixth grades. Neither of these programs or any other bilingual-bicultural program is offered in the other Portales elementary schools nor are any Spanish-surnamed teachers employed in those three schools.

Defendant school district asserts that the programs which have been established at Lindsey and the increase in the number of teachers with a Spanish surname indicate its awareness of the needs of the Spanish-surnamed children and constitutes sufficient affirmative action to remedy whatever deficiencies may have existed. The evidence presented, however, indicates that the achievement of children at Lindsey is consistently lower than that of the children attending the other three elementary schools. I. Q. tests administered to fifth grade students in the four Portales municipal elementary schools reveal that the children at Lindsey scored approximately 13% lower than children at James and approximately 8% lower than children at Steiner. In language expression, Lindsey students were two and one-half years behind James students and 1.3 years behind the national norm.

In I. Q. tests administered to all first graders in the Portales Municipal Schools in October, 1971, Lindsey students scored lowest with 86.7%, which was also below the national norm. While it is recognized that this test was given only one month after Lindsey's bilingual-bicultural program for first graders was inaugurated, the results are indicative of the learning disability with which the Spanish-speaking child comes to school. Testimony by an educational psychologist established that in his opinion language difficulties accounted for 80% to 85% of the differences indicated in achievement testing. He stated that the reading ability of the average child at Lindsey was 1.7 years behind the national norm.

Evidence relating to I. Q. test scores of children in the Portales school system was admitted at the trial with the recognition that such scores are not conclusive indicia of student achievement or failure. What becomes apparent from an examination of these scores, however, is that the performance of the children at every level at Lindsey School is not what it should be when compared with the performance of students at the other schools. Coupled with the testimony of educational experts regarding the negative impact upon Spanish-surnamed children when they are placed in a school atmosphere which does not adequately reflect the educational needs of this minority, as is found to be the situation in the Portales schools, the conclusion becomes inevitable that these Spanish-surnamed children do not in fact have equal educational opportunity and that a violation of their constitutional right to equal protection exists.

The administrators of the Portales school district are aware of these conditions, have taken some steps to alleviate the program, and have made positive improvements. These corrections, however, are not adequate. Under these circumstances, it is incumbent upon the school district to reassess and enlarge its program directed to the specialized needs of its Spanish-surnamed students at Lindsey and also to establish and operate in adequate manner programs at the other elementary schools where no bilingual-bicultural program now exists. The fact that the other three elementary schools have a smaller Spanish-surnamed enrollment than Lindsey does not eliminate the requirement for such programs.

Of particular importance is the recruitment and hiring of more qualified Spanish-speaking teachers and teacher aides at each of the district schools as positions and personnel become available. The presence of qualified teachers who can speak Spanish should be a significant factor toward enabling the Spanish-surnamed students to effectively participate in the educational process.

Defendant argues that the special educational needs of Spanish-surnamed children is not the result of state action and that defendant did not create these problems through any classification or racially motivated discrimination. .   .   .

The promulgation and institution of a program by the Portales school district which ignores the needs of such students does constitute state action.

Defendant school district also contends that it is seriously restricted by its operating budget in expanding its bilingual-bicultural programs. Evidence at the trial established that there are sources of funds available to implement and maintain such programs. Federal funds are available for bilingual-bicultural programs in the elementary and secondary schools under Titles I and VII of the Elementary and Secondary Education Act of 1965 (Title I, 20 U.S.C. § 241a et seq.; Title VII, 20 U.S.C. § 880b et seq.). The State of New Mexico's Bilingual Instruction Act, 11 N.M.S.A. § 77–21–1 et seq., similarly has made funding available for the "special education needs" of students with a limited English-speaking ability caused by living in an environment where the dominant language is not English. These are some of the available sources of funding for a bilingual-bicultural program. Defendant school district is directed to investigate and utilize wherever possible the sources of available funds to provide equality of educational opportunity for its Spanish-surnamed students.

It is also claimed that an obstacle to expanding bilingual-bicultural programs in the Portales school system is the absence of qualified teachers. Defendant school district has made an effort to recruit and has recruited Spanish-speaking teachers. It points to the fact that it has received few applications from such teachers and that the teacher turn-over in the Portales Municipal Schools is relatively low. However great the effort, this is not an acceptable justification for not providing specialized programs where the deprivation of them violates a constitutional right and where funding is available. It is incumbent upon the school district to increase its recruiting efforts and, if those recruiting efforts are unsuccessful, to obtain sufficient certification of Spanish-speaking teachers to allow them to teach in the district.

.   .   .

Plaintiffs did not meet their burden of proof in establishing discrimination by the Portales school district in its employment practices regarding non-teaching personnel. The evidence did prove, however, that the defendant school district is not providing an educational program which affords equality of educational opportunity for all of its students.

Jurisdiction over this action will be retained for ninety (90) days from the date of entry of this memorandum opinion so as to enable the Portales school district to submit to the court its plans for remedial action to be undertaken by the defendant in compliance with the requirements set forth in this opinion.

NOTES AND QUESTIONS

1. The court held that the "school district is not providing an equal educational program which affords equality of educational opportunity for all of its students." What concept of equal educational opportunity has the court embraced?

2. Imagine that you are the lawyer for the local Board of Education of Portales School District, what plan would you have the Board submit to the court? Or instead, would you appeal the case? If so, on what ground?

3. What is the appropriate constitutional conception of equal educational opportunity? Is it appropriate to hold that equal educational opportunity exists whenever the educational opportunities afforded children by the state (1) are such that the opportunities do not depend upon the economic circumstances of the parents of the children nor upon the geographical location of the children within the state; or (2) are such that each child up to a certain age can fulfill all his potentialities regardless of race, creed, social standing or economic position; or (3) are such that they are expressed in dollars with each child representing an expenditure of an equal amount of state funds however allowing local communities to tax themselves further if they should elect to make additional educational opportunities available; or (4) are such that each child is afforded an equal minimum achievement level, although differing amounts of state funds must be allocated to different children in order to produce a common achievement level, but thereafter allowing local communities further to tax themselves in order to make additional educational opportunities available; or (5) are such that the distribution of all funds, state and local, are equal on a per child basis; or (6) are such that the distribution of all state and local funds are in an inverse proportion to the children's abilities in order to insure that all children leave school on an equal footing; or (7) are such that the distribution of all state and local funds are directly in proportion to the various talents and abilities of the children, thereby insuring that those best able to benefit will have the use of the funds; or (8) are such that all state and local funds are distributed equally on a per child basis within a classification, but children might be classified into various groups with differing amounts of state funds being allocated to various classifications even though each classification contains an equal number of children? What are the consequences of each concept? What are the appropriate criteria that should be used in order to select the correct constitutional concept of equal educational opportunity? For discussion see, Wise, Rich Schools, Poor Schools (1972).

4. In United States v. Texas, 342 F.Supp. 24 (E.D.Tex.1971), the court mandated bilingual education for Mexican-American and Anglo-American students in the San Felipe-Del Rio School District of Texas. However, the basis for the court's order was a prior determination that there had been de jure racial segregation and the purpose of the court's order was to "eliminate discrimination root and branch" and to create a unitary school system without separate white and

Mexican schools. In light of Keyes v. School District, supra, how strong is the de jure-de facto distinction?

5. In Lau v. Nichols, 483 F.2d 791 (9th Cir. 1973), cert. granted 412 U.S. 938 (1973), the Court of Appeals decided a case involving two classes of non-English-speaking Chinese children. One class (1,790 of the 2,856 Chinese-speaking children in the school district) was admitted to need special instruction in English but received no help at all. The second class (1,066 Chinese-speaking students) received compensatory-education, 633 on a one-hour per day basis and 433 on a full-time basis. Little more than one-third of the 59 teachers who provided the special education were fluent in English and Chinese. There was no showing of any prior racial segregation practiced by the Board. Plaintiffs-appellants contended that the school district denied the childrens' constitutional rights "to an education and to bilingual education, and disregarded their rights to equal educational opportunity among themselves and with English-speaking students."

In deciding against plaintiffs-appellants the Court of Appeals stated that:

> "Every student brings to the starting line of his educational career different advantages and disadvantages caused in part by social, economic and cultural background, created and continued completely apart from any contribution by the school system. That some of these may be impediments which can be overcome does not amount to a 'denial' by the Board of educational opportunities within the meaning of the Fourteenth Amendment should the Board fail to give them special attention, this even though they are characteristic of a particular ethnic group. Before the Board may be found to unconstitutionally deny special remedial attention to such deficiencies there must be found a constitutional duty to provide them.

> "However commendable and socially desirable it might be for the School District to provide special remedial educational programs to disadvantaged students in those areas, or to provide better clothing or food to enable them to more easily adjust themselves to their educational environment, we find no constitutional or statutory basis upon which we can mandate that these things be done.

> "Because we find that the language deficiency suffered by appellants was not caused directly or indirectly by any State action, we agree with the judgment of the district court and distinguish this case from Brown v. Board of Education, 347 U.S. 483 (1954), and its progeny of de jure cases. Under the facts of this case, appellees responsibility to appellants under the Equal Protection Clause extends no further than to provide them with the same facilities, textbooks, teachers and curriculum as is provided to other children in the district. There is no evidence that this duty has not been discharged.

"Furthermore, the determination of what special educational difficulties faced by some students within a State or School District will be afforded extraordinary curative action, and the intensity of the measures to be taken, is a complex decision, calling for significant amounts of executive and legislative expertise and nonjudicial value judgments. As with welfare, (to which these claims are closely akin), the needs of the citizens must be reconciled with the finite resources available to meet those needs. See Dandridge v. Williams, 397 U.S. 471, at 472.

"As long as there is no discrimination by race or national origin, as has neither been alleged nor shown by appellants with respect to this issue, the States should be free to set their educational policies, including special programs to meet special needs, with limited judicial intervention to decide among competing demands upon the resources at their commands, subject only to the requirement that their classifications be rationally related to the purposes for which they are created."

In dissent Judge Irving Hill stated:

"I would reverse the judgment and remand the case to the trial court for the taking of further evidence on defendants' justification, if any, for their failure to provide the bilingual teaching which plaintiffs seek. The facts already adduced show, in my opinion, that the San Francisco School System withholds from a readily identifiable segment of an ethnic minority the minimum English language instruction necessary for that segment to participate in the educational processes with any chance of success. I view such a deprivation as being *prima facie* within the ambit of the Equal Protection Clause.

"The plaintiffs, and the class they represent, are grade school children of Chinese parents who have recently immigrated to this country. The law requires these children to attend school; so, they come. But they enter the San Francisco School System unable to speak or understand the English language. All the instruction they receive is in English as are all of the books and all of the visual materials which are used. As the *amicus* brief from the Harvard University Center for Law and Education puts it, education for these children becomes "mere physical presence as audience to a strange play which they do not understand." These *amici* correctly stress the fact that the essence of education is communication: a small child can profit from his education only when he is able to understand the instruction, ask and answer questions, and speak with his classmates and teachers. When he cannot understand the language employed in the school, he cannot be said to have an educational opportunity in any sense. As against his English-speaking classmates, his educational opportunity is manifestly unequal even though there is an illusion of equality since the facilities, books, and teachers made available to him are the same as those made available to the rest of the students. It seems clear to me that a pupil knowing only a foreign language cannot be said to have an educational opportunity equal to his fellow students unless and until he acquires some minimal facility in the English language."

Dissenting from a denial of hearing en banc Judge Hufstedler stated that:

". . . the Chinese children made out a prima facie case. A claim of invidious discrimination against those who could speak and write only Chinese came to the Supreme Court almost 50 years ago in Yu Cong Eng v. Trinidad (1926) 271 U.S. 500, 46 S.Ct. 619, 70 L.Ed. 1059. The Philippines had enacted a statute requiring business account books to be kept solely in English, Spanish, or any local dialect. The petitioner, a Chinese, merchant who could neither speak nor write any language except Chinese challenged the statute on due process and equal protection grounds. The Philippine statute, like the California statutes here involved, was facially neutral. Mr. Chief Justice Taft, speaking for a unanimous court, struck down the statute as a denial of equal protection."

What concept of equal educational opportunity is embraced by the court? Judge Hill? This case will be reviewed by the Supreme Court. Assume that you are a Justice on that Court, what decision would you render and for what reason(s)? See, Comment, Linguistic Minorities and Their Right to an Effective Education, 3 C. W. Inter. 112 (1972).

CONSTITUTIONAL FREEDOM AND EDUCATION OF THE "GIFTED" AND "EXCEPTIONAL" CHILD

MILLS v. BOARD OF EDUCATION

United States District Court, D.C.D.C., 1972.
348 F.Supp. 866.

MEMORANDUM OPINION, JUDGMENT AND DECREE

WADDY, District Judge.

This is a civil action brought on behalf of seven children of school age by their next friends in which they seek a declaration of rights and to enjoin the defendants from excluding them from the District of Columbia Public Schools and/or denying them publicly supported education and to compel the defendants to provide them with immediate and adequate education and educational facilities in the public schools or alternative placement at public expense. They also seek additional and ancillary relief to effectuate the primary relief. They allege that although they can profit from an education either in regular class-

rooms with supportive services or in special classes adopted to their needs, they have been labelled as behavioral problems, mentally retarded, emotionally disturbed or hyperactive, and denied admission to the public schools or excluded therefrom after admission, with no provision for alternative educational placement or periodic review.
.   .   .

THE PROBLEM

The genesis of this case is found (1) in the failure of the District of Columbia to provide publicly supported education and training to plaintiffs and other "exceptional" children, members of their class, and (2) the excluding, suspending, expelling, reassigning and transferring of "exceptional" children from regular public school classes without affording them due process of law.

The problem of providing special education for "exceptional" children (mentally retarded, emotionally disturbed, physically handicapped, hyperactive and other children with behavioral problems) is one of major proportions in the District of Columbia. The precise number of such children cannot be stated because the District has continuously failed to comply with Section 31–208 of the District of Columbia Code which requires a census of all children aged 3 to 18 in the District to be taken. Plaintiffs estimate that there are ".   .   . 22,000 retarded, emotionally disturbed, blind, deaf, and speech or learning disabled children, and perhaps as many as 18,000 of these children are not being furnished with programs of specialized education." According to data prepared by the Board of Education, Division of Planning, Research and Evaluation, the District of Columbia provides publicly supported special education programs of various descriptions to at least 3880 school age children. However, in a 1971 report to the Department of Health, Education and Welfare, the District of Columbia Public Schools admitted that an estimated 12,340 handicapped children were not to be served in the 1971–72 school year.

Each of the minor plaintiffs in this case qualifies as an "exceptional" child.   .   .   .

THERE IS NO GENUINE ISSUE OF MATERIAL FACT

Congress has decreed a system of publicly supported education for the children of the District of Columbia. The Board of Education has the responsibility of administering that system in accordance with law and of providing such publicly supported education to all of the children of the District, including these "exceptional" children.

Defendants have admitted in these proceedings that they are under an affirmative duty to provide plaintiffs and their class with publicly supported education suited to each child's needs, including special education and tuition grants, and also, a constitutionally adequate prior hearing and periodic review. They have also admitted that they failed to supply plaintiffs with such publicly supported education and have failed to afford them adequate prior hearing and periodic review. . . .

PLAINTIFFS ARE ENTITLED TO RELIEF

Plaintiffs' entitlement to relief in this case is clear. The applicable statutes and regulations and the Constitution of the United States require it.

Statutes and Regulations

Section 31–201 of the District of Columbia Code requires that:

"Every parent, guardian, or other person residing [permanently or temporarily] in the District of Columbia who has custody or control of a child between the ages of seven and sixteen years shall cause said child to be regularly instructed in a public school or in a private or parochial school or instructed privately during the period of each year in which the public schools of the District of Columbia are in session . . . ."

Under Section 31–203, a child may be "excused" from attendance only when

" . . . upon examination ordered by . . . [the Board of Education of the District of Columbia], [the child] is found to be unable mentally or physically to profit from attendance at school: Provided, however, That if such examination shows that such child may benefit from specialized instruction adapted to his needs, he shall attend upon such instruction."

Failure of a parent to comply with Section 31–201 constitutes a criminal offense. . . . The Court need not belabor the fact that requiring parents to see that their children attend school under pain of criminal penalties presupposes that an educational opportunity will be made available to the children. The Board of Education is required to make such opportunity available. It has adopted rules and regulations consonant with the statutory direction. Chapter XIII of the Board Rules contains the following:

1.1—All children of the ages hereinafter prescribed who are bona fide residents of the District of Columbia are entitled to admission and free tuition in the Public Schools of the District of Columbia, subject to the rules, regulations, and orders of the Board of Education and the applicable statutes.

14.1—Every parent, guardian, or other person residing permanently or temporarily in the District of Columbia who has custody or control of a child residing in the District of Columbia between the ages of seven and sixteen years shall cause said child to be regularly instructed in a public school or in a private or parochial school or instructed privately during the period of each year in which the Public Schools of the District of Columbia are in session, provided that instruction given in such private or parochial school, or privately, is deemed reasonably equivalent by the Board of Education to the instruction given in the Public Schools.

14.3—The Board of Education of the District of Columbia may, upon written recommendation of the Superintendent of Schools, issue a certificate excusing from attendance at school a child who, upon examination by the Department of Pupil Appraisal, Study and Attendance or by the Department of Public Health of the District of Columbia, is found to be unable mentally or physically to profit from attendance at school: Provided, however, that if such examination shows that such child may benefit from specialized instruction adapted to his needs, he shall be required to attend such classes.

Thus the Board of Education has an obligation to provide whatever specialized instruction that will benefit the child. By failing to provide plaintiffs and their class the publicly supported specialized education to which they are entitled, the Board of Education violates the above statutes and its own regulations.

The Constitution—Equal Protection and Due Process

The Supreme Court in Brown v. Board of Education . . .

"Today, education is perhaps the most important function of state and local governments. Compulsory school attendance laws and the great expenditures for education both demonstrate our recognition of the importance of education to our democratic society. It is required in the performance of our most basic public responsibilities, even service in the armed forces. It is the very foundation of good citizenship. Today it is a principal instrument in awakening the child to cultural values, in preparing him for later professional training, and in helping him to adjust normally to his environment. In these days, it is doubtful that any child may reasonably be expected to succeed in life if he is denied the opportunity of an education. *Such an opportunity, where the state has undertaken to provide it, is a right which must be made available to all on equal terms.* (emphasis supplied)

Bolling v. Sharpe .   .   . decided the same day as *Brown,* applied the *Brown* rationale to the District of Columbia public schools by finding that:

> "Segregation in public education is not reasonably related to any proper governmental objective, and thus it imposes on Negro children of the District of Columbia a burden that constitutes an arbitrary deprivation of their liberty in violation of the Due Process Clause." .   .   .

In Hobson v. Hansen, *supra,* Judge Wright found that denying poor public school children educational opportunities equal to that available to more affluent public school children was violative of the Due Process Clause of the Fifth Amendment. *A fortiori,* the defendants' conduct here, denying plaintiffs and their class not just an equal publicly supported education but all publicly supported education while providing such education to other children, is violative of the Due Process Clause.

Not only are plaintiffs and their class denied the publicly supported education to which they are entitled many are suspended or expelled from regular schooling or specialized instruction or reassigned without any prior hearing and are given no periodic review thereafter. Due process of law requires a hearing prior to exclusion, termination of classification into a special program. .   .   .

The Defense

The Answer of the defendants to the Complaint contains the following:

> "These defendants say that it is impossible to afford plaintiffs the relief they request unless:
>
> (a) The Congress of the United States appropriates millions of dollars to improve special education services in the District of Columbia; or
>
> (b) These defendants divert millions of dollars from funds already specifically appropriated for other educational services in order to improve special educational services. These defendants suggest that to do so would violate an Act of Congress and would be inequitable to children outside the alleged plaintiff class."

This Court is not persuaded by that contention.

The defendants are required by the Constitution of the United States, the District of Columbia Code, and their own regulations to provide a publicly-supported education for these "exceptional" children. Their failure to fulfill this clear duty to include and retain these children in the public school system, or otherwise provide them with publicly-supported education, and their failure to afford them due process hearing and periodical review, cannot be excused by the claim

that there are insufficient funds.   In Goldberg v. Kelly, 397 U.S. 254
.   .   .   the Supreme Court, in a case that involved the right of a welfare recipient to a hearing before termination of his benefits, held
that Constitutional rights must be afforded citizens despite the greater
expense involved.   The Court stated   .   .   .   that "the State's interest that his [welfare recipient] payments not be erroneously terminated, clearly outweighs the State's competing concern to prevent
any increase in its fiscal and administrative burdens."   Similarly the
District of Columbia's interest in educating the excluded children
clearly must outweigh its interest in preserving its financial resources.
If sufficient funds are not available to finance all of the services and
programs that are needed and desirable in the system then the available funds must be expended equitably in such a manner that no child
is entirely excluded from a publicly supported education consistent
with his needs and ability to benefit therefrom.   The inadequacies of
the District of Columbia Public School System whether occasioned by
insufficient funding or administrative inefficiency, certainly cannot
be permitted to bear more heavily on the "exceptional" or handicapped
child than on the normal child.   .   .   .

NOTES AND QUESTIONS

1. What concept of equal educational opportunity is implicit in this opinion?

    Do you agree?   For further discussion see, Weintraub and Abeson,
    Appropriate Education for All Handicapped Children: A Growing
    Issue, 23 Syracuse L.Rev. 1037 (1972), and generally see, L. M. Dunn,
    Exceptional Children in the Schools (1963).

2. Pennsylvania Ass'n for Retarded Children v. Commonwealth of Pa., 343
    F.Supp. 279 (E.D.Pa., 1972) involved a statute, common to many states,
    that students can be excluded from schools on the ground that the
    students are "uneducable and untrainable."   The efficacy of this type
    of statute turns on the existence of medical and educational facts.
    Plaintiffs claimed that "the premise of the statutes which necessarily
    assumes that certain retarded children are uneducable and untrainable
    lacks a rational basis in fact."   Unanimous expert opinion showed that
    "all mentally retarded persons are capable of benefitting from a program
    of education and training."   Accepting the expert opinion and plaintiff's
    claim the court held that plaintiffs presented a substantial constitutional
    issue of denial of equal protection of the law.   For additional discussion
    see, Schwartz, The Education of Handicapped Children: Emerging Legal
    Doctrine, 7 Clearinghouse Review 125 (1973).

3. Would the decisions in the cases have been any different if instead of
    involving an "exceptional" child it had involved a "gifted" child of
    unusual ability who had not been recognized but who had been labelled
    "hyperactive," a "behavioral problem" or "uneducable and untrain-
    able," and had been excluded from school?   If not, what remedy could
    the court decree?   In the case of either an "exceptional" or "gifted"
    child can a court decree that teachers' salaries shall vary directly with
    the rate of educational progress shown by their students?

ACKERMAN v. RUBIN

Supreme Court, Special Term, Bronx County, 1962.
35 Misc.2d 707, 231 N.Y.S.2d 112, aff'd 17 A.D.2d 796, 232 N.Y.S.2d 872.

BERNARD NEWMAN, Justice. Petitioner seeks an order of the court (Civil Practice Act, art. 78) compelling respondents to admit his son, who has completed his sixth grade and is now eligible to enter the Junior High School Division, to a two-year special progress class in September of 1962, to be conducted at his Junior High School in The Bronx.

Respondents readily concede that the pupil is academically well qualified, but have denied him admission to the special class on the grounds (a) that he is not of the required age (11.3 years), and (b) that he had been previously "accelerated" in school. These grounds for refusal are in accordance with respondents' established criteria for admission to the special progress class. The latter objection was waived in several similar situations, and hence the respondents' refusal must be predicated on the former ground, viz., that the pupil is younger than the requisite age. Petitioner contends that this criterion applicable to his son (10.7 years of age) is arbitrary, capricious and without legal foundation.

It appears that the Board of Education initiated special progress classes more than forty years ago. Indeed, it has been the experience of the Board and of educators throughout the country that special progress classes and enriched program classes are of great benefit to gifted students, enabling them the better to develop their potential. From time to time the Board has revised the requirements for entrance to such special classes.

The last revision was promulgated by a Board of Education directive in July of 1962—after decades of study and trial by experienced educators—and the Board now offers three different courses comprising the Junior High School curriculum:

(a) regular three-year classes;

(b) three-year special progress classes, embodying a specially enriched curriculum;

(c) two-year special progress classes, accelerated to cover the regular three-year course in two years.

The directive limits eligibility to the b and c courses to pupils with superior scholarship grades. Petitioner's son has been admitted to b, but has been denied admission to c, primarily because of the fact that he will be 10.7 years of age in September—the date of admission —as against the 11.3 years-age requirement. The Board freely acknowledges that the pupil meets all the other detailed requirements; but insists that the norms adopted are not arbitrary, and that the additional year required for younger students will serve to develop them emotionally, socially, and physiologically at the adolescent stage so as to eliminate stress and aid the child's development.

Morris—Const. & Am.Educ. ACB—51

Petitioner, in effect, desires to substitute the judgment of a justly proud parent for that of experienced educators, who seek to apply their observations and experience for the benefit of his son. Contrary to petitioner's contentions, the standards adopted by respondents are based, not on whim or caprice, but on years of study and trial; they are derived from the experience of day-to-day dealings with children and their problems.

In the instant proceeding, it appears to be the considered opinion of those educators who are in close contact with petitioner's son that, although he is a gifted child, nevertheless for reasons specifically outlined in the Board's answering papers, further acceleration might be detrimental to this student's best interests. Indeed, the pupil's teacher for the last two years graciously avers that the pupil "has a great potential and will develop into an exceptional student, if his development is allowed to take a natural course".

Certainly, the court may not hold as arbitrary or capricious the respondents' determination that chronologically determined physical, social and emotional maturity are vital and proper factors to be considered in the development and education of a child. To thrust a youngster into an environment where all his classmates are older may well result in the consequent impairment of the necessary social integration of the child with his classmates. The court proceeds from the hypothesis that these respondents are dedicated to the proper educational development of the whole child; and nothing has been shown to cast the slightest doubt upon the validity of this assumption. It may be that respondents, in the exercise of their continuing concern for the proper development of all their charges, including petitioner's son, will find it possible to afford him all or some of the additional benefits of the accelerated special progress classes. It may be that continuing examination of the emotional, physiological and social maturity of petitioner's son will afford respondents, in the future, a basis for review of their determination challenged herein. Our educational system continually changes and re-examination of procedures and policies is a constant process. In the course of this process, perhaps the respondents will afford intellectually gifted, but chronologically younger children, such as petitioner's son, opportunities for advancement and enrichment supplementing those afforded in the three-year special progress program described above. However, the court will not attempt to invade that area; nor may the court seek to substitute its judgment in that area for respondents' expertise.

Consequently, the court finds the Board's directive (to which petitioner objects) to be proper and in accord with the applicable law (see Sec. 2554 [9], Education Law detailing the "Powers and duties of the board of education"). And the court sincerely believes that petitioner, upon objective reflection, will agree that respondents, in adopting these regulations, have acted in the best interests of his son and all other school children. Furthermore, it is axiomatic that a reasonable administrative determination will not be disturbed by the court. . . . Plainly, then, the directive comes within the familiar rule that the courts will apply the presumption of reasonableness to the acts of public officials taken for the general welfare . . .

Accordingly, the application is denied and the petition is dismissed.

NOTES AND QUESTIONS

1. Is uniformity of age in grades beginning with the first grade a worthy educational goal? A useful administrative device? If you were an instructor in a course of beginning foreign language for adults would you first group them by age for instructional purposes? Can you think of any educational or training program apart from the common schools where children are grouped according to age rather than by level of achievement? Is there justifying reason for schools to be different? Is ability grouping the answer?

CONSTITUTIONAL FREEDOM AND EDUCATIONAL FINANCE

INTRODUCTION

Local government districts raise over half of the school revenue in the United States. While they rely on income and sales taxes, as well as a variety of other type of taxes, the major levy used is the property tax. The property tax is collected from owners of property and is based on the value of that property; for example, a property tax base (say, $1,000) (statutory assessment formulas for property vary: "market value," "actual value," "fair value," "full value," "fair cash value," "true and fair market value," but, basically, they all mean "market value" which, in turn, generally refers to the last sales price), plus a tax (rate say, 1%) giving a tax yield ($10.00).

Usually the "property" that can be subjected to taxation by a local government unit is defined by state constitutions and statutes. Almost all "real property" (land and buildings, bulkheads and other improvements erected onto the land) is taxable. However, many states allow "homestead" and "veteran" tax exemptions. Moreover, since states are constitutionally disallowed from taxing federally owned real property without the consent of Congress, much real property, especially in the American west, escapes state and local taxation. A second category of property subject to the property tax is "tangible personal property." Tangible personal property includes almost everything that is movable, such as cars, trucks, railroad cars, clothing, furniture, business equipment, inventories, farm equipment and animals, jewelry, etc. Some states include tangible personal property under their general property laws and others have special laws applying only to this type of property. Tax exemptions exist here as well. Finally, there is intangible personal property, such as bank accounts, stocks and bonds and other valuable claims of ownership or

control. Intangibles are extremely difficult to locate and to assess.
Only few more than one-third of the states include intangible personal
property in their general property tax. The remainder of the states
tax intangibles by special statute and at very low rates or not at all.
Clearly, the major type of taxable property subject to local government taxation is real estate.

While it is true that the property tax is "paid" by the owner, it
is possible for some property owners to "shift" the tax burden onto
others. For example, the owner of an apartment house may "shift"
the tax burden onto his tenants by charging them higher apartment
rental prices. In these circumstances the tenant bears the "incidence" of the tax while the property owner "pays" it and also receives a federal income tax deduction because he "paid" it. Taxes can
be shifted only by manipulations in the market in one of two ways,
either by charging a higher price ("shifting" forward) or by being
economically strong enough to pay a lower price for what one buys
("shifting" backward). Since ordinary people who own houses do
not function in the housing market, it is generally believed that they
cannot shift their property tax burdens. They "pay" and they also
suffer the "incidence" and burden of the property tax. On the other
hand, when levied on business properties the property tax is generally
believed to be shifted rather easily and quickly onto the consumer.
The tax is simply viewed as a direct expense of doing business and
added to the sales price, especially where sellers have any degree of
market or monopoly power. Also, to the ordinary person the property
tax, like the sales tax, is to be regressive, primarily because high-
priced properties are underassessed. (A regressive tax is one that
falls most heavily on those persons least capable of paying it.)
Estates and mansions are put on the market less frequently than
moderately priced housing; thus, their last "market" value for tax
purposes tends to be lower. Peter Gruenstein ("What's Wrong With
the Property Tax," THE NATION, p. 582, May 7, 1973) states that:

> A large part of the property tax morass stems from
> unprofessional or dishonest assessments which produce tre-
> mendous tax breaks for large corporations and the wealthy.
> For example, a study made by Texas University law students
> found that oil-producing properties in Hector County, Texas,
> were underassessed by about 56 per cent as opposed to about
> 7 per cent for home owners. Union Camp, a large South
> Carolina corporation, sold to the state for $2,000 per acre
> land that was being assessed at $20 per acre. Even after
> the sale, adjoining Union Camp land that was not sold con-
> tinued to be assessed at $20 per acre. In Appalachia, rich
> coal lands are being assessed at $10 per acre or less, even
> though they sell for $200 to $500 per acre on the open mar-
> ket.

Moreover, the property tax properly can be viewed as an excise on housing, perhaps representing, on the average, a figure as high as twenty-five percent. Thus, the property tax is one of the heaviest taxes levied on any single item, or service, in the United States.

Because of the heavy reliance on the property tax local government units usually can get more money only in three ways (1) reassessing existing properties values upward; (2) raising the tax rates if they are not already at the statutory maximum, or (3) by levying taxes on newly built properties, especially industrial properties. The first two are highly unpopular which tends to leave only the third. But the third alternative usually runs into obstacles because local government units compete with each other for the location of new industrial properties by offering prospective industries lower tax rates than those offered by another local government unit. This "beggar-my-neighbor" policy is well known. This type of "competition" produces the unfortunate consequence of concentrating taxable industries within the one or few local government districts that offer the lowest tax rates and of concentrating residential properties in the other districts which soon suffer from high taxes and low services. Given the flight of whites and new industry to the suburbs, more and more a diminishing tax base is becoming the fate of America's core cities. It is clear that equal educational opportunity is denied some children when there are major disparities in per-student expenditures among school districts within a single state.

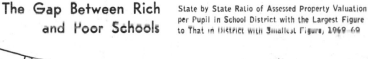

The Gap Between Rich and Poor Schools

State by State Ratio of Assessed Property Valuation per Pupil in School District with the Largest Figure to That in District With Smallest Figure, 1968-69

[A8748]

J. COONS, W. H. CLUNE III, S. SUGARMAN, PRIVATE WEALTH AND PUBLIC EDUCATION

Copyright 1970, Belknap Press of Harvard University Press.
Excerpts from pages xviii-xxii.

. . . A brief tale of two schoolboys will illustrate. They could be any color, but suppose them white in a white neighborhood. One lives on 36th Street in Oakland, California; his friend lives across the street in Emeryville. Every weekday morning at 8:00 they separate, each to attend his assigned public school—one in the Oakland system, one in the Emeryville District. If the reader knows something of California public schools, this trivial event is worth recording. The separation is a fateful one for these children and the millions like them around the nation for whom the accidents of residence and boundary play a decisive role in the character of their formal education. The State of California, like most states, has provided a system guaranteeing to one child a superior education, while to the other it offers mediocrity or worse. Oakland will spend $600–700 on the first child; the Emeryville student will go first class at nearly three times that expense. [The Oakland tax rate is nearly twice that of Emeryville; *California Public Schools Selected Statistics 1967–68,* 24 (Sacramento: Department of Education, 1969).] This example is neither extreme nor extraordinary. The spectrum of school districts in California includes expenditures both higher and considerably lower than these. Nor is the picture radically different in other states: expenditures in Illinois range from under $400 up to $1,600 or more per pupil, and the disparities in Ohio are similar.

Differentials of these magnitudes in per-pupil expenditure within the same state should evoke nothing but outrage. Indeed, there is something incongruous about a differential of any magnitude the sole justification for which is an imaginary school district line between two children. It is the kind of phenomenon that forces its defenders into the dense refuge of "political realities" in search of a rationale. The plain fact is that our state governments have embraced the philosophy that, as a rule, the quality of public education should be in direct proportion to the wealth of the school district; in general this also means that the quality will be in inverse proportion to the needs of children. The primary dependence of public education upon the real property tax and the localization of that tax's administration and expenditure have combined to make the public school into an educator for the educated rich and a keeper for the uneducated poor. There exists no more powerful force for rigidity of social class and the frustration of natural potential than the modern public school system with its systematic discrimination against poor districts.

The remedy is not obvious. Political forces supporting the status quo no doubt vary in strength from state to state, but educational systems themselves are so structured as to be naturally protected from legislative drift toward an egalitarian form. Districts favored by a superior tax base are likely to be opposed to change on all grounds; districts of average affluence are apathetic but can also be opposed to change because they fear potential loss of local control. Poor districts alone have a clear stake in change, but their case is supported only by justice. Hence the persuasiveness of the argument from "reality." Little is to be expected from the political process in its legislative mode.

What, if anything, can be expected from the judicial process? The lawyer's instinct is to recoil from judicial intrusion into the structure of state government. The instinct is sound; but, like most instincts, it can also mislead. Its solid core lies in the mistrust of political change through nonmajoritarian decision-making. It is at ground a democratic impulse which prefers that questions of structure be submitted at least indirectly to the popular will. Under certain conditions its essential benevolence is self-defeating. Legislative malapportionment is a historic instance in which vox populi was simply unavailable in any effective form. The will of the majority required not judicial restraint but judicial rescue.

The goal of equal education may justify heroic judicial measures on a rationale similar in two respects to the reapportionment theme. First, as noted, the deprived child and his subsociety may be and frequently are in a position of political impotence, not because of limited numbers but because of districting structure and other factors organic to the system. Second, education shares with voting the quality of being logically and practically anterior to all other values in democratic society. In fact, as between the two, education arguably deserves precedence as the indispensable preamble of political life.

But there is a third and independent rationale for equality in public education in any capitalist society. At the pinnacle of our economic temple still flies the standard of universal access to the levers of opulence and mobility. Beyond argument, the prime mover in the modern labor market is education. In a free-enterprise system its differential provision by the public school marks the intrusion of economic (if not legal) heresy, for it means that certain participants in the economic race are hobbled at the gate—and hobbled by the public handicapper.

In assessing the propriety of judicial intervention under the Fourteenth Amendment these three factors and others will be elaborated in more detail. They are noted at this preliminary stage to suggest both that systematic discrimination in quality of public education may be viewed as a realistic constitutional issue and that the objection to it is in many respects an intensely conservative one. This latter observation is useful here to parry or at least postpone the natural reaction that equality is once more to become the leveler's stalking horse. The truth is not so simple. The case for equality in public education is a schizophrenic medley of Karl Marx and Barry Goldwater, St. Thomas and Saint-Simon. Reservation of judgment is all that can be asked, but nothing less will do.

The problem is complicated principally by the value that Americans place on local decision-making—a value we shall label "subsidiarity." Few would object in theory to equality of educational opportunity if that result did not seem necessarily to cast out local choice. Some argue simplistically that equality of educational opportunity is flatly inconsistent with local authority. [See, e. g., Phillip Kurland, "Equal Educational Opportunity: The Limits of Constitutional Jurisprudence Undefined," *University of Chicago Law Review*, 35:583 (1968). (See also A. E. Wise, *Rich Schools, Poor Schools: The Promise of Equal Educational Opportunity* (Chicago: University of Chicago Press, 1968).] We are convinced that this supposed antithesis between equality and subsidiarity is overdrawn: that both values can be preserved if only one is willing to struggle with the complexities and fine tuning required of any balanced system. Much of this book involves an analysis of the relation between the two values and of structures designed to achieve such a balance. A moment's reflection will suggest the significance of such structures for the movement toward greater decentralization of control in public education. Until it descends to the level of the family, the drift toward smaller units in education has no natural limit other than the ability of such units to finance themselves. . . .

SERRANO v. PRIEST

Supreme Court of California, 1971.
5 Cal.3d 584, 96 Cal.Rptr. 601, 487 P.2d 1241.

SULLIVAN, Justice. We are called upon to determine whether the California public school financing system, with its substantial dependence on local property taxes and resultant wide disparities in school revenue, violates the equal protection clause of the Fourteenth Amendment. . . .

We begin our task by examining the California public school financing system which is the focal point of the complaint's allegations. At the threshold we find a fundamental statistic—over 90 percent of our public school funds derive from two basic sources: (a) local district taxes on real property and (b) aid from the State School Fund.

By far the major source of school revenue is the local real property tax. Pursuant to article IX, section 6 of the California Constitution, the Legislature has authorized the governing body of each county, and city and county, to levy taxes on the real property within a

school district at a rate necessary to meet the district's annual education budget. . . .   The amount of revenue which a district can
raise in this manner thus depends largely on its tax base—i. e., the
assessed valuation of real property within its borders.   Tax bases
vary widely throughout the state; in 1969–1970, for example, the assessed valuation per unit of average daily attendance of elementary
school children ranged from a low of $103 to a peak of $952,156—a
ratio of nearly 1 to 10,000. . . .

The other factor determining local school revenue is the rate of
taxation within the district.   Although the legislature has placed ceil-
ings on permissible district tax rates . . . these statutory max-
ima may be surpassed in a "tax override" election if a majority of
the district's voters approve a higher rate. . . .   Nearly all districts
have voted to override the statutory limits.   Thus the locally raised
funds which constitute the largest portion of school revenue are
primarily a function of the value of the realty within a particular
school district, coupled with the willingness of the district's residents
to tax themselves for education.

Most of the remaining school revenue comes from the State
School Fund pursuant to the "foundation program," through which
the state undertakes to supplement local taxes in order to provide a
"minimum amount of guaranteed support to all districts   *   *   *."
. . . With certain minor exceptions, the foundation program en-
sures that each school district will receive annually, from state or
local funds, $355 for each elementary school pupil . . . and $488
for each high school student. . . .

The state contribution is supplied in two principal forms.   "Basic
state aid" consists of a flat grant to each district of $125 per pupil
per year, regardless of the relative wealth of the district. . . .
"Equalization aid" is distributed in inverse proportion to the wealth
of the district.

To compute the amount of equalization aid to which a district
is entitled, the State Superintendent of Public Instruction first determines how much local property tax revenue would be generated if
the district were to levy a hypothetical tax at the rate of $1 on each
$100 of assessed valuation in elementary school district and $.80 per
$100 in high school districts. . . .   To that figure, he adds the
$125 per pupil basic aid grant.   If the sum of those two amounts is
less than the foundation program minimum for that district, the
state contributes the difference. . . .   Thus, equalization funds
guarantee to the poorer districts a basic minimum revenue, while
wealthier districts are ineligible for such assistance.

An additional state program of "supplemental aid" is available
to subsidize particularly poor school districts which are willing to
make an extra local tax effort.   An elementary district with an assessed valuation of $12,500 or less per pupil may obtain up to $125

more for each child if it sets its local tax rate above a certain statutory level.   A high school district whose assessed valuation does not exceed $24,500 per pupil is eligible for a supplement of up to $72 per child if its local tax is sufficiently high. . . .

Although equalization aid and supplemental aid temper the disparities which result from the vast variations in real property assessed valuation, wide differentials remain in the revenue available to individual districts and, consequently, in the level of educational expenditures.   For example, in Los Angeles County, where plaintiff children attend school, the Baldwin Park Unified School District expended only $577.49 to educate each of its pupils in 1968–1969; during the same year the Pasadena Unified School District spent $840.19 on every student; and the Beverly Hills Unified School District paid out $1,231.72 per child.   . . .   The source of these disparities is unmistakable: in Baldwin Park the assessed valuation per child totaled only $3,706; in Pasadena, assessed valuation was $13,706; while in Beverly Hills, the corresponding figure was $50,885—a ratio of 1 to 4 to 13.   Thus, the state grants are inadequate to offset the inequalities inherent in a financing system based on widely varying local tax bases.

Furthermore, basic aid, which constitutes about half of the state educational funds . . .   actually widens the gap between rich and poor districts.   . . .   Such aid is distributed on a uniform per pupil basis to all districts, irrespective of a district's wealth.   Beverly Hills, as well as Baldwin Park, receives $125 from the state for each of its students.

For Baldwin Park the basic grant is essentially meaningless. Under the foundation program the state must make up the difference between $355 per elementary child and $47.91, the amount of revenue per child which Baldwin Park could raise by levying a tax of $1 per $100 of assessed valuation.   Although under present law, that difference is composed partly of basic aid and partly of equalization aid, if the basic aid grant did not exist, the district would still receive the same amount of state aid—all in equalizing funds.

For Beverly Hills, however, the $125 flat grant has real financial significance.   Since a tax rate of $1 per $100 there would produce $870 per elementary student, Beverly Hills is far too rich to qualify for equalizing aid.   Nevertheless, it still receives $125 per child from the state, thus enlarging the economic chasm between it and Baldwin Park.   (See Coons, Clune & Sugarman, Educational Opportunity: A Workable Constitutional Test for State Financial Structures (1969) 57 Cal.L.Rev. 305, 315.)

Having outlined the basic framework of California school financing, we take up plaintiffs' legal claims.   Preliminarily, we reject their contention that the school financing system violates article IX, section 5 of the California Constitution, which states, in pertinent part: "The Legislature shall provide for *a system of common schools* by which a free school shall be kept up and supported in each district at least six months in every year * * *." (Italics added.) Plaintiffs' argument is that the present financing method produces separate and distinct systems, each offering an educational program which varies with the relative wealth of the district's residents.

. . .

Having disposed of these preliminary matters, we take up the chief contention underlying plaintiffs' complaint, namely that the California public school financing scheme violates the equal protection clause of the Fourteenth Amendment to the United State Constitution.

As recent decisions of this court have pointed out, the United States Supreme Court has employed a two-level test for measuring legislative classifications against the equal protection clause. "In the area of economic regulation, the high court has exercised restraint, investing legislation with a presumption of constitutionality and requiring merely that distinctions drawn by a challenged statute bear some rational relationship to a conceivable legitimate state purpose. [Citations.]

"On the other hand, in cases involving 'suspect classifications' or touching on 'fundamental interests,' [fns. omitted] the court has adopted an attitude of active and critical analysis, subjecting the classification to strict scrutiny. [Citations.] Under the strict standard applied in such cases, the state bears the burden of establishing not only that it has a *compelling* interest which justifies the law but that the distinctions drawn by the law are *necessary* to further its purpose." .   .   .

Wealth as a Suspect Classification

In recent years, the United States Supreme Court has demonstrated a marked antipathy toward legislative classifications which discriminate on the basis of certain "suspect" personal characteristics. One factor which has repeatedly come under the close scrutiny of the high court is wealth. "Lines drawn on the basis of wealth or property, like those of race [citation], are traditionally disfavored." (Harper v. Virginia State Bd. of Elections (1966) 383 U.S. 663, .   .   .) Invalidating the Virginia poll tax in *Harper*, the court stated: "To introduce wealth or payment of a fee as a measure of a voter's qualifications is to introduce a capricious or irrelevant factor." "[A] careful examination on our part is especially warranted where lines are drawn on the basis of wealth * * * [a] factor which would independently render a classification highly suspect and thereby demand a more exacting judicial scrutiny. [Citations.]" .   .   .

Plaintiffs contend that the school financing system classifies on the basis of wealth. We find this proposition irrefutable. As we have already discussed, over half of all educational revenue is raised locally by levying taxes on real property in the individual school districts. Above the foundation program minimum ($355 per elementary student and $488 per high school student), the wealth of a school district, as measured by its assessed valuation, is the major determinant of educational expenditures. Although the amount of money raised locally is also a function of the rate at which the residents of a district are willing to tax themselves, as a practical matter districts with small tax bases simply cannot levy taxes at a rate sufficient to produce the revenue that more affluent districts reap with minimal tax efforts. . . . For example, Baldwin Park citizens, who paid a school tax of $5.48 per $100 of assessed valuation in 1968–1969, were able to spend less than half as much on education as Beverly Hills residents, who were taxed only $2.38 per $100. . . .

Defendants vigorously dispute the proposition that the financing scheme discriminates on the basis of wealth. Their first argument is essentially this: through *basic* aid, the state distributes school funds equally to all pupils; through *equalization* aid, it distributes funds in a manner beneficial to the poor districts. However, state funds constitute only one part of the entire school fiscal system. The foundation program partially alleviates the great disparities in local sources of revenue, but the system as a whole generates school revenue in proportion to the wealth of the individual district.

Defendants also argue that neither assessed valuation per pupil nor expenditure per pupil is a reliable index of the wealth of a district or of its residents. The former figure is untrustworthy, they assert, because a district with a low total assessed valuation but a miniscule number of students will have a high per pupil tax base and thus appear "wealthy". Defendants imply that the proper index of a district's wealth is the total assessed valuation of its property. We think defendants' contention misses the point. The only meaningful measure of a district's wealth in the present context is not the absolute value of its property, but the ratio of its resources to pupils, because it is the latter figure which determines how much the district can devote to educating each of its students.

But, say defendants, the expenditure per child does not accurately reflect a district's wealth because that expenditure is partly determined by the district's tax rate. Thus, a district with a high total assessed valuation might levy a low school tax, and end up spending the same amount per pupil as a poorer district whose residents opt to pay higher taxes. This argument is also meritless. Obviously, the richer district is favored when it can provide the same educational quality for its children with less tax effort. Furthermore as a statistical matter, the poorer districts are financially unable to raise their taxes high enough to match the educational offerings of wealthier districts. . . . Thus, affluent districts can have their cake and eat it too: they can provide a high quality education for their children while paying lower taxes. Poor districts, by contrast, have no cake at all.

Finally, defendants suggest that the wealth of a school district does not necessarily reflect the wealth of the families who live there. The simple answer to this argument is that plaintiffs have alleged that there is a correlation between a district's per pupil assessed valuation and the wealth of its residents and we treat these material facts as admitted by the demurrers.

More basically, however, we reject defendants' underlying thesis that classification by wealth is constitutional so long as the wealth is that of the district, not the individual. We think that discrimination on the basis of district wealth is equally invalid. The commercial and industrial property which augments a district's tax base is distributed unevenly throughout the state. To allot more educational dollars to the children of one district than to those of another merely because of the fortuitous presence of such property is to make the quality of a child's education dependent upon the location of private commercial and industrial establishments. Surely, this is to rely on the most irrelevant of factors as the basis for educational financing.

Defendants, assuming for the sake of argument that the financing system does classify by wealth, nevertheless claim that no constitutional infirmity is involved because the complaint contains no allegation of purposeful or intentional discrimination. . . . Thus, defendants contend, any unequal treatment is only de facto, not de jure. Since the United States Supreme Court has not held de facto school segregation on the basis of race to be unconstitutional, so the argument goes, de facto classifications on the basis of wealth are presumptively valid.

We think that the whole structure of this argument must fall for want of a solid foundation in law and logic. First, none of the wealth classifications previously invalidated by the United States Supreme Court or this court has been the product of purposeful discrimination. Instead, these prior decisions have involved "unintentional" classifications whose impact simply fell more heavily on the poor. . . .

Other cases dealing with the factor of wealth have held that a state may not impose on an indigent certain payments which, although neutral on their face, may have a discriminatory *effect*. In Harper v. Virginia State Bd. of Elections, supra, . . . the high court struck down a $1.50 poll tax, not because its *purpose* was to deter indigents from voting, but because its *result* might be such. . . . In summary, prior decisions have invalidated classifications based on wealth even in the absence of a discriminatory motivation.

We turn now to defendants' related contention that the instant case involves at most de facto discrimination. We disagree. Indeed, we find the case unusual in the extent to which governmental action *is* the cause of the wealth classifications. The school funding scheme is mandated in every detail by the California Constitution and statutes. Although private residential and commercial patterns may be partly responsible for the distribution of assessed valuation throughout the state, such patterns are shaped and hardened by zoning ordinances and other governmental land-use controls which promote economic exclusivity. . . . Governmental action drew the school district boundary lines, thus determining how much local wealth each district would contain. . . .

Finally, even assuming arguendo that defendants are correct in their contention that the instant discrimination based on wealth is merely de facto, and not de jure, such discrimination cannot be justified by analogy to de facto *racial* segregation. Although the United States Supreme Court has not yet ruled on the constitutionality of de facto racial segregation, this court eight years ago held such segregation invalid and declared that school boards should take affirmative steps to alleviate racial imbalance, however created. . . . Consequently, any discrimination based on wealth can hardly be vindicated by reference to de facto racial segregation, which we have already condemned. In sum, we are of the view that the school financing system discriminates on the basis of the wealth of a district and its residents.

B

Education as a Fundamental Interest

But plaintiff's equal protection attack on the fiscal system has an additional dimension. They assert that the system not only draws lines on the basis of wealth but that it "touches upon," indeed has a direct and significant impact upon, a "fundamental interest," namely education. It is urged that these two grounds, particularly in combination, establish a demonstrable denial of equal protection of the laws. To this phase of the argument we now turn our attention.

Until the present time wealth classifications have been invalidated only in conjunction with a limited number of fundamental interests—rights of defendants in criminal cases. . . . and voting rights. . . . Plaintiff's contention—that education is a fundamental interest which may not be conditioned on wealth—is not supported by any direct authority.

We, therefore, begin by examining the indispensable role which education plays in the modern industrial state. This role, we believe, has two significant aspects: first, education is a major determinant of an individual's chances for economic and social success in our competitive society; second, education is a unique influence on a child's development as a citizen and his participation in political and community life. "[T]he pivotal position of education to success in American society and its essential role in opening up to the individual the central experiences of our culture lend it an importance that is undeniable." (Note, Development in the Law—Equal Protection (1969) 82 Harv.L.Rev. 1065, 1129.) Thus, education is the lifeline of both the individual and society.

The fundamental importance of education has been recognized in other contexts by the United States Supreme Court and by this court. These decisions—while not *legally* controlling on the exact issue before us—are persuasive in their accurate factual description of the significance of learning.

The classic expression of this position came in Brown v. Board of Education . . . which invalidated de jure segregation by race in public schools. The high court declared: "Today, education is perhaps the most important function of state and local governments. Compulsory school attendance laws and the great expenditures for education both demonstrate our recognition of the importance of education to our democratic society. It is required in the performance of our most basic public responsibilities, even service in the armed forces. It is the very foundation of good citizenship. Today it is a principal instrument in awakening the child to cultural values, in preparing him for later professional training, and in helping him to adjust normally to his environment. In these days, it is doubtful that any child may reasonably be expected to succeed in life if he is denied the opportunity of an education. Such an opportunity, where the state has undertaken to provide it, is a right which must be made available to all on equal terms." . . .

The twin themes of the importance of education to the individual and to society have recurred in numerous decisions of this court. . . .

It is illuminating to compare in importance the right to an education with the rights of defendants in criminal cases and the right to vote—two "fundamental interests" which the Supreme Court has already protected against discrimination based on wealth. Although an individual's interest in his freedom is unique, we think that from a larger perspective, education may have far greater social significance than a free transcript or a court-appointed lawyer. "[E]ducation not only affects directly a vastly greater number of persons than the criminal law, but it affects them in ways which—to the state—have an enormous and much more varied significance. Aside from reducing the crime rate (the inverse relation is strong), education also supports each and every other value of a democratic society—participation, communication, and social mobility, to name but a few." . . .

The analogy between education and voting is much more direct: both are crucial to participation in, and the functioning of, a democracy. Voting has been regarded as a fundamental right because it is "preservative of other basic civil and political rights * * *."

.   .   .   At a minimum, education makes more meaningful the casting of a ballot.   More significantly, it is likely to provide the understanding of, and the interest in, public issues which are the spur to involvement in other civic and political activities.

The need for an educated populace assumes greater importance as the problems of our diverse society become increasingly complex. The United States Supreme Court has repeatedly recognized the role of public education as a unifying social force and the basic tool for shaping democratic values.   The public school has been termed "the most powerful agency for promoting cohesion among a heterogeneous democratic people   *   *   *   at once the symbol of our democracy and the most pervasive means for promoting our common destiny."
.   .   .

We are convinced that the distinctive and priceless function of education in our society warrants, indeed compels, our treating it as a "fundamental interest."

First, education is essential in maintaining what several commentators have termed "free enterprise democracy"—that is, preserving an individual's opportunity to compete successfully in the economic marketplace, despite a disadvantaged background.   Accordingly, the public schools of this state are the bright hope for entry of the poor and oppressed into the mainstream of American society.

Second, education is universally relevant.   "Not every person finds it necessary to call upon the fire department or even the police in an entire lifetime.   Relative few are on welfare.   Every person, however, benefits from education   *   *   *."   .   .   .

Third, public education continues over a lengthy period of life—between 10 and 13 years.   Few other government services have such sustained, intensive contact with the recipient.

Fourth, education is unmatched in the extent to which it molds the personality of the youth of society.   While police and fire protection, garbage collection and street lights are essentially neutral in their effect on the individual psyche, public education actively attempts to shape a child's personal development in a manner chosen not by the child or his parents but by the state.   .   .   .   "[T]he influence of the school is not confined to how well it can teach the disadvantaged child; it also has a significant role to play in shaping the student's emotional and psychological make-up."   .   .   .

Finally, education is so important that the state has made it compulsory—not only in the requirement of attendance but also by assignment to a particular district and school.   Although a child of wealthy parents has the opportunity to attend a private school, this freedom is seldom available to the indigent.   In this context, it has been suggested that "a child of the poor assigned willy-nilly to an inferior state school takes on the complexion of a prisoner, complete with a minimum sentence of 12 years."   .   .   .

C

The Financing System is Not Necessary to Accomplish a Compelling State Interest

We now reach the final step in the application of the "strict scrutiny" equal protection standard—the determination of whether the California school financing system, as presently structured, is necessary to achieve a compelling state interest.

The state interest which defendants advance in support of the current fiscal scheme is California's policy "to strengthen and encourage local responsibility for control of public education."   .   .   . We treat separately the two possible aspects of this goal: first, the granting to local districts of effective decision-making power over the administration of their schools; and second, the promotion of local fiscal control over the amount of money to be spent on education.

The individual district may well be in the best position to decide whom to hire, how to schedule its educational offerings, and a host of other matters which are either of significant local impact or of such a detailed nature as to require decentralized determination. But even assuming arguendo that local administrative control may be a compelling state interest, the present financial system cannot be considered necessary to further this interest. No matter how the state decides to finance its system of public education, it can still leave this decision-making power in the hands of local districts.

The other asserted policy interest is that of allowing a local district to choose how much it wishes to spend on the education of its children. Defendants argue: "[I]f one district raises a lesser amount per pupil than another district, this is a matter of choice and preference of the individual district and reflects the individual desire for lower taxes rather than an expanded educational program, or may reflect a greater interest within that district in such other services that are supported by local property taxes as, for example, police and fire protection or hospital services."

We need not decide whether such decentralized financial decision-making is a compelling state interest, since under the present financing system, such fiscal freewill is a cruel illusion for the poor school districts. We cannot agree that Baldwin Park residents care less about education than those in Beverly Hills solely because Baldwin Park spends less than $600 per child while Beverly Hills spends over $1,200. As defendants themselves recognize, perhaps the most accurate reflection of a community's commitment to education is the rate at which its citizens are willing to tax themselves to support their schools. Yet by that standard, Baldwin Park should be deemed far more devoted to learning than Beverly Hills, for Baldwin Park citizens levied a school tax of well over $5 per $100 of assessed valuation, while residents of Beverly Hills paid only slightly more than $2.

In summary, so long as the assessed valuation within a district's boundaries is a major determinant of how much it can spend for its schools, only a district with a large tax base will be truly able to decide how much it really cares about education. The poor district cannot freely choose to tax itself into an excellence which its tax rolls cannot provide. Far from being necessary to promote local fiscal choice, the present financing system actually deprives the less wealthy districts of that option.

It is convenient at this point to dispose of two final arguments advanced by defendants. They assert, first, that territorial uniformity in respect to the present financing system is not constitutionally required; and secondly, that if under an equal protection mandate relative wealth may not determine the quality of public education, the same rule must be applied to all tax-supported public services. . . . We think that two lines of recent decisions have indicated that where fundamental rights or suspect classifications are at stake, a state's general freedom to discriminate on a geographical basis will be significantly curtailed by the equal protection clause. . . .

Defendants' second argument boils down to this: if the equal protection clause commands that the relative wealth of school districts may not determine the quality of public education, it must be deemed to direct the same command to all governmental entities in respect to all tax-supported public services; and such a principle would spell the destruction of local government. We unhesitatingly reject this argument. We cannot share defendants' unreasoned apprehensions of such dire consequences from our holding today. Although we intimate no views on other governmental services, we are satisfied that, as we have explained, its uniqueness among public activities clearly demonstrates that *education* must respond to the command of the equal protection clause.

We, therefore, arrive at these conclusions. The California public school financing system, as presented to us by plaintiff's complaint supplemented by matters judicially noticed, since it deals intimately with education, obviously touches upon a fundamental interest. For the reasons we have explained in detail, this system conditions the full entitlement to such interest on wealth, classifies its recipients on the basis of their collective affluence and makes the quality of a child's education depend upon the resources of his school district and ultimately upon the pocketbook of his parents. We find that such financing system as presently constituted is not necessary to the attainment of any compelling state interest. Since it does not withstand the requisite "strict scrutiny," it denies to the plaintiffs and others similarly situated the equal protection of the laws. If the allegations of the complaint are sustained, the financial system must fall and the statutes comprising it must be found unconstitutional.

. . .

NOTES AND QUESTIONS

1. Did the court in Serrano say that wealth classifications based on property valuations within school districts were "suspect" and that education was a "fundamental" right? Were these the reasons for requiring the state to show that a compelling state interest was served by its acts rather than a showing that a rational relationship existed between the state action and a legitimate state interest?

2. Is the crucial role education plays in the context of other constitutional values, for example, substantial rights protected under the First and Fifteenth Amendments, sufficient justification for holding it a "fundamental interest," requiring a state to demonstrate a "compelling state interest" to justify a classification based on unequal wealth?

3. Is the right to education a "fundamental interest" especially protected under the State and Federal Constitutions? Is it more important to be well housed or well fed? Are the latter interests especially protected? If not, then why education? Was Serrano decided under the state and federal constitutions? Is this important?

4. In Serrano, was the equal protection clause applied to children, taxpayers, or to school districts? Does it make a difference? What concept of equal educational opportunity is involved in Serrano.

5. Under the rationale of Serrano could each school district spend different amounts on education per student if it chose different property tax rates so long as the state guaranteed equal per capita education revenues to students in different school districts taxing at the same rate?

6. Should the allocation of educational resources among students within a state depend upon where a student lives within the state; on his parents wealth, or on how his neighbors within his school district value education? On what should it depend? Why? Suppose, collectively, the parents of students in school district A didn't value education very highly and accordingly voted for a very low property tax rate but that the parents of students in school district B, on the contrary, valued education most highly and, therefore, voted for a very high property tax rate to provide for "the best education that money can buy." Should the "sins" of the parents be visited upon their student children?

7. Is per capita expenditure on education necessarily a true measure of the quality of the education offered? How significant is non-neutral state fiscal policy in education to the student?

8. Does Serrano's rationale rely on the unsupported premise that poor people live in school districts with low property values? Isn't it often true that poor people live in housing near industrial complexes, for example, which could provide a much higher property value base for its school district than, say, middle-class residential suburbs which draw their property tax revenues almost exclusively from moderately valued residential housing?

9. A concept of equal access is that all participants are afforded the same opportunity to enter into participation, but no effort is made to compensate for any of the participant's disabilities which impede his progress. For example, all have an equal opportunity, so far as the state is concerned, to start a business enterprise, but no special state aid is provided to one who is an inadequate businessman so that he can function successfully in the business world. He either stands or falls, as a businessman, on his own ability. But, in the realm of public education consider the President's Commission on School Finance, Final Report, Schools, People & Money (1972). That report states that "[t]he only reasonable and defensible public policy for communities, States, and the Nation is to ensure to all children equal access to education that is good enough to meet their individual needs and the collective demands of a growing economy in a democratic society. . . . To provide necessary resources, children with educational needs greater than others should receive special attention. This can be expected to require more resources, generally in the form of adult classroom staff. While it is difficult to determine absolute needs for any child, the principle of relative or comparative needs should be employed." Thus, the report recommends the dispensing of compensatory and unequal educational resources designed to overcome or minimize the disability of the low achiever. That is, the report recommends allocating educational resources not equally among students but in proportion to their "educational needs." Thus, schools would be unequal, but they would be equalizers. How do you suppose, the commission justified this distribution of public resources? Could such unequal resource allocation be justified on the rationale that the state has a legitimate and compelling interest in assuring that its citizens have the necessary skills for self-government and that even non-egalitarian means which assure that egalitarian end are justified? Would such a rationale justify a state's allocating revenues to a school district in an inverse proportion to the achievement of its students, other factors being equal? Should it? Would our democratic system of self-government be best served by such a scheme of education or by equal access only? Why?

10. If in the near future the states do approximate the Serrano standard, the inevitable next issue will concern inequities between and among the states. If education is truly a fundamental interest, shielded by the Fourteenth Amendment, why should the accident of location in New Mexico or Nevada instead of in California or New York condemn an innocent child to an inferior education? If it is both inappropriate and illegal to use wealth as an educational criterion within states, should it not be equally inappropriate and illegal to allow wealth to define educational opportunity between and among the states? Lawyers can distinguish between the two situations, can you? The disparities of wealth among the states are likely to become the sort of issue that wealth differences within states already are. Would Bolling v. Sharp, supra, provide the needed rationale? Why or why not? See, e. g., Lekachman, "Schools, Money & Politics: Financing Public Education," The New Leader, Sept. 18 (1972).

SAN ANTONIO INDEPENDENT SCHOOL DIST. v.
RODRIGUEZ

Supreme Court of the United States, 1973.
409 U.S. 822, 93 S.Ct. 40, 34 L.Ed.2d 77.

Mr. Justice POWELL delivered the opinion of the Court.

This suit attacking the Texas system of financing public education was initiated by Mexican-American parents whose children attend the elementary and secondary schools in the Edgewood Independent School District, an urban school district in San Antonio, Texas. They brought a class action on behalf of school children throughout the State who are members of minority groups or who are poor and reside in school districts having a low property tax base.   . . .

I

The first Texas Constitution, promulgated upon Texas' entry into the Union in 1845, provided for the establishment of a system of free schools. Early in its history, Texas adopted a dual approach to the financing of its schools, relying on mutual participation by the local school districts and the State.   . . .

Until recent times Texas was a predominantly rural State and its population and property wealth were spread relatively evenly across the State. Sizable differences in the value of assessable property between local school districts became increasingly evident as the State became more industrialized and as rural-to-urban population shifts became more pronounced. The location of commercial and industrial property began to play a significant role in determining the amount of tax resources available to each school district. These growing disparities in population and taxable property between districts were responsible in part for increasingly notable differences in levels of local expenditure for education.   . . .

Recognizing the need for increased state funding to help offset disparities in local spending and to meet Texas' changing educational requirements, the state legislature in the late 1940's undertook a thorough evaluation of public education with an eye toward major reform. [After review, it] establish[ed] the Texas Minimum Foundation School Program. Today this Program accounts for approximately half of the total educational expenditures in Texas.

The Program calls for state and local contributions to a fund earmarked specifically for teacher salaries, operating expenses, and transportation costs. The State, supplying funds from its general revenues, finances approximately 80% of the Program, and the school districts are responsible—as a unit—for providing the remaining 20%. The districts' share, known as the Local Fund Assignment, is apportioned among the school districts under a formula designed to reflect each district's relative taxpaying ability.   . . . .   In the years since this program went into operation in 1949, expenditures for education—from State as well as local sources—have increased steadily. Between 1949 and 1967 expenditures increased by approximately 500%. . . .

The school district in which appellees reside, the Edgewood Independent School District, has been compared throughout this litigation with the Alamo Heights Independent School District. This comparison between the least and most affluent districts in the San Antonio area serves to illustrate the manner in which the dual system of finance operates. . . . Edgewood is one of seven public school districts in the metropolitan area. Approximately 22,000 students are enrolled in its 25 elementary and secondary schools. The district is situated in the core-city sector of San Antonio in a residential neighborhood that has little commercial or industrial property. The residents are predominantly of Mexican-American descent: approximately 90% of the student population is Mexican-American and over 6% is Negro. The average assessed property value per pupil is $5,960—the lowest in the metropolitan area—and the median family income ($4,686) is also the lowest. At an equalized tax rate of $1.05 per $100 of assessed property—the highest in the metropolitan area—the district contributed $26 to the education of each child for the 1967–1968 school year above its Local Fund Assignment for the Minimum Foundation Program. The Foundation Program contributed $222 per pupil for a state-local total of $248. Federal funds added another $108 for a total of $356 per pupil.

Alamo Heights is the most affluent school district in San Antonio. Its six schools, housing approximately 5,000 students, are situated in a residential community quite unlike the Edgewood District. The school population is predominantly Anglo, having only 18% Mexican-Americans and less than 1% Negroes. The assessed property value per pupil exceeds $49,000 and the median family income is $8,001. In 1967–1968 the local tax rate of $.85 per $100 of valuation yielded $333 per pupil over and above its contribution to the Foundation Program. Coupled with the $225 provided from that Program, the district was able to supply $558 per student. Supplemented by a $36 per pupil grant from federal sources, Alamo Heights spent $594 per pupil.

Although the 1967–1968 school year figures provide the only complete statistical breakdown for each category of aid, more recent partial statistics indicate that the previously noted trend of increasing state aid has been significant. For the 1970–1971 school year, the Foundation School Program allotment for Edgewood was $356 per pupil. . . . Alamo Heights enjoyed a similar increase under the Foundation Program, netting $491 per pupil in 1970–1971. These recent figures also reveal the extent to which these two districts' allotments were funded from their own required contributions to the Local Fund Assignment. Alamo Heights, because of its relative wealth, was required to contribute out of its local property tax

collections approximately $100 per pupil, or about 20% of its Founda-
tion grant. Edgewood, on the other hand, paid only $8.46 per pupil,
which is about 2.4% of its grant,   .   .   .   it was these disparities,
largely attributable to differences in the amounts of money collected
through local property taxation, that led the District Court to conclude that Texas' dual system of public school finance violated the
Equal Protection Clause. The District Court held that the Texas system discriminates on the basis of wealth in the manner in which education is provided for its people. Finding that wealth is a "suspect"
classification and that education is a "fundamental" interest, the
District Court held that the Texas system could be sustained only if
the State could show that it was premised upon some compelling state
interest. On this issue the court concluded that "[n]ot only are defendants unable to demonstrate compelling state interests   .   .   .
they fail even to establish a reasonable basis for these classifications."

II

The wealth discrimination discovered by the District Court in
this case, and by several other courts that have recently struck down
school financing laws in other States, is quite unlike any of the forms
of wealth discrimination heretofore reviewed by this Court. Rather
than focusing on the unique features of the alleged discrimination,
the courts in these cases have virtually assumed their findings of a
suspect classification through a simplistic process of analysis: since,
under the traditional systems of financing public schools, some poorer
people receive less expensive educations than other more affluent
people, these systems discriminate on the basis of wealth. This approach largely ignores the hard threshold questions, including whether
it makes a difference for purposes of consideration under the Constitution that the class of disadvantaged "poor" cannot be identified
or defined in customary equal protection terms, and whether the relative—rather than absolute—nature of the asserted deprivation is of
significant consequence. Before a State's laws and the justifications
for the classifications they create are subjected to strict judicial scrutiny, we think these threshold considerations must be analyzed more
closely than they were in the court below.

The case comes to us with no definitive description of the classifying facts or delineation of the disfavored class. Examination of
the District Court's opinion and of appellees' complaint, briefs, and
contentions at oral argument suggests, however, at least three ways
in which the discrimination claimed here might be described. The
Texas system of school finance might be regarded as discriminating
(1) against "poor" persons whose incomes fall below some identifiable
level of poverty or who might be characterized as functionally "indigent," or (2) against those who are relatively poorer than others,
or (3) against all those who, irrespective of their personal incomes,

happen to reside in relatively poorer school districts. Our task must be to ascertain whether, in fact, the Texas system has been shown to discriminate on any of these possible bases and, if so, whether the resulting classification may be regarded as suspect.

The precedents of this Court provide the proper starting point. The individuals or groups of individuals who constituted the class discriminated against in our prior cases shared two distinguishing characteristics: because of their impecunity they were completely unable to pay for some desired benefit, and as a consequence, they sustained an absolute deprivation of a meaningful opportunity to enjoy that benefit. In Griffin v. Illinois, 351 U.S. 12, 76 S.Ct. 585, 100 L. Ed. 891 (1956), and its progeny, the Court invalidated state laws that prevented an indigent criminal defendant from acquiring a transcript, or an adequate substitute for a transcript, for use at several stages of the trial and appeal process. The payment requirements in each case were found to occasion *de facto* discrimination against those who, because of their indigency, were totally unable to pay for transcripts. And, the Court in each case emphasized that no constitutional violation would have been shown if the State had provided some "adequate substitute" for a full stenographic transcript.

Likewise, in Douglas v. California, 372 U.S. 353, 83 S.Ct. 814, 9 L.Ed.2d 811 (1963), a decision establishing an indigent defendant's right to court-appointed counsel on direct appeal, the Court dealt only with defendants who could not pay for counsel from their own resources and who had no other way of gaining representation. *Douglas* provides no relief for those on whom the burdens of paying for a criminal defense are relatively speaking, great but not insurmountable. Nor does it deal with relative differences in the quality of counsel acquired by the less wealthy.

Williams v. Illinois, 399 U.S. 235, 90 S.Ct. 2018, 26 L.Ed.2d 586 (1970), and Tate v. Short, 401 U.S. 395, 91 S.Ct. 668, 28 L.Ed.2d 130 (1971), struck down criminal penalties that subjected indigents to incarceration simply because of their inability to pay a fine. Again, the disadvantaged class was composed only of persons who were totally unable to pay the demanded sum. Those cases do not touch on the question whether equal protection is denied to persons with relatively less money on whom designated fines impose heavier burdens. The Court has not held that fines must be structured to reflect each person's ability to pay in order to avoid disproportionate burdens. Sentencing judges may, and often do, consider the defendant's ability to pay, but in such circumstances they are guided by sound judicial discretion rather than by constitutional mandate.

Finally, in Bullock v. Carter, 405 U.S. 134, 92 S.Ct. 849, 31 L.Ed. 2d 92 (1972), the Court invalidated the Texas filing fee requirement for primary elections. Both of the relevant classifying facts found in the previous cases were present there. The size of the fee, often runing into the thousands of dollars and, in at least one case, as high as $8,900, effectively barred all potential candidates who were unable to pay the required fee.   As the system provided "no reasonable alternative means of access to the ballot" inability to pay occasioned an absolute denial of a position on the primary ballot.

.   .   .   Even a cursory examination, however, demonstrates that neither of the two distinguishing characteristics of wealth classifications can be found here.   First, in support of their charge that the system discriminates against the "poor," appellees have made no effort to demonstrate that it operates to the peculiar disadvantage of any class fairly definable as indigent, or as composed of persons whose incomes are beneath any designated poverty level.   Indeed, there is reason to believe that the poorest families are not necessarily clustered in the poorest property districts.   A recent and exhaustive study of school districts in Connecticut concluded that "[i]t is clearly incorrect   .   .   .   to contend that the 'poor' live in 'poor' districts .   .   .   .   Thus, the major factual assumption of *Serrano*—that the educational finance system discriminates against the 'poor'—is simply false in Connecticut." Defining "poor" families as those below the Bureau of the Census "poverty level," the Connecticut study found, not surprisingly, that the poor were clustered around commercial and industrial areas—those same areas that provide the most attractive sources of property tax income for school districts.   Whether a similar pattern would be discovered in Texas is not known, but there is no basis on the record in this case for assuming that the poorest people—defined by reference to any level of absolute impecunity—are concentrated in the poorest districts.

Second, neither appellees nor the District Court addressed the fact that, unlike each of the foregoing cases, lack of personal resources has not occasioned an absolute deprivation of the desired benefit. The argument here is not that the children in districts having relatively low assessable property values are receiving no public education; rather, it is that they are receiving a poorer quality education than that available to children in districts having more assessable wealth. Apart from the unsettled and disputed question whether the quality of education may be determined by the amount of money expended for it, a sufficient answer to appellees' argument is that at least where wealth is involved the Equal Protection Clause does not require absolute equality or precisely equal advantages.   Nor indeed, in view of the infinite variables affecting the educational process, can any system assure equal quality of education except in the most relative sense.   Texas asserts that the Minimum Foundation Program provides an "adequate" education for all children in the State.   By providing 12 years of free public school education, and by assuring teachers, books, transportation and operating funds, the Texas Legislature has endeavored to "guarantee, for the welfare of the state as a whole, that all people shall have at least an adequate program of education.

This is what is meant by 'A Minimum Foundation Program of Education.' " The State repeatedly asserted in its briefs in this Court that it has fulfilled this desire and that it now assures "every child in every school district an adequate education." No proof was offered at trial persuasively discrediting or refuting the State's assertion.

For these two reasons—the absence of any evidence that the financing system discriminates against any definable category of "poor" people or that it results in the absolute deprivation of education—the disadvantaged class is not susceptible to identification in traditional terms.

As suggested above, appellees and the District Court may have embraced a second or third approach, the second of which might be characterized as a theory of relative or comparative discrimination based on family income. Appellees sought to prove that a direct correlation exists between the wealth of families within each district and the expenditures therein for education. That is, along a continuum, the poorer the family the lower the dollar amount of education received by the family's children. . . . These questions need not be addressed in this case, however, since appellees' proof fails to support their allegations or the District Court's conclusions.

This brings us, then, to the third way in which the classification scheme might be defined—*district* wealth discrimination. Since the only correlation indicated by the evidence is between district property wealth and expenditures, it may be argued that discrimination might be found without regard to the individual income characteristics of district residents. . . . district except the district that has the most assessable wealth and spends the most on education. Alternatively, as suggested in Mr. Justice MARSHALL's dissenting opinion the class might be defined more restrictively to include children in districts with assessable property which falls below the state-wide average, or median, or below some other artificially defined level.

However described, it is clear that appellees' suit asks this Court to extend its most exacting scrutiny to review a system that allegedly discriminates against a large, diverse, and amorphous class, unified only by the common factor of residence in districts that happen to have less taxable wealth than other districts. The system of alleged discrimination and the class it defines have none of the traditional indicia of suspectness: the class is not saddled with such disabilities, or subjected to such a history of purposeful unequal treatment, or relegated to such a position of political powerlessness as to command extraordinary protection from the majoritarian political process.

We thus conclude that the Texas system does not operate to the peculiar disadvantage of any suspect class. But in recognition of the fact that this Court has never heretofore held that wealth discrimination alone provides an adequate basis for invoking strict scrutiny, appellees have not relied solely on this contention. They also assert that the State's system impermissibly interferes with the exercise of a "fundamental" right and that accordingly the prior decisions of this Court require the application of the strict standard of judicial review.   It is this question—whether education is a fundamental right, in the sense that it is among the rights and liberties protected by the Constitution—which has so consumed the attention of courts and commentators in recent years.

Nothing this Court holds today in any way detracts from our historic dedication to public education.   We are in complete agreement with the conclusion of the three-judge panel below that "the grave significance of education both to the individual and to our society" cannot be doubted.   But the importance of a service performed by the State does not determine whether it must be regarded as fundamental for purposes of examination under the Equal Protection Clause.   .   .   .   It is not the province of this Court to create substantive constitutional rights in the name of guaranteeing equal protection of the laws.   Thus the key to discovering whether education is "fundamental" is not to be found in comparisons of the relative societal significance of education as opposed to subsistence or housing.   Nor is it to be found by weighing whether education is as important as the right to travel.   Rather, the answer lies in assessing whether there is a right to education explicitly or implicitly guaranteed by the Constitution.

Education, of course, is not among the rights afforded explicit protection under our Federal Constitution.   Nor do we find any basis for saying it is implicitly so protected.   As we have said, the undisputed importance of education will not alone cause this Court to depart from the usual standard for reviewing a State's social and economic legislation.   It is appellees' contention, however, that education is distinguishable from other services and benefits provided by the State because it bears a peculiarly close relationship to other rights and liberties accorded protection under the Constitution.   Specifically, they insist that education is itself a fundamental personal right because it is essential to the effective exercise of First Amendment freedoms and to intelligent utilization of the right to vote.   In asserting a nexus between speech and education, appellees urge that the right to speak is meaningless unless the speaker is capable of articulating his thoughts intelligently and persuasively.   The "marketplace of ideas" is an empty forum for those lacking basic communicative tools.   Likewise, they argue that the corollary right to receive information becomes little more than a hollow privilege when the recipient has not been taught to read, assimilate, and utilize available knowledge.

A similar line of reasoning is pursued with respect to the right to vote.   Exercise of the franchise, it is contended, cannot be divorced from the educational foundation of the voter.   The electoral process, if reality is to conform to the democratic ideal, depends on an informed electorate: a voter cannot cast his ballot intelligently unless his reading skills and thought processes have been adequately developed.

We need not dispute any of these propositions. The Court has long afforded zealous protection against unjustifiable governmental interference with the individual's rights to speak and to vote. Yet we have never presumed to possess either the ability or the authority to guarantee to the citizenry the most *effective* speech or the most *informed* electoral choice. That these may be desirable goals of a system of freedom of expression and of a representative form of government is not to be doubted. These are indeed goals to be pursued by a people whose thoughts and beliefs are freed from governmental interference. But they are not values to be implemented by judicial intrusion into otherwise legitimate state activities.

Even if it were conceded that some identifiable quantum of education is a constitutionally protected prerequisite to the meaningful exercise of either right, we have no indication that the present levels of educational expenditure in Texas provide an education that falls short. Whatever merit appellees' argument might have if a State's financing system occasioned an absolute denial of educational opportunities to any of its children, that argument provides no basis for finding an interference with fundamental rights where only relative differences in spending levels are involved and where—as is true in the present case—no charge fairly could be made that the system fails to provide each child with an opportunity to acquire the basic minimal skills necessary for the enjoyment of the rights of speech and of full participation in the political process.

Furthermore, the logical limitations on appellees' nexus theory are difficult to perceive. How, for instance, is education to be distinguished from the significant personal interests in the basics of decent food and shelter? Empirical examination might well buttress an assumption that the ill-fed, ill-clothed, and ill-housed are among the most ineffective participants in the political process and that they derive the least enjoyment from the benefits of the First Amendment.

.　.　. The present case, in another basic sense, is significantly different from any of the cases in which the Court has applied strict scrutiny to state or federal legislation touching upon constitutionally protected rights. Each of our prior cases involved legislation which "deprived," "infringed," or "interfered" with the free exercise of some such fundamental personal right or liberty. A critical distinction between those cases and the one now before us lies in what Texas is endeavoring to do with respect to education. Mr. Justice Brennan, writing for the Court in Katzenbach v. Morgan, 384 U.S. 641, 86 S.Ct. 1717, 16 L.Ed.2d 828 (1966), expresses well the salient point:

> "This is not a complaint that Congress　.　.　. has unconstitutionally denied or diluted anyone's right to vote but

rather that Congress violated the Constitution by not extending the relief effected [to others similarly situated] .   .   .   .

> "[The federal law in question] does not restrict or deny
> the franchise but in effect extends the franchise to persons
> who otherwise would be denied it by state law. .   .   .
> We need decide only whether the challenged limitation on
> the relief effected   .   .   .   was permissible. In deciding
> that question, the principle that calls for the closest scrutiny
> of distinctions in laws *denying* fundamental rights   .   .   .
> is inapplicable; for the distinction challenged by appellees is
> presented only as a limitation on a reform measure aimed at
> eliminating an existing barrier to the exercise of the fran-
> chise. Rather, in deciding the constitutional propriety of the
> limitations in such a reform measure we are guided by the
> familiar principles that a 'statute is not invalid under the
> Constitution because it might have gone farther than it did,'
> .   .   .   that a legislature need not 'strike at all evils at the
> same time,'   .   .   .   and that 'reform may take one step
> at a time, addressing itself to the phase of the problem which
> seems most acute to the legislative mind   .   .   .   .' " (Em-
> phasis from original.)

The Texas system of school finance is not unlike the federal legislation involved in *Katzenbach* in this regard. Every step leading to
the establishment of the system Texas utilizes today—including the
decisions permitting localities to tax and expend locally, and creating
and continuously expanding the state aid—was implemented in an effort to *extend* public education and to improve its quality. Of course,
every reform that benefits some more than others may be criticized for
what it fails to accomplish. But we think it plain that, in substance,
the thrust of the Texas system is affirmative and reformatory and,
therefore, should be scrutinized under judicial principles sensitive to
the nature of the State's efforts and to the rights reserved to the States
under the Constitution.

We need not rest our decision, however, solely on the inappropri-
ateness of the strict scrutiny test. A century of Supreme Court
adjudication under the Equal Protection Clause affirmatively supports the application of the traditional standard of review, which requires only that the State's system be shown to bear some rational
relationship to legitimate state purposes. This case represents far
more than a challenge to the manner in which Texas provides for
the education of its children. We have here nothing less than a direct
attack on the way in which Texas has chosen to raise and disburse
state and local tax revenues. We are asked to condemn the State's
judgment in conferring on political subdivisions the power to tax local
property to supply revenues for local interests. In so doing, appellees
would have the Court intrude in an area in which it has traditionally

deferred to state legislatures. This Court has often admonished against such interferences with the State's fiscal policies under the Equal Protection Clause   .   .   .

Thus we stand on familiar grounds when we continue to acknowledge that the Justices of this Court lack both the expertise and the familiarity with local problems so necessary to the making of wise decisions with respect to the raising and disposition of public revenues. Yet we are urged to direct the States either to alter drastically the present system or to throw out the property tax altogether in favor of some other form of taxation. No scheme of taxation, whether the tax is imposed on property, income, or purchases of goods and services, has yet been devised which is free of all discriminatory impact. In such a complex arena in which no perfect alternatives exist, the Court does well not to impose too rigorous a standard of scrutiny lest all local fiscal schemes become subjects of criticism under the Equal Protection Clause.

In addition to matters of fiscal policy, this case also involves the most persistent and difficult questions of educational policy, another area in which this Court's lack of specialized knowledge and experience counsels against premature interference with the informed judgments made at the state and local levels. Education, perhaps even more than welfare assistance, presents a myriad of "intractable economic, social, and even philosophical problems." The very complexity of the problems of financing and managing a statewide public school system suggest that "there will be more than one constitutionally permissible method of solving them," and that, within the limits of rationality, "the legislature's efforts to tackle the problems" should be entitled to respect. On even the most basic questions in this area the scholars and educational experts are divided. Indeed, one of the hottest sources of controversy concerns the extent to which there is a demonstrable correlation between educational expenditures and the quality of education—an assumed correlation underlying virtually every legal conclusion drawn by the District Court in this case. Related to the questioned relationship between cost and quality is the equally unsettled controversy as to the proper goals of a system of public education. And the question regarding the most effective relationship between state boards of education and local school boards, in terms of their respective responsibilities and degrees of control, is now undergoing searching re-examination. The ultimate wisdom as to these and related problems of education is not likely to be divined for all time even by the scholars who now so earnestly debate the issues. In such circumstances the judiciary is well advised to refrain from interposing on the States inflexible constitutional restraints that could circumscribe or handicap the continued research and experimentation so vital to finding even partial solutions to educational problems and to keeping abreast of ever changing conditions.

It must be remembered also that every claim arising under the Equal Protection Clause has implications for the relationship between national and state power under our federal system. . . . it would be difficult to imagine a case having a greater potential impact on our federal system than the one now before us, in which we are urged to abrogate systems of financing public education presently in existence in virtually every State.

III

The State's contribution, under the Minimum Foundation Program, was designed to provide an adequate minimum educational offering in every school in the State. Funds are distributed to assure that there will be one teacher—compensated at the state-supported minimum salary—for every 25 students. Each school district's other supportive personnel are provided for: one principal for every 30 teachers; one "special service" teacher—librarian, nurse, doctor, etc. —for every 20 teachers; superintendents, vocational instructors, counselors, and educators for exceptional children are also provided. Additional funds are earmarked for current operating expenses, for student transportation, and for free textbooks.

By virtue of the obligation to fulfill its local Fund Assignment, every district must impose an *ad valorem* tax on property located within its borders. The Fund Assignment was designed to remain sufficiently low to assure that each district would have some ability to provide a more enriched educational program. Every district supplements its foundation grant in this manner. In some districts the local property tax contribution is insubstantial, as in Edgewood where the supplement was only $26 per pupil in 1967. In other districts the local share may far exceed even the total Foundation grant. . . .
In large measure, these additional local revenues are devoted to paying higher salaries to more teachers. Therefore, the primary distinguishing attributes of schools in property-affluent districts are lower pupil-teacher ratios and higher salary schedules. . . . In its reliance on state as well as local resources, the Texas system is comparable to the systems employed in virtually every other State.

. . . While assuring a basic education for every child in the State, it permits and encourages a large measure of participation in and control of each district's schools at the local level. In an era that has witnessed a consistent trend toward centralization of the functions of government, local sharing of responsibility for public education has survived. . . . In part, local control means, as Professor Coleman suggests, the freedom to devote more money to the education of one's children. Equally important, however, is the opportunity it offers for participation in the decision-making process that determines how those local tax dollars will be spent. Each locality is free to tailor local programs to local needs. Pluralism also affords some opportunity for experimentation, innovation, and a healthy competition for educational excellence. An analogy to the Nation-State relationship in our federal system seems uniquely appropriate. Mr. Justice Brandeis identified as one of the peculiar strengths of our form of government each State's freedom to "serve as a laboratory . . . and try novel social and economic experiments." No area of social concern stands to profit more from a multiplicity of viewpoints and from a diversity of approaches than does public education.

. . . While it is no doubt true that reliance on local property taxation for school revenues provides less freedom of choice with respect to expenditures for some districts than for others, the existence of "some inequality" in the manner in which the State's rationale is achieved is not alone a sufficient basis for striking down the entire system. Nor must the financing system fail because, as appellees suggest, other methods of satisfying the State's interest, which occasion "less drastic" disparities in expenditures, might be conceived. Only where state action impinges on the exercise of fundamental constitutional rights or liberties must it be found to have chosen the least restrictive alternative. It is also well to remember that even those districts that have reduced ability to make free decisions with respect to how much they spend on education still retain under the present system a large measure of authority as to how available funds will be allocated. They further enjoy the power to make numerous other decisions with respect to the operation of the schools. The people of Texas may be justified in believing that other systems of school finance, which place more of the financial responsibility in the hands of the State, will result in a comparable lessening of desired local autonomy. That is, they may believe that along with increased control of the purse strings at the state level will go increased control over local policies.

. . . But any scheme of local taxation—indeed the very existence of identifiable local governmental units—requires the establishment of jurisdictional boundaries that are inevitably arbitrary. It is equally inevitable that some localities are going to be blessed with more taxable assets than others. Nor is local wealth a static quantity. Changes in the level of taxable wealth within any district may result from any number of events, some of which local residents can and do influence. For instance, commercial and industrial enterprises may be encouraged to locate within a district by various actions—public and private.

Moreover, if local taxation for local expenditure is an unconstitutional method of providing for education then it may be an equally impermissible means of providing other necessary services customarily financed largely from local property taxes, including local police and fire protection, public health and hospitals, and public utility facilities of various kinds. We perceive no justification for such a severe denigration of local property taxation and control as would follow from appellees' contentions. It has simply never been within the constitutional prerogative of this Court to nullify statewide measures for financing public services merely because the burdens or benefits thereof fall unevenly depending upon the relative wealth of the political subdivisions in which citizens live.

. . . the system here challenged is not peculiar to Texas or to any other State. In its essential characteristics the Texas plan for financing public education reflects what many educators for a half century have thought was an enlightened approach to a problem for which there is no perfect solution. We are unwilling to assume for ourselves a level of wisdom superior to that of legislators, scholars, and educational authorities in 49 States, especially where the alternatives proposed are only recently conceived and nowhere yet tested. The constitutional standard under the Equal Protection Clause is whether the challenged state action rationally furthers a legitimate state purpose or interest. We hold that the Texas plan abundantly satisfies this standard.

IV

. . . this Court's action today is not to be viewed as placing its judicial imprimatur on the status quo. The need is apparent for reform in tax systems which may well have relied too long and too heavily on the local property tax. And certainly innovative new thinking as to public education, its methods and its funding, is necessary to assure both a higher level of quality and greater uniformity of opportunity. These matters merit the continued attention of the scholars who already have contributed much by their challenges. But the ultimate solutions must come from the lawmakers and from the democratic pressures of those who elect them.

Reversed.

Mr. Justice STEWART, concurring.

The method of financing public schools in Texas, as in almost every other State, has resulted in a system of public education that can fairly be described as chaotic and unjust. It does not follow, however, and I cannot find, that this system violates the Constitution of the United States. I join the opinion and judgment of the Court because I am convinced that any other course would mark an extraordinary departure from principled adjudication under the Equal Protection Clause of the Fourteenth Amendment. . . .

Mr. Justice BRENNAN, dissenting.

Although I agree with my Brother WHITE that the Texas statutory scheme is devoid of any rational basis, and for that reason is violative of the Equal Protection Clause, I also record my disagreement with the Court's rather distressing assertion that a right may be deemed "fundamental" for the purposes of equal protection analysis only if it is "explicitly or implicitly guaranteed by the Constitution." As my Brother MARSHALL convincingly demonstrates, our prior cases stand for the proposition that "fundamentality" is, in large measure, a function of the right's importance in terms of the effectuation of those rights which are in fact constitutionally guaranteed. Thus, "[a]s the nexus between the specific constitutional guarantee and the nonconstitutional interest draws closer, the nonconstitutional interest becomes more fundamental and the degree of judicial scrutiny applied when the interest is infringed on a discriminatory basis must be adjusted accordingly."

Here, there can be no doubt that education is inextricably linked to the right to participate in the electoral process and to the rights of free speech and association guaranteed by the First Amendment. This being so, any classification affecting education must be subjected to strict judicial scrutiny, and since even the State concedes that the statutory scheme now before us cannot pass constitutional muster under this stricter standard of review, I can only conclude that the Texas school financing scheme is constitutionally invalid.

Mr. Justice WHITE, with whom Mr. Justice DOUGLAS and Mr. Justice BRENNAN join, dissenting.

. . . this case would be quite different if it were true that the Texas system, while insuring minimum educational expenditures in every district through state funding, extends a meaningful option to all local districts to increase their per-pupil expenditures and so to improve their children's education to the extent that increased funding will achieve that goal. The system would then arguably provide a rational and sensible method of achieving the stated aim of preserving an area for local initiative and decision.

The difficulty with the Texas system, however, is that it provides a meaningful option to Alamo Heights and like school districts but almost none to Edgewood and those other districts with a low per-pupil real estate tax base. In these latter districts, no matter how desirous parents are of supporting their schools with greater revenues, it is impossible to do so through the use of the real estate property tax. In these districts the Texas system utterly fails to extend a realistic choice to parents, because the property tax, which is the only revenue-raising mechanism extended to school districts, is practically and legally unavailable. . . .

Both the Edgewood and Alamo Heights districts are located in Bexar County, Texas. . . . In order to equal the highest yield in any other Bexar County district, Alamo Heights would be required to tax at the rate of 68¢ per $100 of assessed valuation. Edgewood would be required to tax at the prohibitive rate of $5.76 per $100. But state law places a $1.50 per $100 ceiling on the maintenance tax rate, a limit that would surely be reached long before Edgewood attained an equal yield. Edgewood is thus precluded in law, as well as in fact, from achieving a yield even close to that of some other districts.

The Equal Protection Clause permits discriminations between classes but requires that the classification bear some rational relationship to a permissible object sought to be attained by the statute. It is not enough that the Texas system before us seeks to achieve the valid, rational purpose of maximizing local initiative; the means chosen by the State must also be rationally related to the end sought to be achieved. . . .   Requiring the State to establish only that unequal treatment is in furtherance of a permissible goal, without also requirig the State to show that the means chosen to effectuate that goal are rationally related to its achievement, makes equal protection analysis no more than an empty gesture. In my view, the parents and children in Edgewood, and in like districts, suffer from an invidious discrimination violative of the Equal Protection Clause.

. . .

Perhaps the majority believes that the major disparity in revenues provided and permitted by the Texas system is inconsequential. I cannot agree, however, that the difference of the magnitude appearing in this case can sensibly be ignored, particularly since the State itself considers it so important to provide opportunities to exceed the minimum state educational expenditures. . . .

Mr. Justice MARSHALL, with whom Mr. Justice DOUGLAS concurs, dissenting.

The Court today decides, in effect, that a State may constitutionally vary the quality of education which it offers its children in accordance with the amount of taxable wealth located in the school districts within which they reside. The majority's decision represents an abrupt departure from the mainstream of recent state and federal court decisions concerning the unconstitutionality of state educational financing schemes dependent upon taxable local wealth. More unfortunately, though, the majority's holding can only be seen as a retreat from our historic commitment to equality of educational opportunity and as unsupportable acquiescence in a system which deprives children in their earliest years of the chance to reach their full potential as citizens. The Court does this despite the absence of any substantial justification for a scheme which arbitrarily channels educational resources in accordance with the fortuity of the amount of taxable wealth within each district.

In my judgment, the right of every American to an equal start in life, so far as the provision of a state service as important as education is concerned, is far too vital to permit state discrimination on grounds as tenuous as those presented by this record. Nor can I accept the notion that it is sufficient to remit these appellees to the vagaries of the political process which, contrary to the majority's suggestion, has proven singularly unsuited to the task of providing a remedy for this discrimination. I, for one, am unsatisfied with the hope of an ultimate "political" solution sometime in the indefinite future while, in the meantime, countless children unjustifiably receive inferior educations that "may affect their hearts and minds in a way unlikely ever to be undone." Brown v. Board of Education, . . . the issue in this case is not whether Texas is doing its best to ameliorate the worst features of a discriminatory scheme, but rather whether the scheme itself is in fact unconstitutionally discriminatory in the face of the Fourteenth Amendment's guarantee of equal protection of the laws. When the Texas financing scheme is taken as a whole, I do not think it can be doubted that it produces a discriminatory impact on substantial numbers of the schoolage children of the State of Texas.

. . . Authorities concerned with educational quality no doubt disagree as to the significance of variations in per pupil spending. Indeed, conflicting expert testimony was presented to the District Court in this case concerning the effect of spending variations on educational achievement. We sit, however, not to resolve disputes over educational theory but to enforce our Constitution. It is an inescapable fact that if one district has more funds available per pupil than another district, the former will have greater choice in educational planning than will the latter. In this regard, I believe the question of discrimination in educational quality must be deemed to be an objective one that looks to what the State provides its children, not to what the children are able to do with what they receive. That a child forced to attend an underfunded school with poorer physical facilities, less experienced teachers, larger classes, and a narrower range of courses than a school with substantially more funds—and thus with greater choice in educational planning—may nevertheless excel is to the credit of the child, not the State. . . . Indeed, who can ever measure for such a child the opportunities lost and the talents wasted for want of a broader, more enriched education? Discrimination in the opportunity to learn that is afforded a child must be our standard.

. . . it is difficult to believe that if the children of Texas had a free choice, they would choose to be educated in districts with fewer resources, and hence with more antiquated plants, less experienced teachers, and a less diversified curriculum. In fact, if financing variations are so insignificant to educational quality, it is difficult to understand why a number of our country's wealthiest school districts, who have no legal obligation to argue in support of the constitutionality of the Texas legislation, have nevertheless zealously pursued its cause before this Court.

At the very least, in view of the substantial interdistrict disparities in funding and in resulting educational inputs shown by appellees
to exist under the Texas financing scheme, the burden of proving that
these disparities do not in fact affect the quality of children's education must fall upon the appellants. Cf. Hobson v. Hansen, 327 F.Supp.
844, 860–861 (D.C.D.C.1971). Yet appellants . . . have argued
no more than that the relationship is ambiguous. This is hardly
sufficient to overcome appellees' prima facie showing of state created
discrimination between the school children of Texas with respect to
objective educational opportunity.

Nor can I accept the appellants' apparent suggestion that . . .
the Equal Protection Clause cannot be offended by substantially unequal state treatment of persons who are similarly situated so long
as the State provides everyone with some unspecified amount of
education which evidently is "enough."

. . . this Court has never suggested that because some "adequate" level of benefits is provided to all, discrimination in the provision of services is therefore constitutionally excusable. The Equal
Protection Clause is not addressed to the minimal sufficiency but
rather to the unjustifiable inequalities of state action. It mandates
nothing less than that "all persons similarly circumstanced shall be
treated alike."

Even if the Equal Protection Clause encompassed some theory
of constitutional adequacy, discrimination in the provision of educational opportunity would certainly seem to be a poor candidate for its
application. Neither the majority nor appellants informs us how
judicially manageable standards are to be derived for determining
how much education is "enough" to excuse constitutional discrimination. . . .

In my view, then, it is inequality—not some notion of gross inadequacy—of educational opportunity that raises a question of denial of
equal protection of the laws. I find any other approach to the issue
unintelligible and without directing principle. Here appellees have
made a substantial showing of wide variations in educational funding
and the resulting educational opportunity afforded to the school children of Texas. This discrimination is, in large measure, attributable
to significant disparities in the taxable wealth of local Texas school
districts. This is a sufficient showing to raise a substantial question
of discriminatory state action in violation of the Equal Protection
Clause. . . . This is clear from our decision only last Term in
Bullock v. Carter, 405 U.S. 134, 92 S.Ct. 849, 31 L.Ed.2d 92 (1972),
where the Court, in striking down Texas' primary filing fees as violative of equal protection, found no impediment to equal protection
analysis in the fact that the members of the disadvantaged class could
not be readily identified. The Court recognized that the filing fee
system tended "to deny some voters the opportunity to vote for a

candidate of their choosing; at the same time it gives the affluent the power to place on the ballot their own names or the names of persons they favor." Id., at 144, 92 S.Ct., at 856. The Court also recognized that "[t]his disparity in voting power based on wealth cannot be described by reference to discrete and precisely defined segments of the community as is typical of inequities challenged under the Equal Protection Clause. . . ." Ibid. Nevertheless, it concluded that "we would ignore reality were we not to recognize that this system falls with unequal weight on voters . . . according to their economic status." Ibid. The nature of the classification in *Bullock* was clear, although the precise membership of the disadvantaged class was not. This was enough in *Bullock* for purposes of equal protection analysis. It is enough here.

I believe it is sufficient that the overarching form of discrimination in this case is between the school children of Texas on the basis of the taxable property wealth of the districts in which they happen to live. . . . the children of a district are excessively advantaged if that district has more taxable property per pupil than the average amount of taxable property per pupil considering the State as a whole. By contrast, the children of a district are disadvantaged if that district has less taxable property per pupil than the state average. Whether this discrimination, against the school children of property poor districts, inherent in the Texas financing scheme is violative of the Equal Protection Clause is the question to which we must now turn.

. . . The Court apparently seeks to establish today that equal protection cases fall into one of two neat categories which dictate the appropriate standard of review—strict scrutiny or mere rationality. But this Court's decisions in the field of equal protection defy such easy categorization. A principled reading of what this Court has done reveals that it has applied a spectrum of standards in reviewing discrimination allegedly violative of the Equal Protection Clause. This spectrum clearly comprehends variations in the degree of care with which the Court will scrutinize particular classifications, depending, I believe, on the constitutional and societal importance of the interest adversely affected and the recognized invidiousness of the basis upon which the particular classification is drawn. I therefore cannot accept the majority's labored efforts to demonstrate that fundamental interests, which call for strict scrutiny of the challenged classification, encompass only established rights which we are somehow bound to recognize from the text of the Constitution itself. . . .

The majority is, of course, correct when it suggests that the process of determining which interests are fundamental is a difficult one. But I do not think the problem is insurmountable. . . . Although not all fundamental interests are constitutionally guaranteed, the determination of which interests are fundamental should be firmly rooted in the text of the Constitution.   The task in every case should be to determine the extent to which constitutionally guaranteed rights are dependent on interests not mentioned in the Constitution.   As the nexus between the specific constitutional guarantee and the non-constitutional interest draws closer, the nonconstitutional interest becomes more fundamental and the degree of judicial scrutiny applied when the interest is infringed on a discriminatory basis must be adjusted accordingly.   .   .   .

.   .   .   Procreation is now understood to be important because of its interaction with the established constitutional right of privacy. The exercise of the state franchise is closely tied to basic civil and political rights inherent in the First Amendment.   And access to criminal appellate processes enhances the integrity of the range of rights implicit in the Fourteenth Amendment guarantee of due process of law.   Only if we closely protect the related interests from state discrimination do we ultimately ensure the integrity of the constitutional guarantee itself.   This is the real lesson that must be taken from our previous decisions involving interests deemed to be fundamental.

The effect of the interaction of individual interests with established constitutional guarantees upon the degree of care exercised by this Court in reviewing state discrimination affecting such interests is amply illustrated by our decision last Term in Eisenstadt v. Baird, 405 U.S. 438, 92 S.Ct. 1029, 31 L.Ed.2d 349 (1972).   In *Baird*, the Court struck down as violative of the Equal Protection Clause a state statute which denied unmarried persons access to contraceptive devices on the same basis as married persons.   The Court purported to test the statute under its traditional standard whether there is some rational basis for the discrimination effected.   In the contex of commercial regulation, the Court has indicated that the Equal Protection Clause "is offended only if the classification rests on grounds wholly irrelevant to the achievement of the State's objective.   And this lenient standard is further weighted in the State's favor by the fact that "[a] statutory discrimination will not be set aside if any state of facts reasonably may be conceived [by the Court] to justify it."   But in *Baird* the Court clearly did not adhere to these highly tolerant standards of traditional rational review.   For although there were conceivable state interests intended to be advanced by the statute— e. g., deterrence of premarital sexual activity; regulation of the dissemination of potentially dangerous articles—the Court was not prepared to accept these interests on their face, but instead proceeded to test their substantiality by independent analysis.   Such close scrutiny of the State's interests was hardly characteristic of the deference shown state classifications in the context of economic interests.   Yet I think the Court's action was entirely appropriate for access to and use of contraceptives bears a close relationship to the individual's constitutional right of privacy.

A similar process of analysis with respect to the invidiousness of the basis on which a particular classification is drawn has also influenced the Court as to the appropriate degree of scrutiny to be accorded any particular case. The highly suspect character of classifications based on race, nationality, or alienage is well established. The reasons why such classifications call for close judicial scrutiny are manifold. Certain racial and ethnic groups have frequently been recognized as "discrete and insular minorities" who are relatively powerless to protect their interests in the political process. Moreover, race, nationality, or alienage is " 'in most circumstances irrelevant' to any constitutionally acceptable legislative purpose, Kiyoshi Hirabayashi v. United States, 320 U.S. 81, 100, 63 S.Ct. 1375, 87 L.Ed. 1774." McLaughlin v. Florida, 379 U.S., at 192, 85 S.Ct., at 288. Instead, lines drawn on such bases are frequently the reflection of historic prejudices rather than legislative rationality. It may be that all of these considerations, which make for particular judicial solicitude in the face of discrimination on the basis of race, nationality, or alienage, do not coalesce—or at least not to the same degree—in other forms of discrimination. Nevertheless, these considerations have undoubtedly influenced the care with which the Court has scrutinized other forms of discrimination.

In James v. Strange, 407 U.S. 128, 92 S.Ct. 2027, 32 L.Ed.2d 600 (1972), the Court held unconstitutional a state statute which provided for recoupment from indigent convicts of legal defense fees paid by the State. The Court found that the statute impermissibly differentiated between indigent criminals in debt to the state and civil judgment debtors, since criminal debtors were denied various protective exemptions afforded civil judgment debtors. The Court suggested that in reviewing the statute under the Equal Protection Clause, it was merely applying the traditional requirement that there be " 'some rationality' " in the line drawn between the different types of debtors. Yet it then proceeded to scrutinize the statute with less than traditional deference and restraint. Thus the Court recognized "that state recoupment statutes may betoken legitimate state interests" in recovering expenses and discouraging fraud. The Court, in short, clearly did not consider the problems of fraud and collection that the state legislature might have concluded were peculiar to indigent criminal defendants to be either sufficiently important or at least sufficiently substantiated to justify denial of the protective exemptions afforded to all civil judgment debtors, to a class composed exclusively of indigent criminal debtors.

Similarly, in Reed v. Reed, 404 U.S. 71, 92 S.Ct. 251, 30 L.Ed.2d 225 (1971), the Court, in striking down a state statute which gave men preference over women when persons of equal entitlement apply for assignment as an administrator of a particular estate, resorted to a more stringent standard of equal protection review than that employed in cases involving commercial matters. The Court   .   .   . was unwilling to consider a theoretical and unsubstantiated basis for distinction—however reasonable it might appear—sufficient to sustain a statute discriminating on the basis of sex.

James and *Reed* can only be understood as instances in which the particularly invidious character of the classification caused the Court to pause and scrutinize with more than traditional care the rationality of state discrimination. Discrimination on the basis of past criminality and on the basis of sex posed for the Court the spectre of forms of discrimination which it implicitly recognized to have deep social and legal roots without necessarily having any basis in actual differences. Still, the Court's sensitivity to the invidiousness of the basis for discrimination is perhaps most apparent in its decisions protecting the interests of children born out of wedlock from discriminatory state action.

In summary, it seems to me inescapably clear that this Court has consistently adjusted the care with which it will review state discrimination in light of the constitutional significance of the interests affected and the invidiousness of the particular classification. In the context of economic interests, we find that discriminatory state action is almost always sustained for such interests are generally far removed from constitutional guarantees.   .   .   .   But the situation differs markedly when discrimination against important individual interests with constitutional implications and against particularly disadvantaged or powerless classes is involved. The majority suggests, however, that a variable standard of review would give this Court the appearance of a "superlegislature." I cannot agree. Such an approach seems to me a part of the guarantees of our Constitution and of the historic experiences with oppression of and discrimination against discrete, powerless minorities which underlie that Document. In truth, the Court itself will be open to the criticism raised by the majority so long as it continues on its present course of effectively selecting in private which cases will be afforded special consideration without acknowledging the true basis of its action.

Opinions such as those in *Reed* and *James* seem drawn more as efforts to shield rather than to reveal the true basis of the Court's decisions. Such obfuscated action may be appropriate to a political body such as a legislature, but it is not appropriate to this Court. Open debate of the bases for the Court's action is essential to the rationality and consistency of our decisionmaking process. Only in this way can we avoid the label of legislature and ensure the integrity of the judicial process.

.   .   .   It is true that this Court has never deemed the provision of free public education to be required by the Constitution. Indeed, it has on occasion suggested that state supported education is a privilege bestowed by a State on its citizens. Nevertheless, the fundamental importance of education is amply indicated by the prior decisions of this Court, by the unique status accorded public education by our society, and by the close relationship between education and some of our most basic constitutional values. Education directly affects the ability of a child to exercise his First Amendment interest both as a source and as a receiver of information and ideas, whatever interests he may pursue in life. . . ., in the final analysis, "the pivotal position of education to success in American society and its essential role in opening up to the individual the central experiences of our culture lend it an importance that is undeniable."

. . . Education serves the essential function of instilling in our young an understanding of and appreciation for the principles and operation of our governmental processes. Education may instill the interest and provide the tools necessary for political discourse and debate. Indeed, it has frequently been suggested that education is the dominant factor affecting political consciousness and participation. A system of "[c]ompetition in ideas and governmental policies is at the core of our electoral process and of the First Amendment freedoms." Data from the Presidential Election of 1968 clearly demonstrates a direct relationship between participation in the electoral process and level of educational attainment.

. . . the issue is neither provision of the most *effective* speech nor of the most *informed* vote. Appellees do not now seek the best education Texas might provide. They do seek, however, an end to state discrimination resulting from the unequal distribution of taxable district property wealth that directly impairs the ability of some districts to provide the same educational opportunity that other districts can provide with the same or even substantially less tax effort. The issue is, in other words, one of discrimination that affects the quality of the education which Texas has chosen to provide its children; and, the precise question here is what importance should attach to education for purposes of equal protection analysis of that discrimination. . . .

. . . We are told that in every prior case involving a wealth classification, the members of the disadvantaged class have "shared two distinguishing characteristics: because of their impecunity they were completely unable to pay for some desired benefit, and as a consequence, they sustained an absolute deprivation of a meaningful opportunity to enjoy that benefit." . . . at 1290. I cannot agree. . . .

. . . *Griffin* and *Douglas* refute the majority's contention that we have in the past required an absolute deprivation before subjecting wealth classifications to strict scrutiny. The Court characterizes *Griffin* as a case concerned simply with the denial of a transcript or an adequate substitute therefor, and *Douglas* as involving the denial of counsel.   But in both cases the question was in fact whether "a State that [grants] *appellate review* can do so in a way that discriminates against some convicted defendants on account of their poverty."   In that regard, the Court concluded that inability to purchase a transcript denies "the poor an adequate *appellate review* accorded to all who have money enough to pay the costs in advance," *ibid.*   (emphasis added), and that "the type of an *appeal* a person is afforded   .   .   hinges upon whether or not he can pay for the assistance of counsel."   The right of appeal itself was not absolutely denied to those too poor to pay; but because of the cost of a transcript and of counsel, the appeal was a substantially less meaningful right for the poor than for the rich.   It was on these terms that the Court found a denial of equal protection, and those terms clearly encompassed degrees of discrimination on the basis of wealth which do not amount to outright denial of the affected right or interest.

This is not to say that the form of wealth classification in this case does not differ significantly from those recognized in the previous decisions of this Court.   Our prior cases have dealt essentially with discrimination on the basis of personal wealth.   Here, by contrast, the children of the disadvantaged Texas school districts are being discriminated against not necessarily because of their personal wealth or the wealth of their families, but because of the taxable property wealth of the residents of the district in which they happen to live. The appropriate question, then, is whether the same degree of judicial solicitude and scrutiny that has previously been afforded wealth classifications is warranted here.

.   .   .   That wealth classifications alone have not necessarily been considered to bear the same high degree of suspectness as have classifications based on, for instance, race or alienage may be explainable on a number of grounds.   The "poor" may not be seen as politically powerless as certain discrete and insular minority groups.   Personal poverty may entail much the same social stigma as historically attached to certain racial or ethnic groups.   But personal poverty is not a permanent disability; its shackles may be escaped.   Perhaps, most importantly, though, personal wealth may not necessarily share the general irrelevance as basis for legislative action that race or nationality is recognized to have.   While the "poor" have frequently been a legally disadvantaged group, it cannot be ignored that social legislation must frequently take cognizance of the economic status of our citizens.   Thus, we have generally gauged the invidiousness of wealth classifications with an awareness of the importance of the interests being affected and the relevance of personal wealth to those interests.

When evaluated with these considerations in mind, it seems to me that discrimination on the basis of group wealth in this case likewise calls for careful judicial scrutiny. First, it must be recognized that while local district wealth may serve other interests, it bears no relationship whatsoever to the interest of Texas school children in the educational opportunity afforded them by the State of Texas. Given the importance of that interest, we must be particularly sensitive to the invidious characteristics of any form of discrimination that is not clearly intended to serve it, as opposed to some other distinct state interest. Discrimination on the basis of group wealth may not, to be sure, reflect the social stigma frequently attached to personal poverty. Nevertheless, insofar as group wealth discrimination involves wealth over which the disadvantaged individual has no significant control, it represents in fact a more serious basis of discrimination than does personal wealth. For such discrimination is no reflection of the individual's characteristics or his abilities. And thus— particularly in the context of a disadvantaged class composed of children—we have previously treated discrimination on a basis which the individual cannot control as constitutionally disfavored.

The disability of the disadvantaged class in this case extends as well into the political processes upon which we ordinarily rely as adequate for the protection and promotion of all interests. Here legislative reallocation of the State's property wealth must be sought in the face of inevitable opposition from significantly advantaged districts that have a strong vested interest in the preservation of the status quo, a problem not completely dissimilar to that faced by underrepresented districts prior to the Court's intervention in the process of reapportionment . . . our other prior cases have dealt with discrimination on the basis of indigency which was attributable to the operation of the private sector. But we have no such simple *de facto* wealth discrimination here. The means for financing public education in Texas are selected and specified by the State. At the same time, governmentally imposed land use controls have undoubtedly encouraged and rigidified natural trends in the allocation of particular areas for residential or commercial use, and thus determined each district's amount of taxable property wealth. In short, this case, in contrast to the Court's previous wealth discrimination decisions, can only be seen as "unusual in the extent to which governmental action *is* the cause of the wealth classifications."

. . . I do not question that local control of public education, as an abstract matter, constitutes a very substantial state interest. . . . But I need not now decide how I might ultimately strike the balance were we confronted with a situation where the State's sincere concern for local control inevitably produced educational inequality. For on this record, it is apparent that the State's purported concern with local control is offered primarily as an excuse rather than as a justification for interdistrict inequality. . . . If Texas had a system truly dedicated to local fiscal control one would expect the quality of the educational opportunity provided in each district to vary with the decision of the voters in that district as to the level of sacrifice they wish to make for public education. In fact, the Texas scheme produces precisely the opposite result. Local school districts cannot choose to have the best education in the State by imposing the highest tax rate. Instead, the quality of the educational opportunity offered by any particular district is largely determined by the amount of taxable property located in the district—a factor over which local voters can exercise no control.

The study introduced in the District Court showed a direct inverse relationship between equalized taxable district property wealth and district tax effort with the result that the property poor districts making the highest tax effort obtained the lowest per pupil yield. . . . Clearly, this suit has nothing to do with local decisionmaking with respect to educational policy or even educational spending. It involves only a narrow aspect of local control—namely, local control over the raising of educational funds. In fact, in striking down inter-district disparities in taxable local wealth, the District Court took the course which is most likely to make true local control over educational decisionmaking a reality for *all* Texas school districts.

Nor does the District Court's decision even necessarily eliminate local control of educational funding. The District Court struck down nothing more than the continued interdistrict wealth discrimination inherent in the present property tax. Both centralized and decentralized plans for educational funding not involving such interdistrict discrimination have been put forward. The choice among these or other alternatives remains with the State, not with the federal courts.

The Court seeks solace for its action today in the possibility of legislative reform. The Court's suggestions of legislative redress and experimentation will doubtless be of great comfort to the school children of Texas' disadvantaged districts, but considering the vested interests of wealthy school districts in the preservation of the status quo, they are worth little more. The possibility of legislative action is, in all events, no answer to this Court's duty under the Constitution to eliminate unjustified state discrimination. In this case we have been presented with an instance of such discrimination, in a particularly invidious form, against an individual interest of large constitutional and practical importance. To support the demonstrated discrimination in the provision of educational opportunity the State has offered a justification which, on analysis, takes on at best an ephemeral character. Thus, I believe that the wide disparities in taxable district property wealth inherent in the local property tax element of the Texas financing scheme render that scheme violative of the Equal Protection Clause.

I would therefore affirm the judgment of the District Court.

NOTES AND QUESTIONS

1. What concept of equal educational opportunity is rejected by the Court and which is accepted by it? By Mr. Justices White and Marshall?

2. In Serrano, California's Supreme Court held that education was a fundamental interest and wealth a suspect class, but the Supreme Court of the United States refused to make these holdings. Is wealth a suspect class and is education a fundamental interest? In California? In the United States? What is the validity of Serrano after San Antonio Independent School District?

3. According to the Supreme Court, how can one identify the interest that ranks as "fundamental"? Compare the approach of Serrano and of Mr. Justice Marshall, which approach is best?

4. When considering whether wealth is a suspect class the Court reviewed prior precedents and concluded that a classification based on wealth is suspect only where it functions as a complete deprivation of education because of an absolute inability to pay (indigency), rather than a relative deprivation based on a relative inability to pay. Is the Court's reading of the prior cases correct? For example, in Griffin, Illinois granted a partial appellate review to an indigent but not a full appellate review because it refused to afford an indigent a free copy of the trial transcript of the testimony. Thus, an indigent had a partial review and suffered a relative deprivation. However, the Supreme Court struck Illinois' procedures and required that it afford an indigent a full review equal to that of any other appellant. Is Griffin a precedent for the Court's decision? If not, what should have been the decision based on Griffin? If so, would the decision have been different if Rodiguez had been indigent?

PROBLEM

JOHNSON v. NEW YORK STATE EDUCATION DEPARTMENT

Supreme Court of the United States, 1972.
409 U.S. 75, 93 S.Ct. 259, 34 L.Ed.2d 290.

PER CURIAM. We granted certiorari to review the judgment of the United States Court of Appeals for the Second Circuit, . . . affirming the District Court's . . . dismissal of petitioners' complaint challenging the constitutionality of New York Education Laws § 701 et seq. (1971). . . . However, respondents' brief states that "[o]n May 3, 1972, the qualified voters of the respondent school district elected by majority vote to assess a tax for the purchase of *all* textbooks for grades one through six in the schools of the district." In light of this fact, and given the suggestion at oral argument that the books themselves have a life expectancy of five years, the judgment is vacated and the case is remanded to the United States District

Court for the Eastern District of New York to determine whether this case has become moot.

Mr. Justice MARSHALL, concurring.

While I join the Court's decision, I feel obliged to state somewhat more fully what I view to be the reasons for and meaning of this remand.

The New York statutory scheme here under attack effectively denies textbooks to indigent elementary public school children unless the voters of their district approve a tax especially for the purpose of providing the books.[1] Petitioners who are indigent recipients of public assistance allege, *inter alia*, that the statute, as applied to their children, creates a wealth classification violative of the Equal Protection Clause.

When this action was initiated in September 1970, respondent Board of Education of Union Free School District No. 27 was not providing free textbooks to petitioners' children, although textbooks were available upon the payment of a fee, which petitioners were unable to afford.[2] The practical consequence of this situation was that indigent children were forced to sit " 'bookless, side by side in the same classroom with other more wealthy children learning with purchase[d]   .   .   .   textbooks, [thus engendering] a [widespread] feeling of inferiority and unfitness in poor children [which] is psychologically, emotionally, and educationally disastrous to their well being.' " Indeed, an affidavit submitted to the District Court indicated that in at least one case, an indigent child was told that "he will receive an 'F' for each day because he is without the required textbooks. When the other pupils in the class read from text-books, the teacher doesn't let him share a book with another pupil, instead she gives him paper and tells him to draw." Despite this evidence, the Court of Appeals, with one Judge dissenting, affirmed the District Court's dismissal of the complaint. We granted certiorari.

This case obviously raises questions of large constitutional and practical importance. For two full school years children in elementary grades were denied access to textbooks solely because of the indigency of their families while these questions were considered by the lower courts. After we had granted certiorari, however, a majority of the voters in respondent school district finally agreed to levy a tax for the purchase of textbooks for the elementary grades, and we are told that free textbooks have now been provided.

---

[1] Under New York law, local school districts are required to loan textbooks free to students in grades seven through 12. N.Y.Education Law § 701 (1971). No such provision is made for children in grades one through six; free textbooks are to be made available to children in those grades only upon the vote of the majority of the district's eligible voters to levy a tax to provide funds for the purchase of the textbooks, N.Y.Education Law § 703 (1971).

[2] The fee imposed was $7.50 per child.

I join in the Court's decision to remand the case so that the District Court can assess the consequences of this new development. I do so because I believe that the Court acts out of a proper sense of our constitutional duty to decide only live controversies, and because I believe that the District Judge can best resolve the factual issues upon which proper resolution of the mootness question depends. Certainly, our mere act of remanding in no way suggests any particular view as to whether this case is in fact moot. That decision is for the District Judge in the first instance.

In reaching his decision, the District Judge will, of course, have to take into account the standards which we have previously articulated for resolving mootness problems. On the one hand, "[a] case [may be] moot if subsequent events [make] it absolutely clear that the allegedly wrongful behavior could not reasonably be expected to recur." . . . But on the other, "[m]ere voluntary cessation of [allegedly] illegal conduct does not moot a case; if it did, the courts would be compelled to leave '[t]he defendant . . . free to return to his old ways.'" . . . In the context of constitutional questions involving electoral processes, these principles have generally found expression in the proposition that a case is not moot if "[t]he problem is . . . 'capable of repetition, yet evading review.'" . . .

In applying these standards to this case, the District Judge should ascertain the nature of the textbook problem for the elementary grades in respondent school district. Respondents have not suggested that the problem has been resolved once and for all by the recent purchases. To be sure, they do contend that the new textbooks have a useful life of five years. But does this adequately account for destruction by extraordinary events, for loss due to theft, and for obsolescence due to curriculum changes? And, even accepting the five-year figure, does this make the problem a non-recurring one insofar as the continuing viability of this litigation is concerned?

The District Judge should also investigate the posture in which the legal issues presented by this case might again arise when the books begin to wear out. Will the respondent school district delay holding a new election until the new books are actually needed? Is it possible that litigation would again have to proceed for an entire school year, or more, while indigent children are deprived of books before the constitutionality of that deprivation is finally determined?

These seem to me essential questions for the District Court to consider on remand in disposing of the issue of mootness.

Assume that you are the judge. What decision would you render on the merits and for what reasons?

IS REVENUE SHARING THE ANSWER?

Many people believe that the local tax burdens can be alleviated by the federal government sharing tax revenues with states. If the federal government through revenue sharing is to supply states with tax funds for education, public welfare and other purposes, the federal government will have to get the money through taxation. It is possible that the funds will be derived from the existing sources of federal revenue, primarily the income tax, but it is equally likely that a new source of revenue will be sought. One frequently named candidate is the value-added tax (VAT), which, in reality, is a sales tax. A general sales tax administered at the federal level would produce as much revenue as a greater reliance on the income tax, but its impact would be quite different. The reason is that the income tax is mildly progressive, but a value-added tax is regressive in its impact.

A value-added tax is a tax on consumption expenditures, just like a sales tax, except it is hidden. It would work something like the following hypothetical: a cattle raiser would pay one cent of tax on every ten cents' worth of cattle produced; the butcher would pay one cent on every ten cents' worth of value that he added in butchering, but he would be allowed to subtract the ten cents that he paid the cattle raiser before calculating his value-added basis. The meat packer would pay one cent on each of his ten cents' worth of value added during packing, but first he would be allowed a deduction for the amount paid to the butcher, and finally, the retailer pays one cent on each ten cents' worth of value that he adds during retail distribution. The consumer pays the full, final price. An example of the tax's regressiveness can be seen by comparing its impact on a poor husband and wife with four children and an income of $6,000 and on a more affluent husband and wife with four children and an income of $25,000. Assuming each family buys $5,000 worth of goods subject to the value added tax, the poor family has five-sixths of its income subjected to the value-added tax, but the richer family has only one-fifth. Thus, the general impact of the tax falls heavier on poorer families. The value-added tax is made politically appealing to voters because part of its legislative package includes property tax relief.

Morris—Const. & Am.Educ. ACB—54

David L. Kirp & Mark G. Yudof
REVENUE SHARING AND ITS EFFECT ON THE POOR

Copyright © 1972, by Northwestern University.
Reprinted by permission from THE CLEARING HOUSE REVIEW, Vol. 5, No. 9.
Excerpts from pages 496–97, 529–32.

.   .   .   President Nixon has placed revenue sharing at the top of his list of national priorities, describing it as the heart of the solution to perceived fiscal and political imbalance, namely, the concentration of power and dollars in Washington, to the detriment of the local and state governments primarily responsible for the welfare of the citizenry.   In the context of presidential rhetoric, revenue sharing is not a limited response to the nation's problems, but a necessary element in the revitalization of government: "Power [is] turned back to the people   .   .   .   [so that] government at all levels [is] refreshed and renewed, and made truly responsive."

The most interesting, because the most novel, of the administration's revenue sharing plans would turn back to the states on a population basis 1.3% of the income tax dollars collected by the Internal Revenue Service, an estimated $5 billion for the fiscal year 1972.   The states could use those funds to meet their self-determined, self-described needs;   they would be essentially unencumbered by federal restrictions.   .   .   .

The fiscal arguments for general revenue sharing are straightforward.   Federal revenues, tied to the progressive income tax, rise rapidly as the gross national product increases.   While the federal government has almost preempted income tax as a means of raising money (90% of all income tax dollars are collected by Washington, only 10% by other governmental units), state and local governments are forced to rely on regressive and relatively sluggish property and sales taxes to support their increasing needs.   As a result, the argument continues, Washington rapidly collects dollars while the rest of the country verges on bankruptcy.   Why not address that fiscal mismatch by using the federal government for the one thing it is unmistakably good at doing—raising revenue—while at the same time turning over a portion of that revenue to states, counties and cities so that they can maintain and expand their public services?   .   .   .

Behind the obliquity of the president's pronouncements lies a set of facts more complex and elusive.   An analysis of the *impact* of revenue sharing yields conclusions not obvious on the face of the proposal and detrimental to the interests of the poor.   Revenue sharing undermines the commitment of the national government to poor and minority groups, moving this country in a direction antithetical to their claim for a decent life.   It jeopardizes the role of Washington as the advocate for innovation, reform, and equitable taxation.   It submerges the federal presence to what is at best a revitalized parochialism, a reinforcement of the worst aspects of the status quo. In short, Mr. Nixon's proposals are those of a ward politician, not a revolutionary.

.   .   .

The most notable fiscal failing of general revenue sharing, as Nixon has described it, is that it does not address serious *within-state* inequities in taxing and spending practices. Current state revenue-raising schemes are not merely sluggish. They are regressive: their burden falls unduly on those in our society least able to pay. Sales and excise taxes are relatively more detrimental to the poor than to the rich; even in those states and cities which have adopted income taxes, the practice has generally been to set a uniform rate and not to tax progessively. A revenue sharing bill could address this problem intelligently, providing a $5 billion carrot to coerce states into adjusting their own taxing practices .   .   .

.   .   . If states employed an equitable formula for the distribution of state-collected dollars, a formula based on relative need or even parity, cities would be significantly better off than they are at present. Yet the administration's revenue sharing proposal does nothing to prevent a state from deliberately designing a revenue distribution plan to keep the cities poor. As in the case of the tax structure, revenue sharing could serve as a device to correct distribution inequities by requiring that state spending arrangements be reformed; the Nixon plan, however, provides only a *carte blanche* for states to continue acting as they have in the past.

.   .   . the crucial question is not whether state and local governments are presently responsive to "the people," but to which people they respond. The answer to this question is clear: city and state governments are committed to those middle class constituents who have a political and economic interest in the status quo. State and local governmental control over unrestricted money would inevitably reward the affluent, for it is they who control state houses and city halls. There is little likelihood (and no requirement) that additional dollars would evoke novel behavior; indeed, infusions of new money seem more likely to reinforce their worst habits. With no incentive for these governments to behave otherwise, the David Riesman principle "the more, the more" would apply in full force.

The poor and minority groups, to whom state and local governments have been unresponsive, are the political losers under revenue sharing. Whether measured in terms of welfare eligibility requirements, exclusionary zoning, education dollars, low-cost housing, or municipal services, the cities and states have not hitherto reflected the wishes and interests of these disadvantaged groups. Indeed, the chief impetus for innovation and reform has come from Washington, for poor and black people have historically turned to Washington for support against entrenched, unsympathetic local power structures. The Voting Rights Act, community action agencies, Title I of the Elementary and Secondary Education Act and the Model Cities Program are but a few of the positive federal responses. To be sure, that support has often been reluctant and unwilling. But under the administration's revenue sharing plan, even this impetus will be lost, and the disadvantaged "insular minorities" will once again be subject to the vagaries of state and local politics. . . .

Nor is there much evidence that local school districts are using *local revenue* to provide compensatory programs for the poor or to experiment with new education models. Very few states provide supplemental services for disadvantaged students; none presently require that bilingual programs be offered the non-English speaking. Disparities between rich and poor schools and rich and poor districts abound. Poor and black students, north and south, find themselves locked into dead-end "vocational" or "remedial" groups. No effort is made to nourish non-sectarian alternatives to the public schools, to create the sort of educational diversity which might ultimately improve the quality of education for all children; instead, progress is inextricably linked to the fate of the public school monopoly. Urban school systems "decentralize" without granting any power to the decentralized governing units. Apart from North Dakota's state-wide effort and a handful of experiments in other parts of the country, efforts at informalizing and humanizing the classroom are submerged in a resurgent war against "permissiveness." Test scores continue to serve as the sole criterion for school-measured success. Student self-image, pluralism, diversity, experimentation and even income and status rewards become unimportant in the quest for good achievement test results and the "efficient" management of schools. . . .

It is not difficult to fathom a functional rationale for special revenue sharing. State governments are the big winners; they receive unrestricted dollars which they can divide much as they see fit. City and state education bureaucracies are given another opportunity to expend funds in accordance with their self-described interest, unfettered by the need to attend to the welfare of those without political power. Rich suburbs benefit also, for the relative need standard in practice means equal dollars per child for all districts regardless of need. Those who oppose education reform will also gain; for parochialism, undiminished by federal restraint or by a truly representative governing structure, will be strengthened.

The losers? Urban areas, once again, wil be shortchanged. Children whose native language is not English, or who come to school with physical, mental or emotional problems, will find fewer programs designed to meet their special needs. Poor children—white, black, Chicano, Puerto Rican, Indian—will continue to be discarded by the educational system run by and for the middle class. . . .

Chapter XI

CONSTITUTIONAL FREEDOM AND VOUCHER EDUCATION AND A FINAL PROBLEM

INTRODUCTION

An educational voucher program is a significant departure from the traditional concept of public schools, especially in the areas of finance and management. If a voucher program is adopted it will significantly alter the financial and organizational aspects of public education that have existed since the beginning of the twentieth century. Many variations of a voucher program exist, and they all involve "parental choice."

The basic idea behind vouchers is quite simple. See, generally, C. Jencks, Education Vouchers (1970). The parents of each school-aged child would be given one voucher per child which, in turn, the parents could assign to any school of their choice—public, private, religious, profit making, or what have you. The schools would collect the vouchers and then cash them in for public tax funds at state or federal treasuries. Many variations on the basic scheme have been advanced. In addition to "parental choice," one of the alleged advantages of a voucher program is that it would eliminate the swollen educational bureaucracy consisting of administrators piled on top of administrators. In light of all the materials that have preceeded this chapter, would the following voucher program be constitutional? Wise? Identify each of the constitutional or legal questions presented and give its most probable resolution by a court applying the most relevant precedents and legal or constitutional principles.

VOUCHER PROBLEM

(Adapted from Summary of Key Elements of a Proposed Demonstration of a Voucher Plan in Seattle by Bureau of School Service and Research, University of Washington, 1972).

The Regulated Compensatory Model

The Regulated Compensatory Model has been proposed by the Center for the Study of Public Policy, Cambridge, Massachusetts, and supported by the Office of Economic Opportunity. This model provides that each student in a selected demonstration area receive a basic voucher equal to the current per-pupil cost of instruction in the public schools. Students designated as economically and/or educationally disadvantaged would be granted a voucher worth up to one-third more than the basic voucher value. All voucher schools must accept the voucher value for each participating student as full payment for the cost of education but this provision would not preclude the possibility of private fund-raising by either public or non-public voucher schools.

Determination of Basic Voucher Value

The basic voucher value should be equivalent to the School District's per pupil instructional costs (PPIC) plus per pupil ancillary (supportive) costs (PPAC) for elementary education. Instructional costs include payments to teachers, secretaries, textbooks and supplies; while ancillary costs include central office services, building maintenance and other expenditures required to operate the District. The basic per pupil expenditure is calculated by dividing the total money available by the total number of pupils enrolled. Special funds (e. g., Title I, Urban Rural Racial Disadvantaged and Model Cities) are not included in the calculation of the basic voucher value, for they would be allocated in the same manner as they are presently, with each voucher school receiving special funds in proportion to the number of participating students that these special funds are specifically designated to serve.

At the beginning of the demonstration, the voucher value would represent current per pupil expenditures; however, the value would be re-evaluated in terms of the District budget each succeeding year. Based on the District's budget, the voucher value would equal approximately $750 (PPIC equals about $600 plus PPAC, which equals about $150).

Compensatory Vouchers

In addition to the basic voucher, elementary school children within a demonstration area who fall in the category "disadvantaged" will receive "compensatory" vouchers worth up to one-third the amount of the basic voucher value, or $250. Disadvantaged students will thus present a voucher to the schools worth up to $1,000.

The reasons for providing a "compensatory" increment for disadvantaged students are:

1. To provide additional funds to schools to meet the higher costs of educating disadvantaged students (e. g., lower student-teacher ratio, added tutorial assistance, etc.).

2. To encourage schools to develop programs more attractive to disadvantaged students (e. g., provision of ethnic studies curricula, school breakfast programs, etc.).

The criteria used to determine which children receive compensatory vouchers is an important aspect of the regulated compensatory voucher model. Although the Office of Economic Opportunity suggests that either educational or economic criteria may be used to determine eligibility for these additional funds, we tentatively recommend that eligibility for compensatory vouchers be determined on economic criteria alone because:

1. A workable definition of economically disadvantaged persons is already in use in both federal and state agencies.

2. There is a high degree of correlation between educationally disadvantaged children and low income families in the School District. Therefore, disadvantaged children eligible to receive compensatory vouchers would involve essentially the same population whether defined by educational or economic criteria.

3. The use of an economic definition would reduce administrative costs and involve a more consistently quantitative criterion, e. g., a child's eligibility to receive compensatory vouchers could be quickly determined without waiting for test results.

4. Difficulties would arise in the administration, scoring and interpretation of tests.

5. Tests given to determine whether a child is educationally disadvantaged are often no more indicative of the cost of educating a child than an income figure. For example, certain students with low scores on standardized tests (within a given percentile) may be working at capacity. Compensatory vouchers would not likely be either beneficial or necessary.

Special Education

There has been much discussion of the question of assigning vouchers to children requiring special education. Many citizens feel that these students should be eligible to receive compensatory in addition to regular vouchers. Basic to the voucher concept, however, is the idea that no school can charge more than the amount of the tuition voucher, but may receive private gifts. Since handicapped children require special materials such as large print books, mobility instruction, materials translated into braille, etc., the cost of instruction for these children tends to be significantly higher than the average per pupil expenditure by the School District.

This cost factor leads us to recommend the exclusion of severely handicapped children from a trial voucher plan. It would be advisable, however, to include in the voucher system educational programs for children with less severe learning disorders. To accommodate these children, the School District would operate and finance special classrooms within a school, separate from the school administration. The

School District would pay these schools a specified number of dollars for each hour the special education student spends in the regular classroom. Let us suppose that the student spends two hours per day (⅓ time) in the regular classroom. The School District would then pay the school approximately $250 per year (that is, one-third of the average per pupil expenditure of $750) to cover the cost of regular contact hours.

In addition to those special education students who are severely handicapped and also those with less severe learning disorders, there are many children with mild speech and language difficulties who spend the greater part of their time in regular classrooms. We recommend in these cases that the children receive regular vouchers plus additional help from regular School District specialists who would continue to provide special services as needed.

In summary during a voucher demonstration, students with special needs would be classified according to one of the following categories:

1. *Severely Handicapped Children* (with no interaction): Children in this group are severely handicapped. Examples could include the blind, deaf, and/or mentally retarded. These children would receive *no* voucher and would continue to be educated and financed in the same manner as is currently being used.

2. *Special Classes* (with moderate interaction): Children with less severe learning disorders who spend approximately 50 percent of their time in the regular classroom and 50 percent in special classrooms such as dyslexic and partially visually handicapped comprise this group. These children would receive *no* voucher and their programs would continue to be financed through the School District.

3. *Special Needs* (with high interaction): Children with mild speech and language difficulties who spend most of their time in the regular classroom comprise this group. These students would receive *regular* vouchers and additional help would be provided by the School District as needed. *No* compensatory voucher would be issued unless the child meets the criteria as established for such vouchers.

We recommend that the EVA protect in each voucher school the space currently being used for special education students, and that the School District continue the current on-going pupil personnel services such as psychological counseling, social service, speech and hearing, medical services, etc. in voucher schools.

Admissions Model

We recommend that the following admissions model be used:

1. Any student, already enrolled or once accepted into a voucher school, should be assured continuation in that school during a voucher demonstration or until completing the highest grade level incorporated into the demonstration project;

2. Children entering school for the first time in the demonstration area who have older sibling(s) in one voucher school will be automatically admitted if their first choice is that school. Children entering school who have siblings in more than one voucher school will *not* have admission priority to any voucher school. All members of a family who apply to the same school(s) at the beginning of their participation in a voucher demonstration will be treated as a unit, so that all are admitted to the same school;

3. Following this protection of continuing students and siblings, a school's vacant seats will be open to all applicants on an equal basis;

4. Should the number of applicants exceed the number of seats, all vacancies will be filled on a lottery basis.

There are two exceptions to the above model. The first of these would be schools containing a minority group exceeding 40 percent. Since the voucher demonstration, and therefore the admissions policy, should respect the State Human Rights Commission guideline that no school should exceed more than 40 percent of one minority group, schools with minority enrollment over this percentage would have to determine which students could continue on a lottery basis, not to exceed 40 percent. We clearly recognize that current desegregation efforts are of higher priority than this plan and that any new guidelines established will be equally respected in the admission procedures for voucher schools.

The second exception to the model would be to new schools in their first year of operation. We recommend that new schools be permitted to select up to 50 percent of their first-year enrollment on any basis other than race, religion, sex, and income.

If necessary, both racial and neighborhood quotas could be applied to a lottery process; however, such a determination could only be made after completing a trial application process in a specific demonstration area. Such determination would also, of course, depend upon the desegregation plans of the School District at the time of implementation.

At the time of application to a voucher school, we recommend that each parent make three school choices in order of preference.

A parent would fill out an IBM card with the following information: name, age of child, grade level, income, race, and school choices. Because of the continuity clause, only one choice is necessary for a parent who chooses the child's current school as the first choice (since that first choice guarantees placement in that school). A parent who wishes his child to attend a different school, however, (and a parent whose child is just entering school in the demonstration area and is not protected by sibling protection) must make three choices ranking them in order of preference. After completion of the application process, the EVA will automatically admit children protected by continuation or sibling protection clauses.

Should the number of applicants exceed the number of seats, all vacancies will be filled on a lottery basis. If this is necessary, there are means of operating a lottery which will maximize fairness and opportunity for all students. The lottery could be run by initially selecting all first choices first, then second choices, and finally third choices. The computer would compare the number of first choices given each grade in each school to the number of places remaining in that class. If the number of applicants were less than the number of spaces available, all would be admitted. If the number of applicants exceeded the number of spaces available, the computer would calculate the proportion of first choice applicants who could be admitted and then randomly select (perhaps on the basis of birth dates using the same order of priority as the draft) the appropriate number of students for each class from among those who listed it as their first choice. The name of every student who is admitted to his first choice school would be dropped from the lottery pools of all schools his parents had ranked lower. After the first choice selection, many schools will be filled, but many will not. The computer would then repeat the same process, looking at the second choices of all students who had not been admitted to their first choice. Where the number of second choices given a class exceeded the number of remaining places, a random allocation would again be made. This process would be repeated until every child had been allocated to a school.

In a demonstration involving a large number of applicants to a small number of very popular schools, some students may not be accommodated by the above procedure and may have to be assigned to a school. In a demonstration involving more evenly distributed applications to more of the schools, most students would be admitted to their first choice school, and all would be admitted to their first, second or third choice school.

Each school's capacity should originally be stated as a range (for example, fifty to seventy students for any given grade level) so that flexibility would exist in the case of over or under-application. This would maximize chances of each parent getting his child into the school of his choice, and maximize the schools' ability to accommodate acceptable variations in the number of students.

After the initial lottery process is completed in the spring, parents would commit themselves to the school to which they will be sending their children, perhaps by means of a signed confirmation card. Each school would provide for the EVA information on the number or seats they wish to open for late applicants and the desire to take in transfer students. Most schools would probably be filled in the spring, but as families move out of the area, the space available would increase.

Based on the fact that the number of students leaving most schools exceeds the number of students entering the schools in any one year, we recommend that no seats be reserved for late applicants, but that each school provide for the EVA an up-to-date list of seats available throughout the year.

Located within the proposed demonstration area are 25 public schools and ten private schools, five of the private schools are parochial schools.

THE EDUCATION VOUCHER AGENCY

Description and Composition

The Education Voucher Agency should be responsible for the administration of a voucher demonstration. In executing the various tasks associated with a voucher system, the EVA should operate as a type of "Consumer Protection Agency" to protect the rights of parents.

Authority

The EVA would receive its authority primarily from the School Board of Directors with only such adjustments in State law as are necessary.

Functions

The EVA will both establish and enforce general policies for schools as well as perform administrative duties related to a voucher demonstration. The administration of these responsibilities will be delegated to an EVA administrator. Because of time constraints and to prevent the development of a large bureaucracy, we recommend that the administrator contract with outside groups to perform the necessary administrative functions (e. g., information collection, counseling, etc.). Such an outside group could include the public schools, whose resources such as transportation, counseling, etc. could be beneficial to the operation of a voucher system. We recommend that a division of responsibilities between the EVA board members and administrators be as follows:

EVA Policy Board

1. Select and EVA administrator and delegate to him all the necessary administrative power and authority over the voucher demonstration project.

2. Formulate and adopt policies for the governing of the demonstration.

3. Be responsible for all federal, state, and local education funds to be used during the demonstration.

4. Establish and enforce criteria for the participation of schools in the education voucher project and certify participating voucher schools.

5. Establish and enforce uniform standards for application and admission, transfer, suspension and expulsion of voucher students.

6. Establish and enforce standards for curriculum and instruction, health, and other programs in operation in the voucher schools within the minimum standards set by state codes, statutes, regulations, and guidelines.

7. Establish and enforce a uniform system of accounting and record keeping for the voucher project.

8. Establish and enforce criteria for determining the eligibility of students for basic and compensatory vouchers and certify that eligibility.

9. Establish and enforce procedures for awarding contracts to private and other public organizations for awarding services within the education voucher project and the voucher schools.

EVA Administrator

1. Perform the necessary duties of chief administrative officer for the EVA.

2. Hire a staff to coordinate and administer the policies of the EVA through appropriate administrative regulations.

3. Administer all federal, state and local education funds for the EVA.

4. Administer the process of approving voucher schools for participation.

5. Administer procedures for application, admission, transfer, suspension and expulsion within voucher schools.

6. Administer standards set by the EVA for programs and operations in voucher schools.

7. Administer a system of accounting and record keeping established by the EVA for voucher schools.

8. Administer EVA criteria for determining the eligibility of students for basic and compensatory vouchers.

9. Administer contracts for services in private and other public organizations, that is, transportation, curriculum development, educational planning, evaluation.

EVA Policy Board—Cont'd

10. Approve the capital outlay within the EVDP.

11. Approve bills previously authorized.

12. Require periodic and annual reports on EVDP programs, operations, and progress.

EVA Administrator—Cont'd

10. Direct all capital expenditures within the EVA.

11. Direct all purchases for the EVA over and above those provided to voucher schools by their basic authority.

12. Prepare, coordinate and provide reports to the EVA on the conduct of the voucher demonstration. Evaluate such reports.

13. Plan and prepare measures for the EVA to keep the community and other public bodies and agencies well informed.

14. Inform EVA of appeals and carry out rulings.

15. Ensure that information from participating schools is collected and adequate counseling is provided for parents.

16. Provide technical assistance to new schools.

FINAL PROBLEM

[Adapted from a final examination question of Professor Archibald Cox, Harvard Law School, 1972.]

Like the problem on voucher education this final problem is designed to test a person's ability to apply all the knowledge and insights that have been obtained from the materials in this book. Each possible problem or legal issue should be identified, as well as each constitutional or legal principle and prior case precedent that arguably is relevant to each of the identified legal problems. Then, each arguably relevant principle and case precedent should be carefully evaluated and assessed to determine its applicability to one or more of the legal problems in its context. Finally, a reasoned conclusion on each legal issue should be reached. The hypothetical set of facts are found in the hypothetical State of Feliciana, U.S.A.

PROBLEM

The white population of Baton Noir, Feliciana, is overwhelmingly Roman Catholic. Since Brown v. Board of Education, enrollment in the parochial school system has doubled. There is no racial discrimination, except at Boys' Latin, but the enrollment there is predominantly white because only children of Roman Catholic families are admitted and relatively few black families belong to that church.

By Feliciana law, all property of charitable, educational or benevolent organizations is exempt from taxation. All gifts to a charitable corporation for local educational purposes may be credited against the Feliciana income tax. The church charges no tuition. The parochial schools receive no state or federal grants.

A new Feliciana statute provides for State financial assistance up to $10 per student annually for the provision of secular textbooks to students in the high school grades in both public and private schools, provided that the textbooks are designated for use by the State Board of Education. Another section grants a credit against the state income tax in the amount of $100 in respect of tuition paid for each child enrolled in an approved private or church-supported school. Another section of the same statute authorizes a school district to vote by referendum to levy a tax fully to provide books to students in all private schools on the same basis as to students in public elementary and grammar schools. The Baton Noir school district voted to levy the tax.

Boys' Latin is a superior high school in the parochial school system to which only the most promising students, as shown by previous grades and entrance examinations, are admitted. No black students, no girls and no non-Catholics are admitted.

(a) Adam, an outstanding parochial school student who is black, is denied admission to Boys' Latin. Adam and his parents sue in the U. S. District Court to gain admission. What judgment should the court enter? Why?

(b) Eve, an outstanding parochial school student who is a girl, is denied admission to Boys' Latin. Eve and her parents sue in U. S. District Court to gain admission. What judgment should the court enter? Why?

(c) Calvin, a brilliant scholar who attended the Baton Noir public grammar schools, has been denied admission to Boys' Latin solely upon the ground that he is not a Roman Catholic. Calvin and his parents sue in the U. S. District Court to gain admission. What judgment should the court enter? Why?

(d) David, a brilliant scholar in the parochial schools of Philadelphia, Pennsylvania, applied for admission to Boys' Latin, planning to live with an aunt in Baton Noir while attending school. His parents will continue to keep the family home in Philadelphia. The letter rejecting his application explained, "Unfortunately, we cannot admit even the most talented students from homes outside Baton Noir parish." Is David entitled to judicial relief? Why or why not?

(e) Edward is a fourth grade parochial school student. He and his parents are too poor to buy or rent the textbooks available to students whose parents have greater means. Edward and his parents bring suit in the U. S. District Court against the appropriate parochial school and State authorities alleging that the failure to provide Edward with textbooks violates the Fourteenth Amendment. What judgment should the court enter? Why?

(f) Henry David Thoreau, a state taxpayer, on behalf of himself and the class of those similarly situated, sued in the Federal court to have the new statute declared unconstitutional. What judgment, for what reasons, should be issued?

*

APPENDIX

CLEVELAND BD. OF ED. v. LaFLEUR

COHEN v. CHESTERFIELD CTY. SCH. BD.

Supreme Court of the United States, 1974.
—— U.S. ——, 94 S.Ct. 791, —— L.Ed.2d ——.

Mr. Justice STEWART delivered the opinion of the Court. . . .

I

Jo Carol LaFleur and Ann Elizabeth Nelson are junior high school teachers employed by the Board of Education of Cleveland, Ohio. Pursuant to a rule first adopted in 1952, the school board requires every pregnant school teacher to take a maternity leave without pay, beginning five months before the expected birth of her child. Application for such leave must be made no later than two weeks prior to the date of departure. A teacher on maternity leave is not allowed to return to work until the beginning of the next regular school semester which follows the date when her child attains the age of three months. A doctor's certificate attesting to the health of the teacher is a prerequisite to return; an additional physical examination may be required. The teacher on maternity leave is not promised re-employment after the birth of the child; she is merely given priority in re-assignment to a position for which she is qualified. Failure to comply with the mandatory maternity leave provisions is grounds for dismissal.

Neither Mrs. LaFleur nor Mrs. Nelson wished to take an unpaid maternity leave; each wanted to continue teaching until the end of the school year. Because of the mandatory maternity leave rule, however, each was required to leave her job in March of 1971. The two women then filed separate suits in the United States District Court for the Northern District of Ohio . . . challenging the constitutionality of the maternity leave rule. The District Court tried the cases together, and rejected the plaintiffs' arguments. A divided panel of the United States Court of Appeals for the Sixth Circuit reversed, finding the Cleveland rules in violation of the Equal Protection Clause of the Fourteenth Amendment.

Susan Cohen, was employed by the School Board of Chesterfield County, Virginia. That school board's maternity leave regulation requires that a pregnant teacher leave work at least four months prior to the expected birth of her child. Notice in writing must be given to the school board at least six months prior to the expected birth date. A teacher on maternity leave is declared re-eligible for employment when she submits written notice from a physician that she is physically fit for re-employment, and when she can give assurances that care of the child will cause minimal interferences with her job responsibilities. The teacher is guaranteed re-employment no later than the first day of the school year following the date upon which she is declared re-eligible.

Mrs. Cohen informed the Chesterfield County School Board in November 1970, that she was pregnant and expected the birth of her child about April 28, 1971. She initially requested that she be permitted to continue teaching until April 1, 1971. The school board rejected the request, as it did Mrs. Cohen's subsequent suggestion that she be allowed to teach until January 21, 1971, the end of the first school semester. Instead, she was required to leave her teaching job on December 18, 1970. She subsequently filed this suit in the United States District Court for the Eastern District of Virginia. The District Court held that the school board regulation violates the Equal Protection Clause, and granted appropriate relief. A divided panel of the Fourth Circuit affirmed, but, on rehearing *en banc*, the Court of Appeals upheld the constitutionality of the challenged regulation in a 4–3 decision.

We granted certiorari in both cases in order to resolve the conflict between the Courts of Appeals regarding the constitutionality of such mandatory maternity leave rules for public school teachers.

II

This Court has long recognized that freedom of personal choice in matters of marriage and family life is one of the liberties protected by the Due Process Clause of the Fourteenth Amendment. . . . there is a right "to be free from unwarranted governmental intrusion into matters so fundamentally affecting a person as the decision whether to bear or beget a child."

By acting to penalize the pregnant teacher for deciding to bear a child, overly restrictive maternity leave regulations can constitute a heavy burden on the exercise of these protected freedoms. Because public school maternity leave rules directly affect "one of the basic civil rights of man," . . . the Due Process Clause of the Fourteenth Amendment requires that such rules must not needlessly, arbitrarily, or capriciously impinge upon this vital area of a teacher's constitutional liberty. The question before us in these cases is whether the interests advanced in support of the rules of the Cleveland and Chesterfield County School Boards can justify the particular procedures they have adopted.

The school boards in these cases have offered two essentially overlapping explanations for their mandatory maternity leave rules. First, they contend that the firm cut-off dates are necessary to maintain continuity of classroom instruction, since advance knowledge of when a pregnant teacher must leave facilitates the finding and hiring of a qualified substitute. Secondly, the school boards seek to justify their maternity rules by arguing that at least some teachers become physically incapable of adequately performing certain of their duties during the latter part of pregnancy. By keeping the pregnant teacher out of the classroom during these final months, the maternity leave rules are said to protect the health of the teacher and her unborn child, while at the same time assuring that students have a physically capable instructor in the classroom at all times.

It cannot be denied that continuity of instruction is a significant and legitimate educational goal. Regulations requiring pregnant teachers to provide early notice of their condition to school authorities undoubtedly facilitate administrative planning toward the important objective of continuity. But, as the Court of Appeals for the Second Circuit noted in Green v. Waterford Board of Education, 472 F.2d 629, 635:

> "Where a pregnant teacher provides the Board with a date certain for commencement of leave, however, that value [continuity] is preserved; an arbitrary leave date set at the end of the fifth month is no more calculated to facilitate a planned and orderly transition between the teacher and a substitute than is a date fixed closer to confinement. Indeed, the latter . . . would afford the Board more, not less, time to procure a satisfactory long-term substitute." (Footnote omitted.)

Thus, while the advance notice provisions in the Cleveland and Chesterfield County rules are wholly rational and may well be necessary to serve the objective of continuity of instruction, the absolute requirements of termination at the end of the fourth or fifth month of pregnancy are not. Were continuity the only goal, cut-off dates much later during pregnancy would serve as well or better than the challenged rules, providing that ample advance notice requirements were retained. Indeed, continuity would seem just as well attained if the teacher herself were allowed to choose the date upon which to commence her leave, at least so long as the decision were required to be made and notice given of it well in advance of the date selected.

In fact, since the fifth or sixth months of pregnancy will obviously begin at different times in the school year for different teachers, the present Cleveland and Chesterfield County rules may serve to hinder attainment of the very continuity objectives that they are purportedly designed to promote. For example, the beginning of the fifth month of pregnancy for both Mrs. LaFleur and Mrs. Nelson occurred during March of 1971. Both were thus required to leave work with only a few months left in the school year, even though both were fully willing to serve through the end of the term. Similarly, if continuity were the only goal, it seems ironic that the Chesterfield County rule forced Mrs. Cohen to leave work in mid-December 1970 rather than at the end of the semester in January, as she requested.

We thus conclude that the arbitrary cut-off dates embodied in the mandatory leave rules before us have no rational relationship to the valid state interest of preserving continuity of instruction. As long as the teacher is required to give susbtantial advance notice of her condition, the choice of firm dates later in pregnancy would serve the boards' objectives just as well, while imposing a far lesser burden on the women's exercise of constitutionally protected freedom.

The question remains as to whether the fifth and sixth month cut-off dates can be justified on the other ground advanced by the school boards—the necessity of keeping physically unfit teachers out of the classroom. There can be no doubt that such an objective is perfectly legitimate, both on educational and safety grounds. And, despite the plethora of conflicting medical testimony in these cases, we can assume *arguendo* that at least some teachers become physically disabled from effectively performing their duties during the latter stages of pregnancy.

The mandatory termination provisions of the Cleveland and Chesterfield County rules surely operate to insulate the classroom from the presence of potentially incapacitated pregnant teachers. But the question is whether the rules sweep too broadly.   .   . That question must be answered in the affirmative, for the provisions amount to a conclusive presumption that every pregnant teacher who reaches the fifth or sixth month of pregnancy is physically incapable of continuing. There is no individualized determination by the teacher's doctor—or the school board's—as to any particular teacher's ability to continue at her job. The rules contain an irrebuttable presumption of physical incompetency, and that presumption applies even when the medical evidence as to an individual woman's physical status might be wholly to the contrary.

.   .   .   "permanent irrebuttable presumptions have long been disfavored under the Due Process Clauses of the Fifth and Fourteenth Amendments."   .   .   .

> "[I]t is forbidden by the Due Process Clause to deny an individual the resident rates on the basis of a permanent and irrebuttable presumption of nonresidence, when that presumption is not necessarily or universally true in fact, and when the state has reasonable alternative means of making the crucial determination."

Similarly, in Stanley v. Illinois, 405 U.S. 645, the Court held that an Illinois statute containing an irrebuttable presumption that unmarried fathers are incompetent to raise their children violated the Due Process Clause. Because of the statutory presumption, the State took custody of all illegitimate children upon the death of the mother, without allowing the father to attempt to prove his parental fitness.

.   .   .

Hence, we held that the State could not conclusively presume that any particular unmarried father was unfit to raise his child; the Due Process Clause required a more individualized determination. . . .

These principles control our decision in the cases before us. While the medical experts in these cases differed on many points, they unanimously agreed on one—the ability of any particular pregnant woman to continue at work past any fixed time in her pregnancy is very much an individual matter. . . . The conclusive presumption embodied in these rules . . . is neither "necessarily nor universally true," and is violative of the Due Process Clause.

The school boards have argued that the mandatory termination dates serve the interest of administrative convenience, since there are many instances of teacher pregnancy, and the rules obviate the necessity for case-by-case determinations. Certainly, the boards have an interest in devising prompt and efficient procedures to achieve their legitimate objectives in this area. . . .

While it might be easier for the school boards to conclusively presume that all pregnant women are unfit to teach past the fourth or fifth month or even the first month, of pregnancy, administrative convenience alone is insufficient to make valid what otherwise is a violation of due process of law. The Fourteenth Amendment requires the school boards to employ alternative administrative means, which do not so broadly infringe upon basic constitutional liberty, in support of their legitimate goals.

We conclude, therefore, that neither the necessity for continuity of instruction nor the state interest in keeping physically unfit teachers out of the classroom can justify the sweeping mandatory leave regulations that the Cleveland and Chesterfield County School Boards have adopted. While the regulations no doubt represent a good-faith attempt to achieve a laudable goal, they cannot pass muster under the Due Process Clause of the Fourteenth Amendment, because they employ irrebuttable presumptions that unduly penalize a female teacher for deciding to bear a child.

III

In addition to the mandatory termination provisions, both the Cleveland and Chesterfield County rules contain limitations upon a teacher's eligibility to return to work after giving birth. Again, the school boards offer two justifications for the return rules—continuity of instruction and the desire to be certain that the teacher is physically competent when she returns to work. As is the case with the leave provisions, the question is not whether the school board's goals are legitimate, but rather whether the particular means chosen to achieve those objectives unduly infringe upon the teachers' constitutional liberty.

Under the Cleveland rule, the teacher is not eligible to return to work until the beginning of the next regular school semester following the time when her child attains the age of three months. A doctor's certificate attesting to the teacher's health is required before return; an additional physical examination may be required at the option of the school board.

[LaFleur does] not seriously challenge either the medical requirements of the Cleveland rule or the policy of limiting eligibility to return to the next semester following birth. The provisions concerning a medical certificate or supplemental physical examination are narrowly drawn methods of protecting the school board's interest in teacher fitness; these requirements allow an individualized decision as to teacher's condition, and thus avoid the pitfalls of the presumptions inherent in the leave rules. Similarly, the provision limiting eligibility to return to the semester following delivery is a precisely drawn means of serving the school board's interest in avoiding unnecessary changes in classroom personnel during any one school term.

The Cleveland rule, however, does not simply contain these reasonable medical and next-semester eligibility provisions. In addition, the school board requires the mother to wait until her child reaches the age of three months before the return rules begin to operate. The school boards have offered no reasonable justification for this supplemental limitation, and we can perceive none. To the extent that the three months provision reflects the school board's thinking that no mother is fit to return until that point in time, it suffers from the same constitutional deficiencies that plague the irrebuttable presumption in the termination rules. The presumption, moreover, is patently unnecessary, since the requirement of a physician's certificate or a medical examination fully protects the school's interests in this regard. And finally, the three month provision simply has nothing to do with continuity of instruction, since the precise point at which the child will reach the relevant age will obviously occur at a different point throughout the school year for each teacher.

Thus, we conclude that the Cleveland return rule, insofar as it embodies the three months age provision, is wholly arbitrary and irrational, and hence violates the Due Process Clause of the Fourteenth Amendment. The age limitation serves no legitimate state interest, and unncessarily penalizes the female teacher for asserting her right to bear children.

We perceive no such constitutional infirmities in the Chesterfield County rule. In that school system, the teacher becomes eligible for reemployment upon submission of a medical certificate from her physician; return to work is guaranteed no later than the beginning of the next school year following the eligibility determination. The medical certificate is both a reasonable and narrow method of protecting the school board's interest in teacher fitness, while the possible deferring of return until the next school year serves the goal of preserving continuity of instruction. In short, the Chesterfield County rule manages to serve the legitimate state interests here without employing unnecessary presumptions that broadly burden the exercise of protected constitutional liberty. . . .

Mr. Justice DOUGLAS concurs in the result.

Mr. Justice POWELL, concurring in the result.

I concur in the Court's result, but I am unable to join its opinion. In my view these cases should not be decided on the ground that the mandatory maternity leave regulations impair any right to bear children or create an "irrebuttable presumption." It seems to me that equal protection analysis is the appropriate frame of reference.

These regulations undoubtedly add to the burdens of childbearing. But certainly not every government policy that burdens childbearing violates the Constitution. Limitations on the welfare benefits a family may receive that do not take into account the size of the family illustrate this point. . . . Undoubtedly Congress could, as another example, constitutionally seek to discourage excessive population growth by limiting tax deductions for dependents. That would represent an intentional governmental effort to "penalize" childbearing. . . . The regulations here do not have that purpose. Their deterrent impact is wholly incidental. . . .

I am also troubled by the Court's return to the "irrebuttable presumption" line of analysis . . . As a matter of logic, it is difficult to see the terminus of the road upon which the Court has embarked under the banner of "irrebuttable presumptions." If the Court nevertheless uses "irrebuttable presumption" reasoning selectively, the concept at root often will be something else masquerading as a due process doctrine. That something else, of course, is the Equal Protection Clause. . . .

To be sure, the boards have a legitimate and important interest in fostering continuity of teaching. And, even a normal pregnancy may at some point jeopardize that interest. But the classifications chosen by these boards, so far as we have been shown, are either contraproductive (sic) or irrationally overinclusive even with regard to this significant, nonillusory goal. Accordingly, in my opinion these regulations are invalid under rational basis standards of equal protection review.

. . . I think it important to emphasize the degree of latitude the Court, as I read it, has left the boards for dealing with the real and recurrent problems presented by teacher pregnancies. Boards may demand in every case "substantial advance notice of [pregnancy] . . . ." Subject to certain restrictions, they may require all pregnant teachers to cease teaching "at some firm date during the last few weeks of pregnancy. . . ." The Court further holds that boards may in all cases restrict re-entry into teaching to the outset of the school term following delivery.

In my opinion, such class-wide rules for pregnant teachers are constitutional under traditional equal protection standards. School boards, confronted with sensitive and widely variable problems of public education, must be accorded latitude in the operation of school systems and in the adoption of rules and regulations of general application. . . . A large measure of discretion is essential to the effective discharge of the duties vested in these local, often elective, governmental units. My concern with the Court's opinion is that, if carried to logical extremes, the emphasis on individualized treatment is at war with this need for discretion. Indeed, stringent insistence on individualized treatment may be quite impractical in a large school district with thousands of teachers. . . .

Mr. Justice REHNQUIST, with whom The Chief Justice joins, dissenting.

The Court rests its invalidation of the school regulations involved in these cases on the Due Process Clause of the Fourteenth Amendment, rather than on any claim of sexual discrimination under the Equal Protection Clause of that Amendment. My Brother STEWART thereby enlists the Court in another quixotic engagement in his apparently unending war or irrebuttable presumptions. . . .

Countless state and federal statutes draw lines such as those drawn by the regulations here which, under the Court's analysis, might well prove to be arbitrary in individual cases. The District of Columbia Code, for example, draws lines with respect to age for several purposes. The Code requires that a person to be eligible to vote be 18 years of age, that a male be 18 and a female be 16 before a valid marriage may be contracted, that alcoholic beverages not be sold to a person under age 21 years, or beer or light wines to any person under the age of 18 years. A resident of the District of Columbia must be 16 years of age to obtain a permit to operate motor vehicle, and the District of Columbia delegate to the United States Congress must be 25 years old. Nothing in the Court's opinion clearly demonstrates why its logic would not equally well sustain a challenge to these laws from a 17-year-old who insists that he is just as well informed for voting purposes as an 18-year-old, from a 20-year-old who insists that he is just as able to carry his liquor as a 21-year-old, or from the numerous other persons who fall on the outside of lines drawn by these and similar statutes.

More closely in point is the jeopardy in which the Court's opinion places long-standing statutes providing for mandatory retirement of government employees.   5 U.S.C. § 8335 provides with respect to Civil Service employees:

> "(a) Except as otherwise provided by this section, an employee who becomes seventy years of age and completes fifteen years of service shall be automatically separated from the service . . . ."

. . . In Truax v. Reich, the Court said:

> "It requires no argument to show that the right to work for a living and the common occupations of the community is of the very essence of the personal freedom and opportunity that it was the purpose of the Amendment to secure." 239 U.S. 33, 41.

Since this right to pursue an occupation is presumably on the same lofty footing as the right of choice in matters of family life, the Court will have to strain valiantly in order to avoid having today's opinion lead to the invalidation of mandatory retirement statutes for governmental employees.   In that event federal, state, and local governmental bodies will be remitted to the task, thankless both for them and for the employees involved, of individual determinations of physical impairment and senility.

It has been said before, Williamson v. Lee Optical Co., 348 U.S. 483, but it bears repeating here: All legislation involves the drawing of lines, and the drawing of lines necessarily results in particular individuals who are disadvantaged by the line drawn being virtually indistinguishable for many purposes from those individuals who benefit from the legislative classification. The Court's disenchantment with "irrebuttable presumptions," and its preference for "individualized determination," is in the last analysis nothing less than an attack upon the very notion of lawmaking itself.

The lines drawn by the school boards in the city of Cleveland and Chesterfield County in these cases require pregnant teachers to take forced leave at a stage of their pregnancy when medical evidence seems to suggest that a majority of them might well be able to continue teaching without any significant possibility of physical impairment.   But so far as I am aware, the medical evidence also suggests that in some cases there may be physical impairment at the stage of pregnancy fastened on by the regulations in question, and that the probability of physical impairment increases as the pregnancy advances.   If legislative bodies are to be permitted to draw a general line anywhere short of the delivery room, I can find no judicial standard of measurement which says the ones drawn here were invalid. I therefore dissent.

NOTES AND QUESTIONS

1. The records in these cases indicate that the maternity leave regulations originally may have been inspired by other considerations.

Would any of the following have served to justify the regulations: (1) that they were adopted to save pregnant teachers from the embarrassment of giggling children saying such things as "my teacher swallowed a watermelon"; (2) that their cut-off date at the end of the fourth month was chosen because that is when a teacher "begins to show", or (3) that the regulations insulate the school children from seeing conspicuously pregnant teachers?

2. In footnote 13 the Court states: "We are not dealing in these cases with maternity leave regulations requiring a termination of employment at some firm date during the last few weeks of pregnancy." Suppose medical evidence showed that pregnancy generally impaired a teacher's job performance during the last six or four weeks, would a mandatory cut-off rule for the last six or four weeks be constitutional?

3. Suppose psychological evidence showed that children of mothers who return to work within the first three months develop less rapidly and less well, having feelings of rejection and alienation, would this evidence have justified the return-to-work regulations?

4. The Court did not say that Virginia's rule requiring that the teacher give assurances that care of the child will not unduly interfere with her job duties is unconstitutional. Is it?

5. What are the constitutional requirements of these cases in the situations posed by Mr. Justice REHNQUIST?

LAU v. NICHOLS

Supreme Court of the United States, 1974.
—— U.S. ——, 94 S.Ct. 786, —— L.Ed.2d ——.

Mr. Justice DOUGLAS delivered the opinion of the Court.

The San Francisco California school system was integrated in 1971 as a result of a federal court decree, 339 F.Supp. 1315. See Lee v. Johnson, 404 U.S. 1215. The District Court found that there are 2,856 students of Chinese ancestry in the school system who do not speak English. Of those who have that language deficiency, about 1,000 are given supplemental courses in the English language. About 1,800 however do not receive that instruction.

This class suit brought by non-English speaking Chinese students against officials responsible for the operation of the San Francisco Unified School District seeks relief against the unequal educational opportunities which are alleged to violate the Fourteenth Amendment. No specific remedy is urged upon us. Teaching English to the students of Chinese ancestry who do not speak the language is one choice. Giving instructions to this group in Chinese is another. There may be others. Petitioner asks only that the Board of Education be directed to apply its expertise to the problem and rectify the situation.

The District Court denied relief. The Court of Appeals affirmed, holding that there was no violation of the Equal Protection Clause of the Fourteenth Amendment nor of § 601 of the Civil Rights Act of 1964, which excludes from participation in federal financial assistance, recipients of aid which discriminate against racial groups, 483 F.2d 791. One judge dissented. A hearing en banc was denied, two judges dissenting.

We granted the petition for certiorari because of the public importance of the question presented . . . .

The Court of Appeals reasoned that "every student brings to the starting line of his educational career different advantages and disadvantages caused in part by social, economic and cultural background, created and continued completely apart from any contribution by the school system,". . . . Yet in our view the case may not be so easily decided. . . . § 571 of the California Education Code states that "English shall be the basic language of instruction in all schools." That section permits a school district to determine "when and under what circumstances instruction may be given bilingually." That section also states as "the policy of the state" to insure "the mastery of English by all pupils in the schools." And bilingual instruction is authorized "to the extent that it does not interfere with the systematic, sequential, and regular instruction of all pupils in the English language."

Moreover § 8573 of the Education Code provides that no pupil shall receive a diploma of graduation from grade 12 who has not met the standards of proficiency in "English," as well as other prescribed subjects. Moreover by § 12101 of the Education Code children between the ages of six and 16 years are (with exceptions not material here) "subject to compulsory full-time education."

Under these state-imposed standards there is no equality of treatment merely by providing students with the same facilities, text books, teachers, and curriculum; for students who do not understand English are effectively foreclosed from any meaningful education.

Basic English skills are at the very core of what these public schools teach. Imposition of a requirement that, before a child can effectively participate in the educational program, he must already have acquired those basic skills is to make a mockery of public education. We know that those who do not understand English are certain to find their classroom experiences wholly incomprehensible and in no way meaningful.

We do not reach the Equal Protection Clause argument which has been advanced but rely solely on § 601 of the Civil Rights Act of 1964, 42 U.S.C. § 2000 (d) to reverse the Court of Appeals.

That section bans discrimination based "on the ground of race, color, or national origin," in "any program or activity receiving federal financial assistance." The school district involved in this litigation receives large amounts of federal financial assistance. HEW, which has authority to promulgate regulations prohibiting discrimination in federally assisted school systems, 42 U.S.C. § 2000 (d), in 1968 issued one guideline that "school systems are responsible for assuring that students of a particular race, color, or national origin are not denied the opportunity to obtain the education generally obtained by other students in the system." 33 CFR § 4955. In 1970 HEW made the guidelines more specific, requiring school districts that were federally funded "to rectify the language deficiency in order to open" the instruction to students who had "linguistic deficiencies." 35 Fed. Reg. 11595.

By § 602 of the Act HEW is authorized to issue rules, regulations, and orders to make sure that recipients of federal aid under its jurisdiction conduct any federal financed projects consistently with § 601. HEW's regulations specify, 45 CFR § 80.3(b)(1), that the recipients may not:

> "Provide any service, financial aid, or other benefit to an individual which is different, or is provided in a different manner, from that provided to others under the program;

>   .   .   .   .   .

> "Restrict an individual in any way in the enjoyment of any advantage or privilege enjoyed by others receiving any service, financial aid, or other benefit under the program";

Discrimination among students on account of race or national origin that is prohibited includes "discrimination in the availability or use of any academic . . . or other facilities of the grantee or other recipient."

Discrimination is barred which has that *effect* even though no purposeful design is present: a recipient "may not . . . utilize criteria or methods of administration which have the effect of subjecting individuals to discrimination" or has "the effect of defeating or substantially impairing accomplishment of the objectives of the program as respect individuals of a particular race, color, or national origin."

It seems obvious that the Chinese-speaking minority receives less benefits than the English-speaking majority from respondents' school system which denies them a meaningful opportunity to participate in the educational program—all earmarks of the discrimination banned by the Regulations. In 1970 HEW issued clarifying guidelines (35 Fed.Reg. 11595) which include the following:

"Where inability to speak and understand the English language excludes national origin-minority group children from effective participation in the educational program offered by a school district, the district must take affirmative steps to rectify the language deficiency in order to open its instructional program to these students."

"Any ability grouping or tracking system employed by the school system to deal with the special language skill needs of national origin-minority group children must be designed to meet such language skill needs as soon as possible and must not operate as an educational deadend or permanent track."

Respondent school district contractually agreed to "comply with title VI of the Civil Rights Act of 1964 . . . and all requirements imposed by or pursuant to the Regulations" of HEW (45 CFR Pt. 80) which are "issued pursuant to that title . . ." and also immediately to "take any measures necessary to effectuate this agreement." The Federal Government has power to fix the terms on which its money allotments to the States shall be disbursed. . . . Whatever may be the limits of that power . . . they have not been reached here. Senator Humphrey, during the floor debates on the Civil Rights Act of 1964, said:

"Simple justice requires that public funds, to which all taxpayers of all races contribute, not be spent in any fashion which encourages, entrenches, subsidizes, or results in racial discrimination."

We accordingly reverse the judgment of the Court of Appeals and remand the case for the fashioning of appropriate relief.

Reversed.

Mr. Justice WHITE concurs in the result.

Mr. Justice STEWART, with whom The Chief Justice and Mr. Justice BLACKMUN join, concurring in the result.   . . .

The critical question is,   . . . whether the regulations and guidelines promulgated by HEW go beyond the authority of § 601. Last Term, in Mourning v. Family Publications Service, Inc., 411 U.S. 356, 369, we held that the validity of a regulation promulgated under a general authorization provision such as § 602 of Tit. VI "will be sustained so long as it is 'reasonably related to the purposes of the enabling legislation.'" I think the guidelines here fairly meet that test. The Department has reasonably and consistently interpreted § 601 to require affirmative remedial efforts to give special attention to linguistically deprived children.

For these reasons I concur in the judgment of the Court.

Mr. Justice BLACKMUN, with whom The Chief Justice joins, concurring in the result.   . . .

I merely wish to make plain that when, in another case, we are concerned with a very few youngsters, or with just a single child who speaks only German or Polish or Spanish or any language other than English, I would not regard today's decision, or the separate concurrence, as conclusive upon the issue whether the statute and the guideline require the funded school district to provide special instruction. For me, numbers are at the heart of this case and my concurrence is to be understood accordingly.

INDEX

References are to Pages